Second Edition

PUBLIC FINANCE

A Normative Theory

Second Edition
PUBLIC FINANCE

A Normative Theory

Richard W. Tresch

Department of Economics
Boston College
Chestnut Hill, Massachusetts

ACADEMIC PRESS

An imprint of Elsevier Science

Amsterdam Boston London New York Oxford Paris
San Diego San Francisco Singapore Sydney Tokyo

Academic Press
An Elsevier Science Imprint
525 B Street, Suite 1900, San Diego, California 92101-4495, USA
http://www.academicpress.com

Academic Press
32 Jamestown Road, London NW1 7BY, UK
http://www.academicpress.com

Library of Congress Catalog Card Number: 2002102557

International Standard Book Number: 0–12–699051–4

PRINTED IN THE UNITED STATES OF AMERICA
02 03 04 05 06 07 MM 9 8 7 6 5 4 3 2 1

CONTENTS

2 A General Equilibrium Model for Public Sector Analysis

3 First-Best and Second-Best Analysis and the Political Economy of Public Sector Economics

II THE THEORY OF PUBLIC EXPENDITURES AND TAXATION—FIRST-BEST ANALYSIS

4 The Social Welfare Function in Policy Analysis

7 Production Externalities

8 The U.S. Antipollution Policies: An Application of Externality Theory

9 The Theory of Decreasing Cost Production

10 The First-Best Theory of Taxation

11 Applying First-Best Principles of Taxation—What to Tax and How

15 Taxation Under Asymmetric Information

16 The Theory and Measurement of Tax Incidence

17 Expenditure Incidence and Economy-Wide Incidence Studies

22 General Production Rules in a Second-Best Environment

IV COST–BENEFIT ANALYSIS

23 Introduction: The Issues of Cost–Benefit Analysis

24 The Rate of Discount for Public Investments

25 Uncertainty and the Arrow–Lind Theorem

26 Measurement Problems in Cost–Benefit Analysis

30 Optimal Federalism: The Sorting of People within the Fiscal Hierarchy

PREFACE

The second edition of *Public Finance: A Normative Theory* is a substantial revision of the original text. It incorporates four major lines of development in mainstream public sector theory since the publication of the original text in 1981:

1. The "new, new welfare economics" as described by Joseph Stiglitz in his chapter in the book entitled *The Handbook of Public Economics.* He was referring to the willingness to use flexible-form social welfare functions to incorporate society's concern for equity, in both theoretical and policy analysis.
2. Private information about citizens that the government cannot know, at least not without some cost and effort. This has had an enormous impact on all dimensions of the mainstream normative theory.
3. Social decision theory, by which I am primarily referring to the mechanism design problem that goes hand-in-hand with private information.
4. The increasing use of dynamic models in economic analysis.

The first three receive the most emphasis and have led to entirely new chapters—Chapter 4 on social welfare, Chapter 15 on taxation under asymmetric information, and Chapter 19 on second-best transfer payments—as well as to substantial revisions to most of the other chapters. Dynamic modeling is less featured in the revised text because of my desire to hold down the level of mathematical sophistication and because my impression is that it has had more of an impact on macro analysis than on micro analysis. It is central, however, to the revised Chapter 17 on tax incidence, the one micro area in which dynamic models have had a transforming impact on public sector theory. Overall, 18 of the first 22 chapters are either new or substantially revised, as are Chapter 26 in Part IV: Cost–Benefit Analysis and all three chapters in Part V: Fiscal Federalism.

A fifth line of development since 1981, the new political economy, does not receive much emphasis. The second edition pays more attention to political considerations than the original, but it is not a text on political economy. In my view, the new political economy derives more from the public choice perspective than the mainstream theory and would require a text of its own to receive an adequate treatment.

Despite the many revisions, the second edition will be familiar to users of the original text. It retains all the basic components of the original:

1. The text covers mainstream normative public sector theory and is entirely micro oriented. Positive and empirical studies are mentioned, but only as illustrative of the normative theory. Public choice theory is mentioned where appropriate but generally not developed.
2. The second edition retains the five-part structure of the original: an introduction; first-best public expenditure and tax theory; second-best public expenditure and tax theory; cost- benefit analysis; and fiscal federalism. These are the topics covered in the standard full-year Ph.D. field sequence in public sector economics.
3. The level of mathematical sophistication is designed to be appropriate for all Ph.D. programs in the United States and elsewhere as well as the better Masters programs.
4. Finally, the main thrust of the text is foundational rather than an attempt to present all the latest work in detail. I believe the foundational approach is most useful to the students, and allows the professors to take their courses where they will. Even so, I highlight important recent variations and extensions of the mainstream theory, sometimes with a fair amount of development.

Writing a textbook affords one the opportunity to say thank you. I again want to express my admiration of Peter Diamond and to thank him for his role in my intellectual development, as I had in the Preface to the original text. I had noted Peter's brilliant and innovative lectures on public sector theory at MIT in the late 1960s, as well as his influence in shaping Parts II and III of the text on public expenditure and tax theory. He more than anyone sparked my interest in public sector economics. I also want to acknowledge my gratitude to Nan Friedlaender for her support and mentoring while I was a junior faculty member at Boston College. Nan was a superb empirical public sector economist and a wonderful person who was taken from us much too young. I especially want to thank Rebecca and Leo LeBlanc for undertaking the daunting task of typing the original text to computer files and doing so with remarkable accuracy. I am deeply grateful to them. A final heartfelt thank you goes out to the people at Academic Press for their help and encouragement in producing the text, particularly my editor J. Scott Bentley, production manager Paul Gottehrer, copyeditor Sarah Nicely Fortener, and marketing manager Mara Conner.

Richard W. Tresch
Chestnut Hill, Massachusetts

PART I

INTRODUCTION

The Content and Methodology of Public Sector Theory

INTRODUCTION TO NORMATIVE PUBLIC SECTOR THEORY

Public sector economics is the study of government economic policy. Its primary goal is to determine whether government policies promote a society's economic objectives. This happens to be quite an ambitious goal. The advanced Western market economies experienced enormous growth in the size and influence of their government sectors during the last half of the twentieth century, and economic analysis of the public sector has reflected this growth. No single textbook on public sector economics can possibly hope to capture the variety and richness of the professional economic literature on government policy, even at an introductory level. Consequently, a public sector text must begin by defining its limits.

We have chosen to limit both the subject matter and the approach of this text. The text concentrates on the microeconomic theory of the public sector in the context of capitalist market economies. The macroeconomic theory of the public sector, commonly referred to as fiscal policy, receives little attention. In addition, the text focuses on the normative theory of the public sector rather than the positive theory. The normative theory considers what governments ought to be doing in accordance with norms that are broadly accepted by a society. In contrast, the positive theory of the public sector emphasizes the incentives generated by existing governmental institutions and policies and their resulting economic effects, without necessarily judging their effectiveness in terms of some accepted norms. A complete separation of normative and positive theory is impossible, of course. A normative analysis must make assumptions about how agents will respond to various government polices; otherwise, it cannot predict whether a given policy will achieve particular norms. Therefore, the text pays some attention to the empirical literature on the responses to government policies—for example, how the supply of labor responds to income taxation. In every chapter, though, our primary emphasis is on the normative theory of government policy under standard assumptions about economic behavior, such as utility maximization by consumers and profit maximization by producers.

That a consensus, mainstream, normative theory of the public sector should have evolved at all in Western economic thought is perhaps surprising, yet there is remarkable agreement on the problems the government ought to address and the appropriate course of government action in solving them. The consensus has arisen in part because the vast majority of Western public sector economists embrace the same set of policy norms, even though their political tastes may vary along the entire liberal–conservative spectrum. In addition, most public sector economists have chosen the same basic model to analyze all public sector economic problems. Given the same norms and a common analytical framework, consensus was inevitable.

The only serious competitor to the mainstream view within public sector economics is the theory of public choice, the founding father of which is James Buchanan, a Nobel laureate in economics. Buchanan has garnered an enthusiastic following, and his public choice perspective has been influential in policy analysis. Public choice remains a distinctly minority view, however, and its approach is more positive than normative. For these reasons, this text considers the public choice perspective only when it has been especially influential in challenging mainstream positions.

The first three chapters introduce the mainstream normative theory of the public sector. Chapter 1 begins by describing the four fundamental questions that a normative analysis must address and shows how a particular set of values or norms shared by virtually all Western economists has produced a consensus on how to answer them. The chapter also introduces the public choice perspective on the economic role of the government.

Chapter 2 presents a baseline "textbook" version of the basic general equilibrium model that is used to develop normative public sector decision rules. The chapter emphasizes how the norms described in Chapter 1 are incorporated into the formal model.

Chapter 3 concludes the introductory material with two methodological points. The first point is the distinction between first-best and second-best analysis. First-best analysis assumes that a government is free to pursue whatever policies are necessary to reach society's economic goals. It is restricted only by the two natural fundamentals inherent in any economy: individuals' preferences over goods and factor supplies and the available production technologies for turning inputs into outputs. Second-best theory assumes, more realistically, that a government is constrained beyond the two fundamentals in pursuing society's goals. For example, a government may lack the information it needs about individuals' preferences or production technologies to design first-best policies, or it may be forced to use certain kinds of taxes that distort economic decisions.

The second methodological point relates to the political content of the baseline general equilibrium model developed in Chapter 2. The discussion centers on the General Impossibility Theorem of Kenneth Arrow, another Nobel laureate in economics. Arrow's theorem, which he published in 1951, stands as one of the landmarks results of twentieth-century political philosophy.[1] He proved that, in general, the political decisions needed to achieve any social objective, economic or otherwise, cannot be made in a manner that would be acceptable to a democratic society. This was a devastating blow to the concept of a democratic or representative government. Any normative economic theory of the public sector must acknowledge the huge political shadow cast over it by Arrow's theorem.

THE FUNDAMENTAL NORMATIVE QUESTIONS

A normative economic theory of the public sector addresses four fundamental questions:

1. The primary normative question, upon which all others turn, is the question of *legitimacy:* In what areas of economic activity can the government legitimately become involved? The legitimacy question points to the expenditure side of government budgets, asking what items we should expect to find there and why.

2. Once the appropriate sphere of government activity has been determined, the next question concerns how the government should proceed. What *decision rules* should the government follow in each area?

[1] K. Arrow, *Social Choice and Individual Values*, Wiley, New York, 1951.

Taken together, these two questions comprise the heart of normative public sector theory, commonly referred to as the theory of government expenditures.

3. The theory of government expenditures in turn suggests a third normative question: How should the government finance these expenditures? Analysis of this question provides the basis for a comprehensive *normative theory of taxation* (more generally, a theory of government revenues). The theory of taxation is not necessarily distinct from the theory of government expenditures, however. Frequently the decision rules for government expenditures incorporate taxes as part of the solution. When this occurs the theory of taxation is effectively subsumed within the theory of government expenditures. A common example is the use of taxes to correct for externalities. Often, however, expenditure theory does not specify a payment mechanism for financing particular expenditures, in which case the theory of taxation takes on a life of its own. For example, broad-based taxes such as the federal and state personal income taxes are used to finance a number of different expenditures. The design of these taxes depends on norms developed specifically to address the problem of how general tax revenues should be collected.

4. The fourth normative question arises in the context of a federalist system of governments. A federalist system is a hierarchical structure of governments in which each citizen is, simultaneously, a member of more than one governmental jurisdiction. The United States, with its national government, 50 state governments, and over 89,000 local government entities is but one example. Most countries have a federalist structure.

Having determined the legitimate areas of government activity in answering the first question, the *theory of fiscal federalism* raises two additional questions, both in the nature of assignment or sorting problems. The first concerns the assignment of functions throughout the fiscal hierarchy: Which tasks should each government perform? The second concerns the sorting of people within the fiscal hierarchy: Where should each person live?

A society must assign the legitimate functions of government among the various levels of government so that public policies do not work at cross-purposes in pursuing economic objectives. One can easily imagine potential conflicts arising without proper coordination, such as one government heavily taxing one group of people while another government is simultaneously trying to transfer income to the same group, or one town actively promoting industrial development that damages the environment of neighboring towns. The theory of fiscal federalism, then, accepts as given the normative rules for public expenditures and taxation established in response to the first three questions. It merely tries to ensure that these rules are followed consistently throughout the entire fiscal structure.

The sorting of people by jurisdiction is closely related to the assignment of functions, since people choose where to live partly in response to the expenditure and tax mix in different localities. Once people choose where to live, they then become voters who influence the expenditure and tax mix within that locality. Therefore, the movement of people across localities can affect how well lower level governments perform their assigned functions or, indeed, whether they can perform certain functions at all. The assignment of functions and people are the two main issues in the normative theory of fiscal federalism.

Parts II–IV of the text develop the normative theories of public expenditures and taxation under the assumption of a single government. Part V considers the special problems associated with a federalist system of government.

GOVERNMENT EXPENDITURE THEORY: PHILOSOPHICAL UNDERPINNINGS

The answer a society gives to the first normative question on the legitimate functions of government is culturally determined. It turns on essentially the same set of cultural norms and attitudes that lead to the choice of a particular economic system.

Economic systems are typically characterized as lying along a spectrum whose endpoints are centrally planned socialism and market capitalism in their purest forms. All actual economic systems are mixtures of the two. The four principal characteristics of pure centrally planned socialism are centralized economic decision making undertaken by a bureau of the national government; the use of a national plan developed by the central bureau to process all relevant economic information and coordinate economic exchanges; public ownership of capital, and possibly land as well; and the use of moral suasion to motivate agents to carry out the national plan "for the good of the state." The four principal characteristics of pure market capitalism are decentralized economic decision making undertaken by individuals and firms; the use of markets to process all the relevant information that agents need to engage in exchange and to coordinate their economic exchanges; private ownership of capital and all other resources; and the use of material rewards to motive agents to engage in exchange. A society's view of the legitimate functions of government clearly depends upon whether it has chosen an economic system closer to centrally planned socialism or to market capitalism.

Humanism, Consumer Sovereignty, Capitalism, and the Government

The normative economic theory of the public sector that developed in the West is closely tied to market capitalism. This is hardly surprising, as all the developed market economies in the West are positioned much closer to the capitalist end of the economic spectrum than to the socialism end of the spectrum. On a more basic level, however, the seeds of the preference for capitalism itself were planted when humanism swept through Europe in the fifteenth century and spawned the Reformation. Humanism was the philosophical revolution that replaced the quest for the divine with the quest for individual development and well being as the central purpose of human endeavor. Among other things, humanism established the principle of *consumer sovereignty* (and producer sovereignty) as a fundamental value judgment or norm in the conduct of economic affairs. The principle states that consumers (producers) are the best judges of their own well being and should be allowed to pursue their self interests toward this end. The decentralized nature of market capitalism, coupled with the private ownership of property, gave individuals (and firms) the freedom to pursue their self-interests. From a humanistic perspective, then, decentralization and private property are powerful attractions of capitalism, whatever other economic properties capitalism might possess. Likewise, the mainstream public sector theory became closely tied to market capitalism in the West because it, too, is rooted in humanism and takes the principle of consumer (and producer) sovereignty as a fundamental value judgment. The same can be said of any branch of Western economic theory—consumer economics, industrial organization, international trade, and so forth. Mainstream Western economists are all children of humanism.

The humanistic foundation of public sector theory has produced a consensus among Western economists on three issues related to the role of government in the economy: the legitimate functions of government, the appropriate goals of public policy, and how the government should proceed in pursuing the goals. In other words, there is broad agreement on the answers to the first two fundamental questions of the normative theory, the questions that comprise the theory of public expenditures.

The Legitimate Functions of Government

The government's economic role, broadly speaking, is to enhance the performance of the market economy. The market always takes precedence for solving agents' economic problems and allocating resources, and a perfectly competitive market economy is accepted as the ideal economic system. But even a perfectly competitive economy cannot solve all economic problems, and many markets are far from perfectly competitive. The government, therefore, has a legitimate role to play in a market economy.

Government activity gains its legitimacy through market failure. The government should perform those economic functions that markets cannot perform at all or that markets perform badly enough to warrant government intervention. Reasonable people may disagree in particular instances on whether the market is performing "badly enough" to justify government intervention, but market failure is always the test. Government activity is never justified if markets are performing adequately. Despite the room for disagreement, there happens to be fairly broad agreement on the list of legitimate government functions implied by the market failure criterion. We will consider them below.

The Goals of Government Policy

The goal of any economic system is often loosely stated as promoting the economic well being of a nation's citizens, in keeping with the humanist philosophy. The same goal applies to government policy as well. This goal is difficult to define more precisely, however. It cannot be to maximize each individual's economic well being or even to allow individuals to reach their full economic potential. These goals may sound attractive, but they are meaningless because they violate the Law of Scarcity; only a limited amount of resources are available to promote each individual's economic well being or economic potential. Therefore, Western economists have chosen two proximate goals that are directly related to individual well being as the principal economic objectives: efficiency and equity (fairness). When economists speak of promoting the "public interest," they mean the public's interest in efficiency and equity.

Efficiency

The efficiency criterion is the standard one of *pareto optimality* stated in terms of people: An allocation is efficient if it is impossible to reallocate resources such that one person can be made better off without making at least one other person worse off. Moreover, the people themselves must be the judges of whether they are better or worse off, by the principle of consumer sovereignty. An immediate corollary is that the government should pursue all *pareto-superior* allocations, those that make at least one person better off without making anyone else worse off.

Equity

The equity criterion is more difficult to define because neither economists nor anyone else have reached a consensus on what is equitable or fair in the realm of economic affairs. About all one can point to are some notions of equity that commonly appear in the economic literature. They fall into two categories: process equity and end-results equity. *Process equity* is a judgment about the rules of the economic game: Are the rules fair, independently of the outcomes that result? *End-results equity* is a judgment about the outcomes of the economic game: Are the outcomes fair, independently of how they were achieved?

Process Equity

One widely held norm of process equity is *equal opportunity*, or equal access, which says that all people should be allowed to pursue whatever opportunities they are willing and able to pursue. Equal opportunity rules out inappropriate forms of discrimination, such as denying people access to certain jobs on the basis of their race, religion, or sex. Another widely held norm of process equity is *social mobility*, which refers to the ability of individuals or families to move within the distribution of income or wealth over time. The antithesis of social mobility is the caste system, in which people are born into a certain position within the distribution and must remain there for life. One of the great attractions of a market economy is that it fosters both equal opportunity and social mobility so long as markets are competitive.

The call for process equity is most closely associated with the philosopher Robert Nozick, who believes that equity begins and ends with the rules of the game.[2] He argues that any outcome of a fair game is fair. In particular, if the rules of the economic "game" are fair, then any outcome the economy generates is inherently fair. Societies have tended to reject Nozick's view on economic matters, however. Nations routinely make independent judgments about outcomes, especially about the extremes of poverty and wealth. They have been willing to transfer resources to the poor in cash and in kind to ease the burden of poverty, paid for by taxes on the non-poor. The United States went so far as to declare a war on poverty in 1964 with the intent of eradicating poverty.

The majority of economists worry about end-results equity as well. One reason why may be that the rules governing the game are commonly seen to be inherently unfair. Think of the game as a race to economic well being run within the confines of a market economy. The problem with the race occurs at the starting line. The outcomes in a market economy depend to a considerable extent on the resources that people can bring to the marketplace, and some of these resources are beyond their control. Those born into high-income families with highly educated parents have a much better chance of succeeding than those born into low-income families with poorly educated parents. A person's genetic make-up also matters. Some people are naturally bright, outgoing, and competitive, traits that tend to be rewarded in the marketplace. Others possess special talents such as exceptional athletic ability that are very highly rewarded. Still others lack any of these traits. In effect, then, people are forced to begin the economic race to well being at very different starting lines through no fault of their own. Given the widely unequal chances of success, many people are quite willing to make independ-

---

[2] R. Nozick, *Anarchy, State, and Utopia*, Basic Books, New York, 1974. See also Hal Varian's excellent mainstream critique of Nozick's position in H. Varian, "Distributive Justice, Welfare Economics, and the Theory of Fairness," *Philosophy and Public Affairs*, Vol. 4, 1974–75.

ent judgments of the outcomes according to their perceptions of end-results equity and to adjust the outcomes by redistributing if necessary.

Of course, people may be quite willing to judge economic outcomes without much concern about the underlying process that generated them. For example, they may simply take pity on the poor without caring how they became poor. Whatever the motivation, the quest for end-results equity figures prominently in normative public sector theory.

End-Results Equity

End-results equity has proven to be an extremely elusive concept. The quest for end-results equity is often termed the quest for distributive justice— that is, a just distribution of income—but trying to determine the just distribution of income runs into a fundamental difficulty that can be seen in terms of redistributing income toward the "just" distribution. Suppose the government engages in a tax-transfer program in an attempt to reach the just distribution. How large should the program be? To know when to stop redistributing, the government must somehow compare the losses of the losers (those who are taxed) with the gains of the gainers (those who receive the transfers). Unfortunately, no one, not economists or anyone else, has ever come up with a compelling way to do this. Indeed, economists are skeptical of any attempt to make interpersonal comparisons of well being. Yet some means of comparing gains and losses across people must be made for end-results equity to be operational; otherwise, no one can know how much to redistribute to arrive at the "just" distribution.

In truth, all we have is a range of suggestions to serve as guidelines for end-results equity. To give one example, Lester Thurow argues that there is a strong bias for equality in the United States, so strong that the burden of proof is on inequality—inequality in the distribution of income always has to be justified.[3] The common economic justification for tolerating inequality rests on efficiency grounds, that the taxes and transfers used to redistribute generate inefficiencies in the economy. Most economists would argue that the marginal inefficiency costs of further equalizing the distribution outweigh the marginal benefits in terms of end-results equity at a point well short of full equality.

Thurow's position on the bias toward equality may seem extreme, but we will see in Chapter 4 that it has generally been incorporated into public sector theory. The models commonly used by public sector economists to express a concern for end-results equity have the property that everyone should end up with the mean level of income if taxes and transfers do not generate any inefficiencies.

---

[3] L. Thurow, *Generating Inequality: Mechanisms of Distribution in the U.S. Economy*, Basic Books, New York, 1975, chap. 2, especially pp. 26–27.

The only widely accepted norm within end-results equity is the principle of *horizontal equity*, which calls for equal treatment of equals: Two people who are equal in all relevant economic dimensions, such as ability and productivity, should enjoy an equal amount of well being. We will see that horizontal equity has considerable standing among public-sector economists in the design of tax policy. Horizontal equity also provides a link between process equity and end-results equity. Equal opportunity in the marketplace leads to horizontal equity; equals are treated equally in the long run when there are no barriers to entry.

A related principle of end-results equity is *vertical equity*, which says that unequals may be treated unequally. This principle, even if accepted, begs the difficult question of just how unequally society should treat unequals. We know that people who are unequal in ability and productivity can be treated very unequally in a market economy, even if markets are perfectly competitive. Some earn fabulously high incomes, while others do not earn enough to escape poverty. How much inequality should be tolerated? There is no consensus at all on this question, which is hardly surprising. After all, the quest for vertical equity is the same as the quest for distributive justice.

The Government as Agent

The humanistic value judgment of consumer sovereignty has one final and rather remarkable implication for normative public sector theory that concerns the way the government should proceed in designing its policies. The government is not supposed to have a will of its own, in the sense that government officials are not permitted to interject their own preferences into the design of policy. Instead, the proper role of the government is that of an agent acting on behalf of the citizens. The idea is this. Suppose that the market system fails in some way that legitimizes government intervention. The government is expected to design policies to set the economy back on the path toward efficiency or equity, but in doing so it should follow only the preferences of its citizens. The preferences of the president or the members of the legislature carry no special weight; these people are just more of the many citizens.

The government-as-agent viewpoint has considerable standing in the United States. It is essentially the view expressed by Abraham Lincoln in his Gettysburg Address when he referred to the government being of the people, by the people, and for the people. Lincoln was simply reminding us that the purpose of democratic or representative forms of government is to follow the will of the people. Nonetheless, accepting this view of government severely limits the scope of public sector theory. It implies that the theory is not meant to be a theory of government behavior in the sense of recognizing the state as an organic being with a (political) life of its own. It also consciously removes the theory from the reality that government officials are constantly interjecting their own preferences into the decision-making process. They do not simply follow the preferences of their constituents.

Ignoring the preferences of public officials is clearly a severe limitation for a political theory of the government, but it happens to be a source of richness and subtlety for an economic theory. A normative economic analysis based solely on the preferences of some group of government administrators would be little more than an exercise in the theory of consumer behavior: What are the administrators' objectives? What choices are available to them? What constraints are they operating under? These may be interesting practical questions, but they do not carry much normative weight.

By forcing the government to consider only the preferences of its citizens, however, all sorts of interesting and difficult problems arise. For example, what should the government do if individual preferences clash, as they inevitably will? Suppose one group of citizens wants more spending on national defense, while another group wants less spending. How should the government resolve this conflict? Normative theory must provide answers to questions such as these.

Other puzzling questions arise as well about the appropriateness of government intervention. If the market system cannot solve a particular problem, acting as it does on individual preferences, why should the government be able to do any better, if all it has to work with are the same individual preferences? A strict libertarian economist might insist that government intervention can only be justified if markets fail *and* if it can be demonstrated conclusively that some *viable* government policy will actually improve upon the market results. Most economists have been content to assign to normative theory the lesser task of describing a *potential* improvement through government action. But this does leave open the question of whether some normative policy prescription really is viable, and, if not, whether a different, viable, policy can actually improve social welfare.

This question lies at the heart of *social decision theory*, a rapidly expanding subspecialty within public sector economics. Social decision theory analyzes the problem of designing practical decision rules and procedures that will actually achieve optimal normative policies. One of its main concerns is whether democratic voting procedures are consistent with economic efficiency and equity. Another concern is whether government policies can be decentralized, the alternative being government provision or some form of coercion.

As one might expect, sometimes there are clear answers to practical questions such as these, and sometimes not. In any event, it is the principle of consumer sovereignty and the government-as-agent perspective that makes them all so compelling.

GOVERNMENT EXPENDITURE THEORY AND MARKET FAILURE

The Fundamental Theorems of Welfare Economics

Since legitimacy for government intervention is defined in terms of market failure, the natural question to ask is "In what sense do markets fail?" To determine the answer, let's begin with the problem of achieving an efficient allocation of resources.

The market system is entirely neutral with respect to society's well being, of course. Nonetheless, if conditions are right, competitive markets generate an efficient allocation of resources. The problem for a market economy is that the conditions or assumptions underlying a perfectly functioning market system are far too strong. They typically do not hold in practice, and when they do not a public policy can be described that is pareto superior to the free-market allocation of resources. That is, the public policy can reallocate resources so as to make at least one consumer better off without making any other consumer worse off. This principle underlies all normative policy prescriptions concerned with the allocation of resources.

To determine the subject matter of normative public sector theory, then, consider the assumptions that would allow a market economy to achieve a pareto-optimal allocation of resources. These "best" assumptions fall into two distinct groups: a set of *market assumptions* about the structure of individual markets within the market economy and a set of *technical assumptions* about consumers' preferences and production technologies.

The market assumptions are necessary to assure that all markets are perfectly competitive, so that each economic agent is a price taker and acts on full information. This is the case if four assumptions hold:

    a. There are large numbers of buyers and sellers in each market.
    b. There is no product differentiation within each market.
    c. All buyers and sellers in each market have access to all relevant market information.
    d. There are no barriers to entry or exit in markets.

The technical assumptions are required to assure that both consumption and production activities are "well behaved," so that perfectly competitive markets do generate a pareto-optimal allocation of resources. Consider the following set of technical assumptions:

    1. Preferences are convex.
    2. Consumption possibilities form a convex set.
    3. No consumer is satiated.
    4. Some consumer is not satiated.
    5. Preferences are continuous.
    6. Individual utility is a function of one's own consumption and own factor supplies.

7. An individual firm's production possibilities depend only upon its own inputs and outputs.
8. Aggregate production possibilities are convex.

Assumptions 6 and 7 rule out the possibility of externalities in either consumption or production. Assumptions 1, 2, and 5 on individual preferences are satisfied by the standard assumptions of consumer theory, that utility functions are quasi concave, continuous, and twice differentiable. Assumptions 3 or 4 are commonly employed in economic analysis. Assumption 8 on aggregate production possibilities implies constant or increasing opportunity costs and is satisfied if all individual firms' production functions are continuous, twice differentiable, and exhibit either decreasing or constant returns to scale. Assumption 8 rules out significant increasing returns to scale production, which would imply decreasing opportunity costs, or a production-possibilities frontier convex to the origin.

Gerard Debreu has shown that:[4]

a. If assumptions 1, 2, 3, 6, and 7 hold, then a competitive equilibrium is a pareto optimum.

b. If assumptions 1, 2, 4, 5, 6, 7, and 8 hold, then a pareto optimum can be achieved by a competitive equilibrium with the appropriate distribution of income.

Results (a) and (b) are the *two fundamental theorems of welfare economics*.

Debreu's fundamental theorems of welfare economics have the following implication for public policy. If the four market assumptions hold so that all markets are perfectly competitive, and the combination of technical assumptions specified under (a) or (b) of the fundamental theorems of welfare economics hold as well, then the government sector would not be required to make any decisions regarding the allocation of resources. Indeed, it would not be permitted to do so, according to the normative ground rules.

The Distribution of Income

If all the appropriate market and technical assumptions hold, would there be anything at all for the government to do? The answer is yes, because of societie's concern for end-results equity. A perfectly functioning market system can assure an efficient allocation of resources. Perfect competition also satisfies the process equity norm of equality of opportunity and is likely to ensure a high degree of social mobility. But, even a perfectly functioning market economy cannot guarantee that the distribution of the goods and services will be socially acceptable. As noted above, the market takes the ownership of resources as a given at any point in time. If society deems

---

[4] G. Debreu, *The Theory of Value: An Axiomatic Analysis of Economic Equilibrium*, Wiley, New York, 1959, chap. 6.

the pattern of ownership to be unjust, then it will probably find the distribution of goods and services produced by these resources to be unjust as well. Moreover, there are no natural market mechanisms to correct for distribution imbalances should they occur, nothing analogous to the laws of supply and demand which, under the stringent conditions listed above, automatically select pareto-optimal allocations. Thus, a decision concerning the distribution of income is the first order of business in public sector economics in the sense that it cannot be assumed away. Even in the best of all worlds, with all the appropriate market and technical assumptions holding, the government has to formulate some policy with respect to the distribution of income if society cares about end-results equity. Society might simply choose to accept the market-determined distribution, but this is still a distribution policy requiring a collective decision on the part of the citizens even though it involves no actual redistribution. Moreover, no country has ever made this choice. At a minimum, then, a normative theory of the public sector must address the fundamental question of distributive justice: What is the optimal or just distribution of income?

We have already noted that the search for an optimal income distribution has not achieved a consensus. The only point to add is that any attempt to solve the distribution question is at odds with the preferred government-as-agent ground rule that follows from the principle of consumer sovereignty. By its very nature, a redistribution of income must violate the principle of consumer sovereignty, so long as the losers in the redistribution do not willingly surrender some of their incomes. Therefore, redistribution policy cannot be based entirely on consumers' preferences, with the government simply acting as a passive agent acting on their preferences. It requires a collective decision articulated through some kind of political process, one in which government officials are likely to play a very active role. Normative public sector theory cannot be entirely devoid of political content. Politics necessarily enters the theory through society's attempt to resolve the distribution question.

The collective political decision is troublesome for normative public sector theory, however, because of the lack of a consensus on a set of distribution norms to guide the decision. Furthermore, the theoretical difficulties spread far beyond the distribution question. Since an economic system is a closed system in which all decisions are ultimately interrelated, any public policy decision on the distribution of income necessarily affects all the allocational issues as well. The government cannot simply make a particular redistributional decision, for better or worse, and be done with it.

Public sector economics has never totally come to grips with this problem. Economists have all too often assumed away distributional problems in order to analyze more comfortable allocational issues, knowing full well that separating allocational and distributional decisions is often not legitimate and may produce normative policy prescriptions quite wide of the mark. Some theoretical studies that do incorporate distributional considerations into their models make no attempt to justify particular distributional norms. Rather, the government's distributional preferences are simply taken as given, and normative policies are described with respect to these preferences. The spirit of the analysis is to "have the government provide us with a set of distributional preferences, and we will tell it what it should do." Perhaps this is all economists can hope to do with the distribution question, but it is at least unsettling that the resulting policy decision rules depend upon an assumed pattern of distributional preferences that has no special normative significance.

The Allocation of Resources

The allocational issues in public sector economics follow directly from a breakdown in the market and technical assumptions necessary for a perfectly functioning market system. Many of the market and technical assumptions do fail to hold in practice, so there is broad scope for legitimate government activity. A long tradition within the profession held that the study of failures in the market assumptions typically fell within the domain of industrial organization or consumer economics. These fields analyze such problems as monopolistic behavior and imperfect information, along with the corresponding public policy responses such as antitrust and consumer-protection legislation. Public sector economics, or public finance, traditionally limited its concern to breakdowns in the technical assumptions,[5] concentrating primarily on *externalities* and *increasing returns* or *decreasing cost production*.

Private or Asymmetric Information

This traditional division has broken down in one respect over the past 20 years, around the problem of imperfect information. Economists have been particularly interested in the consequences of asymmetric information, in which some individuals have private information that other individuals do not know. Private or asymmetric information is so common in exchange that

---

[5] The theory of fiscal policy can also be thought of as a response to a breakdown in the market and technical assumptions. For example, externalities play a role in the two main themes of macroeconomic policy, stabilizing the business cycle and promoting optimal long-run economic growth. New Keynesians argue that coordination problems are an important determinant of the wage and price stickiness that gives rise to the business cycle from the demand side. The economy would operate closer to its production frontier, on average, if workers and firms would agree to index wages and prices to the rate of growth in aggregate demand. But individual firms and workers are not willing to index unless they can be assured that all workers and firms will index, and coordinating an economy-wide indexing is difficult to accomplish in practice. Therefore, wages and prices remain largely unindexed. Similarly, externality problems help to explain why a nation's rate of saving might not be optimal, at a rate consistent with the Golden Rule of Accumulation, which maximizes consumption per person over time. Externalities are also central to the newer endogenous theories of long-run economic growth (for instance, all those theories that point to the spread of knowledge as an engine of growth).

it is has become a focus of analysis in all fields of economics, including public sector economics. Some reflection on the relationship of private information to government policy is in order, because economists have come to realize that private information has a profound effect on normative public sector theory.

Private information is, first of all, an important source of market failure that requires government intervention. The general problem with private information is that it tends to undermine market exchanges because it gives an undue advantage to those who have it. They can easily cheat the other parties. This is why even the most libertarian of economists acknowledge the need for a judicial system to enforce contracts and define private property rights. It also leads to agencies such as a bureau of standards to protect consumers from fraud (e.g., to ensure that a gallon of gasoline at the pump really is a gallon), and the Occupational Safety and Health Administration (OSHA) to ensure that workers understand the hazards of their jobs. People want independent certification from the government that producers are telling the truth about products and working conditions.

The widespread provision of public insurance is another important example of a response to market failure caused in part by private information. Private firms are willing to provide insurance against risky events only if a number of conditions hold. Among them is the requirement that they have good information about the insured. Absent good information, the insurance companies are exposed to the *principal–agent problem*. The structure of the problem is that a principal is in charge of a set of agents who have different objectives from the principal. Therefore, the principal has to monitor the agents so that they will behave in accordance with the principal's objectives, and the principal needs good information about the agents to monitor them effectively.

In the case of insurance markets, each insurance company (the principal) needs to be able to monitor the insured (the agents) to write profitable policies. For starters, the companies need to know the riskiness of the insured so that they can adjust their premiums according to risk (e.g., higher auto insurance premiums for the more risky drivers). Otherwise, they are forced to charge one premium for all risk classes, and the low-risk policy holders have an incentive to drop out and form their own group. This phenomenon is called *adverse selection*, because it leaves the insurance companies with an ever-riskier (adverse) pool of the insured, and the companies must charge ever higher premiums to earn a profit. At some point, the premiums may become too high to attract a large enough pool of high-risk policy holders, leaving the high-risk people without any insurance. Insurance companies also have to be confident that their policy holders cannot influence the probability of the event being insured against unbeknownst to the company (e.g., unhealthy live styles that are difficult for the medical insurers to detect). The ability to change the odds of the insured event is called *moral hazard*, and it is a clear threat to the profitability of the insurance companies. Private firms may not provide insurance if either adverse selection or moral hazard is a possibility; consequently, people who want the insurance must turn to the government to provide it. In fact, the governments in most of the developed market economies operate large public insurance programs.

At a deeper level, private information threatens the government-as-agent role that the government is supposed to play when trying to solve allocational problems. The government obviously must know the preferences of the people to be an effective agent on their behalf. But if people have private information, they often have an incentive to hide their true preferences from the government to get a better deal for themselves by having others "play the sucker." The government cannot hope to achieve pareto-optimal allocations if the people will not reveal their preferences, as pareto optimality is defined in terms of each individual's own preferences.

Unfortunately, getting self-interested people to tell the truth is a difficult problem in the context of many allocation issues, as we shall see throughout the text. A major research agenda in social decision theory is the *mechanism design problem*: how to design preference-revealing mechanisms such that the dominant, utility-maximizing strategy is for people to reveal their true preferences. Some truth-revealing mechanisms have been described, but most are not practicable. The one exception has been in the design of auctions used by the federal government to sell rights to oil reserves and telecommunication bandwidths.

Getting people to reveal the truth about themselves is also a central problem in designing tax and transfer policies. Governments do not want people to escape taxes or receive inappropriate transfers by claiming to be something other than what they are. Economists have been successful in designing tax-transfer policies that are truth revealing, but having to design the policies in this way still undermines the government-as-agent ideal because it wastes resources relative to the case of perfect information. (See later discussion of tax theory.)

At the deepest level, private information can be viewed as the fundamental justification for *all* government intervention directed at allocational problems. To see why, suppose that everyone did have full information, as Debreu's fundamental theorems of welfare economics assume. If so, then self-interested individuals would presumably use their knowledge to extract all possible pareto-superior gains from the economy because they have a mutual interest in doing so. They would employ whatever means are necessary—markets, various forms of private negotiation and bargaining, side payments to exploit all the gain–gain opportunities. The economy would naturally achieve a pareto-optimal allocation of resources, without the aid of any kind of government policy. This would be true even if the other market and technical assumptions failed to hold. The economy could be riddled with market power, externalities, and decreasing cost production. Yet self-interested agents with perfect information would discover the pareto-superior allocations for all these problems.

The only limitation on these private exchanges would be the transactions costs of making them, which Debreu's analysis assumed away. In some cases, the transactions costs might exceed the potential gains from an exchange, but to argue that transactions costs are a justification for government intervention under perfect information is not entirely convincing. People are unlikely to have perfect information about each other if significant transactions costs hinder their exchanges and negotiations. The assumptions of perfect information and insignificant transactions costs tend to go hand in hand. Furthermore, if transactions costs prevent private exchanges from occurring they may also prevent government agencies from improving on the private allocations. Why should the government have an advantage in reducing transactions costs over coalitions of private citizens armed with perfect information?

The only obvious role for the government under perfect information would be distributional, to redistribute income if necessary in accordance with society's norms regarding end-results equity. There would be no need for any normative economic analysis relating to allocational problems, not in public sector economics or in any other field of economics. Therefore, private information may well be the ultimate justification for government intervention in correcting all allocational inefficiencies.

THE GOVERNMENT SECTOR IN THE UNITED STATES

Limiting the allocational functions of government to externalities, decreasing cost production, and private information within public sector economics may seem highly restrictive, yet nearly all the exhaustive or resource-using expenditures on goods and services in the United States can be justified in terms of these conditions. We have already noted the justification of the judicial system, various bureaus of standards or safety, and public insurance programs on the basis of private information. Examples of U.S. government programs justified in terms of externalities include defense, the space program, and related activities, which together comprise the overwhelming majority of exhaustive expenditures in the national budget; education, which accounts for nearly 40% of all state and local exhaustive expenditures; and many lesser items such as local public safety and government-supported research and development programs. Public services exhibiting significant increasing returns-to-scale production include many types of public transportation (which frequently generate externalities as well), the public utilities (electricity, water, and sewerage), many recreational facilities (public parks and beaches), and radio, television, and other forms of communication such as the Internet, which may well be among the purest examples of decreasing cost services.

Table 1.1 lists the expenditures of the U.S. federal (FY2001), state (FY1999), and local (FY1999) governments. The data underscore the view

TABLE 1.1 Expenditures by Federal, State, and Local Governments in the United States

	Expenditures ($, billions)	Percentage of Subcategory	Expenditures ($, billions)	Percentage of Total Expenditures (%)
A. Federal government (FY2001)[a]				
Government expenditures on goods and services			411	22
Defense and defense-related	336[b]	82		
Non-defense	75	18		
Domestic transfers to persons (direct expenditures)			923	50
Social insurance and pensions				
Social Security benefits (OASDI)	430	47		
Medicare	238	26		
Civilian and military retirement	87	9		
Unemployment Insurance	26	3		
Agricultural support payments	22	2		
Veterans benefits[c]	45	5		
Public assistance				
Food Stamps	20	2		
Housing assistance	25	3		
Supplemental Security Income (SSI)	26	3		
Earned Income Tax Credit (EITC)	26	3		
Net interest payments			206	11
Grants-in-aid			316	17
Payments to individuals	204	65		
TANF	21	7		
Medicaid	128	41		
Other	112	35		
Total expenditures			1856	100
B. State governments (FY1999)[d]				
Direct expenditures			585	66
Public welfare	182	31		
Education	114	19		
Highways	18	3		
Health and hospitals	54	9		
Other	217	37		
Grants-in-aid			305	34
Total general expenditures			890	100.0

(*Continues*)

TABLE 1.1 (*Continued*)

	Expenditures ($, billions)	Percentage of Subcategory	Expenditures ($, billions)	Percentage of Total Expenditures (%)
C. Local governments (FY1999)^d				
Education			315	45
Housing and community development			23	3
Health and hospitals			63	9
Public safety			45	6
Public welfare			33	5
Highways, airports, other transportation			38	5
Other			186	26
Total general expenditures			703	100

^{a} The data for the federal government are estimated outlays.

^{b} Includes national defense; general science, space, and technology; and international affairs.

^{c} Includes education benefits, medical benefits, insurance benefits, and compensation, pension, and burial payments.

^{d} Data for state and local governments were available only through fiscal year 1999.

Sources: *Budget of the United States Government, Fiscal Year 2002. Supplement, February 2001*, U.S. Government Printing Office, Washington D.C., 2001, Part Five: Historical Tables, Tables 3.1, 3.2, 11.1, 11.2, 12.1, and 12.3. U.S. Census Bureau, http://www.census.gov/govs/estimate/9900us.html. *State and Local Government Finances by Level of Government, 1998–99*, U.S. Summary.

put forth in this introduction chapter that market failure is the primary justification for government intervention in the United States. On the one hand, most of the resource-using purchases of goods and services exhibit either externalities or increasing returns. On the other hand, purchases of goods and serves accounted for only 22% of total federal expenditures in fiscal year 2001. The remainder were transfer payments: transfers to persons or grants-in-aid to state and local governments or interest payments on the national debt. The transfers to persons, the largest category, are primarily redistributive in their impact.[6] As such, they too can be considered a response to market failure, namely the inability of the market system to guarantee an acceptable distribution of income. Also, a large proportion of the grants-

[6] As noted above, the large public insurance programs have an informational justification. Nonetheless, the problems of adverse selection and moral hazard do not disappear with government provision of insurance. Public insurance programs inevitably redistribute from low-risk to high-risk individuals and from the honest to those engaging in moral hazard. These unintended redistributions may help to explain why public insurance programs are strenuously opposed by so many taxpayers.

in-aid help the state and local governments pay for two of the largest public assistance programs targeted to the poor, Temporary Assistance to Needy Families (TANF) and Medicaid. These two programs are administered by the states (and localities in some states). Finally, the largest single government program, Social Security (including Medicare), reflects a mixture of motives based on market failure: redistributional (the elderly are vulnerable to becoming impoverished in a market economy without public pensions); insurance (relating to uncertainty about the timing of death and the problems of private information inherent in medical insurance); and paternalism (without the forced savings through payroll taxes to pay for Social Security benefits, many people might not save enough for their retirement and would risk becoming wards of the state).

THE THEORY OF TAXATION

Most of the remarks thus far have been directed to the theory of public expenditures as opposed to the theory of taxation, because the former is logically prior to the latter. Public expenditure theory defines the legitimate areas of public concern as well as the permissible forms that policy may take. Moreover, as indicated above, public expenditure theory often contains its own theory of taxation in the sense that the expenditure decision rules define a set of taxes and transfers necessary to guide the market system to an optimum. Taxes contribute to the pursuit of efficiency and equity in these instances.

The theory of taxation becomes interesting in its own right only when the expenditure decision rules indicate the need for specific government expenditures without simultaneously specifying how those expenditures are to be financed. When this occurs, the same criteria that guide public expenditure analysis also apply to the collection of tax revenues. In particular, taxes should promote society's microeconomic goals of allocational efficiency and distributional equity.

A natural tension arises between tax policy and the goal of allocational efficiency, however. Most taxes generate distortions in the market system by forcing suppliers and demanders to face different prices. These distortions misallocate resources, thereby generating allocational inefficiencies. Resource misallocation is not desirable, of course, but it is an unavoidable cost of having to raise tax revenues. One goal of normative tax theory, then, is to design taxes that minimize these distortions for any given amount of revenue to be collected. Alternatively, if the government must use one of two or three specific kinds of taxes to raise revenue, normative tax theory should indicate which of these taxes generates the minimum amount of inefficiency.

Normative issues such as these are part of the allocational theory of taxation and, just as with the allocational issues of public expenditure theory, the guiding principle is pareto optimality. According to the pareto criterion, the government should collect a given amount of revenue such that it could not raise the same amount of revenue with an alternative set of taxes that would improve at least one consumer's welfare without simultaneously lowering the welfare of any other consumer. If such pareto improvements are impossible, then tax policy satisfies the pareto criterion of allocational efficiency, even though it necessarily generates inefficiencies relative to a no-tax situation.

The second unavoidable effect of taxes is that they reduce taxpayers' purchasing power so that they necessarily become part of the government's redistributional program. The government naturally wants its taxes to contribute to society's distributional goals, but there are two difficulties here. The first is that the redistributional theory of taxation suffers from all the indeterminancies of redistributional theory in general. Thus, while public sector economists generally agree on normative tax policy with respect to society's allocational goals, there is considerable disagreement as to what constitutes good tax policy in a distributional sense. The second difficulty is the inherent trade-off between equity and efficiency in taxation. Generally speaking, achieving greater redistribution requires levying higher tax rates on the "rich" but, as we shall discover, higher tax rates tend to increase inefficiency. In addition, taxing a particular good might be desirable in terms of society's distributional goals but highly undesirable on efficiency grounds, or vice versa. Understanding the nature of these kinds of equity–efficiency trade-offs has always been a primary goal of normative tax theory.

Two additional subsidiary goals of tax policy are *ease of administration* and *simplicity*, which relate to the practical problem of collecting taxes. The ease-of-administration criterion adopts the tax collectors' point of view. A tax has to be easy for a department of revenue to administer or it will not be used. Private information comes directly into play here. Self-interested taxpayers have a strong incentive to avoid paying taxes, and they can do so if they are able to hide information about themselves from the government's tax collectors. Illegal avoidance of taxes is called *tax evasion*. Legal sanctions or just plain old honesty may prevent some people from cheating on their taxes, but not everyone. Therefore, the design of any tax has to address the problem of potential evasion.

Consider an income tax as an example. Suppose the government wants to tax high-income taxpayers at a higher rate than low-income taxpayers as part of its redistributional policy. It may not be able to do this, however, if high-income taxpayers can hide much of their income from the authorities and thereby evade much of their proper tax liability. Also, the hiding of income forces the government to raise average tax rates to collect a given amount of revenue, which increases the inefficiencies associated with the tax. Finally, some taxes are easier to evade then others. Therefore, the relative ease of evading different taxes has to be considered in determining what mix of taxes to use to meet the government's total revenue requirements.

The goal of simplicity adopts the taxpayers' point of view. Taxpayers have to be able to comply with the tax laws fairly easily for a tax to be used. They must be able to understand the tax laws and not suffer undue record-keeping and filing burdens. A clear example of this principle is the preference in less-developed countries for taxing businesses rather than people. The average person is not educated enough to maintain records on income or prepare and file an income tax form, regardless of how honest or dishonest he or she may be. Therefore, the less-developed countries tax businesses simply because they are able to collect taxes on businesses.

FISCAL FEDERALISM

A hierarchical structure of national, state (provincial), and local governments raises a number of interesting normative issues that cannot arise with a single government. Foremost among them is the question: What is the advantage of having layers of governments as opposed to a single national government? In terms of the prevailing jargon, should government be decentralized or centralized? The conventional wisdom within democratic societies is that a highly decentralized federalism is preferable because local government officials know the preferences of their citizens better than national officials do. Therefore, each legitimate function of government should be provided at the lowest level of government in the fiscal hierarchy, consistent with the requirements of efficiency and equity.

Counterbalancing this conventional wisdom are some difficult problems associated with the ability of people to move from locality to locality in response to local government policies. The ability to move can itself generate inefficiencies that would not be possible with a single government. It also raises the possibility of multiple equilibria or no equilibrium at all as people search for the localities that maximize their utilities. Mobility also severely limits the possibilities for redistributing income at any level in the fiscal hierarchy other than the national level. Suppose a locality undertakes a tax-transfer policy to redistribute income from its high-income citizens to its low-income citizens. The high-income citizens have an incentive to move to another locality that is not redistributing, thereby undermining the original locality's redistribution policy and lowering the average income in the locality as well. At the same time, we shall see that denying a government the distribution function removes its political identity in the mainstream model of the public sector. This leads to another fundamental problem for a normative theory. With each person simultaneously being a citizen of multiple governments and with some of the governments lacking political identities, the notion of an overall social optimum that the various governments are striving for becomes highly problematic.

Information also plays a special role in the normative theory of fiscal federalism. The main issue here is how sophisticated people are within each local government. As they vote on policies in their own localities, do they consider how people in other localities might react to they policies, or do they take the policies elsewhere as given? The answer to this question has important implications for the efficiency of local solutions to allocational problems.

THE THEORY OF PUBLIC CHOICE

The theory of public choice developed by James Buchanan and his followers challenges virtually every tenet of the mainstream public sector theory. Buchanan described the foundations of the public choice perspective in his Nobel lecture delivered in Stockholm, Sweden, in 1986.[7] The disagreements with the mainstream view begin at the most basic level, with the assumptions about how people behave. According to Buchanan, the mainstream theory assumes that people are essentially schizophrenic. They are self-interested in their economic lives, but when they turn to the government in their political lives they suddenly become other-interested and consider the broader social or public interest in efficiency and equity. Nonsense, say the public choice advocates. People do not change their stripes; they remain self-interested in their political lives as well. They turn to government only because they cannot get what they want for themselves in the marketplace, and they view the government as just another venue for seeking their own objectives. Buchanan refers to individuals' interactions with the government as fiscal exchanges, to mirror the self-interested motivations of standard market exchanges. Using the government in the pursuit of self-interest is seen as entirely appropriate and legitimate.

The thrust of public choice theory is positive, not normative. Buchanan scoffs at the notion of an idealized, beneficent government acting as an agent of the people in pursuit of social objectives. Instead, Buchanan argues that public sector economists should be studying actual political and governmental institutions and determining whether they give the people what they want. The test of government efficiency in this positive vein is simply how well the government serves each person's self-interest. Full efficiency requires unanimity under democratic decision making, because only then will no one lose as a result of any government policy. This is as "efficient" as the government can be in helping people get what they want. Notice that the public choice

---

[7] The lecture was reprinted in J. Buchanan, "The Constitution of Economic Policy," *American Economic Review*, June 1987, pp. 243–250.

definition of efficiency in political activity is far stronger than the economic definition of efficiency as pareto optimality, which the mainstream perspective uses to judge public policies.

The public choice perspective does have normative content but it is strictly process oriented, concerned only with the rules that govern political activity. Moreover Buchanan claims that the normative content centers on a single point in time, at the founding of a democratic nation. The norms are embedded in the constitution drafted by the nation's constitutional convention.

In focusing on the constitution, Buchanan was influenced by the Swedish economist Knut Wicksell, who theorized about the legitimate role of in a democratic society at the end of the nineteenth century. It was Wicksell who first thought of government activity in terms of fiscal exchanges and who described the ideal in as unanimous consent for all policies at every point in time. Buchanan concedes that requiring unanimity all the time is asking for too much; it would lead to paralysis. Instead, he points to the constitution. He argues that legitimacy in government requires only a consensus among the framers of the nation's constitution about the rules under which the government is permitted to operate. In designing these rules, the convention members think only of their self-interests and those of their descendants as they perceive them. Unanimous agreement at the constitutional convention about the rules of politics would be the ideal, although Buchanan concedes that a consensus may be all that is possible.

The only valid normative test of government activity at any time after the convention is the following: Could the current rules that guide and constrain government activity have arisen from an agreement at the constitutional convention? If the answer is yes, then the current rules are legitimate and society has forged a legitimate link between the people and their government. Notice that the policies that result from these rules cannot be evaluated directly by any norms. In particular, the outcomes of policies are irrelevant in and of themselves. Process is everything according to this test, namely consistency with the self-interested rules agreed to at the constitutional convention.

Normative policy analysis after the convention is possible, but it is limited to suggestions for constitutional reform and then only if the normative test fails. Normative proposals take the form of recommending changes in the constitutional rules so that people are better able to pursue their self-interests in their fiscal exchanges with the government. For example, Buchanan seriously doubts that the large, prolonged U.S. federal budget deficits of the 1980s and early 1990s would pass his normative constitutional test because of the damage they could inflict upon future generations. He favors a balanced-budget amendment to the constitution.

An interesting question is whether redistributional policies or rules could ever achieve a consensus at a constitutional convention, given that redistributions force some people to pay taxes for the benefit of others. Those who are taxed may well feel that they are not getting what they want from their fiscal exchanges. Buchanan believes that consensus could be reached if the framers of the constitution choose to consider the welfare of future generations and are willing to view the future through a veil of ignorance. The idea is that no one can predict the future, so that no one at a constitutional convention can know with certainty how their descendants will fare for all time. Therefore, they may see it in their self-interest to establish rules that permit redistributions of income on the chance that their descendants might be the ones who fall on hard times. In other words, they are simply allowing for the possibility of future transfers to their own families.

The public choice perspective is persuasive in a number of respects. The assumption of self-interested political behavior is instinctively appealing to economists, and much political behavior is clearly self-interested. The insistence on analyzing actual political institutions and actual political choices is also sensible, as is a focus on the constitutional rules that guide and constrain all political activity. Nonetheless, public choice has not captured the day among public sector economists. It remains a distinctly minority perspective, if the weight of the professional literature is an accurate guide.

Perhaps the mainstream has stood firm against the public choice challenge because the normative basis of public choice theory is so thin. The public choice perspective as articulated by Buchanan lacks any clear sense of good citizenship or empathy, qualities that many people believe are essential ingredients for a society that anyone would want to live in. A narrow focus on self-interested constitutional rules may not be enough to sustain a comprehensive normative economic theory of the public sector. In any event, the majority of economists apparently want to judge the results of specific government policies directly and to do so in terms of the pareto efficiency criterion and commonly accepted equity norms such as equal opportunity or horizontal equity. More generally, government activity motivated entirely by self-interest simply does not have the normative appeal of government activity motivated by the public interest in efficiency and equity.

The battle between public choice and mainstream economists is unlikely to be decided on empirical grounds because ample evidence exists to support both sides. Two recent published reflections by Joseph Stiglitz and Joel Slemrod are instructive.[8]

Stiglitz, a Nobel laureate, has contributed as much as any economist to mainstream public sector theory over the past 30 years. When he was asked to reflect on his years at the Council of Economic Advisors, he responded with a

---

[8] J. Stiglitz, "The Private Uses of Public Interests: Incentives and Institutions," *Journal of Economic Perspectives*, Spring 1998; J. Slemrod, "On Voluntary Compliance, Voluntary Taxes, and Social Capital," *National Tax Journal*, September 1998. See also a set of lectures by Buchanan and Richard Musgrave, dean of the mainstream economists, recently published in J. Buchanan and R. Musgrave, *Public Finance and Public Choice: Two Contrasting Views of the State* MIT Press, Cambridge, MA, 1999.

paper describing why the government has such difficulty enacting policies that are so clearly beneficial from the mainstream perspective. The problem in a nutshell, according to Stiglitz, is that all too many government officials behave as Buchanan said they would. They pursue and protect their self-interests rather than the public interest, such as by keeping their private information secret when it is to their personal advantage to do so. Stiglitz believes that the government is hugely beneficial overall but not nearly so much as it could be if officials were more consistently public spirited.

Joel Slemrod has been a major contributor to mainstream tax theory and policy over the past 20 years. He recently speculated that other-directed, civic-minded behavior may produce much more than just a kinder and gentler society. He points to a few recent studies that show a positive relationship between economic growth and prosperity and what he terms social capital, such things as the degree of trust in others, the propensity to obey society's rules, and civic behavior. The social capital variables in these studies are obtained though surveys. A connection between civic-minded, other-directed behavior and economic growth would be a major boost for the mainstream perspective if it stands up to further analysis.

SUMMARY

To summarize the main points of this wide-ranging overview:

1. Chapter 1 has discussed the predominant themes in the normative economic theory of the public sector as that theory has evolved in Western economic thought. The four foundational elements of the mainstream theory are the following:

    a. Government activity is justified strictly in terms of competitive market failure. In particular, the microeconomic theory of the public sector focuses on the problems caused by externalities, decreasing cost production, asymmetric or private information, and an inequitable distribution of income, none of which can be resolved adequately by the free-market system.

    b. The principle of consumer (and producer) sovereignty is the fundamental value judgment underlying normative public sector theory, that consumers (and producers) are the best judges of their self-interest and should be allowed to pursue their self-interest. Consumer sovereignty ties public sector theory closely to the free-market system, as advocates of market capitalism also embrace the principle of consumer sovereignty.

    c. Government policies should promote the microeconomics goals of allocational efficiency and distributional equity. Allocational efficiency is pareto optimality defined in terms of individuals. Distributional equity includes both process equity and end-results equity. Two widely held norms within process equity are equal opportunity and social mobility. There are no widely held norms within end-results equity other than horizontal equity, which says that equals should be treated equally. Horizontal equity is the one bridge between process equity and end-results equity because equal opportunity promotes horizontal equity in the marketplace. Despite the lack of consensus on other end-results norms, most models used by public sector economists embrace the goal of equality in the sense that inequality has to be justified. The usual justification is the inefficiency of taxing and transferring; at some point, the gains to further equality are offset by the costs of increased inefficiency.

   d. When addressing allocational issues, the government should act as an agent on behalf of the citizens and design policies strictly in accordance with their preferences. The preferences of government officials are irrelevant, other than in their role as citizens. The government-as-agent prescription breaks down if society undertakes redistributional policies in the name of end-results equity. Redistributional policy requires a collective decision through a political process, and it is this collective distributional decision that constitutes the political content of normative public sector theory.

   2. Almost all government expenditures in the United States can be justified as reactions to market failures. Most of the exhaustive or resource-using expenditures are reactions to allocational problems resulting from externalities, decreasing costs, and private information. The transfer payments are largely motivated by concerns about the distribution of income, particularly the problem of poverty. The Social Security pensions and Medicare have a mixture of allocational and redistributional motives.

   3. The theory of public choice is the primary competitor to the mainstream theory. It assumes that people are motivated in their political behavior by self-interest just as in their economic behavior. The main thrust of public choice theory is positive in nature, to study the operation of actual political institutions and determine if they give people what they want. The normative content of public choice is entirely process oriented. It focuses on the rules under which the government operates as set down in that nation's constitution. The only normative test is whether the current rules that guide and constrain political activity could have emerged from a consensus at the constitutional convention. Normative policy analysis is limited to suggestions for constitutional reforms that will better help people to get what they want. Public choice theory remains a minority position among public sector economists, perhaps because its insistence on strictly self-interested political behavior gives it a fairly thin normative base relative to the mainstream theory.

   With the mainstream themes in hand, Chapter 2 presents a baseline version of the basic general equilibrium model of an economy that is used to develop normative public sector decision rules. The chapter emphasizes how the efficiency and equity norms described in Chapter 1 are incorporated into the formal model.

REFERENCES

Arrow, K., *Social Choice and Individual Values*, Wiley, New York, 1951.

Buchanan, J., "The Constitution of Economic Policy," *American Economic Review*, June 1987, pp. 243–250.

Buchanan, J. and Musgrave, R., *Public Finance and Public Choice: Two Contrasting Views of the State*, MIT Press, Cambridge, MA, 1999.

Budget of the United States Government, Fiscal Year 2002, Supplement, February 2001, U.S. Government Printing Office, Washington D.C., 2001, Part Five: Historical Tables, Tables 3.1, 3.2, 11.1, 11.2, 12.1, and 12.3.

Debreu, G., *The Theory of Value: An Axiomatic Analysis of Economic Equilibrium*, Wiley, New York, 1959.

Nozick, R., *Anarchy, State, and Utopia*, Basic Books, New York, 1974.

Slemrod, J., "On Voluntary Compliance, Voluntary Taxes, and Social Capital," *National Tax Journal*, September 1998.

Stiglitz, J., "The Private Uses of Public Interests: Incentives and Institutions," *Journal of Economic Perspectives*, Spring 1998.

Thurow, L. C., *Generating Inequality: Mechanisms of Distribution in the U.S. Economy*, Basic Books, New York, 1975.

U.S. Census Bureau, http://www.census.gov/govs/estimate/9900us.html. *State and Local Government Finances by Level of Government, 1998–99*, U.S. Summary.

Varian, H., "Distributive Justice, Welfare Economics, and the Theory of Fairness," *Philosophy and Public Affairs*, Vol. 4, 1974–75.

2

A GENERAL EQUILIBRIUM MODEL FOR PUBLIC SECTOR ANALYSIS

A BASELINE GENERAL EQUILIBRIUM MODEL
> *Individual Preferences*
> *Production Technologies*
> *Market Clearance in the Aggregate*

EFFICIENCY: THE PARETO-OPTIMAL CONDITIONS

EQUITY: THE SOCIAL WELFARE FUNCTION AND OPTIMAL DISTRIBUTION OF INCOME
> *The Bergson-Samuelson Social Welfare Function*
> *Limitations of the Social Welfare Function*

MAXIMIZING SOCIAL WELFARE
> *Necessary Conditions for Social Welfare Maximization*
> *The First-Best Efficiency-Equity Dichotomy*
> *The Pareto-Optimal Conditions*
> *Pareto Optimality and Perfect Competition*
> *The Interpersonal Equity Conditions*

POLICY IMPLICATIONS AND CONCLUSIONS

Chapter 2 develops a baseline analytical model of an economy, variations of which have been used for almost all mainstream public sector analysis.

A model must possess four attributes to be useful as a framework for a normative theory of the public sector. First, it must be a general equilibrium model of the economy. All general equilibrium models describe the three fundamental elements of any economy: (1) the preferences of every consumer, (2) the production technologies and (3) market clearance for all goods and services and factors of production. A particular model may contain other features as well, but the three fundamentals must be present to have a valid general equilibrium model. Second, the model must be flexible enough to consider a broad spectrum of public sector problems, particularly those associated with externalities, decreasing cost production, asymmetric information, the distribution of income, and various issues in the theory of taxation. Third, the model must be designed to highlight the public interest in efficiency and equity, the two main objectives of normative public sector theory. Finally, the model must be compatible with a market economy, since Western public sector economics assumes that the government operates within the context of a market system.

Paul Samuelson presented a model with exactly these attributes in his 1954 article, "The Pure Theory of Public Expenditure."[1] He happened to use the model to analyze a nonexclusive good such as national defense, which is a particular kind of externality. But Samuelson's model proved to be readily adaptable to the full range of public sector problems, and it quickly became the standard model for virtually all mainstream normative public sector analysis. Indeed, Samuelson's model became the standard normative model used by neoclassical economists in every field of economics. Students will recognize the model in Chapter 2 as the baseline general equilibrium model presented in all intermediate and advanced textbooks on microeconomics.

It is absolutely essential to understand the structure of the Samuelson model and the properties of its solution as a prelude to the study of public sector economics. This is the goal of Chapter 2.

A BASELINE GENERAL EQUILIBRIUM MODEL

A general equilibrium model can be specified in terms of quantities or prices. The quantity model is the simpler one because it requires fewer assumptions. It can be thought of as an exercise undertaken by an omniscient social planner who dictates all consumption and production decisions and whose objective is the public interest in efficiency and equity.

The fiction of a social planner can be dropped by specifying the general equilibrium model in terms of prices so that the model describes the operation of a market economy. This requires three sets of assumptions about market behavior and market structure. The first set relates to the objectives of individuals and firms in their market exchanges. The standard assumptions are utility maximization by consumers and profit maximization by firms, but these may not always be appropriate assumptions. For example, consumers and firms may choose other objectives when operating in highly complex and uncertain environments, such as bounded rationality by consumers and profit satisficing by firms. The second set of assumptions relates to the

---

[1] P. A. Samuelson, "The Pure Theory of Public Expenditure," *Review of Economics and Statistics*, November 1954. The following year Samuelson supplemented the mathematical analysis with a geometric presentation in P. A. Samuelson, "Diagrammatic Exposition of a Theory of Public Expenditure," *Review of Economics and Statistics*, November 1955. No articles have had any greater impact on public sector analysis.

structure of markets: Are they perfectly competitive or something else? The final set relates to the market behavior of the government in its dual role as a consumer of some goods and services and a producer of others. For example, does the government engage in exchange at the market prices or at some other prices that it determines? Whatever the government may do, normative public sector theory always assumes that the government's objective is the public interest in efficiency and equity, just as in the social planner quantity model.

The natural place to begin is with the simpler social planner model specified in terms of quantities. Our baseline model assumes that all the technical assumptions necessary for a well-functioning competitive market system apply, so that we can relate the solution of the model to standard competitive market behavior. This will provide an appropriate analytical foundation for introducing breakdowns in the technical assumptions one at a time in Part II, as we explore public expenditure and tax theory in the context of a competitive market economy. The baseline model is also immediately useful for analyzing the problem of achieving an optimal distribution of income, since the distribution problem exists even if all the technical assumptions hold.

Let's begin, then, with the three fundamental elements of any general equilibrium model: individual preferences, production technologies, and market clearance.

Individual Preferences

As noted in Chapter 1, individuals' preferences are the fundamental demand data for all normative public sector analysis under the government-as-agent ground rule. The individual preferences are defined over all goods and services consumed and all factors supplied. Let there be H individuals (households), G goods and services (hereafter, goods), and F factors. Define:

X_{hg} = the consumption of good g by person h. $h = 1, \ldots, H$
$\phantom{X_{hg} = }$ $g = 1, \ldots, G$

V_{hf} = the supply of factor f by person h. $h = 1, \ldots, H$
$\phantom{V_{hf} = }$ $f = 1, \ldots, F$

and let:

$$U^h = U^h(X_{h1}, \ldots, X_{hG}; V_{h1}, \ldots, V_{hF})$$

or simply:

$$U^h = U^h(X_{hg}; V_{hf}) \qquad h = 1, \ldots, H \qquad (2.1)$$

represent the ordinal utility function for person h, assumed to be "well behaved."[2] The functions $U^h(\;)$ represent a complete description of individual preferences for the economy, defined over $H*G$ individual goods consumed and $H*F$ individual factors supplied.

Two points about the specification of factor supplies are worth noting. The first is that individuals are assumed to view factor supplies as bad, a necessary evil for gaining command over goods and services. Therefore, factor supplies enter the utility function with a negative sign. For example, if X is the only good, and L, labor, is the only factor, the utility of person h might be represented as:

$$U^h = U^h(X_h;\; 24 - L_h)$$

where 24 represents the total hours in the day, L_h is the number of hours worked per day, and $(24 - L_h)$ is leisure time, the "good."

The second point is that our baseline model assumes that the supplies of all factors are variable. Some general equilibrium models assume instead that one or more factors are in fixed supply and treat the fixed factors as separate resource or endowment constraints within the economy. Land is a common example. The fixed factors do not need to enter the utility functions because they are not decision variables for the individuals. They appear only in the market clearance equations and production functions as fixed resources to be allocated among the producers. These resource constraints become a fourth fundamental element of the model. Our assumption that factor supplies are variable is the more realistic one, however, especially for labor and capital (saving).

Production Technologies

Production in a general equilibrium model is completely described by the production technologies that relate inputs of factors to the outputs of goods and services. To remain fairly general at this point, specify a separate production function for each output. Define:

r_{gf} = factor f used in the production of good g. $g = 1, \ldots, G$
$\phantom{r_{gf} = \text{factor f used in the production of good g.}}$ $f = 1, \ldots, F$
X^g = the aggregate amount of good g produced. $g = 1, \ldots, G$

and let:

$$X^g = \phi^g(r_{g1}, \ldots, r_{gF})$$

or simply:

---

[2] Utility functions are always assumed to be continuous, strictly quasi-concave, and twice differentiable, with all goods and factors infinitely divisible.

$$X^g = \phi^g(r_{gf}) \qquad g = 1, \ldots, G \qquad (2.2)$$

represent the "well-behaved" production function relating the factor inputs to aggregate production of goods g.[3] The functions $\phi^g(\ )$ represent a complete description of the economy's production technology, defined over G*F individual inputs and G aggregate goods and services.

Market Clearance in the Aggregate

In a general equilibrium context, market clearance requires that the markets for all goods and factors clear simultaneously. The total purchases of any one good by all consumers must equal the total quantity of the good produced, and the total supply of any one factor by all the consumers must equal the total purchases of that factor by all the firms in the economy. Hence:

$$\text{Goods markets:} \quad \sum_{h=1}^{H} X_{hg} = X^g \qquad g = 1, \ldots, G \qquad (2.3)$$

$$\text{Factor markets:} \quad \sum_{h=1}^{H} V_{hf} = \sum_{g=1}^{G} r_{gf} \qquad f = 1, \ldots, F \qquad (2.4)$$

There are G + F market-clearing equations.

Taken together, Eqs. (2.1) to (2.4) provide a complete general equilibrium model of an economy. They comprise all the economic information available to the fictional omniscient social planner who is trying to achieve an efficient allocation of resources and an equitable distribution of income.

EFFICIENCY: THE PARETO-OPTIMAL CONDITIONS

Having specified consumers' preferences, the production technologies, and market clearance, the general equilibrium model is sufficiently detailed to determine the pareto-optimal or efficiency conditions for the economy as a whole. To see how this is done, recall that pareto optimally requires the existence of an allocation of resources such that no one consumer can be made better off by a reallocation of resources without simultaneously making at least one other consumer worse off. The locus of pareto-optimal allocations thus defines a frontier in utility space, the utility-possibilities frontier. Figure 2.1 illustrates the frontier for the two-person case. The axes are the utility levels achieved by persons 1 and 2, based on one particular utility function for each person that describes their preferences.

---

[3] All production functions are assumed to be continuous, twice differentiable, and well behaved in that their Hessians are negative definite, with all goods and factors infinitely divisible. Notice that our specification of production assumes away intermediate products.

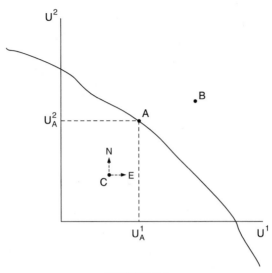

FIGURE 2.1

A point on the frontier such as A satisfies pareto optimality because an increase in the utility of either person from A requires that the utility of the other person must decrease. Conversely, all points under the frontier, such as point C, cannot be pareto optimal because it is possible to move north, east, or northeast from C. That is, either person can be made better off without the other person being made worse off, or both people can be made better off. The region to the north, east, and northeast of C and bounded by the frontier represents the allocations that are pareto superior to C. Points beyond the frontier, such as B, are simply unattainable, given society's production technologies, individuals' preferences regarding the supply of factors of production, and the requirements of market clearance.

Because the locus of pareto-optimal allocations describes a frontier in utility space, all points on the frontier, such as A, have the following interpretation: Given that person 2 is held at utility level U_A^2, U_A^1 is the maximum satisfaction attainable by person 1. Alternatively, given that person 1 is held at utility level U_A^1, U_A^2 is the maximum utility attainable by person 2.

This interpretation indicates that the set of pareto-optimal allocations for all H individuals can be determined by solving the following problem algebraically: Hold everyone's utility constant except for one person, arbitrarily chosen to be person 1. Maximize person 1's utility subject to the constraints that all other utilities are held constant. Include as additional constraints the G production technologies and the G + F market clearance requirements. Formally:

$$\max_{(X_{hg};\, V_{hf};\, X^g;\, r_{gf})} \quad U^1\left(X_{lg};\, V_{lf}\right)$$

$$\text{s.t.} \quad \overline{U}^h = U^h(X_{hg};\, V_{hf}) \qquad h = 2, \ldots, H$$

$$X^g = \phi^g\left(r_{gf}\right) \qquad g = 1, \ldots, G$$

$$\sum_{h=1}^{H} X_{hg} = X^g \qquad g = 1, \ldots, G$$

$$\sum_{h=1}^{H} V_{hf} = \sum_{g=1}^{G} r_{gf} \qquad f = 1, \ldots, F$$

The pareto-optimal conditions follow directly from the first-order conditions of this constrained optimization problem. We will derive them later on in the chapter.

EQUITY: THE SOCIAL WELFARE FUNCTION AND OPTIMAL DISTRIBUTION OF INCOME

Although the model as it stands is sufficiently detailed to analyze the necessary conditions for allocational efficiency, it is entirely neutral with respect to any equity norms. Chapter 1 described two types of equity, process equity and end-results equity. The model is silent regarding process equity. This is not so troubling in a social planning context, however, because the planner simply dictates all economic decisions. Process equity norms such as equal opportunity and social mobility are far more relevant in a market context, in which the degree of process equity depends primarily on the structure of the individual markets. Equal opportunity and a reasonable amount of social mobility are likely to be achieved if markets are highly competitive. Market power and other kinds of market imperfections are the chief enemies of these norms.

The same cannot be said about end-results equity, the quest for a just distribution of income. We saw in Chapter 1 that end-results equity is a fundamental issue for any society, even when all the technical and market assumptions for a well-functioning economy hold.

The baseline, social planning efficiency model described above illustrates the end-results equity problem in the following manner. The first-order conditions for the constrained optimum of the model solve for a single allocation of resources, a single point on the utility possibilities frontier. But the constraints imposed upon utility levels of persons $h = 2, \ldots, H$, the $\overline{U}^h$, are entirely arbitrary. Placing at least one of these consumers at a different utility level and solving the model again generates a different allocation of resources, so long as the new constraints permit a feasible solution $(U^1\,(\,) \geq 0)$. Since the utility constraints can be reset in infinitely many ways, solutions to the constrained optimum problem generate an infinity of feasible solutions in general, all points on the utility-possibilities frontier. Furthermore, the model as it stands has no way of choosing a best allocation among these allocations. According to the pareto criterion, all allocations on the frontier are optimal and therefore equivalent. Pareto optimality is an extremely weak normative criterion in this sense.

The inability of the pareto criterion to choose a best allocation is a glaring weakness for a normative theory of the public sector. For instance, the following allocations are equivalent in a two-person economy in terms of the pareto criterion: Person 2 receives almost all the goods and services, and person 1 almost nothing; each person receives an equal allocation of the goods and services; person 1 receives almost all the goods and services, and person 2 almost nothing. The baseline model is completely neutral regarding these outcomes.

Societies are typically not so neutral, however. They embrace a set of end-results equity norms and devise some method of ranking the possible outcomes according to these norms. At the very least, most societies express a concern about the extremes of wealth and poverty.

The Bergson–Samuelson Social Welfare Function

Because most public sector economists believe economic analysis is properly concerned with end-results equity, they have seen fit to include a representation of distributional rankings in their models. The model requires a function that indicates the desirability from society's perspective, the social welfare, of all the possible distributions of individual utility or well being. The function almost universally chosen for this purpose is the so-called Bergson–Samuelson *individualistic social welfare function*,[4] first described by Abram Bergson and Paul Samuelson in the late 1930s:

$$W = W[U^1(X_{1g}; V_{1f}), \ldots, U^H(X_{Hg}; V_{Hf})]$$

or simply

$$W = W[U^h(X_{hg}; V_{hf})] \tag{2.5}$$

with $\partial W/\partial U^h > 0$, for all h.

The social welfare function is said to be individualistic because its only arguments are the individuals' utility functions. That is, W( ) measures the social welfare attained in each possible state of the economy by considering

---

[4] After Abram Bergson and Paul Samuelson, who first described the function. Samuelson used this construct in his 1954 article, "The Pure Theory of Public Expenditure," referred to in footnote 1. Refer to Samuelson's lucid discussion of the social welfare function in P. A. Samuelson, *Foundations of Economic Analysis*, Atheneum Publishers, New York, 1965, pp. 219–230. See also A. Bergson, "A Reformulation of Certain Aspects of Welfare Economics," *Quarterly Journal of Economics*, 1938.

only the utility level or well being of each individual in that state. Nothing else about the economy matters from a social perspective. Moreover, the individuals themselves determine how well off they are, in keeping with the principle of consumer sovereignty. The Bergson–Samuelson individualistic method of measuring social welfare is therefore consistent with the humanistic view that the goal of an economic system is to promote individual well being.

The social welfare function gives, in effect, the ethical weight that society confers on each individual in its determination of end-results equity. The ethical weights are usually stated in terms of the first partial derivative of $W(\ )$. $\partial W / \partial U^h$ is the *marginal social welfare weight* for person h, the increase in social welfare resulting from a marginal increase in the utility of person h, holding all other utilities constant.

The condition $\partial W / \partial U^h > 0$, for all h, means that the social welfare rankings honor the Pareto principle: If one person's utility increases (decreases), all other utilities held constant, then social welfare must increase (decrease). In other words, all pareto-superior reallocations increase social welfare, and all pareto-inferior reallocations decrease social welfare. Notice, though, that the rankings implied by $W(\ )$ are broader than those implied by the pareto criterion. The function $W(\ )$ can compare two allocations in which a movement from the first to the second increases some utilities while decreasing others' utilities. The pareto criterion cannot make this comparison.

Nobel laureate Wassily Leontief claims that economists can agree on only two principles of distributive justice, that social welfare should be individualistic and that it should satisfy the pareto principle.[5] His remark underscores the popularity of the Bergson–Samuelson social welfare function among economists, because these are the two properties that they thought a social welfare function should possess.

The Bergson–Samuelson social welfare function completes the baseline model by providing a complete ordering of the well being of its individual members, analogous to the complete ordering of goods and factors provided by the utility index of an individual consumer. A complete ordering implies that society can make a pairwise, ordinal ranking of all the points in utility space in terms of preference or indifference. It further implies that the ranking is transitive. For example, if point A is preferred to point B, and point B is preferred to point C, then A must be preferred to C.

Graphically, $W(\ )$ generates a set of *social welfare indifference* curves in $U^1 - U^2$ space, depicted by W_0, W_1, and W_2 in Fig. 2.2, having most of the properties associated with an individual's indifference curves.[6] The slope of a

---

[5] W. Leontief, *Essays in Economics: Theories and Theorizing*, Oxford University Press, New York, 1966, p. 27.

[6] In particular, the curves are everywhere convex to the origin, society is indifferent among the utility distributions along any one curve, higher numbered curves imply higher levels of social welfare, and no two indifference curves may intersect.

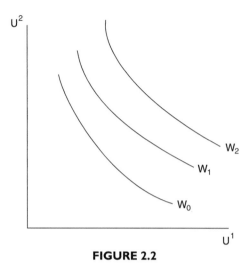

FIGURE 2.2

social welfare indifference curve is the ratio of the marginal social welfare weights of the two individuals.[7]

The objective function of the social planner is to maximize $W(\ )$. In terms of Fig. 2.2, society's goal is to reach the highest possible social welfare indifference curve, just as the consumer's goal is to reach the highest possible indifference curve.

The social welfare function is one of the more convenient analytical constructs in all of economics. It simultaneously solves two of the more difficult normative issues in public sector theory. On the one hand, it represents society's norms regarding end-results equity and thereby answers the distribution question. On the other hand, it resolves the indeterminacy of which of the efficient points society should choose along the utility possibilities frontier.

---

[7] The ordinal property of $W(\ )$ deserves comment because the arguments of the social welfare function, unlike those of individual's utility functions, are ordinal. From consumer theory we know that monotonic transformations of an individual's utility function leave the goods demands and factor supplies unchanged. Since these functions themselves are arguments of the social welfare function, arbitrary (monotonic) transformations of the individual's utility functions could easily change the social welfare rankings. But Samuelson and Bergson assumed that if such transformations occurred, the social welfare function would itself change form to preserve the original rankings. There does exist a method of reformulating $W(\ )$ to preserve the individual rankings for any given set of monotonic transformations of the individual utility functions. For a discussion of the transformations that preserve the ordinality of W, see K. Arrow, "Contributions to Welfare Economics," in E. C. Brown and R. Solow (Eds.), *Paul Samuelson and Modern Economic Theory*, McGraw-Hill, New York, 1983. Also, Samuelson discusses the ordinal properties of W in P. Samuelson, "Bergsonian Welfare Economics," in S. Rosefielde (Ed.), *Economic Welfare and the Economics of Soviet Socialism: Essays in Honor of Abram Bergson*, Cambridge University Press, New York, 1981.

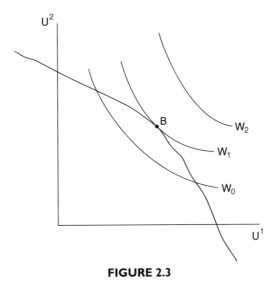

FIGURE 2.3

Refer to Fig. 2.3. The social welfare function selects the distributionally best allocation among the infinity of pareto-optimal allocations along the utility-possibilities frontier. Point B represents this distributionally best allocation in the figure, the point at which the utility-possibilities frontier attains the highest numbered social welfare indifference curve.[8] Francis Bator referred to this point as the "bliss point," a name that has stuck in the public sector literature.[9] The bliss point maximizes social welfare. As such, it represents a complete solution to the social planners' problem, a solution that best meets the public interest in efficiency and (end-results) equity.

Limitations of the Social Welfare Function

The analytical usefulness of the social welfare function is clear enough, but its practical significance for policy analysis is very much an open question. Unfortunately, the social welfare function also happens to be one of the more problematic constructs in all of economic theory. We will mention a few of the difficulties here and return to them in more detail in Chapter 3.

The first difficulty is simply trying to determine what the social welfare function is for any nation. The social welfare function is a political concept, not a market concept. It reflects the collective will of the people regarding their notions of distributive justice expressed through the political process.

[8] Since continuity is not required of either $W(U^h)$ or the utility-possibilities frontier, B may not be a point of tangency.

[9] F. M. Bator, "Simple Analytics of Welfare Maximization," *American Economic Review*, March 1957.

Indeed, the social welfare function is the only explicit element of political content in all of normative public sector economics. The idea of government-as-agent passively representing the desires of the people stops at the social welfare function, because the political process itself is assumed to play a role in shaping the social welfare function.

Deciding what function has evolved from the political process is a difficult question, however. Political signals are often more mixed than market signals and more difficult to test for. Compare, for example, the marginal rate of substitution (MRS) along an individual's indifference curve with the marginal rate of substitution along a social welfare indifference curve. Economists assume that the individual's MRS equals the price ratio of the two goods from the first-order condition for maximizing utility. What, though, is the MRS along a social welfare indifference curve? To what extent is society willing to trade off one person's well being for another person's well being on the margin? Has society reached a consensus on the MRS? If so, how do we test for that MRS? No obvious answers come to mind.

A second difficulty relates to the ethical content of the social welfare function. What should the marginal social welfare weights, $\partial W/\partial U^h$, be for different people? As noted in Chapter 1, no one has come up with a convincing answer to this question. All we have are some suggestions (to be discussed in Chapter 3). This is unsettling, to say the least, since the social welfare function is one of the normative linchpins of economic theory. The marginal social welfare weights are society's norms regarding distributive justice, and a normative theory ought to be able to say something about what those norms should be.

A third difficulty is Arrow's Impossibility Theorem regarding collective decisions of any kind, also noted in Chapter 1. Arrow's Theorem shows that a democratic society may not be able to produce a consistent social welfare function when there is disagreement about the appropriate ethical norms, as there certainly is. A social welfare function may evolve from the political process, but not necessarily in a manner that would be acceptable to a democratic society.

Despite these severe problems, we will follow the conventional practice of using the social welfare function to represent the distributional judgments of society. Societies do care about the distributional implications of their government's policies, and government decision making ought to reflect this concern. Therefore, the prudent course is to incorporate the social welfare function into a general equilibrium model that will be used to develop normative policy rules. This at least allows us to see how the concern for equity might affect the government's decision rules.

At the same time, the social welfare function should not be viewed as anything more than an analytical device representing society's concern for distributive equity. It is not meant to suggest what the distributional judgments should be, other than that they be consistent, individualistic, and satisfy the pareto principle. The alternative of ignoring social welfare rankings entirely because we do not know what they are or should be would simplify the analysis, but it would not produce a meaningful normative theory if society really does care about end-results equity.[10]

MAXIMIZING SOCIAL WELFARE

Adding the social welfare function to the general equilibrium model significantly changes the nature of the model as a foundation for normative policy analysis. The policy objective becomes one of maximizing social welfare, as represented by the social welfare function, rather than simply tracing out the locus of pareto-optimal allocations. Moreover, all individual utilities are allowed to vary, so that the formal model is constrained only by the G production functions and the G + F market clearance equations. The first-order conditions of the model simultaneously determine the set of pareto-optimal and distributional conditions that bring society to the bliss point, the single best allocation and distribution of resources.

Analytically, social welfare maximization is represented as follows:

$$\max_{(X_{hg}; V_{hf}; X^g; r_{gf})} W\left[U^h(X_{hg}; V_{hf})\right]$$

$$\text{s.t.} \quad X^g = \phi^g(r_{gf}) \qquad g = 1, \ldots, G$$

$$\sum_{h=1}^{H} X_{hg} = X^g \qquad g = 1, \ldots, G$$

$$\sum_{h=1}^{H} V_{hf} = \sum_{g=1}^{G} r_{gf} \qquad f = 1, \ldots, F$$

Defining multipliers for each of the constraints and setting up the Lagrangian, the problem becomes:

$$\max_{(X_{hg}; V_{hf}; X^g; r_{gf})} L = W\left[U^h(X_{hg}; V_{hf})\right] + \sum_{g=1}^{G}\mu_g\left[X^g - \phi^g(r_{gf})\right] +$$

$$\sum_{g=1}^{G}\delta_g\left[\sum_{h=1}^{H}X_{hg} - X^g\right] + \sum_{f=1}^{F}\pi_f\left[\sum_{h=1}^{H}V_{hf} - \sum_{g=1}^{G}r_{gf}\right]$$

[10] The comments in this section barely scratch the surface of a voluminous literature on collectively determined decision rules. It is enough for our purposes to establish the central role of the social welfare function in normative public sector analysis. We would recommend D. Mueller, "Public Choice: A Survey," *Journal of Economic Literature*, June 1976, as a starting point for the student interested in the theory of social choice mechanisms. A *Handbook of Social Choice and Welfare Economics*, edited by K. Arrow, A. Sen, and K. Suzumura, is in preparation and scheduled for publication by North–Holland.

Necessary Conditions for Social Welfare Maximization

The first-order conditions for this model are

$$\frac{\partial L}{\partial X_{hg}} = \frac{\partial W}{\partial U^h}\frac{\partial U^h}{\partial X_{hg}} + \delta_g = 0 \qquad \begin{array}{l} h = 1, \ldots, H \\ g = 1, \ldots, G \end{array} \tag{2.6}$$

$$\frac{\partial L}{\partial V_{hf}} = \frac{\partial W}{\partial U^h}\frac{\partial U^h}{\partial V_{hf}} + \pi_f = 0 \qquad \begin{array}{l} h = 1, \ldots, H \\ f = 1, \ldots, F \end{array} \tag{2.7}$$

$$\frac{\partial L}{\partial X^g} = \mu_g - \delta_g = 0 \qquad g = 1, \ldots, G \tag{2.8}$$

$$\frac{\partial L}{\partial r_{gf}} = -\mu_g \frac{\partial \phi g}{\partial r_{gf}} - \pi_f = 0 \qquad \begin{array}{l} g = 1, \ldots, G \\ f = 1, \ldots, F \end{array} \tag{2.9}$$

and the constraints are

$$X^g = \phi^g(r_{gf}) \qquad g = 1, \ldots, G \tag{2.10}$$

$$\sum_{h=1}^{H} X_{hg} = X^g \qquad g = 1, \ldots, G \tag{2.11}$$

$$\sum_{h=1}^{H} V_{hf} = \sum_{g=1}^{G} r_{gf} \qquad f = 1, \ldots, F \tag{2.12}$$

There are $HG + HF + GF + 3G + F$ equations in all, which we assume generate a unique solution to the $HG + HF + GF + 3G + F$ variables of the model, consisting of the $HG + HF + GF + G$ economic variables, X_{hg}, V_{hf}, r_{gf}, X^g, and the $2G + F$ Lagrangian multipliers.[11]

The First-Best Efficiency–Equity Dichotomy

A most useful feature of these equations for policy purposes is that the first $(HG + HF + G + GF)$ first-order conditions can be combined into two distinct sets. One set contains the *pareto-optimal conditions*, the necessary conditions for an efficient allocation of resources. The other set contains the *interpersonal equity conditions*, the necessary conditions for an optimal distribution. The pareto-optimal conditions do not contain any social welfare terms, whereas the interpersonal equity conditions do. This makes intuitive sense considering that the pareto-optimal conditions describe how to achieve the allocations that bring the economy to the utility-possibilities frontier, and

[11] Existence of a unique solution is never guaranteed by simply matching the number of equations with the number of variables, but we do not want to consider the problem of existence in the text. Hence, existence of a unique solution for all maximization problems will be assumed throughout.

we know that they can be determined using a model that does not employ a social welfare function. The interpersonal equity conditions, in contrast, must involve the social welfare function, since that function contains the additional ethical information needed to determine the optimal distribution.

The pareto-optimal conditions themselves divide into three distinct sets: one describing the optimal consumption conditions, one describing the optimal production conditions, and one describing the optimal interrelationships between production and consumption.

To obtain the optimal consumption conditions, standardize on any one person and consider the following pairs of first-order conditions:

1. Any two goods demanded by that person
2. Any two factors supplied by that person
3. Any one good demanded and any one factor supplied by that person

Pairing the first-order conditions in this manner eliminates any terms involving the social welfare function.

Since production does not involve the social welfare function, all pairs of production relationships generate pareto-optimal conditions, including:

4. Any one factor used in the production of any two goods
5. Any two factors used in the production of any one good

The interrelationships between production and consumption are derived by combining the first two sets of pairings. There are three relevant combinations:

6. The rate at which any one person is willing to trade any two goods (P1) with their efficient rate of exchange in production (P4)
7. The rate at which any one consumer is willing to substitute any two factors (P2) with their efficient rate of exchange in production (P5)
8. The rate at which any one consumer is willing to substitute any one good for any one factor (P3) with their efficient rate of exchange in production (P4)

Taken together, these eight pairings generate all the conditions necessary for the economy to be on its utility-possibilities frontier. Should any one of them fail to hold, the omniscient planner can always find a reallocation of resources that will increase the utility of at least one person without making any other person worse off.

To derive the interpersonal equity conditions, the first-order conditions must be paired in such a way as to retain the social welfare terms. Since these terms involve the consumers, there are only two possible ways of doing this. Compare:

1. Any one good demanded by two different people
2. Any one factor supplied by two different people

A final point worth noting by way of an introduction to policy analysis is that this dichotomization of the first-order conditions is not peculiar to the baseline general equilibrium model. As we shall see, it applies to all general equilibrium social planning models that assume government policy is not constrained in any way other than by the fundamental elements of any economy: preferences, production technologies, and market clearance. Policy analysis under this assumption is called *first-best analysis*. This feature is extremely important as a practical matter because it implies that the government can pursue its equity and efficiency goals with distinct sets of policy tools. We will return to this point in Chapter 3.

The Pareto-Optimal Conditions

To demonstrate the derivation and interpretation of the pareto-optimal conditions, we will consider the three conditions most commonly presented in microeconomic analysis, corresponding to the pairings in 1, 5, and 6 above. If all factors of production are supplied by consumers in absolutely fixed amounts, then these conditions are the only necessary conditions for a pareto optimum. The pairings 2, 3, 7, and 8 have no meaning when factor supplies are fixed because the fixed factors are not decision variables for the consumers. In general, however, all eight conditions are necessary for overall economic efficiency.

Condition P1 (= marginal rate of substitution, MRS)

Consider the first-order conditions for any two goods demanded by any one person, say X_{hg} and X_{hg^*}:

$$\frac{\partial L}{\partial X_{hg}} = \frac{\partial W}{\partial U^h} \frac{\partial U^h}{\partial X_{hg}} + \delta_g = 0 \tag{2.13}$$

$$\frac{2L}{\partial X_{hg^*}} = \frac{\partial W}{\partial U^h} \frac{\partial U^h}{\partial X_{hg^*}} + \delta_{g^*} = 0 \tag{2.14}$$

Dividing Eq. (2.13) by (2.14) yields:

$$\frac{\dfrac{\partial U^h}{\partial X_{hg}}}{\dfrac{\partial U^h}{\partial X_{hg^*}}} = \frac{\delta_g}{\delta_{g^*}} \qquad \begin{array}{l} \text{all} \quad h = 1, \ldots, H \\ \text{any} \quad g, g^* = 1, \ldots, G \end{array} \tag{2.15}$$

Notice that the social welfare term $\partial W/\partial U^h$ cancels on the left-hand side (LHS) of Eq. (2.15), so that the LHS is the familiar marginal rate of substitution between goods g and g* for person h. Also, the right-hand side (RHS) of Eq. (2.15) is independent of h. Therefore, condition P1, Eq. (2.15), says that the marginal rate of substitution between any two goods must be the same for all people.

To represent this condition geometrically, consider an economy with two people, persons 1 and 2, and two goods, X^g and X^{g*}. Figure 2.4 is the Edgeworth box for which the axes are society's total production of X^g and X^{g*}. Person 1's indifference curves are drawn with reference to the lower left-hand corner as the origin, and person 2's indifference curves are drawn with reference to the upper right-hand corner as the origin. The equality of marginal rates of substitution is represented by the contract curve AB, the locus of points at which the two sets of indifference curves are tangent. Any point along the contract curve is efficient. Any allocation off the contract locus, such as C, is inefficient since some other allocation exists that can make one or both people better off without making anyone else worse off. For example, suppose at C the slopes of the indifference curves are such that $MRS^1_{x^g, x^{g*}} = 2$ and $MRS^2_{x^g, x^{g*}} = 1.8$. If the social planner forces person 1 to give 1.9 units of X^{g*} to person 2 in exchange for 1 unit of X^g, person 1 is better off, since she is willing to exchange at a 2-for-1 ratio, by the definition of the marginal rate of substitution. Person 2 will accept the 1.9-for-1 exchange as well, since he is willing to trade 1 unit of X^g for only 1.8 units of X^{g*} in return. Any (small) trade between the ratios 2:1 and 1.8:1, including the boundaries, generates an allocation of the goods that is pareto superior to C (at the trade boundaries, only one person gains, but the other is no worse off).

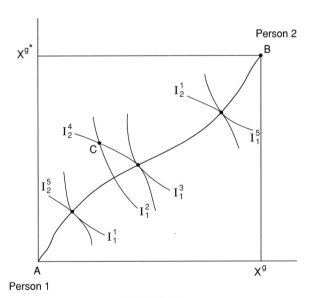

FIGURE 2.4

Only when the two MRS are equal is no such beneficial trade possible, which is true for any point along the contract curve. Note, finally, that the pareto criterion cannot rank points along the contract curve—they are all pareto optimal by condition P1.

Condition P5 (= marginal rate of technical substitution, MRTS)

Consider any two factors used in the production of any one good, say r_{gf} and $r_{gf}*$:

$$\frac{\partial L}{\partial r_{gf}} = -\mu_g \frac{\partial \phi^g}{\partial r_{gf}} - \pi_f = 0 \tag{2.16}$$

$$\frac{\partial L}{\partial r_{gf}*} = -\mu_g \frac{\partial \phi^g}{\partial r_{gf}*} - \pi_{f*} = 0 \tag{2.17}$$

Dividing Eq. (2.16) by (2.17) yields:

$$\frac{\dfrac{\partial \phi^g}{\partial r_{gf}}}{\dfrac{\partial \phi^g}{\partial r_{gf}*}} = \frac{\pi_f}{\pi_{f*}} \qquad \begin{array}{l} \text{all} \;\; g = 1, \ldots, G \\ \text{any} \; f, f* = 1, \ldots, F \end{array} \tag{2.18}$$

The LHS of Eq. (2.18) is the marginal rate of technical substitution of factors f and f* in the production of good g.[12] The RHS of Eq. (2.18) is independent of g. Therefore, condition P5, Eq. (2.18), states that the marginal rate of technical substitution between any two factors in the production of a good must be equal for all goods. The usual way of representing this condition geometrically is to think of the factors f and f* as capital (K) and labor (L) and draw a production box analogous to the Edgeworth consumption box, as in Fig. 2.5.

The axes represent society's total supply of capital and labor, a representation possible only under the assumption of fixed factor supplies. The isoquants $q_g^1, \ldots, q_g^5$ for X^g are drawn with reference to the lower left-hand corner as the origin, and the isoquants $q_{g*}^1, \ldots, q_{g*}^5$ for X^{g*} are drawn with reference to the upper right-hand corner. As before, the contract locus of tangency points represents the pareto-optimal allocations of K and L between the two goods, X^g and X^{g*}, and all points off this locus are dominated according to the pareto criterion by some point on the locus. The pareto criterion is defined in terms of production in this context, but production efficiency is necessary for full pareto optimality defined in terms of individuals' utilities. If society can produce more of at least one good without sacrificing production of some other good, then the planner can

---

[12] Notice that the numerator and denominator of Eq. (2.18) equal the marginal products of factors f and f*, respectively, in the production of g. Hence, the marginal rate of technical substitution between any two factors is the ratio of their marginal products.

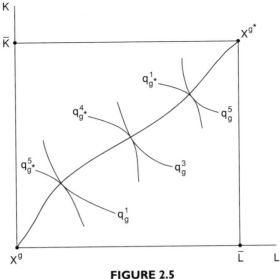

FIGURE 2.5

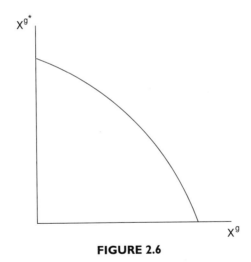

FIGURE 2.6

distribute the bonus to make someone better off without making anyone else worse off.

The contract locus in factor space in turn bears a point-to-point correspondence with the production-possibilities frontier in goods space, depicted in Fig. 2.6. If society is producing along the contract locus in factor space, it cannot realign its resources to produce more of one good without sacrificing some of the other good. But, this is exactly what the production-possibilities frontier represents, the locus of pareto-efficient production of the goods.

Condition P6 (MRS = MRT)

Pareto optimality requires that the rate at which consumers are willing to trade any one good for any other equal their rate of transformation in (efficient) production. The slope of the production-possibilities frontier in Fig. 2.6 is the marginal rate of transformation (MRT) between the two goods, X^g and X^{g*}, in production, assuming efficient production. To derive the MRT algebraically, consider a single factor f switched from the production of good X^g to good X^{g*}.

The first-order conditions for r_{gf} and r_{g*f} are

$$\frac{\partial L}{\partial r_{gf}} = -\mu_g \frac{\partial \phi^g}{\partial r_{gf}} - \pi_f = 0 \tag{2.19}$$

$$\frac{\partial L}{\partial r_{g*f}} = -\mu_{g*} \frac{\partial \phi^{g*}}{\partial r_{g*f}} - \pi_f = 0 \tag{2.20}$$

Therefore,

$$-\mu_g \frac{\partial \phi^g}{\partial r_{gf}} = -\mu_{g*} \frac{\partial \phi^{g*}}{\partial r_{g*f}} \tag{2.21}$$

or

$$\frac{\dfrac{\partial \phi^{g*}}{\partial r_{g*f}}}{\dfrac{\partial \phi^g}{\partial r_{gf}}} = \frac{\mu_g}{\mu_{g*}} \qquad \begin{array}{l} \text{all } f = 1, \ldots, F \\[4pt] \text{any } g, g* = 1, \ldots, G \end{array} \tag{2.22}$$

The LHS of Eq. (2.22) is the marginal rate of transformation between X^g and X^{g*} obtained by switching factor f from good X^g to good X^{g*}. Since the RHS of Eq. (2.22) is independent of f, Eq. (2.22) holds for all factors switched between X^{g*} and X^g. Thus, the LHS is simply *the* marginal rate of transformation between X^{g*} and X^g. (Eq. (2.22) is also production condition P4.)

The $MRT_{g*,g}$ must now be related to each consumer's $MRS_{g*,g}$. From the consumption condition P1, Eq. (2.15),

$$\frac{\dfrac{\partial U^h}{\partial X_{hg}}}{\dfrac{\partial U^h}{\partial X_{hg*}}} = \frac{\delta g}{\delta_{g*}} = MRS^h_{g*,g} \qquad \begin{array}{l} \text{all } h = 1, \ldots, H \\[6pt] \text{any } g*, g = 1, \ldots, G \end{array} \tag{2.23}$$

Consider, next, the first-order conditions with respect to X^g, the aggregate production of good g:

$$\frac{\partial L}{\partial X^g} = \mu_g - \delta_g = 0 \qquad g = 1, \ldots, G \qquad (2.24)$$

Thus, $\mu_g = \delta_g$, $g = 1, \ldots, G$, so that:

$$\frac{\dfrac{\partial U^h}{\partial X_{hg}}}{\dfrac{\partial U^h}{\partial X_{hg^*}}} = \frac{\dfrac{\partial \phi^{g^*}}{\partial r_{g^*f}}}{\dfrac{\partial \phi^g}{\partial r_{gf}}} \qquad \text{any } g^*, g = 1, \ldots, G \qquad (2.25)$$

In other words,

$$MRS^h_{g^*,g} = MRT_{g^*,g} \qquad \text{any } g^*, g = 1, \ldots, G \qquad (2.26)$$

To picture this result, suppose society is at point A on the production-possibilities frontier in Fig. 2.7. Let point A define the dimensions of an Edgeworth consumption box placed inside the frontier, consisting of $X_A^{g^*}$ units of X^{g^*} and X_A^g units of X^g.

Condition P6, Eq. (2.25), says that society must distribute the total product at A between persons 1 and 2 such that the common MRS between the two goods equals their MRT in production. Of all the pareto-efficient points on the consumption contract curve, society must choose A', giving

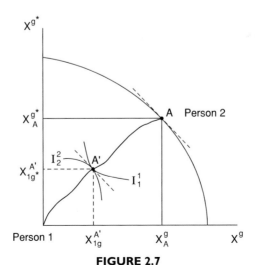

FIGURE 2.7

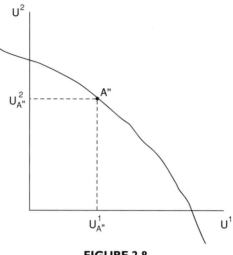

FIGURE 2.8

person 1 $(X^{A'}_{1g}*, X^{A'}_{1g})$ and person 2 the remainder.[13] Notice that while condition P6 has distributional implications, it is not a distributional rule in the sense of an interpersonal equity condition because it does not involve the social welfare function. The distribution $[(X^{A'}_{1g}*, X^{A'}_{1g}), (X^{g*}_{A'} - X^{A'}_{1g}*, X^{g}_{A'} - X^{A'}_{1g})]$ is not determined by interpersonal utility comparisons.

Having satisfied P1, P5, and P6 simultaneously, A′ defines a single point on the utility-possibilities frontier, point A″ in Fig. 2.8, corresponding to A′ in Fig. 2.7. ($U^2_{A''}$ in Fig. 2.8 is the utility achieved by person 2 on indifference curve I^2_2 in Fig. 2.7. $U^1_{A''}$ in Fig. 2.8 is the utility achieved by person 1 on indifference curve I^1_1 in Fig. 2.7.) Thus, conditions P1, P5, and P6 are consistent with an infinity of allocations.

If factor supplies are variable, attaining the utility-possibilities frontier requires satisfying four additional pareto-optimal conditions, corresponding to the pairings of first-order conditions 2, 3, 7, and 8. They are derived following the same procedures used to generate conditions P1, P4, P5, and P6, an exercise that will be left to the reader.

The conditions are as follows:

P2: The marginal rate of substitution between any two factors in supply must be equal for all people.

P3: The marginal rate of substitution between a good and a factor must be equal for all consumers.

---

[13] There may be no point which satisfies Eq. (2.26) given A or many points.

P7: The common marginal rate of substitution between any two factors in supply must equal their common marginal rate of technical substitution in the production of any good.

P8: The common marginal rate of substitution between any good demanded and any factor supplied must equal the marginal product of that factor in producing that good (or the marginal rate of technical substitution between the good and the factor in production).

Pareto Optimality and Perfect Competition

The first fundamental theorem of welfare economics states that if all the technical assumptions listed in Chapter 1 hold, then a perfectly competitive market system generates all eight necessary conditions for full pareto optimality. A formal proof of the theorem requires mathematical techniques beyond the scope of this text, but an intuitive, heuristic argument illustrating the theorem is relatively straightforward. As with the derivation of the conditions themselves, we will illustrate this theorem with reference only to conditions P1, P5, and P6.

That condition P1 is satisfied in a competitive market economy follows immediately from the behavioral assumption that consumers maximize utility subject to their budget constraints and the fact that in a perfectly competitive economy all consumers are price takers facing the same set of prices. Under these conditions, each utility-maximizing consumer sets the marginal rate of substitution between any two goods equal to the ratio of their prices.[14] If all consumers do this, and each faces the same set of prices, then the marginal rate of substitution between any two goods must be equal for all consumers.

---

[14] Formally, each consumer h solves the following problem:

$$\underset{\left(X_{hg}, V_{hf}\right)}{\text{Max}} \quad U^h\left(X_{hg}, V_{hf}\right)$$

$$\text{s.t.} \sum_{g=1}^{G} p_g X_{hg} + \sum_{f=1}^{F} w_f V_{hf} = 0$$

where:

p_g = the price of the gth good.

w_f = the price of the fth factor.

The first-order conditions for any two goods g and g* imply:

$$\frac{\dfrac{\partial U^h}{\partial X_{hg}}}{\dfrac{\partial U^h}{\partial X_{hg^*}}} \equiv MRS^h_{g^*,g} = p_g/p_{g^*} \qquad \text{all } g, g^* = 1, \ldots, G$$

Similarly, condition P5 follows directly from the fact that profit-maximizing firms produce any given output with the least-cost combination of factors of production. If a firm cannot influence factor prices, then it minimizes cost by producing such that the marginal rate of technical substitution between any two of its factors equals the ratio of the factor prices.[15] If markets are perfectly competitive, then all firms will face the same set of factor prices. Consequently, the marginal rate of technical substitution between any two factors is equalized throughout the economy, as required by condition P5.

Condition P6 follows from the result that, in competitive markets, firms produce the output at which price equals marginal cost to maximize profit. If $p_g = MC_g$ and $p_{g*} = MC_{g*}$, then:

$$\frac{p_g}{p_{g*}} = \frac{MC_g}{MC_{g*}} \qquad \text{any } g, g* = 1, \ldots, G \qquad (2.27)$$

Each consumer (h) sets $MRS^h_{g*,g} = p_g/p_{g*}$. Moreover, assuming efficient production (that conditions P4 and P5 hold), the ratio of marginal costs between any two goods is equal to their marginal rate of transformation. MC_g gives the extra cost of (efficiently) producing an extra unit of X^g, and similarly for MC_{g*}. Hence, the ratio MC_g/MC_{g*} gives the rate at which g substitutes for g in production by transferring a dollar's worth of resources from g to $g*$, or vice versa.[16] Therefore, with marginal cost pricing in every market, $MRT_{g*,g} = p_g/p_{g*}$, and condition P6 is satisfied for all goods and services.

That perfectly competitive markets also generate conditions P2, P3, P7, and P8 when factor supplies are variable can be shown by similar reasoning.

The Interpersonal Equity Conditions

The competitive market system can generate the full set of pareto-optimal conditions, but no more. Like the pareto criterion itself, the market is neutral

---

[15] Formally, each firm (g) solves the following problem:

$$\min_{(r_{gf})} \sum_{f=1}^{F} w_f r_{gf}$$

$$\text{s.t. } X^g = \phi(r_{gf})$$

The first-order conditions for any two factors f and $f*$ imply:

$$\frac{\frac{\partial \phi^g}{\partial r_{gf}}}{\frac{\partial \phi^g}{\partial r_{gf*}}} \equiv MRTS^g_{f*,f} = w_f/w_{f*} \qquad \text{all } f*, f = 1, \ldots, F$$

[16] That the marginal rate of transformation between g and g* is equal to the ratio of their marginal costs follows immediately from Eg. (2.22). Switch a dollar of factor f from g* to g. The numerator and denominator measure the per dollar loss and gain in outputs g* and g, respectively. Inverting each term gives the ratio of marginal costs.

regarding the points on the utility-possibilities frontier. If society is not neutral, clearly preferring some distributions of the economy's goods and services to others, it must ask the government to carry out its collective will with respect to the distribution. Assuming that the Bergson–Samuelson social welfare function represents its distributional norms and society wants to maximize social welfare, the government must act according to the dictates of two additional sets of first-order conditions, the interpersonal equity conditions. The interpersonal equity conditions combine with the pareto-optimal conditions to bring the economy to the bliss point on the utility-possibilities frontier.

As indicated above, the interpersonal equity conditions arise from pairings of the first-order conditions Eqs. (2.6) and (2.7) that standardize on a single good or factor. Consider condition IE1, a single good demanded by two different people (say, X_{hg} and X_{h*_g}). The first-order conditions are

$$\frac{\partial L}{\partial X_{hg}} = \frac{\partial W}{\partial U^h} \frac{\partial U^h}{\partial X_{hg}} + \delta_g = 0 \qquad (2.28)$$

$$\frac{\partial L}{\partial X_{h*_g}} = \frac{\partial W}{\partial U^{h*}} \frac{\partial U^{h*}}{\partial X_{h*_g}} + \delta_g = 0 \qquad (2.29)$$

Therefore,

$$\frac{\partial W}{\partial U^1} \frac{\partial U^1}{\partial X_{1g}} = \frac{\partial W}{\partial U^h} \frac{\partial U^h}{\partial X_{hg}} = \cdots = \frac{\partial W}{\partial U^{h*}} \frac{\partial U^{h*}}{\partial X_{h*_g}} = \cdots$$

$$= \frac{\partial W}{\partial U^H} \frac{\partial U^H}{\partial X_{Hg}} = -\delta_g \qquad g = 1, \ldots, G \qquad (2.30)$$

$\frac{\partial W}{\partial U^h} \frac{\partial U^h}{\partial X_{hg}}$ is the *social marginal utility of consumption* of good g for person h, equal to the product of the marginal social welfare weight of person h, $\partial W/\partial U^h$, and the private marginal utility of consumption of good g of person h, $\partial U^h/\partial X_{hg}$. It indicates the marginal increase (decrease) in social welfare from a *ceteris paribus* unit increase (decrease) in person h's consumption of good g. Condition (2.30) says that interpersonal equity is achieved only if all goods are distributed such that, on the margin, the increase in social welfare is the same no matter who consumes the last unit of the good. A similar condition applies to all factor supplies as well.[17] By following this

---

[17] From conditions (2.7),

$$\frac{\partial L}{\partial V_{hf}} = \frac{\partial W}{\partial U^h} \frac{\partial U^h}{\partial V_{hf}} + \pi_f = 0$$

$$\frac{\partial L}{\partial V_{h*_f}} = \frac{\partial W}{\partial U^{h*}} \frac{\partial U^{h*}}{\partial V_{h*_f}} + \pi_f = 0$$

Hence:

$$\frac{\partial W}{\partial U^h} \frac{\partial U^h}{\partial V_{hf}} = -\pi_f \qquad \begin{aligned} &\text{all } h = 1, \ldots, H \\ &\text{any } f = 1, \ldots, F \end{aligned}$$

decision rule and assuming the pareto-optimal conditions are satisfied, society in effect moves along the utility-possibilities frontier to the bliss point, which is distributionally the best of all possible pareto-optimal allocations.

Three policy implications of this rule should be noted.

How Many Goods To Redistribute?

First, there are not really $(G + F)$ *independent* conditions, one for each good and factor. To the contrary, if the pareto-optimal conditions hold and society is able to satisfy the interpersonal equity condition for any one good g, then the interpersonal equity condition is automatically satisfied for all other goods and factors. To see this, suppose that interpersonal equity holds for good g, so that

$$\frac{\partial W}{\partial U^h}\frac{\partial U^h}{\partial X_{hg}} = \frac{\partial W}{\partial U^{h^*}}\frac{\partial U^{h^*}}{\partial X_{h^*g}} \qquad \text{any } h, h^* = 1, \ldots, H \qquad (2.31)$$

Assume, also, that pareto-optimal condition P1 holds for goods g and g^* :

$$\frac{\dfrac{\partial U^h}{\partial X_{hg}}}{\dfrac{\partial U^h}{\partial X_{hg^*}}} = \frac{\dfrac{\partial U^{h^*}}{\partial X_{h^*g}}}{\dfrac{\partial U^{h^*}}{\partial X_{h^*g^*}}} \qquad \begin{array}{l} \text{any } h, h^* = 1, \ldots, H \\ \text{any } g, g^* = 1, \ldots, G \end{array} \qquad (2.32)$$

or

$$MRS^h_{g^*,g} = MRS^{h^*}_{g^*,g} \qquad \text{any } h, h^* = 1, \ldots, H \qquad (2.33)$$

Restore the social welfare terms in condition P1 (from Eqs. (2.13) and (2.14)), maintaining the equality:

$$\frac{\dfrac{\partial W}{\partial U^h}\dfrac{\partial U^h}{\partial X_{hg}}}{\dfrac{\partial W}{\partial U^h}\dfrac{\partial U^h}{\partial X_{hg^*}}} = \frac{\dfrac{\partial W}{\partial U^{h^*}}\dfrac{\partial U^{h^*}}{\partial X_{h^*g}}}{\dfrac{\partial W}{\partial U^{h^*}}\dfrac{\partial U^{h^*}}{\partial X_{h^*g^*}}} \qquad \begin{array}{l} \text{any } h, h^* = 1, \ldots, H \\ \text{any } g, g^* = 1, \ldots, G \end{array} \qquad (2.34)$$

The numerators of the two ratios are equal from the interpersonal equity condition for good g. Therefore, the denominators are also equal, and interpersonal equity is satisfied for g^* as well. Since the choice of g^* was entirely arbitrary, interpersonal equity must hold for all goods if it holds for the gth good.[18]

Thus, the government's task is much easier than it first appears to be. Difficult as it may be to satisfy any of the interpersonal equity conditions, at least they need be satisfied for only one good (or, alternatively, only one factor) in an otherwise competitive economy.

Lump-Sum Redistributions

The second policy implication relates to the actual policies required to satisfy these conditions. The competitive market system is of no help. The interpersonal equity conditions will not hold in general at a competitive general equilibrium, and, if they do not, no natural market forces are at work to bring about the necessary equality. The government must find some other means of satisfying the interpersonal equity conditions. By the same token, government redistributions must not undermine the considerable achievement of the competitive market system—namely, the attainment of full pareto optimality. If social welfare is to be maximized, the government must use the information contained in the social welfare function to move society *along* the utility-possibilities frontier to the bliss point. It cannot take society inside the frontier.

Only one form of redistribution ensures that the pareto-optimal conditions continue to hold. The redistributions must be *lump sum*, meaning that the amount of the good or factor redistributed among the consumers is invariant to the economic decisions of all consumers and producers. An example is a tax or transfer based on a person's age. The tax liabilities under an age tax are clearly invariant to any economic decisions the taxpayers might make.

Another way to define a lump-sum tax or transfer is to say that it does not distort the operation of the market economy. A tax (transfer) is non-distorting if it does not introduce any inefficiency into the economy; that is, it does not drive the economy beneath its utility-possibilities frontier. For this to be true, the tax (transfer) must allow all the pareto-optimal conditions to hold. But this in turn requires that all consumers and producers face the same prices for the same goods or factors; otherwise, some of the pareto-optimal conditions will not hold. Conversely, taxes (transfers) distort economic decisions by causing different agents to face different prices for the same goods or factors.

---

[18] The F additional interpersonal equity conditions for the variable factor supplies will also be satisfied. This follows immediately from the subset of pareto-optimal conditions in P3 relating the marginal rate of substitution between good g and any factor f and the interpersonal equity condition for good g.

An age tax is nondistorting by this definition. Two consumers may pay different amounts of tax under an age tax, but they continue to face the same price ratios for all goods and factors. Therefore, their marginal rates of substitution remain equal for all goods and factors, as required for pareto optimality. In contrast, suppose the government redistributes income using a set of taxes and transfers based on wage income, and consider the tax on wages. The tax drives a wedge between the price of labor paid by the firms and the price of labor received by the consumers. Firms look at the wage *including the tax* when deciding how many workers to hire, whereas workers look at the wage *net of the tax* (their take home pay) when deciding how much labor to supply. Consequently, pareto-optimal conditions P7 and P8 cannot be fully satisfied in the market exchange of labor.

Notice two qualities that lump-sum taxes and transfers *do not* possess. First, it is not true that lump-sum redistributions have no effect on economic activity. Any redistribution program has income effects that tend to change individuals' demands for goods or supplies of factors, with obvious repercussions throughout the entire economy. Second, it is not true that lump-sum redistributions have no effect on the values of the consumers' marginal rates of substitution, producers' marginal rates of technical substitution, and the marginal rates of transformation in production. Prices change in general as demand (and factor supply) curves shift. Therefore, the values of some of the marginal rates of exchange change as well, as consumers and producers equate these margins to relative prices. For instance, the movement along the utility-possibilities frontier occasioned by the government's lump-sum redistribution policy also moves society along its production-possibilities frontier. Since the marginal rate of transformation is the slope of this frontier, marginal rates of transformation necessarily change if the frontier is anything but constant cost (a straight line). Subsequently, all marginal rates of substitution have to change as competitive market forces reestablish the equality between consumers' marginal rates of substitution and the marginal rates of transformation. Lump-sum redistributions only ensure that the pareto-optimal conditions continue to hold, not that they hold at any particular value.[19] A lump-sum redistribution of one of the goods or factors, then, is the absolute minimum policy required of the government even in a world of perfect markets with all the technical assumptions of Chapter 1 holding, so long as society cares about end-results equity.

---

[19] A potential confusion on this point arises from the typical exercises in consumer theory that represent lump-sum taxes and transfers as parallel shifts in the consumer's budget line. The parallel shift does not change the consumer's MRS in the new equilibrium. This representation is valid in a general equilibrium context only if the tax or transfer is so small that it has no effect on the overall economy, for example, if that consumer is only one being taxed or receiving a transfer. Any large tax-transfer redistribution changes prices throughout the economy and causes all consumers' budget lines to rotate. There is no distortion from these price changes, however, since consumers and producers face the same new price ratios.

The Social Marginal Utility of Income

One final point about the interpersonal equity conditions deserves mention. Economists typically refer to the interpersonal equity conditions in terms of "income." The relevant social marginal utilities are written as $\frac{\partial W}{\partial U^h} \frac{\partial U^h}{\partial Y^h}$, where Y^h is the income of person h, and are referred to as the *social marginal utility of income* of person h. The social marginal utility of income is a product of the marginal social welfare weight ($\partial W/\partial U^h$) and the private marginal utility of income ($\partial U^h/\partial Y^h$). The single required interpersonal equity condition is then stated as equalizing the social marginal utilities of income across all individuals and is achieved with lump-sum redistributions of income.

This interpretation of the interpersonal equity condition can be confusing, however, because the meaning of "income" is ambiguous if more than one variable factor is being supplied by consumers. Furthermore, the interpersonal equity conditions of social welfare maximization seem to suggest that physical quantities of some good or factor must be transferred rather than a dollar value of "income." What, then, is the "income" that is being redistributed lump sum?

One possible interpretation is to assume that all consumers possess an initial endowment of some good, say, X^g, which is also produced and sold by some of the firms in the economy. Some consumers may want to consume their entire endowment of X^g and purchase additional quantities either from other consumers or the producers of X^g. Other consumers may consume only a part of their endowment and sell the rest. If the government redistributes the initial endowments the redistribution is clearly lump sum. If it continues to redistribute until

$$\frac{\partial W}{\partial U^h} \frac{\partial U^h}{\partial X_{hg}} = -\delta_g, \text{ for all } h = 1, \ldots, H \qquad (2.35)$$

then the interpersonal equity condition for X^g is satisfied. Assuming a competitive market system with all technical assumptions holding, full pareto optimality is also maintained. Hence, the interpersonal equity conditions are satisfied for all other goods and factors as well. Finally, by evaluating the endowments at either the pre- or posttransfer prices of X^g one can speak of transferring a dollar value of "income," or purchasing power.[20]

Another common interpretation is to associate the "income" with some factor of production that consumers supply in absolutely fixed amounts, such as their land holdings. Transferring physical or dollar amounts of this resource is obviously lump sum, since by definition it is not a decision variable of any consumer. Moreover, these transfers move society along its utility-possibilities frontier as those taxed lose utility and those receiving transfers

---

[20] The same analysis could be applied to the endowment of a primary factor, such as inherited capital.

gain utility. In effect, the government is satisfying the interpersonal equity conditions indirectly. Presumably there exists a redistribution of the fixed resource that satisfies the interpersonal equity condition for one of the variable goods or factors (say, X^g). But if $(\partial W/\partial U^h)(\partial U^h/\partial X_{hg}) = -\partial_g$, all $h = 1, \ldots, H$, and pareto optimality holds, then the interpersonal equity conditions hold for *all* variable goods and factors. Thus, the existence of a fixed factor gives the government the leverage it needs to satisfy the interpersonal equity conditions, even though they are defined in terms of the variable goods and factors.

Finally, it may simply be assumed that the good or factor being transferred is serving as the numeraire, such that its price is equal to one at any general equilibrium. Competitive market economies determine pareto-optimal allocations of resources in terms of relative prices; the absolute price level is entirely arbitrary. Thus, it is always possible to single out a good or factor, set its price equal to one, and solve for the values of all other prices in terms of the one fixed price. If the numeraire good is chosen for redistribution, unit transfers of it are equivalent to unit transfers of purchasing power or "real" income. This is the most general interpretation of "income" and the most common one.

One final comment on equity is in order, a reminder pertaining to the goal of process equity. The interpersonal equity conditions have nothing to do with process equity norms; they relate strictly to the goal of end-results equity, of achieving a just distribution of income. As noted earlier, the competitive market system is relied on to achieve process equity by promoting equal opportunity and social mobility. Our baseline, social planner model has nothing explicit to say regarding process equity, as is true of most models used in public sector economics.

POLICY IMPLICATIONS AND CONCLUSIONS

The principal task in Chapter 2 was to present a baseline version of the standard general equilibrium model used in normative public sector analysis. Nonetheless, the discussion of the interpersonal equity conditions and lump-sum redistributions generated a number of fundamental prepositions relating to the goal of end-results equity:

1. If society cares about distributive equity, it must establish a government to carry out its wishes. A perfectly functioning competitive market economy generates an efficient (pareto-optimal) allocation of resources, but even the most perfect market system is neutral regarding the question of end-results equity.

2. Society's norms regarding distributive justice can be represented analytically by a Bergson–Samuelson individualistic social welfare function,

whose arguments are the utility functions of each individual in the society. The partial derivative, $\partial W/\partial U^h$, is the marginal social welfare weight, society's ethical judgment about the effect on social welfare of a marginal change in the well being of person h. The social welfare function comes from the political process. As such, it is the only explicit political content in normative public sector theory.

3. In the best of all worlds, with all the technical assumptions of a well-functioning market system holding and perfectly competitive markets, distributive equity is achieved by a set of lump-sum redistributions satisfying the first-order interpersonal equity conditions of social welfare maximization. The interpersonal equity conditions require that the social marginal utilities of any one good or factor be equalized across all individuals.

The interpersonal equity conditions represent a complete normative theory of the optimal income distribution and redistribution in this setting. The normative question—What is the optimal distribution of resources?—has a remarkably simple answer, in principle. It is the distribution that satisfies the interpersonal equity conditions, given the distributional rankings implied by the underlying social welfare function. If some other distribution happens to exist, then the interpersonal equity conditions provide a complete normative policy prescription for redistributing resources lump-sum to achieve the optimal distribution. Nothing more need be said about the government's redistributive policies.

The second theorem of welfare economics says that if the technical assumptions hold, then any pareto optimum can be achieved by a competitive equilibrium with a suitable redistribution of resources. The pareto optimum that maximizes social welfare is the bliss point on the utility-possibilities frontier, and society can get there with lump-sum redistributions that satisfy the interpersonal equity conditions.

This result may seem relatively unimportant, as few markets are perfectly competitive and many of the technical assumptions are frequently violated. Actual economies operate under, not on, their utility-possibilities frontiers. The result is actually quite powerful, however, at least in principle. Our subsequent analysis will show that if the government has enough policy tools at its disposal to restore pareto optimality when faced with market imperfections and violations of the technical assumptions and if it can redistribute resources in a lump-sum fashion, then it should use the lump-sum redistributions to satisfy the interpersonal equity conditions. This is a much stronger statement and suggests the vital role of the interpersonal equity conditions in normative public sector theory. Conversely, if the government does not act to satisfy the interpersonal equity conditions, then it should not necessarily try to achieve the pareto-optimal conditions either. The interpersonal equity conditions and the pareto-optimal conditions go hand in hand in maximizing social welfare; they are both first-order conditions for a social welfare maximum in a first-best policy environment.

The requisite policy tools may not exist to reach the bliss point. Governments may not be able to restore pareto optimality nor redistribute lump sum. If so, then the policy environment is second best, and the interpersonal equity conditions no longer provide a theory of optimal income distribution and redistribution. We turn to this important point in Chapter 3.

REFERENCES

Arrow, K., "Contributions to Welfare Economics," in E. C. Brown and R. Solow (Eds.), *Paul Samuelson and Modern Economic Theory*, McGraw-Hill, New York, 1983.

Arrow, K., Sen, A., and Suzumura, K. (Eds.), *A Handbook of Social Choice and Welfare Economics*, North–Holland, Amsterdam, in preparation.

Bator, F. M., "Simple Analytics of Welfare Maximization," *American Economic Review*, March 1957.

Bergson, A., "A Reformulation of Certain Aspects of Welfare Economics," *Quarterly Journal of Economics*, 1938.

Leontief, W., *Essays in Economics: Theories and Theorizing*, Oxford University Press, New York, 1966.

Mueller, D., "Public Choice: A Survey," *Journal of Economic Literature*, June 1976.

Samuelson, P. A., "The Pure Theory of Public Expenditure," *Review of Economics and Statistics*, November 1954.

Samuelson, P. A., "Diagrammatic Exposition of a Theory of Public Expenditure," *Review of Economics and Statistics*, November 1955.

Samuelson, P. A., *Foundations of Economic Analysis*, Atheneum Publishers, New York, 1965.

Samuelson, P. A., "Bergsonian Welfare Economics," in S. Rosefielde (Ed.), *Economic Welfare and the Economics of Soviet Socialism: Essays in Honor of Abram Bergson*, Cambridge University Press, New York, 1981.

3

FIRST-BEST AND SECOND-BEST ANALYSIS AND THE POLITICAL ECONOMY OF PUBLIC SECTOR ECONOMICS

Chapter 3 concludes our introduction to normative public sector economics with a discussion of two issues. One is the distinction between first-best and second-best analysis. The other is the political economy of public sector theory, centered around the social welfare function and Arrow's Impossibility theorem. The social welfare function is the one indispensable political element in normative mainstream public sector models.

LUMP-SUM REDISTRIBUTIONS AND PUBLIC SECTOR THEORY

Are lump-sum redistributions a feasible policy tool for the government? This may appear to be a relatively uninteresting question. One is tempted to answer: "Probably not, but even if they are feasible it hardly matters because few governments use lump-sum taxes and transfers. For instance, no major U.S. tax or transfer program is lump sum." All this is true, yet it is hard to imagine a more important question for normative public sector theory. The answer has a dramatic impact on all normative policy prescriptions in every area of public sector analysis, whether they be directed at distributional or allocational problems. In public sector theory, lump-sum redistributions stand at the border between first-best and second-best analysis.

The issue is not so much the existence of lump-sum redistributions. Lump-sum tax and transfer programs are easy enough to describe. Poll taxes have occasionally been used as revenue sources and they are certainly lump sum from an economic perspective. On the transfer side, many countries have instituted per-person demogrants (e.g., Canada, which provides a grant to all the elderly). The United States has not used demogrants, but it may soon. In his 1996 presidential election campaign, Robert Dole proposed a $500 per child refundable tax credit under the federal personal income tax. It might be argued that decisions on family size are essentially economic and would influence the amount of transfer received. If so, then tax credits and demogrants to children are not strictly lump sum, although the legislation could be drafted such that only children already living at the time of passage would receive the transfers.

The mere existence of lump-sum taxes and transfers is not enough, however, to render them feasible policy tools in the pursuit of equity. The lump-sum taxes and transfers must be flexible enough so that they can be designed to satisfy the interpersonal equity conditions for social welfare maximization, and this is a very tall order indeed. To be effective, the taxes and transfers would almost certainly have to be related to consumption or income or wealth in order to distinguish the haves from the have nots, but then it is doubtful that they would be lump sum.

Income taxes were thought to be essentially lump sum before 1970, because empirical research had been unable to discover any relationship between income tax rates and either work effort or saving. Research since then, employing detailed micro data sets and sophisticated microeconometric techniques, suggests that labor supply does respond to changes in after-tax wages, certainly the female labor supply. The evidence on saving behavior is more mixed, but saving also appears to respond somewhat to changes in after-tax rates of return.[1] In any event, no one today believes that income-

[1] For an excellent review of the early empirical studies on labor supply and savings elasticities, see M. Boskin, "On Some Recent Econometric Research in Public Finance," *AEA*

based taxes and transfers are lump sum. Therefore, the assumption that the government can pursue an optimal lump-sum redistribution policy is heroic in the extreme. Nonetheless, public sector economists have been quite willing to employ the assumption of optimal lump-sum redistributions to analyze allocational policy questions in a first-best framework.

FIRST-BEST ANALYSIS

First-best analysis means that the government has a sufficient set of policy tools for whatever problems may exist to restore the economy to the bliss point on its first-best utility-possibilities frontier. By the 'first-best' utility-possibilities frontier, we mean the locus of pareto-optimal allocations constrained only by three fundamentals of any economy: individual preferences, production technologies, and market clearance.[2]

The required set of policy tools is broad indeed. If the analysis occurs within the context of a market economy, it is understood either that all markets are perfectly competitive or that the government can adjust behavior in noncompetitive markets to generate the perfectly competitive results. Faced with a breakdown in one of the technical assumptions discussed in Chapter 1, the government must be able to respond with a policy that restores first-best pareto optimality. As we shall discover in Part II, the required policy responses may be exceedingly complex, enough so that they have little hope of practical application. Finally, the government must employ optimal lump-sum redistributions to equalize social marginal utilities of consumption (income) at the first-best bliss point.

The Two Dichotomies in First-Best Models

What is the attraction of first-best analysis, given its stringent and unrealistic assumptions? The answer is that first-best analysis is really the only way to analyze the particular allocation problems caused by breakdowns in the technical assumptions and market imperfections in and of themselves. Consider, first, the role of lump-sum redistributions in this regard.

If lump-sum redistributions are feasible, then the problem of social welfare maximization dichotomizes into separate efficiency and distributional

---

Papers and Proceedings, May 1976. The Tax Reform Act of 1986 led to renewed interest in these elasticities. See A. Auerbach and J. Slemrod, "The Economic Effects of the Tax Reform Act of 1986," *Journal of Economic Literature*, June 1997.

[2] If some factors or production are supplied in absolutely fixed amounts, they, too, act as constraints on the set of attainable utility possibilities. Recall that the general equilibrium model of Chapter 2 assumes variable factor supplies so that, formally, consumers' disutility from supplying factors enters as an argument of the social welfare objective function rather than as a constraint.

problems, exactly as the model in Chapter 2 dichotomized into the pareto-optimal and interpersonal equity conditions. The intuition for why this is so can be seen in terms of concepts already developed.

Suppose one of the technical assumptions in Chapter 1 fails to hold—for example, there exists a consumer eternality, meaning that at least one person's utility depends on the goods demanded and/or factors supplied by some other consumer(s). Suppose, further, that the government consists of an allocation branch charged with designing policies to correct for allocational problems such as externalities and a distributional branch charged with creating an optimal distribution of income.[3] If lump-sum redistributions are possible, the allocation branch can ignore the existence of a social welfare function and analyze the externality in the context of the first general equilibrium model presented in Chapter 2, the model in which one consumer's utility is maximized subject to the constraints of all other utilities held constant (and production and market clearance). This model is specifically designed to find the set of pareto-optimal allocations consistent with society's first-best utility-possibilities frontier given the presence of an externality or any other imperfection. All relevant structural elements of the policy necessary to correct for the externality follow directly from the first-order conditions of this model. The allocational branch does not have to worry about social welfare. It knows that the distributional agency is simultaneously designing policies to ensure that social marginal utilities are equalized along the first-best utility-possibilities frontier in accordance with the interpersonal equity conditions. Therefore, it knows that any unwanted distributional consequences of its allocational policies are being fully offset by the distribution branch.

Suppose, instead, that a single superagency concerns itself with both the externality and the original nonoptimal income distribution and develops a full model of social welfare maximization to analyze these two problems simultaneously. Since the first-order conditions of the model dichotomize, this agency would discover one set of pareto-optimal conditions that do not involve the social welfare rankings and one set of interpersonal equity conditions that equalize all social marginal utilities of income (or of one good or factor). These conditions would be identical with those developed independently by the separate allocation and distribution branches. Since the pareto-

---

[3] Richard Musgrave, the dean of living public sector economists, long ago proposed the useful fiction of government policy emanating from three distinct branches of government, an allocation branch, a distribution branch, and a stabilization branch. The allocation branch was dedicated to pursuing efficiency, the distribution branch to pursuing equity, and the stabilization branch to pursuing long-run economic growth and the smoothing of the business cycle. One difficulty with Musgrave's fiction is the extent to which the three branches can design policies independently from one another. They can operate independently in a first-best environment, but not in a second-best environment. See R. Musgrave, *A Theory of Public Finance: A Study in Public Economy*, McGraw-Hill, New York, 1959.

optimal conditions contain no social welfare terms, they must generate the first-best utility-possibilities frontier. No other result is consistent with social welfare maximization under first-best assumptions. Similarly, the interpersonal equity conditions must be identical to those developed by the independent distribution agency. Only one distribution, in general, is consistent with the bliss point on the first-best utility possibilities frontier.

The two independent branches would have to coordinate their efforts. Since an economy is an interdependent system, all allocational decisions have distributional consequences, and vice versa. Consequently, the allocation branch cannot finally set its policies until it knows what the distributional branch has done or is about to do, and vice versa. Continuing with the externality example, suppose the externality is a "bad" such as pollution. Moreover, suppose the correct policy takes the form of a tax on the polluters (a reasonable supposition, as we shall discover in Chapter 6). By following the independent modeling process described above, the allocation branch can determine all the relevant *design* characteristics of the tax, such as what should be taxed and what parameters in the economy affect the level of the tax rates, but the exact *level* of the tax rate cannot be determined. The criterion of pareto optimality admits to an infinity of allocations, all of those on the utility-possibilities frontier. In this example, each allocation has one particular tax rate associated with it, so that the final tax rate cannot be announced until the distribution branch announces its optimal redistributional policy, thereby selecting the allocation consistent with the bliss point.

Turning the example around, the interpersonal equity conditions tell the distributional agency all the relevant *design characteristics* of the optimal lump-sum redistributions, but the exact *levels* of all individual taxes and transfers depend in part upon the gains and losses occasioned by the pollution tax. Thus, while it is possible analytically to distinguish between the design of allocational policies and the design of distributional policies, as first-best analysis does, the exact policies to be followed must be simultaneously determined. In formal terms, the pareto-optimal and interpersonal equity conditions are both necessary conditions for social welfare maximization. They must be solved simultaneously to determine a social welfare maximum.

Despite the ultimate interdependence of allocational and distributional policies, the first-best literature on public expenditure theory typically analyzes only efficiency problems inherent in the breakdown of the technical assumptions (or of market imperfections), ignoring completely the question of distributive equity. The analysis generally proceeds along the following lines. First, the pareto-optimal conditions are derived, given that one of the technical assumptions fails. Then policies are described that generate the pareto-optimal conditions, given the assumption that consumers and firms operate within a perfectly competitive market economy. Perfect competition is the only market environment consistent with first-best analysis. The assumption of perfect competition naturally leads to two further questions:

1. What allocation of resources would the competitive market generate in the absence of government intervention?
2. Can the government restore first-best pareto optimality while maintaining existing competitive markets, or is a complete government takeover of some activity absolutely necessary?

Distributional issues are ignored in the first-best literature not because they are unimportant but rather because they are relatively uninteresting. As noted in the conclusion to Chapter 2, having said that the government should redistribute lump sum to satisfy the interpersonal equity conditions necessary for social welfare maximization, there is little else to say. A breakdown in one of the technical assumptions may alter the precise form of the interpersonal conditions somewhat, but they still have the interpretation that one good (or factor) should be redistributed lump sum to equalize the social marginal utilities of that good (or factor).

In contrast, the pareto-optimal conditions often change substantially when the technical assumptions fail, both in their form *and* their interpretation. Small wonder, then, that first-best analysis tends to emphasize these conditions and often relegates the interpersonal equity conditions to a footnote, if they are mentioned at all. Knowing that the first-order conditions of a full model of social welfare maximization dichotomize, there is no need to use the full model. A simple model highlighting the first-best pareto-optimal conditions for the allocational problem at hand is sufficient.

The first-best analysis in Part II of the text is careful, however, to use full models of social welfare maximization when analyzing allocational problems. Keeping the social welfare function in the models serves to emphasize the importance of lump-sum redistributions to all first-best policy analysis.

First-best models have a second dichotomy property besides the dichotomy between the pareto-optimal and interpersonal equity conditions. The pareto-optimal conditions themselves dichotomize. A breakdown in one of the technical assumptions or a market imperfection alters the pareto-optimal conditions for those goods and factors directly affected but leaves unchanged the form of the pareto-optimal conditions of all the unaffected goods and factors. For example, suppose a competitive market satisfies the pareto-optimal condition for the allocation of some good, with price equal to marginal cost. Price equal to marginal cost continues to the be pareto-optimal pricing rule for that good even if other markets contain externalities or exhibit decreasing cost production, so long as the policy environment is first best. The government's response to the market failure can stay focused on the source of the market failure.

To summarize, the double dichotomy of distributional and allocational problems under first-best assumptions makes first-best analysis especially attractive for the *ceteris paribus* analysis of policy issues. An allocational problem associated with a particular economic activity can be isolated from distributional considerations *and* from all the other conditions within the economy that are required for pareto optimality. This property justifies the use of very simple general equilibrium models that focus exclusively on one source of market failure and describe the rest of the economy by means of a single composite commodity that is assumed to be marketed competitively. Assuming a first-best policy environment is a tremendous analytical convenience.

SECOND-BEST ANALYSIS

Suppose, realistically, that lump-sum taxes and transfers are not available to the government, at least not with sufficient flexibility to generate the interpersonal equity conditions of the standard model. This changes the analysis rather drastically. To see why, consider two government policy strategies in the context of a market economy, one designed to produce distributive equity, the other designed to restore first-best pareto optimality.

Constrained Social Welfare Maximization

Suppose that the government chooses to redistribute income until social marginal utilities are equalized by using taxes and transfers that are not lump sum.[4] The redistribution necessarily introduces distortions into the economy because some consumers and/or producers now face different prices for the same goods and/or factors. Since consumers and producers equate relative prices to their marginal rates of substitution and transformation, respectively, and since pareto optimality requires that the marginal rate of substitution (MRS) equals the marginal rate of transformation (MRT), some of the pareto-optimal conditions no longer hold. The redistribution forces the economy beneath its first-best utility-possibilities frontier.

Suppose instead that the government focuses only on allocational problems and chooses allocational policies designed to bring society to the first-best utility-possibilities frontier.[5] Without simultaneously employing lump-sum redistributions, however, the economy would not be at the bliss point, in general. The government may actually choose some policy mix designed to move the economy somewhat closer to full pareto optimality, and somewhat closer to distributive equity, but the point remains that removing the possibility of feasible lump-sum redistributions restricts the set of solutions available to the government, for example, to the shaded portion in Fig. 3.1. The viable allocations and distributions may or may not include points on the

---

[4] Assume it is possible to equalize social marginal utilities without lump-sum redistributions. It may not be, given the available policy tools.

[5] Again, assume this is possible.

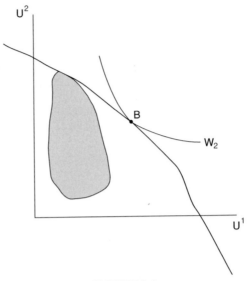

FIGURE 3.1

first-best utility-possibilities frontier, but, importantly, they definitely exclude the bliss point, point B. The policy problem now becomes one of finding the best policy option within this restricted set of opportunities. As such it is part of *second-best analysis*, defined as the analysis of optimal public sector policy given that the bliss point on the first-best utility possibilities frontier is unattainable.

One immediate implication of second-best public expenditure analysis is that government policy should not necessarily try to keep society on its first-best utility-possibility frontier. Points other than those on the first-best frontier may yield greater social welfare within the restricted set of policy alternatives. To see this, refer to Fig. 3.2.

Suppose society is initially at point A in Fig. 3.2, possibly because one of the technical assumptions of Chapter 1 has failed and the competitive market is therefore generating the wrong allocation of resources. If lump-sum redistributions were feasible and the world were otherwise first best, the government should design policies to restore full pareto optimality and redistribute lump sum to achieve the bliss point, point D in the figure. In a second-best environment, without the ability to redistribute lump sum, the policy option that brings society to point B on the first-best frontier is dominated by another option that keeps society below the frontier, point C. Society's goal is still the maximization of social welfare, reaching the highest possible social welfare indifference curve. Point C is the maximum attainable level of social welfare given the restricted set of available options. Point B is pareto

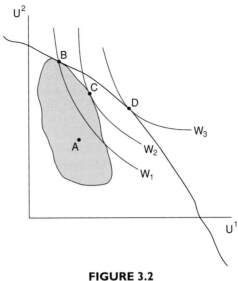

FIGURE 3.2

efficient, point C is not, but the superior distributional attributes of point C prove decisive. In a second-best environment, then, society's efficiency and equity norms are completely interrelated. They cannot be pursued with separate policy tools, unlike in a first-best policy environment.

Figure 3.2 highlights the way we defined second-best policy analysis, as the inability to attain the first-best bliss point. An equivalent definition is the analysis of optimal public sector policy given that additional constraints have been added to the first-best framework of social welfare maximization. The addition of a single binding constraint on the baseline model of Chapter 2 renders the first-best bliss point unattainable, establishing the equivalence of the two definitions of second-best analysis.

As noted above, the first-best constraints consist solely of the fundamental economic constraints of any economy: the production technologies and market clearance equations.[6] The additional constraints are typically either restrictions on the permissible set of government policy tools or maintained imperfections in the market economy. The form of the additional constraint does not matter. Any single additional binding constraint, or any combination of these constraints, renders the analysis second best.

We have been careful throughout this section to refer to the "first-best" utility-possibilities frontier, or the "first-best" bliss point. Given the existence of additional constraints, it is always possible to derive a new utility-possibilities frontier and a new bliss point corresponding to the restricted set

---

[6] And fixed factor supplies, if relevant, see footnote 2.

of feasible allocations. In terms of Fig. 3.2, these would correspond to the outer boundary of the shaded portion and point C, respectively. The government can still be thought of as pursuing the distributionally best allocation among all possible pareto-optimal allocations along the restricted frontier, exactly as in first-best analysis. Although this is technically correct, it tends to obscure the important differences between first-best and second-best analysis, differences that can best be seen in terms of the attainable first-best allocations.

The Most Common Policy and Market Constraints

The inability to redistribute lump-sum is merely one of a large number of possible constraints on the feasible set of government policy tools. It is often one of the constraints chosen, because second-best analysis is an attempt to develop normative policy rules in more realistic policy environments, and denying the government feasible lump-sum redistributions is an obvious step toward realism. Generalizing beyond this is more difficult. The second-best literature has considered an enormous variety of additional constraints on available policy tools. This is hardly surprising, since the set of potential constraints is virtually limitless, given political realities and the staggering complexity of actual market economies. It is fair to say, however, that four kinds of policy restrictions have been most commonly employed in the literature (in addition to restrictions on lump-sum redistributions): the use of distorting taxes and transfers, the existence of legislated budget constraints on individual government agencies or on the government as a whole, the drafting of resources or the offer of certain government services free of charge (or at prices below marginal cost), and asymmetric information in the form of private information about individuals that the government cannot know (at least not without bearing some costs to monitor the individual).

Distorting Taxes and Transfers

Almost no major tax or transfer programs are lump sum. Actual taxes are either *ad valorem* (percentage of price) or per-unit taxes on buyers or sellers of goods and factors, including sales and excise taxes on goods and services, income and payroll taxes on factors of production, and various kinds of wealth or property taxes. In addition, tax rates on income and wealth are often graduated, increasing with income (wealth). All these taxes force buyers and sellers to face different prices in the same markets and are thereby distorting. Most of the major transfer programs condition the transfers on consumption or income, which makes them distorting as well. Therefore, models that analyze actual distorting taxes and transfers directly or assume that distorting taxes are being used to finance public expenditures are necessarily second best. In contrast, taxes used to solve problems such as externalities in a first-best environment promote social welfare. They cannot be distorting in the sense of generating welfare costs.

Analysis of the welfare costs of distorting taxes and transfers has a long history dating back to the very beginnings of public sector economics. The discipline was named public finance until about 30 years ago because the emphasis was more on tax policy than expenditure policy. Public finance economists studied a number of issues related to the efficiency of taxes that have no meaning in a first-best environment, including: If the government must raise revenue using a single distorting tax, such as a particular sales or income tax, what are the efficiency costs to society? Are some taxes less costly (that is, less distorting) than others per dollar of revenue collected? If the government is free to vary a wide set of distorting taxes, what pattern of tax rates minimizes the resulting distortions while raising a required amount of revenue? The allocational theory of taxation has always been a second-best analysis. The main change in tax theory over the past 30 years is that general equilibrium modeling techniques have increasingly replaced partial equilibrium analysis in studying these issues. It is not that assumptions with respect to tax instruments have become more realistic.

The assumption that governments use distorting taxes to finance government expenditures has become commonplace over the past 30 years, and it has had a monumental impact on public expenditure theory. The problems being analyzed are the same as in the older first-best analysis—principally externalities and decreasing cost production—but the second-best optimal policy prescriptions are often dramatically different from their first-best counterparts.

Fixed Budget Constraints

Legislatures usually impose budgetary ceilings on individual government agencies that can be exceeded only by means of special supplemental appropriations. Frequently, the budgets of entire governments are limited as well. In the United States, for instance, many state and local government administrations are required to submit annually balanced operating budgets. Even without this requirement, most state and local governments cannot routinely borrow in the national capital markets to cover annual operating deficits without threatening their credit ratings. Only the federal government enjoys this privilege.

Imposing either agency-by-agency or overall budget constraints is generally not a first-best strategy. Only by chance would legislators set budgets at the expenditure levels consistent with a first-best allocation of resources. Thus, as a further step toward reality, public sector economists have incorporated legislated budget constraints into their models to see how they affect traditional first-best policy rules. Once again, the new second-best policy prescriptions are often quite different from their first-best counterparts.

Drafting Resources or Giving Away Goods

All scarce goods and factors have marginal opportunity costs associated with them. Their prices would reflect these marginal opportunity costs in a first-best world, but governments sometimes choose to set prices well below opportunity costs, often at zero. The military draft is one example on the factor side; citizens are required to serve and many are paid below their market wages. On the goods and services side, governments in the United States often follow an average cost pricing strategy when they do charge for public services. Sometimes they just give public services away, such as the side benefits of hydroelectric projects in the form of flood control protection to homes and irrigation of farmland. These self-imposed government pricing constraints have often been the focus of second-best analysis.

Maintained Monopoly Power

Market imperfections would render the first-best bliss point unattainable even if government policy tools were not restricted in any of the ways described above. One example is monopoly power. Price does not equal marginal cost in markets with monopoly power, so that the pareto-optimal conditions do not hold for these goods and services. Monopoly power could be viewed as a restriction on government policy in the sense that the government is unable to correct the imperfection despite the existence of policies that would do so. In any event, any maintained market imperfection such as monopoly power implies a second-best environment, and the first-best policy rules of public expenditure theory may not be optimal.

Asymmetric or Private Information

Another pervasive market imperfection is asymmetric or private information. We described in Chapter 1 the various ways in which private information leads to a call for government intervention—e.g., to establish a legal system and bureaus of standards and to provide public insurance. We also noted the difficulties it poses for the government's responses to all problems under the government-as-agent ground rules. Recall that the problem of private information is not limited to allocational issues. Private information is a decided handicap to a government interested in redistributing purchasing power in accordance with the interpersonal equity conditions of first-best theory. Redistributional policies can hardly be effective if people can hide their incomes from the government. Suffice it to add here that second-best analysis now commonly includes private information as one of the constraints that prevents government policy from attaining the first-best bliss point.

Further Implications of Second-Best Modeling

Two further distinctions between first-best and second-best modeling are worth emphasizing in these introductory comments, both resulting from the feature that second-best general equilibrium models are basically first-best models modified by the addition of one or more constraints.

The Scope of Government Intervention

As noted earlier, the first-order conditions of first-best models dichotomize in two ways that are especially convenient for *ceteris paribus* policy analysis. Second-best models typically do not dichotomize in either way. As a general rule, all the necessary first-order conditions of a second-best model contain both efficiency and equity considerations, especially if lump-sum distributions are not permitted. This is simply the formal counterpart to a point demonstrated by Fig. 3.2, that the efficiency and equity norms are directly interrelated when the first-best bliss point is unattainable.

This property of second-best models has been especially disheartening for normative analysis because it further limits the government's ability to honor the principle to consumer sovereignty. In a first-best environment, the demand (factor supply) content of all allocational decision rules derives solely from individual's preferences, usually their marginal rates of substitution. The social welfare rankings influence allocational decision rules only indirectly in the sense that any redistribution can be expected to shift aggregate demands. Thus, consumer sovereignty guides the government's intervention into the market economy when addressing allocational problems. In a second-best environment, however, the allocational decision rules contain the social welfare rankings as well as terms representing individuals preferences, so that consumer sovereignty must be partially overridden even in allocational decision making. This property of second-best analysis is doubly disturbing, since there is nowhere near a consensus on what the social welfare rankings should be. It is no longer possible to isolate the uncertainties associated with the social welfare rankings into a single decision on optimal income distribution.

Worse yet, the social welfare terms contaminate *all* markets in general, even those that first-best analysis would leave entirely in the hands of the competitive market system. This is so because a second-best policy environment generally requires broad intervention of the government into the workings of the market economy, unlike the more limited intrusion of first-best analysis. Government intervention remains justified by market failure, but the intervention is no longer limited to the markets containing the failures. Policy prescriptions that require broad government intervention are naturally resisted in capitalist societies.

The broader intrusion of the government in a second-best environment follows directly from a famous theorem published in 1956 by Archibald Lipsey and Kelvin Lancaster. They proved that if the first-best pareto-optimal conditions are assumed not to hold for some goods and factors as a maintained hypothesis, then it is generally not optimal to pursue first-best pareto optimality for the other goods and factors. Their article now stands as a classic in public sector economics, and the Lipsey–Lancaster Theorem is often referred to as *the* theorem of the second best.[7]

Lipsey and Lancaster spoke in terms of the pareto-optimal conditions because the model they used to illustrate the theorem did not contain a social welfare function. Nonetheless, their theorem applies to the broader social welfare model as well. If one of the first-order conditions for a first-best social welfare maximum fails to hold because of an added constraint to the model, then the other first-order conditions do not hold either at the constrained second-best welfare optimum, in general.

Interpreting Second-Best Results

Still another discouraging implication of second-best analysis is that second-best allocational decision rules generally do not have clear intuitive interpretations with obvious analogs to free-market principles. First-best allocational decision rules often do have competitive analogs, because they are usually just simple combinations of consumers' marginal rates of substitution and producers' marginal rates of transformation (marginal rates of technical substitution for factors). Since competitive markets equate price ratios to these margins, a competitive market structure can always be described that would generate first-best pareto-optimal conditions of this type. This result is especially appealing if one believes in competitive markets, consumer sovereignty, and the least possible amount of government interference with the market system. In first-best analysis, the government can often be viewed as an imitator of perfectly competitive behavior in solving allocational problems.

There are two formal reasons why second-best allocational decision rules tend not to have competitive market interpretations. One is that terms from the additional constraints appear in the first-order conditions along with their associated Lagrangian multipliers, and the multipliers are unrelated to standard market concepts. The other has already been noted, that the decision rules generally contain social welfare terms if lump-sum redistributions are forbidden. The social welfare terms certainly have no competitive market analogs.

Model and Policy Sensitivity

A final discouraging property of second-best optimal policy rules is that they tend to be rather sensitive to modifications in constraints or additions of new constraints. This type of model sensitivity is extremely troublesome because the real world is obviously many times more constrained, more imperfect than any analytical model can hope to capture. Second-best analysis can never hope to produce truly definitive government policy rules on anything.

---

[7] R. G. Lipsey and K. Lancaster, "The General Theory of the Second Best," *Review of Economic Studies*, December 1956.

To summarize, second-best public expenditure theory has offered the severest possible challenge to the long-standing first-best orthodoxy in the attempt to make public sector theory more realistic. The second-best rules often bear no clear-cut relationship to their long-standing first-best counterparts. These challenges notwithstanding, the first-best results of public expenditure theory have hardly disappeared. They still dominate undergraduate textbooks on public sector economics and they instruct much actual policy debate. The staying power of first-best analysis is no doubt due to the intuition it provides about allocational and distributional issues and its call for limited government intervention. In contrast, second-best policy rules tend to be resisted as normative policy prescriptions, since they contain the problematic social welfare terms, they tend to call for broad intervention in the economy, and the policy rules are so sensitive to the form and number of constraints. The relative advantages of the first-best results must always be weighed against the blatant unrealism of the first-best models in a policy context.

SIMILARITIES BETWEEN FIRST-BEST AND SECOND-BEST ANALYSIS

The numerous differences between first-best and second-best public sector analysis should not obscure the fact that the two approaches are virtually identical in method and philosophy. The challenge to first-best orthodoxy is contained in the first-order conditions of the second-best models. One would certainly not want to minimize the importance of this challenge, since the first-order conditions translate directly into normative policy rules. But second-best analysis hardly represents a methodological or philosophical departure from first-best theory. All it does is attach some additional constraints to the basic first-best neoclassical general equilibrium model in an attempt to be more realistic. This is not revolutionary. For instance, second-best analysis retains the fundamental notion that the government is interested in social welfare maximization, with social welfare indexed by means of an individualistic Bergson–Samuelson social welfare function. In principle, then, second-best analysis honors consumer sovereignty to the same degree as first-best analysis, even though its results are less clear cut in this regard. Furthermore, second-best research has generally remained closely allied with the competitive market system, so much so that the following standard competitive market assumptions are commonplace in second-best models:

1. Consumers maximize utility subject to a budget constraint and have no control over any prices.
2. Private sector producers are decentralized price-taking profit maximizers such that goods prices equal marginal costs and factor prices equal the values of marginal products.

3. If there is government production, the government buys and sells factors and outputs at the competitively determined private sector producer prices. This is often true even if the second-best decision rules imply that a different set of "shadow" prices should be used to determine the optimal level of government production.

There are two reasons why second-best analysis has emphasized competitive market behavior. The first turns on the *ceteris paribus* condition. Exploring the effects of particular market imperfections or policy restrictions on first-best public sector decision rules requires introducing them as constraints one at a time into an otherwise first-best model. If the analysis proceeds within the context of a market economy, this means that the parts of the market economy not specifically analyzed must be assumed to be competitive. As a result, second-best analysis to date has been much closer to a first-best perfectly competitive market environment than to highly imperfect real-world market economies. It is at best a small, hesitant step toward reality.

The second reason is also a matter of analytical convenience. The competitive market assumptions permit flexibility in model building, a feature that second-best analysis has frequently exploited. As noted in Chapter 2, general equilibrium models can always be defined in terms of quantities of goods and factors, with the economy viewed as being under the control of a social planner. The model developed in that chapter served as an example. General equilibrium models can also be expressed directly in terms of prices by incorporating specific assumptions about market structure and behavior, and the competitive assumptions happen to be the easiest ones to employ. For many second-best problems, the price specification has proven to be the most direct analytical approach.

To gain some preliminary intuition why this is so, consider the common second-best policy restriction that the government must use distorting taxation. As noted above, taxes distort by driving a wedge between the prices faced by different economic agents operating in the same market. If the general equilibrium model is already defined in terms of prices, the gross and net of tax prices (and the tax itself) can be incorporated directly into the model. Furthermore, all of the interesting allocational and distributional implications of the tax follow directly from the first-order conditions of the price/market model. Proceeding in this way turns out to be far more convenient than beginning with a quantity model and reworking the first-order conditions using standard market assumptions to capture the effects of the taxes.

In summary, the transition to the second-best analysis in Part III of the text from the first-best analysis in Part II is fairly easy and straightforward.

THE POLITICAL ECONOMY OF THE SOCIAL WELFARE FUNCTION

The social welfare function is central to mainstream normative public sector theory. It is the only indispensable political element of the theory and it serves two critical analytical purposes: It describes society's views on distributive justice, and it selects the one efficient allocation that maximizes social welfare from the infinity of possible efficient allocations. At the same time it is a highly problematic concept because of the limitations noted in Chapter 2. The two most serious limitations for the normative theory are the lack of a consensus on what the social welfare function should be and the difficulties that a democratic society may have in formulating a consistent social welfare function. Each of these limitations deserves some discussion.

The Form of the Social Welfare Function: From Utilitarian to Rawlsian

Neither economists nor anyone else have been able to agree on what the appropriate end-results ethical rankings of individuals should be—that is, what form the social welfare function should take. The only consensus that has emerged in the economic literature is on the reasonable limits of the ethical rankings. Most economists agree that the ethical spectrum should be bounded by utilitarianism at one end and Rawlsianism at the other end. Utilitarianism implies complete indifference to the distribution; Rawlsianism implies the greatest degree of equality.

Utiltarianism

The utilitarian view reached its height of popularity among social philosophers and political economists in the mid- to late-1800s under the leadership of Jeremy Bentham. Bentham and his followers argued that the goal of society should be to maximize aggregate happiness or satisfaction. Their view implies that social welfare is the sum of the individuals' utility functions:

$$W = \sum_{h=1}^{H} U^h \qquad (3.1)$$

where W is the utilitarian or Benthamite social welfare function. Its social welfare indifference curves for any two individuals are $45°$ straight lines as pictured in Fig. 3.3.

One appealing feature of utilitarianism is its adherence to the ethical principle of impersonality, that all people should have equal ethical weight. The ethical weights of a social welfare function are the marginal social welfare terms $\partial W/\partial U^h$, which are all equal to one under utilitarianism. Societies do not always honor the impersonality principle, however. Affirmative action

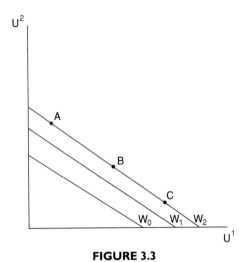

FIGURE 3.3

in the United States is a counter example, with its other-things-equal preference for women and minorities in hiring. Yet, some compelling justification usually lies behind the violations of impersonality in liberal societies, such as the unfair handicaps resulting from current and past discrimination in the case of affirmative action. Another appealing feature of utilitarianism is that it honors the pareto principle. Social welfare increases (decreases) if one person is made better off (worse off) and no other person's utility changes.

These appealing features are more than counterbalanced for most economists by utilitarianism's complete indifference to the distribution of well being. Points A, B, and C on social welfare indifference curve W_2 in the figure all yield the same amount of social welfare. Societies are never indifferent to such extremes in the distribution, and most people are not either.[8]

Rawlsianism

Rawlsianism is named after the ethical position described by Harvard philosopher John Rawls.[9] Rawls argues that people have difficulty thinking about end-results equity because they know where they stand in the distribution and have reasonably firm expectations about their future well being. The only way people can think objectively about distributive justice, according to Rawls, is to assume that they stand behind a veil of ignorance, with no idea at all about their current or future position in the distribution. In other words, people should assume they are truly uncertain about their prospects, unable

---

[8] An excellent discussion of the pros and cons on utilitarianism from both economic and philosophic perspectives is found in S. Gordon, *Welfare, Justice, and Freedom*, Columbia University Press, New York, 1980, pp. 21–37.

[9] J. Rawls, *A Theory of Justice*, Harvard University Press, Cambridge, MA, 1971.

even to attach probabilities about their possible outcomes. As such, they cannot choose to maximize expected utility, the standard assumption about consumer behavior under uncertainty.

What principles of distributive justice would people adopt in the face of true uncertainty about the distribution? Rawls believed that people would become extremely risk averse and adopt a maximin strategy. They would agree that society should always pursue policies that maximize the well being of those who are the worst off, based on the possibility that they could be among the worst off at some future date. Rawls' position implies the Min form for the social welfare function:

$$W = \min_h\left(U^1, \ldots, U^h, \ldots, U^H\right) = \min_h\left(U^h\right) \tag{3.2}$$

where W is the Rawlsian social welfare function. Its social welfare indifference curves for any two individuals are right angles from the 45° line of equality as pictured in Fig. 3.4. Movement from point A to B along W_2 in the figure does not increase social welfare because person 1 is now the worst off at point B, and that person's social welfare has not improved relative to point A. Social welfare can only increase from a position of equality if both peoples' utilities increase, because then the worst-off person becomes better off. In addition, equality is the social welfare maximum for any given aggregate level of utility because then the worst-off person has the highest possible utility.

Rawl's veil of ignorance principle when thinking about distributive justice is very appealing to many people. It is a central tenet of public choice theory. As noted in Chapter 1, Buchanan uses it as the justification for why the self-serving framers of the constitution would allow governments to redistribute

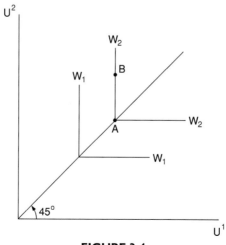

FIGURE 3.4

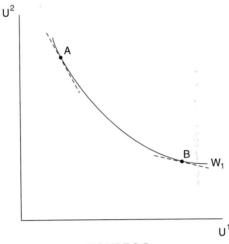

FIGURE 3.5

income. Overall, though, Rawls' position has been rejected by the majority of economists. It is highly problematic from an economic perspective.[10]

To begin with, why should people be so extremely risk adverse in the face of true uncertainty that they favor the maximin strategy? Economists have not been able to develop a consensus theory of behavior under true uncertainty, but maximin is just one of many possible strategies that people might adopt. Also, the maximin strategy has a number of unattractive features. It suggests, for example, that people would forego the possibility of a new situation that makes the worst-off individuals slightly worse off and everyone else substantially better off. A vast majority of people might be willing to accept the new situation on the chance that they would not be among the new worst off. An especially uncomfortable example of this possibility relates to long-run economic growth. Virtually all societies favor economic growth, yet saving for growth is not a maximin strategy in an intergenerational context. The first generation is always the worst-off in a growing economy, and saving for the benefit of future generations makes them even worse off. Still another severe drawback of Rawlsianism is that it does not honor the pareto principle, as the move from point A to B in Fig. 3.4 illustrates.

Most economists believe that social welfare indifference curves should have the standard property of diminishing marginal rate of substitution and be convex to the origin, as shown in Fig. 3.5. Compare points A and B. At point A, when person 2 is much the better off, society should be willing to

---

[10] See Arrow's mainstream critique of Rawlsianism in K. Arrow, "Some Ordinalist-Utilitarian Notes on Rawls' Theory of Justice," *Journal of Philosophy*, Vol. 70, 1973.

sacrifice more of person 2's utility to make person 1 one-util better off than it would be willing to sacrifice at point B, when person 1 is already much better off. The greater the curvature of the indifference curves the more egalitarian social welfare function, with the straight-line curves of utilitarianism and the right-angled curves of Ralwsians defining the reasonable extremes.

A Flexible Social Welfare Function

In theoretical work it is often unnecessary to be specific about the form of W( ). $\partial W / \partial U^h$ is simply understood to represent society's ethical judgment about the social marginal utility of person h, whatever that judgment may be. A specific parameterization of W( ) is essential, however, if one wishes to test the sensitivity of a normative policy rule to society's social welfare rankings. Many different functional forms appear in the literature, but the most common is one suggested independently by Anthony Atkinson and Martin Feldstein in the early 1970s.[11] It has the advantage of being able to represent the full range of possibilities from the utilitarian to the Rawlsian positions. Define W( ) as:

$$W[U_h( )] = \left(\sum_{h=1}^{H} U_h^V \right)^{1/V}, \quad V = [1, -\infty] \qquad (3.3)$$

where V is a constant reflecting society's aversion to inequality. $V = 1$ implies that W is the straight sum of the individuals' utilities, utilitarianism. At the other extreme, $V \rightarrow -\infty$ implies maximizing the utility of the worse-off individual, the Rawlsian maximin criterion.[12] In between the extremes,

---

[11] A. Atkinson, "How Progressive Should the Income Tax Be?," in M. Parkin (Ed.), *Essays on Modern Economics*, Longman Group, London, 1973; M. Feldstein, "On the Optimal Progressivity of the Income Tax," *Journal of Public Economics*, Vol. 2, 1973. These specifications assume the government has chosen particular cardinal representations of the U_h on which to base its social welfare judgments.

[12] To see that $V \rightarrow -\infty$ implies the Rawls maximin criterion, differentiate W with respect to some U_j:

$$\frac{\partial W}{\partial U_j} = \frac{1}{V} \cdot \left(\sum_{h=1}^{H} U_h^V \right)^{(1/V-1)} \cdot V U_j^{(V-1)} \qquad (3.3a)$$

$$\frac{\partial W}{\partial U_j} = \frac{U_j^{(V-1)}}{\left(\sum_{h=1}^{H} U_h^V \right)^{\frac{V-1}{V}}} = \left[\frac{U_j}{\left(\sum_{h=1}^{H} U_h^V \right)^{1/V}} \right]^{(V-1)} \qquad (3.3b)$$

Dividing numerator and denominator inside the brackets by U_j and rearranging terms yields:

$$\frac{\partial W}{\partial U_j} = \frac{1}{\left[\sum_{h=1}^{H} \left(\frac{U_h}{U_j} \right)^V \right]^{(1-1/V)}} \qquad (3.3c)$$

increasingly larger negative values of V imply increasing aversion to extremes in the distribution of utility.[13] The social welfare indifference curves become ever more convex to the origin. Equation (3.3) is an especially convenient flexible functional form for examining the robustness of policy rules to distributional judgments because the various possibilities are contained in the single parameter V, the aversion to inequality.

Arrow's Impossibility Theorem

The social sciences ran headlong into a brick wall in 1951 when Kenneth Arrow published his General Impossibility Theorem. There is no other way to put it. Arrow's Theorem is truly devastating to democratic societies.

Arrow was commissioned by the Department of Defense to develop a theory of how democratic societies should make decisions about public goods such as defense. He approached the problem of social decision making in the manner of cooperative game theory: Develop a minimal set of axioms to guide the social decision process that would be acceptable to a democratic society and then determine the implications of those assumptions. Arrow put forth five axioms that he thought a democratic social decision process should possess. He then proved that, in general, no social decision process can simultaneously satisfy all five axioms.

Arrow's Theorem does not imply that a democratic society cannot make social decisions. They clearly can, and do. But, it does imply that a democratic society cannot, in general, formulate consistent social decisions under a minimal set of conditions that would be acceptable to it. Arrow's Theorem applies to social decisions on any issue, including the attempt to formulate a consistent social welfare function for resolving the problem of distributive justice. All students interested in public sector economics should have at least

---

Letting $V \to -\infty$ yields:

$$\frac{\partial W}{\partial U_j} = \frac{1}{\left(\frac{U_1}{U_j}\right)^{\infty} + \ldots + \left(\frac{U_h}{U_j}\right)^{\infty} + \ldots + 1 + \ldots + \left(\frac{U_H}{U_j}\right)^{\infty}} \qquad (3.3d)$$

If U_j is selected such that $U_j < U_h, j \neq h$, all variable terms in the denominator of Eq. (3.3d) go to zero in the limit, so that

$$\frac{\partial W}{\partial U_j} = 1 \qquad (3.3e)$$

Selecting any other U_j implies that the denominator becomes large without limit. Hence,

$$\frac{\partial W}{\partial U_j} = 0, U_j \neq \min_{(h)} U_h$$

[13] By inspection of Eg. (3.3c), the value of $\partial W/\partial U_j$ increases as V becomes increasingly negative, $U_j < U_h$ for all $j \neq h$.

an intuitive understanding of Arrow's General Impossibility Theorem. It is considered by many to be *the* landmark result in twentieth-century political philosophy.

Arrow's Five Axioms

Arrow proposed the following five axioms as reasonable requirements for social decisions in a democratic society:

1. *Universality*: Individuals should be allowed to have any preferences they wish about social outcomes. Democratic societies should not be willing to impose restrictions on individuals' preferences, presuming of course that the preferences are right minded and not destructive.

2. *A complete ordering*: The social decision process must be able to provide a complete ordering of social outcomes for all possible combinations of the individuals' preferences over those outcomes, just as consumers must be able to provide a complete ordering of all possible consumption bundles. One requirement of a complete preference ordering is that it be transitive.

3. *The pareto principle*: The social decision process must honor the pareto principle: If every individual prefers social outcome X to social outcome Y, then society must prefer X to Y. (This is the strong version of the pareto principle.)

4. *The independence of irrelevant alternatives*: Suppose society prefers X to Y, and it also prefers Y to Z. Then individuals change their minds regarding Y and Z and now prefer Z to Y. The change in preference between Z and Y cannot change the preference between X and Y. Z is considered an irrelevant alternative in the choice between X and Y.

This is the least intuitive of Arrow's assumptions, but it is sensible for a democratic decision process. One huge advantage is that it conserves on information in decision-making. Without this assumption, the ranking of two alternatives may depend on the rankings of all other alternatives, which can become unwieldy for the decision-making process. Also, the assumption sharply reduces the possibilities for strategic behavior. For example, suppose ten possible outcomes are under consideration and individuals are asked to rank-order each one from one to ten. The winning outcome is the one with the highest total score. Suppose one person prefers Y first and X second but is afraid that X will win. That person has an incentive to falsely rank X last to boost Y's chances of winning. The independence assumption rules out such behavior. Suffice it to say that economists have tried to eliminate or replace this assumption without much success in improving the social decision process.

5. *Nondictatorship*: The rankings made by the social decision process cannot always be the same as the ranking of one particular person no matter what the preferences of the other people are. If this were so, the one individual is effectively a dictator.

The nature of the proof is that all five axioms cannot hold simultaneously, in general. The usual way of presenting the proof is to assume axioms one through four hold and then show that these four assumptions imply that one person is a dictator.

To gain an intuition for why one person inevitably becomes a dictator, consider a simple two-person example in which each person has preferences over three social outcomes, X, Y, and Z. There are 36 possible preference pairings over which society must make a choice. To begin, consider the ranking X P Y P Z for person 1 (first column below), paired with all six possible rankings for person 2 (second column):

$$
\begin{array}{cccccc}
XX & XX & XY & XY & XZ & XZ \\
YY & YZ & YX & YZ & YX & YY \\
ZZ & ZY & ZZ & ZX & ZY & ZX
\end{array}
$$

If the preferences are as in column 1, then society chooses X SP Y SP Z by the pareto principle—they both agree (SP means the first variable is socially preferred over the next). The first disagreement occurs in column 2, between Y and Z. Suppose society chooses in favor of person 1, so that Y SP Z when the two disagree. Having decided this one time in favor of person 1, society must favor person 1 forever after when the two disagree. The way to show this is to select pairs of preferences such that they agree on one ranking and disagree on the other two, but society has already settled one of the disagreements. The universality assumption (U) allows us to consider pairings in this manner, because every possible pair of preferences must yield a consistent social decision. Then the pareto principle (PP) and transitivity (T) settle the remaining disagreement in favor of person 1.

To see how this works, look at the fifth column. The two agree on X vs. Y, and disagree on Y vs. Z and X vs. Z. Society must decide that X SP Y because the two agree (PP). Also, from the second column, society ranks Y SP Z whenever person 1 says Y P Z and person 2 says Z P Y, as here. But, if X SP Y and Y SP Z, then by transitivity X SP Z. Therefore, society's rankings are the same as those of person 1.

Next we need to determine what happens when the two people disagree on the ranking of X and Y. Suppose that person 1 says X P Y and person 2 says Y P X. To see that person 1 prevails, select the following pairing with one agreement and two disagreements (with the preferences of person 1 in the first column, as always):

$$
\begin{array}{c}
XZ \\
ZY \\
YX
\end{array}
$$

They agree on Z and Y, so that Z SP Y (PP). Also, when person 1 says X P Z, and person 2 says Z P X, we have seen that X SP Z. Therefore, X SP Z and Z SP Y imply X SP Y (T). Person 1 wins again.

To complete the possibilities, reverse the order of the disagreements. Suppose person 1 says Z P Y and person 2 says Y P Z, the opposite of the first disagreement above which we assumed was decided in favor of person 1. This time select the pair:

Z Y
X Z
Y X

They agree on Z and X, so Z SP X (PP). Also, when person 1 says X P Y and person 2 says Y P X, we have seen that X SP Y. Therefore, Z SP X and X SP Y impliy Z SP Y (T). Person 1 wins again.

Next suppose that person 1 says Z P X and person 2 says X P Z. This time select the pair:

Z Y
Y X
X Z

They agree on Y and X, so Y SP X (PP). Also, when person 1 says Z P Y and person 2 says Y P Z, we have seen that Z SP Y. Therefore, Z SP Y and Y SP X impliy Z SP X (T). Person 1 wins again.

Finally, suppose person 1 says that Y P X and person 2 says that X P Y. This time select the pair:

Y X
Z Y
X Z

They agree on Y and Z, so that Y SP Z (PP). Also, when person 1 says Z P X and person 2 says X P Z, we have seen that Z SP X. Therefore, Y SP Z and Z SP X imply Y SP X (T). Person 1 wins again.

Person 1 wins all possible disagreements over the pairs of outcomes and is therefore is said to be decisive, a dictator, over all pairs of preferences involving X, Y, and Z. (Verify that person 1 must win the remaining pairings that we did not consider in the row of six pairings above, columns 3, 4, and 6. Also, verify that if the first disagreement above is decided in favor of person 2, then person 2 would be the dictator, using the same method of combining one ranking on which they agree and two on which they disagree). Finally, note that the independence of irrelevant alternatives has been used implicitly in the examples. When deciding on any two outcomes, the position of the third outcome within each person's rankings is irrelevant to the social decision on the two outcomes.

Next, add a new outcome to the list, say W. If person 1 is decisive over all pairs of preferences involving X, Y, and Z, then person 1 must also be decisive over all pairs of preferences involving W and X, W and Y, and W and Z. This can be shown by following the same pairings as above. To give one example, suppose person 1 says W P Y and person 2 says Y P W. Select the pair:

$$
\begin{array}{l}
\text{W Y} \\
\text{X W} \\
\text{Y X}
\end{array}
$$

They agree that W P X, so W SP X (PP). Also, when person 1 says X P Y and person 2 says Y P X, we have seen that X SP Y. (That W is now in the mix rather than Z does not matter because of the independence of irrelevant alternatives assumption). Therefore, W SP X and X SP Y imply W SP Y (T). Person 1 wins again.

The final step of our heuristic proof considers the case of more than two people. The key concept here is the notion of a decisive set. A subset of people is said to be decisive in the ranking of two outcomes (say, X and Y), if X SP Y when all members of the decisive set say X P Y and *everyone else* says Y P X. Once a decisive set is established, it can always be further subdivided into smaller decisive sets over other outcomes by suitably reselecting the preferences of the members inside and outside the original decisive set until the decisive set over all outcomes consists of a single person, the dictator.

The two person example above illustrates the ability to subdivide a decisive set down to a single person. Go back to the beginning of the example when the preferences were those in the second column of six pairings and society chose Y SP Z. Think of the two lists of preferences in the second column as belonging to two subsets of the entire population, with one subset having the preferences on the left and the other on the right. Then, the subset on the left is a decisive set regarding the choice of Y and Z when the preferences over Y and Z are in the order of the second column. Perhaps society chose Y SP Z because the members on the left were in the majority.

Once the decision Y SP Z is made, then all the other possibilities in the two-person case are decided only by application of the pareto principle, transitivity, and the independence of irrelevant alternatives. Having a numerical majority, or appealing to any other criterion besides those three axioms, is irrelevant. In other words, the social decisions would hold in each subsequent example if only one person held the winning preferences and everyone else held the opposite preferences. Therefore, once a first decisive set is determined by some method such as majority voting, then some member of the decisive set is in effect a dictator. Each comparison in the examples after the first can be interpreted as person 1 having the one set of preferences and 'person 2' representing everyone else in the society with the opposite set of preferences on the pair under disagreement. Therefore, person 1, a member of the first decisive set, is decisive over all possibilities, a dictator. The universality axiom permits this interpretation, because the social decision process must make consistent decisions for all possible combinations of the individuals' preferences.

The implication of this form of the proof is that a consistent social decision process that generates a complete ordering of social outcomes may not result from democratic voting procedures when people disagree. It may have to be imposed by some agent who is in effect a dictator.

Cycling Preferences

Democracies are not dictators. Therefore, a common variation of the Arrow Theorem is to assume that nondictatorship holds, along with axioms 1, 3, and 4, and then show that axiom 2 requiring a complete social ordering does not hold, in general. This variation implies that social decisions that are democratically determined do not yield a consistent set of social preferences over outcomes in general. In other words, democracies cannot expect to generate clear-cut decisions on social issues.

Consider the example of three people deciding about three different policies to divide $100 between them. The three people could be legislatures representing their constituencies. The three policies are A, B, and C, and they divide the $100 as follows:

	Person 1	Person 2	Person 3
A	$50	$20	$30
B	$30	$50	$20
C	$20	$30	$50

Suppose the three people vote according to their self-interests; they rank the policies in terms of the money they receive from each. Therefore, the individual rankings are

Person 1:	A P B P C
Person 2:	B P C P A
Person 3:	C P A P B

The social decision process is democratic: The majority rules. Unfortunately, majority voting on the three policies does not establish as best policy, even though each person has a clear set of preferences: Two of the three vote A P B (1 and 3), and two of the three vote B P C (1 and 2). Therefore, transitivity requires that A SP C, but two of the three vote C P A (2 and 3). The social preferences under majority voting are intransitive, and no clear winner can emerge when preferences are intransitive.

Often legislatures vote in pairs when there are more than three choices, with the winner of the first pairing going against the next choice. If this were done in our example, the winner would be determined by the order of the vote under majority voting:

A vs. B, A wins. Then A vs. C, C wins.
A vs. C, C wins. Then C vs. B, B wins.
B vs. C, B wins. Then B vs. A, A wins.

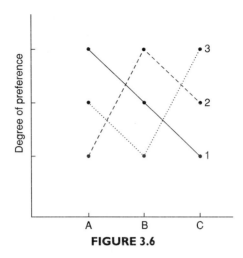

FIGURE 3.6

Again, no clear-cut winner emerges. The legislator who controls the order of the vote determines the winning policy.

The example illustrates a theorem about democratic voter procedures due to Duncan Black, a political scientist. Black proved that democratic voting establishes a consistent set of social preferences when people disagree if and only if the individuals preferences are single-peaked.[14] The problem in this example is that the preferences of person 3 are double peaked. Figure 3.6 illustrates.

An important extension of Black's theorem considers the realistic case of voting for different options that each contain a bundle of at least two services. An example would be a vote on different local budgets that contain different proportions of expenditures on education and public safety. Black's requirement of single-peakness is almost certain to be violated in this case, implying that no consistent social consensus can emerge.

The simple example on the distributional choices gets right to the heart of the problem of determining a social welfare function to resolve distributional questions in a democratic society. It suggests that no consensus social welfare function can be expected to emerge when individuals disagree about the appropriate distribution of income, as they surely do. The social welfare function that is so central to normative public sector theory may not be forthcoming in a democracy.

The Gibbard–Satterthwaite Theorem

Social decision making in democracies took a further battering in 1970 with publication of the Gibbard–Satterthwaite Theorem. Alan Gibbard

---

[14] D. Black, "On the Rationale of Group Decision Making," *Journal of Political Economy*, February 1948.

and Mark Satterthwaite proved that democratic social decisions are vulnerable to manipulation by self-serving individuals. The manipulation takes the form of lying about one's preference to achieve a more favorable social decision.[15]

Their theorem proceeds much like Arrow's. It is an exercise in cooperative game theory that focuses on the problem of choosing a single outcome based on individuals' preferences over three or more social outcomes. They posit four axioms that they believe a social decision process should possess and show that the four axioms cannot all be satisfied, in general:

1. *Universality*: The same as with Arrow; individuals can have any set of preferences over three or more outcomes.

2. *Non-degeneracy*: The social decision process cannot rule out any one outcome from being the winning outcome.

3. *Non-manipulability*: Individuals cannot manipulate the social decision in their favor by lying about their preferences.

4. *Non-dictatorship*: The same as with Arrow; the social outcome chosen cannot always be the same as the preferred outcome of one particular individual, no matter what the preferred outcomes of the other people are.

The Gibbard–Satterthwaite theorem says that these four axioms are incompatible, in general, when society is choosing among three or more outcomes. The nature of their proof can be seen by considering the two-person case above. We will not offer a complete example.

There are 36 possible pairings of the two people's preferences, and three possible social choices for each pairing (X or Y or Z), a total of 3^{36} possible choices for the social decision process to consider over the 36 pairs. Consider the first six pairings, as above:

$$
\begin{array}{cccccc}
X\,X & X\,X & X\,Y & X\,Y & X\,Z & X\,Z \\
Y\,Y & Y\,Z & Y\,X & Y\,Z & Y\,X & Y\,Y \\
Z\,Z & Z\,Y & Z\,Z & Z\,X & Z\,Y & Z\,X
\end{array}
$$

We can say the following about the social choices for each pairing based on these preferences alone:

$$ X \quad X \quad \text{not } Z \quad \text{not } Z \quad \text{not } Y \quad ? $$

The first two pairings generate X because X is the first choice of each. The next two pairings cannot lead to a choice of Z because it is clearly dominated by X and Y. In the third pairing, Z is the third choice of both; in the fourth

---

[15] A.Gibbard, "Manipulation of Voting Schemes: A General Result," *Econometrica*, Vol. 41, 1973; M. Satterthwaite, "Strategy-Proofness and Arrow's Conditions: Existence and Correspondence Theorems for Voting Procedures and Social Welfare Functions," *Journal of Economic Theory*, Vol. 10, 1975. For more detailed discussion of the Arrow and Gibbard-Satterthwaite theorems, and of social choice generally, see A. Feldman, *Welfare Economics and Social Choice Theory*, Martinus Nijhoff, Boston, 1980.

pairing, Z is the second and third choice, which is lower than the combined choices for either X or Y. By the same argument, the fifth pairing cannot lead to a choice of Y. Nothing can be said about the social choice in the last pairing.

Suppose the social choice in the third pairing is X, so that society chooses in favor of person 1. If this is so, then the axiom of non-manipulability requires that society choose X for all the pairings in the row. Person 1 is a dictator.

To see why, suppose society chooses Y for the fourth pairing, having chosen X for the third pairing. If so, then person 2 can lie about his preferences in the third pairing and represent them as Y Z X. This would make the third pairing identical to the fourth pairing, in which Y is chosen. Therefore, to prevent manipulation by person 2, society must choose X for the fourth pairing. Then, having chosen X for the fourth pairing, we now know that the last pairing cannot choose Y. If Y is not chosen in the fourth pairing when ranked second (by person 1) and first (by person 2), it will not be chosen in the last pairing when it is ranked second by both.

Next, suppose society chooses Z for the fifth or sixth pairing. If so, then person 2 can lie about his preferences in the fourth pairing and represent them as Z X Y or Z Y X. Society would then choose Z over X in the fourth pairing, which person 2 prefers. Therefore, to prevent manipulation by person 2, society must choose X for the final two pairings.

In conclusion, the social choices for each of the six pairings that prevent manipulation by person 2 are

X   X   X   X   X   X

Person 1 is a dictator. Conversely, preventing person 1 from being a dictator allows person 2 to manipulate the outcome.

The Gibbard–Satterthwaite Theorem has three troubling implications for normative public sector theory in democratic societies.

The first is its potential devastation of the government-as-agent principle. How accurate is the information that the government collects about individuals' preferences on social issues in its role as agent? How can the government know whether people are manipulating their preferences when they vote?

The second relates to the mechanism design problem of social decision theory, which attempts to design decision-making mechanisms in which people have an incentive to reveal their true preferences. Democracies would hope that people could register their preferences voluntarily through some kind of voting mechanism. The Gibbard–Satterthwaite Theorem tells us, however, that voluntary voting mechanisms can never guarantee that people will register their true preferences. Truth-revealing decision mechanisms may exist, but the theorem implies that they generally require some form of coercion by the government to implement them.

Finally, the Gibbard-Satterthwaite Theorem calls into question the entire thrust of normative public sector theory. The practical value of designing truth-revealing political mechanisms may be clear enough in light of the theorem, but the normative significance is questionable. Self-interested individuals who exploit private information to their own political ends, those who cheat on their taxes and lie to government officials, fail a fundamental test of social behavior, the test of good citizenship. What is the normative significance of having the government spend time and energy designing mechanisms to prevent people from cheating and lying? In what sense is a collection of individuals a society if they are dishonest, self-serving, and manipulative and have no stake in a broader public interest? After all, many people are good citizens, honest and concerned about the public interest. They would never even think of cheating on their taxes. Should they be given higher social welfare weights (assuming they could be identified)? What is the appropriate social objective function when good citizenship is lacking in some or all? Is pareto optimality enough?

These questions underscore the main point of this section, that the politically determined social welfare function is on very shaky ground indeed in democratic societies. At the same time, the analysis of Chapter 2 indicates that mainstream public sector theory is on very shaky ground without the social welfare function.

Reactions to the Arrow and Gibbard–Satterthwaite Theorems

Public sector economists have reacted in one of three ways to the problematic nature of the social welfare function. Two are mainstream reactions; the third is associated with the public choice school.

One mainstream reaction, commonly associated with Paul Samuelson, might be termed the technocratic response: Economists should stop worrying about the social welfare function. A social welfare will emerge from the political process by whatever means; societies do make distributional judgments. Economists should simply ask the government's policy makers what the social welfare function is and then advise them how to maximize social welfare. All policy problems are constrained optimization problems consisting of objectives, alternatives, and constraints for which the given social welfare serves as the objective function. Economists can help the policy makers fill in the remaining elements of each economic policy problem, the relevant alternatives and constraints, and then describe how to solve the problem. Economists know how to solve constrained optimization problems.

A second mainstream reaction sees a more instructive role for the social welfare function. It calls for the use of flexible-form social welfare functions in normative policy exercises that allow for the full range of ethical rankings, from utilitarian to Rawlsian. The purpose of this type of analysis is to show policy makers how different ethical rankings influence optimal policy rules. This approach is not contradictory with the first approach, since the flexible social welfare function could include the government's actual social welfare function as one of the options.

Joseph Stiglitz dubbed the application of flexible form social welfare functions the "New, New Welfare Economics," because he viewed it as a direct reaction to the so-called "New Welfare Economics" of the 1930s and 1940s.[16] The older 'New Welfare Economics' held that interpersonal comparisons of utility are meaningless. Economists can say nothing about situations in which some people gain and others lose, because there is no meaningful way to compare the increased utility of the gainers with the decreased utility of the losers. This older view rules out a social welfare function defined in terms of individuals' utilities and along with it any hope of an economic solution to the quest for distributive justice.

The balancing of gains and losses through redistributions is the central economic issue in achieving distributive justice. The newer breed of economists who subscribe to the "New, New Welfare Economics" want to say something about distributive justice, and in doing so they completely reject the older view. To make the flexible-form approach operational in applied work, the researcher must specify a particular social welfare function and particular utility functions to serve as arguments in the social welfare function. Once the particular functions are specified, utility becomes cardinal and fully comparable across individuals, in direct opposition to the older view.[17]

The third reaction to the problems associated with the social welfare function, commonly associated with the public choice economists, is essentially one of indifference. Public choice economists do not care that the social welfare function is problematic because they do not accept it as a valid concept. They deny that citizens enter the political process to help resolve the public interest in distributive justice. Instead, they argue that a society's distributional policies must be understood as evolving from the desires of self-serving individuals who want to maximize their own utilities. People do not spend their political energies trying to formulate social welfare functions. There is no social welfare function, and no need for one in public sector theory.

CONCLUSION

The discussions in Chapter 3 on the distinction between first-best and second-best analysis and on the problems with the social welfare function conclude

---

[16] J. Stiglitz, "Pareto Efficient and Optimal Taxation and the New New Welfare Economics," in A. Auerbach and M. Feldstein (Eds.), *Handbook of Public Economics*, Vol. 2, North-Holland, New York, 1985, chap. 15, pp. 991–993.

[17] Robin Boadway and David Wildasin have an excellent discussion of restrictions on the social welfare function that make utilities comparable for policy analysis in R. Boadway and D. Wildasin, *Public Sector Economics*, second ed., Little, Brown and Co., Boston, 1984, chap. 10, pp. 269–277.

our introduction to public sector theory. The thrust of the chapter has been appropriately cautionary, a warning that the foundations underlying normative public sector theory are less firm than one would like. The chapter contains three main messages:

1. First-best analysis yields definite policy prescriptions for solving society's allocational and distributional problems but only by adopting patently unrealistic assumptions. The main advantage of first-best analysis is the intuition it gives about the nature of the problems.

2. Second-best analysis adds a dose of realism to public sector analysis by explicitly addressing the policy and market constraints under which governments operate. But second-best analysis can never yield definitive policy prescriptions because a second-best model can incorporate only a few of the underlying constraints. Unfortunately, the results from second-best models tend to be highly sensitive to the number and form of the constraints that the analyst chooses.

3. The social welfare function is a central construct in mainstream public sector theory and the theory's only indispensable political content. It has the dual analytical tasks of resolving the question of distributive justice and selecting the one efficient allocation that maximizes social welfare from the infinity of possible efficient allocations. Yet, the social welfare function is highly problematic. Particularly troublesome are the lack of guidelines about what society's ethical judgments should be, the problem that a consistent social welfare function may not emerge under conditions that would be acceptable to a democratic society, and that democratic decision processes are susceptible to manipulation by self-serving people in the form of lying to bias outcomes in their favor. These three messages apply to all of normative economics.

A fair short summary of the state of mainstream normative public sector economics would be as follows. Virtually all mainstream normative public sector analysis relies on variations of one model, Samuelson's model of social welfare maximization. But the consensus on the underlying model has not yielded a consensus set of optimal policy prescriptions for the allocation and distribution problems that are the legitimate concerns of the government. The lack of a policy consensus stems from the inherent limitations of first-best analysis, second-best analysis, and the social welfare function discussed in Chapter 3. These limitations notwithstanding, normative public sector economics does offer important insights into all the complex allocation and distribution problems that governments have been asked to solve.

Chapters 4 through 11 in Part II turn to the first-best theory of public expenditures and taxation, in which the government is assumed to have all the necessary policy tools to reach the bliss point on the first-best utility-possibilities frontier. The first-best analysis is the core of normative public sector theory. It yields the baseline "best possible" results of public sector economics, against which the more realistic second-best results are always compared.

REFERENCES

Arrow, K., "Some Ordinalist-Utilitarian Notes on Rawls' Theory of Justice," *Journal of Philosophy*, Vol. 70, 1973.

Atkinson, A., "How Progressive Should the Income Tax Be?," in M. Parkin (Ed.), *Essays on Modern Economics*, Longman Group Ltd., London, 1973.

Auerbach, A. and Slemrod, J., "The Economic Effects of the Tax Reform Act of 1986," *Journal of Economic Literature*, June 1997.

Black, D., "On the Rationale of Group Decision Making," *Journal of Political Economy*, February 1948.

Boadway, R. and Wildasin, D., *Public Sector Economics*, second ed., Little, Brown and Company, Boston, 1984.

Boskin, M., "On Some Recent Econometric Research in Public Finance," *AEA Papers and Proceedings*, May 1976.

Feldman, A., *Welfare Economics and Social Choice Theory*, Martinus Nijhoff, Boston, 1980.

Feldstein, M., "On the Optimal Progressivity of the Income Tax," *Journal of Public Economics*, Vol. 2, 1973.

Gibbard, A., "Manipulation of Voting Schemes: A General Result," *Econometrica*, Vol. 41, 1973.

Gordon, S., *Welfare, Justice and Freedom*, Columbia University Press, New York, 1980.

Lancaster, K. and Lipsey, R. G., "The General Theory of the Second Best," *Review of Economic Studies*, December 1956.

Musgrave, R., *A Theory of Public Finance: A Study in Public Economy*, McGraw-Hill, New York, 1959.

Rawls, J., *A Theory of Justice*, Harvard University Press, Cambridge, MA, 1971.

Satterthwaite, M., "Strategy-Proofness and Arrow's Conditions: Existence and Correspondence Theorems for Voting Procedures and Social Welfare Functions," *Journal of Economic Theory*, Vol. 10, 1975.

Stiglitz, J., "Pareto Efficient and Optimal Taxation and the New New Welfare Economics," in A. Auerbach and M. Feldstein (Eds.), *Handbook of Public Economics*, Vol. 2 North–Holland, New York, 1985, chap. 15.

THE THEORY OF PUBLIC EXPENDITURES AND TAXATION— FIRST-BEST ANALYSIS

Part II presents the first-best analysis of public expenditure and tax theory in the context of a market economy. Recall from the discussion in Chapter 3 that a first-best policy environment exists if the market economy is perfectly competitive and the government can use whatever policy tools are necessary to achieve full pareto optimality and the interpersonal equity conditions of a social welfare maximum. In other words, the government can bring the economy to the bliss point on its first-best utility-possibilities frontier.

The first-best policy environment may seem unduly restrictive, but first-best analysis is the appropriate way to begin the study of the public sector. It serves as the baseline for all public sector analysis by indicating the maximum possible increase in social welfare that public policies can achieve. The social welfare implications of second-best policy prescriptions are almost always compared with their first-best counterparts. In addition, the single set of first-best assumptions permits an exploration of the essence of a technical market failure such as an externality, along with the policy required to correct it. All formal first-best analysis uses variations of the general equilibrium model of social welfare maximization developed in Chapter 2, suitably modified to highlight the problem under consideration. In contrast, the restrictions added to the basic model to make the policy second best contaminate the analysis of the market failure and its solutions, with additional factors that have to do with the second-best restrictions. Finally, first-best analysis figures prominently in the history of the discipline and in much of the conventional wisdom on government policy. Virtually all public expenditure analysis before 1970 employed the first-best assumptions, as did much of the huge body of literature concerned with issues of equity in the theory of taxation. Second-best analysis in these two areas has been commonplace since then, but much of the received doctrine on public expenditures and income distribution that appears in the current undergraduate public sector texts comes from first-best analysis. Only the allocational theory of taxation has consistently employed second-best assumptions from the very beginning of public sector economics, simply because the welfare cost of taxation is inherently a second-best topic. As we shall discover in Part II, all interesting first-best efficiency issues relating to taxation are effectively subsumed within the optimal public expenditure decision rules.

The eight chapters in Part II are structured as follows.

Chapter 4 begins with the distribution question, one of the fundamental market failures requiring social decisions. The chapter describes how economists use the social welfare function in applied research to determine the effects of inequality and social mobility on social welfare. Examples are drawn from the U.S. economy.

Chapters 5–9 then turn to the two most important allocational market failures in a first-best environment: externalities and decreasing cost production. Chapters 5–8 consider the theory of externalities, with applications to U.S. policy, and Chapter 9 presents the theory of decreasing cost production, also with U.S. policy applications.

Chapters 10 and 11 conclude Part II with a discussion of taxes and transfers from a first-best perspective. Chapter 10 briefly reviews the first-best optimal tax and transfer rules developed to that point, stressing their limitations as guidelines for actual tax policy. The rest of the chapter is devoted to the theory of pareto-optimal redistribution, which derives normative rules for optimal redistribution without resorting to a social welfare function. Pareto optimal redistribution is the normative distribution theory favored by public choice economists, who reject the concept of a social welfare function. Chapter 11 introduces still another distributional norm, the ability-to-pay principle of taxation and transfer, which dates to Adam Smith and John Stuart Mill. The ability-to-pay principle has always been the primary guideline for tax design and tax reform in the United States and other developed market economies. The chapter begins by comparing the policy implications of the ability-to-pay principles and the interpersonal equity conditions of social welfare maximization. It then presents two applications of the ability-to-pay principle that have been featured in the public sector literature. One is how closely the U.S. federal personal income tax adheres to the principle. The other is whether the ability-to-pay principle favors the taxation of income or consumption. The chapter concludes with two practical issues relating to the taxation of income from capital under an income tax, how to adjust for inflation, and the appropriate taxation of capital gains.

4

THE SOCIAL WELFARE FUNCTION IN POLICY ANALYSIS

One of the more difficult economic questions every society must is the fundamental question of distributive justice: What is the optimal distribution of income? The question cannot be avoided. It must be answered even if the economy performs as well as it possibly can and presents no other economic problems. Moreover the answer must come through the political process, not the market system.

Chapter 2 really began the analysis of public sector economics when it presented the answer to the distribution question given by the mainstream normative public sector model in a first-best policy environment: The government should redistribute any one good or factor lump-sum to satisfy the interpersonal equity conditions of an individualistic social welfare function. For some good (factor) X_k, and H individuals, redistribute such that the social marginal utilities of X are equal for all individuals, or

$$\frac{\partial W}{\partial U^h} \frac{\partial U^h}{\partial Y_{hk}} \qquad h = 1, \ldots, H \qquad (4.1)$$

The interpersonal equity conditions are necessary conditions for a first-best social welfare maximum, along with the pareto optimal conditions. They are the entirety of first-best distribution theory in the mainstream model.

Chapter 4 begins Part II on first-best public sector theory with some common applications of the social welfare function in policy analysis. The applications are in the spirit of the "New, New Welfare Economics," which employs flexible-form social welfare functions to show how ethical judgments ranging from utilitarian to Rawlsian can instruct public policy. Also, because the analysis is first-best, the applications generally focus on the question of distributive justice without worrying about the inefficiencies that actual redistributions of income give rise to. In other words, they assume that the pareto optimal conditions are satisfied, unless specifically stated otherwise.

SOCIAL WELFARE AND THE DISTRIBUTION OF INCOME: THE ATKINSON FRAMEWORK

England's Anthony B. Atkinson was a pioneer of the "New, New Welfare Economics" in the early 1970s. He became interested in the possibility of making social welfare judgments based on the personal income data that England and other developed capitalist countries were collecting from surveys of the population. The U.S. survey is the annual Current Population Survey (CPS), which began in 1947. The CPS surveys approximately 60,000 families and unrelated individuals and is the principal source of the federal government's published statistics on personal income, poverty, and other personal characteristics such as family size and education.

Atkinson's desire to meld social welfare and the income data led him to specify the social welfare function in terms of income. Write each individual's (family's) utility as a function only of income, Y_h, and the social welfare function as:

$$W = W(U^h(Y_h)) \qquad (4.2)$$

The relevant margin for the interpersonal equity conditions is the social marginal utility of income, $\frac{\partial W}{\partial U^h} \frac{\partial U^h}{\partial Y_h}$; the product of the marginal social welfare weight, $\frac{\partial W}{\partial U^h}$; and the private marginal utility of income, $\frac{\partial U^h}{\partial Y_h}$.

The Atkinson Assumptions

Atkinson sought a very simple specification of W, one that could easily be applied to the income data and yet would capture the full range of ethical judgments from utilitarian to Rawlsian. He achieved this with three highly simplified and heroic assumptions: (1) the social welfare function is utilitarian, (2) everyone has identical tastes, and (3) utility exhibits diminishing private marginal utility of income. Atkinson's assumptions were widely adopted in applied social welfare analysis. The assumptions deserve some comment by way of justification simply because they are so strong.

Utilitarian Social Welfare

Atkinson assumed that social welfare should honor the impersonality principle, discussed in Chapter 3. The simplest way to incorporate the principle is to assume that social welfare is utilitarian, with the marginal social welfare weights always equal to one:

$$W = \sum_{h=1}^{H} U^h; \quad \frac{\partial W}{\partial U^h} = 1$$

Other researchers have chosen a less restrictive interpretation of the principle: Individuals with equal utilities should have the same social welfare weights. This variation permits flexible social welfare functions; nonetheless, it retains the strong results that follow from Atkinson's three assumptions. The impersonality principle is especially compelling in a first-best environment. Such practices as discrimination, which are used to justify affirmative action policies, do not arise in a first-best environment.

Same Preferences

This assumption is clearly false, but it can be justified in a modeling context in one of three ways. The first is to view it simply as an assumption by default. If we assume that preferences differ, how should the differences be modeled? No obvious answer comes to mind and, therefore, nothing more really need be said. Still, the assumption can be somewhat justified on other grounds.

A second possible justification is that differences in preferences should not have any influence on policy decisions (so long as tastes are not destructive). Most people would argue that policy decisions should be based on differences in peoples' circumstances rather than differences in their tastes, especially policies related to the distribution question. How much income people have is what matters, not what they choose to buy with their incomes.

A final possible justification is that people's preferences may well be quite similar if viewed from a lifetime perspective. Differences in preferences may be largely determined by different positions in the life-cycle, holding circumstances constant. Single 20-year olds have different preferences from married 50-year olds. But the 50-year-old father may have had much the same tastes as his 20-year-old son when he was 20, and the 20-year-old daughter may have much the same tastes as her 50-year-old mother when she is 50 and a mother.

Whether these last two justifications are convincing is almost beside the point. The assumption of identical tastes remains the only plausible default assumption for modeling purposes.

Diminishing Marginal Utility of Income

The assumption of diminishing marginal utility is difficult for economists to accept because diminishing marginal utility of income is neither a necessary nor a sufficient condition for any result in standard consumer theory. The best case for it is the demand for insurance under expected utility maximization, which assumes invariance only up to linear transformations of the utility function. People who are risk averse act as if they have diminishing marginal utility of income when they pay insurance premiums to avoid exposure to risky future income streams. For example, suppose people face a 50% chance of becoming ill and losing $1000 as a result. The expected loss is $500, yet most people would be willing to pay a premium greater than $500 to insure against the possibility of the $1000 loss. This implies that their utility gain from a $500 increase in income is less than the utility loss from a $500 loss in income; the marginal utility of income is decreasing.

The insurance example refers to a single individual, however. In a social welfare context, the utility comparison is being made across individuals. The equal tastes assumption combined with diminishing marginal utility of income implies that the utility loss to the "rich" of taking $1 from them is less than the utility gain to the "poor" of giving them the $1. The notion that the marginal utility of income to the rich is less than the marginal utility of income to the poor is undoubtedly appealing to many people, especially at the extremes of income. It may even be the primary reason why the majority of people in the United States accept some redistribution of income to help the poor. But this was precisely the kind of interpersonal comparison of utility that the New Welfare Economics rejected as meaningless in the 1930s. The New, New Welfare Economics resurrected the notion of diminishing marginal utility across individuals which had been widely accepted by political economists at the end of the 19th century.

The Bias Toward Equality

Atkinson's three assumptions together imply a very strong result in a first-best environment, the complete equality of incomes. The optimal policy rule from the interpersonal equity conditions is to tax and transfer lump sum to equalize the social marginal utilities of income. With the utilitarian social welfare function, however, the social marginal utilities of income are the private marginal utilities of income:

$$\frac{\partial W}{\partial U^h}\frac{\partial U^h}{\partial Y_h} = \frac{\partial U^h}{\partial Y_h} \tag{4.3}$$

with $\dfrac{\partial W}{\partial U^h} = 1$ for all h. Therefore, the interpersonal equity conditions imply equalizing the private marginal utilities of income:

IE conditions (under Utilitarianism) : $\dfrac{\partial U^h}{\partial Y_h} =$ all h = 1, ..., H

But assumptions 2 and 3 imply that everyone transfers income into utility by means of the same concave function. Therefore, the private marginal utilities of income are equal if and only if everyone has the same income, the mean level of income. The government should lump-sum tax everyone above the mean down to the mean, and lump-sum transfer everyone below the mean up to the mean.

Figure 4.1 illustrates. Everyone transforms income into utility according the function U(Y); the slope of U(Y) is the private marginal utility of income. Suppose there are initially two classes of people, the "rich" with incomes of Y_R above the mean and the "poor" with incomes of Y_P below the mean. The $MU_{Y_R} < MU_{Y_P}$, so that aggregate utility can be increased by taxing the rich and transferring to the poor. The inequality continues to hold, and aggregate utility can be further increased, until each has reached the mean. At that point the marginal utilities are equal, the interpersonal equity conditions are satisfied, and aggregate utility is at a maximum.

Very few people would support the complete leveling of incomes, yet this result is commonplace in public sector modeling. Almost all mainstream public sector models of social welfare reach the conclusion that if redistribution is costless (i.e., lump-sum), then incomes should be equalized after tax and transfer to maximize social welfare. The underlying reason for this

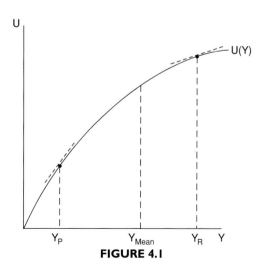

FIGURE 4.1

result is that Atkinson's assumptions, heroic as they may be, have been widely accepted by public sector economists, especially the assumptions of identical preferences and diminishing marginal utility. As noted above, models do often use nonutilitarian social welfare functions with varying social welfare weights. But if the social welfare function honors the impersonality principle by giving equal social marginal welfare weights to those with equal utility levels and the other two assumptions are maintained, then the equal-incomes implication of the interpersonal equity conditions obtains with lump-sum redistributions.

In other words, Thurow's contention that there is a strong bias toward equality in the United States, noted in Chapter 1, has been incorporated into mainstream public sector theory. Thurow also maintains that the bias is so strong that inequality has to be justified. The standard justification for inequality among economists is that redistribution is not costless. Government's are forced to use distorting taxes and transfers to redistribute income, not lump-sum taxes and transfer, so that redistribution causes efficiency losses. At some point short of equality, the additional efficiency losses of further redistribution more than offset the equity gains, and redistribution should stop.

Okun's Leaky Bucket

Arthur Okun described the redistributions as if occurring with a leaky bucket, an image of the efficiency losses that has stuck in the literature.[1] He imagined the rich dropping their tax dollars in a bucket, which a government official then carries to the poor. The bucket leaks, however, so that the poor receive fewer dollars than the rich had placed in the bucket. The leaks take three forms: the administrative costs to the government of taxing and transferring; the costs to the taxpayers and transfer recipients of complying with the laws, such as filing tax returns and applying for public assistance; and the dead-weight efficiency losses in the marketplace as the tax and transfer programs cause buyers and sellers to face different prices for the same goods and factors.

The rich–poor example illustrates the effect of Okun's leaky bucket on the optimal amount of redistribution. With lump-sum taxes and transfers (no leaks), the redistribution continues until:

$$MU_{Y_R} = MU_{Y_P} \tag{4.4}$$

which is full equality. In terms of the effect of the redistribution on social welfare, think of the MU_{Y_R} as the marginal cost and the MU_{Y_P} as the marginal benefit. The redistribution continues until the marginal cost and

---

[1] A. Okun, *Equality and Efficiency, The Big Tradeoff*, The Brookings Institution, Washington, D.C., 1975, pp. 91–100.

marginal benefit are equal, the standard result. Okun's leaky bucket intro-duces an additional marginal cost from the three sources noted above, so that the full marginal cost of redistributing is the sum of the marginal costs borne by the rich plus the leaky bucket. Therefore, with distorting taxes and transfers (a leaky bucket), the redistribution continues until:

$$MU_{Y_R} + MC_{LB} = MU_{Y_P} \qquad (4.5)$$

where MC_{LB} is the marginal cost of the leaky bucket. Since $MU_{Y_R} < MU_{Y_P}$ at the optimum, $Y_R > Y_P$. Referring again to Fig. 4.1, the initial situation pictured there could be the final equilibrium with distorting taxes and trans-fers. In Thurow's terms, the marginal costs of Okun's leaky bucket justify the remaining inequality.

The Atkinson Social Welfare Function

To obtain more specific results than simply equality vs. inequality requires specifying a particular utility function. Atkinson chose the following utility function:

$$U^h = \frac{1}{(1-e)} Y_h^{(1-e)} \qquad e = [0, \infty] \qquad (4.6)$$

where e is a measure of society's aversion to inequality.[2] The utilitarian social welfare function, W, under the assumption of equal tastes for all H individ-uals, is

$$W = \sum_{h=1}^{H} U^h = \sum_{h=1}^{H} \frac{1}{(1-e)} Y_h^{(1-e)} \qquad (4.7)$$

Atkinson chose this utility function because it is especially easy to apply in social welfare analysis. It has the following useful properties.

The Private Marginal Utilities of Income

The private marginal utilities of income, which are relevant to the inter-personal equity conditions, are simple functions of income and society's aversion to inequality:

$$\frac{\partial U^h}{\partial Y_h} = MU_{Y_h} = \frac{1}{Y_h^e} \qquad (4.8)$$

---

[2] This utility function is commonly employed in the theory of risk taking because it exhibits constant relative risk aversion, meaning that the elasiticty of marginal utility with respect to income is constant. The reader can verify that the elasticity equals $-e$ for Atkinson's utility function. See A. Atkinson, *The Economics of Inequality*, second ed., Oxford University Press, New York, 1983, sect. 3.4, pp. 53–59.

Marginal utility decreases with increases in Y, as required. Also, the ratio of the marginal utilities for any two people is a simple ratio of their incomes. Returning to the rich/poor example,

$$\frac{MU_{Y_P}}{MU_{Y_R}} = \left(\frac{Y_R}{Y_P}\right)^e \qquad (4.9)$$

Therefore, the social welfare implications of any small redistribution of income are easily determined.

Society's Aversion to Inequality

Society's aversion to inequality applies directly to individual incomes in Atkinson's specification rather than to the marginal social welfare weights, which are all equal to unity. The limits of the aversion-to-inequality parameter e are the utilitarian and the Rawlsian cases. To see this refer to the ratios of marginal utility above.

If $e = 0$, then $U^h = Y_h$ and $W = \sum_{h=1}^{H} Y_h$. Social welfare is utilitarian in income. All marginal utilities are equal to unity so that redistributing cannot raise social welfare, no matter how large the difference between Y_R and Y_P. Society is indifferent to the distribution of income.

If $e = \infty$, the ratio of marginal utilities is infinite and would be no matter what the discrepancy in income is between the rich and the poor. Because the marginal utility of the poorer of two people receives a relatively infinite weight, the poorest member of society receives an infinitely greater weight than anyone else. In effect, then,

$W = \min(Y_1, \ldots, Y_h, \ldots, Y_H)$. Social welfare is Rawlsian in incomes; society is as egalitarian as possible.

Finally, increases in e between 0 and ∞ increase the ratio of marginal utilities for any given difference in incomes Y_R and Y_P. Society's aversion to inequality increases as e increases.

Okun's Leaky Bucket Again

Atkinson's social welfare function can be applied to the CPS data on income to make social welfare inferences about the distribution of income in the United States. One of the more interesting early applications of Atkinson's framework was due to Arnold Harberger. He combined Atkinson's social welfare function with Okun's leaky bucket to argue that the United States does not care very much about inequality.[3]

At the time Harberger wrote, the average income of those in the top 10% of the income distribution was nine times greater than the average income of

---

[3] A. Harberger, "Basic Needs Versus Distributional Weights in Social Cost-Benefit Analysis," in R. Haveman and J. Margolis (Eds.), *Public Expenditure and Policy Analysis*, third ed., Houghton Mifflin, Boston, 1983, pp. 107–110.

those in the bottom 10%. Designating the average income of those at the top Y_R and the average income of those at the bottom Y_P,

$$\frac{Y_R}{Y_P} = \frac{9}{1} \tag{4.10}$$

Suppose, said Harberger, that the aversion to inequality parameter e were equal to 1/2, fairly close to the utilitarian indifference to inequality (e = 0). Then,

$$\frac{MU_{Y_P}}{MU_{Y_R}} = \left(\frac{Y_R}{Y_P}\right)^{\frac{1}{2}} = \left(\frac{9}{1}\right)^{\frac{1}{2}} = \frac{3}{1} \tag{4.11}$$

With e = 1/2, society believes that $MU_{Y_P} = 3MU_{Y_R}$. In other words, society believes that an additional dollar of income is worth three times as much to the poorest people than to the richest people, yet it stops redistributing at a point which the disparity in incomes between the richest and poorest is very large, 9 to 1. Suppose inequality is justified by the inefficiencies of redistributing as mainstream economists believe. Then these numbers imply that Okun's bucket has a huge leak, 67 cents on the dollar. Society permits a 9-to-1 income disparity because it believes that only 1/3 of each additional dollar taken from the top income group in taxes would reach the bottom income group in transfers.

Harberger thought a leak of 67 cents on the dollar was absurdly large. At the time, the best estimates of the marginal dead weight loss from income taxes were on the order of 10 cents on the dollar, and everyone assumed that the administrative and compliance costs of income taxes were negligible. Therefore, Harberger concluded that the aversion-to-inequality parameter in the United States must be quite a bit less than 1/2 to justify such a large disparity in the richest and poorest incomes; that is, e is very close to zero. The United States does not care very much about inequality.

Harberger may not be correct. Estimates of the marginal costs of redistributing have been steadily increasing since he wrote. Estimates of the marginal dead weight loss from income taxes are now all over the map, but the average estimate in the literature is probably on the order of 30 to 40 cents on the dollar, with the high-end estimates at $1 or more. Also, economists are finding that the compliance costs of income taxes may be fairly substantial, perhaps as much as 10 cents per dollar of revenue collected. The point is that an estimate of a leak in Okun's bucket of 67 cents on the dollar, or even more, would not be considered outlandish today. Had Harberger known of these higher estimates, he might have concluded that the appropriate aversion to inequality parameter for the United States was 1/2, or even higher. At the same time, the disparity in incomes among the richest and poorest groups has also been steadily increasing; it now exceeds 13 to 1. The increasing inequality would tend to lower the estimate of e for the United States. Whatever the true value for e may be, Harberger's calculations illustrate that the Atkinson

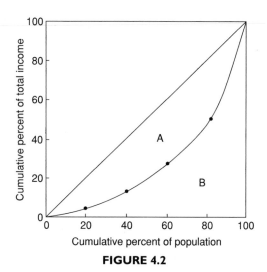

FIGURE 4.2

social welfare framework offers a very convenient first-pass means of think-ing about the equity-efficiency trade off in redistributing income.[4]

Social Welfare Indexes of Inequality

Atkinson was particularly interested in the social welfare implications of inequality. His approach was to incorporate the social parameter e, the aver-sion to inequality, directly into an index of income inequality. He was widely followed in this and spawned a huge new literature on inequality measurement.

The most popular way of presenting data on the distribution of income has always been the Lorenz curve and its associated Gini coefficient. The Lorenz curve compares the cumulative percent of the total income with the cumulative percent of the total population, when individuals (or families) are ordered from lowest to highest income (Fig. 4.2). The Lorenz curve is typically drawn inside a square. The bottom of the square, the horizontal axis, records the cumulative percent of the total population; the sides of the square, the vertical axes, record the cumulative percent of the total income earned by each cumulative percent of the population.

Every Lorenz curve must begin in the lower left-hand corner (0% of the population earns 0% of the total income) and end at the top right-hand corner (100% of the population earns 100% of the total income). The diagonal of the

---

[4] A recent test of students to determine their aversion to inequality found that it was very low, around .25, much as Harberger had surmised. See Y. Amiel, J. Creedy, and S. Hurn, "Measuring Attitudes Towards Inequality," *Scandinavian Journal of Economics*, Vol. 101, No. 1, pp. 83–96, 1999.

square is the line of perfect equality; each x% of the population earns x% of the total income. Actual Lorenz curves lie below the diagonal because incomes are unequally distributed. The further below the diagonal the Lorenz curve lies, the more unequal the distribution of income.

The distribution on income by quintiles for U.S. families and households in 1998 is presented in Table 4.1, and the Lorenz curve in Fig. 4.2 represents the household data.

The Gini coefficient is the ratio of the area A between the Lorenz curve and the diagonal to the entire area under the diagonal, A + B:

$$\text{Gini} = \frac{A}{(A + B)} \tag{4.12}$$

Its values lie between 0 (A = 0, perfect equality) and 1 (B = 0, perfect inequality in the sense that one person has all the income).

Atkinson used his social welfare framework to think about the following problem. Consider two different distributions of income that have the same means:

$$Y^A = (Y_1^A, \ldots, Y_h^A, \ldots, Y_H^A) \text{ and } Y^B = (Y_1^B, \ldots, Y_h^B, \ldots, Y_H^B)$$

Let W^A be the social welfare associated with Y^A, and W^B be the social welfare associated with distribution Y^B. Assume, as above, identical tastes and diminishing private marginal utility of income (that is, social welfare cannot be utilitarian in income). Can anything of a general nature be said about W^A versus W^B?

The answer is yes, under certain conditions. Atkinson proved, in the case of equal means, that $W^B > W^A$ for all values of e $\neq$ 0 if and only if the Lorenz curve for distribution Y^B lies everywhere inside the Lorenz curve for

TABLE 4.1 Personal Distribution of Income in the United States: Families and Households, 1998

	Quintile				
	Bottom 20%	2nd 20%	3rd 20%	4th 20%	Top 20%
Percentage of total income for families	4.2	9.9	15.7	23.0	47.2
Percentage of total income for households	3.6	9.0	15.0	23.2	49.2

Source: U.S. Census Bureau, Current Population Reports, Series P60–206, *Money Income in the United States: 1998*, U.S. Government Printing Office, Washington, D.C., 1999, Table C and Historical Tables, Table F.

distributionY^A.[5] Y^B is said to Lorenz dominate Y^A. The intuition is that under Lorenz dominance the more equal distribution can be obtained from the less equal distribution by a top–down redistribution from those with higher income to those with lower income. Such a top–down redistribution must increase individualistic social welfare under diminishing marginal utility of income, because the utility gains of those with lower income exceed the utility losses of those with higher incomes per dollar of income transferred. Atkinson's theorem was the first direct link between social welfare and the Lorenz curve representation of inequality.

Atkinson's theorem has limited applicability for two reasons. One is that two distributions often have different mean incomes and the other is that the two Lorenz curves may cross.

Generalized Lorenz Dominance

Tony Shorrocks extended Atkinson's theorem to distributions with different mean incomes by defining a "generalized" mean-augmented Lorenz curve of the following form.[6] Represent the standard Lorenz curve for the $100p\%$ poorest individuals as:

$$L(p) = [Y(1) + \ldots + Y(j)]/H\mu \tag{4.13}$$

where H is the total population; $j = 1, \ldots, H$; $p = j/H$; and μ is the mean income. Shorrocks' generalized mean-augmented Lorenz curve is

$$GL(p) = \mu L(p) = [Y(1) + \ldots + Y(j)]/H \tag{4.14}$$

Points on $GL(p)$ are a hybrid per capita income measure in which the numerator is the sum of the incomes of the $100p\%$ poorest individuals and the denominator is the total population. Consequently, the vertical axis of the generalized Lorenz curve runs from 0 to the mean level of income, as pictured in Fig. 4.3. Also, the diagonal is still the line of perfect equality. If income were equally distributed, any $100p\%$ of the population would have a hybrid per capita income equal to $100p\%$ of the mean income.

Shorrocks showed that for two income distributions, Y^A and Y^B, $W^B > W^A$ for all $e \neq 0$ if and only if $GL_B(p) > GL_A(p)$ for all p [0, 1]. That is, the generalized Lorenz curve for Y^B lies everywhere above (Lorenz dominates) the generalized Lorenz curve for Y^A. Notice that one requirement for Y^B to have higher social welfare is that it must have a larger mean: $\mu^B > \mu^A$ at $p = 1$. The intuition behind Shorrocks' theorem, then, is that Y^B has higher social welfare because $100p\%$ of the poorest people always have a higher share of a larger mean income relative to Y^A.

---

[5] A. Atkinson, "On the Measurement of Inequality," *Journal of Economic Theory*, Vol. 2, September 1970.

[6] A. Shorrocks, "Ranking Income Distributions," *Economica*, Vol. 50, 1983.

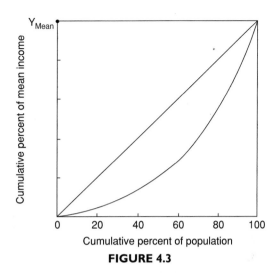

FIGURE 4.3

Crossing Lorenz Curves

Unfortunately, Lorenz and generalized Lorenz curves may cross, in which case Atkinson's and Shorrock's theorems do not apply. Distributions-whose Lorenz curves cross require a specific social welfare function to determine which has higher social welfare because different values of e ($\neq 0$) can generate different social welfare rankings. Figure 4.4 illustrates for the standard Lorenz curve. The Lorenz curves in the figure cross once, at 15% of

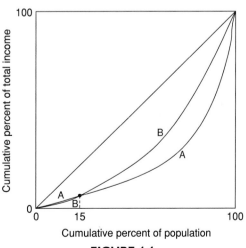

FIGURE 4.4

the total population. A social welfare function that gives a large weight to the bottom 14% of the population might prefer distribution Y^A, because the bottom 14% receive a higher share of the total income under Y^A. Conversely, a social welfare function that gives a large weight to the bottom 16% of the population might prefer distribution Y^B, because the bottom 16% receive a higher share of the total income under Y^B. Society's aversion to inquality matters in ranking the two distributions.

Atkinson's Index of Inequality

Atkinson proposed to rank instances of crossing Lorenz curves by constructing an index of inequality that directly incorporates society's aversion to inequality into the index. As noted earlier, his proposal stimulated a large number of imitators. Social-welfare-based indexes of inequality have been widely used for determining the incidence of government expenditures and taxation from a social perspective, as well as in the analysis of income distributions. We will discuss some of the incidence applications in later chapters.

Atkinson's index of inequality follows directly from his social welfare framework and is constructed as follows. Using Eq. (4.7), calculate the level of social welfare, W^A, implied by the distribution Y^A, for a given value of e. Next, determine the amount of income that, if given equally to everyone, would generate the same level of social welfare, W^A, as the given distribution. Atkinson called this income the "equally distributed equivalent" income, labeled Y_{ede}. For Atkinson's social welfare function, Y_{ede} is a solution to the equation:

$$W^A = \frac{H}{(1-e)} Y_{ede}^{(1-e)} \qquad (4.15)$$

Finally, use Y_{ede} to form the following index of inequality:

$$I(e) = 1 - \left[\frac{Y_{ede}}{Y_{mean}}\right] \quad I(e){:}\,[0,1] \qquad (4.16)$$

Note that the index depends on the aversion to inequality parameter e.

$I(e)$ has two attractive properties. First, $I = 0$ represents "perfect equality" and $I = 1$, "perfect inequality," in line with most indexes of inequality. $I = 0$ *either* if everyone has the same income so that $Y_{ede} = Y_{mean}$, *or if* $e = 0$ and society is indifferent to inequality because social welfare is utilitarian in income. $I = 1$ if social welfare is Rawlsian, with $e = \infty$. Second, $I(e)$ has a natural interpretation of the social cost of inequality for given values of e. Suppose $I(e) = .25$. Then $\left[\frac{Y_{ede}}{Y_{mean}}\right] = .75$. In other words, the index says that society could have the same level of social welfare with only 75% of the total income if income were equally distributed. Twenty-five percent of the total income can be viewed as the social cost of the given inequality. Note, finally, that any two distributions can be ranked using Atkinson's index of inequality.[7]

Inequality versus Social Welfare: Sen's Critique

Amartya Sen, the 1998 Nobel laureate in Economics, is one of the leading economic theorists working on the problems of inequality, poverty, and social justice. He has been highly critical of all attempts to incorporate social welfare into indexes of inequality. Sen argues that social welfare and inequality are both primitive concepts, meaning that one cannot be derived from the other as Atkinson and others have tried to do. This is most easily seen if social welfare is utilitarian in terms of income ($e = 0$). Suppose society consists of two people and consider the two distributions:

$$Y^A = (\$5, \$5) \quad \text{and} \quad Y^B = (0, \$10).$$

Everyone would say that Y^B is the more unequal distribution, yet they both yield the same social welfare with a utilitarian social welfare function.

Sen points out that the fundamental inconsistency between social welfare and inequality is not limited to the knife-edge utilitarian case. It is a more general problem. To see this, suppose that $e > 0$ and the incomes of the two people are unequal. Consider a reverse Robin Hood transfer of $1 from the poorer person to the richer person. Ask what happens as e decreases to: the inequality of income, the inequality of utility, and the change in social welfare. Use Atkinson's social welfare framework to make the comparisons.

Inequality of Income

The inequality of income does not change. All straight measures of income inequality, such as the Gini coefficient, do not incorporate social welfare and are therefore independent of e.

Inequality of Utility

The inequality of utility increases. The change in the inequality of utility from the transfer is the sum of marginal utilities of income, $MU_{Y_R} + MU_{Y_P}$. The utilities of the two people are being driven further apart by the transfer. But $MU_Y = (1/Y^e)$, which increases as e decreases for all Y. Therefore the sum of the marginal utilities increases as e decreases.

Social Welfare

The change in social welfare may decrease. The change in social welfare from the transfer is the difference in the marginal utilities of income,

[7] Peter Lambert has written an excellent survey of the relationship between income measures of inequality and social welfare: P. Lambert, "Estimating Impact Effects of Tax Reforms," *Journal of Economic Surveys*, September 1993.

$MU_{Y_R} - MU_{Y_P}$. Giving the higher income person one more dollar increases social welfare by MU_{Y_R}; taking the dollar from the poor decreases social welfare by MU_{Y_P}. The difference in marginal utilities, $(1/Y_R^e) - (1/Y_P^e)$, can become less negative as e decreases for certain ranges of incomes and e, as the reader can verify.

Sen's examples suggest that attempts to infer changes in social welfare from changes in inequality are problematic, the more so if a nation cannot reach a consensus on its aversion to inequality.[8]

The Atkinson Framework and Inequality in the United States

John Bishop, John Formby, and James Smith (BFS) applied the Atkinson framework to the CPS income data from 1967–1986 to track changes in social welfare over those 20 years. They found that Lorenz curves calculated from the CPS data crossed in 7 of the 20 years. The CPS data are just a sample of the entire U.S. population, however. Given the sample variance of incomes, BFS developed a test of statistical significance for Lorenz curve crossing. They concluded that the Lorenz curves crossed only once, from 1973 to 1974, on the basis on statistical significance. In all other year-to-year comparisons, the new Lorenz curve was either entirely inside or entirely outside the old Lorenz curve in a statistical sense.

The change in social welfare from one year to the next depends on the change in the mean level of income and the change in inequality as measured by the year-to-year positions of the Lorenz curves. An increase in the mean increases social welfare and an increase in inequality decreases social welfare (and vice versa). BFS discovered three distinct periods in the data, each with a consistent pattern in the year-to-year changes:

> 1967–78—Social welfare increased; the mean increased and inequality decreased.
>
> 1979–83—Social welfare decreased; the mean was essentially constant and inequality increased (the increase in inequality was "relatively massive").
>
> 1983–86—Social welfare increased; the mean increased, and inequality was essentially constant.

Their findings produced one major surprise. The deep recession of 1974/75 did not prevent a continuing decrease in inequality that had been ongoing for 7 years, whereas the deeper recession of 1981/82 led to a massive increase in inequality. Why inequality responded so differently to the two recessions remains an intriguing open question.[9]

[8] A. Sen, "Ethical Measurement of Inequality: Some Difficulties," in A. Sen (Ed.), *Choice, Welfare, and Measurement*, MIT Press, Cambridge, MA, 1982.

[9] J. Bishop, Formby, J. and Smith, W., "Lorenz Dominance and Welfare: Changes in the U.S. Distribution of Income, 1967–86," *Review of Economics and Statistics*, February 1991.

SOCIAL WELFARE AND CONSUMPTION: THE JORGENSON ANALYSIS

Dale Jorgenson provided an important extension of Atkinson's social welfare analysis shortly after Atkinson's work appeared. He developed a method for linking measures of social welfare to people's consumption patterns rather than their incomes.[10]

Econometric demand analysis of aggregate consumption data was well established by the mid–1970s, including estimation of the aggregate consumption function and major categories such as food, clothing, transportation, and so forth. Panel data sets that permit more microeconometric demand analysis were not yet available. Jorgenson's idea was to meld econometric demand analysis with the social welfare function by using the estimated demand equations for the major consumption categories to track changes in social welfare over time. His approach has three distinct steps:

1. Posit individual utility functions defined over a set of consumer goods and derive demand equations for the goods from the utility functions.
2. Estimate the demand equations in a manner that allows for recovery of the unknown parameters of the utility functions.
3. Use the estimated utility functions as the arguments of a flexible-form social welfare function that registers society's aversion to inequality, and track changes in social welfare over time.

The Estimating Share Equations

Jorgenson begins by assuming that each household, h, has an indirect utility function, V^h, defined over three sets of arguments: the prices of the various consumer goods, $\vec{P}_k$; the household's income, M^h; and a vector of household characteristics, $\vec{A}^h$, such as family size, age of the head of household, and where the household resides:

$$V^h = V^h(\vec{P}_k; M^h; \vec{A}^h) \qquad h = 1, \ldots, H \qquad (4.17)$$

The parameters of V^h are assumed to be equal for all households and constant over time. That is, households have identical, unchanging tastes. They also face the same vector of consumer prices. Therefore, the differences in households' utilities are due entirely to differences in their circumstances—that is, their incomes and characteristics.

Jorgenson employed the transcendental logarithmic (translog) indirect utility function to approximate the true indirect utility function. The translog is a second-order Taylor series expansion in the logs of the independent variables around their means (each independent variable is scaled by dividing

[10] D. Jorgenson, "Aggregate Consumer Behavior and the Measurement of Social Welfare," *Econometrica*, September 1990.

by its own mean, so that the log at each variable's mean is zero.). For example, the translog approximation of V^h assuming N prices and a single characteristic A^h, is

$$
\ln V^h = \sum_{i=1}^{N} \alpha_i \ln P_i + \alpha_M \ln M^h + \alpha_A \ln A^h + 1/2 \sum_{i=1}^{N} \sum_{j=1}^{N} \beta_{ij} \ln P_i \ln P_j
$$

$$
+ \sum_{i=1}^{N} \beta_{iM} \ln P_i \ln M^h + \sum_{i=1}^{N} \beta_{iA} \ln P_i \ln A^h + 1/2 \beta_{MA} \ln M^h \ln A^h \qquad (4.18)
$$

$$
+ 1/2 \beta_{MM} (\ln M^h)^2 + 1/2 \beta_{AA} (\ln A^h)^2
$$

The estimating equations are obtained by taking log derivatives of the translog function with respect to each of the prices and income:

$$
\frac{\partial \ln V^h}{\partial \ln P_k} = \frac{\partial V^h}{\partial P_k} \frac{P_k}{V^h} \qquad k = 1, \ldots N \qquad (4.19)
$$

From Roy's identity, $(\partial V^h / \partial P_k) = \lambda^h X_{hk}$, where λ^h is the marginal utility of income for household h, and X_{hk} is the consumption of good k by household h. Therefore,

$$
\frac{\partial \ln V^h}{\partial \ln P_k} = \lambda^h \frac{P_k X_{hk}}{V^h} \qquad k = 1, \ldots, N \qquad (4.20)
$$

Similarly,

$$
\frac{\partial \ln V^h}{\partial \ln M^h} = \frac{\partial V^h}{\partial M^h} \frac{M^h}{V^h} = \frac{\lambda^h M^h}{V^h} \qquad (4.21)
$$

Dividing Eq. (4.20) by (4.21) yields:

$$
\frac{\left(\dfrac{\partial \ln V^h}{\partial \ln P_k} \right)}{\left(\dfrac{\partial \ln V^h}{\partial \ln M^h} \right)} = \frac{P_k X_{hk}}{M^h} \qquad k = 1, \ldots, N \qquad (4.22)
$$

the expenditure share of good k for household h. The expenditure shares become the dependent variables in the demand estimation. The advantage of using the expenditure shares is that the researcher does not have to worry about separating out prices from quantities.

Next, write out the price and income derivatives of the translog function to see the full system of estimating equations:

$$
\frac{\partial \ln V^h}{\partial \ln P_k} = \alpha_k + \sum_{i=1}^{N} \beta_{ik} \ln P_i + \beta_{kM} \ln M^h + \beta_{kA} \ln A^h \qquad k = 1, \ldots, N
$$

$$
(4.23)
$$

$$\frac{\partial \ln V^h}{\partial \ln M^h} = \alpha_M + \sum_{i=1}^{N} \beta_{iM} \ln P_i + \beta_{MM} \ln M^h + \beta_{MA} \ln A^h \tag{4.24}$$

Dividing each of the N equations (4.23) by (4.24) yields the entire system of share equations to be estimated. The left-hand sides (LHSs) are the N expenditure shares. The right-hand side (RHS) is a nonlinear combination of the independent variables and the coefficients of the translog utility function. The system can be estimated by nonlinear estimating techniques if the data on the individual households are available.

The required microdata were not available to Jorgenson, however. He had individual household data on income and characteristics from surveys such as the annual CPS, but he only had aggregate U.S. data on the expenditure shares for most years. The question, then, was whether the parameters of the individual household's translog utility function could be recovered from an estimation on the aggregate expenditures shares. The answer in general is no, without further restrictions on the utility parameters beyond the restrictions implied by utility maximization.

The problem without further restrictions can be seen as follows. Think of each coefficient in the share equation as a coefficient in the price derivative equation (4.23) divided by the entire RHS of the income derivative equation (4.24). The share coefficients defined in this way are functions of all the prices, income M^h, and the single individual characteristic A^h. Next, compute the aggregate shares from the individual shares. The aggregate shares are weighted averages of the individual shares, with the weights equal to each household's share of total income:

$$\sum_h \left(\frac{M_h W_{jk}}{\sum_h M_h}\right) = \sum_h \left(\frac{\frac{M_h P_k X_{hk}}{M_h}}{\sum_h M^h}\right) = \frac{\sum_h P_k X_{hk}}{\sum_h M_h} = W_k^{Agg} \tag{4.25}$$

The aggregate share coefficients as defined above would vary depending on the distribution of income and the characteristic across households. They would not be the same as the coefficients from each household's share equation, and they must be the same to recover the individual utility parameters in the estimation.

The weakest restriction that makes the aggregate and individual share coefficients the same is that the individual expenditure shares are linear functions of the household's income and characteristic. This in turn requires that the RHS of Eq. (4.24) be independent of a household's income and characteristic, or that $\beta_{MM} = \beta_{MA} = 0$ for the system as written above. Jorgenson refers to these two restrictions as the exact aggregation restrictions. With these two restrictions, the individual share coefficients defined by dividing Eq. (4.23) by Eq. (4.24) as above are functions only of the prices. Write:

$$W_{hk} = \alpha'_k + \sum_i \beta'_{ik} \ln P_i + \beta'_{kM} \ln M^h + \beta'_{kA} \ln A^h$$

$$k = 1, \ldots, N; \; h = 1, \ldots, H$$

(4.26)

where the α', β' coefficients are the α, β coefficients in Eq. (4.23) divided by Eq. (4.24) with the aggregate aggregation restrictions imposed.

The aggregate shares are

$$W_k^{Agg} = \frac{\sum_h M^h W_k^h}{\sum_h M^h} = \alpha'_k + \sum_i \beta'_{ik} \ln P_i + \beta'_{kM} \frac{\sum_h M^h \ln M^h}{\sum_h M^h}$$

$$+ \beta'_{kA} \frac{\sum_h M^h \ln A^h}{\sum_h M^h} \qquad k = 1, \ldots, N$$

(4.27)

The only difference in the individual and aggregate share equations is the independent variables. The aggregate shares are regressed on income-weighted shares of individual household's income and characteristic, so that the aggregate shares depend on the joint distribution of incomes and characteristics. But, the coefficients in the aggregate and individual share equations are the same. Therefore, the parameters of the individual translog utility function can be recovered from estimates of the aggregate share equations, as required.

The remaining issue is to ensure that the estimated system of share equations, Eq. (4.27), is consistent with consumer theory, so that the system can be derived from a translog indirect utility function of the form of Eq. (4.18). For this to be true, the coefficient estimates must satisfy the integrability conditions on demand functions, which requires imposing a large number of *a priori* restrictions on the coefficients both within and across equations. To give one example, the matrix of the price coefficients B_{pp} must be symmetric. Jorgenson shows that the integrability conditions, combined with the exact aggregation restrictions, lead a translog utility function of the form (in vector notation):

$$\ln V^h = \ln p' \alpha_p + 1/2 \ln p' B_{pp} \ln p - D(P) \ln[M^h / m^0(P, A^h)] \qquad (4.28)$$

where:

$D(p)$ is the denominator of the share equations, Eq. (4.24), with the exact aggregation restrictions imposed, and the normalization $\alpha'_p 1 = -1$. $m^0(P, A^h)$ is a translog household equivalence scale that captures the effect of the household's characteristics on its utility level. It can be interpreted as the number of household equivalent members, so that the bracketed expression at the end of Eq. (4.28) is the per capita expenditure defined in terms of household equivalent members. Equation (4.28) is the central equation used to track changes in social welfare over time.[11]

Social Welfare

Once the translog utility parameters have been estimated, each household's indirect utility is determined by substituting the values of the prices, the household's income, and the household's characteristic(s) in Eq. (4.18). Social welfare is then a function of the households' indirect utility functions, $\ln V^h$.

Jorgenson assumed that social welfare should depend positively on the mean level of utility and negatively on two factors: the inequality of households' utilities around the mean and Atkinson's aversion to the inequality parameter e. He chose a social welfare function of the general form:

$$W = \overline{\ln V} - g\left(\overline{\ln V} - \ln V^h; e\right) \qquad (4.29)$$

$\overline{\ln V}$ is a weighted average of the logs of the indirect utilities, with the weights equal to the household equivalence scale, $m^0(P, A^h)$:

$$\overline{\ln V} = \frac{\sum_h m^0\left(P, A^h\right) \ln V^h}{\sum_h m^0\left(P, A^h\right)} \qquad (4.30)$$

As in Atkinson, $e = [0, \infty]$, with $e = 0$ representing the utilitarian case of no concern for inequality and ∞ representing the most egalitarian Rawlsian case. g() is a complex function with the following properties:

---

[11] The discussion in the text ignores a number of other econometric issues associated with estimating the system of share equations so that the system is consistent with consumer theory, such as the nature of the error-covariance matrix for the entire system, and further coefficient restrictions that Jorgenson imposes to reduce the number of coefficients to be estimated or to allow him to ignore parameters in $\ln V^h$ in Eq. (4.18) that do not appear in the system of share equations (4.26) and (4.27). Our goal is to give an overview of Jorgenson's approach without getting bogged down in the econometric details. A complete discussion of the estimation of the translog indirect utility funtion (4.18) can be found in D. Jorgenson, "Aggregate Consumer Behavior and the Measurement of Social Welfare," *Econometrica*, September 1990, pp. 1007–1049, Another excellent and readily accessible overview of the Jorgenson approach to measuring social welfare is contained in D. Jorgenson, "Efficiency Versus Equity in Economic Policy Analysis," *American Economist*, Vol. 29, No. 1, Spring 1985. See also the cautionary notes by Fisher, Blackorby, and Donaldson on the implicit assumptions behind Jorgenson's use of household equivalence scales and the cardinalization of utility when making interpersonal comparisons: F. Fisher, "Household Equivalence Scales and Interpersonal Comparisons," *Review of Economic Studies*, Vol. LIV, 1987; C. Blackorby and D. Donaldson, "Money Metric Utility: A Harmless Normalization?," *Journal of Economic Theory*, October 1988. A good general reference on social welfare measurement is Section 3 of D. Slesnick, "Empirical Approaches to the Measurement of Welfare," *Journal of Economic Literature*, December 1998.

1. $g_1, g_2 > 0$; g increases and social welfare decreases if either inequality increases or society's concern for inequality increases.
2. $g = 0$ if either $V^h = V$ for all h (there is no inequality) or $e = 0$ (society is unconcerned about inequality). Notice that, under either condition, W is maximized and equal to $\overline{\ln V}$ for a given sum of the households indirect utilities
3. g yields equal-weighted social marginal utilities and satisfies the impersonality principle, in the sense that two people with the same level of indirect utility have the same effect on g and, therefore, on W.

Given W, the researcher can track social welfare over time as a function of prices, P_t; households' incomes, M_t^h; households' characteristics, A_t^h; and society's aversion to inequality, e_t, which might also change over time. The only maintained hypotheses are that individual preferences remain constant over time (the estimated coefficients of the indirect utility function are unchanged) and that the form of W also remains the same.[12]

Income Measures of Social Gain and Loss

Jorgenson's final contribution was to propose income measures of gains and losses in social welfare comparable to the Hicksian Compensating and Equivalent Variations (HCV and HEV, respectively) that are used to measure gains and loses of individual well being. The Hicksian measures are derived from the consumer's expenditure function. Jorgenson derives his income measures from a concept that he calls the social expenditure function. A brief review of the consumer's expenditure function will be useful to understand Jorgenson's analogous social expenditure function and his income measures of social welfare gains and losses.

The Expenditure Function, HCV, and HEV[13]

The expenditure function follows directly from the dual to the standard consumer problem of maximizing utility subject to a budget constraint. The dual problem is to minimize "expenditures" subject to utility being held constant:

[12] The social welfare rankings over time implied by W are invariant to linear transformations of the indirect utility functions of the form $V^{h'} = a + bV^h$, with a and b the same for all households. The indirect utilty functions are cardinal and fully comparable under this condition. The exact form of W, along with a complete discussion of its properties, are in D. Jorgenson, "Aggregate Consumer Behavior and the Measurement of Social Welfare," *Econometrica*, September 1990, p. 1027.

[13] This section can be skipped by students familiar with the expenditure function and the Hicksian compensation measures of individual welfare.

$$\min_{(X_i)} \sum_{i=1}^{N} q_i X_i$$

$$\text{s.t. } U(X_i) = \overline{U}$$

where the X_i are the quantities and the q_i are the prices of the goods and variable factors. "Expenditures" is understood to mean expenditures on all goods and services less income from all variable factors, given that the X_i include all variable factors supplied. The first-order conditions of the dual solve for goods demand and factor supply curves of the form:

$$X_i^c = X_i(\vec{q}; \overline{U}), \text{ for } i = 1, \ldots, N \tag{4.31}$$

These are compensated demand and supply curves; they show they consumer's response to price changes given that utility is held constant at $\overline{U}$. (By contrast, the ordinary market demand curves show responses to price changes given that lump-sum income is held constant.)

To form the expenditure function, replace the X_i in the objective function of the dual with the compensated supply and demand relationships (4.31) to obtain:

$$M(\vec{q}; \overline{U}) = \sum_{i=1}^{N} q_i X_i^c(\vec{q}; \overline{U}) \tag{4.32}$$

The function, M, is the consumer's *expenditure function*, defined solely in terms of prices and a constant utility level. Since the function is derived from the dual of the standard consumer problem, it is certainly a valid representation of consumer's preferences. Furthermore, the relationship between a primal problem and its dual guarantees that the value of the expenditure function equals the consumer's lump-sum income when $\overline{U}$ is set at the maximum utility level obtained from solving the standard utility maximization problem.

Hicks' Compensating and Equivalent Variations

Economists are naturally interested in knowing whether changes in prices increase or decrease the consumer's utility and by how much. Direct utility measures are not useful for this purpose, however, because they require cardinality, the choice of a particular utility index, even though consumer's demands (and factor supplies) are invariant to monotonic transformations of the utility index. Rather, one wants an income measure of gains and losses that is invariant to monotonic transformations of the utility index. The proper income measure is based on the notion of compensation, or indifference: How much lump-sum income (payment) is required to keep the consumer indifferent to the change in prices? The expenditure function provides the basis for this measure, because for *any* price vector $\vec{q}$, $M(\vec{q}; \overline{U})$ gives the minimum expenditures, or lump-sum income, required to keep the consumer at an arbitrarily selected utility level, $\overline{U}$.

To relate the expenditure function to the standard treatment of income-compensation criteria in terms of consumer indifference curves, consider a two-good example in which all factor income is lump sum because of fixed factor supplies. Suppose that the consumer is originally in equilibrium at point A on I_1 in Fig. 4.5, with relative prices q_1/q_2 indicated by the slope of the budget line tangent to I_1 at A. Suppose the price of X_2 increases, resulting in a new equilibrium at point B in Fig. 4.5 (assume the consumer's lump-sum income remains unchanged).

The parallel distance between I_1 and I_0 gives an income measure of the welfare loss caused by this price increase. The distance is invariant to monotonic transformations of the utility index because the indifference curves are invariant to these transformations. In general, there is an infinity of possible income measures since the parallel distance between I_1 and I_0 varies depending on the slope of the parallel lines used to measure the distance. The two most popular, and natural, choices used to measure the parallel distance are the slopes corresponding to the initial and final price vectors.

In Fig. 4.6, the parallel distance from point B to C gives the additional lump-sum income necessary to compensate the consumer for the new set of prices. With this additional income the consumer would remain on I_1 (at point C) despite the higher prices and would therefore be indifferent to the new prices. This income measure is Hicks' Compensating Variation. The parallel distance from point A to D gives the lump-sum income the consumer would be willing to sacrifice to maintain the old set of prices. By giving up this

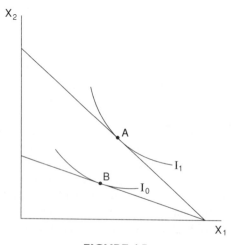

FIGURE 4.5

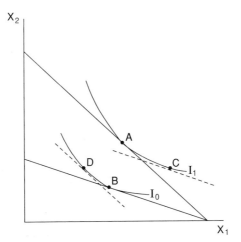

FIGURE 4.6

income, the consumer would remain on I_0 (at point D) despite facing the original prices and would therefore be indifferent to returning to the original prices. This income measure is Hicks' Equivalent Variation.

In general, the value of the expenditure function at the new price vector and the original utility level, $M\left(\vec{q}_1; \overline{U}^0\right)$, measures the lump-sum income necessary for indifference to the new price vector. Subtracting off the consumer's actual amount of lump-sum income, I^0 (assumed unchanged in this example), gives the HCV:[14]

$$\text{HCV} = M\left(\vec{q}_1; \overline{U}^0\right) - I^0 = M\left(\vec{q}_1; \overline{U}^0\right) - M\left(\vec{q}_1; \overline{U}^1\right) \qquad (4.33)$$

The expenditure function defined at the original set of prices and the new utility level, $M\left(\vec{q}_0, \overline{U}^1\right)$, measures the lump-sum income necessary for indifference to the new utility level but at the original price vector. Subtracting off the consumer's actual lump-sum income gives the HEV:

$$\text{HEV} = M\left(\vec{q}_1; \overline{U}^1\right) - I^0 = M\left(\vec{q}_0; \overline{U}^1\right) - M\left(\vec{q}_0; \overline{U}^0\right) \qquad (4.34)$$

The HEV is the preferred measure when comparing three or more situations because it is always calculated using the original price vector. By standardizing on the prices, it gives an unambiguous welfare ordering of the

[14] As defined in Eq. (4.33), the HCV is a loss measure. If, as in this example, goods prices should rise, then the income necessary to compensate the consumer will generally exceed the income actually available, and the HCV as written will be positive. Since the consumer is surely worse off, this positive value gives an income measure of his welfare loss. A welfare gain would be measured negatively. Some writers reverse the signs so that a gain is measured positively.

situations. The HEV is said to be a money metric of utility because of this ordering property. In contrast, the HCV makes pairwise comparisons of the situations using different price vectors each time. The pairwise comparisons at the different prices may not yield a transitive ordering of the utilities.[15]

Jorgenson's Social Expenditure Function

Now return to Jorgenson's problem of constructing an appropriate income measure of the change in social welfare. Consider two social states, 0 and 1, defined by the vectors of prices, households' incomes, and households' characteristics in each situation. The vectors of prices, incomes, and characteristics in turn determine a vector of indirect utilities and a level of social welfare in each situation, given Jorgenson's translog estimates of the indirect utility function and his social welfare function:

$$\left(\vec{P}_0, \vec{M}_0^h, \vec{A}_0^h\right) \Rightarrow \ln\vec{V}_0^h \Rightarrow W^0$$

$$\left(\vec{P}_1, \vec{M}_1^h, \vec{A}_1^h\right) \Rightarrow \ln\vec{V}_1^h \Rightarrow W^1$$

The *social expenditure function* for each social state that corresponds to the individual consumer's expenditure function asks the question: What is the minimum aggregate level of (lump-sum) income required to achieve the actual level of social welfare in that social state? The problem is how to compute the minimum aggregate level of income. Consider social state 0, in which social welfare equals:

---

[15] If both price and lump-sum income change simultaneously, these two HCV and HEV expressions have to be modified as follows. Hicks' Compensating Variation becomes:

$$HCV = M\left(\vec{q}_1; \overline{U}^0\right) - I^1 \tag{4.33a}$$

The HCV is the lump-sum income necessary to keep the consumer at the original utility level, given the new price vector, less the lump-sum income actually available at the new level, I^1. Alternatively, since $M\left(\vec{q}_0; \overline{U}^0\right) = I^0$, from the duality of the consumer problem,

$$HCV = \left(I^0 - I^1\right) - \left[M\left(\vec{q}_0; \overline{U}^0\right) - M\left(\vec{q}_1; \overline{U}^0\right)\right] \tag{4.33b}$$

In terms of changes in lump-sum income, then, the consumer's gain or loss is the actual change in lump-sum income less the additional income required to keep him indifferent to the price changes, measured at the original utility level.

Similarly, the HEV is now the income required to keep the consumer at the new utility level with the old price vector, less the income actually available in the initial situation:

$$HEV = M\left(\vec{q}_0; \overline{U}^1\right) - I^0 \tag{4.34a}$$

Alternatively, since $M\left(\vec{q}_1; \overline{U}^1\right) = I^1$ from duality,

$$HEV = \left(I^1 - I^0\right) - \left[M\left(\vec{q}_1; \overline{U}^1\right) - M\left(\vec{q}_0; \overline{U}^1\right)\right] \tag{4.34b}$$

The HEV is the actual change in lump-sum income less the additional income necessary to compensate the consumer, measured at the final uility level.

$$W^0 = \overline{\ln V_0} - g(\ln V_0 - \ln V_0^h; e)$$

Assume that there is some inequality ($V_0^h \neq \overline{V}_0$, for some h) and some aversion to inequality (e > 0). Under these assumptions, the minimum aggregate level of income necessary to achieve W^0 must be less than the actual aggregate level of income in social state 0. The reason why is that social welfare would be maximized for the given sum of indirect utilities if everyone's utility were equal to the mean, $\overline{V}_0$. With no inequality, g = 0 and $W^0 = \ln\overline{V}_0$. The task, then, is to compute for each household the amount of income that would place the household at the mean level of utility, $W^0 = \overline{\ln V}_0$, given the actual prices and the household's characteristic(s) in social state 0: $\vec{P}_0$ and $\vec{A}_0^h$.

This can be done with the estimated translog utility function for each household, Eq. (4.28), reproduced here as Eq. (4.35):

$$\ln V^h = \ln p' \alpha_p + 1/2 \ln p' \beta_{pp} \ln P - D(P) \ln[M^h/m^0(P, A^h)] \qquad (4.35)$$

Invert the utility function to represent $\ln M^h$ as a function of prices, the household's characteristic(s), and the household's utility. The inversion is possible because of the exact aggregation restrictions defined above, which make $\ln V^h$ linear in $\ln M^h$:

$$\ln M^h = 1/D(P)[\ln p' \alpha_p + 1/2 \ln p' \beta_{pp} \ln P - \ln V^h] + \ln m^0(P, A^h) \qquad (4.36)$$

Finally, substitute $W^0 = \overline{\ln V}_0$ for $\ln V^h$ in Eq. (4.36), along with $\vec{P}_0$ and A_0^h, to find the level of income required to place the household at the mean level of utility. Call the required income M_*^h. M_*^h is less than M_{act}^h for those whose utilities are above the mean and greater than M_{act}^h for those whose utilities are less than the mean. Compute M_*^h for each household. The aggregate social expenditure (income) associated with W^0 is $\Sigma_h M_*^h$. Also, $\sum_h M_*^h$ must be less than $\Sigma_h M_{act}^h$ because the estimated indirect utility functions exhibit diminishing marginal utility of income under the exact aggregation assumption. With $\ln V^h$ linear in $\ln M^h$, V^h is concave in M^h. Therefore, when placing everyone at the mean level of utility the sum of the incomes taken away from those whose utilities are above the mean exceeds the sum of the income given to those below the mean.

Figure 4.7 illustrates the case of two households. V_H^h and V_L^h are equidistant from the mean, $\overline{V}$, but much more income must be taken from the high-utility person than must be given to the low-utility household to bring each to $\overline{V}$. Therefore, the aggregate income required to bring each to the mean is less than the actual aggregate income when the utilities are V_H^h and V_L^h.[16]

---

[16] An alternative and instructive evaluation of the social expenditure function relies on the property that individual utilites are equalized if expenditures per household equivalent member, $M^h/m^0(P, A_0^h)$, are equalized. With expenditures per household equivalent member equalized,

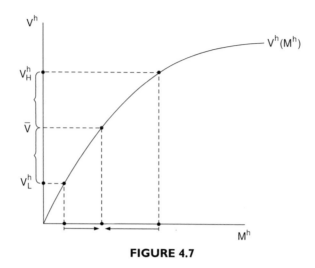

FIGURE 4.7

The minimum social expenditure $\sum_h M_*^h$ associated with social state 0 is a function of the prices, households' characteristics, and the level of social welfare in that state (the level of social welfare implicitly incorporates the distribution of utilities and society's aversion to inequality). Therefore, write the social expenditure function for social state 0 as:

$$M_{soc}^0 = M^0(\vec{P}_0, \vec{A}_0^h, W^0) \tag{4.37}$$

The minimum aggregate income associated with social state 1 is derived in the same manner, using , $\vec{P}_1, \vec{A}_1^h$, and $W^1 = \overline{\ln V}^1$. Therefore, write the social expenditure function for social state 1 as:

$$M_{soc}^1 = M^1(\vec{P}_1, \vec{A}_1^h, W^1) \tag{4.38}$$

$$\overline{\ln V} = \ln P' \alpha_p + 1/2 B_{pp} \ln P - D(P) \ln[M/\sum m_0(P, A^h)] = W, \tag{4.36a}$$

where M is aggregate expenditures. Inverting the equation yields the log of the required minimum aggregate expenditures to achieve W:

$$\ln M = 1/D(P)[\ln p' \alpha_p + 1/2 B_{pp} \ln P - W] + \ln[\sum m^0(P, A^h) \tag{4.36b}$$

The aggregate social expenditure function depends on prices, the level of social welfare W, and the number of household equivalent members. Furthermore, the log of minimum aggregate social expenditures per capita is

$$\ln[M/\sum m^0(P, A^h)] = 1/D(P)[\ln P' \alpha_p + 1/2 B_{pp} \ln P - W] \tag{4.36c}$$

where the per capita measure is defined in terms of household equivalent members.

In general, a social expenditure function can be defined for any vector of prices, household characteristics, and a given level of social welfare, just as the consumer's expenditure function can be defined for any vector of prices and a given level of utility:

$$M_{soc} = M(\vec{P}, \vec{A}^h, W) \tag{4.39}$$

Social HCV and HEV

The social analogs to the individual HCV and HEV income measures of gains and losses follow naturally from the social expenditure function. Comparing a move from social state 0 to social state 1,

$$HCV_{soc} = M(\vec{P}_1, \vec{A}_1^h, W^0) - M(\vec{P}_1, \vec{A}_1^h, W^1) \tag{4.40}$$

The social Hicks' Compensating Variation is the difference between the minimum aggregate income that would be required to achieve the original level of social welfare at the new prices and new household characteristics and the minimum aggregate income that would be required to achieve the new level of social welfare at the new prices and new household characteristics. If prices rose on average or household characteristics changed in such a way as to make households worse off, the HCV_{soc} would be positive. Society would have to receive a gift of income to maintain the level of social welfare:

$$HEV_{soc} = M(\vec{P}_0, \vec{A}_0^h, W^1) - M(\vec{P}_0, \vec{A}_0^h, W^0) \tag{4.41}$$

The social Hicks' Equivalent Variation is the difference between the minimum aggregate income that would be required to achieve the new level of social welfare at the original prices and original household characteristics and the minimum aggregate income that would be required to achieve the original level of social welfare at the original prices and original household characteristics. If prices rose on average or household characteristics changed in a way to make households worse off, the HEV_{soc} would be negative. Society would be willing to sacrifice some income to return to the original prices and household characteristics.

Two Applications for the U.S. Economy

The U.S. Standard of Living

Jorgenson estimated a system of five share equations for the United States from 1947 to 1985 using data from the National Income and Product Accounts, the Current Populations Survey, and the 1972–73 Survey of Consumer Expenditures. The five expenditure categories were energy, food, other nondurable goods, capital services from consumer durables and housing, and consumer services. He chose five household characteristics: family size, age of head of household, region of residence, race, and type of residence (urban, rural). Based on the estimates, he computed the HEV_{soc} for the United States from 1947 to 1985, expressed on a per capita basis using household equivalent members to represent the U.S. standard of living. The per capita HEV_{soc} slightly more than tripled during that period in real terms, with an average annual rate of growth of 2.92. In contrast, the average annual rate of growth of real income per capita, the conventional measure of standard of living, was a much more modest 2.07% from 1947 to 1985.

Jorgenson attributes the overly pessimistic bias of the conventional income measure to three sources (with the percentage of the overall bias in parenthesis):

1. The use of the Consumer Price Index (CPI) to deflate income rather than the price index implied by the Jorgenson approach to measuring social welfare, which Jorgenson calls the social cost of living index.[17] The estimated social cost of living index grew more slowly than the CPI during this period (34.1% of the overall bias).

2. The use of a straight head count in arriving at a per capita measure rather than household equivalent members. The household equivalent member measure assumes that the household is the decision-making unit and takes account of changes in household characteristics over time. The number of household equivalent members grew more slowly than the overall population during this period (17.6% of the overall bias).

3. Ignoring equity entirely. The distribution of estimated utilities across household equivalent members became more equal during this period (48.2% of the overall bias).

Poverty in the United States

The Jorgenson consumption-based approach to measuring social well being also gives a more optimistic picture of the extent of poverty in the United States relative to the official Department of Commerce poverty count, which is based on income. Daniel Slesnick estimated virtually the same expenditure system as Jorgenson using 13 years of data from the Consumer Expenditure Surveys (1961/62, 1972, 1973, and 1980 through 1989). He had the same five expenditure categories but added a sixth household characteristic, the sex of the head of household, to the five characteristics listed above. He then used his estimates to compute a consumption-based poverty head

---

[17] The social cost of living index is based on the notion of the potential level of social welfare attainable in a given year, equal to the level of social welfare if the aggregate income were distributed to equalize utilities. The social cost of living is the ratio of the expenditures required to reach the potential social welfare at current prices to the expenditures required to reach the potential social welfare at base-year prices. The expenditures at base-year prices can be computed from Eq. (4.36)

count for each of the 13 years.[18] The poverty computation involves three steps.

The first step is to define a consumption-based poverty line. Slesnick chose to define his poverty line similar to the method that the Department of Commerce chose to compute the official poverty line in 1964. The Department of Commerce determined the minimum income a family required to purchase a nutritionally adequate diet and then multiplied the food budget by three to arrive at the "official" poverty line level of income. The poverty line varies by family size and composition (but no other characteristics) and is adjusted annually for changes in the CPI.

Slesnick chose a reference family and noted how much the Department of Commerce said it would have to spend on food in 1964 to purchase a nutritionally adequate diet. His reference family had the following six characteristics: four people; headed by a white male 25–34 years old; living in a nonfarm area in the Northeast. Call the vector of reference characteristics A^R. Using the food equation from the estimated demand system, Slesnick determined the total expenditures, M^Z, that would be consistent with purchasing the nutritionally adequate diet at 1964 prices for the reference family with characteristics A^R. Then, using Eq. (4.35), he determined the utility level, V_Z^R, achieved by the reference family at 1964 prices, expenditures M^Z, and characteristics A^R. V_Z^R is the poverty line level of utility for a reference family, and M^Z is the consumption-based poverty line level of expenditures. V_Z^R is assumed to remain constant over time.

Slesnick rescaled M^Z to 1973 prices since 1964 was not a year in his dataset. Therefore, his poverty line M^Z was the individual expenditure function (4.36) evaluated at 1973 prices, characteristics A^R, and utility level V_Z^R:

$$M^Z = M(\vec{P}_{73}, A^R, V_Z^R) \qquad (4.42)$$

The next step is to compute the utility level achieved in each year by each family in his dataset. The utility level for family h at time t, V_t^h, is determined by Eq. (4.35) evaluated at current year prices $\vec{P}_t$, current family income M_t^h, and current family characteristics A_t^h.

The final step is to ask how much total expenditure each family in each year would have required to achieve utility level V_t^h if it could consume at 1973 prices and if it had the reference family characteristics A^R. This expenditure level is given by the individual expenditure function (4.36) evaluated at 1973 prices $\vec{P}_{73}$, characteristics A^R, and utility level V_t^h:

$$M_t^h = M(\vec{P}_{73}, A^R, V_t^h) \qquad (4.43)$$

---

[18] D. Slesnick, "Gaining Ground: Poverty in the Postwar United States," *Journal of Political Economy*, February 1993. See also the articles by D. Jorgenson and R. Triest in the *Journal of Economic Perspectives*, Winter 1998, pp. 79–114.

M_t^h evaluated in this way standardizes both for changes in prices since 1973 and for the needs of families with characteristics different from A^R. The number of poor equals the number of families for which $M_t^h < M^Z$. Alternatively, the number of poor equals the number of families for which $V_t^h < V_Z^R$, the poverty line level of utility, which is constant over time.

Slesnick found that his consumption-based poverty count was lower than the official poverty count in all but 4 years of the sample period and was substantially lower by the end of the period. From 1981 through 1989, Slesnick's estimated poverty rate was approximately four percentage points below the official poverty rate each year. For example, in 1989 Slesnick estimated that 8.4% of all families were poor, whereas the official poverty rate was 12.8%.

The consumption-based poverty rate is below the official income poverty rate primarily for three reasons. One is that 40% of the poor own their own homes, so that they consume a fairly large amount of capital services; capital service flows account for 10 to 13% of the total expenditures of the poor in Slesnick's sample. The second is that a large number of the poor dissave; their incomes are temporarily low and they dissave to maintain their standard of living. The third factor that drove the Slesnick poverty counts down sharply in the 1980s was a change in family characteristics that helped to move families out of poverty, both directly and indirectly by its effect on the composition of family expenditures

Slesnick argues that his consumption-based poverty count is superior to the official count because it better reflects families' permanent economic situations. The poor by his measure are more likely to be permanent income poor than the "official" current income poor. He found that budgets of the consumption poor contain a lower percentage of capital services than the consumption nonpoor because they are less likely to own their own homes. He also found that the consumption poor devote a higher percentage of their budgets to purchases of food.

SOCIAL WELFARE AND SOCIAL MOBILITY

Bergson and Samuelson conceived of their individualistic social welfare function in terms of end-results equity, as a device for evaluating the ethical content of social outcomes. All our applications of the social welfare function so far have been in this vein. Despite its end-results orientation, economists have also used the social welfare function to measure the ethical implications of one common measure of process equity, the degree of social mobility in society.

Social mobility refers to the ability of individuals (families) to move throughout the distribution of income over time. It is closely related to the other widely held notion of process equity, equal opportunity. At one extreme is the caste system, a completely immobile society. People are assigned a position in the distribution at birth and can never move; there is no opportunity for change, much less equal opportunity. At the other extreme is complete mobility, in which people at any point on the distribution have an equal probability of staying there or moving to any other point on the distribution. A completely mobile society would almost certainly have full equality of opportunity along every relevant economic dimension.

The degree of social mobility is described by a *transition probability matrix*, defined as follows. Divide the income distribution into a number of categories (say, three for the purposes of illustration): low, $0 < Y_{low} \leq Y_1$; middle, $Y_1 < Y_{middle} \leq Y_2$; and high, $Y_{high} > Y_2$. Collect data on the position of the individuals (families) at time t and on the position of the same individuals (families) at time $t + 1$, where $t + 1$ may be 5 to 10 years beyond t. On the basis of these data, compute the 3×3 probability transition matrix:

$$P = [p_{ij}] \tag{4.44}$$

Each element, p_{ij}, is the probability that an individual (family) who was in income category i at time t is in income category j at time $t + 1$.

Social Mobility and the Distribution of Income

The idea that movement through the distribution over time is governed by the transition probability matrix leads to a dramatic and well-known theorem. Assume that the matrix has the following three properties:

1. The p_{ij} are constant over time.[19]

2. $p_{ij} > 0$, for all i, j. There is always some probability that a person can move to any point on the distribution from any other point. Movement between two categories is never impossible, as it would be in a caste system.

3. The transition between income categories over time is a Markov process. The probability of a person being in income category j at time $t + 1$ depends only on that person's position in time t. All history before time t is irrelevant to the distribution in time $t + 1$.

These three assumptions are almost universally employed in the analysis of social mobility. They imply that the economy will eventually reach the same steady-state distribution of income *regardless of the initial distribution of income*.

The proof of this result is straightforward. Define the distribution vector $\pi'_t = (\pi^t_1, \pi^t_2, \pi^t_3)$, where π^t_i is the proportion (or number) of people in income category i at time t. Under the Markov assumption,[20]

---

[19] This is a truly heroic assumption given that the p_{ij} are influenced by so many factors, such as labor supply and saving behavior, trends in individual labor and capital markets, education decisions and markets, marriage patterns, social contacts, discrimination, and so forth.

[20] For example, the first term in the multiplication on the RHS of Eq. (4.45) is $\pi^t_1 p_{11} + \pi^t_2 p_{21} + \pi^t_3 p_{31}$, equal to the sum of the proportion of people in the first category at

$$\pi'_{t+1} = \pi'_t P \qquad (4.45)$$

Adding the other two assumptions, the steady-state distribution vector π is the solution to the system of equations:

$$\pi' = \pi' P \qquad (4.46)$$

or

$$\pi'(I - P) = 0 \qquad (4.47)$$

which has a unique solution for π' because $(I - P)$ is singular.

The intuition behind the result is that the spreading effect of P eventually dominates any initial distribution. Suppose the distribution is in the steady state at time $t - 1$. Then, at time t, the government levels everyone to the mean with lump-sum taxes and transfers, in accordance with the first-best interpersonal equity conditions under the assumptions of equal marginal social welfare weights, identical tastes, and diminishing marginal utility of income. Everyone is now in middle income category 2 at t. By time $t + 1$, however, some people will have moved to the other two income categories, the numbers determined by the probabilities p_{21} and p_{23}. In time $t + 2$, the distribution will spread some more, as movement now occurs from all three income categories. The spreading continues until the original steady-state distribution of time $t - 1$ is eventually reestablished.

The theorem points to a sharp tension between the process equity goal of social mobility and end-results equity goal of distributive justice. It implies that any redistribution of income undertaken in the name of end-results equity is ultimately futile. The underlying social mobility in the economy generated by P always returns the economy to the original steady-state distribution.

This tension is tempered by two considerations, however. One is that the government's redistribution policies will change the distribution until the economy returns to the steady state, and the new distributions during the transition periods may be social welfare increasing. The second is that any substantial redistribution of income will almost certainly change some of the elements of P. For instance, a complete leveling of the distribution would at the very least change people's labor supply and saving behavior. Whether the resulting changes in the p_{ij} are desirable, however, is another matter.

These considerations notwithstanding, the idea that the social mobility in the economy tends to undermine the government's redistribution policies strikes at one of the foundations of normative public sector theory, the

---

time t times the probability that they stay in the first categoy, plus the proportion of people in the second categoy times the probability that they move to the first category, plus the proportion of the people in the third category times the probability that they move to the first category. The sum equals π_1^{t+1}.

first-best interpersonal equity conditions. The government may not be able to achieve the distribution implied by the interpersonal equity conditions of social welfare maximization as a steady state distribution even in a first-best policy environment.

Structural Mobility, Circulation Mobility, and Social Welfare

The question remains whether the degree of social mobility itself has any direct bearing on social welfare as measured by the Bergson–Samuelson social welfare function. The answer is yes. Two features of the transition probability matrix P are related to social welfare. One is the steady-state distribution vector implied by P, which is commonly referred to as the *structural mobility* of the economy. Structural mobility is an element of end-results equity and, as such, has an obvious effect on social welfare. The other is the transition of the economy from any given distribution to its steady state, which is commonly referred to as the *circulation mobility* of the economy. The circulation mobility is the pure process equity component of P.

The limits of circulation mobility are given by the transition matrices:

1. $P = I$, the identity matrix
2. $P = [1/n]$, with $p_{ij} = 1/n$ for all i, j, and n = the number of income categories

$P = I$ is the case of no circulation, the caste system. The distribution can never change because the given, initial distribution is the steady-state distribution. $P = [1/n]$ is the case of full circulation. From any initial distribution of income, the economy moves in one period to the steady-state distribution with an equal number of people in each income category.[21]

Valentino Dardanoni has provided an extensive analysis of the social welfare implications of circulation mobility.[22] We will highlight two of his main results, which relate to the question of whether circulation mobility has an independent effect on social welfare.

To focus on circulation mobility per se, Dardanoni begins by considering the set of transition probability matrices that have the same steady-state distribution. Two transition matrices P and Q have the same steady-state distribution if:

$$\pi' = \pi'P = \pi'Q \qquad (4.48)$$

This restriction is not very limiting because transition probability matrices that generate the same steady-state distribution can have very different

---

[21] For example, with $n = 3$, $\pi_1^{t+1} = \pi_1^t(1/3) + \pi_2^t(1/3) + \pi_3^t(1/3) = 1/3$, and likewise for π_2^{t+1} and π_3^{t+1}.

[22] See V. Dardanoni, "Measuring Social Mobility," *Journal of Economic Theory*, Vol. 61, pp. 372–394, 1993.

transitional properties. For example, even the extreme transition matrices $P = I$ and $P = [1/n]$ (no circulation and full circulation), have the same steady state when the initial distribution is $\pi' = (1/n, \ldots, 1/n)$.

Dardanoni then argues that the appropriate arguments of a Bergson–Samuelson social welfare function are the expected discounted lifetime utilities of every individual. Define u_i as the utility received in any time period by people in income category i, the instantaneous utility. Assume that all people in income category i receive utility u_i, that u_i increases with income, and that, for simplicity, u_i remains constant over time. Identify people by the utility they receive in the initial distribution of income: A u_i person is someone in category i in the initial distribution. Define V_i as the expected discounted lifetime utility of a u_i person. Then, in matrix notation, the vector of expected discounted lifetime utilities V^P under the transition probability matrix P equals:

$$V^P = u + \rho P u + \rho^2 P^2 u + , \ldots, + \rho^n P^n u \qquad (4.49)$$

where $\rho = 1/(1 + r_{soc}) = $ the social discount factor applied to future utilities with r_{soc} equal to the social marginal rate of substitution, and u is the vector of instantaneous utilities.[23] In the limit,

$$V^P = [I - \rho P]^{-1} u \qquad (4.50)$$

Dardanoni normalizes the vector V^P by the discount factor, so that

$$V^P = (1 - \rho)[I - \rho P]^{-1} u \qquad (4.51)$$

Define the matrix

$$P(\rho) = (1 - \rho)[I - \rho P]^{-1} \qquad (4.52)$$

so that

$$V^P = P(\rho) u \qquad (4.53)$$

---

[23] For example, the first term of Pu is $p_{11}u_1 + p_{12}u_2 + p_{13}u_3$, which is the expected utility in period 2 of a u_1 person, a person who is initially in category 1 at the bottom of the distribution. The entry in the first row, first column of P^2 is $p_{11}p_{11} + p_{12}p_{21} + p_{13}p_{31}$. It shows every path that a u_1 person can take and be in category 1 two periods from now: remain in category 1 in both periods, move to category 2 in period 1 and then back to category 1 in period 2; move to category 3 in period 1 and then back to category 1 in period 2. Multiplying this sum by u_1 gives the expected utility of these paths for a u_1 person. The element in the first row, second column of P^2 shows every path that a u_1 person can take and be in the second category in period two, and the element in the first row, third column of P^2 shows every path that a u_1 person can take and be in the third category in period two. Multiplying these elements by u_2 and u_3, respectively, indicates the period 2 expected utility of a u_1 person who takes these paths. Therefore, the multiplication of the first row of P^2 and u gives the expected utility of a u_1 person in period 2. Similarly, the elements in the first row of P^n indicate every possible path that a u_1 person can take to be in categories 1, 2, and 3, respectively, in period n. V_1 is the discounted sum of these period-by-period expected utilities of a u_1 person, the lifetime expected utility.

$P(\rho)$ is a lifetime transition probability matrix. Its elements, $p(\rho)_{ij}$, can be interpreted as the discounted lifetime probability of moving from initial category i to final category j.

Utilitarian Social Welfare and Circulation Mobility

The arguments of the Bergson–Samuelson social welfare function are the elements of V^P, which are in turn a function of ρ, P, u, and n. Suppose that social welfare is utilitarian, as is commonly assumed. Then, given the steady-state distribution $\pi' = (\pi_i)'$ as

$$W^P = \sum_{i=1}^{N} \pi_i V_i^P = \pi' V^P = \pi' P(\rho) u \tag{4.54}$$

Consider another transition probability matrix, Q, with the same steady-state distribution $\pi' = (\pi_i')$. Then,

$$W^Q = \sum_{i=1}^{N} \pi_i V_i^Q = \pi' V^Q = \pi' Q(\rho) u \tag{4.55}$$

The first result relating to social welfare is that $W^P = W^Q$. Circulation mobility has no effect on social welfare if the social welfare function is utilitarian. The proof follows immediately from the derivation of the steady-state distribution and the fact that P and Q generate the same steady state:

$$\pi' P(\rho) = \pi' P = \pi' = \pi' Q = \pi' Q(\rho) \tag{4.56}$$

Therefore,

$$W^P = \pi' P(\rho) u = \pi' Q(\rho) u = W^Q \tag{4.57}$$

Utilitarianism is indifferent to circulation mobility because it only cares about aggregate lifetime expected utility. It is completely indifferent to the composition of that aggregate, both in the steady state and as the economy evolves to the steady state over time.

Weighted Social Welfare and Circulation Mobility

The indifference of the utilitarian social welfare function to circulation mobility had been known for some time.[24] Dardanoni's contribution was to show that circulation mobility does have an independent effect on social welfare if social welfare is a weighted sum of the expected lifetime utilities. He also developed an empirical test for determining which of two transition matrices P and Q that generate the same steady state distribution yields the larger social welfare because of its superior transitional properties.

[24] The result was first demonstrated in 1986 by Kanbur and Stiglitz in S. Kanbur and J. Stiglitz, "Intergenerational Mobility and Dynastic Inequality," *Woodrow Wilson Discussion Paper No. 111*, Princeton University, 1986.

Define a nonincreasing vector of social welfare weights, $\lambda' = (\lambda_i)$. Dardanoni argues that a nonincreasing weighting scheme is the natural distributional assumption in the context of social mobility if society cares about the poor and the transition probability matrix is monotonic, as is also commonly assumed. P is monotonic if it exhibits stochastic dominance, in the sense that it is always better in expected value terms to start in a higher income category. For example, P would be monotonic if:

$$p_{11} > p_{21} > p_{31}; p_{11} + p_{12} > p_{21} + p_{22}; p_{21} + p_{22} > p_{31} + p_{32}; \text{and so forth}$$

(The proof of his weighted social welfare result does not require monotonicity; some other results in his paper do, however.)

As before, consider two transition probability matrices P and Q that generate the same steady-state distribution vector $\pi' = (\pi_i)'$. Define Π as the diagonal matrix with the steady-state proportions in each income category on the diagonal. The weighted social welfare under each transition matrix is

$$W^P = \sum_{i=1}^{N} \lambda_i \pi_i V_i^P = \lambda' \Pi P(\rho) u \tag{4.58}$$

and

$$W^Q = \sum_{i=1}^{N} \lambda_i \pi_i V_i^Q = \lambda' \Pi Q(\rho) u \tag{4.59}$$

Dardanoni asks: Under what set of conditions is $W^P > W^Q$?

The necessary and sufficient conditions make use of the summation matrix T, which has ones on and above the diagonal and zeros below the diagonal:

$$T = \begin{vmatrix} 1 & 1 & 1 \\ 0 & 1 & 1 \\ 0 & 0 & 1 \end{vmatrix} \qquad T' = \begin{vmatrix} 1 & 0 & 0 \\ 1 & 1 & 0 \\ 1 & 1 & 1 \end{vmatrix}$$

PT generates the cumulative sums of each row in P, the cumulative density function for each income category. For example, the first row of PT is p_{11}, $p_{11} + p_{12}$, $p_{11} + p_{12} + p_{13}$. Similarly, T'P generates the cumulative sums of each column in P. Also,

$$T^{-1} = \begin{vmatrix} 1 & -1 & 0 \\ 0 & 1 & -1 \\ 0 & 0 & 1 \end{vmatrix}$$

Premultiplying a vector by T^{-1} takes the differences of successive terms except the last term, which retains its value. For example,

$$T^{-1}u = \begin{vmatrix} 1 & -1 & 0 \\ 0 & 1 & -1 \\ 0 & 0 & 1 \end{vmatrix} \begin{vmatrix} u_1 \\ u_2 \\ u_3 \end{vmatrix} = (u_1 - u_2, u_2 - u_3, u_3)$$

Postmultiplying a vector by $(T^{-1})'[= (T')^{-1}]$ produces the same result. For example,

$$\lambda(T^{-1})' = (\lambda_1, \lambda_2, \lambda_3) \begin{vmatrix} 1 & 0 & 0 \\ -1 & 1 & 0 \\ 0 & -1 & 1 \end{vmatrix} = (\lambda_1 - \lambda_2, \lambda_2 - \lambda_3, \lambda_3)$$

Using the matrix T, Dardanoni's main theorem on weighted social welfare is that $W(V^P, \lambda) - W(V^Q, \lambda) \geq 0$ if and only if $T'\Pi[P(\rho) - Q(\rho)] \, T \leq 0$, for λ nonincreasing and u nondecreasing.

To show that the second relationship implies the first, rewrite the first relationship as:

$$\lambda'\Pi P(\rho)u - \lambda'\Pi Q(\rho)u \geq 0 \tag{4.60}$$

or

$$\lambda'\Pi[P(\rho) - Q(\rho)]u \geq 0 \tag{4.61}$$

Insert $I = (T)^{'-1}T' = TT^{-1}$ into the LHS to produce:

$$\lambda'(T)^{'-1}T' \, \Pi[P(\rho) - Q(\rho)]T \, T^{-1}u \geq 0 \tag{4.62}$$

Consider the terms $T'\Pi[P(\rho) - Q(\rho)]T$ for the 3×3 case to illustrate the following properties:

i. The last row of the expression is zero. The last row of $T'\Pi$ is $\pi' = (\pi_1, \pi_2, \pi_3)$, the steady-state distribution vector. But $\pi'P(\rho) = \pi' = \pi'Q(\rho)$. Therefore, the last row of the expression is zero.

ii. The last column of the expression is also zero. The last column of the matrix T sums the rows of $P(\rho)$ and $Q(\rho)$, both of which have to add to 1. Therefore, the last column of the expression is zero.

Next, consider the first two terms and last two terms of Eq. (4.62).

iii. The first two elements of $\lambda'(T)^{'-1} = (\lambda_1 - \lambda_2, \lambda_2 - \lambda_3, \lambda_3)$ are ≥ 0.[25]

iv. The first two elements of $T^{-1}u = (u_1 - u_2, u_2 - u_3, u_3)$ are ≤ 0.

Therefore, the entire expression is positive if $T'\Pi[P(\rho) - Q(\rho)]T \leq 0$, the sufficient condition for $W(V^P, \lambda) - W(V^Q, \lambda) \geq 0$.

To show that $W(V^P, \lambda) - W(V^Q, \lambda) \geq 0$ implies $T' \Pi[P(\rho) - Q(\rho)]T \leq 0$, suppose to the contrary that the ij[th] element of the second expression is

---

[25] Notice that the equal weights of the utilitarian social welfare function implies that the expression is zero, so that $W^P = W^Q$.

positive. The difference in social welfare is given by Eq. (4.62). To establish a contradiction, select the vector λ such that it has ones for its first i elements and zeros thereafter, and select the vector u such that it has zeros for its first j elements and ones thereafter. Then, $\lambda'(T)'^{-1}$ has a 1 in the ith element and zeros everywhere else, and $T^{-1}u$ has a -1 in its jth element and last element and zeros everywhere else (the last element is unimportant). Having selected λ and u this way, the entire expression Eq. (4.62) is negative if the ij^{th} element of the second expression above is positive, a contradiction of $W(V^P, \lambda) - W(V^Q, \lambda) \geq 0$.

Finally, the expression $T'\Pi[P(\rho) - Q(\rho)]T \leq 0$ has a satisfying interpretation in terms of the social welfare implications of circulation mobility. Return to the 3×3 case for purposes of illustration and consider the first two rows and columns of $T'\Pi P(\rho)T$, which are the nonzero rows and columns in the entire expression. Postmultiplying $\Pi P(\rho)$ by T yields the cumulative sums of the rows, and then premultiplying by T' yields the cumulative sums of the columns of the cumulative row sums:

$$T'\Pi P(\rho)T = \begin{vmatrix} \lambda_1 p_{11} & (\lambda_1 p_{11} + \lambda_1 p_{12}) & \cdots \\ (\lambda_1 p_{11} + \lambda_2 p_{21}) & (\lambda_1 p_{11} + \lambda_1 p_{12} + \lambda_2 p_{21} + \lambda_2 p_{22}) & \cdots \\ \cdots & \cdots & \cdots \end{vmatrix}$$

For the entire expression to be negative, the corresponding elements in $T'\Pi Q(\rho)T$ must each be larger than the elements in $T'\Pi P(\rho)T$. Therefore, $Q(\rho)$ has less circulation mobility, and lower social welfare in the following sense: Individuals who start in category k or lower have a higher discounted probability of winding up, lifetime, in category j or lower for all k and j. In the expression $T'\Pi P(\rho)T$ (and $T'\Pi Q(\rho)T$), the row indicates the starting position and the column the ending lifetime position. Therefore, in the 3×3 case above, the first row, first column compares the probabilities of those who start and end in category 1. The first row, second column compares the probabilities of those who start in category 1 and end in either category 1 or 2. The second row, first column compares the probabilities of those who start in category 1 or 2 and end in category 1. And the second row, second column compares the probabilities of those who start in either category 1 or 2 and end in either category 1 or 2. These probabilities are all higher for $Q(\rho)$ if $Q(\rho)$ has lower social welfare than $P(\rho)$. Notice that the difference in welfare is entirely due to the difference in circulation mobility, in process equity, because $Q(\rho)$ and $P(\rho)$ both generate the same steady-state distribution. They have the same structural mobility, the same end results equity.

In summary, Dardanoni has shown that an increase in upward mobility improves social welfare, but only if the social welfare function favors those with lower incomes.

Social Mobility in the United States

Thomas Hungerford measured the amount of social mobility in the United States by computing transition probability matrices over two 7-year time periods, 1969 to 1976 and 1979 to 1986. He divided the population into ten income categories each time. His results were essentially the same in the two periods and tended to undercut the notion that the United States is the land of equal opportunity. The transition matrices were much closer to the no-circulation identity matrix than to the matrix of full circulation, despite the fairly fine gradation of the income categories. Most people stayed at or near to their original position in the distribution over a 7-year period. The p_{ij} declined sharply to very low levels at three or more deciles away from the initial position, at all points in the distribution. Hungerford concludes that there is not very much social mobility in the United States—bad news for process equity.

An offsetting piece of good news in Hungerford's data relates to end-results equity. Redistributional policies are not so quickly undermined by social mobility when the degree of social mobility is small. After all, if the transition probability matrix were the identity matrix, the redistribution would stick forever. Hungerford's data suggest that a social-welfare-improving redistributional policy may retain much of its impact for a very long time.[26]

REFERENCES

Amiel, Y., Creedy, J., and Hurn, S., "Measuring Attitudes Towards Inequality," *Scandinavian Journal of Economics*, Vol. 101, No. 1, 83–96, 1999.

Atkinson, A., "On the Measurement of Inequality," *Journal of Economic Theory*, Vol. 2, 1970.

Atkinson, A., *The Economics of Inequality*, second ed., Oxford University Press, New York, 1983, sect. 3.4, pp. 53–59.

Bishop, J., Formby, J., and Smith, W., "Lorenz Dominance and Welfare: Changes in the U.S. Distribution of Income, 1967–86," *Review of Economics and Statistics*, February 1991.

Blackorby, C. and Donaldson, D., "Money Metric Utility: A Harmless Normalization?," *Journal of Economic Theory*, October 1988.

Buchinsky, M. and Hunt, J., "Wage Mobility in the United States," *Review of Economics and Statistics*, August 1999.

Dardanoni, V., "Measuring Social Mobility," *Journal of Economic Theory*, Vol. 61, pp. 372–394, 1993.

---

[26] See T. Hungerford, "U.S. Income Mobility in the Seventies and Eighties," *Review of Income and Wealth*, December, 1993. See also M. Buchinsky and J. Hunt, "Wage Mobility in the United States," *Review of Economics and Statistics*, August 1999. They found that young wage earners experienced lower social mobility and greater within-category inequality from 1979 to 1991.

Fisher, F., "Household Equivalence Scales and Interpersonal Comparisons," *Review of Economic Studies*, Vol. LIV, 1987.

Harberger, A., "Basic Needs Versus Distributional Weights in Social Cost–Benefit Analysis," in R. Haveman and J. Margolis (Eds.), *Public Expenditure and Policy Analysis*, third ed., Houghton Mifflin Boston, 1983.

Hungerford, T., "U.S. Income Mobility in the Seventies and Eighties," *Review of Income and Wealth*, December 1993.

Jorgenson, D., "Aggregate Consumer Behavior and the Measurement of Social Welfare," *Econometrica*, September 1990.

Jorgenson, D., "Efficiency Versus Equity in Economic Policy Analysis," *American Economist*, Vol. 29, No. 1, Spring 1985.

Jorgenson, D., "Did We Lose the War on Poverty?," *Journal of Economic Perspectives*, Winter 1998.

Kanbur, S. and Stiglitz, J., "Intergenerational Mobility and Dynastic Inequality," *Woodrow Wilson Discussion Paper No. 111*, Princeton University, 1986.

Lambert, P., "Estimating Impact Effects of Tax Reforms," *Journal of Economic Surveys*, September 1993.

Okun, A., *Equality and Efficiency, The Big Tradeoff*, The Brookings Institution, Washington, D.C., 1975.

Sen, A., "Ethical Measurement of Inequality: Some Difficulties," in Sen, A. (Ed.), *Choice, Welfare, and Measurement*, MIT Press, Cambridge, MA, 1982.

Shorrocks, A., "Ranking Income Distributions," *Economica*, Vol. 50, 1983.

Slesnick, D., "Gaining Ground: Poverty in the Postwar United States," *Journal of Political Economy*, February 1993.

Slesnick, D., "Empirical Approaches to the Measurement of Welfare," *Journal of Economic Literature*, December 1998.

Triest, R., "Has Poverty Gotten Worse?," *Journal of Economic Perspectives*, Winter 1998.

U.S. Census Bureau, Current Population Reports, Series P60-206, *Money Income in the United States: 1998*, U.S. Government Printing Office, Washington, D.C., 1999, Table C and Historical Tables, Table F.

5

THE PROBLEM OF EXTERNALITIES—AN OVERVIEW

We begin our study of public expenditure theory with an analysis of externalities, which are a major source of inefficiency in any economy, market or otherwise. Externalities are often loosely defined as third-party effects, meaning that some activity by a set of economic agents affects other economic agents, "third parties," who are not directly engaged in the activity. This common definition is not precise enough for policy analysis, however. Because an economy is a highly interdependent system, almost any (important) economic activity generates repercussions—third party effects—throughout the entire economy. Yet, not all economic activity requires public sector intervention.

POLICY-RELEVANT EXTERNALITIES

Consider the following two examples of externalities:

1. In the middle of the twentieth century, the demand for long-distance passenger travel shifted toward the airplane at the expense of the railroads.

2. A family living on the top of a hill builds a high fence around its property, which restricts the view previously enjoyed by many of its neighbors.

The first situation triggered a huge number of third-party effects as the economy worked to accommodate the shift in demand. Generally speaking, resources specific to air travel gained, and those specific to rail travel lost, signaling a shift of resources away from the railroads and toward the airlines. Since people's tastes presumably differ, and different people received different incomes than before the shift to air travel, the whole pattern of demands for all goods and services tended to shift as well. These changes in demand occasioned still further changes in incomes and additional resource shifts to and from industries that may have been totally unrelated to air or rail travel, and so on, endlessly. Yet, the government did not necessarily have to intervene in this process. To the contrary, the very strength of the competitive market system is its ability to coordinate shifts in demands and resources, while bringing the economy to a new, efficient equilibrium.

In the second situation, however, the third-party effects occur outside the normal market process. There is no natural market mechanism for recording the loss that each neighbor suffers from the fence. Any redress the neighbors might seek would presumably occur through the judicial process.

There is a second crucial difference in these two examples. In the first situation, the demand shifts in and of themselves have no effect on any of the fundamental *technical* relationships in the economy: the consumers' utility functions and the producers' production functions. All third-party gains and losses accrue through changes in prices, both goods prices and factor prices. Some consumers faced new budget constraints and some firms new profit functions, with corresponding gains or losses, all caused by the competitive process of supply and demand which continuously changes consumer and producer prices while searching for a new equilibrium. In the second situation, in contrast, the neighbors lose because the properties of one of the variables in their utility functions, their land, has been altered and not because prices have changed. Each neighbor's ability to enjoy his own property has diminished because of the fence, independently of any price changes generated by building the fence (of course, it is unlikely that prices would change in this case).

These two distinctions are the vital ones for public sector analysis. An externality, or third-party effect, may require government intervention to maintain efficiency if two conditions hold:

1. An activity by a set of economic agents enters ("alters") the utility functions of other consumers or the production functions of other producers not directly involved with the activity.

2. The gains and losses from these effects are not properly reflected in the competitive market system. This second condition is redundant in most cases,

since externalities satisfying the first condition are almost never accounted for properly by the competitive market system.

Given the existence of externalities with these two properties, a perfectly competitive market economy no longer generates a pareto-optimal allocation of resources. Government intervention may be required to keep society on its first-best utility-possibilities frontier. The only other possibility is private bargaining among the affected parties, which can be pareto optimal under certain conditions.

The Terminology of Externalities

Public sector economists struggled for years trying to pinpoint what kinds of third-party effects required government intervention. The puzzle was finally resolved in 1931 when Jacob Viner distinguished between pecuniary and technological externalities, terminology that remains in use today.[1] *Pecuniary externalities* refer to the market price effects illustrated by the first situation, those resulting directly from competitive market adjustments. They do not require public intervention to maintain pareto optimality. *Technological externalities* refer to third-party effects that satisfy the two conditions described above. These are the policy-relevant externalities.

The externality literature is filled with jargon to distinguish among the many different kinds of externalities. For instance, public sector economists distinguish between *external economies* and *diseconomies*: The former term refers to beneficial third-party effects, the latter to harmful third-party effects. Thus, one can speak of a "pecuniary external economy" or a "technological external diseconomy," and so forth. We will keep the distinction between economies and diseconomies in the text but drop the pecuniary/technological distinction. Because our only concern is for policy-relevant externalities, the term *externality* will always mean "technological externality" unless otherwise noted.

Another important distinction is among consumption, production, and consumption-production externalities:

Consumption externality: Economic activity by some consumer enters (alters) the utility function of at least one other consumer but does not enter into (alter) any production relationships. The fence described above is an example of a consumer externality. Consumption of national defense is another more important example.

---

[1] J. Viner, "Cost Curves and Supply Curves," *Zeitschrift fur Nationalokonomie*, III, 1931 (reprinted in *American Economic Association Readings in Price Theory*, Richard D. Irwin, Chicago, 1952). The conceptual distinction was first noted by Allyn Young in 1913, but without Viner's terminology. A. A. Young, "Pigou's Wealth and Welfare," *Quarterly Journal of Economics*, August 1913.

Production externality: Economic activity by some firm enters (alters) the production function of at least one other firm but does not enter (alter) the utility function of any consumer. One firm removing oil from a common pool situated under land owned by more than one firm would be an example. The rate at which any one firm extracts the oil affects the total amount of oil that can be extracted from the pool by all the firms.

Consumption–production externality: Economic activity by some consumer enters (alters) the production function of at least one firm, or vice versa. Water pollution by a firm that affects both recreational and commercial fishing activities is an example of a consumption–production externality.

These distinctions are useful analytically because they generate different optimal policy rules. Chapters 6, 7, and 8 consider each of them in turn, beginning with consumption externalities in Chapter 6.

Still other terminological distinctions appear in the externality literature. We will develop them as needed within each chapter, whenever they are relevant for public policy.[2]

THE ANALYSIS OF EXTERNALITIES: MODELING PRELIMINARIES

Chapter 3 described a useful property of first-best general equilibrium models, that their first-order conditions dichotomize in two ways. One is that they generate distinct sets of interpersonal equity and pareto-optimal conditions. The former incorporate the social welfare function and describe how society can achieve end-results equity through lump-sum redistributions. The latter describe all the efficiency conditions necessary for society to achieve its utility-possibilities frontier. The pareto-optimal conditions do not contain any social welfare terms and can be achieved by competitive markets absent any of the technical market failures such as externalities. The dichotomization of the interpersonal equity and pareto-optimal conditions was demonstrated in Chapter 2. The second dichotomy arises within the set of pareto-optimal conditions. Suppose that a technical market failure such as

---

[2] The treatment of externalities in Chapters 6–8 is comprehensive, with one notable exception. It does not consider an important type of externality called the *club good*, which was first analyzed by James Buchanan. A club good has the property that the extent of the externality can be controlled by the agents who generate the externality. For example, all members of a swim club have equal access to the club's swimming pool, but the club members control the total membership in the club. Buchanan's club good has appeared most prominently in the literature on fiscal federalism because a city or town can be viewed as a type of club. The standard economic model of a local jurisdiction assumes that only the citizens of a locality enjoy the public services offered by that locality, such as fire or police protection, and that the citizens determine the conditions of entry into the locality. We will hold off on presenting the club good until Part V on fiscal federalism. See J. Buchanan, "An Economic Theory of Clubs," *Economica*, February 1965.

an externality exists in some market. The externality changes the pareto-optimal conditions for that market, and government intervention may be required to achieve them. But the market failure has no effect on the form of the pareto-optimal conditions for all the other markets. Therefore, competitive markets can generate the pareto-optimal conditions in the unaffected markets; no government intervention is required in those markets. We will demonstrate the second dichotomy in Chapter 6.

These two dichotomies are useful because they permit formal analysis of policy problems with greatly condensed versions of the general equilibrium model presented in Chapter 2. For example, a consumer externality involves interrelationships among consumers only; producers are unaffected. Therefore, a first-best model analyzing a consumer externality can simply assume that production efficiency results from competitive markets, suppress the production side of the full model, and focus on the consumption externality among the consumers. Conversely, a production externality involves inter-relationships among producers only. Therefore, a first-best analysis of a production externality can focus on the externality by positing a one-consumer equivalent economy, which assumes that competitive markets generate all the pareto-optimal conditions among consumers and that the government is optimally redistributing lump-sum to satisfy the interpersonal equity conditions. These are legitimate assumptions in a first-best policy environment. Having analyzed the full model in Chapter 2, we know what the missing pareto-optimal and interpersonal equity conditions must be in the suppressed portions of the condensed models. Economists exploit these dichotomies all the time to analyze market failures with simple models. We will do the same throughout Part II.

Consider the following condensed version of the Chapter 2 model that is suitable for analyzing consumption externalities. The model deemphasizes production as much as possible while retaining all the essential consumption/utility elements from the full model. We will use it as our basic model in Chapter 6, adding only the particular external effects being analyzed. The condensed model is accomplished with the following modifications:

1. Define all goods and factors in terms of consumption by suppressing, notationally, the use of factors and the supply of goods by firms. Further, ignore the notational distinction between goods and factors, other than the convention that factors enter all utility and production relationships with a negative sign. Let:

$$X_{hi} = \text{good i consumed by or factor i supplied by person h,}$$
$$i = 1, \ldots, N \text{ and } h = 1, \ldots, H$$

Notice that there are N total goods and factors in the economy (instead of the G goods and F factors in the model of Chapter 2).

2. Assume production is efficient and can be represented implicitly as a production-possibilities frontier in terms of the aggregate amount of consumer goods produced and factors supplied. Write:

$$F(X_1, \ldots, X_i, \ldots, X_N) = 0 \tag{5.1}$$

where X_i = the aggregate consumption (supply) of good (factor) i, and $F(\ )$ = an implicit function of all the relevant production relationships, corresponding to the production-possibilities frontier in two-good space.[3]

3. Finally, market clearance requires that

$$\sum_{h=1}^{H} X_{hi} = X_i \qquad i = 1, \ldots, N$$

These constraints can be incorporated directly into the production-possibilities frontier, obtaining:

$$F\left(\sum_{h=1}^{H} X_{h1}, \ldots, \sum_{h=1}^{H} X_{hi}, \ldots, \sum_{h=1}^{H} X_{hN}\right) = 0, \text{ or} \tag{5.2}$$

$$F\left(\sum_{h=1}^{H} X_{hi}\right) = 0 \tag{5.3}$$

with the understanding that producers do not care who receives (supplies) an additional unit of a good (factor). That is,

$$\frac{\partial F}{\partial X_{hi}} = \frac{\partial F}{\partial X_i} = F_i \qquad \text{all } h = 1, \ldots, H$$

With these three condensations, the social welfare maximization problem becomes extremely simple to represent formally:

$$\max_{(X_{hi})} W\left[U^h(X_{hi})\right]$$

$$\text{s.t. } F\left(\sum_{h=1}^{H} X_{hi}\right) = 0$$

where W is the Bergson–Samuelson individualistic social welfare function.

Although this is a drastically condensed version of the original model, it is still perfectly valid as a general equilibrium model in a first-best environment. Furthermore, it is sufficiently general to generate all relevant pareto-

---

[3] Unless otherwise stated, we will always assume that $F(\ )$ describes a regular (convex outwards) transformation surface for the economy. This in turn implies certain restrictions on the individual production functions. Kelvin Lancaster's *Mathematical Economics*, sects. 8.4 through 8.7, contains an excellent analysis of the necessary and sufficient conditions on the individual production functions for a regular transformation surface. See K. Lancaster, *Mathematical Economics*, Macmillan, New York, 1968.

optimal conditions involving consumption, as well as the standard interpersonal equity conditions. As such, it is ideal for analyzing consumer externalities, which essentially involves specifying which goods and factors enter whose utility functions.

The Interpersonal Equity Conditions

Consider first the interpersonal equity conditions. They are obtained from the first-order conditions with respect to any single good (or factor) consumed (supplied) by any two people, say X_{h1} and X_{j1}. Setting up the Lagrangian,

$$\max_{(X_{hi})} L = W\left[U^h(X_{hi})\right] + \lambda F\left(\sum_{h=1}^{H} X_{hi}\right)$$

and differentiating yields:

$$X_{h1}: \quad \frac{\partial L}{\partial X_{h1}} = \frac{\partial W}{\partial U^h} \frac{\partial U^h}{\partial X_{h1}} + \lambda F_1 = 0 \tag{5.4}$$

$$X_{j1}: \quad \frac{\partial L}{\partial X_{j1}} = \frac{\partial W}{\partial U^j} \frac{\partial U^j}{\partial X_{j1}} + \lambda F_1 = 0 \tag{5.5}$$

Therefore:

$$\frac{\partial W}{\partial U^h} \frac{\partial U^h}{\partial X_{h1}} = -\lambda F_1 \qquad \text{all } h = 1, \ldots, H \tag{5.6}$$

The social marginal utility of consumption of good 1 should be equalized across all people. This is the same rule obtained in the more detailed model of Chapter 2.

The Pareto-Optimal Conditions

To derive the pareto-optimal conditions for consumption, consider the first-order conditions with respect to two goods consumed by any one person— say, X_{hi} and X_{hk} (X_{hi} and X_{hk} could also be two factors or any one good and any one factor).

$$X_{hi}: \quad \frac{\partial L}{\partial X_{hi}} = \frac{\partial W}{\partial U^h} \frac{\partial U^h}{\partial X_{hi}} + \lambda F_i = 0 \tag{5.7}$$

$$X_{hk}: \quad \frac{\partial L}{\partial X_{hk}} = \frac{\partial W}{\partial U^h} \frac{\partial U^h}{\partial X_{hk}} + \lambda F_k = 0 \tag{5.8}$$

Rearranging, dividing, and simplifying,

$$\frac{\dfrac{\partial U^h}{\partial X_{hi}}}{\dfrac{\partial U^h}{\partial X_{hk}}} = \frac{F_i}{F_k} \qquad \begin{array}{l} \text{all } h = 1, \dots, H \\[6pt] \text{any } i, k = 1, \dots, N \end{array} \qquad (5.9)$$

The ratio F_i/F_k gives the marginal rate of transformation (substitution) in production between goods (factors) i and k, and the left-hand side is their marginal rate of substitution in consumption. Hence, the single set of relationships, Eq. (5.9), reproduces pareto-optimal conditions P1, P2, P3, P6, P7, and P8 from the full model of Chapter 2. (recalling that i and k can be any two goods, any two factors, or any one good and any one factor.) Only the production efficiency conditions P4 and P5 cannot be reproduced with this model, but they are assumed to hold whenever production is represented as an implicit production-possibilities frontier. Production must occur on the contract locus in factor space for the economy to be on its production-possibilities frontier.

Thus, condensed versions of the standard model such as this one retain a substantial amount of analytical flexibility despite their simplicity. This is why they are so useful for analyzing public sector problems in a first-best framework.

Chapter 6 turns to the analysis of consumption externalities using the condensed model. As we shall see, the analysis of any consumer externality requires only a simple modification of the condensed model. All one need specify is which variables appear in each person's utility function.

REFERENCES

Buchanan, J., "An Economic Theory of Clubs," *Economica*, February 1965.

Lancaster, K., *Mathematical Economics*, Macmillan, New York, 1968.

Viner, J., "Cost Curves and Supply Curves," *Zeitschrift fur Nationalokonomie*, III, 1932 reprinted in *American Economic Association Readings in Price Theory*, Richard D. Irwin, Chicago, 1952.

Young, A. A., "Pigou's Wealth and Welfare," *Quarterly Journal of Economics*, August 1913.

6

CONSUMPTION EXTERNALITIES

    A policy-relevant consumption externality occurs whenever economic activity by some consumer enters (alters) the utility function of at least one other consumer and is not accounted for by the market system. The very definition itself suggests that the fundamental problem in analyzing consumption externalities is deciding exactly what activities enter whose utility functions and in precisely what form. Once the arguments of each consumer's utility function are specified, they determine every relevant feature of the consumer externality, including the proper government policy required to achieve pareto optimality.

We will make use of variations of the condensed general equilibrium model described in Chapter 5. Let X_{ik} represent the consumption (supply) of good (factor) k by person i, where

$k = 1, \ldots, N$ (N total goods and factors)
$i = 1, \ldots, H$ (H people)

Then the basic model for analyzing all consumption externality problems in a first-best policy environment is

$$\max_{(X_{ik})} W\left[U^h()\right]$$

$$\text{s.t.} \quad F\left(\sum_{i=1}^{H} X_{ik}\right) = 0$$

W is the individualistic social welfare function to be maximized, and F is the implicit aggregate production possibility frontier. It assumes production efficiency and incorporates the market clearing equations for the N goods and factors. Also,

$$\frac{\partial F}{\partial X_{ik}} = \frac{\partial F}{\partial X_k} = F_k \qquad \text{all } i = 1, \ldots, H_i; \qquad \text{any } k = 1, \ldots, N$$

Producers do not care who consumes each good (supplies each factor). The nature of the consumer eternality depends entirely on how the X_{ik} enter each person's utility function, the U^h.

HOW BAD CAN EXTERNALITIES BE?

Let's begin by considering the most intractable externality case and ask: How bad can consumption externalities be? The worst possible situation imaginable would require a triple indexing of X, X_{ik}^j, with X_{ik}^j entering the utility function of each person h:

$$U^h = U^h\left(X_{ik}^j\right)$$

X_{ik}^j refers to the consumption (supply) of good (factor) k, by person i, affecting person j, i = 1, \ldots, H; j = 1, \ldots, H; and k = 1, \ldots, N. That is, each person h worries about who consumes (supplies) what good (factor) and how it affects each person.

Return to the example of the fence in Chapter 5, in which each person in a given neighborhood is affected whenever anyone builds a fence. Suppose there are H people in the neighborhood and person i builds a fence, good k. Each person h in the neighborhood notes that person i built the fence (good k) and that the fence affects everyone in the neighborhood differently. Thus, from the point of view of person h, X_{ik}^j is different from X_{ik}^ℓ, for $\ell \neq j$ and $\ell, j = 1, \ldots, H$. Each variable refers to person i's fence, but persons j and ℓ react differently to the fence and each person h in the neighborhood takes note of this difference. Had someone else built a fence (say, person m), then each person's utility function would contain another H argument, X_{mk}^j, $j = 1, \ldots, H$, and so forth. In the worst of all worlds, anything anyone did would affect everyone, and each person would take note of how everyone was affected by any one person's consumption of any good. Hence, each utility function would contain all H^2N elements, X_{ik}^j, as arguments. This would surely be the worst possible consumption externality situation imaginable.

Fortunately, we can at least dispense with the superscript j without disservice to any realistic situation. Continuing with the fence example, when any one person h considers the effects of the fence on himself and his $(H - 1)$ neighbors, we can assume that the H separate effects combine to generate a single overall effect on person h's utility. Thus, person h's utility function need only record that person i built a fence (good k), as opposed to someone else building a fence. At most, then, we need to place HN arguments, X_{ik}, in each person's utility function. Write:

$$U^h = U^h(X_{ik}) \qquad \text{any } h = 1, \ldots, H; \text{ all } i = 1, \ldots, H;$$
$$\text{and } k = 1, \ldots, N \tag{6.1}$$

to indicate that, in the worst of all worlds, each person h is affected by anyone's (i) consumption (supply) of any good (factor) k. The fact that person h considers the effects of some X_{ik} on all people is simply summarized as one effect on his utility, $U^h(X_{ik})$.

The general equilibrium social planner's model in this worst of all worlds becomes:

$$\max_{(X_{ik})} W\left[U^h(X_{ik})\right]$$

$$\text{s.t.} \quad F\left(\sum_{i=1}^{H}X_{ik}\right) = 0$$

Notice that the goods (and factors) in this model are exclusive goods. X_{ik} means that person i physically consumes (supplies) good (factor) k, as indicated by the market clearance relationship $\sum_{i=1}^{H} X_{ik} = X_k$. X_{ik} enters into the utility function of all $(H - 1)$ other persons, but they are merely affected by X_{ik}; they do not physically consume it. Thus, there are $H \cdot (H - 1)$ *external* effects associated with the consumption (supply) of good (factor) k, and $H \cdot (H - 1) \cdot N$ total external effects, counting all N goods and factors in the worst of all possible worlds.

Externalities of this type are referred to as *individualized externalities* because the external effects depend on who is engaged in the exclusive activity that generates the externalities. It matters who builds the fence.

In the context of this model, a natural definition of a *pure public good (factor)* is

$$\frac{\partial U^h}{\partial X_{ik}} \neq 0 \qquad \text{all } i, h = 1, \ldots, H \qquad (6.2)$$

If everyone is affected *on the margin* by anyone's consumption (supply) of good (factor) k, then k is a pure public good. The choice of marginal rather than total utility in the definition makes sense because, as we shall see, it is marginal utilities (more precisely, marginal rates of substitution) that enter into the pareto-optimal decision rules. Person h could be significantly affected by person i's consumption of good k in a total sense, but if the marginal effect is zero, then it turns out that person h's feelings do not matter for purposes of allocational efficiency at the optimum.[1]

Note that our definition of publicness says nothing about the signs of $\partial U^h / \partial X_{ik}$. For some h, the derivative could be positive, for others negative, so long as $\partial U^h / \partial X_{ik}$ is never zero. The smoking of marijuana comes to mind as an example. Some people enjoy the fact that others indulge; other people clearly dislike it. In the terminology of externalities, marijuana generates both external economies and diseconomies.

Correspondingly, a *pure private good (factor)* is one for which

$$\frac{\partial U^h}{\partial X_{ik}} = 0 \qquad i \neq h \qquad (6.3)$$

Only person i is affected on the margin by her consumption (supply) of good (factor) k. We will write $U^h(X_{hk})$ to indicate that good (factor) k is a pure private good (factor), and $U^h(X_{ik})$ to indicate that a consumer externality exists that is *potentially* a pure public good. We say potentially because all the notation implies is that some person h is affected by at least one other person's consumption (supply) of good (factor) k as well as his own consumption of good (factor) k. It is not meant to imply that everyone is necessarily affected by each person's consumption of good (factor) k. $\partial U^h / \partial X_{ik}$ could

---

[1] For the benefit of those somewhat familiar with the externality literature, we should also note that this definition differs from Samuelson's early definition of a pure public good which has gained fairly wide acceptance. Samuelson equated publicness to nonexclusiveness or jointness in consumption, meaning that if any one person consumes the services of a good, then everyone automatically consumes its services. In our model, in contrast, only person i consumes X_{ik}, only person j consumes X_{jk}, and so forth, for any $i, j = 1, \ldots, H$, and X_{ik} does not necessarily equal X_{jk}. (For more on nonexclusive goods, refer to the next section of this chapter.)

equal zero for some i or even most i. All that is required for the existence of a consumption externality is that one person's utility be a function of one other person's consumption (supply) of something.

THE WORST OF ALL WORLDS—ALL GOODS (FACTORS) ARE PURE PUBLIC GOODS (FACTORS)

In the worst of all worlds, all goods (factors) are pure public goods (factors).[2] For policy purposes, this is really a horrendous situation as the government can hardly interpret what the proper decision rules mean let alone have any hope of implementing them. The government's problem is

$$\max_{(X_{ik})} W\left[U^h(X_{ik})\right]$$

$$\text{s.t.} \quad F\left(\sum_{i=1}^{H} X_{ik}\right) = 0$$

with the understanding that each utility function $U^h(\ )$ contains all NH elements, X_{ik} $i = 1, \ldots, H;\ k = 1, \ldots, N$.

The corresponding Lagrangian is

$$\max_{(X_{ik})} L = W\left[U^h(X_{ik})\right] + \lambda F\left(\sum_{i=1}^{H} X_{ik}\right)$$

Before proceeding, notice how deceptively similar this problem is to the problem of social welfare maximization when there are only pure private goods. In our notation, the pure private goods case is represented as:

$$\max_{(X_{hk})} W\left[U^h(X_{hk})\right]$$

$$\text{s.t.} \quad F\left(\sum_{h=1}^{H} X_{hk}\right) = 0$$

In each case, maximization occurs with respect to HN goods and factors, the N goods and factors consumed and supplied by each of H people. The difference is that in the worst of all worlds all HN variables appear in each utility function, whereas in the pure private goods (factors) world only N variables appear in each utility function. This difference matters, because the policy implications are enormously different. In the latter case, the competitive market can achieve full pareto optimality. In the former case, the market cannot be expected to achieve efficiency, and the government is virtually powerless to act in an optimal manner. The problems for the government in the pure public goods case are self-evident upon examination of the

[2] Ng provides an alternative model of this worst of all worlds in Y-K Ng, "The Paradox of Universal Externalities," *Journal of Economic Theory*, April 1975.

first-order conditions for social welfare maximization, both the interpersonal equity conditions and the pareto-optimal conditions.

Interpersonal Equity Conditions

Recall that the interpersonal equity conditions are obtained by comparing the first-order conditions for any one good (factor) consumed (supplied) by any two people, say X_{j1} and X_{i1}. The first-order conditions are

$$X_{j1}: \quad \sum_{h=1}^{H} \frac{\partial W}{\partial U^h} \frac{\partial U^h}{\partial X_{j1}} = -\lambda F_1 \qquad (6.4)$$

$$X_{i1}: \quad \sum_{h=1}^{H} \frac{\partial W}{\partial U^h} \frac{\partial U^h}{\partial X_{i1}} = -\lambda F_1 \qquad (6.5)$$

From conditions (6.4) and (6.5),

$$\sum_{h=1}^{H} \frac{\partial W}{\partial U^h} \frac{\partial U^h}{\partial X_{i1}} = -\lambda F_1 \qquad \text{all } i = 1, \ldots, H \qquad (6.6)$$

The interpretation of the interpersonal equity conditions is identical to that of the standard model in Chapter 2, which contained only pure private goods: The government should redistribute good 1, lump sum, until social welfare is equalized on the margin across all individuals. This task, difficult enough with pure private goods, is now hopelessly complex, however. When the government gives (takes) an extra unit of good (factor) 1 to (from) person i, it must know how *all* people react to that transfer (tax) on the margin, not just how person i's utility is affected, and similarly for units transferred to or from any other person. This is clearly an impossible task, one the government could not even hope to approximate.

Pareto-Optimal Conditions

The pareto-optimal conditions also differ considerably from their counterpart in a world of pure private goods, both in form and interpretation. Recall that the pareto-optimal conditions are obtained from the first-order conditions of any two goods consumed (factors supplied) by any one person, say X_{ik} and X_{i1}. The first-order conditions are

$$X_{ik}: \quad \sum_{h=1}^{H} \frac{\partial W}{\partial U^h} \frac{\partial U^h}{\partial X_{ik}} = -\lambda F_k \qquad (6.7)$$

$$X_{i1}: \quad \sum_{h=1}^{H} \frac{\partial W}{\partial U^h} \frac{\partial U^h}{\partial X_{i1}} = -\lambda F_1 \qquad (6.8)$$

Dividing Eq. (6.7) by (6.8) yields:

$$\frac{\sum\limits_{h=1}^{H} \dfrac{\partial W}{\partial U^h} \dfrac{\partial U^h}{\partial X_{ik}}}{\sum\limits_{h=1}^{H} \dfrac{\partial W}{\partial U^h} \dfrac{\partial U^h}{\partial X_{il}}} = \frac{F_k}{F_l} \qquad \begin{array}{l} \text{all } \ i = 1, \ldots, H \\[4pt] \text{any } k = 2, \ldots, N \end{array} \qquad (6.9)$$

The right-hand side of (6.9) has a standard interpretation, the marginal rate of transformation (MRT) in production between goods (factors) k and 1. The left-hand side has no standard interpretation, however. As written, it is a ratio of marginal impacts on social welfare from consuming (supplying) the two goods (factors), and there is no way to simplify the expression. In particular, the social welfare terms, $\partial W/\partial U^h$, do not cancel, so that the rule is not really a pareto-optimal or efficiency condition at all. Recall that pareto-optimal conditions do not contain social welfare terms. In this worst of all worlds, then, the model does not dichotomize into interpersonal equity and pareto-optimal conditions, the only exception we will encounter in all of Part II. All the decision rules are of the interpersonal equity type and can be achieved only by lump-sum redistributions of all goods and factors, a truly hopeless situation. Moreover, the competitive market system, which equates marginal rates of substitution in consumption to marginal rates of transform-ation, would be absolutely useless. Nothing short of a complete government takeover of the economy would be capable of satisfying the first-order conditions for social welfare maximization, even in principle.

THE EXISTENCE OF AT LEAST ONE PURE PRIVATE GOOD

Fortunately, the real world is not so riddled with consumption externalities. A large number of goods are pure private goods, or close enough to pure private goods that a government would not consider intervening in their markets. To keep the discussion as general as possible, however, let us assume that there is only one pure private good in the economy, the first. Formally, $\partial U^h/\partial X_{il} = 0, i \neq h$. The other $(N - 1)$ goods and factors remain pure public goods. As it turns out, only one private good is needed to resurrect the dichotomy between the pareto-optimal and interpersonal equity conditions that normally exists in first-best analysis and to retain a role for the competi-tive market system in allocating all the goods and factors.

    With a single private good, the social welfare maximization problem becomes:

$$\max_{(X_{ik}; X_{hl})} W\left[U^h(X_{ik}; X_{hl})\right]$$

$$\text{s.t.} \quad F\left(\sum_{i=1}^{H} X_{ik}; \sum_{h=1}^{H} X_{hl}\right) = 0$$

where $k = 2, \ldots, N$. Good 1 has been written separately to indicate specifically that it is a pure private good.

Interpersonal Equity Conditions

Consider the interpersonal equity conditions with respect to good 1, the pure private good. The first-order conditions are[3]

$$X_{h1}: \quad \frac{\partial W}{\partial U^h} \frac{\partial U^h}{X_{h1}} = -\lambda F_1 \tag{6.10}$$

$$X_{i1}: \quad \frac{\partial W}{\partial U^i} \frac{\partial U^i}{X_{i1}} = -\lambda F_1 \tag{6.11}$$

or

$$\frac{\partial W}{\partial U^h} \frac{\partial U^h}{X_{h1}} = -\lambda F_1 \qquad \text{all } h = 1, \ldots, H \tag{6.12}$$

Equation (6.12) is identical to the interpersonal equity conditions in the standard model of Chapter 2. *Assume the government can redistribute X_1 lump sum to achieve this condition as part of its first-best policy strategy.*

Pareto-Optimal Conditions

As above, consider the first-order conditions with respect to two goods (factors) consumed (supplied) by any one person i, say X_{ik} and X_{i1}. The choice of k is arbitrary, but good 1, the private good, must be one of the two goods chosen. The first-order conditions are

$$X_{ik}: \quad \sum_{h=1}^{H} \frac{\partial W}{\partial U^h} \frac{\partial U^h}{X_{ik}} = -\lambda F_k \tag{6.13}$$

$$X_{i1}: \quad \frac{\partial W}{\partial U^i} \frac{\partial U^i}{\partial X_{i1}} = -\lambda F_1 \tag{6.14}$$

Dividing Eq. (6.13) by (6.14) yields:

$$\frac{\sum_{h=1}^{H} \dfrac{\partial W}{\partial U^h} \dfrac{\partial U^h}{\partial X_{ik}}}{\dfrac{\partial W}{\partial U^i} \dfrac{\partial U^i}{\partial X_{i1}}} = \frac{F_k}{F_1}, \text{ for } k = 2, \ldots, N \tag{6.15}$$

Condition (6.15) can be simplified if the government has satisfied the interpersonal equity conditions for good 1. The left-hand side is a summation

[3] λ is the Lagrangian multiplier associated with F ( ).

of social welfare terms over a common denominator, $\dfrac{\partial W}{\partial U^i}\dfrac{\partial U^i}{\partial X_{i1}}$. But, if inter-personal equity holds,

$$\frac{\partial W}{\partial U^i}\frac{\partial U^i}{X_{i1}} = -\lambda F_1 \qquad \text{all } i = 1, \ldots, H \qquad (6.16)$$

Selectively substitute for the denominator term by term, matching up the social welfare terms, and write:

$$\frac{\dfrac{\partial W}{\partial U^1}\dfrac{\partial U^1}{\partial X_{ik}}}{\dfrac{\partial W}{\partial U^1}\dfrac{\partial U^1}{\partial X_{11}}} + , \ldots , + \frac{\dfrac{\partial W}{\partial U^h}\dfrac{\partial U^h}{\partial X_{ik}}}{\dfrac{\partial W}{\partial U^h}\dfrac{\partial U^h}{\partial X_{h1}}} + , \ldots , + \frac{\dfrac{\partial W}{\partial U^H}\dfrac{\partial U^H}{\partial X_{ik}}}{\dfrac{\partial W}{\partial U^H}\dfrac{\partial U^H}{\partial X_{H1}}} = \frac{F_k}{F_1}, \quad (6.17)$$

$$\text{any } k = 2, \ldots, N$$

$$\sum_{h=1}^{H} \left[\frac{\dfrac{\partial W}{\partial U^h}\dfrac{\partial U^h}{\partial X_{ik}}}{\dfrac{\partial W}{\partial U^h}\dfrac{\partial U^h}{\partial X_{h1}}} \right] = \frac{F_k}{F_1} \qquad \begin{array}{l} \text{all } i = 1, \ldots, H \\ \text{any } k = 2, \ldots, N \end{array} \qquad (6.18)$$

The social welfare indexes, $\partial W/\partial U^h$ cancel term by term, yielding:

$$\sum_{h=1}^{H} \left[\frac{\dfrac{\partial U^h}{\partial X_{ik}}}{\dfrac{\partial U^h}{\partial X_{h1}}} \right] = \frac{F_k}{F_1} \qquad (6.19)$$

The left-hand side of Eq. (6.19) has a standard pareto-optimal interpretation, devoid of social welfare terms. It is a sum of marginal rates of substitution, each person's marginal rate of substitution (MRS) between person i's consumption of good k and her own consumption of the pure private good. Thus, the rule can be written as:

$$\sum_{h=1}^{H} MRS^h_{X_{ik}, X_{h1}} = MRT_{k,1} \qquad \begin{array}{l} \text{for all } i = 1, \ldots, H \\ \text{any } k = 2, \ldots, N \end{array} \qquad (6.20)$$

Note carefully that the ability to cancel the social welfare terms is not just a formal "trick." It implies an optimal first-best policy action, a lump sum redistribution that satisfies the interpersonal equity conditions for good (factor) 1. Without the optimal redistribution, the terms would not cancel and all the policy implications of the pareto-optimal conditions which we are about to discuss become irrelevant. Conditions (6.19) would not be the necessary conditions for a social welfare maximum. We will employ this cancellation technique repeatedly throughout the chapter, with the same policy implications understood each time. Without the ability to achieve correct lump-sum redistributions, none of the standard first-best policy prescriptions apply, even those ostensibly related only to allocational issues.[4]

Note, finally, that only good 1 need be redistributed lump sum, exactly as in the baseline private goods model of Chapter 2. If the government correctly redistributes good 1 and designs policies to achieve all the pareto-optimal conditions, then the interpersonal equity conditions automatically hold for goods (and factors) $k = 2, \ldots, N$ as well. To see this, plug the social welfare terms back into the left-hand side of Eq. (6.19), obtaining Eq. (6.18). If Eq. (6.18) holds and the denominators are also equal from interpersonal equity, then the numerators are also equal:

$$\sum_{h=1}^{H} \frac{\partial W}{\partial U^h} \frac{\partial U^h}{\partial X_{ik}} = -\lambda F_k \qquad \begin{array}{l} \text{all } i = 1, \ldots, H \\ \text{any } k = 2, \ldots, N \end{array} \qquad (6.21)$$

as required by the interpersonal equity conditions for goods $k = 2, \ldots, N$.

Because the pareto-optimal rules for externality-generating exclusive goods are combinations of marginal rates of substitution and marginal rates of transformation, they have the following properties:

1. One can always describe a market structure with competitive prices that will achieve the correct pareto-optimal conditions without government intervention. This is so because producers and consumers equate market prices to marginal rates of transformation and substitution under perfect competition. The necessary market structure is far more complex than the normal competitive market structure, however. It requires an entire new set of competitive market transactions among consumers that correctly account for all the external effects. In other words, the market failure associated with externalities can be thought of as a problem of nonexistent markets, namely the required competitive side markets among consumers.[5]

2. The government can achieve the pareto-optimal conditions within the standard decentralized competitive markets for each of the goods (factors) by

---

[4] Notice that conditions (6.19) can be derived without reference to the social welfare function by solving the following problem: Maximize the utility of any one person, subject to holding the utilities of the remaining $(H - 1)$ people constant, and the production frontier and market clearance. But, the first-order conditions for this problem are not the necessary conditions for a social welfare maximum if the distribution is not optimal, in general. The first-order conditions for externalities with a nonoptimal distribution are derived in Chapter 20.

[5] Kenneth Arrow argues for this view of the externality problem in K. J. Arrow, "The Organization of Economic Activity: Issues Pertinent to the Choice of Market Versus Nonmarket Allocation," in R. H. Haveman and J. Margolis (Eds.), *Public Expenditure and Policy Analysis*, second ed., (Rand-McNally College Publishing, Chicago, 1977).

levying a set of taxes or subsidies that direct competitive behavior to the correct pareto-optimal conditions.

These two properties are worth extended discussions.

Externalities as Market Failure: The Missing Side Markets

The property that pareto-optimal decision rules for exclusive activities that generate externalities can always be achieved by an appropriate set of competitive markets follows directly from the assumptions of profit and utility maximization. Suppose, as above, that goods (factors) $k = 2, \ldots, N$ are pure public goods and that good 1 is a private good. Suppose, also, that the markets for all the goods (factors) are competitive, and that $P_1 = 1$ (good 1 is the numeraire). The standard competitive markets generate the conditions:

$$MRS^h_{X_{hk}, X_{hl}} = MRT_{k, 1} \qquad \text{all } h = 1, \ldots, H \qquad (6.22)$$
$$\text{any } k = 2, \ldots, N$$

because both consumers and producers face the identical prices P_k and P_1 for goods (factors) k and 1, respectively. $MRS^h_{X_{hk}, X_{hl}}$ refers to person h's MRS between his own consumption of goods k and 1 (supply of factors k and 1). These are not the pareto-optimal conditions given by Eq. (6.20). Additional competitive side markets are needed to achieve conditions (6.20).

To understand the nature of these side markets, consider again person i's consumption of public good k, X_{ik} (assume both X_k and X_1 are goods). The competitive market structure that would generate the pareto-optimal condition,

$$\sum_{h=1}^{H} MRS^h_{X_{ik}, X_{hl}} = MRT_{k, 1}$$

is as follows. Producers insist on a price P_k, equal to $MRT_{k, 1}$ (MC_k), to supply good k. If consumer i wants to buy X_k, she has to pay the producer this price. Suppose X_{ik} generates an external economy (a "good") for all other consumers. In this case, person i and all the others have a mutual interest in developing side markets to influence the final value of X_{ik}, the others because they would be willing to pay something to have person i increase her consumption of good k, and person i because she can extract side payments that effectively lower the price to her below the producer price, P_k.

Consider next Fig. 6.1, which shows the set of indifference curves for some person $h \neq i$, between X_{ik}, person i's consumption of good k, and X_{hl} person h's own consumption of good 1. X_{ik} is a parameter for person h, but he determines his own consumption of good 1. Suppose their independent decisions place consumer h at point B on indifference curve I_1. The slope of I_1 at B is $MRS^h_{X_{ik}, X_{hl}}$. If these were two purely private goods both under the control of person h, then he would pay a competitive price for X_{ik} equal to

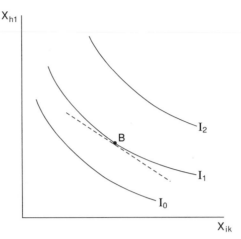

FIGURE 6.1

$MRS^h_{X_{ik}, X_{h1}}$. Call this price P^h_{ik} (with $P_1 \equiv 1$). Suppose person h actually paid person i the competitive price $P^h_{ik} = MRS^h_{X_{ik}, X_{h1}}$, and all other consumers did likewise, having formed identical "competitive" side market relationships with person i. This set of competitive side markets could achieve the desired pareto-optimal condition.

The effective price of good k to person i is

$$P^i_k = P_k - \sum_{h \neq i} P^h_{ik} \tag{6.23}$$

which she equates to her own personal marginal rate of substitution between goods k and 1, $MRS^i_{X_{ik}, X_{i1}}$. With the "competitive" side payments received from the $(H - 1)$ other consumers equal to

$$P^h_{ik} = MRS^h_{X_{ik}, X_{h1}}, \text{ for all } h \neq i \tag{6.24}$$

the external effect of person i's consumption of good k, and with the producers setting

$$P_k = MRT_{k, 1} \tag{6.25}$$

this expanded competitive market structure satisfies the pareto-optimal condition:

$$\sum_{h=1}^{H} MRS^h_{X_{ik}, X_{h1}} = MRT_{k, 1}$$

Notice that $(H - 1)$ "competitive" side markets (prices) are required just for person i's consumption of good k, plus the usual market between the producer and consumer i, or H markets (prices) in all. By a similar analysis,

$H(H-1)$ additional side markets (prices) would be necessary to allocate X_k correctly among all H consumers, with $(H-1)$ side markets (prices) for each of the H consumers, a formidable set of markets indeed. Adding the H markets (prices) between the producers and each consumer, there would be H^2 markets (prices) in all. Furthermore, $H(H-1)$ distinct side markets (prices) and H^2 total markets (prices) are necessary for *each* pure public good.

The same analysis applies if the externality is a diseconomy (a "bad"), although the mutual gains come about indirectly. Achieving pareto optimality increases aggregate real income by moving the economy to the first-best utility-possibilities frontier, and the additional income can then be redistributed to everyone's mutual gain. Each person i might be skeptical of this argument, however, and refuse to make "competitive" side payments equal to the marginal damage he is causing other people. These payments have the obvious direct effect of lowering his utility, and he may doubt that he will receive adequate compensation when the additional real income is distributed.

Relating the problem of externalities to market failure in this way suggests why the market system breaks down in their presence even when it is mutually beneficial for people to form the necessary side markets. The existence of potential mutual gains from trade is the motivation that normally causes markets to form. For these externalities, however, three difficulties hinder the development of the proper side markets.

The first is that legal and/or political constraints may preclude formation of the side markets, especially in the case of external diseconomies. Suppose industry in New York state is polluting Vermont air. Even if New Yorkers are convinced that side payments to Vermonters can increase the combined welfare of both states, they certainly have no guarantee that sufficient tax revenues (and other necessary income) will be transferred back to New York to make the potential gain for New Yorkers a real one. Without proper redistributions, New Yorkers may well be better off continuing to pollute, especially if most of the costs of pollution are borne by Vermonters because of prevailing westerly winds. These same circumstances pose difficulties for government intervention in the form of corrective taxes, the textbook solution to externalities to be described in the next section. Who will levy these taxes? Certainly not New York state, and Vermont cannot tax New York citizens for pollution damage. Moreover, the Constitution of the United States may well proscribe levying federal taxes on New York citizens based on damage caused to Vermont citizens. As will be argued in more detail in Part V, a federalist system of governments causes problems for any policy designed to correct for externalities when the externalities spill over jurisdictional lines.

Transactions costs are a second potential hindrance to developing side markets, especially when the external effects are extensive. Suppose people benefit from other people's education but differentially depending on just who is educated (for example, bright people versus dull people). Furthermore, suppose all other people do not benefit equally from any one person's education. In short, education may have the properties of a (virtually) pure public exclusive good, with many different values to the marginal rates of substitution that comprise the external effects. If so, then the sheer number of side markets required to achieve an optimal amount of education for anyone is staggering (H is a very large number) and the costs of even trying to get everyone together are clearly prohibitive, meaning that they would almost surely offset any efficiency gains from achieving or even approaching pareto optimality. Put another way, normal competitive markets permit all consumers and producers to face the same price, an enormous advantage in terms of information requirements. In contrast, externalities of the type under consideration generally require negotiations and differential prices among all consumers in the market, a huge increase in structural complexity. Small wonder, then, that such side markets almost never form, even when the mutual gains, ignoring transactions costs, are obvious to all, such as for external economies. Unfortunately, all important examples of externalities associated with private activity, such as education, pollution, and research and development, affect a very large number of people. After all, their broad scope is what makes them important.

Finally, mutually beneficial side payments might not obtain even if the externality were relatively simple, affecting only a few people, and none of the problems mentioned above existed. There remains the problem that the affected parties have an incentive not to reveal their true preferences. Suppose person i's consumption of good k generates an external economy for persons j and m. Despite the benefits she receives, person j might decide not to subsidize i's consumption, hoping instead that the other person, m, will do so. In the parlance of the literature, j desires to be a "free rider." Person m reasons similarly, and because no one wants to play the sucker, no side payments occur, despite the obvious gains to all. Various tax schema exist for avoiding the free-rider problem, but we will defer discussion of them until the next section on nonexclusive goods since the revelation problem has been most closely associated with these goods. It could just as easily apply to exclusive goods, however.

Bargaining and the Coase Theorem

Ronald Coase felt differently about the possibilities for side payments, at least when the externalities involve a small number of consumers or firms. He argued that the appropriate side bargains would take place so long as the property rights to the external effects were established (for instance, someone held the rights to the benefits from a research and development project). His reasoning was simply that bargaining to achieve the pareto-optimal conditions represents a pareto-superior move, and rational, utility-maximizing consumers can be counted on to realize the mutual gains, by the definition of rationality. Some of the gains may have to be redistributed among the parties to ensure that everyone is better off, but this too is in everyone's mutual interest. Also, the bargained solution does not necessarily have to set each price equal to the MRS, as the competitive market analog suggests. All it must do is select the levels of private activity that satisfies the pareto-optimal conditions, Eq. (6.20), and possibly redistribute some of the gains to ensure that everyone is better off relative to the status quo. Coase's argument became universally known as the Coase Theorem.[6]

The Coase Theorem was a provocative challenge to received public sector theory at the time, which stressed incentives to free ride and presumed that government intervention would always be necessary to achieve pareto optimality in the presence of externalities. The theorem has generated a huge literature, sometimes favorable, sometimes critical. The most recent literature has concentrated on the validity of the Coase Theorem when people have private information about the external effects, and the results have generally been unfavorable to the theorem. This is so even when the external effects are extremely limited, such as to one or two "third parties." Private information is a second-best problem, however, so we will defer most discussion of the Coase Theorem until Chapter 20 in Part III. For now it is enough to note that the Coase Theorem was never assumed to apply when the external effects were extensive. (We will return to it briefly in Chapter 7.)

The Tax/Subsidy Solution

Society does not have to rely on private bargaining to correct for externalities. The government has the option of taxing (subsidizing) externality-generating activities to achieve the pareto-optimal conditions. The tax (subsidy) scheme is simpler than the required competitive market structure, by a factor of H. To see why, consider again the decision by person i to consume (supply) good (factor) k, X_{ik}. As before, assume that all markets are competitive in line with first-best analysis, and that $P_1 = 1$, the numeraire. Person i's decision to purchase good k affects all other people, but for these people it is essentially a lump-sum event. Only person i decides the quantity; the others must accept it as a parameter. Thus, the government need only adjust person i's behavior with respect to X_{ik}, as follows.

Before government intervention, all producers and consumers face the same price P_k, which producers set equal to the MRT (marginal cost) and consumers to their personal-use MRS. The government does not want this, but it knows that if it establishes another set of prices for person i (say, P_k^i),

[6] R. Coase, "The Problem of Social Cost," *Journal of Law and Economics*, October 1960. The assignment of property rights to the activities associated with the external effects is crucial to the theorem. A counterexample is water or air pollution. Private bargaining cannot work here because air and most bodies of water are common-use resources. No one can hold the property rights to clean air and clean water on the public bodies of water.

then consumer i will set this price to $\text{MRS}^i_{X_{ik}, X_{il}}$, her own personal use MRS. The goal, then, is to design a tax for person i, t^i_k that simultaneously:

1. Drives a wedge between P^i_k and P_k such that:

$$P^i_k = P_k + t^i_k$$

2. Achieves the desired pareto-optimal condition,

$$\sum_{h=1}^{H} \text{MRS}^h_{X_{ik}, X_{hl}} = \text{MRT}_{k,1}$$

The proper tax is $t^i_k = -\sum_{h \neq i} \text{MRS}^h_{X_{ik}, X_{hl}}$, equal to the sum of the marginal effects on all others of person i's consumption (supply) of good (factor) k. With this tax, the price person i pays for good k, P^i_k, differs from the producer's marginal cost price of k by exactly the summation of his marginal effects on all other consumers:

$$P^i_k = \text{MRS}^i_{X_{ik}, X_{il}} = P_k + t^i_k = \text{MRT} - \sum_{h \neq i} \text{MRS}^h_{X_{ik}, X_{hl}} \qquad (6.26)$$

Thus, the tax establishes the correct pareto-optimal condition on X_{ik}. It is referred to as the Pigovian tax after the British economist A. C. Pigou, who first proposed taxes (subsidies) equal to the sum of the external marginal effects to correct for externalities.[7]

Using the convention that the MRS between two goods is positive if these side effects are beneficial (an external economy), then the "tax" t^i_k is negative, a subsidy, so that person i pays less than the marginal cost price of producing good k. Conversely, if the side effects are harmful (external diseconomies), the tax is positive and person i pays more than the marginal cost price of producing good k.

Furthermore, the government can adjust the tax to the desired level, at least in principle. Suppose at first the tax is zero, and X_{ik} generates external economies. Without benefit of the subsidy, person i consumes (supplies) too little of good (factor) k, and $t^i_k > -\sum_{h \neq i} \text{MRS}^h_{ik, hl}$. A subsidy to person i lowers p^i_k increases X_{ik}, and thereby decreases the absolute value of each other person's $\text{MRS}^h_{X_{ik}, X_{hl}}$. Thus, it is possible to find the t^i_k such that $t^i_k = -\sum_{h \neq i} \text{MRS}^h_{i k, hl}$ as required.

To allocate the aggregate amount of X_k correctly requires H separate taxes, t^i_k, $i = 1, \ldots, H$, one for each consumer (supplier) of X_k, determined exactly as above. Pareto optimality requires:

$$\sum_{h=1}^{H} \text{MRS}^h_{X_{ik}, X_{hl}} = \text{MRT}_{k,1} \qquad \text{all } i = 1, \ldots, H$$

[7] A.C. Pigou, *The Economics of Welfare*, fourth ed., Macmillan & Co., London, 1932.

The effects of the tax can also be considered in terms of supply and demand curves (with $P_1 = 1$). Think of k as a good. The aggregate supply curve for good k has the usual interpretation. It is the horizontal summation of the marginal cost curves for the individual producers of k. The aggregate demand curve for the good k is, similarly, the horizontal summation of the individual consumers' demand curves for good k, with this important difference. Before the individual curves are summed horizontally, they are each adjusted vertically downward (upward) by the amount of the tax (subsidy), t_k^i. Because of the way the taxes (subsidies) are defined, the vertical adjustments just equal $\sum_{h \neq i} MRS_{ik,hl}^h$ at each unit of X_{ik}, person i's combined marginal impact on all other people. Thus, the resulting individual demand curve for person i reflects the entire $\sum_{h=1}^{H} MRS_{X_{ik},X_{hl}}^h$, including person i's own MRS between goods k and 1. Because these adjusted curves are then summed *horizontally* to be equated with aggregate supply,

$$\sum_{h=1}^{H} MRS_{X_{ik},X_{hl}}^h = MRT_{k,1} = P_k \qquad \text{all } i = 1, \ldots, H \qquad (6.27)$$

in aggregate equilibrium, as required for pareto optimality. The taxes, t_k^i, if set optimally, determine the effective price for each person i and their individual contribution, X_{ik}, to the aggregate X_k at the equilibrium.

Designing the proper set of H taxes for any one pure public good is obviously a hopeless task. For *each* of the taxes the government must know $(H - 1)$ separate pieces of information, the $MRS_{ik,hl}^h$. The full set of H taxes, therefore, requires $H(H - 1)$ independent pieces of information, all of which may differ. In general, $MRS_{ik,hl}^h \neq MRS_{ik,jl}^j$, for $j \neq h$. (Think of the fence example. The external MRS effect on each third party depends on how their view is affected by whoever builds the fence). Finally, a world consisting of one pure private good and $(N - 1)$ pure public goods would require $H(N - 1)$ taxes and $H(H - 1)$ $(N - 1)$ independent observations on the external marginal effects.

Limited Externalities

Only a small subset of people is likely to be affected by the consumption of some good; that is, the good is somewhere on the continuum between pure publicness and pure privateness. (For example, a fence is likely to affect only the neighbors on the adjacent properties and perhaps not all of them.) As is immediately obvious from the construction of the model, the pareto-optimal rule:

$$\sum_h MRS_{ik,hl}^h = MRT_{k,1}$$

applies only to the subset of H people affected by person i's consumption of good k. The subset could number as few as two people (person i and one other), and pareto optimality would still be described by this rule. Furthermore, the subset of people whose consumption generates consumer externalities could number far fewer than H people. There may only be one such person. As a practical matter, the government would only intervene if the number of people affected by a particular externality was fairly large and/or the externalities generated in any one instance were deemed to be "substantial" in some sense. Very few goods (factors) are likely to meet this practical criterion. That is, most goods are certainly well toward the pole of pure privateness. Private bargaining may be the preferred solution when the numbers affected are small if, indeed, any action can hope to improve the private market outcomes given the transactions costs of bargaining or government intervention.

All these considerations serve to mitigate the actual policy problems caused by consumption externalities. Nonetheless, if, for example, J people were affected by each of L goods as described by the model, then $J \cdot L$ taxes (subsidies) are required for allocative efficiency, a formidable task even if both J and L are "fairly small" relative to all the people and all the goods and factors in the economy.

We have been analyzing the case of *individualized externalities*, in which the external effects associated with private sector activity depend not only on what the activity is but who is doing it: It matters who builds a fence. The inescapable conclusion is that neither government taxes and subsidies nor private bargaining can be expected to achieve the pareto-optimal conditions for any individualized externality in which the external effects are widespread.

Not all externalities are individualized, however. The final two sections of the chapter consider two common types of externalities that are not individualized: the nonexclusive good and the aggregate externality. The aggregate externality is the more hopeful of the two from a policy perspective.

NONEXCLUSIVE GOODS—THE SAMUELSON MODEL

Paul Samuelson was the first economist to analyze the problem of externalities using a formal general equilibrium model of social welfare maximization for his analytical framework. He developed his model in the two articles mentioned in Chapter 2,[8] and it is safe to say that no other single work has been more influential to the development of public expenditure theory. For this reason alone, his model deserves special attention in any treatise on public sector economics. It also happens to be a useful vehicle for exploring a number of important issues, including:

---

[8] P. A. Samuelson, "The Pure Theory of Public Expenditure," *Review of Economics and Statistics*, November 1954; P. A. Samuelson, "Diagrammatic Exposition of a Theory of Public Expenditure," *Review of Economics and Statistics*, November 1955. See also P. A. Samuelson, "Aspects of Public Expenditure Theories," *Review of Economics and Statistics*, November 1958.

1. The special problems caused by nonexclusive goods, Samuelson chose the nonexclusive good for his example of an externality.
2. A method for introducing the government into the standard general equilibrium model, given that the government's preferences are not supposed to count other than in providing the social welfare function.
3. The important first-best dichotomy property that a competitive market system correctly allocates pure private goods, This property could have been developed above by considering a model with at least two pure private goods. It always holds under first-best assumptions.
4. An initial presentation of the *benefits-received* principle of taxation, one of the two widely accepted normative criteria for judging whether or not a particular tax is fair.

A nonexclusive good (a service, really) has the property that if any one person consumes it, everyone necessarily consumes its services in equal amounts. Nonexclusivity works both ways. On the one hand, if one person consumes the good, he cannot exclude others from consuming it. On the other hand, once someone consumes the good, no individual within the domain of the good can exclude himself from consuming the services of the good even if he should want to. Consumption is truly joint. These goods cause terrible problems for any society dedicated to competitive market principles and consumer sovereignty. Unfortunately, they are hardly theoretical curiosities to be found only in obscure economics journals. Defense and the exploration of outer space are two very important examples of nonexclusive goods.[9]

The free-rider problem undermines the ability of markets to allocate nonexclusive goods. Markets work for exclusive goods because people must purchase the goods to receive any utility from them. They reveal their preferences when they purchase the goods. In contrast, people do not have to purchase a nonexclusive good to receive its services. The strategy of free riding is a viable, and preferred, option. People have an incentive not to reveal their preferences, hoping that someone who wants the good will actually buy it. If someone does play the "sucker," everyone immediately consumes its services as free riders. Therefore the government is forced to purchase the good on behalf of society for there to be any hope of achieving the proper allocation of resources to the good, and perhaps to have any of the good at all, even though everyone might desire the services of the good. This is why Samuelson labeled nonexclusive goods "public goods." As we shall

---

[9] The terminology "nonexclusive" introduced by Samuelson is somewhat misleading as some good might have the properties described above over a subset of individuals yet not be available at all to still other people. Compare national defense with local police protection. Jointness of consumption is perhaps a more accurate description, leaving open the possibility that some consumers may be excluded. At this point, however, we will use *nonexclusiveness* and *jointness* in consumption interchangeably and assume the entire population is affected.

see, these goods satisfy our definition of public goods, which can also apply to exclusive goods. Samuelson's equation of "publicness" with "nonexclusivity" (joint consumption) is the one most often employed in the externality literature, however.

Having decided to purchase the good, the government is faced with two difficult questions:

1. How much of the good should it buy?
2. How should people be taxed to pay for the good?

One can provide answers to both questions consistent with the standard criteria of consumer sovereignty, pareto optimality, and competitive market principles, but these answers depend upon consumers revealing their true preferences to the government. Unfortunately, consumers have no more incentive to relate their true preferences to the government than they do to the marketplace. In answering these questions, therefore, the government confronts the mechanism design problem. It must find a tax scheme that induces consumers to reveal their preferences.

The Government in a General Equilibrium Model

To focus on the problems peculiar to nonexclusivity, assume that there is one nonexclusive good, the kth, and that all other $(N - 1)$ goods are pure private goods. Assume further that the market for nonexclusive goods is inoperative because of the free-rider problem, so that the government must decide how much of the good to buy and how to ask people to pay for it. The immediate problem, then, is to incorporate the government into the formal model of social welfare maximization.

One method of proceeding is to assume the government has a preference function for nonexclusive goods derived through some sort of political process, exactly the approach taken for the government's social welfare function. If this government preference function also includes the overall size of the private sector as one of its arguments, then the private sector defines the opportunity costs of public expenditures on the nonexclusive good, and finding the optimal amount of the "public" good becomes a simple exercise in consumer theory. The government would solve a problem of the general form:

$$\max_{\text{(public expenditures, private sector)}} \text{G(public expenditures, private sector)}$$

$$\text{s.t.} \quad \text{Public expenditures} + \text{Private sector} = Y$$

where G = the government's preference function, and Y = total national product, to be split among the private and public sectors.

As was stressed in Chapter 1, however, the government is not supposed to interject its own preferences into the decision-making process according to the mainstream normative theory. Rather, it is supposed to play the part of agent, acting solely upon consumers' preferences for its demand data whenever possible—that is, to honor the principle of consumer sovereignty.

The government has no choice but to violate consumer sovereignty when faced with the distribution question. Society must develop a set of social welfare rankings through some political process that establish the criteria for achieving end-results equity. Individual preferences, by themselves, are not sufficient to determine the interpersonal equity conditions for the optimal distribution of income. But such is not the case with allocational issues. Consumer preferences are sufficient to determine the demand component of the pareto optimal conditions for allocational efficiency, and consumers have preferences over *all* goods and services, including nonexclusive goods. There is no reason why their preferences cannot be honored, at least in principle. Thus, mainstream normative theory has rejected the construct of a distinct government preference function for nonexclusive goods, or, indeed, for any expenditures arising for allocational reasons. Only consumers' preferences enter the optimal normative policy rules.

A simple analytical device for introducing government purchases into the standard general equilibrium model without generating a distinct government demand for these purchases is to define a fictitious individual (say, the first) to represent the government.[10] By fictitious we mean that $U^1(\vec{X}_1) \equiv 0$, where $\vec{X}_1$ is a vector of government purchases. The vector $\vec{X}_1$ enters into the production-possibility frontier and market clearance—the goods themselves are real and use up scarce resources—but government preferences never count for social welfare, as $\partial U^1 / \partial X_{1k} \equiv 0$, for any k.

Allocating a Nonexclusive Good

If good k is the only nonexclusive good, social welfare maximization can be represented as:

$$\max_{\left(X_{1k}; X_{hj}\right)} W\left[U^1(X_{1k}); U^h\left(X_{hj}; X_{1k}\right)\right]$$

$$\text{s.t.} \quad F\left(\sum_{h=2}^{H} X_{hj}, X_{1k}\right) = 0$$

where:

X_{1k} = the nonexclusive good, purchased only by the government.
X_{hj} = good (factor) j consumed (supplied) by person h, h = 2, ..., H_j
$\quad$ j = 1, ..., k − 1, k + 1, ..., N.
U^1 = the (fictitious) preference function of the government.

---

[10] This technique was first demonstrated to us by Peter Diamond in a set of unpublished class notes.

The corresponding Lagrangian is

$$\max_{(X_{1k};X_{hj})} L = W\left[U^1(X_{1k}); U^h(X_{hj}; X_{1k})\right] + \lambda F\left(\sum_{h=2}^{H} X_{hj}, X_{1k}\right)$$

Notice that even though only the government purchases good k, X_{1k} enters into each person's utility function since everyone automatically consumes the entire services of the nonexclusive good. Compare this with the case of an exclusive good that generates externalities. With the exclusive good, there is a distinct difference between the services it provides privately to each individual who purchases it and the flow of external services received by other consumers in the form of external economies or diseconomies. Think once again of the fence. The person who built the fence receives a flow of services that are distinct from the "services" bestowed upon his neighbors. With nonexclusive goods, however, there is no such distinction. Whatever services are available to the purchaser, these identical services are automatically available to all others, whether they want the services or not.

Interpersonal Equity Conditions

Consider the necessary conditions for a social welfare maximum for the model with nonexclusive goods, beginning with the interpersonal equity conditions for good 1. Take the first-order conditions with respect to X_{h1} and X_{21}, the consumption of good 1 by persons h and 2:

$$X_{h1}: \quad \frac{\partial W}{\partial U^h} \frac{\partial U^h}{\partial X_{h1}} = -\lambda F_1 \tag{6.28}$$

$$X_{21}: \quad \frac{\partial W}{\partial U^2} \frac{\partial U^2}{\partial X_{21}} = -\lambda F_1 \tag{6.29}$$

Consequently,

$$\frac{\partial W}{\partial U^h} \frac{\partial U^h}{\partial X_{h1}} = -\lambda F_1 \quad \text{all } h = 2, \ldots, H \tag{6.30}$$

Equation (6.30) is the standard result that good 1 should be distributed lump-sum across all individuals to equalize the social marginal utility of good 1.

Pareto-Optimal Conditions

The pareto-optimal conditions are obtained somewhat differently in this model. We have to compare the government's purchase of good k, X_{1k}, with any other consumer's purchase of any private good—say, the purchase of good 1 by person j, X_{j1}. The first-order conditions are

$$X_{1k}: \quad \sum_{h=2}^{H} \frac{\partial W}{\partial U^h} \frac{\partial U^h}{\partial X_{1k}} = -\lambda F_k \tag{6.31}$$

(Recall that $\partial U^1/\partial X_{1k} \equiv 0$.)

$$X_{j1}: \quad \frac{\partial W}{\partial U^j} \frac{\partial U^j}{\partial X_{j1}} = -\lambda F_1 \tag{6.32}$$

Dividing Eq. (6.31) by (6.32),

$$\frac{\sum_{h=2}^{H} \frac{\partial W}{\partial U^h} \frac{\partial U^h}{\partial X_{1k}}}{\frac{\partial W}{\partial U^j} \frac{\partial U^j}{\partial X_{j1}}} = \frac{F_k}{F_1} = MRT_{X_k, X_1} \tag{6.33}$$

But, if the government has correctly redistributed good 1 such that the interpersonal equity conditions hold, then

$$\frac{\partial W}{\partial U^j} \frac{\partial U^j}{\partial X_{j1}} = \quad \text{all } j = 2, \ldots, H$$

Selectively substituting for the denominators in each term on the left-hand side of Eq. (6.33) and canceling $\partial W/\partial U^h$ term by term yields:

$$\sum_{h=2}^{H} \left(\frac{\frac{\partial U^h}{\partial X_{1k}}}{\frac{\partial U^h}{\partial X_{h1}}} \right) = MRT_{X_k, X_1} \tag{6.34}$$

or

$$\sum_{h=2}^{H} MRS^h_{X_{1k}, X_{h1}} = MRT_{X_k, X_1} \tag{6.35}$$

Condition (6.35) gives the familiar result that the sum of each person's marginal rates of substitution between the nonexclusive good and good 1 equals the marginal rate of transformation between X_k and X_1 in production. Samuelson was the first to demonstrate formally the summation rule for externalities. Subsequent research showed that this same type of rule also applies to exclusive goods that generate externalities, as already demonstrated above.

The First-Best Dichotomy: The Private Goods and Factors

Before discussing the government's prospects of satisfying the pareto-optimal conditions, consider the following important proposition: In a first-best policy environment, pure private goods and factors can be allocated efficiently by the competitive market system despite the presence of externalities elsewhere in the economy. To see this, consider the pareto-optimal conditions for any two pure private goods (or factors). Compare, for example, the first-order conditions for X_{hm} and X_{h1}, two private goods (factors) consumed (supplied) by person h. The first-order conditions are

$$X_{hm}: \quad \frac{\partial W}{\partial U^h} \frac{\partial U^h}{\partial X_{hm}} = -\lambda F_m \qquad (6.36)$$

$$X_{h1}: \quad \frac{\partial W}{\partial U^h} \frac{\partial U^h}{\partial X_{h1}} = -\lambda F_1 \qquad (6.37)$$

Dividing Eq. (6.36) by (6.37),

$$\frac{\dfrac{\partial U^h}{\partial X_{hm}}}{\dfrac{\partial U^h}{\partial X_{h1}}} = \frac{F_m}{F_1} \qquad \begin{array}{l} \text{all} \ \ h = 2, \dots, H \\[4pt] \text{any} \ \ m \neq k \end{array} \qquad (6.38)$$

or

$$MRS^h_{X_m, X_1} = MRT_{X_m, X_1} \qquad (6.39)$$

These are the standard pareto-optimal conditions for private goods developed in Chapter 2 and they are achieved by competitive markets for m and 1. Therefore, the existence of nonexclusive goods does not upset the competitive allocations of the other pure private goods, at least with first-best assumptions. That this property applies to our model of externality-generating exclusive goods should be clear from the structural similarities of the two models.

Policy Problems with Nonexclusive Goods

Knowing that it should purchase a nonexclusive good to the point at which $\sum_{h=2}^{H} MRS^h_{X_{1k}, X_{h1}} = MRT_{X_k, X_1}$ may not be very helpful to the government in practice, as it still has the vexing problem of determining each person's MRS under the handicap of nonrevelation. The problem is not that a MRS is a special theoretical construct that cannot be observed in practice. For pure private goods its value is easily determined. Assuming rational behavior, the marginal rate of substitution between any two goods for any consumer simply equals the price ratio of the two goods. Rather, the problem is nonexclusivity itself, which leads to the incentive to free ride. Competitive market analogs to private goods are of little help to the government.

The government cannot simply set a price (tax), ask consumers how much they would be willing to buy at that price, and compare quantities demanded with quantities supplied at the producer price to check for equilibrium. Consumers might well hide their preferences if they thought they might actually have to buy the stated amounts at the going price. Furthermore, this competitive process would not generate the pareto-optimal quantity even if revelation were not a problem. The market process is reversed for nonexclusive goods: the single output selected by the government is the given for each consumer, not the price. Therefore, the proper method of reaching equilibrium is for the government to select an *output*, ask consumers how much they would be willing to pay for the last unit of the output, add each consumer price, and compare the aggregate consumer demand price with the marginal cost (the producer's supply price) at the selected output. The optimum quantity occurs at the output for which the aggregate demand price equals the supply price.

In terms of the standard supply and demand diagram, every consumer has a demand curve for the nonexclusive good even if he won't reveal it. Just as with the externality portion of exclusive goods, these demand curves must be added *vertically*, not horizontally, to arrive at aggregate market demand. (There is no further horizontal summation, however, as the quantity selected by the government *is* the aggregate quantity.) The quantity at which the vertical summation of individual demand curves intersects the supply curve satisfies the pareto-optimal condition, Eq. (6.35).

This reversed competitive process is illustrated in Fig. 6.2 for the two-person case. In the diagram:

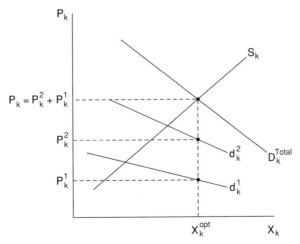

FIGURE 6.2

1. d_k^1 and d_k^2 are the individual's demand curves for X_k, reflecting their respective $MRS_{k,i1}^i$ at every X_k ($P_1 = 1$, the numeraire).
2. D_k^{total} is the vertical summation of d_k^1 and d_k^2.
3. S_k is a normal supply curve for X_k reflecting the $MRT_{k,1}(MC_k)$ at every X_k.
4. P_k is the producer's supply price at X_k^{opt}.
5. $P_k^2 = MRS_{X_k,X_{21}}^2$ at X_k^{opt}.
6. $P_k^1 = MRS_{X_k,X_{11}}^1$ at X_k^{opt}.

At X_k^{opt},

$$P_k = P_k^1 + P_k^2 \qquad (6.40)$$

or

$$MRT_{X_k,X_1} = MRS_{X_k,X_{11}}^1 + MRS_{X_k,X_{21}}^2 \qquad (6.41)$$

Thinking in terms of defense, if the last weapon system costs \$20 billion and in the aggregate consumers are willing to pay \$20 billion based on their marginal rates of substitution, then the defense budget is optimal.

Thus, it is possible to describe a competitive analog for establishing the optimum quantity of nonexclusive goods, but the analog is not terribly useful in practice as consumers have little incentive to reveal their demand prices at each quantity. The government has to design a different mechanism to induce consumers to reveal their preferences for nonexclusive goods. Otherwise, the government has little choice but to select a quantity and hope that its choice is correct without benefit of the normal market signals to aid its judgment.

Paying for the Public Good

The question "How should people be taxed to pay for a nonexclusive good such as defense?" can be viewed as uninteresting from a normative perspective. It has no normative significance for social welfare maximization in the mainstream perspective. The only normative requirement for the government is to select the optimal quantity of the good. Suppose it has. The government's output choice is exogenous from each consumer's point of view and, since the government is not interfering in any other market, the pareto-optimal conditions for all other goods (factors) hold as well. Therefore, all the government need do to preserve efficiency is raise taxes on a lump-sum basis to finance the good. Any lump-sum tax will do—for example, a head tax based on age scaled up or down until sufficient revenues have been collected.

The only caveat is that the optimal quantity of the nonexclusive good depends in part on the particular lump-sum tax chosen. Any tax shifts people's demands for the nonexclusive good simply because their incomes have changed. The new pattern of after-tax incomes therefore dictates a new output choice to satisfy the pareto-optimal condition for the nonexclusive good. But any pattern of lump-sum taxes allows all the pareto-optimal conditions to hold, by the definition of a lump-sum tax. The "only" allocational problem for the government remains selecting the correct output for the chosen tax. Furthermore, any adverse distributional consequences of a particular tax such as an age tax would be fully offset by the lump-sum redistributions that satisfy the interpersonal equity conditions. In this sense, then, the question of how people should pay for the good is uninteresting; it can be entirely subsumed within the distribution question.

Public sector economists have nonetheless expressed considerable interest in the payments mechanism, for equity and efficiency reasons. The equity motivation is that citizens may not accept any pattern of lump-sum taxation to pay for these goods, especially if no strong consensus has emerged regarding the social welfare function. They may well insist that the taxes satisfy commonly held notions of equity, that they be fair as well as efficient. The efficiency motivation is the mechanism design problem. Finding a tax scheme that induces people to reveal their true preferences for the nonexclusive good is essential. Avoiding the free-rider problem removes the principal barrier towards achieving the pareto-optimal allocation. Should these taxes also be deemed equitable, so much the better. Let's consider the question of equity first.

The Benefits-Received Principle of Taxation

Although there are no equity norms agreed upon by everyone, two general principles of fair taxation have gained remarkably wide acceptance in Western economic thought as practical guidelines for tax policy. Taxes are deemed fair if they are related to the benefits received from public goods and services, or if they are closely related to each person's ability to pay.

The benefits-received principle of taxation is the older of the two principles. It dates back at least to the fourteenth and fifteenth centuries in European feudal societies, when the nobles paid a tribute to the king in return for protection from foreign enemies. The benefits-received principle is meant to apply to all resource-using public expenditures, such as nonexclusive goods. It is especially compelling in capitalist societies as a natural and fair way to pay for public services because the payment for goods in the marketplace is on a benefit-received basis. The rationale for taxing according to the benefits received from public services runs as follows:

> The government is engaged in allocational activities only because one of the technical assumptions underlying a well-functioning market system fails to hold and the competitive market system is signaling an incorrect allocation of resources. Because the government is merely substituting for the competitive market system

in these instances, taxes raised to finance these activities should imitate the *quid pro quo* feature of market prices. Competitive markets in effect exact payments from consumers and producers reflecting the benefits received from their market transactions. Thus, taxes should reflect the benefits received from the government services.

The benefits-received principle is obviously limited to the allocational, or resource-using, part of the government's budget. Transfer payments designed to achieve distributional goals cannot possibly be financed by the benefits principle because the transfer recipients are the primary beneficiaries of the transfers. Consequently, public sector economists have developed a second practical guideline for equitable taxation, the ability-to-pay criterion, first proposed by Adam Smith and John Stuart Mill in the late 1700s and early 1800s.[11] Smith and Mill viewed taxes as a necessary sacrifice that citizens undertake to support the commonweal, the common good. In their view, people should be asked to sacrifice in accordance with their ability to pay. Their ability-to-pay principle was meant to apply to transfer programs and also serve as the default option for allocational expenditures whenever taxes cannot easily be related to benefits received.

The ability-to-pay principle is clearly related to society's distributional norms and bears a kinship to the modern social welfare view of distributive justice. We will discuss it in detail in Chapter 11. Our present goal is to consider tax schemes designed to finance expenditures on nonexclusive goods, for which the benefits-received principle is meant to apply.

Saying that taxes should be related to the benefits received from public expenditures is still too general for policy purposes. It begs the immediate question of exactly what benefits should be used as the basis for taxation: total benefits? average benefits? marginal benefits? and so forth. There is less agreement on this question than on the general principle itself, but one can make an excellent case for choosing marginal benefits as the appropriate tax base. If society firmly believes in competitive market principles and views the government as an agent merely substituting for the market in any of these allocational areas, then a tax system that duplicates competitive pricing principles is likely to be considered fair by that society. Competitive prices equal marginal benefits, more accurately consumers' (producers') marginal rates of substitution (marginal rates of transformation) between any two goods (factors). Therefore, taxes that equal marginal rates of substitution are truly pseudo-competitive prices. Whether one labels them taxes or prices hardly matters.

Following this competitive interpretation of the benefits-received principle, the government ideally should levy a set of H differential taxes to

---

[11] A. Smith, *The Wealth of Nations*, Vol. II, E. Cannon (Ed.), G. P. Putnam's Sons, New York, 1904, p. 310, J. S. Mill, *Principles of Political Economy*, W. J. Ashley (Ed.), Longmans Green & Co., London, 1921.

pay for the nonexclusive good, equal to each person's marginal rate of substitution between the good and a private (numeraire) good at the quantity selected by the government. In terms of Fig. 6.2, person 2 would pay a tax $t_k^2 = P_k^2$, and person 1 a tax $t_k^1 = P_k^1$. At the optimum, these taxes would add exactly to the supply price P_k, equal to the marginal cost of producing X_k. Taxing or pricing in this way is known as Lindahl pricing after the Swedish economist Eric Lindahl, who first proposed this method of taxation.[12] Lindahl prices have the dual properties of preserving allocational efficiency *and* satisfying widely held notions of tax equity because of their direct correspondence with competitive market pricing.

Notice the kinship between Lindahl prices and Pigovian taxes levied on externality-generating exclusive goods. Pigovian taxes are also benefits-received taxes in the sense that they equal the aggregate marginal external benefit (damage) resulting from the consumption of the exclusive good. These taxes (subsidies) *have* to be equal to the aggregate marginal damage (benefit) to achieve pareto optimality.

Interpreting benefits received as marginal benefits received is required for most allocation problems, as one would suspect. Nonexclusive goods happen to be an exception, however. We have seen that Lindahl prices are not necessary for achieving pareto optimality with nonexclusive goods; any lump-sum tax also supports the optimum. But Lindahl prices do support the efficient allocation and their basic appeal is one of equity, that they represent a competitive interpretation of the benefits-received principle of taxation.

One might ask how Lindahl prices can be said to imitate competitive pricing, since everyone faces the same price in the market system, whereas Lindahl prices generally differ for each person. The answer lies in the peculiar way in which nonexclusive goods must be marketed, described above. For exclusive goods, price is the parameter faced by all consumers in common. Each person buys the quantity for which price equals the marginal rate of substitution (with the numeraire good as the basis of comparison). Hence, in equilibrium, marginal rates of substitution are equal for all consumers, but the quantities purchased generally differ. The situation is reversed for the nonexclusive good. Everyone is forced to consume the one quantity selected by the government. Because people's tastes differ, their marginal rates of substitution generally differ at that quantity, implying that the price (tax) each should pay differs as well. The competitive pricing principle common to

[12] E. Lindahl, *Die Gerechtigkeit der Besteverung*, Lund, 1919; reprinted (in part) in R. A. Musgrave and A. T. Peacock (Eds.), *Classics in the Theory of Public Finance*, Macmillan, New York, 1958. See also subsequent developments in L. Johansen, "Some Notes on the Lindahl Theory of Determination of Public Expenditures," *International Economic Review*, September 1963; P. A. Samuelson, "Pure Theory of Public Expenditures and Taxation," in J. Margolis and H. Guitton (Eds.), *Public Economics*, (St. Martin's Press, New York, 1969).

both goods is that price equals the marginal rate of substitution, each person's willingness to pay on the margin.

Virtually any pattern of differential taxes is consistent with competitive pricing applied to nonexclusive goods, since the prices depend only on the individual demands for the good. Return to the two-person example of Fig. 6.2. Person 1 may well place a value of zero on the marginal unit at the optimal quantity, as pictured in Fig. 6.3. If the quantity X_k^{opt} is pareto optimal, then $t_k^2 = P_k$ as drawn. Person 2 would pay the entire cost of the good, and person 1 would pay nothing, even though in a total or average sense she benefits from having the good, as evidenced by her willingness to pay positive prices for inframarginal units of the good. In fact, depending on the slopes of d_k^1 and d_k^2, person 1 may actually be willing to pay more for X_k on an average, per-unit basis than person 2, even though her marginal evaluation of the good is zero. Thus, a tax schema based on marginal benefits can produce completely different results from one based on total or average benefits received.

It could also happen that, at the optimum, person 1 believes the government has purchased too much X_k; the marginal units are harmful in her view. If this were true, then $t_k^1 < 0$ and $t_k^2 > P_k$, as shown in Fig. 6.4. Person 2 pays *more* per unit than competitive producers require to supply the good, and subsidizes person 1 for the harm caused her on the margin at the equilibrium. Notice that the subsidy has nothing whatsoever to do with standard distributional issues. It simply reflects taxes set equal to marginal rates of substitution.

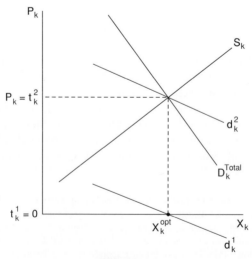

FIGURE 6.3

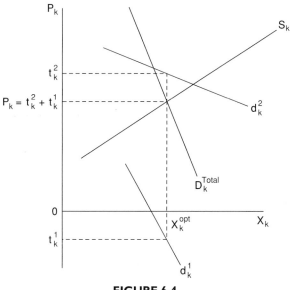

FIGURE 6.4

This situation is hardly an anomaly—it almost certainly applies to defense spending, at least in the United States. Some people believe the defense budget is much too large and causes them harm on the margin. Others just as clearly believe that the defense budget is too low. They would accept an increase in their current tax burdens if they could be assured that the taxes would be spent on defense.

In the late 1960s, some people refused to pay their federal income taxes in protest against the war in Vietnam. Their protest highlighted one of the problems peculiar to nonexclusive goods. If consumers do not want an exclusive good, they simply choose not to buy it. This choice does not exist for the nonexclusive goods, but at the very least these protesters felt entirely justified in not paying to support the U.S. effort in Vietnam. On the whole, these people were probably not staunch believers in competitive market principles, yet these principles supported their protest rather well. One wonders how much of a subsidy would have been required to offset the harm done to them, and whether the war effort really was pareto optimal. Some of these people obviously had extremely negative marginal rates of substitution. In principle, even a relatively few negative marginal rates of substitution could generate an $X_k^{opt} \approx 0$ according to the pareto-optimal rule, if they were extremely negative. The war protest turned on other ethical issues; the protesters did not use the principles of competitive market pricing to support their cause, but they could have.

At the same time, many who supported an even stronger U.S. military effort in Vietnam undoubtedly believed very strongly in competitive pricing principles. Would they have been willing to pay a Lindahl subsidy to the protesters consistent with these principles? Probably not, the point being that the commitment to a competitive market interpretation of the benefits-received principle may not be very strong, despite its underlying rationale. It can easily be overridden by other ethical principles, such as the principle that everyone ought to support the country in time of U.S. military involvement.

People's commitments to various ethical principles may well become confused even on more narrow economic grounds. For instance, people may simply reject the notion of differential payments for goods commonly consumed. A principle of equal payment for equal consumption may appeal to many people's sense of equity, even though this criterion bears no close relationship to competitive market pricing principles in which marginal benefit, not consumption, is what counts. Moreover an appeal to pure economic theory cannot resolve these confusions. Recall that *any* payment schema for nonexclusive goods is consistent with pareto optimality, so long as it is lump sum. A benefits-received principle consistent with competitive market principles is required in other contexts to promote economic efficiency, but not here.

In conclusion, the discussion of Lindahl pricing as a benefits-received tax points out that, strictly speaking, the benefits-received principle has no standing as an equity principle in the mainstream neoclassical model of social welfare maximization. Its only function is to promote efficiency. *All* end-results equity considerations in the mainstream neoclassical model are contained in the social welfare function and the corresponding interpersonal equity conditions.[13] The social welfare function bears no relationship at all to any benefits-received tax, including Lindahl prices. Nonetheless, benefits received as an equity principle was well established in the public sector literature before Samuelson formalized the neoclassical model, and it undoubtedly retains its appeal among the general public as a fair method of taxation.

Preference Revelation and Taxation: The Mechanism Design Problem

In 1971, Edward Clarke achieved a significant theoretical breakthrough by describing a set of taxes that would, in principle, avoid the free-rider problem with nonexclusive goods.[14] His schema of necessity breaks with the competi-

---

[13] We are grateful to Robin Broadway for emphasizing this point.

[14] E. H. Clarke, "Multipart Pricing of Public Goods," *Public Choice*, Fall 1971; E. H. Clarke, "Multipart Pricing of Public Goods: An Example," in S. Mushkin (Ed.), *Public Prices for Public Products*, Urban Institute, Washington, D.C. 1972. The discussion in the text closely

tive pricing model, which, as we have seen, offers no incentive for people to reveal their preferences. Rather, his taxes are based on the premise that individuals will reveal their true preferences if they are forced to accept the consequences of their actions on everyone else. The so-called *Clarke taxes* are designed as follows.

Suppose the nonexclusive good, X_k, is competitively supplied at constant cost, with $P_k = MC_k$. Without loss of generality, set $P_k \equiv \$1$. The government begins by assigning arbitrary per-unit tax shares t_h to each person, with $\sum_{h=1}^{H} t_h = 1$. It then asks everyone to announce their demand curves for the public good, d_k^h. Ordinarily, the intersection of the horizontal price line, \$1, and the vertical summation of the individual d_k^h would determine the optimal quantity of the public good, but the government has no reason to believe that the consumers have revealed their true demand curves. This is where Clarke's tax scheme comes into play. It is a mechanism for extracting the individuals' true preferences one person at a time.

Suppose the government begins with person i. All announced demand curves except person i's are summed vertically, and the government selects the quantity given by the intersection of this new aggregate demand curve and ($\$1 - t_i$), the combined tax share of the other $(H - 1)$ individuals (refer to Fig. 6.5):

AD = vertical summation of all H announced demand curves.

$AD - d_i$ = vertical summation of all but person i's announced demand curve.

t_i = assigned tax share of person i.

$\$1 - t_i$ = combined assigned tax shares of the other $(H - 1)$ individuals. The initial quantity chosen is X_k^A, at the intersection of ($AD - d_i$) and ($\$1 - t_i$).

Person i is then given the following choice. He can accept X_k^A with a total tax payment $t_i X_k^A$. Alternatively, the government will increase (decrease) the amount of X_k, providing person i pays an additional Clarke tax (receives an additional Clarke subsidy) equal to the amount required to make all the other individuals indifferent to the change given their announced demands. For instance, should person i vote an increase to X_k^1, his Clarke tax would be equal to the triangle abc. Triangle abc is the difference between the total taxes paid by all the other people for the increment ($X_k^1 - X_k^A$), less the total value of the increment to them as measured by the area under ($AD - d_i$) between

follows the presentation of "Clarke taxes" by Nicolaus Tideman and Gordon Tullock in T. N. Tideman and G. Tullock, "A New and Superior Process for Making Social Choices," *Journal of Political Economy*, December 1976. By now, a number of preference revelation mechanisms have appeared in the literature. For an alternative tax schema applicable to many public goods simultaneously, see T. Groves and M. Loeb, "Incentives and Public Inputs," *Journal of Public Economics*, August 1975.

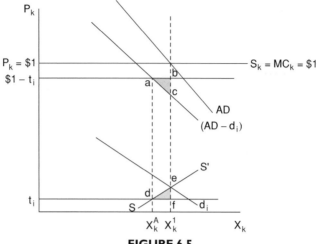

FIGURE 6.5

X_k^1 and X_k^A.[15] Draw SS′ through X_k^A as the mirror image of $(AD - d_i)$, so that the area between ($\$1 - t_i$) and $(AD - d_i)$ equals the area between SS′ and t_i. Using SS′, person i's Clarke tax (subsidy) equals the area between SS′ and t_i, area def in the example.

Person i always chooses to reveal his true preferences and pay the Clarke tax (subsidy) [unless d_i is horizontal at t_i]. As drawn in Fig. 6.5, if d_i is his true demand curve, person i chooses X_k^1 and pays the Clarke tax def, in addition to the assigned tax share $t_i X_k^1$. The marginal benefits and marginal costs of X_k to person i are equal at X_k^1. Any other choice reduces the net benefits from consuming X_k. For example, if d_i were false it would benefit person i to select the intersection of the true d_i and SS′ and pay the corresponding Clarke tax (receive the corresponding Clarke subsidy) along with the assigned tax share. Hence, self-interest dictates true revelation of preferences.

What holds for person i holds for everyone. Place the true d_i in AD and go on to the next person. Offer X_k^1 or any other output the person wants, subject to paying the Clarke tax. That person has the same incentive as person i to reveal her true demand curve and pay the Clarke tax. Continue until all but one person have been given this option, and let Fig. 6.5 represent the situation at this point. The aggregate demand curve $(AD - d_i)$ now contains the true demand curves for the other $(H - 1)$ individuals, not the original announced demand curves. Therefore, when the last individual has chosen, all the true demand curves have been revealed and the intersection of AD and S^k is the pareto optimum.

---

[15] We are assuming no income effects, in which case the actual and compensated demand curves are the same, and triangle abc is an appropriate measure of loss suffered by all the other individuals.

The Clarke tax schema bears no necessary relationship to Lindahl prices or any other tax schema that might be deemed equitable, because the assignment of initial tax shares is entirely arbitrary. Tideman and Tullock argue, however, that Clarke taxes could be made consistent with Lindahl prices by letting one citizen assign the tax shares under the condition that the assignor pays a penalty equal to some proportion of the aggregate Clarke taxes at the optimum.[16] Presumably this person would have an incentive to minimize Clarke taxes, which implies reassigning tax shares as closely as possible to each person's true marginal evaluation. Referring to Fig. 6.5, person i's tax share would be reassigned to the intersection of d_i and SS'. With the Tideman and Tullock modification, then, people reveal their true preferences by means of the Clarke tax schema, the government chooses the pareto-optimal allocation of X_k, and tax payments correspond to Lindahl pricing, the competitive interpretation of the benefits-received principle of taxation.

Clarke's tax schema was a significant breakthrough in the theory of mechanism design, which is concerned with the problem of how to induce people to tell the truth when they have private information. At the same time, his schema is unlikely to have much practical significance. A government could hardly be expected to administer the Clarke taxes even approximately over a large population; the computational requirements are enormous. And even if it could, Tideman and Tullock note that each individual Clarke tax is likely to be quite small, enough so that many people might actually abstain from voting for a new allocation. They also show how coalitions might form to undermine its revelation properties.[17] Finally, the Clarke tax schema ignores income effects. One must conclude that Clarke taxes do not resolve the free-rider problem as a practical matter.

Do People Free Ride?

The question remains whether people do attempt to free ride on the good will of others when they have an incentive to do so. The mainstream normative public sector theory would dearly prefer that they do not. Truth telling and cooperation in the name of good citizenship are fundamental to the mainstream theory. The notion of the government acting as an agent to promote efficiency when markets fail requires that people tell the truth about their preferences. And the social welfare function, which is so central to the mainstream theory, also presumes cooperative, other-directed behavior when people enter the political sphere to confront the problem of distributive justice.

[16] T. N. Tideman and G. Tullock, "A New and Superior Process for Making Social Choices," *Journal of Political Economy*, December 1976, p. 1156.

[17] T. N. Tideman and G. Tullock, "A New and Superior Process for Making Social Choices," *Journal of Political Economy*, December, 1976, pp. 1156–1158.

A number of economists have explored the extent of free riding with nonexclusive goods in experimental settings. They often choose undergraduate economics majors as their test subjects, presumably because economics majors ought to understand the personal advantages of free riding. The results of these experiments are somewhat encouraging to the mainstream theory.

The standard experiment consists of a group of N players who are each given a fixed number of tokens, W, which they can allocate to a private good, X, or a public good, G, during each round of play. One token buys one unit of either good. The private good yields a return of R per unit to the individual who purchases it. The public good yields a return of V per unit to all players. The players keep the profits they have earned at the end of each round, equal for player i to:

$$\Pi_i = RX_i + VG_i + V\sum_{j\neq i}G_j$$

(6.42)

$$\text{with } W_i = X_i + G_i$$

The game may be played for one or more rounds. If more than one round is played, the players know at the start of the game how many rounds will be played. Also, the players allocate their tokens independently of one another during each round. They are not permitted to collude, and they only learn what the others players did after each round (or after the game concludes in some versions of the experiment).

The returns on the goods are set so that:

$$R > V \quad \text{and} \quad NV > R$$

With these returns, the pareto-optimal strategy is for all to behave cooperatively and purchase nothing but the public good each round. In this way, they maximize both the group profits and their individual profits. Cooperation is not the Nash strategy, however, given the way the experiment is set up. The Nash strategy is based on the other-things-equal assumption by each player that his play has no effect on the play of the other players. This is the only reasonable assumption in an independent game of this nature, and it leads to a clear-cut strategy given the returns on the private and public goods: Attempt to free ride on the good will of others and buy only the private good. The reason is that expected marginal profit under the Nash strategy is the partial derivative of the profit function, or

$$\partial\Pi_i/\partial X_i = R - V > 0$$

(6.43)

Put differently, the only equilibrium outcome of the game in which no player would want to change his decision, other things equal, is for everyone to purchase only the private good. Furthermore, this is true whether the game is played once or repeatedly for a fixed and known number of rounds. The incentive to free ride in a one-shot game is clear. That the same incentive exists in every round of a multiround game follows from backward induction. There is a clear incentive for everyone to purchase the private good in the final round of the game. Because everyone knows this, the incentive to free ride extends to the next-to-last round and, given that, to the round before that and so on, back to the first round. In summary, the experiments are designed to induce free riding as the rational strategy.

The results from these experiments are far different, however. The students are much more cooperative than expected. In multiround games, they typically contribute about 50% of their tokens to the public good in the first round. Cooperation does diminish as the game continues, but nowhere close to zero. After ten rounds, students still contribute from 15 to 25% of their tokens to the public good. Furthermore, the degree of cooperation is relatively insensitive to all the following variations of the experiments:

1. The size of each group: N is usually in a range of 4 to 10. Mark Isaac, James Walker, and Arlington Williams ran the experiment with groups ranging from 4 to 100 and found that group size had little effect on the results. If anything, cooperation increased slightly the larger the group.[18]

2. The number of rounds: Most of the experiments are multiround games, but some students cooperate even in one-shot games.

3. Whether the subjects know the outcomes from previous rounds or not as the game progresses: The one exception was a study by Joachim Weimann, in which cooperation declined sharply when the other players were perceived to be very selfish. Weimann noted that the subjects apparently expect their cooperation to be reciprocated.[19]

4. Whether the same groups play each round and come to know one another or the groups are randomly reformed each round: The experiments show no evidence of reputation building; in fact, James Andreoni found that "strangers" cooperated more than "partners" in his experiments.[20]

5. The amount of the return to the public good: There does appear to be more cooperation the larger V is, but the difference is slight. And V cannot be larger than R if the incentive to free ride is to be maintained.

Kindness, Confusion, or a Warm Glow from Giving?

Andreoni conducted two separate and widely-cited experiments to try to understand the motivation behind the excessive cooperation.[21] The first experiment was designed to determine the extent to which cooperation was

[18] M. Isaac, J. Walker, and A Williams, "Group Size and the Voluntary Provision of Public Goods," *Journal of Public Economics*, May 1994.

[19] J. Weimann, "Individual Behavior in a Free Riding Experiment," *Journal of Public Economics*, June 1994.

[20] J. Andreoni, "Cooperation in Public-Goods Experiments: Kindness or Confusion?," *American Economic Review*, September 1995.

[21] J. Andreoni, "Warm Glow vs. Cold Prickly: The Effects of Positive and Negative Framing on Cooperation Experiments," *Quarterly Journal of Economics*, February 1995.

the result of kindness towards others or confusion about the incentive structure. He had the students play three different versions of the game, which he called the Regular Game, the Rank Game, and the Regular/Rank game. Each game lasted ten rounds. The Regular game is the standard game described above, in which the students keep the profits from each round of the game. The Rank game offers the students a fixed payoff that is based on the rankings of their profits over the course of the entire game. The students learn the rankings after each round. The Regular/Rank game is the standard Regular game with one difference: The students are told their rankings after each round.

The idea behind the Rank game is to place the students in a zero-sum situation that gives them absolutely no incentive to cooperate out of kindness. A student who cooperates knows that this helps the noncooperators even more. The noncooperators get their own private returns plus the public return and move ahead of the cooperators in the rankings. This becomes clear as the rankings are announced each round. Reciprocal kindness is out of the question. Therefore, Andreoni argues that any cooperation in the Rank game must be the result of confusion about the nature of the game.

The only difference between the Regular/Rank and Rank games is the method of payment. The former is a positive-sum game and the latter is a zero-sum game. Therefore, Andreoni argues that any increase in cooperation in the Regular/Rank game over the Rank game is a measure of cooperation resulting from kindness.

Andreoni's experiments produced the expected results. The amount of cooperation in rounds one and ten for each of the games was as follows:

Game	Percent of tokens to the public good		Percent of subjects contributing zero to the public good	
	Round 1	Round 10	Round 1	Round 10
Regular	56	26.5	20	45
Rank	32.7	5.4	35	92.5
Regular/Rank	45.8	9.0	10	65

The Regular game yielded the typical outcomes for these experiments. The Rank game produced a huge decrease in cooperation and students were more cooperative in the Regular/Rank game than in the Rank game. Looking at the outcomes over all ten rounds, Andreoni concluded that about half of the cooperation was the result of kindness and half was the result of confusion. Moreover there was a distinct change in both effects from the early rounds (1–6) to the later rounds (7–10). Throughout the early rounds, kindness increased and confusion decreased. Throughout the later rounds kindness decreased and confusion remained fairly constant. He concluded from this that the typical pattern of decay in cooperation in the later rounds in these experiments is due to the frustration that kindness is not reciprocated. It is not the result of learning the incentive structure, which is a common explanation in the literature.

Positive Versus Negative Framing

In a second experiment, Andreoni discovered that the way in which the game was framed for the students had an enormous impact on the outcome. In the standard game, the students are told in the instructions that if they invest in the public good every member of the group benefits, and this is true no matter who invests in the public good. Andreoni refers to this instruction as positive framing because it emphasizes the benefit of doing something good. It suggests that each student is endowed with tokens of private goods and the issue for them is how many of the private tokens they will exchange for the public good to benefit everyone. Andreoni then ran a second experiment in which the students were told that if they invest in the private good they reduce the earnings of all the other people by an amount V, the return on the public good, and this is true no matter who invests in the public good. Andreoni refers to this instruction as negative framing because it emphasizes the costs of doing something bad. The negative frame in effect rewrites the profit function, Eq. (6.42), as:

$$\Pi_i = RX_i + VG_i + V\sum_{j\neq i}(W_j - X_j), \text{ or} \tag{6.44}$$

$$\Pi_i = RX_i + VG_i - V\sum_{j\neq i}X_j + VW_j(N - 1) \tag{6.45}$$

It suggests that each student is endowed with their opponents' tokens in public goods, $V*W_j*(N - 1)$, which endowment is lost only if they go into private goods.

The two games were identical, of course, with the same clear-cut incentive to free ride. Yet, the outcomes were quite different, with the negative frame game yielding only about half the amount of cooperation over the ten rounds as the positive frame game. The students apparently enjoy doing a good deed more than they enjoy not doing a bad deed.

Andreoni's previous research on charitable giving had shown that the amount and extent of charitable giving in the United States far exceed what would be expected from altruism alone. This led him to conclude that people experience a "warm glow" from the act of giving to others in and of itself, in addition to whatever impulse they may have to be altruistic. He views these two experiments as further support for his "warm glow" hypothesis. We will return to Andreoni's research on charitable giving in Chapter 10.

Following up on Adreoni's research, Thomas Palfrey and Jeffrey Prisbrey recently made an important contribution to our understanding of the motivation behind excessive cooperation.[22] Their innovation was to introduce far more variation in the payoffs than in previous experiments. They ran four sessions with ten rounds per session. The value of the public good, V, varied over the four sessions. In addition, the value of the private good, R, was determined by a random draw from a distribution in each round of each session. The variation in R was such that at times $R < V$, giving the subjects a clear incentive to invest in the public good, and at other times $R > NV$, giving the subjects an equally clear incentive to invest in the private good. In some sessions, the students were given one token per round; in other sessions, they were given nine tokens to test for irrational splitting of the tokens between the private and public goods each round. The variation in the payoffs allowed for a probit analysis of the results to test for heterogeneity among the subjects.

The experimental framework of Palfrey and Prisbrey allowed them to conduct the following tests:

1. *Kindness towards others* (*altruism*): Kindness exists if the subjects contribute more to the public good as V increases, other things equal. They found no evidence of kindness, unlike Andreoni.

2. *A warm glow effect*: The tested for a warm-glow threshold, g, such that when $R > V$ so that the incentive was to free ride, if

$R - V < g$, then the subjects contributed to the public good.
$R - V > g$, then the subjects contributed to the private good.
$R - V = g$, then the subjects contributed to either good.

They found a warm-glow threshold in line with Andreoni's hypothesis about the motivation for excessive cooperation. But Palfrey and Prisbey also found that the threshold varied considerably among the subjects.

3. *Gross errors as evidence of confusion*: The test for confusion was whether the subjects committed one or more of three gross errors that the structure of their experiment made possible:

a. Splitting the tokens between the public and private good when they were given nine tokens.
b. "Spite:" contributing to the private good when $R < V$.
c. "Sacrifice:" contributing to the public good when $R > NV$.

They found evidence of these errors early on but they virtually disappeared in the later rounds. The eventual elimination of gross errors led Palfrey and Prisbey to conclude that the decline in cooperation over time in these free-riding experiments is most likely due to a reduction in confusion as the subjects begin to understand the game. They found no evidence of attempts to build reputation or of an increase in selfishness as the game progressed— that is, no noticeable change in the subjects' preferences.

---

[22] J. Palfrey and J. Prisbrey, "Anomalous Behavior in Public Goods Experiments: How Much and Why?," *American Economic Review*, December 1997.

Staged experiments must always be viewed with caution, especially when the subjects are shown to be somewhat confused by the experiments. Nonetheless, the overwhelming weight of the free-rider experiments is that people are willing to behave cooperatively even when it is clearly in their interests to behave selfishly. And, as Andreoni points out, the real world is likely to be more conducive to acts of kindness than these experimental settings are. These findings are somewhat encouraging for the mainstream normative public sector theory.

AGGREGATE EXTERNALITIES

Thus far we have considered two kinds of externalities that are likely to cause severe practical problems for the government: (1) individualized externalities arising from exclusive activities for which the identity of each individual consumer matters and (2) nonexclusive goods. Fortunately, a number of important externalities have a special form that is much more amenable to corrective public policy action

Consider the example of highway congestion. An additional car on a congested highway generates an external diseconomy to anyone driving on the highway because it adds to the total number of vehicles on the road, to the total amount of congestion. But no one cares who is actually driving the additional car. This is an example of an *aggregate externality*, meaning that the external effect depends only upon the aggregate level of some exclusive economic activity. The identity of the individuals within the aggregate is irrelevant.

To formalize the idea of an aggregate externality, let X_{ik} = person i's driving on a particular highway, good k. Write:

$$C = C\left(\sum_{i=1}^{H} X_{ik}\right) = C(X_k), \quad \frac{\partial C}{\partial X_{ik}} = \frac{\partial C}{\partial X_k} \qquad \text{all } i = 1, \ldots, H \qquad (6.46)$$

where:

C = congestion on the highway.
X_k = aggregate number of cars on the highway at any given time (assuming one person per car).

The condition $\partial C/\partial X_{ik} = \partial C/\partial X_k$ implies that a decision by anyone to drive on the highway has an identical marginal effect on total congestion.

If consumers only care about the aggregate level of congestion, then they each have a utility function of the form:

$$U^h = U^{*h}[X_{hn}; X_{hk}; C(X_k)] = U^h\left(X_{hn}; X_{hk}; \sum_{i=1}^{H} X_{ik}\right) \qquad (6.47)$$

where:

X_{hn} = good (factor) n consumed (supplied) by person h,

n = 1, ..., k − 1, k + 1, ..., N, each assumed to be a pure private good (factor).

X_{hk} = use of the highway by person h.

C and X_k, as above.

U^h ( ) has the following properties:

$$\frac{\partial U^{*h}}{\partial X_{ik}} = \frac{\partial U^h}{\partial X_k}, \text{ for } i \neq h \tag{6.48}$$

$$\frac{\partial U^{*h}}{\partial X_{ik}} = \frac{\partial U^h}{\partial X_{hk}} + \frac{\partial U^h}{\partial X_k}, \text{ for } i = h \tag{6.49}$$

If anyone but person h uses the road, his utility is affected simply because aggregate road use increases, thus increasing congestion. When person h uses the road, however, there are two distinct effects. On the one hand, person h has some private reason for choosing to drive on the road that is totally unrelated to the congestion problem. On the other hand, he is adding to the congestion exactly as any other driver would and with the same consequences for his utility. He may or may not consciously understand that his choice to drive on the road necessarily contributes to the congestion and thereby lowers his utility (a point we will return to later), but he certainly views his own use of the road differently from anyone else's use of the road. This is why the derivative of U^h with respect to X_{hk} has two separate terms. A private-use term and a congestion term. Note, finally, that congestion must be a function of aggregate road use and not a general function of individual road use such as $C^* = C^*(X_{1k}, ..., X_{ik}, ..., X_{Hk})$. With this more general formulation, $\partial U^{*h}/\partial U_{ik} \neq \partial U^{*h}/\partial X_{jk}$ for $i \neq j$, and we are back in a situation of individualized externalities in which the identity of the individual consumer matters.

Congestion is not the only important example of an aggregate externality by any means. Virtually all pollution externalities affecting consumers, whether caused by other consumers or by producers, can be thought of as aggregate externalities arising from exclusive economic activities. Smog, airport noise, and industrial air and water pollution usually exhibit this property.

The Pigovian Tax

Aggregate externalities are far more amenable to government policy than are the individualized externalities or nonexclusive goods. The government need not design a set of H taxes, one specific to each individual. They can be corrected by a single tax levied on the externality-causing activity. The single tax solution requires one additional behavioral assumption, that when an individual engages in the activity for his own personal reasons, he ignores the effect of his activity on the aggregate externality. This is certainly a plausible assumption.

To derive the single tax result, consider social welfare maximization when a single exclusive good (factor) X_k gives rise to an aggregate externality affecting all consumers. Assume all other $(N - 1)$ goods and factors are purely private. The government's problem becomes:

$$\max_{(X_{hn}; X_{ik})} W\left[U^h\left(X_{hn}; X_{hk}; \sum_{i=1}^{H} X_{ik}\right)\right]$$

$$\text{s.t.} \quad F\left(\sum_{h=1}^{H} X_{hn}; \sum_{i=1}^{H} X_{ik}\right) = 0$$

where:

$n = 1, \ldots, k - 1, k + 1, \ldots, N.$
The corresponding Lagrangian is:

$$\max_{(X_{hn}; X_{ik})} L = W\left[U^h\left(X_{hn}; X_{hk}; \sum_{i=1}^{H} X_{ik}\right)\right] + \lambda F\left(\sum_{h=1}^{H} X_{hn}; \sum_{i=1}^{H} X_{ik}\right)$$

Interpersonal Equity Conditions

As always in the first-best analysis of consumer externalities, we need the interpersonal equity to obtain the pareto-optimal conditions. Consider the first-order conditions with respect to two different people's consumption (supply) of good 1, say X_{h1} and X_{j1}. The first-order conditions are

$$X_{h1}: \quad \frac{\partial W}{\partial U^h}\frac{\partial U^h}{\partial X_{h1}} = -\lambda F_1 \tag{6.50}$$

$$X_{j1}: \quad \frac{\partial W}{\partial U^j}\frac{\partial U^j}{\partial X_{j1}} = -\lambda F_1 \tag{6.51}$$

Thus,

$$\frac{\partial W}{\partial U^i}\frac{\partial U^i}{\partial X_{i1}} = -\lambda F_1 \qquad \text{all} \quad i = 1, \ldots, H \tag{6.52}$$

the standard result.

Pareto-Optimal Conditions

To derive the efficiency conditions, compare the first-order conditions for person i's consumption of the externality good (factor) k and his consumption of any other good (factor), say good 1 (X_{i1}). The first-order conditions are

$$X_{ik}: \quad \frac{\partial W}{\partial U^i} \frac{\partial U^i}{\partial X_{ik}} + \sum_{h=1}^{H} \frac{\partial W}{\partial U^h} \frac{\partial U^h}{\partial X_{ik}} = -\lambda F_k \tag{6.53}$$

$$X_{i1}: \quad \frac{\partial W}{\partial U^i} \frac{\partial U^i}{\partial X_{i1}} = -\lambda F_1 \tag{6.54}$$

Condition (6.53) for X_{ik} reflects both the personal enjoyment that person i receives from good (factor) k (the first term) and the externality from his consumption that affects everyone, *including himself* (second term). Because the externality is of the aggregate form, condition (6.53) can be rewritten:

$$\frac{\partial W}{\partial U^i} \frac{\partial U^i}{\partial X_{ik}} + \sum_{h=1}^{H} \frac{\partial W}{\partial U^h} \frac{\partial U^h}{\partial X_k} = -\lambda F_k \tag{6.55}$$

where:

$$X_k = \sum_{i=1}^{H} X_{ik}$$

Next, follow the usual procedure for obtaining the pareto-optimal conditions by dividing Eq. (6.55) by (6.54) to obtain:

$$\frac{\dfrac{\partial W}{\partial U^i} \dfrac{\partial U^i}{\partial X_{ik}} + \sum_{h=1}^{H} \dfrac{\partial W}{\partial U^h} \dfrac{\partial U^h}{\partial X_k}}{\dfrac{\partial W}{\partial U^i} \dfrac{\partial U^i}{\partial X_{i1}}} = \frac{F_k}{F_1} \qquad i = 1, \ldots, H \tag{6.56}$$

Assuming the interpersonal equity conditions have been achieved for good (factor) 1, separate the left-hand side of Eq. (6.54) into $(H+1)$ terms, selectively substitute the interpersonal equity conditions term by term to match the marginal social welfare terms $\partial W / \partial U^h$ in the numerator and denominator, and cancel the social welfare terms to yield:

$$\frac{\dfrac{\partial U^i}{\partial X_{ik}}}{\dfrac{\partial U^i}{\partial X_{i1}}} + \sum_{h=1}^{H} \left(\frac{\dfrac{\partial U^h}{\partial X_k}}{\dfrac{\partial U^h}{\partial X_{h1}}} \right) = \frac{F_k}{F_1} \qquad i = 1, \ldots, H \tag{6.57}$$

Condition (6.55) can be written as:

$$MRS^i_{X_{ik}, X_{i1}} + \sum_{h=1}^{H} MRS^h_{X_k, X_{h1}} = MRT_{X_k, X_1} \qquad i = 1, \ldots, H \tag{6.58}$$

Pareto optimality requires that the marginal rate of transformation between goods (factors) k and 1 be equal to each person's marginal rate of substitution between his personal use of k and good 1, plus the summation of everyone's (his own included) marginal rate of substitution between the externality and good 1. Bringing all the externality terms over to the right-hand side,

$$\text{MRS}^i_{X_{ik}, X_{il}} = \text{MRT}_{X_k, X_l} - \sum_{h=1}^{H} \text{MRS}^h_{X_k, X_{hl}} \qquad i = 1, \ldots, H \qquad (6.59)$$

Notice that the right-hand side of Eq. (6.59) is independent of i. That is, each consumer's "personal use" marginal rate of substitution differs from the marginal rate of transformation by the same amount, the summation of all the marginal external effects. This differs significantly from the result when the externality depends upon who consumed good k, the individualized externality. In that case, pareto optimality required:

$$\sum_{h=1}^{H} \text{MRS}^h_{X_{ik}, X_l} = \text{MRT}_{X_k, X_l} \qquad (6.60)$$

or

$$\text{MRS}^i_{X_{ik}, X_{il}} = \text{MRT}_{X_k, X_l} - \sum_{h \neq i} \text{MRS}^h_{X_{ik}, X_{hl}} \qquad (6.61)$$

Hence, the personal use marginal rates of substitution differ from the marginal rate of transformation by a variable amount, depending upon whose personal use is being considered. Consequently, H Pigovian taxes are required to correctly allocate good k, one for each consumer.

In contrast, only a single Pigovian tax is necessary in the aggregate case. Let good (factor) 1 be the numeraire, $P_1 \equiv 1$. Faced with a producer price P_k, the producers set $P_k = \text{MRT}_{X_k, X_l}$ by profit maximization. Faced with a consumer price q_k, each person consumes good k such that his personal use $q_k = \text{MRS}^i_{X_{ik}, X_{il}}, i = 1, \ldots, H$, assuming he ignores the marginal external effect of his consumption (supply). Therefore, to achieve pareto optimality place a unit tax, t_k, on each consumer equal to $-\sum_{h=1}^{H} \text{MRS}^h_{X_k, X_{hl}}$, the sum of the marginal external effects. With the unit tax and assuming utility and profit maximization,

$$q_k = P_k + t_k \qquad (6.62)$$

and

$$\text{MRS}^i_{X_{ik}, X_{il}} = \text{MRT}_{X_k, X_l} - \sum_{h=1}^{H} \text{MRS}^h_{X_k, X_{hl}} \qquad (6.63)$$

as required. $t_k > 0$ if the external effects are diseconomies such as congestion, following the convention that MRS > 0 for goods, < 0 for bads. External economies are subsidized ($t_k < 0$).

Note that the single Pigovian tax is correct only under two conditions: (1) the externality has a simple, aggregate formulation, and (2) consumers ignore all external effects when maximizing utility. The behavioral assumption is crucial because if any consumer considers so much as a single external effect, the single Pigovian tax is no longer pareto optimal. Suppose, for example, that consumer i considered both the direct personal effect and the indirect externality effect on himself when deciding how much of good k to consume. He would then equate the gross of tax price q_k to $MRS^i_{X_{ik}, X_{il}} + MRS^i_{X_k, X_{il}}$ to maximize utility, and the single tax scheme breaks down. The government would need an additional tax for each consumer who considered external effects in this way, and the aggregate externality would be just as difficult to correct as an individualized externality.

The aggregate externality case is easy to represent with standard supply and demand analysis. In Fig. 6.6, S_k is a normal supply curve, representing the marginal costs of X_k (the MRT in terms of good 1, the numeraire). D^P_k is the "private" aggregate demand curve, obtained by horizontal summation of the individuals' personal use demand curves reflecting their personal use marginal rates of substitution. D^{soc}_k is the true "social" demand curve equal, at every X_k, to D^P_k plus the (negative) aggregate marginal external effects, $\sum_{h=1}^{H} MRS^h_{X_k, X_{hl}}$. The Pigovian tax forces consumers onto D^{soc}_k, establishing the pareto-optimal equilibrium at the intersection of D^{soc}_k and S_k.

Finding the Optimum by Trial and Error

Figure 6.6 highlights an important property of the tax: It must equal the sum of the marginal external effects $\left(-\sum_{h=1}^{H} MRS^h_{X_k, X_{hl}}\right)$ at the optimal level of X_k. Setting the tax equal to the aggregate marginal damage at the initial output X^c_k, the competitive equilibrium without the tax, is not correct.

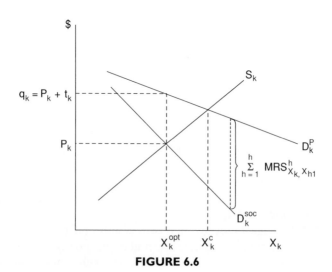

FIGURE 6.6

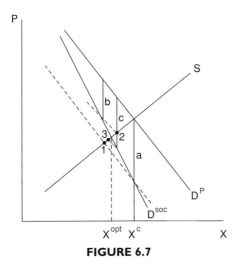

FIGURE 6.7

Given that only a single tax is necessary, however, the government may be able to reach the correct tax (approximately) by trial and error even if its initial choice in incorrect. The effectiveness of any trial and error solution depends upon four factors: the nature of the trial and error process used, the government's ability to assess aggregate marginal damages, the shape of the marginal damage function ($\sum_{h=1}^{H} MRS_{X_k, X_{h1}}^{h}$, the difference between D^P and D^{soc} at each X_k), and the stability of the competitive market being taxed.

Refer to Fig. 6.7. Assume the curves S, D^P, and D^{soc} in the figure accurately describe the competitive market for some activity and the aggregate marginal damages stemming from the activity. The following trial and error process is stable and generates t_k^{opt} in the limit:[23] The government sets an initial tax equal to the marginal damages at the no-tax equilibrium and recomputes the tax to equal the marginal damages at each successive equilibrium. The resulting pattern of equilibria converge to X_k^{opt}.

The tax, t_k, is initially set at a, equal to the marginal damages at X^c. With $t_k = a > t_k^{opt}$, the market overshoots X^{opt}, establishing a new equilibrium at point 1 on S. The marginal damages have been reduced to b, however, so t_k is adjusted to equal b. This tax overshoots X^{opt} in the opposite direction, bringing the economy to point 2 on S. Readjusting the tax to equal c, the

[23] See M. Kraus and H. Mohring, "The Role of Pollutee Taxes in Externality Problems," *Economica*, May 1975; W. J. Baumol, "On Taxation and the Control of Externalities," *American Economic Review*, June 1972, for further discussion of the suitability of sequential pollution taxes in determining a global optimum.

new higher marginal damages, brings the economy to point 3 on S, and so forth. The trial and error process approaches X^{opt} in the limit.

The trial and error process works in this market because it is stable and the marginal damages are positively related to the level of economic activity. Most markets with externalities are likely to have the same properties. Therefore, it is reasonable to assume that simple trial and error processes can generate results that are at least approximately optimal for a broad range of aggregate externalities.[24]

Two Caveats to the Pigovian Tax

The Pigovian single tax solution comes with two caveats. The first caveat is the usual one of all first-best analysis. If the government cannot achieve the interpersonal equity conditions by means of lump-sum redistributions of income, and there is no reason to suppose that it can, then a tax equal to $-\sum_{h=1}^{H} MRS_{X_k, X_{hl}}^h$ may not be consistent with the (constrained) social optimum. We will return to this point in Chapter 20, which discusses externality theory in a second-best framework.

The second caveat is a more narrow distributional point. Optimally correcting for an aggregate externality with a Pigovian tax is potentially pareto superior to the initial situation without the tax. Everyone can be made better off by moving to the first-best utility possibilities frontier from an inefficient point below the frontier. But whether everyone actually is better off with the Pigovian tax depends on what the government does with the tax revenues collected. The highway congestion example is a good case in point. The Pigovian tax is supposed to benefit the drivers on the congested highway, but the drivers could be made worse off if the revenues are not returned to them, in which case the very people the government is trying to help with the tax will oppose it.

Figure 6.8 illustrates. As in Fig. 6.6, D^p is the private market demand curve, reflecting only the private-use value of driving on the highway. D^{soc} is the social demand curve; it lies below D^P at every output by the aggregate losses to the drivers on the margin resulting from the congestion. The supply curve, S_k, assumes constant marginal cost of P_k to focus on the drivers' problem. The optimal Pigovian tax is t_k. Without a tax, the competitive equilibrium is (X_k^c, P_k), at the intersection of S_k and D^p. With the optimal Pigovian tax, the equilibrium road use drops to X_k^{opt}, at the intersection of S_k and D^{soc}. The price to the drivers rises to $P_k + t_k$, and the tax revenue collected from them is $t_k X_k^{opt}$.

Assume no income effects so that consumer surplus is an appropriate income measure of the drivers' welfare. The potential consumer surplus at

---

[24] There are other means besides taxes for achieving the optimum. We will consider some of the alternatives in Chapter 7 in the context of a production externality.

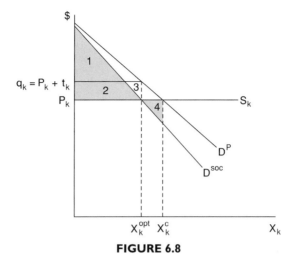

FIGURE 6.8

any output is the area between D^{soc} and S_k to that output. At the no-tax equilibrium X_k^c, the drivers' consumer surplus equals areas $1 + 2 - 4$. Area 4 represents the loss caused by excessive congestion at the no-tax equilibrium. At the pareto optimal output X_k^{opt}, the potential consumer surplus available to the drivers equals area $1 + 2$, but the drivers obtain this surplus only if the tax revenue, equal to area $2 + 3$ is returned to them. The drivers are clearly better off at X_k^{opt} if they receive the tax revenue; they avoid the excessive congestion at the no-tax equilibrium, represented by area 4. If the tax revenue is not returned, however, the drivers' actual consumer surplus is only area $1 - 3$. Whether they are now better off at X^{opt} depends on the relative size of areas $1 + 2 - 4$ and $1 - 3$. If the tax revenue $(2 + 3)$ exceeds area 4, the drivers are worse off at the optimum and they will resist the tax.[25]

This analysis may explain why commuters tend to resist tolls that are intended to reduce highway congestion by diverting some of them to other means of transportation. The commuters know they will not receive the toll revenue. In their view, they will simply face higher commuting costs that exceed the value to them of the reduced congestion.

We should note that this second caveat is not entirely consistent with the first-best policy assumptions. First-best analysis assumes that the government engages in allocational policies to bring society to the first-best utility possibilities frontier *and* that it redistributes lump-sum to reach the bliss point on the frontier. The caveat ignores the distributional part of the policy. Whether the drivers are better or worse off at the bliss point ultimately depends on society's social welfare rankings and the interpersonal equity

---

[25] We were made aware of this caveat by Russell Roberts in a seminar that he gave at Boston College.

conditions that are derived from them. The disposition of Pigovian tax revenues may be taken into consideration by the government when it redistributes, but it is irrelevant to determining the final distribution of income. Nonetheless, resistance to tolls and other forms of externality taxes is quite vocal, perhaps because people do not believe that the government has a fully articulated distributional policy. Therefore, they react more to their direct gains and losses from the government's allocational policies than to the efficiency gains from the policies.

REFERENCES

Andreoni, J., "Warm Glow vs. Cold Prickly: The Effects of Positive and Negative Framing on Cooperation Experiments," *Quarterly Journal of Economics*, February 1995.

Andreoni, J., "Cooperation in Public-Goods Experiments: Kindness or Confusion?," *American Economic Review*, September 1995.

Arrow, K. J., "The Organization of Economic Activity: Issues Pertinent to the Choice of Market Versus Nonmarket Allocation," in R. Haveman and J. Margolis (Eds.), *Public Expenditure and Policy Analysis*, second ed., Rand McNally College Publishing, Chicago, 1977.

Baumol, W. J., "On Taxation and the Control of Externalities," *American Economics Review*, June 1972.

Buchanan, J., "An Economic Theory of Clubs," *Economica*, February 1965.

Clarke, E. H., "Multipart Pricing of Public Goods," *Public Choice*, Fall 1971.

Clarke, E. H., "Multipart Pricing of Public Goods: An Example," In S. Mushkin (Ed.), *Public Prices for Public Products*, Urban Institute, Washington, D. C., 1972.

Coase, R. H., "The Problem of Social Cost," *Journal of Law and Economics*, October 1960.

Groves, T. and Loeb, M., "Incentives and Public Inputs," *Journal of Public Economics*, August 1975.

Isaac, M., Walker, J., and Williams, A., "Group Size and the Voluntary Provision of Public Goods," *Journal of Public Economics*, May 1994.

Johansen, L., "Some Notes on the Lindahl Theory of Determination of Public Expenditures," *International Economic Review*, September 1963.

Johansen, L., "The Theory of Public Goods: Misplaced Emphasis?," *Journal of Public Economics*, February 1977.

Kamien, M., Schwartz, N., and Roberts, D., "Exclusion, Externalities, and Public Goods," *Journal of Public Economics*, Vol. 2, 1973.

Kraus, M. and Mohring, H., "The Role of Pollutee Taxes in Externality Problems," *Economica*, May 1975.

Lindahl, E., *Die Gerechtigkeit der Besteverung*, Lund, 1919, reprinted (in part,) in R. Musgrave and A. Peacock (Eds.), *Classics in the Theory of Public Finance*, Macmillan, London, 1958.

Mill, J. S., *Principles of Political Economy*, W. J. Ashley (Ed.), Longmans Green & Co., London, 1921.

Ng, Y-K., "The Paradox of Universal Externalities," *Journal of Economic Theory*, April 1975.

Pigou, A. C., *The Economics of Welfare*, fourth ed., Macmillan, London, 1932.

Palfrey, J. and Prisbrey, J., "Anomalous Behavior in Public Goods Experiments: How Much and Why?," *American Economic Review*, December 1997.

Samuelson, P. A., "The Pure Theory of Public Expenditure," *Review of Economics and Statistics*, November 1954.

Samuelson, P. A., "Diagrammatic Exposition of a Theory of Public Expenditure," *Review of Economics and Statistics*, November 1955.

Samuelson, P. A., "Aspects of Public Expenditure Theories," *Review of Economics and Statistics*, November 1958.

Samuelson, P. A., "Pure Theory of Public Expenditures and Taxation," in H. Guitton and J. Margolis (Eds.), *Public Economics*, St. Martin's Press, New York, 1969.

Smith, A., *The Wealth of Nations*, Vol. II, E. Cannan (Ed.), G. P. Putnam's Sons, New York, 1904.

Tideman, T. N. and Tullock, G., "A New and Superior Process of Making Social Choices," *Journal of Political Economy*, December 1976.

Weimann, J., "Individual Behavior in a Free Riding Experiment," *Journal of Public Economics*, June 1994.

7

PRODUCTION EXTERNALITIES

A policy-relevant, technological production externality has two properties: Production activity by some firm directly enters into (or "alters") the production function of at least one other firm, and the external effect is not captured in the marketplace. These properties are completely analogous to those of a policy-relevant, technological consumption externality. Therefore, having analyzed various consumption externality models in some detail, the treatment of production externalities can be fairly brief. The production models and the resulting pareto-optimal decision rules for production externalities are virtually identical to their consumption counterparts, with the roles of consumption and production reversed. In particular, there are these important similarities:

1. The pareto-optimal decision rules for consumption externalities require equating marginal rates of transformation in production to summations of marginal rates of substitution in consumption. For production externalities, summations of marginal rates of transformation in production (or the marginal rates of technical substitution equal marginal rates of substitution in consumption.

2. In both instances, the government can achieve pareto optimality by retaining decentralized markets and taxing (subsidizing) an externality-generating exclusive activity.

3. We saw that public policy is problematic in the case of individualized consumption externalities because the government must design a set of H corrective taxes, one for each of H people consuming the good. In contrast, when the external effect depends only on aggregate consumption a single tax paid by all consumers can achieve the pareto-optimal conditions. The same distinction applies for production externalities.

Because of these similarities, Chapter 7 presents only the aggregate production externalities model. The aggregate model is by far the one most widely used in policy applications, and it provides a simple analytical framework for considering a number of policy implications that could have been discussed in the preceding chapter but are especially intuitive in a production framework. Most of the policy examples in Chapter 7 center on pollution control, as industrial pollution is a particularly appropriate and important application of the aggregate production externalities model. Chapter 8 then discusses U.S. antipollution policy as an extended example incorporating both production and consumption externalities.

Having analyzed aggregate production externalities and noted their similarities with aggregate consumption externalities, the reader should have no difficulty modeling other types of production externalities. The other production cases are also closely analogous to their consumption counterparts.

THE CONDENSED MODEL FOR PRODUCTION EXTERNALITIES

The analysis of consumption externalities used a condensed version of the general equilibrium model in Chapter 2 for its analytical framework of the form:

$$\max_{(X_{ik})} W\left[U^h(\ )\right]$$

$$\text{s.t. } F\left(\sum_{i=1}^{H} X_{ik}\right) = 0$$

where X_{ik} was defined as the consumption of good k by person i. The way in which the X_{ik} entered each person's utility function determined the appropriate policy response by the government.

Production externalities can also be analyzed with a condensed version of the full general equilibrium model, the only difference being that the model must highlight possible interdependencies in production rather than in consumption. To achieve this, we will ignore once again any notational distinction between goods and factors but define the arguments, X, in terms of production. Let X_{ji} = good (factor) i supplied (demanded) by firm j, with factors measured negatively, $j = 1, \ldots, J$ and $i = 1, \ldots, N$. There are J firms and N goods and factors.

Since we are now interested in production interrelationships, writing production as a single production-possibilities frontier is no longer useful. The model must retain the individual-firm production functions. Define $f^k() = 0$ as the implicit production function for firm k, k = 1, ..., J. Write:

$$f^k(X_{ji}) = 0 \qquad k = 1, ..., J \tag{7.1}$$

as the most general notation. This allows for the worst possible case of individualized externalities, in which each of the J production relationships has JN arguments: The production (use) of any of the N goods (factors) by any of the J firms in the economy affects every firm. In this model, each firm could produce multiple outputs, rather than a single output as in the Chapter 2 model. The model also permits each good and factor to be produced, although this is not necessary. J can be larger or smaller than N.[1]

Analogous with consumption externalities, define a pure public good (factor) as one for which:

$$\frac{\partial f^k}{\partial X_{ji}} \equiv f^k_{ji} \neq 0 \qquad \text{all } k, j = 1, ..., J \tag{7.2}$$

That is, production (use) of good (factor) i affects all production relationships on the margin no matter where activity i occurs. This is the worst case described above. Similarly, a pure private good (factor) is one for which:

$$\frac{\partial f^k}{\partial X_{ji}} \equiv f^k_{ji} = 0 \qquad k \neq j \tag{7.3}$$

Firm k's use or production of i affects only itself on the margin. Production with private goods and factors is represented notationally as $f^k(X_{ki}) = 0$, analogous with the notation of Chapter 6.

The condensation occurs in the household sector of the Chapter 2 model. Interrelationships among consumers are irrelevant to the study of production externalities, so that it is no longer necessary to retain a many-consumer economy along with the social welfare function to resolve distributional questions. These could be retained, to be sure, but the existence of production externalities does not alter any of the pareto-optimal consumption conditions or the interpersonal equity social welfare conditions that are necessary for reaching the first-best bliss point. No loss of generality occurs, then by assuming a one-consumer-equivalent economy in which the consumer supplies all factors of production and receives all the produced goods and services, *providing it is understood that one-consumer equivalence arises because the government is optimally redistributing lump sum to satisfy the interpersonal equity conditions of social welfare maximization.* Without this

[1] J is much larger than N in actual economies—the number of firms far exceeds the number of goods and factors.

assumption (or one of the severe restrictions on preferences that are sufficient for one-consumer equivalence) the pareto-optimal conditions developed in this chapter would literally apply only to an economy with one consumer. They would not have any normative policy significance.

With this understanding, the household sector of the model can be represented as:

$$U(X_1; \ldots, X_i, \ldots, X_N) = U(X_i) \tag{7.4}$$

where X_i = aggregate production of (demand for) good (factor) i. Finally, market clearance implies:

$$X_i = \sum_{j=1}^{J} X_{ji} \qquad i = 1, \ldots, N \tag{7.5}$$

Equation (7.5) can be incorporated directly into the utility function as:

$$U = U\left(\sum_{j=1}^{J} X_{ji}\right) \tag{7.6}$$

with the understanding that:

$$\frac{\partial U}{\partial X_{ji}} = \frac{\partial U}{\partial X_i} = U_i \qquad j = 1, \ldots, J; \text{ all } i = 1, \ldots, N$$

That is, the consumer does not care where the production activity occurs.

Thus, the complete general model for analyzing production externalities is

$$\max_{(X_{ji})} U\left(\sum_{j=1}^{J} X_{ji}\right)$$
$$\text{s.t. } f^k(\ ) = 0 \qquad k = 1, \ldots, J$$

The arguments of the individual production functions $f^k(\ )$ depend on the exact form of the production externality.

AGGREGATE PRODUCTION EXTERNALITIES

Industrial water pollution offers an appropriate context for the analysis of the aggregate externality case. Suppose that all firms are located on the shore of a lake and that they all use the water as a coolant for their production processes. Using the water in this manner heats it up, so that each firm returns the water to the lake at a higher temperature than it was originally received. The hotter the water, the less effective it is as a cooling agent. The heat, then, is the source of a technological production externality (a diseconomy), because each firm's production function is directly affected. Furthermore, suppose the firms do not care who is heating the water. All that matters is the amount that the water temperature increases, which is a function only of the total amount of water used by all the firms as a cooling agent. The heat pollution is an example of an aggregate externality.[2]

To model this example, let factor i be water and assume that all other goods and factors are purely private. The production relationships in this case are

$$f^{*k}(X_{kn}; X_{ki}; H) = 0 \quad n = 1, \ldots, i-1, i+1, \ldots, N \quad (7.7)$$

$$k = 1, \ldots, J$$

with

$$H = H\left(\sum_{j=1}^{J} X_{ji}\right) \quad (7.8)$$

where H = the water temperature, and $\dfrac{\partial H}{\partial X_{ji}} = \dfrac{\partial H}{\partial X_i}$, all $j = 1, \ldots, J$. Substituting for H in f^{*k} yields:

$$f^k\left(X_{kn}; X_{ki}; \sum_{j=1}^{J} X_{ji}\right) = 0 \quad k = 1, \ldots, J \quad (7.9)$$

These production relationships distinguish between each firm's private use of water as a coolant, represented by the argument X_{ki}, and the external effect of the heat, represented by the argument $\sum_{j=1}^{J} X_{ji}$. Thus,

$$\frac{\partial f^{*k}}{\partial X_{ji}} = \frac{\partial f^k}{\partial X_i} \quad j \neq k \quad (7.10)$$

$$\frac{\partial f^{*k}}{\partial X_{ji}} = \frac{\partial f^k}{\partial X_{ki}} + \frac{\partial f^k}{\partial X_i} \quad j = k \quad (7.11)$$

When some other firm uses water, firm k is affected on the margin only because the water temperature has increased. When firm k uses water, its production function is twice affected on the margin, once by the cooling effect of the water and once by the increased heat to which it contributes.

Combining Eqs. (7.6) and (7.9), the complete model of social welfare maximization is

---

[2] Notice that if the firms were situated along a river, as is often the case, the aggregate model would not apply. The firm farthest upstream would be unaffected by how any of the remaining firms use the water; the second firm would be affected only by the first firm's use of the water; and so on, so that it matters to each firm who uses the water. Unfortunately, industrial water and air pollution sometimes do take the form of individualized externalities, in which case the optimal public policy becomes much more difficult to implement, as we have seen with consumption externalities.

$$\max_{(X_{jn};X_{ji})} U\left(\sum_{j=1}^{J}X_{jn}, \sum_{j=1}^{J}X_{ji}\right)$$

$$\text{s.t. } f^k\left(X_{kn}; X_{ki}; \sum_{j=1}^{J}X_{ji}\right) = 0 \qquad n = 1, \ldots, i-1, i+1, \ldots, N$$

$$k, j = 1, \ldots, J$$

Supplying Lagrangian multipliers λ^k for each of the production functions, the Lagrangian is

$$\max_{(X_{jn};X_{ji})} L = U\left(\sum_{j=1}^{J}X_{jn}, \sum_{j=1}^{J}X_{ji}\right) + \sum_{k=1}^{J}\lambda^k f^k\left(X_{kn}; X_{ki}; \sum_{j=1}^{J}X_{ji}\right)$$

The First-Order Conditions—Pareto Optimality

Production models of this type, with one-consumer equivalent economies, generate only the pareto-optimal conditions necessary to bring the economy to its first-best production possibilities frontier. They are derived by considering any two activities by any one firm. Let us first establish the important result that the presence of production externalities in some markets implies intervention only in those markets. The perfectly competitive allocation is correct for all other activities. To see this, consider the purely private goods (factors) m and 1 supplied (demanded) by firm j, X_{jm}, and X_{jl} for $m \neq i$. The first-order conditions are

$$X_{jm}: \qquad \frac{\partial U}{\partial X_m} = -\lambda^j \frac{\partial f^j}{\partial X_{jm}} \qquad \text{all } j = 1, \ldots, J$$
$$\text{any } m \neq i \qquad (7.12)$$

$$X_{jl}: \qquad \frac{\partial U}{\partial X_1} = -\lambda^j \frac{\partial f^j}{\partial X_{jl}} \qquad \text{all } j = 1, \ldots, J \qquad (7.13)$$

Dividing Eq. (7.12) by (7.13):

$$\frac{\dfrac{\partial U}{\partial X_m}}{\dfrac{\partial U}{\partial X_1}} = \frac{\dfrac{\partial f^j}{\partial X_{jm}}}{\dfrac{\partial f^j}{\partial X_{jl}}} \equiv \frac{f^j_{jm}}{f^j_{jl}} \qquad \text{all } j = 1, \ldots, J \qquad (7.14)$$

This is the standard competitive result. The left-hand side (LHS) is the MRS between m and 1. There are three possible interpretations of the production derivatives, depending on whether m and 1 are goods or factors. Differentiating $f^j(\ ) = 0$ with respect to X_{jl} and X_{jm} yields:

$$\frac{f^j_{jm}}{f^j_{j1}} = -\frac{d\,X_{j1}}{d\,X_{jm}} \tag{7.15}$$

with all other goods and factors constant.

If both m and 1 are goods, the ratio is their marginal rate of transformation. If both are factors, the ratio is their marginal rate of technical substitution in production. Finally, if 1 is a good and m a factor, the ratio is the marginal product of factor m in producing good 1 (recall that factors are measured negatively). Since 1 and m can be goods or factors, conditions (7.14) reproduce pareto-optimal conditions P4 to P8 from the full model of Chapter 2. We will refer to the ratio generally as a marginal rate of transformation throughout Chapter 7 and switch to one of the other interpretations when a specific example warrants it.

To derive the pareto-optimal rules for factor i (water), which generates the aggregate externality, consider the use of water by firm j and its supply of good 1, X_{ji} and X_{j1}, (assume X_1 is a good for purposes of interpretation). The first-order conditions are

$$X_{ji}: \quad \frac{\partial U}{\partial X_i} = -\lambda^j \frac{\partial f^j}{\partial X_{ji}} - \sum_{k=1}^{J} \lambda^k \frac{\partial f^k}{\partial X_i} = -\lambda^j f^j_{ji} - \sum_{k=1}^{J} \lambda^k f^k_i \tag{7.16}$$

$$X_{j1}: \quad \frac{\partial U}{\partial X_1} = -\lambda^j \frac{\partial f^j}{\partial X_{j1}} = \lambda^j f^j_{j1} \qquad j = 1, \ldots, J \tag{7.17}$$

Dividing Eq. (7.16) by (7.17):

$$\frac{\dfrac{\partial U}{\partial X_i}}{\dfrac{\partial U}{\partial X_1}} = \frac{\lambda^j f^j_{ji} + \sum_{k=1}^{J} \lambda^k f^k_i}{\lambda^j f^j_{j1}} \tag{7.18}$$

The left-hand side has a standard interpretation as the marginal rate of substitution between the consumption of good 1 and the supply of factor i (water). To interpret the right-hand side (RHS), the λ^k multipliers must be removed. To do this, note that:

$$\frac{\partial U}{\partial X_{j1}} = \frac{\partial U}{\partial X_1} = -\lambda^j f^j_{j1} \qquad \text{all } j = 1, \ldots, J \tag{7.19}$$

from the first-order conditions. Eq. (7.19) says that the marginal "kick" to utility from the production of good 1 must be the same no matter which firm produces it. This condition holds automatically under the assumption that the consumer is indifferent to the identity of the firms. Using this result, the RHS can be cleared of the λ^k terms by separating the RHS into $J + 1$ terms, making the appropriate substitution for $\lambda^j f^j_{j1}$ in the denominators to match up the corresponding λ^k in the numerators, and canceling each λ term by term. This procedure is analogous to the one used to simplify expressions for consumer externalities, with one important difference. For the consumer case, the procedure was legitimate only under the assumption that the proper lump-sum redistributions were carried out to satisfy the interpersonal equity conditions of social welfare maximization. In the production case, all that matters is that the consumer does not care which firm supplies (uses) a good (factor).[3]

Having applied this procedure, the first-order conditions become:

$$\frac{\frac{\partial U}{\partial X_i}}{\frac{\partial U}{\partial X_1}} = \frac{f^j_{ji}}{f^j_{j1}} + \sum_{k=1}^{J} \left(\frac{f^k_i}{f^k_{k1}} \right) \qquad \text{all } j = 1, \ldots, J \qquad (7.20)$$

The marginal rate of substitution between good 1 and factor i in consumption must equal, for each firm, the private-use marginal product of factor i in the production of good 1 (the cooling property of the water) *plus* the additional aggregate marginal effect that increased use of factor i has on the production of good 1 through the externality (i.e., the combined adverse effects on every firm's production of good 1 resulting from the increased water temperature). For firm k, the ratio $f^k_i/f^k_{k1} = -d\,X_{k1}/d\,H$, the (negative) marginal product of heat on its production of good 1. These two effects combined are the true social marginal product of factor i in the production of good 1. For purposes of further discussion, rewrite the condition (7.20) as:

$$MRS_{i,1} = MP^j_{ji,j1} + \sum_{k=1}^{J} MP^k_{i,k1} \qquad j = 1, \ldots, J \qquad (7.21)$$

The Pigovian Tax

Consistent with our analysis of an aggregate consumption externality, suppose that each firm considers only the private cooling properties of water when deciding how much to use. It ignores the external heat affect, not only on all others but on itself. Under this assumption, the government can achieve pareto-optimal condition (7.21) by retaining a decentralized market for factor i and setting a unit tax on the use of i equal to the sum of its external effects on the margin. Define consumer prices q_i and q_1, producer prices p_i and q_1, and a tax t_i such that:

$$\frac{q_i}{q_1} = \frac{p_i}{q_1} + \frac{t_i}{q_1} \qquad (7.22)$$

[3] We are, however, implicitly assuming that the interpersonal equity conditions are satisfied in specifying a one-consumer equivalent economy. The only way to avoid the interpersonal equity conditions is by assuming that preferences take one of the highly restrictive, and unrealistic, forms that generate one-consumer equivalence at any income distribution.

(We assumed that good 1 was the numeraire when analyzing consumption externalities. Here we choose to retain the price q_1 because it often aids in the interpretation of production externalities.) The consumer sets $q_i/q_1 = MRS_{i,1}$. Each firm sets $p_i/q_1 = MP^j_{ji,j1}$, its private-use marginal product. Alternatively, $p_i = MP^j_{ji,j1} \cdot q_1$, which says that firms equate the price of an input to the value of its marginal product. This assumes, of course, that each firm ignores the external effects of using factor i. Without any government intervention, $p_i = q_i$, and the $MRS_{i,1}$ would equal the private marginal product for each firm in equilibrium. To achieve the correct pareto-optimal conditions, the government must set $t_i = \left(\sum_{k=1}^J MP^k_{i,k1}\right) \cdot q_1$, equating the tax rate to the marginal value of the external effects at the optimum. With this tax and competitive behavior,

$$\frac{q_i}{q_1} - \frac{t_i}{q_1} = MRS_{i,1} - \sum_{k=1}^k MP^k_{i,k1} = \frac{p_i}{q_1} = MP^j_{ji,j1} \qquad j = 1, \ldots, J$$

(7.23)

or

$$MRS_{i,1} = MP^j_{ji,j1} + \sum_{k=1}^J MP^k_{i,k1} \qquad j = 1, \ldots, J \qquad (7.24)$$

as required for pareto optimality.

A single Pigovian tax is sufficient because the marginal damage to any firm depends only on the aggregate use of factor i. The divergence between the marginal rate of substitution and the marginal external effects, $MRS_{i,1} - \sum_{k=1}^J MP^k_{i,k1}$ from Eq. (7.21), is independent of j. The only difference from the consumer externality is that the tax equals the value of the marginal external effects rather than the negative of this value, simply because the firm is paying the tax. If the marginal external effect is adverse as in the heat example, the tax is negative (each marginal product $MP^k_{i,k1}$ is negative); the producer price p_i must exceed the consumer supply price q_i. Conversely, for external economies each firm is subsidized in an amount equal to the aggregate marginal external benefit of the activity. With the single tax then, the consumer's marginal rate of substitution is correctly equated to the full social marginal product of factor i in the production of good 1.

Note, finally, that the production model has been written in its most general form. Realistically, any source of pollution affects only a small subset of firms in the economy. In terms of the general model, this simply means that $MP^k_{i,k1} = 0$ for most k in the summation of the external effects.

Three Geometric Interpretations of the Pareto-Optimal Conditions

Three equivalent geometric interpretations have been commonly used in the literature to depict the optimal solution for aggregate production externalities, especially in the context of industrial pollution.

The Market for the Pollutant

The most straightforward representation is in terms of the factor market for i (water), since this is where the external effect actually occurs. In Fig. 7.1, factor demand curve D^{priv} is the horizontal summation of each firm's private demand curve for i, equal to the firm's common private-use value of marginal product between good 1 and water. The supply curve S represents consumer's marginal rate of substitution between i and 1. Without government intervention, the market clears at (X_i^c, p_i^c) with $q_c = MRS_{i,1} \cdot q_1 = MP_{ji,j1}^j q_1 = p_i^c$. The curve D^{soc} represents the true social value of marginal product between 1 and i. It differs from D^{priv} at each level of input by a vertical distance equal to the value of the aggregate external marginal damage, $\sum_{k=1}^{J} MP_{i,k1}^k \cdot q_1$. The optimum quantity of i occurs at the intersection of D^{soc} and S, the point at which the social marginal product equals the marginal rate of substitution. If a tax is levied on the use of factor i exactly equal to the aggregate external marginal damage at the optimum X_i^{opt}, then the decentralized market selects X_i^{opt}, with producer and consumer prices p_i^{opt} and q_i^{opt}, and $q_i^{opt} = p_i^{opt} - t_i^{opt}$.

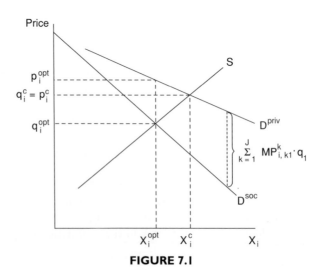

FIGURE 7.1

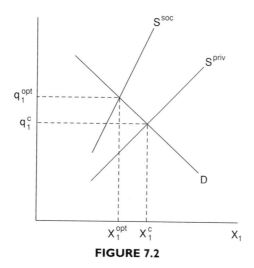

FIGURE 7.2

The Market for Goods That Pollute

An alternative supply-demand interpretation focuses on the market for good 1. Figure 7.2 represents the idea that production of goods generating external diseconomies should be reduced relative to the no-intervention competitive equilibrium, X_1^c. The supply curve S^{priv} is the horizontal summation of each firm's private marginal cost $\left(q_i/MP_{ji,j1}^j \right)$, the ratio of the price of the input to its marginal product. S^{soc} represents the true social marginal cost of producing good 1, equal to:

$$\left(\frac{q_i}{MP_{ji,j1}^j + \sum_{k=1}^{J} MP_{i,k1}^k} = \frac{q_i}{MP_{i,1}^{soc}} \right)$$

Since $\sum_{k=1}^{J} MP_{i,k1}^k < 0$ for external diseconomies, S^{soc} lies above S^{priv}, as drawn. D is the standard aggregate demand for good 1. In equilibrium, the price q_1 should reflect the social marginal cost of producing good 1, as it does at (X_1^{opt}, q_1^{opt}), and not the private marginal cost, as at (X_1^c, q_1^c). This is equivalent to saying that input prices must equal the value of the social marginal products, not the value of private marginal products.

Extreme care must be taken with this interpretation, however, for two reasons. First, the diagram appears to suggest that a tax on good 1 equal to the divergence between the private and social marginal cost at the optimum X^{opt} can generate a pareto-optimal allocation of resources. This is not true, in general. The Pigovian tax must be on the direct source of the externality to

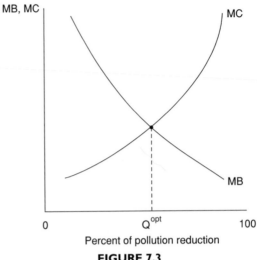

FIGURE 7.3

generate the pareto-optimal conditions, in this case on the use of factor i. The purpose of the tax is to change the firms' incentive to use water. Any output effects from the tax on water happen indirectly as the result of increasing the marginal cost to the firms of using water. Second, output effects in the presence of externalities are not as straightforward as this partial equilibrium diagram might suggest. William Baumol and Wallace Oates have demonstrated that with combined production and consumption externalities, which may well exist with industrial pollution, the conditions required to guarantee output reductions for activities that generate external diseconomies are fairly restrictive.[4]

The Optimal Reduction in Pollution

A final geometric interpretation, especially common in pollution analysis, says that the external damage should be reduced until the marginal benefit just equals the marginal cost of the reduction. In Fig. 7.3, Q^{opt} represents the optimal amount of external damage. The diagram is a useful device for showing that, in general, zero damage (zero pollution) is typically not the pareto-optimal solution.

[4] W. J. Baumol and W. Oates, *The Theory of Environmental Policy*, Prentice-Hall, Englewood Cliffs, NJ, 1975, chap. 7. For a similar comprehensive analysis with consumer externalities, see P. A. Diamond and J. Mirrlees, "Aggregate Production with Consumer Externalities," *Quarterly Journal of Economics*, February 1973; also, E. Sadka, "A Note on Aggregate Production with Consumer Externalities," *Journal of Public Economics*, February 1978. The earliest recognition of possible output anomalies with externalities is generally credited to Buchanan and Kafolgis in J. Buchanan and M. Kafolgis, "A Note on Public Goods Supply," *American Economic Review*, June 1963.

Figure 7.3 can be directly related to Fig. 7.1 in the following manner. The marginal benefit of reducing external damage is the negative of the marginal cost of increasing the external damage. In Fig. 7.1, this marginal cost is $\sum_{k=1}^{J} MP_{i,kl}^{k} \cdot q_{l}$, the value of the reduction in output of good 1 through the externality caused by a marginal increase in factor i. Therefore, the marginal benefit curve of Fig. 7.3 equals the vertical distance between D^{priv} and D^{soc} in Fig. 7.1. The marginal cost of reducing damage is an opportunity cost. It equals, at each quantity of factor input, the marginal private-use value of factor i in production of good 1 (D^{priv} in Fig. 7.1), less the value at which consumers are willing the supply factor i (curve S in Fig. 7.1). Therefore, the marginal cost curve in Fig. 7.3 equals the vertical distance between curves D^{priv} and S in Fig. 7.1. Q^{opt} in Fig. 7.3 thus corresponds to X_{i}^{opt} in Fig. 7.1: MB = MC in terms of external damage reduction when the distance between D^{priv} and D^{soc} equals the distance between D^{priv} and S in the market for factor i.

Internalizing the Externality

Correcting for an externality does not necessarily require a Pigovian tax. There could be other options.

Suppose that a single conglomerate owned all the firms affected by a particular externality. In terms of our general model, this would include every single firm in the economy, but externalities will be much less pervasive in actual cases. If one firm does own all affected firms, then its desire to maximize profits gives it the proper incentive to account for the externality. The government need not intervene because the firm effectively takes on the role of the omniscient social planner.

Our model may be unduly general, but it can be used to illustrate this point quite effectively. The single firm would solve the following problem: Allocate the goods and factors among all production sites to maximize joint profits. Formally,[5]

$$\max_{(X_{kn})} \sum_{k=1}^{J} \sum_{n=1}^{N} p_n X_{kn}$$

$$\text{s.t. } f^k \left(X_{kn}; \sum_{j=1}^{J} X_{ji} \right) = 0$$

with the corresponding Lagrangian:

$$\max_{(X_{kn})} L = \sum_{k=1}^{J} \sum_{n=1}^{N} p_n X_{kn} + \sum_{k=1}^{J} \lambda^k f^k \left(X_{kn}; \sum_{j=1}^{J} X_{ji} \right)$$

[5] Here, n = 1, ..., N and includes i.

The first-order conditions for this problem are

$$X_{kn}: \quad p_n = -\lambda^k f_{kn}^k \qquad n \neq i, \, k = 1, \, \ldots, \, J \tag{7.25}$$

$$X_{ki}: \quad p_i = -\lambda^k f_{ki}^k - \sum_{j=1}^{J} \lambda^j f_i^j \qquad k = 1, \, \ldots, \, J \tag{7.26}$$

Expressing the pareto-optimal conditions in terms of good 1 yields:

$$\frac{p_n}{p_1} = \frac{f_{kn}^k}{f_{k1}^k} \qquad n \neq i; \, k = 1, \, \ldots, \, J \tag{7.27}$$

$$\frac{p_i}{p_1} = \left(\frac{f_{ki}^k}{f_{k1}^k} \right) + \sum_{k=1}^{J} \left(\frac{f_i^k}{f_{k1}^k} \right) \qquad k = 1, \, \ldots, \, J \tag{7.28}$$

If all markets are perfectly competitive and there are no taxes, then:

$$q_n = p_n \qquad n = 1, \, \ldots, \, N$$

Thus, combining utility and profit maximization,

$$\frac{q_n}{q_1} = \frac{U_n}{U_1} = \frac{f_{kn}^k}{f_{k1}^k} = \frac{p_n}{p_1} \qquad n \neq i; \, k = 1, \, \ldots, \, J \tag{7.29}$$

and

$$\frac{q_i}{q_1} = \frac{U_i}{U_1} = \left(\frac{f_{ki}^k}{f_{k1}^k} \right) + \sum_{k=1}^{N} \left(\frac{f_i^k}{f_{k1}^k} \right) = \frac{p_i}{p_1} \qquad k = 1, \, \ldots, \, J \tag{7.30}$$

the required pareto-optimal conditions.

This example illustrates two important points. The first relates to modeling strategy. Any situation involving only production externalities does not require a full general equilibrium model to determine the pareto-optimal conditions. All one need assume is that society is trying to maximize total profits in the economy at fixed producer prices, subject to all the production constraints. A number of researchers have exploited this property and ignored the demand side entirely. The only caveat is that the optimal prices, p_n, cannot be determined without specifying consumer preferences as well. Hence, all profit-maximizing specifications implicitly assume that the prices in the objective profit function are set equal to their values at the full pareto optimum.

The second point is that *some* decision-making unit has to internalize an externality in order to achieve pareto optimality. This is a fundamental prerequisite for any solution to a technological externality, whatever form the externality may take.

One possibility is a bargaining solution among the affected firms. The nature of the bargain is cartel like. In our example, the firms agree to adjust the production of the externality-generating activity to maximize group profits and then further agree on how to divide the increased profits among themselves. This is the solution envisioned by Coase in his famous theorem. Firms certainly have an incentive to internalize the externality in this way because it is potentially a pareto-superior outcome. We will see in Chapter 20, however, that private information about the externality can undermine the incentive to bargain efficiently.

A number of practical problems remain for Coase-style bargaining even with perfect information. One is that a bargaining solution is undoubtedly infeasible if large numbers of firms are affected by the externality. The second concerns the nature of their bargain. The bargaining solution requires that the firms behave in cartel-like fashion in accounting for the externality, but they cannot also use their new-found monopoly power to raise prices to consumers. The firms must remain price takers, or some of the first-order conditions, Eq.(7.27), will not hold. Finally, the bargaining envisioned by Coase requires collusion by the firms and may run afoul of the U.S. antitrust laws.

If the firms cannot or will not internalize the externalities by themselves, then the government must force society to "see" the correct pattern of interrelationships by setting Pigovian taxes (or subsidies). In practice, however, effective internalization by the government sector may also be difficult to achieve. This is especially likely with a federalist system of national, state, and local governments. As will be discussed in detail in Part V, one of the main theoretical problems with a federalist system of governments is that the jurisdictional boundaries of any one government seldom correspond to the pattern of externalities present in the economy. This is particularly true for most forms of air and water pollution. Individual state and local governments often cannot internalize all the external effects simply because many of the affected citizens or firms are not located within their jurisdictions. The national government could theoretically internalize all externalities, but it seldom has the flexibility to offer variable policy solutions tailored to specific local pockets of external effects, especially if the externalities cut across lower level jurisdictions. This jurisdictional dilemma may well go a long way towards explaining why the United States has never been able to mount a very effective antipollution policy. We will return to the United States' antipollution policies in Chapter 8.

Additional Policy Considerations

A number of additional policy considerations can best be analyzed in the context of a simpler model in which only one firm is the source of the externality. This may actually be a more realistic model for many externalities, such as single-source industrial pollution.

Suppose firm 1 produces a product or byproduct, call it z_1, that enters the production function of all other firms in the economy but is a decision variable only for the first firm. z_1 has no effect on consumers. Assume, further, that all other goods and factors X are purely private, and that all firms are price takers operating in competitive markets. An example might be a firm situated on a river and engaging in some polluting activity that affects all other firms located downstream from it.

In this model, the production functions can be represented as:

$$f^1(X_{1n}; z_1) = 0 \tag{7.31}$$

$$f^k(X_{kn}; z_1) = 0 \qquad n = 1, \ldots, N; \ k = 2, \ldots, J \tag{7.32}$$

The government's problem is

$$\max_{(X_{1n}; X_{kn}; z_1)} U\left(\sum_{j=1}^N X_{jn}\right)$$

$$\text{s.t.} \qquad f^1(X_{1n}; z_1) = 0$$
$$\qquad f^k(X_{kn}; z_1) = 0$$

with the corresponding Lagrangian:

$$\max_{(X_{1n}; X_{kn}; z_1)} L = U\left(\sum_{j=1}^N X_{jn}\right) + \lambda^1 f^1(X_{1n}; z_1) + \sum_{k=2}^J \lambda^k f^k(X_{kn}; z_1),$$
$$k = 2, \ldots, J; \ n = 1, \ldots, N$$

The first-order conditions for this problem are

$$U_n = \lambda^k f^k_{kn} = \lambda^1 f^1_n \qquad n = 1, \ldots, N; \ k = 2, \ldots, J \tag{7.33}$$

$$\lambda^1 f^1_{z_1} + \sum_{k=2}^J \lambda^k f^k_{z_1} = 0 \tag{7.34}$$

Expressing the pareto-optimal conditions in terms of good 1 yields:

$$\frac{U_n}{U_1} = \frac{f^k_{kn}}{f^k_{k1}} = \frac{f^1_{1n}}{f^1_{11}} \qquad n = 1, \ldots, N; \ k = 2, \ldots, J \tag{7.35}$$

and

$$\frac{f^1_{z_1}}{f^1_{11}} + \sum_{k=2}^J \left(\frac{f^k_{z_1}}{f^k_{k1}}\right) = 0 \tag{7.36}$$

Equation (7.36) follows from the consumer's indifference to which firms supply goods or buy factors: $\lambda^j f^j_{j1} = \lambda^1 f^1_{11} = U_1 \neq 0$, $j = 2, \ldots, J$. This assumption can then be used to remove the Lagrangian multipliers from Eq. (7.34) by selective substitution in the denominators, as demonstrated in the aggregate externality case. A number of important policy implications follow from the first-order conditions.

Taxing the Externality

The government can achieve the pareto-optimal conditions by setting a unit tax on firm 1's production of z_1, such that:

$$t_z = -\sum_{k=2}^{J} \left(\frac{f_{z1}^k}{f_{k1}^k} \right) \cdot q_1 \tag{7.37}$$

equal to the value of the aggregate marginal external effect from producing z_1. All other goods and factors are untaxed. This is the standard Pigovian tax; it achieves the pareto-optimal conditions because the firm sets $q_1 \cdot \dfrac{f_{z1}^1}{f_{11}^1} = t_z$.

Taxing and Subsidizing Everything Else

A unit tax (subsidy) on the externality-generating activity works by changing the vector of *relative* prices in the economy from their values in the no-intervention competitive situation to the values necessary to support the pareto optimum. Only relative prices determine the allocation of resources. This implies that any set of absolute prices that maintains the unique vector of pareto-optimal relative prices is an admissible solution to the externality problem. An infinity of absolute prices satisfy the optimal relative price vector, including a vector of prices in which the externality-generating activity is not taxed. An interesting problem, then, is to find the set of taxes (and subsidies) that generates the pareto-optimal allocation given that, for some reason, the externality-generating activity cannot be taxed.

The following set of taxes on firm 1 achieves the pareto optimum:

$$t_1^1 = a = \left(\frac{f_{11}^1}{f_{z1}^1} \right) \cdot \sum_{k=2}^{J} \left(\frac{f_{z1}^k}{f_{k1}^k} \right) q_1$$

$$t_n^1 = a \left(\frac{f_{1n}^1}{f_{11}^1} \right) \qquad n = 1, \dots, N \tag{7.38}$$

$$t_z^1 = 0$$

The tax on good 1, a, equals the marginal increase in z_1 resulting from a unit increase in good 1 by firm 1 (first term), times the marginal decrease in good 1 across all firms per unit increase in z_1. The tax on one of the private goods n equals the marginal increase in good 1 by firm 1 per unit increase in good (factor) n, multiplied by the aggregate marginal external effect of an increase in good 1, given by a. As such, the two taxes account for the aggregate external effects of all firm 1's activities except its production of z_1. In other words, the taxes indirectly account for the externality caused by firm 1.

To see that these taxes generate the pareto-optimal conditions, consider firm 1's use of any good or factor n and good 1. Firm 1 equates:

$$q_n + t_n^1 = \frac{f_{1n}^1}{f_{11}^1}(q_1 + a) \tag{7.39}$$

or

$$q_n = \frac{f_{1n}^1}{f_{11}^1}q_1 \tag{7.40}$$

as required for conditions (7.35).
Next consider the firm's use of z_1 and good 1. The firm equates:

$$(q_1 + a)\frac{f_{z_1}^1}{f_{11}^1} = t_z = 0 \tag{7.41}$$

as required for condition (7.36).

Notice that the government should not levy any taxes on firms $k = 2, \ldots, J$. Since z_1 is not a decision variable for firms $k = 2, \ldots, J$, their production of the other goods and factors can be left untaxed.

This exercise emphasizes the importance of taxing the source of the externality if possible, a point mentioned above in the discussion of Fig. 7.2. Otherwise, the government must tax (or subsidize) all goods and factors that directly substitute for the externality-causing activity in production, and that can be a very large number.

Subsidizing or Compensating the Victims

The tax analysis also shows that the government cannot merely subsidize (tax) firms $k = 2, \ldots, J$ for the damage (gain) caused by firm 1's production of z_1. No matter what form the subsidy (tax) may take, society cannot possibly satisfy the pareto-optimal condition, Eq. (7.36), if firm 1 is not taxed appropriately, Firm 1, if untaxed, will produce z_1 until $f_{z_1}^1/f_{11}^1 = 0$, contrary to the requirements of pareto optimality. Furthermore, if the government chooses to subsidize the other firms by means of a unit subsidy (tax) of any of the other firm's outputs or inputs or any other type of subsidy that changes their first-order profit-maximizing conditions, then a subset of conditions (7.35) must fail as well. Firms $k = 2, \ldots, J$ and firm 1 would face different prices for at least one of the N goods and factors. Consequently,

$$\frac{f_{kn}^k}{f_{k1}^k} \neq \frac{f_{1n}^1}{f_{11}^1} \tag{7.42}$$

for some good or factor n and some firm k, contrary to the pareto-optimal conditions.

Furthermore, suppose the government chooses to tax firm 1's use of z_1 and does so correctly (assume the externality is a diseconomy). The government can use the tax revenues to compensate some or all of the remaining firms $k = 2, \ldots, J$ (the "victims" of the externality), but it must do so in a lump-sum fashion. z_1 is a lump-sum event from the point of view of the other firms, and the subsidy must be, too. Otherwise some of the pareto-optimal conditions, Eq. (7.35), will fail to hold.

Partial Taxes and Subsidies

Regarding the policy of taxing z_1, the government need not place a unit tax on the entire production of z_1. It can instead tax the production of z_1 only above some arbitrary minimal level $\bar{z}_1$, perhaps, using the pollution example again, a level judged to be harmless. Alternatively, it can subsidize firm 1 for reducing z_1 below some other arbitrary level, $\bar{\bar{z}}_1$, perhaps the level of z_1 at the untaxed, prepolicy, competitive equilibrium. The objective profit function for firm 1 with each of these alternatives is

$$\text{Option a:} \quad \sum_{n=1}^{N} p_n X_{1n} - t_z z_1 \quad \text{(tax entire } z_1) \tag{7.43}$$

$$\text{Option b:} \quad \sum_{n=1}^{N} p_n X_{1n} - t_z(z_1 - \bar{z}_1) \quad \text{(tax } z_1 \text{ above } \bar{z}_1) \tag{7.44}$$

$$\text{Option c:} \quad \sum_{n=1}^{N} p_n X_{1n} + s_z(\bar{\bar{z}}_1 - z_1) \quad \text{(subsidize reduction of } z_1 \text{ below } \bar{\bar{z}}_1) \tag{7.45}$$

where $s_z = $ a unit subsidy.

These profit functions all lead to the same first-order conditions if firm 1 maximizes any one of them subject to its production constraint $f^1(X_{1n}; z_1) = 0$. We know that profit function (7.43) generates the proper pareto-optimal conditions with:

$$t_z = -\sum_{k=2}^{J} \left(\frac{f_{z_1}^k}{f_{k1}^k} \right) \tag{7.46}$$

Therefore, so too must Eqs. (7.45) and (7.46) so long as:

$$s_z = t_z = -\sum_{k=2}^{J} \left(\frac{f_{z_1}^k}{f_{k1}^k} \right) \tag{7.47}$$

$\bar{z}_1$, $\bar{\bar{z}}_1$, t_z, and s_z in Eqs. (7.44) and (7.45) are all parameters fixed by the government. Thus, the terms $t_z \cdot \bar{z}_1$ and $s_z \cdot \bar{\bar{z}}_1$ in Eqs. (7.44) and (7.45) cannot affect the first-order conditions for profit maximization.

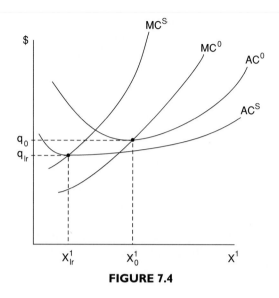

FIGURE 7.4

Entry, Exit, and Optimality in the Long Run

Policy options b and c may cause problems in the long run if the government is not careful, however—a point first demonstrated by Baumol and Oates in their book *The Theory of Environmental Policy*.[6] Consider the subsidy, option c. In the unlikely event that $\bar{\bar{z}}_1$ happens to equal the value of z_1 at the full pareto optimum, firm 1 receives no net subsidy and no problem arises. One would expect $\bar{\bar{z}}_1$ to be set at a value greater than z_1^{opt}, however, in which case firm 1 actually receives a subsidy. If so, and the economy was at a zero-profit competitive equilibrium before the subsidy, other firms now have an incentive to enter the industry represented by firm 1 to receive the same subsidy. In effect, policy option c raises the marginal costs of firm 1 by an amount related to the unit subsidy s_z, while simultaneously *lowering* its average costs because of the lump-sum subsidy, $s_z \bar{\bar{z}}_1$. The average cost lowering effect occurs so long as $\bar{\bar{z}}_1 > z_1^{opt}$. The situation is depicted in Fig. 7.4. To interpret the diagram, think of good 1 as the output of firm 1 and that a large number of such firms comprise industry 1. The original no tax (subsidy) long-run equilibrium each firm in for the industry is at (X_0^1, q_0).

With policy option c, each firm's marginal costs shift upward from MC^0 to MC^s, as required for optimality. But their average costs fall from AC^0 to AC^s because, net, they are subsidized by amount $s_z \cdot (\bar{\bar{z}}_1 - z_1)$. The new long-run equilibrium is at (X_{lr}^1, q_{lr}). Although each firm's production has decreased

[6] W. J. Baumol and W. Oates, *The Theory of Environmental Policy*, Prentice-Hall, Englewood Cliffs, NJ, 1975, chap. 12.

from X_0^1 to X_{1r}^1, entry of new firms leads to the lower price and an increase in industry output. As a result, total production of z_1 may actually rise, surely an unwanted result.

The problem is that a subsidy given to producers in industry 1 is not truly a lump-sum subsidy for the economy as a whole in the long run, if other firms have the option of entering the industry. As discussed in Chapter 2, a lump-sum subsidy has the property that economic decisions cannot alter the size of the subsidy. Thus, to make these subsidies truly lump sum in the long run, they must either be offered to all firms whether or not they actually enter the first industry or be given only to the *original* firms in the industry and not to new entrants. Because governments are probably not going to do either of these, the safest policy is simply a unit tax on the full amount of z_1, policy option a.

Strictly speaking, the Baumol–Oates subsidy problem cannot arise in the model as presented above because of our implicit assumption that only firm 1 can produce z_1. Hence, the other firms $k = 2, \ldots, J$ are not even potential entrants into industry 1. One can imagine a different model, however, in which firms $k = 2, \ldots, J$ can produce z_1 in the long run but choose not to without a subsidy, given the going market prices $(p_1, \ldots, p_N)$, and the form of the $(J - 1)$ production functions $f^k(\ )$. This is the type of model Baumol and Oates have in mind.

Policy option b also fails if the alternative Baumol–Oates model really applies in the long run. It raises average costs so long as $Z_1^{opt} > \overline{Z}_1$, but not by the same amount as a tax on the full amount of z_1. If type 1 firms can become other kinds of firms, not enough of them will exit industry 1 in the long run. In effect, the term $t_z \cdot \overline{z}_1$ acts as a locational subsidy and is not consistent with pareto optimality.

The original conclusion stands: The safest policy is a straight unit tax of the full amount of z_1. With this policy it does not matter which of the two models actually applies. It is always pareto optimal.

Bargaining in the Long Run with Entry and Exit

Free entry has troubling implications for Coase-style bargaining solutions to externalities. It turns out to make efficient bargaining extremely problematic. Earlier we showed that joint profit maximization among all the firms associated with the externality, both the generators or receivers of the externality, satisfies the first-best pareto optimal conditions, as Coase had surmised in his theorem. The efficient bargain rests on four assumptions:

1. The property rights to control the extent of the externality and the disposition of the profits are assigned to some decision maker.
2. Prices are taken as given.
3. Bargaining among the firms is costless.
4. The number of firms in each industry is fixed.

The fourth assumption is crucial to the Coasian efficiency result. The possibility of entry into the externality generating or receiving industries adds a new dimension to the bargain process that severely limits the chances for an efficient solution. Unfortunately, the assumption of free entry in the long run goes hand in hand with the assumption of competitive, price-taking behavior, which is also necessary for efficient bargains.

Jonathan Hamilton, Eytan Sheshinski, and Steven Slutsky (HSS) explored the problems of bargaining in a general equilibrium model with a production externality that is about as simple as such a model can be.[7] Their model consists of just two goods, X and Y, with the production of X conferring an aggregate external diseconomy in the form of pollution on Y. Labor is the only factor of production, and the consumers' utility is additively separable in labor to remove income effects from the model. Producers operate in competitive markets with free entry (exit) in the long run. They take prices as fixed.

HSS consider three types of property rights that might be associated with the externality: a liability rule, a complete property right, and an ultra-complete property right. Under a *liability rule*, agents are assigned property rights only by entering an industry. The rule might take the form of a right of X producers to collect bribes from Y producers for reducing pollution in the X industry, or a right of Y producers to collect damages resulting from the externality. A *complete property right* exogenously assigns the rights to fees or compensation associated with the externality which can then be purchased from the owner. A complete property right would give the owner the right to determine the amount of pollution. Ownership of the property right is independent of entry into one of the industries. An *ultra-complete property right* extends the complete property right by also granting the owner control over entry in both the industries. The owner can collect entry fees from firms in either industry.

A liability rule leads to inefficient bargains with entry for the same reason that partial taxes and subsidies do. The number of firms in one or both industries is nonoptimal. For example, a liability rule encourages too much entry into the X industry if X producers have the right to collect bribes or too much entry into the Y industry if Y producers have the right to collect damages.

Assignment of complete property rights is also incompatible with the efficient solution in the long run. Consider the right to control the amount of pollution in the X industry, which in the HSS model is the same as controlling the total output of X. Efficiency requires that the Y industry reach its zero-profit equilibrium without interference of any kind (the complete property right cannot be an exogenous right to damages in the Y industry). The zero-profit equilibrium also implies that the property right owners cannot extract

[7] J. Hamilton, E. Sheshinski, and S. Slutsky, "Production Externalities and Long-run Equilibria: Bargaining and Pigovian Taxation," *Economic Inquiry*, Vol. XXVII, July, pp. 453–471, 1989.

any income from the Y producers, such as through bribes. Therefore, the owners' incentive is to ignore the Y industry and maximize profits in the X industry at the fixed competitive price P_x. But, ignoring the Y industry ignores the external damage caused by the production of X, so that the profit maximizing solution cannot be the efficient solution.

Assignment of ultra-complete property rights also cannot sustain an efficient equilibrium with positive production of X and Y under the assumptions of price-taking behavior, costless bargaining among firms, and free entry. The problem is that the externality causes the second-order conditions to fail at the efficient allocation.

The essence of the failure here concerns the relation of the fixed prices to the minimum long-run average costs in each industry ($LRAC_{min}$). Industry X has a unique $LRAC_{min}$, say at P_x^{min}. The $LRAC_{min}$ in industry Y depends on the value of X; the lowest $LRAC_{min}$ occurs at $X = 0$, say at a value P_y^{min}. Suppose the fixed competitive prices are the minimum possible values P_x^{min} and P_y^{min}. Then, one of the following is true:

1. $X = 0$ and there are zero profits in the Y industry.
2. $X > 0$, and $Y = 0$ (since $P_y^{min} < LRAC_{min}$ in the Y industry with $X > 0$); also, there are zero profits in the X industry (since $P_x^{min} = LRAC_{min}$).

In either case the property rights owner earns zero profit.

Suppose that the first-best efficient equilibrium is an interior solution with $X, Y > 0$. Then $P_x > P_x^{min}$ and $P_y > P_y^{min}$. In addition, profits in the Y industry must be zero at the efficient equilibrium. HHS show that the efficient solution fails the second-order conditions for maximizing the fees collected by the property rights owner. The solution is a saddle point, with profit (fee) maximizing in Y (at zero profit) but profit (fee) minimizing in X. Hence, the efficient equilibrium is not sustainable in the long run even with ultra-complete property rights.

The intuition as to why X is a profit minimum is as follows:

1. An increase in X increases profits in the X industry at fixed P_x and $P_x > LRAC_{min}$.[8] The efficient solution reduces the profits in X below the maximum possible profit because it accounts for the externality on the Y producers. True, the increase in X increases costs in Y and drives Y producers out of business at the fixed P_y. But the property rights owner earns zero profits from the Y industry anyway at the efficient equilibrium, so no fees are lost from the Y industry.

2. A reduction in X reduces the profits in X. But it also lowers the costs of producing Y and leads to profits in the Y industry at the fixed P_y. It turns

---

[8] The assumption of fixed prices is crucial for efficiency. If the owners of the ultra-complete property rights see the demand curves of the consumers and can manipulate prices, they will act as profit-maximizing monopolists, which certainly cannot yield the efficient solution.

out that the profit-increasing effect in the Y industry dominates in the HHS model.

HSS show that costless Coase bargaining can be efficient in their model, but only if the owners of the property rights, whether complete or ultra-complete, can engage in costless, all-or-none bargains with the consumers as well as the firms. The owners bargain to keep prices at the social optimum and take from the consumers all their utility (consumer surplus) above the utility they would receive if the owners behaved as monopolists. In other words, the owners engage in first-degree price discrimination. The ability to capture the extra consumer surplus provides the owners with the incentive to produce at the social optimum since it maximizes total consumer surplus.

This is hardly the decentralized bargaining that Coase envisioned, however. To the contrary, the knowledge and market power of the property rights owners would have to be equivalent to that of an omniscient socialist planner. The conclusion to be drawn from HSS's analysis is clear: Efficient *decentralized* bargaining solutions to externalities in a competitive market environment are patently unrealistic.[9] This is discouraging, the more so because the government's ability to design optimal Pigovian taxes is also highly problematic. Externalities pose difficult problems indeed for market economies.

Bargaining Costs Versus Property Rights

Dan Usher offers an appropriate concluding general perspective on Coasian bargains.[10] In his view, the key assumption behind the Coase theorem is that bargaining is costless and not the assignment of property rights. If bargining were truly costless, then economic agents would naturally come together and make whatever arrangements were required to reach a mutually advantageous pareto optimum. The assignment of property rights would be irrelevant. In terms of the HHS model, consumers would join with firms and the owners of the property rights in the all-or-none bargains required for economic efficiency. Indeed one can imagine economic agents worldwide bargaining to maximize, and divide, total world income. The Coase Theorem is a tautology under costless bargaining.

---

[9] HHS also consider the combination of bargaining with Pigovian taxation. They imagine that the government attempts to set optimal Pigovian taxes under the assumption that the producers in each industry are independently maximizing profits. In fact, bargaining is occurring to maximize the income of the property rights owners and the government is unaware of this. This policy environment is second best because the behind-the-scenes bargaining is private information from the government's perspective. Not surprisingly, the Pigovian tax is no longer efficient in the presence of bargaining. Efficiency requires a highly complex and nonlinear tax scheme even in the simple HHS model. Moreover, the tax revenues must be returned lump sum to the producers to support the efficient solution. The Pigovian tax revenues are returned lump sum to the consumers in the first-best policy environment.

[10] D. Usher, "The Coase Theorem Is Tautological, Incoherent, or Wrong," *Economic Letters*, October 1998.

The truth is that bargaining is almost always costly and generally the more so as the number of agents in the bargain increases. This explains why societies have chosen markets and command systems to allocate resources rather than relying exclusively on bargaining. Under costly bargaining, the assignment of property rights mostly determines who gets to join the bargaining process. It does not necessarily determine whether the bargains will be (second-best) efficient. Governments establish property rights primarily because they agree to enforce contracts, and enforcement is easier if property rights have been assigned.

We will return to Coasian bargains one last time in Chapter 20, when we consider the effects of imperfect information on bargaining outcomes. Imperfect information can lead to inefficient bargains even when only two agents are bargaining and the bargaining process is otherwise costless.[11]

CONCLUDING COMMENTS: THE PROBLEM OF NONCONVEX PRODUCTION POSSIBILITIES

The analysis in Chapter 7 has assumed that aggregate production possibilities are strictly convex. This is a crucial assumption, for without it the tax policies and their equivalents offered as a means of achieving pareto optimality may be only locally optimal. They may not represent a global optimum. Unfortunately, production externalities themselves can generate significant nonconvexities, so that the assumption may not be valid.[12]

Analyzing the special problems caused by nonconvex production possibilities (increasing returns—decreasing costs) is premature, as the general theoretical treatment of nonconvexities appears in Chapter 9. But the crux of the problem can be seen with reference to a simple two-good, one-factor economy.

Suppose that goods X_1 and X_2 are produced with linear technology by a single factor of production, L (labor). If there are no externalities, then the production- possibilities frontier is a straight line, AB, reflecting constant opportunity costs, as depicted in Fig. 7.5. If X_1 generates an external diseconomy for X_2, however, then the quantity of X_2 must lie below AB at each X_1, except at the endpoints. Hence, assuming the frontier is continuous, it must contain a nonconvex segment near the endpoint B, as depicted in Fig. 7.6.

---

[11] Coasian bargaining has fared well in experimental settings in which the subjects are well informed and bargaining is relatively costless. As one example of bargaining in the presence of an aggregate externality, consult G. Harrison, E. Hoffman, E. Rutstrom, and M. Spitzer, "Coasian Solutions to the Externality Problem in Experimental Markets," *Economic Journal*, June 1987.

[12] See W. J. Baumol and W. Oates, *The Theory of Environmental Policy*, Prentice-Hall, Englewood Cliffs, NJ, 1975, chap. 8, for an excellent detailed analysis of the nonconvexity issue and the important distinction between local and global solutions to externality problems.

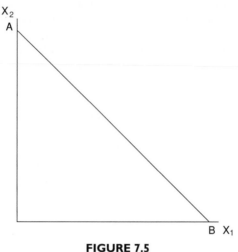

FIGURE 7.5

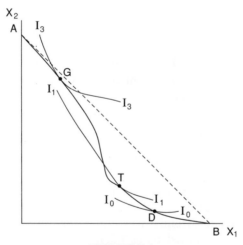

FIGURE 7.6

To see the potential local-global problem, suppose society initially ignores the externality, thereby underestimating the true costs of producing X_1, and achieves an equilibrium at D on indifference curve I_0 in Fig. 7.6, on the nonconvex region of the frontier. Opportunity costs are incorrectly measured by the slope of I_0 at D. A Pigovian tax reduces production of X_1 and moves society to point T, where indifference curve I_1 is tangent to the frontier. Although T is an improvement over D, it is only a local optimum.

The global optimum is at point G, the tangency of I_3 with the frontier, and a Pigovian tax cannot possibly achieve G starting from D. A similar demonstration applies to the case of external economies.

A common example is a laundry (X_2) sitting downwind from a factory (X_1). A Pigovian tax on the smoke emitted by the factory may benefit the laundry by reducing the smoke pollution. The least-cost solution, however, may simply be to have the laundry move upwind from the factory and thereby avoid all (or almost all) of the smoke pollution.

The laundry–factory example is a specific instance of a more general question: How must optimal policies be adjusted if the victims of an external diseconomy such as pollution can partially or completely defend themselves from the external effects? The example illustrates one wrinkle, that defensive strategies can themselves give rise to nonconvexities. We will consider the question of defensive expenditures in more detail in Chapter 8 as part of the discussion of U.S. antipollution policy. Waste treatment, a defensive strategy, is an important part of the United States' fight against pollution, and it is justified on the basis of decreasing cost (nonconvex) production.

REFERENCES

Baumol, W. J. and Oates, W., *The Theory of Environmental Policy*, Prentice-Hall, Englewood Cliffs, N.J., 1975.

Buchanan, J. and Kafolgis, M., "A Note on Public Goods Supply," *American Economic Review*, June 1963.

Diamond, P. and Mirrlees, J., "Aggregate Production with Consumer Externalities," *Quarterly Journal of Economics*, February 1973.

Hamilton, J., Sheshinski, E., and Slutsky, S., "Production Externalities and Long-Run Equilibria: Bargaining and Pigovian Taxation," *Economic Inquiry*, Vol. XXVII, July 1989.

Harrison, G., Hoffman, E., Rutstrom, E., and Spitzer, M., "Coasian Solutions to the Externality Problem in Experimental Markets," *Economic Journal*, June 1987.

Sadka, E., "A Note on Aggregate Production with Consumer Externalities," *Journal of Public Economics*, February 1978.

Usher, D., "The Coase Theorem Is Tautological, Incoherent, or Wrong," *Economic Letters*, October 1998.

8

THE U.S. ANTIPOLLUTION POLICES: AN APPLICATION OF EXTERNALITY THEORY

The federal government has been waging an all-out battle against water and air pollution since the early 1970s. The two main targets have been stationary-source industrial polluters and the automobile, the most important nonstationary source of air pollution. The government's antipollution strategy is broad based. It attempts to reduce pollution at the source as well as clean up existing pollution, and it has targeted both conventional and toxic (hazardous) pollutants

Economists have been highly critical of the federal antipollution legislation because it pays almost no attention to the theory of externalities. For example, the legislation aimed at reducing pollution at the source ignores the principle that water and air pollution is essentially a pricing problem, one that results from the inability of the market system to establish a price for these common-use resources. The theory tells us that the government should use pricing incentives such as taxes that force manufacturers to consider the value of clean air and water in their production decisions. Instead the government has chosen a command-and-control (CAC) approach in which polluters are forced to adopt certain abatement technologies approved by the federal Environmental Protection Agency (EPA) and/or the states' regulatory agencies to meet legislated air- or water-quality standards. Moreover the CAC approach is not informed by careful cost–benefit analyses of the possible abatement technologies. To the contrary, abatement costs are often ignored as a matter of law. The only major exception to the CAC approach is the control of sulfur dioxide (SO_2) emissions from the electric utilities which, since 1990, is being achieved by means of marketable pollution permits. The marketable permits are similar to taxes and subsidies, and can in principle lead to efficient reductions of pollution.

The CAC approach has produced considerable improvements in air and water quality since the 1970s. The problem, though, is that the reductions in pollution have not been cost effective. Properly designed pricing incentives could have achieved the same reductions much more cheaply.

The strategy of cleaning up pollution after the fact is justified in terms of economies of scale: Large government clean-up efforts may be less expensive than individual clean up by firms. But a clean-up strategy is suspect nonetheless. The efficient method of fighting pollution relies fundamentally on reducing pollution at the source. Cleaning up pollution is almost never an efficient strategy by itself. Also, knowing that the government will clean up pollution after the fact can weaken incentives to reduce pollution at the source.

Chapter 8 analyzes the federal government's antipollution strategy by drawing on the theoretical principles developed in the last two chapters. The Appendix provides a chronological history of the major antipollution legislation for the benefit of those unfamiliar with U.S. policies.

PRELIMINARY THEORETICAL CONSIDERATIONS IN ANALYZING POLLUTION

Two preliminary considerations must be noted before analyzing the advantages of pricing/incentives over CAC in reducing pollution. One is that many of the leading examples of industrial air and water pollution are combined consumption–production externalities. The other is that the federal government does not try to achieve the full social optimum in its fight against pollution. Instead, its goal is to achieve a legislated, target reduction in pollution at least cost. An analytical model of pollution must incorporate both features.

Consumption–Production Externalities

A policy-relevant, technological, consumption–production externality is an externality in which some production (consumption) activity enters the utility function (production function) of a least one consumer (producer). The externality may affect other producers (consumers) as well.

Some instances of pollution are essentially pure consumption externalities, such as the smog created by automobile emissions. Others may be pure production externalities, such as the destruction of commercial fishing grounds by disposing of industrial wastes and garbage in the ocean. But, many important examples of industrial pollution obviously affect consumers, perhaps more so than other producers. The dumping of industrial wastes into lakes and rivers often destroys recreational uses of the water even if it has no effect on commercial fishing. Industrial air pollution increases mortality and morbidity, dirties homes, corrodes public monuments, and destroys freshwater game fishing (through acid rain). These are clearly examples of consumption–production externalities, and they require broader analytical models than were provided in Chapters 6 and 7.

Unfortunately, even very simple examples of consumption–production externalities require the full general equilibrium model of Chapter 2 or its equivalent to capture the extent of the external effects. Condensing the model as we did for consumption and production externalities would hide essential features of the externality. The notational requirements alone are formidable in a complete general equilibrium model. But, having worked through the general equilibrium model of Chapter 2 and the pure consumption and production externality models of Chapters 6 and 7, the analysis of consumption–production externalities is reasonably straightforward and predictable.

Consider the general case of an aggregate consumption–production externality, in which the aggregate use of some factor in production (e.g., water) enters into every person's utility function and every firm's production function, with all other goods and factors purely private. This is the most extensive possible example of an aggregate consumption–production externality. The scope of the external effects is admittedly unrealistic, but we saw in the previous chapters that the pareto-optimal rules for the general case are easily modified if some people or firms are unaffected by the externality. Also, some forms of industrial pollution may approximate this kind of aggregate externality within a small geographic region, such as water pollution by firms situated on a lake or bay.

The main advantage of the general model is that it is easily compared with our models of aggregate consumption and production externalities in Chapters 6 and 7. As it turns out, the policy rules are virtually identical in form.

Following the notation of Chapter 2, let:

X_{hg} = consumption of good g by person h   g = 1, ..., G
    h = 1, ..., H

V_{hf} = factor f supplied by consumer h (measured negatively)
    f = 1, ..., F; h = 1, ..., H

r_{gf} = factor f used in the production of good g   g = 1, ..., G
    f = 1, ..., F

X^g = the aggregate output of good g   g = 1, ..., G

Assume that the aggregate quantity of factor i (e.g., water) used in production enters the utility function of every consumer and every firm in the economy because its use causes pollution that affects all agents. Let:

$$P = P\left(\sum_{g=1}^{G} r_{gi}\right) = \text{pollution as a function of the aggregate} \qquad (8.1)$$
$$\text{use of factor i by the firms}$$

$$X^g = \phi^{*g}\left(r_{gf}; r_{gi}; P\right) = \phi^g\left(r_{gf}; r_{gi}; \sum_{g=1}^{G} r_{gi}\right) \qquad (8.2)$$

$$g = 1, ..., G; f = 1, ..., i-1, i+1, ..., F$$

$$U^h = U^{*h}\left(X_{hg}; V_{hf}; P\right) = U^h\left(X_{hg}; V_{hf}; \sum_{g=1}^{G} r_{gi}\right) \qquad (8.3)$$

$$h = 1, ..., H; g = 1, ..., G; f = 1, ..., F$$

where $\phi^g(\ )$ = the production function for X^g, and $U^h(\ )$ = the utility function of person h. Notice that the each production function, $\phi^g(\ )$, incorporates each firm's "personal use" of factor i, r_{gi} (e.g., water used as a cooling agent or as a convenient disposal for waste products), as well as the pollution externality $\sum_{g=1}^{G} r_{gi}$.

The usual assumptions about aggregate externalities apply:

$$\partial\phi^{*g}/\partial r_{ji} = \partial\phi^g/\partial \sum_{g=1}^{G} r_{gi} \qquad\qquad j \neq g \qquad (8.4)$$

$$\partial\phi^{*g}/\partial r_{ji} = \partial\phi^g/\partial r_{ji} + \partial\phi^g/\partial \sum_{g=1}^{G} r_{gi} \qquad j = g \qquad (8.5)$$

$$\partial U^h/\partial r_{gi} = \partial U^h/\partial \sum_{g=1}^{G} r_{gi} \qquad\qquad g = 1, ..., G \qquad (8.6)$$

Society's problem is to maximize social welfare subject to the production constraints and market clearance:

$$\max_{\{X_{hg};\, V_{hf};\, X^g;\, r_{gf};\, r_{gi}\}} W\left[U^h\left(X_{hg}; V_{hf}; \sum_{g=1}^{G} r_{gi} \right) \right]$$

$$X^g = \phi^g\left(r_{gf}; r_{gi}; \sum_{g=1}^{G} r_{gi} \right)$$

$$\text{s.t.} \quad \sum_{h=1}^{H} X_{hg} = X^g \qquad g = 1, \ldots, G$$

$$\sum_{h=1}^{H} V_{hf} = \sum_{g=1}^{G} r_{gf} \qquad f = 1, \ldots, F \ (\text{including } i)$$

The model can be solved in the usual manner by defining Lagrangian multipliers for each of the production and market clearance constraints and taking derivatives of the resulting Lagrangian with respect to all the variables and the multipliers.

Generating and manipulating the first-order conditions so that they have the standard interpretations is tedious and will be left for the interested reader. We will simply note the principal results, which are entirely familiar thanks to the two dichotomies that apply to all first-best models. In particular, the usual interpersonal equity and pareto-optimal conditions are required to achieve a social welfare maximum at the bliss point.

The Interpersonal Equity Conditions

The government should redistribute one good or factor lump sum to equalize its social marginal utility of consumption (supply) across all consumers. The interpersonal equity conditions have the standard form:

$$\frac{\partial W}{\partial U^h} \frac{\partial U^h}{\partial V_{h1}} = \qquad \text{all } h = 1, \ldots, H \qquad (8.7)$$

with factor 1 chosen for redistribution. Assuming the interpersonal equity conditions hold, then the usual pareto-optimal conditions hold at the bliss point.

The Pareto-Optimal Conditions

The Purely Private Goods and Factors

The pareto-optimal conditions for all the purely private goods and factors have the standard form. For example,

$$MRS^h = MRT \qquad h = 1, \ldots, H \qquad (8.8)$$

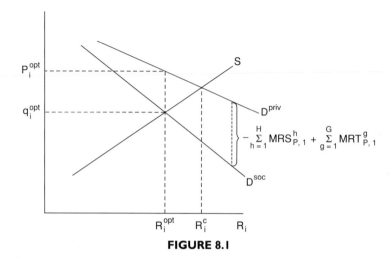

FIGURE 8.1

for any two goods.[1] They can be achieved by competitive markets without any government intervention.

The Externality

The pareto-optimal condition for the eternality-generating factor i also has the standard form expressed in terms of factor 1. The difference between the private supply, $MRS^h_{i,1}$, and the private use, $MRT^g_{i,1}$, should equal the aggregate external effects of factor i on the margin. The only modification from previous models is that the external effects apply to all consumers and all firms. The pareto-optimal condition has the form:

$$MRS^h_{i,1} - MRT^g_{i,1} = -\sum_{h=1}^{H} MRS^h_{P,1} + \sum_{g=1}^{G} MRT^g_{P,1} \qquad (8.9)$$

Because the aggregate external effects on the right-hand side (RHS) are independent of the firm using factor i, a single Pigovian tax on the use of factor i can achieve condition (8.9), with

$$t_i = -\sum_{h=1}^{H} MRS^h_{P,1} + \sum_{g=1}^{G} MRT^g_{P,1} \qquad (8.10)$$

and $P_1 = q_1 = 1$, the numeraire.

The standard supply and demand analysis applies as well to factor i, as depicted in Fig. 8.1. Aggregate use of factor i, R_i, is on the horizontal axis. S represents the horizontal summation of each consumer's $MRS^h_{i,1}$ in supply.

---

[1] Recall that MRT is interpreted as a marginal rate of transformation for two goods, a marginal product for a good and a factor, and a marginal rate of technical substitution for two factors. The last interpretation applies in our example of water pollution with both i and 1 factors of production.

Similarly, D^{priv} represents the horizontal summation of each firm's private use $MRT^g_{i,1}$. D^{soc} corrects D^{priv} by vertically subtracting the aggregate marginal external diseconomy at every aggregate R_i.

At the optimum, the difference between the private MRS and MRT, represented by the vertical distance $D^{priv} - S$, just equals the value of the marginal external effects,

$$-\sum_{h=1}^{H} MRS^h_{P,1} + \sum_{g=1}^{G} MRT^g_{P,1}$$

represented by the vertical distance $D^{priv} - D^{soc}$. The Pigovian tax, t_i, drives the appropriate wedge between the producer demand price, P^{opt}_i, and the consumer supply price, q^{opt}_i, at the optimum. Thus, the only modification of our Chapter 6 and 7 analysis required by the consumption–production externality is in the terms reflecting the extent of the marginal damage, which now include both consumers and producers. Otherwise, the analysis is identical to that of the earlier models, not only for aggregate externalities but also for all other forms of externalities, as could easily be verified.

A final point is that the same alternative solutions are open to the government should it choose not to levy a direct tax on the source of the externality. For example, firms could be subsidized for reducing the amount of the externality below the uncontrolled amount. In summary, the presence of a combined consumption–production externality changes none of the policy insights gained from analyzing the simpler consumption and production externalities.

Legislating Pollution Standards

A second preliminary consideration centers around the severe practical difficulties that so often arise with externalities. Societies cannot be expected to find the full social optimum when combating pollution. Governments have no real hope of even approximating the first-best social optimum in the face of industrial pollution and they do not even try. The main problem comes in trying to evaluate the marginal benefits of pollution reduction (the distance between D^{priv} and D^{soc} in Fig. 8.1). This is especially true for the portion of the marginal benefits received by the consumers. Researchers and policymakers face three serious handicaps in determining the benefits.

The first is the enormous uncertainty about the harm caused by various pollutants, especially the conventional pollutants. Which pollutants are carcinogens, and at what concentrations? What is the precise relationship between the concentrations of the various pollutants in the atmosphere and the resulting increase in morbidity or mortality? Definite answers to questions such as these must await further scientific research.

Second, even if the effects of all pollutants were known, how does one evaluate the costs of pollution (benefits of less pollution). What values should be placed on such things as decreased visibility, increased morbidity, and the loss of life? Economists have developed some ingenious survey and indirect market price techniques to estimate the benefits of reducing pollution that we will discuss in the cost–benefit section of the text. Despite their ingenuity, however, the benefit estimates from these techniques remain problematic and controversial. Also, the government must aggregate each person's marginal loss to arrive at the aggregate marginal damage on which the pollution tax is to be levied, and do so without the benefit of markets in which people are forced to reveal their preferences for cleaner air or water.[2]

A final problem, noted in Chapter 7, is that the government must measure the marginal benefits at the optimum, not at the original pre-intervention equilibrium. In terms of Fig. 8.1, the tax should equal the divergence between D^{priv} and D^{soc} at R_i^{opt}, not at R_i^c. Even if the marginal benefits at R_i^c were known with reasonable accuracy, their value at R_i^{opt} may well be subject to great uncertainty, especially if R_i^{opt} is far from R_i^c. (A trial-and-error process may discover R_i^{opt}, however, a point discussed in Chapter 7.)

Given all these difficulties, governments have thrown in the towel and turned to a second-best "standards" approach for controlling pollution. They somewhat arbitrarily select a desired target level for each pollutant and then legislate policies to meet the target. The standards approach is evident in the U.S. antipollution policies described in the Appendix. Examples include the automobile emissions standards, the regional ambient-air-quality standards, the targeted 10-million-ton reduction in the SO_2 emissions of the electric utilities, and the CAC approach to reducing water pollution.

The analytical question is how to modify our first-best model to incorporate the standards approach. The modification turns out to be straightforward. Once a standard is selected, the proper economic criterion is to achieve the standard at minimum opportunity cost to society. Alternative antipollution strategies would be evaluated strictly in terms of the least-cost criterion in an otherwise first-best environment, since any unwanted distributional effects of a given policy would be offset by the lump-sum redistributions that satisfy the interpersonal equity conditions.

Minimizing the opportunity costs of achieving a given pollution standard is formally equivalent to maximizing social welfare subject to the additional constraint that the standard is satisfied. The reason why is that the opportunity costs are simply the losses in social welfare from satisfying the constraint.

---

[2] Cropper and Oates have an excellent discussion of attempts to measure the benefits (and costs) of pollution reduction in M. Cropper and W. Oates, "Environmental Economics: A Survey," *Journal of Economic Literature*, Vol. XXX, part IV, June 1992.

Adding the pollution constraint makes the analysis second best so long as the target level of pollution differs from its first-best optimum level. Nonetheless, we will briefly sketch out the constrained model here because of its relevance to U.S. pollution policy and because the solution to the constrained social welfare optimum problem is also a single tax, the properties of which are virtually identical to the unconstrained Pigovian tax.

To analyze the constrained social welfare optimum, let us continue with the same aggregate consumption–production externality as above, in which:

$$\text{Pollution (P)} = P\left(\sum_{g=1}^{G} r_{gi}\right) \tag{8.11}$$

Assume the government arbitrarily targets the pollution standard at $\overline{P}$. Since P is assumed to be a monotonic function of $\sum_{g=1}^{G} r_{gi}$, reinterpret the constraint to be

$$\overline{R}_i = \sum_{g=1}^{G} r_{gi} \tag{8.12}$$

where $\overline{R}_i$ corresponds to $\overline{P}$. Assume further that the pollution target is the only additional constraint in an otherwise first-best policy environment. In other words, the formal aggregate externality model above applies with the addition of the pollution constraint.

The Lagrangian of the formal problem becomes:

$$\max_{\{X_{hg};\, V_{hf};\, X^g;\, r_{gf};\, r_{gi}\}} L = W\left[U^h\left(X_{hg};\, V_{hf};\, \sum_{g=1}^{G} r_{gi}\right)\right] +$$

$$\sum_{g=1}^{G} \mu_g\left(X^g - \phi^g\left(r_{gf};\, r_{gi};\, \sum_{g=1}^{G} r_{gi}\right)\right) +$$

$$\sum_{g=1}^{G} \delta_g\left(\sum_{h=1}^{H} X_{hg} - X^g\right) +$$

$$\sum_{f=1}^{F} \pi_f\left(\sum_{h=1}^{H} V_{hf} - \sum_{g=1}^{G} r_{gf}\right) + \lambda\left(\overline{R}_i - \sum_{g=1}^{G} r_{gi}\right)$$

By inspection, the first-order conditions for all pure private goods and factors are identical to those of the unconstrained model. As before, the government need not intervene in any market except the market for factor i. Similarly, the interpersonal equity conditions remain unchanged since they are unaffected by r_{gi}. The only difference is the first-order condition for the r_{gi}, which now includes the term $-\lambda$, the multiplier applied to the pollution constraint. λ equals the marginal increase in social welfare from relaxing the pollution constraint, measured at the second-best optimum. Alternatively, λ is the marginal social cost of reducing the use of R_i to $\overline{R}$.

The pareto-optimal condition for r_i, expressed in terms of factor 1, is now:

$$MRS_{i,1}^h - MRT_{i,1}^g = -\sum_{h=1}^{H} MRS_{P,1}^h + \sum_{g=1}^{G} MRT_{P,1}^g + \lambda/\pi_1 \qquad (8.13)$$

which differs from Eq. (8.9) only by the presence of the term λ/π_1. The terms on the left-hand side (LHS) represent the private marginal rates of substitution in use and supply. The first two terms on the RHS represent the marginal social costs of the pollution externality to the consumers and producers. The final term on the RHS is an additional marginal social cost from imposing the resource constraint on the solution. (The division by π_1 expresses the loss of social welfare in terms of factor 1, since $\pi_1 = \dfrac{\partial W}{\partial U^h} \dfrac{\partial U^h}{\partial V_{h1}}, h = 1, \ldots, H$, from the first-order condition for V_{h1}.)

Given the legislated constraint $\overline{R}(\overline{P})$, therefore, the divergence between the private use MRT and MRS now equals the aggregate external effects on the margin *plus* the social marginal cost of the constraint at $\overline{R}_i$. Note also that the RHS is independent of g; it does not matter which firm pollutes on the margin. Therefore, a single Pigovian-style tax can achieve the second-best optimum, as illustrated in Fig. 8.2.

R_i^{opt} is the unconstrained first-best optimum and $\overline{R}_i$ is the pollution standard imposed by the government. The producer and consumer prices as the constrained optimum are p_i^{const} and q_i^{const}, with the difference between them equal to the tax t_i. The government imposes $\overline{R}_i$ by adjusting the tax until $R_i = \overline{R}$. As in Fig. 8.1, the vertical distance between D^{priv} and D^{soc} equals the third and fourth terms in Eq. (8.11), the direct marginal social costs on the producers and consumers caused by the externality. The additional distance

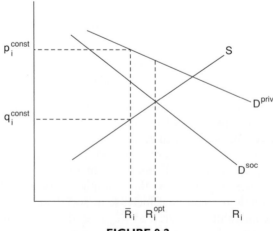

FIGURE 8.2

between D^{soc} and S at $\overline{R}_i$ is a measure of λ/π_1, the marginal social cost of the pollution constraint. Notice that λ/π_1 is a residual cost, in effect. Once the government sets the tax to obtain $\overline{R}_i$, the tax automatically represents the full marginal social cost of using factor i at the second-best optimum. The diagram also indicates that the marginal constraint cost is zero only if $\overline{R}_i = R_i^{opt}$.[3]

The final point is that this tax must minimize the opportunity costs of achieving the resource constraint. This could be demonstrated by setting up a cost minimization problem but that is not necessary. Since the tax satisfies the pareto-optimal conditions of the constrained social welfare maximization problem, it must be cost minimizing in a production sense. If production were inefficient, a reallocation of resources could increase outputs without additional resources and the bonus could be given to consumers to increase social welfare. But this contradicts the fact that social welfare is maximized given the arbitrary pollution standard. $\overline{R}_i(\overline{P})$ may be a terrible choice, far from the first-best optimum, but given that society chose it, taxing the use of resource i such that $\overline{R}_i$ is met is the least cost way of achieving $\overline{R}_i(\overline{P})$.

As we have noted, the federal government has overwhelmingly rejected economists' advice to use taxes or equivalent pricing incentives to reduce air and water pollution. Instead, it has favored the CAC regulatory strategy to combat air pollution and a combination of CAC and waste treatment to combat water pollution. The single major exception is the use of marketable permits to reduce the SO_2 emissions of the electric utilities. The CAC and waste-treatment strategies have succeeded in improving air and water quality, but the same improvement could have been achieved at a fraction of the cost by using taxes or equivalent price incentives.

Taxing Pollution: The Least-Cost Strategy

Further intuition for the cost advantage of a pollution tax over the CAC approach can be gained from the simple textbook least-cost production rule. Consider the example of industrial water pollution. Water is a productive resource for many firms (even excluding those firms whose product contains water such as soft-drink manufacturers). Firms situated along rivers and lakes may use the water as a cooling agent, a cleansing agent, or most often as a convenient disposal for their waste products.

Think of some firm producing its output (Q) with the use of capital (K), labor (L), and water (W), according to the production function:

$$Q = Q(K, L, W)$$

The least-cost production rule says that to produce any given amount of Q at least cost the firm must equalize the ratios of marginal product to price across all three inputs:

---

[3] As in the unconstrained case, whether a single tax or separate taxes on each source of the pollution is least cost depends on whether the externality is aggregate (single tax) or individualized (separate taxes).

$$MP_k/P_k = MP_L/P_L = MP_W/P_W$$

The ratios represent the extra output per dollar from using each of the factors. If the ratios are unequal, the firm should substitute toward the factors with the higher ratios (the higher marginal output per dollar) until the ratios are equalized.

Industrial water pollution is certain to be a problem for a market economy because clean water is a common-use resource that no one owns; hence, firms can use water virtually free of charge. (The same is true of air pollution; the atmosphere provides free disposal for industrial wastes.) With $P_W \to 0$, the ratio MP_W/P_W becomes large without limit. Firms have an incentive to think of every conceivable way to use water for cooling, cleaning, or as a disposal, until the MP_W is driven down to zero. The profit motive under capitalism works to maximize the pollution of common-use resources.

The least-cost production rule highlights the general principle that a quantity complaint ("there is too much pollution") is symptomatic of a pricing problem. As such, a tax (or equivalent pricing mechanism) gets right to the heart of the problem. A tax on water forces a positive price on polluters that reflects the scarcity value of clean water (or air). If the firms have driven the MP_W to zero before the tax, the value of the ratio is now zero with the tax:

$$MP_W/(P_W + t_W) = 0$$

Since zero is less than the ratios $MP_k/P_k = MP_L/P_L$, firms now have an incentive to substitute away from water and toward capital and labor to clean, cool, or dispose of wastes, in order to minimize their production costs. In other words, the tax combats pollution by appealing to the same profit motive that led to the pollution in the first place. It also gives firms flexibility to respond to the tax depending on their ability to substitute away from water. For example, firms that are highly profitable and have difficulty substituting for water may simply pay the tax and continue to pollute as before. Other firms that can easily find substitutes for water may find that substituting capital and labor for water is less expensive than paying the tax and polluting.

The cost-minimizing (social-welfare-optimizing) properties of taxing pollution at the source to meet a pollution standard should now be clear. A correctly designed tax forces firms to consider the full social costs of their decisions, and the tax is easy to design correctly. Simply adjust the tax until the standard is met. In addition, a tax permits each firm to respond as flexibly as possible to these social costs. The tax raises the costs for each polluting firm because they now pay to use a resource that they previously used free of charge. Each firm reacts by trying to minimize these additional costs. With each firm seeking its own least-cost reaction to the tax, society's costs of reaching the standard are minimized in the aggregate. This is the essence of a tax or pricing strategy for combating pollution.[4]

U.S. ANTIPOLLUTION POLICIES

Having established the optimality of taxing polluters to meet a pollution standard, the remainder of the chapter compares and contrasts the CAC, marketable permits, and waste treatment strategies with the tax strategy.

The CAC Approach to Industrial Water and Air Pollution

The CAC regulatory approach to industrial polluters that dominates U.S. antipollution policy is seriously flawed relative to a tax or incentive policy. In principle, regulation can be designed to be equivalent to the tax for any given standard, but only if it duplicates the exact pattern of resource use and production occasioned by the tax. This is clearly not practicable. Instead regulation invariably takes the form of simple rules that are decidedly worse than the tax. For example, suppose society wants a 50% reduction in some industrial pollutant. The preferred solution is to tax the sources of the pollutant until the pollutant is reduced 50% *in the aggregate*. If direct regulation is used instead, the government may have little choice other than to dictate a 50% reduction by each polluter. The government may even dictate the methods used to achieve the reduction, as the federal government typically does with its BACT, BCT, and BAT requirements for reducing air and water pollutants (see the Appendix). The regulation may achieve the desired 50% reduction, but it does so at opportunity costs far in excess of the tax policy.

The flaw in the regulatory strategy is that it ignores the differences in costs and substitution possibilities across firms. The tax strategy, in contrast, exploits these differences in a least-cost manner. Asking firms to reduce their pollution equally in the name of fair play may strike some people as equitable. If so, it is a very costly notion of equity and one that has no standing in the quest to maximize social welfare. Yet, this notion of even-handed fair play appears to dominate antipollution policy in the United States.

A second practical drawback to regulation, stressed long ago by Edwin Mills,[5] is that the incentive structure is literally backwards. With pollution taxes, firms have an incentive to substitute away from water to minimize their tax burdens. With regulation, firms have a profit-motivated incentive to cheat

---

[4] Production possibilities must also remain convex in the presence of the externality. Refer to the discussion of this point at the end of Chapter 7.

[5] See E. Mills, "Economic Incentives in Air-Pollution Control," in M. Goldman (Ed.), *Controlling Pollution: The Economics of a Cleaner America*, Prentice-Hall, Englewood Cliffs, NJ, 1967.

because the direct price of using water or air remains at zero. Rational firms will weigh the cost advantages of continuing to pollute against the probability of being caught and the penalty for cheating. Moreover, it is up to the government prosecutors to bring suit, and under U.S. law the burden of proof is on the government. With taxes, in contrast, the firms bear the burden of proving that they deserve a lower tax bill because they have reduced their pollution.

A judicial system of conviction and punishment almost certainly does deter cheating to some extent. The CAC approach has obviously had some impact because air and water quality have improved, but the question remains as to why the United States should bear the increased costs of the CAC approach when a simple Pigovian-style tax is the better alternative.

Direct regulation makes sense as a standby weapon for short-term emergencies. If air pollution becomes extremely dangerous because of unusual atmospheric conditions, then a temporary ban on some air pollutants may be the only effective short-term solution. Also, if the United States had maintained its original goal of zero water pollution then the choice of taxes versus regulation is irrelevant. The only way to achieve zero pollution in the aggregate is for each polluter to stop polluting entirely—taxes or CAC necessarily lead to the same solution firm by firm.

CAC, Taxes, and Uncertainty

Another consideration that could favor CAC over taxes relates to the uncertainties surrounding the marginal benefits and marginal costs of reducing pollution. The optimal amount of pollution occurs when the marginal benefits and costs are equal, as depicted in Fig. 7.3. The government is unlikely to be able to measure either the marginal benefits or marginal costs for any pollutant with much precision, however. At best it might only have some intuitive sense of the relative shape of the marginal benefit and marginal cost curves. For example, the government might reasonably assume that the MB curve becomes quite steep for many toxic substances at some threshold level of pollution reduction simply because high concentrations of these substances can be so dangerous. (The marginal benefits of reducing pollution are the same as the marginal damages of increasing pollution.) Alternatively, the government might just as reasonably assume that the MC becomes quite steep for all pollutants beyond some very high level of pollution reduction. Reducing pollution any more beyond that point may require extremely costly abatement techniques. Even rough guesses about the relative shape of the MB and MC curves turn out to be important information for they can lead to a preference for CAC or taxes.

Suppose the government assumes that the MB curve is quite steep and the MC curve is quite flat in some region of pollution reduction, as is likely for toxic substances. CAC is the preferred strategy under this scenario because it is better able to control the quantity of the pollutant, assuming it can be enforced. Pollution can be set at a safe level below the danger threshold. If this happens to be beyond the optimal MB = MC point, at least it avoids the steep portion of the MB curve without incurring large increases in cost. Using taxes, in contrast, runs the risk that the tax will be set too low, there will be too little pollution reduction, and society will remain exposed to dangerous concentrations of the pollutant.

Suppose, instead, that the government assumes the MC curve is quite steep and the MB curve is relatively flat in the region near the target level of pollution. This combination is highly likely with conventional pollutants if the target levels are fairly stringent. A pollution tax is the preferred strategy under this scenario since the tax allows tighter control over the costs of reducing pollution. Errors in setting the tax too high or too low have rather modest effects on marginal damages. CAC, in contrast, runs the risk of setting a much too stringent target, which sharply raises the marginal costs of pollution reduction without much offset from the marginal benefits.[6]

Congress has generally favored very stringent standards for many of the conventional air and water pollutants. Antipollution legislation has targeted 90% reductions in automobile emissions of hydrocarbons, carbon monoxide, and nitrous oxides; the ambient-air-quality standards are stringent enough that they have not been met in many of the regions; the original standard for water pollution called for zero pollution; and the current abatement standard requires the use of the best available technology (BAT) economically achievable. Most studies have found that the marginal costs are very steep at the standards chosen, much steeper than the marginal benefits. Therefore, these studies implicitly favor pollution taxes over CAC approaches for meeting the conventional pollutant standards.

Automobile Emissions Control Equipment

Practical considerations may also dictate a CAC approach. Practicality was clearly a motivating factor in the federal government's response to automobile emissions. The government requires all cars to be equipped with expensive antipollution equipment which in turn requires more expensive unleaded gasoline (some high-pollution states require even more expensive reformulated gasoline).

This particular CAC policy suffers from two glaring theoretical deficiencies. One is that automobile emissions are likely to be harmful only in the large urban areas where traffic is highly concentrated, and even then the effects vary depending on the prevailing atmospheric conditions. Requiring

---

[6] The general preference for quantity or price controls under uncertainty was first analyzed by Martin Weitzman in M. Weitzman, "Prices vs. Quantities," *Review of Economic Studies*, Vol. 41, pp. 477–491, 1974.

people who drive in cities only infrequently or not at all to reduce their automobile pollution to the same extent as city drivers cannot possibly be close to an optimal solution. It forces high costs on people that may not produce any corresponding benefits. A policy of taxing people when they drive in cities would appear to be far more cost effective. Another deficiency is that the equipment approach lacks the flexibility of a tax policy. It assumes that the antipollution equipment is the least-cost method of reaching a given standard, an assumption that may not be true. For example, people faced with a city driving tax may simply choose not to drive in cities.

In summary, a tax based on where and when people drive and the amount of pollutants emitted from their automobile is the policy suggested by externality theory. Such a tax may not have been feasible in 1965, when the auto emission control policies were instituted. Monitoring technology has improved considerably since then, to the point where it may now be feasible to monitor driving patterns and tax accordingly. The economic advantages of monitoring and taxes are such that a reconsideration of the auto emissions policies might well be in order.

Marketable Permits for SO_2 Emissions

Economists were heartened by the 1990 Amendments to the Clean Air Act, which introduced the system of marketable permits to reduce the emissions of sulfur dioxide by the electric utilities. It marked the first significant movement away from the CAC approach to controlling pollution.

Marketable permits are equivalent to pollution taxes in principle. To see why, recall the model from Chapter 7 in which a firm (firm 1) produces a byproduct, z_1, that affects the production of all other firms. Part of the discussion there compared various kinds of taxes and subsidies for reducing the firms' output of z_1 by seeing how each affects the profit function of firm 1.

Under a straight tax on z_1, t_z, the profit function of the firm is

$$\text{Profits} = \sum_{n=1}^{N} P_n X_{1n} - t_z z_1 \qquad (8.14)$$

where X_{1n} are the purely private goods and factors supplied and purchased by firm 1. Think of z_1 as tons of SO_2 emissions for our current purposes.

Under a marketable permit scheme, the electric utilities must buy permits for whatever amount of SO_2 they choose to emit. Define z_p as the number of permits purchased by a utility, with each permit allowing one ton of SO_2 emissions. The permits are traded in a national market which has established a price of P_p for each permit. Letting firm 1 represent an electric utility, the utility's profit function under the marketable permit scheme becomes:

$$\text{Profits} = \sum_{n=1}^{N} P_n X_{1n} - P_p z_p$$

$$\text{s.t.} \quad z_1 \leq z_p$$

Assuming the constraint is binding (firms will not buy permits they do not intend to use), the profit function is

$$\text{Profits} = \sum_{n=1}^{N} P_n X_{1n} - P_p z_1 \tag{8.15}$$

Therefore, the permits and tax are identical from the perspective of firm 1 providing $t_z = P_p$.

That the tax and permit price are equal for a given reduction in pollution can be seen from Fig. 8.2. Think of $\overline{R}_i$ as the legislated target for SO_2 emissions, and $t_i = t_z$. The tax is set such that it induces firms to emit exactly the target level of emissions, $\overline{R}_i$. Thus, if the government issues a total number of permits equal to $\overline{R}_i$ and the permits are traded in a competitive market, the equilibrium price P_p must equal the tax. If $P_p > t_z$, the firms would want to purchase fewer than $\overline{R}_i$ permits, the permit market would be in excess supply, and the price would fall to t_z. Similarly, P_p would be driven up to t_z if it were originally less than t_z and the permit market were in excess demand. With $P_p = t_z$, the permit and tax schemes are identical.[7]

Practical considerations may favor permits or taxes, however. Permits have the advantage of assuring that the legislated target is met at the outset of the program, whereas taxes have to be adjusted until the target is reached. Also, the price of permits automatically adjusts to the general level of inflation. A pollution tax, in contrast, would have to be increased every year to maintain the appropriate relative value of the tax. Countering these advantages is the possibility that existing utilities could hoard the permits. We assumed above that $z_1 = z_p$. A utility could, however, buy more permits than it intended to use for the sole purpose of preventing other firms from obtaining them. Hoarding could be a very effective barrier to entry, either by preventing new utilities from entering the market or by forcing existing utilities to reduce their production or increase their costs if they cannot obtain their profit-maximizing number of permits.

---

[7] The government initially allocated the permits to the utilities and allowed them to trade the permits. This is equivalent to the tax case discussed in Chapter 7 of levying a tax on an amount of pollution above some set amount if the utility chooses to buy more permits, or to the case of subsidizing pollution reduction below an existing amount if the utility chooses to sell some of its permits. It leads to the same potential long-run entry problems as partial taxes and subsidies. In fact, the SO_2 permits have worked quite well. See R. Schmalensee *et al.*, "An Interim Evaluation of Sulfur Dioxide Emissions Trading," *Journal of Economic Perspectives*, Summer 1998.

Imperfect Marketable Permits

Although a nationwide system of marketable permits may be an improvement over the CAC approach for reducing the electric utilities' SO_2 emissions, it is far from optimal. By establishing a single price for the permits in a national auction market, the program treats the SO_2 emissions as an aggregate externality when they really are an individualized externality.

The utilities' SO_2 emissions follow the same general pattern of most forms of stationary-source industrial air pollution: Each production facility emits a pollutant that finds it way into a number of air-quality regions. With the pollutant cutting across regions, the identity of the source matters in determining the damages caused by the pollutant. The externality is individualized.

To see this, consider the following simple formal model of stationary-source air pollution. Suppose there are M stationary sources (production facilities) that emit a pollutant and N air-quality regions, with one receptor site per region that measures the amount of the pollutant in the region. Define:

e_i = amount of pollutant emitted by source i $i = 1, \ldots, M$.
q_j = total amount of pollutant measured at receptor j $j = 1, \ldots, N$.

Let the spread of the pollutant from the sources to the regions be governed by the fixed M × N diffusion matrix:

$$D = [d_{ij}]$$

with elements d_{ij} the amount of pollutant measured at receptor j per unit of pollutant emitted by source i. The pattern of pollution can be represented in matrix notation as:

$$eD = q \tag{8.16}$$

where:

$e = (e_1, \ldots, e_i, \ldots, e_M)$, a 1 × M row vector of source emissions.
$q = (q_1, \ldots, q_j, \ldots, q_N)$, a 1 × N row vector of the amount of pollutant measured at each receptor.

Finally, define:

$$C^i = C^i(e_i), \quad i = 1, \ldots, M$$

as the cost to source i of holding emissions to level e_i.

The government's problem is to minimize the total cost of abatement given that the amount of the pollutant at each air quality receptor is at or below a target level, q_j^*:

$$\min_{\{e_i\}} \sum_{I=1}^{M} C^i(e_i)$$
$$\text{s.t. } eD \leq q_j^*$$

where $q^* = (q_1^*, \ldots, q_j^*, \ldots, q_N^*)$, the $1 \times N$ row vector of air quality targets for each region. The corresponding Lagrangian is

$$\min_{\{e_i\}} L = \sum_{i=1}^{M} C^i(e_i) + \lambda(eD - q^*)'$$

where $\lambda = (\lambda_1, \ldots, \lambda_j, \ldots, \lambda_N)$, the $1 \times N$ vector of Lagrangian multipliers. Assuming that the pollutant target is just satisfied at each receptor ($eD = q^*$), the first-order conditions for cost minimization are

$$\partial C^i/\partial e_i - \sum_{j=1}^{N} \lambda_j d_{ij} = 0 \qquad i = 1, \ldots, M \qquad (8.17)$$

along with the N relationships (in vector notation):

$$eD = q^* \qquad (8.18)$$

The Lagrangian multipliers λ_j equal the shadow value of target levels q_j^* with the target constraints binding, the savings in total abatement cost of relaxing q_j^* by one unit. Assume that the marginal damage of relaxing a target constraint is at least as large as the marginal cost. Then, the second term in the M relationships (8.17) can be interpreted as the marginal damage of an additional unit of pollutant from source i, equal to the sum of its damages on the margin across all N regions. Therefore, each firm should set pollutant emissions such that its marginal abatement cost just equals the marginal damage of its pollutant (or the marginal benefit of reducing its pollutant). Since the marginal damage varies by firm, satisfying the M first-order conditions requires separate taxes for each firm (even if each firm has the same cost-abatement function, which is unlikely).

Now return to the utilities' SO_2 emissions. The national auction for permits establishes a single price for emitting a ton of SO_2. This is equivalent in our simple model to setting one tax on all firms such that the most stringent target level is just binding, which is not cost minimizing.

In fairness to the marketable permits, though, their goal is to obtain an overall nationwide reduction in SO_2 emissions at minimum total abatement cost, which can be achieved by a single price. Nonetheless, this SO_2 target is inconsistent with the EPA's general goal of meeting targeted pollutant standards in every air quality region, which is the more sensible goal and the one captured by our simple model. The national auction, by viewing SO_2 emissions as an aggregate externality, makes the following error: A pollution permit purchased by a utility in Los Angeles from a utility in Maine treats the marginal damage of the increased emissions in the populous Los Angeles area as equal to the marginal benefit of the decreased emissions in rural Maine. This can hardly be true.

Imperfect Taxes Versus the CAC Approach

The argument against nationwide marketable permits ignores an important practical consideration, that optimal taxes by firm are simply not feasible. A single price (tax) for reducing stationary source pollutants such as the utilities' SO_2 emissions may be the only practical alternative to a CAC approach. The relevant policy question, then, is whether a nonoptimal single price (tax) dominates a nonoptimal CAC approach to reducing stationary-source air pollution.

Wallace Oates, Paul Portney, and Albert McGartland attempted to answer the question with a study of total suspended particulates (TSPs) in the Baltimore area.[8] Their dataset included 400 sources of TSP emissions in the area, and 23 receptor points at which TSP levels were monitored. Their study was quite sophisticated. They estimated cost-of-abatement functions for each source. They also computed the benefit of reducing TSP to different targeted levels at each receptor based on estimates in the literature of the effects of TSP on premature mortality, increased morbidity, soiling of houses, and reduced visibility. They then used their cost and benefit estimates to compare two TSP reduction programs:

1. An incentive-based (IB) approach that minimizes the aggregate costs for meeting the most stringent constraint across the 23 receptors for each targeted level of TSP reduction. This IB approach is equivalent to setting a single tax that meets the most stringent constraint.

2. A CAC approach in which all firms are required to reduce their emissions using specified abatement technologies until the most stringent constraint is satisfied across the 23 receptors. The CAC approach they employed is somewhat cost sensitive. The 400 sources were sorted into subgroups that used similar abatement technologies and the reductions were specified uniformly within each group. As the target levels were tightened, the groups with the lowest abatement costs would reduce their emissions uniformly until the most stringent target level of TSP reduction was met. This is similar to the actual CAC approach used in the Baltimore area.

Oates *et al.* termed the comparison as one between a "feasible" incentive-based approach and a "well-designed" CAC approach. The target levels of TSP were determined by computing the marginal benefit and marginal cost of reducing the target in small increments from the uncontrolled level. The optimal target level under each approach was the lowest level for which the marginal benefit of abatement equaled or exceeded the marginal cost. Their study produced a number of interesting results:

---

[8] W. E. Oates, P. Portney, and A. McGartland, "The Net Benefits of Incentive-Based Regulation: A Case Study of Environmental Standard Setting," *American Economic Review*, Vol. 79, No. 5, pp. 1233–1242, 1989. They used the model in the preceding section to develop their empirical estimates.

1. The IB approach led to a more stringent maximum standard, 90 mg/m^3 vs. 100 mg/m^3 of TSP. The advantage derived from the superior cost properties of the approach which allowed the marginal benefits and costs to equate at a lower TSP level.

2. At the same time, the CAC approach provided substantially better average overall air quality throughout the area for any given maximum standard because it leads to larger TSP reductions in the regions for which the constraint is not binding. An IB approach is more forgiving of pollution in the nonbinding regions. Consequently, at the optimal maximum standard under each approach (90 and 100 mg/m^3), the improvement in the area-wide average air quality from the IB approach was negligible (62.9 vs. 63.7 mg/m^3).

3. The net benefits in going from a "baseline" standard of 120 mg/m^3 of TSP to the maximum standards under each approach were similar. The IB approach had only a $6 million advantage in net benefits over the CAC approach.

Oates, *et al.* concluded that there may not be much difference between a feasible IB approach (i.e., a single tax) and a well-designed CAC approach. They concede, however, that a CAC approach that pays no attention to differences in abatement costs and applies uniform controls on all firms may be much worse than a feasible IB approach.

4. A final result of interest is that the marginal costs of abatement are quite steep and the marginal benefits fairly flat in the region of the 90-mg/m^3 optimal standard under the IB approach. This suggests a preference for the IB over CAC approach for reducing TSP given the large uncertainties associated with the marginal cost and marginal benefit estimates, particularly the marginal benefits.

MUNICIPAL WASTE-TREATMENT FACILITIES AND THE SUPERFUND: DEFENSIVE ANTIPOLLUTION STRATEGIES

Pollution taxes, marketable permits, and CAC are strategies designed to reduce pollution at its source. In contrast, municipal waste-treatment facilities and the Superfund are defensive strategies. They simply remove the pollution that has already occurred.

Cleaning up pollution after the fact is certainly a policy worth considering. Suppose someone invented a method for removing vast amounts of water pollutants or hazardous wastes for only a few pennies. Clearly an antipollution policy would want to make liberal, perhaps exclusive, use of this technology. Recall the factory–laundry example from Chapter 7, which suggested that simply moving the laundry upwind from the factory may be less expensive and more effective than a Pigovian tax designed to reduce the factory's smoke emissions. Generally speaking, any technology or solution is attractive so long as it is "cheap enough." But whether the government should subsidize defensive antipollution strategies is a complex question that depends on the exact form of the externality, available policy options, and the nature of the waste-treatment technology.

All our models of pollution externalities so far have reached the same conclusion, that the government must reduce pollution at its source to achieve pareto optimality. These models, however, have not included the possibility of defensive measures by individuals or firms to reduce their exposure to pollution. A number of interesting questions arise once defensive measures are admitted:

1. Does the government still have to reduce pollution at the source or can it rely exclusively on defensive measures?[9]
2. Is a mixed strategy of reducing pollution at the source and removing pollution after the fact pareto optimal, in general?
3. Does the government have to subsidize defensive measures to achieve pareto optimality or can individuals and firms be counted on to respond optimally on their own?

To explore these questions in a relatively simple framework, let us return to the single-source production externality model of Chapter 7, in which firm 1 produces a substance, z_1, that enters into all other firms' production functions. Think of z_1 as a pollutant that harms the firms. There are J firms and N goods and factors besides z_1, and all the other goods and factors, X_{jn}, are purely private.

To incorporate the possibility of defensive measures, assume that each of the other firms can reduce its exposure to z_1 with the use of factor k, according to the function $h^j(X_{jk})$. Firm 1 can also use factor k to reduce its own exposure to z_1 should it want to.

Firm j's exposure to the externality is

$$z_{jl} = z_1 - h^j(X_{jk}) \qquad j = 1, \ldots, J \qquad (8.19)$$

with $\partial h^j / \partial X_{jk} > 0$.

Define the production functions for each of the J firms to be

$$f^j(X_{jn}; z_1 - h^j(X_{jk})) = 0 \qquad j = 1, \ldots, J; n = 1, \ldots, N \qquad (8.20)$$

This formulation assumes that input X_{jk} may have some direct use for firm j besides its use in reducing z_{j1}. An example might be an all-purpose cleaning agent or a cooling technology that has many uses to firms besides reducing the harmful effects of z_1.

---

[9] Superfund and waste-treatment efforts are obviously necessary to remove existing pollutants that resulted because no attempt was made to reduce them at their sources and that would remain harmful if not treated or removed. Our question is meant to be forward looking, when all strategies are possible.

Assume a one-consumer equivalent economy because the interpersonal equity conditions hold. Let $U\left(\sum_{j=1}^{J} X_{jn}\right)$ = the utility function of the single consumer, incorporating the N market clearance equations, with $\partial U/\partial X_{jn} = \partial U/\partial X_n$, all $J = 1, \ldots, N$. The consumer is indifferent about the identity of firm j. Note, also, that the consumer is unconcerned about the production of z_1 since it generates only a production externality.

The government's problem is

$$\max_{(X_{jn}; z_1)} U\left(\sum_{j=1}^{J} X_{jn}\right)$$

$$\text{s.t. } f^j\left(X_{jn}; z_1 - h^j\left(X_{jk}\right)\right) = 0$$

with corresponding Lagrangian:

$$\max_{(X_{jn}; z_1)} L = U\left(\sum_{j=1}^{J} X_{jn}\right) + \sum_{j=1}^{J} \lambda_j f^j\left(X_{jn}; z_1 - h^j\left(X_{jk}\right)\right)$$

The first-order conditions are:

$$\partial L/\partial X_{jm} = \partial U/\partial X^m + \lambda_j \partial f^j/\partial X_{jm} = 0 \qquad j=1, \ldots, J; \ m \neq k \qquad (8.21)$$

$$\partial L/\partial X_{jk} = \partial U/\partial X_k + \lambda_j(\partial f^j/\partial X_{jk} - \partial f^j/\partial z_{j1} \cdot \partial h^j/\partial X_{jk}) = 0 \\ j = 1, \ldots, J \qquad (8.22)$$

$$\partial L/\partial z_1 = \lambda_1 \partial f^1/\partial z_1 + \sum_{j=2}^{J} \lambda_j \partial f^j/\partial z_{j1} = 0 \qquad (8.23)$$

Express the first-order conditions as ratios in terms of X_1, and assume X_1 is a good for purposes of interpretation. From conditions (8.21) for m and 1,

$$U_m/U_1 = \dfrac{\dfrac{\partial f^j}{\partial X_{jm}}}{\dfrac{\partial f^j}{\partial X_{j1}}} \qquad j = 1, \ldots, J; m \neq k \qquad (8.24)$$

Adding the possibility of defensive measures does not change the result that the government need not intervene in the markets of the purely private goods and factors that are unrelated to the externality. They can be marketed competitively, with the consumer and producer prices equal for all the private goods: $q_m = p_m$, $m \neq k$.

Consider, next, the allocation of z_1 expressed in terms of good 1. Dividing Eq. (8.23) by the first-order conditions for good 1 in Eq. (8.21) and selectively eliminating all the λ_j in the usual manner, yields:

$$\frac{\dfrac{\partial f^1}{\partial z_1}}{\dfrac{\partial f^1}{\partial X_{11}}} + \sum_{j=2}^{J} \frac{\dfrac{\partial f^j}{\partial z_{j1}}}{\dfrac{\partial f^j}{\partial X_{j1}}} = 0 \tag{8.25}$$

Condition (8.25) can be satisfied by a pollution tax on firm 1, t_z, such that:

$$t_z/q_1 = -\sum_{j=2}^{J} \frac{\dfrac{\partial f^j}{\partial z_{j1}}}{\dfrac{\partial f^j}{\partial X_{j1}}} \tag{8.26}$$

where t_z is the standard Pigovian tax, equal to the aggregate damage of z_1 on the margin to all the affected firms. Faced with the optimal tax, firm 1 sets the tax equal to the value of marginal product of z_1 in its production of X_{11}:

$$t_z = \left(\frac{\dfrac{\partial f^1}{\partial z_1}}{\dfrac{\partial f^1}{\partial X_{11}}} \right) q_1, \text{ or } t_z/q_1 = \frac{\dfrac{\partial f^1}{\partial z_1}}{\dfrac{\partial f^1}{\partial X_{11}}}$$

Therefore,

$$t_z/q_1 = \frac{\dfrac{\partial f^1}{\partial z_1}}{\dfrac{\partial f^1}{\partial X_{11}}} = -\sum_{j=2}^{J} \frac{\dfrac{\partial f^j}{\partial z_{j1}}}{\dfrac{\partial f^j}{\partial X_{j1}}} \tag{8.27}$$

as required for pareto optimality. The answer to the first question above, then, is that the government should continue to tax the pollutant at its source in the presence of defensive measures.

Consider, next, the optimal allocation of the defensive factor X_k expressed in terms of good 1. Dividing Eq. (8.22) by the first-order conditions for good 1 in Eq. (8.21) and selectively eliminating all the λ_j in the usual manner, yields:

$$U_k/U_1 = \frac{\dfrac{\partial f^j}{\partial X_{jk}}}{\dfrac{\partial f^j}{\partial X_{j1}}} - \left(\frac{\dfrac{\partial f^j}{\partial z_{j1}}}{\dfrac{\partial f^j}{\partial X_{j1}}} \right) \frac{\partial z_{j1}}{\partial X_{jk}} \quad j = 1, \ldots, J \tag{8.28}$$

The RHS of Eq. (8.26) is for each firm j, the full marginal product of factor k in the production of good 1. The first term is the direct effect of factor k on good 1, and the second term is the indirect effect on good 1 acting through the reduction of exposure to z_{j1}.

Suppose that X_k is marketed competitively so that $q_k = p_k$. The consumer sets q_k/q_1 equal to the LHS of Eq. (8.28), and each producer sets p_k/p_1 equal to the RHS of Eq. (8.26). Therefore, competitive markets optimally allocate each affected firm's use of the defensive factor X_k.[10]

The answers, then, to the second and third questions above in this model are

1. A mixed strategy of taxing a pollutant at its source and using defensive measures to reduce exposure to the pollutant is pareto optimal. Also, the availability of defensive measures lowers the required Pigovian tax at the source because it reduces the other firms' exposure to the pollutant.

2. The government should *not* subsidize the use of defensive measures, providing the pollutant has been taxed (optimally) at its source. The intuition is that the full value of using a defensive measure is internal to each of the affected firms and is therefore a purely private good.

Equalizing Marginal Costs in Reducing Pollution

Another important result follows immediately from Eqs. (8.27) and (8.28): When there is more than one strategy for reducing pollution, all strategies should be employed such that the marginal costs of each strategy are equal. Equalizing marginal costs across strategies ensures that any given reduction of pollution exposure is achieved at minimum total cost to society. This result is analogous to the standard competitive result of equalizing marginal costs across firms in an industry to minimize the total costs of supplying a good or service.

The equal-marginal-cost interpretation comes from rearranging the profit-maximizing conditions for the firms. The tax raises firm 1's marginal cost of using z_1 from zero to

$$t_z / \left(\frac{\dfrac{\partial f^1}{\partial z_1}}{\dfrac{\partial f^1}{\partial X_{11}}} \right) = q_1$$

---

[10] One interesting variation of the model would be an assumption that the use of X_{1k} by firm 1 benefits the other firms as well. Since firm 1 generates z_1, its attempts to reduce its own exposure could also reduce the amount of z_1 emitted from its site of production. This might be realistic for some kinds of pollution. Under this assumption, firm one is exposed to $z_{11} = z_1 - h^1(X_{1k})$, and the other J–1 firms are exposed to $z_{j1} = z_{11} - h^j(X_{jk})$. X_{1k} thus gives rise to an externality just as z_1 does. The interested reader can verify that competitive marketing of X_{1k} would still be pareto optimal providing the government sets the optimal tax t_z on the production of z_1. The optimal tax not only guides firm 1 to the optimal production of z_1. It also causes the firm to incorporate correctly the external effect of X_{1k} when making its private decision regarding the use of X_{1k}. The intuition is that using X_{1k} reduces the firm's tax revenues (among its effects) by reducing its effective emission, z_{11}. Given t_z, the revenue reduction just equals the marginal external benefits to the other firms from the reduction in z_{11}.

On the LHS, t_z is the price of z_1, the denominator is the marginal product of z_1 in the production of X_{11}, and the ratio is the marginal cost of using z_1 expressed in terms of X_{11}. The marginal cost of X_{11} equals its price q_1 given competitive markets. Also,

$$\left(\frac{\dfrac{\partial f^1}{\partial z_1}}{\dfrac{\partial f^1}{\partial X_{11}}} \right) = - \sum_{j=2}^{J} \frac{\dfrac{\partial f^j}{\partial z_{j1}}}{\dfrac{\partial f j}{\partial X_{j1}}}$$

Therefore,

$$t_z / - \sum_{j=2}^{J} \frac{\dfrac{\partial f^j}{\partial z_{j1}}}{\dfrac{\partial f j}{\partial X_{j1}}} = q_1$$

The LHS equals the social marginal external cost of z_1 on the other firms, or the social marginal benefit of reducing z_1. In other words, the tax generates the standard $MB = MC$ result for reducing pollution.

The marginal cost of X_{jk} for firm j is

$$q_k / \left(\frac{\dfrac{\partial f^j}{\partial X_{jk}}}{\dfrac{\partial f^j}{\partial X_{j1}}} - \frac{\dfrac{\partial f^j}{\partial z_{j1}}}{\dfrac{\partial f^j}{\partial X_{j1}}} \frac{\partial z_{j1}}{\partial X_{jk}} \right) = q_1 \qquad j = 1, \ldots, J$$

the ratio of the price of X_{jk} to the full marginal product of X_{jk}.

Notice that the marginal cost to firm 1 of producing z_1, given the tax t_z and the marginal costs of using X_k are both equal to q_1. Therefore, the marginal costs of the tax and defensive strategies are equal, as required for reducing z_1 at minimum total cost to society.

Additional Complicating Issues

Our simple model ignores a number of complicating issues that are likely to be important in practice:

1. *Defensive measures as externalities*—In some instances, the defensive measures by affected agents may themselves generate an externality and require a Pigovian tax or subsidy on that account. A common example is vaccinations against diseases. People who receive vaccinations not only protect themselves from the disease, they also reduce the likelihood that others who are not vaccinated will contract the disease. This may explain

why governments frequently subsidize vaccinations.[11] Our model could incorporate this feature by having the h^j be a function of each firm's X_{jk}, either individually or in the aggregate. Pareto optimality would then require a Pigovian subsidy on each firm's use of X_{jk}. This will be left as an exercise for the interested reader.

2. *Defensive measures as a medium for externality*—Suppose that the effectiveness of the defensive measures depends on the level of the pollutant. We could represent this in our model as:

$$z_{j1} = z_1 - h^j(X_{jk}, z_1)$$

This dependence generates two externality channels for z_1, one related to the damages inflicted on the other firms by the production of z_1 and the other related to the firms' costs in defending themselves. The second channel implies that the marginal costs of using X_{jk} depend on the level of z_1, which may often be the case. If so, then the marginal costs of defensive measures are more likely to be inversely rather than directly related to the level of the pollutant. A common pattern is that the first units of a pollutant can be removed relatively inexpensively, but then the costs of removal rise sharply once the pollutant reaches some low level. The inverse relationship can lead to nonconvexities and multiple equilibria for the abatement technology.

3. *Very inexpensive defensive measures*—Suppose the marginal costs of the defensive measures are so low that they can remove all exposure to the pollutant at a marginal cost below the marginal cost of reducing any pollution at its source. The laundry–factory example comes to mind. The paretooptimal solution is to employ only defensive measures and not have any reduction of the pollutant at its source. Even so, the government should set a per-unit pollution tax on the polluters equal to the marginal cost of the defensive measures to prevent unwanted entry into the polluting industry. The reason for maintaining a pollution tax in this case is as follows: Since the tax, by definition, is less than the marginal cost of any abatement by the source, the polluter has no incentive to reduce the pollutant to save tax revenues. There is still no reduction of the pollutant at the source, as required for pareto optimality. At the same time, the pollutant does require costly defensive measures, and the tax acts as an entry fee into the industry. It discourages the entry of more polluters in the long run whose pollution would require still more defensive measures. In the laundry–factory example, the government does not want to encourage the building of more smoke-belching factories that might place still more moving costs on the laundries.[12]

---

[11] See D. Brito, E. Sheshinski, and M. Intriligator, "Externalities and Compulsory Vaccinations," *Journal of Public Economics*, June, 1991.

[12] These last two points, along with additional analysis of defensive strategies, are contained in W. E. Oates, "The Regulation of Externalities: Efficient Behavior by Sources and Victims," *Public Finance*, Vol. XXXVIII, No. 3, 1983.

Municipal Waste-Treatment Plants and Superfunds

Our model does not suggest that the government should be subsidizing and building large municipal waste-treatment plants. On the contrary, it implies that the affected firms and individuals should undertake defensive measures on their own. Large waste-treatment facilities subsidized by the government do make sense, however, if waste treatment exhibits significant economies of scale. This is true even if pollution is taxed at its source. Economies of scale in waste treatment is an entirely separate issue from the externality point and will be analyzed in Chapter 9. The crux of the matter is that each agent affected by a pollutant should not be undertaking defensive measures at high marginal costs when a single large facility can be operated at much lower marginal costs to provide the protection. In fact, waste treatment does exhibit substantial scale economies. Nonetheless, the federal grant program that leaves the option of building up to each individual municipality does not necessarily provide the proper amount of waste treatment. Nor should polluters be untaxed in the first place. The equal-marginal-cost rule for reducing pollution still applies in the presence of scale economies.

The same points apply to the Superfund program. Once hazardous wastes accumulate at a site, a single removal facility is probably a much less expensive option than having the affected individuals and firms trying to protect themselves forever from the hazard. Also, hazardous wastes should be controlled at their sources.

CONCLUDING COMMENTS

Economists are accused of being a contentious lot, unable to agree on much of anything. One thing they do agree on, though, is that the federal government's antipollution efforts are much more costly and less effective than they need be. The assumptions of first-best analysis may be highly restrictive, but the theoretical evidence against the CAC bias of the federal antipollution programs is fairly overwhelming.

In favoring a tax- or price-incentive-based approach to reducing pollution, economists have long held up as an example one of the most effective antipollution campaigns ever, the program to clean up the Ruhr River Basin in the 1960s in what was then West Germany.[13] The Ruhr River Basin consists of five rivers on which a significant portion of West Germany's heavy industry was located in the 1960s. All five rivers were choked with industrial pollutants at the time. West Germany established a separate jurisdictional

---

[13] For an excellent overview and analysis of the water quality management program on the Ruhr, see A. Y. Kneese, "Water Quality Management by Regional Authorities in the Ruhr Area," in M. Goldman (Ed.), *Controlling Pollution*, Prentice-Hall, Englewood Cliffs, NJ, 1967.

body to regulate the Basin, decided the quality of water it wanted for each of the rivers, and used a combination of taxes on polluters and waste-treatment facilities to achieve the new pollution standards. Although the program might not have been pareto optimal (taxes, for example, were based on average and not marginal damage levels), the results were dramatic nonetheless. The standards were achieved fairly rapidly, and the taxes did induce firms to substitute other resources for water as theory predicts. On average, West German firms on the Ruhr River used far less water after the program than their counterparts in other countries.[14] Water is apparently highly substitutable in production, a fact that makes the federal government's reluctance to tax polluters or use permits all the more frustrating to economists.

REFERENCES

Baumol, W. J. and Oates, W., *The Theory of Environmental Policy*, Prentice-Hall, Englewood Cliffs, N. J., 1975.

Baumol, W. J. and Oates, W., *The Theory of Environmental Policy*, second ed., Cambridge University Press, New York, 1988.

Brito, D., Sheshinski, E., and Intriligator, M., "Externalities and Compulsory Vaccinations," *Journal of Public Economics* June, 1991.

Cropper, M. and Oates, W., "Environmental Economics: A Survey," *Journal of Economic Literature*, Vol. XXX, part IV, June 1992.

Freeman, III, A., *Air and Water Pollution Control: A Benefit–Cost Assessment*, Wiley, New York, 1982.

Goldman, M. I., (Ed.) "Pollution: The Mess Around Us," in *Controlling Pollution: The Economics of a Cleaner America*, Prentice-Hall, Englewood Cliffs, N. J., 1967.

Kneese, A., "Water Quality Management by Regional Authorities in the Ruhr Area," in M. Goldman (Ed.), *Controlling Pollution: The Economics of a Cleaner America*, Prentice-Hall, Englewood Cliffs, N. J., 1967.

Mills, E., "Economic Incentives in Air-Pollution Control," in M. Goldman (Ed.), *Controlling Pollution: The Economics of a Cleaner America*, Prentice-Hall, Englewood Cliffs, NJ, 1967.

Oates, W., "The Regulation of Externalities: Efficient Behavior by Sources and Victims," *Public Finance*, Vol. XXXVIII, No. 3, 1983.

Oates, W., Portney, P., and McGartland, A., "The Net Benefits of Incentive-Based Regulation: A Case Study of Environmental Standard Setting," *American Economic Review*, Vol. 79, No. 5, December 1989.

Schmalensee, R. *et al.*, "An Interim Evaluation of Sulfur Dioxide Emissions Trading," *Journal of Economic Perspectives*, Summer 1998.

Tietenberg, T., *Environmental and Natural Resource Economics*, Harper-Collins College Publishers, New York, 1996.

Weitzman, M., "Prices vs. Quantities," *Review of Economic Studies*, Vol. 41, 1974.

[14] For instance, steel production on the Ruhr used 2.6 cubic yards or water per ton of steel on average following the antipollution campaign, whereas the industry average worldwide was 130 cubic yards per ton. See M. I. Goldman, (Ed.), "Pollution: The Mess Around Us," *Controlling Pollution: The Economy of a Cleaner America*, Prentice-Hall, Englewood Cliffs, NJ, 1967, p. 36.

APPENDIX: HISTORY OF U.S. ANTIPOLLUTION LEGISLATION

Controlling water and air pollution was entirely a state and local responsibility until the last half of the twentieth century. The federal government joined the effort shortly after World War II with the passage of the Water Pollution Control Act of 1948 and the Air Pollution Control Act of 1955. These were hesitant first steps that did little more than assist states in researching the harmful effects of various pollutants and identifying polluters.[15]

Municipal Waste Treatment

The federal government's first substantial antipollution program appeared in 1956. The Water Pollution Control Act of 1956 authorized grants-in-aid to subsidize the construction of municipal waste treatment facilities. Municipalities applied for the grants, which were allocated on a first-come, first-served basis. The federal government paid 55% of the construction costs. The federal subsidy was increased to 75% of the construction costs in 1972, and then was returned to 55% in 1981. The appropriations were modest at first, about $50 million per year, but grew to $25 billion by 1977.

The waste-treatment program has suffered from a number of handicaps that have reduced its effectiveness. An immediate problem was beginning the fight against water pollution with a clean-up strategy without any attempt to reduce water pollution at its sources. As shown in this chapter, incentives must be in place to encourage polluters to reduce pollution before attempting to clean up the pollution. Otherwise, the burden on the facilities to combat pollution is well beyond the optimum. A second problem was allocating the funds on a first-come, first-served basis rather than according to the severity of the pollution. Finally, by choosing to subsidize only the construction costs the federal government did not have any leverage over the operation of the waste-treatment facilities once they were built. All too often the operation of the treatment plants suffered from insufficient local funding.

The government tried to address the first two problems in 1977. It established a set of pretreatment standards for wastes entering the municipal facilities. These standards applied to pollutants not covered by the source standards that were in place by then (see below). The government also began

---

[15] For an excellent, comprehensive history and analysis of the U. S. antipollution legislation, see T. Tietenberg, *Environmental and Natural Resource Economics*, Harper-Collins College Publishers, New York, 1996, chaps. 15–19. This appendix draws liberally from these five chapters in Tietenberg. Another excellent overview of environmental policy from an economics perspective is M. Cropper and W. Oates, "Environmental Economics: A Survey," *Journal of Economic Literature*, Vol. XXX, pp. 675–740, 1992. The seminal modern analysis of the economics of the environment is W. Baumol and W. Oates, *The Economics of Environmental Policy*, Prentice-Hall, Englewood Cliffs, NJ, 1975 and the second edition (Cambridge University Press, New York, 1988).

allocating the grants on a priority basis. Operating costs have never been subsidized, however.

Automobile Emissions

The federal government next turned its attention to automobile emissions. By 1965, it had targeted six conventional air pollutants for reduction: sulfur oxides, particulate matter, carbon monoxide, ozone, nitrogen dioxides, and lead. The automobile is the principal source of three of the six pollutants— carbon monoxide, ozone, and nitrogen dioxide—and a major source of lead emissions. The Clean Air Acts of 1965 set automobile emissions standards for hydrocarbons and carbon monoxide, to take effect in 1968. Hydrocarbons are a precursor for the production of ozone in the atmosphere (along with nitrogen oxides).

The 1965 emissions standards were ineffective, however, so the government responded with a new and very tough set of standards under the 1970 Amendments to the Clean Air Act. The 1970 Amendments called for a 90% reduction of hydrocarbon, carbon monoxide, and nitrogen dioxide emissions below uncontrolled levels. The hydrocarbon and carbon monoxide standards were to be met by 1975; the nitrogen dioxide standards, by 1976. The new standards were so severe that the technology did not exist to meet them, so the deadlines kept being pushed back. The 1977 amendments granted states delays in meeting the standards until 1987 if they agreed to establish regular vehicle inspection maintenance programs. The 1970 Amendments also targeted lead in gasoline, mandating that new cars manufactured from 1973 and later use only unleaded gasoline.

The auto emissions standards have led to impressive reductions in automobile emissions. The EPA reported that from 1982 to 1991 lead emissions decreased by 90% and carbon monoxide emissions by 30%, despite a 30% increase in vehicle miles driven. The battle against ozone has been less impressive. In 1991, 101 air-quality regions had ozone levels above the 1987–88 standards. On the positive side, the number of "exceedance" regions declined by 38% from 1982 to 1991. Much of the automobile emissions legislation in the 1990s has focused on the further reduction of ozone in the nonattainment regions, by requiring states in those regions to sell cleaner burning, reformulated gasoline.[16]

Industrial Air Pollution

The 1970 Amendments to the Clean Air Act did much more than establish extremely tough auto emissions standards. The Amendments created the

---

[16] See T. Tietenberg, *Environmental and Natural Resource Economics*, Harper-Collins College Publishers, New York, 1996, pp. 419–420.

Environmental Protection Agency and marked the federal government's serious entry into the war against stationary-source air pollution. The EPA established ambient air-quality standards for each of the six conventional pollutants noted above: a primary standard to protect human health and a secondary standard to protect such things as aesthetic quality (visibility), physical objects such as statues and buildings, and vegetation. The states retained the responsibility for meeting the standards, but they were required to develop State Implementation Plans (SIPs) indicating how they would meet the standards by controlling the emissions of the six pollutants at their sources.

The first task of the SIPs was to define distinct air-quality regions within each state, then the polluters and the individual state regulators would agree on an appropriate abatement technology on a case-by-case basis. (The legislation presumed that the states would continue to use the CAC approach of dictating certain abatement technologies that they had always used.) The degree of abatement required depended on the air quality in the region and where the source was located. The 1970 Amendments also essentially guaranteed that the states' CAC approach would be inefficient because they ruled out the use of cost–benefit analysis in determining how best to meet the standards. In particular, the states could not consider the costs of meeting the standards.

The stationary-source component of the 1970 Amendments was an ambitious program, to say the least. The air quality in many regions of the country was nowhere close to the EPA standards at the time, and there are today over 27,000 stationary sources emitting one or more of the six pollutants. As in the case of automobile emissions, the deadlines for meeting the standards were often pushed back, and many regions today are still well above the standards.

Two subsequent amendments to the Clean Air Act were noteworthy: the 1977 Amendments and the 1990 Amendments. The 1977 Amendments were somewhat schizophrenic. On the one hand, they strengthened the federal CAC approach by dictating that all new source polluters meet one of two abatement standards. In nonattainment areas, new sources had to achieve the least achievable emission rate (LAER), defined as the lowest emission rate appearing in any SIP whether or not the technology to achieve that rate had ever been installed. In attainment areas, new sources had to install the best available control technology (BACT). The EPA also established uniform floors for LAER and BACT technologies in the SIPs so that polluters could not play off one state against the other. These were very tough standards indeed, given that the effect on a polluter's costs (profits) were not to be considered in determining the LAER or BACT for each source.

On the other hand, the 1977 Amendments took the first steps towards a more rational price-incentive-based approach to controlling pollution. Legislators can ignore costs but economic agents cannot. The EPA, properly fearful that the LAER and BACT requirements might hinder economic growth, introduced an Emissions Trading Program in which polluters who more than met the standards would receive pollution credits to be used to offset other sources of pollution. The credits could be banked by the source for use in the future or they could be sold to other sources. The sources buying additional credits could then pollute in excess of the LAER or BACT standards.

The three programs under which credits could be exchanged were called offsets, bubbles, and netting. Under the offset program, a new source polluter in a nonattainment had to purchase 20% more credits than the pollution it would add. The bubble exchange took place among different sources owned by the same firm. The firm could treat its combined sources as if they were under one "bubble" and achieve the required abatement for the entire bubble. This permitted firms to reduce pollution where less costly and continue to pollute where more costly. The netting program was an offset arrangement that applied to modifications or expansions of existing sources.

Some states did experiment with the Emissions Trading Program. By the early 1990s, the EPA estimated that between 7000 and 12,000 exchanges of credits had occurred under the three programs. Much of the recent data cited later on the cost advantage of an incentive-based approach over the CAC approach to reducing pollution come from the states' experiences with the Emissions Trading Program.

The 1990 Amendments took the Emissions Trading Program one step further. They established a national program of marketable permits to control the emissions of sulfur dioxide (a primary cause of acid rain) from the electric utilities. The goal is to reduce SO_2 emissions by 10 million tons from 1980 levels; each permit allows one ton of emissions. The utilities are given a certain number of permits each year. Those utilities who choose to emit less SO_2 than their permits allow can sell excess permits to utilities who wish to emit more SO_2 than their permits allow. Permits are exchanged periodically in a nationwide action run by the Chicago Board of Trade. The EPA can assure that the targeted reduction of 10 million tons of SO_2 emissions is met by the number of permits that it issues each year.

We showed in Chapter 8 that marketable permits are very similar to Pigovian taxes and share the same optimal properties. There are some important practical differences between the two, however, and it is not entirely clear which is the better option for controlling SO_2 emissions of the electric utilities. Nonetheless, marketable permits dominate a CAC approach to reducing the emissions because they implicitly recognize that the costs of abating a given amount of SO_2 emissions differ across utilities.

Earlier we noted that the automobile emissions program had made some impressive strides against the conventional pollutants caused by the automobile. The CAC approach to stationary-source pollution has also improved the nation's ambient air quality. The 1994 EPA Report noted that particulate matter had been reduced by 20% from 1984–93.[17] It did not report progress against sulfur oxides, but the marketable permit program reduces SO_2 emissions with certainty given the nature of the program.

Industrial Water Pollution

The federal government's serious entry into the battle against stationary-source water pollution came 2 years after it moved against air pollution, with the passage of the Water Pollution Control Act of 1972. The 1972 Act introduced extremely stringent standards for the pollution of surface water, much more stringent than the air pollution standards. It stipulated that there would be *no* discharge of pollutants into navigable waters by 1985. Before 1985, all stationary sources of pollution would require permits to discharge pollutants, which they would receive only if they met technologically based effluent standards approved by the EPA. By 1977, dischargers had to use the best available control technology (BACT). By 1983, they had to use the best available technology (BAT) economically achievable. Also, wherever possible, the water quality in all waterways must be clean enough to support fish and recreation by June 1, 1983. These new standards superseded a set of ambient water quality standards for interstate waterways that had been established by the Water Quality Act of 1965 to be implemented by the states. Little progress had been achieved by 1972, however, so the EPA decided to take matters into its own hands.

The standards under the 1972 Act were absurdly excessive. No economic model would suggest anything close to a zero-pollution goal for conventional pollutants. Moreover, the standards amounted to the most heavy-handed CAC approach as they were imposed uniformly nationwide.

Not surprisingly, the 1977 Amendments to the Water Pollution Control Act backed off somewhat from the 1972 standards. They removed most of the deadlines in the 1972 Amendments and introduced a distinction between conventional and toxic pollutants. The new standards were that, by 1974, dischargers had to install the best conventional technology (BCT) to abate conventional pollutants, with BAT applied only to toxic pollutants.

The technology-based CAC approach to reducing water pollution at the source remains in effect to this day. No price/incentive program comparable to the Emissions Trading Program or the SO_2 marketable permits exists in the fight against water pollution. The progress made against water pollution is difficult to determine because pollutants in waterways are much more difficult to monitor than pollutants in the air. One common measure of water quality is the amount of dissolved oxygen (DO) in the water, and by that measure there does appear to have been considerable progress in a

---

[17] See T. Tietenberg, *Environmental and Natural Resource Economics*, Harper-Collins College Publishers, New York, 1996, p. 364.

number of waterways. Still, the government is far from achieving its fishing and recreational objectives nationwide.

Toxic Substances

Reducing risks to health is the obvious motivation for the control of toxic emissions. Not all health risks are treated equally, however. The EPA has been most concerned with substances known to cause cancer or birth defects.

The federal government's strategy for controlling toxic pollutants relies heavily on private lawsuits against polluters under the common and strict liability laws. Otherwise, specific federal legislation directed against toxic pollutants is guided by the same three general principles that apply to conventional water pollutants: (1) a combination of reducing pollution at the source and cleaning up existing pollution; (2) total reliance on the CAC approach for reducing pollution at the source, with uniform standards applied to all polluters; and (3) virtually no attempt to balance costs of abatement against the benefits of reducing pollution.

The EPA distinguishes between airborne pollutants and all other pollutants. It had identified eight airborne carcinogens by 1989: asbestos, beryllium, mercury, vinyl chloride, benzene, radionuclides, inorganic arsenic, and radon-222. The Clean Air Act Amendments of 1990 mandated controls on all eight, but little action has been take to date. One problem is that scientists have not been able to agree on the safe threshold level for any of the airborne carcinogens.

Toxic pollutants that make their way into the water and ground are covered by a number of separate laws, the following of which are the most important:

1. *Federal Food, Drug, and Cosmetic Act of 1938*—Monitors the safety of food additives among its many provisions and is administered by the Food and Drug Administration (FDA). Amendments in 1958 forbid any food additive that is known to cause cancer.

2. *Occupational Safety and Health Act of 1970*—Established the Occupational, Safety, and Health Administration (OSHA) whose functions include regulating exposure to toxic pollutants in the workplace.

3. *Federal Environmental Pesticide Control Act of 1972*—Provides for the pretesting of all pesticides and the registering and certifying of all commercial users of pesticides.

4. *Safe Drinking Water Act of 1974*—Applies to community water systems and sets maximum levels for bacteria, turbidity, and chemical and radiological contaminants. Communities must use BAT to meet all the standards.

5. *Resource Conservation and Recovery Act of 1976 and the Toxic Substances Control Act of 1976*—The first act establishes standards for handling,

shipping, and disposing of toxic wastes. The second act empowers the EPA to inventory over 55,000 chemical substances used in commerce and to control the introduction of new substances to ensure they are safe, with the burden of proof of safety placed on the manufacturer. The average time to test new chemicals has been 8 years.

6. *Comprehensive Environmental Response, Compensation, and Liability Act of 1980 (the Superfund Act)*—Authorized the establishment of a $1.6 billion fund to clean up existing toxic waste sites from 1980 to 1985. A $9 billion reauthorization bill was passed in 1986. The Superfund is financed mostly by taxes on chemicals. Cleaning up all known toxic waste sites would be an enormous task. By 1992, the EPA had identified 1275 sites. It had constructed 149 cleanup facilities and fully cleaned up only 40 of the sites, despite an expenditure of $13 billion. The EPA estimates that $750 billion ($1992) would be necessary to clean up all 1275 sites.[18]

Two other antipollution initiatives are worth noting, one related to ozone depletion in the stratosphere and the other to oil spills.

1. A 1978 EPA regulation banned any fully halogenated chlorofluoro-alkane, the chemical used at the time in almost all aerosol propellants. The United States has since signed agreements with other nations in 1988 and 1990 to ban the use of other chemicals responsible for ozone depletion.

2. Efforts to prevent oil spills in the ocean are contained in regulations under the Clean Water Act of 1990 and the Oil Pollution Act of 1990. The Clean Water Act permits private suits against oil spills to encourage enforcement. Regulations to prevent oil spills in all other bodies of water are covered by the Marine Protection Research and Sanctuaries Act of 1972, which also regulates other forms of toxic pollutants in the nation's waters.

The current "hot" antipollution issue is the problem of global warming caused by the emission of the so-called greenhouse gases, primarily carbon dioxide (CO_2). Scientists have not yet reached agreement on such fundamental questions as to whether the earth is getting significantly warmer and, if it is, whether greenhouse gas emissions or other factors beyond the control of humankind are the principal cause of the warming. Furthermore, even assuming that global warming exists and that it can be reduced significantly by controlling greenhouse gas emissions, there remains the question of how best to respond to global warming. Possible strategies include reducing greenhouse gas emissions, engaging in climatic engineering such as by planting forests to absorb CO_2, or simply adapting to the warmer temperatures. No one is certain which of these strategies is the most costeffective, whether applied alone or in combination.

---

[18] See T. Tietenberg, *Environmental and Natural Resource Economics*, Harper-Collins College Publishers, New York, 1996, p. 481.

Finally, any strategy requires full international cooperation because the warming phenomenon truly is global in scope. Past efforts to secure full international cooperation against ozone depletion do not bode well for global warming. One problem is that developing nations are understandably reluctant to trade off desperately needed economic growth for a reduction in any form of pollution.

The Effectiveness of U. S. Antipollution Policies

Air Pollution

As noted above, the government's CAC approach against automobile and stationary-source air pollutants had led to substantial reductions by the early 1990s in five of the six conventional pollutants targeted by the EPA (the exception is SO_2, which the marketable permits program targeted in the 1990s, successfully). Moreover, the government's battle against air pollution appears to be cost effective overall. To cite one example, A. Myrick Freeman attempted to calculate the net benefits of controlling stationary-source air pollution, primarily the reduction in particulate matter. Estimating the benefits of pollution reduction is problematic; Freeman produced a range of estimates from \$4.8 billion to \$49.4 billion, with a "best" estimate of \$21.4 billion. He estimated the costs at \$9.0 billion, so that the overall net benefits appear to be positive and substantial using his best estimate of the benefits.[19]

Even granting that air quality has improved and the net benefits are positive, the typical economist's complaint is that the government's policies are not nearly as cost effective as they could be. Replacing the CAC approach with efficient price/incentive approaches such as marketable permits or Pigovian taxes could generate the same reduction in pollution at much lower cost. Tietenberg summarized the results of nine studies that compared the CAC and price/incentive approaches to achieving a given reduction in pollution. Although the studies varied by pollutant and region of the country, their overall message was clear. Only one study reported essentially the same costs with either method. The other eight studies found that the CAC approach was anywhere from 1.78 to 22 times more costly than an efficient price/incentive approach. Cost savings of this magnitude are important given the scope of the government's antipollution efforts.[20]

Water Pollution

Cost comparisons of water pollution strategies yield the same message. Tietenberg summarized the results of 14 studies that compared the CAC and

---

[19] Freeman's estimates are reported by T. Tietenberg, *Environmental and Natural Resource Economics*, Harper-Collins College Publishers, New York, 1996, p. 459. See also A. M. Freeman, III, *Air and Water Pollution Control: A Benefit-Cost Assessment*, Wiley, New York, 1982.

[20] T. Tietenberg, *Environmental and Natural Resource Economics*, Harper-Collins College Publishers, New York, 1996, p. 363.

price/incentive approaches to achieving certain dissolved oxygen targets. The CAC approach was between 1.12 and 3.13 more costly.[21]

At present the marketable permit program for controlling the SO_2 emissions of the electric utilities is the only important federal example of a price/incentive approach to reducing pollution in the United States. Every other major federal initiative uses the CAC approach. Economists are close to unanimous in pushing for an expansion of price/incentive approaches where feasible, as the analysis in Chapter 8 would suggest.

---

[21] Freeman's estimates are reported by T. Tietenberg, *Environmental and Natural Resource Economics*, Harper-Collins College Publishers, New York, 1996, p. 441. See also A. M. Freeman, III, *Air and Water Pollution Control: A Benefit-Cost Assessment*, Wiley, New York, 1982.

9

THE THEORY OF DECREASING COST PRODUCTION

Production of some goods and services exhibits significant decreasing cost or increasing returns to scale, meaning that unit or average cost for an individual firm continues to decline up to a substantial proportion of total market demand. Whenever this occurs, government intervention is almost certainly required to ensure a social welfare optimum.

Public sector economics has traditionally concerned itself only with the most extreme example of decreasing cost, in which a single firm's average cost declines all the way to total market demand. This is referred to as a *natural monopoly*, because a single firm can supply the entire industry output most cheaply. The problems arising in less extreme instances of decreasing cost production that lead to oligopolistic market structures have traditionally been covered in courses on industrial organization. In keeping with this tradition, Chapter 9 analyzes only the natural monopoly, so that "decreasing cost" means decreasing unit cost to total market demand.

Decreasing cost industries are not at all rare. They typically occur in the production of services rather than products—in particular, services that require relatively large setup costs, after which large numbers of users can be served at relatively low marginal cost. The combination of high startup costs and low marginal cost causes unit cost to decline even as the number of users becomes large. Services having these attributes include many forms of transportation, especially highways, bridges, tunnels, and rail transit; the so-called public utilities, such as telephone service, electricity, water supply, and sewage; first-class mail delivery; some recreational facilities such as beaches and parks; some forms of entertainment such as radio, television, and the commercial use of songs; and the software, data, and other services available on the Internet.

The entertainment examples and the Internet are among the purest instances of decreasing cost services. Think of the viewing of television programs. Considerable resources are required to produce, transmit, and receive any one television program. But once the program is produced and the transmitting and receiving facilities (televisions) are in place, the cost of another viewer turning on his television set is essentially zero no matter how many people are watching. Because the number of viewers is the relevant unit of output, average cost decreases continuously as the number of viewers increases. The same properties apply as well to the Internet. Software and data services are most often sold commercially on CD-ROMs, with accompanying manuals, so that their producers can earn a profit, but the software and data could be provided over the Internet (and sometimes are), where they would simply be downloaded by whoever wants them. Clearly the lowest marginal cost of providing software and data is virtually zero. They are exactly like songs in this respect. All the cost and effort are in the creation of the work (i.e., the setup cost).

Marginal costs are greater than zero for each of the other services listed above, but they are nonetheless relatively unimportant compared with the fixed costs of establishing the services. For example, the decreasing cost property of the public utilities or first-class mail arises in the distribution of the services, the need to set up a network of telephone and electric lines (or satellites), water pipes, or post offices to reach every household. Similarly, a large percentage of the costs of providing and maintaining highways, bridges, rail transit, beaches, and parks are essentially fixed costs, unrelated to the number of users.[1]

Decreasing cost production requires government intervention in a market economy for the simple reason that it is totally incompatible with a competitive market structure. Decreasing cost industries cannot possibly have a competitive structure, with large numbers of price-taking firms. Moreover, even if the competitive structure were possible, it would not be desirable. In order to capture the benefits of increasing returns production, the

---

[1] Marginal costs do rise considerably for these services when they become congested, but congestion is an example of an externality. It is unrelated to the phenomenon of significant scale economies or decreasing cost.

entire output must be produced by a single firm. This is why decreasing cost industries are referred to as "natural monopolies" and why they necessarily violate the technological assumption of well-behaved production required for a well-functioning competitive market system.

Chapter 9 explores the pareto-optimal conditions for efficient production with decreasing cost industries. It shows why the competitive market system cannot achieve them and considers the pricing and investment rules implied by the efficiency conditions. The pricing rules imitate standard competitive principles and are therefore relatively straightforward. The investment rules are far from standard, however. Investment in decreasing cost industries has a lumpy, all-or-none quality to it that is absent in the usual marginal investment analysis applied to the small competitive firm. Also, profitability is not necessarily a reliable investment guideline for decreasing cost services, and there may not be any other practicable criteria to determine whether an investment in these services is worthwhile. As a result, investment decisions for these industries are frequently among the more difficult decisions the government has to make, even under the simplifying assumptions of first-best theory.

The chapter concludes with a discussion of actual U.S. policy with respect to the decreasing cost services. Governments in the United States have not embraced the first-best price and investment decision rules for decreasing cost services. They tend to favor some form of average cost pricing and the standard private-sector profitability criteria for investment decisions, neither of which is pareto optimal. The policy discussion speculates on the popularity of these policies and analyzes their properties relative to the first-best decision rules.

DECREASING COST IN GENERAL EQUILIBRIUM ANALYSIS

The problems caused by a decreasing cost natural monopoly are directly related to the particular form of its production function, nothing more. Therefore, the general equilibrium model required to analyze decreasing cost production can be extremely simple. There is no need to model explicitly the interrelationships among consumers or producers, unlike in the analysis of externalities. Also, the model can exploit the dual dichotomies of all first-best models. The demand side of the model can be adequately represented by a single consumer. Were the model to include many consumers and a social welfare function, the first-order conditions would merely reproduce the interpersonal equity conditions and the pareto-optimal consumption conditions of the full model in Chapter 2. Assuming optimal redistributions implies a one-consumer equivalent economy. Similarly, positing many "well-behaved" firms would reproduce the standard pareto-optimal production conditions for those firms. Hence, a single producer is also sufficient so long as its production exhibits increasing returns to scale. Finally, there is no need to specify N goods and factors. A one-good, one-factor economy is sufficient to represent increasing returns/decreasing cost production. Consequently, a general equilibrium model consisting of one person with one source of (decreasing cost) production at which a single output is produced by means of a single input is sufficiently general to capture both the nature of the decreasing cost problem and the decision rules necessary to ensure full pareto optimality. Keeping the model this simple has the additional advantage of permitting a two-dimensional geometric analysis, a welcome relief from the notational complexities of the various externality models. Therefore, let us assume:

1. A single consumer with utility function:

$$U = U(X, L) \qquad (9.1)$$

where

X = the single output.
L = labor, the only factor of production.

By the usual convention, L enters U( ) with a negative sign (leisure is the good). The indifference curves corresponding to $U(X, L)$ are represented in Fig. 9.1.

2. A single firm produces X according to the production function:

$$X = f(L) \qquad (9.2)$$

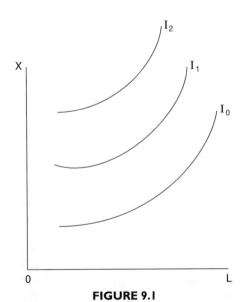

FIGURE 9.1

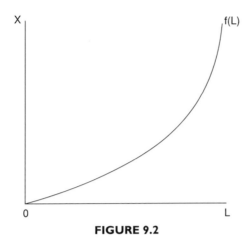

FIGURE 9.2

with $\partial f/\partial L \equiv f' > 0$, $\partial^2 f/\partial L^2 \equiv f'' > 0$ and $f(0) = 0$. The increasing returns production function is represented in Fig. 9.2.

f(L) is a homogeneous function exhibiting increasing returns to scale. As such, average cost continuously decreases. This follows because $Lf' > f$ from Euler's equation on homogeneous functions; thus, $f' > f/L$ (the slope of f at any point is greater than the slope of a ray from the origin), and

$$AC = P_L/f/L > P_L/f' = MC \tag{9.3}$$

everywhere. Average cost (AC) and marginal cost (MC) decrease continuously, with $MC < AC$.[2]

Market clearance automatically holds in this model since it is understood that the consumer supplies all the labor used by the firm and consumes all the output produced by the firm. In a market context, the consumer also receives (pays) all pure economic profits (losses) arising from production at prices P_X and P_L, as well as earning all the labor income.

The Pareto-Optimal Conditions

Society's problem is the standard one:

$$\max_{(X,L)} U(X, L)$$

$$\text{s.t.} \ \ X = f(L)$$

To derive the pareto-optimal conditions, substitute the production function into the utility function and solve the unconstrained maximum:

---

[2] The appendix demonstrates the relationship between increasing returns to scale and decreasing cost for the general case of more than one factor of production.

$$\max_{(L)} \ U(f(L); L)$$

The first-order conditions are

$$U_X f' + U_L = 0 \tag{9.4}$$

or

$$U_X f' = -U_L \tag{9.5}$$

Condition (9.5) gives the standard result that labor should be used to produce X until the marginal utility of X just equals the marginal disutility of further work.

The second-order conditions cannot be ignored with increasing returns-to-scale production, as both the indifference curves and the production function have the same general curvature. To ensure that condition (9.5) represents a utility maximum, the derivative of Eq. (9.5) with respect to L must be negative. Thus,

$$\frac{d\left(f' + \dfrac{U_L}{U_X}\right)}{dL} < 0 \tag{9.6}$$

or

$$\frac{df'}{dL} + \frac{d\left(\dfrac{U_L}{U_X}\right)}{dL} < 0 \qquad \text{(Note: } U_L < 0\text{)} \tag{9.7}$$

Equation (9.7) implies that the curvature of the indifference curves for X and L must be greater than the curvature of the production function. If the reverse is true, Eq. (9.5) represents a utility *minimum* along the production frontier. Refer to panels (a) and (b) in Fig. 9.3.

Decreasing Cost and Competitive Markets

A competitive industry cannot achieve condition (9.5) even if the second-order conditions for a welfare maximum are satisfied. A price-taking competitive firm would solve the following problem:

$$\max_{(L)} \ P_X f(L) - P_L L$$

The first-order conditions are

$$P_X f' - P_L = 0 \tag{9.8}$$

Alternatively,

$$P_X = P_L / f' \equiv MC_X \tag{9.9}$$

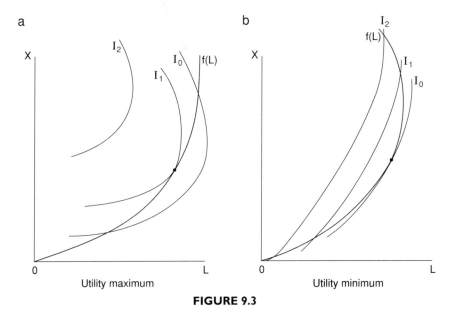

FIGURE 9.3

Conditions (9.8) and (9.9) are the familiar results that the competitive firm hires labor such that the value of the labor's marginal product equals the price of the labor or, equivalently, supplies X such that price equals marginal costs.

On the surface this result would appear to satisfy the full pareto-optimal conditions. The consumer maximizes utility by equating:

$$\frac{U_X}{P_X} = \frac{-U_L}{P_L} \tag{9.10}$$

or

$$P_X = -\frac{U_X}{U_L} \cdot P_L \tag{9.11}$$

Substituting for P_X in Eq. (9.9) yields:

$$-\frac{U_X}{U_L} \cdot P_L \cdot = P_L/f' \tag{9.12}$$

or

$$U_X f' = -U_L \tag{9.13}$$

the pareto-optimal condition (9.5).

Perfect competition cannot be pareto optimal, however, because setting the price of labor equal to the value of its marginal product is *not* profit

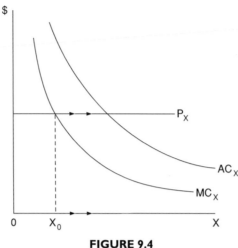

FIGURE 9.4

maximizing for a decreasing cost firm. Since $P_X f'' > 0$, the second-order conditions for a maximum fail to hold. Thus, Eq. (9.9) is the profit-*minimizing* condition.

The perfectly competitive, decreasing marginal cost firm would maximize profits by increasing output indefinitely, as depicted in Fig. 9.4. Since marginal cost P_L/f' declines continuously,[3] the firm loses on every unit up to X_0, but that is the output given by Eq. (9.9). Marginal profits begin at $X_0 + 1$ and increase indefinitely as X increases. The industry would finally consist of a single firm producing the entire market demand.

Competition and decreasing costs are incompatible in another sense. Even if the government were able to subsidize the losses suffered by each firm producing at X in Fig. 9.4, society would not want this solution. One firm has to become the entire industry to exploit the scale economies and minimize production costs, resulting in a natural monopoly. Figure 9.5 is the relevant diagram, with a single firm facing the entire market demand curve.

The Optimal Pricing Rule

Efficiency requires that pareto-optimal condition (9.5) hold; it is the first-order condition for a pareto optimum. But, this implies that the monopoly firm must set price equal to marginal cost. Only if $P_X = P_L/f' = MC_X$ will $U_X f' = -U_L$ Referring to Fig. 9.5, the monopolist must produce at X_{opt}, the point at which the market demand and marginal cost curves intersect.

---

[3] $d(P_L/f') = -P_L f''/(f')^2 < 0$. Strictly speaking, marginal costs could be constant or rising because the term *decreasing cost* refers to decreasing unit cost. But, since MC < AC when AC is declining, any P = MC "equilibrium" implies losses for the competitive firm.

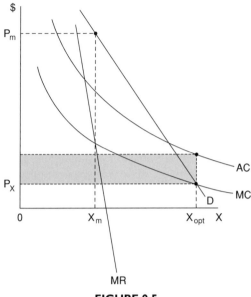

FIGURE 9.5

There are two problems with the pareto-optimal solution, however. First, an unregulated, profit-maximizing monopoly would not produce X_{opt}; instead, it would choose X_m, at which $MR = MC$, and set $P_m > P_X$. Thus, the government must either force the monopoly to select (P_X, X_{opt}) through regulation or operate the industry itself. Second, a regulated monopoly (or the government) makes perpetual losses if forced to produce at $P_X = MC$, with $AC > MC$. Since the monopoly must cover its full costs in the long run, it must be subsidized by an amount equal to $X_{opt} \cdot (AC - MC)$, the shaded area in Fig. 9.5. Moreover the subsidy must not generate inefficiencies elsewhere in the economy. It must be lump sum. In this simple economy the consumer would transfer the required income to the firm. Such a transfer is possible, because the excess of the consumer's earned income over her expenditures, $P_L L - P_X X$, exactly matches the firm's deficit.

In a many-person economy, the transfers to decreasing cost firms become part of the lump-sum redistributions necessary to satisfy the interpersonal equity conditions. The only difference from the optimal lump-sum redistributions described in Chapter 2 is that the taxes collected must be sufficient to cover both the transfers to other individuals and the transfers to decreasing cost firms. Social marginal utilities are still equalized at the first-best optimum.

To summarize, the first-best pricing rule is $P = MC$, with a lump-sum subsidy to cover the deficit with marginal-cost pricing.

The Optimal Investment Rules

When confronted with decreasing cost production, society must make a fundamental investment decision that does not present itself in "normal" industry situations. If the firm is forced to price optimally at P = MC, it cannot cover the opportunity costs of investing in that industry. The lump-sum subsidy does allow the firm to cover opportunity cost, but this in itself is not especially helpful since profit (loss) is not performing its customary function as a signal for investment. Society is, instead, presented with an all-or-none decision: Is providing the service at P = MC, with a subsidy to cover the operating deficit, preferable to not having the service at all? This is obviously quite different from the standard investment decision, in which the present value formula is used to determine the profitability of a marginal increment to the capital stock evaluated at current (and expected) market prices.

One can usefully distinguish two cases in analyzing the investment decision, which we shall refer to as the "easy" case and the "hard" case. The distinction between them turns on whether a profit maximizing monopolist could at least break even *if* it were allowed to do so.[4]

The Easy Case

Suppose we know that demand is sufficiently high so that a monopolist, if allowed to profit maximize, could at least break even by charging a single price for its product. In other words, the market demand curve is at least tangent to the firm's AC curve, as in the two panels of Fig. 9.6. This case would certainly apply to most public utilities; urban highways, bridges and tunnels; television and radio; many Internet services; and many recreational facilities.

We will show that if (at least) breakeven production is possible, the service should be produced. Potential profitability is thus a sufficient condition for having the service. The monopolist must not be allowed to capture these potential profits, however. Price must be set at marginal cost, with a lump-sum subsidy to cover the resulting losses at that price.

The Hard Case

The ability to break even is not a necessary condition for providing the service, however. Suppose demand is everywhere below AC, as in Fig. 9.7, such that there is no single price at which a profit maximizing monopolist could break even. Clearly, no private firm would be interested in this market

[4] Because capital is suppressed in the simple geometric analysis, we are implicitly assuming that the capital stock is optimal for any given X; that is, AC and MC are minimum long-run costs. The all-or-none test is an additional question, asking whether first-best optimal production and pricing is preferred to having no service at all. Our analysis of the all-or-none test follows that of P. Diamond and D. McFadden, "Some Uses of the Expenditure Function in Public Finance," *Journal of Public Economics*, February 1974.

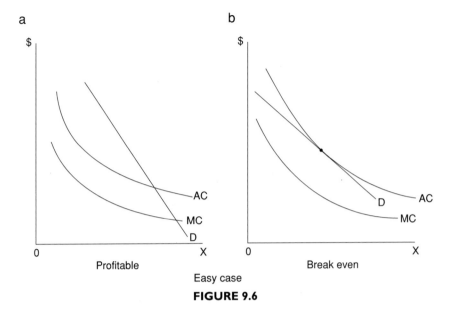

a

b

Profitable   Break even

Easy case

FIGURE 9.6

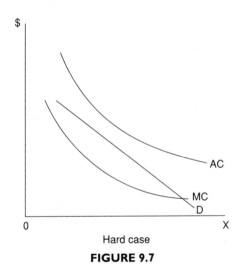

Hard case

FIGURE 9.7

unless heavily subsidized. Society may be interested in having the government provide the service, however, once again at the intersection of price and marginal cost. Then again, society may not be interested. Demand may be so low that the service is not worth having.

Notice that even potential profitability is not a useful investment guideline for the hard case. As we shall see, the necessary conditions involve willingness-to-pay criteria that do not have close market analogs.

The hard case is not merely a theoretical *curiosum*. Many, if not most, rural highways would certainly fall into this category, as well as a number of recreational facilities such as national parks in remote areas. Urban rail transit systems may also be examples of the hard case. Rail transit deficits have been the rule rather than the exception in the United States. Despite a history of continual real fare increases, rail transit deficits continue to grow in most U.S. cities. Perhaps no single fare would cover full rail transit costs.

The Suffcient Condition: The Easy Case

Let us first establish the sufficient condition for decreasing cost production.

Proposition: If a profit-maximizing monopolist can at least break even by charging a single price, then society should produce the good. Utility is maximized, however, by setting $P = MC$, and covering the resulting deficit with a lump-sum transfer. ∎

A geometric proof will suffice, providing we use the consumer's indifference map and the production-possibilities frontier in $(X-L)$ space. The demand curve–average cost diagrams are useful for illustrating certain points but are illegitimate as a representation of general equilibrium. They rely on inappropriate measures of consumer's surplus.[5]

Breakeven Production

The first step in the proof is to characterize breakeven production in $(X-L)$ space. Refer to Fig. 9.8. Think of production as occurring somewhere along the ray 0R from the origin, say at point B. Suppose the monopolist were to set the relative prices P_L/P_X equal to the slope of 0R. Let the slope equal k. The monopolist would then just break even, since at any point along the ray:

$$X = P_L/P_X \cdot L \quad \text{or} \quad P_X X = P_L L \qquad (9.14)$$

This example is *not* to suggest a monopolist would actually set relative prices equal to k, but only to depict the limiting, breakeven, $P = AC$ case.

The Price–Consumption Locus

The ray 0R through B, with relative prices $P_L/P_X = k$, also serves as a budget line for the consumer with no lump-sum taxes or transfers. Suppose the consumer happens to be in equilibrium at point B as shown in Fig. 9.9.

[5] The geometric proofs of the necessary and sufficient conditions were demonstrated to us by Peter Diamond in his graduate Public Finance class at MIT. See also P. Diamond and D. McFadden, "Some Uses of the Expenditure Function in Public Finance," *Journal of Public Economics*, February 1974, especially for the hard case.

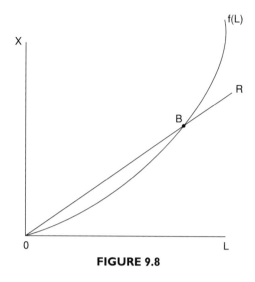

FIGURE 9.8

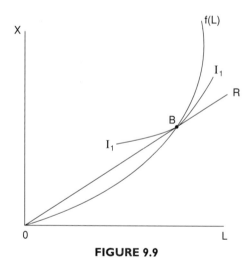

FIGURE 9.9

Then, point B represents an actual general equilibrium for the economy with prices such that production is breakeven.

We can trace out a price–consumption line for the consumer by varying the slope of the ray through the origin, as in Fig. 9.10, with P_L/P_X always equal to the slope. Every point on the price–consumption locus represents a potential general equilibrium for the economy, in which the consumer is in equilibrium and the firm is breaking even.

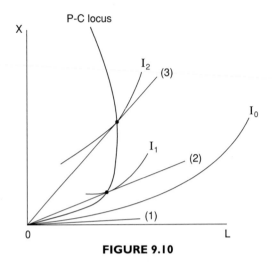

FIGURE 9.10

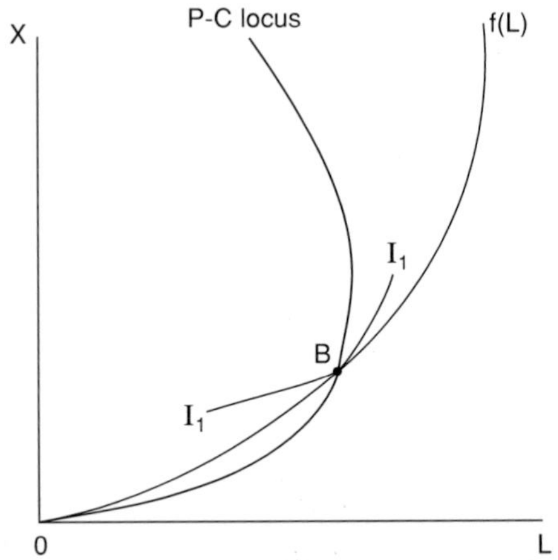

FIGURE 9.11

The only remaining question is whether a general equilibrium with breakeven production is feasible. The answer is yes if the price–consumption locus intersects the production-possibilities frontier, such as at point B in Fig. 9.11. Furthermore, breakeven production at point B is preferred to the origin, the point of zero production. This follows because the consumer is in equilibrium at B, so that the indifference curve on which point B lies is tangent to the ray through the origin. Therefore, B must lie above the indifference curve that passes through the origin, I_0, establishing the first part of the proposition: Feasibility of breakeven production is a sufficient condition for having the service.

Production is not pareto optimal at B, however. The problem with point B is that P_X equals the average cost of producing X, not the marginal cost. The slope $k = X/L$ is the average product of labor at B. Therefore,

$$P_X = P_L/k = P_L/AP_L = AC_X \tag{9.15}$$

The marginal product of labor at B is f', which is greater than k, the average product. Therefore:

$$P_L/f' = MC_X < P_L/k = AC_X = P_X \tag{9.16}$$

in violation of the pareto-optimal condition (9.5).

The utility from the service is maximized by producing at point A in Fig. 9.12, at which the production-possibilities frontier is just tangent to one of the consumer's indifference curves, I_2.

The remaining question is how to establish point A as a marketed general equilibrium. This is done by setting P_L/P_X equal to the slope of the production-possibilities frontier at A, so that $P_X = MC_X \equiv P_L/f'$. This price ratio is the slope of a ray intersecting the L-axis at point b, not the origin. This ray can be a budget line for the consumer only if the consumer first surrenders b units of labor lump sum, so that:

$$P_X X - P_L \cdot L = -P_L b \tag{9.17}$$

Similarly, with $P_X = MC_X$ at A, the firm makes pure economic losses equal to $P_L b$, since the ray is also the firm's profit line. Therefore, with a lump-sum transfer of $P_L \cdot b$ from the consumer to the firm and with marginal

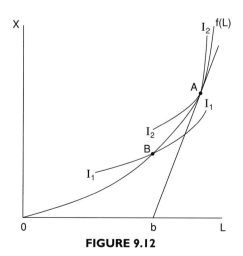

FIGURE 9.12

cost pricing, the firm covers its full costs and the consumer attains the highest possible indifference curve. This is the price-with-transfer general equilibrium market solution that satisfies pareto-optimal condition (9.5), in line with the second part of the proposition.

The Necessary Condition: The Hard Case

The existence of a breakeven production point such as B in Fig. 9.11 implies the existence of a preferred pareto-optimal point such as A, but a pareto-optimal point A preferred to zero production does not imply B. Suppose the price–consumption line lies everywhere above f(L) (except at the origin), as in Fig. 9.13. Since the price–consumption locus defines all possible breakeven general equilibrium points, breakeven production is not feasible. This corresponds, in $(P_X - X)$ space, to the situation in which the demand curve for X is everywhere below the AC curve.

Society may still prefer production at $P_X = MC$ to not having the service, however. The all-or-none test turns on the position of the indifference curve passing through the origin, I_0. If I_0 lies everywhere above the production-possibilities frontier as in Fig. 9.14, society should not produce X. The consumer prefers zero production to any of the feasible choices lying on or below f(L).

If I_0 crosses f(L) as in Fig. 9.15, then there exists a higher indifference curve tangent to the frontier, such as I_2 in Fig. 9.15. Society should produce at the tangency point A in Fig. 9.15, set $P_X = MC_X$, and transfer b units of

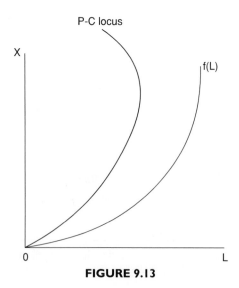

FIGURE 9.13

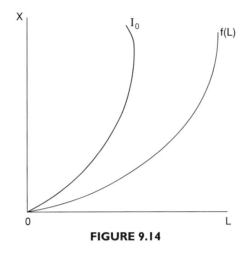

FIGURE 9.14

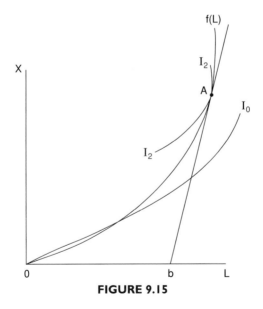

FIGURE 9.15

labor lump sum from the consumer to the firm, exactly as in the easy case. This is the only way to satisfy pareto-optimal condition (9.5).

Notice that even potential profitability is no guideline in the hard case. Even if the firm were allowed to maximize profits it could not so much as break even by setting a single price. The government must rely instead on

willingness-to-pay lump-sum income measures of welfare, such as Hicks'
Compensating Variation (HCV), to determine whether production is worthwhile.

Consider the indifference curve through the origin I_0 in Fig. 9.16 and the
lines (1), (2), and (3) tangent to I_0. The tangency lines (1), (2), and (3)
represent budget lines for the consumer, in which:

1. P_X is decreasing such that the ratio of prices P_L/P_X equals the slope of
   the corresponding line.
2. The consumer first sacrifices (lump sum) $0, 0d_2$, and $0d_3$ units of labor,
   respectively, to remain on I_0.

For example, P_X is so high (relative to P_L, assumed constant) on budget
line (1) that the consumer purchases no X. Consider line (3). Since utility is
being held constant along I_0, the distance $0d_3$ can be interpreted as the lump-
sum income (in terms of labor) the consumer is willing to pay for the
opportunity to purchase X at the lower P_X (equal to $P_L/$ slope of (3)). The
income sacrificed keeps utility constant by exactly offsetting the utility gains
resulting from the reduction in P_X. Hence, $0d_3$ is the HCV for this P_X,
measured relative to a P_X so high that quantity demanded is zero. Also, X_3
is a point on the consumer's compensated demand curve for X, compensated
to equal the utility level represented by I_0.

The HCV can then be compared with the actual amount of income the
consumer must sacrifice for feasible decreasing cost production. Consider
Fig. 9.17. At point A on I_2 with marginal cost pricing, the firm requires $0b$
units of L to break even. But, at the marginal-cost price, the lump-sum

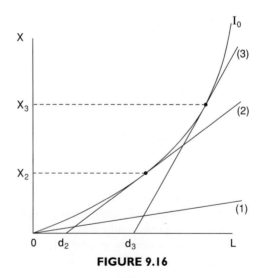

FIGURE 9.16

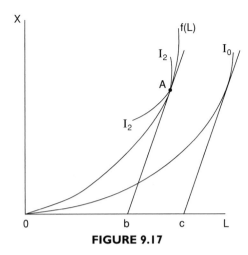

FIGURE 9.17

amount the consumer is willing to pay is 0c, the HCV measured along I_0. The consumer only has to pay 0b as a lump-sum transfer, so society should provide the service. In contrast, with I_0 everywhere above the f(L) as in Fig. 9.14, the consumer would never be willing to sacrifice the lump-sum income required for the firm to cover its cost with marginal cost pricing. Hence, the service should not be provided.

To summarize, the necessary condition for providing the service is that the consumer's HCV, evaluated at $P_X = MC_X$ and the utility level with zero production, exceed the firm's deficit at the marginal cost price.

This test can also be represented in $(P_X - X)$ space, an interpretation worth analyzing because it appears in many sources, especially intermediate-level texts. Consider the market for X_1 as represented by the demand and cost curves in Fig. 9.18. The necessary condition is often stated as follows: If the area $EP_1^B A$ exceeds the fixed-cost subsidy, area $CBAP_1^B$, then society should operate the service at X_1. This test is flawed because the measure of the consumer's benefit is Marshallian consumer surplus, which has no willing-ness-to-pay interpretation. But, if the demand curve is the compensated demand curve and only P_1 varies, then this test is equivalent to the necessary condition derived in $(X - L)$ space.

The Necessary Condition and Compensated Demand Curve

To see this, suppose the government is considering whether or not to operate a new, decreasing cost industry at $P = MC$. Should the government decide not to produce, the consumer remains at the status quo (call it A), with a utility level equal to U^A. Should the government produce, the consumer is in situation B, at a utility level of U^B. The question is whether $U^B \gtreqless U^A$.

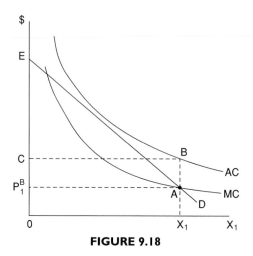

FIGURE 9.18

The expenditure function provides the answer, since

$$U^B > U^A \text{ iff } M\left(\vec{P}; U^B\right) > M\left(\vec{P}; U^A\right) \quad \text{for any price vector } \vec{P}$$

That is, for any price vector $\vec{P}$, situation B costs more if it represents greater utility.[6]

To see how the expenditure function generates the all-or-none tests described above, begin by defining T^A as the lump-sum payment required of the consumer to support the equilibrium at A. Therefore,

$$M\left(\vec{P}^A; U^A\right) = -T^A \tag{9.18}$$

or

$$\sum_i P_i^A X_i^A\big|_{\text{comp}} = -T^A \tag{9.19}$$

Note that $-T^A$ could well be 0. It measures lump-sum income from taxes, transfers, fixed factors, and pure economic profits. With no decreasing cost production and all income earned income, it is reasonable to assume $-T^A = 0$, although this is not required.

Situation B with decreasing cost production requires an additional transfer from the consumer to the firms, thereby increasing the total payments by the consumer to T^B. Therefore,

$$M\left(\vec{P}^B; U^B\right) = -T^B \tag{9.20}$$

---

[6] The sufficient condition follows directly from the assumption of nonsatiation, which implies a positive marginal utility of income. The necessary condition follows from the property that well-behaved indifference curves cannot cross. Thus, given two market situations with identical prices, the one with higher income must generate higher utility.

To determine whether $U^B > U^A$, evaluate the expenditure functions at $\vec{P} = \vec{P}^B$, the new prices.[7] $U^B > U^A$ iff:

$$M\left(\vec{P}^B; U^B\right) > M\left(\vec{P}^B; U^A\right) \tag{9.21}$$

$$-T^B > M\left(\vec{P}^B; U^A\right) \tag{9.22}$$

or

$$T^B < -M\left(\vec{P}^B; U^A\right) \tag{9.23}$$

But,

$$-T^A = M\left(\vec{P}^A; U^A\right) \tag{9.24}$$

Thus, $U^B > U^A$ iff:

$$T^B - T^A < M\left(\vec{P}^A; U^A\right) - M\left(\vec{P}^B; U^A\right) \tag{9.25}$$

The left-hand side of Eq. (9.25) is the additional lump-sum subsidy required for the decreasing cost service to cover its full costs. It corresponds to distance 0b in Fig. 9.16. The right-hand side gives the income the consumer is willing to sacrifice to face prices $\vec{P}^B$ instead of $\vec{P}^A$. Thus, it corresponds to distance 0c in Fig. 9.17.

The right-hand side also represents a summation of areas under compensated demand (supply) curves. This interpretation follows from Shepard's lemma, that the partial derivative of the expenditure function with respect to the ith price is the compensated demand (supply) for good (factor) i. Therefore, letting all prices change one at a time,

$$M\left(\vec{P}^A; U^A\right) - M\left(\vec{P}^B; U^A\right) = \int_{i=1}^{N} \int_{P_i^B}^{P_i^A} \frac{\partial M(\vec{P}; U^A)}{\partial s} ds$$

$$= \sum_{i=1}^{N} \int_{P_i^B}^{P_i^A} X_i^c dP \tag{9.26}$$

When the ith compensated demand (supply) is integrated, it is evaluated at the prices P^B for the 1 to $(i-1)$ goods and factors that have already been integrated, and at prices P^A for the $(i+1)$ to N goods and factors that have yet to be integrated. Since the X_i are the compensated demands (supplies), the order of integration makes no difference.

If the new product is the first good and it is "small" so that prices P_i for $i \geq 2$ remain unchanged, then:

---

[7] The expenditure functions could also be evaluated at $\vec{P}^A$ which would involve Hicks' Equivalent Variation rather than Hicks' Compensating Variation.

$$M\left(\vec{P}^A; U^A\right) - M\left(\vec{P}^B; U^A\right) = \int_{P_1^B}^{P_1^A} X_1^c dP_1 \tag{9.27}$$

where P_1^A is the price at which the demand curve intersects the price axis, and P_1^B is the marginal cost price. Hence, the area defined by Eq. (9.27) is EP_1^B A in Fig. 9.18, providing D refers to the compensated demand curve. Note, also, that the compensated demand curve lies to the left of the actual demand curve because the consumer sacrifices income as price is lowered to remain at the initial utility level. Thus the area behind the compensated demand curve corresponding to EP_1^BA in Fig. 9.18 is less than area EP_1^BA, in general.

Marshallian Consumer's Surplus and Hicks' Compensating Variation

Needless to say, the hard case poses a number of practical difficulties for the policy maker. Operating the service at *any* single price generates losses, and justifying its continued operation in the face of these losses requires knowing a hypothetical willingness-to-pay income measure, such as Hicks' Compensating Variation, that the general public will not understand. The public thinks in terms of profitability.

In addition, the HCV may not be easy to estimate even if it were understood. At best, the policymaker may know the aggregate market demand curve, although even this is extremely unlikely for many decreasing cost services. The all-or-none test requires knowing the demand relationship over the entire range of prices, from $P = MC$ up to a price high enough to preclude any demand for the service. Yet, some of the hard-case decreasing cost services such as rural highways and some of the national parks have never been priced, so the quantities demanded at higher prices are unknown. In these cases, the econometrician is forced to use indirect methods to estimate the value of these services to consumers. When prices do exist, such as for mass rail transit, econometric analysis typically provides information on just a portion of the curve estimated over a relatively narrow range of historical prices. In some instances, there may be reasonable ways to extrapolate the estimated relationship back to the price axis, but even so one is left with the actual demand curve, not the compensated demand curve.

Suppose enough price data exist to estimate the market demand curve along the full range of prices with a reasonable degree of confidence. Additional assumptions are still required to estimate the HCV. First and foremost is the assumption that income is continuously and optimally redistributed so that the first-best interpersonal equity conditions are satisfied and the economy is one-consumer equivalent. This assumption justifies the estimation of an aggregate market demand curve rather than individual demand curves because it assumes a well-defined set of social indifference curves defined over aggregate goods and services. Conversely, without this assumption the policy environment is second best and an appropriate second-best model would have to be specified and solved to determine the proper all-or-none second-best test. The literature offers a number of choices under the one-consumer equivalent assumption.

Jorgenson–Slesnick Expenditure Shares

One possibility is the Jorgenson–Slesnick approach to demand estimation discussed in Chapter 4, in which expenditure shares are estimated in such a way as to recover the underlying (aggregate) indirect utility function in prices and income. Once the indirect utility function is obtained, it can be used to calculate the income required to hold utility constant as prices vary. The Jorgenson–Slesnick approach requires estimating an entire demand system, however, for which the data may not be available.

Roy's Identity

Another approach is to estimate a single market demand curve for the decreasing cost service and then make use of Roy's identity to recover the corresponding indirect utility function. Roy's identity states:

$$\partial V(P, Y)/\partial P_i = \lambda X_i(P, Y) = \partial V(P, Y)/\partial Y \cdot X_i \qquad (9.28)$$

where V is the indirect utility function, and X_i is the actual demand curve. Equation (9.28) is a differential equation in P_i and Y which has a closed-form solution for V for certain demand functions. For example, the linear demand curve $X_i = \alpha + \beta P_i + \gamma Y$ yields the indirect utility function:

$$V(P, Y) = e^{\gamma P}[\alpha/\gamma - \beta/\gamma^2 + \beta/\gamma P + Y] \qquad (9.29)$$

This example assumes that only the price of the service, P_i, is changing.[8] The remaining prices are part of the constant term α. Unfortunately, large projects such as mass rail transit systems or highways are likely to cause many prices to change. The single price assumption is highly suspect for the hard-case decreasing cost services.

Marshallian Consumer Surplus

Still another popular approach is to assume away income effects so that the actual and compensated demand curves are one and the same. In this case, Marshallian consumer surplus and the appropriate willingness-to-pay income measures such as the HCV are identical, so there is no need to uncover the underlying indirect utility function. Assuming away income effects is hardly an attractive assumption, however. Almost all goods have some income elasticity of demand, and for services such as highways and recreational facilities it may well be substantial. The higher the income elasticity of demand, the more these two benefit measures will diverge.

---

[8] We first saw this approach applied in J. Hausman, "Labor Supply," in H. Aaron and J. Pechman (Eds.), *How Taxes Affect Economic Behavior*, Brookings, Washington, D.C., 1981; see p. 40, fn. 19.

Nonetheless, Marshallian consumer surplus has remained a popular measure of the value of price changes thanks to an approximation formula due to Robert Willig. Willig demonstrated that Marshallian consumer surplus is likely to be a close approximation of the HCV, even for fairly large income elasticities. Specifically, he proved that, for a single price change,[9]

$$\frac{C - A}{A} \approx \frac{\eta A}{2M^0} \tag{9.30}$$

where:

C   = Hicks' Compensating Variation due to the price change.
A   = Marshallian consumer surplus.
η = income elasticity of demand.
M^0 = income in the original, no-service situation.

As Willig points out, if the surplus (A) is 5% of total income (M^0), even with an income elasticity (η) as high as .8, the error in using A for C is approximately 2%, well within the range of demand estimation error.

Willig's approximation formula is not without its problems. The assumption of a single price change is crucial to Willig's proof. If more than one price changes so that Eq. (9.26) applies, the Marshallian measure is not path dependent and is therefore not well defined. As noted above, the single-price-change assumption is highly suspect.

Roy's Identity Again

Peter Hammond has argued strongly, and persuasively, that applied economists should reject Marshallian consumer surplus measures of willingness-to-pay, Willig's approximation formula notwithstanding. Suppose an estimated demand curve does not lead to a closed-form solution for the indirect utility function or one of the willingness-to-pay income measures. Even so, Roy's identity can be used to construct an ordinary differential equation in prices and income from any estimated actual demand curve. The equation can then easily be solved by today's computers using standard numerical methods. Hammond demonstrates the technique in terms of a solution that yields Hicks' Equivalent Variation, which is a valid income measure of the change in utility. Furthermore, the technique can be applied to any number of price changes. Modern computing has simply rendered Marshallian consumer surplus obsolete.[10]

---

[9] R. D. Willig, "Consumer's Surplus Without Apology," *American Economic Review*, September 1976.

[10] P. Hammond, "Theoretical Progress in Public Economics: A Provocative Assessment," *Oxford Economic Papers*, January 1990, sects. 10, 11, and 12. Hammond also discusses aggregation problems when the distribution of income is not optimal so that the economy is not one-consumer equivalent.

Note, finally, that the problem of estimating the HCV or HEV to justify a decreasing cost service arises only for the hard case. Simply knowing that the service could break even or make a profit at a single price is sufficient in the easy case. As such, the profitability test that the public is familiar with applies even if the service is priced at marginal cost and operated at a deficit.

Decreasing Cost Services and Public Goods

A brief discussion of the relationship between decreasing cost services and nonexclusive public goods would be useful at this point because there is some confusion between the two in the professional literature. Decreasing cost goods with zero (or approximately zero) marginal costs are sometimes referred to as "public goods" because consumption is nonrival: Any one person's consumption of the good does not diminish the quantity available for others to consume.[11] The uncongested highway, bridge, or tunnel; national wildlife preserves; television viewing; and downloaded software are all reasonably good examples. Yet, referring to these services as "public goods" because marginal costs are (approximately) zero is extremely misleading. Samuelson coined the phrase "public good" for a particular kind of externality-generating activity, the nonexclusive good, for which consumption is nonrival because everyone necessarily consumes its services in equal amounts. In Chapters 6 and 7 we suggested an alternative definition of a public good that could also be applied to exclusive goods, providing the externalities generated by their consumption (production) affect everyone.

People are free to call things what they wish, but we believe the term "public good" ought to be reserved for certain kinds of externalities and not brought into the realm of decreasing cost theory. To apply it as well to decreasing costs, even when marginal cost is zero and consumption is nonrival, is bound to cause confusion. The problem is that the pareto-optimal rules for externality-generating activities differ substantially from their decreasing cost counterparts.

Consumption externalities lead to pareto-optimal rules of the form $\sum MRS = MRT$. Decreasing cost services, in contrast, require the normal competitive rules, $MRS = MRT$, for pareto optimality. Furthermore, the marginal production costs of externality-type "public goods" need not be zero. The marginal costs for weapons systems are obviously considerable. And even if the marginal cost of a nonexclusive good happened to be zero, it would not be allocated the same way as a decreasing cost good with zero marginal cost.

[11] Francis Bator describes "publicness" in this manner in *The Question of Government Spending*: "There are activities, however, where the additional cost of extra use are literally zero. The economist labels the output of such activities 'public'." See F. M. Bator, *The Question of Government Spending*, Harper Brothers, New York, 1960; p. 94. (See pp. 90–98 for an extended discussion of zero marginal cost and decreasing cost services, especially pp. 94 and 96.)

To see that these two rules imply two distinct allocation mechanisms, compare the pareto-optimal allocations of an externality-type "public good" and a decreasing cost service in a two-person economy given that:

1. The marginal costs of providing each good are zero at every output.
2. The individual demand curves for each good are identical (but the two people have different demand curves).

These relationships are shown in Fig. 9.19.

If marginal costs (MRT) are zero for the decreasing cost good, then both people should be allowed to consume the good until their personal MRSs are zero. The aggregate demand curve D_{DC}^{Total} is the *horizontal* summation of d_1 and d_2, and the optimum quantity is X_{DC}^{opt}, the point at which D_{DC}^{Total} intersects the X axis. If marginal costs (MRT) are zero for the externality-type "public good," then the proper allocation occurs when $MRS^1 + MRS^2 = 0$. The aggregate demand curve D_{PG}^{Total} is the *vertical* summation of d_1 and d_2, and the optimum quantity is X_{PG}^{opt}, the point at which D_{PG}^{Total} intersects the x axis.

Finally, the decreasing cost good can be marketed more or less normally since each consumer should face the same price ($= 0$). Of course, the government does have to ensure that the fixed costs are covered with a lump-sum subsidy, but this is true of any properly marketed decreasing cost service, even those with nonzero marginal costs. In contrast, "marketing" the non-exclusive public good requires that the government select the single quantity.

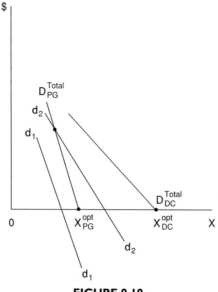

FIGURE 9.19

The consumers may then be charged their demand prices (Lindahl prices) at the chosen quantity, but this is not necessary. Any lump-sum tax preserves pareto optimality.

In conclusion, the nonrivalry quality that "any one person's consumption does not diminish the quantity available to anyone else" is not precise enough to be useful. It could refer to a nonexclusive good or it could imply nothing more than zero marginal costs (MRT). To avoid this ambiguity, we believe the term "public good" should be reserved for instances of pervasive externalities, more or less as Samuelson originally intended. If the term is also used to characterize zero marginal cost, decreasing cost services, it loses its particular analytical significance. It might as well refer to any good requiring government intervention, since there is no analytical reason to distinguish between zero and nonzero marginal cost, decreasing cost services.

REFLECTIONS ON U.S. POLICY REGARDING DECREASING COST SERVICES: THE PUBLIC INTEREST IN EQUITY AND EFFICIENCY

Suppose a decreasing cost service satisfies the requirements of the "easy case," that a profit-maximizing monopolist could at least break even. The easy case presents three obvious pricing options for the government, each depicted in Fig. 9.20.

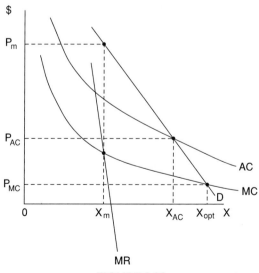

FIGURE 9.20

The simplest option is to preserve free enterprise, offer the natural monopoly to private investors, and let them operate the service as a monopolist. The expectation is that the owners will choose to maximize profits by producing output X_m at which $MR = MC$, setting price equal to P_m, and earning pure profits of $(P_m - AC) \cdot X_m$.

The other two options involve government intervention, either in the form of a direct government takeover of the service or private ownership with government regulation. In either case, the government has two natural choices:

1. Follow the dictates of first-best theory, charge the marginal cost price P_{MC}, and subsidize the operation out of general tax revenues in the amount of $(AC - MC) \cdot X_{opt}$.
2. Charge a price equal to average costs, P_{AC}, and produce X_{AC}, in which case the service covers its full costs.

United States governments at all levels have overwhelmingly adopted the average cost pricing strategy, or some close approximation to it, whether the service is publicly or privately owned. For example, fees for recreational facilities such as beaches and parks are usually set to cover the full costs of operating these facilities. Tolls on urban highways, bridges, and tunnels are often designed to cover the full costs of the entire network of transportation facilities under the jurisdiction of a local transportation authority. The federal gasoline tax was originally established to defray the expenses of constructing the interstate highway system. Similarly, state gasoline tax rates are determined primarily by the anticipated expenses of state highway departments. Public utility rates are generally designed to cover all expenses including a fair rate of return to the private investors. Admittedly, unless the "fair return" equals the opportunity cost of capital services, this is not strictly average cost pricing, but its philosophy is more or less identical. One can think of the utility regulatory commissions as constructing an average cost curve that includes the "fair" rate of return and setting rates equal to these constructed average costs.

In some instances, governments have not insisted on average cost pricing for decreasing cost services. Examples include some national and state parks and beaches financed out of general revenues, over-the-air commercial television financed by advertising revenues, and sales of rights to use recorded music through agencies such as ASCAP and BMI, which charge users a one-time annual fee for access to their music inventories. Notice that in each of these examples the per-use price of the service is essentially zero. Since the marginal cost of these services is likely to be near zero, where the quantity axis defines the number of users or viewers, the zero price can be thought of as roughly consistent with optimal pricing (as long as the service remains uncongested). The use of general revenues, advertising, or one-time fees to cover costs may not be optimal, however.

The preference for average cost pricing may seem surprising, given the general support for free enterprise in the United States or the first-best theoretical arguments favoring marginal cost pricing with government intervention. The question arises as to why average cost pricing is so common in the United States. What are its perceived advantages and to what extent are these perceptions reasonable?

In our view, the United States accepts the average cost option as a reasonable compromise between the other policy options on both equity and efficiency grounds. We would also hazard a guess that equity issues are the more compelling to the general public, but efficiency arguments are at least considered in most public deliberations on price setting.

Equity Considerations

The interesting equity issue concerns the choice between average cost pricing and marginal cost pricing. U.S. citizens will not willingly permit a private owner to "exploit" a natural monopoly position and earn monopoly profits. Dissatisfaction in the United States over public price increases that are ostensibly justified by cost increases is often severe. One can well imagine the public's outrage over a charge of profiteering at the public's expense.

Perhaps the outstanding example of the government hedging against profiteering occurs in defense contracting.[12] Complex weapon systems routinely experience huge cost overruns. One of the more obvious reasons why is that the government negotiates cost-plus-fixed-fee contracts through the research and development stages of the production cycle, so that there is little incentive for contractors to hold down cost. An equally obvious solution is to insist on fixed-fee contracts from the beginning, but given initial uncertainties over cost and quality parameters the government has been willing to use them only sparingly. Apparently, the federal government considers the risk of huge profits (and huge losses) for its few large weapons suppliers less acceptable than the cost overruns, despite incessant public disfavor with the latter.[13]

Although the defense contractors are not decreasing cost industries, the same principle undoubtedly applies to the decreasing cost services as well. The fear of the private owners profiteering at the public's expense is probably

---

[12] The classic references on defense contracting are M. Peck and F. Scherer, *The Weapons Acquisition Process: An Economic Analysis*, Division of Research, Graduate School of Business Administration, Harvard University, Boston, MA, 1962; F. Scherer, *The Weapons Acquisition Process: Economic Incentives*, Division of Research, Graduate School of Business Administration, Harvard University, Boston, MA, 1964.

[13] The same issues are being revisited in the debate over the best way to provide health care. The fee-for-service payment for hospitals and physicians has undoubtedly coontributed to the steady rise in medical costs. The HMO single-payment alternative does better at containing costs, but critics complain that the HMOs cut corners on care to increase the profits of their investors.

sufficient to rule out the private monopoly option. One might argue that a natural monopoly would not fully exploit its monopoly power knowing that excessive profits would not be tolerated. For example, although ticket prices are usually raised for important sporting events (e.g., baseball's World Series, football's Super Bowl), public pressure clearly keeps owners from setting even higher, market-clearing prices. In any event, average cost pricing avoids profiteering, at least in principle. As a practical matter, it is questionable whether a monopoly such as a public utility can be effectively regulated to avoid all monopoly profit.

The more subtle question is why governments favor average cost over marginal cost pricing, despite the obvious efficiency advantages of the latter. We believe the answer lies in the public's belief in the benefits-received principle of taxation or public pricing, a principle that was first discussed in Chapter 6 in the context of paying for nonexclusive goods.

Recall that the benefits-received principle is commonly accepted as an equity principle[14] which, broadly interpreted, states that consumers should pay for a public service in direct proportion to the benefits they receive. A natural corollary is that those who receive no benefits should not have to pay for the service. Suppose the government chooses the marginal cost pricing option for a decreasing cost service that it operates or regulates. The marginal cost price itself is consistent with the benefits-received principle: Only users pay the price and more intensive users pay it more often. The problem comes with the subsidy required to cover the losses, which is presumably paid out of general tax revenues. Consumers no longer pay for the full costs of the service in proportion to their use of the service when a substantial portion of the costs are covered by general tax revenues. Contributions to the subsidy are more likely to be proportional to income or consumption than to the use of the service. Worse yet, some nonusers may end up paying part of the costs with their taxes.

As indicated in Chapter 6, the benefits-received principle begs the issue of which benefits the payments ought to be related to. Even so, the easy case decreasing cost services are perfect candidates for pricing according to benefits received. They are exclusive goods for which nonusers can easily be distinguished from users and more intensive users from less intensive users. Moreover, a single price can cover the full costs of the service. Therefore, one could reasonably argue that average cost pricing satisfies the intent of the benefits-received principle, whereas marginal cost pricing does not. If people adopt this point of view and believe that the equity gains from average cost pricing outweigh its efficiency losses relative to marginal cost pricing, then average cost pricing is entirely reasonable.

---

[14] Recall also from the discussion of Chapter 6 that the benefits-received principle is not a valid equity principle within the formal neoclassical model, despite its long standing within the profession.

Economists can easily attack this position by appealing to first-best theoretical principles, but it is not at all clear that the general public will find the economic case very compelling. Recall that the economic argument runs as follows. The benefits-received principle is meant to be applied to all exhaustive or resource-using government expenditures, those undertaken to correct for misallocations of resources within a competitive market system. The public may view it as an equity principle in the sense that it imitates the *quid pro quo* payment mechanism of the free-market system, but its real purpose is to support an efficient allocation of resources, exactly as competitive prices do in markets for which all the technical and market assumptions hold.

For nonexclusive goods, an infinity of payment schemes preserve pareto optimality, but not for decreasing cost services. Only if the benefits-received principle is interpreted to mean marginal cost pricing is its efficiency function upheld. Marginal cost pricing is, of course, also consistent with the equity criterion that it should imitate competitive pricing. Each person is allowed to consume the good until price equals MRS (assume the other good is the numeraire), which in turn is equated to the MRT in production. According to this interpretation, then, payment is related to use only to the point at which price covers marginal cost.

Although the benefits-received principle so interpreted does not cover the full costs of decreasing cost services, this is simply irrelevant. According to first-best theory, payment of the required subsidy through lump-sum taxes depends only on the interpersonal equity conditions of social welfare maximization. It has nothing to do with use or nonuse of the service. Those people who ultimately support these services through lump-sum taxes are simply those who originally have relatively low social marginal utilities of income (i.e., the rich). Conversely, the people whose use of the service is implicitly subsidized by the set of lump-sum taxes and transfers receive implicit subsidies only because they have relatively high social marginal utilities of income (i.e., the poor).

To clarify this point, suppose a decreasing cost service is paid for by an efficient two-part tariff consisting of a marginal cost price for actual use and a one-time, lump-sum fee collected from all actual and potential users of the service.[15] This one-time fee may seem desirable from a benefits-received perspective because the users pay the full costs.[16] But the government's distribution bureau will effectively override the lump-sum payments if they do not square with the interpersonal equity conditions.

---

[15] The one-time fee must be collected from potential users, or an economic choice to use or not use the service would dictate the amount of payment, contrary to the notion of a lump-sum payment. We saw this same problem when considering subsidies for nonpolluting behavior in Chapter 7.

[16] Potential but not actual users can be thought of as purchasing an option to use the service, which, if they pay the fee, must have value to them.

Suppose, for example, that only poor people use rail transit and that the interpersonal equity conditions require a net redistribution from the rich to the poor. The lump-sum user fees drive the social marginal utilities of income of the rich and the poor further apart. The distribution bureau simply offsets this, however, by taking even more income from the rich and transferring it to the poor until their social marginal utilities are equalized. Although the poor users appear to be covering the transit costs, the rich actually are, precisely because they are rich. The interpersonal equity conditions always take precedence in social welfare maximization.

The marginal cost interpretation of the benefits-received principle may be consistent with first-best principles, but the general public is not likely to accept it, especially its equity implications. Subsidizing a public service out of general revenues would undoubtedly be highly unpopular, even though it would permit lower prices for using the service. The benefits-received principle is deeply ingrained as an equity principle in the United States.

In summary, we are quite prepared to admit that an average cost interpretation of the benefits-received principle squares best with the public's notion of equity in the provision of decreasing cost services. First-best theory to the contrary, economists should perhaps concede that average cost pricing has certain appealing equity properties.

Efficiency Considerations

The efficiency advantages of marginal cost pricing over average cost pricing are unambiguous in a first-best environment, since the marginal cost price is pareto optimal. Nonetheless an 'easy case' service at least passes an all-or-none efficiency test if priced at average cost. We saw that operating the service at the breakeven output is preferable to having no service at all. When the average cost pricing philosophy is applied to a 'hard case' service, however, society risks having the service fail even this gross efficiency test.

Strict average cost pricing is impossible in the hard case, of course, because demand is everywhere below average cost. In lieu of covering the full costs, the public may insist on minimizing the deficit as the next-best alternative: If the users cannot cover the full costs of the service, they at least should pay for as much of the costs as possible.

Unfortunately, minimizing the deficit may not be a harmless extension of the average cost principle. The minimum deficit solution may be grossly inefficient (refer to Fig. 9.21).

Minimizing the deficit is the same as maximizing profits in the hard case. Therefore, the level of service that minimizes the deficit is X_{MD}, at the intersection of the MR and MC curve, with a price of P_{MD}. The shaded area is the minimum deficit.

Suppose the service passes the all-or-none test if priced at marginal costs and operated at X_{opt}. Even so, it could fail the all-or-none necessary

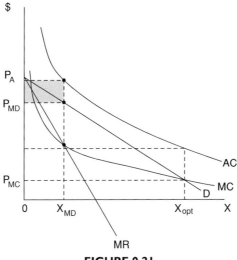

FIGURE 9.21

condition at (P_{MD}, X_{MD}). That is, it is possible for Hicks' Compensating Variation from P_A to P_{MC} to exceed the lump-sum subsidy required to cover the deficit at X_{opt}, whereas the HCV from P_A to P_{MD} fails to cover the deficit at X_{MD}.[17] The mere potential for satisfying the all-or-none test at the optimum is not enough. Unless society actually operates the service at a level sufficient to pass this test, it is simply wasting resources. Minimizing the deficit is not the same principle as maximizing the difference between total benefit and total cost, because total benefit equals total revenue plus the HCV.

Rail transit in a number of urban areas could be an example of the dangers of the minimum deficit philosophy, although we do not know enough about either transit demand or costs to say for sure. Despite numerous fare increases designed specifically to eliminate deficits (presumably demand is inelastic in the relevant range), the deficits persist and, predictably, ridership diminishes. We speculated earlier that rail transit may be an example of the 'hard case' such that no single fare can avoid an operating deficit. In addition, if ridership continues to decline as fares are increased to lower the deficit, the transit system may not be worth operating at all. The trains may run too empty too often.

One can imagine the public outcry at a suggestion to lower fares and incur even larger deficits, even if this were the only way that the transit service could pass the all-or-none test. The general public is unlikely to understand

---

[17] For the purposes of this discussion, assume zero income effects, so that $D^{actual} = D^{compensated}$.

the subtleties associated with the hard case decreasing cost services. Their belief in profitability as the proper guide for the use of scarce resources is deeply held, and understandably so. They see the profitability test applied every day in the marketplace.

REFERENCES

Bator, F. M., *The Question of Government Spending*, Harper Brothers, New York, 1960.

Diamond, P. and McFadden, D., "Some Uses of the Expenditure Function in Public Finance," *Journal of Public Economics*, February 1974.

Hammond, P., "Theoretical Progress in Public Economics: A Provocative Assessment," *Oxford Economic Papers*, January 1990.

Hausman, J., "The Effect of Taxes on Labor Supply," published as a chapter entitled "Labor Supply" in H. Aaron and J. Pechman (Eds.), *How Taxes Affect Economic Behavior*, Brookings, Washington, D.C., 1981.

Peck, M. and Scherer, F., *The Weapons Acquisition Process: An Economic Analysis*, (Division of Research, Graduate School of Business Administration, Harvard University, Boston, MA, 1962).

Scherer, F., *The Weapons Acquisition Process: Economic Incentives*, (Division of Research, Graduate School of Business Administration, Harvard University, Boston, MA, 1964).

Willig, R., "Consumer's Surplus Without Apology," *American Economic Review*, September 1976.

APPENDIX: RETURNS TO SCALE, HOMOGENEITY, AND DECREASING COST

Since *increasing returns to scale* imply *decreasing average cost*, the two terms are used interchangeably in the chapter. To see that the former implies the latter, consider the homogeneous production function:

$$Y = f(X_1, \ldots, X_N) = f(X_i) \tag{9A.1}$$

where $X_i =$ input i, $i = 1, \ldots, N$, and $Y =$ output. By the definition of homogeneous functions,

$$\lambda^\beta Y = f(\lambda \cdot X_i) \tag{9A.2}$$

Increasing returns to scale implies that $\beta > 1$, or a scalar increase (decrease) in each of the factors generates a more-than-proportionate increase (decrease) in output. Furthermore, if the production function is homogeneous of degree β, then the marginal product functions, $\partial Y / \partial X_k \equiv f_K(X_i)$ are homogeneous of degree $\beta - 1$. This follows immediately by differentiating $\lambda^\beta Y = \lambda^\beta f(X_i) = f(\lambda X_i)$ with respect to X_k:

$$\lambda^\beta f_k(X_i) = \frac{\partial f(\lambda X_i)}{\partial X_K} = \lambda f_K(\lambda X_i) \tag{9A.3}$$

Hence:

$$\lambda^{\beta-1}f_K = f_K(\lambda X_i) \qquad k = 1, \ldots, N \qquad (9A.4)$$

To minimize production costs for any given output, the firm solves the following problem:

$$\min_{(X_i)} \sum P_i X_i$$
$$\text{s.t. } Y = f(X_i)$$

The first-order conditions imply:

$$\frac{P_i}{P_1} = \frac{f_i(X_i)}{f_1(X_i)} \qquad i = 2, \ldots, N \qquad (9A.5)$$

The ratio of factor prices equals the marginal rate of technical substitution of the factors in production. Suppose the firm increases (decreases) its use of all factors X_i by the scalar λ. Since $f_i(\lambda X_i) = \lambda^{\beta-1} f_i(X_i)$, this scalar increase (decrease) continues to satisfy the first-order conditions:

$$\frac{f_i(\lambda X_i)}{f_1(\lambda X_i)} = \frac{\lambda^{\beta-1}f_i(X_i)}{\lambda^{\beta-1}f_1(X_i)} = \frac{f_i(X_i)}{f_1(X_i)} = \frac{P_i}{P_1} \qquad (9A.6)$$

Hence, if a vector of inputs $\vec{X_i^*}$ minimizes cost, so too will any vector $\lambda\vec{X_i^*}$. But, if all inputs are increased by the scalar λ, total costs increase by λ and output increases by a factor λ^{β}. Thus, the total cost function must be of the form:

$$TC = kY^{1/\beta} \qquad (9A.7)$$

since $k \cdot (\lambda^{\beta}Y)^{1/\beta} = \lambda \cdot k \cdot Y^{1/\beta} = \lambda \cdot TC$.
Finally,

$$AC = TC/Y = k \cdot Y^{((1/\beta)-1)} = k \cdot Y^{((1-\beta)/\beta)} \qquad (9A.8)$$

Differentiating,

$$\frac{\partial AC}{\partial Y} = \left(\frac{1-\beta}{\beta}\right)k \cdot Y^{((1-\beta)/\beta-1)} < 0, \text{ for } \beta > 1 \qquad (9A.9)$$

Hence, average cost declines continuously as output increases with increasing returns to scale.

10

THE FIRST-BEST THEORY OF TAXATION

Having covered the mainstream normative theory of public expenditures in Chapters 2 through 9, the mainstream first-best theory of taxation is easy to describe. We saw that first-best public expenditure theory addresses two fundamental questions:

1. In what area of economic activity can the government legitimately became involved?
2. What decision rules should the government follow in each area?

In answering these questions, public expenditure theory provides both a complete prescription for government expenditures and a complete normative theory of taxation. There is no first-best theory of taxation distinct from the first-best theory of public expenditures. All we need do is review the main results from the previous chapters.

The first point to recall is that taxes can only enhance social welfare in a first-best environment. They are not at all the necessary evil that the public sometimes makes them out to be. To the contrary, first-best taxes promote the public interest in efficiency and equity as they support society's quest for a social welfare maximum at the bliss point. They have no other purpose in the mainstream first-best theory.

Regarding efficiency, either public expenditure theory describes some particular tax necessary to achieve a pareto-optimal allocation of resources or it does not. If not, then taxes have no further role to play in promoting economic efficiency. For example, we found that exclusive goods that generate either consumption or production externalities can be allocated correctly with a set of Pigovian taxes (subsidies) equal to the aggregate marginal damage (benefit) resulting from the externality. Similarly, decreasing cost services require marginal-cost pricing for pareto optimality. Whether one refers to these publicly set prices as admission "fees,", highway and bridge "tolls," or transit "fares" hardly matters. The marginal cost charges for these services can always be thought of as taxes set according to the competitive interpretation of the benefits-received principle of taxation, the only interpretation consistent with economic efficiency.

One can analyze the efficiency costs of distorting taxation, of course. In fact, the analysis of distorting taxation dates from the very beginnings of modern public finance when taxes received far more attention than expenditures. But distorting taxation is inherently part of second-best theory.

At times first-best public expenditure theory requires certain government expenditures without specifying exactly how to collect the revenues to finance these expenditures. Leading examples are Samuelsonian nonexclusive public goods and subsidies to cover the deficits of decreasing cost services when prices (taxes) are set equal to marginal costs. The only efficiency criterion in these instances is that the taxes be *lump sum* to avoid generating distortions that would prevent the first-best pareto-optimal conditions from holding. Any pattern of lump-sum taxation preserves the efficient allocation of these goods.

As we have also seen, first-best theory solves the problem of how to collect the lump-sum taxes to finance these expenditures. The required taxes (transfers) simply become part of the pattern of lump-sum taxes and transfers that satisfy the interpersonal equity conditions of social welfare maximization of the form

$$\frac{\partial W}{\partial U^h} \frac{\partial U^h}{\partial I^h} = \qquad \text{all } h = 1, \ldots, H$$

where I^h can loosely be thought of as lump-sum income.[1] Whether the requirement of equalizing the social marginal utilities of income is viewed as part of first-best expenditure theory or first-best tax theory is a matter of semantics. Either way, the interpersonal equity conditions are the only equity

---

[1] More precisely, it is a good or factor (presumably the numeraire) singled out for taxation and transfer.

criterion for taxes and transfers in a first-best policy environment. They represent, simultaneously, a complete prescription for the optimal distribution of income and for the optimal redistribution of income when starting from a nonoptimal distribution.

Having considered how taxes and transfers help achieve the pareto-optimal and interpersonal equity conditions of first-best social welfare maximization, mainstream public sector theory has nothing more to say about first-best tax policy.

PUBLIC CHOICE AND PARETO-OPTIMAL REDISTRIBUTION

The policy implications associated with the interpersonal equity conditions are perhaps the least convincing component of the mainstream first-best theory. On the one hand, any tax or transfer that is related to an individual's well being, such as a personal income tax or a means-tested transfer payment, is unlikely to be lump sum. On the other hand, the interpersonal equity conditions rely on the social welfare function which, although a useful analytical construct, is problematic in the extreme as a practical guide to distributional policies. As noted in Chapter 3, there is no convincing theory to determine what the marginal social welfare weights should be, and Arrow proved that a democratic society may not be able to articulate a consistent social welfare function when individuals disagree about the appropriate weights.

Mainstream public sector economists have responded to the difficulties of the social welfare function in one of two ways, for the most part. The first might be called the technocractic response, most closely associated with Paul Samuelson. The idea here is to concede that economic theory has nothing useful to say about the form of the social welfare function. At the same time, an operative social welfare function undoubtedly exists; the ruling politicians are setting their policies with some set of marginal social welfare weights in mind. Therefore, simply ask the policymakers what their social welfare function is and then tell them what the optimal policies are given that function. Economists can solve constrained optimum problems once they know what the objective function is. The second mainstream response, and the more common one, is to retain the social welfare function in normative analysis but use a flexible form of the function that permits a wide range of social welfare weights. The Atkinson and Jorgenson social welfare functions described in Chapter 4 are examples. They each employ Atkinson's aversion-to-inequality parameter, which admits the full range of social welfare weights that people are likely to prefer, from utilitarian indifference to Rawlsian egalitarianism. The idea behind the flexible-form approach is to see how optimal policies vary with the social welfare weights.

A third, and very different, response to the social welfare function comes from the public choice economists following James Buchanan. They are unconcerned about the difficulties surrounding the social welfare function because they reject it out of hand. They see it as an illegitimate construct based on the patently false assumption that people are self-interested in their economic affairs and yet other-interested in their political affairs as they think about an appropriate social welfare function for resolving the distribution question. In their view, people are just as self-interested in their political affairs; they simply do not think in terms of a social welfare function.

The public choice position raises an interesting question. The United States spends approximately $350 billion a year (FY2001) in public assistance to the poor through such programs as Supplemental Security Income (SSI), Temporary Assistance to Needy Families (TANF), Medicaid, Food Stamps, Housing Assistance, and the Earned Income Tax Credit (EITC). Can such a large a public assistance effort possibly be explained without something like an other-interested, politically determined social welfare function? Yes, say the public choice economists. Just think of public assistance as a natural extension of private charity that is undertaken because of certain limitations in private giving. Their view of public assistance is as follows.

Private donations to the poor indicate that people are not narrowly self-interested in their private lives. They do have altruistic impulses toward the poor and are willing to help them. Moreover the private donations meet the test of a policy-relevant, technological consumption externality. The donations result because the plight of the poor directly affects the nonpoor donors (enters their utility functions), and the voluntary donations occur outside the normal market channels. Therefore, the optimal pattern of donations is determined by the standard kind of pareto-optimal conditions that apply to consumer externalities, not by the interpersonal equity conditions of an illegitimate social welfare function. According to the public choice perspective, the quest for end-results equity is entirely subsumed within the quest for efficiency.

Harold Hochman and James Rodgers were the first to formalize the notion of redistributive taxes and transfers from the perspective of a consumer externality. They referred to the optimal policy as a *pareto-optimal redistribution*, a label that has stuck in the literature.[2]

The public choice economists see a distinct advantage in viewing the optimal distribution as an efficiency rule. It presumes that distributional policy is a self-interested gain–gain policy rather than an other-interested,

---

[2] H. Hochman and J. Rodgers, "Pareto-Optimal Redistributions," *American Economic Review*, September 1969.

lose–gain policy, consistent with economic rationality. The taxes and transfers driven by the interpersonal equity conditions of social welfare maximization imply that those who are taxed are willing to lose, to sacrifice some of their own utility for the greater good in supporting the poor. Pareto-optimal redistribution, in contrast, is a gain–gain proposition—the donors gain as well as the recipients. This may seem like an unimportant distinction when donors are altruistic, but there are important differences from a political perspective. A lose–gain policy runs into the difficulties of determining how to compare the losses of the losers with the gains of the gainers. It is also vulnerable to Arrow's Impossibility Theorem in a democracy if people vary in their willingness to sacrifice for the poor. A gain–gain redistribution, in contrast, would presumably receive unanimous consent in a democratic election.

Pareto Optimality and the Overall Distribution of Income

The view of redistribution as a consumer externality applies so long as any concerns about the distribution of income enter into people's utility functions, not necessarily just concerns about the poor. Therefore, let's begin with the more general model of pareto-optimal redistribution specified in terms of the overall distribution, as Hochman and Rodgers did.

To keep the analysis as simple as possible, imagine an exchange economy in which each individual, h, has an endowment of two goods (factors), $\overline{Y}_h$ and $\overline{Z}_h$. The total supply of Y and Z is assumed fixed, equal to $\overline{Y} = \sum_{h=1}^{H} \overline{Y}_h$ and $Z = \sum_{h=1}^{H} \overline{Z}_h$.[3]

Suppose each person's utility is a function of Y, Z, and the distribution of Y among all members of the society. That is,

$$U^h = U^h(Y_h, Z_h, X)$$

where $X = X(Y_h)$ represents an index of the distribution of Y among all H individuals. Assume there is no social welfare function, in keeping with the public choice perspective. Instead, society's goal is to achieve the pareto-optimal allocation of Y_h and Z_h given the total fixed endowments of $\overline{Y}$ and $\overline{Z}$.

The pareto-optimal conditions are derived by maximizing the utility of any one person, say person 1, subject to holding the utility of all other people constant and to the endowment constraints. Formally,

---

[3] There is no need to model production since we are only concerned with distribution rules. Were production included it would have no effect on the optimal distributional decision rules in a first-best economy.

$$\max_{(Y_1, Z_1, Y_h, Z_h)} U^1(Y_1, Z_1, X)$$

$$\text{s.t.} \quad U^h(Y_h, Z_h, X) = \overline{U}^h \qquad h = 2, \ldots, H$$

$$\sum_{h=1}^{H} Y_h = \overline{Y}$$

$$\sum_{h=1}^{H} Z_h = \overline{Z}$$

The corresponding Lagrangian is

$$\max_{(Y_1, Z_1, Y_h, Z_h)} L = U^1(Y_1, Z_1, X) + \sum_{h=2}^{H} \lambda^h \left(U^h(Y_h, Z_h, X) \right) + \pi \left(\overline{Y} - \sum_{h=1}^{H} Y_h \right)$$

$$+ \delta \left(\overline{Z} - \sum_{h=1}^{H} Z_h \right)$$

The first order conditions are

$$Y_1: \quad \frac{\partial U^1}{\partial Y_1} + \frac{\partial U^1}{\partial X} \frac{\partial X}{\partial Y_1} + \sum_{h=2}^{H} \lambda^h \frac{\partial U^h}{\partial X} \frac{\partial X}{\partial Y_1} = \pi \tag{10.1}$$

$$Y_i: \quad \frac{\partial U^1}{\partial X} \frac{\partial X}{\partial Y_i} + \lambda^i \frac{\partial U^i}{\partial Y_i} + \sum_{h=2}^{H} \lambda^h \frac{\partial U^h}{\partial X} \frac{\partial X}{\partial Y_i} = \pi \qquad i = 2, \ldots, H \tag{10.2}$$

$$Z_1, Z_h: \quad \frac{\partial U^1}{\partial Z_1} = \delta = \lambda^h \frac{\partial U^h}{\partial Z_h} \qquad h = 2, \ldots, H \tag{10.3}$$

Dividing Eq. (10.1) or (10.2) by Eq. (10.3), with appropriate selection of h in Eq. (10.3) yields:

$$\frac{\partial U^i}{\partial Y_i} \bigg/ \frac{\partial U^i}{\partial Z_i} + \sum_{h=1}^{H} \left(\frac{\partial U^h}{\partial X} \frac{\partial X}{\partial Y_i} \bigg/ \frac{\partial U^h}{\partial Z_h} \right) = \pi/\delta \qquad i = 1, \ldots, H \tag{10.4}$$

Equation (10.4) has the standard form for a consumption externality. It says that the government should equate each person's personal-use marginal rate of substitution between Z and Y, plus the sum of everyone's marginal rate of substitution between their own consumption of Z and the effect of Y_i on the distributional index X. These rules are identical to the pareto-optimal rules for allocating exclusive pure public goods. The only difference is in their interpretation. They are distribution rules, the optimal policy for redistributing Y across the population. In other words, they are the recipe for a pareto-optimal redistribution.

Note, too, that because the optimal distribution rule is described in terms of marginal rates of substitution (MRSs), it can be achieved by competitive markets for Y and Z buttressed by a set of H personalized Pigovian taxes or subsidies on good (factor) Y:

$$t_i = \sum_{h=1}^{H} \left(\frac{\partial U^h}{\partial X} \frac{\partial X}{\partial Y_i} \middle/ \frac{\partial U^h}{\partial Z_h} \right) \qquad i = 1, \ldots, H^4 \qquad (10.5)$$

The taxes (subsidies) equal the aggregate marginal external effect of an additional unit of consumption of Y by person i, the standard interpretation of a Pigovian tax, with the external effect arising through the concern for the distribution.

The taxes and subsidies would be difficult to implement because the distribution is an example of an individualized externality. In principle, H taxes are required to achieve the pareto-optimal conditions. The policy burden would be lessened, however, if society thought of the distribution in terms of, say, deciles of the population and assumed that everyone within a given decile had the same effect on X.

Pareto-Optimal Redistribution and the Poor

The United States is unlikely to try to implement rules such as Eq. (10.4) because it has never articulated a policy regarding the overall distribution of income. There has always been a concern for helping the poor, however, which reached its zenith in 1964 when President Johnson declared a War on Poverty. The goal of the war effort was nothing less than the eradication of poverty in the United States, a goal that remains elusive. Over 30 million people in the United States live in poverty.

The implications of pareto-optimal redistributions on antipoverty policies are best seen with a simpler version of the general distribution model above. Suppose that society consists of two classes of people, the rich (non-poor) and the poor. The rich are concerned about the economic state of the poor, but are unconcerned about the distribution generally. The poor care only about their own consumption and utility; they have no concerns about distributional matters. A model of this form captures the motivation for private charity towards the poor.

Begin with the simplest possible two-person, two-good endowment model, consisting of one rich person, one poor person, and the two goods Y and F. Y is a composite commodity and F is food. The poor person's utility is a function of his own consumption of Y and F:

$$U^p = U^p(Y_p, F_p)$$

The rich person's utility is a function of her own consumption of Y and F and the poor person's consumption of food:

---

[4] $\partial X/\partial Y_i$ would be positive for some people (i.e., more equalizing) and negative for others (i.e., less equalizing). Z is the numeraire.

$$U^r = U^r\left(Y_r, F_r, F_p\right)$$

That is, when the rich person considers the plight of the poor person, her concern is that the poor person has enough to eat.

The first-order, pareto-optimal conditions for this simple model are easily shown to be

$$MRS^r_{Y_r, F_r} = MRS^p_{Y_p, F_p} + MRS^r_{Y_r, F_p} \qquad (10.6)$$

When the rich person consumes Y and F, only her personal use MRS matters, the left-hand side (LHS) of Eq. (10.6). Her consumption does not generate an externality. When the poor person consumes Y and F, however, two MRSs come into play: his personal-use MRS, the first term on the right-hand side (RHS) of Eq. (10.6), and the rich person's MRS between the poor person's consumption of food and her own consumption of Y, the second term on the RHS of Eq. (10.6). The second term indicates the amount of Y the rich person would be willing to sacrifice for the poor person to consume one more unit of food. The sum of the two terms on the RHS is the full social MRS of the poor person's consumption of Y and F, which must equal the rich person's personal-use MRS for a pareto optimum. The rich person would presumably transfer food to the poor person to achieve the pareto optimum in this simple world. Private charity would suffice without the need for government intervention.

The problems with private charity motivated by altruism arise because there are many rich people who care about the poor person. To see this, expand the model to include many rich people, each with the same utility function defined above. The pareto-optimal conditions for the expanded model are

$$MRS^r_{Y_r, F_r} = MRS^p_{Y_p, F_p} + \sum_r MRS^r_{Y_r, F_p} \qquad \text{all } r \, \varepsilon \, R \qquad (10.7)$$

where R is the set of rich people. The second term on the RHS of Eq. (10.7) is the aggregate marginal external effect on the rich of the poor person's consumption of food.

Condition (10.7) runs afoul of the free-rider problem when altruistic people are otherwise self-serving. Each rich person receives a boost in utility when the poor person consumes another unit of food, regardless of who supplies the food. Therefore, every rich person has an incentive to free ride: Let someone else supply the food and thereby capture the utility gain at no cost. Think of this as altruism without citizenship, again in the spirit of the public choice perspective.

The incentive to free ride drives charity into the public sector in the form of public assistance. The government can achieve the pareto optimum by following the standard Pigovian subsidy prescription for beneficial consumption externalities. Suppose the markets for Y and F are competitive, in line with first-best assumptions, with competitive prices P_F and P_Y, and $P_Y = 1$, the numeraire. The optimal rules for public assistance are as follows. First, have the rich buy food at the competitive price P_F so that $MRS^r_{Y_r, F_r} = P_F$. Second, subsidize the food purchases of the poor person with a per-unit subsidy so that he buys food at the discounted price $P_F - s$, and allow him to consume as much food as he wants at the subsidized price. The poor person consumes Y and F such that his $MRS^p_{Y_p, F_p} = P_F - s$. With $s = \sum_r MRS^r_{Y_r, F_p}$, the Pigovian subsidy, the consumption of Y and F by rich and poor satisfies the pareto-optimal condition, Eq. (10.7). Finally, tax the rich in a lump-sum manner to pay for the food subsidies. Any pattern of lump-sum taxes on the rich maintains the pareto-optimal condition.

The tax-transfer policy of a Pigovian subsidy paid for with lump-sum taxes avoids the free-rider problem by forcing all the rich to participate in the program. Also, since this tax-subsidy policy moves society to the utility-possibilities frontier from somewhere under the frontier, there must exist a pattern of lump-sum taxes on the rich such that every rich person is better off with the policy. The increased utility to them of the poor person receiving more food exceeds the decreased utility from the taxes with the appropriate lump-sum taxes. The rich should not object to being forced to participate in an everyone-gains policy.

The model is easily extended to large numbers of poor and even different classes of the poor, say the near-poor (np), the poor (p) , and the desperately poor (dp). As one possibility, assume that the utility of the rich is

$$U^r\left(Y_r, F_r, F_{np}, F_p, F_{dp}\right)$$

and add the assumption that every poor person within any one class is viewed identically by each rich person. The pareto-optimal policy now calls for three different Pigovian per-unit subsidies, with the subsidies presumably increasing the poorer are the poor.

What Motivates Charity: Should Aid Be In-Kind or Cash?

The model we have been using calls for in-kind food subsidies to the poor because it is the consumption of food by the poor that concerns the altruistic rich. The Food Stamp program could be justified by this kind of model. Other in-kind public assistance programs such as Housing Assistance and Medicaid also suggest an underlying model of this form, with concerns about the housing and medical care of the poor added to the utility function of the rich. Over two thirds of all public assistance in the United States is in-kind, and the in-kind percentage has been steadily increasing over time.

At the same time, however, approximately one third of public assistance is in the form of cash, primarily monthly benefit checks, and cash was the principal means of supporting the poor when the federal government entered the public assistance arena during the Great Depression with the passage of the Social Security Act of 1935. The Act established three public assistance programs: Old Age Assistance, Aid to the Blind, and Aid to Dependent Children (later renamed Aid to Families with Dependent Children, AFDC). These programs gave monthly benefit checks to the poor who were also either elderly, blind, or single parents (primarily widows in 1935). They also provided for payments to vendors of medical care to the recipients. Aid to the Disabled was added in 1951. In 1965, Medicaid consolidated all the medical vendor payments under the original programs and has since greatly expanded. In 1974, the federal government combined Old Age Assistance, Aid to the Blind, and Aid to the Disabled into one federal program, Supplemental Security Income. In 1996, Congress replaced AFDC with TANF.

Explaining monthly benefit payments under the original public assistance programs, and now under SSI, TANF, and the EITC, requires a different model from the one described above. Cash assistance suggests a motivation in which the altruistic rich look at the poor and see that they are lacking all kinds of goods and services, not just food or housing or medical care. They decide that the poor need more income to reach even a minimally adequate standard of living, to be spent as the poor see fit. Returning to the simple two-person model, the utility function of the rich would include the entire utility function of the poor as one of its arguments:

$$U^r = U^r\left(Y_r, F_r, U^p\left(Y_p, F_p\right)\right)$$

The utility of the rich person is greatest when the utility of the poor person is as high as possible for any given amount of aid, and the utility of the poor person is highest with a cash transfer in general, not an in-kind transfer.

Recipients' Preference for Cash

Figure 10.1 illustrates the advantage of a cash transfer from the vantage point of the poor recipient. It assumes that the market prices of F and the composite commodity Y are both equal to one. AB is the budget line of the poor person (P) given his own resources, without any transfer from the rich (R). P is initially in equilibrium at point E on AB and reaches indifference curve I_0. A food subsidy rotates the budget line outward from point A to line AC. P achieves a new equilibrium at point M on budget line AC, reaching indifference curve I_1. At M, P spends GH of his own resources on F and receives a subsidy of HM. The percentage subsidy is $(HM/GM) \cdot 100$.

Compare the in-kind food subsidy HM with a cash transfer equal to HM. The cash transfer causes the budget line AB to shift out parallel by an amount HM, to the new budget line JK. P achieves a new equilibrium at point N on budget line JK and reaches indifference curve I_2.

In general, N contains more Y and less F than M and is on a higher indifference curve, as shown in the figure. The first point follows because the in-kind food subsidy generates a substitution effect in favor of purchasing F that is missing with the cash grant. They both have the same income effect, represented as the value of the transfer HM. The second point follows by a

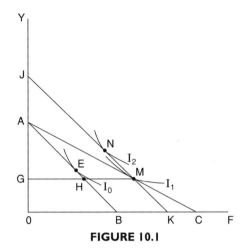

FIGURE 10.1

revealed preference argument. When P purchased the combination of Y and F at N with the cash subsidy, he could have purchased the combination at M; when he purchased the combination at M with the food subsidy, he could not have purchased the combination at N. Therefore, N is revealed preferred to M. Intuitively, P has to bias his purchases toward F to generate the transfer of HM under the in-kind food subsidy, whereas he receives HM under the cash transfer no matter what he buys. The subsidy acts as an additional constraint on P's options and lowers his utility relative to a cash transfer of equal value.

Another way to see that cash is preferred under the new model is to ask how the rich person responds to the poor person's purchases of Y and F. The relevant MRS from the point of view of the rich person is

$$\frac{\partial U^r}{\partial U^p}\frac{\partial U^p}{\partial Y_p} \bigg/ \frac{\partial U^r}{\partial U^p}\frac{\partial U^p}{\partial F_p} = \frac{\partial U^p}{\partial Y_p} \bigg/ \frac{\partial U^p}{\partial F_p} = MRS^p_{Y_p, F_p} \qquad (10.8)$$

the poor person's own MRS. Therefore, the utility of the rich is maximized if the poor person buys Y and F at the going market prices, implying that the transfer should be in cash.

The mixture of in-kind and cash public assistance in the United States gives mixed signals about how the nonpoor view the poor. The in-kind aid suggests that altruistic impulses are moderated by paternalism, that the nonpoor give in-kind aid of basic goods and services because they want accountability for their charity. They fear that the poor would tend to spend cash transfers irresponsibly, against the best interests of themselves and their families.[5] The cash transfers suggest a purer form of altruism, a willingness

[5] The professional literature has analyzed other nonaltruistic reasons for preferring in-kind aid that are based on imperfect information, such as the inability to moniter the behavior of the

to extend the principle of consumer sovereignty to the poor. The non-poor give cash because they believe that the poor, like themselves, are best able to judge their own self interests and will spend any additional income they receive responsibly.[6] Do the nonpoor believe that poor have fundamentally different preferences from them or that they simply have less income? The nonpoor in the United States have not given a clear answer this question.

Limited Aid: Cash-Equivalent In-Kind Transfers

The desire for accountability through in-kind transfers may be difficult to achieve if, as is often the case, the amount of aid per person or family is limited. The model above that justifies in-kind aid calls for unlimited subsidies of F: Let the poor buy as much food as they want at the discounted price. Yet, governments almost always put limits on the amount of aid that can be received.

One reason for limiting aid is budgetary accountability. Refer again to Fig. 10.1. With the unlimited subsidy, legislators cannot know the amount of aid they will be giving until the poor make their spending decisions. In terms of the diagram, the amount of aid HM is unknown until the poor select point M on the subsidized budget line AC. Legislators do not like that kind of uncertainty so they place a limit on the amount of aid to have a better sense in advance what their commitment will be.

A second reason for limits is to avoid the possibility of resales. Under an unlimited-subsidy food stamp program, for example, the poor could buy the stamps at a given discount and resell the coupons to anyone at a slightly higher price, but one that is still well below the market price. The demand for food stamps would be unlimited, a powerful incentive for imposing limits on the amount of stamps any one person can receive. Housing assistance and Medicaid are less prone to resales than food stamps, but the desire for budgetary accountability still applies and leads to limits on these very expensive items.

The problem with placing a limit on in-kind aid is that it can make the in-kind aid equivalent to a cash transfer and undermine the nonpoor's desire for accountability. To see this refer to Fig. 10.2. The figure reproduces the same initial conditions as in Fig. 10.1. The budget line without aid is AB, and the poor person is initially in equilibrium at point E. The government offers a food subsidy at the same rate as in Fig. 10.1 (HM/GM · 100), but this time

---

aid recipients. A world of imperfect information is inherently a second-best environment, so we will consider these other motives for in-kind aid in Chapter 19.

[6] A decidedly less noble spin on the willingness to give cash has been suggested by Gordon Tullock. He argues that giving cash may be motivated out of fear, namely that the poor will rise up against the nonpoor and try to seize their property. The nonpoor respond by trying to buy off the poor with aid, and the most effective way to do this is to maximize the satisfaction of the poor per dollar of aid. That is, give them cash. See G. Tullock, *The Economics of Income Redistribution*, Kluwer-Nijhoff, Boston, MA, 1983, chap. 1.

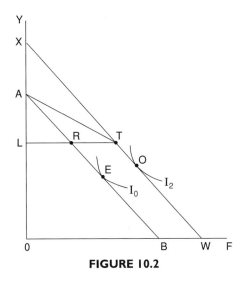

FIGURE 10.2

with a limit on the total amount of aid equal to RT. Once the limit is reached, the with-aid budget line continues parallel to AB at a horizontal distance RT beyond AB. The with-aid budget line is ATW. The poor person reaches a new equilibrium at point O on ATW. Suppose, instead, the government offered a cash transfer in amount RT. This would shift the budget line to XW, and the poor person would again reach a new equilibrium at point O, the same point as with the limited in-kind aid.

Limited in-kind aid is always equivalent to a cash transfer as long as the recipient spends more on the aided item than the total amount spent when the subsidy reaches its maximum. This amount is LT in Fig. 10.2, less than the amount of F purchased at O. Alternatively, in-kind aid is equivalent to cash if *marginal* purchases of the aided item occur at the full market price. This applies to virtually all families who receive food stamps, which is why economists view the Food Stamp program as just another cash transfer to the poor.

The intuition for cash-equivalence is that the substitution effect under the subsidy program ends beyond point T, leaving only the same income effect as under a cash transfer. Therefore, recipients can undo the in-kind condition by reducing expenditures from their own incomes on the aided item until they reproduce what they would have done under an equal-value cash grant. Put differently, limited in-kind aid differs from a cash transfer only if the recipient does not reach the limit—in terms of Fig. 10.2 if the recipient ends up somewhere on line segment AT under the in-kind program. Only then has the in-kind aid imposed some accountability on the poor by biasing their expenditures toward the aided item relative to a cash grant. The bias is due to the substitution effect, which does apply below the limit.

Are Pareto-Optimal Redistributions Enough?

Pareto-optimal redistributions cannot by themselves fully resolve society's quest for distributive justice, for end-results equity. They may be part of the recipe for the optimal distribution, but they cannot be the entire recipe. The reason why not is that a gain–gain redistribution motivated by altruism only serves to restrict the range of the first-best utility possibilities frontier. The efficient pareto-optimal redistribution selects one point on the restricted frontier but, as with all efficiency rules, it cannot judge whether it has chosen the best point on the frontier. Selecting the first-best bliss point still requires a social welfare function.

To see this, refer to the utility possibilities frontier in Fig. 10.3. Suppose the two people whose utilities are pictured in the figure are altruistic toward one another. Begin at point A, at which person 2 has everything. Because person 2 is altruistic, he is presumably willing to transfer some income to person 1. Therefore, both people gain from the transfer and the utility possibilities frontier moves in a northeast direction from A. At some point though, say at point B, person 2 decides that person 1 has enough and is unwilling to transfer more income to her. Any further (forced) transfers are lose–gain propositions, and the utility frontier moves in the usual southeast direction from B. The same argument applies in reverse at point D, at which person 1 has everything. The utility possibilities frontier moves in a northeast direction from D until some point C, when person 1's willingness to transfer to person 2 ends. Any further (forced) transfers from person 1 to 2 are lose–gain propositions, and the utility frontier moves in the usual

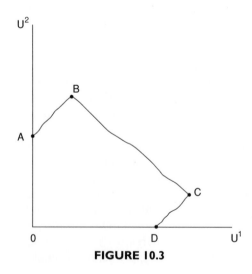

FIGURE 10.3

northwest direction from C. Therefore, pareto-optimal redistribution restricts the utility-possibilities frontier to the line segment BC.[7]

If the economy begins to the left of point B or the right of point C, a pareto-optimal redistribution would bring the economy to B or C. The economy can achieve points between B and C on the frontier starting from other initial distributions, and a pareto-optimal redistribution may or may not be part of the complete set of pareto-optimal conditions on the interior segment.

Which is the best point, the bliss point, on the restricted frontier? Society cannot answer this question without recourse to the social welfare function. The pareto-optimal conditions are never sufficient by themselves to determine which of the efficient allocations is distributionally the best, even if the efficiency conditions themselves imply some redistribution motivated by altruism. It is always the interpersonal equity conditions from social welfare maximization that bring the economy to the bliss point.

Formally, the general equilibrium model described at the beginning of this section would have to be specified as a social welfare maximization in the usual manner to determine the first-best bliss point. The model would then describe two types of redistribution: one pareto-optimal redistribution, either cash or in-kind depending on the nature of the altruism; and one set of lump-sum taxes and transfers of some good or factor to satisfy the interpersonal equity conditions. The two redistributions depend on one another and are determined simultaneously.

An argument can be made that one set of redistributions is enough (namely, the pareto-optimal redistribution), but the argument is not entirely convincing. It presumes, first of all, that society is willing to accept the initial distribution of resources whatever it may be. It also allows the nonpoor donors to have complete say over the amount of distribution that takes place; the poor are effectively disenfranchised in the quest for distributive justice. The poor in such a society may not fare very well if the initial distribution of resources is highly skewed and the nonpoor are not very charitable.

The social welfare function brings two distinct advantages to society's quest for end-results equity: It implicitly gives everyone a vote through the political process on the distribution question, and it adjusts for perceived inequities in the initial distribution of resources through the interpersonal equity conditions. In truth, the social welfare function is not so easy to discard from a normative theory of the public sector, however problematic it may be.[8]

---

[7] This analysis appears in R. Boadway and D. Wildasin, *Public Sector Economics*, second ed., Little, Brown & Company, Boston, MA, 1984, pp. 66–69 and 113–118.

[8] Readers interested in models of altruism might consult E. Ley, "Optimal Provision of Public Goods with Altruistic Individuals," *Economic Letters*, January 1997. Ley cautions against

ALTRUISM, FREE RIDING, AND CROWDING OUT OF PRIVATE CHARITY

The notion of pareto-optimal redistribution has practical as well as theoretical difficulties when private charity and public assistance exist side by side. Gain–gain redistributions motivated by altruism have two very strong properties. One is the powerful incentive for donors to free ride on the gifts of other donors. The other is that public assistance crowds out (reduces) private charity dollar for dollar under altruism. Neither property is even roughly consistent with the facts in the United States.

James Andreoni has developed a simple endowment model with altruism to illustrate the effects of these two properties for large economies. He begins with the case of only private charity and explores the propensity to free ride on the gifts of others.[9]

Do People Free Ride?

Assume a nation of N people in which everyone has the same tastes, with utility defined over a composite commodity good y and the total amount of charitable giving, G:

$$U^i = U^i(y_i, G) \qquad i = 1, \dots, N$$

$P_y = 1$, the numeraire, and a unit of G is \$1, a cash grant. Each person i has an endowment w_i.

Define g_i as person i's own charitable contribution, and G_{-i} as the total charitable contributions of everyone except person i. Assume a Nash environment in which person i takes G_{-i} as given. Under the Nash assumption each person i solves the problem:

$$\max_{(y_i, g_i)} U^i(y_i, G) \qquad \text{equivalently} \qquad \max_{(y_i, G)} U^i(y_i, G)$$

$$\text{s.t. } y_i + g_i = w_i \qquad g_i \geq 0 \qquad\qquad \text{s.t. } y_i + G = w_i + G_{-i} \qquad G \geq G_{-i}$$

Using the equivalent formulation on the right, the demand for G can be written as

---

the potential pitfalls of simple linear utility representations of altruism of the form $V_i = \beta_{ii} U_i + \sum_{j \neq i} \beta_{ij} U_j, \beta_{ij} \geq 0$. To give one example, he considers the case in which utility is a function of one private composite good and one public good and shows that all pareto-optimal allocations in the altruistic economy are pareto-optimal allocations in the egoistic economy in which utility is a function only of one's own consumption. The linear representation of altruism does not buy anything.

[9] J. Andreoni, "Privately Provided Public Goods in a Large Economy: The Limits of Altruism," *Journal of Public Economics*, February 1988.

$$G = \max\{\gamma(w_i + G_{-i}), G_{-i}\} \qquad i = 1, \ldots, N \qquad (10.9)$$

where $\gamma( )$ is i's Engel curve for charitable giving, identical for all individuals. Assume y and G are both normal goods, so that $0 < \gamma' = a < 1$. If person i is at an interior solution, then:

$$G = \gamma(w_i + G_{-1}) \qquad (10.10)$$

Invert γ and then add g_i to both sides to obtain:

$$\gamma^{-1}(G) = w_i + G_{-1} \qquad (10.11)$$

and

$$g_i = w_i + G - \gamma^{-1}(G) = w_i - \phi(G) \qquad (10.12)$$

with

$$\phi(G) = \gamma^{-1}(G) - G \qquad (10.13)$$

Note for future reference that $\phi' = 1/a - 1$, and $\phi^{-1'} = a/(1-a) < \infty$.

Let $w^* = $ the amount of endowment at which the individual is just indifferent between giving and not giving. From Eq. (10.12),

$$g_i = 0 = w^* - \phi(G) \qquad (10.14)$$

or

$$w^* = \phi(G) \qquad (10.15)$$

Therefore, also from Eq. (10.12),

$$g_i = w_i - w^*, \text{ for } w_i > w^*$$
$$g_i = 0, \text{ for } w_i \leq w^* \qquad (10.16)$$

and

$$G = \sum_{w_i > w^*} (w_i - w^*) \qquad (10.17)$$

But, $G = \phi^{-1}(w^*)$ from Eq. (10.15). Therefore,

$$\phi^{-1}(w^*) = \sum_{w_i > w^*} (w_i - w^*) \qquad (10.18)$$

Next consider the average amount of charity per person, H_N, equal to

$$H_N = \phi^{-1}(w^*)/N = 1/N \sum_{w_i > w^*} (w_i - w^*) \qquad (10.19)$$

and ask what happens to the average as N becomes large.

Note, first, that the level of wealth at which an individual is just indifferent to giving varies with N. Thus, the general expression for the average amount of charity per person, H_N, is

$$H_N(s) = \phi^{-1}(s)/N = 1/N \sum_{w_i > s} (w_i - s) \tag{10.20}$$

As N becomes large without limit, total giving $G = \phi^{-1}(s)$ is bounded if wealth is bounded because $\phi^{-1'} = a/(1 - a) < \infty$. Therefore: $H_N(s)$, the average gift per person, goes to zero.

To see what happens to the distribution of giving as N becomes large without limit, define an income distribution density function $f(w)$ over the continuum of individuals. The average gift per person is the expected value over the range of giving, or

$$\lim_{N \to \infty} H_N(s) = H(s) = \int_{s}^{\overline{w}} (w - s)f(w)dw \tag{10.21}$$

where $\overline{w}$ is maximum value of wealth in the economy.

But, the expected value is zero, so that the level of wealth, w^{**}, that divides those who give from those who do not give is the solution to the equation:

$$H(s) = \int_{w^{**}}^{\overline{w}} (w - w^{**})f(w)dw = 0 \tag{10.22}$$

The only solution to Eq. (10.22) is $w^{**} = \overline{w}$: Only the wealthiest individuals give to private charity.

In conclusion, this simple model of altruistic behavior yields two very strong conclusions for large economies:

1. Although total giving, G, grows as the economy grows, the average gift per person goes to zero.
2. Only the wealthiest individuals give anything to private charity; the propensity to free ride is almost universal.

Neither of these conclusions is remotely close to the truth in the United States. Andreoni reports that about 85% of U.S. households donate to private charities. The vast majority of people do not free ride on the gifts of others. Moreover, the average gift per household was $200 in 1971, with a range of $70 per person for those in the lowest fifth of the income distribution to $350 per person for those in the highest fifth of the income distribution. Pure altruism simply cannot explain the pattern of donations to private charity in the United States.

Does Public Assistance Crowd Out Private Giving?

To test the crowding out hypothesis, Andreoni posits a simple form of public assistance operating entirely through the tax system. Donors are subsidized at a rate s to give to charity, with the subsidies paid for by lump-sum taxes, τ, on each individual. Both the subsidy rate and the lump-sum tax can vary by individual. This form of assistance roughly imitates the subsidies to private donations under the federal personal income tax: Taxpayers can deduct a portion of their private donations in computing their taxable income. The net contribution to public assistance by person i, a_i, is the difference between his lump-sum tax and the subsidy he receives on his private donations:

$$a_i = \tau_i - s_i g_i \qquad (10.23)$$

The total amount of public assistance given to charity is

$$A = \sum_i (\tau_i - s_i g_i) \qquad (10.24)$$

Each person's utility is now defined over the composite commodity y and the total amount of private plus public giving, $G + A$. $U^i = U^i(y_i, G + A)$.

Person i now solves the following problem:

$$\max_{(y_i, g_i)} U^i(y_i, G + A)$$

$$\text{s.t.} \quad y_i + g_i + \tau_i - s_i g_i = w_i$$

Alternatively, define the total giving by person i, c_i, as the sum of her private and public giving:

$$c_i = g_i + a_i \qquad (10.25)$$

Then total giving for the entire economy is

$$C = \sum_i c_i$$

Define C_{-i} as the total giving by everyone except person i. Under the Nash assumption, an alternative formulation of the utility maximization problem is

$$\max_{(y_i, C)} U^i(y_i, C)$$

$$\text{s.t.} \quad y_i + C = w_i + C_{-i}$$

Under the assumption that wealth after taxes, $w_i - \tau_i$, is always positive, this problem is identical in structure to the problem above with only private charity, with C replacing G. The economy achieves the same equilibrium and has the same strong free-riding properties.

Adding public assistance does not change the equilibrium because people can adjust their private giving to offset fully any changes in public assistance caused by changes in either taxes or the subsidy rate. Totally differentiate Eq. (10.23) and set $da_i = -dg_i(dc_i = 0)$ to determine how g_i adjusts to hold total net giving constant for changes in τ_i and s_i. In other words: Increases in public assistance crowd out private giving dollar for dollar under pure altruism.

Once again the facts are quite different. Andreoni reported that econometric estimates of the degree of crowding out of private giving by public assistance in the United States ranged from $.05 and $.28 per dollar of public assistance. A more recent estimate by Donald Cox and George Jakubson is also within this range. They found the crowding-out effect of public transfers on private transfers to be around $.12 on the dollar.[10]

Andreoni speculates that other motives besides altruism drive donations to private charity, such as envy, sympathy, a sense of fairness, and a perceived duty to give. His preferred explanation for the large amount of private giving in the United States is what he calls a "warm glow" effect: People simply feel good about the act of giving to private charities, and the presence of public assistance cannot entirely undo this effect.

In conclusion, the public choice model of pareto-optimal redistribution motivated by altruism cannot be a complete model of the optimal distribution of income, either in theory or in practice. It does not remove the need for a social welfare function to answer the end-results equity question of distributive justice, and it cannot provide an explanation of the patterns of private or public charity in the United States. Nonetheless, the concept of a pareto-optimal redistribution is an important contribution to first-best distributional analysis. Charitable impulses that occur independently of any political process or social welfare function are an important phenomenon, and they do have the properties of a consumer externality.

OTHER MOTIVATIONS FOR REDISTRIBUTIVE TRANSFERS

We conclude the chapter with brief discussions of some other motivations for redistributive transfers that appear in the literature.

Public Insurance

Redistributive transfers motivated by a desire for income insurance are consistent with the public choice perspective. Buchanan argued in his Nobel address that the framers of a nation's constitution might permit redistributive public insurance programs such as unemployment insurance and public assistance if they choose to view the future behind a veil of ignorance in which the future is truly uncertain.[11] This vantage point raises the possibility that some of the framers or their descendants may become

---

[10] J. Andreoni, "Warm Glow vs. Cold Prickly: The Effects of Positive and Negative Framing on Cooperation in Experiments," *Quarterly Journal of Economics*, February 1995, D. Cox and G. Jakubson, "The Connection Between Public Transfers and Private Interfamily Transfers," *Journal of Public Economics*, May 1995.

[11] J. Buchanan, "The Constitution of Economic Policy," *American Economic Review*, June 1987.

impoverished, in which case allowing for redistributive public insurance can be viewed as self-serving.[12]

Thomas Husted attempted to distinguish between altruistic and insurance motives for public assistance in the United States on the basis of survey data collected as part of the 1982 American National Election Study.[13] The participants were asked whether spending on food stamps and on AFDC was too much, about right, or too little. Husted hypothesized that the motives for food stamps were likely to be purely altruistic, with accountability. In contrast, the motives for AFDC were likely to be a mixture of altruism and insurance because the majority of the spells on AFDC are very short term, often only a month or two. Using econometric techniques suitable for survey responses (described in Chapter 26), Husted obtained estimates that support his hypotheses. The demand for food stamps was uniformly upward sloping in income, whereas the demand for AFDC was U-shaped in income. An upward sloping relationship between public assistance and income is consistent with an altruism motive. The inverse relationship between AFDC and income at the lower incomes is consistent with an insurance motive among the near-poor.

Husted's interpretation of the insurance motive is reasonable but open to question. One wonders how the poor and near-poor were able to muster support for insurance-based transfers as they tend to have little political influence. A possibility is that the rich also support public assistance at least partially for its insurance properties as Buchanan had suggested, but that the regression equation cannot separate insurance and altruistic motives among the rich.

Social Status

Amihai Glazer and Kai Konrad have raised the possibility that charity may be motivated by the donors' desire to achieve status among their peers rather than from any altruistic or warm-glow feelings.[14] Donors understand that income confers status and that a charitable gift acts as a signal of a person's income. The larger the gift, the larger the presumed income of the donor and the greater the status achieved.

---

[12] This motivation differs from the standard information problems of moral hazard and adverse selection that can undermine the formation of private insurance markets for some contingencies such as ill health and lead to a demand for public insurance. These information problems are second-best instances of market failure. Note that public insurance arising from poor information will also be redistributive, and in a particularly distressing fashion—from the well-behaved to the misbehaving. Simply bringing the insurance into the public sector does not eliminate the moral hazard incentives.

[13] T. Husted, "Micro-Based Estimates of the Demand for Income-Redistribution Benefits," *Public Finance Quarterly*, April 1990.

[14] A. Glazer and K. Konrad, "A Signaling Explanation for Charity," *American Economic Review*, September 1996.

Glazer and Konrad present a model in which individuals' utility is a function of their own consumption and their income as perceived by others, net of their charitable donation. Their perceived income is directly related to the size of their charitable donation. The model can explain a number of features of private charitable giving that pose difficulties for models based on altruism, in particular: why so many people give to charities, why the vast majority of gifts are not anonymous, and why, when charitable organizations report gifts in ranges such as $500–$999, the majority of gifts are bunched at or near the low end of the range.

Status seeking may well be an important motive for private charitable giving but it has difficulty explaining the tolerance for public transfers, which are necessarily anonymous. In any event, charitable gifts motivated by status seeking are obviously self-serving in the extreme.

Equal Access

Edgar Olsen and Diane Rogers have speculated that in-kind transfers may be motivated in part by the idea that people ought to have (approximately) equal access to certain social necessities such as medical care.[15] The call for equal access falls more within the realm of process equity than end-results equity.

Complete equal access would require that each individual's purchase of the social good is subsidized such that everyone can afford the same maximum amount of the good. Think in terms of a two-good model, one the social good (necessity) and the other a composite commodity of all the other goods. Equal access for the social good implies that all budget lines are rotated by the subsidies such that they start at the same point on the social-good axis.

Olsen and Rogers present a model of altruism in which each person's utility depends on own consumption and a function defined over the maximum amount of the social good that each person can consume. The function is zero under equal access and causes reductions in utility that increase with the differences among individuals in their maximum possible consumption of the social good. The government policy is a combination of income subsidies and price subsidies for the social good. One of their central results is that all efficient allocations that are pareto superior to some initial allocation below the utility possibilities frontier reduce the original inequality of access.

REFERENCES

Andreoni, J., "Privately Provided Public Goods in a Large Economy: The Limits of Altruism," *Journal of Public Economics*, February 1988.

[15] E. Olsen and D. Rogers, "The Welfare Economics of Equal Access," *Journal of Public Economics*, June 1991.

Andreoni, J., "Warm Glow vs. Cold Prickly: The Effects of Positive and Negative Framing on Cooperation in Experiments," *Quarterly Journal of Economics*, February 1995.

Boadway, R. and Wildasin, D., *Public Sector Economics*, second ed., Little, Brown & Company, Boston, MA, 1984.

Buchanan, J., "The Constitution of Economic Policy," *American Economic Review*, June 1987.

Cox, D. and Jakubson, G., "The Connection Between Public Transfers and Private Interfamily Transfers," *Journal of Public Economics*, May 1995.

Glazer, A. and Konrad, K., "A Signaling Explanation for Charity," *American Economic Review*, September 1996.

Hochman, H. and Rodgers, J., "Pareto-Optimal Redistributions," *American Economic Review*, September 1969.

Husted, T., "Micro-Based Estimates of the Demand for Income-Redistribution Benefits," *Public Finance Quarterly*, April 1990.

Ley, E., "Optimal Provision of Public Goods with Altruistic Individuals," *Economic Letters*, January 1997.

Olsen, E. and Rogers, D., "The Welfare Economics of Equal Access," *Journal of Public Economics*, June 1991.

Tullock, G., *The Economics of Income Redistribution*, Kluwer-Nijhoff, Boston, MA, 1983.

II

APPLYING FIRST-BEST PRINCIPLES OF TAXATION—WHAT TO TAX AND HOW

Chapter 11 moves from theory to practice. It concludes our first-best analysis with a discussion of the practical problems that legislators and administrators wrestle with in designing broad-based taxes such as income, wealth, sales, and value added taxes. The focus throughout is the extent to which mainstream first-best principles can inform tax policy in the United States.

DESIGNING BROAD-BASED TAXES: THE ECONOMIC OBJECTIVES

Economists have proposed five economic objectives that governments should strive for in designing broad-based taxes:

1. Ease of administration and taxpayer compliance
2. Minimize dead-weight loss
3. Promote long-run economic growth
4. Maintain flexibility
5. Honor society's norms of fairness or equity

The first objective takes precedence in the sense that if a tax does not meet both parts of this objective it simply will not be used. Ease of administration refers to the ability of a department of revenue to collect the taxes due easily and economically, at a small fraction of the cost of the revenues raised. Ease of taxpayer-compliance refers to the taxpayers' ability to understand the tax code and pay the taxes owed with minimal effort, record keeping, and cost. The two are closely related, as taxpayers must be able and willing to pay their taxes for them to be collected easily. The need to satisfy the first objective explains why less developed countries rely mostly on sales taxes, import duties, and other forms of business taxes rather than personal income and wealth taxes to raise revenue. Broad-based personal taxes such as in income tax cannot be used if a large percentage of the population cannot read or write.

Objectives two and three refer to the efficiency properties of taxes, the second to static efficiency, and the third to dynamic efficiency. Regarding static efficiency, we saw in Chapter 2 that buyers and sellers must face the same market prices to achieve the pareto-optimal conditions. Taxes distort markets by driving a wedge between the prices faced by buyers and sellers, thereby generating dead-weight efficiency losses. The goal of tax design is to minimize the dead-weight efficiency losses for any given amount of revenues collected. The dynamic efficiency problem is that taxes may also reduce incentives to save and invest, to the detriment of long-run economic growth. The goal is to maintain incentives for saving and investment to the fullest extent possible. A related problem is to ensure that tax policy keeps the economy as close as possible to the Golden Rule of Accumulation, the capital/labor ratio that maximizes consumption per person for any given rate of growth.

The flexibility objective is usually associated with the macroeconomic stabilization goal of smoothing the business cycle to keep the economy close to its production possibilities frontier. Taxes are the main instrument of fiscal policy. As such, they must be flexible enough to be adjusted up or down as needed to smooth the business cycle.

The final objective calling for equity in taxation is a reminder that taxes must be consistent with society's norms in its quest for end-results and process equity.

Chapter 11 addresses only the final objective of achieving equity in taxation, for two reasons. One is that the pursuit of equity is a fundamental problem for a market economy that even a first-best perspective cannot assume away. The second is that the other tax design objectives are either less compelling or inapplicable in a first-best environment. The static and dynamic efficiency objectives, although very important to the design of broad-based taxes, are necessarily second-best objectives and will be considered in Part III of the text. So, too, will the first objective. Ease of administration is generally not a serious issue for any of the broad-based taxes in the United States. All the major U.S. taxes are collected fairly easily and at very low cost. Taxpayer compliance is an important issue for some of the taxes, with the most serious problems resulting from private information. Taxpayers who are unwilling to pay their taxes may be able to hide information about themselves from the tax authorities. Private information is inherently a second-best issue, however. Finally, the macro flexibility issues are beyond the scope of this text

We have seen in the previous chapters that first-best public sector theory does not provide much guidance to policymakers charged with designing broad-based taxes that the public will view as fair. The prescription for distributive equity in taxation (and transfer payments) is entirely contained within the interpersonal equity conditions for a social welfare maximum, yet these conditions beg the prior question of what the social welfare function should be. We also considered the benefits-received principle of taxation. It appears to have great appeal as a principle of tax equity in the United States, but its role in first-best theory is strictly as an efficiency principle. In any event, the benefits-received principle can only be narrowly applied to certain resource-using expenditures whose pattern of benefits is clearly defined. It cannot serve as the basis for designing broad-based taxes.

As it happens, tax practitioners have never been bothered by the difficulties surrounding the social welfare function or the limitations of the benefits-received principle. Attempts to design fair broad-based taxes have always been grounded in another principle of tax equity called the *ability-to-pay principle*, which dates from the beginnings of modern economics, having first been proposed by Adam Smith in the late 1700s and then further developed by John Stuart Mill in the early 1800s. The only established principle of tax equity before Smith and Mill was the benefits-received principle, which had originated in the 14th and 15th centuries under feudalism. The feudal lords would pay a tribute (tax) to the Crown in return for protection from foreign enemies. Smith and Mill recognized the need for another principle of tax equity for general taxes that were not so clearly tied to particular benefits received by the taxpayers.

The remainder of Chapter 11 focuses on the ability-to-pay principle, indicating how to proceed from the principle to the design of broad-based taxes. The U.S. federal personal income tax will serve as the primary application throughout the chapter. Of all the broad-based taxes, it is the tax most closely grounded in the ability-to-pay principle.

The Smith–Mill ability-to-pay principle and the Bergson–Samuelson interpersonal equity conditions of first-best theory are also compared and contrasted. The older ability-to-pay principle would appear to bear a close kinship to the newer interpersonal equity conditions. The taxes and transfers implied by the interpersonal equity conditions surely depend on individuals' economic well being, that is, on their ability to pay. Even so, the two principles are not as closely related as one might think. They derive from fundamentally different views of taxation and, as such, they do not necessarily imply that the government should collect the same tax revenues from individuals or even use the same taxes.

ABILITY TO PAY: THEORETICAL CONSIDERATIONS

Smith and Mill recognized the limitations of the benefits-received principle as public expenditures became more varied and their benefits more diffused throughout the population. They reacted by introducing the concept of taxes as a necessary evil, a sacrifice that individuals have to make for the common good to support desired public expenditures. Given their perspective, they saw the fundamental question of tax equity as being one of how the government should ask people to sacrifice for the commonweal, the common good. Their answer was that people should be asked to sacrifice in accordance with their ability to pay. In addition, the pattern of sacrifice should honor the two principles of *horizontal equity* and *vertical equity*. Horizontal equity says that equals should be treated equally. Two people judged to have equal ability to pay should bear the same tax burden. Vertical equity allows for the unequal treatment of unequals; that is, two people with unequal abilities to pay can properly be asked to bear unequal tax burdens. This new Smith–Mill ability-to-pay principle was a sacrifice principle, pure and simple. Taxpayers should not expect a *quid pro quo* from general or broad-based taxes, in direct contrast to taxes paid according to benefits received.[1] Ability-to-pay

[1] Adam Smith, *The Wealth of Nations*, E. Cannan, Ed., G. P. Putnam's Sons, New York, 1904, Vol. II, pp. 300–310. John Stuart Mill, *Principles of Political Economy*, W. J. Ashley Ed., Longmans, Green Co., Ltd., London, 1921, p. 804. For an excellent history of the development of ability-to-pay principles, see R. A. Musgrave, *The Theory of Public Finance*, McGraw-Hill, New York, 1959, chap. 5.

was viewed as a default principle, to be used whenever the narrower benefits-received principle could not be applied.

The ability-to-pay principle quickly gained virtual unanimous acceptance as the appropriate equity norm for broad-based tax design. Its intellectual origins were familiar, dating from Aristotle and perhaps even further back, but a huge gap remained in applying the principles of horizontal and vertical equity to the actual design of a tax.

The requirements of horizontal and vertical equity beg two important and difficult questions. The first is the definition of equality: In what sense are two people equal or unequal for the purposes of taxation? Both principles require an answer to this question. The second is the fundamental question in applying vertical equity: How unequally should unequals be treated under the tax laws? This is part of the broader question of end-results equity, or distributive justice, related to the distribution of income.

The quest for horizontal equity in taxation has typically been associated with the goal of defining the *ideal tax base*. A person's tax liability is computed by multiplying a tax rate times the tax base. Therefore, two people with the same value of the tax base necessarily pay the same tax and are treated equally in terms of taxation. The ideal tax base applies to vertical equity as well, since it defines the extent to which people are judged to be unequal for purposes of taxation.

Once the ideal tax base has been determined, the quest for vertical equity is then concerned with the design of the *tax structure*, which has two main components. One is the pattern of rates to be applied to different levels of the tax base. The second is the pattern of allowable exemptions, deductions, credits, and other adjustments to the tax base in computing the tax liability. These adjustments are justified in terms of promoting certain social goals that the government deems important. Two examples under the federal personal income tax are the personal exemptions that prevent the poor from having to pay taxes, which are permitted in the name of equity, or the deduction of interest payments on mortgages, which are permitted to encourage home ownership.

Two Preliminary Considerations

Two points should be noted before turning to the ideal tax base and tax structure. The first point is the fundamental difference in perspective between the Bergson–Samuelson interpersonal equity conditions of first-best theory and the Smith–Mill ability-to-pay principle. The taxes called for by the interpersonal equity conditions are inherently viewed as a good in and of themselves, since the interpersonal equity conditions are one of the two sets of first-order conditions necessary for maximizing social welfare. They promote social welfare by helping society reach the best distribution of income or utility on the utility possibilities frontier. Taxes are not at all the necessary evil that Smith and Mill saw them to be. This sharp difference in perspective helps to explain why these two theoretical principles do not necessarily imply the same taxes, even if the taxes required by the interpersonal equity conditions are levied on the basis of ability to pay. We will return to this point after developing the implications of the ability-to-pay principle for the design of taxes.

The second point is that the ability-to-pay principle can properly be considered part of first-best theory. Ability-to-pay as a sacrifice principle relates specifically to the goal of distributive justice. Second-best tax theory is concerned, first and foremost, with the efficiency costs of distorting taxation. In a many-person second-best environment, efficiency considerations must be tempered by the equity implications of alternative distorting taxes, so that second-best theory has an interest in ability-to-pay principles. But the principles themselves have nothing whatsoever to do with questions of efficiency. Hence, ability-to-pay principles are analyzed most conveniently in a first-best environment, one in which efficiency and equity issues are separable. This is precisely what happened in the professional literature.

Careful distinctions between first-best and second-best analysis are a fairly recent phenomenon, but it is clear that early ability-to-pay theorists were implicitly assuming a first-best environment. We have two clues on this. The first is that the ability-to-pay literature generally ignores efficiency considerations altogether. This would be impossible in a second-best framework. The second is that ability-to-pay theory has traditionally equated tax payments with tax burdens. This, too, implies a first-best environment, for reasons that can only be sketched at this point in the text.

Tax incidence theory, the subject matter of Chapter 16, distinguishes between the burden of a tax (who sacrifices as a result of the tax) and the impact of a tax (who physically pays the tax—writes the check—to the government). We were careful earlier when defining horizontal and vertical equity to refer to "tax burdens." This is not always done. The two principles are often defined in terms of "tax payments" as follows:

- *Horizontal equity:* Equals should pay equal taxes.
- *Vertical equity:* Unequals should pay unequal taxes.

The difference is significant. Tax incidence theory shows that under certain conditions in a first-best policy environment, lump-sum tax payments are an appropriate measure of individual welfare losses, or burdens, using standard willingness-to-pay criteria such as Hicks' Compensating or Equivalent Variations. With distorting taxes, however, the tax payments are never entirely accurate measures of welfare loss. These points are fairly subtle and will be discussed in detail in Chapters 13 and 16. What matters here in terms of the ability-to-pay principles is that equal tax payments may yield unequal burdens with distorting taxes simply because of the distortions. Alternatively, unequal tax payments may entail equal burdens. Hence, once the possibility of distorting taxation is recognized, horizontal and vertical equity must be more broadly defined in terms of tax burdens, as we have done. Conversely, equating tax payments with tax burdens must imply both a first-best policy environment *and* lump-sum taxation.

We will adopt a first-best framework and equate tax payments with tax burdens to focus strictly on the equity issues involved with the ability-to-pay principles. This is at best an uneasy convenience, however. The problem is that the ability-to-pay principles lead to choices of broad-based taxes that are almost certainly not lump sum, so that it is impossible to ignore distortions entirely. In particular, the federal personal income tax contains a number of second-best distortions whose equity implications can only be understood in terms of the broader tax-burden interpretation of horizontal and vertical equity. Thus, we will occasionally stray from the first-best assumptions.

HORIZONTAL EQUITY

From Horizontal Equity to the Ideal Tax Base

Mainstream public sector economists do not agree on which tax base best satisfies the principle of horizontal equity. They do agree, however, on the proper way to think about what the ideal tax base should be. The line of reasoning from horizontal equity to the ideal tax base always relies on the same three principles of tax design. The disagreement occurs in applying the third principle, which describes the final step to the tax base.

The Three Principles of Tax Design

People Bear the Tax Burden

The first principle of tax design is that people ultimately bear the burden of any tax no matter what is actually taxed. For example, corporate income taxes and sales taxes are levied on business firms in the United States, but the fact that a business firm pays $X million in taxes is of little consequence. The interesting questions in terms of tax equity are which people finally bear the burden of these taxes. Is some or all of the burden "passed forward" to the consumers of the final product through higher prices, "passed back" to labor employed by the firm through lower wages, borne by the stockholders of the firm, or borne by third parties not directly associated with the firm? Social well being is directly related to individuals' utility functions, not to production relationships, and any tax eventually burdens people in their roles as consumers or as suppliers of factors, or both.

Individuals Sacrifice Utility

The second principle of tax design is that individuals ultimately sacrifice utility when they pay general taxes, so that the ideal tax base would be individual utility levels. In 1976, Martin Feldstein clarified what horizontal equity must mean to mainstream, neoclassical economists.

FELDSTEIN'S HORIZONTAL EQUITY PRINCIPLE: *Two people with the same utility before tax must have the same utility after tax.*

This is the only sensible economic interpretation of equal treatment of equals under a sacrifice principle of taxation.

Feldstein also proposed a minimum condition for the unequal treatment of unequals—no reversals—that has also gained universal acceptance among neoclassical economists.

FELDSTEIN'S VERTICAL EQUITY PRINCIPLE (NO REVERSALS): *If person i has greater utility than another person j before tax, then person i must have greater utility than person j after tax.*[2]

Feldstein's two principles can only be guaranteed if utility is the tax base.

The Ideal Tax Base as the Best Surrogate Measure of Utility

Taxing utility is impossible, of course, but it still serves as a goal to strive for. Therefore, in lieu of taxing utility, the third principle of tax design is that the tax base should be the best practical surrogate measure of utility. Under this "ideal" tax base, the best surrogate for utility, two people with an equal value of the tax base are equals and should tax pay the same tax. This is as close as the tax practitioner can come to Feldstein's principle of equal utility before tax: equal utility after tax in the quest for horizontal equity.

Mainstream economists agree on the three principles, but they have not reached a consensus on what constitutes the best surrogate measure of utility. The two main contenders are income and consumption.

Haig–Simons Income

Neither Smith nor Mill was able to produce a convincing argument for an ideal tax base from their ability-to-pay principles. The first proposed tax base that caught on appeared over 100 years later, in the 1920s and 1930s. Robert Haig of Columbia and Herbert Simons of Chicago, following the line of reasoning above, independently concluded that a certain broad-based measure of income was the ideal tax base.[3] Their proposal was almost universally

[2] M. Feldstein, "On the Theory of Tax Reform," *Journal of Public Economics*, July–August 1976. Feldstein's no-reversals principle is more than an equity principle. It also has important efficiency implications in a second-best world of imperfect information in which the government might not know how well off certain people are. Some people would have a powerful incentive to hide private information about themselves if the tax laws permitted reversals of utility. We will return to this point in Chapter 15 when analyzing optimal second-best taxes.

[3] H. C. Simons, *Personal Income Taxation*, University of Chicago Press, Chicago, 1938; R. M. Haig, "The Concept of Income: Economic and Legal Aspects," in R. M. Haig, Ed., *The Federal Income Tax*, Columbia University Press, New York, 1921.

adopted, and "Haig–Simons income" remained essentially unchallenged among mainstream economists as the best surrogate measure of utility until the 1960s, when consumption began to gain favor as a better surrogate measure. The majority of mainstream economists today may view consumption as the better choice.

Haig and Simons argued that purchasing power is the best surrogate measure of utility. This led them to propose income defined as the *increase in purchasing power during the year* as the ideal tax base for a tax levied annually. Using standard national income accounting terminology, Haig–Simons income can be defined as:

$$\text{Haig–Simons income} \equiv \text{consumption} + \text{the increase in net worth}$$

Consumption is the additional purchasing power actually taken, and the increase in net worth is additional potential purchasing power that has been deferred for future consumption. Net worth can be increased either by new saving or by an increase in the value of the individual's assets existing at the beginning of the year, the individual's *capital gains*. Therefore,

$$\text{Haig–Simons income} \equiv \text{consumption} + \text{saving} + \text{capital gains}$$

or

$$\text{Haig–Simons income} \equiv \text{personal income} + \text{capital gains}[4]$$

Haig–Simons income is also called the *accretion standard* or, more commonly, the *comprehensive tax base*, a label so widely used now that it is often just referred to by the initials CTB.

Having determined that Haig–Simons income is the best surrogate measure of utility, horizontal equity is then defined as follows:

Horizontal equity: Two people with identical amounts of Haig–Simons income are equals and should pay the same tax.   ∎

Similarly, two people with different amounts of Haig–Simons income are unequals and should pay different taxes by the principle of vertical equity. The difference in their taxes depends on the tax structure applied to Haig–Simons income.

The Sources and Uses of Income

All components of Haig–Simons income are equivalent in terms of increasing purchasing power, so that the sources of income should not affect the amount of tax paid. The uses of the income are also irrelevant to the tax payment. Therefore, distinctions of the following kind should *not* matter in computing a person's tax liability, although they happen to matter

---

[4] Notice that the Haig–Simons definition uses personal income rather than disposable income because the former includes personal income taxes which are originally part of the tax base.

under the federal personal income tax (violations of the Haig–Simons stand-ard under the federal personal income tax are noted in brackets).

Sources of Income:

1. Whether income is derived from personal income or capital gains. [Capital gains are taxed at a substantially lower rate.]

2. Whether personal income is earned (wages, rents, etc.) or unearned (transfer payments). [Many transfer payments are untaxed, such as public assistance.]

3. Whether income is received in cash or in kind. [Many fringe benefits received by employees are untaxed, such as employer contributions to pensions and insurance.]

4. Whether earned income derives from labor, capital, or land. [Interest income on many forms of saving for retirement are exempt from income tax, such as the interest on Individual Retirement Accounts (IRAs).]

Uses of Income:

1. Whether income is consumed or saved. Both consumption and saving increase utility. In terms of tax policy, the only relevant consideration is the increase in purchasing power, whether realized currently as consumption or postponed through saving. [Income used to purchase IRAs and some other retirement accounts is deductible from income in computing taxable income.]

2. Within capital gains, whether a gain is realized by selling an asset or simply accrues in value without a sale. Allowing gains to accrue is merely one particular form of saving. Also, capital losses should be fully offset against other income. [Capital gains are taxed only when realized, and there is only partial offset of capital losses.]

3. Consumption choices are also irrelevant, since all consumption decisions are viewed as voluntary and thereby utility-increasing. These include contributions to private charities and tax payments to other governments to pay for the services they offer. [The following expenditures are deductible from income in computing taxable income (sometimes above some minimum level): medical expenses, contributions to charities and other nonprofit institutions such as colleges, state and local income and property taxes, and interest on a first mortgage.]

The only legitimate deduction from Haig–Simons income are expend-itures necessary for earning income in the first place, so-called *business expenses*. Presumably income used in this manner does not represent an increase in utility-enhancing purchasing power.[5]

---

[5] The only issue is what constitutes a legitimate business expense, and this is often fought out in the courts. Purchase of a uniform required for work is deemed a legitimate business expense. Commuting expenses typically are not. They are considered part of the overall consumption package when people choose to live in a particular community.

Real Versus Nominal Income

Haig–Simons income should be indexed for inflation so that inflation alone does not affect a taxpayer's real tax liability. Real income, not nominal income, is the better surrogate measure of the increase in purchasing power during the year. This point is important for an income tax since it taxes income from capital, which can differ greatly in real and nominal terms. Indexing for inflation matters for all sources of income when a tax uses a set of graduated rates that increase with income, as the federal personal income tax does. (The tax rates varied from 0 to 39.6% in 2000). Inflation itself can move a taxpayer into a higher tax bracket and increase the real tax liability. (Only some components of the personal income tax, such as the personal exemptions and the income defining the tax rate brackets are indexed for inflation.)

Other Tax Bases

A final point is that *all* tax bases other than Haig–Simons income are inappropriate because they are not the best surrogate measures of utility. These include: all broad-based taxes such as sales taxes, gift and estate (inheritance) taxes, and value-added taxes; selective excise taxes (except when required by the benefits-received principle); and taxes on specific sources of income, such as the payroll (Social Security) tax and the corporation income tax. Also inappropriate is taxing wealth in any form, such as local property taxes. The increase in purchasing power during the year, not accumulated purchasing power, is the appropriate annual tax base. The flaw with all these other taxes is that they cannot guarantee that two people with the same Haig–Simons income before tax bear the same tax burden as required for horizontal equity. In fact, equals in terms of Haig–Simons income are very likely to be treated unequally under these other taxes.

Criticisms of Haig–Simons Income

Although Haig–Simons income is a reasonable choice for a tax base under the ability-to-pay principle, it could not be expected to gain unanimous acceptance among economists and policymakers, and it has not. Haig–Simons income is vulnerable to both negative and positive attacks. The negative attack is that Haig–Simons income may be a terrible surrogate measure of utility, in which case it loses its appeal as the ideal tax base. The positive attack is simply the belief that there is a better alternative to Haig–Simons income as the ideal tax base. The increasing support among neoclassical economists for consumption or expenditures as the ideal tax base is an argument of this kind. Finally, economists who do not accept the neoclassical perspective are likely to believe that some tax base other than Haig–Simons income is the better alternative.

A Flawed Surrogate Measure of Utility?

The negative view that Haig–Simons income may be a poor surrogate measure of utility is worth some discussion because the same argument can be applied to all proposed tax bases under the ability-to-pay principle. Haig–Simons income does not necessarily suffer relative to other tax bases on these matters. We will simply use it to illustrate the nature of these attacks.

Haig–Simons income is a perfect surrogate measure of utility if people have the same tastes, abilities, and opportunities; otherwise, it may be a very poor surrogate. This is easily seen by means of the simple labor–leisure model in which people exchange hours of leisure for income at a constant hourly wage, w. The budget constraint is

$$Y = w(24 - \text{leisure})$$

where Y is income, w is the hourly wage, and there are 24 hours in the day. Labor is the only source of income.

The two panels in Fig. 11.1 illustrate the difficulties with Haig–Simons income (wage income here) when tastes and opportunities differ. Tastes differ in the left-hand panel. One person is a leisure lover with indifference curves given by I_{LL}. The other person is a work lover (relatively speaking) with indifference curves given by I_{WL}. They face the same wage rate, w, the slope of the budget line. The diagram is meant to indicate that they have the same utility before tax because they reach the same numbered indifference curve, I^2. Therefore, they should have the same utility after tax by the principle of horizontal equity. But they have different incomes, Y_{LL} and Y_{WL}, so that

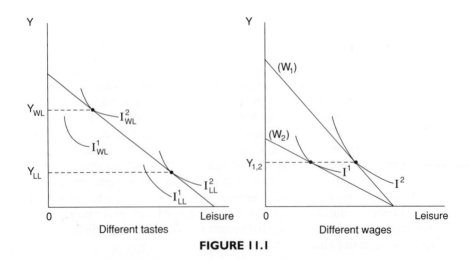

Different tastes   Different wages

FIGURE 11.1

they would pay different taxes with Haig–Simons income as the tax base. Consequently, their after-tax utilities may well differ, in violation of horizontal equity.

Opportunities differ in the right-hand panel. The two people, 1 and 2, have the same tastes but face different wages, w_1 (the steeper slope) and w_2. The person facing the higher wage w_1 is assumed to take all the additional purchasing power as increased leisure, to sharpen the point about income as a surrogate measure of utility. Person 1 is clearly better off, but they both earn the same income and therefore pay the same tax. Unequals are treated equally, in possible violation of both horizontal and vertical equity.

The failure of Haig–Simons income as a surrogate measure of utility in these examples is that it captures only one of the two variables that confer utility. The narrowness of income would not matter if the two people were identical in every respect. It would then be a perfect surrogate for utility. These points are not peculiar to (Haig–Simons) income; they apply as well to anything chosen as the tax base. Income, consumption, or any component of income or consumption serves as a perfect surrogate for utility when people are identical in every respect, providing it is something purchased or earned by everyone (as opposed to an either/or choice of, say, a house or an apartment, which otherwise identical people may choose with indifference). Conversely, any one item that generates utility can be wide of the mark as a utility surrogate when tastes, abilities, and/or opportunities differ, because then all items may matter in comparing utility.

A Better Alternative to Haig–Simons Income?

Is there a better alternative to Haig–Simons income as the ideal tax base for broad-based taxes? Many economists would say that there is.

To begin with, nonmainstream economists would not necessarily accept the three principles of tax design above as the path to the ideal tax base. Marxist economists, for example, would surely opt for differential treatment of wage and profit income for reasons that have nothing to do with surrogate measures of utility. As another example, Nicholas Kaldor is credited with the first serious proposal for a consumption or expenditures tax. He favored consumption not because of its relation to individual utility but from a broader social perspective. Kaldor agreed that consumption and saving are both self-serving choices by individuals designed to increase their utility, either now or in the future, but he argued that society can meaningfully distinguish between the two, as follows. When individuals consume they use up scarce resources for their own personal satisfaction, to the sacrifice of others' well-being. In contrast, when individuals save they provide funds for investment that leads to a more productive economy, to the potential future benefit of all citizens. Therefore, Kaldor argued that society can properly discriminate against consumption in taxation even if taxes are based on a sacrifice principle, providing sacrifice is viewed from a social rather than an individual perspective.[6]

Consumption or Expenditures as the Preferred Alternative

The growing support among neoclassical economists for consumption or expenditures as the ideal tax base is in part based on Kaldor's argument. The only twist is that Kaldor's argument is seen today as a dynamic efficiency argument, not an equity argument. Simple, stylized, overlapping generations models with perfect foresight that track the economy out for 100 periods and more find that replacing an income tax with a consumption tax leads to huge steady-state increases in output per person. Some models report increases on the order of 10 to 20%. The increased output results from the increase in saving, investment, and productivity under the consumption tax, exactly as Kaldor argued. This is seen as a powerful efficiency argument in favor of a consumption tax.

Many neoclassical economists add to this efficiency argument an equity argument that follows the standard three-step argument to an ideal tax base. They accept Feldstein's principle of horizontal equity—equal utility before tax, equal utility after tax—and the notion that the ideal tax base is the best surrogate measure of utility. But, they part company with the traditional Haig–Simons conclusion because they believe that the proponents of Haig–Simons income have the time frame wrong.

The break with the traditional view began in the 1960s following the development of Friedman's Permanent Income Hypothesis and Modigliani–Brumberg's Life Cycle Hypothesis (LCH), which themselves broke from the traditional Keynesian view of the consumption decision. The new theories viewed consumers as determining their consumption decisions over a longer period of time than a single year, indeed, over an entire lifetime in the case of the Life Cycle Hypothesis.

The newer mainstream view of the ability-to-pay principle was that taxation should also be viewed in a lifetime context. Haig–Simons income is flawed as the ideal tax base because it relates only to a single year. Feldstein's equal utility before tax/equal utility after tax is the correct principle, but it should be applied to lifetime utility, appropriately discounted to present value: Two people with equal present value of lifetime utility before tax should have equal present value of lifetime utility after tax. Therefore, the ideal tax base is the best surrogate measure of (discounted) lifetime utility.

The lifetime perspective argues for consumption, not income, as the ideal tax base by the following line of reasoning. The act of consumption is most closely related to the generation of utility. The Haig–Simons proponents have to think in terms of purchasing power because they adopt an annual perspec-

---

[6] N. Kaldor, *An Expenditure Tax*, George Allen & Unwin, Ltd., London, 1955.

tive in which some purchasing power can be saved for future consumption. This is unnecessary in a lifetime perspective, however, because all income is eventually consumed (counting bequests to heirs as the final act of consumption). People receive income over their lifetimes in three forms: labor market earnings, inheritance, and other transfers from individuals and government.[7] They eventually consume all the their income (again, counting the final bequest) such that the lifetime budget constraint holds: The present value of lifetime income equals the present value of lifetime consumption.[8]

From a lifetime perspective, therefore, the best surrogate for the present value of lifetime utility is the present value of lifetime consumption. Consequently, horizontal equity requires that two people with identical present value of lifetime consumption before tax should have the same present value of lifetime consumption after tax. If taxes were levied on a lifetime basis it would not matter whether consumption or income was the tax base, because the present value of lifetime consumption and income are equal. But taxes are levied on an annual basis, and this matters. Only an *annual* consumption tax can guarantee that two people with the same present value of lifetime consumption before tax have the same present value of lifetime consumption after tax.

An annual income tax breaks the equality between lifetime (discounted) consumption before and after tax because it effectively taxes saving twice. The income out of which the saving occurs is taxed, and any returns to the saving are also taxed. In other words, the pattern of consumption and saving matters in determining after-tax lifetime (discounted) consumption under an annual income tax, but not under an annual consumption tax. The following simple example illustrates this point.

Consumption Versus Income Taxes: An Example

Suppose that two people each live for two periods and earn a fixed amount of income Y in each period. Person 1 consumes the entire amount of income each period. Person 2 saves all of the first-period income and consumes everything in the second period. The savings earn a rate of interest, r, the same rate that the people use to discount their second period income and consumption to present value.

The top half of Table 11.1 gives the present value of lifetime consumption before tax, which is equal for both people. Under an annual consumption tax

---

[7] Income from capital is not a source of lifetime income, at least not in an expected present value sense. Income from capital is expected to grow at the same rate of return, r, that is used as the discount rate to compute the present value of income. Therefore, any savings out of three sources of lifetime income cannot grow in expected present value terms. Saving only changes the timing of consumption, not the overall present value of consumption, from a lifetime perspective.

[8] In fact, most people lead virtually self-contained economic lives. The vast majority of people inherit very little wealth, which is the same as saying that most people bequeath very little wealth to their heirs.

TABLE 11.1

	Period 1 consumption	Period 2 consumption	Present value of lifetime consumption before tax
Person 1	Y	Y	$Y + Y/(1 + r)$
Person 2	0	$Y(1 + r) + Y$	$[Y(1 + r) + Y]/(1 + r)$ $= Y + Y/(1 + r)$

	Tax payments (income tax)		Present value of lifetime tax payments (income tax)
	Period 1	Period 2	
Person 1	$t_y Y$	$t_y Y$	$t_y[Y + Y/(1 + r(1 - t_y))]$
Person 2	$t_y Y$	$t_y Y + t_y r Y(1 - t_y)$	$t_y[Y + Y/(1 + r(1 - t_y)) +$ $rY(1 - t_y)/(1 + r(1 - t_y))]$

levied at rate t_c, the present value of lifetime taxes is the same for both people: Taxes$_{PV} = t_c[Y + Y/(1 + r)]$. The only difference is that person 1 pays the tax in two installments and person 2 pays the tax all at once in the second period. Their present values of consumption are the same after tax, as required for horizontal equity.

The present value of taxes differs under an income tax at rate t_y, however, as illustrated by the bottom half of Table 1.1. Notice first, that the discount rate changes from $(1 + r)$ to $(1 + r(1 - t_y))$ under an income tax because interest income is taxed. The double taxation of saving occurs because the income of person 2 is taxed first period, so that only $Y(1 - t_y)$ is available as saving for second period consumption, and then the interest on the saving is taxed again (assumed to be taxed in the second period here). The taxing of the interest income is what drives a wedge between the present value of taxes for the two people. Horizontal equity is thus violated under an annual income tax. The two people have equal present value of consumption before tax but unequal present value of consumption after tax.

The simple example also illustrates two ways to make an income tax equivalent to a consumption tax. One possibility is to allow taxpayers to deduct saving from income in computing their taxable income. This is an *expenditures tax*, which would be levied exactly as the personal income tax but with a deduction allowed for saving in computing taxable income. Since income is taxed only if consumed, an expenditures tax is the same as a consumption tax. In terms of the bottom half of Table 11.1, the deduction of saving removes the first period tax from person 2 and also removes the tax on the interest income until it is consumed. With accumulating interest untaxed until consumed, the relevant discount factor reverts to $(1 + r)$, and the income tax with the savings deduction is fully equivalent to the consumption tax (assuming $t_y = t_c$).

The second possibility is to remove the double taxation of saving by allowing the taxpayer to deduct all interest income in computing taxable income (in general, any returns to saving/income from capital, whatever its form). This deduction also causes the discount rate to be $(1 + r)$ and removes the second tax term in period 2 for person 2. The income tax and consumption tax are once again equivalent.

Note finally, that an expenditures tax is equivalent to a tax on wage income in this simple example because it is an income tax in which all income from capital is deductible. As this text is being written, some members of Congress are proposing a vastly simplified U.S. personal income tax code along the lines of a 1983 proposal by Robert Hall and Alvin Rabushka in their book *Low Tax, Simple Tax, Flat Tax*.[9] Hall and Rabushka proposed a single-rate tax that could be filled out on a postcard: The taxpayers list their wage income, apply the one tax rate, and compute their tax liability. This tax on wage income is much easier to administer and especially to comply with than the equivalent expenditures tax. A pure expenditures tax requires all the record keeping of an income tax to list all sources of income and register all forms of savings, which are deductible from income in computing taxable income.

An expenditures and a wage tax are not equivalent in actual economies, however. The difference is that a wage tax is paid only during the working years, whereas an expenditures tax is paid in all years of life, including the retirement years. Neoclassical overlapping generations (OLG) models show that switching from a wage tax to an expenditures tax increases saving and investment because it hits the retired elderly particularly hard. They paid the wage tax while working and now they have to pay a tax on the consumption during retirement that they are financing from their accumulated savings while working. They also have the highest marginal propensity to consume of all the cohorts. The equivalent taxes in an OLG framework are an expenditures tax and a wage tax that includes a one time capital levy on the retired elderly generation.

TRA86: Income Taxation Versus Expenditures Taxation

The Tax Reform Act of 1986 (TRA86) was the largest single reform of the federal personal income tax ever undertaken. It made significant changes in the definition of taxable income and in the graduated rate structure applied to taxable income. The Reagan administration considered the possibility of replacing the income tax with an expenditures tax when preparing its initial proposal to Congress. The tax at the time was a mixture of the two kinds of

---

[9] R. Hall and A. Rabushka, *Low Tax, Simple Tax, Flat Tax*, McGraw-Hill, New York, 1983.

taxes: essentially an income tax but with many features of an expenditures tax. The most important expenditures tax features were the treatment of various forms of pension savings such as IRA accounts and contributions to employer-sponsored pension plans. Contributions to these accounts and plans are deductible from income when made, and the accrued interest income until retirement is also excluded from taxable income. The pension incomes are taxed when received during retirement. This is exactly how savings of all kinds would be treated under an expenditures tax (provided that the pension income is consumed).

The administration decided to stay with the income tax, in large part because of the administrative headaches involved in switching from an income to an expenditures tax.[10] A particular sticking point was what to do about the elderly. They had already been double-taxed on their nonpension forms of saving. Under the income tax, they are not taxed again when they draw down their savings for consumption during retirement. If an expenditures tax were substituted for an income tax, the elderly would be taxed a third time as they consumed their savings. In truth, the large dynamic efficiency gains of switching from an income to an expenditures tax in an OLG framework come at an enormous cost to one group, the elderly at the time of the switch. Burdening the elderly in this way was naturally considered grossly unfair, yet it was not clear how to protect the elderly (and near elderly) during the changeover.[11]

Haig–Simons Income Versus Expenditures: Musgrave's Perspective

Richard Musgrave believes that economists should call a halt to the income tax versus expenditures tax debate regarding horizontal equity. In his view, either Haig–Simons income or expenditures is an acceptable tax base. Neither one is a perfect surrogate measure of utility, but nothing else is either, and continuing to debate which is the better utility surrogate is pointless. Musgrave believes that vertical equity is far more important than horizontal equity in any event. Distributive justice is less affected by the choice of Haig–Simons income or expenditures as the tax base than by the tax structure applied to either.

According to Musgrave, the most useful way to interpret the call for horizontal equity in taxation is in a legalistic sense, the same way it is applied

---

[10] The expenditure tax treatment of pension savings was retained, however, and still exists today.

[11] The academic debate over income versus expenditures first heated up in the 1970s. See the articles by Richard Goode, David Bradford, and Michael Graetz in *What Should Be Taxed? Income or Expenditure*, J. Pechman, Ed., The Brookings Institution, Washington, D.C., 1980. Goode favors retaining the income tax, Bradford favors the expentifures tax, and Graetz offers an excellent discussion of the practical difficulties of changing from the income tax to an expenditures tax.

in other economic contexts. Equal treatment of equals should simply mean that the tax laws must never discriminate against people in inappropriate ways, such as on the basis of sex or race or religion. Both Haig–Simons income or expenditures are admissible tax bases by this test. Therefore, Musgrave's position is that the federal government should simply choose one of them as the tax base and then worry about the appropriate tax structure.[12]

Horizontal Equity and the Interpersonal Equity Conditions

Neoclassical economists would presumably want a tax designed in accordance with ability-to-pay principles to bear a fairly close relationship with the interpersonal equity conditions, since the interpersonal equity conditions are the ultimate guidelines for end-results equity in first-best public sector theory. Unfortunately, the ability-to-pay principle and the interpersonal equity conditions do not lead to the same pattern of taxation in general, even though the interpersonal equity conditions pay attention to peoples' economic circumstances, their ability to pay. The differences between them begin with the quest for horizontal equity.

Under the ability-to-pay principle, two people are necessarily treated equally if they have the same tastes, abilities, and opportunities. Equal treatment under the interpersonal equity conditions also requires that people be identical over these three attributes but adds a fourth attribute as well: They must have the same marginal social welfare weights at equal levels of Haig–Simons income.[13] Two people with equal utility before tax necessarily have equal utility after tax under the interpersonal equity conditions only if they are equal across all four attributes. Furthermore, if two people with equal utility before tax are not identical over the first three attributes then they are not necessarily treated the same under the two principles even if they have equal marginal social welfare weights.

To illustrate, compare the interpersonal equity conditions and Feldstein's equal-utility-before, equal-utility-after criterion of horizontal equity within the context of a two-person, two-good exchange economy with fixed endowments of the two goods. Let X_{ij} = consumption of good j by person i, for i, j = 1, 2. The first-order conditions for a social welfare maximum in this economy are

$$\textit{Pareto optimality:} \quad \frac{\dfrac{\partial U^1}{\partial X_{11}}}{\dfrac{\partial U^1}{\partial X_{12}}} = \frac{\dfrac{\partial U^2}{\partial X_{21}}}{\dfrac{\partial U^2}{\partial X_{22}}} \tag{11.1}$$

[12] R. Musgrave, "Horizontal Equity, Once More," *National Tax Journal*, June 1990.

[13] For the purposes of this discussion, assume that Haig–Simons income is chosen as the ideal tax base to satisfy horizontal equity and is the item redistributed lump sum to satisfy the interpersonal equity conditions.

$$\textit{Interpersonal equity:} \quad \begin{aligned} \frac{\partial W}{\partial U^1} \frac{\partial U^1}{\partial X_{11}} &= \frac{\partial W}{\partial U^2} \frac{\partial U^2}{\partial X_{21}} \\ \frac{\partial W}{\partial U^1} \frac{\partial U^1}{\partial X_{12}} &= \frac{\partial W}{\partial U^2} \frac{\partial U^2}{\partial X_{22}} \end{aligned} \qquad (11.2)$$

If the two otherwise identical people have unequal social welfare weights, $\partial W/\partial U^1 \neq \partial W/\partial U^2$, evaluated at equal utility levels, the equal-utility-before-tax, equal-utility-after-tax criterion is inconsistent with Eq. (11.2), in general. This possibility can arise under an affirmative action policy that corrects for past injustices, as exists in the United States for women and minorities. The social welfare function can incorporate such a policy through the marginal social welfare weights. The ability-to-pay principle cannot because it depends only on individuals' utilities.

Suppose the social welfare weights are equal so that Eq. (11.2) becomes:

$$\begin{aligned} \frac{\partial U^1}{\partial X_{11}} &= \frac{\partial U^2}{\partial X_{21}} \\ \frac{\partial U^1}{\partial X_{12}} &= \frac{\partial U^2}{\partial X_{22}} \end{aligned} \qquad (11.3)$$

Even Eq. (11.3) differs from the horizontal equity criterion if people's tastes and/or initial endowments are unequal. If the two consumers happen to enjoy the same level of utility at an initial pareto optimum before the government redistributes one of the goods to satisfy the interpersonal equity conditions, there is no guarantee they will enjoy equal utility levels after the socially optimum tax and transfer has been effected. The following simple model in which the two people have different tastes provides a counter example. Let:

$$U^1 = X_{11}(3 + X_{12}) + 27$$
$$U^2 = \frac{1}{2} \cdot X_{21}(1 + 2X_{22})$$
$$X_{11} + X_{12} = 10$$
$$X_{21} + X_{22} = 10$$

The reader can verify that an initial equal-utility pareto optimum occurs at:

$$(X_1, X_2)$$

Person 1 $(4, 2.4)$

Person 2 $(6, 7.6)$

The social welfare optimum, satisfying both Eqs. (11.1) and (11.3), occurs at:

$$(X_1, X_2)$$

Person 1   (5, 15/4)
Person 2   (5, 25/4)

with unequal utilities. The difference occurs because the interpersonal equity requires equal after-tax *marginal* utilities, whereas the Feldstein criterion requires equal after-tax utility *levels*. Even ignoring differences in social welfare weights, these two rules are consistent only if preferences and endowments are identical.

The unsettling conclusion is that the ability-to-pay principle of taxation is unlikely to be consistent with the interpersonal equity conditions of social welfare maximization. There are three differences between the two that cannot be fully reconciled.

The most important difference is that the interpersonal equity conditions add a new piece of information, the social welfare function, that is missing from the ability-to-pay principle. This alone is enough to generate inconsistencies between the two principles. The presence of the social welfare function also underscores their fundamentally different views of broad-based taxes: as promoters of social welfare on the one hand and as a necessary evil on the other hand.

A second difference is that horizontal equity under the ability-to-pay principle involves a before and after comparison of individuals' utility *levels*: equal utility before, equal utility after. The interpersonal equity conditions, in contrast, are concerned only with individuals' positions after tax (and transfer), and the comparison is in terms of margins, not levels: equal social *marginal* utilities.

A final, and most striking difference between them is that the quest for horizontal equity under the ability-to-pay principle is concerned with determining the ideal tax base, whereas the choice of the tax base is *irrelevant* under the interpersonal equity conditions. As we saw in Chapter 2, if pareto optimality holds and the interpersonal equity conditions are satisfied for any one good or factor, then the interpersonal equity conditions are automatically satisfied for all goods and factors, as required for a social welfare maximum. Any good or factor can be chosen for lump-sum redistribution; that is, *any* tax base will do. The only concern of the interpersonal equity conditions is vertical equity, the choice of the tax structure to be applied to whatever tax base is chosen. In summary, the ability-to-pay principles and the interpersonal equity conditions are quite different principles of taxation.

The question remains whether the ability-to-pay principle is a useful addition to neoclassical tax theory, given that the interpersonal equity conditions of social welfare maximization are *the* neoclassical statement of distributive equity. Might it not be better for policymakers to announce their preferred social welfare function, design a tax (and transfer) system that roughly corresponds to the requirements of the interpersonal equity conditions, and let citizens judge whether they are willing to accept the policymakers' social welfare function? What is gained by adding a completely different set of equity principles to the design of tax policy? These questions are in the spirit of Musgrave's suggestion to worry much more about the tax structure than the choice of an ideal tax base.

The practical answer appears to be that people are generally satisfied with the ability-to-pay principles. The Bergson–Samuelson social welfare function has had an enormous impact on the economic theory of the public sector but almost no impact at all on the design of broad-based taxes so far as equity itself is concerned. The only impact of social welfare analysis has been on the level of the tax rates, and then only when efficiency considerations are intermingled with equity considerations in a second-best environment. The interaction of efficiency and equity principles in taxation will be discussed in Chapters 14 and 15. The next step in this chapter is to consider the principle of vertical equity.

VERTICAL EQUITY

Once the ideal tax base has been determined, the quest for vertical equity centers on the design of the tax structure. Should the tax be levied at a single rate—a flat tax—or should the rates be graduated, rising with income? Should some minimum amount of income be exempt from taxation (assuming Haig–Simons income is the tax base)? Should taxpayers be allowed to deduct certain items of income or expenditure in computing their taxable income? The answers to these questions determine exactly how unequally unequals are treated under the tax laws, which is the central issue of vertical equity.

Progressive, Proportional, and Regressive Taxes

Actual policy discussions almost never get much further than the debate over whether taxes should be progressive, proportional, or regressive, three very broad indexes of vertical equity. Economists have devised various methods of defining these terms, but the most common definition is in terms of the average tax burden across individuals. Let:

Y_i = value of the ideal tax base for individual i
T_i = burden of the ideal tax on individual i

The average tax burden on individual i is the ratio T_i/Y_i. Rank order individuals on the basis of Y_i and ask how the average tax burden varies as Y_i increases:

The tax is *progressive* if T_i/Y_i increases as Y_i increases.
The tax is *proportional* if T_i/Y_i remains constant as Y_i increases.
The tax is *regressive* if T_i/Y_i decreases as Y_i increases.

A number of points are worth stressing in applying this measure. The numerator should be the tax burden rather than the tax payment if the two differ, because the implicit standard is the relative loss in utility from the tax. By the same token, although the measure can be applied to any tax, the denominator should always be the ideal tax base for the purposes of assessing the vertical equity of the tax. The ideal tax base is the surrogate measure of an individual's utility and not anything else that might happen to be taxed. Additionally, the time frame should correspond to the time frame used to determine the ideal tax base. For example, proponents of Haig–Simons income as the ideal tax base should use it for the Y_i and the annual tax burden of a particular tax for the T_i. Proponents of consumption or expenditures should use the expected present value of lifetime consumption or income for the Y_i and the expected present value of the lifetime tax burden of a particular tax for the T_i.

A final point is that the three broad characterizations of vertical equity are not very limiting. Suppose, for example, that Haig–Simons income is chosen as the ideal tax base and society decides that it wants to collect more taxes from the rich than the poor under the ability-to-pay principle. A wide range of tax structures—progressive, regressive, or proportional—can satisfy the vertical equity criterion of unequal treatment of unequals and collect more taxes from higher income individuals. For example, a tax structure that applies a 10% rate to an income of $50,000 and a 5% rate to an income of $200,000 is regressive. Yet, it collects more tax from the richer individual, in broad concordance with the ability-to-pay principle.

About all one can say with confidence for the United States is that there appears to be an overwhelming consensus in favor of progressive or proportional taxes over regressive taxes. Studies of the overall U.S. tax system tend to show that the burden of all taxes is roughly proportional over all but the lowest income levels, within which they are slightly progressive. The U.S. tax system does not appear to redistribute much purchasing power in and of itself.

Vertical Equity and the Interpersonal Equity Conditions

In principle, the interpersonal equity conditions solve the problem of achieving vertical equity in tax design as part of determining the optimal distribution of income (assuming, again, that Haig–Simons income is the ideal tax base). Suppose that $Y^B = (Y^B_1, \ldots, Y^B_h, \ldots, Y^B_H)$ is the vector of Haig–Simons incomes across individuals before tax and transfer, and $Y^A = (Y^A_1, \ldots, Y^A_h, \ldots, Y^A_H)$ is the vector of Haig–Simons incomes across individuals after taxing and transferring to satisfy the interpersonal equity conditions. The difference between the corresponding elements in Y^B and Y^A defines the exact rate of tax (or transfer) to apply to each individual.

As usual, however, the interpersonal equity conditions are not very helpful to the tax practitioner. In addition to the uncertainties surrounding the social welfare function, the pattern of taxation may require that different tax rates be applied to people with the same Y_h^B if, say, the social welfare function incorporates a policy of affirmative action. Taxing different people differently on some basis other than their incomes may well be illegal in the United States. It also violates Musgrave's interpretation of horizontal equity as a proscription against taxation on the basis of inappropriate personal characteristics, a compelling proscription in matters of taxation.

Finally, we saw in Chapter 4 that attempts to apply the social welfare function typically assume: 1. equal marginal social welfare weights at equal incomes; 2. everyone has the same tastes; and 3. diminishing private marginal utility of income. The implication of the interpersonal equity conditions under these three assumptions is that everyone should have the mean level of income after tax and transfer. Hardly anyone accepts this view of vertical equity, perhaps because it is so difficult to ignore the efficiency implications of leveling everyone's income to the mean.

Sacrifice Principles of Vertical Equity

Public sector economists had long worked on the problem of vertical equity from the sacrifice perspective of the ability-to-pay principle, but without much success until 1988. This line of research had pretty much died out by the 1980s. The main suggestions for vertical equity in the tax literature at that time dated from the late 1800s and early 1900s. Then, in 1988, H. Peyton Young achieved a substantial breakthrough. Building on one of the earlier principles, Young used the methods of cooperative game theory to develop specific recommendations for the tax structure. Young's game-theoretic approach appears to be a promising avenue for future research.[14]

The two long-standing principles of vertical equity in taxation before Young wrote were minimum aggregate sacrifice and equal sacrifice.

Minimize Aggregate Sacrifice

The call to minimize the aggregate sacrifice from taxation came from the utilitarian school led by Jeremy Bentham, which believed that the economic goal of society should be to maximize aggregate happiness or utility. Their social welfare function was the straight sum of individual utilities. With

---

[14] H. Young, "Distributive Justice in Taxation," *Journal of Economic Theory*, April 1988. His companion empirical exercise related to the U.S. personal income tax is H. Young, "Progressive Taxation and Equal Sacrifice," *American Economic Review*, March 1990.

broad-based taxes viewed as a necessary sacrifice for the common good, the corresponding utilitarian goal for tax policy was to minimize the aggregate sacrifice from collecting the taxes. Under the assumptions of identical tastes and diminishing marginal utility of income, aggregate sacrifice is minimized by levying taxes in a top-down, highly progressive manner until the required total tax revenue is collected.

To see this, suppose there are three groups of consumers whose pretax incomes are Y_1, Y_2, and Y_3, with $Y_1 < Y_2 < Y_3$. Incomes are equal within each group. Assume further that their pre-tax marginal utilities of income are, respectively:

$$\frac{\partial U^1}{\partial Y_1} = 10 \qquad \frac{\partial U^2}{\partial Y_2} = 9 \qquad \frac{\partial U^3}{\partial Y_3} = 8$$

reflecting diminishing marginal utility.

If the government wants to collect a given amount of tax revenue, the minimum aggregate sacrifice principle requires that the government tax people in the third group until either their marginal utility rises to 9 or the required tax revenue has been collected. If the first case applies, then the government taxes both the second and third groups until either their marginal utility rises to 10 or the required tax revenue has been collected. If the former applies, then the government taxes all three groups, maintaining equality on the margin, until the revenue requirement has been met. This pattern of tax collections is highly progressive in terms of the tax burdens.

Equal Sacrifice

The other main suggestion called for equal sacrifice in terms of utility, the only debate being whether the government should require equal absolute sacrifice or equal proportional sacrifice. Letting Y_h be pretax income and T_h be the tax for person h, the two candidates are

Equal absolute sacrifice : $U(Y_h) - U(Y_h - T_h) = c$ all $h = 1, \ldots, H$

Equal proportional sacrifice : $[U(Y_h) - U(Y_h - T_h)] / U(Y_h - T_h) = k$
all $h = 1, \ldots, H$

The equal-proportional-sacrifice variation was a modern restatement of Aristotle's belief that proportional taxation was the just way to raise tax revenues.

Neither the utilitarian nor equal-sacrifice versions of vertical equity ever gained much standing among economists as a prescription for the design of a tax structure. One problem at the outset was the cardinality of the measures. The utilitarian prescription relies on diminishing marginal utility, which is neither a necessary nor sufficient condition for diminishing marginal rates of substitution, the condition for a well-behaved consumer indifference map.

Even if marginal utility is diminishing with respect to one utility index, there exists an admissible monotonic transformation of the utility function that leaves demands (and factor supplies) unchanged and implies either constant or increasing marginal utility. That is, given a utility index $\phi(X)$ and its transformation $F[\phi(X)]$, $F' > 0$,

$$\frac{\partial^2 F[\phi(X)]}{\partial X_i^2} = F' \frac{\partial^2 \phi}{\partial X_i^2} + \left(\frac{\partial \phi}{\partial X}\right)^2 F'' \geq 0 \qquad (11.4)$$

is consistent with $\partial^2 \phi / \partial X_i^2 < 0$ for $F'' > 0$.

The same problem plagues the equal sacrifice principles. Equal absolute or proportional sacrifice with respect to $\phi(X)$ does not necessarily imply equal absolute or proportional sacrifice with respect to $F[\phi(X)]$. Needless to say, economists are skeptical of any economic principles based on cardinal utility measures.

Finally, suppose the government picked one cardinal representation of the utility index that satisfies diminishing marginal utility for each person in order to design a tax structure. Unfortunately, the pattern of taxes implied by any of the sacrifice principles could be just about anything. Even the utilitarian tax program need not be progressive. Using a simple general equilibrium model with one good and one factor, Efriam Sadka was able to show that lump-sum taxes consistent with the utilitarian social welfare function would not necessarily be progressive, where factor income is used as the basis of comparison. Whether the taxes are progressive or not turns on a number of parameters, including the elasticity of the consumers' indifference curves between the factor and the good, third derivatives of the utility function, and the like. Certainly no conclusions can be drawn *a priori*.[15]

Young's Prescription for Vertical Equity

H. Peyton Young revived the equal sacrifice ability-to-pay principle of vertical equity by introducing a new and thoroughly modern view of the problem of tax design. Young reasoned that if society views broad-based taxes as a necessary evil, a sacrifice made for the common good, then the levying of these taxes ought to be viewed as a cooperative game played by all members of the society. The design of the tax structure becomes the standard exercise in cooperative game theory of establishing a set of sharing rules for splitting up the profits or costs of the game. In this instance, the design problem is to posit a set of sacrifice principles that society could agree to in the levying of a broad-based tax and see what the principles imply for the tax structure. Arrow used the same cooperative game theory approach in proving his General Impossibility Theorem for social decisions in a democratic society.

[15] E. Sadka, "On Progressive Taxation," *American Economic Review*, December 1976.

Young posited six principles that he thought a democratic society could agree to in the levying of a broad-based tax. He then proved that they imply equal sacrifice in terms of one of two utility functions commonly used in the theory of risk taking. They also imply very simple tax systems.

We will assume that Haig–Simons income has been chosen as the tax base in demonstrating his result. Also everyone is assumed to have the same tastes; individuals vary only in the amount of income they have. We saw that the same-tastes assumption is necessary when selecting a tax base as a surrogate measure of utility. It is also necessary in order to say anything definite about vertical equity.

Young's Six Principles of Taxation

Young proposed the following six principles as the bases for an equitable tax structure:

1. *The consistency principle*—If a method of taxation is considered to be fair for the entire group of taxpayers, then it must also be considered fair for any subgroup of the taxpayers. The force of this principle is to ensure that people cannot alter their tax liabilities simply by joining different subgroups. As such, it satisfies the requirement of coalition stability for solutions of cooperative games. The consistency principle is automatically satisfied if the tax is levied on individuals, since different subgroupings or coalitions of taxpayers cannot possibly alter individual tax liabilities.[16]

2. *Monotonicity*—If the government is forced to increase total tax revenues, then everyone's tax liability must increase. This is the strong version of the principle. The weak version is that if total tax revenues increase, then no individual's tax liability can decrease. The monotonicity principle captures the spirit of ability-to-pay as a sacrifice principle, namely that the taxpayers are all in this game together. Notice that the strong version might not be satisfied by the utilitarian aggregate minimum sacrifice principle with its highly progressive, top–down tax collections.

3. *The composition principle*—The method used to raise a given amount of tax revenue must also be used to raise any increment in tax revenue. In other words, society should stick with the method that it believes is fair. This principle is satisfied by surtaxes, which raise additional revenue by requiring taxpayers to pay an additional percentage of their existing tax liability.

Feldstein's principles of horizontal and vertical equity:

---

[16] It is not satisfied by the federal personal income tax, however, because the IRS cannot decide if it wants to tax on an individual or a family basis. As a result, taxpayers within a family have the option of filing as individuals or pooling their incomes and filing jointly as members of a family. The individual and joint filing income cut-offs at which the different graduated rates apply differ, which means that taxpayers' liabilities can vary if they marry or divorce. Young's principle would permit only individual filing and thereby avoids the marry/divorce problem.

4. *Horizontal equity*—Two people with equal utility before tax should have equal utility after tax.

5. *Vertical equity*—No utility reversals. For any two people, the person with higher utility before tax must have higher utility after tax.

These two principles can also be stated in terms of Haig–Simons income since it is assumed to be an appropriate surrogate measure of utility.

6. *Scale invariance or the homogeneity principle*—Suppose everyone's incomes and the revenue requirement increase by a scalar θ. Then, everyone's tax liability must increase by θ. This principle is standard in income distribution theory, where it is applied to measures of income inequality. The idea is that an index of inequality should be invariant to scalar increases or decreases in everyone's income. It applies to relative tax burdens in this context.

The results of cooperative game theory rely on accepting the underlying principles, which may or may not be persuasive. If a democratic society were to accept Young's six principles of tax design, however, then the results are rather striking. Young proved that the first five principles hold if and only if the tax collections imply equal sacrifice with respect to some utility function, without specifying what that function should be. By adding the homogeneity principle, Young' six principles hold if and only if tax collections imply equal sacrifice with respect to one of two utility functions:

$$U^h = a\ln(Y_h) + b \qquad \text{or}$$
$$U^h = aY^P + b \qquad a, P < 0$$

These are the utility functions commonly used in the theory of risk taking because they exhibit constant relative risk aversion (CRRA), meaning that the elasticity of marginal utility with respect to income is constant (as the reader can easily verify). Equal sacrifice under these two utility functions in turn implies very simple tax functions, the first a proportional tax and the second a progressive tax.

An important point to note before demonstrating Young's results is that the distinction between equal absolute sacrifice and equal proportional sacrifice is irrelevant to modern economic theory. The reason is that equal absolute sacrifice with respect to some utility function, U, is equivalent to equal proportional sacrifice with respect to the function e^U, which is a valid monotonic transformation of U and would have no effect on individual choice. To see this, suppose equal absolute sacrifice exists with respect to U, such that $U(Y_h) - U(Y_h - T_h) = C$. Equal proportional sacrifice with respect to e^U is

$$\left[e^{U(Y_h)} - e^{U(Y_h - T_h)}\right]/e^{U(Y_h - T_h)} = K \tag{11.5}$$

Simplifying Eq. (11.5) and rearranging terms, equal proportional sacrifice implies:

$$e^{[U(Y_h)-U(Y_h-T_h)]} = K + 1 = K' \qquad (11.6)$$

which can only hold if $U(Y_h) - U(Y_h - T_h)$ is constant.

We will consider the sufficient conditions to see what Young's principles imply for the tax structure.[17] The first task is to show that each of Young's first five principles hold if the tax collections satisfy equal sacrifice with respect to some utility function. (Equal absolute sacrifice is easier to work with.) Therefore, suppose $U(Y_h) - U(Y_h - T_h) = C$, for all $h = 1, \ldots, H$, and consider each of the first five principles.

1. *Consistency*—This holds by definition assuming that the tax base is each individual's Haig–Simons income.

2. *Monotonicity*—The strong version of monotonicity must hold under equal absolute sacrifice assuming positive marginal utility of income. Let total tax collections rise and assume person i is taxed more. Then $U(Y_i) - U(Y_i - T_i) > C$. To maintain equal absolute sacrifice, everyone else must pay more taxes to increase their difference between $U(Y_h)$ and $U(Y_h - T_h)$ and restore equal sacrifice.

3. *Composition*—Assume that $U(Y_h) - U(Y_h - T_{1h}) = C$ for given total tax collections T_1. Suppose that tax collections rise to T_2 and equal absolute sacrifice is maintained for the increment of taxes between T_1 and T_2: $U(Y_h - T_{1h}) - U(Y_h - T_{1h} - T_{2h}) = C'$. Adding the two results: $U(Y_h) - U(Y_h - T_{1h} - T_{2h}) = C + C' = C''$. Equal absolute sacrifice is also maintained for the new higher tax collections T_2.

4. and 5. *Feldstein's principles of horizontal and vertical equity*—These two principles must hold under equal absolute sacrifice so long as the marginal utility of income is positive. Regarding horizontal equity, if $U(Y_i) = U(Y_j)$ and $U(Y_i) - U(Y_i - T_i) = C = U(Y_j) - U(Y_j - T_j)$, then $U(Y_i - T_i) = U(Y_j - T_j)$. Regarding the principle of no reversals, if $U(Y_i) > U(Y_j)$ and $U(Y_i) - U(Y_i - T_i) = C = U(Y_j) - U(Y_j - T_j)$, then $U(Y_i - T_i) > U(Y_j - T_j)$. Therefore, equal absolute sacrifice with respect to any valid utility function U satisfies each of Young's first five principles of taxation.

Now add the scale-invariance or homogeneity principle, which generates Young's two proposed tax structures. The sufficient conditions on the tax structures involve two steps. First, determine the tax structure implied by equal absolute sacrifice with respect to the two CRRA utility functions noted above, then show that the tax structures are scale invariant.

Proportional Taxation

Consider the utility function $U^h = a\ln Y_h + b$. Equal absolute sacrifice implies $a\ln Y_h - a\ln(Y_h - T_h) = C$, for $h = 1, \ldots, H$. The left-hand side

---

[17] The necessary conditions are much more difficult to prove and will be left to a reading of Young's paper.

(LHS) is constant at any income if (and only if) $T_h = tY_h$, that is, under a flat-rate, proportional tax:

$$a[\ln Y_h - \ln(1 - t)Y_h] = a \ln(1 - t) = C \qquad (11.7)$$

A proportional tax clearly satisfies the homogeneity principle; the ratio $\theta T_h / \theta Y_h$ is independent of θ. Young's six principles of taxation have resurrected Aristotle's call for proportional taxation, assuming log-linear utility.

Progressive Taxation

Now consider the utility function $U^h = a Y_h^P + b$. Equal absolute sacrifice implies:

$$a Y_h^P - a(Y_h - T_h)^P = C \qquad h = 1, \ldots, H \qquad (11.8)$$

Rearranging terms and solving for T_h yields,

$$Y_h^P - (Y_h - T_h)^P = C/a = -\lambda, \text{ with } a < 0 \qquad (11.9)$$

$$(Y_h - T_h)^P = \left(Y_h^P + \lambda\right) \qquad (11.10)$$

$$T_h = Y_h - \left(Y_h^P + \lambda\right)^{1/P} \qquad (11.11)$$

Under this tax, individual tax collections can be multiplied by a scalar as needed for total revenues. Therefore, the tax is a flat rate tax applied to a tax base in which taxpayers exempt an amount $(Y_h^P + \lambda)^{1/P}$ from their Haig–Simons income (Y_h) in determining their taxable income. The tax has a number of interesting properties.

First, T_h/Y_h is independent of θ. This follows from dividing Eq. (11.11) by Y_h, and noting from Eq. (11.9) that scaling T_h and Y_h by θ scales λ by θ^P.

Second, the tax is progressive in terms of the standard average tax burden measure of progressivity. The average tax burden increases as Y_h increases (divide Eq. (11.11) by Y_h and recall that $P < 0$ and $\lambda > 0$).

Third, and most unusual, the exemption from the income in computing taxable income, $(Y_h^P + \lambda)^{1/P}$, *increases* as income increases. In all actual taxes with exemptions, the exemption either remains constant or decreases as income increases. Even so, the increasing exemption does not prevent the tax from being progressive.

Fourth, the homogeneity principle rules out graduated tax rates (although not progressive taxes).

In conclusion, Young has provided a rationale for either proportional or progressive broad-based taxes using the methods of cooperative game theory. In doing so, he has brought the old equal-sacrifice principle of taxation into the realm of modern economic theory. Whether he has done so successfully depends on a society's willingness to accept his six principles of fair taxation.

Perhaps some other set of sacrifice principles would be viewed as more attractive and imply quite different tax structures.

Vertical Equity in the United States

The five major broad-based taxes in the United States give a mixed reading on how unequally the United States is willing to treat unequals. As we will see in Chapter 17, some of the taxes are progressive and others regressive. One can argue that the federal personal income tax gives the clearest signal of the U.S. view of vertical equity since it is designed on ability-to-pay principles. Unfortunately, it gives mixed signals as well.

The federal personal income tax appears to be fairly progressive on paper, with a graduated rate structure ranging from 10 to 39.6% and a large exemption of the first dollars of income to protect the poor from taxation. It turns out to be much less progressive in practice, however, because capital gains and some other forms of income from capital receive highly favorable tax treatment, in some cases no tax at all. Capital income is highly concentrated among the richer taxpayers.

The recent history of the federal personal income tax has not clarified matters. The Tax Reform Act of 1986 reduced the number and range of the graduated rate schedule from 11 categories ranging from 14 to 50% to three categories ranging from 15 to 33%. The reduction of the top rate to 33% was done in large part to improve the dynamic efficiency of the tax. At the same time, TRA86 sharply increased the personal exemption to protect the poor from taxation. Subsequent reforms under President George Bush's administration lowered the top rate once again, to 28% but then further reforms under President Clinton's administration added new rates on high incomes ranging from 31 to 39.6%. The 2001 George W. Bush tax cut is scheduled to lower the top rate to 35% by 2006.

The message from all these reforms is unclear, except for a desire to protect the poor from taxation. The Earned Income Tax Credit (EITC), which grew rapidly during the 1990s, also greatly reduces the federal tax burden on the poor. At the same time, however, three of the other major U.S. taxes—the federal payroll tax, the state sales taxes, and the local property taxes—do not protect the poor from taxation.

A widely cited study of the U.S. tax system by Joseph Pechman and Benjamin Okner, last updated in 1984, estimated that the overall U.S. tax structure is mildly progressive at the lowest incomes and then roughly proportional over all remaining income levels. The low-end progressivity is due largely to the exemptions under the federal and state personal income taxes. (Other studies have reached approximately the same conclusion.) The U.S. tax system does not redistribute much purchasing power in and of itself.[18]

---

[18] B. Okner and J. Pechman, *Who Bears the Tax Burden?*, The Brookings Institution, Washington, D.C., 1974, p. 10. We will take a closer look at tax incidence studies in Chapter 17.

REFLECTIONS ON THE HAIG–SIMONS CRITERION IN PRACTICE: THE FEDERAL PERSONAL INCOME TAX

Despite its appeal to many public-sector economists, the Haig–Simons income measure has not fared well in the United States. Only the federal and state personal income taxes pay so much as lip service to the Haig–Simons criterion. State governments rely heavily on sales taxes and local governments rely primarily on the property taxes, neither of which is valid according to the Haig–Simons criterion.

State sales taxes may appear to be consistent with the view that consumption is the ideal tax base. In practice, however, sales taxes are far removed from an ideal consumption tax. Sales taxes often exclude broad classes of expenditures from taxation, they usually tax all included items at one fixed rate, and they are levied on businesses. What expenditures tax proponents have in mind is a tax levied on individuals exactly as the federal income tax is, except that it would exclude saving from the tax base. A graduated rate schedule could easily be applied to individual expenditures, removing the stigma from sales taxes that they may be regressive.[19]

The federal personal income tax is the single largest tax in the United States. Of all the broad-based taxes, it comes closest to the Haig–Simons income measure as its tax base, but not really all that close. Recall that, according to the Haig–Simons criterion, the federal income tax base should include personal income and capital gains on assets held from the beginning of the tax year, without regard to the sources or uses of income. The only permitted deductions from Haig–Simons income are legitimate business expenses, meaning expenses required to earn the income. The actual tax base falls far short of the Haig–Simons ideal, both the personal income and capital gains components.

Personal Income

Taxable income is only about half of personal income. The main discrepancies between taxable income and personal fall into three categories: exemptions, exclusions, and deductions.

An *exemption* is income that is recognized as taxable income by the Internal Revenue Service (IRS) but is simply not taxed. The main example is the personal exemption given to the taxpayer and all the taxpayer's dependents. The exemption was $2800 per person in 2000, and it is adjusted each year for increases in the consumer price index (CPI).

Exclusions are sources of income that are counted as personal income by the U.S. Department of Commerce in the National Income and Product

---

[19] This stigma may be more myth than reality. See the discussion in Chapter 17 on the incidence (burden) of the sales tax.

Accounts but are not counted as taxable income by the IRS. The principal exclusions are employee fringe benefits (primarily employer contributions to pension plans [along with the accrued interest on the investments under these plans], health insurance, and life insurance); interest income on Individual Retirement Accounts and Roth IRA Accounts, which are earmarked for retirement income; many federal, state, and local transfer payments; imputed rental income on owner-occupied homes and imputed income on farm produce consumed on the farm; and interest received on state and local bonds, commonly referred to as "municipals."

Deductions are not sources of income at all, but rather certain expenditures that can be deducted from personal income in computing taxable income. The most important itemized deductions are extraordinary medical payments and other uninsured losses, state and local income and property taxes (but not sales taxes), interest payments on mortgages for the principal residence, contributions to charities and other nonprofit organizations, and business expenses. Taxpayers can elect to take a "standard deduction" (equal to $7350 in 2000 for married taxpayers filing jointly) instead of itemizing deductions.

The various exemptions, exclusions, and deductions exist because Congress and the administration cannot avoid the temptation to use the income tax to pursue other social ends, such as protecting low-income families and individuals from taxation, promoting home ownership, helping people save for their retirement years, subsidizing state and local governments, encouraging charitable giving, and so forth. These may all be worthy goals, but they come at a cost. The exemptions, exclusions, and deductions can undermine the horizontal and vertical equity of the tax. They also introduce inefficient distortions into the income tax. (We will return to these points below.)

Capital Gains

The capital gains portion of the tax base is also far from the Haig–Simons ideal. Recall that capital gains should be taxed as they accrue and at the same rate applied to personal income. Also, capital losses should be fully offset against other income because they represent equal dollar decreases in purchasing power. Finally, the tax base should reflect increases in real purchasing power only. Increases in income arising solely from inflation should not be taxed. If nominal income is used as the tax base, then at least all sources of income should be treated equally with respect to the effects of inflation on purchasing power.

Capital gains taxation is deficient on all counts. Capital gains are taxed on a realized basis (that is, only when an asset is sold) and then at a lower rate than the rates applied to personal income (for assets held for more than one year as of 2000; in effect, part of the realized gains are excluded from the tax base). The ability to offset losses against income is mostly limited to offsets against capital gains. Finally, the tax is levied on nominal capital gains, with no adjustment for the effects of inflation on purchasing power. As a result, capital and wage income are treated very differently in times of inflation.

Equity judgments about the income tax would be easiest if Haig–Simons income were the tax base (except for business expenses, which we will ignore from now on). Since Haig–Simons income is assumed to be the surrogate measure of utility, the tax payments themselves would be the appropriate basis for judgment. Horizontal equity would be satisfied if two people with the same Haig–Simons income paid the same tax. Similarly, vertical equity would be appropriately measured by the difference in taxes paid by people with different amounts of Haig–Simons income.

Given the exemptions, exclusions, and deductions, however, the tax payments are no longer accurate measures of either horizontal or vertical equity. The problem is that markets react to any differences from the ideal tax base, and the market reactions have to be factored into any assessment of horizontal and vertical equity. They are sources of gains and losses to the taxpayers that matter every bit as much as the tax payments themselves. Tax burdens, not tax payments, determine the equity of the tax, and Feldstein's versions of horizontal and vertical equity defined in terms of utility are the only appropriate basis of judgment. For example, the proper statement of horizontal equity is that two people with the same utility before tax should have the same utility after tax. That is, they should bear the same tax burden, the same loss of utility.

Unfortunately, judgments based on before and after utility comparisons can be problematic and are likely to confuse the general public. People tend to see the individual incomes and the tax payments, not the additional market-induced gains and losses. As a result, the exemptions, exclusions, and deductions are branded pejoratively as "tax loopholes." People see two taxpayers with the same Haig–Simons income who do not pay the same tax. Even worse, they see higher income people paying less tax than lower income people, an apparent equity reversal. The public's sense of horizontal and vertical equity is offended.

The Taxation of Personal Income: The Tax Loopholes

Not all tax loopholes in the personal income portion of the tax base are equally distasteful. The personal exemptions, for example, do not generate much complaint from the public. Protecting low-income people from taxation is an accepted goal in a nation that has declared a war on poverty. One of the oft-stated criticisms of sales taxes, property taxes, and the payroll tax is that they do not offer such protection. Even proponents of a single, flat-rate income tax favor including a personal exemption for the taxpayers and their dependents.

Exemptions are a simple way to ensure that a tax is progressive, if progressivity is desired. Figure 11.2 illustrates the case of a taxpayer with three other dependents It assumes a flat-rate tax of 18% on all income beyond a personal exemption of $4000, or $16,000 for a family of four ($16,000 was approximately equal to the poverty line for a family of four in 1998). The vertical axis pictures the marginal and average tax rates. The marginal rates are 0 up to $16,000 and 18% thereafter. The average rates are also 0 up to $16,000 but then rise steadily beyond $16,000 as tax payments begin, approaching 18% asymptotically. (For example, at an income of $116,000, the tax is $18,000, and the average tax rate is 18/116 = 15.5%). The tax is progressive by the usual average tax rate measure.

The exclusions and deductions are far more contentious "loopholes," as perhaps they should be. They violate the pattern of vertical equity implicit in the tax structure, and they generate market and other forms of inefficiency. They may not be a source of horizontal inequity, however, despite the common perception that they are. The relationship between tax loopholes and horizontal equity is a particularly subtle issue that illustrates the importance of the market's reaction to the loopholes.

Tax Loopholes, Tax Capitalization, and Horizontal Equity

Consider the three large tax breaks to homeowners relative to those who rent an apartment: the exclusion of imputed rent on the home, the deduction for the interest payments on the mortgage, and the deduction for the local property tax on the home. Figure 11.3 illustrates the market's reaction to the tax break. The left-hand panel depicts the market for owner-occupied homes purchased by people within a certain income range (housing markets

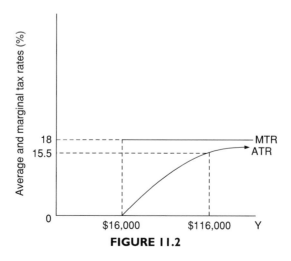

FIGURE 11.2

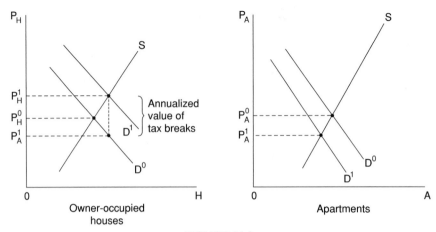

FIGURE 11.3

segment by income.) The right-hand panel depicts the market for rental apartments purchased by people within the same income range. The apartments are assumed to provide the same housing services as the owner-occupied homes, and the people in these markets are assumed to have identical tastes.

The equilibrium before these three tax breaks were introduced into the federal tax is given by the intersection of D^0 and S in each market. Since the housing services are identical, the prices are the same in each market, P_H^0 and P_A^0. (P_H^0 is the annualized price of a home, the implicit rental value). The people are indifferent to owning or renting.

The introduction of the three tax breaks makes the owner-occupied homes more attractive. Demand shifts out in the owner-occupied market and down in the apartment market, driving the (annualized) price of the homes up and the rentals on the apartments down. The new equilibrium occurs at the intersection of D^1 and S in each market, with the new equilibrium prices P_H^1 and P_A^1.

At the new equilibrium, the difference in prices $P_H^1 - P_A^1$ must equal the annualized value of the three tax breaks to the home owner. The market is said to *capitalize* the tax breaks into the relative prices of the two forms of housing. The implication of the market capitalization is that once the new equilibrium has been reached, the people in this income range are once again indifferent to owning or renting. If they choose to buy a house, the higher price less the value of the tax breaks equals the rent they would have to pay for the apartment, P_A^1. This has to be the case, since the housing services are the same for the homes and the apartments, the people have identical tastes, and they are free to purchase a home or rent. Indifference to owning or renting is the only possible long-run equilibrium, regardless of the tax system.

This example illustrates the principle that any two people in these markets who had equal utility before the tax breaks were introduced must have equal utility once the market returns to equilibrium in response to the tax breaks. The tax breaks do not violate horizontal equity in the new equilibrium. The homeowners get the tax breaks but no gain in utility relative to the renters. The same analysis applies to any tax loophole and for the same reason: The value of the loophole is eventually fully capitalized by the market system.

Feldstein summarized this fundamental principle of *tax design* as follows:[20]

> "Once the market system establishes a long-run equilibrium in response to a given tax system, the tax system *per se* cannot be a source of horizontal inequity, where horizontal equity is defined in terms of burden or utility."

A corollary to this fundamental principle of tax design is an equally fundamental principle of *tax reform*:

> "Any reform of an existing tax code will create horizontal inequities through unanticipated gains and losses, and will continue to do so until a new long-run equilibrium obtains in the market place."

Continuing with the housing example, suppose the three loopholes favoring home ownership were suddenly removed in the name of promoting horizontal equity. Assuming the long-run equilibrium had been achieved, current home owners surely lose, but not necessarily because they lose a tax advantage that had been unfairly given them, as the reformers intend. Rather, some of them will lose because they never received any gain in the first place at the higher prices they paid for their homes. These pure losses are an unavoidable consequence of any tax reform that removes the "loopholes."

A final point is that determining who gains from the three tax breaks is difficult once the market has reached its new equilibrium and the homes have changed hands a few times. Tax loopholes can even be capitalized in anticipation of the loopholes, before they become part of the law.[21] In conclusion, simply looking at tax payments gives a very misleading picture of horizontal equity when the tax contains various exclusions and deductions from Haig–Simons income.

---

[20] See M. Feldstein, "On the Theory of Tax Reform," *Journal of Public Economics*, July–August, 1976, pp. 94–97.

[21] For further analysis of the owner-occupied tax breaks that includes supply adjustments, see L. J. White and M. J. White, "The Tax Subsidy to Owner-Occupied Housing—Who Benefits?", *Journal of Public Economics*, February 1977. Boris Bittker tells an amusing anecdote illustrating the principle of capitalization. It concerns an eager young law student who searches in vain for the beneficiary of a tax-sheltered apartment building in his hometown known as Rainbow Gardens. The tax shelter had been in existence since the inception of federal income taxation under the Revenue Act of 1913. Rainbow Gardens was for sale, but the law student

Tax Loopholes, Vertical Equity, and Inefficiency

Although tax loopholes may not be a source of horizontal inequity, tax reformers can still make a good case for removing them. They are likely to give rise to vertical inequities, and they lead to various kinds of inefficiencies. Therefore, the gains to vertical equity and efficiency from removing the loopholes may exceed any temporary horizontal inequities plus the lost benefits associated with whatever social goals the loopholes are trying to promote. This is especially so if there are more effective ways of promoting the social goals.

The housing example above illustrates the possibility of vertical inequity. Both homeowners and apartment renters gain equally from the three tax breaks. Their annual costs fall from $P_A^0 (= P_H^0)$ to P_A^1 because of the tax breaks, whether they own or rent. But, as noted above, housing markets segment by income. It is possible, therefore, that the decrease in their housing costs is greater than the decrease in the housing costs of other people in a lower income range. If so, the larger break to the higher income people is likely to offend people's sense of vertical equity.

Exclusions and deductions always generate this kind of vertical inequity under an income tax with graduated rates. Since the exclusion or deduction is taken off the tax base, it reduces the taxpayer's liability by t cents per dollar of exclusion or deduction, where t is the taxpayer's marginal tax rate. Under a graduated tax, the value of the tax savings rises with income. For example, every dollar given to charity that can be deducted from taxable income costs the taxpayer only $ (1 − t)$. The richer the taxpayers, the lower their costs of contributing to their favorite charity, or church, or school. This is why economists tend to favor tax credits over exclusions or deductions if the tax system is to be used to encourage certain activities. A 10% tax credit is taken directly against the tax liability, after the tax has been computed, so that it is 10% for all taxpayers.

---

quickly surmised that at the asking price he would only realize a normal return on his investment. He also learned that the current owners were selling because they, too, were only able to earn a normal return despite the existence of the tax shelter. The same had been true of the previous owners, and the ones before them, and so on. Alas, they all paid too much to realize an economic profit from the tax shelter. The persistent student was able to trace the line of ownership all the way back to one R. E. Greison, who had purchased Rainbow Gardens in 1896. Greison possessed remarkable foresight. In 1896 he was clerking for a U.S. Supreme Court justice when the Court ruled that a federal income tax was unconstitutional. Greison nonetheless correctly predicted that the Court's decision would eventually be overturned by a constitutional amendment (the 16th), and further that the income tax law, when drafted, would tax shelter apartment buildings. Based on these predictions, Greison bought Rainbow Gardens. Sad to say, the capitalization of the tax shelter predated Greison. His epitaph read: "Sacred to the memory of R. E. Greison, who learned that before every early bird, there is an earlier bird." See B. Bittker, "Tax Shelters and Tax Capitalization or Does the Early Bird Get a Free Lunch," *National Tax Journal*, December 1975.

The housing example also illustrates the market inefficiencies of tax loopholes. As we will learn in Chapter 13, anything that drives a market away from its normal supply and demand equilibrium generates a dead-weight efficiency loss. In the example above, the natural equilibria in the two markets are at the intersection of S and D^0 in the two markets, without the tax breaks. The tax breaks lead to too many homes and too few apartments, with resulting dead-weight efficiency losses in both markets. Tax loopholes inevitably lead markets away from their natural equilibria as the markets capitalize the loopholes. Thus, they necessarily generate efficiency losses (unless supply or demand is perfectly inelastic, which is rare in the long run).

Tax loopholes lead to other inefficiencies as well. Consider the exclusion for interest received on state and local bonds, the municipals. The exclusion acts as a subsidy to the lower-level governments, equal to the reduction in debt service made possible by the municpals' tax-free status, but this is a particularly inefficient form of subsidy from the federal government's point of view. Suppose a state government can offer an interest rate of 8% rather than 10% because of the exclusion, a savings of $20 of interest income on each $1000 bond. The problem is that only investors who can save more than $20 in taxes will purchase the municipals. For example, at the assumed interest rates a person in the 28% tax bracket can earn interest of $80 net of tax on the municipal at 8% but only $72 net of tax on the taxable bond at 10%. Therefore, the U.S. Treasury loses more than $1 in tax revenue for every $1 of interest subsidy received by a state or locality, $28 of lost revenue for a $20 subsidy in this example. In contrast, a direct federal subsidy (grant-in-aid) for capital expenditures would give $1 of subsidy for every $1 of tax revenue collected, a more efficient subsidy from the federal government's viewpoint. Also, the direct subsidy avoids the dead-weight loss inefficiencies in the bond market as the tax break to the municipals is capitalized into a lower interest rate relative to the taxable bonds.

Another source of efficiency gain from removing the loopholes is that the tax becomes much simpler, which saves on administrative and compliance costs. In addition, a broader tax base means that the same tax revenues can be collected with lower tax rates, which sharply reduces the size of the dead-weight loss in the marketplace. We will see in Chapter 13 that the dead-weight efficiency loss from a tax varies directly with the square of the tax rate.

Would the gains to vertical equity and efficiency from removing the exclusions and deductions more than offset any temporary horizontal inequities that may arise and the social benefits of the loopholes? This remains an open question, but many economists favor removing most of the exclusions and exemptions. The economists in the Treasury Department during the Reagan administration put forth such a plan in their proposal for TRA86. The administration's proposal called for almost a textbook version of an income tax based on Haig–Simons income, with little more than the personal exemptions and legitimate business expenses as reductions to the tax base. The administration's proposal could not stand up to the special interest groups favoring the loopholes, however, and all the major exclusions and deductions were retained.

The Taxation of Capital Gains: Inflation Bias and Realization

Two long-standing issues in the taxation of capital gains are that capital gains (and other sources of income from capital) are not protected from inflation in computing taxable income and that capital gains are taxed on a realized rather than an accrued basis. The failure to index income from capital for inflation can lead to a huge bias against income from capital in an inflationary economy, a troubling situation for the United States given its relatively low rates of saving and investment. Taxing capital gains on a realized rather than an accrued basis generates further sources of inefficiencies and vertical inequities. The chapter concludes with a discussion of these two issues.

THE INFLATIONARY BIAS AGAINST INCOME FROM CAPITAL[22]

The U.S. Tax Codes were written for a noninflationary economy. This, in itself, generates an extra tax burden on income from capital relative to wage income, simply because inflation causes nominal asset income to grow more rapidly than nominal wage income. Consequently, equal growth in nominal income from these two sources reflects unequal growth in real purchasing power, so that equal taxation implies unequal treatment, in violation of horizontal equity.[23] The inequity is compounded by the graduated rate schedule, because the artificially expanded tax base of asset income may be taxed at higher rates.

To see how the differential inflation effect arises, suppose an economy has been experiencing inflation since time $t = 0$. Define the accumulated inflation to time t as:

$$I(t) = \exp \int_0^t i(s)ds \qquad (11.12)$$

where $i(t) =$ the instantaneous rate of inflation at time t. Assume further that inflation is fully anticipated so that $i(t)$ represents both the actual and

---

[22] The analysis in this section follows P. Diamond, "Inflation and the Comprehensive Tax Base," *Journal of Public Economics*, August 1975, pp. 228–230.

[23] Vertical equity is also necessarily violated by the inflation bias, presumably in an anti-rich, pro-poor direction. Horizontal equity may not be violated if investments in physical and human capital are perfect substitutes. In that case, the inflation bias would drive investment towards human capital, lowering wages and raising the return to physical capital until the difference just equaled the value of the inflation bias against physical capital.

expected rate of inflation. If W(t) represents wage income at time t without inflation, then:

$$W'(t) = W(t) \cdot I(t) \tag{11.13}$$

is wage income with inflation.

Let Y(t) represent income from capital in the absence of inflation:

$$Y(t) = r(t) \cdot V(t) \tag{11.14}$$

where $r(t)$ = the real rate of return, and $V(t)$ = the value of an asset without inflation. The basis arises because expected inflation affects income from capital in two ways. It increases both the value of assets *and* the rate of return on assets. Let:

$$V'(t) = V(t) \cdot I(t) \tag{11.15}$$

represent the value of assets with inflation, and

$$n(t) = r(t) + i(t) \tag{11.16}$$

represent the nominal rate of return. Hence,

$$Y'(t) = n(t) \cdot V'(t) = [r(t) + i(t)]V(t) \cdot I(t) \tag{11.17}$$

where $Y'(t)$ = income from capital with inflation. Dividing Eq. (11.17) by (11.13), using Eqs. (11.14) and (11.15), and rearranging terms yields:

$$\frac{Y'(t)}{W'(t)} = \frac{(r(t) + i(t)) \cdot V(t) \cdot I(t)}{W(t) \cdot I(t)} = \frac{Y(t)}{W(t)} + \frac{i(t) \, V'(t)}{W'(t)} > \frac{Y(t)}{W(t)} \tag{11.18}$$

Therefore, capital income grows more rapidly then wage income simply because of the inflation factor. If the tax base is nominal income, capital income is overly taxed. By inspection of the right-hand side (RHS) of Eq. (11.18), the inflationary bias can be removed by subtracting from nominal asset income the expected rate of inflation times the value of assets with inflation, $i(t) \cdot V'(t)$, before applying the tax rates.

The inflation adjustment should be applied to all sources of capital income, but the nature of the adjustment varies depending upon the particular form of the asset. For example, if the income derives from an interest-bearing asset, the taxable income should include only the proportion of the interest resulting from the real rate of return. That is, if $Y'(t) = (r(t) + i(t)) \cdot V'(t)$, then

$$Y'(t) - i(t) \cdot V'(t) = r(t)V'(t) \tag{11.19}$$

But,

$$r(t)V'(t) = \frac{r(t)}{n(t)} \cdot n(t) \cdot V'(t) = \frac{r(t)}{n(t)} \cdot Y'(t) \tag{11.20}$$

Thus, the taxpayer would report actual interest payments times the ratio of the real to the nominal rate of return.

For a straight capital gain without interest payments, the taxpayer would increase the purchase price by the accumulated inflation factor before subtracting it from the current value to compute the capital gain. For these assets,

$$Y'(t) = CV - PV \qquad (11.21)$$

where

CV = current value, inclusive of inflation.
PV = original purchase value.

Adjusting $Y'(t)$ yields:

$$Y'(t)_{adjusted} = (CV - PV) - (CV - PV)_{inflation} \qquad (11.22)$$

$$Y'(t)_{adjusted} = (CV - PV) - (PV \cdot I(t) - PV) \qquad (11.23)$$

$$Y'(t)_{adjusted} = CV - PV \cdot I(t) \qquad (11.24)$$

Finally, money holdings would receive a credit equal to $i(t) \cdot V'(t)$, since there is no nominal return from which to subtract this adjustment factor. Diamond recommends ignoring this adjustment on the grounds that the bookkeeping for cash assets would be especially difficult and that the liquidity services from holding cash are untaxed anyway.[24]

These inflation adjustments are correct as given only if inflation is always fully anticipated and all income inflates at the same rate over time. In actuality, of course, neither of these is true, and it is not clear what should be done to correct for discrepancies. As a practical matter, governments would surely have to use actual rather than expected rates of inflation for any adjustment. Economic research has not even been able to determine how inflationary expectations are formed. Yet nominal interest rates and capital values almost certainly adjust to some degree for anticipated inflation. Thus, it is probably more accurate to adjust capital income by some long-run smoothed inflation index than to make no adjustment at all. People who anticipate inflation incorrectly will either make windfall gains or losses relative to the theoretical ideal, but this is unavoidable.

The practical question remains as to which long-run series to use, since assets and other sources of income inflate at different rates. A broad series such as the consumer price index is probably a reasonable choice for practical

---

[24] See P. Diamond, "Inflation and the Comprehensive Tax Base," *Journal of Public Economics*, August, 1975, p. 232.

purposes, although again some people will receive (suffer) windfall gains (losses) in purchasing power relative to the ideal.

TAXING REALIZED GAINS: AUERBACH'S RETROSPECTIVE TAXATION PROPOSAL

Economists have long understood the equity and efficiency problems caused by taxing capital gains on a realized basis rather than an accrued basis. The equity problem is that deferring taxes on the capital gains until they are realized places the government in the position of offering interest-free loans each year to the asset holders. The loans equal the amount of the tax liability that would have been paid on an accrued basis. Since assets that generate capital gains, such as common stocks, are disproportionately held by the rich, the pattern of loans is likely to violate the public's sense of vertical equity. The efficiency problem is that taxing capital gains on a realized basis alters the pattern of buying and selling of assets that would occur if the gains were taxed properly on an accrued basis. By taxing on a realized basis, investors have an incentive to "lock-in" the gains on successful assets (choose not to sell) to defer the tax payment and to sell unsuccessful assets early to deduct the losses against other sources of income. A related inefficiency is the incentive to take income as capital gains to defer the tax, an example being executives who take stock options in lieu of salary.

The inequities and inefficiencies notwithstanding, no one has seriously proposed taxing capital gains on an accrued basis. The difficulty comes with assessing the accrued gains on real assets that are infrequently traded. How much capital gain accrued last year on the house that has not been on the market since 1980 or the painting that has been hanging in the den since 1985? Tax authorities have no good way of estimating the gains (or losses) for these assets. Even if they could evaluate the accrued gains, people whose wealth consisted primarily of real assets may have to sell some of their assets to pay the accrued tax liability. The public would tend to view this as unfair. (An analogous situation is the elderly couple that is forced to sell their house they have lived in for 50 years because they can no longer pay the local property taxes out of their retirement pension.) For all these reasons, capital gains will almost certainly continue to be taxed on a realized basis.

In 1991, Alan Auerbach achieved a substantial breakthrough in solving the problems of taxing gains on a realized basis. He proposed a tax reform that avoids the lock-in and early sales effects by leaving investors always indifferent between: (1) holding an asset for one more period, or (2) selling the asset and investing the after-tax proceeds in a risk-free asset for one period. His proposal also protects the government from making interest-free loans, at least on an expected value basis. The beauty of the Auerbach proposal is its practicality. It continues to tax capital gains on a realized basis and makes use of data that are readily available at the time the asset is sold.

A Two-Period Example

The following simple two-period example provides the intuition for the nature of the realization problem and how Auerbach proposes to overcome it. Consider two options for investing $1 at the start of the first period.

Option 1: Hold the asset for one period, realize the gain at the end of the period, and invest the after tax proceeds in a risk-free asset during the second period.

Option 2. Hold the asset for two periods and then realize the capital gain over the two periods.

Assume:

g = the capital gain during the first period
i = the one-period return on the risk-free asset
r = the (uncertain) capital gain during the second period
t = the income tax rate

Option 1: Sell and Invest Risk Free

The value of the asset at the end of the first period is $(1 + g)$. The realized gain g is taxed at rate t, leaving net of tax proceeds of $[1 + g(1 - t)]$ to be invested in the risk-free asset during the second period. The proceeds grow at rate i, and the interest is taxed at rate t. Therefore, the net-of-tax value of the asset at the end of period 2 is

$$[1 + g(1 - t)][1 + i(1 - t)]$$

For comparison with option 2, rewrite the net-of-tax value as:

$$[(1 + g) - tg][(1 + i) - it] =$$
$$[(1 + g)(1 + i)] - t[(1 + g)i + g(1 + i(1 - t))]$$

The first bracketed term is the gross-of-tax value and the second bracketed term is the tax liability.

Option 2: Hold for Two Periods

The value of the asset at the end of period 2 is $(1 + g)(1 + r)$, and a tax is paid on the capital gain, leaving a net-of-tax value at the end of period 2 equal to:

$$[(1 + g)(1 + r)] - t[(1 + g)(1 + r) - 1] =$$
$$[(1 + g)(1 + r)] - t[(1 + g)r + g]$$

In comparing the two outcomes, note that r is an uncertain return at the end of period 1. Assume that the certainty equivalent of r is i. That is, investors are indifferent between investing at the uncertain return r or the certain return i.[25] Under this assumption, the certainty equivalent net-of-tax value of option 2 is

$$(1 + g)(1 + r) - t[(1 + g)i + g]$$

Thus, option 2 is more valuable by the amount $(tg)i(1 - t)$, equal to the after-tax interest on the portion of the accrued tax liability that is avoided by taxing the capital gain on a realized basis. The tax savings can be thought of as an interest-free loan by the government of (tg) made at the end of period 1. The taxpayer invests the loan risk free at rate i during the second period, pays a tax on the interest at rate t, and pays back the principal on the loan, for a net gain of $(tg)i(1 - t)$, the after-tax interest on the loan.

The value to the asset holder of taxing on a realized basis follows the same pattern for any number of periods. The value equals the net-of-tax interest on the current value of the taxes that would have been collected each year if capital gains were taxed on an accrued basis. (Note that the tax is paid once, when the asset is sold. The deferred tax liabilities, the "loans," accumulate at untaxed interest until the sales date.)

The Vickrey Proposal

In 1939, William Vickrey proposed the following tax on capital gains to remove the interest-free loan advantage from taxing on a realized basis: Tax the gain in the final period on a realized basis, and add to the tax the interest on the current value of accrued tax liabilities to date, with the interest being tax deductible.[26] The combined tax plus interest payment would make asset holders indifferent at any given time between holding the asset for one more period or selling the asset and investing the after-tax proceeds in a risk-free asset.

Under the Vickrey scheme, the instantaneous *increase* in the tax at time s if the asset is held one more period is, in general,

$$\dot{T}_s = i(1 - t)T_s + tr_sA_s \tag{11.25}$$

where:

T_s = the current value of the accumulated deferred tax liabilities to date at time s

r_s = the gain in period $s + 1$

A_s = the current value of the asset at time s

In terms of the two-period example above, s is the end of period 1, $T_s = gt$, and $tr_sA_s = tr(1 + g)$.[27]

---

[25] $i = E[r]$ under risk neutrality.

[26] W. Vickrey, "Averaging Income for Income Tax Purposes," *Journal of Political Economy*, 47, June 1939, 379–397.

[27] The part of the realized tax liability gt in the two-period example is the tax on the first-period gain. It is not part of the tax increase.

The problem with Vickrey's scheme is that it is as impractical as taxing on an accrued basis. It requires knowing the entire pattern of accrued tax liabilities to the time of sale, which is the same as knowing the entire pattern of gains. The current value of the total accrued taxes due on a asset held for ten years is quite different if all the gains came in the first year, or in the last year, or evenly over time. In other words, the data requirements are the same as they would be under an accrued tax, data that would be unavailable for infrequently sold real assets.

The Auerbach Proposal

Auerbach proposed a variation of the Vickrey scheme that is practicable for all assets.[28] It is based on the certainty equivalence operator, $V(\ )$, which gives the value that an investor would require, with certainty, to be indifferent to an uncertain return that is the argument of the function V. The idea is that investors make their portfolio choices prospectively. They are indifferent to holding an uncertain asset for one more period if the certainty equivalence of the after-tax return on the asset is equal to the risk-free after-tax return. In terms of the operator V, indifference requires that at time s:

$$V(\dot{A}_S - \dot{T}_S)/(A_s - T_s) = i(1 - t) \tag{11.26}$$

where $\dot{A}_s$ is the uncertain next period return on the asset and the other terms are as defined above. Multiplying both sides of Eq. (11.26) by $(A_s - T_s)$ yields:

$$V(\dot{A}_S - \dot{T}_S) = i(1 - t)[A_s - T_s] \tag{11.27}$$

$V(\ )$ is a linear operator. Therefore,

$$V(\dot{A}_S) - V(\dot{T}_S) = iA_s - i(1 - t)T_s - itA_s \tag{11.28}$$

But $V(\dot{A}_S) = iA_s$, the certainty equivalent next period return on the asset. Thus, indifference to holding or selling requires that

$$V(\dot{T}_s) = i(1 - t)T_s + itA_s \tag{11.29}$$

Auerbach's proposal is Vickrey's proposal from an *ex ante* rather than an *ex post* perspective. $V(\dot{T}_s)$, the *ex ante* certainty equivalence of the increase in the taxes, is the net-of-tax risk-free interest on the deferred tax liabilities plus the tax on the certainty equivalent return for the next period.

Auerbach proves that the required $V(\dot{T}_s)$ is achieved if and only if the accumulated tax liability upon realization, T_s, is

$$T_s = (1 - e^{-its})A_s \tag{11.30}$$

---

[28] A. Auerbach, "Retrospective Capital Gains Taxation," *American Economic Review*, March 1991.

Note that T_s depends only on current data at the time the asset is sold: the risk-free market interest rate, i; the number of periods that the asset has been held, s; the marginal tax rate, t; and the current value of the asset, A_s. The taxpayer could easily determine the tax liability by looking it up in a table. Note, also, that $T_s = 0$ when $s = 0$ (an asset bought and sold immediately yields no income and incurs no tax); and $T_s \to A_s$ as $s \to \infty$ (the accumulated deferred tax approaches the value of the asset as the holding period extends into the future without limit).

We will demonstrate the sufficient conditions and leave the necessary conditions to the interested reader.[29] Suppose $T_s = (1 - e^{-its})A_s$. Then, the instantaneous increase in taxes from holding one more period is

$$\dot{T}_S = \left(1 - e^{-its}\right)\dot{A}_s + it\, e^{-its}A_s \qquad (11.31)$$

Add and subtract itA_s to the RHS and multiply and divide the first term by A_s:

$$\dot{T}_s = \left(1 - e^{-its}\right)\left(\dot{A}_s/A_s\right)A_s - \left(1 - e^{-its}\right)it\, A_s + it\, A_s \qquad (11.32)$$

$$\dot{T}_s = \left(1 - e^{-its}\right)A_s\left[(\dot{A}_s/A_s) - it\right] + it\, A_s \qquad (11.33)$$

But, $\dot{A}_s/A_s = i + e$, where e is a random variable with mean zero. Thus,

$$\dot{T}_s = \left(1 - e^{-its}\right)A_s[i + e - it] + it\, A_s \qquad (11.34)$$

$$\dot{T}_s = \left(1 - e^{-its}\right)A_s[e + i(1 - t)] + it\, A_s \qquad (11.35)$$

But $V(e) = 0$, by definition of the certainty equivalence operator. Therefore

$$V\left(\dot{T}_s\right) = \left(1 - e^{-its}\right)A_s[i(1 - t)] + it\, A_s \qquad (11.36)$$

or

$$V\left(\dot{T}_s\right) = T_s[i(1 - t)] + it\, A_s \qquad (11.37)$$

as required for investor indifference to holding the asset one more period or realizing and investing in the risk free asset.[30]

The only caveat to Auerbach's proposal is that the tax is essentially a prospective tax because it is based on the certainty equivalence of the next period return rather than the actual return. Many proponents of income taxation tend to believe that the fair way to tax is on the *ex post* actual returns and not the *ex ante* expected returns. From the *ex post* perspective,

---

[29] The necessary conditions establish that Eq. (11.30) is the only possible T_s that is a function only of i, s, t, and A_s. See A. Auerbach, "Retrospective Capital Gains Taxation," *American Economic Review*, March, 1991, pp. 172–173.

[30] Auerbach also presents more complicated cases, such as the appropriate tax for indifference when there are both capital gains and dividends.

exceptionally good assets are undertaxed and exceptionally poor assets are overtaxed under Auerbach's proposal. Nonetheless, investors do base their decisions on prospective returns, so that Auerbach's proposal does avoid the lock-in effect. Whether it is entirely fair or not depends on the *ex post* versus *ex ante* point of view, and this is largely a matter of taste.

Economists who favor expenditure taxes based on lifetime utility arguments tend to be indifferent between taxing on an *ex post* or *ex ante* basis. For example, they are indifferent between taxing the value of a house when it is purchased or the stream of housing services as they accrue, because the purchase price of the house equals the *expected* present value of the stream of housing services. The IRS would tax the value of the house when purchased under an expenditures tax because it is the only practical alternative. Whatever one's view of its equity implications, Auerbach's proposal for taxing realized capital gains must be considered a landmark in the theory of tax design for having solved the capital gains lock-in problem in a practical manner.

Capital Gains Taxation: A Postscript

Congress has never protected income from capital from inflation nor even remotely considered adopting Auerbach's tax scheme. The most favored policy is excluding a portion of "long-term" capital gains, the gains on assets held for more than one year, thereby effectively taxing the gains at a lower rate. This is done in the name of encouraging saving. It is also justified as a way of offsetting the inflationary bias against capital gains. At the same time, however, it has the effect of giving another tax break to high-income taxpayers in addition to the interest-free loans they receive from deferring the tax until realization.

The issues surrounding the taxation of capital gains and other sources of income from capital may become moot if Congress replaces the income tax with a flat-rate wage or expenditures tax, as some politicians want to do. The call for a simpler tax system is gaining momentum as this is written, and the only truly simple personal tax is one that excludes all income from capital from the tax base.

The Taxation of Human Capital

Louis Kaplow has taken a provocative position regarding the appropriate taxation of wage income under an ideal income tax if one views wages as the returns to a person's stock of human capital.[31] His point is simply that physical and human capital should be treated identically under an ideal

---

[31] L. Kaplow, "On the Divergence Between 'Ideal' and Conventional Income-Tax Treatment of Human Capital," *American Economic Review*, May 1996.

income tax. If this were done, however, it would lead to a sharp increase in the share of taxes collected from income received by labor.

Wages are not treated as returns to human capital in the standard Haig–Simons version of the ideal income tax presented earlier in this chapter. Instead wages are viewed as arising completely and concurrently with the supply of labor and are therefore taxed in full as they are realized each year, exactly as they would be taxed under an ideal wage or payroll tax. Viewing wages as returns to human capital would lead to very different tax treatment.

Compare, for example, the decision to save and the decision to invest in human capital. Under an ideal income tax, the saving is taxed immediately (not deducted from taxable income) and the returns to the saving are taxed as they *accrue*, whatever form they may take (e.g., interest, capital gains, a stream of returns from a real, depreciable asset). In the case of a real asset, the taxable returns are the gross returns less the depreciation on the asset each year, with the depreciation equal to the decline in the value of the asset. An investment in human capital is most directly equivalent to an investment in a real, depreciable asset. The initial investment costs should be taxed, that is, not deducted from taxable income. Also, the net returns from the investment—equal to the increase in the wages less the annual depreciation of the stock of human capital—should be taxed each year. Neither requirement is met under the standard income tax. Investment in the human capital may well be expensed, that is, deducted in full from taxable income, if it takes the form of lower wages received while participating in an on-the-job training program. Also, no deduction is allowed for the depreciation of a person's human capital. The wages are taxed in their entirety each year as they are realized. Notice that, from the human capital perspective, the full taxation of wages each year is completely wrong in the person's last year of work because the stock of human capital necessarily depreciates to zero in the last year, and always by an amount equal to the wages earned in that year. The final-year tax liability should be zero under an ideal accrued income tax.

Kaplow takes the taxation of human capital one step further by assuming that all wages can be thought of as a return to human capital. Under this view, the stock of human capital is a gift received at birth that should be subjected to two forms of taxation if treated symmetrically to physical capital.

First, the receipt of a gift of physical capital, or of any financial asset that is ultimately a claim against the earnings of physical capital, is treated as income under an ideal income tax and subject to full taxation. Therefore, the initial gift of human capital should be treated as income and subject to full taxation at birth. The value of the gift is the present value of a person's lifetime stream of wages less any expenses/investments incurred to generate the wage stream. In a world of perfect certainty, all future expenses/investments associated with the maintaining and increasing the stock of human capital would be known at birth, as would the entire stream of future wages arising from the human capital. The cash flow from the human capital would be lower in years when future investments were made and higher in the noninvestment years. In other words, the initial gift of human capital at birth is the capacity to engage in certain kinds investments in human capital throughout one's lifetime, along with the lifetime wages that result from the investments.

In addition, any accrued income (net of depreciation) earned by the physical capital gift in subsequent years is subject to taxation each year. Similarly, the stream of wages each year net of depreciation resulting from the gift of human capital should also be taxed under an ideal income tax. Given the usual pattern of depreciation of human capital, the present value of the depreciation is likely to be less than the present value of the wage stream because wages will far exceed depreciation except in the last working years. Thus, the annual stream of wages and depreciation represents a second source of taxable income.

To summarize, the appropriate tax base for human capital under an ideal, accrued income tax consists of: (1) the initial gift of human capital at birth, equal to the present value of lifetime wages less any lifetime expenses/ investments; and (2) the annual stream of wages less the depreciation of the stock of human capital. This tax treatment is equivalent to the ideal tax treatment of a gift of physical capital.

In fact, gifts of physical capital (or financial assets) are stepped up in basis when passed on to heirs, so that the initial value of the capital escapes taxation. This is not supposed to happen under an ideal income tax, but because it does happen one could argue for exempting the initial gift of human capital from taxation. If so, then the tax base for human capital is just the annual stream of wages less depreciation of the human capital stock. Since the standard "ideal" income tax calls for full taxation of wages, it actually over-taxes wage income when it is viewed as a return to human capital.

Suppose the income tax were reformed to include all gifts of capital as income, as called for by an ideal income tax. Then, if human capital escapes taxation at birth, the Auerbach/Vickrey method of retrospective taxation could be employed to capture the escaped tax liability when the wages (returns to human capital) are realized. The taxes due on the wages each year would include tax-deductible interest since birth on the taxes that should have been collected on those wages at birth. The later in life that the wages occur the higher the tax due on them, because the taxes due on them at birth have been receiving implicit interest tax free since then.

For example, the present value at birth of $1 of wages received at time i equals $\dfrac{1}{(1+r)^i}$, where r is the annual gross-of-tax interest rate, assumed constant over time. Had a tax been collected on that wage at birth, the value of the human capital at time i would have been $(1-t)\left[\dfrac{(1+r_a)}{(1+r)}\right]^i$ where t is the tax rate and r_a is the after-tax rate of interest, both assumed constant over time. Therefore, the *current value* of the taxes that should have been collected at birth, increased by the after-tax interest rate since birth, is

$$\left[1-(1-t)\left[\frac{(1+r_a)}{(1+r)}\right]^i\right]$$

If the escaped taxes are to be collected retrospectively at rate t in period i, then the \$1 of wages has to be scaled by $\left[\dfrac{1}{t}-\dfrac{(1-t)}{t}\left[\dfrac{(1+r_a)}{(1+r)}\right]^i\right]$ to collect this portion of the tax due under the ideal income tax.

Kaplow presents some calculations to show that wages received in the last few working years would have to be increased by a factor of 2 to 3 to capture retrospectively the escaped taxes since birth. Such scaling of the wages would be equivalent to scaling the returns on tax-deferred pension instruments such as IRAs if the taxes were collected retrospectively when the returns were realized. Under an ideal accrued income tax, savings for retirement should not be deducted from income as IRAs are.

Taxing human capital at birth, or scaling wages later on in life to account for taxes that should have been paid, would undoubtedly lead to horrendous problems of evaluation and liquidity—people might not trust how the tax liabilities were calculated or be able to pay the taxes when they are due. The fact remains, however, that Kaplow's suggested treatment of human capital is the proper one under an ideal accrued income tax if wages are viewed as the returns to human capital.

The discussion so far has assumed perfect certainty. The taxation of uncertain income streams would be resolved as the uncertainty is resolved: Unexpected favorable (unfavorable) returns to human capital would increase (decrease) its value and the taxes due.

In conclusion, the only three ways that taxable income from human capital can arise are at birth, over time (the steam of wages less depreciation), and as uncertainties about future income streams are resolved. Proponents of the ideal taxation of physical capital should favor similar taxation of human capital if they view wages as a return to human capital. This point takes on special force given the widely cited estimate by James Davies and John Whalley that the stock of human capital in the United States is on the order of three times the stock of physical capital.[32] If gifts of human and

---

[32] J. Davies and J. Whalley, "Taxes and Capital Formation: How Important is Human Capital?" in B. D. Bernheim and J. Shoven, Eds., *National Saving and Economic Performance*,

physical capital were counted as income as they should be, then the share of tax revenues collected from labor income would rise substantially.

SUMMARY

Chapter 11 has emphasized that the problem of designing equitable broad-based taxes is one of the more vexing in all of public sector economics. First-best theory offers two guidelines for tax design: the interpersonal equity conditions of social welfare maximization and the ability-to-pay principle. The interpersonal equity conditions are preferred by the mainstream theory, yet the ability-to-pay principle has won the day in terms of informing tax policy. Even so, ability-to-pay principles are subject to various interpretations. Furthermore, even if ability-to-pay principles can be agreed upon, it is extremely difficult to determine who has actually gained or lost from a given tax system and who will gain or lose from particular tax reforms.

A brief review of the federal personal income tax served to highlight these problems. The tax pays lip service to the ability-to-pay principle on paper, but there are many slips in application. The chapter considered a number of reforms that would make the tax conform more closely to traditional ability-to-pay principles, such as removing certain exclusions and deductions. But we were forced to admit that these reforms would not necessarily make the tax more equitable under a proper utility-based interpretation of these same principles, since reforms themselves generate inequities. Equity in taxation is as difficult to achieve as equity in any other context.

REFERENCES

Auerbach, A., "Retrospective Capital Gains Taxation," *American Economic Review*, March 1991.

Bittker, B., "Tax Shelters and Tax Capitalization or Does the Early Bird Get a Free Lunch," *National Tax Journal*, December 1975.

Davies, J. and Whalley, J., "Taxes and Capital Formation: How Important Is Human Capital?," in B. D. Bernheim and J. Shoven, Eds., *National Saving and Economic Performance*, University of Chicago Press, Chicago, 1991.

Diamond, P., "Inflation and the Comprehensive Tax Base," *Journal of Public Economics*, August 1975.

University of Chicago Press, Chicago, 1991. Kaplan is definitely not proposing that the personal income tax be reformed to treat wages as returns to human capital. To the contrary, he does not believe that the ability-to-pay perspective is a useful addition to tax theory. He prefers the modern social welfare function perspective on taxes, transfers, and distributive equity generally which, as discussed earlier in the chapter, is concerned much more with issues of the tax structure (vertical equity) than with precisely defining the tax base.

Feldstein, M., "On the Theory of Tax Reform," *Journal of Public Economics*, July–August 1976 (International Seminar in Public Economics and Tax Theory).

Haig, R. M., "The Concept of Income: Economic and Legal Aspects." In R. M. Haig, Ed., *The Federal Income Tax*, Columbia University Press, New York, 1921.

Hall, R. and Rabushka, A., *Low Tax, Simple Tax, Flat Tax*, McGraw Hill, New York, 1983.

Kaldor, N., *An Expenditure Tax*, George Allen & Unwin, Ltd., London, 1955.

Kaplow, L., "On the Divergence Between 'Ideal' and Conventional Income-Tax Treatment of Human Capital," *American Economic Review*, May 1996.

Mill, J. S., *Principles of Political Economy*, W. J. Ashley, W. J., Ed., Longmans, Green Co., Ltd., London, 1921.

Musgrave, R., *The Theory of Public Finance*, McGraw-Hill, New York, 1959.

Musgrave, R., "Horizontal Equity, Once More," *National Tax Journal*, June 1990.

Okner, B. and Pechman, J., *Who Bears the Tax Burden?*, The Brookings Institution, Washington, D.C. 1974.

Pechman, J., Ed., *What Should Be Taxed? Income or Expenditure*, The Brookings Institution, Washington, D.C., 1980.

Sadka, E., "On Progressive Taxation," *American Economic Review*, December 1976.

Simons, H. C., *Personal Income Taxation*, University of Chicago Press, Chicago, 1938.

Smith, A., *The Wealth of Nations*, Vol. II, E. Cannan, Ed., G. P. Putnam's Sons, New York, 1904.

Vickrey, W., "Averaging Income for Income Tax Purposes," *Journal of Political Economy*, 47, June 1939.

White, L. J., and White, M. J., "The Tax Subsidy to Owner-Occupied Housing—Who Benefits?", *Journal of Public Economics*, February 1977.

Young, H., "Distributive Justice in Taxation," *Journal of Economic Theory*, April 1988.

Young, H., "Progressive Taxation and Equal Sacrifice," *American Economic Review*, March 1990.

THE THEORY OF PUBLIC EXPENDITURES AND TAXATION: SECOND-BEST ANALYSIS

12

INTRODUCTION TO SECOND-BEST ANALYSIS

A BRIEF HISTORY OF SECOND-BEST THEORY
Second-Best Tax Theory
Second-Best Expenditure Theory
Private Information
PHILOSOPHICAL AND METHODOLOGICAL UNDERPINNINGS
PREVIEW OF PART III

First-best analysis offers us a complete, internally consistent normative theory of the public sector, yet the theory is far from satisfactory. It is often quite unrealistic and therefore unresponsive to the needs of policymakers. First-best models ignore a number of important real-world phenomena that the policymaker cannot ignore.

The strengths and weaknesses of first-best theory derive from a common source, that the only restrictions on a first-best policy environment are the two sets of restrictions inherent in any economic system: the underlying production relationships and market clearance for all goods and factors. In particular, those sectors of the market economy not subject to government intervention are assumed to be perfectly competitive, and the admissible set of government policy tools includes anything necessary to achieve a social welfare maximum. The government can redistribute any good or factor lump sum; it can change the price of any good or factor to consumers or firms; it can commandeer inputs and supply outputs at will, subject as always to given production relationships and market clearance; and it has perfect information about preferences, technologies, and markets. In short, the government has sufficient degrees of freedom to achieve Bator's bliss point, the social welfare maximum. It can design whatever policies are necessary to restore

pareto optimality and bring society to its first-best utility-possibilities frontier. Then it can move society along the frontier to the bliss point by means of
lump-sum redistributions that satisfy the interpersonal equity conditions.

Second-best analysis is a reaction to these heroic first- best assumptions.
In an attempt to be more realistic, it posits at least one additional constraint
on the policy environment. The constraint(s) can be on the underlying market
environment, on the set of admissible government policy tools, or on the
information available to the government. An immediate implication is that
the search for the social welfare maximum covers a restricted set of allocations and distributions relative to first-best theory, illustrated by the shaded
portion in Fig. 12.1. The defining difference from first-best analysis is that the
restricted set cannot include point B, Bator's bliss point, because adding
binding restrictions must reduce the maximum attainable level of social
welfare. Whether or not any points on the first-best utility-possibilities frontier are feasible depends on the nature of the additional constraints, but such
points might not be policy relevant anyway. As illustrated in Fig. 12.1, point
A on $U^2 - U^1$ is dominated by any point within the shaded portion and
above the social welfare indifference curve W_1.

The entire thrust of second-best analysis is toward increased realism. For
instance, second-best theory recognizes that governments cannot redistribute
income lump-sum. Taxes and transfers conditioned on income are almost
always distorting. Similarly, all market economies contain some monopoly or
monopsony elements that are unlikely to disappear in the foreseeable future.

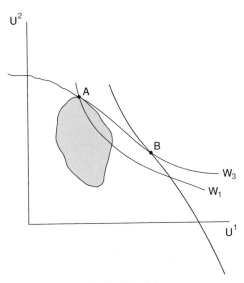

FIGURE 12.1

In addition, individuals and firms possess private information about themselves that others, including the government, do not know. Policy analysis should incorporate these real-world phenomena, which appear as additional constraints in a formal general equilibrium model.

As noted in Chapter 3, the most common government policy restrictions employed to date in the professional literature have been the inability to make lump-sum redistributions, the necessity of raising tax revenue in a distorting manner, the requirement that government agencies or entire governments operate within a legislated budget constraint, the not uncommon practice of governments either drafting some production inputs or offering some outputs of public projects free of charge (or at least at prices below opportunity costs), and the existence of private information. The most common market restriction assumes the existence of maintained monopoly power somewhere in the private sector, so that at least one private sector price does not equal marginal opportunity costs.

The potential set of policy, market, and information restrictions is limited only by the imagination, and individual constraints can always be combined, each additional constraint further restricting the set of feasible allocations and distributions. Thus, the possibilities for second-best analysis are virtually endless. There can never be *a* second-best normative theory of the public sector as there is with first-best theory.

Public sector economists thus face something of a dilemma in trying to inform public policy. They can recommend that policymakers try to approximate the definitive results from first-best theory, knowing that the underlying first-best model is patently unrealistic, or they can recommend that policymakers try to approximate the results from one or more second-best models, knowing that the results depend on the particular constraints that have been chosen in the name of realism and that the real world is many times more constrained than any one model can hope to capture.

Peter Hammond, in a brilliant review of the state of public sector economics published in 1990, came down firmly on the side of the second-best models. He urged public sector economists to dismiss out of hand the "delusions" of first-best theory, particularly its reliance on lump-sum redistributions.[1] He recommended instead that they push on with second-best theorizing if they wished to be taken seriously by policymakers, especially the most recent theory associated with private information. One wonders, however, whether Hammond believes that second-best theory will eventually achieve a conventional wisdom, an agreed-upon set of results that policymakers can rely on. His article gave no hint that second-best theory had yet come anywhere near this goal.

---

[1] P. Hammond, "Theoretical Progress in Public Economics: A Provocative Assessment," *Oxford Economic Papers*, 42, 1990, pp. 6–33.

A BRIEF HISTORY OF SECOND-BEST THEORY

Second-best theorizing swept into public sector economics to stay in the 1970s and has been at the forefront of the discipline ever since. The impetus was provided by two seminal articles that appeared about ten years apart: "The General Theory of Second-Best," by Archibald Lipsey and Kelvin Lancaster, and "Optimal Taxation and Public Production," by Peter Diamond and James Mirrlees.[2] The two articles approached second-best analysis from different perspectives and each became a template for distinct branches of the second-best literature that followed.

The Lipsey–Lansacter paper took the natural first step away from the Samuelson's first-best general equilibrium model. Their model assumes that price exceeds marginal cost in at least one market, either because of private monopoly power or distorting government taxes, and that the government is unwilling or unable to remove the distortion. Otherwise, the government has as much freedom to act as it has in the first-best model, including the ability to redistribute income lump sum.

Lipsey and Lancaster were specifically interested in the following question: Given maintained distortions in some markets, are the first-best pareto-optimal rules for other markets still consistent with social welfare maximization? The answer turned out to be "no" in general, a result that became known as the "theorem of the second best." Subsequent research has expanded their analysis to consider the effects of maintained distortions on first-best public expenditure decision rules and on the welfare implications of changing the pattern of distorting taxes. One can ask, for example, whether substituting one set of distorting taxes for another while holding tax revenue constant increases social welfare, given the existence of still other distortions. These are issues of *policy reform* in a second-best environment, by now a huge body of literature in the Lipsey–Lancaster mold.

The Diamond–Mirrlees model was also only one step removed from Samuelson's first-best model, but they asked a different question from Lipsey–Lancaster. The only maintained restriction in their model is that the

---

[2] R. Lipsey and K. Lancaster, "The General Theory of Second-Best," *Review of Economic Studies*, Vol. 24 (1), No. 63, pp. 1956–57; P. Diamond and J. Mirrlees, "Optimal Taxation and Public Production," *American Economic Review*, March, June 1971 (2 parts; Part I: Production Efficiency, Part II: Tax Rules). The Diamond/Mirrlees paper was completed in 1968 and widely circulated as an MIT Working Paper. It was well known and widely cited by the time it was published in 1971. Two other early articles are worth mentioning, one on production and one on taxation: M. Boiteux, "On the Management of Public Monopolies Subject to Budgetary Constraints," *Journal of Economic Theory*, September 1971 (Boiteux's article first appeared in the January 1956 *Econometrica* in French); and J. Stiglitz and P. Dasgupta, "Differential Taxation, Public Goods, and Economic Efficiency," *Review of Economic Studies*, April 1971. These articles are frequently referenced in the second-best literature. For an excellent (but difficult) summary of second-best methodology, see H. Green, "Two Models of Optimal Pricing and Taxation," *Oxford Economic Papers*, November 1975.

government must raise some tax revenue by means of distorting taxation; otherwise, the government is free to vary all price–cost margins, exactly as in first-best analysis. Because all tax rates are under the government's control, Diamond–Mirrlees were able to consider the optimal pattern of distorting taxation for raising a given amount of revenue. As such, their paper spawned another huge body of literature on *optimal policy* in a second-best environment. These two seminal papers, and the literature that has followed, have taken the normative analysis of tax and expenditure theory in many new directions.

Second-Best Tax Theory

The allocational theory of taxation, which analyzes the welfare losses caused by distorting taxes, dates from the very beginning of public sector economics. It has, by its very nature, always been part of the theory of the second best. The application of formal, second-best, general equilibrium models to tax problems over the past 30 years has mainly served to sharpen normative tax theory. The most notable extensions have been in the context of many-person economies. We now have a much better understanding of the trade-offs between equity and efficiency in a second-best environment. Tax theory has also become more tightly integrated with public expenditure theory.

Second-Best Expenditure Theory

The impact of second-best modeling on public expenditure theory has been nothing short of revolutionary. Until the 1960s, the received doctrine on public expenditures was the first-best theory of Part II. Since then, public expenditure theory has literally been rewritten by second-best theorizing. One might have anticipated this. Adding constraints to a general equilibrium model obviously changes its first-order conditions and the resulting policy decision rules. The changes have hardly been trivial, however. Second-best public expenditure decision rules often bear little relationship to their first-best counterparts, to the point that economists now seriously question the policy relevance of such cherished old "standards" as $\sum \text{MRS} = \text{MRT}$ for consumption externalities, or marginal cost pricing with subsidy for decreasing cost firms. Worse yet, it is now painfully obvious that the very latest, "state-of-the-art" second-best policy rules may not have much policy relevance either. As researchers invent new ways to constrain economic systems, they necessarily develop new and different, perhaps quite different, policy guidelines for the standard problems. As noted earlier, second-best theory is inherently a theory in flux, its policy implications always vulnerable to further variations in the models.

Second-best analysis has uncovered still other difficulties. To begin with, second-best public expenditure rules typically lack the comfortable intuitive appeal of the first-best rules. As we discovered throughout Part II, first-best policy rules always have close competitive market analogs. The correct price for decreasing cost services is a pseudo-competitive price, and externality problems can be viewed as instances of market failure, meaning that a competitive market structure can always be described that will generate the correct pareto-optimal rules. These interpretations arise precisely because all first-best decision rules are simple combinations of marginal rates of substitution and transformation. Such is not the case for the second-best rules. The marginal rates of substitution and transformation are present, to be sure, but so are a number of terms embedded in the additional constraints that do not have natural competitive market interpretations or analogs. This is a discouraging outcome for believers in the competitive market system.

A second disappointment is that the first-order conditions of second-best general equilibrium models do not generally dichotomize into distinct sets of pareto-optimal and interpersonal equity conditions. Recall that first-best models dichotomize because the government is assumed to be able to lump-sum redistribute in order to satisfy the interpersonal equity conditions of social welfare maximization. In their quest for realism, second-best models usually deny the government that option, with the result that *all* second-best optimality conditions combine elements such as marginal rates of substitution (transformation), which appear only in first-best efficiency rules, *and* social welfare terms, which first-best theory isolates in the interpersonal equity conditions. Normative prescriptions such as "place a unit tax on each person's consumption of this particular good" tend to be replaced or modified by rules such as "tax those goods that are consumed relatively more by people with low social welfare weights." But, because we have no useful theory of interpersonal equity comparisons, these policy rules tend not to be terribly compelling. Economists can take some comfort in the knowledge that the second-best policy rules are useful to public officials so long as the officials are willing to provide the social welfare weights, but this is a far cry from having a complete normative theory of the public sector.

Economists sometimes avoid the social welfare terms altogether by resorting to the fiction of the one-consumer equivalent economy. These models, however, can do little more than highlight the efficiency aspects of public sector problems. We will use one-consumer models for this purpose as well, but it should be understood that their policy implications are uncertain, unless it is assumed that distributional equity has been achieved. This can occur only by chance, however, without lump-sum redistributions. (Alternatively, does anyone seriously believe that preferences are identical and homothetic?) Furthermore, given the likelihood of unequal social welfare weights, it is always possible to specify some pattern of weights such that the efficiency aspects of any given policy rule become relatively unimportant. Needless to say, the presence of the social welfare terms in the optimal decision rules for allocational problems such as externalities is extremely troublesome for normative public sector theory.

A final discouragement is that second-best restrictions tend to affect *all* markets, not just those in which public expenditures occur. First-best models have the property that government intervention in any one market does not change the form of the pareto-optimal rules for other goods and factors. They can be allocated in competitive, decentralized markets. The important implication is that instances of market failure can be corrected with policies targeted solely at the failure. This is no longer true in a second-best environment. The Lipsey–Lancaster theorem says that if price–cost margins are distorted in some markets, then first-best competitive efficiency rules are no longer optimal for other markets, in general. Roughly the same result applies in the Diamond–Mirrlees framework. If the government must raise revenue by means of distorting taxation, it is generally optimal to tax all goods and factors (except one). The thrust of second-best analysis, therefore, is toward pervasive rather than limited government intervention, a discouraging result indeed for decentralized capitalist economies and the government-as-agent principle of government intervention.

Private Information

The constraint that people possess private information about themselves that other people and/or the government do not know deserves separate mention in this brief history of second-best theory. Private information is also commonly referred to as asymmetric information. It has been one of the more important focal points of public sector analysis over the past 25 years, if not the most important. The intense interest in the implications of private or asymmetric information is understandable. It opens up a whole new range of possibilities for public sector economists to consider, possibilities that challenge much of the received doctrine in public sector theory.

Private information is different from the other second best constraints because it is not simply a technological or practical assumption tacked on to an otherwise first-best model. It is in part an assumption about how people behave, that they are willing to use their private information for their own personal gain and to deceive if need be. As such, it leads normative public sector theory down a very slippery slope.

On the one hand, the idea that people are willing to deceive the government for their own ends tears at the very fabric of society. It belies the expectation of good citizenship and makes a mockery of the traditional notion that the government's proper economic function is as an agent of the people acting to correct market failures by pursuing the public interest in efficiency and equity. What is the normative appeal of maximizing an individualistic social welfare function when some people are willing to deceive and others are honest? Should the deceivers receive zero marginal social welfare weights? How much deception does it take before the society collapses? The objective function of public policy is not at all obvious when people are prone to act selfishly to exploit their private information.

On the other hand, some people certainly do use private information to their own advantage, and such behavior is entirely consistent with the economic view of individuals as self-interested utility maximizers. The willingness to exploit private information is not just a matter for positive economic analysis, however. It matters for normative analysis as well. All normative policy prescriptions must make assumptions about people's behavior and about how they will respond to the policies, and the prescriptions are only useful if the behavioral assumptions are reasonably accurate. Normative theory cannot simply ignore the issue of private information. The problem, though, is that the existence of private information can be extremely constraining for a government dedicated to the public interest in efficiency and equity, to social welfare maximization.[3]

The force of the private information constraint turns on the very meaning of an equilibrium in the social sciences, as a situation from which no one has any incentive to change. The particular requirement of an equilibrium in the presence of private information is that no one has any incentive to deceive or to represent their private information as other than what it really is. The only feasible public policies are those that are consistent with this notion of equilibrium. To be feasible, therefore, a public policy must be such that everyone's best strategy is to tell the truth about themselves given the policy; deception cannot lead to personal gain. For example, high-income people cannot pretend to have low income in order to reduce their taxes.

In the parlance of game theory, public policies must honor the revelation principle or, equivalently, be incentive compatible. In terms of formal modeling, private information necessitates adding one or more incentive compatibility constraints to a social welfare maximization problem to assure that the resulting policy prescription is feasible.

Incentive compatibility constraints can indeed place severe restrictions on the set of feasible policies. To begin with, they rule out almost all lump-sum redistributions unless they can be targeted to readily observable characteristics that an individual cannot hide or change, such as age. The feasible redistributions are unlikely to have much distributional bite, however. In truth, the government really has no chance of satisfying the first-best interpersonal equity conditions in a world of private information. And, as we have seen, the entire body of first-best theory rests on shaky foundations when the scope of lump-sum redistributions is limited.

---

[3] The implications of private information for public sector analysis are masterfully set out in the overview article by Peter Hammond for the *Oxford Economic Papers*. He discusses the points raised here plus the implications of limited information for applied cost-benefit analysis. Hammond also references the most important journal articles in these areas. See P. Hammond, "Theoretical Progress in Public Economics: A Provocative Assessment," *Oxford Economic Papers*, Vol. 42, 1990.

It turns out that economists have been unable to find very many public sector policies that are both efficient and equitable for which truth telling is the dominant strategy. The most obvious inventive-compatible distributional policy in the face of private information is to do nothing; simply accept the initial distribution of resources. This policy may be consistent with efficiency but it is likely to be seen as unjust.

Another variation of private information is the ability to engage in market exchanges in the underground, informal sector of the economy, out of sight of the government. The possibility of underground exchanges can severely limit the government's ability to do much of anything if escape to the informal sector is relatively easy. For example, the government may not be able to collect taxes or enforce sanctions against illegal activities.

Notice, too, how the presence of an underground economy changes the perception of markets. The traditional view of markets is that they are the best mechanisms yet devised for promoting efficient exchanges. The relatively few exceptions are the instances of market failure that require government intervention, such as nonexclusive goods or decreasing cost services. Markets in the underground economy, even highly competitive markets there, are destructive to efficiency, however. They sharply constrain the feasible set of government policies that can be used to promote efficiency (and equity).

Still another variation of private information that causes problems for normative public sector theory is the limited information that consumers and the government have about their relevant opportunity sets. Regarding the consumers, traditional microeconomic analysis assumes that consumers maximize their utilities with full information about their opportunity sets, including perfect foresight about future events. In fact, consumers often have very limited information about their opportunity sets and little economic incentive to obtain much more information. Instead, they engage in some form of bounded rationality, often basing their decisions on simple rules of thumb consistent with the limited information available to them. Normative policy analysis typically assumes that consumers maximize under full information because it is the convenient assumption to make. If consumers instead use simple rules of thumb, questions arise as to what rules they follow, and how they change their behavior as their information sets change. There are no obvious answers to these questions, yet a normative theory has to know how consumers will respond to public policies. Regarding the government, public policies often result in large changes in the economy that affect many people and many prices. Policymakers are hard pressed to keep track of all the general equilibrium changes in the economy, to say the least. They, too, have only limited information, not enough to know for sure whether any given policy increases or decreases social welfare.[4]

---

[4] For an expanded discussion of the problems caused by limited information, see P. Hammond, "Theoretical Progress in Public Economics," *Oxford Economic Papers*, Vol. 42, 1990.

In summary, the presence of private or asymmetric information offers any number of challenges to traditional normative public sector theory. The challenges are especially strong if private information takes a form that utility-maximizing individuals can use for their personal gain. For then the government has to be concerned with designing incentive-compatible policies that may severely limit its ability to pursue the public interest in efficiency and equity, which mainstream economists view as its primary function. At some point the willingness to deceive may so restrict the government's options that economic policy is hardly worth doing. The social contract is broken and the goal of developing a normative public sector theory is no longer compelling.

We will demonstrate the implications of private information at various points in this part of the text. The underlying assumption throughout is that the government's pursuit of efficiency and equity remains a worthwhile endeavor.

PHILOSOPHICAL AND METHODOLOGICAL UNDERPINNINGS

Second-best theory shares the same philosophical and methodological foundations as first-best theory. The added constraints of second-best theory are the only important differences between them. For instance, consumer sovereignty remains the fundamental value judgment of second-best theory, and distributional considerations are most often represented by a Bergson–Samuelson individualistic social welfare function. Second-best analysis is also closely tied to the competitive market system. This is best illustrated by the observation that much of the second-best literature uses general equilibrium models expressed in terms of competitive market prices, not quantities. Analytical constructs such as indirect utility functions, expenditure functions, production functions expressed in terms of market supply (input-demand) functions, and generalized profit functions are commonplace in second-best analysis, and they all implicitly assume competitive market behavior.

There is an obvious reason why this has happened. The second-best literature has been centrally concerned with restrictions in the form of price–cost differentials, most often resulting from distorting taxation. Models already specified in terms of prices can incorporate these distortions more readily than models specified in terms of quantities. In turn, the easiest way to convert a general equilibrium quantity model into a price model is by assuming competitive price-taking behavior. Thus, in nearly all second-best models consumers are assumed to maximize utility subject to a fixed-price budget constraint. They have no monopoly or monopsony power. Producers are typically viewed as decentralized, perfectly competitive profit maximizers, often with simple production relationships exhibiting either constant costs or constant returns to scale. Even the government is assumed to transact at the competitive producer prices to the extent it buys and sells inputs and outputs. A second-best model might posit constraints in the form of noncompetitive behavior in a small subset of markets, but the underlying market economy is almost always competitive. Second-best results may not have competitive interpretations, but the majority of models used to date have been competitive through and through.

The newer literature on private information is somewhat of an exception because it applies the techniques of game theory, and the games being played may not occur in a market setting. Even so, the decentralized nature of the competitive market has a correspondence in the public sector allocation mechanisms that honor the revelation principle. A standard requirement of truth-revealing mechanisms is that individuals have no control over their opportunity sets. The public sector mechanisms must be decentralizable in this sense.

In summary, although second-best theory has severely challenged all first-best policy rules, it has taken only the smallest, most hesitant steps away from the highly stylized first-best policy environment. Second-best analysis is more realistic, but only slightly so.

PREVIEW OF PART III

With these reflections in mind, we will begin our second-best analysis with the allocational theory of taxation, thereby reversing the order of presentation in Part II. This happens to coincide with the historical development of second-best theory, but that is really beside the point. There are two good analytical reasons for considering tax theory first.

One is that second-best tax theory is inherently simpler than second-best expenditure theory, in this sense. Public expenditure theory requires the specification of a distinct problem (e.g., an externality) and one or more distinct constraints (e.g., distorting taxation), whereas tax theory requires only the specification of a constraint. Saying that all taxes must be distorting is at once an additional constraint on the system and the source of the problem being analyzed in tax theory. Consequently, problems in tax theory can be analyzed with much simpler general equilibrium models. This is an important advantage. Second-best models specified in terms of prices are quite different from the first-best quantity model of Part II, enough so that it pays to begin the analysis as simply as possible. Thus, the initial chapters on tax theory have two goals. Their main purpose is to demonstrate some important theorems in the allocational theory of taxation, but they also serve as an introduction to second-best methodology.

Second-best tax theory also logically precedes public expenditure theory, so long as distorting taxes are one of the policy constraints. Having studied the effects of distorting taxation in isolation, the implications for externalities or decreasing cost production are that much more apparent. Chapters 13–17 contain a detailed analysis of the theory of distorting taxes, often without any consideration of how governments actually spend tax revenues. Chapters 18–22 then rework selected public expenditure problems from Part II within a second-best framework—transfer payments, aggregate externalities, nonexclusive goods, decreasing costs—using the constraints most commonly employed in the literature.

REFERENCES

Boiteux, M., "On the Management of Public Monopolies Subject to Budgetary Constraints," *Journal of Economic Theory*, September 1971 (translation from French, *Econometrica*, January 1956).

Diamond, P. A., and Mirrlees, J., "Optimal Taxation and Public Production" (2 parts; Part I: Production Efficiency and Part II: Tax Rules), *American Economic Review*, March, June 1971.

Green, H., "Two Models of Optimal Pricing and Taxation," *Oxford Economic Papers*, November 1975.

Hammond, P., "Theoretical Progress in Public Economics: A Provocative Assessment," *Oxford Economic Papers*, Vol. 42, 1990.

Lancaster, L., and Lipsey, R., "The General Theory of Second- Best," *Review of Economic Studies*, Vol. 24 (1), No. 63, 1956–1957.

Stiglitz, J., and Dasgupta, P., "Differential Taxation, Public Goods, and Economic Efficiency," *Review of Economic Studies*, April 1971.

13

THE SECOND-BEST THEORY OF TAXATION IN ONE-CONSUMER ECONOMIES WITH LINEAR PRODUCTION TECHNOLOGY

The second-best theory of taxation explores the effects of distorting taxes on social welfare. A distorting tax is one that prevents at least one of the first-best pareto-optimal conditions from holding; that is, it forces society inside its first-best utility-possibilities frontier. The first-best pareto-optimal conditions are equalities between marginal rates of substitutions and marginal rates of transformation. As such, they require that agents face the same prices in a market economy. Distorting taxes prevent the equalities from holding because they force at least two economic agents in the same market to face different prices in an otherwise perfectly competitive economy. Virtually all taxes actually employed by governments introduce some distortion into the economy, whether they be sales, excise, income, or wealth taxes. (Transfer payments are automatically included in the analysis because transfers are analytically equivalent to negative taxes.)

Because tax distortion is defined relative to pareto optimality, much of the literature on second-best tax theory has treated it strictly as an allocational issue, concerned only with questions of economic efficiency. Consequently, the analysis often occurs within the context of one-consumer economies, a simplification that makes sense if one is willing to ignore distributional concerns. As Chapter 12 noted, however, second-best analysis has shown that allocational and distributional issues do not dichotomize in a second-best environment without lump-sum taxes and transfers, thereby raising questions about the policy relevance of considering the efficiency aspects of distorting taxes independently from their distributional consequences. Probably no one today would recommend a set of taxes simply on the basis of their efficiency properties. Nonetheless, it is analytically convenient to isolate the efficiency effects of taxes by using one-consumer economy models. We can then consider the tax rules in many-person economies as combinations of efficiency and distributional elements, with the latter represented by the social welfare weights derived from an individualistic social welfare function. This is the approach we will take in developing the second-best theory.

The theory of distorting taxation addresses three main questions, one associated with welfare loss, another with optimality, and a third with tax reform:

1. *Welfare loss*—Relative to the first-best optimum, what is the loss in social welfare associated with any given set of distorting taxes (including a single tax)? Harold Hotelling provided the first rigorous analysis of this issue in his 1938 article, "The General Welfare in Relation to Problems of Taxation and of Railway and Utility Rates."[1] Arnold Harberger rekindled interest in this question in two separate articles appearing in 1964, "Taxation, Resource Allocation and Welfare" and "The Measurement of Waste."[2] By now the literature is voluminous, with these three articles standing as the seminal contributions.

2. *Optimality*—Relative to the first-best optimum, what pattern of distorting taxes minimizes the loss in social welfare for any given amount of tax revenue the government might wish to raise? This question has been explored under two separate assumptions: (a) that the government can tax all goods and factors, and (b) that a subset of goods and factors must remain untaxed. The study of optimal taxation under the first assumption is commonly referred to as the optimal commodity tax problem, with seminal contributions by Frank Ramsey in "A Contribution to the Theory of Taxation" (1927), and Peter Diamond and James Mirrlees' "Optimal Taxation and Public Produc-

---

[1] H. Hotelling, "The General Welfare in Relation to Problems of Taxation and of Railway and Utility Rates," *Econometrica*, July 1938.

[2] A. Harberger, "Taxation, Resource Allocation and Welfare," in National Bureau of Economic Research and the Brookings Institution, *The Role of Direct and Indirect Taxes in the Federal Revenue System*, (Princeton University Press, Princeton N.J., 1964; A. Harberger, "The Measurement of Waste," *American Economic Association Papers and Proceedings*, May 1964. An excellent recent reference for the early literature is J. Green and E. Sheshinski, "Approximating the Efficiency Gains of Tax Reforms," *Journal of Public Economics*, April 1979.

tion" (1971).[3] Explorations of optimal taxation under the second assumption are a more recent phenomenon.[4] We will defer discussion of restricted optimal taxation until Chapter 15 when we consider an important subset of that literature, the theory of optimal income taxation. Mirrlees' "An Exploration in the Theory of Optimum Income Taxation" is the seminal article on optimal income taxation.[5]

3. *Tax reform*—Holding tax revenues (or the government budget constraint) constant, what is the change in social welfare from substituting one set of distorting taxes for another? Once again, the literature on this question is voluminous, with the seminal article by Corlett and Hague, "Complementarity and the Excess Burden of Taxation."[6]

Most of the formal analysis of these three questions employs general equilibrium models specified in terms of prices. Therefore, we will switch at this point from quantity models to price models in order to familiarize the reader with the most common second-best methodology.

GENERAL EQUILIBRIUM PRICE MODELS

General equilibrium price models can be rather complex or extremely simple depending upon the assumptions made regarding the nature of demand and the underlying production technology for the economy and whether the economy is static or dynamic. Choices on demand range from one-consumer-equivalent economies to many-person economies with interpersonal equity rankings determined by a Bergson–Samuelson social welfare function. The key choice with respect to production technology is whether production exhibits linear or general technology and, if the latter, whether or not the technology is constant returns to scale. The choice of production technology also has direct implications for the way in which market clearance

---

[3] F. P. Ramsey, "A Contribution to the Theory of Taxation," *Economic Journal*, March 1927; P. Diamond and J. Mirrlees, "Optimal Taxation and Public Production" (2 parts; Part I: Production Efficiency and Part II: Tax Rules), *American Economic Review*, March, June 1971. Two excellent surveys of the optimal tax literature are A. Sandmo, "Optimal Taxation," *Journal of Public Economics*, July–August 1976; D. Bradford and H. Rosen, "The Optimal Taxation of Commodities and Income," *American Economic Association Papers and Proceedings*, May 1976. Finally, P. Diamond and D. McFadden, "Some Uses of the Expenditure Function in Public Finance," *Journal of Public Economics*, Vol. 3, 1974, contains an excellent analysis of some of the second-best tax issues analyzed in this chapter.

[4] Dixit presents a lucid analysis of restricted taxation using the model to be developed in this chapter in A. Dixit, "Welfare Effects of Tax and Price Changes," *Journal of Public Economics*, February 1975. Also see A. Dixit and K. Munk, "Welfare Effects of Tax and Price Changes: A Correction," *Journal of Public Economics*, August 1977.

[5] J. Mirrlees, "An Exploration in the Theory of Optimum Income Taxation," *Review of Economic Studies*, April 1971.

[6] W. Corlett and D. Hague, "Complementarity and the Excess Burden of Taxation," *Review of Economic Studies*, Vol. 21(1), No. 54, 1953–1954.

is specified. Moving from static to dynamic analysis raises a whole new set of modeling issues, such as how different cohorts of people behave (e.g., the working young and the retired elderly), how people form expectations about the future, how asset markets clear as capital accumulates, and how technology changes over time.

In order to highlight the economic intuition of tax distortions, we will begin with the simplest possible general equilibrium model, a static one-consumer-equivalent economy with linear aggregate production technology. The one-consumer assumption removes all distributional considerations, so that welfare loss means efficiency loss and the theory of distorting taxation is purely an allocational theory. Positing a linear technology is enormously convenient because it exhibits constant marginal (opportunity) costs along the linear production-possibilities frontier. Since the economy is assumed to be perfectly competitive, this means that all relevant production parameters can be described by a vector of fixed producer prices, assumed equal to the constant marginal costs (or value of marginal products for factors). Furthermore, output supply (and input demand) curves are perfectly elastic at the fixed prices within the boundaries of the aggregate production frontier. Hence, market clearance is implicit because supplies (input demands) automatically expand or contract to meet the consumer's demands (factor supplies). That is, output (and factor supply) is completely determined by the consumer's preferences at the given prices within the boundaries of the frontier. Market clearance is also irrelevant to the determination of prices, which are solely a function of the production technology.

The one main drawback to the linear technology assumption is that its simplicity tends to mask the role of production in determining the welfare costs of distorting taxes. Fortunately, however, a fair number of properties of distorting taxes do carry over virtually intact from linear to general technologies, especially if the latter exhibit constant returns to scale. In any event, we will relax the assumption of linear technology in Chapter 14.

THE MEASUREMENT OF LOSS FROM DISTORTING TAXES

The first question of distorting taxation concerns the measurement of welfare loss: Relative to the first-best optimum, what is the social welfare loss resulting from any given pattern of distorting taxes, within the context of a one-consumer, linear production economy? With one consumer, loss in social welfare is equivalent to the consumer's loss in utility. To be concrete, assume that the distorting taxes (transfers) take the form of unit taxes on both the consumer's purchases of goods and services and his supply of factors, levied on the consumers. In principle, then, the taxes include most forms of sales and excise taxes on the product side and income taxes on the factor side. In practice, only income taxes are typically paid by consumers; sales and excise taxes are paid by firms. As we shall discover, however, it makes no difference to loss measurement whether the government levies a tax on the demand or supply side of any market. Therefore, the assumption that consumers pay a sales or excise tax is of no consequence. The only distorting taxes specifically ruled out at this point are so-called partial taxes paid by certain firms (consumers) but not others, such as the corporation income tax.

The Geometry of Loss Measurement: Partial Equilibrium Analysis

The analysis of welfare loss from distorting unit taxes dates from the beginnings of public sector theory and has long appeared in economic texts at all levels, including introductory Principles texts. Figure 13.1 depicts the standard textbook analysis of the loss from a single tax under linear technology. S and D represent the zero-tax market supply and demand curves for a particular product. The no-tax equilibrium price is p, the constant supply price. A unit tax levied on the consumer shifts the demand curve down everywhere by the amount of the tax, to D' in the figure. As a result of the tax, equilibrium output drops from X_0 to X_T, and the price to the consumer rises to $q = p + t$, where t is the unit tax. With constant producer prices, the price to the consumer rises by the full amount of the tax. The government collects revenue equal to $X_T \cdot t$.

The *dead-weight* or *efficiency* loss of the tax is measured by the triangle abc, by the following argument. Because the tax causes the consumer price to rise from p to q, the consumer loses Marshallian consumer surplus in amount equal to the trapezoidal area qpac. Some of this loss is captured by the government as revenue $X_T \cdot t$, the rectangle qpbc, which presumably is used to finance socially beneficial expenditures. But the loss of triangle abc is

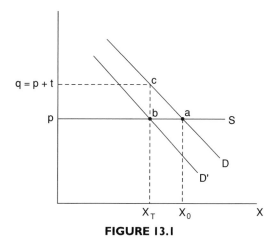

FIGURE 13.1

captured by no one. It is a pure or dead-weight welfare loss, generated by the distorting tax which forces consumers and producers to face different prices for the product. The consumer price q is called the *gross-of-tax* price, and the producer price p is the *net-of-tax* price. The loss triangle is an indication that the pareto-optimal condition MRS = MRT no longer holds in this market. Consumers equate their MRS to q, and producers equate their MRT to p (relative to the numeraire good). Without the tax, both the MRS and MRT are equated to p.

The traditional analysis is intuitively instructive, but it is not a valid general equilibrium presentation of the loss question. We saw in Chapter 9 that Marshallian consumer's surplus is not a meaningful compensation measure of loss, in general.[7] Moreover, it can be seriously misleading. For instance, one "theorem" commonly derived from the supply and demand framework is that the government should tax products (factors) whose demand (supply) is perfectly inelastic to avoid deadweight loss. If either the demand or supply curve in Fig. 13.1 were vertical, output would remain constant, and there would be no deadweight loss triangle resulting from the unit tax. Unfortunately, this proposition is not accurate. Unit taxes can generate welfare loss, properly measured, even if demand or supply is perfectly inelastic.

Another limitation of the standard textbook discussion is that it is partial equilibrium analysis. As such, it cannot capture the effects on loss of further price changes in other markets.

The Geometry of Loss Measurement: General Equilibrium Analysis[8]

The first task, then, is to develop a proper and unambiguous measure of the welfare loss resulting from distorting taxes in a full general equilibrium context. To capture the intuition behind the measure, we will continue with a graphical analysis but switch from the partial equilibrium supply–demand framework to a valid general equilibrium representation using the consumer's indifference curves and the economy's production-possibilities frontier.

Suppose the consumer buys a single good, X_1, and supplies a single factor, X_2 (e.g., labor, measured negatively), with preferences $U(X_1, X_2)$, represented by the indifference curves I_1, I_2, and I_3 in Fig. 13.2. In addition, assume producers can transform X_2 into X_1 according to the linear technology $X_1 = a \cdot X_2$, where a is the marginal product of X_2 (labor). The production-possibilities frontier is depicted as line segment 0b in Fig. 13.2. All feasible (X_1, X_2) combinations lie on or to the southwest of 0b. Given the

---

[7] Chapter 9 has a detailed discussion of this point.

[8] The analysis in this section draws heavily on unpublished class notes provided to us by Professors Peter Diamond and Paul Samuelson of MIT. See also P. A. Diamond and D. McFadden, "Some Uses of the Expenditure Function in Public Finance," *Journal of Public Economics*, Vol. 3, 1974.

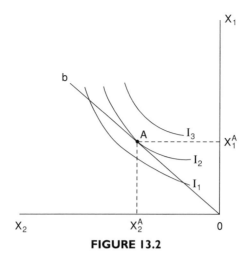

FIGURE 13.2

consumer's preferences and the economy's production possibilities, point A is the first-best welfare optimum for the economy. Point A can be achieved by a competitive equilibrium, with relative prices P_{x_2}/P_{x_1} equal to the slope of the production frontier. That is, $P_{x_1} = P_{x_2}/a = MC_{x_1}$, the standard competitive result. To see that this is a general market equilibrium, note that with $P_{x_2}/P_{x_1} = a$, the production-possibilities frontier 0b is also a budget line for the consumer, with zero lump-sum income (payment):

$$\frac{P_{x_2}}{P_{x_1}} = a = \frac{X_1}{X_2} \tag{13.1}$$

$$P_{x_1} \cdot X_1 = P_{x_2} \cdot X_2 \tag{13.2}$$

Thus, the consumer can purchase the optimal bundle $\left(X_2^A, X_1^A\right)$. Furthermore, 0b represents the profit function for the firm with competitive pricing and indicates that the firm just breaks even. There are no pure economic profits (losses) to distribute to the consumer. Thus, Eq. (13.2) holds for both the consumer and producer, and point A is the pretax competitive general equilibrium for the economy.

The first point to stress is that *any* tax on the consumer generates a loss in utility. Suppose the government places a lump-sum tax on the consumer in an amount equivalent to T_1 and forces him to a new equilibrium, point B in Fig. 13.3. Clearly the utility at B is less than the utility at A; the consumer has suffered a loss. Yet because lump-sum taxes are nondistorting, they cannot possibly generate a dead-weight loss. Hence, the loss $U(A) - U(B)$ must be considered an unavoidable consequence of any tax and should not be included in the measure of loss arising from tax distortion.

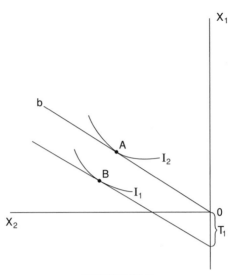

FIGURE 13.3

To see that a distorting tax generates loss in addition to this unavoidable loss, place a unit tax, t_1, on the consumption of X_1 such that it raises the same amount of revenue as the lump-sum tax. This tax changes the relative prices faced by the consumer from P_{x_2}/P_{x_1} to $P_{x_2}/(P_{x_1} + t_1)$, while leaving the relative producer prices at P_{x_2}/P_{x_1}. Since the consumer and producers now face different relative prices, $MRS_{x_1, x_2} \neq MRT_{x_1, x_2} \left(\equiv MP_{x_2}^{x_1} \right)$, pareto optimality cannot obtain, and the tax is distorting, by definition. The consumer chooses a new equilibrium, point C in Fig. 13.4.

Notice that the lump-sum and unit taxes raise the same amount of revenue, T_1 units of X_1 , but that the equilibrium points B and C differ.[9] In general, C will be to the southeast of B, as drawn. The reason is that the unit tax introduces a *substitution effect* because of the relative price change that is absent from the lump-sum tax. The *income effects* of the two taxes are identical by construction, each measured by the lost tax revenue, but the added substitution effect causes the consumer to purchase less X_1 and less X_2 than with the lump-sum tax (more negative X_2, the "good"—for example, leisure). Also, C provides less utility than B, as drawn. This follows from revealed preference. When the consumer purchased B with the lump-sum tax, he was able to purchase C. Conversely, when he purchased C with the unit tax, he was unable to purchase B. Hence, B is revealed preferred to C. Only if

---

[9] It is always possible to construct equal-revenue taxes by positing any given unit tax, finding the new equilibrium, and constructing a line through this equilibrium parallel to the no-tax budget line to represent the equivalent lump-sum tax.

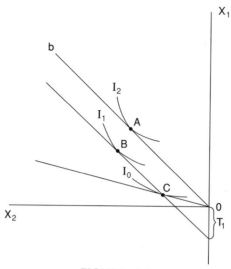

FIGURE 13.4

the indifference curves are right angled, so that there is no substitution effect with the unit tax, do the two taxes generate the same after-tax equilibrium and thus the same loss in utility.

The additional loss in utility from B to C, then, can be considered the *avoidable loss* of the distorting unit tax, the loss corresponding to the dead-weight loss triangle in the supply and demand presentation of Fig. 13.1. This is the loss society is interested in minimizing. Furthermore, the graphical analysis suggests that the amount of the avoidable loss for any distorting tax depends upon two factors: (1) the level of the tax rate, and (2) the magnitude of the substitution effect between goods and factors.

Of course, we would not want to measure the avoidable loss as the difference in utility levels $U(B) - U(C)$, since this measure is not invariant to monotonic transformations of the utility index. What is required is an unambiguous income measure of the avoidable utility loss. As discussed in Chapter 9 when considering the "hard case" for decreasing cost services, such income measures involve the notion of compensation or willingness to pay. There is an infinite number of acceptable income compensation measures because they are all based on parallel distances between indifference curves, which can be computed at an infinity of points. One particularly intuitive income measure of tax loss is obtained from the following conceptual experiment:

1. Place a unit tax on the consumer's purchases of one of the goods or factors (say, X_1).

2. Simultaneously transfer to the consumer enough income, lump sum, to keep him on the original zero-tax indifference curve.
3. Include in this income the tax revenue collected from the unit tax.
4. Ask if the tax revenue alone is sufficient compensation. If not, then measure the loss as the difference between the lump-sum income necessary to compensate the consumer less the tax revenue collected and then returned lump sum.

Because utility is being held constant at the original no-tax equilibrium and the income computed at the with-tax price, this measure utilizes Hicks' Compensating Variation resulting from the (relative) price change.

Consider first the lump-sum tax by this measure of loss. No matter what the size of the tax, if the consumer receives the revenue back lump sum simultaneously as it is collected from him, he remains at the original no-tax equilibrium. No further lump-sum income is necessary as compensation, and the loss measure is zero, as it must be. With the unit tax, however, the tax revenue is not sufficient compensation and the loss measure is positive, providing that the substitution effect is nonzero. This case is illustrated in Fig. 13.5.

Given the lump-sum compensation, the consumer remains on indifference curve I_2 as the budget line rotates in response to the tax. Suppose the consumer winds up at point D. D is a compensated market equilibrium in which the consumer faces the with-tax price line HE and simultaneously receives income lump-sum equal to 0E (in terms of X_1). The tax revenue collected (and returned) at the compensated equilibrium D equals EF units of X_1, the difference between the no-tax and with-tax price lines at D projected

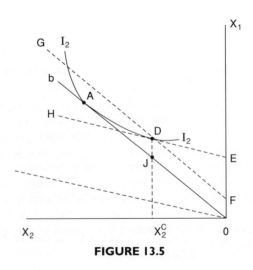

FIGURE 13.5

back to the X_1 axis. Hence, the distance OF measures the loss, the income (in units of X_1) required in excess of the tax revenue to compensate the consumer for the tax. OF is positive as long as the tax generates a substitution effect.

Note, finally, that society cannot produce the compensated equilibrium D because it lies outside the production-possibilities frontier 0b. This is another useful way of conceptualizing the notion of dead-weight or avoidable loss, that society cannot satisfy the entire set of compensated goods demands and factor supplies from its own resources given distorting taxes. Suppose the consumer supplies the amount of labor at the compensated equilibrium, X_2^C. Producers can only supply J units of X_1 on 0b given X_2^C. Hence, the vertical distance $(D - J)$ provides an alternative measure of loss, equal to OF, the amount of X_1 that the government would have to obtain from an outside source to compensate the consumer fully for the unit tax.[10]

It should be understood that these compensation experiments are merely conceptual exercises, useful for deriving certain analytical properties of distorting taxes. They are not indicative of actual government policies. There is no reason to suppose a compensated equilibrium would ever actually be observed, and normative theory surely does not require that governments simply return whatever taxes they collect lump sum.

The Analytics of General Equilibrium Loss Measurement

Extending the concept of efficiency loss from distorting taxation to N goods and factors and any given pattern of existing taxes can be accomplished quite easily by means of the expenditure function from the theory of consumer behavior:

$$M(\vec{q}; \overline{U}) = \sum_{i=1}^{N} q_i X_i^C(\vec{q}; \overline{U})$$

where

$\vec{q} =$ the vector of consumer prices, with element q_i.

$X_i^C(\vec{q}; \overline{U}) =$ the compensated demand (supply) for good (factor) i.

$M(\vec{q}; \overline{U})$ gives the lump-sum income for any vector of consumer prices necessary to keep the consumer at utility level $\overline{U}$. But, if $\overline{U}$ is set equal to the original zero-tax utility level, that is, $\overline{U} = U^0$, then $M(\vec{q}; \overline{U}^0)$ is precisely the income measure required for the conceptual experiment described above.[11]

---

[10] Alternatively, the dotted line GF represents a production-possibilities frontier in which producers receive a lump-sum transfer of OF units of X_1 from an outside source. Given this transfer, and with the ratio of *producer* prices $P_{X_2}/P_{X_1} = a$, competitive production can achieve the compensated equilibrium D.

[11] It should be noted that the choice of $\overline{U}$ is arbitrary since any constant utility level generates the same analytical expressions for total and marginal loss. Setting $\overline{U} = U^0$ is a natural

Furthermore, there can be no pure profits or losses in the economy with linear technology. Hence, it is reasonable to assume that

$$M\left(\vec{p}; \overline{U}^0\right) \equiv 0$$

where:

$\vec{p}$ = the vector of producer prices, assumed fixed and equal to marginal costs.

With the zero-profit assumption, the loss for any given tax vector is the value of the expenditure function at the gross-of-tax consumer price vector less the tax revenues collected and returned (conceptually) lump sum, or

$$L(\vec{t}) = M\left(\vec{q}; \overline{U}^0\right) - \sum_{i=1}^{N} t_i \cdot X_i^C\left(\vec{q}; \overline{U}^0\right) \tag{13.3}$$

where

$\vec{q} = \vec{p} + \vec{t}$, and $\vec{t}$ is the vector of unit taxes, with element t_i.

The tax revenue is the only source of lump-sum income available to the consumer.

Notice that the tax revenue is the revenue that would be collected at the fully compensated equilibrium, corresponding to point D in Fig. 13.5. To be consistent, the conceptual experiment must assume that compensation is actually paid, in which case the tax revenues collected from the vector of rates $\vec{t}$ is $\vec{t} \cdot X\left(\vec{q}; \overline{U}^0\right)$. Actual tax collections, equal to $\sum_{i=1}^{N} t_i X_i(\vec{q}; 0)$ where $X(\vec{q}; 0)$ represents the consumer's ordinary or Marshallian demand (supply) curves, are irrelevant to this conceptual loss experiment.

Relating Eq. (13.3) to Fig. 13.5, $M(\vec{q}; U^0)$ corresponds to the distance 0E, $\sum_{i=1}^{N} = t_i X_i^C\left(\vec{q}; \overline{U}^0\right)$ corresponds to the distance EF, and $L(\vec{t})$ corresponds to the distance 0F.

Note before proceeding further that the expenditure function $M\left(\vec{q}; \overline{U}^0\right) \equiv M\left(\vec{p} + \vec{t}; \overline{U}^0\right)$ is, *by itself,* a valid general equilibrium model of a one-consumer economy with linear technology, when coupled with the standard assumption of perfectly competitive markets. On the demand side, the expenditure function incorporates all relevant aspects of the consumer's behavior.[12] On the supply side, the price vector $\vec{p}$ specifies all relevant

---

choice when measuring the loss from distorting taxation, since loss is then defined explicitly with reference to the zero-tax, nondistorted economy. As noted in the text, setting $\overline{U} = U^0$ coincides with the conceptual loss experiment described above. Another intuitive choice would be to set $\overline{U}$ equal to the utility level obtained with lump-sum taxation. This would correspond to our introductory discussion of loss as represented in Fig. 15.4, in which loss is defined in terms of U(C) versus U(B), two equal-tax-revenue equilibria.

[12] The compensated demands (factor supplies) come from the dual of the consumer's utility maximization problem: Minimize expenditures, $\sum_{i=1}^{N} q_i X_i$, subject to utility being held constant (at U^0).

production parameters, since relative producer prices equal marginal rates of transformation with perfect competition. Market clearance is implicit. It is understood that supplies (input demands) respond with perfect elasticity to the consumer's demands (factor supplies) at the specified price vector $\vec{p}$ and that the consumer automatically supplies all factors used in production and receives all the goods produced. Also, the resource limitations defining the outward limits to these supply responses depend entirely on the consumer's willingness to supply factors, which is already incorporated in $M\left(\vec{q}; \overline{U}^0\right)$. Finally, once $\vec{t}$ is set by the government, $\vec{q}$ is determined by the relationships $\vec{q} = \vec{p} + \vec{t}$. Separate market clearance equations are not needed to determine equilibrium price vectors. Thus, given that $M(\vec{q}; \overline{U})$ is a valid general equilibrium specification of a one-consumer economy with linear technology, it follows immediately that Eq. (13.3), along with the relations $\vec{q} = \vec{p} + \vec{t}$, is a valid general equilibrium specification of the conceptual loss experiment described in the preceding section.

Marginal Loss

As a first step in determining the policy implications of distorting taxation, consider the marginal loss from a small change in one of the unit taxes, t_k, all other taxes held constant:

$$\frac{\partial L(\vec{t})}{\partial t_k} = \frac{\partial M\left(\vec{q}; \overline{U}^0\right)}{\partial t_k} - \frac{\partial \left[\sum\limits_{i=1}^{N} t_i X_i^C\left(\vec{q}; \overline{U}^0\right)\right]}{\partial t_k} \qquad k = 1, \ldots, N \qquad (13.4)$$

$$\frac{\partial L(\vec{t})}{\partial t_k} = M_k - M_k - \sum\limits_{i=1}^{N} t_i M_{ik} \qquad k = 1, \ldots, N \qquad (13.5)$$

$$\frac{\partial L(\vec{t})}{\partial t_k} = -\sum\limits_{i=1}^{N} t_i M_{ik} \qquad k = 1, \ldots, N \qquad (13.6)$$

where:

$$M_k = \frac{\partial M}{\partial q_k}$$

$$M_{ik} = \frac{\partial X_i^C}{\partial q_k} \text{ , the substitution terms in the Slutsky equation.}$$

The derivatives take on these values because of the assumption of linear technology, which fixes the vector of producer $\vec{p}$. In the kth market, represented by Fig. 13.6, the demand curve shifts down by the amount of the tax, and the consumer price q_k increases by the full amount of the tax in the new equilibrium. Thus, $dq_k = dt_k$, with p_k constant. The change t_k may well affect demand (factor supply) in some other markets, say, the market for good j, as

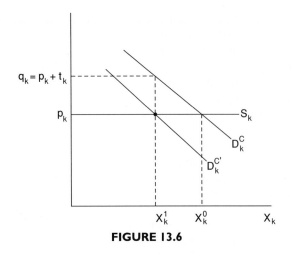

FIGURE 13.6

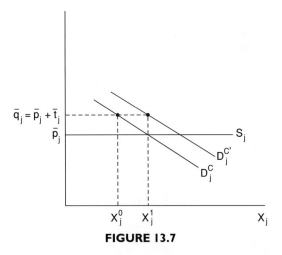

FIGURE 13.7

represented in Fig. 13.7. Output increases from X_j^0 to X_j^1, but there is no change in the equilibrium price q_j, since neither p_j nor t_j can change as t_k is varied. p_j is constant because technology is linear, and t_j is a control variable for the government, assumed constant. Hence, the derivative $\partial M/\partial t_k = \sum_{i=1}^{N}(\partial M/\partial q_i)(\partial q_i/\partial t_k)$ contains the single term $(\partial M/\partial q_k)\ (\partial q_k/\partial t_k) = \partial M/\partial q_k = M_k$; similarly, $\partial X_i^C\left(\vec{q}; \overline{U}^0\right)/\partial t_k = M_{ik}$.

Notice that Eq. (13.6) for marginal loss confirms the results suggested by the one-good, one-factor graphical analysis: The additional loss from a marginal change in a distorting tax depends only upon the level of taxes already in existence and the Slutsky substitution effects between all pairs of goods and factors, the M_{ik}.

Total Loss for Any Given Pattern of Taxes

Equation (13.3) gives one valid general equilibrium measure of the total loss from any given vector of distorting taxes, $\vec{t}$. An alternative expression for total loss can be derived by integrating the N expressions for marginal loss and summing over all markets:

$$L(\vec{t}) = \sum_{i=1}^{N} \int_0^{t_i} \frac{\partial L}{\partial t_i}\, dt_i = \sum_{i=1}^{N} \int_0^{t_i} \frac{\partial L(q_1, \cdots, q_{i-1}; s; p_{1+1}, \cdots, P_N)}{\partial s}\, ds \quad (13.7)$$

Substituting Eq. (13.6) into (13.7) yields:

$$L(\vec{t}) = \sum_{i=1}^{N} \sum_{j \leq i} \int_0^{t_i} t_j M_{ij}\, dt_i \qquad (13.8)$$

The inside summation before the integral sign of Eq. (13.8) indicates that the taxes are being introduced market by market. Thus, $t_j = 0, j > i$. Moreover, since $M_{ij} = M_{ji}$ from the symmetry of the Slutsky substitution terms, the order of integration is irrelevant. That is, the order in which the government actually levies the given vector of taxes does not affect the value of the total welfare loss resulting from the entire set of taxes. Equation (13.8) is an exact measure of total welfare loss for a one-consumer economy with linear technology. It can be related to the standard geometric representation of dead-weight loss triangles, properly measured using compensated demand curves, if the compensated demand derivatives, $M_{ik} = \partial X_i^C(\vec{q}; \overline{U}^0)/\partial q_k$, are assumed constant—that is, if the compensated demand curves are assumed to be linear over the relevant range of prices. With this assumption, the M_{ij} can be taken outside the integrals so that Eq. (13.8) becomes:

$$L(\vec{t}) = \sum_{i=1}^{N} \left(-\sum_{j=1}^{i-1} t_j M_{ji} \int_0^{t_i} dt_i - M_{ii} \int_0^{t_i} t_i dt_i \right) \qquad (13.9)$$

Performing all N integrations yields:

$$L(\vec{t}) = -\sum_{i=1}^{N} \left(\sum_{j=1}^{i-1} t_j t_i M_{ji} + \frac{1}{2} M_{ii} t_i^2 \right) \qquad (13.10)$$

Rearranging terms:

$$L(\vec{t}) = -\frac{1}{2} \sum_i \sum_j t_i t_j M_{ij} \qquad (13.11)$$

Arnold Harberger first derived an expression of this form in his 1964 articles "Taxation, Resource Allocation and Welfare" and "The Measurement of Waste."[13]

To relate this expression to deadweight loss triangles, rewrite Eq. (13.11) as:

$$
\begin{aligned}
L(\vec{t}) &= -\frac{1}{2}\sum_{i=1}^{N}t_i\sum_{j=1}^{N}t_jM_{ij} = -\frac{1}{2}\sum_{i=1}^{N}t_i\sum_{j=1}^{N}t_j\frac{\Delta X_i^C}{\Delta q_j} \\
&= -\frac{1}{2}\sum_{i=1}^{N}t_i\Delta X_i^C
\end{aligned}
\tag{13.12}
$$

under the assumptions of constant M_{ij} and $dq_j = dt_j$ for a linear technology economy. Equation (13.12) appears to suggest that the total loss from a given vector of taxes can be approximated as the sum, over all markets, of deadweight loss triangles in each market, as taxes are added one by one. This is misleading, however, since the quantity base of these triangles, the ΔX^C in Eq. (13.12), represents the total general equilibrium change in each X_i in response to the *entire set* of tax distortions t_j, for $j \leq i$. Thus, it is not correct to sum dead-weight loss triangles as they are traditionally presented in partial equilibrium analysis, even with the proper compensated demand curves.

Consider a two-tax example in which the imposition of t_1 precedes the imposition of t_2.[14] As t_1 is imposed, the loss at that point is correctly approximated by the shaded triangle in Fig. 13.8. D_1 and D_1' are the pre- and post-tax compensated demand curves for X_1 (at the zero-tax utility level) under the assumption that $q_2 = p_2$, the producer price of good 2. D_2 may shift in response to t_1, but with no resulting addition to (subtraction from) loss since its price equals marginal cost. (The same is true of all other goods.) Hence, loss is properly measured as:

$$
\frac{1}{2}t_1^2\frac{\partial X_1^C}{\partial q_1} = \frac{1}{2}\cdot t_1\cdot\frac{\partial X_1^C}{\partial q_1}\cdot\Delta q_1 = \frac{1}{2}\cdot t_1\cdot\Delta X_1^C
$$

---

[13] See A. Harberger, "Taxation, Resource Allocation and Welfare," in *The Role of Direct and Indirect Taxes in the Federal Revenue System*, Princeton University Press, Princeton, N.J., 1964; A. Harberger, "The Measurement of Waste," *American Economic Association Papers and Proceedings*, May 1964. Harberger refers to the Slutsky substitution terms specifically in each article, but only as special cases. Generally, his $\partial X_i/\partial q_j$ refer to the general equilibrium response of the X_i along the production-possibilities frontier, not the movement along the consumer's zero-tax indifference curve. See Chapter 26 for additional discussion. Harberger clarifies the meaning of his "demand" derivatives in A. Harberger, "Three Basic Postulates for Applied Welfare Economics," *Journal of Economic Literature*, September 1971; A. Harberger, *Taxation and Welfare*, Little, Brown and Co., Boston, MA, 1974. 86–90.

[14] Harberger presents a similar geometric analysis of adding losses across markets in A. Harberger, "Taxation, Resource Allocation and Welfare," in *The Role of Direct and Indirect Taxes in the Federal Reserve System*, Princeton University Press, Princeton, NJ, 1964.

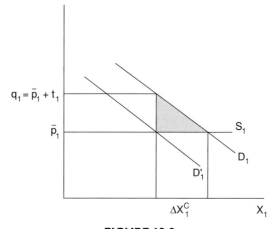

FIGURE 13.8

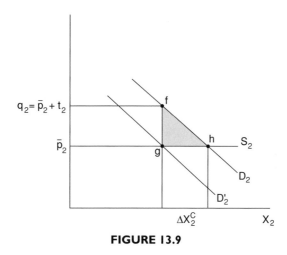

FIGURE 13.9

the shaded triangle. It immediately follows that the traditional representation of loss as a triangle on a demand and supply diagram is accurate for a single tax, providing the compensated demand curves are employed and they are linear.

When t_2 is imposed, it creates an additional loss in the market for good 2 which can be represented by the shaded triangle in Fig. 13.9. The compensated pre- and post-tax demand curves D_2 and D_2' assume that $q_1 = p_1 + t_1$, the gross of tax price for good 1. The triangle equals $\frac{1}{2} \cdot t_2 \cdot M_{22} \cdot t_2 = \frac{1}{2} t_2 \cdot \Delta X_2^C$. However, if we simply add this loss triangle to the loss triangle in Fig. 13.8 for good 1 and stop, we will have ignored a third term in the expression for loss in Eq. (13.11) or (13.10), equal to $(-)t_1 \cdot t_2 \cdot M_{12}$, or $t_1 \cdot \partial X_1^C / \partial q_2 \cdot \Delta q_2$. Given that t_1 exists, the response of X_1 to a change in the price of X_2 entails a further source of loss since price no longer equals marginal cost for good 1. This additional loss equals the change in tax revenue collected from good 1 as its demand shifts. Recall that loss is the income required to compensate for the taxes less any tax revenue available for compensation. If the tax revenue collected in other markets changes as a new tax is imposed, there is more or less revenue available for compensation. Thus, if demand shifts to D_1'' as depicted in Fig. 13.10 (the two goods are Slutsky complements), then the shaded rectangular area (abcd) must be added to the standard dead-weight loss triangle (cde) to compete the total loss associated with the market for good 1 resulting from the entire set of taxes t_1 and t_2. Note that D_1'' assumes $q_2 = p_2 + t_2$, whereas D_1' (D_1) assumes $q_2 = p_2$. Thus, total loss from both markets is the trapezoidal area abed in Fig. 13.10 plus the triangle (fgh) in Fig. 13.9.

X_1 and X_2 could be Slutsky complements if there are more than two goods. They must be Slutsky substitutes ($M_{ij} > 0$) if they are the only two goods, however, from the homogeneity of the M_i. In this case, D'' shifts to the right of D' and the resulting rectangle represents a reduction in loss. The government collects more tax revenue from X_1 as t_2 is imposed, and the additional tax revenue is available to compensate the consumer for the increase in q_2. The additional tax revenue reduces the total loss.

The geometric analysis generalizes directly to N goods (and factors) in which rectangles of the form $t_i \cdot \Delta X_i$ in markets for which taxes already exist are added (subtracted) to the standard dead-weight loss triangles $\frac{1}{2} t_k \cdot \Delta X_k$ as

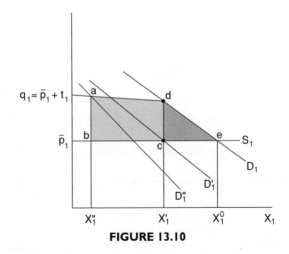

FIGURE 13.10

taxes t_k are added one by one. The triangles correspond to the terms $-\sum_i \frac{1}{2} M_{ii} t_i^2$ in Eq. (13.10); the rectangles, to the terms $-\sum_{i=1}^{N} \sum_{j=1}^{i-1} t_j t_i M_{ji}$. [15]

Policy Implications of the Loss Measures

The expressions (13.6) and (13.11) for marginal and total loss reveal a number of important policy implications on distorting taxation, despite the simplicity of the one-consumer, linear technology model. They all follow from the property that both marginal and total loss depend only upon the level of existing tax rates and the Slutsky substitution effects. Here are eight such implications as a representative sampling. [16]

Zero-Tax Economy Versus Existing-Tax Economy

An immediate implication from the expression for marginal loss, Eq. (13.6), is that if there are no tax distortions in the economy, then the imposition of a marginal tax on one of the goods or factors does not generate a dead-weight loss even to a second order of approximation. The level of all tax rates is either exactly or approximately equal to zero near the initial no-tax equilibrium so that marginal loss is also (approximately) zero. In other words, the first marginal distortion is free. The intuition behind this result is that all resource transfers in response to the new marginal tax occur at values (approximately) equal to their marginal costs. If so, then returning the tax revenue is sufficient compensation for the distortion.

---

[15] The loss measure (13.11) can be directly related to our earlier discussion of the gain or loss to the consumer for any given change in consumer prices. In Chapter 9 we showed that the gain or loss for any price change can be represented as a summation of areas behind the consumer's compensated demand (and supply) curves between the old and new prices in each market. The result followed from the fact that

$$M(q^1; \overline{U}) - M(q^0; \overline{U}) = \sum_{i=1}^{N} \int_{q_i^0}^{q_i^1} \frac{\partial M\left(q_1^1, ..., q_{i-1}^1; s; q_{i+1}^0, ..., q_N^0; \overline{U}\right)}{\partial s} ds \qquad (13.1n)$$

$$= \sum_{i=1}^{N} \int_{q_i^0}^{q^1} X_i^C\left(q_1^1, ..., q_{i-1}^1; s; q_{i+1}^0, ..., q_N^0; \overline{U}\right) ds \qquad (13.2n)$$

where $X_i^C\left(\bar{q}^1; s; \bar{q}^0; \overline{U}\right)$ is the demand for X^i compensated at utility level $\overline{U}$ and evaluated at $q_j = q_j^1$, for $j < i$, and $q_j = q_j^0$, for $j > i$. With $\overline{U} = U^0$, these areas measure Hicks Compensating Variation. In the tax problem $t_i = q_i^1 - q_i^0$ and $M(\bar{q}_0; \overline{U}) = 0$, so the loss measure from distorting taxes corresponds directly to this earlier loss measure. The original measure gives the entire area behind each demand curve—for example, area $p_1 edq_1$ in Fig. 13.10. As such, it captures only the change in the value of the expenditure function in response to the tax; that is, it ignores the disposition of the tax revenue. The tax loss measure recognizes that the revenue $p_1 baq_1$ can be put to some socially useful purpose. Conceptually, it is simply returned lump sum to the consumer. Hence, the net or dead-weight loss caused by the distortion is just the trapezoidal area *abed*.

[16] Paul Samuelson discusses a number of the implications presented here in P. Samuelson, "Theory of Optimal Taxation," *Journal of Public Economics*, June 1986.

Of course, the zero-tax, zero-loss result is just a theoretical *curiosum*. All developed countries have complex tax structures that raise substantial amounts of revenue. Thus, the policy relevant conclusion to be drawn from Eq. (13.6) is that even a marginal tax change can generate substantial losses in welfare, precisely because resources are shifting from an initial position in which marginal values may be far from their marginal costs. The government cannot choose to ignore the efficiency implications of minor changes in the tax structure simply because the changes are "small."

Proportional Taxes Generate No Dead-Weight Loss

Equations (13.6) and (13.11) indicate that the dead-weight loss from distorting taxes depends fundamentally on the Slutsky substitution terms, the M_{ij}. But, substitution effects can only arise from changes in relative prices which move the consumer along a given indifference curve. Thus, if all prices change in the same proportion, relative prices remain unchanged, and there can be no dead-weight loss from these taxes. The compensated with-tax equilibrium is the original zero-tax equilibrium.

This can be seen directly from rewriting Eq. (13.11) as:

$$L(\vec{t}) = -\frac{1}{2}\sum_{i=1}^{N} t_i \sum_{j=1}^{N} t_j M_{ij} \tag{13.13}$$

Suppose $t_j = \alpha q_j^0$, for all $j = 1, \ldots, N$, so that all prices change in the same proportion, $(1 + \alpha)$.[17] Equation (13.13) becomes:

$$L(\vec{t}) = -\frac{1}{2}\sum_{i=1}^{N} t_i \sum_{j=1}^{N} \alpha \cdot q_j^0 M_{ij} = -\frac{1}{2}\sum_{i=1}^{N} t_i \alpha \sum_{j=1}^{N} q_j^0 M_{ij} \tag{13.14}$$

But, compensated demands (factor supplies), $M_i = X_i^C(\vec{q}; \overline{U}^0)$, are homogeneous of degree zero in all prices. Thus $M_i[(1 + \alpha)\vec{q}^0; \overline{U}^0] = M_i(\vec{q}^0; \overline{U}^0)$ and, from Euler's theorem on homogeneous functions, $\sum_{i=1}^{N} q_j M_{ij} = 0$, for all $\vec{q}$. Hence, $L(\vec{t}) = 0$.

Unfortunately, governments may not be able to use proportional taxation. With no pure profits in the system, the value of the expenditure function at the zero-tax equilibrium $M(\vec{p}; \overline{U}^0)$ could well be zero, as we have been assuming. In this case, a proportional tax on all goods and factors raises no revenue because:

$$\sum_{i=1}^{N} t_i X_i^C(\vec{q}; \overline{U}) = \alpha\sum_{i=1}^{N} q_i^0 X_i^C(\vec{q}; \overline{U}^0) = \alpha\sum_{i=1}^{N} q_i^0 X_i(\vec{q}_0; \overline{U}^0) = 0$$

Since variable factor supplies enter the expenditure function with a negative sign, the rule "set $t_j = \alpha q_j^0$, all $j = 1, \ldots, N$" implies taxing goods and

---

[17] $q_j = \overline{p}_j + t_j = \overline{p}_j + \alpha q_j^0$. Hence, $q_j = \overline{p}_j + \alpha\overline{p}_j = (1 + \alpha)\overline{p}_j$.

subsidizing factors, the net effect of which raises no revenue for the government.

If, instead, $M(\vec{q}^0; \overline{U}^0) = k, k > 0$, then a proportional tax (subsidy) on all goods and factors at rate α collects revenue equal to $\alpha \cdot k$. But, since $M(\vec{q}^0; \overline{U}^0)$ includes both goods and variable factor supplies, k must be a source of lump-sum income—most likely, income from a factor in absolutely fixed supply, meaning that both its substitution and income effects are identically zero. Thus, a simpler alternative would be to tax the income from the fixed factor at rate α, a tax that cannot possibly be distorting. Henry George once proposed a tax on land rents for just this reason.[18]

In conclusion, the ability to levy proportional taxes is essentially the ability to tax lump sum. For this reason, proportional taxation is hardly an interesting policy for second-best tax theory. The allocational theory of taxation ought properly concern itself only with taxes that generate distortions by changing the vector of relative prices.

Efficiency Properties of Income Taxes

Thirty years ago income taxes were held in very high regard by public sector economists. We noted in Chapter 11 that Haig–Simons income was once almost universally regarded as the ideal tax base in the ability-to-pay tradition of equity in taxation. In addition, the income tax was viewed as a highly efficient tax. The direct market effects of an income tax are on labor supply and saving behavior, and the older empirical studies found low to negligible labor and savings elasticities with respect to after-tax wages and interest rates, respectively. These studies suggested that the income tax generated very little dead-weight loss.

Support for the income tax has since faded considerably. On the one hand, many neoclassical economists now prefer an expenditure tax to an income tax on ability-to-pay grounds, as discussed in Chapter 11. On the other hand, the efficiency argument in favor of an income tax was seen to be faulty.

Nearly all the early empirical studies measured $\partial X_i/\partial q_i$, the derivative of the ordinary market supply curves with respect to changes in supply prices, whereas the relevant derivatives for efficiency loss are the Slutsky substitution effects $M_{ii} = \partial X_i^C/\partial q_i$. These two derivatives are related through the Slutsky equation, $(\partial X_i/\partial q_i) = (\partial X_i^C/\partial q_i) - X_i(\partial X_i/\partial I)$. If one observes $\partial X_i/\partial q_i = 0$, the crucial question is whether the ordinary price derivative is zero because both the substitution and income effects are zero, or because the substitution and income effects cancel one another out. If the former is true, then indifference curves are right angled, the compensated factor supply is invariant to changes in relative prices, and taxing the factor does not produce any dead-weight loss. Income from these factors is truly lump sum. If, however, the

[18] H. George, *Progress and Poverty*, Doubleday & Co., New York, 1914, Book VII.

ordinary market elasticity merely reflects a canceling of income and substitution effects, the market supply curve may be vertical, but taxing the factor can nonetheless generate a considerable amount of deadweight loss.

Unfortunately, the canceling story is quite possible for both the supply of labor and capital, since in each case the income and substitution effects work in opposite directions. Consider the case of labor, using the standard income–leisure model of neoclassical theory in which the consumer equates his marginal rate of substitution between income and leisure with the wage rate. Refer to Fig. 13.11. The slope of the budget line equals the net-of-tax wage rate. Suppose the consumer is initially in equilibrium at point A, with no tax on wages. If the government imposes a wage tax, the budget line rotates downward and the consumer reaches a new equilibrium, at point B. The question is whether B is to the right or left of A—that is, whether work effort has increased or decreased. The substitution effect of the tax says that the consumer substitutes leisure for income because the relative marginal cost of leisure (earning income) has decreased (increased). In turn, more leisure implies *less* work effort. Intuitively, marginal effort is penalized, so why work harder? The income effect says that because the price of one of the goods (income) has risen, real purchasing power has diminished. Consequently, the consumer tends to "buy" less of both goods, income and leisure. But less leisure implies *more* work effort. Intuitively, the consumer has to work harder to maintain his standard of living. Thus, the overall effect of the tax on work effort is ambiguous.

The same analysis applies to saving. A decrease in the after-tax rate of interest generates a substitution effect that favors current consumption over future consumption, and an income effect that goes against both current and

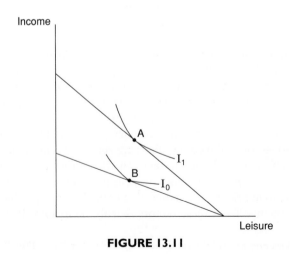

FIGURE 13.11

future consumption. Thus, the effect on current consumption (hence saving) is ambiguous.

The empirical breakthrough regarding labor supply behavior was Jerry Hausman's 1981 paper on "Labor Supply."[19] Hausman's analysis brought a number of improvements to the estimation of labor supply, two of which were essential. He developed an estimation technique that took into account the highly nonlinear budget set that the federal personal income tax generates as a result of the personal exemption, the itemized and standard deductions, and the graduated tax rates. He also showed how to derive the indirect utility function from the estimated ordinary labor supply equation using Roy's Identity. With the indirect utility function in hand, he could solve for the compensated labor supply curve and compute appropriate measures of dead-weight loss.[20]

Hausman found that the ordinary labor supply elasticity for prime aged male heads of households was indeed very small, essentially zero, but the low elasticity was the net result of fairly substantial substitution and income effects nearly canceling one another. His point estimates of the Slutsky substitution and income elasticities were approximately 15%. The fairly high substitution elasticity led to an estimated dead-weight loss of 22 to 54% of revenue collected, depending on income level, relative to an equal-revenue lump sum tax. His estimates also generated a dead-weight loss of 12 to 25% for an equal-revenue, proportional income tax. The overall estimated dead-weight loss from the income tax was 28.7% of tax revenues collected.

The revised view of saving behavior came from research using neoclassical growth models in the early 1980s. Dynamic efficiency is the proper criterion for judging the effects of tax policy on saving behavior, not the static one-period effects on saving that had been the norm before 1980. Lawrence Summers (1981) was the first to suggest that taxing saving can generate large dynamic efficiency losses.[21] He found that replacing a consumption tax with an income tax generates substantial intertemporal substitutions of consumption even if the initial effect on current consumption is quite low. His intertemporal substitution elasticities were huge, on the order of 1.2. The large intertemporal substitutions in turn generate very large dynamic efficiency losses in the long run because they induce a large reduction in the capital stock, with corresponding reductions in productivity and output. The

---

[19] J. Hausman, "Labor Supply," in H. Aaron and J. Pechman, Eds., *How Taxes Affect Economic Behavior*, The Brookings Institution, Washington, D.C., 1981. The estimates of elasticities and dead-weight loss reported below are found on pp. 52–54, including Table 3 on p. 54, and p. 61. For an update, see J. Hausman and P. Rudd, "Family Labor Supply with Taxes," *American Economic Association Papers and Proceedings*, May, 1984.

[20] We discussed Hausman's derivation of compensated consumer demand and supply functions from the ordinary estimated demand and supply functions in Chapter 9.

[21] L. Summers, "Capital Taxation and Accumulation in a Life Cycle Growth Model," *American Economic Review*, September 1981.

steady-state output loss in his model was on the order of 18% of national product.

Direct Versus Indirect Taxation

There is a large literature on the relative inefficiencies caused by direct versus indirect taxes, where direct taxes refer to taxes on factor supplies and indirect taxes to taxes on consumer goods and services. The earlier literature, which relied on static models, tended to favor direct taxation on efficiency grounds.[22] More recent literature, which employs neoclassical growth models, tends to favor indirect consumption or expenditure taxes over income taxes.[23]

In theory, Eqs. (13.6) and (13.11) convey everything we need to know to settle the issue of which taxes are best. No general presumption in favor of direct taxes over indirect taxes, or vice versa, emerges from the equations. One can always postulate a set of M_{ij} (static and intertemporal) and tax rates t_k that would tip the balance one way or the other.

The issue is ultimately an empirical one. We would need to know the entire set of M_{ij} over time to resolve the issue, but our current knowledge of intertemporal Slutsky terms is virtually nil. The neoclassical growth models rely on highly simplified assumptions about the intertemporal terms, not sophisticated econometric estimates. As an empirical matter, then, statements in favor of either direct or indirect taxes must be largely conjectural, given current econometric knowledge. Furthermore, as the next section will demonstrate, the optimal pattern of taxes for raising any given amount of tax revenue is generally a mix of both direct and indirect taxes, not one or the other.

If the Government Chooses To Collect All Revenue by Imposing a Single Distorting Tax, Which Good or Factor Should It Tax?

Equation (13.11) provides the answer to this question. Consider the use of a single tax on good (factor) k versus a single tax on the good (factor) j to raise a given amount of revenue, $\overline{T}$. The loss using tax t_k is $(-)\frac{1}{2}t_k^2 M_{kk}$, assuming $t_i = 0$, for $i \neq k$. Similarly, the loss with the single tax t_j is $(-)\frac{1}{2}t_j^2 M_{jj}$. Which one dominates depends entirely on two factors: the values of M_{kk} and M_{jj} and the tax rates t_k and t_j necessary in each instance to raise

[22] For example, see M. Friedman, "The Welfare Effects of an Income and Excise Tax," *Journal of Political Economy*, February 1952; E. Browning, "The Excess Burden of Excise vs. Income Taxes: A Simplified Comparison," *Public Finance*, 3, 1975. Clearly, the bias in favor of income taxes results from special assumptions in the models which, in effect, place restrictions on the values of certain M_{ij} terms.

[23] Overlapping generations (OLG) growth models, in particular, make a strong case for an expenditures tax on efficiency grounds. Two seminal contributions were L. Summers, "Capital Taxation and Accumulation in a Life Cycle Growth Model," *American Economic Review*, September 1981; L. Kotlikoff, "Taxation and Savings: A Neoclassical Perspective," *Journal of Economic Literature*, December 1984.

the required revenue $\overline{T}$. At issue, then, is the standard empirical question: What confidence do we place in our estimates of M_{kk} and M_{jj}?

The Issue of Tax Avoidance

People tend to favor taxes that they can avoid fairly easily, meaning taxes on goods with high price elasticities for which substitutes are readily available. But, these are precisely the taxes governments should avoid if they are concerned about dead-weight loss, especially if the high price elasticities reflect large substitution effects as opposed to income effects. One immediate implication is that, on efficiency grounds alone, taxes on goods and services ought to be levied by higher rather than lower level governments in the fiscal hierarchy, that is, by the national government rather than the state governments and by state governments rather than the local governments. If a city taxes some good such as cigarettes, substitutes are readily available in the form of cigarettes sold outside the city limits. The tax artificially creates two goods in effect—city cigarettes and non-city cigarettes—that are very close substitutes.[24] A national cigarette tax is least likely to generate artificial distinctions of this type.

Single-Market Measures of Loss

Because of data limitations, empirical research is often forced to adopt partial equilibrium techniques and focus entirely on the market directly under consideration. Unfortunately, partial equilibrium measures of tax loss can be quite misleading. They would compute the loss from a tax, t_k, as $(-)\frac{1}{2}t_k^2 M_{kk}$, ignoring all cross-product terms in Eq. (13.11). This would be appropriate if t_k were the only tax, but because many goods and factors are taxed it is not clear that the cross-product terms can be safely ignored.

One assumption commonly employed in empirical research to "justify" partial equilibrium analysis is that all cross-price elasticities are zero, but this assumption can only hold for ordinary demand (factor supply) derivatives. It cannot be imposed on the M_{ij}. Consumer theory tells us that $M_{kk} \leq 0$, and $\sum_{i=1}^{N} q_i M_{ik} = 0$, for all $k = 1, \ldots, N$. These results imply that at least one $M_{kj} \geq 0$, for $j \neq k$. In other words, if the compensated demand (supply) for one good (factor) changes in response to a relative price change, then the compensated demand (supply) for at least one other good (factor) must change as well. As always it is the substitution terms that are relevant to second-best tax questions.[25]

---

[24] City residents would also waste resources by traveling outside the city to purchase cigarettes. This waste is in addition to the standard dead-weight loss.

[25] Researchers will also frequently assume away all income effects, so that $\partial X_i/\partial q_j = \partial X_i^C/\partial q_j$, all $i, j = 1, \ldots, N$, in order to justify the use of ordinary demand (factor supply) derivatives in their loss measures. Given this assumption, one cannot then assume away all ordinary cross-price derivatives.

Despite these lessons from consumer theory, public sector economists have been willing to employ the assumption that $M_{ij} = 0$, for $i \neq j$, to get some rough indication of tax loss even though there is no way of judging how accurate the resulting estimate is. Ignoring the cross-product terms leads to a convenient back-of-the-envelope approximation of the marginal loss per dollar of tax revenue. Write:

$$dL = -t_i M_{ii} dt_i \qquad (13.15)$$

absent the cross-product terms. Assume the tax is an *ad valorem* percent or price tax of the form $t_i = \alpha q_i$. Therefore,

$$dL = -\alpha q_i M_{ii} d(\alpha q_i) \qquad (13.16)$$

Because this is an approximation, calculate the marginal loss at the original equilibrium before the marginal change in the tax rate:

$$dL = -\alpha q_i M_{ii} q_i d\alpha \qquad (13.17)$$

Multiply and divide by the original X_i to express the marginal loss in terms of the elasticity of demand for X_i, yielding:

$$dL = -\alpha E_{ii}(d\alpha q_i X_i) \qquad (13.18)$$

The last term in the parentheses is the change in the tax revenue, dT, given the marginal change in the tax rate α, computed at the original equilibrium. Therefore,

$$dL/dT = -\alpha E_{ii} \qquad (13.19)$$

The marginal loss per dollar of tax revenue is approximately equal to the *ad valorem* tax rate times the price elasticity of demand.

Edgar Browning used this approximation to compute one of the first marginal loss estimates of the federal personal income tax, published in 1976. The relevant elasticity was the supply of labor with respect to the wage rate, which he assumed was approximately .2. The "average" marginal tax rate was .35. Therefore, his back-of-the-envelope approximation was that the federal personal income tax led to about a $.07 increase in loss per additional dollar of revenue raised.[26]

Browning also provided more complicated estimates based on the following considerations: (1) consumers with different incomes face different marginal tax rates; (2) exemptions and deductions in the federal income tax increase the marginal rates necessary to raise a dollar of revenue; and (3) a person's marginal tax rate is in part determined by other federal, state, and local taxes. With these additional considerations Browning was able to derive

---

[26] E. Browning, "The Marginal Cost of Public Funds," *Journal of Political Economy*, April 1976.

a range of estimates for dL/dT bounded by the values $|.07|$ and $|.16|$. These marginal losses were considered to be comfortably low at the time.

Feldstein's Estimate of Total and Marginal Dead-Weight Loss

Martin Feldstein has recently suggested another back-of-the envelope calculation of the deadweight loss from income taxes that is based on the elasticity of taxable income with respect to one minus the tax rate.[27] His calculations produce higher estimates of total loss per dollar of revenue than Browning-style calculations based on the labor supply elasticity, and much higher estimates of the marginal loss per dollar of additional revenue. Feldstein's calculation is based on five premises.

First, the behavioral responses to changes in personal income tax rates go far beyond changes in labor supply (and saving). They include changes in the form of compensation between taxed wages and salaries and untaxed (or more lightly taxed) fringe benefits such as contributions to pension and stock options; changes in the composition of portfolio investments; changes in itemized deductions and other expenditures that reduce taxable income; and changes in tax compliance. Feldstein believes that these other behavioral changes are potential sources of dead-weight loss. His back-of-the-envelope calculation highlights tax avoidance through exclusions and deductions.[28]

Second, the simple utility maximizing model behind the back-of-the-envelope calculations based on labor supply responses is

$$\max U(C, L)$$
$$\text{s.t. } C = (1 - t)w(1 - L)$$

where C = consumption, for which the price is assumed to be one; L = leisure; w = the wage rate; and t = the income tax rate, assumed constant for all taxpayers. Feldstein argues for an expanded model that includes exclusions (E) and deductions (D):

$$\max U(C, L, E, D)$$
$$\text{s.t. } C = (1 - t)(w - wL - E - D)$$

Third, leisure, exclusions, and deductions can be considered as one composite commodity in this simple model since an income tax does not change the relative prices of L, E, and D.

---

[27] M. Feldstein, "Tax Avoidance and the Deadweight Loss of the Income Tax," *Review of Economics and Statistics*, November 1999.

[28] Joel Slemrod had noted in an earlier paper that the hierarchy of responses to TRA86 was (1) changes in the timing of transactions, particularly the realization of capital gains; (2) financial and accounting responses, especially the shift from nondeductible forms of debt to deductible mortgage debt; and (3) responses in "real" activities—in labor supply, saving, and investment. The real activities were a distant third in order of importance. See J. Slemrod, "Do Taxes Matter?," *American Economic Review*, May 1992.

Fourth, the budget constraint under a consumption (sales) tax would be $(1 + \tau)C = (w - wL - E - D)$, where τ is the consumption tax rate. Therefore, a consumption tax is equivalent to the income tax if $(1 + \tau)$ $(1 - t) = 1$.

Fifth, the dead-weight loss (dwl) from the consumption tax equals:

$$dwl = -.5\tau dC = -.5\tau \frac{dC}{d(1 + \tau)} d\tau \tag{13.20}$$

Refer to Figure 13.12.

Rewriting Eq. (13.20) in elasticity form and substituting $d\tau = \tau$ yields:

$$dwl = -.5\left(\frac{\tau}{1 + \tau}\right)\left(\frac{1 + \tau}{C}\right)\frac{dC}{d(1 + \tau)}\tau C = -.5\left(\frac{\tau}{1 + \tau}\right)E_{C,P}\tau C \tag{13.21}$$

But, $\dfrac{\tau}{1 + \tau} = t$ and $\tau = \dfrac{t}{1 - t}$. Therefore,

$$dwl = -.5t^2 E_{C,P} \frac{C}{(1 - t)} \tag{13.22}$$

expressed in terms of the consumption elasticity and the income tax rate.

The objective is to express Eq. (13.22) in terms of the elasticity of taxable income (TI) with respect to $(1 - t)$. To do so, note that:

$$E_{C,P} = \left(\frac{1 + \tau}{C}\right)\frac{dC}{d(1 + \tau)} = -\left(\frac{1 - t}{C}\right)\frac{dC}{d(1 - t)} \tag{13.23}$$

by replacing $(1 + \tau)$ with $\dfrac{1}{1 - t}$ and differentiating w.r.t. $\dfrac{1}{1 - t}$.

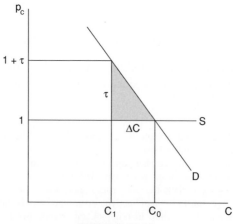

FIGURE 13.12

The elasticity in terms of taxable income is

$$E_{TI,(1-t)} = \left(\frac{1-t}{TI}\right)\frac{dTI}{d(1-t)} \tag{13.24}$$

From the budget constraint, the only difference between the uncompensated derivatives $\dfrac{dC}{d(1-t)}$ and $\dfrac{dTI}{d(1-t)}$ is the change in tax revenue. If the tax revenue is returned to the consumer, then the income-compensated derivatives are equal, or

$$\left(\frac{dC}{d(1-t)}\right)_{comp} = \left(\frac{dTI}{d(1-t)}\right)_{comp} \tag{13.25}$$

Compensating to hold income constant is not the same as compensating to hold utility constant. Nonetheless, Feldstein is following Harberger here. Harberger recommended using income-rather than utility-compensated elasticities in applied work.[29]

Combining Eq. (13.25) with the definitions of the two elasticities, Eq. (13.23) and (13.24), implies:

$$-CE_{C,P} = (1-t)\left(\frac{dC}{d(1-t)}\right)_{comp} = (1-t)\left(\frac{dTI}{d(1-t)}\right)_{comp} = TI \cdot E_{TI,(1-t)} \tag{13.26}$$

Therefore, from Eq. (13.22), dead-weight loss in terms of taxable income is

$$dwl = +.5t^2 E_{TI,(1-t)}\frac{TI}{(1-t)} \tag{13.27}$$

This is the back-of-the-envelope formula Feldstein recommends for calculating the dead-weight loss and comparing it with the total tax revenue. Further, the difference in the dead-weight loss for two different tax rates is the estimate of the marginal dead-weight loss from replacing one tax rate with the other. The marginal dead-weight loss can then be compared with the change in taxable income from the tax change.

In previous work analyzing the Tax Reform Act of 1986 (TRA86), Feldstein estimated that the average $E_{TI,(1-t)} = 1.04$ across all taxpayers.[30] He believes this can be considered an income-compensated elasticity because TRA86 was designed to be revenue neutral across households. This elasticity yields the following total and marginal dead-weight loss estimates:

1. In 1994, the dead-weight loss of the personal income tax was 32.2% of the total tax revenues.

---

[29] A. Harberger, "Three Basic Postulates for Applied Welfare Economics," *Journal of Economic Literature*, September 1971.

[30] M. Feldstein, "The Effects of Marginal Tax Rates on Taxable Income: A Panel Study of the 1986 Tax Reform Act," *Journal of Political Economy*, June 1995.

2. Raising all marginal tax rates in 1994 by 10% would generate a dead-weight loss of $43 billion.

Tax revenues, however, would only increase by $26 billion, and only by $21 billion counting the reduction in payroll taxes caused by the reduction in labor supply. Using the $21 billion produces an incremental dead-weight loss of $2.06 per dollar of additional tax revenue. This estimate far exceeds the usual estimates in the previous literature. Nonetheless, Feldstein cautions that tax increases that primarily affect the highest income taxpayers, such as the 1993 tax reform, are likely to generate even larger increases in dead-weight loss per dollar of additional tax revenue. His analysis of TRA86 suggested that $E_{TI,(1-t)}$ was on the order of 3 for the highest income taxpayers. Therefore, increasing their tax rates generates very high dead-weight losses and very little additional tax revenue, leading to extremely high incremental dead-weight losses per dollar of revenue collected.

The accuracy of Feldstein's suggested back-of-the-envelope calculation is difficult to judge. First, income-compensated elasticities are not the same as utility-compensated elasticities, and the latter can only be determined by specifying how specific elements of E and D enter the utility function.[31] Second, the elasticity of consumption with respect to income tax rates could be quite low, especially among high-income taxpayers. One wonders how accurate Feldstein's calculation would be relative to a richer intertemporal model that allows for saving. On the one hand, the equivalence of the income and consumption tax is not as simple as in the static model. The income tax would have to allow for deductions of all income from capital to establish equivalence. Second, income shifting between untaxed and taxed items may not have much effect on consumption and saving, just on the form of saving. If the principal changes are to households' budget constraints and not directly to their utilities, then the total and (especially) the marginal dead-weight losses from the personal income tax may be far less than Feldstein's simple calculations suggest. One's intuition is that responses of the real activities—of labor supply, saving, and investment—are the major sources of dead-weight loss arising from an income tax. Nonetheless, the other behavioral responses that Feldstein mentions are important reactions to income taxes and they may well increase the dead-weight loss from income taxes to the extent that Feldstein's measure suggest.

Efficiency Cost of the Personal Income Tax

No consensus exists on the total or marginal dead-weight loss from the federal personal income tax. As noted earlier, Hausman estimated the total

---

[31] An excellent analysis of the potential pitfalls of substituting income-compensated for utility-compensated elasticities in loss measures is D. Richter, "Games Pythagoreans Play," *Public Finance Quarterly*, October 1977.

loss per dollar of revenue collected at 28.7% looking only at the labor supply response. Feldstein's estimate considering other behavioral responses of 32.2% is in the same ballpark. The accuracy of these numbers is subject to debate, however. Thomas MaCurdy has shown that Hausman's estimating procedure can produce an upward bias in the estimate of the substitution effect, suggesting the dead-weight loss was overstated.[32] Other researchers have noted that estimates of female labor supply elasticities are typically much higher than those of males, suggesting that the dead-weight loss has increased as more women entered the labor market. A recent study of female labor supply responses in England by Richard Blundell, et al., however, found compensated wage elasticities ranging from .14 to .44, much smaller than in most previous studies.[33] Therefore, to claim a consensus has arisen of about 30% of the revenue collected may not be warranted.

Whatever the estimate of dead-weight loss, it should be increased by the costs of complying with income tax, the second potential source of inefficiency. Marsha Blumenthal and Joe Slemrod have estimated the compliance costs at about 5 to 7% of the revenue collected.[34] The administrative costs of collecting the revenue, the third potential source of inefficiency, are minuscule and can be ignored. There is no controversy on this point.

The estimates of the marginal dead-weight loss per additional dollar of revenue collected are all over the lot. The weight of the evidence suggests that the marginal loss is larger than the average loss, and perhaps much larger, but few studies have estimated marginal losses above $1 per dollar of additional revenue. Feldstein's $2.06 estimate is well above the typical estimate in the literature.

THE OPTIMAL PATTERN OF COMMODITY TAXES

The second main question of distorting taxation is that of optimality. Suppose the government has to raise a given amount of tax revenue $\overline{T}$, subject to the constraint that it must use distorting unit taxes paid by the consumer. If the government is free to tax or subsidize any good (or factor), what pattern of taxes raises the required revenue in such a way as to minimize dead-weight loss in the economy? This is commonly referred to as the optimal commodity tax problem, with the understanding that "commodities" include both goods and factors.

[32] T. MaCurdy, "Work Disincentive Effects of Taxes: A Reexamination of Some Evidence," *American Economic Review*, May 1992.

[33] R. Blundell, A. Duncan, and C. Meghir, "Estimating Labor Supply Responses Using Tax Reforms," *Econometrica*, July 1998. The elasticity estimates are from Table IV, p. 846.

[34] M. Blumenthal and J. Slemrod, "The Compliance Cost of the U.S. Individual Income Tax System: A Second Look After Tax Reform," *National Tax Journal*, June 1992.

Having defined the appropriate loss function for a one-consumer, linear technology economy, the optimal commodity tax problem is a straightforward, constrained, loss-minimization problem of the form:[35]

$$\min_{(t_k)} L(\vec{t})$$

$$\text{s.t.} \sum_{i=1}^{N} t_i X_i^C = \overline{T}$$

Two assumptions are necessary to ensure that the first-order conditions yield interesting results. First, we will continue to assume that the value of the consumer's expenditure function in the pretax equilibrium is zero; that is, $M(\vec{p}; \overline{U}^0) = 0$. If, to the contrary, $M(\vec{p}; \overline{U}^0) = k$, the loss-minimizing strategy is to tax the lump-sum income k at rate α such that $\overline{T} = \alpha k$, thereby avoiding any loss at all. If $k < \overline{T}$, the loss-minimizing strategy is to tax away the entire k and then using distorting taxes to collect revenue equal to $(\overline{T} - k)$. Because the problem can always be redefined in this way, it is convenient to assume $k = 0$ at the outset so that lump-sum income taxation is impossible.

Second, with zero lump-sum income, both demand and supply are homogeneous of degree zero in prices $\vec{q}$ and $\vec{p}$. Hence, we are permitted two separate normalizations, one for $\vec{q}$ and one for $\vec{p}$. For convenience, normalize both on the same good, the first. Therefore, set $q_1 \equiv p_1 \equiv 1$, which in turn implies $t_1 = 0$, or that the government does not tax the first good. These normalizations also remove the uninteresting possibility of proportional taxation, which is equivalent to lump-sum taxation and would entail no dead-weight loss. Proportional taxes also raise no revenue given the assumption of zero lump-sum income and constant producer prices. With good one untaxed, however, any set of tax rates on the remaining $(N - 1)$ goods and factors necessarily changes the vector of *relative* prices and generates loss.[36]

Given these two assumptions, define the Lagrangian[37] for the optimal tax problem as:

$$\min_{(t_k)} L = L(\vec{t}) + \lambda \left(\sum_{i=1}^{N} t_i X_i^c - \overline{T} \right) = M\left(\vec{q}; \overline{U}^0 \right) - \sum_{i=1}^{N} t_i X_i^c$$

$$- \lambda \left(\sum_{i=1}^{N} t_i X_i^c - \overline{T} \right)$$

with $t_1 \equiv 0$. The first-order conditions are

[35] The optimal tax problem can also be modeled using the consumer's utility function as the objective function, in which the goal is to maximize utility subject to a revenue constraint and distorting taxation. The resulting tax rules are identical upon using the Slutsky equation to substitute the compensated demand (and factor supply) derivatives for the ordinary derivatives.

[36] We assume further that the revenue requirement $\overline{T}$ is feasible.

[37] Whether the tax revenue summations go from $1, \ldots, N$ or $2, \ldots, N$ is immaterial as $t_1 \equiv 0$.

$$\frac{\partial L}{\partial t_k} = X_k^C - X_k^C - \sum_{i=1}^{N} t_i \frac{\partial X_i^C}{\partial q_k} - \lambda \left(X_k^C + \sum_{i=1}^{N} t_i \frac{\partial X_i^C}{\partial q_k} \right) = 0, \text{ for } k = 2, \ldots, N$$

$$(13.28)$$

(recall that $\partial q_k = \partial t_k$ with linear technology). Rearranging terms:

$$-(1 - \lambda) \left(\sum_{i=1}^{N} t_i \frac{\partial X_i^C}{\partial q_k} \right) - \lambda X_k^C = 0, \text{ for } k = 2, \ldots, N, \text{ or} \qquad (13.29)$$

$$\frac{\sum_{i=1}^{N} t_i \frac{\partial X_i^C}{\partial q_k}}{X_k^C} = \frac{-\lambda}{1 - \lambda} \qquad k = 2, \ldots, N \qquad (13.30)$$

Also,

$$\sum_{i=1}^{N} t_i X_i^C = \overline{T} \qquad (13.31)$$

Notice that the right-hand side (RHS) of Eq. (13.30) is independent of k. Furthermore, since $\partial X_i{}^C / \partial q_k = M_{ik} = M_{ki} = \partial X_k^C / \partial q_i$ from the symmetry of the Slutsky substitution terms, Eq. (13.30) can be rewritten as:

$$\frac{\sum_{i=1}^{N} t_i M_{ki}}{X_k^C} = C \qquad k = 2, \ldots, N \qquad (13.32)$$

The numerator, $\sum_{i=1}^{N} t_i (\Delta X_k^C / \Delta q_i) = \sum_{i=1}^{N} t_i (\Delta X_k^C / \Delta t_i)$ approximates the total change in X_k in response to marginal changes in all the taxes, $2, \ldots, N$. Hence, the left-hand side (LHS), $\Delta X_k^C / X_k^C$, is the percentage change in X_k^C, in response to the tax package. The first-order conditions, then, require a set of taxes that produce equal percentage changes in the compensated demands and supplies for all goods and factors.[38,39]

Notice that Eq. (13.32) describes percentage changes in terms of quantities and not the tax rates themselves. Unfortunately, the pattern of tax rates cannot be described by an equivalently simple rule. Their general pattern is

---

[38] If all the taxed goods and factors, $k = 2, \ldots, N$, undergo equal percentage changes, then the first untaxed good also undergoes the same percentage change, although the base for computing the percentage change differs.

[39] The equal percentage change interpretation applies, strictly speaking, only to marginal changes in each of the tax rates from the no-tax position, that is, to a marginal revenue package. For discrete tax changes, the rule implies that there must be an equal percentage change in quantity demanded in response to a further infinitesimal proportional change in all the tax rates from their optimum values. This interpretation is necessary because the compensated demand curves in the discrete case are all evaluated at the gross-of-tax consumer prices existing at the optimum when solving for the optimal pattern of the t_k. If all the M_{ik} are constant in the relevant range, however, then the rule needs no modification for the discrete case. This follows because:

clear, however: Goods (factors) whose compensated demands (supplies) are relatively inelastic should be subjected to relatively higher rates of taxation. This is the only way the "equal-percentage-change" rule can possibly be satisfied.

A rough intuitive explanation of the rule can be obtained by considering the optimal tax problem as one of minimizing the sum of the dead-weight loss triangles in each market (this ignores the cross-substitution terms $M_{ij}, j \neq i$, and their corresponding loss rectangles depicted in Fig. 13.10).[40]

If the compensated demand for one good is highly inelastic and the compensated demand for another highly elastic, most of the required revenue should be raised from the inelastic good. Its quantity demanded does not change much even with a relatively high tax rate. Consequently, it raises a relatively large amount of revenue with a relatively small dead-weight loss triangle. Conversely, placing an equal tax rate on a good with a relatively elastic demand causes a larger change in quantity demanded. Hence, the revenue collected is smaller and the dead-weight loss triangle larger. Per dollar of revenue then, it pays to tax the relatively inelastic goods (factors). In the limit, if one good (factor) has a perfectly inelastic compensated demand (supply), it should be used to collect all the revenue. There can be no dead-weight loss, and the percentage change in output is equalized across all goods at a value equal to zero.

Policy Implications of the Optimal Tax Rule

The equal-percentage-change rule is a deceptively simple representation of the optimal tax equilibrium. Computing the actual tax rates involves solving N first-order conditions for λ and the t_k, $k = 2, \ldots, N$, a prodigiously complex task, especially given limited econometric knowledge of the crucial Slutsky substitution terms. Furthermore, all goods and factors (except the untaxed numeraire) are either taxed or subsidized at the optimum, in general. Thus, it is extremely unlikely that any government could ever even approximate the *optimal* pattern of tax rates. Nonetheless, the equal-percentage-charge rule yields a number of useful qualitative insights for tax policy.

$$\Delta X_k{}^c = \sum_{i=1}^{N} \int_0^{t_i} M_{ik}\,dq_i = \sum_{i=1}^{N} \int_0^{t_i} M_{ki}\,dq_i = \sum_{i=1}^{N} M_{ki} \int_0^{t_i} dq_i$$

$$= \sum_{i=1}^{N} t_i M_{ki} = \sum_{i=1}^{N} t_i M_{ik}$$

when the M_{ik} are constant (and $t_1 \equiv 0$).

[40] See W. Baumol and D. Bradford, "Optimal Departures from Marginal Cost Pricing," *American Economic Review*, June 1970, on this point. Their article offers an excellent intuitive feel for the optimal tax problem and the properties of its solutions.

Broad-Based Taxation

The optimal commodity tax rule, (Eq. 13.32), offers a strong presumption against broad-based taxes such as general sales or general income taxes, which tax a broad range of goods or factors at a single rate. Additional restrictions on preferences are clearly required to generate the result that $t_k = aq_k$ with k defined over two or more goods (or factors).

Public sector economists have been particularly interested in the restrictions on preferences required for uniform taxation, in which all goods are taxed at the same proportional rate, the broadest general sales tax. Understanding the conditions for uniform taxation is especially compelling because of a theorem we will prove in Chapter 16, that the efficiency implications of an equal proportional tax on all the goods can be duplicated by replacing it with a proportional tax on all factors. Hence, if a uniform sales tax is optimal, it need not be used. A uniform income tax is also optimal. Income taxes are generally preferred to sales taxes on equity grounds because they are easier to tailor to the personal circumstances of individuals and families.

The public sector literature contains a number of sufficient conditions for uniform taxation in a model with $(N - 1)$ goods and labor as the untaxed numeraire. The first results appeared in the early 1970s. In 1995, Timothy Besley and Ian Jewitt were finally able to establish the necessary and sufficient conditions for uniform taxation in terms of a concept called the wage-compensated labor supply.[41] A sketch of the proof follows.

Distinguishing between the goods and labor is useful. Define $\vec{X}$ as the N-vector of goods, with element X_k; L, as labor, the untaxed numeraire; $\vec{q}$, as the N-vector of goods prices with element q_k and w, as the wage.

Necessary Conditions

If taxes are optimal, then Eq. (13.32) holds for all $k = 1, \ldots, N$:

$$\sum_{l=1}^{N} t_i M_{ik} = -\theta M_k \qquad (13.33)$$

Suppose also that taxes are uniform, so that $t_i = \rho q_i$, $i = 1, \ldots, N$. Therefore,

$$\sum_{l=1}^{N} \rho q_i M_{ik} = -\theta M_k, \text{ or} \qquad (13.34)$$

---

[41] Their model is identical to our simple model with the exception that it allows for general technology with constant returns to scale production. As we will see in Chapter 14, however, the first order conditions for optimal taxation with general technology continue to be Eq. (13.32) as long as there are no pure profits, which is true under constant returns to scale (CRS) production (and perfect competition). See T. Besley and I Jewitt, "Uniform Taxation and Consumer Preferences," *Journal of Public Economics*, September 1995.

$$\sum_{l=1}^{N} q_i M_{ik} = (-\theta/\rho) M_k \qquad (13.35)$$

Homogeneity of the compensated demands and supplies implies:

$$\sum_{l=1}^{N} q_i M_{ki} + w M_{kw} = 0 \qquad (13.36)$$

Therefore,

$$w M_{kw} = (\theta/\rho) M_k, \text{ or} \qquad (13.37)$$

$$M_{kw} = [\theta/(\rho w)] M_k = \alpha M_k \quad k = 1, \ldots, N \qquad (13.38)$$

where α is a scalar. The necessary conditions for uniform taxation are that the derivatives of the compensated demand for each good with respect to the wage are proportional to the compensated demand for the good.

Sufficient Condition

The sufficient condition relies on the property that the producer and consumer prices of all the goods must be collinear for Eqs. (13.32) and (13.38) to hold simultaneously. That is, $p_i = k q_i$, for $i = 1, \ldots, N$. But, $t_i = q_i - p_i$. Therefore, the collinearlity condition implies uniform taxes. (See their article for the details surrounding the collinearity condition on the prices.)

Consider, next, the wage-compensated labor supply. *Wage-compensated* means that the wage adjusts to maintain utility at a given level. That is, $w = w(q, \overline{U})$ such that $V(q, w(q, \overline{U})) = \overline{U}$, where V is the indirect utility function. The wage-compensated labor supply is the derivative of the expenditure function with $w = w(q, \overline{U})$:

$$L(q, \overline{U}) = -\partial M(q, w(q, \overline{U}), \overline{U})/\partial w \qquad (13.39)$$

To obtain the necessary and sufficient conditions in terms of the wage-compensated labor supply, differentiate $L(q, \overline{U})$ with respect to q_k:

$$\partial L/\partial q_k = -\partial M^2/\partial w \partial q_k + \partial^2 M/\partial w^2 \cdot \partial w/\partial q_k \qquad (13.40)$$

$$= -\partial M^2/\partial w \partial q_k + \partial^2 M/\partial w^2 \cdot (\partial M/\partial q_k/\partial M/\partial w) \qquad (13.41)$$

$$= -\partial M^2/\partial w \partial q_k + (\partial^2 M/\partial w^2/\partial M/\partial w) \cdot \partial M/\partial q_k, \\ k = 1, \ldots, N \qquad (13.42)$$

The RHS of Eq. (13.42) has the same form as Eq. (13.38). Therefore, the necessary and sufficient conditions for uniform taxation are that the RHS of Eq. (13.42) equal zero, or $\partial L(q, \overline{U})/\partial q_k = 0$, all $k = 1, \ldots, N$. The wage-compensated labor supply curve must be independent of all commodity prices for uniform taxation to be optimal.

An immediate implication of the Besley–Jewitt theorem is that uniform taxation is optimal if:[42]

$$\partial(\partial M/\partial q_i /\partial M/\partial q_j)/dw = 0 \quad \text{all } i, j = 1, \ldots, N \quad (13.43)$$

or

$$\partial\left(\frac{X_i^C}{X_j^C}\right)/\partial w = 0 \quad (13.44)$$

The ratio of the compensated demands is independent of the wage at the optimum. The literature has developed a number of sufficient conditions for the optimality of uniform taxation based on the separability of either the expenditure function or the utility function, all of which imply condition (13.44). For example, an expenditure function of the form $M(q, w, U) = F(g(q, U), w, U)$ satisfies Eq. (13.44).[43,44]

The Exemption of "Necessities"

The optimal commodity tax rule also gives a strong presumption against the common practice of exempting necessities such as food and clothing from sales tax bases. If anything, these items can be expected to have relatively low substitution effects (along with their income elasticities being less than one). Therefore, by the efficiency criterion, they should be taxed at *higher* than average rates, not exempted from taxation. But, governments exempt these items anyway for equity reasons, in an attempt to make sales taxes somewhat less regressive. For example, 26 states in the United States exempt food purchased for home consumption from their sales taxes.

Analysis of optimal commodity taxation within the context of a many-consumer economy, the subject of Chapter 14, can reconcile the equity–efficiency trade-off, but only in principle. Many-person tax rules are

---

[42] $\partial(\partial M/\partial q_i /\partial M/\partial q_j)/\partial w = (\partial M/\partial q_j \cdot \partial^2 M/\partial q_i \partial w - \partial M/\partial q_i \cdot \partial^2 M/\partial q_j \partial w)/(\partial M/\partial q_j)^2$. But, with uniform optimal taxation, $\partial^2 M/\partial q_i \partial w = \alpha \partial M/\partial q_i$ and $\partial^2 M \partial q_j \partial w = \alpha \partial M/\partial q_j$, so that the numerator is zero.

[43] See Besley and Jewitt, *op. cit.*, for a complete analysis of why separability of the expenditure function is sufficient but not necessary for uniform taxation to be optimal.

[44] Atkinson and Stiglitz were the first to derive sufficient conditions for uniform taxation in the simple model with $N - 1$ goods and labor the untaxed numeraire. Atkinson and Stiglitz prove that uniform taxation is optimal if either (a) labor is in absolutely fixed supply (see pp. 319–320) or (b) preferences are homothetic. They also proved that if preferences have an additive representation (i.e., $U(X_1, \ldots, X_{n-1}, L) = g_1(X_1) + \ldots + g_{n-1}(X_{n-1}) + g_n(L)$, then tax rates are inversely proportional to each commodity's income elasticity of demand. This implies uniform taxation if preferences are additive in logarithms with equal coefficients, in which case all income elasticities equal one. They also proved that if preferences have an additive representation, and the marginal disutility of labor is constant (i.e., $\partial g_n/\partial L = k$), then the optimal tax rates are inversely proportional to each commodity's own price elasticity of demand (refer to the discussion of the inverse elasticity rule, below). See A. Atkinson and J. Stiglitz, "The Structure of Indirect Taxation and Economic Efficiency," *Journal of Public Economics*, Vol. 1, 1972.

extremely difficult to apply. Nonetheless, it is clear that many governments have been swayed more by equity than by efficiency arguments in designing their sales taxes. This is often the case whenever equity and efficiency goals conflict. Favoring equity over efficiency considerations is not peculiar to tax policy.

Percentage Charge Rules for Ordinary Demand (Factor Supply) Relationships

Some additional qualitative policy information can be obtained by re-writing Eq. (13.32) in terms of the ordinary price and income derivatives by means of the Slutsky equation:

$$\frac{\partial X_k}{\partial q_i} = M_{ki} - X_i \frac{\partial X_k}{\partial I} \tag{13.45}$$

or

$$M_{ki} = \frac{\partial X_k}{\partial q_i} + X_i \frac{\partial X_k}{\partial I} \tag{13.46}$$

Substituting Eq. (13.46) into (13.32) yields:

$$\frac{\sum_{i=1}^{N} t_i \left(\frac{\partial X_k}{\partial q_i} + X_i \frac{\partial X_k}{\partial I} \right)}{X_k} = C \quad k = 2, \ldots, N \tag{13.47}$$

Rearranging terms:

$$\frac{\sum_{i=1}^{N} t_i \frac{\partial X_k}{\partial q_i}}{X_k} = C - \sum_{i=1}^{N} t_i X_i \frac{\frac{\partial X_k}{\partial I}}{X_k} \quad k = 2, \ldots, N \tag{13.48}$$

Multiplying and dividing the second term on the RHS of Eq. (13.48) by I yields:

$$\frac{\sum_{i=1}^{N} t_i \frac{\partial X_k}{\partial q_i}}{X_k} = C - \frac{\sum_{i=1}^{N} t_i X_i}{I} (E_{k,I}) \quad k = 2, \ldots, N \tag{13.49}$$

where $E_{k,I}$ is the income elasticity for good k.

Assuming the $\partial X_k / \partial q_i$ are constant in the relevant range, the LHS of Eq. (13.49) gives the percentage change in the ordinary demand (supply) of the kth good (factor). Notice that these percentage changes are not equal. Goods with higher income elasticities should change by the greater amount (in absolute value; C is presumably negative for goods). The intuition is to exploit income effects, since they do not contribute to dead-weight loss. Of course, the optimal tax rates are no more easily solved by Eq. (13.49) than by Eq. (13.32) (including the revenue constraint in each instance). At the same time, common sense often suggests which goods tend to have relatively high income elasticities. Notice, for example, that Eq. (13.49) gives a partial efficiency justification for taxing necessities lightly.

The Inverse Elasticity Rule

An approximation to the equal-percentage-change rule that is often used in policy analysis is the inverse elasticity rule (IER). The IER says that tax rates should be increased in inverse proportion to a good's (factor's) price elasticity of demand.[45] The basis for this interpretation of Eq. (13.32) is as follows.

Suppose, as an approximation, that all income effects are ignored as being empirically unimportant and, further, that all cross-price derivatives are set equal to zero on the grounds that their own price effects dominate the cross-price effects. With these two assumptions, Eq. (13.32) reduces to:

$$\frac{t_k M_{kk}}{X_k} = C \qquad k = 2, \ldots, N \tag{13.50}$$

where:

M_{kk} = the own price derivative for *both* compensated and ordinary demand (supply) curves, since there are no income effects.

Multiplying and dividing the LHS of Eq. (13.50) by q_k yields:

$$\left(\frac{t_k}{q_k}\right) \cdot \left(\frac{\partial X_k}{\partial q_k} \cdot \frac{q_k}{X_k}\right) = C \qquad k = 2, \ldots, N \tag{13.51}$$

Alternatively,

$$\left(\frac{t_k}{q_k}\right) = \frac{C}{E_{kk}} \qquad k = 2, \ldots, N \tag{13.52}$$

where:

E_{kk} = the own-price elasticity of demand.

The tax rate as a percentage of the gross of tax price, q, should be inversely proportional to the own-price elasticity of demand (supply) for each good (factor), hence the inverse elasticity rule.

The IER is an intuitively appealing interpretation of the optimal tax rules, especially if one thinks in terms of minimizing dead-weight loss triangles, but the assumptions supporting this interpretation are heroic, to say the least. As noted in the preceding section on marginal loss, if all income

---

[45] A. Kahn, *The Economics of Regulation: Principles and Institutions*, Wiley, New York, 1970, Vol. I, pp. 144–145, contains a discussion of the inverse elasticity rule in the context of price discrimination. Kahn's analysis reflects the importance of the IER in the industrial organization literature. As we shall discover in Chapter 21, second-best pricing rules for multiproduct decreasing cost industries with profit constraints are virtually identical to the optimal tax rule.

effects are zero, then ordinary price derivatives must follow the same laws as compensated price derivatives, in particular the homogeneity result that $\sum_{i=1}^{N} q_i M_{ik} = 0$, all $k = 1, \ldots, N$. But, this implies $M_{ki} \neq 0$ for some i, $i \neq k$ (because $M_{ii} < 0$). One legitimate possibility is to assume that $M_{ki} = 0, i \neq k$, for all *taxed* goods (factors). This implies that all cross-price effects occur with respect to the untaxed numeraire; that is, $M_{k1} \neq 0$, all $k = 2, \ldots, N$. In particular, with $q_1 \equiv 1$ (the numeraire),

$$M_{k1} = -q_k M_{kk} \quad k = 2, \ldots, N \tag{13.53}$$

Unfortunately, Eq. (13.53) can hardly be expected to be true. Thus, the IER may not be very useful even as a rough guideline to the policymaker.

A more sensible alternative for policy analysis may be to select one or two $M_{ki}, i \neq k$, that are likely to be nonzero, place reasonable values on them that satisfy the homogeneity condition $\sum_{i=1}^{N} q_i M_{ik} = 0$, and apply a simplified version of the equal percentage change rule, Eq. (13.32). It will still have nearly an inverse elasticity interpretation. For example, suppose one assumes that only M_{kk} and M_{kj} are nonzero when evaluating the first-order condition for t_k. The kth relation in Eq. (13.32) becomes:

$$\frac{t_k M_{kk} + t_j M_{kj}}{X_k} = C \tag{13.54}$$

Multiplying and dividing the two terms on the LHS by q_k and q_j, respectively, yields:

$$\frac{t_k}{q_k} \cdot E_{kk} + \frac{t_j}{q_j} E_{kj} = C \tag{13.55}$$

Rearranging terms,

$$\frac{t_k}{q_k} E_{kk} = C - \frac{t_j}{q_j} E_{kj} \tag{13.56}$$

and

$$\left(\frac{t_k}{q_k} \right) = \frac{1}{E_{kk}} \left[C - \left(\frac{t_j}{q_j} \right) E_{kj} \right] = \left[C/E_{kk} + t_j/q_j \right] \tag{13.57}$$

with $E_{kj} = -E_{kk}$. In this form, the IER says that the percentage tax on good (factor) k is inversely related to its own-price elasticity corrected by a term equal to the percentage tax (at the optimum) on the other good.

This simplification at least avoids having to impose patently unrealistic assumptions on the compensated cross-price elasticities. Also, the resulting simultaneous system of equations would not be much more difficult to solve than the standard IER applied to all goods and factors.[46]

---

[46] The IER has figured prominently in public hearings concerned with setting prices in the regulated industries. The reason for this is that second-best pricing rules for multiproduct,

SUBSTITUTIONS AMONG TAXES: IMPLICATIONS FOR WELFARE LOSS

The third main question of distorting taxation is that of tax reform: What is the implication on social welfare of substituting one set of taxes for another while holding revenue constant? This tax substitution experiment is perhaps the most compelling of all second-best exercises within the pure allocational theory of taxation, if only because governments occasionally engage in such tax substitutions. We continue to assume a one-consumer equivalent economy with linear technology.

As long as the tax changes are "small," the expressions for marginal loss and total tax revenue are all that are needed to determine the efficiency implications for any given equal-revenue substitution among taxes. Begin with the total differential of dead-weight loss, Eq. (13.11), with respect to all the taxes:

$$dL = -\sum_{k=1}^{N} \sum_{i=1}^{N} t_i M_{ik} dt_k \qquad (13.58)$$

(there is no need to assume an untaxed good in this exercise). Equation (13.58) is an appropriate measure of marginal loss for any given change in the vector of tax rates. The reason why is that a substitution can always be viewed as a multistep series of individual loss experiments, in which one tax is reduced and the revenue returned to the government lump sum, after which a second tax is imposed, with its revenue returned to the consumer lump sum, and so on, for any number of tax changes. Because $M_{ik} = M_{ki}$, the order of substitution is irrelevant.

Next, add the values of dt_k that hold revenue constant. These can be determined by totally differentiating the tax revenue equation:

$$dT = \sum_{k=1}^{N} \left(M_k + \sum_{i=1}^{N} t_i M_{ik} \right) dt_k \qquad (13.59)$$

Setting $dT = 0$, Eq. (13.59) determines all possible tax substitutions that keep revenue unchanged. Once the appropriate values for dt_k have been determined from Eq. (13.59), they can be substituted back into Eq. (13.58) to determine the resulting change in dead-weight loss.

When only two taxes change, Eq. (13.59) describes the exact relationship between the two changes necessary to hold revenue constant. Suppose,

---

decreasing-cost industries with profit constraints are virtually identical to the optimal tax rule, as we shall discover in Chapter 21. One common example is the U.S. postal service, which has long used the IER to justify its policy of covering its cost increases primarily by increasing rates on first-class mail (relatively inelastic demands) rather than on the other classes of mail such as parcel post (relatively elastic demands). We will return to the postal service example in Chapter 21.

for example, t_j and t_k are to be changed, $dt_i = 0$, for $i \neq j, k$. From Eq. (13.59),

$$dT = 0 = \left(M_k + \sum_{i=1}^{N} t_i M_{ik} \right) dt_k + \left(M_j + \sum_{i=1}^{N} t_i M_{ij} \right) dt_j \qquad (13.60)$$

or

$$\frac{dt_k}{dt_j} = -\frac{\dfrac{\partial T}{\partial t_j}}{\dfrac{\partial T}{\partial t_k}} \qquad (13.61)$$

As expected, the two rates must change in direct ratio to the marginal changes in tax revenue with respect to each of the taxes. Presumably, one tax is increased and the other is decreased. Notice also that the relevant marginal revenue changes are the changes at the compensated equilibria, not the actual equilibria. This is consistent with the definition of loss in terms of compensated equilibria.

To complete the analysis, the marginal loss with respect to changes in t_j and t_k is

$$dL = - \left(\sum_{i=1}^{N} t_i M_{ik} dt_k + \sum_{i=1}^{N} t_i M_{ij} dt_j \right) \qquad (13.62)$$

from Eq. (13.58). Substituting in the equal-revenue constraint, Eq. (13.61), and recalling that $\partial L / \partial t_k = -\sum_{i=1}^{N} t_i M_{ik}$ yields:

$$dL = \left[\frac{\partial L}{\partial t_k} \left(-\frac{\dfrac{\partial T}{\partial t_j}}{\dfrac{\partial T}{\partial t_k}} \right) dt_j + \frac{\partial L}{\partial t_j} dt_j \right] \qquad (13.63)$$

Rearranging terms:

$$\frac{dL}{dt_j} = \left[\frac{\partial L}{\partial t_k} \left(-\frac{\dfrac{\partial T}{2t_j}}{\dfrac{\partial T}{\partial t_k}} \right) + \frac{\partial L}{\partial t_j} \right] = \left[\frac{\partial L}{\partial t_k} \left(+\frac{dt_k}{dt_j} \bigg|_{R=\overline{R}} \right) + \frac{\partial L}{\partial t_j} \right] \qquad (13.64)$$

Equation (13.64) gives an entirely plausible result. The change in loss from increasing one tax (say, t_j) and lowering another tax (say, t_k) to keep total tax revenue constant is a linear combination of the marginal losses from changing t_k and t_j individually. The marginal loss for the revenue-compensating tax, t_k, is weighted by the amount that t_k must be changed per unit change in t_j in order to keep revenue unchanged. Put another way, the second term on the RHS of Eq. (13.64) measures the direct effect on loss because of a change in t_j. The first term measures the indirect effect on loss working through the required change in t_k in response to dt_j so that $dT = 0$. In the two-tax case, then, Eq. (13.64) gives an exact expression for the change in loss arising from a "small" equal revenue tax substitution.

When more than two taxes change, an infinity of combinations for the dt can satisfy Eq. (13.59). The natural way to proceed in this case is to impose values on all but one of the tax changes, use Eq. (13.59) to solve for the remaining tax change, and then substitute for the dt in Eq. (13.58).

Other than the obvious point that, given approximately equal revenue effects, taxes that generate small changes in loss should replace taxes that generate large changes in loss to reduce loss, equations such as Eq. (13.64) are not particularly illuminating for policy purposes. Equation (13.64) can yield some interesting results, however, with additional restrictions added to the model in the form of limited possibilities for substitution and/or limitations in the number of taxed goods.

The Corlett and Hague Analysis

Corlett and Hague presented one of the more famous exercises along these lines, and one of the first. They examined the efficiency implications of moving from equal proportional taxes on two goods in the context of a three-good economy in which leisure is the third good and is incapable of being taxed.[47] Label the two goods k and j, and let good 1 be leisure, the untaxed numeraire ($q_1 \equiv 1 \equiv p_1; t_1 \equiv 0$). Assume initially that $t_j = \alpha \bar{p}_j$ and $t_k = \alpha \bar{p}_k$, with α the equal proportional rate of tax. Consider the efficiency implications of a marginal increase in t_j coupled with a marginal decrease in t_k that holds revenue constant—that is, an equal revenue movement away from proportionality.

With proportional taxes α,

$$q_j = \bar{p}_j + \alpha \bar{p}_j = (1 + \alpha)\bar{p}_j \qquad (13.65)$$

$$q_k = \bar{p}_k + \alpha \bar{p}_k = (1 + \alpha)\bar{p}_k \qquad (13.66)$$

Substituting the expressions for marginal loss into Eq. (13.64) yields:

$$\frac{dL}{dt_j} = -\left[+ \sum_{i=k,j} t_i M_{ik} \left(\frac{dt_k}{dt_j} \Big|_{R=\bar{R}} \right) + \sum_{i=k,j} t_i M_{ij} \right] \qquad (13.67)$$

[47] See W. Corlett and D. Hague, "Complementarity and the Excess Burden of Taxation," *Review of Economic Studies*, Vol. 21(1), No. 54, 1953–1954. See also P. A. Diamond and D. McFadden, "Some Uses of the Expenditure Function in Public Finance," *Journal of Public Economics*, Vol. 3, 1974.

To replace the terms $\sum_{i=k,j} t_i M_{ik}$ and $\sum_{i=k,j} t_i M_{ij}$, make use of the homogeneity condition and the symmetry of the Slutsky derivatives:

$$\sum_{i=1}^{3} q_i M_{ik} = \sum_{i=1}^{3} q_i M_{ij} = 0 \tag{13.68}$$

Rewrite $\sum_{i=1}^{3} q_i M_{ik} = 0$ as:

$$M_{1k} = -q_j M_{jk} - q_k M_{kk}, \text{ with } q_1 \equiv 1 \tag{13.69}$$

But, from Eqs. (13.65) and (13.66),

$$M_{1k} = -\left[(1 + \alpha)\bar{p}_j M_{jk} + (1 + \alpha)\bar{p}_k M_{kk}\right] \tag{13.70}$$

Furthermore,

$$t_j M_{jk} + t_k M_{kk} = \alpha \bar{p}_j M_{jk} + \alpha \bar{p}_k M_{kk} \tag{13.71}$$

Hence, from Eqs. (13.70) and (13.71),

$$\sum_{i=k,j} t_i M_{ik} = -\left(\frac{\alpha}{1 + \alpha}\right) M_{1k} \tag{13.72}$$

Similarly,

$$\sum_{i=k,j} t_i M_{ij} = -\left(\frac{\alpha}{1 + \alpha}\right) M_{1j} \tag{13.73}$$

Therefore, Eq. (13.67) becomes:

$$\frac{dL}{dt_j} = +\left(\frac{\alpha}{1 + \alpha}\right)\left(M_{1k}\frac{dt_k}{dt_j}\bigg|_{R=\bar{R}} + M_{1j}\right) \tag{13.74}$$

Next, totally differentiate M_1, the demand for leisure, with respect to t_j, subject to the total revenue constraint and $q_1 \equiv 1$:

$$\frac{dM_1}{dt_j} = M_{1k}\frac{dt_k}{dt_j}\bigg|_{R=\bar{R}} + M_{1j} \tag{13.75}$$

Substituting Eq. (13.75) into (13.74) yields:

$$\frac{dL}{dt_j} = +\left(\frac{\alpha}{1 + \alpha}\right)\frac{dM_1}{dt_j} \tag{13.76}$$

Thus, if leisure decreases (work increases) in response to the changes in $t_j(+)$ and $t_k(-)$, loss decreases, in which case equal proportional taxes are dominated by a system of nonproportional taxes on goods k and j.[48]

---

[48] By similar manipulations it can be demonstrated that $dL/dt_k = +\left(\frac{\alpha}{1+\alpha}\right)(d\, M_1/d\, t_k)$. Hence, if either dM_1/dt_k or dM_1/dt_j is negative, nonproportional taxes dominate proportional taxes.

Whether or not dM_1/dt_j is negative depends on the Slutsky substitution terms M_{ij} and M_{ik}. To see this, write Eq. (13.75) as:

$$\frac{dM_1}{dt_j} = M_{1k}\left[-\frac{\dfrac{\partial T_j}{\partial t_j}}{\dfrac{\partial T_k}{\partial t_k}}\right] + M_{1j} \tag{13.77}$$

$$\frac{dM_1}{dt_j} = M_{1k}\left[-\frac{M_j + \displaystyle\sum_{i=k,j} t_i M_{ij}}{M_k + \displaystyle\sum_{i=k,j} t_i M_{ik}}\right] + M_{1j} \tag{13.78}$$

Substitute Eqs. (13.72) and (13.73) into Eq. (13.78) to obtain:

$$\frac{dM_1}{dt_j} = M_{1k}\left[-\frac{\left(M_j - \left(\dfrac{\alpha}{1+\alpha}\right)M_{1j}\right)}{\left(M_k - \left(\dfrac{\alpha}{1+\alpha}\right)M_{1k}\right)}\right] + M_{1j} \tag{13.79}$$

Equation (13.79) assumes proportional taxes initially. Placing Eq. (13.79) over a common denominator and rearranging terms yields:

$$\frac{dM_1}{dt_j} = \frac{-M_j M_{1k} + M_k M_{1j}}{\left[M_k - \left(\dfrac{\alpha}{1+\alpha}\right)M_{1k}\right]} \tag{13.80}$$

Multiplying the first term in the numerator by M_k/M_k and the second term by M_j/M_j yields:

$$\frac{dM_1}{dt_j} = \frac{M_k M_j}{\left(M_k - \left(\dfrac{\alpha}{1+\alpha}\right)M_{1k}\right)} \cdot \left(\frac{M_{1j}}{M_j} - \frac{M_{1k}}{M_k}\right) \tag{13.81}$$

Assuming the first term on the RHS of Eq. (13.81) is positive, the sign of Eq. (13.81) depends upon the relative magnitudes of M_{1j}/M_j and M_{1k}/M_k. Consider the various possibilities. With $M_{11} < 0$, one possibility is $M_{1k} > 0$ and $M_{1j} < 0$. In the Slutsky sense, goods k and 1 are substitutes; goods j and 1, complements. If this is the case, then $dM_1/dt_j < 0$ as required for a decrease in loss. Hence, the government should raise the tax on the good that is complementary with leisure. If $M_{ik} < 0$ and $M_{1j} > 0$ then t_k should be raised.[49] If both are substitutes, such that M_{1k} and $M_{ij} > 0$, then Eq. (13.81)

---

[49] If the analysis is carried out with respect to dt_k, the equation replacing Eq. (13.81) would be

$$\frac{dM_1}{dt_k} = \frac{M_k M_j}{\left[M_j - \left(\frac{\alpha}{1-\alpha}\right)M_{1j}\right]} \cdot \left(\frac{M_{1k}}{M_k} - \frac{M_{1j}}{M_j}\right) \tag{13.81n}$$

implies raising the tax on the good relatively more complementary (less substitutable) with leisure—for example, raising t_j if, roughly speaking, $M_{1j} < M_{1k}$ and vice versa. The only other possibility in a three-good world is for one of the goods to be a Slutsky substitute for leisure (say, $M_{1k} > 0$) while the other is neither a substitute nor a complement ($M_{1j} = 0$). In this case, the tax should be increased on the good for which the cross-price derivative is zero, since it is *relatively* more complementary with leisure. (Both goods cannot be Slutsky complements, since $\sum_{k=1}^{3} q_k M_{1k} = 0$ from homogeneity of the compensated demand functions and $M_{11} < 0$.)

Note, finally, that the Corlett–Hague analysis applies, strictly speaking, only for small changes in taxes. Using the homogeneity conditions to obtain expressions in terms of M_{1k} and M_{1j} requires evaluating all demand relationships (M_k, M_{jk}, etc.) at the original proportional tax prices. The larger the tax changes, the more inaccurate this evaluation becomes. There are no longer any simple relationships between M_{1k} and $\sum_{i=k,j} t_i M_{ik}$ or between M_{1j} and $\sum_{i=k,j} t_i M_{ij}$.

REFERENCES

Atkinson, A., and Stiglitz, J., "The Structure of Indirect Taxation and Economic Efficiency," *Journal of Public Economics*, Vol. 1, 1972.

Atkinson, A., and Stiglitz, J., "The Design of Tax Structure: Direct vs. Indirect Taxation," *Journal of Public Economics*, July / August 1976.

Baumol W., and Bradford, D., "Optimal Departures from Marginal Cost Pricing," *American Economic Review*, June 1970.

Besley, T., and Jewitt, I., "Uniform Taxation and Consumer Preferences," *Journal of Public Economics*, September 1995.

Blumenthal, M., and Slemrod, J., "The Compliance Cost of the U.S.Individual Income Tax System: A Second Look After Tax Reform," *National Tax Journal*, June 1992.

Blundell, R., Duncan, A., and Meghir, C., "Estimating Labor Supply Responses Using Tax Reforms," *Econometrica*, July 1998.

Boskin, M., "On Some Recent Econometric Research in Public Finance," *American Economic Association Papers and Proceedings*, May 1976.

Bradford, D., and Rosen, H., "The Optimal Taxation of Commodities and Income," *American Economic Association Papers and Proceedings*, May 1976.

Browning, E., "The Excess Burden of Excise vs. Income Taxes: A Simplified Comparison," *Public Finance*, 3, 1975.

Browning, E., "The Marginal Cost of Public Funds," *Journal of Political Economy*, April 1976.

Corlett, W., and Hague, D., "Complementarity and the Excess Burden of Taxation," *Review of Economic Studies*, Vol. 21(1), No. 54, 1953–1954.

Diamond, P. A., and McFadden, D., "Some Uses of the Expenditure Function in Public Finance," *Journal of Public Economics*, Vol. 3, 1974.

Diamond, P. A., and Mirrlees, J., "Optimal Taxation and Public Production" (2 parts; Part 1: 'Production Efficiency,' Part II: 'Tax Rules'), *American Economic Review*, March, June 1971.

Dixit, A., "Welfare Effects of Tax and Price Changes," *Journal of Public Economics*, February 1975.

Dixit, A., and Munk, K., "Welfare Effects of Tax and Price Changes: A Correction," *Journal of Public Economics*, August 1977.

Feldstein, M., "The Effects of Marginal Tax Rates on Taxable Income: A Panel Study of the 1986 Tax Reform Act," *Journal of Political Economy*, June 1995.

Feldstein, M., "Tax Avoidance and the Deadweight Loss of the Income Tax," *Review of Economics and Statistics*, November 1999.

Friedman, M., "The Welfare Effects of an Income and an Excise Tax," *Journal of Political Economy*, February 1952.

George, H., *Progress and Poverty*, Doubleday & Co., New York, 1914, Book VIII.

Green, J., and Sheshinski, E., "Approximating the Efficiency Gains of Tax Reforms," *Journal of Public Economics*, April 1979.

Harberger, A., "Taxation, Resource Allocation and Welfare," in *The Role of Direct and Indirect Taxes in the Federal Revenue System*, The National Bureau of Economic Research and The Brookings Institution, Princeton University Press, Princeton, N.J., 1964.

Harberger, A., "The Measurement of Waste," *American Economic Association Papers and Proceedings*, May 1964.

Harberger, A., "Three Basic Postulates for Applied Welfare Economics," *Journal of Economic Literature*, September 1971.

Harberger, A., *Taxation and Welfare*, Little, Brown and Co., Boston, MA, 1974.

Hausman, J., "Labor Supply," in H. Aaron and J. Pechman, Eds., *How Taxes Affect Economic Behavior*, The Brookings Institution, Washington, D.C., 1981.

Hausman, J., and Rudd, P., "Family Labor Supply with Taxes," *American Economic Association Papers and Proceedings*, May, 1984.

Hotelling, H., "The General Welfare in Relation to Problems of Taxation and of Railway and Utility Rates," *Econometrica*, July 1938.

Kahn, A., *The Economics of Regulation: Principles and Institutions*, Wiley, New York, 1970, Vol. 1.

Kotlikoff, L., "Taxation and Savings: A Neoclassical Perspective," *Journal of Economic Literature*, December 1984.

MaCurdy, T., "Work Disincentive Effects of Taxes: A Reexamination of Some Evidence," *American Economic Review*, May 1992.

Mirrlees, J., "An Exploration in the Theory of Optimum Income Taxation," *Review of Economic Studies*, April 1971.

Ramsey, F. P., "A Contribution to the Theory of Taxation," *Economic Journal*, March 1927.

Richter, D., "Games Pythagoreans Play," *Public Finance Quarterly*, October 1977.

Samuelson, P. A., "Theory of Optimal Taxation," *Journal of Public Economics*, June 1986.

Sandmo, S., "Optimal Taxation," *Journal of Public Economics*, July–August 1976.

Slemrod, J., "Do Taxes Matter?," *American Economic Review*, May 1992.

Summers, L., "Capital Taxation and Accumulation in a Life Cycle Growth Model," *American Economic Review*, September 1981.

14

THE SECOND-BEST THEORY OF TAXATION WITH GENERAL PRODUCTION TECHNOLOGIES AND MANY CONSUMERS

The second-best analysis of Chapter 13 must be extended in two directions to make it more responsive to real-world economies. One is to incorporate general production technologies, with increasing cost production-possibilities frontiers. Another is to consider the case of many consumers with different tastes and different marginal social welfare weights. Neither extension is analytically trivial.

With general technologies, producer prices vary as government policy variables move society along (or inside of) its production-possibilities frontier. Also, pure economic profits or losses are possible and have to be accounted for in a general equilibrium framework. As a consequence of these features, the marginal loss from taxation depends on production derivatives as well as consumption derivatives.

The many-consumer economy brings the social welfare function back into the analysis in a fundamental way, such that distinctions between the equity and efficiency implications of government policy become blurred. In addition, the concept of a general aggregate income measure of tax loss becomes problematic.

The modeling implications of either extension are sufficiently complex that Chapter 14 considers each separately before combining them into a fully general model. The first section of the chapter reworks two of the main results of Chapter 13 in the context of a one-consumer, general-technology economy. The second section considers the many-consumer economy with fixed producer prices. The third and final section then presents the full general model and emphasizes how the results of Chapter 13 must be modified to accommodate a more realistic economic environment.

A ONE-CONSUMER ECONOMY WITH GENERAL TECHNOLOGY

Dead-Weight Loss from Taxation

Replacing the assumption of linear technology with the more realistic assumption of general technology affects the analysis of tax loss in two ways. The most direct implication is that production terms enter into the loss function in a nontrivial manner. In addition, general technology reintroduces market clearance explicitly into the analysis because the full set of market clearance equations is necessary to determine the relationship between producer and consumer prices. Each point deserves careful attention.

Pure Profits and Losses

With linear technology, the loss resulting from a vector of commodity taxes is defined as the lump-sum income necessary to keep the consumer indifferent to the taxes less the tax revenue collected at the compensated equilibrium and returned lump sum to the consumer, or $L(\vec{t}) = M(\vec{q}; \overline{U}) - \sum_{i=2}^{N} t_i X_i^C(\vec{q}; \overline{U})$. There is no need to keep track of production because as society moves along a linear production frontier there can never be any pure profits in the system that could also be given to the consumer. If, as we assumed, the competitively determined producer prices for the goods and factors generate no pure profits in the initial equilibrium, then there can never be pure profits because these prices never change. With general technologies, however, the competitively determined producer prices may well generate pure profits and losses, both at the initial zero-tax equilibrium and at the final with-tax equilibrium, and the pure profits may vary from one equilibrium to another. Consider, for example, the one-input, one-output, decreasing-returns-to-scale technology depicted in Fig. 14.1, in which input X_2 (measured negatively) produces output X_1.

The competitive price ratio P_{X_2}/P_{X_1} at the initial no-tax equilibrium A equals the slope of the line ab. Notice that at these prices the factor payments

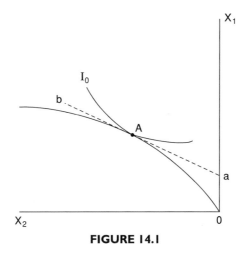

FIGURE 14.1

$P_{X_2} \cdot X_2$ do not exhaust the product $P_{X_1} \cdot X_1$. The firm earns pure profits equal to 0a (in units of X_1) which presumably accrue to the single consumer. Note, also, that the value of the pure profits changes as society moves along the frontier in response to commodity taxes. As a result, loss must be reinterpreted more generally as the lump-sum income necessary to keep the consumer indifferent to the new consumer prices less *all* sources of lump-sum income available to the consumer at the new with-tax equilibrium. These include both the tax revenue that is returned lump sum *and* any pure profits existing at the new equilibrium.

Figure 14.2 shows the dead-weight loss from a unit tax on X_1 that changes the slope of the consumer's budget line to that of line segment cd. The income necessary to compensate the consumer for the new price vector is 0c (in units of X_1). The tax revenue collected and returned at the compensated equilibrium is cg, equal to the difference between the consumer prices (slope of cd) and the producer prices (slope of ef or gh) at the compensated equilibrium D, projected back to the X_1 axis. But loss is no longer the difference, 0g, because production at the compensated equilibrium gives rise to pure profits equal to 0e at the net-of-tax producer prices. These profits are also available to the consumer. Hence, the consumer's loss is only eg, equal to the difference between the consumer's required lump-sum compensation and the lump-sum income received from all sources within the economy. Notice that eg also equals the difference between the amount of X_1 required to compensate the consumer at D, less the amount of X_1 society is able to produce at E given the compensated supply of X_2, X_2^C.

The first requirement for retaining the loss-minimizing approach in general equilibrium analysis, then, is to develop a valid production relationship, specified in terms of producer prices, that measures the pure economic

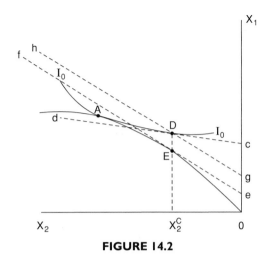

FIGURE 14.2

profits in the economy for any given vector of production prices. The proper analytical construct is the general equilibrium profit function. Assuming perfectly competitive goods and factor markets, the profit function, $\pi(\vec{p}) = \sum_{i=1}^{N} p_i Y_i(\vec{p})$ is derived by assuming that a planner maximizes aggregate profits at fixed producer prices subject to the aggregate production-possibilities frontier $f(\vec{Y}) = 0$. The resulting aggregate goods supply and input demand functions $Y_i(\vec{p})$ are then substituted back into the profit function $\sum_{i=1}^{N} p_i Y_i$. Analogous to the consumer's expenditure function, $\partial \pi(p)/\partial p_k = Y_k(\vec{p})$, the supply of (demand for) the kth good (factor), a property known as Shepard's lemma.[1]

The general equilibrium profit function $\pi(\vec{p})$ incorporates all relevant aspects of production for the economy. Therefore, the expression:

$$L(\vec{t}) = M(\vec{q}; \overline{U}) - \sum_{i=1}^{N} t_i M_i(\vec{q}; \overline{U}) - \pi(\vec{p}) \tag{14.1}$$

is a valid general equilibrium expression for the dead-weight loss resulting from any given vector of taxes, $\vec{t}$, assuming competitive market structures, general production technology, and tax revenues measured at the new with-tax compensated equilibrium. The expenditure function $M(\vec{q}; \overline{U})$ measures the income necessary to compensate the consumer, and the final two expressions measure the (lump-sum) income actually available at the new compensated

[1] Shepard's lemma is derived as follows. $\partial \pi(p)/\partial p_k = \partial \sum_i p_i Y_i(p)/\partial p_k = Y_k(p) + \sum_i p_i \partial Y_i/\partial p_k$. But $p_i = \lambda f_i$ from the first-order conditions for profit maximization. Therefore, $\partial \pi(p)/\partial p_k = Y_k + \lambda \sum_i f_i \partial Y_i/\partial p_k$. The second expression equals zero with $f(Y) = 0$, so that $\partial \pi/\partial p_k = Y_k$.

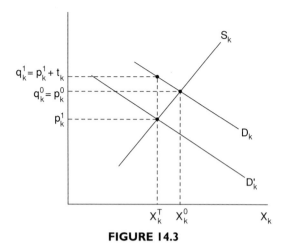

FIGURE 14.3

equilibrium.[2] As before, $\vec{q}$, is the vector of gross-of-tax consumer prices, $\vec{p}$ is the vector of net-of-tax producer prices, and $\vec{q} = \vec{p} + \vec{t}$.

Market Clearance

Equation (14.1) is not a complete general equilibrium specification of the economy, however, unlike the loss expression with a linear technology. Although $M(\vec{q}; \overline{U})$ completely specifies the preferences of the consumer and $\pi(\vec{p})$ completely specifies the production technology under perfect competition, $L(t)$ does not incorporate market clearance. Recall that market clearance was implicit with linear technology. There was only one consumer, and aggregate production and producer prices were fixed. Therefore, once $\vec{t}$ was specified, $\vec{q}$ was determined through the identities $\vec{q} = \vec{p} + \vec{t}$. There is still only one consumer and aggregate production with general technology, but the crucial difference is that producer prices are no longer fixed. In general, goods supply curves (input demand curves) are upward (downward) sloping so that any given producer price p_i is now a function of the entire vector of taxes, $\vec{t}$, that is, $p_i = p_i(\vec{t})$. To see this, consider the response to a tax, t_k, in both the market for k and the market for some other good, i. In the market for good k, depicted in Fig. 14.3, the tax t_k generates a new equilibrium X_k^T, with new consumer *and* producer prices q_k^1 and p_k^1. Similarly, in some other market i, if D_i shifts in response to the tax t_k (as pictured in Fig. 14.4, the goods i and k are substitutes), both the consumer

---

[2] As in Chapter 13, $\overline{U}$ is arbitrarily set at U^0, the utility level attainable without any taxation. Refer to Chapter 13 for a discussion of this choice.

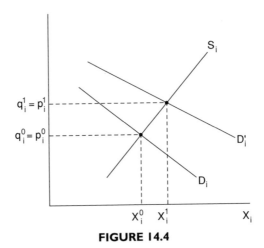

FIGURE 14.4

and the producer prices change, from $q_i^0 = p_i^0$ to $q_i^1 = p_i^1$.[3] With linear technologies, in contrast, all supply (input demand) curves are horizontal so that a tax t_k could only change the consumer price q_k by the full amount of the tax. p_k could not change, nor could any other producer or consumer price, even if the tax t_k caused demand shifts in these other markets.

With general technology, therefore, market clearance relationships of the form:

$$M_i(\vec{q}; \overline{U}) = M_i[\vec{p}(\vec{t}) + \vec{t}; \overline{U}] = Y_i[\vec{p}(\vec{t})] \qquad i = 1, \dots, N \qquad (14.2)$$

become necessary to determine the vector of producer prices $\vec{p}$ for any given vector of taxes $\vec{t}$. Once $\vec{p}$ has been determined through these relationships, $\vec{q}$ is determined by the identities $\vec{q} = \vec{p} + \vec{t}$.

The market clearance relationships, Eq. (14.2), can be incorporated into the analysis in one of two ways. One possibility is to replace either M_i or Y_i in Eq. (14.1), the expression for loss. The other choice is to keep Eq. (14.1) exactly as it is and use the market clearance relationships to simplify derivatives of $L(t)$. We will use the second method throughout the chapter.

There is one additional complication. The loss expression, Eq. (14.1), is specified in terms of *compensated* goods demands and factor supplies. To be consistent, the market clearance relationships, Eq. (14.2), must also be specified in terms of the compensated demands and supplies, the $M_i(\vec{q}; \overline{U})$, as written. But, market clearance cannot possibly hold in terms of *all* N compensated supplies and demands, because the consumer would not suffer any loss as a result of the commodity taxes if society could provide the full vector

---

[3] This diagrammatic analysis ignores further price changes as D_k shifts in response to the changes in q_i, which changes q_k and further shifts D_i, and so on.

of *compensated* supplies and demands. As noted above, the compensated equilibrium for the consumer in Fig. 14.2, point D (the $M_i(\vec{q}; \overline{U})$), is not attainable with the given production technology. Production at the compensated equilibrium (the $Y_i(\vec{p})$) is represented by point E. Thus, specifying that $M_i = Y_i$, for all $i = 1, \ldots, N$, would require that E and D coincide, which cannot possibly occur if there is dead-weight loss.

A natural resolution of the market clearance problem is to impose market clearance on all but one of the goods and factors, say, the first, and assume that compensation occurs through this good. It is also natural to let good one serve as the untaxed numeraire, with $q_1 \equiv p_1 \equiv 1$, and $t_1 = 0$. From the discussion of loss in Chapter 13 we know that loss requires a change in *relative* prices, and setting $t_1 = 0$ ensures that any tax vector must change the vector of relative prices. Moreover, with $q_1 \equiv p_1 \equiv 1$, units of X_1 can be interpreted as units of purchasing power. These assumptions are consistent with Fig. 14.2 in which loss is depicted as eg (or DE), equal to the units of X_1 demanded at the compensated equilibrium less the amount of X_1 actually produced given the producer prices at that equilibrium. In fact, given that $M_i = Y_i$, $i = 2, \ldots, N$, and $q_1 \equiv p_1 \equiv 1, t_i \equiv 0$, the loss from taxation can be written as:

$$L(\vec{t}) = M_1(\vec{q}; \overline{U}) - Y_1(\vec{p}) \tag{14.3}$$

the amount of excess demand for good 1 at the compensated equilibrium. Equations (14.3) and (14.1) are equivalent specifications of dead-weight loss for analytical purposes.

The choice of the untaxed numeraire and the corresponding uncleared market is immaterial since it has no effect on the vector of relative prices and therefore on the compensated equilibrium. The numerical value of loss changes as it gets expressed in different units of the chosen numeraire good, but not the compensated equilibrium. Nonetheless, the discussion so far suggests that the concept of dead-weight loss in general technology is not as useful as we might like. The problem is that the vector of (relative) prices $\vec{p}$ solved through the $(N - 1)$ market clearing equations differs, in general, from the actual $\vec{p}$ observed in the economy in response to any given $\vec{t}$.

The issue of compensation thus points to a dilemma between actual and compensated equilibria. If we want to define dead-weight loss for a general technology economy, all components of the loss function must be defined in terms of the compensated equilibrium resulting from any given tax vector. If the actual and compensated equilibria are mixed together by, say, returning the *actual* tax revenue collected, then the loss minimization specification of a particular problem does not generate the same analytical results as a welfare maximum specification. Thus, to be an entirely consistent general equilibrium exercise, the conceptual loss experiment must assume, in effect, that the consumer is actually compensated by some outside agent and that the compensation takes place in terms of some particular good. Were such compensation to occur, the price vector $\vec{p}$ solved for by this experiment would be the actual price vector observed in the economy. The dilemma arises because the compensation does not actually occur, so that the price vector $\vec{p}$ resulting from the conceptual loss experiment is neither the same as, nor does it bear any necessary relationship to, the actual $\vec{p}$ resulting from any given pattern of taxes, $\vec{t}$. The actual $\vec{p}$ are irrelevant to a carefully designed conceptual experiment defining dead-weight loss.

There appears to be no way out of this dilemma as long as one remains interested in defining a legitimate loss measure. One can avoid the dilemma by modeling all second-best tax issues as welfare maximization problems using the indirect utility function, in which case everything is defined in terms of the actual post- and pretax equilibria. There is no need to define a loss function to analyze second-best tax (or expenditure) issues. The loss minimization framework is compelling, however, since dead-weight loss has been the traditional notion of tax inefficiency.

This dilemma does not arise with the same force under linear technologies because producer prices are fixed. The conceptual loss experiment still involves the compensated rather than actual tax collections and is therefore somewhat removed from the actual equilibrium. But, the loss experiment at least employs the observed vector of prices, both $\vec{q}$ and $\vec{p}$, for any given vector of tax rates, $\vec{t}$. The fixed vector $\vec{p}$ is the same in each equilibrium.

Marginal Loss: General Technology

With these comments in mind, we can analyze the loss from taxation in a one-consumer economy with general technology. Begin by computing the marginal loss with respect to the k_{th} tax, t_k. Use the loss expression, Eq. (14.1), $L(\vec{t}) = M(\vec{q}; \overline{U}) - \sum_{i=1}^{N} t_i M_i(\vec{q}; \overline{U}) - \pi(\vec{p})$, along with the $(N-1)$ market clearance relationships:

$$M_i(\vec{q}; \overline{U}) = Y_i(\vec{p}) \qquad i = 2, \ldots, N \qquad (14.4)$$

and the pricing identities:

$$q_i = p_i + t_i \qquad i = 2, \ldots, N \qquad (14.5)$$

plus:

$$q_1 \equiv p_1 \equiv 1, \qquad t_1 \equiv 0 \qquad (14.6)$$

Given that $p_i = p_i(\vec{t})$, $i = 2, \ldots, N$, $\partial \pi / \partial p_i \equiv Y_i$, and noting that $p_1 \equiv 1$,

$$\frac{\partial L}{\partial t_k} = M_k + \sum_{i=2}^{N} M_i \frac{\partial p_i}{\partial t_k} - M_k - \sum_{i=2}^{N} t_i \left(M_{ik} + \sum_{j=2}^{N} M_{ij} \frac{\partial p_j}{\partial t_k} \right) - \sum_{i=2}^{N} Y_i \frac{\partial p_i}{\partial t_k} \qquad (14.7)$$

$$\frac{\partial L}{\partial t_k} = \sum_{i=2}^{N} M_i \frac{\partial p_i}{\partial t_k} - \sum_{i=2}^{N} t_i \left(M_{ik} + \sum_{j=2}^{N} M_{ij} \frac{\partial p_j}{\partial t_k} \right) - \sum_{i=2}^{N} Y_i \frac{\partial p_i}{\partial t_k} \qquad (14.8)^4$$

Equation (14.8) can be simplified further by means of the market clearance equations, Eq. (14.4). Multiplying Eq. (14.4) by $\partial p_i/\partial t_k$ yields:

$$M_i \frac{\partial p_i}{\partial t_k} = Y_i \frac{\partial p_i}{\partial t_k} \qquad i = 2, \ldots, N \qquad (14.9)$$

Next, sum Eq. (14.9) over all $(N-1)$ relationships to obtain:

$$\sum_{i=2}^{N} M_i \frac{\partial p_i}{\partial t_k} = \sum_{i=2}^{N} Y_i \frac{\partial p_i}{\partial t_k} \qquad (14.10)$$

Hence, Eq. (14.8) simplifies to:

$$\frac{\partial L}{\partial t_k} = -\sum_{i=2}^{N} t_i \left(M_{ik} + \sum_{j=2}^{N} M_{ij} \frac{\partial p_j}{\partial t_k} \right) \qquad (14.11)$$

Equation (14.11) is similar to Eq. (13.6), the expression for marginal loss with linear technology. With $q_i = p_i + t_i$, for $i = 2, \ldots, N$, Eq. (14.11) can be rewritten as:

$$\frac{\partial L}{\partial t_k} = -\sum_{i=2}^{N} t_i \frac{\partial X_i^{comp}}{\partial q_j} \frac{\partial q_j}{\partial t_k} = -\sum_{i=2}^{N} t_i \frac{\partial X_i^{comp}}{\partial t_k} \qquad k = 2, \ldots, N \qquad (14.12)$$

Once again, we see that marginal loss depends upon the pattern of existing taxes and the change in compensated demands (factors supplies) in response to the tax. With a linear technology, $\partial q_k = \partial t_k$ and $\partial q_j/\partial t_k = 0$, $j \neq k$, so that Eq. (13.6) is just a special case of the general expression (14.11). The major qualitative difference between the two expressions is that the derivative $\partial X_i^{comp}/\partial t_k$ depends on both consumption *and* production responses, since $\partial q_j/\partial t_k$ depends upon all the consumption and production elasticities through the $(N-1)$ market clearance equations, Eq. (14.4). This is hardly a trivial difference, of course.

To see the roles of the consumption and production derivatives, rewrite the $(N-1)$ market clearance relationships, Eq. (14.4), and the expression for loss, Eq. (14.11), in vector notation:[5]

$$dL = -(t')(M_{ij})\left(\frac{dq}{dt}\right)(dt) \qquad (14.13)$$

$$M_i(q; \overline{U}) = \pi_i(q - t) \qquad (14.14)$$

---

[4] $q_i = p_i(t) + t_i$;   therefore, $\partial q_i/\partial t_k = \partial p_i/\partial t_k$, $i \neq k$. $\partial q_k/\partial t_k = \partial p_i/\partial t_k + \partial t_k/\partial t_k = \partial p_k/\partial t_k + 1$.

[5] This technique was first demonstrated to us by Peter Diamond in a set of unpublished class notes.

where:

(t) = the $(N - 1) \times 1$ column vector $\begin{bmatrix} t_2 \\ \vdots \\ t_N \end{bmatrix}$

(M_{ij}) = the $(N - 1) \times (N - 1)$ matrix:

$$\begin{bmatrix} M_{22} \ldots M_{2N} \\ \vdots \quad\quad \vdots \\ M_{N2} \ldots M_{NN} \end{bmatrix}$$

$\left(\dfrac{dq}{dt} \right)$ = the $(N - 1) \times (N - 1)$ matrix of differentials:

$$\begin{bmatrix} \dfrac{dq_2}{dt_2} \ldots \dfrac{dq_2}{dt_N} \\ \vdots \quad\quad \vdots \\ \dfrac{dq_N}{dt_2} \ldots \dfrac{dq_N}{dt_N} \end{bmatrix}$$

(dt) = the $(N - 1) \times 1$ column vector of differentials:

$$\begin{bmatrix} dt_2 \\ \vdots \\ dt_N \end{bmatrix}$$

M_i = the $(N - 1) \times 1$ column vector of compensated demands (factor supplies):

$$\begin{bmatrix} M_2 \\ \vdots \\ M_N \end{bmatrix}$$

π_i = the $(N - 1) \times 1$ column vector of supplies (input demands):

$$\begin{bmatrix} Y_2 \\ \vdots \\ Y_N \end{bmatrix}$$

q, p = the $(N - 1) \times 1$ column vectors of prices.

Totally differentiating Eq. (14.14) yields:

$$M_{ij}dq = Y_{ij}(dq - dt) \qquad (14.15)$$

Solving for dq/dt and substituting the notation X for M_i and Y for π_i yields:

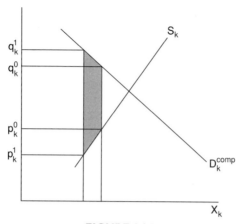

FIGURE 14.5

$$\frac{dq}{dt} = \frac{-\left(\dfrac{\partial Y}{\partial p}\right)}{\left(\dfrac{\partial X}{\partial q} - \dfrac{\partial Y}{\partial p}\right)} \tag{14.16}$$

Substituting Eq. (14.16) into (14.13), the expression for loss becomes:

$$dL = -(t')\left(M_{ij}\right)\left[\frac{-\dfrac{\partial Y}{\partial p}}{\dfrac{\partial X}{\partial q} - \dfrac{\partial Y}{\partial p}}\right] dt \tag{14.17}$$

Hence, marginal loss depends upon both consumption and production derivatives.

As one additional comparison of marginal losses in general versus linear technology economies, consider the simple (and unlikely) case in which t_k is the only existing tax, only the kth prices, q_k and p_k, vary in response to a marginal change in the kth tax, t_k, and that all cross-price derivatives are zero.[6] With these assumptions, Eq. (14.13) (or Eq. (14.17)) simplifies to:

$$dL = -t_k \frac{\partial X_k}{\partial q_k}\frac{dq_k}{dt_k} dt_k = -t_k \frac{\partial X_k}{\partial q_k} dq_k = -t_k \Delta X_k \tag{14.18}$$

The marginal loss occurs entirely within the market for good (factor) k and is approximately equal to the shaded trapezoidal area in Fig. 14.5. This area can

[6] Assuming $M_{ij} = 0$, for all $i \neq j$ is improper, but the example is meant to be illustrative only. This analysis, along with the result, Eq. (14.17), can be found in R. Boadway, "Cost–Benefit Rules and General Equilibrium," *Review of Economic Studies*, June 1975. Boadway derives Eq. (14.17) in a utility-maximizing framework.

be thought of as the combined (marginal) decrease in consumer's and producer's surplus from consuming and producing good k, where the former is measured with reference to the compensated demand for good k and the latter with reference to the generalized supply function $Y_k = \partial\pi(\vec{p})/\partial p_k$. By contrast, with linear technology loss was approximated by a set of triangles, equal in each market to the loss in consumer's surplus measured with reference to the set of compensated demand (factor supply) curves. A generalized producer's surplus cannot arise in a linear technology with its perfectly elastic output supplies (input demands) at constant producer prices.

Optimal Commodity Taxation

One of the more important results in the allocational theory of taxation is that the equations describing the optimal pattern of commodity taxes in a one-consumer, general-technology economy are *identical* to their linear technology counterparts if the technology exhibits constant returns to scale (CRS). The first-order conditions for optimal taxation continue to depend *only* upon compensated demand (factor supply) derivatives despite the fact that marginal tax loss in general technology with CRS depends upon consumption and production derivatives. Having already discussed the notion of loss from taxation with general technologies, this result is easily derived.

The optimal commodity tax problem in a one-consumer general technology economy can be represented as:

$$\min_{(t_k)} L(t) = M(\vec{q}; \overline{U}) - \sum_{i=2}^{N} t_i M_i - \pi(\vec{p})$$

$$\text{s.t. } \sum_{i=2}^{N} t_i M_i(\vec{q}; \overline{U}) = \overline{T}$$

along with the market clearance equations, Eq. (14.4), and the pricing identities, Eqs. (14.5) and (14.6). Notice once again that tax revenue is measured at the compensated equilibrium. The corresponding Lagrangian is

$$\min_{(t_k)} \xi(t) = M(\vec{q}; \overline{U}) - \sum_{i=2}^{N} t_i M_i - \pi(\vec{p}) - \lambda\left(\sum_{i=2}^{N} t_i M_i(\vec{q}; \overline{U}) - \overline{T}\right)$$

The first order conditions are

$$\frac{\partial L}{\partial t_k} - \lambda\frac{\partial T}{\partial t_k} = 0 \qquad k = 2, \ldots, N \qquad (14.19)$$

and

$$\sum_{i=2}^{N} t_i M_i = T \qquad (14.20)$$

But,

$$\frac{\partial L}{\partial t_k} = -\sum_{i=2}^{N} t_i \left(M_{ik} + \sum_{j=2}^{N} M_{ij} \frac{\partial p_j}{\partial t_k} \right) \tag{14.21}$$

and

$$\frac{\partial T}{\partial t_k} = M_k + \sum_{i=2}^{N} t_i \left(M_{ik} + \sum_{j=2}^{N} M_{ij} \frac{\partial p_j}{\partial t_k} \right) \tag{14.22}$$

Therefore, Eq. (14.19) becomes:

$$(1 + \lambda)\frac{\partial L}{\partial t_k} - \lambda M_k = 0 \qquad k = 2, \ldots, N \tag{14.23}$$

or

$$-(1 + \lambda)\left[\sum_{i=2}^{N} t_i \left(M_{ik} + \sum_{j=2}^{N} M_{ij} \frac{\partial p_j}{\partial t_k} \right) \right] - \lambda M_k = 0 \qquad k = 2, \ldots, N \tag{14.24}$$

Without imposing the assumption of CRS, all we can do is rewrite Eq. (14.24) in a form corresponding to, but not identical to, the optimal tax rules for a linear technology:

$$\left(M_{ik} + \sum_{j=2}^{N} M_{ij} \frac{\partial p_j}{\partial t_k} \right) = \sum_{j} \frac{\partial X_i^{comp}}{\partial q_j} \cdot \frac{\partial q_j}{\partial t_k}$$

$$= \frac{\partial X_i^{comp}}{\partial t_k} \qquad \text{all } i = 2, \ldots, N \tag{14.25}$$

Therefore, the first-order conditions, Eq. (14.24), are equivalent to:

$$\frac{-\sum_{i=2}^{N} t_i \frac{\partial X_i^{comp}}{\partial t_k}}{M_k} = \frac{\lambda}{1 + \lambda} = C \qquad k = 2, \ldots, N \tag{14.26}$$

As was true with the expression for marginal loss, the linear technology rules, Eq. (13.30), are a special case of the general equations (14.26), with $\partial q_k = \partial t_k$ and $\partial q_j/\partial t_k = 0, j \neq k$. But, with general technology the derivatives $\partial X_i^{comp}/\partial t_k$ in Eq. (14.26) refer to the general equilibrium changes in X_i^{comp} in response to the tax which in turn depend upon the changes in the full set of producer and consumer prices as t_k changes. And, as demonstrated above, these price changes are functions of both demand and supply price derivatives through the market clearance equations.

It is not immediately obvious why the assumption of CRS should reduce the general equations (14.26) to their linear technology counterparts. After all, even with CRS the output supply (input demand) curves are generally upward (downward) sloping, which means that producer prices vary in response to variations in government taxes.[7] But the key is that there can be no pure profits in the economy with CRS technology and perfectly competitive market structures. $\pi(\vec{p}) \equiv 0$, so that:

$$\frac{\partial \pi}{\partial t_k} = \sum_{i=1}^{N} \pi_i \frac{\partial p_i}{\partial t_k} = 0$$

With $p_1 \equiv 1$ as the numeraire, $\sum_{i=1}^{N} \pi_i(\partial p_i/\partial t_k) = 0$ as well. But this implies, from market clearance, that:

$$\sum_{i=2}^{N} M_i \frac{\partial p_i}{\partial t_k} = \sum_{i=2}^{N} \pi_i \frac{\partial p_i}{\partial t_k} \equiv \sum_{i=2}^{N} Y_i \frac{\partial p_i}{\partial t_k} = 0 \tag{14.27}$$

Using this result, subtract $\lambda \sum_{i=2}^{N} M_i(\partial p_i/\partial t_k)(= 0)$ from Eq. (14.24), obtaining:

$$-(1 + \lambda)\sum_{i=2}^{N} t_i \left(M_{ik} + \sum_{j=2}^{N} M_{ij}\frac{\partial p_j}{\partial t_k} \right) - \lambda \left(M_k + \sum_{i=2}^{N} M_i\frac{\partial p_i}{\partial t_k} \right) = 0, \tag{14.28}$$

$$k = 2, \ldots, N$$

Writing all $(N - 1)$ of these equations in matrix notation,

$$-(1 + \lambda)(t')(M_{ij})\left[I + \left(\frac{\partial p}{\partial t}\right) \right] - \lambda (M_i')\left[I + \left(\frac{\partial p}{\partial t}\right) \right] = 0' \tag{14.29}$$

where:

t, M_{ij}, and M_i are defined as above.
λ and $(1 + \lambda)$ are scalars.
I is the $(N - 1) \times (N - 1)$ identity matrix.
$\left(\dfrac{\partial p}{\partial t}\right) = $ the $(N - 1) \times (N - 1)$ matrix of price derivatives:

$$\begin{bmatrix} \dfrac{\partial p_2}{\partial t_2} & \cdots & \dfrac{\partial p_2}{\partial t_N} \\ \vdots & & \vdots \\ \dfrac{\partial p_N}{\partial t_2} & \cdots & \dfrac{\partial p_N}{\partial t_N} \end{bmatrix}$$

0 = an $(N - 1)$ column vector of zeros.

Since $[I + (\partial p/\partial t)]$ is nonsingular, Eq. (14.29) implies:

$$-(1 + \lambda)(t')(M_{ij}) - \lambda (M_i') = 0' \tag{14.30}$$

Equation (14.30) holds for each of the $(N - 1)$ relationships. Hence:

[7] CRS generates an increasing-cost production-possibilities frontier so long as production of the various goods is unequally factor intensive, meaning that the optimal factor proportions across goods differ at the same relative factor prices.

$$-(1 + \lambda)\sum_{i=2}^{N} t_i M_{ik} - \lambda M_k = 0 \qquad k = 2, \ldots, N \qquad (14.31)$$

Rearranging terms:

$$\frac{\sum_{i=2}^{N} t_i M_{ik}}{M_k} = -\frac{\lambda}{1 + \lambda} = C \qquad k = 2, \ldots, N \qquad (14.32)$$

with C independent of k. Equations (14.32) are identical to Eqs. (13.30). They imply that the pattern of optimal taxes depends only upon the compensated demand (factor supply) derivatives $\partial X_i^{comp}/\partial q_k$. Moreover, the equal percentage change interpretation applies to Eq. (14.32) exactly as it applies to Eq. (13.30).[8]

The assumption of CRS, then, greatly simplifies the application of second-best results. Admittedly Eq. (14.32) would be difficult to apply in practice given our limited econometric knowledge of the relevant Slutsky substitution terms, but at least the general equilibrium supply responses to the tax can be ignored.

That the assumption of CRS for private production simplifies the optimal commodity tax rules is not unique to that problem. CRS tends to simplify all second-best results in both tax and expenditure theory. Whether CRS is an appropriate assumption for the US economy is an open question. CRS is often assumed for aggregate production in empirical analysis, but this is mostly because aggregate production data are collected by the government and are constructed under the assumption of CRS (exhaustion of the product). The same is true of production analysis at the two-digit industry level.

Another difficulty in applying this, and other, second best results is the market assumption of perfect competition. It is certainly violated for a number of important goods and services. At the same time, perfect competition is the natural default assumption for second-best public sector analysis. One could hardly attempt to model the various forms that market imperfections take industry by industry throughout the economy.

MANY-PERSON ECONOMIES: FIXED PRODUCER PRICES

Social Welfare Maximization Versus Loss Minimization

Before 1970, public sector economists chose to analyze second-best tax theory almost exclusively within the context of one-consumer economies to

---

[8] The independence of the optimal tax rules to supply responses with constant returns-to-scale production was first pointed out to us by Paul Samuelson in a set of unpublished class notes. Refer to J. Stiglitz and P. Dasgupta, "Differential Taxation, Public Goods, and Economic Efficiency," *Review of Economic Studies*, April 1971, for an alternative derivation of this result.

highlight the efficiency aspects of that theory. The results derived in Chapters 13 and 14 provide a representative sampling of the received theory in the professional journals up to 1970. During the 1970s, however, a number of the leading public sector theorists—Boadway, Diamond, Feldstein, Green, Hartwick, and Mirrlees, to name just a few[9]—reworked second-best tax theory within the more realistic context of many-person economies. These first papers showed that it might not be very useful to consider efficiency aspects of various taxes independently of their distributional effects, at least not for the purposes of practical application. Economists had long known that distributional considerations would modify the standard one-consumer results of second-best tax theory, but the many-person models made it painfully obvious just how hopelessly intertwined distributional and efficiency terms become in many second-best tax (and expenditure) decision rules. This is especially disturbing because arbitrary assignment of the distributional weights embodied in an underlying social welfare function can generate quite different policy implications from these decision rules.

Along these same lines, it may not be very useful to think of the effects of distorting taxes in terms of dead-weight loss, even though public sector economists have characterized distortion as loss since the very beginnings of the discipline. Unambiguous notions of efficiency loss involve the use of the expenditure function, which is best suited to one-consumer economies. Loss minimization and welfare minimization generate identical results in second-best analysis if the objective function is the welfare or loss of a single individual. In a many-person economy, however, loss minimization and *social* welfare maximization are no longer equivalent except under the highly restrictive assumptions that render the many-person economy essentially equivalent to the one-person economy. Indeed the concept of loss is not generally well defined in a many-person economy. This point is worth considering before analyzing a specific second-best problem in a many-person context.[10]

Loss measures using the expenditure function model the economy in terms of market prices. Therefore, loss can be directly compared with social welfare expressed in terms of each consumer's indirect utility function, $V^h(\vec{q}; I^h)$. The indirect utility function is obtained by solving for the consumer's demand (input supply) functions $X_{hk} = X_{hk}(\vec{q}; I^h)$ from utility maxi-

---

[9] R. Boadway, "Integrating Equity and Efficiency in Applied Welfare Economics," *Quarterly Journal of Economics*, November 1976; P. Diamond, "A Many Person Ramsey Tax Rule," *Journal of Public Economics*, November 1975; M. Feldstein, "Distributional Equity and the Optimal Structure of Public Prices," *American Economic Review*, March 1972; J. Green, "Two Models of Optimal Pricing and Taxation," *Oxford Economic Papers*, November 1975; J. Hartwick, "Optimal Price Discrimination," *Journal of Public Economics*, February 1978; J. Mirrlees, "Optimal Commodity Taxation in a Two-Class Economy," *Journal of Public Economics*, February 1975.

[10] This point was discussed in Chapter 4. Here we assume a CRS, zero-profit economy.

mization and substituting them for the arguments of the direct utility function $U^h(X_{h\,k})$. Let:

$$W^*\left[V^h\left(\vec{q};I^h\right)\right] = V\left(\vec{q};I^1,\ldots,I^h,\ldots,I^H\right) \tag{14.33}$$

represent the Bergson–Samuelson individualistic social welfare function expressed as a function of the vector of consumer prices, $\vec{q}$, and the distribution of lump-sum incomes, $(I^1,\ldots,I^H)$.

The problem is that, in general, there exists no aggregate expenditure function of the form $M(\vec{q};\overline{V}^1,\ldots,\overline{V}^H)$ corresponding to the social welfare function, which can be incorporated into a many-person loss measure, because there is no unambiguous method for specifying the vector of constant utilities, $\overline{V}_1,\ldots,\overline{V}_H$, to be inserted into M. Suppose, for example, that the government were to change the vector of consumer prices, $\vec{q}$, by instituting a set of distorting taxes, $\vec{t}$. A natural way of defining M would be to hold each consumer at his pretax utility level and ask how much lump-sum income in the aggregate would be required to do this given the new gross of tax consumer prices. In effect, each consumer would be fully compensated for the tax, with Eq. (14.33) evaluated at the pretax utility levels $(\overline{V}_0^1,\ldots,\overline{V}_0^H)$. Imagine that the government actually borrowed (at no cost) the required income from some third country and compensated each consumer. Clearly, this amount of income would differ from the income required to keep *social welfare* constant in response to the tax, because by returning *each* consumer to his pretax utility the government has foregone the possibility of exploiting differences in the social welfare weights $\partial W^*/\partial V^h$. By judiciously offering more income to people with high marginal social utilities and less to those with low marginal social utilities, the government can restore the pretax level of social welfare without necessarily returning each consumer to his pretax utility level. The only appropriate vector of utilities $(\overline{V}_1,\ldots,\overline{V}_H)$ to plug into M, therefore, is the vector of individual utilities that would exist once social welfare has been "compensated" at its pretax level, but there is no general method of solving for this vector. In particular, a many-person loss measure of the form:

$$L(\vec{t}) = \sum_{h=1}^H L^h(\vec{t}) = \sum_{h=1}^H \left[M^h\left(\vec{q};\overline{U}^h\right) - \sum_{i=2}^N t_i X_{hi}\right],$$

the straight sum of each individual's loss, bears no necessary relationship to the social welfare function $V(\vec{q};I^1,\ldots,I^H)$.

One might think that weighting each $L^h(\vec{t})$ by the marginal social welfare terms $\partial W^*/\partial V^h$ and defining aggregate loss as:

$$L(\vec{t}) = \sum_{h=1}^H \frac{\partial W^*}{\partial V^h} \cdot L^h(\vec{t})$$

would be equivalent to Eq. (14.33), but that is not so. It turns out that the proper weighting scheme for individual losses is problem specific. Terms from second-best constraints must be incorporated into the vector of weights to make loss minimization equivalent to social welfare maximization.

The aggregate expenditure function is unambiguously defined for a many-consumer economy only if the economy is equivalent to a single-consumer economy in the sense that the level of social welfare is independent of any distributional considerations, including both the distribution of lump-sum income and the pattern of consumption (and factor supply) among the various consumers. Three sufficient conditions have been described that will generate one-consumer equivalence, two by Samuelson and one by Green, as follows:[11]

1. Lump-sum income is continuously and optimally redistributed in accordance with the interpersonal equity conditions of first-best social welfare maximization. That is, the social marginal utility of income is always equal for all consumers.

2. Consumers have identical and homothetic tastes so that for any given consumer price vector, $\vec{q}$, and all lump-sum income distributions $I^1, \ldots, I^H$, the aggregate Engel's (income–consumption) curves are straight parallel lines.

3. The covariance of person h's social marginal utility of income and his proportion of aggregate consumption of any one good (X_{hk}/X_k) is identical for all goods (and factors) $k = 1, \ldots, N$ (Green's condition).

Under any of these conditions, the function $V(\vec{q}; I^1, \ldots, I^H)$ is equivalent to $V(\vec{q}; I)$, which in turn is identical to the specification of indirect utility for a single consumer. Moreover, if social welfare can be expressed as $V(\vec{q}; I)$, then the problem

$$\max_{(q)} V(\vec{q}; I)$$

$$\text{s.t. } \vec{q} \cdot \vec{X} = I$$

where:

$\vec{X}$ = the vector of aggregate quantities.
I = aggregate lump-sum income.

has the dual form:

$$\min_{(X)} \vec{q} \cdot \vec{X}$$

$$\text{s.t. } V = \overline{V}$$

The dual can be solved unambiguously for an aggregate expenditure function:

---

[11] P. Samuelson, "Social Indifference Curves," *Quarterly Journal of Economics*, February 1956; J. Green, "Two Models of Optimal Pricing and Taxation," *Oxford Economic Papers*, November 1975.

$$\sum_{i=1}^{N} q_i X_i^{comp}(\vec{q}; \overline{U}) = M(\vec{q}; \overline{U}) \qquad (14.34)$$

In this case, then, aggregate deadweight loss from taxation is also unambiguously defined as:

$$L(\vec{t}) = M(\vec{q}; \overline{U}) - \sum_{k=2}^{N} t_k X_k^{comp}(\vec{q}; \overline{U}) \qquad (14.35)$$

exactly analogous to the one-consumer economy.

Unfortunately, none of the sufficient conditions is particularly compelling. Thus, it would seem more realistic to analyze second-best tax (and expenditure) problems within the context of social welfare maximization and *actual* general equilibria using Eq. (14.33) as the maximand, and under the assumptions of nonidentical individual preferences, a fixed distribution of lump-sum incomes $(I^1, \ldots, I^H)$ and unequal social welfare weights, $\partial W^*/\partial V^h$. We will adopt this approach for the remainder of the chapter.[12]

Optimal Commodity Taxation in a Many-Person Economy

As one illustration of the differences in second-best analysis between one-person (equivalent) and many-person economies, let us reconsider the optimal commodity tax problem in a many-person context, while retaining the assumption of fixed producer prices. As in the one-consumer economies, assume good 1 is the untaxed numeraire to ensure that relative prices change as tax rates are varied, with resulting losses in social welfare. Note also that with fixed producer prices, $\vec{p}$, the social welfare function:

$$W^*\left[V^h\left(\vec{q}; \overline{I}^h\right)\right] = V\left(\vec{q}; \overline{I}^1, \ldots, \overline{I}^H\right)$$

along with the pricing identities $\vec{q} = \vec{p} + \vec{t}$, provides a complete general equilibrium description of the economy. Production is entirely specified by

[12] Recall from Chapter 4 that Jorgenson defined a social expenditure function as the minimum aggregate income required to reach a given level of social welfare. In his model, the minimum income occurs when utilities are equal if society has any aversion to inequality. He then compares the value of the social expenditure function at different general equilibria to obtain an aggregate income measure of gain or loss. For purposes of describing optimal policy rules, however, minimizing Jorgenson's social expenditure function is not equivalent to maximizing social welfare when utilities are unequal and the distribution of income is fixed. Also, Jorgenson's social expenditure function assumes that the government can costlessly redistribute, which is best suited to a first-best environment. Harris and Wildasin described the true dual of the social welfare maximization problem in a second-best environment when redistribution is costly. Their model requires specifying the form that the government redistribution must take to hold social welfare constant, which depends on the nature of the underlying constraints. It is much more straightforward to work directly with the social welfare function. See R. Harris and D. Wildasin, "An Alternative Approach to Aggregate Surplus Analysis," *Journal of Public Economics*, April 1985.

the producer price vector, $\vec{p}$. Market clearance is implicit, as production is perfectly elastic at the prices $\vec{p}$, expanding or contracting as needed to meet the aggregate vector of consumer demands (factor supplies). Moreover, $\vec{q}$ is determined by the pricing identities given $\vec{t}$.

The government's problem, then, is to:

$$\max_{(t_k)} W^* \left[V^h \left(\vec{q}; \vec{I}^h \right) \right] = V \left(\vec{q}; \vec{I}^1, \ldots, \vec{I}^H \right)$$

$$\text{s.t.} \sum_{h=1}^{H} \sum_{i=2}^{N} t_i X_{hi} = \overline{T}$$

along with the identities $\vec{q} \equiv \vec{p} + \vec{t}; q_1 \equiv p_1 \equiv 1; t_1 \equiv 0,$
where:

> $\overline{T}$ = the fixed amount of revenue to be collected with distorting taxes.
> X_{hi} = good (factor) i demanded by (supplied by) person h, for
> $h = 1, \ldots, H; i = 1, \ldots, N$ (The X_{hi} are the actual goods demands
>   and factor supplies and $\overline{T}$ is the actual tax revenue).

The corresponding Lagrangian is

$$\max_{(t_k)} L = W^* \left[V^h \left(\vec{q}; \vec{I}^h \right) \right] + \lambda \left(\sum_{h=1}^{H} \sum_{i=2}^{N} t_i X_{hi} = \overline{T} \right)$$

Assuming the distribution of lump-sum income is fixed, the first-order conditions are[13]

$$t_k: -\sum_{h=1}^{H} \frac{\partial W^*}{\partial V^h} \alpha^h X_{hk} + \lambda \sum_{h=1}^{H} \left(X_{hk} + \sum_{i=2}^{N} t_i \frac{\partial X_{hi}}{\partial q_k} \right) = 0 \tag{14.36)[14]}$$

$$k = 2, \ldots, N$$

and

$$\sum_{h=1}^{H} \sum_{i=2}^{N} t_i X_{hi} = \overline{T} \tag{14.37}$$

where

> α^h = the private marginal utility of income for person h.

---

[13] The derivation of Eq. (14.36) employs Roy's Identity on individual's indirect utility functions, $\partial V^h / \partial q_k = -\alpha^h X_{hk}, k = 1, \ldots, N$. The identity follows from differentiating the consumer's indirect utility function and making use of the first-order conditions from utility maximization:

$$\frac{\partial V^h(X_{hi}(q, I^h))}{\partial q_k} = \sum_i \frac{\partial V^h}{\partial X_{hi}} \cdot \frac{\partial X_{hi}}{\partial q_k} = \sum_i \alpha^h q_i \frac{\partial X_{hi}}{\partial q_k} = \alpha^h \sum_i q_i \frac{\partial X_{hi}}{\partial q_k}$$

But, $\sum_i q_i \frac{\partial X_{hi}}{\partial q_k} = -X_{hk}$ from differentiating the consumer's budget constraint, $\sum_i q_i X_{hi} = I^h$, with respect to q_k, generating Roy's Identity.

[14] Recall that with fixed producer prices, $\partial q_i / \partial t_k = 0, i \neq k$.

Let $\beta^h = (\partial W^*/\partial V^h)\alpha^h$ represent the social marginal utility of income for person h, the product of the marginal social welfare weight and the private marginal utility of income. Rewrite Eq. (14.36) as:

$$-\sum_{h=1}^{H}\beta^h X_{hk} + \lambda\sum_{h=1}^{H}\left(X_{hk} + \sum_{i=2}^{N}t_i\frac{\partial X_{hi}}{\partial q_k}\right) = 0$$

$$k = 2, \ldots, N \tag{14.38}$$

Equation (14.38) cannot be manipulated into simple and intuitive equal percentage change rules as in the one-consumer case, even in terms of individual's compensated demands (factors supplies). All one can say by way of a simple general interpretation is that, at the optimum, the marginal change in social welfare resulting from a change in any given tax rate must be proportional to the change in tax revenues resulting from changing the tax rate or:

$$\frac{\partial W^*}{\partial t_k} = \lambda\frac{\partial T}{\partial t_k} \tag{14.39}$$

To see how the equal percentage change rule must be modified, substitute the individual consumer's Slutsky equations:

$$\frac{\partial X_{hi}}{\partial q_k} = S_{ik}^h - X_{hk}\frac{\partial X_{hi}}{\partial I^h} \qquad h = 1, \ldots, H$$

$$k = 1, \ldots, N \tag{14.40}$$

into Eq. (14.38) to obtain:

$$-\sum_{h=1}^{H}\beta^h X_{hk} + \lambda\sum_{h=1}^{H}X_{hk} + \lambda\sum_{h=1}^{H}\sum_{i=2}^{N}t_i S_{ik}^h$$

$$-\lambda\sum_{h=1}^{H}\sum_{i=2}^{N}t_i X_{hk}\frac{\partial X_{hi}}{\partial I^h} = 0 \qquad k = 2, \ldots, N \tag{14.41}$$

Rearranging terms, dividing through by $\lambda\sum_{h=1}^{H}X_{hk} = \lambda X_k$, and noting that $S_{ik}^h = S_{ki}^h$, yields:

$$\frac{\sum_{i=1}^{H}\sum_{i=2}^{N}t_i S_{ki}^h}{X_k} = -1 + \frac{\frac{1}{\lambda}\sum_{h=1}^{H}\beta^h X_{hk}}{X_k} + \frac{\sum_{i=2}^{N}\sum_{h=1}^{H}t_i X_{hk}\frac{\partial X_{hi}}{\partial I^h}}{X_k} \tag{14.42}$$

Martin Feldstein defined the *distributional coefficient for good k* as:

$$\lambda^k = \sum_{h=1}^{H}\beta^h X_{hk}/X_k$$

The distributional coefficient is a weighted average of the individual social marginal utilities of income, with the weights equal to the proportion of total X_k consumed by each person. Using Feldstein's distributional coefficient, Eq. (14.42) becomes:

$$\frac{\sum\limits_{h=1}^{H}\sum\limits_{i=2}^{N}t_{i}S_{ki}^{h}}{X_{k}}=-1+\frac{\lambda^{k}}{\lambda}+\frac{\sum\limits_{h=1}^{H}\sum\limits_{i=2}^{N}t_{i}\frac{\partial X_{hi}}{\partial I^{h}}X_{hk}}{X_{k}} \qquad k=2,\ldots,N \qquad (14.43)$$

The left-hand side (LHS) of Eq. (14.43) gives the percentage change in the aggregate compensated demand for good k (approximately), but the right-hand side (RHS) is no longer independent of k. Rather, the percentage changes depend in a complicated manner on Feldstein's distributional coefficients and the change in tax revenue in response to changes in the pattern of lump-sum incomes. Furthermore, the right-hand side cannot readily be divided into two distinct sets of terms, with one set containing all relevant efficiency considerations and the second containing all relevant distributional information.

One can shed some additional light on the pattern of optimal taxes by considering changes in actual demands, even though these changes cannot be described in a simple way either. From the individual Slutsky equations:

$$S_{ki}^{h}=\frac{\partial X_{hk}}{\partial q_{i}}+X_{hi}\frac{\partial X_{hk}}{\partial I^{h}} \qquad (14.44)$$

Substituting for the S_{ki}^{h} in Eq. (14.43) and rearranging terms:

$$\frac{\sum\limits_{h=1}^{H}\sum\limits_{i=2}^{N}t_{i}\frac{\partial X_{hk}}{\partial q_{i}}}{X_{k}}=-1+\frac{\lambda^{k}}{\lambda}+\frac{\sum\limits_{h=1}^{H}\sum\limits_{i=2}^{N}t_{i}\frac{\partial X_{hi}}{\partial I^{h}}X_{hk}}{X_{k}}$$
$$-\frac{\sum\limits_{h=1}^{H}\left(\sum\limits_{i=2}^{N}t_{i}X_{hi}\right)\frac{\partial X_{hk}}{\partial I^{h}}}{X_{k}} \qquad k=2,\ldots,N \qquad (14.45)$$

$$\frac{\sum\limits_{h=1}^{H}\sum\limits_{i=2}^{N}t_{i}\frac{\partial X_{hk}}{\partial q_{i}}}{X_{k}}=-1+\frac{\lambda^{k}}{\lambda}+\frac{\sum\limits_{h=1}^{H}\sum\limits_{i=2}^{N}t_{i}\frac{\partial X_{hi}}{\partial I^{h}}X_{hk}}{X_{k}}$$
$$-\sum\limits_{h=1}^{N}\left(\frac{\sum\limits_{i=2}^{N}t_{i}X_{hi}}{I^{h}}\cdot\frac{\partial X_{hk}}{\partial I^{h}}\cdot\frac{I^{h}}{X_{hk}}\right) \qquad k=2,\ldots,N \qquad (14.46)$$

Equation (14.46) says that the actual percentage changes in demand (factor supply) resulting from the optimal pattern of commodity taxes should be greater:

    1. The lower its distributional coefficient λ^{k} or the more it is demanded by people with low social marginal utilities of income ($\Delta X_{k}/X_{k}$ is expected to be negative for goods, and λ is positive). Presumably, the people with low λ^{k}

are the rich. If so, the rule says that, other things equal, taxes should be heaviest on those goods consumed most heavily by the rich.

2. The more it is demanded by people whose total taxes change least as lump-sum income changes.

3. The more it is demanded by people for whom, other things equal, the product of the fraction of income paid as taxes and the income elasticity of demand for the good is highest.

Unfortunately, there is no clear presumption as to whom the people referred to in items 2 and 3 might be, so that rewriting the first-order conditions in terms of actual demand changes still fails to provide any really clear intuitive feel for the optimal pattern of taxation.

A Covariance Interpretation of Optimal Taxation

Peter Diamond provided an ingenious interpretation of these rules that does give one a better intuitive appreciation of the tax rules.[15] Suppose the government, in addition to the commodity taxes, has the ability to offer a single head or poll subsidy of equal value to all consumers. Although this is admittedly a lump-sum subsidy, it is not the sophisticated variable subsidy necessary to satisfy the interpersonal equity conditions of first-best theory. With the additional head subsidy, the government's problem becomes:

$$\max_{(\vec{t}, I)} V(\vec{q}; I^1, \dots, I^H)$$

$$\text{s.t.} \ \sum_{h=1}^{H} \sum_{i=2}^{N} t_i X_{hi} = \overline{T} + H \cdot I$$

where:

I = the equal per-person subsidy.

The first-order conditions with respect to the t_k are obviously unchanged by the presence of the subsidy. Reproducing Eq. (14.41):

$$-\sum_{h=1}^{H} \beta^h X_{hk} + \lambda \sum_{h=1}^{H} X_{hk} + \lambda \sum_{h=1}^{H} \sum_{i=2}^{N} t_i S_{ik}^h$$
$$-\lambda \sum_{h=1}^{H} \sum_{i=2}^{N} t_i X_{hk} \frac{\partial X_{hi}}{\partial I^h} = 0 \quad k = 2, \dots, N \tag{14.47}$$

The first-order condition with respect to the head tax, I, is

$$\sum_{h=1}^{H} \beta^h + \lambda \left(\sum_{h=1}^{H} \sum_{i=2}^{N} t_i \frac{\partial X_{hi}}{\partial I} - H \right) = 0 \tag{14.48}$$

with $\partial I = \partial I^h$, all $h = 1, \dots, H$. Diamond then defines:

[15] P. Diamond, "A Many Person Ramsey Tax Rule," *Journal of Public Economics*, February 1975.

$$\gamma^h = \beta^h + \lambda \sum_{i=2}^{N} t_i \frac{\partial X_{hi}}{\partial I^h} \tag{14.49}$$

as the full social marginal utility of income for person h, consisting of the conventional direct increase in social utility when I^h increases, the β^h term, plus the social marginal utility of the increased tax revenues when I^h increases, equal to $\lambda \sum_{i=2}^{N} t_i (\partial X_{hi}/\partial I^h)$. With γ^h defined in this manner, the first-order conditions, Eq. (14.47), can be rewritten as:

$$\lambda \sum_{i=2}^{N} \sum_{h=1}^{H} t_i S_{ik}^h = \sum_{h=1}^{H} (\gamma^h - \lambda) \cdot X_{hk} \qquad k = 2, \ldots, N \tag{14.50}$$

Furthermore, Eq. (14.48) becomes simply:

$$\lambda H = \sum_{h=1}^{H} \gamma^h \tag{14.51}$$

or

$$\lambda = \frac{\sum_{h=1}^{H} \gamma^h}{H} \tag{14.52}$$

Thus, λ can be interpreted as the *average* full social marginal utility of income given that the government employs an optimal head subsidy. Furthermore, once λ is expressed in this form, the first-order conditions, Eq. (14.50), have a simple covariance interpretation. To see this, divide Eq. (14.50) by $\lambda X_k = \lambda \sum_{h=1}^{H} X_{hk}$ (and note that $S_{ik}^h = S_{ki}^h$) to obtain:

$$\frac{\sum_{h=1}^{H} \sum_{i=2}^{N} t_i S_{ki}^h}{X_k} = \frac{\sum_{h=1}^{H} (\gamma^h - \lambda) X_{hk}}{\lambda X_k} \qquad k = 2, \ldots, N \tag{14.53}$$

But, from Eq. (14.51), $\sum_{h=1}^{H} (\gamma^h - \lambda) = 0$. Hence, $\sum_h (\gamma^h - \lambda) \cdot \overline{X}_k = 0$, where

$$\overline{X}_k = \frac{\sum_{h=1}^{H} X_{hk}}{H}$$

so that Eq. (14.53) can be rewritten as:

$$\frac{\sum_{i=1}^{H} \sum_{i=2}^{N} t_i S_{ki}^h}{X_k} = \frac{\sum_{h=1}^{H} (\gamma^h - \lambda)(X_{hk} - \overline{X}_k)}{H \lambda \overline{X}_k} \qquad k = 2, \ldots, N \tag{14.54}$$

Equation (14.54) says that the aggregate percentage change in the compensated demand (supply) of good (factor) k should be proportional to the covariance between the full marginal social utility of income and the consumption (supply) of good (factor) k. This is the simplest interpretation of the many-person optimal tax rule to date. (Although it requires the simultaneous imposition of a uniform head subsidy/tax.)

A Two-Class Tax Rule

Defining an optimal per-person income subsidy and the full social marginal utility of income yields some additional intuition into the pattern of optimal taxes. Consider again the first-order conditions, Eq. (14.50), with λ interpreted as the average full social marginal utility of income given an optimal head subsidy. Multiply each equation by t_k and sum over $k = 1, \ldots, N$ to obtain:[16]

$$\sum_{h=1}^{H} \left[(\gamma^h - \lambda) \sum_{k=1}^{N} t_k X_{hk} \right] = \lambda \sum_{h=1}^{H} \sum_{i=1}^{N} \sum_{k=1}^{N} t_i S_{ik}^h t_k \qquad (14.55)$$

Because S_{ik}^h is negative semidefinite,

$$\sum_{i=1}^{N} \sum_{h=1}^{H} \sum_{k=1}^{N} t_i S_{ik}^h t_k \leq 0$$

Therefore,

$$\sum_{h=1}^{H} \left[(\gamma^h - \lambda) \sum_{k=1}^{N} t_k X_{hk} \right] \leq 0 \qquad (14.56)$$

Suppose the government is willing to think of the H consumers as divided into two subsets, the rich and the poor, such that all rich people are identical and all poor people are identical (equal preferences and equal full social marginal utilities of income). Let there be R rich people each with full social marginal utility γ^R, and $(H - R)$ poor people each with full social marginal utility of income γ^P, such that $\gamma^P > \gamma^R$ and $\gamma^P > \lambda$, where λ is the average full social marginal utility of income over all H people.[17] With an optimal head subsidy (Eq. (14.51) satisfied):

$$\sum_{h=1}^{H} \gamma^h = \lambda H = R \cdot \gamma^R + (H - R)\gamma^P \qquad (14.57)$$

Substituting Eq. (14.57) into (14.56) yields:

$$R(\gamma^R - \lambda) \sum_{k=1}^{N} t_k X_{Rk} + (H - R)(\gamma^P - \lambda) \sum_{k=1}^{N} t_k X_{Pk} \leq 0 \qquad (14.58)$$

But, from Eq. (14.57),

$$[R + (H - R)]\lambda = R\gamma^R + (H - R)\gamma^P \qquad (14.59)$$

---

[16] With $t_1 = 0$, k or i can be summed from 1 or 2 to N.
[17] Refer to Eq. (14.52) and its derivation.

Rearranging terms:

$$R(\gamma^R - \lambda) = -(H - R)(\gamma^P - \lambda) \tag{14.60}$$

Substituting for $R(\gamma^R - \lambda)$ in Eq. (14.58) yields:

$$-(H - R)(\gamma^P - \lambda)\sum_{k=1}^{N} t_k X_{Rk} + (H - R)(\gamma^P - \lambda)\sum_{k=1}^{N} t_k X_{Pk} \leq 0 \tag{14.61}$$

Rearranging terms:

$$(H - R)(\gamma^P - \lambda)\left(\sum_{k=1}^{N} t_k X_{Pk} - \sum_{k=1}^{N} t_k X_{Rk}\right) \leq 0 \tag{14.62}$$

Hence, assuming $(\gamma^P - \lambda) > 0$ implies that $\sum_{k=1}^{N} t_k X_{Rk} \geq \sum_{k=1}^{N} t_k X_{Pk}$, or that the optimal pattern of commodity taxes should, in general, collect more taxes from the rich than the poor.

This result is certainly consistent with one's intuitive sense of the effect of social welfare considerations on the optimal pattern of commodity taxes. Nonetheless, Eq. (14.56) does not necessarily yield such simple guidelines when there are more than two classes of people. Also, Eq. (14.62) is more or less compelling depending on how one defines the poor. If the "poor" refers to those in poverty, roughly 11% of the population in the United States, then Eq. (14.62) would be satisfied by almost any tax or set of taxes, not just optimal taxes. If, however, the "poor" refers to those with incomes below the median and $(\gamma^P - \lambda)$ is assumed to be positive for them, then Eq. (14.62) suggests that the optimal taxes might be progressive with respect to the two groups.

U.S. Commodity Taxes: How Far From Optimal?

Balcer *et al.* applied a many-person, fixed-producer-price model to U.S. data to get a feel for how optimal commodity tax rates would vary with the government's revenue needs and society's aversion to inequality.[18] Using data from the 1972 and 1973 Consumer Expenditure Surveys, they calculated expenditures for nine commodity groups for each of ten income classes. The specific model they used to calculate optimal commodity taxes for these data had the following features:

1. Preferences given by the Stone–Geary utility function $U = \sum_{i=1}^{9} (X_i - \gamma_i)^{\beta_i}$, where the γ_i are the subsistence quantities of each good (the minimum quantities above which utility is positive) and the β_i are the marginal budget shares of each good. The γ_i are assumed to be the expenditures

---

[18] Y. Balcer, I. Garfinkel, K. Krynski, and E. Sadka, "Income Redistribution and the Structure of Indirect Taxation," in E. Helpman, A. Razin, and E. Sadka, Eds., *Social Policy Evaluation: An Economic Perspective*, Academic Press, New York, 1983, chap. 13.

of the poorest income class calculated at the net of tax producer prices. The β_i vary by income class. The poorest income class is assumed to receive subsidies that just place them at the subsistence level, so that class is dropped from the analysis. Labor is in fixed supply, and there is no saving.

2. An Atkinson social welfare function:

$$W = \frac{1}{(1-e)} \sum_{h=1}^{H} \left[V^h\left(q_i; I^h\right) \right]^{(1-e)}$$

where

V^h = the indirect utility function for income class h

$q_i = 1 + t_i$, the gross-of-tax consumer price for good i (producer prices are set equal to unity, so that expenditures equal quantities at the net of tax prices);

e = society's aversion to inequality, ranging from 0 (utilitarian) to 2. They believe that e is likely to be in the neighborhood of .5 for the United States with an outside range of .25 to .75, much as Harberger conjectured (see the discussion in Chapter 4). Like Harberger, they believe that the United States does not have much aversion to inequality.

3. A government budget constraint of the form $\sum_{h=1}^{H} \sum_{i=1}^{N} t_i X_{hi} = R$, where R represents the revenue needs of the government. R varied from -5 to 30% of total disposable income in their exercises. The actual revenues collected from U.S. sales and excise taxes at the time were slightly in excess of 4% of disposable income.

The optimal commodity taxes are those that maximize W subject to the government budget constraint. The exercise produced results that were generally consistent with the theory and gave fairly high marks to the actual tax rates on the nine commodity groups. Among their more interesting results:

1. For the baseline case of e = .5 and R slightly in excess of 4%, the optimal tax rates range from -10.8% (housing) to 11.4% (recreation). They vary directly with the ratio of marginal budget shares of the rich to the poor, as predicted by the theory. The variation in rates increases as e and R increase, also as predicted by the theory.

2. Changing the U.S. tax rates from their (then) current values to the optimal values that generate the same revenue would produce only a small increase in social welfare (asserted by the authors on p. 292, but with no data given). It would also have a negligible effect on the Gini coefficient. The reductions in the Gini range from 0.68 to 2.96% for the values of e (positive) and R tested. The reason for the small distributional gain is that only one tax deviated substantially from the optimal rate, the tax on gasoline (39.6% versus a baseline optimal rate of 8.8%). (The high gasoline tax could be justified as a benefits-received tax since its revenues are typically earmarked to highway funds.)

3. They also considered the welfare loss of moving to uniform taxes from the optimal tax rates, with the loss defined as the amount that the government would have to lower its revenue to maintain social welfare at its value with the optimal rates. The welfare cost is negligible, only .17% of disposable income for the baseline case and never higher than 2.28% across all values of R and e. (The welfare cost is zero in the utilitarian case, e = 0, since that is equivalent to a one-consumer economy and the Stone–Geary utility function satisfies the sufficient condition for uniform taxation to be optimal in the one-consumer model.)

MANY-PERSON ECONOMY WITH GENERAL TECHNOLOGY

Synthesizing the separate analyses of a one-person economy with general technology and the many-person economy with linear technology (constant producer prices) is relatively straightforward, especially under the assumption of CRS production.

Let us begin by considering the optimal commodity tax problem. We saw that assuming CRS in the context of a one-consumer economy generates the same optimal tax rules that result when production technology is characterized by fixed producer prices. The key to this result is that there can never be pure economic profits or losses under CRS and perfect competition, so that the value of the general equilibrium profit function $\pi(\vec{p})$ is identically zero for all values of the producer price vector $\vec{p}$.

The same correspondence exists in the many-person economy. As long as we assume CRS, the original distribution of lump-sum incomes $(I^1, \ldots, I^H)$ remains unchanged as producer prices vary in response to taxation. Hence, the many-person optimal tax rule is identical to its linear technology counterpart. In fact, Diamond used a general-technology CRS model to generate the many-person optimal tax rules.

A model appropriate for analyzing second-best tax (and expenditure) problems in a many-person, general-technology economy has four components: the social welfare function, consumer preferences, a general production technology, and market clearance.

Social Welfare and Preferences

The object of government policy is to maximize a social welfare function of the form:

$$W\left[V^h(\vec{q}; I^h)\right] = V(\vec{q}; I^1, \ldots, I^H)$$

specified in terms of consumer prices, exactly as in the many-person, linear-technology case. (We drop the * on W here.)

Production Technology

Production must be specified in terms of prices and actual general equilibria to be compatible with social welfare. The specification must also be flexible enough to allow for various kinds of technologies. But the general technology production can no longer be specified by means of the generalized profit function, $\pi(\vec{p})$, as in the one-consumer economy, because social welfare is not measured in terms of lump-sum income. Instead, the natural choice is to return to an implicit aggregate production frontier of the form $F(\vec{Y}) = 0$, as in first-best analysis, where $\vec{Y}$ = the vector of aggregate goods supplies (factor demands). Then, replace the quantities $\vec{Y}$ with the general equilibrium market supply (input demand) functions $Y_i = Y_i(\vec{p})$, $i = 1, \ldots, N$ (the same functions that would result from a social planner maximizing aggregate profits at given competitive prices). The resulting function, $F[\vec{Y}(\vec{p})] = 0$, which is called the production-price frontier, specifies all relevant production parameters assuming competitive market behavior.

Market Clearance

General technology requires explicit market clearance equations of the form:

$$\sum_{h=1}^{H} X_{hi}\left(\vec{p} + \vec{t}, I^h\right) = Y^i(\vec{p}) \quad i = 1, \ldots, N \tag{14.63}$$

to solve for the vector of producer prices given a vector of tax rates. All N market clearance equations apply because the model describes an actual general equilibrium, not a compensated general equilibrium. The pricing identities $\vec{q} = \vec{p} + \vec{t}$ then solve for the vector of consumer prices.

The Model

Thus, a full general equilibrium model useful for analyzing any problem in the second-best theory of taxation can be represented as:

$$\max_{(\vec{q}, \vec{t}, \vec{p})} W\left[V^h\left(\vec{q}; \bar{I}^h\right)\right]$$

$$\text{s.t.} \quad F[\vec{Y}(\vec{p})] = 0$$

$$\sum_{h=1}^{H} X_{hi}\left(\vec{q}; I^h\right) = Y_i(\vec{p}) \quad 1, \ldots, N$$

$$q_i = p_i + t_i \quad i = 2, \ldots, N$$

$$q_1 \equiv p_1 \equiv 1 \quad t_1 = 0$$

As always, setting $t_1 = 0$ ensures that the tax vector $\vec{t}$ changes the vector of relative consumer and producer prices and thereby generates distortions.

The model can be greatly simplified by incorporating market clearance directly into the production frontier and thinking of the government as solving directly for the vector of consumer prices, $\vec{q}$, rather than the vector of taxes, $\vec{t}$, as follows:

$$\max_{(\vec{q})} W\left[V^h\left(\vec{q}; I^h\right)\right]$$

$$\text{s.t. } F\left[\sum_{h=1}^{H} X_{hi}\left(\vec{q}; I^h\right)\right] = 0$$

The vector of producer prices $\vec{p}$ can then be determined through the market clearance equations, after which the $(N-1)$ optimal tax rates are given by the pricing identities $t_i = q_i - p_i$, $i = 2, \ldots, N$.

Walras' Law and the Government Budget Constraint

The final point is that there is no need to include the government's budget constraint,

$$\sum_{h=1}^{H} \sum_{i=2}^{N} t_i X_{hi}\left(\vec{q}; I^h\right) = \overline{T}$$

explicitly in the model because of Walras' law. The model describes an actual market general equilibrium, for which Walras' law can have either of two interpretations:

1. *The common interpretation*: If each economic agent is on its budget constraint (firms are profit maximizing) and all but one market is in equilibrium, the final market must also be in equilibrium.

2. *An alternative interpretation*: If all but one economic agent are satisfying their budget constraints and *all* markets are in equilibrium, then the last economic agent must also be on its budget constraint. This is the interpretation that allows us to exclude the government's budget constraint since the model: (a) explicitly posits market clearance in all markets, (b) implicitly assumes all consumers are on their budget constraints as a prerequisite for defining their indirect utility functions, and (c) implicitly assumes all producers are maximizing profits when substituting the general equilibrium supply (input demand) functions $\vec{Y}(\vec{p})$ into the aggregate production frontier $F(\vec{Y}) = 0$.

This is the model specification used by Diamond to generate many-person optimal taxes rules identical to Eqs. (14.50) and (14.52).[19]

---

[19] The model is not identical to Diamond's model, since he included a Samuelson non-exclusive public good and assumed all consumers had identical initial endowments of lump-sum income.

Optimal Taxation

To see that the assumption of general technology makes no difference as long as the technology exhibits constant returns to scale, consider the first-order conditions of the model with respect to q_k and an equal head subsidy, I:

$$\sum_{h=1}^{H} \frac{\partial W}{\partial V^h} \frac{\partial V^h}{\partial q_k} = \lambda \sum_{i=1}^{N} \sum_{h=1}^{H} F_i \frac{\partial X_{hi}}{\partial q_k} \qquad k = 2, \ldots, N \qquad (14.64)$$

$$\sum_{h=1}^{H} \frac{\partial W}{\partial V^h} \frac{\partial V^h}{\partial I} = \lambda \sum_{i=1}^{N} \sum_{h=1}^{H} F_i \frac{\partial X_{hi}}{\partial I} \qquad (14.65)$$

Equation (14.64) implicitly embodies the assumption of CRS production because the initial distribution of lump-sum income, $(I^1, \ldots, I^H)$, is assumed unchanged by a marginal change in the kth consumer price.

From Roy's Identity on indirect utility functions, the definition of marginal social utility β^h, and the assumption of profit maximization with $p_1 \equiv 1$, Eq. (14.64) can be written as:[20]

$$-\sum_{h=1}^{H} \beta^h X_{hk} = \lambda \sum_{h=1}^{H} \sum_{i=1}^{N} p_i \frac{\partial X_{hi}}{\partial q_k} \qquad k = 2, \ldots, N \qquad (14.66)$$

But $p_i = q_i - t_i$, for $i = 1, \ldots, N$. Hence,

$$-\sum_{h=1}^{H} \beta^h X_{hk} = \lambda \sum_{h=1}^{H} \sum_{i=1}^{N} \left(q_i \frac{\partial X_{hi}}{\partial q_k} - t_i \frac{\partial X_{hi}}{\partial q_k} \right) \qquad k = 2, \ldots, N \qquad (14.67)$$

Further, if consumers are on their budget constraints,

$$\sum_{i=1}^{N} q_i \frac{\partial X_{hi}}{\partial q_k} = -X_{hk} \qquad h = 1, \ldots, H \qquad (14.68)$$

Therefore:

$$-\sum_{h=1}^{H} \beta^h X_{hk} = \lambda \sum_{h=1}^{H} \left(-X_{hk} - \sum_{i=1}^{N} t_i \frac{\partial X_{hi}}{\partial q_k} \right) \qquad k = 2, \ldots, N \qquad (14.69)$$

which is identical to Eq. (14.38).[21]

Turning to the optimal head tax, make use of profit maximization, the definition of marginal social utility, and the definitional relationships among prices and taxes, to rewrite Eq. (14.65) as:

---

[20] From profit maximization $F_i/F_1 = p_i/p_1$, but $p_1 \equiv 1$ and F can be scaled such that $F_1 = 1$, so that $F_i = p_i$, $i = 2, \ldots, N$.

[21] $\sum_{i=1}^{N} t_i \frac{\partial X_{hi}}{\partial q_k} = \sum_{i=2}^{N} t_i \frac{\partial X_{hi}}{\partial q_k}$, with $t_1 = 0$.

$$\sum_{h=1}^{H} \beta^h = \lambda \sum_{h=1}^{H} \sum_{i=1}^{N} (q_i - t_i) \frac{\partial X_{hi}}{\partial I} \qquad (14.70)$$

If consumers are on their budget constraints,

$$\sum_{i=1}^{N} q_i \frac{\partial X_{hi}}{\partial I} = 1 \quad h = 1, \ldots, H \qquad (14.71)$$

Hence,

$$\sum_{h=1}^{H} \beta^h = \lambda H - \lambda \sum_{h=1}^{H} \sum_{i=1}^{N} t_i \frac{\partial X_{hi}}{\partial I} \qquad (14.72)$$

But

$$\gamma^h = \beta^h + \lambda \sum_{i=1}^{N} t_i \frac{\partial X_{hi}}{\partial I}$$

the full social marginal utility of income. Therefore:

$$\lambda = \sum_{h=1}^{H} \frac{\gamma^h}{H} \qquad (14.73)$$

the average full social marginal utility of income, as in Eq. (14.52). Consequently, the many-person optimal tax rules continue to have a simple covariance interpretation.

THE SOCIAL WELFARE IMPLICATIONS OF ANY GIVEN CHANGE IN TAXES

Once the optimal commodity tax problem had been fully developed by Diamond and Mirrless in the late 1960s, public sector economists turned their attention to more realistic forms of restricted taxation. This opened up two new major lines of reasearch in the 1970s. One group of economists adopted the basic model for optimal commodity taxation and attempted to develop theorems on optimal changes (or levels) of taxes for a subset of the goods and factors (e.g., Dixit, Guesnerie, and Hatta).[22] A second group, following the lead of James Mirrlees and Ray Fair in 1971, concentrated specifically on optimal income taxation (e.g., Mirrlees, Fair, Sheshinski, Atkinson, Stiglitz,

---

[22] The seminal articles were A. Dixit, "Welfare Effects of Tax and Price Changes," *Journal of Public Economics,* February 1975 (also A. Dixit, and K. Munk, "Welfare Effects of Tax and Price Changes: A Correction," *Journal of Public Economics,* August 1977); R. Guesnerie, "On the Direction of Tax Reform," *Journal of Public Economics,* April 1977; R. Guesnerie, "Financing Public Goods with Commodity Taxes: A Tax Reform Viewpoint," *Econometrica,* March 1979; and T. Hatta, "A Theory of Piecemeal Policy Recommendations, *Review of Economic Studies,* February 1977.

Sadka, Stern, and Seade).[23] The chapter concludes with a general example representative of the first line of research. Chapter 15 discusses optimal income taxation.

The general method for analyzing restricted tax changes can been seen by considering the social welfare implications of a marginal change in a single tax, or of substituting one vector of tax rates for another, equal-revenue vector of rates in the context of a many-person, general technology economy.[24] Begin by totally differentiating the social welfare function $W^* = W[V^h(\vec{q}; I^h)]$ with respect to prices and income. Using Roy's Identity and the definition of social marginal utility of income β^h:

$$dW = -\sum_{h=1}^{H}\sum_{i=1}^{N}\frac{\partial W}{\partial V^h}\alpha^h X_{hi}dq_i + \sum_{h=1}^{H}\frac{\partial W}{\partial V^h}\alpha^h dI^h \tag{14.74}$$

$$dW = -\sum_{h=1}^{H}\sum_{i=1}^{N}\beta^h X_{hi}dq_i + \sum_{h=1}^{H}\beta^h dI^h \tag{14.75}$$

Next, totally differentiate the production-price frontier $F(\sum_{h=1}^{H} X_{hi}) = 0$, in which the market clearance equations have been used to substitute consumers' demands and factor supplies for the production aggregates Y_i:

$$\sum_{i=1}^{N}F_i\sum_{h=1}^{H}dX_{hi} = 0 \tag{14.76}$$

Assuming perfect competition, $p_1 \equiv 1$, and that the identity of person h is irrelevant to production, Eq. (14.76) becomes:

$$\sum_{i=1}^{N}p_i\sum_{h=1}^{H}dX_{hi} = 0 \tag{14.77}$$

But, $q_i = p_i + t_i$, for $i = 1, \ldots, N$. Multiplying each price by dX_{hi}, and summing over all goods and people yields:

[23] The seminal articles were J. Mirrlees, "An Exploration in the Theory of Optimum Income Taxation," *Review of Economic Studies*, April 1971 (*the* seminal article); J. Mirrlees, "Optimal Tax Theory: A Syntheses," *Journal of Public Economics*, November 1976; R. Fair, "The Optimal Distribution of Income," *Quarterly Journal of Economics*, November 1971; E. Sheshinski, "The Optimal Linear Income Tax," *Review of Economic Studies*, July 1972; A. Atkinson, "How Progressive Should Income Tax Be?," in M. Parkin, Ed., *Essays in Modern Economics*, Longman Group, Ltd., London, 1973; A. Atkinson and J. Stiglitz, "The Design of Tax Structure: Direct vs. Indirect Taxation," *Journal of Public Economics*, July/August 1976; E. Sadka, "On Income Distribution, Incentive Effects, and Optimal Income Taxation, *Review of Economic Studies*, June 1976; N. Stern, "On the Specification of Models of Optimum Income Taxation," *Journal of Public Economics*, July/August 1976; J. Seade, "On the Shape of Optimal Tax Schedules," *Journal of Public Economics*, April 1977; D. Bradford and H. Rosen, "The Optimal Taxation of Commodities and Income," *American Economic Association Papers and Proceedings*, May 1976.

[24] The analysis in this section draws heavily from R. Boadway, "Integrating Equity and Efficiency in Applied Welfare Economics," *Quarterly Journal of Economics*, November 1976.

$$\sum_{i=1}^{N}\sum_{h=1}^{H}q_i dX_{hi} = \sum_{i=1}^{N}\sum_{h=1}^{H}(p_i + t_i)dX_{hi} \qquad (14.78)$$

which, from Eq. (14.78), becomes:

$$\sum_{i=1}^{N}\sum_{h=1}^{H}q_i dX_{hi} = \sum_{i=1}^{H}\sum_{h=1}^{H}t_i d\,X_{hi} \qquad (14.79)$$

Next, totally differentiate each consumer's budget constraint and sum over all consumers to obtain:

$$\sum_{h=1}^{H}dI^h = \sum_{h=1}^{H}\sum_{i=1}^{N}q_i dX_{hi} + \sum_{h=1}^{H}\sum_{i=1}^{N}X_{hi}dq_i \qquad (14.80)$$

Combining Eqs. (14.79) and (14.80) yields:

$$\sum_{h=1}^{H}dI^h - \sum_{h=1}^{H}\sum_{i=1}^{N}X_{hi}dq_i = \sum_{h=1}^{H}\sum_{i=1}^{N}t_i dX_{hi} \qquad (14.81)$$

Thus, Eq. (14.75) can be written as:

$$dW = -\sum_{h=1}^{H}\sum_{i=1}^{N}\beta^h X_{hi}dq_i + \sum_{h=1}^{H}\beta^h dI^h - \sum_{h=1}^{H}dI^h$$
$$+ \sum_{h=1}^{H}\sum_{i=1}^{N}X_{hi}dq_i + \sum_{i=1}^{N}\sum_{h=1}^{H}t_i dX_{hi} \qquad (14.82)$$

Finally, the dX_{hi} in the last term of Eq. (14.82) can be eliminated by noting that:

$$X_{hi} = X_{hi}(\vec{q}; I^h) \quad h = 1, \ldots, H; \quad i = 1, \ldots, N \qquad (14.83)$$

Totally differentiating Eq. (14.83) yields:

$$dX_{hi} = \sum_{j=1}^{N}\frac{\partial X_{hi}}{\partial q_j}dq_j + \frac{\partial X_{hi}}{\partial I^h}dI^h \quad h = 1, \ldots, H$$
$$i = 1, \ldots, N \qquad (14.84)$$

Substituting Eq. (14.84) into (14.82) and combining terms yields:

$$dW = \sum_{h=1}^{H}\left(\beta^h - 1 + \sum_{i=1}^{N}\sum_{h=1}^{H}t_i \frac{\partial X_{hi}}{\partial I^h}\right)dI^h$$
$$+ \sum_{h=1}^{H}(1 - \beta^h)\sum_{i=1}^{N}X_{hi}dq_i + \sum_{h=1}^{H}\sum_{i=1}^{N}t_i \sum_{j=1}^{N}\frac{\partial X_{hi}}{\partial q_j}dq_j \qquad (14.85)$$

Equation (14.85) highlights the importance of CRS in second-best analysis. With general technology, pure profits or losses can occur in production, thereby changing the pattern of lump-sum incomes $(I^1, \ldots, I^H)$ received by the consumers. As indicated by the first term in Eq. (14.85), the government would then have to keep track of these changes and their subsequent effects on social welfare. With CRS, however, the first term can be ignored since pure profits and losses are zero and the vector of lump-sum income remains unchanged.

Even with CRS, however, it is clear that production derivatives affect second-best decision rules, in general, even if they do not do so in the optimal tax problem. The change in the vector of consumer prices, $\vec{q}$, in Eq. (14.85) is determined by the combined interaction of general equilibrium demand and supply schedules. To see this explicitly, ignore changes in lump-sum income and use market clearance to express the change in welfare in terms of changes in taxes rather than prices, exactly as we did for the one-consumer, general-technology case. Totally differentiating the market clearance equations,

$$\sum_{h=1}^{H} X_{hi}\left(\vec{q}; \overline{I}^h\right) = Y_i(\vec{p}) = Y_i(\vec{q} - \vec{t}) \qquad i = 1, \ldots, N$$

yields:

$$\sum_{h=1}^{H} \sum_{j=1}^{N} \frac{\partial X_{hi}}{\partial q_j} dq_j = \sum_{j=1}^{N} \frac{\partial Y_i}{\partial p_j} (dq_j - dt_j) \qquad i = 1, \ldots, N \qquad (14.86)$$

Solving for $d\vec{q}$ and expressing the N equations, Eq. (14.86), in vector notation yields:

$$dq = E^{-1}\left(-\frac{\partial Y}{\partial p}\right) dt \qquad (14.87)$$

where $E = \left(\frac{\partial X}{\partial q} - \frac{\partial Y}{\partial p}\right)$ in vector notation.[25]

Finally, substitute Eq. (14.87) into (14.85), with $dI^h \equiv 0$, to obtain, in vector notation,

$$dW = \left[-((1 - \beta)'X) - t'\frac{\partial X}{\partial q}\right] E^{-1} \frac{\partial Y}{\partial p} dt \qquad (14.88)$$

where:

$$\beta = \begin{bmatrix} \beta^1 \\ \vdots \\ \beta^H \end{bmatrix},$$ an $(H \times 1)$ column vector of marginal social utilities of income.

$X = [X_{hi}]$, an $(H \times N)$ matrix of individual consumer demands and factor supplies.

$1 =$ an $(H \times 1)$ unit column vector.

---

[25] Each element ij in X is the partial derivative of the aggregate X_i with respect to q_j, the sum of the H individual derivatives.

Equation (14.88) is the fundamental equation for evaluating tax changes in a many-consumer economy with CRS general production technology. By inspection, the supply responses ($\partial Y/\partial p$) affect the change in social welfare.

Equation (14.88) can also be compared directly with the results from a one-consumer equivalent economy. Equation (14.17), reproduced here as Eq. (14.89), calculated the change in loss as:

$$dL = (t')(M_{ij})E^{-1}\frac{\partial Y}{\partial p}\,dt \qquad (14.89)$$

The second term in Eq. (14.88) is very close to Eq. (14.89) but not identical. A trivial difference is the minus sign, resulting from the fact that $dW = -dL$. More importantly, the demand derivatives ($\partial X/\partial q$) in Eq. (14.89) are the compensated Slutsky terms, not the actual demand derivatives, reflecting the fact that Eq. (14.89) derives from a conceptual compensation experiment that is not particularly meaningful in a many-person environment. In practical applications, however, it may prove useful to think of the change in social welfare resulting from any change in tax rates as a linear combination of social welfare considerations and dead-weight efficiency loss, with the former embodied in the first term of Eq. (14.88) and the latter in the second term. This interpretation maintains the dichotomy between equity and efficiency that exists in first-best analysis, but it can only be viewed here as a rough "interpretative" approximation. Whether it is useful or not depends on the particular problem under consideration. We saw, for example, that equity and efficiency terms are tightly intertwined in the many-person optimal commodity tax rules. But it could be more compelling for simple tax change problems, such as in the Corlett and Hague analysis. The welfare effects of such changes can be evaluated directly by Eq. (14.88),[26] once the equal-revenue pattern of tax changes, $d\vec{t}$, has been determined.

REFERENCES

Atkinson, A., "How Progressive Should Income Tax Be?," in M. Parkin, Ed., *Essays in Modern Economics*, Longman Group, Ltd., London, 1973.

Atkinson, A., and Stiglitz, J., "The Design of Tax Structure: Direct vs. Indirect Taxation," *Journal of Public Economics*, July/August 1976.

Balcer, Y., Garfinkel, I., Krynski, K., and Sadka, E., "Income Redistribution and the Structure of Indirect Taxation," in E. Helpman, A. Razin, and E. Sadka, Eds., *Social Policy Evaluation: An Economic Perspective*, Academic Press, New York, 1983.

Boadway, R., "Cost–Benefit Rules and General Equilibrium," *Review of Economic Studies*, June 1975.

[26] Alternatively, Eq. (14.85) with nonconstant returns to scale production. In this case, the vector of income changes dI^h would have to be specified and incorporated into the total differential of the market clearance equations, Eq. (14.83).

Broadway, R., "Integrating Equity and Efficiency in Applied Welfare Economics," *Quarterly Journal of Economics*, November 1976.

Bradford, D., and Rosen, H., "The Optimal Taxation of Commodities and Income," *American Economic Association Papers and Proceedings*, May 1976.

Diamond, P. A., "A Many Person Ramsey Tax Rule," *Journal of Public Economics*, February 1975.

Dixit, A. "Welfare Effects of Tax and Price Changes," *Journal of Public Economics*, February 1975.

Dixit, A., and Munk, K., "Welfare Effects of Tax and Price Changes: A Correction," *Journal of Public Economics*, August 1977.

Fair, R., "The Optimal Distribution of Income," *Quarterly Journal of Economics*, November 1971.

Feldstein, M., "Distributional Equity and the Optimal Structure of Public Prices," *American Economic Review*, March 1972.

Green, J., "Two Models of Optimal Pricing and Taxation," *Oxford Economic Papers*, November 1975.

Guesnerie, R., "On the Direction of Tax Reform," *Journal of Public Economics*, April 1977.

Guesnerie, R., "Financing Public Goods with Commodity Taxes: A Tax Reform Viewpoint," *Econometrica*, March 1979.

Harris, R., and Wildasin, D., "An Alternative Approach to Aggregate Surplus Analysis," *Journal of Public Economics*, April 1985.

Hartwick, J., "Optimal Price Discrimination," *Journal of Public Economics*, February 1978.

Hatta, T., "A Theory of Piecemeal Policy Recommendations," *Review of Economic Studies*, February 1977.

Mirrlees, J., "An Exploration in the Theory of Optimal Income Taxation," *Review of Economic Studies*, April 1971.

Mirrlees, J., "Optimal Commodity Taxation in a Two-Class Economy," *Journal of Public Economics*, February 1975.

Mirrless, J., "Optimal Tax Theory: A Synthesis," *Journal of Public Economics*, November 1976.

Sadka, E., "On Income Distribution, Incentive Effects, and Optimal Income Taxation," *Review of Economic Studies*, June 1976.

Samuelson, P. A., "Social Indifference Curves," *Quarterly Journal of Economics*, February 1956.

Seade, J., "On the Shape of Optimal Tax Schedules," *Journal of Public Economics*, April 1977.

Sheshinski, E., "The Optimal Linear Income Tax," *Review of Economic Studies*, July 1972.

Stern, N., "On the Specification of Models of Optimum Income Taxation," *Journal of Public Economics*, July/August 1976.

Stiglitz, J., and Dasgupta, P., "Differential Taxation, Public Goods and Economic Efficiency," *Review of Economic Studies*, April 1971.

15

TAXATION UNDER ASYMMETRIC INFORMATION

The text so far has ignored an important market imperfection, the presence of private or asymmetric information. Chapter 15 explores the implications of asymmetric information on taxation, and later chapters extend the analysis to transfer payments and other public expenditures. Analysis under the assumption of asymmetric information is inherently second best because first-best analysis requires that agents have perfect information about everything relevant to their economic decisions and exchanges.

The problem of asymmetric information has been a focal point of public sector analysis for the past 15 or 20 years, just as it has been in almost all fields of economics. The recent interest in asymmetric information is understandable, first and foremost because it is so common. Agents often possess private information about themselves that other agents, including the government, do not or cannot know, at least not without undertaking considerable effort and cost to monitor behavior. In addition, optimizing agents have obvious incentives to exploit private information to their own advantage, and economists quite naturally assume they will do so to the fullest extent possible. Finally, the assumption of asymmetric information often produces results that are very different from those obtained under the assumption of perfect information. This has been especially true in public sector economics.

Regarding the theory of taxation, old standards such as the Ramsey tax rule for one-consumer equivalent economies or the Diamond–Mirrlees many-person tax rule are no longer prescriptions for optimal taxation under private information. This is so even if the government can in principle tax (almost) everything as the Ramsey and Diamond–Mirrlees models assume. In fact, governments may be quite restricted in what they can tax under private information. They may not have sufficient information about some economic variables to use them as a tax base. What *can* the government tax? is an important policy question in a world of private information. A final point is that private information can severely constrain a government's ability to redistribute purchasing power through taxes and transfers.

The last comment on redistribution points to a special difficulty with private information: It is not simply a technological or structural imperfection. Rather, it has certain uncomfortable behavioral characteristics that are absent from other market imperfections such as distorting taxes, or monopoly power, or legislated budget constraints. Agents who exploit private information for their own self-interest at the expense of broader social goals tear at the fabric of society. They violate the spirit of good citizenship that is necessary to hold a society together. An obvious example is people who evade paying taxes that would have been transferred to the poor.[1]

Such behavior also strikes at the foundations of normative public sector theory. What is normative theory to make of the tax evaders, especially when the norms include a concern for equity as well as efficiency? In formal terms, should the social welfare function give dishonest taxpayers the same ethical weight as honest taxpayers who could also exploit private information but do not? If unequal weights are chosen, how unequal should they be? Should the dishonest receive zero weight? If the dishonest are to receive a positive weight, should society be expected to spend its scare resources on monitoring their behavior or on punishing them? Should the government significantly alter its tax policies to discourage dishonest behavior? These are difficult, open questions that have profound implications for any normative analysis. Different answers can lead to very different policy recommendations.

As it happens, much of the recent normative public sector analysis has continued the long-established tradition of using the equal-weight utilitarian

---

[1] The same could be said of agents who exploit monopoly power, but their behavior is not different in kind from profit maximizing under perfect competition, unlike the distinction between honest and dishonest taxpayers. It is also less secretive than something like tax evasion.

social welfare function as the objective function, in essence simply adding the assumption of asymmetric information to existing models. This strategy makes sense for studying the other-things-equal implications of asymmetric information. At the same time, however, it implicitly condones the incentive to exploit private information as natural and socially acceptable behavior. Is this sensible as a basis for normative policy analysis? If not, what should the social objective function be? The foundations of normative theory, always vulnerable at best, become shaky indeed in the face of private information.

Private information can greatly complicate the quest for end-results equity, so let us begin with the distribution question.

LUMP-SUM REDISTRIBUTIONS AND PRIVATE INFORMATION

In a first-best environment, with perfect information, the government should transfer one good or factor lump-sum to satisfy the interpersonal equity conditions for a social welfare maximum. Presumably high-ability, high-income people would be taxed and low-ability, low-income people would receive transfers.

Lump-sum redistributions on the basis of ability could raise serious objections, however. Suppose, as is commonly assumed, that everyone has the same tastes and the social welfare function is equal weighted in the sense that everyone has the same social marginal utility at the same commodity bundle. People differ only in their abilities. Under these assumptions, the optimal lump-sum redistributions may violate Feldstein's vertical equity principle of no reversals. The high-ability individuals, who are clearly better off before the redistributions, may be worse off at the social welfare optimum after the redistributions. The following simple example illustrates the possibility of reversals.[2]

Suppose there are two types of people: high-ability people (H) who receive a wage W_H and low-ability people (L) who receive a wage $W_L, W_H > W_L$. The two types of people have identical utility functions defined over a composite commodity, C, and labor, L, with L measured negatively. Assume further that utility is separable in consumption and labor:

$$U(C, L) = f(C) + g(L) \qquad (15.1)$$

with L measured negatively. Markets are competitive, consistent with a first-best environment, and $P_C = 1$, the numeraire.

---

[2] The example is taken from J. Stiglitz, "Pareto Efficient and Optimal Taxation and the New New Welfare Economics," in A. Auerbach and M. Feldstein, Eds., *Handbook of Public Economics*, Vol II, Elsevier Sciences Publishers B.V. (North-Holland), Amsterdam, 1987, chap. 15.

- *Pareto optimality*: The two types of people equate their marginal rates of substitution between consumption and leisure to their wages, as required for pareto optimality:

$$\frac{g_{L_H}}{f_{C_H}} = W_H; \quad \frac{g_{L_L}}{f_{C_L}} = W_L \tag{15.2}$$

- *Interpersonal equity*: Assuming that the good C is redistributed lump-sum, the redistribution equalizes the social marginal utility of consumption across the two types of people (and within each type):

$$\frac{\partial W}{\partial U^H} f_{C_H} = \frac{\partial W}{\partial U^L} f_{C_L} \tag{15.3}$$

With an equal-weighted social welfare function and the same tastes, Eq. (15.3) implies and $f_{C_H} = f_{C_L}$ and $C_H = C_L$ at the social welfare optimum. But equal consumption, coupled with the pareto-optimal condition, Eq. (15.2), implies $g_{L_H} > g_{L_L}$. The marginal disutility of work is greater for the high-ability types; they work harder. Therefore, the high-ability people have the same level of consumption as the low-ability people and work harder at the social welfare optimum. They are worse off after the lump-sum redistributions, in violation of Feldstein's no-reversals principle.

The reversal solution is guaranteed in this example because of the separability assumption. It may not happen with more general, nonseparable utility, but it could, as illustrated in Fig. 15.1. A and A' are the equilibria for each high-ability person before and after the lump-sum tax, and B and B' are the corresponding equilibria for each low-ability person before and after the lump-sum transfer. A reversal is more likely the larger the redistributions required to satisfy the interpersonal equity conditions.

Almost everyone would object to a tax-transfer policy that leads to utility reversals. Therefore, although taxes and transfers based on ability are lump-sum and first-best optimal, high-ability people have a strong incentive to hide their ability from the government. Assume they can do so. Given this incentive, a natural modeling strategy is to assume that the government can at best know people's incomes but not the separate components of their incomes, their wages or their hours worked. The wage is an index of ability, and knowing the hours worked, given income, would reveal the wage. But income is endogenous, so that taxes and transfers of income cannot be lump sum. Thus, the incentive and the means to hide ability force the government into a second-best trade-off between equity and efficiency, in which the equity gains of redistributing income must be balanced against the efficiency losses of both taxing and transferring the income. The redistributions of income must also guard against the possibility of reversals; if not, high-income, high-ability people have an incentive to represent themselves as low-ability people who have high incomes because they work extra hard.

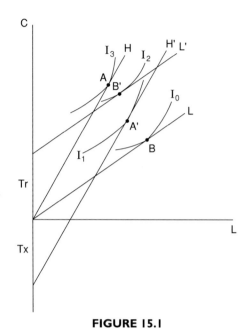

FIGURE 15.1

In summary, private information forces the government to rely on more restricted forms of taxation than are required to achieve the first-best interpersonal equity conditions. Bator's first-best bliss point is unattainable under private information, in general.

REDISTRIBUTION THROUGH COMMODITY TAXATION

One way to reduce the probability of reversals, and the resulting incentive to hide information from the government, is to rely solely on commodity taxes and subsidies.[3] Excise and sales taxes (subsidies) are levied on firms, not individuals, and firms' revenues may be easier to monitor than individual abilities or incomes. Collecting taxes from business is really the only choice when countries are in the early stages of economic development and literacy rates are low. A broad-based income tax requires that the population can keep the records and file the forms associated with an income tax. In contrast, the highly developed industrialized nations can easily use income taxes if they wish. Literacy rates exceed 90%, a very high percentage of economic activity is marketed, and firms can help administer the tax through withholding of income tax liabilities as the income is earned. The interesting question,

---

[3] In this chapter "commodities" has the standard meaning as goods and services.

however, is whether an industrialized nation should prefer commodity taxation to income taxation in a world of imperfect information.

A potential drawback to commodity taxation and subsidy is that it might not have much redistributional bite. The only way to redistribute purchasing power under a pure commodity tax/subsidy scheme is to tax the goods and services favored relatively more by high-income people and subsidize the goods and services favored relatively more by low-income people. This is clearly not as redistributive as directly taxing and transferring incomes unless the rich and poor buy vastly different goods and services.

Raaj Sah developed a simple and ingenious method for determining the limits of redistribution under commodity taxation that relies only on the government's budget constraint.[4] His method led him to conclude that commodity taxes and subsidies are unlikely to have much equalizing effect on the distribution of income.

Sah employs a standard many-person commodity tax model with linear technology (fixed producer prices). Labor, the only factor of production, is in fixed supply and is the untaxed numeraire. The taxes and subsidies are levied per unit, such that $q_i = p_i + t_i$, where the q_i are the consumer prices and the p_i the producer prices. The government budget constraint is $\sum_{i=1}^{N} t_i X_i = 0$, with X_i the aggregate quantity of good i, $t_i > 0$ for the taxed goods, and $t_i < 0$ for the subsidized goods. Setting total taxes equal to total subsidies is a convenience that highlights the distributional impact of the taxes and subsidies. Finally, Sah assumes a Rawlsian social welfare function, which has two advantages. As the most egalitarian of the social welfare functions, it generates the greatest possible incentive to redistribute. It also provides an unambiguous measure of the improvement in the distribution because all that matters is how much the real income of the worst off individual has increased.

Sah chooses the Hicks' Equivalent Variation as the measure of real income improvement, defined as:

$$HEV^1 = M^1(p, V(q, I^1)) - I^1 \qquad (15.4)$$

$M^1(\ )$ is the expenditure function, V is the indirect utility function, and I^1 is the fixed labor income of the worst-off individual, person 1.[5] The HEV is the lump-sum income the worst-off individual would be willing to pay to return to the pretax prices, p. The metric of distributional improvement is the proportional increase in the real income of the worst-off person,

$$HEV^1/I^1 = M^1(p, V(q, I^1))/I^1 - 1 \qquad (15.5)$$

The limits to the distributional improvement rely on the property that the expenditure function is quasi-concave in prices. Thus,

[4] R. Sah, "How Much Redistribution Is Possible Through Commodity Taxes?," *Journal of Public Economics*, February 1983.

[5] p and q are vectors of prices here.

$$M^1(q, V^1(q, I^1)) + \nabla_q M^1(q, V^1(q, I^1))(p - q) \geq M^1(p, V^1(q, I^1)) \qquad (15.6)$$

See Fig. 15.2. Starting from q, a movement along the slope of M to p leaves the consumer above the value of the expenditure function at p. The first term on the left-hand side (LHS) of Eq. (15.6) is the value of the expenditure function at the actual with-tax equilibrium, equal to the worst-off individual's fixed income, I^1. The second term is $-Xt$, the net subsidy received by the worst-off individual, $-T^1$. Therefore,

$$I^1 - T^1 \geq M(p, V(q, I^1)) \qquad (15.7)$$

Dividing by I^1 and using Eq. (15.5) yields:

$$-T^1/I^1 \geq HEV^1/I^1 \qquad (15.8)$$

Equation (15.8) says that the proportional improvement in the real income of the worst-off individual must be less than or equal to the ratio of his net subsidy to income.

Sah establishes limits on the ratio of net subsidy to income in terms of the overall government budget constraint, $\sum_{i=1}^{N} t_i X_i = 0$, written in terms of budget shares as follows.

Define $\phi_i = t_i/q_i$ as the proportional tax (subsidy) rate on good i in terms of the gross of tax price. Note for future reference that $\phi_i < 1$, since $t_i = q_i - p_i$. Also, define $I = \sum_{h=1}^{H} I^h$ as the total fixed labor income in the economy.

Multiplying and dividing each term in the government budget constraint by q_i and dividing the entire budget constraint by I, yields:

$$\sum_{i=1}^{N} \frac{t_i X_i}{I} = \sum_{i=1}^{N} \frac{t_i q_i X_i}{q_i I} = \sum_{i=1}^{N} \frac{\phi_i q_i X_i}{I} = \sum_{i=1}^{N} \phi_i W_i \qquad (15.9)$$

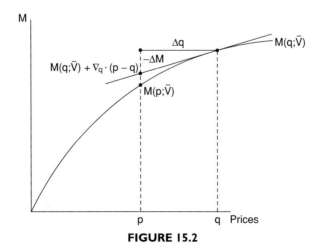

FIGURE 15.2

where W_i = the aggregate budget share for good i.

Next divide the goods into the subsets of taxed goods T, with $\phi_i > 0$, and subsidized goods S, with $\phi_i < 0$:

$$\sum_{i \in T} \phi_i W_i = -\sum_{i \in S} \phi_i W_i \tag{15.10}$$

But,

$$1 > \sum_{i \in T} W_i > \sum_{i \in T} \phi_i W_i \tag{15.11}$$

since $\phi_i < 1$. Therefore,

$$1 > -\sum_{i \in S} \phi_i W_i \tag{15.12}$$

Next consider the $\min_j\{W_j\}$ such that $W_i/\min_j\{W_j\} \geq 1$, for all i. Then,

$$-\sum_{i \in S} \phi_i W_i / \min_j\{W_j\} \geq -\sum_{i \in S} \phi_i \tag{15.13}$$

Therefore, from Eq. (15.12),

$$1 / \min_j\{W_j\} > -\sum_{i \in S} \phi_i \tag{15.14}$$

Return to the worst-off individual, person l:

$$-T^1/I^1 = -\sum_{i=1}^{N} \phi_i W_i^l = -\sum_{i \in T} \phi_i W_i^l - \sum_{i \in S} \phi_i W_i^l \tag{15.15}$$

where W_i^l is person 1's budget share of good i. Therefore,

$$-T^1/I^1 < -\sum_{i \in S} \phi_i W_i^{\,l} \tag{15.16}$$

Also, $W_i^l \leq \max_j\{W_j^l\}$. Therefore,

$$-T^1/I^1 \leq -\sum_{i \in S} \phi_i \max_j\{W_j^l\} \tag{15.17}$$

and from Eq. (15.14):

$$-T^1/I^1 < [1/\min_j\{W_j\}] \max_j\{W_j^l\} \tag{15.18}$$

Comparing Eq. (15.18) with Eq. (15.8), the proportional improvement in the real income of the worst-off individual must be less than the ratio of his maximum budget share to the minimum economy-wide budget share. To push this limit as high as possible, assume that the richest person r has infinite income so that $W_i = W_i^r$, for all i. Then the limit depends on the maximum budget share of the worst-off individual and the minimum budget share of the richest individual. Suppose some necessity item is 80% of person l's budget and 20% of r's budget. Then the limit of the worst-off's gain in real income is four times his income. This may appear to be a large gain, but it is made under the extreme assumption of the richest person having infinite income. The minimum economy-wide budget share is likely to be much more than 1/4 as large as the maximum budget share of the worst-off individual. Also, this is the limit of gain for the worst-off individual, not the average poor person.

Sah conducts a number of simple exercises to get some feeling for the amount of redistribution that is likely though commodity taxes and subsidies. The variations include optimal taxation with a Rawlsian social welfare function; CES utility functions with varying degrees of elasticity of substitution, from Cobb–Douglas to Leontief; two classes of people with different preferences; uniform preferences with an arbitrary number of classes; wide differences in the range of incomes from richest to poorest; and one experiment using actual data for the U.K. and the linear expenditure system. The exercises almost always produce very modest proportional gains in the real income of the worst-off individual(s), usually less than 1.5 and often much less. Sah concludes that not much redistribution is likely to be possible through commodity taxes and subsidies.

The only caveat is if the rich consume some goods that the poor do not consume and vice versa. Then indirect taxes and subsidies can be targeted to the rich and poor just as income taxes can, with much greater redistributional impact. The only natural limitation on the amount of redistribution is the size of the tax base on the items consumed exclusively by the rich. For instance, how much revenue can the government raise from a tax on yachts?[6]

OPTIMAL TAXATION, PRIVATE INFORMATION, AND SELF-SELECTION CONSTRAINTS

Suppose society decides that it has to resort to direct taxes on income to achieve the redistributional bite that it wants from its tax system. It then has to confront the two problems with income taxes mentioned above. One is the trade-off between the distributional gains and the efficiency losses of taxing endogenous income. The other is the potential of violating Feldstein's vertical equity principle of no reversals. This section focuses on the second

---

[6] The analysis in this section should not leave the impression that commodity taxes necessarily avoid problems of imperfect information. The diversion of goods to black markets in an effort to escape taxation is always a potential problem, especially in low-income countries. John McLaren has recently published an analysis of optimal commodity taxes when evasion through black markets is possible. His model generates a number of interesting conclusions. One of the more compelling is that the government might want to tax just one good rather than used a broader based sales tax to save on enforcement costs. This is exactly what many of the poorer developing economies choose to do when they begin to levy taxes. Later on in this chapter we present an analysis of tax evasion under an income tax. Space limitations prevent a presentation of McLaren's model as well, but interested readers should consult J. McLaren, "Black Markets and Optimal Evadable Taxation," *Economic Journal*, May 1998.

problem since it is a fundamental problem for income taxation in a world of private information no matter what norms the government is trying to pursue.

The principle of no reversals is so deeply held that the government might want to design its tax system to prevent reversals from occurring. Taxpayers have an incentive to hide income from the tax authorities under the best of circumstances. The incentive becomes especially strong if taxpayers fear that their ranking in the income distribution would be lower after taxes. An income tax might not even be viable if the potential for reversals is widespread.

No-reversal constraints take the form that each taxpayer prefers his after-tax bundle of goods and factors to anyone else's after-tax bundle. As such, they are called *self-selection constraints*, because they ensure that taxpayers will reveal who they are to the tax authorities. Taxpayers may still try to hide income, but at least they will not claim to be someone else to reduce their tax liability. Self-selection constraints are also called *incentive compatibility constraints* because the utility maximizing strategy under the constraints is for taxpayers to reveal their true identities. That is, the incentive to tell the truth is compatible with utility maximization. Incentive compatibility is a fundamental goal of the theory of mechanism design in the presence of imperfect information.

Once the government designs self-selection constraints into the tax system, the problem of reversals is no longer just a matter of equity. The constraints become part of whatever second-best problem the government is trying to solve, whether it be maximizing social welfare or a more restricted goal such as second-best pareto efficiency or revenue maximization. We will consider the problem of achieving second-best pareto efficiency under self-selection constraints to highlight the effects of the constraints on the design of optimal taxes.

Elements of the Model

The no-reversal, self-selection constraints happen to have a profound effect on the design of taxes. This can be seen by modifying one of the many-person models in Chapter 14 to include income taxation and the self-selection constraints. The simplest choice is a model with N commodities (goods and services), labor as the only factor of production, and linear technology with fixed producer prices. For convenience, the quantities of each commodity are defined such that all producer prices equal 1. Defining producer prices for each commodity would add no insights, and the notational demands of the model are heavy enough as is. As in the earlier discussion of lump-sum taxation, there are two classes of people, those with high ability (H) and those with low ability (L), who receive wages W_H and W_L, respectively. Everyone has identical preferences; people differ only in their abilities.

Regarding taxation, the tax authorities can monitor income perfectly but not ability—that is, not the wages or the hours worked. Therefore, they cannot know who has high ability and who has low ability. Taxes can be levied on any of the commodities and on income (but not labor or wages separately). Moreover, all taxes can potentially be nonlinear to enhance their distributional power.[7] Finally, the model incorporates the self-selection constraints to ensure that the two classes of people reveal themselves to the tax authorities.

Preferences

Given that income is taxed, define preferences in terms of income rather than labor:

$$V^h = V^h(X_{hj}; Y^h) \qquad h = H, L; j = 1, \ldots, N$$

where

X_{hj} = commodity j purchased by a person of ability h
Y^h = the income of a person of ability h, with $Y^h = W_h L_h$

Four properties of V are worth noting:

1. Income is a bad, not a good, in this specification because each person has to supply more labor at the fixed wages to earn more income. Therefore, the indifference curves for one of the commodities X_{hj} and Y^h are upward sloping as they would be if labor were on the horizontal axis.

2. The assumption that everyone has the same tastes implies that the indifference curves in $X_j - L$ space are the same for both classes of people. But the indifference curves in $X_j - Y$ space differ for the two classes. They are flatter for the high-ability people at a given (X_j, Y), as pictured in Fig. 15.3. This follows because:

$$V^h = V^h(X_{hj}; Y^h) = U^h(X_{hj}; W_h L_h/W_h) = U^h(X_{hj}; Y^h/W_h)$$

Therefore, the marginal rate of substitution in terms of one of the commodities X_j and Y is

$$-\left(dX_{hj}/dY^h\right)_{V=\overline{V}} = -\frac{1}{W_h}\left(dX_{hj}/dL_h\right)_{U=\overline{U}} \tag{15.19}$$

Consumers require only $1/W_h$ as much additional X_{hj} to be indifferent to a unit increase in Y^h as they would to a unit increase in L_h. Also, since

---

[7] A model of this nature with self-selection constraints was first developed by A. Atkinson and J. Stiglitz in 1976. See A. Atkinson and J. Stiglitz, "The Design of Tax Structure: Direct Versus Indirect Taxation," *Journal of Public Economics*, July–August 1976. The analysis here closely follows the presentation by Stiglitz in the *Handbook of Public Economics*. See J. Stiglitz, "Pareto-Efficient and Optimal Taxation and the New New Welfare Economics," in A. Auerbach and M. Feldstein, Eds., *Handbook of Public Economics*, Elsevier Science Publishers B.V. (North Holland), Amsterdam, 1987, Chap. 15, pp. 991–1041

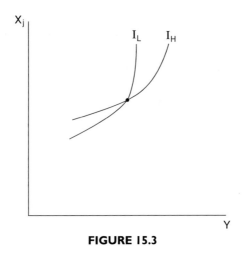

FIGURE 15.3

$W_H > W_L$, the MRS is flatter for the high-ability people at the same (X_j, Y) point. Intuitively, the high-ability people are willing to accept less additional X_j to compensate for an additional unit of Y because they have to supply less labor (can enjoy more leisure) to obtain the same amount of Y.

3. The zero-tax consumer equilibrium requires that the marginal rate of substitution between any commodity and *labor* be equal to the wage (with all commodity prices equal to one):

$$-(dX_{hj}/dL_h)_{U=\overline{U}} = W_h \tag{15.20}$$

Therefore, the zero-tax equilibrium condition in terms of any commodity and *income* is

$$-(dX_{hj}/dY^h)_{V=\overline{V}} = 1 \tag{15.21}$$

A possible zero-tax equilibrium is pictured in Fig. 15.4. Notice that the zero-tax competitive equilibrium is incentive compatible, as would be a first-best equilibrium with lump-sum (nondistorting) taxes.

Self-Selection Constraints

The self-selection constraints require that each class prefers its own bundle of commodities and income:

$$V^H(X_{Hj}; Y^H) \geq V^H(X_{Lj}; Y^L) \tag{15.22}$$

and

$$V^L(X_{Lj}; Y^L) \geq V^L(X_{Hj}; Y^H) \tag{15.23}$$

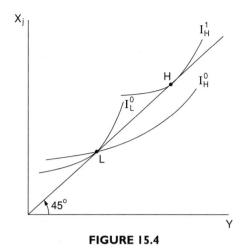

FIGURE 15.4

The realistic concern is that the high-ability class will prefer the low-ability bundle to avoid tax liability. The low-ability class is unlikely to pretend to be of high ability because they would have to sacrifice too much leisure to earn Y^H at a wage of W_L. Therefore, only the high-ability constraint is likely to bind in a tax equilibrium.

Government Budget Constraint

Suppose the government has to raise a fixed amount of revenue, R. If there are N^H high-ability people and N^L low-ability people, then the government's budget constraint is

$$N^H(Y^H - \sum_{j=1}^{N}X_{Hj}) + N^L(Y^L - \sum_{j=1}^{N}X_{Lj}) = R \qquad (15.24)$$

in terms of the X_{hj} and Y^h. The government has access to all income that is not consumed.[8]

Pareto-Efficient Taxation

The goal is to determine the pareto-efficient pattern of commodity and income taxes that raise a given amount of revenue, such that the self-selection constraints hold. The search is for a utility-possibilities frontier rendered second best by the private information on abilities that forces the government to impose the self-selection constraints. Since everyone within each ability class is identical, the frontier is the set of allocations that maximizes the utility

---

[8] Dollars of pretax income and the quantities of the commodities are in the same dollar units given the pricing convention.

of a representative person in one of the classes subject to holding the utility of a representative person in the other class constant and subject to the self-selection and revenue constraints. Formally, the problem is to

$$\max_{\{X_{Hj}; X_{Lj}; Y^H; Y^L\}} V^H(X_{Hj}; Y^H)$$

$$\text{s.t.} \quad V^L(X_{Lj}; Y^L) = \overline{V}^L$$

$$V^H(X_{Hj}; Y^H) \geq V^H(X_{Lj}; Y^L)$$

$$V^L(X_{Lj}; Y^L) \geq V^L(X_{Hj}; Y^H)$$

$$N^H(Y^H - \sum_{j=1}^{N} X_{Hj}) + N^L(Y^L - \sum_{j=1}^{N} X_{Lj}) = R$$

Defining multipliers for the constraints, the Lagrangian is

$$\max_{\{X_{Hj}; X_{Lj}; Y^H; Y^L\}} L = V^H(X_{Hj}; Y^H) + \mu(V^L(X_{Lj}; Y^L) - \overline{V}^L)$$

$$+ \lambda^H(V^H(X_{Hj}; Y^H) - V^H(X_{Lj}; Y^L))$$

$$+ \lambda^L(V^L(X_{Lj}; Y^L) - V^L(X_{Hj}; Y^H))$$

$$+ \gamma(N^H(Y^H - \sum_{j=1}^{N} X_{Hj}) + N^L(Y^L - \sum_{j=1}^{N} X_{Lj}) - R)$$

The first-order conditions are

$$X_{Hj}: \; \partial V^H/\partial X_{Hj} + \lambda^H \partial V^H/\partial X_{Hj} - \lambda^L \partial V^L/\partial X_{Hj} - \gamma N^H = 0$$
$$j = 1, \dots, N \tag{15.25}$$

$$X_{Lj}: \; \mu \partial V^L/\partial X_{Lj} - \lambda^H \partial V^H/\partial X_{Lj} + \lambda^L \partial V^L/\partial X_{Lj} - \gamma N^L = 0$$
$$j = 1, \dots, N \tag{15.26}$$

$$Y^H: \; \partial V^H/\partial Y^H + \lambda^H \partial V^H/\partial Y^H - \lambda^L \partial V^L/\partial Y^H + \gamma N^H = 0 \tag{15.27}$$

$$Y^L: \; \mu \partial V^L/\partial Y^L - \lambda^H \partial V^H/\partial Y^L + \lambda^L \partial V^L/\partial Y^L + \gamma N^L = 0 \tag{15.28}$$

Rearrange terms and divide pairs of the first-order conditions in the usual manner to derive the four relevant sets of marginal rates of substitution (MRS):

$$MRS^H_{X_{Hj}, X_{Hk}} = \frac{\partial V^H/\partial X_{Hk}}{\partial V^H/\partial X_{Hj}} = \frac{-\lambda^H \partial V^H/\partial X_{Hk} + \lambda^L \partial V^L/\partial X_{Hk} + \gamma N^H}{-\lambda^H d V^H/\partial X_{Hj} + \lambda^L \partial V^L/\partial X_{Hj} + \gamma N^H}$$
$$\text{all } j, k \tag{15.29}$$

$$MRS^L_{X_{Lj}, X_{Lk}} = \frac{\partial V^L/\partial X_{Lk}}{\partial V^L/\partial X_{Lj}} = \frac{+\lambda^H \partial V^H/\partial X_{Lk} - \lambda^L \partial V^L/\partial X_{Lk} + \gamma N^L}{+\lambda^H \partial V^H/\partial X_{Lj} - \lambda^L \partial V^L/\partial X_{Lj} + \gamma N^L}$$
$$\text{all } j, k \tag{15.30}$$

$$MRS^H_{x_{Hj}, Y^H} = \frac{\partial V^H/\partial Y^H}{\partial V^H/\partial X_{Hj}} = \frac{-\lambda^H \partial V^H/\partial Y^H + \lambda^L \partial V^L/\partial Y^H - \gamma N^H}{-\lambda^H \partial V^H/\partial X_{Hj} + \lambda^L \partial V^L/\partial X_{Hj} + \gamma N^H}$$

$$\text{all } j, k \qquad (15.31)$$

$$MRS^L_{x_{Lj}, Y^L} = \frac{\partial V^L/\partial Y^L}{\partial V^L/\partial X_{Lj}} = \frac{+\lambda^H \partial V^H/\partial Y^L - \lambda^L \partial V^L/\partial Y^L - \gamma N^L}{+\lambda^H \partial V^H/\partial X_{Lj} - \lambda^L \partial V^L/\partial X_{Lj} + \gamma N^L}$$

$$\text{all } j, k \qquad (15.32)$$

Consider the following two cases.

Self-Selection Constraints Not Binding

Suppose that neither self-section constraint is binding so that $\lambda^H = \lambda^L = 0$. Then all the relevant MRS = 1.[9] There should be no distorting taxation, the first-best result, because the private information does not truly constrain the government. This does not necessarily rule out taxation of the commodities and income if taxes are nonlinear, only that the marginal tax rates must be zero. Average rates of tax could be positive, in which case they would be equivalent to lump-sum taxes because they do not affect decisions on the margin.

Self-Selection Constraint on the High-Ability Class Binding

As noted above, the realistic case is for the self-selection constraints to bind on the high-ability class but not the low-ability class so that $\lambda^H > 0$ and $\lambda^L = 0$.

High-Ability Class

Consider, first, the marginal rates of substitution for the high-ability class. A remarkable result is immediately evident. $MRS^H_{x_{Hj}, x_{Hk}} = MRS^H_{x_{Hj}, Y^H} = 1$. All marginal tax rates on the high-ability class should be zero; they should face no distorting commodity or income taxation. Again, this does not rule out taxation of the rich if taxes are nonlinear, just nonzero marginal taxes. The average rates of tax could be positive. This result is quite robust, applying to models with many classes of taxpayers and even a continuum of taxpayers. The marginal tax rates on the highest ability, highest income taxpayers should be zero.

The intuition for the zero marginal income tax rate is as follows. We have seen that the high-ability taxpayer would set $MRS^H_{x_{Hj}, Y^H} = 1$. With a positive marginal tax rate, T', the taxpayer would set $MRS^H_{x_{Hj}, y^H} = (1 - T') < 1$. Suppose the marginal tax rate is very small, so that by setting it equal to zero the taxpayer essentially moves along the

---

[9] In absolute value. The MRS between two goods and between any one good and income have opposite signs, since income is a "bad."

indifference curve. Since the slope is less than one, income rises more than consumption, which generates some tax revenue to give to the low-ability taxpayer. Therefore, the move from a positive to a zero marginal tax rate leaves the high-ability taxpayer indifferent while increasing the utility of the low-ability taxpayer. The positive tax rate cannot be pareto efficient. (The same argument applies in reverse for a small marginal subsidy. Removing it is pareto improving.)

The zero-marginal-tax-rate result stands in direct contrast to the result obtained in the many-person linear commodity tax model in Chapter 14. In that model, commodities consumed relatively more by the high-income classes (lower social marginal utilities of income) are taxed at higher (marginal) rates.[10] The result also begins to suggest some of the difficulties that private information causes for public policy. Although people undoubtedly want to avoid after-tax reversals, they are unlikely to embrace a tax system with zero marginal tax rates on the richest citizens.

Low-Ability Class

The same results do not apply to the low-ability taxpayers.

Income Taxation. Consider first income taxation, which is based on the marginal rate of substitution between one of the goods and income. With $\lambda^H > 0$ and $\lambda^L = 0$, Eq. (15.32) becomes:

$$\frac{\partial V^L/\partial Y^L}{\partial V^L/\partial X_{Lj}} = \frac{+\lambda^H \partial V^H/\partial Y^L - \gamma N^L}{+\lambda^H \partial V^H/\partial X_{Lj} + \gamma N^L} \qquad \text{all } j \qquad (15.33)$$

Suppose the government levies a general income tax $T = T(Y)$, with marginal tax rate T'. The low-ability taxpayer would set:

$$(-)\frac{\partial V^L/\partial Y^L}{\partial V^L/\partial X_{Lj}} = (1 - T') \qquad (15.34)$$

The question, then, is what does the right-hand side (RHS) of Eq. (15.33) imply about T'? To sign the RHS of Eq. (15.33), define:

$$a^h = -(\partial V^h/\partial Y^L)/(\partial V^h/\partial X_{Lj}) = (dX_{Lj}/dY^L)_{V^h = \bar{V}^h} \qquad h = H, L$$

and

$$v = \lambda^H (\partial V^H/\partial X_{Lj})/\gamma N^L$$

Note that $v > 0$ since every term in v is positive. Divide the numerator and denominator of the RHS of Eq. (15.33) by γN^L and note the sign change in the numerator to obtain:

---

[10] Recall that the taxes considered in Chapter 14 were linear.

$$(-)\frac{\partial V^L/\partial Y^L}{\partial V^L/\partial X_{Lj}} = \frac{-\lambda^H(\partial V^H/\partial Y^L)/\gamma N^L + 1}{+\lambda^H(\partial V^H/\partial X_{Lj})/\gamma N^L + 1} \qquad (15.35)$$

Substituting for a^h and v, Eq. (15.35) becomes:

$$a^L = (1 + va^H)/(1 + v) \qquad (15.36)$$

Adding and subtracting a^H in the numerator and simplifying yields:

$$a^L = a^H + (1 - a^H)/(1 + v) \qquad (15.37)$$

But $a^L > a^H$ since the marginal rate of substitution is steeper for the low-ability individual at the same (Y^L, X_{Lj}). Therefore, $(1 - a^H)/(1 + v) > 0$, so that $a^H < 1$. But $a^H < 1$ implies $a^L < 1$ from Eq. (15.36), and $a^L = (1 - T')$. Hence, $T' > 0$. The marginal income tax rate on the low-ability class should be positive.

Commodity Taxation. Consider, finally, the marginal rates of substitution between the commodities:

$$\frac{\partial V^L/\partial X_{Lk}}{\partial V^L/\partial X_{Lj}} = \frac{\lambda^H \partial V^H/\partial X_{Lk} + \gamma N^L}{\lambda^H \partial V^H/\partial X_{Lj} + \gamma N^L} \qquad (15.38)$$

The marginal tax rates are nonzero, in general. One notable exception is the case in which preferences are weakly separable between labor and the commodities, such that $\partial^2 V^h/\partial X_{hk}\partial L_h = 0$, all k, and h = H, L. Since everyone has identical preferences, weak separability implies that $\partial V^L/\partial X_{Lk} = \partial V^H/\partial X_{Lk}$ and $\partial V^L/\partial X_{Lj} = \partial V^H/\partial X_{Lj}$ at any given X_{Lk} and X_{Lj}. Substituting these equations into Eq. (15.38) implies:

$$\frac{\partial V^L/\partial X_{Lk}}{\partial V^L/\partial X_{Lj}} = 1 \qquad (15.39)$$

The low-ability class should not face distorting commodity taxes, nor should the high-ability class (whether preferences are separable or not). Therefore, weakly separable utility in labor is a sufficient condition for levying only distorting income taxes, and then only on the low-ability class.

In the general case of nonseparable utility, the first-order conditions can be manipulated to show that the relative taxation of commodity j to commodity k depends upon the relative values of the marginal rates of substitution between j and k for the high- and low-ability classes. The higher the relative MRS for the high-ability class, the higher the relative tax on j.[11] The intuition turns on the nature of the self-selection constraint. Only

---

[11] The manipulations are tedious. They can be found in J. Stiglitz, "Pareto-Efficient and Optimal Taxation and the New New Welfare Economics," in A. Auerbach and M. Feldstein, Eds., *Handbook of Public Economics*, Elsevier Sciences Publishers B. V. (North-Holland), Amsterdam, Vol. II, Chap. 15, pp. 1025–1026.

the low-ability class faces distorting taxes. Nonetheless, taxing more heavily the commodities favored relatively more by the high-ability class makes the low-ability class's commodity bundle less attractive to the high-ability class. This has the effect of relaxing the self-selection constraint and pushing out the second-best utility-possibilities frontier. Note how different this justification for higher or lower taxes is from the justification in the many-person Diamond–Mirrlees optimal commodity tax problem with its linear taxes and perfect information regarding people's ability. About the only point of similarity between the two models is their agreement that the pattern of commodity taxes depends importantly on the relationship between labor (leisure) and commodities in the consumers' preferences.

An Extension: The Direct–Indirect Tax Mix

Governments in the developed market economies typically choose a mix of indirect and direct taxes, for reasons that are not at all obvious. A common explanation is that a mix of taxes allows the governments to keep the rates low on each set of taxes, but consumers presumably understand that the combined weight of the indirect and direct taxes is what affects their welfare. The fact that each of the rates is low is more or less irrelevant. Furthermore, the Atkinson–Stiglitz model is not a helpful guideline for determining the optimal mix of indirect and direct taxes in the presence of private information. It has two main results to offer the policymaker. One is that only an income tax should be used if preferences are weakly separable between labor and the commodities. The other is that a mix of indirect and direct taxes should be used, but then the model only provides information on the marginal tax rates, not the average rates. Many different combinations of nonlinear commodity and income taxes could be used to meet the government's revenue needs.

Robin Boadway *et al.* developed a simple extension of the Atkinson–Stiglitz model that shows promise as a first step toward developing a theory of the optimal indirect–direct tax mix.[12] They note that a mix of taxes may be desirable because the income tax is easier to evade. They extend the two class model to include the possibility that the high-ability class can evade a portion of their income tax liability with no risk that the evasion can be detected. (The standard analysis of tax evasion assumes there is a chance of being caught; see later discussion). Evaders do, however, bear a cost that depends on the proportion of the income evaded.

The model becomes extremely complicated with the addition of tax evasion, so much so that we will simply note three results of interest:

---

[12] R. Boadway, M. Marchaud, and P. Pestieu, "Towards a Theory of the Direct-Indirect Tax Mix," *Journal of Public Economics*, September 1994.

1. If commodity taxes are not used, then the possibility of evasion does not change the standard result that the marginal tax rate is zero on the high-ability people and positive on the low-ability people.

2. Starting from zero commodity taxes, the imposition of a uniform commodity tax is welfare improving.

3. Given an income tax, a uniform commodity tax is optimal if preferences are separable between the commodities and leisure and also quasi-homothetic in the commodities. The model is too complex to lead to a simple characterization of the optimal pattern of commodity taxes when this condition is not satisfied and differentiated commodity taxation is called for.

In conclusion, the analysis in the section underscores the important point that the design of a tax system depends crucially on what the government can tax and what form the taxes can take. Both issues depend in large part on the information available to the government.

OPTIMAL INCOME TAXATION

The analysis of optimal income taxation was a natural research topic in the 1970s for economists interested in the properties of restricted taxation. The personal income tax had become the single most important tax in most of the developed market economies, as well as the main tax instrument for redistributing purchasing power. As such, the income tax was the obvious candidate for exploring the equity–efficiency trade-off in taxation.[13]

On the equity side, the income tax has considerable redistributive power because it can be so easily tailored to the personal and economic characteristics of individuals and families through such features as personal exemptions to protect the poor and graduated tax rates that tax high incomes in a very progressive manner. On the efficiency side, the income tax suffers from Okun's leaky bucket with its three main sources of leaks:

---

[13] The mainstream view of redistribution was (and still is) that it is a negative sum game because of the efficiency losses from the distorting taxes and transfers (i.e., Okun's leaky bucket). Some recent literature is trying to recover an older notion in political economy that redistribution can be a positive sum game because the transfers improve the productivity of the poor. This idea is particularly persuasive in some less-developed countries in which the poor may have such nutritionally poor diets absent redistribution that they do not have the strength to work. The possibility of positive-sum redistribution is also gaining support in the context of developed market economies as well. Hoff and Lyon recently developed a model in which the distortions from wage taxation are more than offset by the productivity gains of the subsidies they finance, at least at sufficiently low levels of taxes and subsidies. The subsidies increase productivity because they are targeted to the education of the poor, who would otherwise be shut out of the market for higher education by market imperfections. See K. Hoff and A. Lyon, "Non-Leaky Buckets: Optimal Redistributive Taxation and Agency Costs," *Journal of Public Economics*, November 1995.

1. Dead-weight losses in labor and capital markets caused by the distorting nature of the tax
2. Administrative costs of collecting the revenues, including the costs of monitoring taxpayers and enforcing the tax laws
3. Compliance costs incurred by the taxpayers, both the costs of keeping records and filing the tax forms, whether by the taxpayer or a third-party tax preparer, and the costs incurred by taxpayers to reduce their tax liabilities, whether legally or illegally

The *optimal income tax* is the one that achieves the optimal balance between the gains from redistribution as measured by some social welfare function and the three inefficiency costs from raising the tax revenue.

The first complete formal analysis of optimal income taxation was by James Mirrlees, and it stands as one of the classics in the public sector literature. It was the first formal model to incorporate the inefficiencies of the income tax in a social welfare framework. It was also the seminal article on the implications of private information on taxation. Mirrlees modeled only the labor market inefficiencies of the three leaks in Okun's bucket. He assumed that people varied by ability, but that the government could not know an individual's ability for the purposes of taxation. Instead, it was forced to tax income, not wages (ability) or labor supply separately. His model also implicitly honored the self-selection constraint because it explicitly incorporated the assumption that individuals would maximize their utility subject to the income tax funtion. Hence, they would necessarily prefer their own bundles of consumption and leisure to anyone else's bundle.

Mirrlees, and much of the literature that followed, specified a model with a continuum of taxpayers. These continuous models require the calculus of variations to solve, which is beyond the scope of this text. Nonetheless, the structure of the standard optimal income tax model pioneered by Mirrlees is easy enough to understand.

Stripped to its bare essentials, the optimal income tax problem can be represented as follows. Suppose each consumer has a preference function defined over the consumption of a composite commodity, c, and labor, l:

$$U = U(c, l) \qquad (15.40)$$

All individuals have identical preferences but varying abilities or skills indexed by the parameter n.[14] n transfers one unit of labor, l, into nl efficiency units, which are assumed to be perfect substitutes in the production of c. Let w be the wage rate per efficiency unit of labor. Hence, an n-person's income is equal to:

$$y = wnl \qquad (15.41)$$

---

[14] For our purposes it does not matter whether these differing abilities are innate or the result of different educational experiences, so long as N is exogenous to each individual.

Assume further that the index of skills N is distributed across the population in accordance with a probability density function $\int_0^\infty f(n)dn$.

The government is interested in maximizing the Atkinson version of the continuous Bergson–Samuelson social welfare function of the form:

$$W = \frac{1}{v} \int_0^\infty U^v(c, \ell)f(n)dn \qquad (15.42)$$

where v defines society's aversion to inequality. $v = 1$ implies utilitarianism and $v = -\infty$ implies the Rawls criterion of maximizing the utility of the individual with lowest utility.

The policy instrument is an income tax schedule of the general form:

$$T = T(y) \qquad (15.43)$$

with $T' > 0$. $T(y)$ is assumed to be a general nonlinear schedule with, possibly, graduated marginal tax rates and subsidies to consumers below some threshold income level. In other words, the standard optimal income tax model is really a fully specified redistribution model of optimal income taxation and transfer. A common variation of $T(y)$ is the so-called credit income tax, a two-part schedule consisting of a fixed subsidy ("credit") and a constant marginal tax rate, $T = -\alpha + \beta y$. The government levies the income tax schedule to satisfy an aggregate budget constraint of the form:

$$\int_0^\infty T(wnl)f(n)dn = R \qquad (15.44)$$

R could reflect some public goods or the deficits from decreasing cost production. $R = 0$ implies that the government is solely interested in redistributing income.

Under the income tax, each individual has after-tax or transfer income available for consumption equal to:

$$c = y - T(y) = wnl - T(wnl) \qquad (15.45)$$

Each person maximizes utility (15.40) with respect to l, given Eq. (15.45). The first-order condition is

$$wn(1 - T')U_c + U_1 = 0 \qquad (15.46)$$

so that the marginal rate of substitution between consumption and labor equals the after-tax (transfer) marginal wage. As noted earlier, Eq. (15.46) is essentially the incentive compatibility constraint in the model.

The government's problem, then, is to maximize the social welfare function, Eq. (15.42), with respect to the parameters of $T(y)$, subject to the government budget constraint, Eq. (15.44), and the consumer equilibrium condition, Eq. (15.46). Equation (15.46) highlights the second-best nature of the problem, that the marginal tax rate T' distorts each consumer's choice between consumption and labor (leisure). With an Atkinson equal-weighted social welfare function and consumers having identical preferences, the first-best interpersonal equity conditions would imply equal post-tax (transfer) income for all. If the income tax were lump sum, either because the labor supply was fixed or the government could tax and transfer on the basis of ability, the optimal marginal tax rate would be 100%. But, with variable labor supply and private information about ability, increases in marginal tax rates increase the distortion or efficiency loss, thereby partially offsetting the gains from an improved distribution. The optimal solution, then, finds the tax parameters that just equalize the efficiency losses and distributional gains on the margin.

Even the simplest optimal income tax model yields a number of interesting results. The components of the optimal tax schedule clearly depend on the structure of the tax schedule (e.g., linear or general) and the values of the parameters of the model, including the aversion to inequality, v; the distribution of skills throughout the population; the elasticity of labor supply; and the revenue requirement, R. Numerical analysis with a *linear* tax schedule has yielded a number of intuitively appealing results. Generally speaking, the marginal tax rate is higher:

1. The higher society's aversion to inequality (Atkinson and Stern):[15] The more to be gained from redistribution, the more inefficiency society can tolerate.

2. The greater the dispersion of skills (Mirrlees and Stern):[16] With an individualistic social welfare function, increased dispersion increases the gains from redistribution.

3. The lower the labor supply elasticity (Stern):[17] Generally speaking, the efficiency loss implied by a given marginal tax rate varies directly with the labor supply elasticity. Nicholas Stern's simulation experiments showed that the marginal rate is extremely sensitive to the elasticity parameter, much more so than to any of the other parameters.

4. The higher the revenue requirement R (Stern):[18] Roughly, a given tax rate entails less redistribution when some of the revenues must be used for other purposes. But this tends to increase the marginal returns from still further redistribution, implying a higher marginal rate.

[15] A. Atkinson, "How Progressive Should Income Tax Be?" in Parkin, M., (Ed.,) *Essays in Modern Economics*, Longman Group, Ltd., London 1973; N. Stern, "On the Specification of Models of Optimum Income Taxation," *Journal of Public Economics*, July/August 1976.

[16] J. Mirrlees, "An Exploration in the Theory of Optimum Income Taxation," *Review of Economic Studies*, April 1971; N. Stern, "On the Specification of Models of Optimum Income Taxation," *Journal of Public Economics*, July/August 1976.

[17] N. Stern, "On the Specification of Models of Optimum Income Taxation," *Journal of Public Economics*, July/August 1976.

[18] N. Stern, "On the Specification of Models of Optimum Income Taxation," *Journal of Public Economics*, July/August 1976.

The sensitivity of the optimal marginal tax rates to the labor supply elasticity deserves further comment. Mirrlees, and many of the other early income tax studies, assumed simple utility functions such as the Cobb–Douglas to get a feeling to the optimal tax rate. The utility functions chosen had very high labor supply elasticities (unity for Cobb–Douglas) that implied a relatively low marginal tax rate, on the order of 30%. This was much lower than the highest marginal tax rates in most of the developed market economies (70% in the United States at the time). Stern was the first to add a note of caution. He believed that the (compensated) labor supply elasticity was approximately .4, much lower than in the earlier models, which led him to propose a marginal tax rate of 54% for his most-preferred set of simulation parameters. The literature has never reached a consensus value for the labor supply elasticity, or therefore, for the dead-weight loss in the labor market for raising an additional dollar of income tax.

Subsequent studies of optimal income taxation have added the Okun leaks in the market for saving in a dynamic framework and in compliance costs in a static framework. No consensus has emerged on the marginal dead-weight loss from taxing income from saving for the same reason as labor. The estimates of the intertemporal elasticity of consumption are all over the place, from near zero to as high as 3. There is an emerging consensus on the combined administrative and compliance costs, which Joel Slemrod reports to be in the 5 to 10% range.[19]

What, then, is the marginal dead-weight loss from income taxation? As the discussion in Chapter 13 noted, no one knows for sure. The conventional wisdom is that the labor and capital market losses are likely to be the main leaks in Okun's bucket, but Feldstein's proposal to measure dead-weight loss by means of the elasticity of taxable income with respect to the after-tax rate is a powerful challenge to that wisdom.[20] Also, the compliance leaks are large enough not to be ignored; they should figure prominently in any debate on tax reform, whether of the income tax or presumably of any other tax.[21]

---

[19] J. Slemrod, "Did the Tax Reform Act of 1986 Simplify Tax Matters?" *Journal of Economic Perspectives*, Winter 1992, p. 46. An excellent review of the literature on tax compliance is J. Andreoni, B. Erard, and J. Feinstein, "Tax Compliance," *Journal of Economic Literature*, June 1998.

[20] M. Feldstein, "Tax Avoidance and the Deadweight Loss on the Income Tax," *Review of Economics and Statistics*, November 1999.

[21] The Tax Reform Act of 1986 (TRA86) was the largest reform of the federal personal income tax ever undertaken, and it included some reform of the corporation income tax as well. It served as a large natural tax experiment for which the efficiency and equity effects have been intensely studied. Three excellent surveys of TRA86 are "Symposium on Tax Reform," *Journal of Economic Perspectives*, Summer 1987; "Symposium on the Tax Reform Act of 1986," *Journal of Economic Perspectives*, Winter 1992; A. Auerbach and J. Slemrod, "The Economic Effects of the Tax Reform Act of 1986," *Journal of Economic Literature*, December 1997.

The Shape of the Tax Schedule

The most unusual result with general tax schedules is that the marginal rates are not uniformly increasing throughout the range of income, in contrast to many actual tax schedules. Efraim Sadka was the first to demonstrate the by-now familiar result that the marginal tax rate at the top of the income scale should be zero.[22] This follows because the positive marginal tax rate at the top may reduce the labor supply of the highest income individuals. If the rate is dropped to zero and their labor supply increases, the government collects no revenue on this labor. But there was not any revenue on this marginal labor supply at the positive rate. So the only effect of setting the rate at zero is to increase the utility of the highest income individuals, which raises social welfare.

J. K. Seade demonstrated a similar result for the lowest incomes,[23] namely that as long as everyone who faces a positive wage chooses to work, the optimal marginal rate for the lowest income level is also zero. This follows because the only reason to levy positive rates at any income level, given that inefficiency will arise, is to redistribute the revenue to people below that income level. But no one is below the lowest income level. Hence, there is only an efficiency loss from taxing that income. Combining the Sadka and Seade results, the optimal general tax schedule must have a segment of rising marginal rates near the bottom and a segment of falling marginal rates near the top, contrary to the standard practice.

Another result of interest is the emerging consensus that not too much can be gained distributionally by a schedule of graduated tax rates relative to the linear income tax. This has practical significance because a flat-rate tax has much lower administrative and compliance costs. For example, it avoids the incentive to engage in tax arbitrage across tax brackets and the need to income average when incomes fluctuate over time.[24]

A U-Shaped Tax Schedule?

Diamond has recently made an important contribution to the optimal income tax literature. He has shown that if the government chooses a non-

---

[22] E. Sadka, "On Income Distribution, Incentive, Effects, and Optimal Income Taxation," *Review of Economic Studies*, June 1976.

[23] J. Seade, "On the Shape of Optimal Tax Schedules," *Journal of Public Economics*, April 1977.

[24] An excellent overview of the income tax literature is provided in J. Slemrod, "Do We Know How Progressive the Income Tax System Should Be?," *National Tax Journal*, September 1983. In addition to the results reported here, Slemrod considers various extensions such as uncertain incomes, for which marginal tax rates have an added gain of providing social insurance against income losses; endogenous labor supply, in which taxation can lead to before-tax wage changes that imply a marginal subsidy on the highest income; and optimal income taxation in a dynamic framework which brings into play factors such as the treatment of future generations in the social welfare function and the Golden Rule of Accumulation, in addition to the intertemporal elasticity of substitution in consumption.

linear tax schedule, then the optimal pattern of marginal tax rates could well be U-shaped, with marginal tax rates falling in a region below the modal level of skills and then rising in the region above the modal level. He also demonstrated that the optimal tax rates should probably continue to rise right up to the highest skill level, when they are then dropped to zero. That is, the result that the top marginal tax rate should be zero is of little practical importance.[25]

Diamond's demonstration of the likelihood of U-shaped marginal tax rates is based on a decomposition of the first-order conditions of the Mirrlees model that highlights the three main factors that determine the optimal pattern of marginal tax rates:

1. The compensated elasticity of the labor supply with respect to the wage (skill level), along with the probability density function at a given skill level and the skill level itself: These elements combine to determine the deadweight loss from raising the marginal tax rate on an individual with a given skill level.

2. The difference between the social marginal utility of an additional dollar of government revenue and each individual's social marginal utility of income: This difference determines the social marginal benefit of increasing the tax rate on each individual.

3. The number of people with skills higher than the skill level on which the marginal tax rate is being raised: For the people with higher skills, the increase in the marginal tax rate is an inframarginal event. It raises their taxes but does not affect their supply of labor on the margin. Hence, it has the potential of raising revenue from the higher skilled individuals without increasing efficiency loss.

Diamond's main contribution is in showing the effect of the distribution of skills on the optimal pattern of tax rates. To highlight the effect of the skills distribution, Diamond assumes that utility has the quasi-linear form $U = x + v(1 - y)$, where x is consumption, y is the supply of labor, and v is a concave function. With utility linear in x, the supply of labor is independent of income. This has two important implications for the optimal pattern of marginal tax rates. First, changes in the marginal tax rates on lower skilled individuals have no effect on the labor supply of the higher skilled individuals. The inframarginal effect on the higher skilled individuals is simply to raise revenue from them; there is no increase in efficiency loss from raising this revenue. Further, a per-unit lump-sum subsidy given to everyone also would have no effect on labor supply. This has the effect of setting the social marginal utility of an additional dollar of government revenue equal to the average value of the individuals' social marginal utilities of income. To

---

[25] P. Diamond, "Optimal Income Taxation: An Example with a U-Shaped Pattern of Optimal Marginal Tax Rates," *American Economic Review*, March 1998.

simplify the analysis further for the sake of intuition about the distribution of skills, Diamond assumes a form of v that implies a constant labor supply elasticity.

Under these assumptions, consider the skill level of the person who has the average social marginal utility of income, which Diamond calls the critical skill level. For all people above that skill level, the difference between the marginal value of resources to the government and an individual's marginal utility of income is positive and ever increasing, assuming diminishing social marginal utility of income. Consequently, as skill levels increase, the average difference between the marginal value of resources to the government and individuals' social marginal utility of income over all the people at or above a given skill level continually increases as skills increase. This factor alone calls for steadily increasing marginal tax rates as skills increase. But the second factor that determines the pattern of tax rates is the ratio $(1 - F(n))/nf(n)$, that is, $1/n$ times the ratio of people with skill levels higher than n to the people with skill level n. Between the critical skill level and the modal skill level, this ratio is rapidly falling, sharply enough that it overrides the first factor and leads to falling marginal tax rates. The advantages of taxing the lower skilled people at higher marginal rates in that range are twofold. First, the government can raise proportionately more revenue from the inframarginal higher skilled individuals with no efficiency loss. Second, the direct efficiency loss of a given marginal tax rate is lower at lower n and lower $f(n)$.

Above the mode, Diamond assumes in one of his examples that the distribution of skills is the Pareto distribution, for which $(1 - F(n))/nf(n)$ is constant. Only the first factor is relevant, and it implies that the marginal tax rates should be increasing. Therefore, the pattern of marginal tax rates is U shaped above the critical skill level, with the lowest marginal tax rate at or just above the modal skill level.

Diamond further shows that the marginal tax rates continue to increase at very high skill levels, so that the optimal switchover to a zero marginal tax rate at the highest skill level is likely to occur sharply at or near that skill level.[26] Moreover the marginal tax rates near the top of the distribution can be very high, above 50% for some plausible values of the compensated labor supply elasticity, the distribution of marginal social welfare weights, and the Pareto distribution over the range of high incomes in the United States.

Diamond's demonstration that the optimal pattern of marginal tax rates could be U shaped is particularly relevant in the United States because of a transfer program called the Earned Income Tax Credit (EITC). The EITC

---

[26] Diamond also shows that at two points in the distribution at which $f(n)$ is equal, one above the modal skill and one below the modal skill, the marginal tax rate should be higher for the lower skilled individuals. This turns out to happen because the factor $(1 - F(n))/nf(n)$ is sufficiently larger at the lower skill level to overcome the higher value of the first factor at the higher skill level.

offers a wage subsidy to the poor that reaches a maximum amount below the poverty level of income. The subsidy remains constant for the next few thousand dollars approaching the poverty line and then is phased out at 21 cents on the dollar until the subsidy goes to zero. The phase-out range covers over $10,000 of income, applicable mostly to people with incomes just above the poverty line. The phase-out adds 21 percentage points to their effective marginal tax rate, bringing the total marginal tax rate to 36% for many of these low-income taxpayers. Only the highest income taxpayers face a higher rate, at 39.6% (in 2000). In other words, the EITC has generated a U-shaped pattern of marginal federal tax rates, a pattern that has led to criticism of the EITC. Diamond's analysis, however, suggests that this type of pattern may be optimal. The critics miss the point that the phase-out of the EITC is an inframarginal event for the higher income taxpayers, in effect raising additional tax revenue from them at no efficiency loss (assuming no income effects on labor supply). Still, a U-shaped tax schedule violates the spirit of Feldstein's no reversals principle, if only on the margin.

Concluding Observations

A caveat to all the results reported here is that an income tax by itself is not the optimal way to raise revenues unless preferences have certain separability properties that they are unlikely to have. Sufficient separability conditions for the optimality of a general income tax were given in the preceding section and in Chapter 14. Atkinson and Stiglitz also showed that a *linear* income tax is optimal if preferences are additively separable and the marginal disutility of labor is constant, very strong conditions indeed.[27]

A final point worth noting is a methodology proposed by Erik Plug, Bernard van Praag, and Joop Hartog (PPH) for taxing ability, if a society were serious about trying to do this.[28] In 1993, they surveyed people in the Noord–Brabant province of Holland who had taken IQ tests as sixth graders in 1952. The idea was to regress current income on the 1952 IQ scores to obtain an estimate of earnings capacity (they also included years of education in the estimating equation in one version). They also used the survey to determine people's attitudes about income by asking them what levels of after-tax incomes they would place into six categories, from very bad to very good. The responses can be thought of as measuring the utility they receive from the different levels of income. The mean of the six income levels (in logs) is then regressed on family size, IQ, and income (to account for attitude drift related to income). The purpose of this regression is to standardize the utility

---

[27] See A. Atkinson and J. Stiglitz, "The Design of Tax Structure: Direct Versus Indirect Taxation," *Journal of Public Economic*, July/August 1976.

[28] E. Plug, B. van Praag, and J. Hartog, "If We Knew Ability, How Would We Tax Individuals?," *Journal of Public Economics*, May 1999.

received from mean attitudinal income levels across the respondents so they are comparable.

The next step in the methodology is to propose a utility function whose arguments are the individual's earnings capacity after tax and standardized mean attitudinal utility income. PPH chose the Leyden Welfare Function of Income (Ability) for the utility function.[29]

The final step is to use the utility function to design tax schedules on earnings capacity according to standard ability-to-pay sacrifice principles. PPH chose four sacrifice principles: (1) absolute equality of utility, (2) equality of marginal utilities, (3) equal proportional sacrifice, and (4) equal absolute sacrifice.

The most surprising result of this exercise is that the differences between the respondents' actual and optimal tax payments were fairly small, with the biggest differences arising from the equal marginal utility principle. The main advantage from taxing abilities in this manner is to eliminate discrepancies among people with equal earnings capacities.

The methodology of PPH is a reasonable way to proceed to design a tax on ability, and they suggest various ways of improving the estimates of earnings capacities. Even so, the idea seems politically infeasible. In our view, the main value of their exercise is to underscore the likelihood that existing broad-based taxes will always be distorting. One especially uncomfortable implication of their approach is that a person's lifetime tax liability is at least partly determined by an IQ test taken as a youngster, whatever other adjustments PPH propose for the equation that estimates earnings capacity.

TAX EVASION

Private information raises the possibility of tax evasion, a problem that plagues all the developed nations. The IRS estimated in 1987 that 20% of the tax liability under the federal personal and corporate income taxes went uncollected.[30]

Tax experts and economists distinguish between tax avoidance and tax evasion. *Tax avoidance* refers to taxpayers taking advantage of the provisions of the tax laws to reduce their tax liability, such as arranging to take income in the form of lightly taxed capital gains or untaxed fringe benefits rather than as fully taxed wages and salaries. Avoiding taxes is legal and its consequences

---

[29] The Leyden Welfare Function is a log-normal distribution function of the log difference between the individual's after-tax earnings and standardized mean attitudinal utility income, divided by the standard deviation of the attitudinal utility income over its six categories of incomes. The standard deviation is set equal to the sample average standard deviation and therefore assumed to be constant across individuals.

[30] The estimate was reported in J. Slemrod, "Optimal Taxation and Optimal Tax Systems," *Journal of Economic Perspectives*, Vol. 4, No. 1, Winter 1990, pp. 152–178.

are certain. *Tax evasion* refers to hiding sources of taxable income from the tax authorities to reduce one's tax liability, such as not reporting gambling winnings or failing to file a tax return when required to do so. Evading taxes is illegal and its consequences are uncertain; they depend on the probability of the taxpayer being caught.

Sometimes the line between avoidance and evasion is fuzzy given the complexities of the tax law. For example, a taxpayer may be unclear whether a certain expenditure is deductible under the personal income tax but takes the deduction anyway. Is this avoidance or evasion? In any event, the traditional distinction between the two—legal and certain (avoidance) versus illegal and uncertain (evasion) will suffice for our purposes. We begin with the problem of tax evasion.

The standard economic model of tax evasion is essentially identical to the economic model of criminal activity. The dishonest tax evader weighs the gains from evasion in the form of higher after-tax income against the costs, which depend on the probability of being caught and the penalties for evasion. The following very simple model captures the essentials of the economics of tax evasion.

Suppose a taxpayer has a fixed income Y that is subject to a personal income tax at a constant rate t. If the taxpayer is honest, his after-tax income is $Y_{AT} = (1 - t)Y$. If the taxpayer is dishonest and chooses to hide some of his income to evade taxes, the probability of being caught is p and the penalty is a fine equal to s times the amount of the undeclared tax liability. The fine is in addition to the tax at rate t on the undeclared income. Suppose the dishonest taxpayer declares income of Y^D, with $Y^D < Y$. The possible outcomes are

If not caught: $Y'_{AT} = Y - tY^D$

If caught: $Y''_{AT} = Y - tY - st(Y - Y^D) = Y(1 - t - st) + stY^D$

The usual assumption in tax evasions models is that the dishonest taxpayers are Von Neuman–Morgenstern expected utility maximizers, with

$$E(U) = (1 - p)U(Y'_{AT}) + pU(Y''_{AT}) \tag{15.47}$$

The dishonest taxpayer's problem is to determine the level of income to declare, Y^D, that maximizes E(U), given the opportunity locus between being caught and not being caught.

The opportunity locus as a function of Y^D is depicted in Fig. 15.5, with Y''_{AT} (being caught) on the vertical axis and Y'_{AT} (not being caught) on the horizontal axis.[31] The 45° line is a convenient frame of reference. The

---

[31] From this point on, the analysis follows the presentation in F. Cowell, "The Economic Analysis of Tax Evasion," *Bulletin of Economic Research*, September 1985. Cowell's article is an excellent, wide-ranging review of the literature on tax evasion up to 1985 and offers insightful comments on a large number of issues surrounding tax evasion.

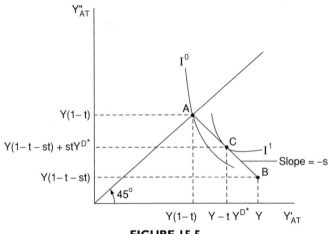

FIGURE 15.5

opportunity locus is the line segment AB. Point A on the 45° line applies if the taxpayer is honest and declares all his income. Y_{AT} equals $Y(1 - t)$. Point B applies if the taxpayer declares none of his income. If he is not caught, $Y'_{AT} = Y$. If he is caught, $Y''_{AT} = Y(1 - t - st)$, because he pays the penalty rate s on the entire tax liability tY. The slope of AB is $-s$, which is immediately evident from the expressions for Y'_{AT} and Y''_{AT} above. An additional dollar of declared income Y^D reduces Y'_{AT} if not caught by t, and raises Y''_{AT} by st if caught. Therefore, the slope $dY''_{AT}/dY'_{AT} = (-)$ st/t $= -s$ along AB.

Regarding preferences, note that the slope of an expected utility indifference curve equals $(1 - p)/p$ at the intersection of the 45° line, with $Y''_{AT} = Y'_{AT}$.[32]

The dishonest taxpayer maximizes expected utility at point C, declares Y^{D*}, and winds up with either $Y'_{AT} = Y - tY^{D*}$ or $Y''_{AT} = Y(1 - t - st) + stY^{D*}$.

Readers familiar with the finance literature will notice that the analysis of tax evasion, and of criminal behavior generally, is closely related to the analysis of risk taking in finance. But there is one important difference. Risk under tax evasion is not exogenous. The government influences both s and p, the former directly and the latter indirectly by the efforts it takes to monitor taxpayers and enforce the tax laws. Consequently, two comparative static exercises of particular interest in the tax-evasion model are the effects on Y^D of changes in s and p. Both can be seen from Fig. 15.6.

---

[32] Along an indifference curve $dE(U) = 0 = (1 - p)U'(Y'_{AT})dY'_{AT} + pU'(Y''_{AT})dY''_{AT}$. $Y''_{AT} = Y'_{AT}$ along the 45° line, so that $(-)dY''_{AT}/dY'_{AT} = (1 - p)/p$.

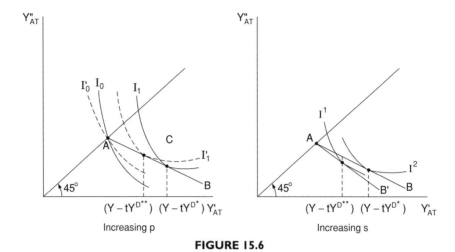

FIGURE 15.6

Increasing the Penalty

An increase in the penalty s rotates the opportunity locus around point A, making it steeper. Y^D increases, since Y''_{AT} and Y'_{AT} are both normal goods. Indeed, the incentive to hide income disappears entirely if s is raised to $(1 - p)/p$, since the equilibrium would then be at A, with all income declared. This is a common result in the analysis of criminal activity: A high enough penalty deters all criminal activity providing utility is unbounded from below.

Increasing Monitoring

An increase in p flattens the indifference curves at their point of intersection with the 45° line and therefore everywhere along the curves, assuming continuity. Once again Y^D increases. An increase in monitoring activity reduces the incentive to hide income, as expected. Raising p such that $(1 - p)/p = s$ removes all incentive to hide income.

The tax authorities thus have two effective methods of deterring tax evasion, but they are not equivalent. Increasing monitoring and enforcement efforts to increase p are likely to be far more expensive than increasing the penalty s, especially if s simply involves a fine and not incarceration. Society might not be willing to increase s high enough to reduce tax evasion, however. We have seen that s must be at least as large as $(1 - p)/p$ to eliminate evasion. Suppose p is small, on the order of 0.10. Then the penalty has to be nine times the tax liability, a hefty fine indeed. The legal principle that "the penalty must fit the crime" might explain why tax authorities (and other policing authorities) engage in costly monitoring and enforcement efforts in lieu of imposing extremely harsh penalties.

A final comment on the model of tax evasion is that the assumption of fixed income does not bias the results in an important manner. A number of models with endogenous income exist in the literature. A common strategy is to tie evasion to the labor supply decision, in which people decide how much to work in the regular economy and how much in the underground economy where their labor income is hidden from the tax authorities. The analysis typically includes a social welfare function and attempts to determine the social welfare maximizing levels of monitoring and enforcement activities or penalties.

Models that assume a utilitarian social welfare function can produce a counter-intuitive result, that reducing enforcement activity may be social welfare enhancing. The reason is that the dishonest taxpayers are given the same weight as the honest taxpayers under utilitarianism, and reduced enforcement makes the dishonest taxpayers better off. If dishonesty is widespread, social welfare increases with reductions in enforcement. This result underscores the problem that private information poses for a normative public sector theory which was mentioned in the introduction to the chapter: It can make the choice of appropriate norms, the social objective function, somewhat problematic. Why, exactly, does society want to reduce tax evasion? Mainstream normative public sector models do not give us a clear-cut answer.

Revenue-Raising Strategies

Increasing monitoring and enforcement activities and increasing penalties are not just means to reduce illegal activity. They also have the effect of raising tax revenues, and in this regard they become an alternative to raising tax rates. Joel Slemrod developed a simple and intuitive model to analyze how the interaction of these different revenue-raising strategies affects social welfare.[33]

Slemrod posits the standard two-class society consisting of one (representative) high-ability person and one low-ability person who are otherwise identical. The high-ability person receives a wage W_H and the low-ability person a wage of W_L which are also their incomes because the supply of labor is fixed at one. The government's principal activity is a tax-transfer redistribution from the high-ability person to the low-ability person to maximize an Atkinson social welfare function. Secondarily, it also expends an amount E on enforcement activity to prevent the high-ability taxpayers from evading taxes. The high-ability person is assumed to have private information about her income that allows her to hide any amount of income from the tax authorities that she wishes.

---

[33] J. Slemrod, "Fixing the Leak in Okun's Bucket: Optimal Tax Progressivity When Avoidance Can Be Controlled," *Journal of Public Economics*, September 1994.

The driving element of Slemrod's model is a cost function that the high-ability person faces if she choose to evade taxes. The cost function has the form:

$$C = 1/2(EA^2/a) \qquad (15.48)$$

where

E = enforcement expenditures by the government
A = the amount of income hidden from taxation
a = a technological parameter that represents the ease of avoiding or evading taxes.

Slemrod refers to A as tax avoidance, but it could be either avoidance or evasion.[34]

Consider first the high-ability person. Her only economic decision in this simple model is to determine the amount of income to hide from the government to maximize her after-tax income, given a, E, and t:

$$\max_{(A)} Y_{AT}^H = W_H - t(W_H - A) - 1/2(EA^2/a)$$

The first-order condition for A is

$$t - EA/a = 0, \text{ or} \qquad (15.49)$$

$$A^* = at/E \qquad (15.50)$$

Therefore,

$$Y_{AT}^{H*} = (1 - t)W_H + at^2/E - 1/2(at^2/E) = (1 - t)W_H + 1/2(at^2/E) \qquad (15.51)$$

Now consider the government's decision. The government budget constraint is

$$R = t(W_H - A) - E \qquad (15.52)$$

with all the R transferred to the low-ability person. The government's objective is to maximize an Atkinson social welfare function with respect to t and E, given the high-ability person's optimal response to any given t and E. Formally,

$$\max_{\{t, E\}} W = 1/\alpha\{[Y_{AT}^{H*}]^\alpha + [Y_{AT}^L]^\alpha\} =$$

$$1/\alpha\{[(1 - t)W_H + 1/2(at^2/E)]^\alpha + [W_L + t(W_H - at/E) - E]^\alpha\}$$

Slemrod simulates the model for $W_H = 3$, $W_L = 1; \alpha = -1, -2, -3$; and $a = .5, 1.0,$ and 1.5.

---

[34] Avoidance is costly because of the record keeping required on deductible items and either the time spent learning the tax laws or the fees paid to a tax preparer.

A result of particular interest is the response of t and E to different values of a, given α. Technological change relating to the ability to monitor and hide income has been an increasingly important factor in tax policy since the 1980s. Computer technology has greatly enhanced the IRS's ability to monitor income, but the monitoring gains have undoubtedly been more than offset by a number of developments in financial markets that have made it much easier to hide income from capital. These include the Monetary Decontrol Act of 1980 which broke down most of the regulatory barriers in financial markets, coupled with that same computer technology that internationalized financial markets and facilitated the development of many new kinds of sophisticated assets and liabilities. For one thing, it is now much easier to move income "offshore" to escape taxation.

The net effect of these changes can be viewed as an increase in the technological parameter a in Slemrod's simple model, which lowers the cost of evasion. For $\alpha = -1$, the most realistic of the three aversion-to-inequality values for the United States, Slemrod found that t should decrease and E should increase. For $\alpha = -3$, however, he found that both t and E should increase. t decreases only if E is held constant.

Slemrod also conducted simulations in which he imbedded the avoidance cost function and his government budget constraint in the Mirrlees optimal income tax problem. The findings on t and E were much the same as in his simple model. In particular, if avoidance (evasion) is concentrated among the high-income people, as is likely, then the optimal t is lower for a given E because the tax rate is a less effective redistributive instrument. But the elasticity of avoidance with respect to the tax rate has an important role to play. A higher elasticity implies a lower t, as expected. At the same time, however, a higher E lowers the elasticity, which implies a higher t. The point is that t cannot be set independently of E.

These results led Slemrod to an interesting observation about the dramatic tax policy of the 1980s. The Tax Code was significantly amended twice in the 1980s, once in 1981 and again in 1986, with the result that the marginal tax rate on the highest incomes rate fell from 70% in 1980 to 28% percent in 1980. The decline in the highest marginal tax rate was widely viewed by economists as a triumph for the optimal income tax model. The consensus result from the model at the time was that the highest marginal tax rate should be on the order of 30% percent. These models only incorporated the dead-weight losses associated with labor supply and savings, however. Research that incorporated the administrative and compliance costs in the face of private information was yet to come. Slemrod observes, based on his model, that a sharp decrease in the tax rate was called for, given the increasing ease of avoidance/evasion (the increase in a) and also that monitoring and enforcement activity (E) was not increased. But if E had been adjusted optimally, then perhaps t should not have been cut so drastically. The increase in the highest marginal tax rate to 39.6% during the Clinton administration may be called for, providing monitoring and enforcement efforts are also increased. Whatever the truth of the matter, the new lesson in tax theory is that the option of increasing revenues through increased monitoring and enforcement should not be ignored.

Tax Amnesties

Tax amnesties are an attempt by the tax authorities to deal with the problem of tax evasion after the fact. A Department of Revenue declares an amnesty period of a few months in which taxpayers can declare previously hidden income and pay taxes on it without an additional penalty. Tax amnesties have been popular with state governments; the states declared 34 amnesties from 1981 to 1992.

The effectiveness of tax amnesties has been the subject of sharp debate. Those in favor of amnesties believe that they bring taxpayers out of the cold and turn them into law-abiding taxpayers from then on. According to this view, amnesties will reduce future tax evasion. Those opposed to amnesties claim that they are likely to backfire among the honest taxpayers, who will resent the break given to the dishonest taxpayers. Even worse, the honest taxpayers will realize how widespread tax evasion is and, given their resentment, be more prone to cheating themselves. The net effect will be an increase in tax evasion.

James Alm and William Beck used times-series econometric techniques to test the effects of a tax amnesty in Colorado in 1985 that ran from September 15 to November 15, 1985. They analyzed monthly state income revenue collections from January 1980 through December 1989 and found that the amnesty had no effect on monthly revenue collections whatsoever, neither after the amnesty nor even during the amnesty period. Perhaps the incentives noted above for amnesties to decrease and increase dishonesty essentially cancel one another, although this is pure conjecture.[35]

CONCLUDING REMARKS

The formal second-best analysis of taxation that combines the dual concerns for efficiency and equity dates from the 1960s. It has gone through two distinct stages. The first stage is represented by Chapters 13 and 14. It explored optimal taxation under the assumption that the tax instruments chosen by the government were fixed and that monitoring and enforcement were not an issue. The government may or may not levy lump-sum taxes; it may tax virtually everything or only a restricted subset of goods and factors.

---

[35] J. Alm and W. Beck, "Tax Amnesties and Compliance in the Long Run: A Time Series Analysis," *National Tax Journal*, March 1993.

Whatever the government choose to tax, however, it knows exactly how much revenue it will collect. The second stage, beginning in the early 1970s, introduced private information into the formal analysis, which has been the subject of this chapter. The concerns about the effects of private information have more or less won the day. As Slemrod notes in a recent review article on optimal taxation, the leading questions surrounding tax policy today are all rooted in the problem that taxpayers have private information. He mentions three of the more important ones.[36]

The first is whether the government should tax consumption or income, in terms of which tax is easier to administer. Most of the complications of an income tax are associated with the taxation of income from capital (saving), which is avoided under a consumption tax. Is it really possible, for example, to tax all income from capital at the same rate, when some of the returns take the form of unrealized capital gains or in-kind services from real assets such as houses or rare paintings? Whether a consumption tax is really simpler is unclear, however. Taxpayers would have to register all their savings to verify the deduction taken from income in determining their tax liability, and this may not be straightforward either. One way to avoid registering saving is to assume that a tax on wages and salaries is approximately equivalent to a consumption tax. Then taxpayers need only report their labor income, which they could do on a postcard. The wage tax has been the long-standing proposal of Robert Hall and Alvin Rabushka, dating from 1983 with the publication of their monograph *Low Tax, Simple Tax, Flat Tax*.[37] The wage tax has a number of proponents in Congress today.

A second issue, assuming Congress retains the income tax, is whether the graduated rates should be replaced by a flat rate. On the one hand, the flat rate would be less redistributive beyond the low end of the income distribution. Low-income families and individuals would presumably still be protected from taxation by an initial exemption. On the other hand, the flat rate would remove the incentives for tax arbitrage that exist under graduated rates. Roughly speaking, graduated rates give high-income taxpayers an incentive to be long in (own) lightly taxed assets and be short in (borrow) heavily taxed assets even if the assets have the same risk and return characteristics.

A final issue is the one addressed earlier, whether the government should increase its revenues by increasing tax rates or beefing up its monitoring and enforcement efforts.

[36] J. Slemrod, "Optimal Taxation and Optimal Tax Systems," *Journal of Economic Perspectives*, Vol. 4, No. 1, Winter 1990.

[37] R. Hall and A. Rabushka, *Low Tax, Simple Tax, Flat Tax*, McGraw-Hill, New York, 1983. (More recently, R. Hall, and A. Rabushka, *The Flat Tax*, Hoover Institution Press, Stanford, CA, 1995.) Recall from the discussion in Chapter 11 that wage and consumption taxes are approximately equivalent in a static context, but not in a dynamic overlapping generations (OLG) context.

In summary, the new issues are related to the search for the optimal tax system in the presence of private information rather than the optimal set of tax rates within an assumed tax system. They recognize that the efficiency costs of taxation are much larger that the dead-weight losses associated with labor supply and saving that were the focus of the first-stage analysis. Administration and compliance costs may not be as large as the market distortions, but they are large enough to force tax experts to think about what kinds of taxes ought to be used. The tax system should not be taken as a given in normative tax analysis.

REFERENCES

Alm, J., and Beck, W., "Tax Amnesties and Compliance in the Long Run: A Time Series Analysis," *National Tax Journal*, March 1993.

Andreoni, J., Erard, B., and Feinstein, J., "Tax Compliance," *Journal of Economic Literature*, June 1998.

Atkinson, A., "How Progressive Should Income Tax Be?," in M. Parkin, Ed., *Essays in Modern Economics*, Longman Group, Ltd., London, 1973.

Atkinson, A., and Stiglitz, J., "The Design of Tax Structure: Direct Versus Indirect Taxation," *Journal of Public Economics*, July/August 1976.

Auerbach, A., and Slemrod, J., "The Economic Effects of the Tax Reform Act of 1986," *Journal of Economic Literature*, December 1997.

Boadway, R., Marchaud, M., and Pestieu, P., "Towards a Theory of the Direct–Indirect Tax Mix," *Journal of Public Economics*, September 1994.

Cowell, F., "The Economic Analysis of Tax Evasion," *Bulletin of Economic Research*, September 1985.

Diamond, P., "Optimal Income Taxation: An Example with a U- Shaped Pattern of Optimal Marginal Tax Rates," *American Economic Review*, March 1998.

Feldstein, M., "Tax Avoidance and the Deadweight Loss on the Income Tax," *Review of Economics and Statistics*, November 1999.

Hall, R., and Rabushka, A., *Low Tax, Simple Tax, Flat Tax*, McGraw-Hill, New York, 1983.

Hall, R., and Rabushka, A., *The Flat Tax*, Hoover Institution Press, Stanford, CA, 1995.

Hoff, K., and Lyon, A., "Non-Leaky Buckets: Optimal Redistributive Taxation and Agency Costs," *Journal of Public Economics*, November 1995.

McLaren, J., "Black Markets and Optimal Evadable Taxation," *Economic Journal*, May 1998.

Mirrlees, J., "An Exploration in the Theory of Optimum Income Taxation," *Review of Economic Studies*, April 1971.

Plug, E., van Praag, B., and Hartog, J., "If We Knew Ability, How Would We Tax Individuals?," *Journal of Public Economics*, May 1999.

Sadka, E., "On Income Distribution, Incentive, Effects, and Optimal Income Taxation," *Review of Economic Studies*, June 1976.

Sah, R., "How Much Redistribution Is Possible Through Commodity Taxes?," *Journal of Public Economics*, February 1983.

Seade, J., "On the Shape of Optimal Tax Schedules," *Journal of Public Economics*, April 1977.

Slemrod, J., "Do We Know How Progressive the Income Tax System Should Be?," *National Tax Journal*, September 1983.

Slemrod, J., "Optimal Taxation and Optimal Tax Systems," *Journal of Economic Perspectives*, Vol. 4, No. 1, Winter 1990.

Slemrod, J., "Did the Tax Reform Act of 1986 Simplify Tax Matters," *Journal of Economic Perspectives*, Winter 1992.

Slemrod, J., "Fixing the Leak in Okun's Bucket: Optimal Tax Progressivity When Avoidance Can Be Controlled," *Journal of Public Economics*, September 1994.

Stern, N., "On the Specification of Models of Optimum Income Taxation," *Journal of Public Economics*, July/August 1976.

Stiglitz, J., "Pareto Efficient and Optimal Taxation and the New New Welfare Economics," in A. Auerbach, and M. Feldstein, Eds., *Handbook of Public Economics*, Vol. II, Elsevier Sciences Publishers B. V. (North-Holland), Amsterdam, chap. 15.

"Symposium on Tax Reform," *Journal of Economic Perspectives*, Summer 1987.

"Symposium on the Tax Reform Act of 1986," *Journal of Economic Perspectives*, Winter 1992.

16

THE THEORY AND MEASUREMENT OF TAX INCIDENCE

When a tax is levied on an economic agent, the agent is said to bear the *impact* of the tax, equal to the amount of the tax payment. Economists distinguish the impact of a tax from the *incidence* or burden of a tax. The distinction is important, because the pattern of tax payments may not be a very good measure of the true economic burdens arising from a tax. The problem is that a tax initiates an entire chain of general equilibrium market effects that can change consumer and producer prices. These price changes, in turn, generate welfare losses and gains throughout the economy that affect, potentially, all economic agents, not just those who paid the tax. The incidence or burden of a tax incorporates both the initial impact of the tax and the gains and losses associated with the general equilibrium market reactions to the tax. As such, the incidence and not the impact of a tax is the central concept of interest in either a normative or a positive distributional theory of taxation.

TAX INCIDENCE: A PARTIAL EQUILIBRIUM ANALYSIS

All students of economics are introduced to the distinction between the impact and incidence of a tax at the principles level, at least in a partial equilibrium context. Recall the standard analysis of a unit sales tax paid by all producers in a competitive market, depicted in Fig. 16.1. The unit tax shifts the supply curve up vertically by the amount of the tax because each producer's marginal cost at any given output rises by the amount of the tax. The shift in the supply curve can be thought of as the suppliers' attempt to pass the tax on to the consumers through higher prices. Whether or not they succeed depends upon the elasticities of both supply and demand. As drawn in Fig. 16.1, the price to the consumer rises, but only from q_0 to q_T, less than the full amount of the tax. The producer price falls from p_0 to p_T $(= q_T - t)$. The new equilibrium output is X_T, and the tax revenue is $X_T \cdot t = X_T(q_T - p_T)$.

The impact of the tax falls on the producers and is equal to the total tax payment, but the incidence, or true burden, of the tax is shared by the producers and consumers in the example. Because the consumer price (the

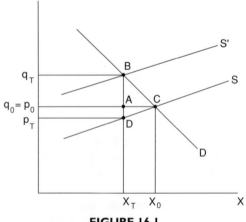

FIGURE 16.1

"gross-of-tax" price) rises from q_0 to q_T, the consumers suffer a loss of consumer surplus (ignoring income effects) equal to $q_T BCq_0$. Because the producer price (the "net-of-tax" price) falls from p_0 to p_T the producers suffer a loss of producer surplus equal to $p_0 CDp_T$. Using the impact, or tax revenue, as a measure of the true burdens, then, would overstate the producers' true economic losses by $(q_T BAp_0 - CAD)$ and understate the consumer's true economic losses by $q_T BCq_0$.[1]

Even though this example is only a partial equilibrium analysis of tax incidence, it illustrates a fundamental point: The market's reactions to a tax are a crucial determinant of its ultimate pattern of burdens.

FIRST-BEST THEORY, SECOND-BEST THEORY, AND TAX INCIDENCE

We have delayed discussing the general theory of tax incidence until this part of the text since the most interesting questions in tax incidence are inherently second best in nature, precisely because they depend on the market's response to distorting taxation. In first-best theory, all questions of distributional equity are incorporated into the interpersonal equity conditions,

$$\frac{\partial W}{\partial U^h} \frac{\partial U^h}{\partial I^h} = \frac{\partial W}{\partial U^j} \frac{\partial U^j}{\partial I^j} \qquad \text{all } h, j = 1, \ldots, H \qquad (16.1)$$

which the government satisfies through a set of lump-sum taxes and transfers among the consumers. As a general rule, these lump-sum redistributions affect equilibrium market prices, contrary to the common assumption that they do not, and these price changes in turn affect people's utilities. The incidence, or burden, on the consumers could presumably be measured as the difference in their utility levels before and after government redistribution, but computing the change in utility for each person is not especially interesting. Consider the various possibilities.

On the one hand, the equilibrium market prices may *not* change if, for example, aggregate production technology is linear with constant marginal opportunity costs. If producer prices remain unchanged, so too will the vector of consumer prices with lump-sum redistributions. In this case, the tax and transfer payments are perfect income proxies for the change in utility in this sense—if any one person received (paid) the tax (transfer) back from (to) the government, his original utility level would be restored. Therefore, the impact and incidence of the redistribution are identical, so that the incidence question is trivial. In practice, tax theorists have often been willing

---

[1] This example is meant only as an illustration of the distinction between tax impact and tax incidence. As we have noted in other contexts, partial equilibrium Marshallian consumer and producer surpluses are generally not valid measures of consumer and producer losses.

to define the incidence of a tax (transfer) solely in terms of the distribution of tax payments (transfer receipts) if they believe the tax (transfer) is approximately lump sum. For example, many incidence studies of the personal income tax commonly allocate the tax on the basis of the tax payments by income class.

On the other hand, equilibrium prices do change in response to a lump-sum redistribution under general technology, the more realistic case. The redistribution moves society along the production-possibilities frontier as well as the utility-possibilities frontier. Now if the government restores the original income level for any *one* person, that person will not be able to achieve his original utility level, in general. The tax payment (transfer receipt) is not necessarily an accurate proxy for the change in utility.

Even so, the pattern of incidence is still not an especially compelling question, for two reasons. In the first place, the relevant alternative to a given program of lump-sum taxes and transfers can always be viewed as the complete unraveling of the redistribution, in which the government restores everyone's original income level *simultaneously*. If this were done, the original general equilibrium and utility levels would also be restored. Under this assumption, then, the payments (receipts) by any one person can be viewed as a perfect proxy for the pattern of burdens since the price changes are irrelevant. Impact and incidence are again identical.

Suppose, however, that one insisted on viewing the problem strictly at the individual level, asking what the consequences would be to some individual of restoring his original income level while leaving the remaining taxes and transfers intact. The utility effects of the price changes are still not very interesting. Presumably the government's redistribution has taken account of the price-induced effects on individual marginal utilities in reaching the final equilibrium, at which the marginal social utilities of income are equalized. That the actual taxes and transfers may not be good proxies for any individual's utility gain or loss is really beside the point, because whatever changes in utility have occurred are the optimal changes required for a first-best social welfare maximum. There is no compelling reason to measure the incidence of the redistributions from a normative perspective, because no other pattern of redistributions could possibly dominate the given redistributions in the sense of being more equitable.

The same cannot be said for second-best taxes. In a second-best environment, taxes are raised in a distorting manner to meet certain revenue requirements. Particular taxes may be chosen simply on the basis of convenience or by some efficiency criterion such as minimizing dead-weight loss, in which case it may well be possible to design more (or less) equitable taxes. If so, then measuring the incidence of the tax is important. Only if the taxes are optimally designed to maximize social welfare in accordance with an equation such as Eq. (14.38) would the question of tax incidence be more or less irrelevant, as it is in a first-best environment. But equations such as

Eq. (14.38) are unlikely to hold in practice. Also, there is no most preferred second-best social welfare optimum because the optimum depends on the underlying constraints that make the environment second best. Therefore, economists have a clear motivation for developing accurate measures of incidence in a second-best environment.

In fact, the theory and measurement of tax incidence have been a central focus of public sector economics since the very beginning of the discipline, with the result that there exists a voluminous literature on the subject. The incidence of every major tax has been studied in detail, both theoretically and empirically. Rather than address each tax separately, Chapter 16 discusses the fundamental methodological issues underlying the theory and measurement of tax incidence in a second-best environment, issues applicable to all taxes.

METHODOLOGICAL DIFFERENCES IN THE MEASUREMENT OF TAX INCIDENCE

The tax incidence literature is bound to be confusing to the beginning student of public sector economics. Empirical studies of individual taxes are fraught with controversy, in part because the empirical analysis of tax incidence is inherently so difficult, but also because there exist serious methodological differences among experts in the field on the appropriate theoretical approaches to the measurement of incidence.

By way of illustration, consider the incidence of the U.S. corporate income tax, which a large number of researchers have studied Their results could not possibly be more divergent. They range all the way from Richard Musgrave's early finding that the tax is borne at least 100% by the consumers of corporate output, to Arnold Harberger's estimate that corporate stockholders almost certainly bear virtually the entire burden of the tax, to Joseph Stiglitz' conjecture that the tax may be nondistorting. To confuse matters further, Ann Friedlaender and Adolph Vandendorpe showed that the analytical framework Harberger used to determine the incidence of the tax should have generated the result that no one bears a burden.[2] This was an important qualification, because Harberger's model is frequently used to study the general equilibrium incidence of taxes.

The corporation income tax may be the most dramatic instance of empirical uncertainty with regard to tax incidence, but the incidence of most other important taxes has hardly been settled either. To give one other example,

[2] M. Krzyzaniak and R. Musgrave, *The Shifting of the Corporation Income Tax*, Johns Hopkins Press, Baltimore, MD., 1963; A. C. Harberger, "The Incidence of the Corporation Income Tax," *Journal of Political Economy*, June 1962; J. Stiglitz, "Taxation, Corporate Financial Policy, and the Cost of Captal," *Journal of Public Economics*, Vol. 2, 1973; A. Friedlaender and A. Vandendorpe, "Differential Incidence in the Presence of Initial Distorting Taxes," *Journal of Public Economics*, October 1976.

most public sector economists had long believed that local property taxes were at least mildly regressive. In the 1970s, a "new view" consensus emerged that the property tax is almost certainly progressive.[3]

Perhaps it is not surprising that empirical estimates of the incidence of any tax should vary considerably, given the nature of the problem. Empirical researchers must select what they think are the most important market reactions to the tax from a staggering set of possibilities, and methods of selection are bound to differ. Unfortunately, empirical tax incidence analysis appears not to be especially robust to assumptions made about sectors of the economy not explicitly under examination. Another confounding factor, mentioned earlier, is that researchers often employ different *theoretical* measures of incidence as a basis for their empirical work, and it is the theoretical differences that we wish to focus on here.

THEORETICAL MEASURES OF TAX INCIDENCE

Three distinct theoretical measures of incidence commonly appear in the literature: incidence as impact, incidence as changes in certain relative prices, and incidence as changes in welfare.

Impact Equals Incidence

Some research merely reports the pattern of tax payments by income class and judges the equity of the tax on this basis alone, thereby equating the impact and incidence of the tax. As noted above, most incidence studies of the personal income tax employ this measure, on the assumption that income taxes are essentially lump sum. For example, Joseph Pechman and Bernard Okner allocate personal income tax burdens in this manner in their widely cited Brookings studies, *Who Bears the Tax Burden* and *Who Paid the Taxes, 1966–85?*,[4] which appeared in 1974 and 1985.

Changes in Relative Prices

At the other end of the spectrum, a large group of incidence studies base their measures of incidence on changes in certain market prices in response to a tax. The change in the wage–rental ratio is the usual choice. Actual tax payments influence this incidence measure because their impact and size

---

[3] M. Feldstein, "Incidence of a Capital Income Tax in a Growing Economy with Variable Savings Rates," *Review of Economic Studies*, October 1974. Refer also to the *American Economic Review Papers and Proceedings*, May 1974, articles by H. Aaron, "A New View of Property Tax Incidence," R. Musgrave, "Is a Property Tax on Housing Regressive?," and comments. Also, H. Aaron, *Who Pays the Property Tax?*, The Brookings Institution, Washington, D. C., 1975.

[4] J. A. Pechman and B. A. Okner, *Who Bears the Tax Burden?*, The Brookings Institution, Washington, D. C., 1974; J. A. Pechman, *Who Paid the Taxes, 1966–85?*, The Brookings Institution, Washington, D. C., 1985.

affect both the pattern of general equilibrium price changes and the degree to which they change, but the tax payments themselves are not a part of the final incidence measure. Arnold Harberger pioneered this approach in his 1962 classic, *The Incidence of the Corporation Income Tax*,[5] and numerous other tax theorists have followed his lead. Changes in relative prices are featured prominently in dynamic tax incidence studies within the context of growth models, whether the models employ the Ramsey representative consumer assumption (e.g., Martin Feldstein) or the overlapping generations (OLG) with life-cycle consumers (e.g., Larwence Kotlikoff and Alan Auerbach).[6] Harberger's paper has certainly been one of the most influential works on the incidence question.

Changes in Welfare

A third approach is to relate tax incidence to changes in welfare, measured either directly as changes in individual's utility levels or indirectly as compensated income changes using the expenditure (and profit) function. John Shoven and John Walley, who pioneered the use of static computable general equilibrium (CGE) models to study tax incidence, follow this approach. So do Don Fullerton and Diane Rogers in their dynamic CGE analysis of tax incidence. Kotlikoff and Auerbach also provide welfare measures of gains and losses in their dynamic OLG models of tax incidence.[7] All these studies also report changes in general equilibrium price ratios as an intermediate step, following the spirit of Harberger's analysis.

Can such different incidence measures be reconciled? In our opinion they cannot be, at least not fully, since they view the problem of measuring the burden of taxation from different perspectives that are some respects irreconcilable. Moreover, there appears to be no clear-cut presumption in favor of any one of them, or some other candidate not currently in vogue. They each have their advantages and disadvantages, and choosing among them ultimately depends on the researcher's personal preferences. No consensus best model or method has emerged for measuring tax incidence.

---

[5] A. Harberger, "The Incidence of the Corporation Income Tax," *Journal of Political Economy*, June 1962.

[6] M. Feldstein, "Incidence of a Capital Income Tax," *Review of Economic Studies*, October 1974; A. Auerbach and L. Kotlikoff, Eds., *Dynamic Fiscal Policy*, Cambridge University Press, New York, 1987.

[7] J. Shoven, "The Incidence and Efficiency Effects of Taxes on Income from Capital," *Journal of Political Economy*, December 1976. Also, J. Shoven and J. Whalley, "A General Equilibrium Calculation of the Effects of Differential Taxation of Income from Capital in the U.S.," *Journal of Public Economics*, November 1972; D. Fullerton and D. Rogers, *Who Bears the Lifetime Tax Burden?*, Brookings Institution, Washington, D.C., 1993.

General Principles of Tax Incidence

Despite differences in the way they measure tax incidence, nearly all tax theorists agree on two general principles. The first is that people ultimately bear the burden of taxation, so that any notion of burden must relate either directly or indirectly to individual utilities. The second is that tax incidence must be analyzed within a general equilibrium framework.

That individuals bear the burden of taxation is merely a specific application of the first principle in all of normative public sector economics, that the government's task is to promote the interests of its constituents. Thus, although the government may levy a corporation income or sales tax on General Motors (GM), the interesting question in tax incidence is not the harm done to General Motors as a legal entity but rather which *people* bear the burden of the tax—GM stockholders, GM workers, consumers of GM products, other consumers, other stockholders, other workers, and so forth—and how much of a burden each of them suffers. This principle also implies that any measure of burden should incorporate each individual's own perception of the burden he or she suffers as a result of the tax. As always in public sector theory, individual preference is a fundamental datum for public sector decision making.

Regarding the general equilibrium framework, the overwhelming majority of tax incidence models assume a fully employed economy with competitive markets, although there has been some work done on tax incidence in the presence of noncompetitive markets and/or unemployed resources.[8] In keeping with the rest of the text, we will adopt the full-employment, competitive-market assumptions unless otherwise stated.

That tax theorists insist on general equilibrium modeling is altogether appropriate, given that the final burden of a tax depends directly on the pattern of the general equilibrium market responses to the tax. At the same time, however, this poses some sticky conceptual problems for tax incidence measurement.

The Disposition of the Tax Revenues

In the first place, general equilibrium analysis challenges the notion that it is possible to consider unambiguously the incidence of a single tax. The heart of the matter is that the disposition of the tax revenue must be accounted for explicitly in a proper general equilibrium framework. Tax revenue collected by the government cannot simply disappear without continued repercussions throughout the economy. The government most likely will spend the

---

[8] Refer to A. Asimakopulos and J. Burbridge, "The Short-Period Incidence of Taxation," *Economic Journal*, June 1974; M. Kalecki, "A Theory of Commodity, Income and Capital Taxation," *Economic Journal*, September 1937.

revenues in some manner, but it could simply save them. In any case, the disposition of the revenues generates its own pattern of welfare gains and losses. In what sense, then, can "the incidence of *a* tax" have meaning as an isolated phenomenon within a general equilibrium, interdependent market economy? This question deserves some careful thought.

Save the Tax Revenues

Suppose one assumes that the government simply saves the tax revenues, in an attempt to isolate the incidence of a particular tax. This would appear to be the spirit of the many income tax studies that assume the taxes are lump sum and thereby equate the impact of the tax with its incidence, without reference to the disposition of the revenues. As noted above, however, if the vector of general equilibrium prices changes in response to the tax, then impact and incidence are not generally equivalent for any one individual. Moreover, if one also assumes continued full employment, as is common with incidence analysis, then at least one price must change.

Suppose, for purposes of illustration, one chooses the simple standard IS–LM model of macroeconomics with competitive factor markets, depicted in Fig. 16.2, to analyze the consequences of taxation when the tax revenues are saved. According to this model, the real rate of interest changes from the pre- to post-tax equilibrium. The tax shifts the IS curve to IS', resulting in excess supply in the goods market. As a consequence, the absolute price level declines, increasing real money balances and shifting the LM curve to LM'. The full employment level of real income is restored, but r has dropped from r_0 to r_1. Thus, in this model, the final burden of the tax depends not only on

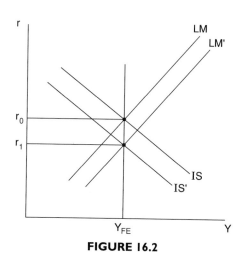

FIGURE 16.2

the pattern of tax payments but also on the welfare consequences of the decline in the real rate of interest. The impact and incidence of the tax are not identical, and the tax payments may be a poor proxy for the true pattern of welfare changes even when the tax revenues are saved.

Balanced-Budget Incidence

Suppose, more realistically, that the tax revenue is used to finance government expenditures. The combined distributional effect of the tax-and-expenditure policy is commonly referred to as *balanced-budget incidence*, which obviously depends upon the particular expenditures being financed. A number of possibilities exist. If the expenditures are lump sum transfer payments and the taxes are also lump-sum, then the tax and transfer program is first best, a case we have already considered. If the taxes are not lump sum, then the analysis is second best, even though the transfers happen to be lump sum. We will return to this point below.

If the expenditures take any other form, including distorting transfers or exhaustive expenditures, then the measure of balanced budget incidence requires specific measures of the incidence of the expenditure programs as well as that of the taxes, a problem that we will consider in Chapter 17. Furthermore, these expenditure programs change the vector of equilibrium prices in general, which means that even a lump-sum tax payment may not be an accurate measure of the tax burden suffered by any individual consumer.

In conclusion, tax studies that use income tax payments as the measure of incidence ought to be assuming that the taxes are lump sum *and* that they are being used to finance lump-sum transfer payments in a balanced-budget manner (no shift in the IS curve). To be absolutely unambiguous, these studies should also assume a linear technology with unchanged producer prices. Then, as was also discussed above, if any *one* consumer received his tax payment back (returned his transfer), that payment would restore the consumer's original utility level. Otherwise, incidence and impact are identical only in the aggregate sense described above, in which the alternative to the tax-transfer program is assumed to be a return to the original pretax and transfer equilibrium.

Pure Tax Incidence: Differential Incidence

Is there any way of focusing on the incidence of taxes *per se* in a general equilibrium framework without complicating the analysis with difficult questions of expenditure incidence? Theoretically the answer is yes, but one should keep in mind that taxes are usually changed in response to particular expenditure initiatives. Therefore the empirical relevance of pure tax incidence measures may be limited.

The Incidence of a Single Tax

One very popular method of analysis, initiated by Harberger, is to assume that the revenues collected are returned lump sum.[9] In a one-consumer or one-consumer-equivalent economy, there is no ambiguity over who receives the lump-sum returns. But the pattern of returns is crucial in a many-person economy, whether one considers the incidence effects from the aggregate viewpoint of social welfare or from each individual's perspective of the loss he suffers as a result of the tax with redistribution. The natural assumption for analytical purposes is that each person receives a lump-sum transfer exactly equal to his tax payment, so that the impact of the tax-and-transfer program on each individual is zero. While this assumption is surely a disservice to reality, it is a useful analytical device for considering the incidence of a single tax within the context of a general equilibrium framework. Assuming lump-sum returns of the revenues at least neutralizes the expenditure side of the budget as much as possible.

Differential Incidence

The other, more realistic, possibility is to consider the incidence of substituting one tax for another, while holding constant either total tax revenues or the entire government budget surplus (taxes − expenditures). This method of analysis is referred to as *differential incidence*, and since governments might actually do this many researchers find it especially appealing. The method of returning tax collections lump sum to analyze the incidence of a single tax can be considered a specific case of differential incidence, in which the taxes being substituted for are head taxes levied on each individual consumer.

It is important to note that whether one chooses to hold tax revenues or the entire government budget surplus constant in a differential incidence analysis is a matter of some consequence. In order to focus strictly on differential tax incidence the tax-revenue-constant assumption might appear to be the preferred alternative, but it may well violate the dictates of a full general equilibrium analysis. Suppose, for example, the government buys and sells goods and factors in the competitive market system either at the producer or consumer prices. With general-technology production, both producer and consumer prices change in response to a tax substitution, thus changing both the level of government expenditures and the amount of revenue from the new tax necessary to balance the overall government budget. If tax collections are held constant in the process of substituting one tax for another, then the

---

[9] Harberger and others actually assume that the government spends the revenue exactly as the consumer(s) would have had they received it, but this is equivalent to redistributing the revenue lump sum and letting the consumer(s) spend it.

overall budget surplus may also change and this change has to be considered as part of the incidence analysis. Adding an assumption that government expenditures are also held constant simply poses different problems, for then government inputs and outputs must change, with corresponding changes in consumers' welfare. Only if the overall budget surplus (deficit) is held constant can the incidence analysis properly focus on the differential effects of the taxes. Government expenditures may change, but as long as the government does not vary the vector of government inputs and outputs there can be no change in consumer(s) welfare arising from the expenditure side of the budget. Thus, the government-budget-surplus-constant assumption is preferred, even though total tax collections vary as one set of taxes is substituted for another.

The tax-revenue-constant and government-budget-surplus-constant assumptions are equivalent only if one assumes that linear production technologies exist in both the private and public sectors *and* that government purchases (sales) are at producer prices. Since producer prices cannot change in response to taxation, neither does the level of government expenditures.

These considerations highlight the care that must be taken in order to specify a well-defined tax incidence analysis within a general equilibrium framework.[10] One must always specify what is being assumed about the disposition of the tax revenues and what effects the use of the revenues has on the general equilibrium of the economy.

Welfare Measures of Tax Incidence: One-Consumer Economy

Having determined that taxation with selective lump-sum return and, more generally, differential incidence are the only appropriate methods for considering tax incidence independently from expenditure incidence in a general equilibrium framework, there remains the difficult theoretical problem of actually measuring the resulting incidence effects. Recall that three measures have been commonly employed: the impact of a tax, the change in (some) general equilibrium prices, and changes in utility or equivalent income compensation measures. The theoretical issues of measurement are sufficiently complex to warrant a preliminary discussion within the context of a one-consumer or one-consumer-equivalent economy, before turning to the more relevant many-person economy.

The first principle of tax incidence is that it should measure the burden on the consumer for any given pattern of taxation. This implies that the natural interpretation of burden in the one-consumer-equivalent economy is the dead-weight loss measure developed in Chapter 13. For instance, if it is assumed that any tax revenue collected is simply returned to the consumer

---

[10] For an excellent general discussion of alternative equivalent taxes, see J. Shoven and J. Whalley, "Equal Yield Tax Alternatives: General Equilibrium Computational Techniques," *Journal of Public Economics*, October 1977.

lump sum and that there are no government expenditures, the incidence of any given (set of) tax(es) would be appropriately measured as:

$$L(\vec{t}) = M\left(\vec{q}; \overline{U}^0\right) - \sum_{i=1}^{N} t_i X_i^{comp} \quad \text{(linear technology)} \quad (16.2)$$

$$L(\vec{t}) = M\left(\vec{q}; \overline{U}^0\right) - \sum_{i=1}^{N} t_i X_i^{comp} - \pi(\vec{p}) \quad \text{(general technology)} \quad (16.3)$$

identical to the measure of dead-weight loss from taxation. With linear technology, recall that $M(\vec{q}; \overline{U}^0)$ measures the lump-sum income necessary to compensate the consumer for a given vector of taxes, $\vec{t}$, with $\overline{U}^0$ equal to the zero-tax level of utility. With general technology, there may be pure profits or losses from production as producer prices, $\vec{p}$, vary in response to the tax rates. In this case, the appropriate income measure of welfare loss is $M(\vec{q}; \overline{U}^0) - \pi(\vec{p})$, where $\pi(\vec{p})$ is the general equilibrium profit function. With the tax revenues returned lump sum, Eqs. (16.2) and (16.3) measure the consumer's loss.

Tax incidence and tax inefficiency are equivalent because, with the taxes returned lump sum, the *only* source of welfare loss is the change in the vector of consumer (and producer) prices resulting from the taxes. The tax payment, the impact of the tax, affects this measure only indirectly. The level of the tax rates, $\vec{t}$, in part determines the amount by which the consumer (and producer) price vectors change, exactly as in loss measurement.

The loss measure is also appropriate for the measure of differential incidence. The substitution of one tax for another with revenue held constant can be thought of as follows: Impose one set of taxes and return the revenues lump sum. Then impose a different set of taxes with its revenues returned lump sum. In short, differential *incidence* is equivalent to differential *efficiency* in a one-consumer economy. It follows exactly the framework developed for the Corlett–Hague analysis presented in Chapter 13. Recall that the relevant equations for marginal changes in tax rates are , in vector notation:

$$dL = \frac{\partial L}{\partial t} dt \quad (16.4)$$

and

$$dT = 0 = \frac{\partial (tX)}{\partial t} dt \quad (16.5)$$

Equation (16.5) determines the changes in tax rates necessary to maintain tax revenues constant, and Eq. (16.4) computes the resulting change in the consumer's welfare in terms of the lump-sum income required to hold utility constant.

In the case of general technologies, the market clearance equations relevant to the compensated equilibrium,

$$X_i\left(\vec{q}; \overline{U}^0\right) = X_i\left(\vec{p} + \vec{t}; \overline{U}^0\right) = \pi_i(\vec{p}) \qquad i = 2, \ldots, N \qquad (16.6)$$

are also necessary to relate market price changes to the tax changes in computing Eq. (16.4). (Recall that compensation is assumed to occur in terms of the numeraire good, the first good as written, which is also assumed to be untaxed. These assumptions have already been discussed in the development of the dead-weight loss from taxation. For linear technologies, $dq = dt$ and $dp = 0$, so that market clearance is unnecessary.) Note, finally, that the incidence or loss from lump-sum taxes is zero according to these measures, precisely because they entail zero dead-weight loss. Clearly, collecting lump-sum taxes and returning the revenues lump sum cannot give rise to an economic burden in a one-consumer or one-consumer-equivalent economy.

The equivalence between incidence and dead-weight loss from taxation carries over in the presence of government expenditures. Suppose the government's budget constraint is

$$\sum_{i=1}^{N} t_i X_i + \sum_{i=1}^{N} p_i Z_i = S \qquad (16.7)$$

where:

S = the fixed government surplus (possibly equal to zero or negative, a deficit).

Z_i = the government purchase (supply) of input (good) i, with all government transactions at competitive producer prices.

As long as any government surplus, S, is returned to the consumer lump sum, an appropriate assumption for general equilibrium analysis, then the dead-weight-loss measures for any given pattern of government decision variables $(\vec{t}; \vec{Z})$ are

$$L\left(\vec{t}; \vec{Z}\right) = M\left(\vec{q}; \overline{U}^0\right) - \sum_{i=1}^{N} t_i X_i - \sum_{i=1}^{N} p_i Z_i \quad \text{(linear technology)} \qquad (16.8)$$

$$L\left(\vec{t}; \vec{Z}\right) = M\left(\vec{q}; \overline{U}^0\right) - \sum_{i=1}^{N} t_i X_i - \sum_{i=1}^{N} p_i Z_i - \pi(\vec{p}) \quad \text{(general technology)}$$

$$(16.9)$$

For Z constant, these are also the appropriate measures for the incidence of any given vector of taxes $\vec{t}$ providing the government surplus is returned lump sum. Moreover, the equations (in vector notation):

$$dL = \frac{\partial L}{\partial t}\, dt \qquad (16.10)$$

and

$$dS = 0 = \frac{\partial(tX - pZ) \cdot dt}{\partial t} \qquad (16.11)$$

determine the differential incidence of any tax substitutions that leave the overall government budget surplus unchanged.[11] If the surplus is held constant, one can think of differential incidence as replacing one set of taxes with the surplus returned lump sum with another set of taxes also with the (same) surplus returned lump sum.

The Relative Price Measure of Differential Tax Incidence: One-Consumer Economy

Although the notion of income compensation provides a nice theoretical bridge between tax inefficiency as represented by dead-weight loss and tax incidence, the loss measures may well have limited applicability to the practical requirement of deriving empirical measures of tax incidence. The problem, which was also addressed in Chapter 13, is that loss measures require knowledge of compensated equilibria and they are not observed in practice. This is not so serious with linear production technologies, since any pattern of tax rates generates the same set of producer and consumer prices at both the compensated and actual with-tax equilibria. Even so, the amount of tax revenues collected for any given set of rates differs between the two equilibria. Therefore, the incidence of a given set of taxes can be thought of as the incidence of establishing a given set of tax *rates* and then returning the resulting revenues lump sum. The loss measure is then unambiguously defined for the given tax rates, but not for a given amount of revenue. Differential incidence would be measured analogously. Presumably one would determine a set of tax rates as an alternative to a given set of tax rates that held *actual* tax collections (or the overall budget surplus) constant and then use those changes to compute Eqs. (16.4) or (16.10). Since dq = dt, and dp = 0 in both the actual and compensated equilibria, the loss can be evaluated unambiguously for the given pattern of dt. Of course the vector dt that keeps actual tax revenues constant does not, in general, hold compensated tax revenues constant, but it is still possible to mix compensated and actual equilibria in the manner suggested.

With general technologies, however, it is not clear how to use the loss measure. Consider the problem of measuring the incidence of a given set of tax rates when the tax revenue has been returned lump sum to the consumer. Presumably one wants to measure the loss implied by the given set of tax

[11] The market clearance equation, Eq. (16.6), are also required with general technology.

rates, $\vec{t}$, and the market prices, $\vec{q}_A$ and $\vec{p}_A$, observed in the actual with-tax equilibrium. With general technologies, however, any given vector $\vec{t}$, generates one set of market prices $(\vec{q}_A, \vec{p}_A)$ in the actual equilibrium and a different set of prices $(\vec{q}_c, \vec{p}_c)$ in the compensated equilibrium. This follows because the market clearance equations for the actual and compensated equilibria,

$$X_i^{actual}\left(\vec{p} + \vec{t}\right) = \pi_i(\vec{p}) \qquad i = 1, \dots, N \qquad (16.12)$$

and

$$X_i^{comp}\left(\vec{p} + \vec{t}; \overline{U}^0\right) = \pi_i(\vec{p}) \qquad i = 2, \dots, N \qquad (16.13)$$

produce different vectors of producer prices $\vec{p}$ for any given $\vec{t}$. Moreover, the compensated $\vec{p}$ depends as well on the good picked for compensation (good 1 in all of our examples). Notice, too, that the level of pure profits also differs in the two equilibria, equal to $\pi(\vec{p}_A)$ in the actual equilibrium and $\pi(\vec{p}_c)$ at the compensated equilibrium. (So will the tax revenues collected, but this is true even for the linear technology case.) For the loss measure to be well defined, then, compensation in some stated good must actually be paid by some agent outside the economy so that the compensated price vectors are observed. Without actual compensation, it is not clear how to evaluate loss. In particular, evaluating loss using Eq. (16.3) (Eq. (16.9)) at actual tax and price vectors $(\vec{t}, \vec{p}_A \vec{q}_A)$ the only vectors actually observed, is not a well-defined theoretical measure.

HCV Versus HEV Welfare Measures

A final comment concerns the choice of compensation. Our analysis has made use of Hicks' Compensating Variation (HCV), defining the compensated equilibrium at the new prices and the original, before-tax utility level. Most incidence studies are presented in the spirit of Hicks' Equivalent Variation (HEV), defining the compensated equilibrium at the original before-tax prices and the new, with-tax utility level. The justification for using the HEV is that it is a money index of utility, since compensation is always measured at the same set of relative prices.

The problems in mixing actual and compensated equilibria discussed above still apply to the HEV framework, however. The expenditure function measures the income the consumer would be willing to sacrifice to return to the original before-tax prices. Placing the consumer on the actual new after-tax indifference curve at the tangency of the original, before-tax prices would bring the economy to a different point on the production possibilities frontier than the actual with-tax equilibrium, with a different vector of producer prices under general technology. Therefore, if taxes were levied and the consumer paid compensation to remain on the new actual after-tax utility level at the before-tax prices, the economy would reach a compensated general equilibrium with vectors of consumer and producer prices different from either the actual before-tax or actual after-tax price vectors. Equation (16.13) would be needed to solve for the compensated price vectors given t, with actual after-tax U instead of U^0, and the discussion surrounding Eq. (16.13) applies. Mixing actual and compensated equilibria is still not legitimate, although it is commonly done in the incidence literature.

The Relative Price Change Measure of Incidence

Because of the difficulties in mixing actual and compensated equilibria, many researchers have been content to compute actual changes in consumer prices as *the* measure of incidence, stopping short of relating the price changes directly to changes in welfare in any formal manner. This is obviously a pragmatic compromise. The resulting measures have no particular theoretical justification, but at least they can be computed fairly easily from the actual data.

Using the profit function to represent production, the procedure for computing price changes for differential incidence can be represented as a three-step process, already outlined earlier. First, totally differentiate the actual government budget constraint with respect to the tax rates being changed (usually two of them) to determine the exact changes required to hold the budget surplus constant; for example:

$$dS = 0 = \frac{\partial (tx^A + pZ)dt}{\partial t} \quad \text{(in vector notation)} \tag{16.14}$$

Second, totally differentiate the actual market clearance relationships:

$$X_i^{\text{actual}}(\vec{p}_A + \vec{t}; I) = \pi_i(\vec{p}_A) + Z_i \qquad i = 1, \ldots, N \tag{16.15}$$

with respect to the tax rates to solve for the producer price changes given the changes in taxes determined from differentiating the government budget constraint. (The demand curve should have an income term to allow for the possibility of dead-weight loss which reduces real income, even if there is zero pure profit or loss from production. If pure profits exist, it is natural to assume they are received by the consumer as income.)

Finally, use the relationships:

$$dq_i = dp_i + dt_i \qquad i = 1, \ldots, N \tag{16.16}$$

to determine the resulting changes in consumer prices.

The price changes could be directly related to welfare losses by positing an indirect utility function of the form $V(\vec{q})$ and totally differentiating it to obtain (in vector notation):

$$dV = -\lambda Xdq, \tag{16.17}$$

with λ = the marginal utility of income. dV/λ represents a money index of utility, but it is path dependent and therefore not uniquely valued for nonmarginal price changes, in general. Consequently, incidence analysis using the change-in-relative-prices measure often concludes the formal analysis with the price changes. The link to consumer's welfare is then simply presented in heuristic terms, in the form of general statements about who gains and who loses (with many consumers).

In summary, then, the theory of tax incidence presents a quandary even for simple one-consumer-equivalent economies. Despite the obvious motivation for developing empirical measures of tax incidence, there appear to be no obvious candidates for the task unless production technology is linear. With general technologies, unambiguous measures of welfare loss involve compensated equilibria that cannot be observed in practice, and observed tax and price vectors offer at best only intuitive guidance to welfare losses. As a practical matter, economists may have to be content with measures of price changes in response to different sets of taxes that leave the government budget surplus unchanged, especially given that production technologies are general and not linear.

The only firm conclusion one can draw is that if the incidence of a given set of taxes is to have any meaning in a general equilibrium context, tax incidence must be defined in such a way as to render the impact of a tax only indirectly relevant to the incidence measure. Tax revenues (or the resulting budget surplus) from distorting taxes must be returned lump sum to the consumer to have a well-defined problem focusing on a single tax. The actual tax payment can affect incidence only through its influence on the amount that market prices change in response to the tax. Regardless of whether one chooses the income compensation or change-in-relative-price approach, the final incidence measure is fully determined by the resulting changes in the general equilibrium price vectors.

THE EQUIVALENCE OF GENERAL TAXES

Although the income compensation and change-in-actual-price measures of incidence approach the problem from different perspectives, they each imply the following important result: In a perfectly competitive, profitless economy, in which tax revenues (or the budget surplus) are always returned lump sum, any two sets of taxes have identical incidence if they generate the same changes in relative prices.

Consider, first, the relative price measure of incidence. If production is profitless and tax revenues are returned to the consumers, actual consumer demands (factors suppliers) are functions only of relative prices. Producers' supply (input demand) relationships are also functions only of relative prices. Therefore, two sets of taxes that generate the same vector of relative prices generate the same with-tax general equilibrium. Consequently, they must have the same incidence by the relative price criterion.

That two sets of taxes generating the same vector of relative prices have the same incidence using the income compensation measure can be most easily demonstrated as follows. Suppose compensation is paid in good 1 so that the market for good 1 remains uncleared in the compensated equilibrium. With compensation defined in terms of good 1, loss can be represented as:

$$L(t) = M_i(\vec{q}; \overline{U}) - \pi_i(\vec{p}) \qquad (16.18)$$

Equation (16.18) measures the difference between the amount of good 1 required for compensation less the amount of good 1 available to the consumer from production, given that all other compensated demands (factor supplies) have been satisfied ($M_i(\vec{q}; \overline{U}) = \pi_i(\vec{p})$, $i = 2, \ldots, N$). But both M_1 and π_1 are homogenous of degree 0 in prices. Therefore, any two taxes creating the same vector of relative prices must generate the same dead-weight loss or incidence.[12]

These considerations lead to a well-known theorem on the equivalence of general taxes that applies to a competitive, profitless economy. A general tax has the following properties: (1) if levied on a single consumer good (factor supply), all consumers pay the same tax rate; (2) if levied on more than one good (and/or factor), property (1) holds for each taxed good (factor), and all the taxed goods (factors) are taxed at the same rate.

Theorem: The Equivalence of General Taxes

Let $(X_1, \ldots, X_N)$ be the vector of goods and factors for a competitive, profitless economy with producer prices $(p_1, \ldots, p_N)$. Levy a general *ad valorem* tax at rate t, paid by consumers, on any subset of the goods and factors, say $X_1, \ldots, X_k$, such that the consumer prices are $q_i = P_i(1 + t)$, $i = 1, \ldots, K$, and $q_j = p_j$, $j = k + 1, \ldots, N$. It is always possible to replace the tax with another general *ad valorem* tax at rate t* on the remaining goods and factors $(X_{k+1}, \ldots, X_N)$ such that the two taxes have the same incidence.

Notice that if $(X_1, \ldots, X_k)$ is the subset of goods and $(X_{k+1}, \ldots, X_N)$ the subset of factors, the theorem establishes the equivalence between a general sales tax and a general income tax (or general value-added tax). Dividing the goods and factors in this way is not necessary, however; any two-way division will do. For example, the theorem also establishes the equivalence between a tax on any one good (or factor) and a tax on all the remaining goods and factors, a specific example of which was discussed in Chapter 13.

---

[12] The government's purchase and sale of Z_i can be included in Eq. (16.18) and the market clearance equations without affecting the result. The Z_i are under the control of the government and therefore exogenous. Also, they do not alter the homogeneity properties of the M_i and π_i.

Proof: With the *ad valorem* tax t on the subset $(X_1, \ldots, X_k)$ the following relationships hold in equilibrium: ∎

$$MRS_{ij} = \frac{p_i}{p_j} = MRT_{ij} \qquad i, j \text{ both in } (k+1, \ldots, N) \qquad (16.19a)$$

$$MRS_{ij} = \frac{p_i(1+t)}{p_j(1+t)} = \frac{p_i}{p_j} = MRT_{ij} \qquad i, j \text{ both in } (1, \ldots, k) \qquad (16.19b)$$

$$MRS_{ij} = \frac{p_i(1+t)}{p_j} = (1+t)MRT_{ij} \qquad \begin{array}{l} i \text{ in } (1, \ldots, k) \\ \\ j \text{ in } (k+1, \ldots, N) \end{array} \qquad (16.19c)$$

With the *ad valorem* tax t* on the subset $(X_{k+1}, \ldots, X_N)$, the following relationships hold:

$$MTS_{ij} = \frac{p_i}{p_j} = MRT_{ij} \qquad i, j \text{ both in } (1, \ldots, k) \qquad (16.19a')$$

$$MRSij = \frac{p_i(1+t^*)}{p_j(1+t^*)} = \frac{p_i}{p_j} = MRT_{ij} \qquad i, j \text{ both in } (k+1, \ldots, N) \qquad (16.19b')$$

$$MRS_{ij} = \frac{p_i}{p_j(1+t^*)} = \frac{1}{(1+t^*)} MRT_{ij} \qquad \begin{array}{l} i \text{ in}(1, \ldots, k) \\ \\ j \text{ in } (k+1, \ldots, N) \end{array} \qquad (16.19c')$$

In a profitless economy, only relative prices matter in determining the general equilibrium. For the taxes to be equivalent, then, Eq. (16.19c) must equal Eq. (16.19c'), which requires that t* be set such that:

$$\frac{p_i(1+t)}{p_j} = \frac{p_i}{p_j(1+t^*)} \qquad (16.20)$$

or

$$(1+t)(1+t^*) = 1 \qquad (16.21)$$

with t and t* defined as decimal fractions.

Implications

1. If $t > 0$, then $t^* < 0$. For example, if $t = 100\%(t = 1)$, t* must be set equal to $-50\%(t^* = -1/2)$. Thus, a general sales tax of 100% on all goods is equivalent to a 50% tax on all factors (factors are measured negatively, so that a negative t* applied to a factor supply is a tax). If the subsets $X = 1, \ldots, k$ and $i = k+1, \ldots, N$ each include a mix of goods and factors,

then some elements of *each* subset are taxed and others subsidized, depending on whether they are goods or factors.

2. The numerical example illustrates that one of the *ad valorem* rates, in the case t*, is applied to the gross-of-tax price and the other, in this case t, to the net-of-tax price. This merely reflects the fact that the producer price for factors is a gross-of-tax price, while the producer price for goods is a net-of-tax price. To see this, consider Fig. 16.3 (goods market) and Fig. 16.4 (factor market) and assume the economy consists of a single good and a single factor. An *ad valorem* tax paid by the consumer shifts the demand curve down in the goods market and the supply curve up in the factor market. For q_i/q_2 to be the same for either tax, the tax rate applied to p_1 must exceed the tax rate applied to p_2 in absolute value. In the graphical example, t raises q_1 100% above p_1, the net-of-tax price, and t* lowers q_2 50% below p_2, the gross-of-tax price. At these rates,

$$\frac{q_1}{q_2} = \frac{p_1(1+1)}{p_2} = \frac{p_1}{\left(1-\frac{1}{2}\right)p_2} = 2\left(\frac{p_1}{p_2}\right) \qquad (16.22)$$

3. In these examples, the consumers actually pay the tax. The same theorem applies if the producers paid the tax, the only difference being that:

$$p_i = (1+t) \cdot q_i \qquad i = 1, \ldots, k \qquad (16.23)$$

$$p_i = (1+t^*) \cdot q_i \qquad i = k+1, \ldots, N \qquad (16.24)$$

$(1+t)(1+t^*) = 1$ is still required for equivalence. In Figs. 16.3 and 16.4, the opposite curves would shift, with t applied to the gross-of-tax price in

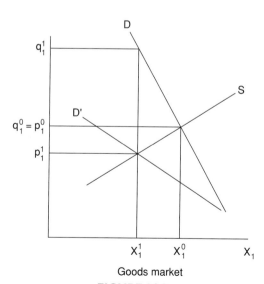

Goods market

FIGURE 16.3

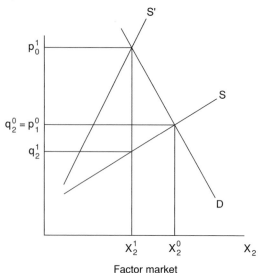

Factor market
FIGURE 16.4

the goods market and t* to the net-of-tax price in the factor market. Whether the impact of a general tax falls on the buyer or supplier in any market can never affect its incidence. This is a particular instance of the general principle that it does not matter which side of a market is taxed. Any tax levied on consumers can in principle be duplicated by a tax levied on producers. In practice, however, the government may prefer to tax one side or the other. For instance, an income tax can more easily take into account the personal characteristics of families and individuals then can a sales tax.

4. The two taxes generate the same tax revenue in either the compensated or actual general equilibria. Consider, first, the compensated equilibrium. By design, the two taxes generate the same relative prices, the same compensated equilibria, and the same dead-weight loss. Thus,

$$L(t) = M\left(\vec{q}^t; \overline{U}^0\right) - \sum_{i=1}^{k} tp_i X_i^{comp} - \pi(\vec{p}^t) = \tag{16.25}$$

$$L(t^*) = M\left(\vec{q}^{t^*}; \overline{U}^0\right) - \sum_{i=k+1}^{N} t^* p_i X_i^{comp} - \pi(\vec{p}^{t*}) \tag{16.26}$$

and $M(\vec{q}^t; \overline{U}^0) - \pi(\vec{p}^t) = M(\vec{q}^{t^*}; \overline{U}^0) - \pi(\vec{p}^{t^*})$. Therefore,

$$\sum_{i=1}^{k} t \cdot p_i X_i^{comp} = \sum_{i=k+1}^{N} t^* p_i X_i^{comp} \tag{16.27}$$

Turning to the actual equilibrium, the tax revenues with each tax are

$$T_t^A = \sum_{i=1}^{k} t \cdot p_i^A X_i^A = t \cdot \sum_{i=1}^{k} p_i^A X_i^A \tag{16.28}$$

$$T_{t*}^A = \sum_{i=k+1}^{N} t^* p_i^A X_i^A = t^* \cdot \sum_{i=k+1}^{N} p_i^A X_i^A \tag{16.29}$$

With perfect competition and zero profits, the actual goods demands and factor supplies are functions only of relative prices. Therefore, t and t* generate the same general equilibria with the same producer prices. Also, $\sum_{i=1}^{N} p_i Y_i = 0$, where Y_i is the supply of (demand for) good (factor) i. Therefore, from market clearance, $\sum_{i=1}^{N} p_i X_i = 0$,

$$\sum_{i=1}^{k} p_i X_i = - \sum_{i=k+1}^{N} p_i X_i \tag{16.30}$$

Given the design of the taxes, under t, $\sum_{i=k+1}^{N} q_i^t X_i = \sum_{i=k+1}^{N} p_i X_i$; under t*, $\sum_{i=1}^{k} q_i^{t*} X_i = \sum_{i=1}^{k} p_i X_i$. The value to the consumer of the non-taxed goods is the same under both taxes (except for sign). But the X_i include all the goods and factors and there is no lump-sum income. Therefore, the consumer's budget constraint is $\sum_{i=1}^{N} q_i X_i = 0$ under t and t*, which implies that the value to the consumer of the taxed goods and factors is also equal under the two taxes (except for sign). $\sum_{i=1}^{k} q_i^t X_i = \sum_{i=k+1}^{N} q_i^{t*} X_i$. Finally, $q^t = (1+t)p_i$, $i = 1$ to k, and $q^{t*} = (1+t^*)p_i$, $i = k+1$ to N. Therefore, subtracting Eq. (16.30) from the value of the taxed goods yields:

$$\sum_{i=1}^{k} t p_i X_i = \sum_{i=k+1}^{N} t^* p_i X_i \tag{16.31}$$

The tax revenues are equal under the two taxes (recall that t and t* have opposite signs).

The only difference between the two taxes is the absolute value of the consumer prices. For example, comparing a sales tax with an income tax, the goods and factor prices to the consumer are *both* higher under the sales tax. The different absolute prices have no effect on the consumer's welfare or on the tax revenues collected, however.

5. The theorem applies only to a one-period, profitless economy. If there were pure profits or losses in production, they would have to be accounted for to define incidence equivalence. And designing equivalent taxes in a multi-period model is much more difficult, since all contemporaneous and inter-temporal price ratios have to be equal with the two sets of taxes. For example, we saw in Chapter 11 that interest income would have to be deductible under an income tax to make it equivalent to an expenditures (sales) tax. Despite these qualifications, the theorem on the equivalence of any two general taxes that span the entire set of goods and factors is one of the more powerful results in all of tax incidence theory, especially since it applies for either measure of tax incidence.

MEASURING TAX INCIDENCE: A MANY-CONSUMER ECONOMY

Our discussion of tax incidence measures and methodology in a one-consumer economy is all preliminary. Tax incidence theory is ultimately concerned with the relative burdens from taxation suffered by various consumers or groups of consumers within the economy. As such it requires analysis within the context of a many-person consumer economy.

Unfortunately, it is not entirely clear how to conceptualize a valid incidence analysis for the many-person economy. There is, at the outset, a fundamental and ambiguous issue centered around the question of point of view: What matters to incidence theory in a many-person economy—the losses suffered by each of the (H) consumers in the economy as *individually* perceived or the *aggregate* loss from a social welfare perspective? Optimal second-best policy analysis certainly requires the aggregate viewpoint, as was demonstrated for the many-person optimal tax problem in Chapter 14. Nonetheless, one could reasonably argue that incidence analysis merely tries to describe the pattern of burdens as perceived by each individual (group of) consumer(s). This view, in effect, says that tax incidence is meant to fall within the domain of the positive theory of the public sector, not the normative theory.

The Individual Perspective on Incidence

Although the individual perspective on tax incidence is certainly appealing, how to maintain an individual perspective in a many-person economy is not at all clear. The same issue arose in Chapter 14 when we discussed dead-weight loss in the context of a many-person economy, because incidence and loss are equivalent under the theoretically appropriate measure of incidence in the one-consumer case. Consider, for example, the problem of measuring the incidence of a single tax from the viewpoint of each individual's loss. Determining the incidence of a single tax requires, at the outset, a specific assumption about how the revenue is given back to the consumers. The natural assumption for incidence analysis is that each consumer receives lump-sum exactly the revenue he or she pays. Any other distribution of the revenues blurs the focus on the incidence of the tax in and of itself.

There are three possible ways to view each individual's loss with this assumption, two of them virtually identical with the one-consumer case: the individuals' dead-weight losses, the change in relative prices, and any one person's dead-weight loss.

Individual Dead-Weight Loss

One possibility is to compute the loss function for each individual as:

$$L^h(\vec{t}) = M^h\left(\vec{q}; \overline{U}^0\right) - \sum_{i=1}^{N} t_i X_{hi}^{comp} - \pi^h(\vec{p}) \qquad (16.32)$$

where $\pi^h(\vec{p})$ = person h's share of pure profits (losses) from private production, and $(\vec{q}, \vec{p})$ are the consumer and producer price vectors at the compensated equilibrium. Then compare individual losses. Although this would give unambiguous individual measures of loss that could be compared across consumers, it suffers the same defects as its one-consumer counterpart, with one additional problem. As already noted in the discussion of one-person measures, it implies a conceptual experiment in which not only are all the tax revenues returned lump-sum to each individual exactly as collected, but also one in which each person simultaneously receives additional lump-sum income (from an agent outside the economy) to fully compensate him for the given pattern of tax rates. Moreover, the compensated equilibrium would not exhibit the same vector of market prices as the actual general equilibrium under general technology unless the compensation actually takes place. It suffers the further handicap in a many-person context that the government would generally not be interested in compensating individuals in this way even if it could, since compensating each individual fully for his or her self-perceived loss requires more resources than are needed to restore the original level of social welfare. This last point was discussed in Chapter 4.

Change in Relative Prices

The second option is to compute the actual change in market prices $(\vec{q}_A, \vec{p}_A)$ and infer the pattern of burdens from these changes, although how such inferences are to be made is difficult to see. As noted in the one-consumer case, the government could use each individual's indirect utility function to compute individual money indexes of utility loss, although the value of such indexes is questionable.[13]

One Person's Dead-Weight Loss

A third option, not open in the one-consumer case, is to focus on the welfare loss of a single person (or one "small" group of consumers) and ask how much income this person (group) would require as compensation for the actual change in market prices resulting from the tax. That is, compute for some person, *but only for that person*,

$$L^h(\vec{t}) = M^h\left(\vec{q}_A; \overline{U}^0\right) - \sum_{i=1}^{N} t_i X_{hi}^{comp}\left(\vec{q}_A; \overline{U}^0\right) - \pi^h(\vec{p}_A) \qquad (16.33)$$

where the loss function is evaluated at the actual with-tax market prices. Since only one person (or one "small" group) is conceptually being compensated, this compensation would presumably leave the actual market prices unchanged, so that this conceptual experiment is well defined. Thus, we can consider the loss suffered by one person (group) as he (it) perceives the loss,

[13] Peter Diamond takes this approach in P. Diamond, "Tax Incidence in a Two-Good Model," *Journal of Public Economics*, June 1978.

although we cannot do this for all people (groups) and compare results. Compensating everyone simultaneously at the actual market prices is *not* a well-defined conceptual experiment with general technologies. This could only be done unambiguously if technology were linear, in which case the observed vector of consumer prices obtains no matter how a conceptual compensation experiment is defined.

The same three options apply to differential incidence, in which one tax is substituted for another. Presumably one would be interested in computing the tax changes necessary for a constant government budget surplus at the actual equilibrium. Given these tax changes, the question remains whether compensation tests could be mixed with actual market results, a question that has been fully discussed in the context of a one-consumer (equivalent) economy.

The Aggregate Social Welfare Perspective on Incidence

There is no ambiguity if the aggregate social welfare point of view is adopted. One would then compute changes in actual market equilibria and their resulting effects on the social welfare function. The aggregate differential incidence problem has already been presented at the end of Chapter 14 for a profitless, competitive economy with no government production. Recall that there are two key relationships. One is the government budget constraint:

$$\sum_h \sum_i t_i X_{hi} = \overline{T} \tag{16.34}$$

which can be totally differentiated to determine the change in tax rates necessary to hold tax revenues constant.[14] The other is Eq. (14.88) (in vector notation):

$$dW = \left| [-(1-\beta)'X] - t' \frac{\partial X}{\partial q} \right| E^{-1} \frac{\partial Y}{\partial p} dt \tag{16.35}$$

which relates changes in social welfare to changes in tax rates.

$\beta = \begin{bmatrix} \beta^1 \\ \beta^h \\ \beta^H \end{bmatrix}$ is the vector of social marginal utilities of income.

The aggregate perspective thus formulates the differential incidence question as determining which of two sets of taxes generates the higher level of social welfare. Although this is certainly a well-defined general equilibrium problem, economists have typically adopted an individual perspective when analyzing the incidence of taxes.

---

[14] With government production, the overall surplus should be held constant.

THE HARBERGER ANALYSIS

Arnold Harberger's 1962 analysis of the incidence of corporate income tax stands as a landmark without rival in the literature on tax incidence theory. Its contributions were twofold. In the first place, his study firmly established the fundamental principle that incidence analysis, properly conceived, requires a full general equilibrium model of the underlying economy. Second, Harberger developed the methodology of measuring incidence in terms of changes in actual general equilibrium consumer and producer prices, focusing primarily on changes in factor prices. Although, as noted above, this measure cannot possibly be the definitive measure of tax incidence, no other single measure is infallible either. Many tax theorists have chosen Harberger's method of analysis in their own studies, regardless of the tax being analyzed. They do so because Harberger's model gives a good intuitive sense of how the market economy spreads the burden of a tax beyond its point of impact in determining the incidence of the tax. For all these reasons, Harberger's study of the corporate income tax deserves careful attention. It also happens to be, somewhat ironically, an excellent vehicle for demonstrating the limitations of the change-in-actual-prices measure of incidence as a measure of true economic burdens. Thus, it serves as an appropriate conclusion to the chapter.

For his analytical framework, Harberger chose a one-consumer (equivalent), profitless, perfectly competitive market economy with general, constant returns to scale (CRS) production technology. His basic methodology can be stated very simply in terms already outlined in the preceding sections of this chapter. First, he chose to analyze the incidence of a single "small" tax in which the revenues were returned to the consumer lump sum. Specifically, Harberger posited a single tax on the use of capital services by all firms in one of two sectors within the economy, the 'corporate sector,[15] the proceeds of which are spent by the government exactly as the consumer would have spent them. This assumption is equivalent to returning the taxes lump sum, and it automatically maintains budgetary balance (at level zero) and consumers' lump-sum income (also at zero with CRS).[16] Once the tax rate is specified, all that is required to determine the resulting price changes is differentiating the market clearance equations of the form:

$$D^i[p(t) + t] = \pi_i[p(t)] \qquad i = 1, \ldots, N \qquad (16.36)$$

where

$D^i(\ ) =$ demand (supply) for good (factor) i by the consumer.

---

[15] Notice that this is a "specific" or "selective" tax as opposed to a "general" tax, since only a subset of all the demanders of capital is taxed.

[16] For a more careful discussion of the effect of this tax and transfer on the consumer's income, see page 563.

$\pi_i =$ the supply (demand) of good (factor) i, the first derivative of the competitive profit function for the economy.

These equations incorporate all the relevant information on preferences (through the demand relations), production technologies (through the profit function), and market clearance, the three elements needed to determine the full general equilibrium. They solve for the producer price changes, after which the consumer price changes follow directly from the price relationships, $q_i = p_i + t_i$, for all $i = 1, \ldots, N$.

With N goods and factors it is impossible to determine *a priori* how these prices will change, in general. In much simpler economies, however, the pattern of price changes is often predictable. Harberger chose the standard two-good, two-factor model used in most geometric presentations of general equilibrium analysis and was able to describe precisely how the various demand and production parameters of this model determine the changes in the wage–rental ratio resulting from the corporate tax. He concluded that the capitalists would bear all or nearly all of the tax burden under most reasonable values of these parameters.

Harberger's analytics are much more complicated than solving Eqs. (16.36). He works directly with the underlying production functions for the economy, rather than the profit functions, in order to highlight the manner in which production parameters influence the pattern of tax incidence. Most other researchers have followed his lead in this regard. Consequently, Harberger's general equilibrium model contains five basic sets of assumptions:

1. There are two goods, X and Y, each produced by two factors of production, capital (K) and labor (L). Consumers supply the factors in absolutely fixed amounts, a standard assumption that permits one to draw the pareto-optimal production frontier in capital–labor space, because the boundaries of the K–L Edgeworth box are fixed.

2. Production is CRS for each good, according to the production relationships:

$$X = X(K_X, L_X) \tag{16.37}$$

$$Y = Y(K_Y, L_Y) \tag{16.38}$$

Furthermore, the two industries are unequally factor intensive, meaning that $K_X/L_X > K_Y/L_Y$ (X being relatively capital intensive) *or* $K_X/L_X < K_Y/L_Y$ (Y being relatively capital intensive) at any given feasible factor price ratio, P_K/P_L. This assumption, along with CRS, generates a production-possibility frontier that is uniformly concave to the origin, so that general equilibrium price ratios vary systematically as the economy moves along the frontier. The CRS assumption rules out the possibility of pure profits or losses at any competitive equilibrium.

3. The model is static; there is no saving in the economy even though capital is one of the factors of production. Also, all markets are competitive, an assumption that[17] has two very important implications:

    a. The equilibrium is characterized by full employment of all resources so that $K_X + K_Y = \overline{K}$ and $L_X + L_Y = \overline{L}$, where $\overline{K}$ and $\overline{L}$ are the fixed factor supplies.

    b. In equilibrium, all consumers pay the same prices for X and Y no matter where purchased, and they must receive the same returns for their factors of production whether they are supplied to industry X or industry Y. Also, the equilibrium factor prices equal the value of their marginal products in each industry.

4. The government levies a "small" tax on the use of capital services in industry X, identified as the corporate sector. There are no other taxes in the economy. To dispose of the revenue, the government spends the proceeds exactly as the consumers would have had they kept the revenue but were confronted with the new general equilibrium vector of prices. As mentioned, this is equivalent to returning the tax revenues lump sum. It also preserves the total level of national income within the economy.

5. Since Harberger does not introduce a social welfare function, he implicitly assumes a one-consumer equivalent economy.

Geometric-Intuitive Analysis

With these five sets of conditions, Harberger is able to describe the change in the factor price ratio P_K/P_L in response to the tax. The changes in factor incomes accruing to capital and labor as a result of the changes in P_K/P_L measure, for Harberger, the true economic burdens of the tax borne by capital and labor. Before turning to his analytical equations, which are fairly complex, let us first develop a feel for Harberger's results by undertaking a geometric-intuitive analysis of the general equilibrium response to the tax in a simple two-good, two-factor economy.

A tax on the use of capital in industry X has the immediate effect of driving a wedge between the returns to capital in the two sectors. Investors in industry X receive the net-of-tax return $(P_K^0 - T_{KX})$, where T_{KX} is the unit tax on capital in industry X. Investors in industry Y continue to receive the gross of tax return P_K^0. Presumably firms in industry X try to increase P_X by an amount sufficient to restore the original rate of return P_K^0. Whether or not they succeed depends upon the demand elasticity for good X. In a two-good economy, one would expect the demand for X to have some price elasticity and that X and Y would be substitutes. Therefore, the demand for Y could

---

[17] Harberger relaxes this assumption in the last part of his article by permitting monopoly power in the market for X, the taxed corporate sector.

increase in response to a rise in the price of X. If this is true, then P_X does not rise sufficiently to cover the tax in the short run, generating losses in industry X. At the same time, profits arise in industry Y, and firms have an incentive to shift resources from X to Y in order to equalize the returns to capital in both industries.

What happens then depends on relative factor intensities. Suppose X is relatively capital intensive. If so, then at the initial factor price ratio P_K^0/P_L^0, industry X is releasing capital and labor in different proportions from those desired by industry Y, generating excess supply in the capital market and excess demand in the labor market. The factor price ratio P_K/P_L begins to fall, and *both* industries respond by becoming more capital intensive as factor markets continue to equate factor prices with values of marginal products. Equilibrium is achieved only when full employment is restored in *both* factor markets. The amount of factor price change required to bring this about depends not only on the relative factor intensities but also on elasticities of substitution between capital and labor in both industries.

To give one extreme example indicating how elasticities of substitution matter, if the elasticity of substitution between capital and labor is infinite (straight-line isoquants) in the untaxed sector, then there can be only one equilibrium factor price ratio for industry Y, the original P_K^0/P_L^0. For a given P_L, the demand schedule for capital in industry Y is perfectly elastic at the original P_K^0. Hence, capital shifts until $(P_K - T_{KX})$ in industry X just equals P_K^0 in industry Y, and the return to capital does not fall as a result of a tax on capital in industry X. This case is depicted in Fig. 16.5.

Finally, returning to the goods markets, the shift in resources to industry Y tends to lower the goods price ratio P_X/P_Y. This follows because the price of capital has fallen relative to the price of labor, and industry X is the relatively capital intensive industry. Consequently, production (marginal)

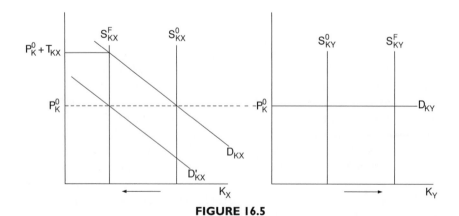

FIGURE 16.5

costs should fall in industry X and rise in Y. What this says, in effect, is that the long-run supply curves (marginal costs) for both goods are expected to be upward sloping with CRS and unequal factor intensities. Overall, the final change in the goods price ratio is indeterminant *a priori*.

Figure 16.6 gives one possible outcome in which there is no change in P_X/P_Y. The shift in the demand curve for Y in response to the original increase in the price of X is just enough to restore (the posited) equality of P_Y and P_X, so that the ratio of these prices remains unchanged. The tax tends to increase P_X relative to P_Y because costs are rising (relatively) in X, but the demand response moves the prices in the other direction. In fact, because Harberger focuses entirely on the changes in the factor price ratio P_K/P_L for his measure of incidence, he is implicitly assuming that there is no change in the equilibrium goods price ratios, exactly as depicted in Fig. 16.6 (or at least that the final change is "small" and can be ignored).

In general, as the economy moves along its productions-possibilities frontier from capital-intensive X to labor-intensive Y, P_K/P_L falls to maintain full employment and P_Y/P_X rises to reflect the relative cost changes in the two industries. The wrinkle with a tax on capital used only in one industry is that it distorts factor markets and drives the economy beneath the production-possibilities frontier. This explains why P_Y/P_X does not have to rise in the new equilibrium in Harberger's analysis.

The descriptive analysis indicates that the incidence of the corporate tax (a tax on the use of capital in sector X) depends on three sets of parameters: the relative factor intensities of the two sectors, the elasticity of substitution between capital and labor in each sector, and the price elasticities of demand for goods X and Y. The analytics uncover a fourth determinant as well, the shares of both capital and labor income originating in each sector. The descriptive analysis also indicates that it is generally not possible to isolate

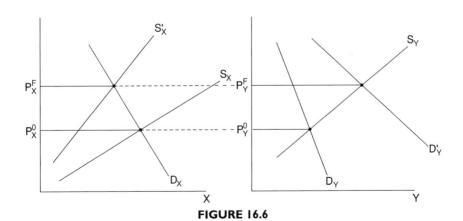

FIGURE 16.6

the burden of a tax to one sector of an economy even though the tax is placed selectively within one sector. If investors in the taxed sector suffer a decrease in the return to capital, investors elsewhere suffer the same burden as well, since competitive factor markets equalize returns to capital everywhere in the economy. Furthermore, since markets are interdependent, the tax burdens could spread to other untaxed factors and to consumers through changes in goods prices. In general, then, a selective tax is selective only in its impact, not in its incidence. The market ultimately determines the incidence of a tax, not the legislature.

The Harberger Analytics

Harberger describes the demand, supply, and market clearance equations for his economy with ten equations designed to highlight changes in the equilibrium values of factor prices and factor supplies in response to the tax on the use of capital in sector X. Since he selects the price of labor as the numeraire, the change in the factor price ratio equals the change in the price of capital, dP_K. The only special feature of his analysis is that all goods and factors are defined in units such that the value of all goods and factor prices in the original pretax equilibrium is one. This is done strictly as a matter of convenience. It implies no loss of generality.

The Demand Equations

Harberger describes the demand side of the general equilibrium model with a single demand equation for X of the form:

$$X = X\left(\frac{P_X}{P_Y}\right) \tag{16.39}$$

With fixed factor supplies, once the change in X is determined in response to the tax, the change in Y follows immediately, since all income is spent on either X or Y. Thus, a separate demand equation for Y is redundant. Also, there is no need to write the demand for X as a function of P_L and P_K. Production is CRS so that factor income exhausts the product—there can be no pure profits or losses. And since the government essentially returns all tax revenue to the consumers, there is no change in the consumers' disposable income even if P_L and P_K change.[18] Finally, given Harberger's one-consumer equivalent assumption, there is only a single demand relationship for X.

Totally differentiating the demand for X yields:

$$dX = \frac{\partial X}{\partial\left(\dfrac{P_X}{P_Y}\right)} \frac{P_Y\,dP_X - P_X\,dP_Y}{P_Y^2} \tag{16.40}$$

---

[18] There may be an income effect in the form of deadweight loss, but Harberger ignores this. We will return to this point later.

Divide by X to express the change in percentage form:

$$\frac{dX}{X} = \frac{\partial X}{\partial \left(\frac{P_X}{P_Y}\right)} \frac{1}{X} \left[\frac{dP_X}{P_Y} - \frac{P_X}{P_Y^2} dP_Y \right] \tag{16.41}$$

Finally, by multiplying and dividing by P_X/P_Y and with quantity units defined such that $P_X = P_Y = 1$, Eq. (16.41) can be rewritten as:

$$\frac{dX}{X}\bigg|_{demand} = E[dP_X - dP_Y] \tag{16.42}$$

where:

$$E = \frac{\partial X}{\partial (P_X/P_Y)} \frac{P_X/P_Y}{X} \tag{16.43}$$

is the demand elasticity for X in terms of the relative prices P_X/P_Y, and dP_X and dP_Y are proportional changes in P_X and P_Y.

The Goods-Supply and Input-Demand Equations

From market clearance, the percentage changes in demand for X must equal the percentage change in supply of X. To determine the percentage change in the supply of X, totally differentiate the production function $X = f(K_X, L_X)$, obtaining:

$$dX = \frac{\partial f}{\partial K_X} dK_X + \frac{\partial f}{\partial L_X} dL_X \tag{16.44}$$

Therefore:

$$\frac{dX}{X}\bigg|_{supply} = \frac{\frac{\partial f}{\partial K_X}}{f} dK_X + \frac{\frac{\partial f}{\partial L_X}}{f} dL_X \tag{16.45}$$

$$\frac{dX}{X}\bigg|_{supply} = \frac{\frac{\partial f}{\partial K_X} K_X}{f} \frac{dK_X}{K_X} + \frac{\frac{\partial f}{\partial L_X} L_X}{f} \frac{dL_X}{L_X} \tag{16.46}$$

$$\frac{dX}{X}\bigg|_{supply} = \theta_{KX} \frac{dK_X}{K_X} + \theta_{LX} \frac{dL_X}{L_X} \tag{16.47}$$

where:

$\theta_{KX} =$ the share of capital's income in industry X.

$\theta_{LX} =$ the share of labor's income in industry X.

Equation (16.47) follows from Eq. (16.46) because: (1) with CRS, factor payments exhaust the product; and (2) factors are paid the value of their marginal products in competitive factor markets. Hence:

$$\frac{\partial f}{\partial K_X}\frac{K_X}{f} = \frac{P_K}{P_X}\frac{K_X}{X} = \theta_{KX}$$

capital's share of income in industry X, and similarly for labor's share. By Walras' law, both the demand and supply equations for Y are redundant.

Turning next to the industries' demands for factors, changes in factor demands can be specified in terms of their direct elasticities of substitution. Define:

$$S_Y = \frac{d\log\left(\frac{K_Y}{L_Y}\right)}{d\log\left(\frac{f_{K_Y}}{f_{L_Y}}\right)} \tag{16.48}$$

$$S_X = \frac{d\log\left(\frac{K_X}{L_X}\right)}{d\log\left(\frac{f_{K_X}}{f_{L_X}}\right)} \tag{16.49}$$

where:

S_Y = direct elasticity of substitution between capital and labor in industry Y.

S_X = direct elasticity of substitution between capital and labor in industry X.

But, with competitive markets and CRS production,

$$d\log\left(\frac{f_{K_X}}{f_{L_X}}\right) = d\log\left(\frac{f_{K_Y}}{f_{L_Y}}\right) = d\log\left(\frac{P_K}{P_L}\right) \tag{16.50}$$

Therefore:

$$d\log\left(\frac{K_Y}{L_Y}\right) = S_Y\, d\log\left(\frac{P_K}{P_L}\right) \tag{16.51}$$

and

$$d\log\left(\frac{K_X}{L_X}\right) = S_X\, d\log\left(\frac{P_K}{P_L}\right) \tag{16.52}$$

Consider Eq. (16.51):

$$d\log\left(\frac{K_Y}{L_Y}\right) = \frac{1}{\frac{K_Y}{L_Y}}d\left(\frac{K_Y}{L_Y}\right) = \frac{1}{\frac{K_Y}{L_Y}}\left[\frac{L_Y dK_Y - K_Y dL_Y}{L_Y^2}\right]$$
$$= \frac{dK_Y}{K_Y} - \frac{dL_Y}{L_Y} \tag{16.53}$$

Similarly,

$$d\log\left(\frac{P_K}{P_L}\right) = \frac{dP_K}{P_K} - \frac{dP_L}{P_L} = dP_K - dP_L, \quad \text{with } P_K = P_L = 1$$

(16.54)

Substituting Eqs. (16.53) and (16.54) into Eq. (16.51) yields:

$$\frac{dK_Y}{K_Y} - \frac{dL_Y}{L_Y} = S_Y(dP_K - dP_L) \tag{16.55}$$

Similarly,[19]

$$\frac{dK_X}{K_X} - \frac{dL_X}{L_X} = S_X(dP_K + T_{KX} - dP_L) \tag{16.56}$$

Market Clearance

Since capital and labor are in fixed supply, capital and labor must move between sectors in equal amounts to maintain full employment. Therefore:

$$dK_Y = -dK_X \tag{16.57}$$

$$dL_Y = -dL_X \tag{16.58}$$

Also, the market for X must remain in balance so that:

$$\left.\frac{dX}{X}\right|_{\text{demand}} = \left.\frac{dX}{X}\right|_{\text{supply}} \tag{16.59}$$

As indicated earlier, a market clearance equation for Y is redundant given the formulation of the model.

Additional Price Relationships

Because Harberger is interested in changes in relative factor prices as the measure of tax incidence, he presents two additional equations relating changes in the goods prices to changes in the factor prices. Consider, first, the market equilibrium for industry X:

$$P_X X = P_L L_X + (P_K + T_{KX})K_X \tag{16.60}$$

from product exhaustion with CRS. Totally differentiating:

$$P_X dX + X dP_X = P_L dL_X + L_X dP_L + (P_K + T_{KX})dK_X + (dP_K + T_{KX})K_X \tag{16.61}$$

---

[19] Recall that Harberger begins with zero taxes, so that $T_{KX} = dT_{KX}$ and $T_{KX} \approx 0$. Equations (16.47), (16.50), and (16.52) implicitly include T_{KX} in P_K for industry X.

But with competitive pricing,

$$\frac{\partial f}{\partial L_X} = \frac{P_L}{P_X} \text{ and} \tag{16.62}$$

$$\frac{\partial f}{\partial K_X} = \frac{P_K + T_{KX}}{P_X} \tag{16.63}$$

Moreover from differentiating the production function:

$$dX = \frac{\partial f}{\partial L_X} dL_X + \frac{\partial f}{\partial K_X} dK_X \tag{16.64}$$

Therefore, from Eq. (16.62):

$$P_X dX = P_L dL_X + (P_K + T_{KX}) dK_X \tag{16.65}$$

and

$$X \, dP_X = L_X dP_L + K_X (dP_K + T_{KX}) \tag{16.66}$$

Thus

$$dP_X = \frac{L_X}{X} dP_L + \frac{K_X}{X} (dP_K + T_{KX}) \tag{16.67}$$

With all prices equal to 1, and the level of taxes equal to 0 to a first order of approximation,

$$\frac{P_L}{P_X} = \frac{P_K + T_{KX}}{P_X} = 1 \tag{16.68}$$

so that Eq. (16.67) can be rewritten as:

$$dP_X = \theta_{LX} \, dP_L + \theta_{KX} (dP_K + T_{KX}) \tag{16.69}$$

By similar analysis,

$$dP_Y = \theta_{LY} \, dP_L + \theta_{KY} \, dP_K \tag{16.70}$$

Finally, labor is chosen as the numeraire. Thus, $P_L \equiv 1$, and

$$dP_L = 0 \tag{16.71}$$

Summary

Equations (16.42), (16.47), (16.55) to (16.59), and (16.69) to (16.71) describe the comparative static changes in the general equilibrium quantities and prices. Plugging Eqs. (16.69) and (16.70) into Eq. (16.42) and employing Eqs. (16.57), (16.58), (16.59), and (16.71), the ten-equation system can be collapsed into the following three-equation system, with dP_K, dL_X/L_X, and dK_X/K_X as the dependent variables:

$$E(\theta_{KY} - \theta_{KX})dP_K + \theta_{LX}\frac{dL_X}{L_X} + \theta_{KX}\frac{dK_X}{K_X} = E\theta_{KX}T_{KX} \tag{16.72}$$

$$S_Y\,dP_K - \frac{L_X}{L_Y}\frac{dL_X}{L_X} + \frac{K_X}{K_Y}\frac{dK_X}{K_X} = 0 \tag{16.73}$$

$$-S_X\,dP_K - \frac{dL_X}{L_X} + \frac{dK_X}{K_X} = S_X T_{KX} \tag{16.74}$$

For purposes of tax incidence, the variable of interest is dP_K ($= d(P_K/P_L)$, with $P_K = P_L = 1$ and $dP_L = 0$). Using Cramer's rule and combining terms:

$$dP_K = \frac{\left[E\theta_{KX}\left(\dfrac{K_X}{K_Y} - \dfrac{L_X}{L_Y}\right) + S_X\left(\dfrac{\theta_{LX}K_X}{K_Y} + \dfrac{\theta_{KX}L_X}{L_Y}\right)\right]T_{KX}}{E(\theta_{KY} - \theta_{KX})\left(\dfrac{K_X}{K_Y} - \dfrac{L_X}{L_Y}\right) - S_Y - S_X\left(\dfrac{\theta_{LX}K_X}{K_Y} + \dfrac{\theta_{KX}L_X}{L_Y}\right)} \tag{16.75}$$

All the relevant information necessary to determine the incidence of the corporate tax is contained in Eq. (16.75).

Comments on the Solution

1. As indicated in the preliminary intuitive analysis, the change in relative factor prices depends upon the demand elasticity for X, the elasticities of substitution between capital and labor in each industry, the relative capital (labor) intensities in the two sectors, and the share of capital and labor income in each sector. Once the change in the price of capital is obtained, it can then be used to compute changes in capital's income relative to changes in national income as a summary measure of incidence, with all changes measured in units of labor, the numeraire. Because the overall supply of capital is fixed, the change in capital's income is simply dP_K. With $P_K = 1$, dP_K also equals the percentage change in income to capital. National income equals the sum of all factor payments, or

$$I = (P_K + T_{KX})K_X + P_K K_Y + P_L L_X + P_L L_Y \tag{16.76}$$

Totally differentiating and recalling that $T_{KX} = dT_{KX}$ (with $T_{KX} = 0$ initially):

$$\begin{aligned}dI = {}&(dP_K + T_{KX})K_X + dP_K K_Y + dP_L L_X + dP_L L_Y \\ &+ (P_K + T_{KX})dK_X + P_K dK_Y + P_L dL_X + P_L dL_Y\end{aligned} \tag{16.77}$$

But $P_X = P_Y = P_L = P_K = 1$, $dP_L = 0$, $dL_X = -dL_Y$, and $dK_X = -dK_Y$. Hence:

$$dI = T_{KX}K_X + (K_X + K_Y)dP_K \tag{16.78}$$

and

$$\frac{dI}{I} = \frac{T_{KX}K_X + (K_X + K_Y)dP_K}{K_X + K_Y + L_X + L_Y} \tag{16.79}$$

Three cases are of special interest:

a. Suppose, first, that $dP_K = -T_{KX}K_X/(K_X + K_Y)$. This would leave national income unchanged measured in units of labor, whereas capital's share would fall by the entire amount of the tax revenue. In this case, then, capital can be said to bear the entire burden of the tax.

b. Suppose, second, that $dP_K = 0$. Since $dP_L \equiv 0$, the income of both capital and labor would fall in proportion to their initial share in national income. This would imply equal sharing of the tax burden.

c. Finally, suppose the percentage change in the price of capital net of tax (dP_K) just equals the percentage change in national income. This would imply that labor bears the entire burden of the tax. It occurs if:

$$dP_K = \frac{dI}{I} = \frac{[T_{KX}K_X + (K_X + K_Y)dP_K]}{L_X + L_Y + K_X + K_Y}, \text{ or} \tag{16.80}$$

$$dP_K = \frac{T_{KX}K_X}{L_X + L_Y} \tag{16.81}$$

2. How the burden is shared between capital and labor depends upon the solution to Eq. (16.75), which in turn depends upon the four demand and production parameters embedded in the right-hand side of the equation. Furthermore, the specific cases mentioned above do not place limits on the possible results. Capital could bear a burden greater than its share of the tax revenue $(dP_K < -T_{KX}K_X/(K_X + K_Y))$; similarly, capitalists could actually gain at the expense of labor despite being taxed $(dP_K > T_{KX}K_X/(L_X + L_Y))$. Harberger presents ten theorems derived from Eq. (16.75), each highlighting how the four supply and demand parameters determine the final incidence of the tax. We will present three of them, indicating how the three special cases mentioned above might occur. The first two theorems were also suggested by the introductory descriptive analysis of the corporate tax.

a. Labor can bear most of the burden of the tax only if the taxed sector is relatively labor intensive.

Proof: For labor to bear most of the burden of the tax, dP_K must be positive. But examination of Eq. (16.75) reveals that this can only occur if industry X is relatively labor intensive. To see this, consider the denominator. The last two terms can be expected to be positive, by inspection. The first term is also generally positive. E can be expected to be negative. $(\theta_{KY} - \theta_{KX})$ and $[K_X/K_Y - L_X/L_Y]$ must have opposite signs, since if capital's share of income is greater in industry Y, $((\theta_{KY} - \theta_{KX}) > 0)$, then industry Y must be relatively capital intensive, or $(K_X/K_Y -$

$L_X/L_Y) < 0$. Thus, the denominator is positive. Turning to the numerator, its second term can be expected to be negative. Hence, for dP_K to be positive, the first term must be positive and greater in absolute value than the second term. Since $E < 0$, and $\theta_{KX} > 0$, this can only occur if $(K_X/K_Y - L_X/L_Y) < 0$, or if the taxed sector, X, is relatively labor intensive.

The exact conditions for which labor bears precisely the full burden of the tax are not easily stated and will not be derived.

b. If the elasticity of substitution between capital and labor in the untaxed industry is infinite, then capital and labor share equally the burden of taxation.

Proof: Equal sharing of the tax burden requires that $dP_K = 0$. But if S_Y, the elasticity of substitution between capital and labor in the untaxed sector, is infinitely large, dP_K must $= 0$.

c. If both industries are initially equally factor intensive and each has the same elasticity of substitution between capital and labor, then capital bears the full burden of the tax.

Proof: Capital bears the full burden of the tax if $dP_K = -T_{KX} K_X/(K_X + K_Y)$. If both industries are equally intensive, then $K_X/K_Y = L_X/L_Y$ and Eq. (16.75) reduces to:

$$dP_K = \frac{S_X\left(\theta_{LX}\dfrac{K_X}{K_Y} + \theta_{KX}\dfrac{L_X}{L_Y}\right)T_{KX}}{-S_Y - S_X\left(\theta_{LX}\dfrac{K_X}{K_Y} + \theta_{KX}\dfrac{L_X}{L_Y}\right)} =$$

$$-\frac{S_X\dfrac{K_X}{K_Y}(\theta_{LX} + \theta_{KX})T_{KX}}{S_Y + S_X\dfrac{K_X}{K_Y}(\theta_{LX} + \theta_{KX})} \tag{16.82}$$

But, $\theta_{LX} + \theta_{KX} = 1$. Therefore,

$$dP_K = -\frac{S_X\dfrac{K_X}{K_Y}T_{KX}}{S_Y + S_X\dfrac{K_X}{K_Y}} \quad \text{or} \tag{16.83}$$

$$dP_K = \frac{-S_X K_X T_{KX}}{S_Y K_Y + S_X K_X} \tag{16.84}$$

If, in addition, $S_X = S_Y$, then

$$dP_K = \frac{-T_{KX}K_X}{K_Y + K_X} \tag{16.85}$$

3. Harberger presents a large number of conditions for which capital bears the full burden of the tax. Suppose that the elasticity of substitution

between capital and labor equals -1, and further that the elasticity of substitution in demand is also -1. These assumptions are often made in empirical research that builds simple models of the economy and simulates them to determine the effects of some public policy, at least for one of the simulations. Capital bears the full burden of the tax under these assumptions. In fact, Harberger shows that capital bears the full burden of the tax if the elasticities of substitution between capital and labor are equal in both industries and equal as well to the elasticity of substitution in demand between the two goods. The proof of this theorem requires extensive manipulation of Eq. (16.75) so we have chosen not to present it, but this is one of the more striking of the ten Harberger theorems.

In the final section of his paper, Harberger performs a sensitivity analysis on the U.S. economy, computing $dP_K^{U.S.}$ for what he believes to be a plausible range of estimates for the various elements on the right-hand side of Eq. (16.75). His analysis leads him to the following conclusion:[20]

> It is hard to avoid the conclusion that plausible alternative sets of assumptions about the relevant elasticities all yield results in which capital bears very close to 100 percent of the tax burden. The most plausible assumptions imply that capital bears more than the full burden of the tax.

Harberger also reworks the analysis to include the special taxation of capital gains and the existence of monopoly elements in the corporate sector. Neither of these considerations affects his basic result, that in all likelihood the incidence of the corporate tax in the United States falls substantially upon capital.

4. Harberger's analysis brings into sharp focus the possible differences between tax incidence measured as changes in actual general equilibrium prices and tax incidence measured as changes in welfare or, equivalently, the lump-sum income required to compensate consumers for a given pattern of taxation. A suitable welfare measure would indicate that the tax described by Harberger generates no burden at all, precisely because his tax is an infinitesimally small change from a zero-tax general equilibrium. With the tax revenues (effectively) returned lump sum to the consumer(s), dead-weight loss is an appropriate welfare measure, and we saw in Chapter 13 that dead-weight loss is zero for a single, infinitesimally small tax. The first marginal distortion is always free.[21]

5. Harberger had to posit a selective tax in order to have an interesting problem given his framework. Had he chosen a general tax on the use

---

[20] A. Harberger, "The Incidence of the Corporation Income Tax," *Journal of Political Economy*, June 1962, pp. 235–236.

[21] The analysis in Chapter 13 is not strictly relevant since it applies only to general taxes paid by consumers. Harberger considers instead a selective tax paid by some, but not all, of the firms for the use of a specific factor. Nonetheless, it can be easily shown that the dead-weight loss is still zero.

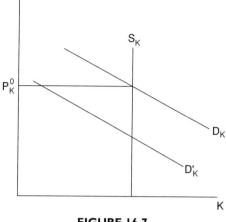

FIGURE 16.7

of capital in both sectors the tax could not possibly have generated a burden even using the change-in-actual-price measure of incidence. Clearly a tax on the *supply* of a factor in absolutely fixed supply in a one-consumer-equivalent, static economy cannot generate a burden if the revenues are returned. Any tax on a fixed factor is equivalent to a lump-sum tax, and returning all the revenues would return the economy to its original equilibrium. But a tax has the same incidence effects if applied to either side of a market. Hence, a tax, with transfer, on the total demand for capital would also keep the economy at its original equilibrium.

Figure 16.7 depicts the case of a tax on all capital. The price of capital remains at P_K^0 whether the suppliers are taxed and S remains unshifted or all firms are taxed and demand shifts to D_K' with the shift equal to the full amount of the tax. Assuming the tax revenue is returned in each case, the consumers suffer no loss in income and no dead-weight loss.

6. Harberger's assumption that the corporate tax represents an infinitesimal movement away from a world of zero taxes may be an analytical convenience for illustrating his approach to the measurement of tax incidence, but it is certainly an extreme departure from reality. J. Gregory Ballentine and Ibrahim Eris reworked the original Harberger analysis to include an existing corporate tax, while retaining the assumption of zero taxes elsewhere in the economy.[22] The assumption of an existing tax changes such calculations as the share of income going to capital in the taxed industry and the change in tax revenues in response to a marginal change in the tax rate. But the major analytical distinction occurs in the equation determining the percentage

[22] J. Ballentine and I. Eris, "On the General Equilibrium Analysis of Tax Incidence," *Journal of Political Economy*, June 1975, pp. 663–644.

change in the demand X (Eq. (16.42)). Because there is now a marginal dead-weight loss from the tax change, the consumers' real income declines, and the change in the demand for X includes this income effect as well as Harberger's relative price effect. When Ballentine and Eris reworked Harberger's empirical sensitivity analysis for the U.S. economy to include the income effect, they found that the burden on capital fell somewhat for plausible values of the income elasticity of demand, although not enough to alter the conclusion that capital bears the major portion of the tax burden.

7. Harberger's equations are easily modified to analyze per-unit commodity taxes on X or Y or other selective factor taxes such as a tax on the use of capital or labor in Y or a tax on the use of labor in X. For instance, a per-unit commodity tax on X involves adding $T_X(= dT_X)$ to the right-hand side of Eq. (16.69), with all other equations unchanged (and, of course, removing all T_{KX} terms). A tax on the use of labor in Y requires replacing dP_L by $(dP_L + T_{LY})$ in Eqs. (16.56) and 16.70), with all other equations unchanged, and similarly for the other taxes.[23] More than one tax change can also be considered with the addition of a government budget constraint, whose derivatives determine the relationship among equal-yield tax alternatives.

8. Finally, Harberger's analysis assumes that the U.S. corporation income tax actually does change the opportunity cost of capital and hence the investment margin within the corporate sector, thereby distorting investors' preferences away from the corporate sector in favor of the unincorporated sector. No attention is given to the characteristics of the tax itself, yet it happens to be a fairly complex tax. For instance, firms are allowed to deduct interest payments on debt and an estimate of depreciation from total returns in computing taxable returns. Moreover net-of-tax returns are taxed again under federal (and state) personal income tax(es), but differentially depending on the exact form of the returns. Dividends and interest income from bonds are taxed as ordinary income, but retained earnings which ultimately generate capital gains are taxed at preferential rates, and only when realized. There are also reasonably complex provisions relating to the offset of losses against income. Many other provisions affect the net-of-tax returns as well, too numerous to cite here. The point, however, is that the distortionary effects of this or any other tax depend crucially on its particular design characteristics.

Suppose the corporate tax turned out to be a tax on pure economic profits. In this case the tax would be lump sum *and* nondistortionary. Corporate investors would simply pay the tax without any adjustment in their investment plans. They would have no incentive to shift resources to the unincorporated sector, and there would be no change in relative prices.

---

[23] Refer to P. Mieszkowski, "On the Theory of Tax Incidence," *Journal of Political Economy*, June 1967, for an analysis of the various possibilities.

This point has long been understood, yet most economists believe that the corporate income tax is not simply a tax on pure economic profits. Joseph Stiglitz is a notable exception. He argued in a widely cited paper that the tax may well approximate a pure profits tax. This is especially so in a world of certainty, which the Harberger analysis assumes. Given that interest payments on debt and depreciation are both deductible, corporate investment decisions may be independent of the tax.[24]

To see this, consider a firm's decision to borrow $1 in time $(t-1)$ to finance an additional unit of capital in time t, all other investment plans being unchanged (and optimal). Let

r = the one period rate of interest on borrowing.
δ = the true rate of economic depreciation.
t_c = the corporate profits tax rate.
$(\partial\pi)/(\partial K_t)$ = the increased operating profits arising from a marginal increase in the capital stock, the gross-of-tax returns to capital.

The decision to invest an additional dollar in time $(t-1)$ leads to $\partial\pi/\partial K_t$ of gross returns in time t, less r dollars of interest costs and δ dollars of depreciation. If both interest payments and the true economic rate of depreciation are tax deductible, the net-of-tax returns from the investment are $(\partial\pi/\partial K_t - r - \delta)(1 - t_c)$. Hence, the firm should borrow invest to long as $(\partial\pi/\partial K_t - \delta) \geq r$. Similar analysis for a unit decrease in investment shows that the appropriate disinvestment margin is $(\partial\pi/\partial K_t - \delta) \leq r$. Therefore, the optimal investment plan occurs when $(\partial\pi/\partial K_t - \delta) = r$. The opportunity cost of capital is just r, equal to the gross-of-tax returns net of depreciation; it is independent of t_c. Therefore, if actual depreciation allowances are reasonably close approximations to true economic depreciation, the interest deductibility feature of the corporate tax renders it nondistortionary.[25]

Harberger's analysis turns out to be most compatible with a corporate tax without interest deductibility, in which the net-of-tax returns equal $(1 - t_c)(\partial\pi/\partial K_t - \delta) - r$, or $(\partial\pi/\partial K_t - \delta) = r/(1 - t_c)$ on the margin. The cost of capital is directly proportional to increases in t_c, as Harberger intended.

---

[24] The seminal paper is J. Stiglitz, "Taxation, Corporate Financial Policy, and the Cost of Capital," *Journal of Public Economics*, Vol. 2, 1973, 1–34, but the following papers are far simpler and more accessible: J. Stiglitz, "The Corporation Tax," *Journal of Public Economics*, April–May 1976; M. King, "Taxation, Corporate Financial Policy and the Cost of Capital: A Comment," *Journal of Public Economics*, August 1975; J. Flemming, "A Reappraisal of the Corporate Income Tax," *Journal of Public Economics*, July–August 1976. The analysis in the text borrows heavily from Stiglitz (1976) and King (1975).

[25] The same result obtains without interest deductibility but with immediate depreciation of full investment costs. In this case, the firm only needs to borrow $(1 - t_c)$ dollars to finance a dollar of additional investment. The remainder can be financed out of tax savings. Hence, the firm's net returns in period t are $(1 - t_c)(\partial\pi/\partial K_t - \delta) - r(1 - t_c)$, with the investment margin again defined by $(\partial\pi/\partial K_t - \delta) = r$, independent of t_c.

Determining whether or not the tax is actually distortionary would require a full analysis of all its design characteristics, as well as the underlying market environment. For instance, some firms may be subject to borrowing constraints that would change their investment margins. Also, estimated depreciation allowances may not reflect true economic depreciation as assumed above. All things considered, the tax is undoubtedly distortionary to some extent. But in light of Stiglitz' analysis, assuming that the U.S. corporate tax is nondistortionary may be a good approximation to reality.

IMPORTANT MODIFICATIONS OF THE HARBERGER MODEL

The basic Harberger model makes a number of very strong assumptions that need to be modified to extend the usefulness of the model. Three especially useful modifications are variable rather than fixed factor supplies, imperfect rather than perfect competition, and heterogeneous rather than homogenous consumers. We conclude the chapter with brief discussions of each of them.

Variable Factor Supplies

The assumption of fixed factor supplies simplifies an already complex analytical model, but it needs to be modified for the sake of reality. Factor supplies are certainly variable in the long run, with the single possible exception of land, and the supply responses to a tax matter in determining the incidence of the tax. As a general rule, they tend to reduce the change in the price of the taxed factors, which spreads more of the burden to the untaxed factors. For example, a reduction in the supply of capital in the Harberger model would raise the return to capital and thereby transfer some of the tax burden to labor.

The assumption of variable factor supplies is essential in long-run dynamic models of tax incidence, which we will consider in Chapter 17. Changes in the supply of capital in response to a tax alter the time path of capital accumulation, both physical and human capital, which in turn affects the marginal products of capital, labor, and all other factors of production. The resulting changes in marginal products are often the most important determinants of the ultimate incidence of a tax as the economy moves to its new long-run steady state. For example, a tax on capital that slows the rate of capital accumulation and reduces the capital/labor ratio can shift much of the long-run incidence of the tax to labor as the marginal product of labor and therefore the real wage fall over time.

Variable supply responses to taxation can be important as well in static models of tax incidence. To see this, consider the opposite extreme from the Harberger model. Assume that the supply of capital is perfectly elastic to the taxing jurisdiction, as depicted in Fig. 16.8. This is a realistic assumption for state (provincial) and local governments, and for all but the largest countries

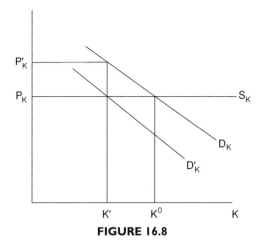

FIGURE 16.8

with the most highly developed financial markets. The supply price of capital, P_K, is a given for these smaller jurisdictions, determined in capital and financial markets whose scope extends far beyond their boundaries. As a consequence, taxes on capital have very different implications for them than the Harberger model would suggest. The following three implications have received attention in the tax incidence literature.

Mobile Versus Immobile Factors

In the first place, a tax on the firms' use of capital in these jurisdictions cannot be borne by capital (refer to Fig. 16.8). The tax shifts D_K down by the full amount of the tax. Since the supply price of capital, the required rate of return, is set on the "world" market, the rate of return within the jurisdiction rises by the full amount of the tax to P'_K. The capitalists escape the burden, passing it on to other factors of production or to consumers. The general principle illustrated here is this: If a jurisdiction contains both mobile factors (e.g., capital) and immobile factors (e.g., land and possible labor), then the immobile factors bear the burden of any factor tax levied on the firms. (If all factors are perfectly mobile, with their prices fixed outside the jurisdiction, then consumers bear the entire burden in the form of higher prices.)

Taxing the Demand Versus the Supply Side

Another implication of the perfectly elastic assumption is that it matters which side of the market is taxed. Earlier we had noted the principle that it did not matter which side of the market the legislature chose to tax: All the effects of a tax on one side of a market can be duplicated by a tax on the other side of the market. The case of perfectly elastic supply is the exception to this principle, and an important one, if the government cannot tax all the suppliers.

Suppose the jurisdiction levies a tax on its own suppliers of capital through, say, a personal income tax. The citizens of the jurisdiction may reduce their saving because the after-tax return to their saving has been reduced. But they represent such a small proportion of the overall supply of saving to the "world" financial markets that they cannot possibly affect the given price of capital, P_K. The tax has no effect whatsoever on the allocation of capital to the jurisdiction. The citizens' after-tax return simply falls by the full amount of the tax, and they bear the entire burden of the tax. The implication is clear. State governments that wish to tax returns to capital in the interests of fairness without harming investment in the state should do so through their personal income tax and not through a corporation income tax or any other business tax on capital. The former has no effect on investment and the incidence sticks where the tax is levied. The latter reduces the equilibrium capital stock, and the burden of the tax is passed on to other factors of production or to consumers.

The Incidence of Local Property Taxes

The supply elasticity of capital has figured prominently in the literature on the incidence of local property taxes in the United States. The local property tax is a combined tax on land and capital. The taxes are levied on the total value of each parcel of land, which includes both the value of the land itself and the value of the structure on the land. The value of the structure is usually much greater than the value of the land, so that the local property tax is primarily a tax on capital.

The original, or "old" view of the incidence of the local property tax had long held that it was a regressive tax overall. The portion of the tax on the value of the land itself is progressive. The supply of land is virtually perfectly inelastic, so that landowners bear the entire burden of this portion of the tax, and the distribution of land ownership is skewed heavily toward high-income households.

The progressivity of the land portion is overwhelmed by the regressivity of the much larger capital portion, according to the old view. The local capital market was seen as in Fig. 16.8, with the supply price of capital given to the locality. The tax on the structures was therefore assumed to be passed on to others by the apartment owners to their renters and by the commercial and industrial firms to their consumers or to labor. The property owners escaped, and the larger portion of the tax was regressive.

The "old" view came to be replaced about 25 years ago by the so-called "new" view, which held that local property taxes were progressive after all. The new view accepts the old view's characterizations of the markets for land and capital. The supply of land is perfectly inelastic, therefore, landowners bear the incidence of the land portion of the tax. The market for capital within localities is as pictured in Fig. 16.8, with the supply of capital perfectly elastic to each locality. What the old view failed to consider, however, is that all localities have property taxes. Therefore, capitalists cannot escape the *average* rate of the property taxes across localities. Since the overall supply of capital in the nation is viewed as fixed, the capitalists bear the average rate of the local property taxes, and the incidence of the capital portion is therefore progressive.

The germ of truth in the old view of the capital market, according to the new view, is that capitalists respond to *differences* in tax rates across localities. Capital would move from jurisdictions with above-average property taxes to jurisdictions with below-average property taxes, until the returns to capital were equalized in all localities. Renters and (immobile) labor in the high-tax jurisdictions lose as the capital leaves, and renters and labor in the low-tax jurisdictions gain as new capital enters. But the differences in local property tax rates are typically much smaller than the overall average tax rates. Also, the incidence resulting from differences in the rates is at least partially a wash, since some renters and consumers gain while others lose. Therefore, the incidence of the capital portion is almost certainly progressive. Since the land portion is also progressive, the local property taxes are progressive, perhaps even highly progressive.

The "new" view of 25 years ago was itself challenged by the advent of dynamic models of tax incidence, which showed that even taxes on land could be regressive. We will return to the property tax in Chapter 17 when we analyze dynamic tax incidence.

Oligopoly and the Corporation Income Tax

Many important industries in the corporate sector in the United States and other developed market economies are better modeled as oligopolies than as perfect competitors (or pure monopolies at the other extreme). This is unfortunate for the study of tax incidence because economists have not been able to develop a general theory of oligopoly, nor are they likely to. Also, the game theoretic approach to oligopoly that has dominated the industrial organization literature for the past 20 years has not paid much attention to taxation.

Nonetheless, the suspicion lingers that the incidence of taxes levied on oligopolies could be quite different from their incidence if levied on perfect competitors or pure monopolies. The primary basis for the suspicion is that oligopolies are likely to produce more output and charge lower prices than would be required to maximize group profits under an industry cartel. On the one hand, noncooperative strategic considerations in a game theoretic environment may drive them away from the cartel profit maximum. On the other hand, they may simply have different goals in the short run, such as maximizing sales (market share) rather than profits, that lead them to set lower prices.

Suppose the firms are operating away from the cartel profit maximum, for whatever reason. A tax such as a corporation income tax could then cause them to raise prices and restrict output in concert, which moves them closer to the cartel profit maximum. The owners may escape the burden of the tax entirely if they have enough unexploited profits to call upon, such that the after-tax profits with the tax equal the profits without the tax. Indeed, the tax may actually make the firms better off if profits before tax rise by more than the tax liability. This particular escape route is not possible for perfect competitors or profit-maximizing monopolists.

The possibility that oligopolists might escape the burden of taxation in this way was first explored by Harvey Rosen and Michael Katz in 1985.[26] They developed a simple conjectural variation model of an industry in which each firm conjectures (guesses) about how the other firms will respond to changes in its prices or output. The conjectures are symmetric—all firms make the same guess, and their model does not allow for entry or exit. One attractive feature of conjectural variation models is that they permit the full range of possible outcomes from the $P = MC$ perfectly competitive result to the $MR = MC$ cartel result, depending on the nature of the conjectures and the number of firms in the industry.

Rosen and Katz illustrated the possibility of escaping the burden of a tax using a very simple example of a duopoly with linear demands and symmetric conjectures. They were particularly interested in the range of consistent, or rational, conjectures, meaning that each firm assumes that the other firm will respond in a profit-maximizing manner to its changes in price or output. They introduced a factor tax that increases marginal cost and found that unexploited profits did rise by more than the tax liabilities under consistent conjectures. The firms more than escaped the tax burden by moving closer to the cartel price and output. Whether actual oligopolies can escape tax burdens in this way remains a wide-open question.

Heterogeneous Consumers

A final important modification of the Harberger model is the assumption of heterogeneous consumers. An obvious implication of heterogeneity is that the incidence of taxation depends on the ownership of factors of production and expenditure patterns across consumers, as well as the amounts by which relative factor and goods prices change.

Although a number of economists have introduced heterogeneity into the Harberger framework, the more recent literature is moving in a different direction. The increase in income inequality in the United States over the past 20 years (and in many of the other developed market economies) is mostly due to an increase in inequality within earnings and not to an increase in the share of national income going to capital. Therefore, in accounting for heterogeneity, economists have been turning their attention toward the

---

[26] M. Katz and H. Rosen, "Tax Analysis in an Oligopoly Model," *Public Finance Quarterly*, January 1985.

effects of the major taxes on the personal distribution of income. They are no longer so interested in how taxes affect the relative shares of capital and labor income. We will discuss the newer incidence studies in Chapter 17.

REFERENCES

Aaron, H. J., "A New View of Property Tax Incidence," *American Economic Association Papers and Proceedings*, May 1974.

Aaron, H. J., *Who Pays the Property Tax?*, The Brookings Institution, Washington D.C., 1975.

Asimakopulos, A., and Burbidge, J., "The Short-Period Incidence of Taxation," *Economic Journal*, June 1974.

Auerbach, A., and Kotlikoff, L., *Dynamic Fiscal Policy*, Cambridge University Press, New York, 1987.

Ballentine, J. G., and Eris, I., "On the General Equilibrium Analysis of Tax Incidence," *Journal of Political Economy*, June 1975.

Diamond, P., "Tax Incidence in a Two-Good Model," *Journal of Public Economics*, June 1978.

Feldstein, M., "Incidence of a Capital Income Tax in a Growing Economy with Variable Savings Rates," *Review of Economic Studies*, October 1974.

Fleming, J., "A Reappraisal of the Corporation Income Tax," *Journal of Public Economics*, July–August 1976.

Friedlaender, A. F., and Vandendorpe, A., "Differential Incidence in the Presence of Initial Distorting Taxes," *Journal of Public Economics*, October 1976.

Fullerton, D., and Rogers, D., *Who Bears the Lifetime Tax Burden?*, Brookings Institution, Washington, D.C., 1993.

Harberger, A., "The Incidence of the Corporation Income Tax," *Journal of Political Economy*, June 1962.

Kalecki, M., "A Theory of Commodity, Income and Capital Taxation," *Economic Journal*, September 1937.

Katz, M., and Rosen, H., "Tax Analysis in an Oligopoly Model," *Public Finance Quarterly*, January 1985.

King, M., "Taxation, Corporate Financial Policy, and the Cost of Capital: A Comment," *Journal of Public Economics*, August 1975.

Krzyzaniak, M., and Musgrave, R. A., *The Shifting of the Corporation Income Tax*, Johns Hopkins University Press, Baltimore, MD, 1963.

Mieszkowski, P., "On the Theory of Tax Incidence," *Journal of Political Economy*, June 1967.

Musgrave, R. A., "Is a Property Tax on Housing Regressive?," *American Economic Association Papers and Proceedings*, May 1974.

Pechman, J., *Who Paid the Taxes, 1966–85?*, The Brookings Institution, Washington, D.C., 1985.

Pechman, J., and Okner, B., *Who Bears the Tax Burden?*, The Brookings Institution, Washington, D.C., 1974.

Shoven, J., "The Incidence and Efficiency Effects of Taxes on Income from Capital," *Journal of Political Economy*, December 1976.

Shoven, J., and Whalley, J., "A General Equilibrium Calculation of the Effects of Differential Taxation of Income from Capital in the U.S.," *Journal of Public Economics*, November 1972.

Shoven, J., and Whalley, J., "Equal Yield Tax Alternatives: General Equilibrium Computational Techniques," *Journal of Public Economics*, October 1977.

Stiglitz, J., "Taxation, Corporate Financial Policy, and the Cost of Capital," *Journal of Public Economics*, Vol. 2, 1973.

Stiglitz, J., "The Corporation Tax," *Journal of Public Economics*, April–May 1976.

17

EXPENDITURE INCIDENCE AND ECONOMY-WIDE INCIDENCE STUDIES

Taxes are most often raised to finance government expenditure programs, not just to substitute for other taxes. Once this obvious point is conceded, it is no longer as compelling to speak only of the incidence of the tax revenues. The policy-relevant incidence measure is clearly balanced-budget incidence, the entire tax-and-expenditure package. One might still argue that tax incidence itself remains relevant since different sets of taxes could have financed the given expenditure program. Still, ignoring the expenditure side is always dangerous since the very existence of a new expenditure program affects the evaluation of the single tax and differential incidence measures discussed in Chapter 16. Government inputs and outputs enter into the market clearance and government budget equations, thereby influencing the price responses to any change in tax rates. Also, the distributional consequences of expenditure programs are likely to be as important as the distributional consequences of the tax revenues raised to finance them. Thus, to the extent incidence analysis is an aid to governmental distributional policies, considering the incidence of an entire tax-and-expenditure package would appear to be the most useful strategy.

This is bound to be a difficult assignment, however, even in theory, because balanced-budget incidence theory is fraught with the same difficulties as the theory of tax incidence, *plus* some other problems as well. At the very least, an analysis of various balanced-budget alternatives must confront these issues at the outset:

1. What measure of incidence will be employed? The three most likely candidates are income compensation or welfare loss measures applied to individuals, the change-in-relative-prices measure in the Harberger tradition, or the change in a many-person social welfare function, the same as for the theory of tax incidence.

2. For any given set of taxes, what expenditure programs are being financed? The obvious candidates are transfer payments, Samuelsonian non-exclusive public goods or other externality-generating goods, and government-operated decreasing-cost services, although the government might be buying goods and services that could have been supplied by a perfectly competitive private sector.

3. Will the analysis consider marginal, balanced-budget changes in taxes and expenditures, or must it focus on a total package of finite taxes and expenditures? Marginal analysis might make sense for transfer payments but surely not for decreasing cost services.

4. For any given expenditure program, how are the taxes being raised? The point that the choice of expenditures affects the measurement of tax incidence is reversible. The method of financing the expenditures dictates the approach to the measurement of expenditure incidence. Are the expenditures assumed to be financed with lump-sum taxes or with a set of distorting taxes? If resource-using government expenditure programs are assumed to be financed with lump-sum taxes, then the incidence analysis could take place within a first-best context, so long as other appropriate assumptions are made, such as perfectly competitive private production and marginal-cost pricing of government services. Lump-sum financing would also provide an unambiguous method for considering the incidence of a single (set of) government programs (s), or a separate theory of expenditure incidence, analogous to the incidence of a single-tax program when the revenues are returned lump sum. This is an important consideration, since first-best expenditure incidence is more compelling than first-best tax incidence. Resource-using expenditures are undertaken solely for efficiency reasons in a first-best

environment. Nonetheless, they do have distributional consequences, and knowing these aids the government in its search for the optimal pattern of lump-sum redistributions.

If, realistically, governments are assumed to use distorting taxes to finance their expenditures, then the analysis is inherently second best, and tax and expenditure incidence cannot be separated (unless the expenditures happen to be self-financing using benefits-received taxes). As we saw in the discussion of tax incidence in a many-consumer world, one may have no choice but to adopt the aggregate-social-welfare approach to have a theoretically sound analysis.

We will not attempt an exhaustive analysis of all possible tax-and-expenditure combinations with all possible incidence measures. Rather, we will highlight some of the problems involved with introducing specific expenditure programs into an analysis of incidence. Thus, to keep the discussion manageable, the numerous possibilities will be limited in three ways:

1. Tax-and-expenditure packages will be evaluated by the income compensation or loss measure of incidence.[1] Hence, we will assume a one-consumer-equivalent economy, with an optimal income distribution.

2. Only three expenditure programs will be considered: transfer payments, decreasing costs services, and nonexclusive Samuelsonian public goods.

3. We will assume that lump-sum tax revenues finance the two *resource-using* expenditure programs—decreasing cost services and Samuelsonian public goods—and analyze their incidence in a first-best environment. Since the theory of resource-using public expenditures in a second-best environment will not be considered until the next chapter, a discussion of second-best expenditure incidence at this point in the text would be premature. In contrast, all the tools necessary for a comprehensive analysis of the incidence of transfer payments in a second-best environment have already been developed.

THE INCIDENCE OF GOVERNMENT TRANSFER PAYMENTS

Transfer payments, or subsidies, are analytically equivalent to negative taxes. Consequently, the theory of tax incidence is fully applicable to government transfer payments, with the single exception that all signs are reversed. All we need do, then, is review the major results of the previous chapter as they apply to subsidies:

[1] The many-person social welfare measure of incidence will be discussed in Chapter 22. For an analysis of expenditure incidence in the Harberger tradition, see C. McClure and W. Thirsk, "A Simplified Exposition of the Harberger Model, II: Expenditure Incidence," *National Tax Journal*, June 1975.

1. If lump-sum taxes finance lump-sum transfers, there is no burden or incidence in a one-consumer-equivalent economy. In a many-person economy, the tax paid or transfer received by any one person will be an appropriate income proxy for the welfare gain or loss by that person under either one of two assumptions: (a) technology is linear so that the taxes and transfers cannot change the equilibrium vector of consumer and producer prices; or (b) the policy relevant alternative to a given transfer-tax program is for the government to completely undo the program, recalling all transfers and returning all taxes, thereby restoring the original pretax and transfer equilibrium. Otherwise the tax-transfer program changes relative prices, and an individual's gain or loss would be measured by the value of his expenditure function evaluated at, say, the new prices and original utility level, less the lump-sum tax paid or transfer received.

2. A set of distorting subsidies offered to consumers and financed by lump-sum taxes is formally equivalent to the single-tax incidence problem of levying a set of distorting taxes and returning the revenues lump sum. The distorting subsidy-with-lump-sum tax generates a deadweight loss measured, in the case of linear technology, by:

$$L(\vec{s}) = M\left(\vec{q}; \overline{U}^0\right) + \sum_{i=1}^{N} s_i X_i^{comp} \tag{17.1}$$

where:

$\vec{s}$ = the vector of per-unit subsidies with element s_i.
$\vec{q}$ = the vector of consumer prices net of subsidy.

The appropriate measure in the case of general technology is:

$$L(\vec{s}) = M\left(\vec{q}; \overline{U}^0\right) + \sum_{i=1}^{N} s_i X_i^{comp} - \pi(\vec{p}) \tag{17.2}$$

The conceptual experiment described by Eq. (17.1) is a comparison between the lump-sum income necessary to reach the original utility level at the new lower prices less the amount of the subsidy, which is returned lump sum, everything measured at the compensated equilibrium. (Eq. (17.2)) subtracts the pure profits available at the compensated income from the required income.) Hence, Eq. (17.1) measures the payment the consumers are willing to make as a consequence of the subsidies less the required lump-sum income payment (the return of the subsidy).[2]

---

[2] Since, from the consumer's point of view, goods prices are falling and factor prices are rising, $M(q; \overline{U}^0)$ measures the income consumers are willing to pay for the subsidies and is a negative number. Hence, loss is the addition of $M(q; \overline{U}^0)$ and $\sum_{i=1}^{N} s_i X_i^{comp}$, where $s_i > 0$ for goods, < 0 for factors. Similarly, good prices are rising and factor prices are falling from the firm's point of view, both of which tend to increase profits. Hence, $\pi(\vec{p})$ must be subtracted from the subsidy payment in Eq. (17.2) under general technology. This HCV measure is conceptually equivalent to the HEV measure for a distorting tax.

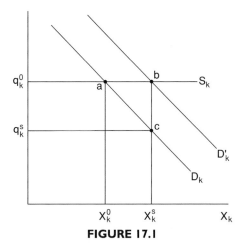

FIGURE 17.1

Figure 17.1 illustrates the measure of loss created by a unit subsidy s_k on the consumption of X_k, with linear technology. The subsidy shifts D_k upward by s_k, reduces the price X_k to the consumer from q_k^0 to q_k^s, and increases consumption from X_k^0 to X_k^s. The gain to the consumer is the area $acq_k^s q_k^0$, the area behind the original compensated demand curve (compensated at utility level $\overline{U}^0$) between the old and new prices, Hicks' Compensating Variation (HCV). The subsidy at the new compensated equilibrium is $s_k \cdot X_k^s$, the area $bcq_k^s q_k^0$, which the consumer must pay for with lump-sum taxes. The net loss, therefore, is the triangle abc. Under the income-compensation measure of incidence, this dead-weight loss is the incidence of the subsidy.[3]

Similarly, the incidence of marginal changes in an entire set of distorting subsidies is measured by summing the changes in dead-weight loss each time, equal (for linear technologies) to:

$$dL = \sum_k \sum_i s_i M_{ik} ds_k \qquad (17.3)$$

where:

M_{ik} = the Slutsky substitution terms.

Likewise, the expression for the total loss from a set of unit subsidies is

$$L = \frac{1}{2} \sum_i \sum_j s_i s_j M_{ij} \qquad (17.4)$$

analogous to the total loss from a set of unit taxes.

---

[3] In single-market partial equilibrium analysis, the dead-weight loss from any distortion is always the area between the compensated demand curve and the general equilibrium supply curve measured from the distorted to the undistorted equilibrium quantities.

3. One set of distorting subsidies may be substituted for another while holding the total subsidy constant, a case of differential expenditure analysis. This is exactly analogous to differential tax incidence. Here, the substitution is viewed as removing one set of subsidies, returning the tax savings lump sum, and then instituting a second set of subsidies, paid for by lump-sum taxes. As in the tax case, the first step involves totally differentiating the government's budget constraint:

$$\sum_{i=1}^{N} s_i X_i^{comp} = \overline{S} \tag{17.5}$$

with $dS = 0$, to determine the changes in the s_i necessary to maintain a balanced budget. The resulting changes are then substituted into Eq. (17.3) to evaluate the change in loss (for linear technologies). Finally, the practical difficulties of applying these compensated measures, especially for general technologies, which were discussed in Chapter 16, apply to transfer incidence as well. Recall that an important issue was whether production is constant returns to scale.

TAX AND EXPENDITURE INCIDENCE WITH DECREASING-COST SERVICES

As long as decreasing-cost services are being analyzed within the context of first-best theory, the government is assumed to charge a price equal to the marginal cost of providing the service and to finance with lump-sum taxes the deficits arising because $MC < AC$. The appropriate comparison is an all-or-none test in which having the service with these characteristics is compared to not having the service at all. Marginal incidence analysis is not relevant for decreasing-cost services.

The income-compensation measure of incidence was developed in Chapter 9. Assuming linear or constant-returns-to-scale (CRS) general production technology elsewhere in the economy, the net benefit of providing the decreasing-cost service with lump-sum financing of its deficit is[4]

$$B = -M\left(\vec{q}; \overline{U}^0\right) - T \tag{17.6}$$

where:

$\vec{q} =$ vector of consumer prices with the service.
$\overline{U}^0 =$ the utility level without the service.

[4] Alternatively,

$$B = \left[M\left(\vec{q}^0; \overline{U}^0\right) - M\left(\vec{q}; \overline{U}^0\right)\right] - T, \text{ with } M\left(\vec{q}^0; \overline{U}^0\right) = 0 \tag{17.6N}$$

The term in brackets is Hicks' Compensating Variation measure of the willingness to pay for the price change, where $\vec{q}^0 =$ the vector of consumer prices without the service.

T = the lump-sum payment required to finance the deficit.

$-M(\vec{q}; \overline{U}^0)$ = the amount consumers are willing to pay for the new prices, $\vec{q}$.

SAMUELSONIAN NONEXCLUSIVE GOODS

Chapter 6 developed the standard pareto-optimal decision rule for a non-exclusive good in a first-best environment, $\sum_{h=1}^{H} MRS^h = MRT$, but did not consider the incidence of the good. The incidence is the gain in welfare to each consumer from being able to consume the good at its optimal level, less the loss in welfare from having to finance the good.

As a first step in deriving an incidence measure, recall that all government decisions with respect to financing and providing the good are lump-sum events from any one consumer's point of view. Since the market system completely breaks down because of the revelation problem, the government has no choice but to select a given quantity of the good that will be available in equal amounts to all consumers, hope that it satisfies the $\sum MRS = MRT$ rule, and then finances its purchases with lump-sum taxes to preserve efficiency in all other markets.

For the purposes of this discussion, assume that the government has selected the optimal quantity, so that $\sum_{h=1}^{H} MRS^h = MRT$. Assume further that production of the nonexclusive good and all other goods and services exhibits either CRS or linear technology.

Consumers react in two ways to the existence of a nonexclusive good. On the one hand, the good enters each consumer's utility function directly as one of the arguments, although the sign of the argument is uncertain. Some consumers may view it as a "good," others as a "bad," especially at the margin. On the other hand, consumers may well adjust their own goods demands and factor supplies in response to the nonexclusive good. That is, the nonexclusive good may be a substitute for or complement to other goods and factors.

A representation of the consumer's indirect utility function that captures these features is

$$V(\vec{q}; \bar{I}; e) = U\left[X_i(\vec{q}; \bar{I}; e); e\right] \tag{17.7}$$

with

$$\frac{\partial V}{\partial e} = \sum_{i=1}^{N} \frac{\partial U}{\partial X_i} \frac{\partial X_i}{\partial e} + \frac{\partial U}{\partial e} \tag{17.8}$$

where:

$\vec{q}$ = the vector of consumer prices.

X_i = good (factor) i demanded (supplied) by the consumer.

$\bar{I}$ = a source of lump-sum income other than profits from production, assumed constant unless taxed by the government.

e = the quantity of the nonexclusive good selected by the government.

Two results useful for the measure of incidence follow directly from the first-order conditions of utility maximization. First, differentiate the budget constraint with respect to e to obtain:

$$\sum_{i=1}^{N} q_i \frac{\partial X_i}{\partial e} = 0 \tag{17.9}$$

From the primal of the consumer problem,

$$\frac{\partial U}{\partial X_i} = \lambda \, q_i \qquad i = 1, \ldots, N \tag{17.10}$$

Substituting Eq. (17.10) into (17.9) yields:

$$\frac{1}{\lambda} \sum_{i=1}^{N} U_i \frac{\partial X_i}{\partial e} = 0 \tag{17.11}$$

Thus, Eq. (17.8) simplifies to:

$$\frac{\partial V}{\partial e} = \frac{\partial U}{\partial e} \tag{17.12}$$

The change in utility from a marginal change in the nonexclusive good equals its direct marginal effect on utility. Although consumers may change their other purchases and factor supplies in response to the change in e, these changes have no further effect on utility.

Second, Eq. (17.12) implies that the marginal rate of substitution between e and ith good or factor, MRS_e, X_i, is defined exactly as it would be for any exclusive good:

$$MRS_{e, X_j} = -\frac{\dfrac{\partial U}{\partial e}}{\dfrac{\partial U}{\partial X_i}} \tag{17.13}$$

If good i is the numeraire, then

$$MRS_{e, X_j} = -\frac{1}{\lambda} \frac{\partial U}{\partial e} = -\frac{dU}{de} \Big/ \frac{dU}{dI} = -dI/de_{U=\bar{U}} \tag{17.14}$$

Thus, the marginal rate of substitution establishes the value of a marginal increase in the public good to the consumer, as it does for any good.

The value of a finite amount of the public good can be derived from the consumer's expenditure function. In the presence of a nonexclusive good, the dual to the standard consumer problem is

$$\min_{(X_i)} \sum_{i=1}^{N} q_i\, X_i$$

$$\text{s.t.} \quad U = \overline{U}\left(\vec{X}; e\right)$$

The first-order conditions yield compensated demand (supply) functions of the form:

$$X_i^{\text{comp}} = X_i\left[\vec{q}; \overline{U}\left(\vec{X}; e\right)\right] \qquad i = 1, \ldots, N \tag{17.15}$$

and the expenditure function:

$$M\left[\vec{q}; \overline{U}\left(\vec{X}; e\right)\right] = \sum_{i=1}^{N} q_i\, X_i^{\text{comp}}\left[\vec{q}; \overline{U}\left(\vec{X}; e\right)\right] \tag{17.16}$$

Thus, even though the consumer does not purchase e, the expenditure function has e as an argument because e appears in the utility function, which is being held constant. All we need establish, then, is that $\partial M / \partial e \neq 0$, so that as e changes the income required to keep the consumer at the same utility level also changes.

$$\frac{\partial M}{\partial e} = \sum_{i=1}^{N} q_i\, \frac{\partial X_i^{\text{comp}}\left[\vec{q}; \overline{U}\left(\vec{X}; e\right)\right]}{\partial e} \tag{17.17}$$

Substituting Eq. (17.10) into (17.17) yields:

$$\frac{\partial M}{\partial e} = \frac{1}{\lambda} \sum_{i=1}^{N} \frac{\partial U_i}{\partial X_i}\, \frac{\partial X_i^{\text{comp}}\left[\vec{q}; \overline{U}\left(\vec{X}; e\right)\right]}{\partial e} \tag{17.18}$$

But $U = \overline{U}(\vec{X}; e)$. Thus,

$$\sum_{i=1}^{N} \frac{\partial U_i}{\partial X_i}\, \frac{\partial X_i^{\text{comp}}}{\partial e} + \frac{\partial U}{\partial e} = 0 \tag{17.19}$$

if utility is held constant, or:

$$\sum_{i=1}^{N} \frac{\partial U_i}{\partial X_i}\, \frac{\partial X_i^{\text{comp}}\left[\vec{q}; \overline{U}\left(\vec{X}; e\right)\right]}{\partial e} = -\frac{\partial U}{\partial e} \tag{17.20}$$

Hence:

$$\frac{\partial M}{\partial e} = -\frac{1}{\lambda}\, \frac{\partial U}{\partial e} = -\frac{dI}{de}\bigg|_{U=\overline{U}} \tag{17.21}$$

As expected, the derivative of the expenditure function with respect to the nonexclusive good yields the change in lump-sum income that makes the consumer indifferent to a change in the nonexclusive good. From Eq. (17.19), this is nonzero, in general. Also, from Eq. (17.14), $\partial M/\partial e$ is the marginal rate of substitution between e and the numeraire good.

An appropriate income measure of the gain from having a finite amount of a nonexclusive good is[5]

$$B = M\left[\vec{q}; \overline{U}^0\left(\vec{X}; e = 0\right)\right] - M\left[\vec{q}; \overline{U}^0\left(\vec{X}; e\right)\right] = \overline{I} - M\left[\vec{q}; \overline{U}^0\left(\vec{X}; e\right)\right] \tag{17.22}$$

where:

$\vec{q}$ = the vector of consumer prices in the presence of the nonexclusive good.
$\overline{U}^0$ = the consumer's utility when e = 0,
$\overline{I}$ = the consumer's lump-sum income, assumed constant.

Notice that Eq. (17.22) would measure the benefit (harm) of any lump-sum event that affects the consumer.

If consumers are asked to make a lump-sum tax payment to finance e or changes in e, then the incidence of the entire tax-income-expenditure package is straightforward. Since the expenditure function expresses welfare changes in terms of lump-sum income, the lump-sum tax is just subtracted from Eq. (17.22) to obtain the incidence of the entire package. Thus, the net benefit is

$$B^N = -M\left[\vec{q}; \overline{U}^0\left(\vec{X}; e\right)\right] + (\overline{I} - T) \tag{17.23}$$

For marginal charges:

$$\frac{\partial B^N}{\partial e} = -\frac{\partial M}{\partial e} - \frac{\partial T}{\partial e} = MRS_{e,\,numeraire} - \partial T/\partial e \tag{17.24}$$

where:

$\dfrac{\partial T}{\partial e}$ = the change in lump-sum taxes per unit change in e.

Equation (17.24) establishes the following result. Suppose the government is able to establish Lindahl prices for each person equal to the MRS, in accordance with the competitive interpretation of the benefits-received principle of taxation as discussed in Chapter 6. If $\sum MRS = MRT$ and all production exhibits CRS, the Lindahl prices are sufficient to cover the full costs of the public good. Lindahl pricing also guarantees positive net benefits

---

[5] If I varies as e varies because of general technology, then:

$$B = (I_e - I_0) + M\left(\vec{q}^0; \overline{U}^0(e = 0)\right) - M\left(\vec{q}; \overline{U}^0(e)\right) \tag{17.22N}$$

The gain equals $(I_e - I_0)$, the actual change in lump-sum income as e moves from 0 to e, plus the amount the consumer is willing to pay to have e increased from 0 to e. Recall that $I_0 = M\left[\vec{q}^0; \overline{U}^0(e = 0)\right]$. Therefore, $B = I_e - M\left[\vec{q}; \overline{U}^0\left(\vec{X}; e\right)\right]$, Eq. (17.22).

to all consumers as long as the MRS declines as e increases or the compensated demand for e is downward sloping. Even consumers who think e is a "bad" on the margain gain net benefits with Lindahl pricing. Since their MRS > 0, they would receive subsidies, and these per-unit subsidies would be greater than required on the inframarginal units of e (their MRS is increasing in e). On the margin, however, changes in e accompanied by Lindahl prices generate no net benefits or losses. This is true for any good for which the price equals its MRS (defined in terms of the numeraire good).

The Incidence of Nonexclusive Goods: Empirical Evidence

Although theoretical formulas for the total or marginal incidence of nonexclusive goods are easy enough to derive, they are always very difficult to apply in practice. The problem is the familiar one that consumers have no incentive to reveal their true demand for nonexclusive goods. In particular, we saw that the marginal benefit to the consumer, $dM/de = -\dfrac{dI}{de}\bigg|_{U = \overline{U}}$, is the marginal rate of substitution between the nonexclusive good and an exclusive numeraire good. Yet, no market or political mechanism exists through which the government can accurately measure each consumer's MRS, and incentive-revealing schemes such as Clarke taxes have never been used. Thus, empirical analysis must resort to indirect methods to determine the incidence of these goods.

Researchers often use extremely simple rules to allocate the benefits of public goods such as defense for want of any better alternatives. Examples include allocating the total expenditures per person or per family or in proportion to income per person or per family. In 1970, Henry Aaron and Martin McGuire published an attempt to go beyond these simple allocation methods by incorporating the $\sum MRS = MRT$ pareto-optimal rules. Even so, they were forced to make some extremely strong assumptions, most notably that everyone has the same preferences and that utility is additively separable in defense. Therefore, everyone is assumed to derive the same utility from defense expenditures. Also, they based the incidence of the public good, e, on the "pseudo-market value" of the good, $MRS \cdot e$, rather than making use of the expenditure function.[6]

A modest literature proposing different methods for distributing the benefits of public (nonexclusive) goods evolved in response to Aaron and

[6] The seminal article is W. Gillespie, "Effect of Public Expenditures on the Distribution of Income," in R. Musgrave, Ed., *Essays in Fiscal Federalism*, The Brookings Institution, Washington, D. C., 1965. Gillespie uses a number of simple allocation formulas for different kinds of public expenditures. H. Aaron and M. McGuire, "Public Goods and Income Distribution," *Econometrica*, November, 1970. See also the public choice view represented by S. Maital, "Apportionment of Public Goods Benefits to Individuals," *Public Finance*, 3, 1975. Notice that the MRS for e will vary across people with different incomes even though the total utility they receive from e is the same in the Aaron-McGuire model.

McGuire. The proposals are motivated by the following problem with Lindahl pricing. Let p be the price of a private composite commodity, y_i be the after-tax income of consumer i, and p_i^e be the Lindahl price paid by consumer i. Ask what amount of lump-sum income, M_i, person i would require under Lindahl pricing to be indifferent to receiving the public good free of charge. The required M_i is the solution to $V(p, p_i^e, y_i + M_i) = U(y_i, e)$, where $V(\ )$ is the indirect utility function, $U(\ )$ is the direct utility function, and y_i is spent on the composite commodity. M_i is the benefit received by i for public good e.[7]

The problem is that the p_i^e are endogenous; they depend on consumers' tastes and incomes. Consequently, with heterogeneous consumers facing different p_i^e, the M_i are generally not comparable across consumers as income measures of utility differences. Thus, the goal became to develop some method of standardizing the pseudo-marketing of the public good so that the M_i are comparable utility compensation measures.

James Hines has one of the latest proposals, in the form of a linear pricing scheme. Suppose each consumer could purchase e at the same (linear) price p_e. Ask, as above, what M_i would set $V(p, p_e, y_i + M_i) = U(y_i, e)$, with p_e set such that $\sum_{i=1}^{H} M_i = e$. That is, the sum of the benefits equals the cost of supplying e. The M_i less the actual taxes paid by consumer i to finance e equal the net fiscal benefit (burden) of the public good. The benefits M_i under this proposal are valid income measures of the difference between the utility each consumer would receive if required to purchase e at p_e and the utility at the e chosen by the government (and offered free of charge). Put differently, the benefits defined by the M_i would allow each consumer to achieve the utility at the actual e if instead they were required to purchase e at a common price. Hines argues that taxes set according to M_i would define taxation according to the benefits-received principle in a manner most closely imitative of the usual single-price market mechanism. It is a cost-based mechanism for distributing the benefits, not a surplus-based mechanism, just as is the pseudo-market value at Lindahl prices.[8]

Applying his method to a sample of U.S. households, Hines finds that the M_i first rise and then fall with income when the direct utility function is assumed to be Cobb–Douglas. The benefits are low for low-income consumers because they place a relatively low value on e. The benefits are low again for high-income consumers because their desired e at p_e is far removed from the actual e provided. Since actual federal income tax payments are progressive, the net fiscal burdens are highly progressive at the higher income levels. Aaron and McGuire's pseudo-market-value measure of benefits produced a much less progressive pattern of net fiscal burdens.

---

[7] In the Lindahl equilibrium with constant returns to scale, the M_i are the pseudo-market values of the good, $p_i^e e$.

[8] J. Hines, "What Is Benefit Taxation?," *Journal of Public Economics*, March 2000. Hines also demonstrates that, under his proposed linear pricing scheme, the consumers' incentives are to have the government set p_e such that the allocation of e is optimal.

Whether any such counterfactual cost-based experiments for distributing public goods benefits are persuasive is undoubtedly a matter of taste. In any event, no consensus has been achieved in measuring the incidence of public goods. As we shall see in the remainder of the chapter, economy-wide studies of incidence that include a public good often focus exclusively on the tax side of the government budget. Two approaches to the incidence of the public good are commonplace. One is to simply ignore the effect of the public good on utility. The other is to adopt the Aaron–McGuire assumption of identical preferences with additively separable public goods, and then argue either that the commonly provided public good cannot lead to a difference in welfare across individuals, or that a unit of public good is equivalent to a unit of lump-sum income to each consumer. Neither position is consistent with the expenditure function measure of individual welfare, $M[\vec{q}; \overline{U}(\vec{X}; e)]$ without further simplifying assumptions on M.

ECONOMY-WIDE INCIDENCE STUDIES

In 1980, Alan Blinder published a study of the personal distribution of income in the United States covering the 30-year period from 1947 to 1977.[9] 1947 was the year that the federal government began collecting data on the personal distribution. Blinder's main conclusion was that the distribution was essentially unchanged during those 30 years, a conclusion that surprised him given the economic and demographic turmoil during those years and the rapid growth of the government sector into domestic areas.

The timing of Blinder's study was somewhat ironic, because subsequent research revealed that the personal distribution of income started to become more unequal sometime in the mid- to late 1970s, a trend that continued at least until 1994. Roughly speaking, the families and individuals at the top of the distribution gained at the expense of those at or near the bottom of distribution in the 1970s and 1980s. In the early 1990s, those at the top gained relative to everyone else.

The two very different trends in the personal distribution of income in the last half of the century ignited a huge body of research on the determinants of the distribution. Public sector economists have contributed to this research agenda with a variety of economy-wide tax incidence studies that attempt to measure the impact of the five major U.S. taxes on the personal distribution.[10] They are, in descending order of importance ($ billions, 1999, the last

[9] A. Blinder, "The Level and Distribution of Economic Well-Being," in M. Feldstein, Ed., *The American Economy in Transition*, University of Chicago Press, Chicago, 1980, pp. 415–479.

[10] The incidence of public expenditures has not received the same attention, with the exception of Social Security and public assistance transfer payments. Similar trends in the distribution in the other developed market economies have led to the same kinds of incidence studies of their major taxes.

year data are available for state and local governments): federal and state personal income taxes ($1069); federal payroll tax that finances the Social Security system ($612); general sales (state and local) and selective excise (all governments) taxes ($360); local property taxes ($240); and federal and state corporation income taxes ($216).[11]

The tax incidence studies have for the most part employed one of three quite different modeling strategies: a heuristic sources and uses approach; computable general equilibrium (CGE) models; and dynamic models of tax incidence. Each strategy has its strengths and weaknesses. None is entirely convincing as a model for determining the overall incidence of a nation's tax system.

We will begin with the sources and uses approach because it appeared first in the literature. Indeed, it was the only method available to economists for economy-wide incidence analysis until the 1970s, when advances in computer technology and computing algorithms gave birth to the other two methods.

THE SOURCES AND USES APPROACH

The sources and uses approach to economy-wide tax incidence is essentially *ad hoc*. The incidence of the five major taxes is determined by a set of assumptions that allocate the burdens to either the sources or the uses of income. The assumptions pay some attention to general equilibrium tax theory, but only some. The approach accepts the principles that individuals bear the burden of taxation and that the changes in prices in response to taxation ultimately determine the incidence of the tax. At the same time, however, it ignores the dead-weight loss arising from taxation. The approach also considers the incidence of each tax in isolation, ignoring potential interdependencies among the taxes. Finally, the alternative against which the current tax system is being compared is usually treated casually. The general equilibrium with the current tax system should be compared with the general equilibrium that would exist with an alternative tax system that raises the same amount of revenue. The usual comparison, however, is with an equal-revenue, single-rate comprehensive income tax, which is simply as-

---

[11] A few cities also levy personal income taxes, and the revenues from these taxes are included in the data. The sales and excise tax revenues consist of $200 billion from general sales taxes ($164 billion state, $36 billion local) and $160 billion of from selective excise taxes ($75 billion states, $70 billion federal and $15 billion local). General sales and excise taxes tend to be treated similarly in economy-wide incidence studies. The property tax data include revenues from the few states that levy property taxes. The state and local tax data are from the U.S. Bureau of the Census website: www.census.gov/govs/estimate/99stlss1.xls. The federal tax data are from the *Budget of the United States Government, Fiscal Year 2001, Supplement*, U.S. Government Printing Office, Washington D.C., 2000, part Five: Historical Tables, Table 2.1.

sumed to generate a pattern of tax burdens proportional to income. This may not be true. For instance, a flat-rate income tax could generate very unequal dead-weight losses per dollar of revenue in the markets for labor and capital if the (compensated) supply and demand elasticities for labor and capital are quite different.

Annual Incidence Studies

The first sources and uses studies adopted an annual perspective on tax incidence. Lifetime incidence studies did not appear until the 1980s. The sources of personal income on an annual basis are transfer receipts (mostly public), income from labor, and income from capital (income from land is inconsequential). The uses of income are consumption and saving. The goal in allocating the tax burdens to these sources and uses is a modest one, to give a rough idea of whether the overall tax system is progressive, proportional, or regressive in terms of individuals' or families' comprehensive income. This is the best the method can hope to achieve given the *ad hoc* nature of its assumptions.[12]

The "play" in the assumptions about the allocations of annual tax burdens comes from transfers and income from capital on the sources side and from the uses of income. Government transfer receipts are concentrated among the elderly and the low-income young. Therefore, allocations of tax burden to transfer income tend to be regressive. Conversely, income from capital is highly concentrated among the wealthy. The Gini coefficient for holdings of financial wealth in the United States is on the order of .80, compared with an annual income Gini of approximately .44. Therefore, allocations of tax burden to income from capital are highly progressive. On the uses side, the ratio of annual consumption to income falls sharply as income rises; therefore, allocations of tax burden to consumption tend to be highly regressive.

[12] The evolution of the sources and uses approach followed the development of the large micropanel datasets that began to appear in the 1970s. Public sector economists had two choices prior to the microdata sets. They could construct "typical" families with given incomes, expenditure patterns, and sizes and use the tax laws and price-shifting assumptions to allocate the burdens of the five taxes to these constructed families. Alternatively, they could allocate the aggregate tax revenues on the basis of the price-shifting assumptions to income classes broadly defined, such as by deciles or quintiles. The microdatasets permitted the allocation of the tax burdens to tens of thousands of actual families and unrelated individuals on the basis of their personal incomes and other characteristics. Some studies went even further, merging IRS data on tax revenues collected from individuals and families with data on individuals and families from one of the panel datasets to get an even more accurate picture of micro-level tax burdens. For further discussion on the evolution of the data used in tax incidence studies, see A. Atkinson, "The Distribution of the Tax Burden," in J. Quigley and E. Smolensky, E., Eds., *Modern Public Finance*, Harvard University Press, Cambridge, MA, 1994, chap. 2. Atkinson also has further discussion and analysis of the appropriate alternative against which to compare the current tax system.

The distribution of income from labor tends to follow the overall personal distribution of income. Thus, the incidence of tax burdens allocated to labor income depends largely on the structure of the particular tax—for example, the nature of its exemptions, exclusions, or deductions from the tax base and whether it has graduated tax rates.

The Pechman–Okner Studies

The two most widely cited annual sources and uses incidence studies were produced by the Brookings Institution. The first was by Joseph Pechman and Benjamin Okner, published in 1974. The second was an update of the first study in 1985, authored by Pechman alone.[13] Pechman and Okner merged the panel data on families and individuals from the Survey of Income and Education with IRS tax files on individual taxpayers to compile a massive dataset on incomes, expenditures, personal characteristics, and tax liabilities for U.S. families and unrelated individuals.

Central Variant Assumptions

Pechman and Okner's most preferred, "central variant" assumptions for allocating the burdens of the five taxes are as follows:

Personal Income Taxes

They assume that the impact equals the incidence, on the grounds that approximately 80% of the tax base is labor income and that the overall supply of labor was assumed at the time to be almost perfectly inelastic. Their assumption that the tax liability is a reasonable measure of the burden ignores the differences in supply elasticities among men and women that empirical analysis has uncovered over the past 20 years. It also ignores the substantial amount of dead-weight loss from the federal and state income taxes that was discovered by Hausman and others. Recall that the loss is due to a substantial substitution effect that is offset by an income effect of approximately equal magnitude (thereby accounting for the near-zero actual supply elasticity).

Allocating the tax burden by tax liability leads to the conclusion that the personal income taxes are fairly progressive overall and highly progressive at low incomes. The overall progressivity is due to the graduated federal tax rates, and the steep low-end progressivity is due to the personal exemptions and the standard deduction in the federal tax. (Many state income taxes incorporate these same features.)

---

[13] J. Pechman and B. Okner, *Who Bears the Tax Burden?*, The Brookings Institution, Washington, D.C., 1974. J. Pechman, *Who Paid the Taxes, 1966–85?*, The Brookings Institution, Washington, D.C., 1985.

Payroll Tax for Social Security

Labor is assumed to bear the entire burden of the payroll tax, even though Congress levies half the tax rate on the employers and half on the employees. Also, the tax burden equals the total tax liability, as with the personal income tax. These assumptions follow because the payroll tax is levied only on wage and salary income, and the overall supply of labor is assumed to be perfectly inelastic.[14]

Figure 17.2 illustrates this point. The equilibrium without the tax is (L_0, W_0). The half of the tax levied on the employers shifts the demand for labor D_L down by the full amount of their tax liability, to D'_L. With S_L perfectly inelastic, the wage falls to W_1. The employers fully escape the tax by lowering the wage against the perfectly inelastic supply. Then, the half of the tax on the employees reduces their after-tax wage to W_2, again by the full amount of their liability. Therefore, the employees bear the entire burden of the payroll tax, equal to the combined tax liabilities of the employers and the employees.

The payroll tax is highly regressive under these assumptions because the tax was levied at a flat rate on wage and salary income below a maximum income limit in 1974 and 1985. Income above the maximum was untaxed. Therefore, a person earning \$200,000 or \$2,000,000 per year paid the same tax as another person earning the maximum amount of taxable income.[15]

Sales and Excise Taxes

Pechman and Okner assume that the markets for goods and services are perfectly competitive, and that the long-run supply curves are perfectly elastic at constant average and marginal costs. Therefore, prices rise by the full amount of the taxes in the long-run, so that the burdens are allocated on the uses side on the basis of consumption. The sales and excise taxes are highly regressive under these assumptions on an annual basis. They tend to be flat-rate taxes such that tax collections are roughly proportional to consumption, and the ratio of annual consumption to income falls sharply as income

---

[14] The Social Security system operated strictly on a pay-as-you-go basis until 1983, in which all taxes collected from current employers and employees were paid out to current retirees. There was no explicit benefits-received link between the tax payments and future pension benefits, although the promise of future benefits was certainly implicit. Reforms in 1983 allowed for an accumulation of some of the tax revenues in a trust fund that would eventually finance the retirement benefits of the Baby Boom generation. Even so, viewing the payroll tax as a benefits-received tax would require a lifetime perspective, not an annual perspective.

[15] In 1994, Congress removed the income limit from the Medicare portion of the payroll tax. The Medicare portion now applies to all wage and salary income earned in occupations covered by Social Security. The tax is still highly regressive under the Pechman–Okner assumptions, however, as the Medicare portion is only 2.9 percentage points of the combined 15.3% tax rate (in 2000). The Medicare portion will rise over time, however, making the payroll tax less regressive. The maximum income against which the remaining 12.4% applies was \$76,200 in 2000.

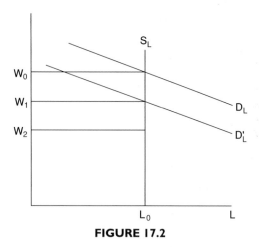

FIGURE 17.2

rises.[16] The 10% of the population with the highest incomes account for about 80% of the total personal saving in the United States.

Local Property Taxes

Pechman and Okner adopt the new view of the property tax, which assumes that the vast proportion of the property tax burden falls on the owners of land and capital. They assign the entire burden to land and capital in their central variant, which makes these taxes highly progressive.

Corporation Income Taxes

Pechman and Okner accept Harberger's view that the corporation income tax is borne by capital as their most preferred assumption and assign the entire burden to income from capital in their central variant. These taxes are therefore highly progressive. Notice that the Harberger model, which has only one kind of capital, implicitly assumes that all forms of capital are perfect substitutes in production and thus earn the same after-tax rate of return.

The Pechman–Okner central variant assumptions led them to essentially the same conclusions about the incidence of the overall U.S. tax system in 1974 and 1985. Table 17.1 presents their central variant tax burdens as a proportion of income by deciles in 1980, reported in Pechman's 1985 study. The overall incidence is mildly progressive throughout the distribution. The mildly progressive personal income taxes and the highly progressive property and corporation taxes slightly dominate the highly regressive payroll and

[16] Twenty-six of the 44 states that levy general sales taxes exempt food purchased for home consumption from the tax bases to lessen the perceived regressivity of these taxes. Even so, the state sales taxes are highly regressive under the Pechman–Okner assumptions.

TABLE 17.1 Effective Average Tax Rates by Income Deciles Under the Central Variant Assumptions

	Decile									
	1	2	3	4	5	6	7	8	9	10
Effective tax rate (%)	20.6	20.7	21.1	22.3	23.4	23.8	24.2	25.5	26.4	27.1

Source: Adapted from J. Pechman, *Who Paid the Taxes, 1966–85?*, The Brookings Institution, Washington, D.C., 1985, Table 4.4, p. 48.

sales and excise taxes. The Pechman–Okner central variant has become the consensus view of the incidence of the U.S. tax system. For instance, it is the one reported in most of the Principles textbooks written for the U.S. market.

Alternative Assumptions

Pechman and Okner present a number of alternative assumptions concerning the local property and corporation income taxes that might be plausible from an annual perspective.

Local Property Taxes

The new view of property tax incidence argues that some of the incidence of the tax could be passed on to nonmobile labor or renters as capital moves in response to differences in the effective tax rates across localities. In light of this argument, Pechman and Okner provide an alternative allocation in which 1/2 of the property tax burden is allocated to capital income, 1/4 of the burden is allocated to labor income, and 1/4 of the burden is allocated to consumption of housing services. This allocation makes the property tax much less progressive than the central variant, in which all of the burden is borne by land and capital. It also seems excessive, however, as nonmobile workers and renters gain in the localities with lower than average property tax rates.

Another possibility is to argue that the local property tax is simply a benefits-received tax, a price that the citizens pay for the locally provided public services. Benefits-received taxes are never part of an incidence calculation because they cannot be a net burden. This assumption is also extreme. It might apply in a frontier environment in which people are highly mobile and towns are continually forming and reforming, expanding and contracting. In such a world, people of like tastes for public services would join together, form a town, provide exactly the public services they want, and levy taxes to pay for the public services.[17] The taxes would be benefits-received taxes. But,

---

[17] Chapter 30 presents a formal version of the frontier model.

in a more realistic setting of fixed communities and limited mobility, most people are unlikely to obtain their most preferred bundle of public services. If not, then their property taxes are not benefits-received taxes, and the incidence of the property taxes remains a relevant question. In any event, viewing the local property tax as a benefits-received tax would also make the overall U.S. tax system less progressive.

Corporation Income Taxes

The implicit Harberger assumption that all forms of capital are perfect substitutes in production and therefore earn the same rate of return is fairly extreme. An alternative is to concede that there is some segmentation among capital markets. One obvious possibility that Pechman and Okner consider is a segmentation between housing and other kinds of physical capital: They may not earn the same after-tax returns because they serve such different purposes. This distinction, if applicable, is particularly relevant for the United States because housing is taxed much more lightly than other forms of capital. Pechman and Okner allocate corporation income taxes to dividends rather than all income from capital under this assumption, which makes the corporation income taxes slightly more progressive than under the central variant.

Another possibility is to assume that corporations are profit satisficers rather than profit maximizers and have leeway to pass the tax on to consumers in the forms of higher prices and reduced output. This is the avenue of escape modeled by Rosen and Katz and discussed in Chapter 16. The ability to pass the tax forward to consumers changes the corporation income taxes from highly progressive taxes under the central variant to highly regressive taxes on an annual basis.

Yet another possibility is to assume that the corporation income tax is essentially a benefits-received tax, a special levy on corporations that the stockholders pay for the privilege of limited liability against losses. The corporation income tax drops out of the incidence calculations under this view, and the overall tax incidence becomes less progressive.

The various alternative assumptions concerning the local property and corporation income taxes can change the incidence of these taxes rather dramatically. But they still do not have much effect on the Pechman–Okner central-variant pattern of tax incidence in the United States because they are the smallest of the five main taxes, much less important than the personal income, payroll, and sales and excise taxes. Researches would have to make very different assumptions about the incidence of the other three taxes to have a substantial impact on the central-variant pattern. Quite different assumptions are possible for the other taxes, but they require a change from an annual to a lifetime perspective. Many public sector economists, perhaps even the majority, would favor switching to a lifetime perspective on tax incidence, and the sources and uses literature has been moving in the direction of lifetime incidence over the past 15 to 20 years.

Mixing Annual and Lifetime Incidence

The first break from the annual perspective came from Edgar Browning and William Johnson in 1979. They used a lifetime perspective to argue that the incidence of sales and excise taxes is likely to be slightly progressive rather than highly regressive, as was universally assumed at the time.[18]

Their argument begins with two facts about the U.S. economy. First, the present value of lifetime consumption is approximately proportional to the present value of income for the vast majority of people. Only a small percentage of people leave substantial bequests or, conversely, receive substantial inheritances. Second, many government transfer payments are indexed to the Consumer Price Index (CPI), including Social Security benefits and, implicitly, in-kind public assistance such as food stamps and medical care. These two facts considerably alter the implications of assuming that these taxes are passed on to consumers through higher prices. On the one hand, allocating the tax burden in proportion to consumption is equivalent to allocating the tax burden in proportion to income from a lifetime perspective. On the other hand, transfer income is protected from the tax burden by the CPI indexing. Therefore, the tax burden should be allocated in proportion only to *earned* income from a lifetime perspective. This implies that the incidence of sales and excise taxes is slightly progressive because transfer income is received disproportionately by the poor. Browning and Johnson conclude that the incidence of the U.S. tax system is somewhat more progressive than suggested by Pechman and Okner's central-variant assumptions.

Whalley's Critique of the Sources and Uses Approach

John Whalley offered a blistering critique of the sources and uses approach to tax incidence in his 1984 Presidential address to the Canadian Economic Association.[19] The fundamental weakness in the approach, according to Whalley, is its reliance on *ad hoc* assumptions and theorizing. By suitably mixing assumptions from annual and lifetime perspectives and selectively borrowing from tax incidence theory, researchers can generate almost any result they want.

In particular, Whalley applied the Pechman–Okner central variant assumptions to the Canadian tax system, which is similar to the U.S. tax system, and produced essentially the same mildly progressive annual pattern of incidence that Pechman and Okner found for the United States. The burden of the Canadian taxes by income deciles ranged from 27.5% at the low end to 43% at the high end, with most of the other deciles in the 30 to 40% range. By selectively varying the assumptions, however, Whalley was able to

---

[18] E. Browning and W. Johnson, *The Distribution of the Tax Burden*, American Enterprise Institute for Public Policy Research, Washington, D.C., 1979.

[19] J. Whalley, "Regression or Progression: The Taxing Question of Incidence," *Canadian Journal of Economics*, November 1984.

generate either a steeply progressive overall tax burden ranging from 11 to 70% or a hugely regressive overall tax burden ranging from nearly 100% to 16%. The assumptions chosen were always consistent with some plausible underlying model of the economy.

To make the overall tax system look highly progressive, Whalley selected assumptions that removed the regressive taxes and made the progressive taxes more progressive. Three assumptions mattered the most, two related to the regressive taxes and one to the progressive taxes. Regarding the regressive taxes, he adopted the Browning–Johnson lifetime argument for the sales taxes that makes them slightly progressive. He also assumed that the payroll tax for Social Security was a benefits-received tax. The argument here is that the payment of the tax comes with an implied promise by the government that employees will receive a public pension during their retirement years, so that people view the tax as equivalent to a contribution to a private pension plan. This is not an implausible assumption. Many economists have argued that political support for the U.S. Social Security system rests on just such an implied promise, even though the system was never designed to be actuarially sound, unlike private plans. Regarding the progressive taxes, Whalley noted that neither the personal nor corporate income taxes correct for inflation in calculating the tax liability on income from capital. The failure to adjust for inflation led to extremely high effective tax rates on income from capital during the 1970s and 1980s when inflation was fairly high, and thereby made each tax much more progressive in real terms, especially the corporation income tax.

To make the overall tax system highly regressive requires the reverse strategy: remove the progressive taxes and make the other taxes as regressive as possible. The way to remove the progressive taxes is to eliminate any tax burden on capital. One plausible assumption for the Canadian economy is that the return to capital is set on the world market, so that all taxes on the demanders of capital are passed on either to consumption or labor. This assumption alone sharply reduces the progressivity of the corporation income taxes and the local property taxes. Regarding the other taxes, Whalley adopts the annual perspective on sales taxes, which makes them highly regressive. He further assumes that labor income consists of a base level of income equal for all workers, augmented by income in the form of a return to a worker's accumulated human capital. Further, he assumes that physical and human capital are perfect substitutes in production so that they must receive the same rate of return. But the return to physical capital is set in the world market and escapes any burden of taxation. Therefore, the return to human capital must also escape the burden of all taxes. This implies that all taxes on labor income are borne entirely by the base component of income. Since the ratio of the base component to total income falls sharply as total income rises, taxes on labor income are highly regressive. Notice also that the assumptions on consumption and income combine to change the corporation income and local property taxes from progressive to highly regressive, since they are now allocated either to *annual* consumption or *base* labor income. Small wonder then that the overall tax burden on low-income taxpayers approaches 100% under this set of assumptions.

Assuming perfect substitutability of physical and human capital may be extreme, but if the return to physical capital is effectively untaxed then it is reasonable to assume that at least some portion of the return to human capital is protected from taxation. If so, then the central variant assumptions could well be wide of the mark and make the tax system seem far more progressive than it is. This conjecture is tempered by the *ad hoc* nature of all the assumptions in the sources and uses approach. One is hard pressed to know what to believe, which is the principal message that Whalley wanted to convey.[20]

Pure Lifetime Tax Incidence

The final stage in the evolution of the sources and uses approach was to move entirely to a lifetime perspective. Switching from an annual to a lifetime perspective has two immediate effects on the sources and uses of income.

The first is that the sources and uses are quite different in a lifetime context. The only three sources of income in a lifetime perspective are inheritances, the present value of labor income, and the present value of public and private transfer income. Income from capital drops out of the sources side, because any income from capital is assumed to grow at the same rate of return as the discount rate used to compute the present value of the income stream. The main item on the uses side is the present value of consumption, including bequests as the final act of consumption. Income from capital also appears on the uses side because saving affects the timing of consumption. Also, taxes on income from capital reduce the after-tax rate of discount which

---

[20] Gilbert Metcalf has published an interesting analysis of pollution taxes from the sources and uses perspective. Pollution taxes are trumpeted as leading to a "double dividend" of efficiency gains. They promote efficiency directly by correcting for the pollution externality and indirectly because the revenues collected can replace revenues from other distorting taxes. The problem, however, is that pollution taxes tend to increase the prices of consumer goods, so that they are highly regressive from an annual sources and uses perspective (less so from a lifetime perspective). Metcalf considers various offsetting tax reductions to reduce the overall tax regressivity. In one experiment, he replaced 10% of personal income tax receipts with taxes on carbon emissions, gasoline consumption, air pollution, and the use of virgin materials in production. Using standard sources-and-uses data sources and methodology, he showed that the (annual) regressivity of the pollution taxes can be mostly offset if the 10% reduction in personal tax receipts is achieved by: (1) removing the first $5000 of the tax base under the payroll tax; (2) offering a $150 refundable credit for each personal exemption taken under the personal income tax; and (3) cutting all personal income tax rates by 4%. He notes that cutting the corporation income tax may generate the biggest double efficiency dividend, but that it is highly regressive from an annual sources and uses perspective. See G. Metcalf, "A Distributional Analysis of Green Tax Reforms," *National Tax Journal*, December 1999.

individuals use to calculate present values and thereby affect the total value of lifetime resources or consumption.

A second effect of switching to a lifetime perspective is that the variation in both the sources and uses of income across families and individuals is sharply reduced. On the sources side, the Gini coefficient for the present value of lifetime labor earnings is about half the value of the Gini coefficient for annual labor earnings. Also, because transfer receipts are concentrated among the young and the elderly, they too show much less variation over lifetimes. On the uses side, the ratio of lifetime consumption to income is approximately equal to one. The only exceptions are those families and individuals who leave substantial bequests, a very small minority. An important implication of the reduced variation in lifetime sources and uses is that selecting different incidence assumptions makes much less of a difference than in an annual context. The only way that a tax can be highly progressive or regressive is if the structure of the tax itself makes it so. Thus the overall tax system is expected to be at most only mildly progressive or regressive from a lifetime perspective.

This expectation was borne out by James Davis *et al.* in their 1984 study of the Canadian tax system, the first truly lifetime incidence analysis in the sources and uses tradition.[21] They began by collecting a sample of 500 lifetime income profiles, spanning the full range on incomes, from the Survey of Consumer Finances. The profiles included lifetime labor earnings and transfer receipts, to which they added initial inheritances simulated from the actual pattern of mortality and bequests among Canadians. The individuals were then assumed to be life-cycle consumers with a bequest motive, choosing an optimal pattern of lifetime consumption over the years from 20 to 75, with death and the bequest occurring in the 75th year. The authors also took into account actual patterns of social mobility across income levels. The lifetime income profiles, combined with all the other assumptions, generated lifetime series for each of the 500 individuals on labor earnings, transfer receipts, and inheritances on the sources side and consumption and income from capital on the uses side. Finally, Pechman–Okner-style assumptions on the incidence of the major Canadian taxes were applied to the lifetime series to compute a central-variant lifetime incidence measure of the overall tax system.

The Canadian taxed system proved to be mildly progressive throughout: moderately progressive in the lowest four income deciles, only slightly but steadily progressive from deciles 5 through 8, and then a bit more steeply progressive over deciles 9 and 10. This was essentially the same pattern as the Pechman–Okner central variant for the U.S. tax system and the Whalley central variant for the Canadian tax system, both from an annual perspective.

---

[21] J. Davies, F. St. Hilaire, and J. Whalley, "Some Calculations of Lifetime Tax Incidence," *American Economic Review*, September, 1984.

As expected, the Davis *et al.* pattern of lifetime incidence was not very sensitive to changes in the central variant assumptions.

A major caveat of the lifetime perspective is the assumption that individuals consume and save according to the Life-Cycle Hypothesis (LCH). The LCH has not been supported in empirical studies of consumption and saving behavior, even when a bequest motive is added as in Davies *et al.* Nor has any other model of consumption and saving behavior stood up to empirical testing. Economists have not been able to reach a consensus on the best way to model consumption and saving.

In conclusion, the sources and uses approach suggests that the U.S. (and Canadian) tax system is mildly progressive throughout, especially if one adopts a lifetime perspective. The annual incidence is more problematic in light of Whalley's caution about knowing which *ad hoc* incidence assumptions are the most plausible for each of the major taxes. The lifetime perspective is not without its problems, however, given the uncertainties surrounding consumption and saving behavior.

Lorenz–Gini Measures of Tax Incidence

A final development in the sources and uses tradition has been to summarize the overall effect of the tax system on the distribution of income using variations of standard Lorenz curve/Gini coefficient measures of inequality. Three popular measures are the tax concentration curve, differences in before-tax and after-tax Gini coefficients, and differences in before-tax and after-tax indexes of inequality that incorporate a social welfare function.[22]

Tax Concentration Curve

A tax concentration curve is a Lorenz style curve with the cumulative percentage of population, ordered by before-tax income, on the horizontal axis, and the cumulative percentage of the total tax burden suffered by the ordered population on the vertical axis. The tax burdens are determined by the sources and uses approach.[23]

The tax concentration curve measures the disproportionality of the tax system. Taxes are progressive, proportional, or regressive depending on whether the Gini coefficient associated with the curve is greater than zero (the curve is below the diagonal), zero (the curve coincides with the diagonal), or less than zero (the curve is above the diagonal). Nanak Kakwani proposed

---

[22] Lorenz curves, Gini coefficients, and indexes of inequality were discussed in Chapter 4. For an overview of the early work using this approach see D. Kiefer, "Distributional Tax Progressivity Indexes," *National Tax Journal*, December, 1984. See also his empirical companion piece in D. Kiefer, "A Comparative Analysis of Tax Progressivity in the United States: A Reexamination," plus "Comments" and "Reply," *Public Finance Quarterly*, January 1991.

[23] A tax concentration curve could apply to a single tax or any combination of taxes including the entire tax system.

subtracting the standard before-tax Gini coefficient from the tax concentration Gini to measure the extent of the disproportionality of the tax system.[24] Using now-standard notation,

$$K = C_T - G_{BT} \qquad (17.25)$$

where:

K = Kakwani's extent of disporportionality index
C_T = the Gini coefficient of the tax concentration curve
G_{BT} = the Gini coefficient corresponding to the Lorenz curve with the cumulative percentage of population ordered by before-tax income on the horizontal axis, and the cumulative percentage of before-tax income on the vertical axis.

Change in the Before-Tax and After-Tax Gini Coefficients

A natural measure of the overall effect of the tax system on the distribution of income is the difference in the standard before-tax and after-tax Gini coefficients:

$$\text{Overall distributional effect} = G_{BT} - G_{AT} \qquad (17.26)$$

where:

G_{BT} is as defined above
G_{AT} = the Gini coefficient corresponding to the Lorenz curve with the cumulative percentage of population ordered by after-tax income on the horizontal axis, and the cumulative percentage of after-tax income on the vertical axis. (After-tax income refers to income minus the tax burden, not necessarily the tax payments.)

Pechman and Okner favored the proportionate version of this measure in reporting the overall distributional effect of the tax system, $(G_{BT} - G_{AT})/G_{BT}$. In his 1985 study, Pechman reported a proportionate reduction in inequality ranging from .8% for the most regressive variant to 2.5% for his most progressive variant.[25]

Change in a Before-Tax and After-Tax Social Welfare Index of Inequality

This measure makes use of indexes of inequality that incorporate society's social welfare judgments. An example is Atkinson's index of inequality discussed in Chapter 4, which is based on the equally distributed, equivalent level of income defined with reference to society's aversion to inequality. The difference in Atkinson's index using before-tax and after-tax incomes,

---

[24] N. Kakwani, "Measurement of Tax Progressivity: An International Comparison," *Economic Journal*, March 1977.

[25] J. Pechman, *Who Paid the Taxes, 1966–85?*, The Brookings Institution, Washington, D.C., 1985, p. 60.

$I_{BT} - I_{AT}$, measures the change in inequality resulting from the tax system as filtered through society's aversion to inequality. For instance, if society did not care about inequality (the utilitarian case), then the difference would be zero no matter what the pattern of tax burdens.

Recall that $(1 - \text{Atkinson's index})$ measures the proportion of mean income that would yield the same level of social welfare as the actual distribution of income if incomes were equally distributed. Therefore, the difference in Atkinson's index before and after tax can be interpreted as an income measure of the social welfare gain from the equalizing effect of the tax system, assuming $I_{AT} < I_{BT}$.

Vertical and Horizontal Inequities

The Lorenz/Gini approach to determining the overall effect of the tax system can also be used to measure the extent of vertical and horizontal inequities. Of the two, vertical inequity is the more straightforward in the Lorenz–Gini framework.

Vertical Inequity

The problem of measuring the extent of vertical inequity can be seen with reference to the overall distributional effect $= G_{BT} - G_{AT}$. One difficulty with this measure is that any tax or tax system is likely to violate the Feldstein vertical equity principle of no reversals. That is, the ordering of the population on the basis of before-tax income may differ from the ordering of the population on the basis of after-tax income, which makes $G_{BT} - G_{AT}$ an incomplete measure of the distributional effect of a tax or tax system. The question arises as the extent of the reranking—that is, the extent of vertical inequity.

Measuring the extent of the reranking makes use of a concept called the *income concentration curve*, which is a Lorenz-style curve with the cumulative percentage of population, ordered by before-tax income on the horizontal axis and the cumulative percentage of after-tax income received by the ordered before-tax population on the vertical axis. The Gini coefficient associated with the income concentration curve is labeled C_Y. The extent of reranking, R, is the standard before-tax Gini coefficient minus the income concentration curve, or

$$R = G_{BT} - C_Y > 0 \qquad (17.27)$$

R must be greater than zero in the presence of reranking because the income concentration curve is closer to the diagonal than the before-tax Lorenz curve. Reranking places a greater proportion of income lower down in the distribution when after-tax income is on the vertical axis rather than before-tax income, and the before-tax income is used to order the population on the horizontal axis for each curve. R can be thought of as a measure of the degree of vertical inequity in the tax system.

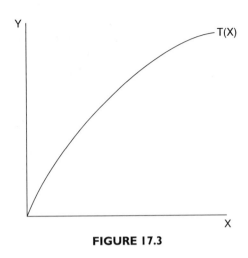

FIGURE 17.3

Horizontal Inequity

Horizontal inequity occurs when equals are treated unequally. Measuring the extent of horizontal inequity requires first defining the ideal tax base to determine whether equals have been treated unequally. J. Richard Aronson, Paul Johnson, and Peter Lambert (A/J/L) have proposed that the ideal tax base be comprehensive or Haig–Simons income adjusted for family size to account for different needs across families with the same incomes.[26] Following A/J/L, call the adjusted Haig–Simons income the *equivalized income*. Thus, two taxpayers with the same level of equivalized income before tax should pay the same tax. Any differences in their after-tax incomes are an indication of horizontal inequity, the result of inappropriate deductions, exclusions, and other "loopholes" in the tax structure.

A/J/L measure the extent of horizontal equity as follows. Define the idealized tax function, pictured in Fig. 17.3, as:

$$Y_i = T(X_i) \tag{17.28}$$

where:

X_i = the equivalized before-tax income of taxpayer i
Y_i = the equivalized after-tax income of taxpayer i, assuming no loopholes in the tax structure (i.e., all equivalized Haig–Simons income is subject to tax). The curve is concave because the rate structure is graduated.

[26] J. Aronson, P. Johnson, and P. Lambert, "Redistributive Effect and Unequal Income Tax Treatment," *Economic Journal*, March 1994. See also J. Aronson, and P. Lambert, "Decomposing the Gini Coefficient to Reveal the Vertical, Horizontal, and Reranking Effects of Income Taxation," *National Tax Journal*, June 1994.

Consider three levels of before-tax equivalized income—X_1, X_2, and X_3,—and refer to Fig. 17.4. The presence of unwarranted tax loopholes produces a fan pattern of after-tax equivalized incomes for each before-tax level of income, as indicated in the figure. Horizontal inequity exists within each fan because equals are being treated unequally by the tax structure. Vertical inequity occurs in the regions of overlap between two fans, the regions in which taxpayers with higher equivalized incomes before tax end up with lower equivalized incomes after tax.

Aronson, Johnson, and Lambert developed the following decomposition of the overall distributional effect that includes both the horizontal and vertical inequities:

$$G_{BT} - G_{AT} = (G_{BT} - G_0) - \sum_X \alpha_x G_{Fx} - R \qquad (17.29)$$

where:

G_0 = the after-tax Gini that would exist if there were no fans and therefore no horizontal or vertical inequity.

G_{Fx} = the Gini coefficient within the fan associated with before-tax income X (the Gini is calculated using the after-tax order of population within the fan).

$\alpha_x = (N_x/N)(N_x\mu_x/N\mu)$,

N_x = the number of taxpayers within the fan associated with before-tax income X

N = total population

μ_x = the mean after-tax income within the fan associated with before-tax income X

μ = the mean after-tax income over all taxpayers

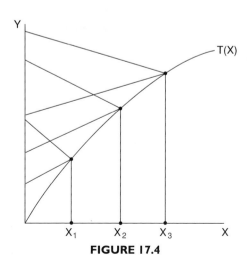

FIGURE 17.4

The second term on the right-hand side (RHS) of Eq. (17.29), $\sum_X \alpha_x G_{Fx}$, measures the extent of horizontal inequity. It equals the sum of the income-share- and population-weighted Gini coefficients within the fans. The third term, R, is the extent of the reranking described above, the regions of overlap across the fans. It is the measure of vertical inequity.[27]

Aronson and Lambert applied their formula to the British personal income tax, using intervals of 5 Ł /week in measuring before-tax income to get enough variation in the data to produce fans. They found that horizontal inequity accounted for only about .2% of the overall distributional effect and vertical inequity accounted for anywhere from 4 to 6% of the overall distributional effect for the years they studied.

A caveat applicable to the A/J/L decomposition is Feldstein's observation that a tax system cannot give rise to horizontal inequities after the market system has fully adjusted to it. Only tax reforms generate horizontal inequities, and then only temporarily. One could counter that the economy is unlikely to be in its long-run equilibrium under a given tax system. Alternatively, A/J/L's finding of very little horizontal inequity could imply that the British economy has almost completely adjusted to its tax structure, in line with Feldstein's observation. Either interpretation is a stretch, however, since the A/J/L decomposition ignores market responses to taxation and characterizes horizontal inequities only in terms of tax payments relative to their view of ideal equivalized incomes.[28]

Lorenz Measures and Tax Progressivity

The analysis of tax progressivity has long been grounded in the Lorenz tradition. We conclude this section with a brief discussion of the progressivity literature.

A tax is considered to be unambiguously distributionally progressive if the distribution of after-tax incomes weakly Lorenz dominates the before-tax distribution, that is, the distribution of average tax incomes is always at least as equal as the distribution of before-tax incomes. This notion of progressivity justifies the use of the distribution of after-tax rates (burdens) to measure progressivity, since the condition of weak Lorenz dominance is satisfied if the average tax rate is nondecreasing. Notice that proportionality is included under progressivity using weak Lorenz dominance.

---

[27] The decomposition is only approximately correct because the within-fan Gini coefficients are of necessity based on the after-tax ordering of the population within each fan, whereas the other Gini coefficients are based on the before-tax ordering of the overall population.

[28] For a full discussion of the A/J/L approach and analysis of taxation in the Lorenz–Gini tradition, consult P. Lambert, *The Distribution and Redistribution on Income: A Mathematical Analysis*, second ed., University Press, Manchester, 1993. A shorter, but excellent overview of this literature by Lambert is P. Lambert, "Evaluating Impact Effects of Tax Reforms," *Journal of Economic Surveys*, September 1993.

Anthony Shorrocks and a number of co-authors have recently explored the question of designing income tax schedules to be distributionally progressive for *all* possible distributions of income. The range of choices turns out to be remarkably limited for realistic income taxes. For example:

1. In one paper, the authors show that increasing the exemptions under an income tax may not increase the progressivity of the tax if the tax has graduated marginal tax rates. It will always be progressivity increasing only under a single proportional tax rate.[29] The intuition behind the result is that an increase in the exemption is worth more to taxpayers with higher marginal tax rates.

2. In another paper, the authors consider a heterogeneous taxpaying population that varies by income and need (e.g., family size). They use well-established extensions of the Lorenz dominance criterion for heterogeneous populations and analyze tax schedules that attempt to adjust for need. The federal personal income tax is an example; it allows a personal exemption based on family size and extends the tax brackets for married couples. They show that the only way to guarantee progressivity for all possible distributions is if the tax structure does not adjust for need. Further, if society wants to ensure that the proportion of taxes paid by the neediest group never increases, then the tax must be a proportional tax. It cannot be redistributive.[30]

The requirement that progressivity hold for all possible distributions may be overly restrictive. The authorities may know that a given tax reform is distributionally more progressive for the existing distribution. Then again, it may well be difficult to ensure that a given tax reform is uniformly progressive in the Lorenz sense throughout the entire distribution of income, if this is what society desires.

COMPUTABLE GENERAL EQUILIBRIUM MODELS OF TAX INCIDENCE

The computable general equilibrium (CGE) approach to modeling an economy was made possible by Herbert Scarf's algorithm for solving complete general equilibrium models of a stylized economy, which Scarf published in 1967.[31]

---

[29] M. Keen, H. Papapanagos, and A. Shorrocks, "Tax Reform and Progressivity," *Economic Journal*, January 2000.

[30] P. Moyes and A. Shorrocks, "The Impossibility of a Progressive Tax Structure," *Journal of Public Economics*, July 1998. Interested readers should also see U. Ebert and P. Moyes, "Consistent Income Tax Structures When Households Are Heterogeneous," *Journal of Economic Theory*, January 2000.

[31] H. Scarf, "On the Computation of Equilibrium Prices," in *Ten Economic Studies in the Tradition of Irving Fisher*, Wiley, New York, 1967. Also see H. Scarf, "An Example of an Algorithm for Calculating General Equilibrium Prices," *American Economic Review*, September 1969.

The application of CGE techniques to overall tax incidence became popular in the 1970s, with John Shoven and John Whalley leading the way,[32] and CGE modeling is still very much in use today.

CGE models of tax incidence are the discrete version of Harberger's general equilibrium marginal analysis. Their appeal is that they can consider very broad incidence questions, such as the overall incidence of the federal and state personal income taxes or the incidence of replacing income taxes with expenditure taxes, within the context of quite detailed models of actual economies.

The typical CGE models that have been used for incidence analysis are impressively complex, even the earliest models. They contain a number of different consumers and commodities. The consumers span the full range of the income distribution, with identical consumers or a single representative consumer within each income class. The commodities are a combination of final consumer goods and intermediate inputs. The consumers' utility functions are usually specified as CES, defined over leisure and the final goods. The commodities are produced with aggregate production functions, also usually of the CES form, using labor, a given stock of capital, and a subset of the intermediate inputs.[33] The selection of inputs for each production function is guided by input/output tables of the actual economies under investigation. The I/O tables are also used to determine the distribution of the final goods among the various income classes. The underlying market environment is assumed to be perfectly competitive.

The government sector typically consists of a Samuelsonian public good and one or more of the major taxes and transfer programs. The public good is usually not well specified. It either has no effect on consumers' utilities or it enters the utility functions in an additively separable manner so that it does not affect the various marginal rates of substitution between the commodities and leisure. The main function of the public good is to determine the resources available for private consumption. The taxes and government transfer payments, in contrast, tend to be more realistic approximations of actual taxes and transfers. The one exception is the existence of a lump sum tax, which can be varied to consider the incidence of a single tax or transfer program in the Harberger manner. The government's budget is assumed to be balanced.

The parameters of the preference and production functions are determined in one of three ways. Some parameters are taken from existing econo-

---

[32] For an overview of these models and the related literature, see J. Shoven and J. Whalley, "Applied General Equilibrium Models of Taxation and International Trade," *Journal of Economic Literature*, September 1984.

[33] The first CGE models were one-period static models, without saving and investment decisions or capital markets. The extension of these models to a lifetime context with some dynamics appeared in the 1990s. The lifetime-CGE modeling approach is discussed in the final section of this chapter.

metric studies. Other parameters (but not all others) are set by assumption so that they can be varied as part of a sensitivity analysis of the results. The final set of parameters are residuals, determined as part of a calibration exercise. Given the first two sets of parameters, the residual parameters take on whatever values are necessary such that the private and public sector variables are initially equal to their values in the actual economy being investigated. The model is said to be calibrated to an actual economy in this way.

The standard incidence exercise is to vary some combination of the public good, the taxes, and the transfers and compute the new general equilibrium. The fiscal variables are changed so as to maintain a balanced budget. The relative incidence of the tax and expenditure changes is then measured by computing Hicks' Compensating or Equivalent Variations for each class of consumers. For example, the HEV is the lump sum income each consumer is willing to give up to return to the original prices (assuming a tax increase). These incidence measures typically mix actual and compensated equilibria because the consumers do not return (receive) the income lump sum required for compensation as part of the fiscal policy exercise. The new general equilibrium is the actual equilibrium, not the new compensated equilibrium. Thus, the incidence measure can be thought of as focusing on each individual income class one at a time, under the implicit assumption that if only one consumer were compensated lump sum it would have no significant effect on the new general equilibrium. This is not quite accurate, as all consumers are affected simultaneously by the fiscal experiment. Nonetheless, the HEV measures give a sense of the relative burdens suffered by each income class, which is the purpose of the exercise.

The big advantage of the CGE approach to tax incidence relative to the sources and uses approach is that it can approximate the dead-weight losses of the distorting taxes and transfers as wages and prices change from one general equilibrium to another. It does not compute them exactly because the new general equilibrium is not the compensated equilibrium. Even so, having a sense of the relative dead-weight losses is important because each individual's dead-weight loss is the proper measure of incidence or burden in a compensation experiment.

Despite their very different approaches, the CGE models and the sources and uses approach have reached roughly the same conclusions about the overall incidence of the five major taxes in the United States. They agree that the overall U.S. tax system is mildly progressive. The agreement of the two approaches is convenient because otherwise researchers and policy makers would be forced into making a choice in the nature of the lesser of two evils. Are they willing to accept the heuristic and sometimes problematic incidence assumptions of the sources and uses approach? Alternatively, are they willing to accept the many assumptions required to specify and parameterize the preferences, production functions, and public sector variables in the CGE models, as well as the assumption of perfectly competitive markets? Which set of assumptions to prefer is unclear, especially since the CGE models are highly simplistic representations of actual economies despite their mathematical complexity.

DYNAMIC TAX INCIDENCE

The early models of tax incidence were static, one-period models. Dynamic models were sure to follow, however, because the dynamic analysis of tax incidence has three huge advantages over static analysis.

First, and foremost, a dynamic model can track the *evolution of the capital stock* in response to tax policies. Changes in the capital stock through time affect the marginal products of capital, labor, and all other factors of production, which determine the real returns to the factors in a competitive environment. These capital-induced changes in the returns to factors over time tend to swamp any direct short-run effects that tax policies might have on factor returns.

Second, a dynamic model can consider *intergenerational tax* and *expenditure incidence*—that is, the relative effects of government policies on people of different ages, such as the young who are still working and the elderly who are retired. Dynamic models have shown that these intergenerational effects can be very large and also very important to the evolution of the economy.

The third advantage, related to the second, is that a dynamic model can analyze the incidence of the *asset revaluations* that immediately follow changes in government policies. The asset revaluations occur because capital is costly to adjust, so that capital assets of different vintages are not perfect substitutes in production. In fact, the short-run supply elasticities of many kinds of capital are quite low. Therefore, as changes in tax policy change the demands for different kinds of capital, fairly large changes in capital prices may be required in the short run to maintain equilibrium in the capital markets. An example is an investment tax credit, which favors new capital over existing ("old") capital and thereby lowers the relative price of new versus old capital. These asset revaluations matter in a dynamic context because people of different ages tend to hold different proportions of old and new capital. For example, the retired elderly have a much higher proportion of claims to old capital in their portfolios than do the working young. Dynamic tax analysis has suggested that the most important incidence effect of tax policy in the short run may well be the intergenerational transfers of wealth through asset revaluations following the change in taxes. (We will return to this point below.)

The two growth models most commonly used in dynamic incidence analysis are the Ramsey model with an infinitely lived representative consumer and the overlapping generations (OLG) model with two or more cohorts of finitely lived consumers. The Ramsey model appeared first, but it was soon overtaken by the OLG model as the preferred model for tax incidence. Only the latter can analyze intergenerational incidence and, as indicated, the early OLG models showed just how important the intergenerational effects of tax and expenditure policies can be.

Peter Diamond's 1965 article comparing and contrasting the burdens of internal and external public debt was the seminal application of the OLG model to a fiscal policy issue.[34] Once Diamond had demonstrated the advantages of the OLG framework, other economists were quick to apply it to other fiscal issues, including tax and expenditure incidence.[35] Foremost among them were Alan Auerbach and Lawrence Kotlikoff, who subsequently became the economists most closely identified with OLG incidence analysis. They published their complete OLG model with applications to a number of fiscal policy issues in *Dynamic Fiscal Policy*.[36]

The basic Auerbach–Kotlikoff model and its variations are far more complex than Diamond's original model, so much so that we will only provide a sketch of the main features of the model. Our goal is simply to give a sense of the various kinds of incidence channels that can occur in an OLG framework. Even the simplest Auerbach–Kotlikoff-style OLG models are so complex that they must be solved with simulation techniques.

The Auerbach–Kotlikoff OLG Model

Structure of the Model

The baseline Auerbach–Kotlikoff model has five essential elements that determine how the economy evolves over time: production, consumption, the government sector, the underlying market environment, and assumptions about how people form expectations of the future and what they know at any time.

Production

The production side of the model is highly simplified. A single all-purpose good, Y, is produced each period using capital and labor. The aggregate production function is CES. Y is either purchased by consumers as their one consumption good or purchased by the government, in which case it becomes a Samuelsonian nonexclusive public good.

---

[34] P. Diamond, "National Debt in a Neoclassical Growth Model," *American Economic Review*, December 1965.

[35] The OLG model also quickly gained favor with macro economists for analyzing long-run macroeconomic issues.

[36] A. Auerbach and L. Kotlikoff, *Dynamic Fiscal Policy*, Cambridge University Press, New York, 1987. See also L. Kotlikoff, "Taxation and Savings: A Neoclassical Perspective," *Journal of Economic Literature*, December 1984; L. Kotlikoff and L. Summers, "Tax Incidence," in A. Auerbach and M. Feldstein, Eds., *Handbook of Public Economics*, North-Holland, Elsevier New York, 1985, Vol. II, chap. 16.

The cost of adjusting the capital stock each period is a function of the level of investment and the investment/capital ratio, such that the marginal cost of investment is a linear function of the investment/capital ratio. The investment decision follows Tobin's q theory of investment with costly adjustment of capital. The marginal cost of investment incorporates tax variables such as a tax on capital income and an investment tax credit.

Consumption

Consumers make economic decisions for 55 years, from ages 21 through 75, after which they die. The model is simulated for 155 years (represented by ∞ below), so that a large number of cohorts (generations) are alive at any one time. Consumers maximize lifetime utility according to the Life-Cycle Hypothesis, with utility a function of their consumption and leisure during each period of their economic lives. (There are no bequests in the baseline model.) The utility function is CES within each period and additively separable over time, discounted by a rate of time preference that is the same for everyone. Consumers are endowed with one unit of time each period that they allocate between labor and leisure. The amount of leisure taken each period and the time of retirement are endogenous.

One of the three main equations of the model that drive its results is each consumer's intertemporal budget constraint. Assuming no borrowing or lending constraints, the most basic intertemporal budget constraint for a consumer of cohort j, one without taxes, is

$$\sum_{t=0}^{T} \left(\frac{C_{jt}}{(1+r_t)} - \frac{we_t(1-l_t)}{(1+r_t)} \right) = 0 \tag{17.30}$$

where:

0, T = the initial and final periods of consumer j's economic life
C_{jt} = consumption by consumer j and period t
r_t = the t-period interest rate for money received in period t; $(1+r_t)$
   equals $\prod_{s=0}^{t} (1+r_s)$,
where r_s is the one-period interest rate in period s.
w = the wage for an unskilled unit of labor
e_t = a skill parameter that permits an age-earnings profile to be built into
   the model
l_t = the amount of leisure taken in period t; $l_t = 1$ indicates retirement.

The Government Sector

The government exogenously sets the value of the public good and the structure of taxes and transfers each period subject to an intertemporal budget constraint that satisfies the no-Ponzi condition. The public debt must be bounded; debt cannot grow indefinitely at a rate above the rate of interest (which is greater than the growth of the economy in the long run in the Auerbach–Kotlikoff model). The government can run a deficit in any one period, however, which it covers by issuing bonds that mature after one period. These assumptions lead to a single-period government budget constraint of the form (assuming no money):

$$D_{t+1} - D_t = G_t + r_t D_t - T_t \qquad (17.31)$$

where:

D_t = debt issued in period t
G_t = the public good in period t
r_t = the government's one-period borrowing rate
T_t = taxes – transfers in period t

Adding the single-period budget constraint over all periods yields the government's intertemporal budget constraint under the no-Ponzi condition:

$$\sum_{t=0}^{\infty} \left(\frac{T_t - G_t}{(1 + r_t)} \right) = D_0 \qquad (17.32)$$

where r_t once again refers to the t-period interest rate for money received in period t. The government's intertemporal budget constraint is the second of the three main equations that drive the results.

The third main equation is the aggregate intertemporal consumption possibilities for the economy.

$$\sum_{j=1}^{J} \sum_{t=0}^{\infty} \frac{Z_{jt}}{(1 + r_t)} + \sum_{t=0}^{\infty} \frac{G_t}{(1 + r_t)} = H_{PV} + A_0 \qquad (17.33)$$

where:

Z_{jt} = consumption of goods and leisure by person j in period t
H_{PV} = the present value of the aggregate lifetime labor endowment, discounted to time zero (the endowment includes the time available for labor or leisure)
A_0 = the economy's initial endowment of physical capital to be used in production.

All resources are ultimately used to produce the consumption good or the public good.

The Market Environment

The economy is assumed to be perfectly competitive. As noted earlier, this implies that the real returns to labor and capital equal their marginal products. Further, labor and capital are fully employed each period, even while the economy is in transition moving from one steady state to another steady state following a change in government policy. The transition to the new steady state takes 150 periods.

Consumers' Expectations and Their Information Set

The guesses consumers and producers make about the future values of all the variables that are exogenous to them—prices, endowments, and tax (transfer) rates—determine their behavior currently and in all future periods and thus the general equilibrium in the economy period by period. This is why an assumption about how people form expectations of the future is a crucial element of any dynamic model. Auerbach and Kotlikoff assume that people have perfect foresight regarding these variables, meaning that their predictions lead to general equilibria each period that generate precisely the values they predicted.

People are not omniscient in the Auerbach–Kotlikoff model, however. Changes in the government's policies catch them by surprise as they occur and cause them to reoptimize from that time forward, again with perfect foresight about prices, endowments, and tax (transfer) rates. Since utility is additively separable over time, all past behavior is irrelevant to their reoptimizations. Also, consumers are partially myopic. They do not see the aggregate consumption possibilities or the government's intertemporal budget constraint embedded within it. Hence, they do not understand how the government will adjust to their reactions to fiscal policies. These informational assumptions are crucial because if people did know the aggregate consumption possibilities and the government's intertemporal budget constraint then fiscal policies would not have any effect. Having once determined an optimal lifetime path of consumption and leisure and knowing the time path of G, consumers would know how to reoptimize from that time forward in such a way as to offset fully anything the government might try to do with its tax (and transfer) policies. Having internalized the government's responses to their decisions, all taxes would become in effect lump sum taxes that consumers could offset.

Fiscal Policy Options

Given the structure of the model, fiscal policies can have real effects on the economy only by changing the consumers' intertemporal budget constraints and thereby altering consumer behavior. Their budget constraints depend upon the net-of-tax prices, wages, and interest rates; labor earnings; capital endowments; and lump-sum taxes and transfers. With this in mind, fiscal policy can essentially do four things in an OLG framework:

1. Change marginal incentives, the net-of-tax prices, wages, and interest rates.
2. Increase or decrease spending on the public good G, which changes the aggregate endowments available for consumption through the aggregate intertemporal consumption possibilities frontier.

3. Redistribute resources across generations (intertemporal redistribution).
4. Redistribute resources within generations (intratemporal redistribution).

Some comments on the first three options are in order.

Changing Marginal Incentives

A change in net-of-taxes prices, wages, and interest rates affects consumers in three ways. It changes the relative prices of present and future consumption and leisure that consumers equate to the marginal rates of substitution between these variables. It changes the present value of labor and capital endowments by changing the net-of-tax wages and interest rates. And, finally, it changes the incentive to invest in human capital and therefore affects the evolution of future wage rates.

Changes in the Public Good

The treatment of the public good in the Auerbach–Kothikoff model is similar to that in the CGE models. G does not generate utility; its only effect is to increase or decrease the resources available for consumption. G could be modeled to have a direct effect on utility without changing the general implications of the model. The only requirement then would be that G not be a perfect substitute for consumption. If it were, it essentially disappears from the aggregate intertemporal consumption possibilities relationship. Public goods are unlikely to be perfect substitutes for private goods, however.

Intertemporal Redistributions

Intertemporal redistributions can have major effects in OLG models with LCH consumers, especially if there is no bequest motive. The reason why is that consumers react to one-time changes in their endowments by spreading the higher or lower consumption possibilities over their remaining lives. Older consumers naturally have higher marginal propensities to consume out of changes in endowments than do younger consumers, simply because their consumption is spread over fewer remaining years. The differences in their MPCs imply that transfers from younger to older generations increase aggregate consumption and reduce saving and investment. Conversely, transfers from older to younger generations decrease aggregate consumption and increase saving and investment. The natural increase in MPCs as cohorts age is a central feature of the OLG model.

With these thoughts in mind, Auerbach and Kotlikoff describe four specific kinds of dynamic fiscal policies:

1. *Tax substitutions*—In a pure tax substitution, one tax is reduced and another tax increased such that there is no change in total tax receipts at the

time of the tax substitution nor for any period thereafter. The new tax always raises the same amount of revenue that the old tax would have raised. The public good also remains unchanged over time. Although tax substitutions involve no aggregate redistribution from the private to the public sector, they do have income effects as well as substitution effects in an OLG framework because different cohorts are affected differently. For example, the substitution of a wage (payroll) tax by a consumption (expenditures) tax disproportionately burdens the elderly, because a wage tax is paid only until retirement whereas a consumption tax is paid until death.

2. *Balanced budget changes in expenditures and taxes*—A one-time change in G is matched by a change in taxes or transfers each period such that $(G_t - T_t)$ remains constant, equal to its value before the change in G.

3. *Temporary deficits or surpluses (intergenerational redistributions)*—A pure temporary deficit consists of a decrease in a particular tax (increase in a transfer) for a number of periods, followed eventually by an increase in that same tax (decrease in the same transfer) such that the accumulated debt per person during the temporary period remains constant forever after. Permanent deficits are not allowed because they would violate the no-Ponzi condition on the government's intertemporal budget constraint. A temporary surplus is the reverse of a temporary deficit.

In an OLG framework, temporary government deficits and surpluses are defined as intergenerational redistributions. A temporary deficit is any fiscal policy that causes a redistribution from the younger to the older generations. In the case of a temporary tax cut, the older generations gain more from the temporary reduction in their taxes than they lose later on when the taxes are increased. The reverse is true for the younger generations. Furthermore, since the older generations have higher MPCs than the younger generations, a temporary deficit increases aggregate consumption, thereby reducing aggregate saving, investment, the future stock of capital, and the productivity of the economy in the long run. A particularly relevant example of a temporary deficit policy for the United States is the pay-as-you-go Social Security system, which operates initially at a deficit to pay the current retirees and then requires higher taxes later on to maintain benefits for future retirees.

Conversely, a temporary surplus is any fiscal policy that causes a redistribution from the older to the younger generations. In the case of a temporary tax increase, the older generations lose more from the temporary increase in their taxes than they gain later on when the taxes are reduced. The reverse is true for the younger generations. Consequently, a temporary surplus such as the United States is currently experiencing decreases aggregate consumption, thereby increasing saving, investment, the future stock of capital, and the productivity of the economy in the long run.

The analysis of temporary surpluses and deficits has three important implications for fiscal policy in the long run:

a. *Annual deficit/surplus measures*—Measures of annual government budget deficits and surpluses are irrelevant in a dynamic framework. The productivity of the economy in the long run is determined entirely by the amount of spending on the public goods and the extent of the redistributions across generations.

b. *Richardian equivalence*—The potentially large impact of intergenerational redistributions on productivity arises only because the young and the old have different marginal propensities to consume, as they surely would without a bequest motive. Robert Barro has proposed an alternative model with bequests that removes these differences.[37] He assumes that the older generations are altruistic towards the younger generations and will not allow them to be affected by temporary deficits and surpluses. For example, instead of consuming all of a temporary decrease in taxes over their remaining lifetimes, the elderly save just enough of the decrease to pass on a bequest to the younger generations that removes the relative disadvantage the young would otherwise suffer. With the relative burdens across generations equalized through the bequests, the temporary deficit has no effect. The same argument holds in reverse for temporary surpluses: The elderly reduce their bequests to remove the relative burden they themselves would otherwise suffer under a temporary surplus. This ineffectiveness of intertemporal redistributions is known as Ricardian equivalence. Barro's OLG model with altruism and bequests implies that the amount of the public good (i.e., public consumption or investment) is the only fiscal policy variable that has a real endowment effect on the economy in the long run. Although Ricardian equivalence is possible, it is extremely unlikely to hold in practice. Most public sector economists believe that intertemporal redistributions have real and important effects on the productivity of the economy in the long run.

c. *Investment versus savings incentives*—The analysis of temporary deficits and surplus leads to a related distinction between investment and savings incentives. The distinction matters under the realistic assumption that adjusting the stock of capital is costly, so that different vintages of capital are not perfect substitutes in production.

Investment incentives are policies that favor new capital over existing capital, such as accelerated depreciation allowances and an investment tax credit. These types of incentives act as hidden temporary surpluses because the older generations hold a disproportionate share of the claims to the existing capital stock. Thus, investment incentives redistribute resources from the older to the younger generations, thereby reducing aggregate consumption and increasing the productivity of the

[37] R. Barro, "Are Government Bonds Net Wealth?" *Journal of Political Economy*, 82 (November / December), 1974.

economy in the long run. A tax on land also acts as an investment incentive because land is held disproportionately by the older generations. Finally, a tax substitution of replacing an income tax with a consumption tax can be thought of as a self-financing investment incentive since the older retired generations lose under the substitution. They have already paid income taxes while working, and they will now pay taxes again on their consumption during retirement.

Savings incentives are policies that favor new and old capital equally, such as lower taxes on capital gains, tax exemptions on municipal bonds, and tax-deferred pensions funds and individual retirement accounts (IRAs). A tax substitution of replacing an income tax with a wage (payroll) tax can be thought of as a self-financing savings incentives since the return to all capital becomes untaxed under this substitution. Because savings incentives favor both kinds of capital equally, they are less potent stimulants to saving and investment per dollar than are investment incentives. They do not hit the older generations as hard.

4. *Intratemporal redistributions*—These are balanced-budget redistributions within each generation, such as an annual redistribution from the non-poor to the poor. Intratemporal redistributions are the only fiscal policies that do not have special effects in a dynamic OLG setting because they do not transfer resources across generations.

A Selection of Results

Realistic fiscal policy changes tend to have fairly potent long-run effects in the Auerbach–Kotlikoff model. Here are some examples:

Tax Substitutions

Auerbach and Kotlikoff consider the replacement of a 15% income tax with a consumption tax, a wage tax, and a capital income tax. The first substitution raises average welfare each year in the new steady state, and the last two lower average welfare:[38]

---

[38] The ultimate interest in the policy simulations is the change in consumers' welfare, which can be handled in a number of different ways in a dynamic context. Suppose a policy generates productivity gains and increased national output. Auerbach and Kotlikoff choose a dynamic HEV measure constructed as follows. First, they introduce a distributional authority that continually redistributes income lump sum to all cohorts born before a certain date so that their utility remains constant, unaffected by the policy change. It then distributes all the remaining gains lump sum and equally to the cohorts born after that date. Having redistributed all the increased output, they measure the gain in welfare as the HEV for the latter cohorts, equal to the lump-sum income each cohort would require at the original prices before the policy change to be as well off as they are following the policy change. This method of compensating the two sets of cohorts from the productivity gains tends to reduce the changes in welfare resulting from the policy simulations. The tax substitution results are taken from L. Kotlikoff, "Taxation and Savings: A Neoclassical Perspective," *Journal of Economic Literature*, December 1984, pp. 1601–1603.

1. *Consumption tax*—Replacing an income tax with a consumption tax sharply favors the young and future generations over the older generations. As such, it leads to large increases in saving, investment, capital stock, productivity, and wages before tax. Overall welfare increases by 2.22% per year in the new steady state.

2. *Wage tax*—In this substitution, the elderly gain relative to the young and future generations. Nonetheless, saving, investment, capital stock, and productivity increase because returns to capital are no longer taxed. Overall welfare declines by 0.89% per year in the new steady state, however, primarily because after-tax wages decrease. The wage tax does not enhance productivity as much as the consumption tax because it favors rather than hurts the elderly. In an OLG context, a consumption tax is equivalent to a wage tax plus a one time levy on existing capital of the elderly. The levy equals the present value of the taxes the elderly would have paid under a consumption tax.

3. *Capital income tax*—This substitution lowers overall welfare by 1.14% per year in the new steady state. By increasing the burden on future consumption over current consumption relative to the income tax, a tax on capital income lowers saving, investment, the capital stock, and productivity.

Balanced Budget Increases in the Public Good

The principal conclusion of the Auerbach–Kotlikoff model is that the tax used to finance an increase in G matters quite a bit. For example, financing an increas in G with a consumption tax leads to a big decrease in consumption. Financing the increase with a wage tax mostly decreases the supply of labor; the decrease in consumption is much smaller.

The one drawback of this particular exercise is that G has no direct effect on utility. Therefore, the model cannot consider the possibility that a tax-financed increase in a public good may be welfare enhancing no matter which tax is used. A true balanced-budget incidence experiment would require a complete specification of the public good, including its effects on consumers' utilities, and the use of the incidence measure for a Samuelsonian nonexclusive public good discussed in the first part of the chapter.

Temporary Deficits

Perhaps the most important insight of the Auerbach–Kotlikoff model is the huge real effect of temporary deficits and surpluses. In one exercise, they reduce the income tax from 15 to 10% for 20 years. This requires an income tax rate of approximately 30% in the 21st year to hold the additional debt per person accumulated in years 1–20 constant from then on. As a result, the capital stock falls by 49%, the before-tax wage falls by 14%, and the interest rate increases by 4 percentage points in the new steady state. Keep in mind, however, that the cost of a temporary deficit is not simply that taxes eventually have to be increased, as is often alleged. Rather, it is that a temporary deficit combined with the subsequent tax increase redistributes purchasing power from the younger to the older generations, thereby increasing aggregate consumption.

Auerbach and Kotlikoff also find that asset revaluations following a change in tax policy can be very large. For example, the 1981 Tax Reform Act introduced a number of new investment incentives into the federal corporation income tax, most notably an investment tax credit on equipment and more accelerated depreciation allowances on different classes of assets. Auerbach and Kotlikoff estimated that the resulting asset revaluations led to a $260 billion loss in the value of existing capital. These tax reforms thus represented a huge stimulus to life-cycle saving by redistributing purchasing power from the older to the younger generations.[39]

Intratemporal Redistributions

Auerbach and Kotlikoff find that intratemporal redistributions tend to have fairly modest effects. This is true even if the poor are liquidity constrained and immediately spend whatever transfers they receive each period. There appears to be an approximate balancing each year of the poor's extremely high MPC of their (relatively) small transfers and the non-poor's quite low MPC of the (relatively) large present value of their taxes required to pay for the annual transfers.

The fiscal policy experiments with the OLG model point to an extremely unsettling trade-off between efficiency and equity in the long run. The largest gains in productivity are achieved by policies that exploit the differences in the MPCs of the younger and older generations. In other words, much of the gains in overall efficiency come at the expense of the older generation. The converse is also true. Policies designed to favor the elderly in the name of equity are likely to be harmful to productivity and overall welfare. Finally, if society simply chooses not to hurt its elderly and designs its fiscal policies to be fairly neutral towards them, then it may not be able to realize much gain in productivity or average welfare.

Concluding Caveats

Although the Auerbach–Kotlikoff OLG model has yielded many new insights about the incidence of tax and expenditure incidence relative to the older static models of incidence, the model is not without its problems. For one, the informational assumptions behind the model are highly suspect: Consumers have perfect foresight about future prices but at the same time are fooled by changes in government policy and are myopic regarding aggregate consumption possibilities. Equally problematic is the assumption of perfect competition in labor markets, that labor is always fully employed in the long transition to the steady state. Third, economists do not really

---

[39] L. Kotlikoff, "Taxation and Savings: A Neoclassical Perspective," *Journal of Economic Literature*, December 1984, p. 1613 (the 1981 Tax Reform Act) and p. 1616 (the temporary deficit).

understand saving behavior. The Life-Cycle Hypothesis of consumption and saving is a natural choice for a long-run policy model, with or without bequests, but the LCH has not been supported by empirical research. Fourth, the empirical analysis of investment has not yielded a consensus on the determinants of investment demand. Finally, the introduction of human capital into these models can have fairly dramatic effects. Some brief observations on the last three points follow.

Saving

The chief competitor to the LCH is precautionary saving, which is a response to uncertain income streams. Precautionary saving is known to be less sensitive to changes in after-tax rates of return than life-cycle saving. Eric Engen and William Gale introduced uncertain incomes and precautionary saving into a long-run OLG model and found that replacing the U.S. personal income tax with a flat-rate consumption tax would increase saving by only 1/2%, and steady-state GDP by only 1 to 2%. The elasticity of saving with respect to after-tax income in their model is .39. When they remove the income uncertainty and the precautionary motive for saving, the elasticity rises to 1.94.[40]

Investment

The majority of studies find that the response of investment to changes in the cost of capital are quite low and operate with fairly long lags. Austan Goolsbee has suggested that these results may be due to a low supply response of many kinds of capital goods. He finds that a 10% investment tax credit on equipment raises equipment prices almost immediately by 3.5 to 7%, and that the price effects lasts for a couple of years.[41] Therefore, much of the tax incentive to stimulate investment demand is captured at first by the suppliers of capital as increased rents. The short-run price response is important, because from 1959–1988 Congress changed the tax laws affecting the cost of capital at least once every 4 years. Goolsbee believes that the price response explains why capital goods suppliers lobby for tax reductions, lags are important in investment demand equations, and the estimated demand elasticities of capital are so low. By taking into account the price responses, he obtains very high estimates of the demand elasticity, in the range of 0.95 to 2.15. Still, the

[40] E. Engen and W. Gale, "Consumption Taxes and Saving: The Role of Uncertainty in Tax Reform," *American Economic Review*, May 1997. Part of the small saving response is also explained by the exemption from tax, or the reduced taxation, of many forms of saving under the personal income tax, such as saving for retirement, imputed rents, and capital gains.

[41] A. Goolsbee, "Investment Tax Incentives, Prices, and the Supply of Capital Goods," *Quarterly Journal of Economics*, February 1998. The supply response is especially low for equipment that has large backorders at the time of a tax change or that faces low competition from imports. For an overview of the empirical literature on investment demand, see R. Chirinko, "Business Fixed Investment Spending," *Journal of Economic Literature*, December 1993; R. Chirinko, S. Fazzari, and A. Meyer, "How Responsive Is Business Capital Formation to Its User Cost? An Exploration With Micro Data," *Journal of Public Economics*, October 1999.

response of the capital stock to tax changes is sharply reduced in the short and medium run by the low supply elasticities.

Human Capital

Human capital is a very important resource. Economists frequently cite the estimate by Davies and Whalley that the stock of human capital is three times the stock of physical capital in the United States.[42] Moreover, incorporating human capital into an OLG growth model can dramatically alter the effects of different kinds of tax policies.

Human capital has a number of distinctive features relative to physical capital. First, it depreciates completely at retirement, so that it cannot be passed on to heirs. Second, the taxation of human capital arises primarily from taxes on wages and salaries that reduce the returns to human capital. Whether it is heavily or lightly taxed under an income tax depends in part on how human capital is acquired. It is potentially vulnerable to heavier taxation than physical capital because there is no depreciation allowance for human capital to be taken against wage income. Thus, both the principal and returns to human capital are taxed. But, if human capital is received through an on-the-job training program and "paid for" by a reduction in wages during the training period, than the investment in human capital may be effectively expensed, in which case there is no marginal tax on human capital. Much of human capital is received through formal education, however, which is only partially subsidized. Therefore, human capital is taxed under an income tax, and potentially quite heavily. Consider the relative effects of a comprehensive income tax on physical and human capital. The taxation of interest income and other returns to capital is borne directly by physical capital but not human capital. Conversely, the taxation of wage and salary income is borne directly by human capital but not physical capital. On net, a comprehensive income tax discriminates against human capital in favor of physical capital because the majority of human capital is not expensed so that the remaining principal is taxed as well as the returns. Finally, although human capital cannot be bequeathed directly, it does contribute to the overall stock of knowledge which has a lasting and important effect on the productivity of the economy.

Marc Nerlove *et al.* added human capital to Diamond's original OLG model and compared the zero-tax steady state with the steady state under various tax policies.[43] None of the human capital was expensed in their model. Among their findings:

---

[42] J. Davies and J. Whalley, "Taxes and Capital Formation: How Important Is Human Capital?," *NBER Working Paper #2899*, National Bureau of Economic Research, Cambridge, MA, March 1989.

[43] M. Nerlove, A. Razin, E. Sadka, and R. von Weizsacker, "Comprehensive Income Taxation, Investments in Human and Physical Capital, and Productivity," *Journal of Public*

1. A proportional 50% comprehensive income tax led to a big increase in the ratio of physical to human capital and reduced productivity by 90%, but the tax increased welfare because it moved the economy closer to the Golden Rule steady state.

2. Human capital has such an important effect on productivity in their model that a wage tax *lowers* productivity because of its bias against human capital and a tax on capital income *raises* productivity because of its bias in favor of human capital. Human capital does not escape a tax burden under a capital income tax because the reduction in the stock of physical capital reduces wages. Nonetheless, the relative bias in favor of human capital under the capital tax is sufficient to increase productivity in their model.

Despite the modeling uncertainties, the OLG framework is useful for comparing the potential long-run effects of different kinds of fiscal policies. Also, its analysis of intergenerational redistributions is an important contribution to the public sector literature.

The Fullerton–Rogers Lifetime CGE Model

The last stage in the evolution of tax incidence models came in 1993. Don Fullerton and Diane Rogers developed a lifetime CGE model for a study of the U.S. tax system produced for the Brookings Institution.[44] They sought to combine the strengths of the three main models of economy-wide tax incidence at the time: the complex representation of the economy made possible by the CGE model, the lifetime perspective and some of the dynamics of the OLG model, and the use of detailed data on families and individuals that characterizes the sources and uses approach. Their model is far too complex to discuss in any detail. We will only highlight some of its novel features and the main incidence findings.

The principal innovations in their model were on the consumption side. Fullerton and Rogers began with a sample of 838 individuals from the Panel Study of Income Dynamics (PSID), which had collected economic, social, and demographic data on families and individuals for 18 years by the time of their study. They used the sample to estimate a wage equation as a function of age and other demographic variables and then combined the estimates with actual data to construct lifetime wage profiles for everyone in the sample. The lifetime wage profiles are then used to compute the present value of the labor endowment for each of the individuals in the sample, their potential lifetime incomes. The labor endowment equals the sum of the estimated wages at each

---

Economics, March 1993. A more recent analysis of the taxation of human capital using a Ramsey growth model is P. Trostel, "The Effect of Taxation on Human Capital," *Journal of Political Economy*, April 1997.

[44] D. Fullerton and D., Rogers, *Who Bears the Lifetime Tax Burden?*, The Brookings Institution, Washington, D.C., 1993.

age of their economic lives times 4000 hours, the number of hours assumed to be available for labor or leisure each year, discounted to present value. The people are divided into 12 income classes on the basis of their potential incomes. Thus, everyone in the sample is characterized by age and income class. These constitute the consumers in their GCE model.

The other elements of the model are highly complex but in line with existing static and dynamic CGE models in the early 1990s. There are 17 different consumer goods, 5 different classes of assets (equipment, structures, land, inventories, and intangibles), 37 representative firms divided into corporate and noncorporate sectors, and production functions for each good whose arguments are capital, labor, and intermediate inputs. The choice of variables in the production functions was guided by intput/output tables for the U.S. economy. The firms' behavior is not dynamic in the sense that they make no investment decisions. The dynamics in the model center on the consumers' saving decisions, with investment set equal to saving each period.

The government produces one of the 17 consumer goods for sale to consumers, and a public good that it supplies free of charge. The public good enters separably into consumers' utility functions. The government also gives lump-sum transfer payments to consumers, which are estimated for each consumer based on the actual pattern of government transfers by age and income class. Government revenues are collected from the five major U.S. taxes, and the government's budget is balanced each period.

Markets are assumed to be perfectly competitive. A foreign sector is added to close the model with exports equal to imports, and the model is calibrated to the U.S. economy.

The individuals are LCH consumers with a bequest motive included, with 60-year economic lives from ages 20–79. The exogenous variables for each person are an inheritance, which Fullerton and Rogers estimate from actual data on inheritances by income class; the lifetime wage profile; a set of tax rules; and a lifetime profile of lump-sum transfer payments received from the government. Given these variables, which they know with perfect foresight, consumers maximize their lifetime utilities in a three-stage sequence. First, they decide how much of their potential income to "spend" each period on consumption and leisure versus how much to save, in accordance with a CES utility function. Next, they decide on the allocation of their "spending" between leisure time and consumer goods each period, again in accordance with a CES utility function. Finally, they determine their purchases of the 17 consumer goods each period so as to maximize a Stone–Geary utility function over the goods. The model also allocates the consumers' purchases of private goods to each of the industries, and then to the corporate and non corporate sectors within each industry

The tax incidence simulations are pure tax substitutions. They consist of changing one or more of the existing taxes and replacing the revenue gained (lost) with a proportionate tax cut (tax) on the consumers' potential income.

Because the revenue-compensating tax is levied on potential income, it is a lump-sum tax. The CGE model simulates the effects of the tax change on the evolution of the supply of labor, saving, capital, outputs, and prices. The incidence comparisons are based on the lifetime consequences of the new evolution of the economy for the individuals within each income class. The measure of the change in economic welfare is the consumers' lifetime HEV which, for a tax cut, is the present value of the lump-sum income that the consumer would be willing to accept to forego the price changes. The relative burdens are computed for each income class. A tax is progressive if the HEV is proportionately higher for the higher income classes. Finally, since the incidence of each of the five major taxes is determined by removing it and replacing it by the proportionate tax on potential income, the incidence of each tax is being compared relative to the incidence of a proportionate, equal-yield, lump-sum tax.

Only some of Fullerton and Rogers' results were consistent with those of the static CGE and sources and uses models at the time. In line with existing studies, F/R found that the personal income tax was progressive, with the burden in terms of lifetime potential income ranging from 5% for the lowest income class to 19% for the highest income class. They also found that the sales and payroll taxes were regressive.

The surprises were the property tax and the corporation income tax. The incidence of the property tax fell on all capital in their model because of the competitive assumptions, which tended to increase the burden on the higher income classes. But it also increased housing costs, which disproportionately burdened the lower income classes. Thus, the property tax had a U-shaped pattern of lifetime incidence. The corporation income tax was so small that it had no noticeable effect on the sources side of the model. It did, however, lead to a reallocation of production towards items that used lightly taxed forms of capital, with some resulting adjustments in the relative costs and prices of the consumer goods. The relative price adjustments turned out to be anti-poor, so that the corporation income tax was slightly regressive overall.

Overall, the Fullerton–Rogers results appear to be roughly consistent with the general consensus that the overall U.S. tax system is mildly progressive even in a lifetime context, largely because the federal and state personal income taxes are progressive.[45]

---

[45] As this book went to press, Altig et al. published an expanded version of the Auerbach-Kotlikoff model that includes many features of the Fullerton-Rogers lifetime CGE model. Their hybrid model has 12 income classes, but not as many goods and factors as the Fullerton-Rogers model. The multiple income classes allow them to analyze the effect of various tax substitutions by cohort and income class. For instance, they found that substituting an ideal expenditures tax for the current U.S. federal personal income tax hurts the high income elderly proportionately more than the low income elderly. A noteworthy prediction of their model is that switching to an expenditures tax would raise steady state output in the United States by 9%. D. Altig, A. Auerbach, L. Kotlikoff, K. Smetters, and J. Walliser, "Simulating Fundamental Tax Reform in the United States, *American Economic Review*, June 2001.

REFERENCES

Aaron, H., and McGuire, M., "Public Goods and Income Distribution," *Econometrica*, November 1970.

Altig, D., Auerbach, A., Kotlikoff, L., Smetters, K., and Walliser, J. "Simulating Fundamental Tax Reform in the United States," *American Economic Review*, June 2001.

Aronson, J., and Lambert, P., "Decomposing the Gini Coefficient To Reveal the Vertical, Horizontal, and Reranking Effects of Income Taxation," *National Tax Journal*, June 1994.

Aronson, J., Johnson, P., and Lambert, P., "Redistributive Effect and Unequal Income Tax Treatment," *Economic Journal*, March 1994.

Atkinson, A., "The Distribution of the Tax Burden," in J. Quigley and E. Smolensky, Eds., *Modern Public Finance*, Harvard University Press, Cambridge, MA, 1994, chap. 2.

Auerbach, A., and Kotlikoff, L., *Dynamic Fiscal Policy*, Cambridge University Press, New York, 1987.

Barro, R., "Are Government Bonds Net Wealth?" *Journal of Political Economy*, 82 (November / December), 1974.

Blinder, A., "The Level and Distribution of Economic Well-Being," in M. Feldstein, Ed., *The American Economy in Transition*, University of Chicago Press, Chicago, 1980.

Browning, E., and Johnson, W., *The Distribution of the Tax Burden*, American Enterprise Institute for Public Policy Research, Washington, D. C., 1979.

Budget of the United States Government, Fiscal Year 2001, Supplement, U.S. Government Printing Office, Washington, D.C., 2000, part Five: Historical Tables, Table 2.1.

Chirinko, R., "Business Fixed Investment Spending," *Journal of Economic Literature*, December 1993.

Chirinko, R., Fazzari, S., and Meyer, A., "How Responsive Is Business Capital Formation to Its User Cost? An Exploration with Micro Data," *Journal of Public Economics*, October 1999.

Davies, J., and Whalley, J., "Taxes and Capital Formation: How Important Is Human Capital?," *NBER Working Paper #2899*, National Bureau of Economic Research, Cambridge, MA, March 1989.

Davies, J., St. Hilaire, F., and Whalley, J., "Some Calculations of Lifetime Tax Incidence," *American Economic Review*, September 1984.

Diamond, P., "National Debt in a Neoclassical Growth Model," *American Economic Review*, December 1965.

Ebert, U., and Moyes, P., "Consistent Income Tax Structures When Households Are Heterogeneous," *Journal of Economic Theory*, January 2000.

Engen, E., and Gale, W., "Consumption Taxes and Saving: The Role of Uncertainty in Tax Reform," *American Economic Review*, May 1997.

Fullerton, D., and Rogers, D., *Who Bears the Lifetime Tax Burden?*, The Brookings Institution, Washington, D.C., 1993.

Gillespie, W., "Effect of Public Expenditures on the Distribution of Income," in R. Musgrave, Ed., *Essays in Fiscal Federalism*, The Brookings Institution, Washington, D. C., 1965.

Goolsby, A., "Investment Tax Incentives, Prices, and the Supply of Capital Goods," *Quarterly Journal of Economics*, February 1998.

Hines, J., "What Is Benefit Taxation?," *Journal of Public Economics*, March 2000.

Kakwani, N., "Measurement of Tax Progressivity: An International Comparison," *Economic Journal*, March 1977.

Keen, M., Papapanagos, H., and Shorrocks, A., "Tax Reform and Progressivity," *Economic Journal*, January 2000.

Kiefer, D., "Distributional Tax Progressivity Indexes," *National Tax Journal*, December, 1984.

Kiefer, D., "A Comparative Analysis of Tax Progressivity in the United States: A Reexamination," plus "Comments" and "Reply," *Public Finance Quarterly*, January 1991.

Kotlikoff, L., "Taxation and Savings: A Neoclassical Perspective," *Journal of Economic Literature*, December 1984.

Kotlikoff, L., and Summers, L., "Tax Incidence," in A. Auerbach and M. Feldstein, Eds., *Handbook of Public Economics*, North-Holland Elsevier, New York, 1985, Vol. II, chap. 17.

Lambert, P., "Evaluating Impact Effects of Tax Reforms," *Journal of Economic Surveys*, September 1993.

Lambert, P., *The Distribution and Redistribution on Income: A Mathematical Analysis*, second ed., University Press, Manchester, 1993.

Maital, S., "Apportionment of Public Goods Benefits to Individuals," *Public Finance*, Vol. 3, 1975.

McGuire, M., "Public Goods and Income Distribution," *Econometrica*, November 1970.

McLure, C., and Thirsk, W., "A Simplified Exposition of the Harberger Model, II: Expenditure Incidence," *National Tax Journal*, June 1975.

Metcalf, G., "A Distributional Analysis of Green Tax Reforms," *National Tax Journal*, December 1999.

Moyes, P., and Shorrocks, A., "The Impossibility of a Progressive Tax Structure," *Journal of Public Economics*, July 1998.

Nerlove, M., Razin, A., Sadka, E., and von Weizsacker, R., "Comprehensive Income Taxation, Investments in Human and Physical Capital, and Productivity," *Journal of Public Economics*, March 1993.

Pechman, J., *Who Paid the Taxes, 1966–85?*, The Brookings Institution, Washington, D.C., 1985.

Pechman, J., and Okner, B., *Who Bears the Tax Burden?*, The Brookings Institution, Washington, D.C., 1974.

Scarf, H., "On the Computation of Equilibrium Prices," in *Ten Economic Studies in the Tradition of Irving Fisher*, Wiley, New York, 1967.

Scarf, H., "An Example of an Algorithm for Calculating General Equilibrium Prices," *American Economic Review*, September 1969.

Shoven, J., and Whalley, J., "Applied General Equilibrium Models of Taxation and International Trade," *Journal of Economic Literature*, September 1984.

Trostel, P., "The Effect of Taxation on Human Capital," *Journal of Political Economy*, April 1997.

U.S. Bureau of the Census website: www.census.gov/govs/estimate/99st/ss.xls.

Whalley, J., "Regression or Progression: The Taxing Question of Incidence," *Canadian Journal of Economics*, November 1984.

18

THE SECOND-BEST THEORY OF PUBLIC EXPENDITURES: OVERVIEW

Second-best public expenditure theory has been at the forefront of theoretical developments in public sector economics for the past 40 years. The latest wave of research is exploring the effects of private information on public sector decision rules, just as private information has dominated recent developments in tax theory.

In extending the methodology of second-best tax theory to expenditure theory, public sector theorists have shattered the received doctrine of first-best expenditure theory that is still featured in the undergraduate textbooks. No longer is it possible to accept, even as approximations, such time-honored decisions rules as $\sum \text{MRS} = \text{MRT}$ for externalities, and marginal cost pricing for decreasing cost services, rules that bear close intuitive relationships to competitive markets. As it now stands, public expenditure theory is more than a little chaotic, each new journal article pushing in new directions and offering new insights, with little in the way of synthesis to provide some clues as to where second-best expenditure theory will eventually lead. Perhaps this is as it must be.

The essence of second-best analysis is the addition of constraints to the basic first-best general equilibrium model beyond the fundamental constraints of production technologies and market clearance (and possibly resource limitations). The promise of second-best theory is its move toward realism, that the additional constraints capture important features of actual economies such as the existence of monopoly elements in the private sector, distorting taxes, and private information. The drawback of the theory is that the second-best decision rules necessarily vary depending upon both the number of constraints added to the model and the precise form that each constraint takes. Unlike first-best analysis, then, the set of policy prescriptions is virtually unlimited. Furthermore, no second-best theory can possibly incorporate all the additional constraints that would be necessary to approximate reality. As was noted in Chapter 12, current second-best models accurately portray only a very few specific distortions operating in the economy. They model the remaining parts of the economic system along standard first-best lines. Hence, the state of the art is still but a hesitant first step or two toward reality despite 40 years of analysis. Even so, virtually none of the old first-best decision rules has remained standing. Needless to say, the goal of developing a widely accepted normative economic theory of the public sector appears increasingly less plausible.

A few chapters in a broad text such as this one cannot do justice to all the ways that public sector theorists have chosen to rework public expenditure theory in a second-best context, much less provide a comprehensive synthesis of this large and varied literature. In lieu of this, the next few chapters undertake a far more modest task. We merely want to highlight a few of the principal second-best public expenditure results to date and to demonstrate the more common methodological tools used to analyze public expenditure theory in a second-best context.

The topics have been chosen to lend some coherence to the overall text. We hope to achieve this by limiting the analysis for the most part to the specific public expenditure problems discussed in Part II under first-best theory. In addition, we will concentrate on the two most common second-best constraints employed in the literature. One is the existence of private information. The other is the government's need to rely on distorting unit "commodity" taxes (subsidies) on consumer goods and factors to finance its expenditures. The market environment, in contrast, is assumed to be perfectly competitive and therefore first best, unless specifically stated otherwise. We will also usually assume that the government's budget must balance. These additional assumptions are commonly employed in the second-best literature.

Structuring the public expenditure models in this way allows us to draw directly upon the models developed in Chapters 13–16 for analyzing the second-best theory of taxation. More often than not, these tax models require only slight modifications to incorporate public expenditure questions. This is why it made sense to reverse the development of Part II and consider second-best tax theory before second-best expenditure theory. It is natural to introduce distorting taxes as the additional constraint necessitating a second-best approach to public expenditure questions. The tax models also prove convenient as an analytical framework for developing two of the strongest results in all of second-best theory. The first is that the optimal commodity tax rules are unaltered by the presence of government expenditures. The second is that second-best public expenditure decision rules tend to have their most appealing and simplest interpretations when distorting taxes are set optimally to maximize social welfare or minimize loss.

Regarding methodology, some of the expenditure problems will be analyzed from the perspective of social welfare maximization, others from the perspective of utility maximization or loss minimization of a representative consumer. The latter is especially useful when distributional considerations are not central to the point being developed. Switching the analytical framework in this manner will allow us to demonstrate a variety of models suitable for analyzing second-best expenditure questions. It should not be confusing since both approaches have been fully explored in the preceding chapters on second-best tax theory. With these goals in mind, a selection of second-best public expenditure results will be presented in four relatively brief and self-contained chapters.

Chapter 19 analyzes transfer payments under second-best assumptions, with an emphasis on the ways that private information affects the optimal design of government transfer programs. We saw in Chapter 17 that the theory of distorting transfers under perfect information is essentially subsumed within second-best tax theory, because transfers are analytically equivalent to negative taxes. Not so the theory of transfers under private information. Private information raises many important issues with the design of transfer programs that are absent with taxation. Taxpayers are particularly concerned that transfer recipients might use their private information to undermine the intent of the transfer programs, such as able-bodied people accepting public assistance instead of working. Much of the recent theoretical work on transfers has focused on the mechanism design problem of preventing potential recipients from misrepresenting themselves to the government. Two central design issues are whether transfers should be cash or in-kind to prevent cheating and whether transfers can be decentralized or must instead be provided directly by the government. The chapter also considers some second-best design issues associated with transfers that are unrelated to private information.

Chapter 20 reworks the first-best theory of externalities contained in Chapters 6–8. The chapter begins with the question of how of distorting taxation affects standard first-best decision rules, under the assumption of perfect information. In a first-best environment, whether one considers a nonexclusive Samuelsonian public good or exclusive activities that generate either "individualized" or "aggregate" externalities, we saw that the government should achieve an allocation in which $\sum_{h=1}^{H} MRS^h = MRT$.[1] For

---

[1] This applies, of course, only to consumption externalities. The standard production-externality rule is that $MRS = \sum_{j=1}^{J} MRT^j$ for J firms.

exclusive goods, the government can, in principle, tax (subsidize) the externality-generating activity to achieve the desired result.

The summation rule fails to hold for any of these cases in a second-best
environment. Chapter 20 will demonstrate this for Samuelsonian nonexclusive
goods when the revenues to pay for this good must be raised with distorting
commodity taxes. This problem was first considered by A. C. Pigou in 1947 but
formalized more precisely in the 1970s, first by Anthony Atkinson and Nicholas Stern and then separately by Peter Diamond and David Wildasin.[2] The
main question of interest is whether applying the first best $\sum \mathrm{MRS} = \mathrm{MRT}$
rule would lead to too much or too little of the public good when taxes are
distorting.[3]

The effect of private information on externalities is difficult to characterize because it depends upon the nature of the private information and the
form of the externality. Rather than attempt a comprehensive analysis, the
chapter shows how private information can alter the efficiency properties of
two time-honored externality policy prescriptions for externalities from first-
best theory, Pigovian taxes, and Coasian bargains.

Chapter 21 turns to a well-known second-best result for decreasing cost
industries. We saw in Chapter 9 that these services should be provided at
marginal cost prices in a first-best policy environment, with lump-sum taxes
covering the resulting losses to the firm. We noted, however, that these
services are typically priced at average cost in the United States, and considered a number of equity issues arising from this practice. Chapter 21
expands upon the average-cost-pricing philosophy by applying it to a multiproduct firm. Marcel Boiteux wrote the classic article on this issue in 1956. He
considered the pricing and investment implications of requiring that a multiservice decreasing-cost industry cover its full costs out of total revenues. Price
does not necessarily equal average cost for each service,[4] but the prices on all
the services combined must raise enough total revenue to cover all costs. The
Boiteux problem is especially intriguing for public sector economics because

---

[2] A. C. Pigou, *A Study in Public Finance*, third ed., Macmillan, London, 1947; A. Atkinson and
N. Stern, "Pigou, Taxation, and Public Goods," *Review of Economic Studies*, January 1974; P.
Diamond, "A Many Person Ramsey Tax Rule," *Journal of Public Economics*, November 1975; D.
Wildasin, "On Public Good Provision with Distortionary Taxation," *Economic Inquiry*, April 1984.

[3] Leuthold derived the second-best tax rules for an aggregate externality when society
cannot redistribute lump sum to satisfy the first-best interpersonal equity conditions. He showed
that the failure to satisfy interpersonal equity destroys the optimal properties of competitive
markets even for purely private goods that are not generating any external effects. The government must tax (subsidize) these goods as well. The pervasiveness of government intervention in
the market economy is obviously a discouraging result for capitalist societies. See J. Leuthold,
"The Optimal Congestion Charge When Equity Matters," *Economica*, February 1976. Also see
J. Hartwick, "Optimal Price Discrimination," *Journal of Public Economics*, February 1978.

[4] If two or more services commonly use one or more resources, it is not always possible to
define average costs for each of them, even in the long run. See M. Boiteux, "On the Management
of Public Monopolies Subject to Budgetary Constraints," *Journal of Economic Theory*, September 1971 (translated from the original version in French, *Econometrica*, January 1956).

it closely parallels the optimal commodity tax problem of Chapter 13 and 14 in which the government has to set taxes (consumer prices) to collect a given amount of revenue. As we shall see, the optimal pricing rules for the multiproduct decreasing-cost firm have virtually the same interpretation as the optimal tax rules. They also apply to any government agency that operates under a legislated budget constraint, whether or not the agency's output exhibits decreasing cost production.

Chapter 22 concludes the second-best public expenditure analysis by considering the general problem of government production in a second-best environment. There are no specific constraints on government production possibilities; they can exhibit decreasing, increasing, or constant returns to scale. Furthermore, the government is permitted to produce anything that the private sector produces. The analysis places only two realistic constraints on government activity. First, if government producers buy and sell inputs and outputs, they must do so at the (competitive) prices faced by the private sector producers. Otherwise, they may not be able to compete effectively with the private sector for scarce inputs or the sale of their outputs. Second, if government production incurs a deficit (surplus) at these prices, the government must use distorting commodity taxes (subsidies) to cover the deficit (return the surplus). This type of general expenditure model was first explored in depth in the 1970s, most notably by Peter Diamond and James Mirrlees and Robin Boadway.[5] Diamond and Mirrlees asked the following questions in their seminal article entitled "Optimal Taxation and Public Production:"

1. Does the existence of government production alter the optimal commodity tax rules derived in the context of raising revenue simply for the sake of raising revenue? The answer turned out to be no.
2. What production rules should the government follow in the presence of optimal commodity taxation to cover production deficits (return surpluses)? Their answer to this question was especially surprising. They showed that if the distorting taxes are optimal, then the government should follow standard *first-best* production rules.

Boadway generalized their analysis to consider the welfare effects of raising additional taxes (subsidies) and/or marginally increasing government production from *any* initial values of distorting taxes and government production, not necessarily the optimal values. As might be imagined, the resulting tax and expenditure rules are extremely complex. One nice result, however, is that the addition of government production does not affect the nonoptimal marginal tax loss rules developed in Chapters 13 and 14.

[5] P. Diamond and J. Mirrlees, "Optimal Taxation and Public Production," *American Economic Review*, March June 1971 (2 parts; Part I: Production Efficiency, Part II: Tax Rules); R. Boadway, "Cost-Benefit Rules and General Equilibrium," *Review of Economic Studies*, June 1975; R. Boadway, "Integrating Equity and Efficiency in Applied Welfare Economics," *Quarterly Journal of Economics*, November 1976.

Chapter 22 develops each of these results and sets the stage for Part IV, Cost–Benefit Analysis. Cost–benefit analysis asks how one can apply the results of normative public sector theory to the analysis of government investment projects. In applying the theory, the predominant issue is the underlying policy environment that one is willing to assume. Is it "approximately" first best or second best? If second best, exactly what constraints make it so? The answers given to these questions are always compromises of sorts, since the real world is many times more complex than any of our theoretical models. But the answers are crucial, nonetheless, for any subsequent cost–benefit study and its policy recommendations. With the conclusion of Chapter 22, all the major first- and second-best results of public expenditure theory will be in hand, ready for application.

REFERENCES

Atkinson, A., and Stern, N., "Pigou, Taxation, and Public Goods," *Review of Economic Studies*, January 1974.

Boadway, R. "Cost–Benefit Rules and General Equilibrium," *Review of Economic Studies*, June 1975.

Boadway, R., "Integrating Equity and Efficiency in Applied Welfare Economics," *Quarterly Journal of Economics*, November 1976.

Boiteux, M., "On the Management of Public Monopolies Subject to Budgetary Constraints," *Journal of Economic Theory*, September 1971 (translated from French in *Econometrica*, January 1956).

Diamond, P. A., "A Many Person Ramsey Tax Rule," *Journal of Public Economics*, November 1975.

Diamond, P. A., and Mirrlees, J., "Optimal Taxation and Public Production" (2 parts; Part I: Production Efficiency, Part II: Tax Rules), *American Economic Review*, March, June 1971.

Hartwick, J., "Optimal Price Discrimination," *Journal of Public Economics*, February 1978.

Leuthold, J., "The Optimal Congestion Charge When Equity Matters," *Economica*, February 1976.

Pigou, A. C., *A Study in Public Finance*, third ed., Macmillan, London, 1947.

Wildasin, D., "On Public Good Provision with Distortionary Taxation," *Economic Inquiry*, April 1984.

19

TRANSFER PAYMENTS AND PRIVATE INFORMATION

Our second-best analysis of transfer payments began with the discussion of expenditure incidence in Chapter 17. We noted there that transfers are fully equivalent to negative taxes when the distortions take the form of distortions in prices from their first-best values. The equivalence of taxes and transfers is more general. Because transfers are just negative taxes, taxes and transfers are, in principle, analytically equivalent except for sign in any policy environment. Nonetheless, transfer payments raise a different set of practical issues from taxes in an environment made second best because of private or asymmetric information.

The practical differences arise because the government's mechanism design problem differs for taxes and transfers under private information. The problem for taxes is to prevent people from evading their tax liabilities. The problem for transfers is to prevent people from accepting transfers that are not meant for them. To this end, the analysis of transfer payments under private information has yielded a number of insights on three issues: whether transfers should be cash or in-kind, whether transfers can be decentralized through market-based subsidies rather than provided directly by government agencies, and the limits of redistribution in the presence of private information. Chapter 19 discusses these three issues, after considering a number of other practical design issues related to cash transfers.

FIRST-BEST INSIGHTS

A quick review of what first-best analysis has to say about transfer payments will be useful as a starting point. The two main decision rules for first-best transfers are the interpersonal equity (IE) conditions of social welfare maximization and pareto-optimal redistributions. The IE conditions are always applicable in the mainstream public sector model since they are among the necessary conditions for a social welfare maximum. The pareto-optimal conditions are applicable if people are altruistic.

Interpersonal Equity Conditions

The IE conditions are indifferent between cash or in-kind transfers or taxes. The only requirement is that the transfers (taxes) be lump sum. The operative principle is that if any one good or factor is redistributed to satisfy the IE conditions *and* the pareto-optimal conditions for a social welfare maximum hold, then the IE conditions are necessarily satisfied for all the other goods and factors. (A cash redistribution can be thought of as a redistribution of income earned by a factor in fixed supply.)

The lump-sum redistributions cannot be decentralized; they must be undertaken by the government. Only the pareto-optimal conditions can be decentralized under first-best social welfare maximization, and then only in the absence of externalities, decreasing cost production, monopoly power, and other such problems that may require more direct government intervention.

Finally, the range of possible redistributions through lump-sum taxes and transfers is as broad as possible, limited only by the boundaries of the first-best utility possibilities frontier.

Pareto-Optimal Redistributions

Both the form of the transfers and the ability to decentralize depend on the nature of people's altruistic impulses. Think in terms of the rich being altruistic toward the poor.

One possibility is that the utility of the rich depends on some item(s) of consumption by the poor, such as the amount of food they have. In this case the pareto-optimal conditions call for in-kind transfers and decentralization. The poor's purchases of food are directly subsidized and the poor can buy as much food they want at the subsidized price. The subsidy equals the sum of each rich person's MRS between the poor's consumption of food and his or her consumption of the numeraire good. The only caveat is if the poor's purchase are restricted for some reason, such as to discourage resales of the subsidized item by the poor. The food subsidy is equivalent to a cash transfer if the restriction is binding.

The other possibility is that the utility of the rich depends on the entire utility of the poor, that is, on the amount of resources the poor have. In this case, the transfers should be cash because a cash transfer maximizes the utility of the poor for a given dollar amount transferred. The cash transfers (and taxes on the rich) have to be centralized.

Finally, pareto-optimal redistributions are gain–gain propositions— both the donors and the recipients gain. As such, they restrict the range of the utility possibilities frontier to the region along which all gain–gain redistributions have been exhausted. The pareto-optimal conditions cannot determine the optimal position on the restricted frontier, however. In the social welfare maximizing context of the mainstream model, the interpersonal equity conditions must be applied as a second layer of redistribution to reach Bator's bliss point on the restricted frontier.

The Samaritan's Dilemma

A dynamic variation of the pareto-optimal redistribution model that we did not discuss in Chapter 10 is the *Samaritan's dilemma*, a phrase coined by James Buchanan. The dilemma can arise whenever the donor and recipient interact for at least two periods. The central feature of the dynamic model is moral hazard on the part of the recipient who, having received a transfer in the first period, can influence the probability of receiving transfers in subsequent periods by relying on the good will of the donor. The model calls for an in-kind transfer in the first period to avoid the moral hazard.

Think of parents and their teenaged son. Suppose the parents are purely altruistic toward their son and give him a large amount of cash. The son has an incentive to squander the cash on consumption goods rather than put it to some productive use such as an education if he is confident that the parents will never allow him to suffer. The son knows that the parents are "Samaritans" who will provide more cash transfers in the future even though he has behaved badly in the past.

The parents' dilemma is that they want what is best for their son. On the one hand, they know that the son would prefer a cash transfer that he can spend as he wishes. On the other hand, they can override the moral hazard incentive if they tie the gift first period to a productive endeavor, such as paying the son's tuition for a college education. By tying the aid in this way, the parents prevent the son from using the gift inefficiently and they also reduce or eliminate the need for future gifts.

In fact, a large percentage of *inter vivos* giving from parents to their children is in-kind rather than cash. One explanation for this is simple paternalism, that the parents think they know what is best for their children and they control the resources. Another possibility, however, is simply the desire to avoid the moral hazard associated with a gift of cash. Hence, the dynamic model suggests that in-kind transfers may be efficient even if altruistic donors consider the entire utility of the recipients, whereas the static model would call for cash transfers in that case.[1]

CASH TRANSFERS: BROAD-BASED OR TARGETED?

Any society that chooses to redistribute income (cash) to alleviate poverty faces an immediate practical difficulty. It must decide between a broad-based or targeted approach to redistributing, and each has its strengths and weaknesses.

The simplest broad-based approach is to use a so-called *credit income tax* of the form Tax $= -C + T(Y)$. Everyone receives a credit of $C and then pays tax on their entire income according to the function $T(Y)$. The credit is refundable, meaning that it is received even if $T(Y) < C$.

The targeted approach offers subsidies only to people with low incomes and also exempts low levels of income from taxation under the income tax. This is the approach chosen by the United States. It targets subsidies to the poor under various public assistance programs: Temporary Assistance to Needy Families (TANF), Supplemental Security Income (SSI), Medicaid, Food Stamps, the Earned Income Tax Credit (EITC), and a number of smaller programs. Then the federal and state income taxes exempt the first dollars of income from taxation through a combination of personal exemptions and standard deductions, such that taxpayers with incomes below the poverty line usually have no tax liability.

A simple example offered by Edgar and Jacquelene Browning illustrates the trade-offs between the broad-based and targeted approaches.[2] Suppose there are five income classes, with equal numbers of people in each income class: $5000, $10,000, $15,000, $20,000, and $25,000. Suppose also that society wants to distribute $3000 to the lowest income group. Two policies that accomplish this are

1. A (linear) credit income tax, $T = -\$4500 + .3Y$.
2. A $3000 subsidy to the lowest income class, paid for by a (linear) income tax that exempts the first $10,000 of income and taxes income above $10,000 at a flat rate of 10%.

[1] J. Buchanan, "The Samaritan's Dilemma," in E. Phelps, Ed., *Altruism, Morality and Economic Theory*, Russell Sage Foundation, New York, 1975, pp. 71–85. For a more recent discussion, see N. Bruce and M. Waldman, "Transfers in Kind: Why They Can Be Efficient and Nonpaternalistic," *American Economic Review*, December 1991, pp. 1345–1351.

[2] E. Browning and J. Browning, *Public Finance and the Price System*, second ed., Macmillan, New York, 1983, pp. 276–284.

TABLE 19.1   Subsidies and Taxes Paid by Income Class

	Income Class				
	$5000	**$10000**	**$15000**	**$20000**	**$25000**
Credit income tax					
$(T = -C + .3Y)$					
Subsidy ($)	4500	4500	4500	4500	4500
Tax ($)	1500	3000	4500	6000	7500
Net tax (subsidy) ($)	(3000)	(1500)	0	1500	3000
Targeted subsidy ($3000)					
$(T = .1(Y - 10,000))$					
Subsidy ($)	3000	0	0	0	0
Tax ($)	0	0	500	1000	1500
Net tax (subsidy) ($)	(3000)	0	500	1000	1500

Table 19.1 provides the subsidies and taxes paid by each income class under these alternatives.

The credit income tax leads to a lot of churning. It collects and distributes $22,500, with a net redistribution of only $4500. It also requires a fairly high marginal tax rate of 30%, which could generate substantial dead-weight losses. The example shows that the credit income tax is not a very effective redistributive mechanism. Even a modest amount of redistribution to the poor can require a very large tax-transfer program that may generate a large amount of dead-weight loss.

The targeted approach appears to be much more effective on the surface. It collects and transfers only $3000 and the marginal tax rate on the taxpayers is only 1/3 as high as the credit income tax, leading to much less dead-weight loss. (Recall that dead-weight loss increases with the square of the tax rate.) The drawback, however, is that the low-income people who are subsidized face an extremely high marginal tax rate. A person at $5000 who works hard and increases her income to $10,000 is only $2000 better off ($8000 versus $10,000). The loss of the $3000 subsidy is in effect a 60% marginal *tax* on the additional $5000 of earnings. A targeted approach thus places a society in the uncomfortable position of expecting the able-bodied poor to work their way out of poverty rather than accept a public subsidy while at the same time subjecting them to very high marginal tax rates. The marginal tax rates can be enormous with multiple targeted public assistance programs such as those in the United States. Some poor families receive aid under five or six different programs. If they work their way out of poverty they not only face a high marginal tax rate because they lose their monthly cash subsidy. They may also lose access to Food Stamps, Medicaid, housing assistance, and other subsidies so that their combined marginal tax rate is well in excess of 100%. Indeed, the marginal rates can be so high for some families that they are actually worse off if they earn additional income, in violation of Feldstein's no-reversals principle of vertical equity.

The potential for reversals under targeted assistance is referred to as the *notch problem*. Notch problems always arise at the cut-off points at which the assistance ends. Taxes levied on incomes immediately above the notch are likely to make those taxpayers worse off than people with incomes just before the notch who are still receiving subsidies. The only way to avoid the notch problem near the cut-off is to decrease the subsidies as incomes approach the notch and exempt a range of incomes above the notch from tax. The example, though discrete, illustrates this principle. The subsidies stop at $5000, whereas the taxes begin at $15000. If incomes were continuous rather than discrete, the notch problem would arise from $5001 to $7999. People with incomes in that range would be worse off than people with incomes of $5000.

An Acceptable Public Assistance Program?

High marginal tax rates and notch problems are not specific to this example. They are inherent in all targeted transfer programs, which helps to explain why people in the United States and other countries never seem to be satisfied with their public assistance programs. In our view, targeted public assistance programs can never be entirely acceptable. The problem is twofold. On the one hand, we believe that people will be satisfied with public assistance only if it satisfies three goals:

1. It removes virtually everyone from poverty. (The poverty gap, the aggregate amount of income by which the poor fall below the poverty line, is less than $100 billion in the United States.)
2. It is not too costly to the taxpayers.
3. It preserves incentives to work (and maintain families intact)

On the other hand, the only sensible way to design a income subsidy is to define a cut-off level of income, $Y_{cut-off}$, below which the family (individual) is subsidized, and then set the subsidy equal to some proportion of the difference between the cut-off and actual levels of income. That is,

$$S = x\,(Y_{cut-off} - Y_{actual}),\ \text{where}\ Y_{actual} \leq Y_{cut-off} \qquad (19.1)[3]$$

with

$$Y_{total} = Y_{actual} + S \qquad (19.2)$$

---

[3] $Y_{cut-off}$ would also vary with family size.

The proportion x has to be fairly large, between .5 and 1, to generate a large enough subsidy for people with very low incomes. Subsidies of this form have a guaranteed minimum level of income equal to $xY_{cut-off}$, the subsidy for a family with no income. The subsidy decreases by xY_{actual} as income increases up to $Y_{cut-off}$, when it becomes zero. All the cash public assistance programs except the EITC (see below) take this form.

The problem is that a subsidy of this form cannot satisfy all three goals. Suppose $Y_{cut-off}$ is set equal to the poverty line, approximately \$17,000 for a family of four in the United States. The program will not be "too costly," in line with the second goal, but it miserably fails the first goal—no one escapes poverty. Everyone below the poverty line remains below the poverty line after receiving the subsidy. To satisfy the first goal, $Y_{cut-off}$ has to be set at $Y_{poverty\ line}/x$, so that the guaranteed minimum income equals the poverty line and everyone with $Y_{actual} > 0$ ends up with Y_{total} above the poverty line. This could be very costly in terms of lost tax revenues, however, if x is much less than one. Many families with incomes above the poverty line would be subsidized rather than taxed, and the first dollars of taxable incomes above $Y_{cut-off}$ must be exempt from tax to avoid the notch problem.

Regardless of the trade-offs between the first two goals, the third goal is impossible to achieve with a subsidy of this form. It has the strongest possible disincentives for work (and maintaining families intact, for that matter).[4] A person who earns extra income in the subsidized range below the cut-off still receives a subsidy: $Y_{total} > Y_{actual}$. Hence, there is an income effect from the total subsidy that favors leisure over work. At the same time, additional earned income is subject to a marginal tax rate of x percent because of the loss of subsidy at rate x per dollar. Hence, there is a substitution effect that again favors leisure over work. The combination of a subsidy on average and tax on the margin is doubly destructive for work incentives.

The federal government tried to avoid the work-incentive problem when it established three public assistance programs as part of the Social Security Act of 1935. It chose a categorical approach, giving aid only to those who were deemed to have well-below-average prospects for work and were therefore not expected to lift themselves out of poverty. Thus, the first three programs targeted aid only to the elderly, the blind, and single-parent families (primarily widows, who usually had little or no insurance and thus were in desperate straits if their husbands died). Aid to the Disabled was added in 1951. An obvious drawback to categorical targeting is that poor families who do not fall into one of the four categories receive no aid at all, such as the majority of poor two-parent families. The United States apparently felt in 1935, and long afterwards, that keeping large numbers of families out of the

---

[4] The family has a strong financial incentive for one spouse to leave home and send back income in a manner that cannot be detected, thereby avoiding the high marginal tax rates built into the public assistance formulas.

public assistance safety net was an acceptable price to pay to avoid incentive problems.

Incentives problems appeared anyway in the 1960s when the single-parent program, Aid to Families with Dependent Children, exploded. The nuclear family was weakening, and single women with children began seeking public assistance because their husbands had deserted them, not because they had died. Taxpayers felt cheated for the first time and searched for ways to improve incentives to work and to keep low-income families together.

The Earned Income Tax Credit

The best one can do in terms of work incentives is a wage subsidy of the form:

$$S = xY_{actual} \qquad (19.3)$$

Unfortunately, the income effect remains in effect and favors leisure over work. But at least the substitution effect favors work, since additional earnings are subsidized at rate x rather than being taxed at rate x. The basic public assistance programs cannot take this form, however, because then people with no income starve to death. But a supplemental antipoverty program could take this form to alleviate the high marginal tax rates of the basic program(s).

This is exactly what the EITC was designed to do. As noted above, the combined marginal tax rates under the other public assistance programs were enormous for some of the poor. The EITC offset this somewhat by offering wage subsidies to the poor that varied by family size. For example, two-person families receive a wage subsidy of 34 cents per dollar up to an income of $6680 (1998), a maximum subsidy of $2271 at the cut-off. Notice, however, that the subsidy cannot simply end without generating an enormous notch problem, an inherent drawback with wage subsidies. Thus, the subsidy remains fixed at $2271 for incomes between $6680 and $12,300. Beyond, $12,300, the subsidy is phased out at the marginal rate of 21 cents on the dollar until it reaches zero, at $23,114. The income ranges are increased each year by the rate of inflation.

The EITC became a very large program in the 1990s, reaching $26 billion by FY2000 (by comparison, TANF was $30 billion that year). It helped considerably to reduce the marginal tax rates on poor families and thereby encourage their work effort. The EITC is not without its drawbacks, however. The program discourages work effort in the flat-subsidy range, given the income effect, and doubly discourages work effort in the phase-out range. The marginal tax rate increases by 21% in the phase-out range. The combination of the 15% income tax rate, the 21% phase-out rate, the 15+% payroll tax rate (assuming labor bears the entire burden), and state income tax rates (in 44 states) saddles many low-income families with marginal tax rates in excess of 50%. Also, the vast majority of the subsidies under the EITC go to the non-poor. In summary, the need to avoid the notch problem under a wage subsidy sharply reduces its attractiveness as a means of fighting poverty.[5]

The United States decided during the Reagan administration to give up on trying to preserve work incentives under the basic public assistance program benefit formulas. The subsidy proportion x was set equal to 1 on all income after the first four months, thereby completely destroying any incentive to work below $Y_{cut-off}$. Families receive $Y_{cut-off}$ no matter what their actual incomes are. Setting x = 1 does well by the first two goals, so long as $Y_{cut-off}$ is the poverty line.[6] But it requires a stick approach to maintain the work incentive called *workfare*, in which the single parent is forced to work (or receive education or job training) in order to receive benefits. Workfare was applied hesitantly by some of the states until 1996, when it became the cornerstone of the TANF program that replaced Aid to Families with Dependent Children. TANF removed public assistance as an entitlement. States were allowed to remove families from the welfare rolls after two years of receiving benefits. They were also encouraged to force able-bodied welfare parents to undertake job training or work in order to maintain their benefits during the first two years. Both provisions provide a strong incentive to prepare for and seek steady employment.

The resolve to maintain the stick approach of workfare will not really be tested until the U.S. economy goes into a recession and low-income jobs become difficult to find. Low-income jobs have been plentiful since 1996 thanks to the booming economy. Also, workfare is not entirely comforting since the stick is being applied primarily to women with very low incomes who are trying to raise their children on their own. The work incentive problem associated with targeted income subsidies to the poor has no obvious solution.

Special Needs, In-Kind Transfers, and Universality

Suppose the government decides to offer in-kind transfers to pay for special needs, such as insulin shots for diabetics, eyeglasses, or hearing aids. Nicholas Rowe and Frances Wooley have argued that these transfers should probably be universal—offered to everyone with these special needs—rather than targeted to the poor.[7] The case for universal transfers follows from thinking of them in the context of the Mirrlees optimal income tax (transfer) problem with utilitarian social welfare that we discussed in Chapter 15.

[5] For further discussion and analysis of the EITC, see E. Browning, "Effects of the EITC on Income and Welfare," *National Tax Journal*, March 1995; J. Schloz, "The EITC: Participation, Compliance, and Anti-Poverty Effectiveness," *National Tax Journal*, March 1994.

[6] In fact, $Y_{cut-off}$ is set below the poverty line under TANF and SSI in all states, and often well below the poverty line.

[7] N. Rowe and F. Wooley, "The Efficiency Case for Universality," *Canadian Journal of Economics*, May 1999.

Suppose the needs are observable, so that the only information problem in the optimal income-tax framework remains the inability to know people's skill level. Suppose further that a special need reduces effective consumption dollar-for-dollar by the expenditures required to offset the need and does so equally for everyone. Also, the special needs are independent of the skill level, as is likely for the examples given above and many other special needs. Under these assumptions, the common utility function in the optimal income tax problem is $U^{ij}(C_{ij} - N_i, 1 - L_{ij})$,
where:

C_{ij} = consumption of person j with special need i
N_i = expenditures required to address special need i, equal for everyone with the special need
$1 - L_{ij}$ = labor supplied by person j with special need i

Define the "poor" as everyone below a given skill level and the "rich" as everyone at or above that skill level. Suppose in-kind transfers equal to N_i are targeted to the needy poor, with a phase-out extending into the non-poor range. Targeting in this way is suboptimal in two respects in the context of optimal income taxation. First, the unneedy rich have higher effective consumption than the needy rich at each skill level and, therefore, a lower marginal utility of consumption. Social welfare would be increased if their marginal utilities of consumption were equalized under utilitarian social welfare. This is the inequity of targeting. Second, the loss of benefits in the phase-out range causes the needy and unneedy in that skill range to face different effective marginal tax rates. Assuming they have equal compensated labor supply elasticities, they should face the same marginal tax rates. That some people of equal skills face unequal marginal tax rates is the inefficiency of targeting.

Both the inequity and inefficiency of targeting are avoided if the tax-transfer function has the universal form $T_i = f(Y_{ij}) - N_i$. That is, the in-kind transfer is given to everyone who is needy. Rowe and Wooley define universality in the presence of special needs as a tax-transfer function that is additively separable in income and needs.

One obvious condition under which universality would be suboptimal in the context of the optimal income tax problem is if the compensated labor supply elasticities were correlated with the special need. This may apply for certain kinds of disabilities, but probably not for many other kinds of special needs such as those given above. In any event, Rowe and Wooley argue that universality should be the benchmark for special needs transfers against which exceptions have to be justified.

Many people would argue that targeting in-kind transfers to the poor is equitable in the sense that it transfers purchasing power from the rich to the poor, but this argument does not apply to special needs. Here the potential for inequity is between the unneedy and needy rich, which targeting gives rise to and universality avoids. The optimal income tax does transfer purchasing power from the rich to the poor, but Rowe and Wooley's point is that in-kind transfers to offset special needs should probably not be part of the rich-to-poor transfer of purchasing power.

PRIVATE INFORMATION AND IN-KIND TRANSFERS

The federal government has always enhanced its cash public assistance transfers with in-kind subsidies to the poor, primarily for medical care, food, and housing assistance. The original three cash-assistance programs, and later Aid to the Disabled, included medical vendor payments—that is, payments to physicians and hospitals that provided medical care to the recipients. The medical assistance was consolidated into a single program, Medicaid, in 1965. Medicaid grew rapidly in the 1970s and 1980s, in part because medical costs experienced high inflation and in part because Medicaid was expanded to cover so-called medically needy families. These are families with low incomes who are not on public assistance but who have large medical expenses. Medicaid was considerably expanded in the 1990s, primarily to cover children and pregnant women in families with incomes as much as twice the poverty line. Housing assistance is another in-kind program that has long subsidized poor families. Food Stamps were added in the early 1970s. The in-kind subsidies are now much larger than the cash subsidies. Spending under Medicaid alone is approaching $200 billion per year, more than all the other public assistance programs combined, cash and in-kind.

Recall that the first-best pareto-optimal redistribution model provides a justification for in-kind aid and suggests that it should be decentralized. The government should ideally subsidize the poor's purchases of food, or housing, or medical care and let them buy as much as they wish in the private market at the subsidized rate. This is presumably what the citizens in a capitalist country would want the government to do. They would not want government agencies providing these goods using some kind of non-market-rationing device.

The Blackorby–Donaldson Model of In-Kind Transfers

Unfortunately, the decentralized subsidy approach becomes vulnerable in the presence of private information. Charles Blackorby and David Donaldson developed a very simple model of the provision of medical care that shows that government provision (rationing) is quite likely to be preferred to decentralized subsidies if the government cannot be certain who really needs medical care.[8]

---

[8] C. Blackorby and D. Donaldson, "Cash Versus Kind, Self-Selection, and Efficient Transfers," *American Economic Review*, September 1988. Note the difference relative to Rowe and Wooley, who assume that the need for medical care is known to the government.

We saw in Chapter 15 how private information limits the government's tax options. The limitations on transfers imposed by private information can be even more severe. The Blackorby–Donaldson model clearly demonstrates why private information limits the government's ability to target transfers to the needy no matter what form they take, cash or in-kind, and if in-kind whether by rationing or by subsidy.

The model consists of two classes of individuals. One class, H, is healthy, so that the utility of class H individuals is a function only of their income (consumption of private goods—in the model, a numeraire composite commodity):

$$U_H = Y_H \qquad (19.4)$$

The second class, I, has an illness, the disutility of which can be reduced by medical services Z; therefore, the utility of class I individuals depends on both their income (consumption of private goods) Y_I and Z according to the utility function:

$$U_I = Y_I - e^{-(1-Z)} \qquad (19.5)$$

Individuals within each class are identical.

The individuals possess private information about the state of their health. The government knows that there are two classes of consumers and knows the utility functions for each class, but it cannot know whether any one individual is healthy or ill. Since the individuals are identical within each class, we will consider the simplest case of a two-person economy with one H person and one I person.

The economy is endowed with 6 units of a resource, K, and a unit of K can be transferred into either a unit of private goods or a unit of Z. Therefore, the production possibilities frontier for the economy is

$$Y_H + Y_I + Z = 6$$

The First-Best Frontier

The first task is to establish the first-best utility-possibilities frontier, which the government could achieve if it had perfect information about individuals' health. The first-best frontier serves as a baseline for comparing the rationed and subsidy approaches to the provision of Z under private information.

The necessary condition for the economy to be on its first-best frontier is that $MRS_{Y,Z} = MRT_{Y,Z}$. The $MRT_{Y,Z} = 1$, and the $MRS_{Y,Z}$ applies only to those who are ill. Thus, first-best pareto optimality requires that:

$$MRT_{Y,Z} = \partial U_I/\partial Z / \partial U_I/\partial Y_I = e^{(1-Z)} = 1 \qquad (19.6)$$

or that $Z = 1$.

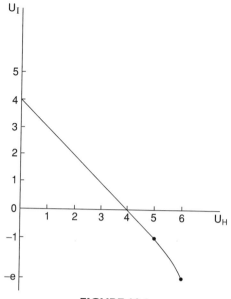

FIGURE 19.1

The first-best utility possibilities frontier is pictured in Fig. 19.1. At one extreme I gets all the resources, purchases 1 unit of Z and 5 units of Y_I, and has $U_I = 4$. Given that $Z = 1$, the other extreme consists of H receiving 5 units of Y_H, in which case $U_H = 5$, and $U_I = -1$. The region from $U_H = 5$ to $U_H = 6$ implies that Z is less than one. I prefers Z to Y in that region because Z has the higher marginal utility with $Z < 1$. Therefore, U_I falls along the curved line to the limit of $-e$, when I has no resources.

Now introduce the private information and consider two government policies: (1) government provision—rationing—of the medical care, and (2) subsidizing the purchase of medical care by I, the decentralized solution.

Government Provision of Medical Care

The most straightforward way to consider government provision in this simple model is to assume that the government allocates Y as well as I. Therefore, it has complete control to place the economy anywhere on the second-best utility possibilities frontier under private information.

Private information gives rise to the mechanism design problem of ensuring that the medical care is given only to those who are ill. The self-selection constraints are

$$Y_H \geq Y_I \text{ for person H} \tag{19.7}$$

$$U_I(Y_I, Z) \geq U_I(Y_H, 0) \text{ for person I} \tag{19.8}$$

H has no use for Z; therefore, she will identify herself correctly as long as the government gives more Y to the healthy. I will identify himself correctly unless H receives so much more Y that it pays for I to forego Z and declare himself as healthy. Equation (19.8) gives the combinations of Y_I and Z for which he will correctly identify himself as ill.

The first point to note is that some of the first-best frontier is preserved under government provision. Z must equal 1 to be on the first-best frontier. This leaves 5 units of Y to be distributed between H and I. Equation (19.7) sets a lower bound for Y_H equal to 2.5, since H must always have at least half of the total Y. Equation (19.8) sets the upper bound of Y_H as follows:

$$Y_I - 1 \geq Y_H - e \qquad (19.9)$$

$$(5 - Y_H) - 1 \geq Y_H - e \qquad (19.10)$$

$$Y_H \leq (2 + e/2) \qquad (19.11)$$

$$Y_H \leq 3.4 \text{ (approximately)} \qquad (19.12)$$

Refer to Fig. 19.2. Within the region $2.5 \leq Y_H \leq 3.4$, the second-best utility-possibilities frontier with private information coincides with the first-best frontier. Outside that region, the frontier with private information must be below the first-best frontier. If $Y_H < 2.5$, then Y_I must also be < 2.5 to satisfy the self-selection constraint Eq. (19.7). But this implies $Z > 1$, in violation of the first-best pareto-optimal condition, Eq. (19.6). At the upper

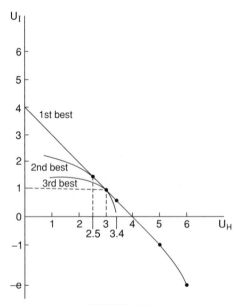

FIGURE 19.2

boundary of $Y_A = 3.4$, I has 2.6 units to divide between Y_I and Z. The division $Y_I = 1.6$, $Z = 1$, yields the same utility (approximately) for I that he would have by declaring himself healthy and taking 3.4 units of Y with no Z:

$$U_I = 1.6 - 1 = .6 = 3.4 - e \qquad (19.13)$$

If the government tried to set $Y_H > 3.4$, then the ill would declare themselves healthy. There is no combination of Z and Y_I with total resources less than 2.6 that yields them as much utility as taking Y_H, since Z and Y are both normal goods. But society does not have enough resources to give both people 3.4 units of Y, so the second-best frontier stops at $Y_H = 3.4$.

Subsidizing Medical Care

Private information severely constrains the decentralized subsidy approach. With the government unable to determine who is healthy and who is ill, the individuals will always choose the option with the highest purchasing power and use it as they wish. Therefore, the government has no choice but to equalize purchasing power under the subsidy plan. The single self-selection constraint is

$$Y_H = Y_I + qZ \qquad (19.14)$$

where q is the subsidized price of Z.

Refer again to Fig. 19.2. The only attainable point on the first-best frontier is equal resources with $q = 1$. Setting the subsidy to zero ($q = 1$) is necessary to satisfy the first-best pareto-optimal condition, Eq. (19.6); equalizing the resources is necessary to satisfy the self-selection constraint, Eq. (19.14). Thus, the only feasible first-best allocation is

$$\{Y_H = 3; Y_I = 2, Z = 1; U_A = 3; U_I = 1\}.$$

Subsidizing medical care ($q < 1$) favors I, and taxing medical care ($q > 1$) favors the H with Eq. (19.14) holding, but in either case society is below the first-best frontier as shown in the figure. Furthermore, the frontier with subsidy must be below the second-best frontier with rationing in the subsidy region. It is clearly below the rationing frontier above $Y_H = 2.5$, since the rationing frontier is the first-best frontier in that region. It is also below the second-best rationing frontier when $Y_H < 2.5$ since it adds the binding equal-purchasing-power constraint that is absent under rationing.

In conclusion, the Blackorby–Donaldson model demonstrates that private information generates a preference for rationing (government provision) over decentralized subsidies when society's charitable impulse is to give people in-kind aid. The intuition is that rationing prevents people from claiming a subsidy to treat some illness that they do not have. Rationing may be the only way of verifying the illness. This result overturns the conclusion of the first-best model of pareto-optimal redistribution, which calls for decentralized subsidies when the charitable impulse is for in-kind aid. Even so, rationing preserves some of the first-best allocations.

The model also points to a more general problem that private information poses for the mainstream public sector model in its attempt to achieve end-results equity. Suppose the government tries to satisfy the first-best interpersonal equity conditions with lump-sum cash subsidies to the poor. If the government cannot know who is poor and who is non-poor, then everyone will claim to be poor in order to receive a subsidy. The only way to prevent people from hiding their true identities is to impose equal incomes for everyone. No other income redistribution is feasible.

We saw in Chapter 4 that the first-best model does imply complete equality under the three assumptions of equal social welfare weights (at equal utilities), identical tastes, and diminishing marginal utility of income. The private information result is stronger, however, since equal income is the only feasible outcome regardless of the assumptions one chooses to make about the social welfare function, tastes, and marginal utility. People's willingness to exploit their private information can clearly be devastating to the mainstream ideal of the government sector acting as an agent for the citizens in the pursuit of the public interest in efficiency and equity. Remember that if the first-best interpersonal equity conditions cannot be satisfied, then in general the first-best pareto-optimal conditions are not optimal either. Also, second-best interventions are generally all-pervasive rather than limited in scope, not at all in the spirit of the government-as-agent ideal.[9]

The Besley–Coate Model of Workfare

As discussed above, workfare was adopted as a centerpiece of TANF to force welfare parents to prepare for and accept jobs in an attempt to overcome the strong work disincentives of the benefit formula. Workfare responds to a principle of long standing in the United States, that the able-bodied should

---

[9] P. Bearse *et al.* offer another possible explanation for the well-documented preference for in-kind aid in less developed countries: the difficulties these governments have in raising tax revenues. They present a simple model in which people have preferences over a composite commodity and education. The government raises taxes to provide either a universal transfer or universal public education, free to all. Families can opt out of public education in favor of private education. People vote in a direct democracy for the level of the tax rate and also for the shares of tax revenues devoted to the transfer and to public education. In their model, as taxes become more difficult to collect the proportion of revenues devoted to public education increases. The main reason is that with lower tax collections the quality of public education suffers and more of the higher income people opt out for private education. The opting out of public education by the rich increases the return of tax dollars spent on education relative to the universal transfer from the point of view of the poor. This leads the majority of voters, who are poor, to prefer an increase in the share of tax revenues devoted to public education. See P. Bearse, G. Glomm, and E. Janeba, "Why Poor Countries Rely Mostly on Redistribution In-Kind," *Journal of Public Economics*, March 2000.

work rather than simply accept a handout from the government. It also tries to help welfare parents become self sufficient by improving their prospects in the labor market.

Timothy Besley and Stephen Coate have shown that workfare can be useful even if the work enforced by the government is entirely unproductive to society or the individual. In particular, unproductive workfare can serve as a signaling device that allows the government to target cash subsidies to the poor in a world of private information in which it would otherwise be difficult to distinguish the poor from the non-poor. Besley and Coate were responding to models such as Blackordy and Donaldson's which conclude that targeting cash subsidies to the poor is impossible if the government cannot distinguish among individuals. Its only option is to equalize incomes. In the Besley–Coate model, workfare acts as a self-selection mechanism that prevents the non-poor from accepting the public assistance subsidies.[10]

The Besley–Coate model has the following elements:

Individuals

There are two classes of individuals, those with high ability (H) and those with low ability (L). The high-ability individuals receive a wage of W_H, the low-ability individuals a wage of W_L. All individuals have the same additive separable utility functions:

$$U_i = Y_i - h(l_i), \quad \text{for } i = H, L \tag{19.15}$$

where Y_i is the numeraire composite commodity (income), and l_i is labor. The proportions of low- and high-ability individuals are γ and $(1 - \gamma)$. Labor markets are competitive, so that $W_H = h'(l_H)$ and $W_L = h'(l_L)$. Letting $\hat{l}_i$ represent the equilibrium labor supplies,

$$Y_L = W_L\hat{l}_L = Y_L(0, W_L) \tag{19.16}$$

and

$$Y_H = W_H\hat{l}_H = Y_H(0, W_H) \tag{19.17}$$

The zeros in Y( ) indicate the absence of government transfers.

The Government

The government has a Rawlsian social welfare function. It wants to ensure that everyone has at least a minimum acceptable level of income Z, with $Z > W_L\hat{l}_L$ (and $Z < W_H\hat{l}_H$). It considers two public assistance plans:

[10] T. Besley and S. Coate, "Workfare Versus Welfare: Incentive Arguments for Work Requirements in Poverty Alleviation Programs," *American Economic Review*, March 1992. They extended and generalized the analysis in T. Besley and S. Coate, "The Design of Income Maintenance Programs," *Review of Economic Studies*, April 1995.

1. A straight welfare plan with lump-sum subsidies b_L and b_H targeted to the low- and high-ability individuals
2. Workfare, which includes a forced work requirement of C units of labor in order to receive the lump-sum subsidies b_L or b_H

The enforced work is entirely unproductive. Its only purpose is to serve as a self-selection device. Also, workfare has no effect on the total amount of labor supplied by either type of person because utility is additively separable. C substitutes one-for-one for market work, so that incomes under workfare are

$$Y_L = W_L\left(\hat{l}_L - C\right) = Y_L(C, W_L) \tag{19.18}$$

and

$$Y_H = W_H\left(\hat{l}_L - C\right) = Y_H(C, W_H) \tag{19.19}$$

Finally, straight welfare and workfare are costless to administer.

The government's goal is to minimize the cost of public assistance subject to satisfying the Rawlsian minimum income constraint:

$$\min \gamma b_L + (1 - \gamma) b_H$$
$$\text{s.t. } Y_i + b_i \geq Z, \text{ for } i = L, H$$

An additional requirement is that participation in straight welfare or workfare has to be voluntary. This requirement is most easily represented in terms of the indirect utility function, with the lump-sum subsidies, workfare, and the market wages as parameters:

$$V_i(b_i, C, W_i) \geq V_i(0, 0, W_i), \text{ for } i = L, H \tag{19.20}$$

First-Best Optimum

The cost-minimizing option with perfect information would clearly be a straight welfare program that only subsidizes the low-ability people such that they achieve Z:

$$b_L = Z - W_L\hat{l}_L; b_H = 0; C = 0; \text{ with a cost of } \gamma b_L.$$

Workfare cannot be first best because C is unproductive.

Private Information

Besley and Coate consider two degrees of private information:

1. Earnings are unobservable. This is most likely to apply to a less-developed country.
2. Earnings are observable, but effort is not, that is, the government knows Y_i and W_i, but not l_i. The inability to observe effort allows a

high-ability individual to claim to have low ability by working just hard enough to earn Y_L with a wage of W_H.

Either type of private information introduces two self-selection (incentive compatibility) constraints:

$$V(b_H, C, W_H) \geq V(b_L, C, W_H) \tag{19.21}$$

$$V(b_L, C, W_L) \geq V(b_H, C, W_L) \tag{19.22}$$

Equations (19.21) and (19.22) require that class H and L individuals prefer their own public assistance options to those of the other class. Equation (19.21) is the operative constraint, because society wants to prevent high-ability individuals from accepting public assistance.[11]

Unobservable Earnings

We will demonstrate how workfare can promote the government's goals in the first case since it is the easier one.

Straight Welfare

With earnings unobservable, the government cannot target cash subsidies to those with low ability. If it tried to set $b_L > b_H$ (with b_H likely equal to zero), the high-ability individuals would claim to have low ability and take b_L. Therefore, the only straight welfare policy is equal subsidies to both, in an amount sufficient to bring those with low ability to Z:

$$b_L = b_H = Z - W_L \hat{l}_L$$

Workfare

Low- and high-ability individuals react differently to workfare:

1. *Low ability individuals:*—The low-ability individuals will accept workfare as long as $C < \hat{l}_L$. Their total labor supply is unchanged, so the disutility of working, $h(\hat{l}_L)$, remains the same. Also, their income is increased to Z, which is better than they can do on their own. The required subsidy is

$$b_L = Z - Y_L(C, W_L) = Z - W_L\left(\hat{l}_L - C\right) \tag{19.23}$$

Notice that b_L is larger than under straight welfare because the individuals' earnings are reduced by the unproductive workfare requirement.

2. *High ability individuals*—High-ability individuals may claim to have low ability in order to receive the subsidy. Whether they do or not depends on the size of the subsidy relative to the cost of accepting the workfare requirement.

---

[11] The information set is somewhat unrealistic since the government knows individuals' common utility functions even though it cannot fully distinguish between people with high and low ability.

If they tell the truth and turn down the subsidy, their utility is $U_H = W_H\hat{l}_H - h(\hat{l}_H)$. The government's mechanism design problem is to find a level of workfare, C^*, such that the high-ability individuals have an incentive to tell the truth. Their utility under workfare is $U_H = W_H(\hat{l}_H - C) - h(\hat{l}_H) + b_L = W_H(\hat{l}_H - C) - h(\hat{l}_H) + Z - W_L(\hat{l}_L - C)$. Therefore, the level of workfare that just makes the high-ability individuals indifferent to accepting the subsidy is the solution to:

$$W_H\hat{l}_H - h\left(\hat{l}_H\right) = W_H\left(\hat{l}_H - C^*\right) - h\left(\hat{l}_H\right) + Z - W_L\left(\hat{l}_L - C^*\right) \quad (19.24)$$

or

$$W_HC^* = Z - W_L\left(\hat{l}_L - C^*\right) \quad (19.25)$$

The left-hand side (LHS) of Eq. (19.24) is the cost of claiming to be low ability, the sacrificed income to workfare, and the right-hand side (RHS) is the benefit b_L under workfare. With $C > C^*$, the workfare subsidy, Eq. (19.23), is effectively targeted only to the low-ability individuals.

Notice that, from Eq. (19.25), $Z - W_L\hat{l}_L = (W_H - W_L)C^*$ is the subsidy b_L under straight welfare, a subsidy that would have to be given to everyone. Therefore, workfare with a requirement of C^* is the least-cost public assistance strategy if:

$$(W_H - W_L)C^* > \gamma W_HC^* \quad (19.26)$$

or

$$(1 - \gamma)W_H > W_L \quad (19.27)$$

Equation (19.27) indicates that workfare is the preferred strategy if either (1) γ is low, so that there are not so many low-ability individuals to target, or (2) $W_H \gg W_L$. The lower (relatively) W_L is, the more costly it is to subsidize everyone. Also, the additional subsidy required because of workfare, W_LC^*, is that much smaller.

The more complex case of observable earnings but unobservable effort, which is more likely for developed countries, yields two additional results of interest. The first is that workfare is less likely to be cost minimizing relative to the earnings-unobservable case. The reason is that the high-ability individuals have to sacrifice much more to receive the subsidy—they have to earn $W_L\hat{l}_L$. The second is that workfare is better if earnings are low because W_L is low rather than because h(l), the disutility of work, is high. A high h(l) would apply to people who are unemployable or who have a number of children at home to care for. For these people it is better to target aid in some other way, such as government provision of medical care as in the Blackorby–Donaldson model or targeting on the basis of observable characteristics. (Interested readers should consult the Besley and Coate article.)

As noted earlier in the chapter, targeting on observable characteristics was the strategy followed by the United States in the Social Security Act of

1935. It targeted cash subsidies only to those poor who were also likely to have poor employment prospects, such as the elderly and widows. The federal government was well aware of the perils of private information when it entered the public assistance fray. Indeed, public assistance was originally allocated entirely to local governments because towns were generally small and local officials were likely to know the poor. Hence, they would know who was truly deserving of aid and who was shirking. They would not face the problems of private information that beset the states and the federal government when trying to help the poor.

The Besley–Coate model is more sanguine than the Blackorby–Donaldson model about the government's ability to use targeted cash transfers in a world of private information. Yet, it has not entirely rescued the mainstream view of the government from the difficulties of private information. That the government has to resort to enforced workfare of the poor to prevent the non-poor from taking public assistance is unsettling to the notion of the government acting as an agent for the citizens in pursuit of end-results equity. One wonders if the poor are indifferent between market work and workfare as in the Besley–Coate model, especially if they view workfare as unproductive. If they are not indifferent, then the potential least-cost property of workfare is less compelling. In any event, workfare should be an effective deterrent to the non-poor falsely claiming public assistance benefits, which is the main point of the Besley–Coate model.

Welfare Stigma

Robert Moffitt's 1983 empirical study of public assistance in the United States found strong evidence that welfare recipients suffer from a stigma that reduces their utility from public assistance.[12] Nine years later, Besley and Coate developed a simple theoretical framework for analyzing welfare stigma.[13] An important feature of their model is that stigma is endogenous, determined by such things as the level of public assistance payments and the percentage of "undeserving" poor who accept welfare.

Besley and Coate speculated that the stigma of being on welfare may arise in one of two ways:

1. As a form of statistical discrimination, in which the knowledge that some able-bodied poor choose to accept public assistance rather than work leads to a perception among the non-poor that all welfare recipients are lazy. All the poor who accept public assistance, even those who are deserving, feel stigmatized by this perception.

---

[12] R. Moffitt, "An Economic Model of Welfare Stigma," *American Economic Review*, December 1983.

[13] T. Besley and S. Coate, "Understanding Welfare Stigma: Taxpayer Resentment and Statistical Discrimination," *Journal of Public Economics*, July 1992.

2. From taxpayer resentment, in which some of the non-poor simply resent having to pay taxes to support the poor. That some taxpayers feel this way is enough to generate a sense of stigma among the poor.

Besley and Coate's model of welfare stigma can accommodate both types of stigma, and they have different implications. We will present the analysis of statistical discrimination here.

Elements of the Model

The population consists of N individuals, n of whom are poor, and (N − n) non-poor. The poor are of two kinds: the deserving ("needy") poor, who cannot work and have been targeted to receive public assistance, and the undeserving poor, who are able to work. The proportions of deserving and undeserving poor are γ and $(1 - \gamma)$. The non-poor have altruistic feelings toward the deserving poor that lead them to support a public assistance program, but the intensity of their altruism varies. Their (common) utility function is

$$U = U(C) - \mu\gamma nP(C_n) \tag{19.28}$$

where:

C = the consumption of each non-poor
μ = the altruism parameter, which is distributed among the non-poor according to the continuous distribution function $G(\mu)$
γn = the number of deserving poor
C_n = the consumption of a deserving poor person
P( ) = an index of hardship suffered by a deserving poor person, with $P' < 0$.

A welfare payment b is given to all the poor who do not work. The non-poor can tell who among the poor are working, but they cannot tell whether a welfare recipient is deserving or undeserving. This is the information problem in the model.

Let M = the number of poor who accept public assistance. Then the per-person tax payment by the non-poor, T, is

$$T = \frac{Mb}{(N - n)} \tag{19.29}$$

The undeserving poor who choose to work earn a wage w and receive utility of:

$$U = V(w) - \theta \tag{19.30}$$

θ indicates the disutility of working, which varies among the poor. It is distributed according to the uniform distribution function from 0 to 1.

Any poor person who accepts public assistance receives utility of:

$$U = V(b) - s \qquad (19.31)$$

where s is a measure of the stigma they suffer as recipients of public assistance. The deserving poor have to accept this option because they are unable to work and earn w.

The border of indifference for an undeserving poor person to accept public assistance, given s, is the disutility of work $\hat{\theta}$ that solves:

$$V(w) - \hat{\theta} = V(b) - s \qquad (19.32)$$

The undeserving poor with $\theta > \hat{\theta}$ choose public assistance. Therefore, the total number of the poor on welfare is

$$M = n \left[\gamma + (1 - \gamma)(1 - \hat{\theta}) \right] \qquad (19.33)$$

The utility of the non-poor with the public assistance program is

$$U = U \left(C - \frac{Mb}{(N - n)} \right) - \mu \gamma n P \left(C_n \right) \qquad (19.34)$$

Statistical Discrimination

The statistical discrimination motive for stigmatizing the poor depends on the distribution of the disutility from work among the poor. The average disutility to work among the poor is

$$\bar{\theta} = \int_0^1 \theta d\theta \qquad (19.35)$$

which is also assumed to be the average disutility to work among the non-poor. In other words, $\bar{\theta}$ is the accepted social norm relating to the distaste for work. The average disutility of work among the undeserving poor who choose public assistance is

$$\bar{\theta}_u = \int_{\hat{\theta}}^1 \theta d\theta / \left(1 - \hat{\theta} \right) \qquad (19.36)$$

Therefore, the average disutility of work among all the poor on public assistance is

$$\bar{\theta}_w = \pi \bar{\theta} + (1 - \pi)\bar{\theta}_u \qquad (19.37)$$

where

$$\pi = \frac{\gamma n}{M} \qquad (19.38)$$

which is the proportion of the poor on public assistance who are deserving. Notice that $\pi < 1 \Rightarrow \bar{\theta}_w > \bar{\theta}$.

The stigma based on statistical discrimination arises from the difference between the average disutility of work among the poor, $\bar{\theta}_w$, and the accepted social norm $\bar{\theta}$. Let $g(\bar{\theta}_w - \bar{\theta})$ be the function that generates stigma, such that $g' > 0$ and $g(0) = 0$. $\bar{\theta}_w$ is a function of b and s through the work/accept-public-assistance relationship, Eq. (19.32). Therefore,

$$s^* = g(\bar{\theta}_w(b, s^*) - \bar{\theta}) \tag{19.39}$$

solves for the equilibrium level of stigma given the exogenous variables b and w, the public assistance payment and the wage. s* closes the model by determining the number of poor who accept welfare, M, and thus the tax payments of the non-poor.

An immediate problem is that s* may not be unique. To see why not, differentiate Eq. (19.39) wrt s and note that $g'\dfrac{\partial\bar{\theta}_w}{\partial s}$ must be less than 1 to ensure that s* is unique.

But

$$\frac{\partial\bar{\theta}_w}{\partial s} = (1 - \pi)\frac{\partial\bar{\theta}_u}{\partial s} + (\bar{\theta} - \bar{\theta}_u)\frac{\partial\pi}{\partial s} \tag{19.40}$$

$\bar{\theta} < \bar{\theta}_u$ and $\dfrac{\partial\pi}{\partial s} > 0$ (the proportion of deserving poor on public assistance increases with stigma as more of the undeserving poor choose to work). Therefore, the second term is negative. The first term is positive because as some undeserving poor choose to work the average disutility from work of the undeserving poor who remain on public assistance rises. Thus, $\dfrac{\partial\bar{\theta}_w}{\partial s}$ could be greater than 1. Besley and Coate assume that $g'\dfrac{\partial\bar{\theta}_w}{\partial s} < 1$ to ensure that s* is unique.

Comparative static exercises using Eq. (19.39) show how stigma that arises from statistical discrimination responds to changes in various exogenous variables. For example, Besley and Coate show that $\dfrac{\partial s^*}{\partial b}$ can be positive or negative depending on the value of $\hat{\theta}$. The algebra is tedious and will be left to the interested reader.

A comparative static exercise that relates directly to Besley and Coate's analysis of workfare is the response of stigma to a change in the proportion of the deserving poor, γ. Differentiating Eq. (19.39) wrt γ and rearranging terms yields:

$$\frac{\partial s^*}{\partial \gamma} = \frac{g'\dfrac{\partial\bar{\theta}_w}{\partial \gamma}}{\left(1 - g'\dfrac{\partial\bar{\theta}_w}{\partial s}\right)} \tag{19.41}$$

The denominator is positive by assumption. Also,

$$\frac{\partial \bar{\theta}_w}{\partial \gamma} = (\bar{\theta} - \bar{\theta}_u) \frac{\partial \pi}{\partial \gamma} \qquad (19.42)$$

which is negative since π is increasing in γ. Therefore, stigma decreases as the proportion of the deserving poor on public assistance increases, the expected result.

The government can directly affect γ in two ways. One is to engage in monitoring the welfare rolls in an effort to detect the undeserving poor. Suppose monitoring can detect a proportion λ of the undeserving poor. Then,

$$M(\lambda) = n \left[\gamma + (1 - \lambda)(1 - \gamma)(1 - \hat{\theta}) \right] \qquad (19.43)$$

Also,

$$\frac{\partial s^*}{\partial \lambda} = \frac{g' \dfrac{\partial \bar{\theta}_w}{\partial \lambda}}{\left(1 - g' \dfrac{\partial \bar{\theta}_w}{\partial s}\right)} \qquad (19.44)$$

which has the same negative sign as $\dfrac{\partial s^*}{\partial \gamma}$. The government can reduce stigma through monitoring.

Workfare is another possibility. If it were designed effectively as described in the previous section, then it would remove all the undeserving poor from the welfare rolls. With $\bar{\theta}_w = \bar{\theta}, g(0) = 0$ and stigma disappears.

These examples introduce some doubt about the wisdom of reducing or eliminating welfare stigma when compared with the alternatives. Monitoring is costly and can generate its own form of psychic costs to the poor. Workfare forces the deserving poor to work, which may make them much worse off. (Recall that the government cannot distinguish the deserving from the undeserving poor without monitoring). In the United States at least, the deserving poor are deserving precisely because they are not expected to work. Stigma is undesirable because it lowers the utility of all the poor, but it has the beneficial effect of keeping some of the undeserving poor off the welfare rolls. Therefore, the non-poor may well prefer stigma to either monitoring or workfare as a means of reducing the number of undeserving poor on welfare, at least if stigma arises from this kind of statistical discrimination.

Note, finally, that neither the preferences of the non-poor nor the total number of poor affect stigma when it results from statistical discrimination. The preferences of the non-poor only come into play in the Besley–Coate model if taxpayer resentment is the source of the stigma.

A Political Note

Assar Lindbeck *et al.* published a variation of the Besley–Coate model in 1999, in which their main contribution was to add a political dimension.[14] Their model assumes that individuals have identical preferences but a continuum of skills (wages). There is no sharp distinction between the poor and non-poor as in Besley–Coate. The stigma in their model depends on the number of people who choose to accept transfers rather than work. The polity is a direct democracy in which the transfer-tax policy is decided by a simple majority of voters. Lindbeck *et al.* assume that everyone votes, so that the voter with the median preferences is decisive.[15] With identical preferences and a continuum of skills, the person with the median skill level is the decisive voter.

Their model yields a number of interesting results, particularly regarding the possibility of multiple equilibria. But we mention it primarily to highlight the additional difficulties economists face as they try to bring political considerations into their models. In the baseline model of Lindbeck *et al.*, with stigma but no altruism, the only possible equilibria under simple majority voting are

1. Zero taxes and transfers if the majority of voters choose to work and pay taxes
2. A tax-transfer equilibrium if the majority of voters choose not to work

Either outcome is far from the reality in any of the highly developed market economies. Also, the poor do not vote in anywhere near the same proportion as the non-poor in the United States, so that a direct democracy with full voting would not seem to be the appropriate political model for determining transfer payments in the United States. Unfortunately, no other obvious alternative comes to mind. Lindbeck *et al.* do obtain more realistic possibilities with extensions of their baseline model. But the point remains that the assumed political environment can have a dramatic impact on the implications of any economic model, which makes the uncertainties surrounding the appropriate political model all the more troublesome for normative public sector theory.

REFERENCES

Bearse, P., Glomm, G., and Janeba, E., "Why Poor Countries Rely Mostly on Redistribution In-Kind," *Journal of Public Economics*, March 2000.

Besley, T., and Coate, S., "The Design of Income Maintenance Programs," *Review of Economic Studies*, April 1995.

Besley, T., and Coate, S., "Understanding Welfare Stigma: Taxpayer Resentment and Statistical Discrimination," *Journal of Public Economics*, July 1992.

[14] A. Lindbeck, S. Nyberg, and J. Weibull, "Social Norms and Economic Incentives in the Welfare State," *Quarterly Journal of Economics*, February 1999.

[15] Chapter 31 has a discussion of the median voter political model.

Besley, T., and Coate, S., "Workfare Versus Welfare: Incentive Arguments for Work Requirements in Poverty Alleviation Programs," *American Economic Review*, March 1992.

Blackorby, C., and Donaldson, D., "Cash Versus Kind, Self-Selection, and Efficient Transfers," *American Economic Review*, September 1988.

Browning, E., "Effects of the EITC on Income and Welfare," *National Tax Journal*, March 1995.

Browning, E., and Browning, J., *Public Finance and the Price System*, second ed., Macmillan, New York, 1983.

Bruce, N., and Waldman, N., "Transfers in Kind: Why They Can Be Efficient and Nonpaternalistic," *American Economic Review*, December 1991.

Buchanan, J., "The Samaritan's Dilemma," in E. Phelps, Ed., *Altruism, Morality and Economic Theory*, Russell Sage Foundation, New York, 1975.

Lindbeck, A., Nyberg, S., and Weibull, J., "Social Norms and Economic Incentives in the Welfare State," *Quarterly Journal of Economics*, February 1999.

Moffitt, R., "An Economic Model of Welfare Stigma," *American Economic Review*, 1983.

Rowe, N., and Wooley, F., "The Efficiency Case for Universality," *Canadian Journal of Economics*, May 1999.

Schloz, J., "The EITC: Participation, Compliance, and Anti-Poverty Effectiveness," *National Tax Journal*, March 1994.

20

EXTERNALITIES IN A SECOND-BEST ENVIRONMENT

THE SECOND-BEST ALLOCATION OF SAMUELSONIAN
NONEXCLUSIVE GOODS
  Relationships Between First-Best and Second-Best Allocations
  Concluding Comment
THE COASE THEOREM, BARGAINING, AND
PRIVATE INFORMATION
  Bargaining Set Stability and the Coase Theorem
  Private Information
  Concluding Comment

We saw in Chapters 6–8 that first-best models of externalities dichotomize in two important respects for policy purposes. One is that the government can pursue appropriate tax or expenditure policies to restore pareto optimality in the presence of externalities without regard to distributional considerations. All distributional issues are embodied in the interpersonal equity conditions, which can be satisfied by an appropriate set of lump-sum taxes and transfers. The other is that externalities arising within a subset of all goods and factor markets can be corrected independently of behavior in the other markets, in the sense that the perfectly competitive allocations in these markets remain pareto optimal. These two properties greatly facilitate policy design when correcting for externalities.

Unfortunately, neither of these dichotomies holds in a second-best environment. As a consequence, even the simplest externalities may require highly complex forms of government intervention, so complex in fact that it is entirely implausible to expect governments to achieve them. To illustrate this fundamental point, we will consider the example of providing a Samuelsonian nonexclusive consumption good in a many-person economy made second best because the government does not have the ability to tax and transfer lump sum to achieve the first-best interpersonal equity conditions.

THE SECOND-BEST ALLOCATION OF SAMUELSONIAN NONEXCLUSIVE GOODS

The first-best analysis of a Sameulsonian nonexclusive public good yielded three specific policy prescriptions:

1. The government should provide the good such that $\sum_{h=1}^{H} MRS^h = MRT$. The government has to provide the good because the incentive to free ride prevents the market system from allocating nonexclusive goods.

2. If the government happens to select the quantity that satisfies the optimal decision rule, then it can finance the good with any lump-sum tax. The lump-sum tax keeps the economy on the first-best utility possibilities frontier. Any unwanted distributional consequences of the tax are overcome by the lump-sum taxes and transfers that satisfy the first-best interpersonal equity conditions for a social welfare maximum.

3. The competitive market economy can be counted on to generate the pareto-optimal allocations of all the purely private goods and factors.

None of these prescriptions applies in a second-best environment in general, although the ways in which the first-best optimal decision rules change depend upon the nature of the additional constraints placed on the system. This is always true in second-best analysis. A natural way to pose a second-best problem is to let the government freely choose the quantity of the nonexclusive good but constrain it to finance the good with distorting unit commodity taxes. This implicitly precludes lump-sum redistributions to satisfy the first-best interpersonal equity conditions by equalizing marginal social utilities of income, because if lump-sum taxes could be used for distributional purposes they should also be available to finance the public good. Otherwise, assume that the economy is perfectly competitive with all other goods (factors) being purely private. In other words, the need to use distorting taxes is the only constraint that makes the analysis second best.

Given this particular second-best environment, there are two compelling policy questions to be asked:

1. How does the required distorting taxation affect the optimal decision rule for providing the public good?
2. How does the presence of the public good affect the optimal tax rules when revenue is raised for its own sake?

These questions can be addressed with a general equilibrium model that is a straightforward extension of the many person model used in Chapter 14 to analyze optimal commodity taxation under general technology.

Preferences and Social Welfare

Let e stand for the nonexclusive good, defined in units such that its price equals 1. Since the government is selecting the quantity of e, consumers treat e as a parameter even though e enters their utility functions. Therefore, each individual solves the following utility maximization problem:

$$\max_{(X_{hi})} U^h(X_{hi}; e)$$

$$\text{s.t. } \sum_{i=1}^{N} q_i X_{hi} = \bar{I}^h$$

where:

q_i = the consumer price of good (factor) i, i = 1, ..., N

X_{hi} = good (factor) i consumed (supplied by) person h, i = 1, ..., N

h = 1, ..., H.

$\bar{I}^h$ = the fixed amount of lump-sum income for person h, which the government cannot change through lump-sum redistributions.

The consumer's maximization problem leads to demand (factor supply) functions of the form:

$$X_{hi} = X_{hi}\left(\vec{q}; \bar{I}^h; e\right) \qquad i = 1, \ldots, N; \qquad h = 1, \ldots, H \qquad (20.1)$$

and indirect utility functions:

$$U^h\left[X_{hi}\left(\vec{q}; \bar{I}^h; e\right)\right] = V^h\left(\vec{q}; \bar{I}^h; e\right) \qquad h = 1, \ldots, H \qquad (20.2)$$

Social welfare, then, is

$$W^*\left[U^h\left(X_{hi}\left(\vec{q}; \bar{I}^h; e\right)\right)\right] = W\left[V^h\left(\vec{q}; \bar{I}^h; e\right)\right] \qquad (20.3)$$

where W( ) is the Bergson–Samuelson individualistic social welfare function.

Production and Market Clearance

e must also enter the aggregate production function F because it uses real resources.[1] Therefore, write the aggregate production function implicitly as:

$$F(X_i; e) = 0 \qquad i = 1, \ldots, N \qquad (20.4)$$

where X_i is the aggregate demand (supply) for good (factor) i. Assume that F( ) exhibits constant returns to scale so that there are no pure profits in the economy. Finally, incorporate market clearance directly into the aggregate production function:

$$F\left[\sum_{h=1}^{H} X_{hi}\left(\vec{q}; \bar{I}^h; e\right); e\right] = 0$$

---

[1] e could be privately produced, as missiles and military aircraft are.

Social Welfare Maximization

Society's problem, then, is[2]

$$\max_{(q_i;\, e)} W\left[V^h\left(\vec{q};\vec{I}^h;e\right)\right]$$

$$\text{s.t. } F\left[\sum_{h=1}^{H} X_{hi}\left(\vec{q};\vec{I}^h;e\right);e\right] = 0$$

with the corresponding Lagrangian:

$$\max_{(q_i\ e)} L = W\left[V^h\left(\vec{q};\vec{I}^h;e\right)\right] - \lambda \cdot F\left[\sum_{h=1}^{H} X_{hi}\left(\vec{q};\vec{I}^h;e\right);e\right]$$

Recall from the discussion of this type of model in Chapter 14 that the government's budget constraint,

$$\sum_{h=1}^{H}\sum_{i=2}^{N} t_i X_{hi} = e$$

is implied by Walras' Law under the assumptions of utility maximization, profit maximization, and market clearance in all markets.

Consider the first-order conditions with respect to the consumer prices, q_i:

$$\sum_{h=1}^{H} \frac{\partial W}{\partial V^h}\frac{\partial V^h}{\partial q_k} = \lambda\sum_{i=1}^{N} F_i \frac{\partial X_i}{\partial q_k} \qquad k = 2, \ldots, N \qquad (20.5)$$

Conditions (20.5) are identical to conditions (14.64); therefore, the existence of a nonexclusive good does not affect the form of the many-person optimal tax rule relative to the case in which the government simply raises revenue for its own sake. Of course, the choice of e determines the amount of revenue required, which in part determines the level of tax rates, but otherwise the optimal tax rules have the identical interpretations developed in Chapter 14.

The reappearance of the optimal tax rules is very discouraging in one respect. It implies that the need to finance the public good with distorting taxes forces the government to intervene pervasively into the market economy. In general, the government must tax or subsidize *all* goods and factors (except the numeraire) to achieve the second-best optimum. The provision and financing of the public good cannot be isolated from rest of the economy as it can in a first-best environment. It could be argued that the problem resides with the commodity taxes and not with the public good itself. Re-

---

[2] Recall that maximizing W with respect to $\vec{q}$ is equivalent to maximizing W with respect to $\vec{t}$, with $\vec{q} = \vec{t} + \vec{p}$ and the market clearance equations establishing the relationships among $\vec{q}$, $\vec{t}$, and $\vec{p}$ in equilibrium. Also, good 1 is the untaxed numeraire, with $q_1 = p_1 = 1$, $t_1 = 0$. This is the model used by Peter Diamond in P. Diamond, "A Many Person Ramsey Tax Rule," *Journal of Public Economics*, November 1975.

member, though, that the optimal decision rule for the public good that we are about to develop requires that Eq. (20.5) hold for the distorting taxes. Otherwise, the first-order condition for the public good that follows would not be the necessary condition for a social welfare optimum, in general.

With these comments in mind, consider the first-order condition with respect to e:

$$\sum_{h=1}^{H} \frac{\partial W}{\partial V^h} \frac{\partial V^h}{\partial e} = \lambda \sum_{h=1}^{H} \sum_{i=1}^{N} F_i \frac{\partial X_{hi}}{\partial e} + \lambda F_e \qquad (20.6)$$

Defining F such that $\partial F / \partial X_1 = 1$, assuming profit maximization under perfect competition, and given that $p_1 \equiv q_1 \equiv 1$, the untaxed numeraire, Eq. (20.6), can be rewritten as:

$$\sum_{h=1}^{H} \frac{\partial W}{\partial V^h} \frac{\partial V^h}{\partial e} = \lambda \sum_{h=1}^{H} \sum_{i=1}^{N} p_i \frac{\partial X_{hi}}{\partial e} + \lambda F_e \qquad (20.7)$$

But $p_i = q_i - t_i$, $i = 1, \ldots, N$. Therefore,

$$\sum_{h=1}^{H} \frac{\partial W}{\partial V^h} \frac{\partial V^h}{\partial e} = \lambda \sum_{h=1}^{H} \sum_{i=1}^{N} (q_i - t_i) \frac{\partial X_{hi}}{\partial e} + \lambda F_e \qquad (20.8)$$

Next, differentiate each consumer's budget constraint, $\sum_{i=1}^{N} q_i X_{hi} \left(\vec{q}; \bar{I}^h; e \right) = \bar{I}^h$, with respect to e:

$$\sum_{i=1}^{N} q_i \frac{\partial X_{hi}}{\partial e} = 0 \qquad h = 1, \ldots, H \qquad (20.9)$$

Substituting Eq. (20.9) into (20.8) yields:

$$\sum_{h=1}^{H} \frac{\partial W}{\partial V^h} \frac{\partial V^h}{\partial e} = -\lambda \sum_{i=1}^{N} t_i \frac{\partial X_i}{\partial e} + \lambda F_e \qquad (20.10)$$

Peter Diamond proposed the following $\sum_{h=1}^{H} MRS^h = MRT$ interpretation of condition (20.10).[3] Rewrite Eq. (20.10) as:

$$\sum_{h=1}^{H} \frac{\partial W}{\partial V^h} \frac{\partial V^h}{\partial e} + \lambda \sum_{i=1}^{N} t_i \frac{\partial X_i}{\partial e} = \lambda F_e \qquad (20.11)$$

The right-hand side (RHS) of Eq. (20.11) measures the marginal social cost, through production, of increasing the public good. The left-hand side (LHS) is the social marginal value of increasing the public good. The first term represents the social marginal value of having each person consume an additional unit of nonexclusive e; the second term represents the social value of the increased tax revenues resulting from a marginal increase in e. Thus,

[3] P. Diamond, "A Many Person Ramsey Tax Rule," *Journal of Public Economics*, November 1975, p. 341.

Eq. (20.11) has the natural interpretation that e should be increased until its social marginal value just equals its social marginal cost. To change this to a $\sum_{h=1}^{H} MRS^h = MRT$ form, define:

$$\delta^h = \frac{\partial W}{\partial V^h}\frac{\partial V^h}{\partial e} + \lambda\sum_{i=1}^{N} t_i\frac{\partial X_{hi}}{\partial e} \tag{20.12}$$

Recall that the social marginal utility of income, β^h, is a product of the marginal social welfare weight and the private marginal utility of income, or $\beta^h = (\partial W/\partial V^h)\alpha^h = (\partial W/\partial V^h)(\partial V^h/\partial I^h)$. Therefore, δ^h can be expressed as:

$$\delta^h = \beta^h\left(\frac{\frac{\partial V^h}{\partial e}}{\frac{\partial V^h}{\partial I^h}}\right) + \lambda\sum_{i=1}^{N} t_i\frac{\partial X_{hi}}{\partial e} = \beta^h MRS^h_{e,X_{h1}} + \lambda\sum_{i=1}^{N} t_i\frac{\partial X_{hi}}{\partial e} \tag{20.13}$$

the social marginal value of letting person h consume an additional unit of e.[4] Substituting Eq. (20.13) into (20.11) yields:

$$\sum_{h=1}^{H}\delta^h = \lambda F_e \tag{20.14}$$

or

$$\sum_{h=1}^{H}\frac{\delta^h}{\lambda} = F_e \tag{20.15}$$

With F defined such that $F_1 = 1$, and $p_1 \equiv q_1 \equiv 1$, the RHS of Eq. (20.15) is the marginal rate of transformation between the public good and the numeraire good. To interpret the LHS, recall from Chapter 14 that if the government offers an optimal equal-value head subsidy to all individuals, λ can be interpreted as the average social marginal utility of income, equal to $\sum_{h=1}^{H}\gamma^h/H$, where $\gamma^h = \beta^h + \lambda\sum_{i=1}^{N} t_i(\partial X_{hi}/\partial I)$, the social marginal utility of giving additional income to person h. Given this interpretation of λ, the LHS of Eq. (20.15) can be interpreted as a $\sum_{h=1}^{H} MRS^h$, the sum of the *social* marginal rate of substitution between consumption of e by each individual and income (or, equivalently, the numeraire good) averaged over the population.

Relationships Between First-Best and Second-Best Allocations

Diamond's interpretation of the social marginal rate of substitution is obviously far removed from the usual notion of a social marginal rate of substi-

[4] $MRS^h_{e,X_{h1}} \equiv \frac{\frac{\partial V^h}{\partial e}}{\frac{\partial V^h}{\partial X_{h1}}} = \frac{\frac{\partial V^h}{\partial e}}{\alpha^h q_1} = \frac{\frac{\partial V^h}{\partial e}}{\frac{\partial V^h}{\partial I^h}}$, from utility maximization and $q_1 = 1$.

tution for nonexclusive goods from first-best analysis. There is no obvious quantitative relationship between the first-best and second-best decision rules for the allocation of e. Clearly, the true social MRS (the Diamond measure) could be arbitrarily larger or smaller than the first-best social MRS depending upon the choice of the β^h, the social marginal utilities of income.

It has long been common wisdom that a nonoptimal income distribution requires dividing the benefits (and costs) of public projects into socially relevant components and weighting each component by the appropriate social marginal utilities of income. But notice that even if the income distribution is optimal, such that $\beta^h = \beta$, for all $h = 1, \ldots, H$, the straight summation of individual MRS^h still misrepresents the true social marginal rate of substitution if distorting taxes are used to finance these public projects, since the tax term $\lambda \sum_{i=1}^{N} t_i \dfrac{\partial X_i}{\partial e}$ remains as part of the true social marginal rate of substitution. This point was established formally by Anthony Atkinson and Nicholas Stern and elaborated on by David Wildasin, although A. C. Pigou presented an intuitive analysis as early as 1947.[5]

To isolate the effect of the tax term on the social valuation of nonexclusive goods, assume all consumers have identical tastes and endowments, $\bar{I} = \bar{I}^1, \ldots, \bar{I}^h, \ldots, \bar{I}^H$. Further, let $\partial W / \partial V^h = 1$, all $h = 1, \ldots, H$, so that the distribution is optimal from society's point of view. Hence, $\beta^h = \beta = \alpha = \partial V^h / \partial I^h$, all $h = 1, \ldots, H$, the common private marginal utility of income. Under these assumptions, Eq. (20.15) becomes (using Eq. (20.13)):

$$\frac{\alpha}{\lambda} \left(H \cdot MRS^h_{e, X_{hl}} \right) + \sum_{i=1}^{N} t_i \frac{\partial X_i}{\partial e} = F_e = MRT_{e, X_l} \qquad (20.16)$$

where:

$(H \cdot MRS^h_{e, X_{hi}})$ = the standard first-best interpretation of the social marginal rate of substitution for a nonexclusive good.

According to Eq. (20.16), the true second-best social MRS (the entire LHS of Eq. (20.16)) tends to exceed the first-best social MRS the more increasing the public good increases tax revenues through its effect on the demands (supplies) of all other goods (factors), and vice versa. Assuming that the revenues increase, this provides an additional source of marginal social value that the first-best measure misses.

Suppose, however, that all purely private demands (and factor suppliers) are independent of e ($\partial X_i / \partial e = 0$, all $i = 1, \ldots, N$), so that the revenue effect vanishes. The true social MRS still differs from the first-best measure by the

[5] A. Atkinson and N. Stern, "Pigou, Taxation, and Public Goods," *Review of Economic Studies*, January 1974; A. C. Pigou, *A Study in Public Finance*, third ed., Macmillan, London, 1947. D. Wildasin, "On Public Good Provision with Distributionary Taxation," *Economic Inquiry*, April 1984.

factor α/λ in a world with distorting taxes. The question remains, then, whether the first-best measure under- or overstates the true measure; that is, whether $\alpha/\lambda \gtrless 1$.

α/λ can be evaluated if we assume the government is raising tax revenue optimally. With identical consumers and $\beta^h = \beta = \alpha$, and using Roy's Identity, the first-order conditions for optimal taxation, Eq. (20.5), become:

$$-H\alpha X_{hk} = \lambda \sum_{h=1}^{H}\sum_{i=1}^{N} F_i \frac{\partial X_{hi}}{\partial q_k} = \lambda H \cdot \sum_{i=1}^{N} F_i \frac{\partial X_{hi}}{\partial q_k} \qquad k = 2, \ldots, N \qquad (20.17)$$

Reproducing the derivation of the optimal rule in Chapter 14:

$$-\alpha X_{hk} = \lambda \sum_{i=1}^{N} F_i \frac{\partial X_{hi}}{\partial q_k} \qquad (20.18)$$

$$-\alpha X_{hk} = \lambda \sum_{i=1}^{N} p_i \frac{\partial X_{hi}}{\partial q_k} \qquad (20.19)$$

$$-\alpha X_{hk} = \lambda \sum_{i=1}^{N} (q_i - t_i) \frac{\partial X_{hi}}{\partial q_k} \qquad (20.20)$$

$$-\alpha X_{hk} = \lambda \left(-X_{hk} - \sum_{i=1}^{N} t_i \frac{\partial X_{hi}}{\partial q_k} \right) \qquad (20.21)$$

$$-\alpha X_{hk} = \lambda \left(-X_{hk} - \sum_{i=1}^{N} t_i S_{ik}^h + X_{hk} \sum_{i=1}^{N} t_i \frac{\partial X_{hi}}{\partial I} \right) \qquad (20.22)$$

where:

$S_{ik}^h = \dfrac{\partial X_{hi}}{\partial q_k}\bigg|_{compensated}$, the Slutsky substitution term.

Dividing both sides by $-\lambda X_{hk}$ and rearranging terms:

$$\left(\frac{\alpha}{\lambda} - 1 + \sum_{i=1}^{N} t_i \frac{\partial X_{hi}}{\partial I} \right) = \frac{\sum_{i=1}^{N} t_i S_{ik}^h}{X_{hk}} \qquad k = 2, \ldots, N \qquad (20.23)$$

Next, multiply the numerator and denominator of the RHS of Eq. (20.23) by t_k and sum over $k = 1, \ldots, N$ to obtain:

$$N \cdot \left(\frac{\alpha}{\lambda} - 1 + \sum_{i=1}^{N} t_i \frac{\partial X_{hi}}{\partial I} \right) = \frac{\sum_{i=1}^{N}\sum_{k=1}^{N} t_i S_{ik}^h t_k}{\sum_{k=1}^{N} t_k X_{hk}} \qquad (20.24)$$

As long as total tax revenue $\left(\sum_{k=1}^{N} t_k X_{hk} \right)$ is positive,[6] the RHS of Eq. (20.24) is negative because the Slutsky matrix is negative definite. Other

---

[6] It may not be, given that factors are subsidized.

things equal, therefore, the RHS tends to lower the value of α/λ and thereby reduce the value of the true social MRS. Pigou identified this as the "indirect damage" of having to raise additional revenues with distorting taxes to finance increases in the public good.[7] The second effect involves the term $\sum_{i=1}^{N} t_i(\partial X_{hi}/\partial I)$, which Atkinson and Stern call the "revenue effect" of distorting taxes.[8] If this term is positive (that is, if tax collections rise with increases in lump-sum income), then α/λ must be less than one and the first-best social MRS overstates the true social MRS. The tax term could well be negative, however, because factor supplies are subsidized if goods are taxed (recall that factors enter the analysis with a negative sign). If so, then α/λ may be greater than, less than, or equal to one despite the (negative) distortionary effect of second-best taxes. Hence, there is no way of knowing, *a priori*, whether the true social MRS is less than, greater than, or equal to the first-best social MRS in the presence of distorting taxes, even if: (1) the distribution of income is optimal, (2) there are no direct revenue effects of increasing the nonexclusive good, and (3) the distorting taxes used to raise revenue are optimally set.[9,10]

Concluding Comment

The public good example emphasizes an important yet discouraging point: Even small departures from a first-best environment can generate staggering problems for public sector decision making. All we did was introduce distorting taxation into an otherwise first-best policy environment. When one

[7] See A. C. Pigou, *A Study in Public Finance*, third ed., Macmillan, London, 1947, p. 34.

[8] A. Atkinson and N. Stern, "Pigou, Taxation, and Public Goods," *Review of Economic Studies*, January, 1974, p. 123. The analysis of α/λ closely follows their derivation. See D. Wildasin, "On Public Good Provision with Distortionary Taxation," *Economic Inquiry*, April 1984, for a complete analysis of the effect of the two tax terms on the allocation of the public good. He considers the cases in which some private goods are complements or substitutes to the public good.

[9] Karen Conway examined the effect of government expenditures on the supply of labor using a sample of males and females from the 1980 PSID. She achieved variation in government expenditures across individuals by using combinations of state, state and local, and state, local, and federal spending as the government variable. She tried both aggregate expenditures and various individual expenditure categories. The estimates proved to be highly sensitive to sample size and attempts to control for state fixed effects. Conway concludes that labor supply and government spending are neither ordinary nor compensated independents for men and unmarried women. She could not reject the hypothesis that labor supply and government spending are compensated and ordinary independents for married women. See K. Conway, "Labor Supply, Taxes, and Government Spending: A Microeconometric Analysis," *Review of Economics and Statistics*, February 1997.

[10] Cost-benefit practitioners might consult A. Sandmo, "Redistribution and the Marginal Cost of Public Funds," *Journal of Public Economics*, December 1998. In this article, Agnar Sandmo presents a simple model of heterogeneous consumers consisting of a composite consumer good, labor, and one non-exclusive public good. Social welfare is utilitarian. He uses the model to demonstrate the effect of four factors on the marginal cost of public funds in line with equations

considers that the number of real-world distortions is far greater than simply the need to use distorting taxes, the prospects for achieving a unified normative theory of the public sector are indeed discouraging.

THE COASE THEOREM, BARGAINING, AND PRIVATE INFORMATION

The Coase Theorem holds out hope that government intervention might not always be required to solve market failures such as externalities. Its premise is that in the absence of private information and transaction costs, private agents have an incentive to bargain with one another and write whatever contracts are necessary to extract all pareto-superior gains and thereby reach the pareto optimum. The only prior requirement is the assignment of property rights, so that ownership of the activities giving rise to or receiving the externalities is clearly established.

No one expected the Coase Theorem to apply to instances of widespread externalities because the transaction costs of bringing large numbers of agents into a bargaining setting were likely to be formidable. But the hope was that externalities involving only a few agents could be settled efficiently through bargaining rather than by government intervention.

Coase published his Theorem in 1960. Since that time, developments in bargaining theory have pretty much dashed the hopes of the Theorem even in the case of small numbers of agents. There are two main problems. One is that the formation of coalitions through cooperative bargaining requires that certain conditions be satisfied for the coalitions to be stable. Unfortunately, the set of stable coalitions may not include the pareto-optimal allocation, and even if it does the bargaining process may not settle on the pareto-optimal coalition. The other problem is that private information may limit the payments that agents are willing to make to other parties as part of a bargain. The acceptable range of payments may preclude the payment that is necessary to achieve the pareto optimum.

The Coase Theorem can get around these problems in principle by assuming them away. Rational agents may be seen as rejecting any pareto-inferior coalitions simply because they are pareto inferior. Or, rational agents may be presumed to reveal their private information willingly if doing so would lead to pareto-superior allocations. Assumptions such as these effect-

---

(20.11) or (20.15): 1). the sources of tax revenues, particularly whether there is the possibility of a lump-sum tax equal for everyone; 2). whether taxes are set optimally; 3). the distributional characteristic of the public good, defined in terms of the covariance between individuals' MRS and their marginal utility of income; and 4). the effect of changes in the public good on tax revenues. Sandmo argues that (1) and (2) should be considered in calculating a marginal cost of public funds but not (3) and (4), since they are specific to particular public goods.

ively turn the Theorem into a tautology. But, if agents act independently and self-interestedly and enter into bargains voluntarily, then the difficulties posed by the requirements of bargaining stability and the presence of private information should not be assumed away. They should be considered in deciding whether government intervention can improve upon a private sector that includes bargaining as well as market exchange.

Bargaining Set Stability and the Coase Theorem

A simple example developed by Varouj Aivasion, Jeffrey Callen, and Irwin Lipnowski illustrates the problems of achieving efficient solutions through cooperative bargaining even in the case of perfect information and small numbers.[11] Suppose there are three agents: two factories (agents 1 and 2) and a laundry (agent 3). Smoke from the factories is an external diseconomy to the laundry. The net values of the factories and laundry if they act alone or form two-agent coalitions or form a three-agent coalition are as follows:

Acting alone	Two-party coalitions	Three-party coalition
$V(1) = 1$	$V(1, 2) = 8$	$V(1, 2, 3) = 12$
$V(2) = 2$	$V(1, 3) = 9$	
$V(3) = 3$	$V(2, 3) = 10$	

All two-party coalitions improve upon the stand-alone outcomes, always providing a net value of 11 for the three agents combined. The three-party coalition yields the most net value; it is the pareto-optimal solution in this example. A story behind these net values might be that the two factories enjoy synergies if merged that are absent if they act alone; the merger of either one of the factories and the laundry internalizes the externality, which increases the attainable net value relative to acting alone; and the three-party coalition has the advantage of realizing the factory synergies and internalizing both externalities.

Bargaining Set Stability

Two commonly-accepted requirements for stable bargaining sets are individual rationality and coalition stability. *Individual rationality* says that agents will not accept an outcome as part of a coalition that is worse than the outcome they can achieve by acting on their own. Thus, the net values in the first column above set a floor on the values the agents will accept as part of any coalition. *Coalition stability* says that any credible objection to a coalition by one of the members must be able to be met by a credible counter objection by another member of the collation to ensure that the coalition is stable. A credible objection is an announcement by one member (say, agent i)

---

[11] V. Aivasian, J. Callen, and I. Lipnowski, "The Coase Theorem and Coalitional Stability," *Economica*, November 1987.

that he can form another coalition consisting of himself, some members of the current coalition, and perhaps some agents currently outside the coalition such that he is better off under the new coalition and no member of the new coalition is worse off. If this is true, then he will break away and form the new coalition unless someone else can mount a credible counter objection of the same kind. For example, agent j might counter object that if agent i were to do this, she could form yet another coalition consisting of all the members in agent i's new coalition, except person i, and perhaps some other people such that she is better off and no one else is worse off relative to their position with agent i's new coalition. Faced with counter objections of this kind, no one can gain by breaking away from the coalition and the coalition is stable.

The coalitions that meet the objection/counter-objection test for coalition stability in Aivasion *et al.*'s example are[12]

$$\{(\$\text{Net Values}): [\text{Coalition}]\}$$
$$\text{One} - \text{agent: } \{(1; 2; 3): [1, 2, 3]\}$$
$$\text{Two} - \text{agent: } \{(3.5; 4.5; 3): [(1, 2), 3]\}$$
$$\{(3.5; 2; 5.5): [(1, 3), 2]\}$$
$$\{(1; 4.5; 5.5): [(2, 3), 1]\}$$
$$\text{Three} - \text{agent: } \{(3; 4; 5): [(1, 2, 3)]\}$$

Consider the first two-agent coalition as an example. Suppose agent 1 objects and proposes to form a new two-agent coalition with agent 3, with the values:

$$\{(3.5 + e; 2; 5.5 - e): [(1, 3), 2]\}$$

Agent 2 can counter object with the following proposed coalition:

$$\{(1; 4.5 + e; 5.5 - e): [(2, 3), 1)]\}$$

Thus, each can credibly block the other's attempt to break away from the coalition.

Similarly, any attempt by one of the agents in the three-agent coalition to break away and form a two-agent coalition is subject to a credible counter objection. For example, if agent 1 objects and wants to break away with agent 3, offering $\{(3.5 + e; 2; 5.5 - e): [(1, 3), 2)]\}$, then agent 2 can counter object and break away with agent 3, offering $\{(1; 4.5 + e; 5.5 - e): [(2, 3), 1]\}$.

That a three-agent coalition with one division of the combined net value is stable may seem encouraging, but the bargaining process may never get there. One problem is that any pareto-superior move from one of the two-agent coalitions does not produce a stable coalition. Consider the move from

---

[12] The values are the solution to a set of linear inequalities that satisfy the conditions for coalition stability. The equations are in Footnote 6 of the A-C-L paper. We will illustrate coalition stability by some examples here.

the two-agent coalition $\{(3.5; 4.5; 3): [(1, 2), 3)]\}$ to the pareto-superior three-agent coalition $\{(3.75, 4.75, 3.5): [(1, 2, 3)]\}$. Suppose agent 3 objects to the new coalition and wants to join agent 1 in a two-agent coalition, $\{(3.75 + e, 2, 5.25 - e): [(1, 3), 2)]\}$. Agent 2 cannot credibly counter object because with only \$8 to split up between agents 1 and 2 it would have to accept $\{(3.75 + e, 4.25 - e, 3.5): [(1, 2), 3)]\}$. The pareto-superior coalition is not stable. Agent 2 might make this counter proposal out of spite, but adding a spite motive makes it unclear what the final bargaining equilibrium might be or, indeed, if any coalition is stable.

An additional problem is that each agent is better off as part of one of the stable two-agent coalitions than in the stable three-agent coalition. Thus, any two agents have a strong incentive to form one of the stable two-agent coalitions as a preemptive move rather than join the three-agent coalition. [13] Therefore, despite the presence of a pareto-optimal and stable three-agent coalition, the bargaining process in this example is highly likely form a two-agent coalition with a combined net value of 11 rather than 12 for the three-agent coalition.

Economists have proposed a number of different equilibrium concepts in cooperative bargaining settings. There is not one accepted definition of equilibrium. Nonetheless, individual rationality and coalition stability are fairly compelling concepts, and the example of Aivasion *et al.* shows that imposing them on the bargaining process can undermine the Coase theorem.

Private Information

The existence of private information makes the chances of achieving an efficient bargaining outcome highly unlikely. Even bargains between two agents can fail to achieve an efficient outcome. A two-agent example provided by Peter Klibanoff and Jonathan Morduch illustrates the nature of the problem. [14]

Suppose that production of firm 1 generates an external economy of size w for firm 2. The externality w is a constant independent of the size of firm 1's output. Firm 2 cannot be certain whether firm 1 will produce. All it knows is that the net value of firm 1 is a random variable, v, ranging from a low of α to a high of β, $\alpha < 0$ and $\beta > 0$, with density function $f(v)$ and cumulative density function $F(v)$. Firm 2 is free to engage in a voluntary negotiation with firm 1 and offer a subsidy to encourage firm 1 to produce. The question is how high the subsidy should be.

---

[13] More generally, the three-agent coalition violates coalition rationality, another widely accepted concept for bargaining set stability. *Coalition rationality* says that any subgroup of agents in a coalition will never accept another coalition in which the total payments to the subgroup are smaller.

[14] P. Klibanoff and J. Morduch, "Decentralization, Externalities, and Efficiency," *Review of Economic Studies*, April 1995.

The pareto-optimal solution is for firm 1 to produce as long as $w + v > 0$. If firm 2 had perfect information about firm 1 and knew that $v < 0$, then it would negotiate a subsidy to firm 1 as long as $w > |v|$. If it knew that $v > 0$, then it would let firm 1 produce without negotiating a subsidy. The pareto-optimal solution obtains in either case.

With uncertainty about v, however, firm 2 has to weigh the expected benefits and costs of any subsidy it gives to firm 1. Suppose it offers a subsidy of x. Then its expected cost is $x(1 - F(-x))$, the subsidy times the probability that firm 1 will produce given the subsidy. The expected benefit is $w[(1 - F(-x)) - (1 - F(0))]$, the value of the externality times the *increase* in the probability that firm 1 will produce given the subsidy. The increase in the probability is the probability that firm 1 will produce given the subsidy x less the probability that firm 1 will produce without a subsidy. Thus, firm 2 offers a subsidy if:

$$w[(1 - F(-x)) - (1 - F(0))] - x[1 - F(-x)] \geq 0, \text{ or} \qquad (20.25)$$

$$w[F(0) - F(-x)] \geq x[1 - F(-x)] \qquad (20.26)$$

The probability that firm 1 will produce without a subsidy greatly reduces the probability that firm 2 will subsidize firm 1. To see this, assume $f(v)$ is the uniform distribution over the interval $[\alpha, \beta]$, such that $F(x) = (x - \alpha)/(\beta - \alpha)$. Substituting for $F(-x)$ into Eq. (20.26) yields:

$$w[(-\alpha + x + \alpha)/(\beta - \alpha)] \geq x[1 + (x + \alpha)/(\beta - \alpha)] \qquad (20.27)$$

Multiplying by $(\beta - \alpha)$ and rearranging terms,

$$wx \geq x(\beta + x) \qquad (20.28)$$
$$w \geq \beta + x \qquad (20.29)$$

The externality has to be very large, larger than the highest net value of firm 1's production, for firm 2 to subsidize firm 1. Smaller externalities will preclude a subsidy even though $w + v$ might be greater than 0. For example, suppose that $\alpha = -1/2$, $\beta = 1$, and $w = 1$. Since $w = \beta$, there will be no negotiation and subsidy even though a subsidy of $1 > x > 1/2$ would guarantee that firm 1 produces and would make both firms better off. Firm 1 would have positive net value inclusive of the subsidy and firm 2 would enjoy a positive externality net of the subsidy. Private information undermines the Coase theorem.

The government can guarantee the first-best outcome if it makes a side deal with firm 1 that it will not produce unless firm 2 gives it a subsidy of w. This is in effect the Pigovian tax solution, since w is the marginal as well as the total external benefit to firm 2 given that firm 1 is making a produce/do not produce decision. Firm 1 will produce under this subsidy as long as $w > |v|$. Also, firm 2 will agree to pay the subsidy because it knows that firm 1 will not produce without the subsidy. Consequently, the term $(1 - F(0))$ drops out from the expected benefits in Eq. (20.25), and firm 2 offers a subsidy x as long as $w \geq x$. The point is that the Coase Theorem can be rescued in the face of private information, but only if the government asserts itself in some coercive fashion. Another example of achieving the first best through government coercion is the Clarke tax scheme, described in Chapter 6, which the government forces people to participate in to get them to reveal their demand curves for a nonexclusive good.

If, however, the negotiations remain voluntary and both agents honor the individual rationality condition on bargains, then the first best outcome is not guaranteed under private information. In the Klibanoff–Morduch example, under the uniform distribution, the first best can be guaranteed only if the externality is so large that firm 2 is willing to ensure that firm 1 produces by giving it a subsidy $x = |\alpha|$, the smallest possible value of v. Plugging $-x = \alpha$ into Eq. (20.26), noting that $w \geq x = -\alpha$ for firm 2 to offer the subsidy, and solving for w:

$$w[F(0) - F(\alpha)] \geq -\alpha[1 - F(\alpha)] \tag{20.30}$$

or

$$w \geq -\alpha/F(0) \tag{20.31}$$

If $-\alpha = \beta$, so that the uniform distribution of v is symmetric around 0, then $F(0) = 1/2$ and

$$w \geq -2\alpha = 2\beta \tag{20.32}$$

The externality has to be greater than *twice* the highest net value of firm 1's production to ensure the first-best solution under private information. This is undoubtedly an unrealistically large externality in most practical applications.

A final question is whether a negotiated subsidy is better than autonomy, even if it is not first best. The answer turns on whether Eq. (20.25) is satisfied for some $v^* < 0$, rewritten here as:

$$K(v^*) = w[(1 - F(v^*)) - (1 - F(0)] + v^*[1 - F(v^*)] \geq 0 \tag{20.33}$$

Note that $K(0) = 0$, and

$$dK(v^*)/dv^* = 1 - F(v^*) - (w + v^*)f(v^*) \tag{20.34}$$

The sign of $dK(v^*)/dv^* = \text{sign}\left[\dfrac{(1 - F(v^*))}{f(v^*)} - (w + v^*)\right]$

$\dfrac{(1 - F(v^*))}{f(v^*)}$ is non-increasing for many distributions, including the uniform distribution. Therefore, a $v^* < 0$ satisfying Eq. (20.25) exists if and only if $dK(v^*)/dv^*|_{v^* = 0} \leq 0$, which is equivalent to:

$$w \geq \frac{(1 - F(0))}{f(0)} \tag{20.35}$$

For the uniform distribution symmetric around 0,

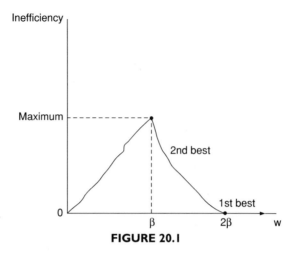

FIGURE 20.1

$$w \geq \frac{(1 - 1/2)}{\dfrac{1}{2\beta}} = \beta = -\alpha \qquad (20.36)$$

We have already seen that firm 2 will offer firm 1 a subsidy as long as $w \geq \beta$, and that the subsidy will be first best if $w \geq 2\beta$. Equation (20.36) establishes that a negotiated subsidy is better than autonomy when $\beta \leq w \leq 2\beta$. It reduces inefficiency, but it is a second-best solution. Finally, the inefficiency of autonomy rises in the range of $0 \leq w \leq \beta$. Fig. 20.1 summarizes the outcomes for different values of w (again assuming a uniform distribution of v symmetric around 0).

Market Power and Private Information

Eric Maskin has noted that the bargaining inefficiencies brought on by private information in two-agent externality models such as the Klibanoff–Morduch model are inherent in *any* exchange between two or more agents.[15] The externality is not the source of the problem. Instead, the inefficiency arises only because one or more of the parties has market power: In the Klibanoff–Morduch model, firm 2 has the ability to set the subsidy x. If all firms were price takers, then the combination of externalities and private information would not necessarily prevent pareto-optimal bargaining even among a large number of agents.

The essence of the problem when an externality is involved is the following. Suppose the beneficiary of an external economy receives a marginal benefit of w as in the Klibanoff–Morduch model. If the beneficiary pays

---

[15] E. Maskin, "The Invisible Hand and Externalities," *American Economic Association Paper and Proceedings*, May 1994.

the generator of the externality a fee equal to w, the Pigovian tax or pseudo-competitive price, and w exceeds the marginal cost of providing the externality, then the externality will be provided in an efficient manner. If, however, the beneficiary has market power, then it will set its offer below w to try to reap some gain on the margin. The generator of the externality cannot be certain that w is the marginal benefit so it cannot insist on w in payment. The problem is that the beneficiary's offer may be less then the marginal cost to the generator even if w is not, in which case the externality is not provided and the outcome is not pareto optimal.

Maskin uses a famous externality example of long standing—the bee-keepers and the apple growers, first described by James Meade—to illustrate the efficiency of price-taking behavior in the presence of private information. The beekeepers keep bees to produce honey, but the bees provide an external economy to the apple growers by pollinating the apple trees. The problem is to efficiently account for the pollination externality by increasing the number of bees kept by the beekeepers.

To provide a competitive setting, Maskin assumes that there are a large and equal number of beekeepers and apple orchards, n. In the baseline example, each beekeeper is adjacent to one apple orchard, and its pollination externality is experienced only by the adjacent apple orchard. Also, the beekeepers have the power of exclusion. They can prevent the bees from pollinating the apple trees if the price they are offered for the externality is below their marginal cost. The apple orchards are identical, as are the beekeepers.

The beekeepers' costs, c_j, are private information to the beekeepers. c_j is a random variable drawn from the uniform distribution over the interval from 1 to 3. The apple growers' external economy from the number of bees, x, is given by the utility function $U = \theta_i x - x^2$, where the θ_i are private information to the apple growers. θ_i is a random variable also drawn from the uniform distribution over the interval from 1 to 3.

Write the supply and demand functions for bees as $s(c_j, p)$ and $d(\theta_i, p)$. Given a competitively determined price, p, the beekeepers' supply decision for the marginal bee is.

$$s(c_j, p) = 1, c_j \leq p$$
$$= 0, c_j > p \qquad (20.37)$$

The producer surplus of the apple growers from the bees, given the price p, is $U(x) = \theta_i x - x^2 - px$, so that the surplus on the margin is $U' = \theta_i - 2x - p$. $U' = 0$ when $x = (\theta_i - p)/2$. Therefore, their demand for bees is

$$d(\theta_i, p) = \max((\theta_i - p)/2, 0) \qquad (20.38)$$

The price is determined in the competitive marketplace. It is the solution to:

$$\frac{1}{n}\sum_{i=1}^{n}d(\theta_i, p^*) = \frac{1}{n}\sum_{j=1}^{n}s(c_j, p^*) \qquad (20.39)$$

written from the perspective of each individual apple orchard and beekeeper. For large n, Eq. (20.39) is approximately equivalent to:

$$E[d(\theta_i, p^*)] = Pr(s(c_j, p^*) = 1) \qquad (20.40)$$

The uniform density function over which θ_i and c_j are drawn is $f(z) = 1/2$. Therefore,

$$E[d(\theta_i, p^*)] = \int_{p}^{3}\left(\frac{\theta_i - p}{2}\right) \cdot \frac{1}{2}\,d\theta = |_p^3 \frac{(\theta_i - p)^2}{8} = \frac{9 - 6p - p^2}{8} \qquad (20.41)$$

and

$$Pr\,(s\,(c_j, p^*) = 1) = \int_{1}^{p}\frac{1}{2}\,dc = |_1^p\frac{1}{2}c = \frac{p - 1}{2} \qquad (20.42)$$

Therefore, p* is the solution to:

$$\frac{9 - 6p - p^2}{8} = \frac{p - 1}{2} \qquad (20.43)$$

$$p^* = 5 - 2\sqrt{3} \qquad (20.44)$$

Competitive pricing is *ex ante* efficient assuming the agents want to maximize their producer surpluses. It calls forth the correct amount of bees even in the presence of private information.[16] The Coase Theorem is vindicated, all the more surprising because the number of agents is large.

This result is tempered by a number of considerations, however. First, the one-on-one nature of the externality makes these transactions not really different in kind from any transaction of a private good between two agents. Second, the ability of the beekeeper to exclude the pollination services of the bees prevents the government from having to assign property rights to the beekeepers. Third, the model ignores transaction costs, which in most many-agent settings are likely to be nontrivial. Finally, the result does not hold if the externalities generated by any one beekeeper extend beyond a single apple orchard.

Nonexclusive Externalities

Maskin develops the final point by considering the nonexclusive case in which the bees can fly to any orchard. Therefore, one bee can be expected to provide 1/n units of service to each apple orchard. The efficient solution in this case is that beekeeper j should keep an additional bee as long as:

---

[16] The solution is only approximately efficient since Eq. (20.40) is only an approximation of Eq. (20.39) for large n. Some beekeepers would have to be chosen at random and required either to keep or not to keep an additional bee to satisfy the supply = demand equilibrium.

$$\frac{1}{n}\sum_{i=1}^{n}(\theta_i - 2x) \geq c_j \tag{20.45}$$

That is, the sum of the marginal benefits equals the marginal cost.

The LHS of Eq. (20.45) is approximately equal to its expected value for large n. Hence,

$$E(\theta_i) - 2E(x) = 2 - 2\frac{(p-1)}{2} = 3 - p \tag{20.46}$$

where E(x) is given by (20.42), the expected supply of bees. Hence,

$$3 - p \geq c_j = p \tag{20.47}$$

$$p^* = 3/2 \tag{20.48}$$

Therefore, beekeepers with $c_j < 3/2$ produce a bee, about 1/4 of the beekeepers given that the uniform distribution for c_j is defined over the interval from 1 to 3. The average cost to the beekeepers who keep a bee is the expected value of c_j over the interval of 1 to 3/2, which equals 5/4. Thus, for large n, every apple grower should pay a price of $5/16 \left(= \frac{1}{4} \cdot \frac{5}{4}\right)$ to ensure the efficient number of bees. But, the free-rider problem prevents this solution: Each apple grower has an incentive not to pay and free ride on the good will of the other growers.

The government can enforce the efficient outcome by having agents sign a contract in which: (1). each beekeeper agrees to announce whether it is willing to supply a bee if paid a fee of 3/2; (2). a random selection of (approximately) 3/4 of the apple growers agree to pay a fee of $1/2\left(\frac{1}{2} \cdot \frac{3}{4} = \frac{3}{8} = \frac{3}{2} \cdot \frac{1}{4}\right)$; and (3) nonparticipating apple growers have to pay the fee. This last condition ensures that apple growers will sign the contract: If they sign, they may not be selected to pay the fee, yet they enjoy the same amount of services. One problem with this solution is that the government may not know what the proper fees should be. In any event, this is yet another example of government coercion being required to overcome the free-rider problem with nonexclusive externalities.

Concluding Comment

Although Maskin's analysis clarifies the nature of the bargaining problems in the presence of externalities and private information, it hardly rescues the Coase Theorem. On the one hand, when the number of agents is small, some or all of them are likely to have market power. They may not agree to pseudo-competitive fees, in which case the bargains are unlikely to be pareto efficient.

On the other hand, externalities that affect a large number of agents are likely to give rise to the free-rider problem. (Transaction costs are also likely to prevent efficient bargains.) The models presented in this section indicate that the solution in either case involves some form of government coercion. The combination of voluntary bargaining, individual rationality, and private information is unlikely to produce pareto-efficient outcomes, contrary to Coase's expectations for bargained solutions to market failures.[17,18]

REFERENCES

Aivasian, V., Callen, J., and Lipnowski, I., "The Coase Theorem and Coalitional Stability," *Economica*, November 1987.

Atkinson, A., and Stern, N., "Pigou, Taxation, and Public Goods," *Review of Economic Studies*, January 1974.

Conway, K., "Labor Supply, Taxes, and Government Spending: A Microeconometric Analysis," *Review of Economics and Statistics*, February 1997.

Diamond, P., "A Many Person Ramsey Tax Rule," *Journal of Public Economics*, November 1975.

Dixit, A., and Olson, M., "Does Voluntary Participation Undermine the Coase Theorem?," *Journal of Public Economics*, June 2000.

Farrell, J., "Information and the Coase Theorem," *Journal of Economic Perspectives*, Fall 1987.

Klibanoff, P., and Morduch, J., "Decentralization, Externalities, and Efficiency," *Review of Economic Studies*, April 1995.

Maskin, E., "The Invisible Hand and Externalities," *American Economic Association Papers and Proceedings*, May 1994.

Pigou, A. C., *A Study in Public Finance*, third ed., Macmillan, London, 1947.

Sandmo, A., "Redistribution and the Marginal Cost of Public Funds," *Journal of Public Economics*, December 1998.

Wildasin, D., "On Public Good Provision with Distortionary Taxation," *Economic Inquiry*, April 1984.

[17] An excellent discussion of this last point can be found in J. Farrell, "Information and the Coase Theorem," *Journal of Economic Perspectives*, Fall 1987. Be mindful, however, that Maskin was responding to Farrell's article in clarifying the source of the bargaining problem with private information.

[18] Avinash Dixit and Mancur Olson constructed a simple model to emphasize the difficulties that the combination of voluntary participation and transactions costs causes for the Coase theorem. A group of citizens agree to meet and provide a non-exclusive good if the sum of the benefits of the good to the people at the meeting exceeds its cost. There are no problems reaching agreement at the meeting since there is no private information and no transactions costs to hinder the negotiation of a pareto improvement. The problem is getting people to come to the meeting in the first place, since nonparticipants share the benefits of the good but do not have to pay any of its costs. Asking nonparticipants to pay would be coercive. If the number of citizens exceeds the number required at a meeting to provide the good, then people have a strong incentive to free ride and not attend, and the good may not be provided. Dixit and Olson describe some options in which everyone must participate for the good to be provided that would be pareto optimal, but show that these options are undermined by small transactions costs of attending the meeting (or impatience, if the call to meet can be infinitely repeated should it fail to attract everyone). The Coase theorem rests on shaky grounds even without private information, at least for the provision of non-exclusive goods. A. Dixit and M. Olson, "Does Voluntary Participation Undermine the Coase Theorem?," *Journal of Public Economics*, June 2000.

21

DECREASING COSTS AND THE THEORY OF THE SECOND-BEST— THE BOITEUX PROBLEM

THE BOITEUX PROBLEM: THE MULTIPRODUCT DECREASING-COST FIRM
Analytics of the Boiteux Problem
Public Agencies and Private Markets
The U.S. Postal Service
CONSTRAINED GOVERNMENT AGENCIES

Chapter 9 developed the three first-best decision rules for decreasing cost services:

1. *A decreasing cost industry is a natural monopoly.* It should consist of a single firm to minimize the total cost of producing any given output.

2. *Price must equal marginal cost for pareto optimality.* Achieving this result requires either government regulation or government provision of the service, since a profit-maximizing monopolist would presumably set marginal revenue equal to marginal cost.

3. *Marginal-cost pricing implies operating losses with decreasing unit costs.* Therefore, the government must subsidize the firm's losses with a lump-sum transfer so that the investors can earn a return equal to the opportunity cost of capital. This transfer simply becomes part of the first-best interpersonal equity conditions for optimal income distribution. That is, in satisfying interpersonal equity, the government must collect enough taxes from one subset of consumers to subsidize all decreasing cost producers as well as provide transfers to the remaining subset of consumers.[1]

---

[1] A final point common to all first-best expenditure theory is that the government should allow competitive allocations in all other nondecreasing cost markets. The simple model of

The chapter concluded by pointing out that the United States tends to favor average-cost pricing rather than marginal-cost pricing for the decreasing-cost services. The public apparently views average-cost pricing as being fully consistent with the benefits-received principle of public pricing and therefore more equitable. In contrast, mainstream public sector theory has no use for the benefits-received principle as an equity principle.

Chapter 21 extends the analysis of decreasing cost firms by considering a common property of these firms that Chapter 9 ignored: They are often multiproduct firms that offer a variety of services to different customers (e.g., the U.S. Postal Service and most public utilities).

THE BOITEUX PROBLEM: THE MULTIPRODUCT DECREASING-COST FIRM

We begin with an analysis of the multiproduct, decreasing-cost firm developed by Marcel Boiteux in the 1950s.[2] Boiteux's analysis is one of the seminal contributions to second-best public expenditure theory. He is as closely associated with the decreasing-cost firm as Paul Samuelson is with the nonexclusive public good.

Boiteux considered the optimal pricing and investment rules for multiproduct decreasing-cost monopolies that are required to raise a given amount of revenue. His model is particularly appropriate for the United States. When faced with multiproduct decreasing-cost firms, the U.S. regulatory agencies simply extend their average-cost pricing philosophy to them. They require that the firm's total revenue equal its total cost across all the products in the aggregate rather than for each product individually. The total cost includes an allowable return to capital. Requiring that total revenue equal total cost (or any other arbitrary amount as in the Boiteux model) renders the analysis second best. The firm's total revenue would be less than its total cost in a first-best environment.

Chapter 9 would have had to add one other good to show this formally, but it was clear from the previous analysis of externalities in Chapters 6–8 that marginal cost pricing of all other goods is pareto optimal.

[2] M. Boiteux, "On the Management of Public Monopolies Subject to Budgetary Constraints," *Journal of Economic Theory*, September 1971 (translated from the original in French, *Econometrica*, January 1956). Jacques Dreze presents a useful interpretation of Boiteux's results in J. Dreze, "Some Post-War Contributions of French Economists to Theory and Public Policy," *American Economic Review*, June 1964 (suppl.), pp. 27–34. Our analysis closely follows these two papers. We would also recommend W. Baumol and D. Bradford, "Optimal Departures from Marginal Cost Pricing," *American Economic Review*, June 1970, for an excellent intuitive discussion of the Boiteux problem, including its relationship to the optimal tax literature. The article also presents a brief historical account of the early second-best price and tax literature.

Boiteux analyzed this regulatory problem in the context of a many-person, N goods and factors, general equilibrium model in which all other markets are perfectly competitive and the government has the ability to redistribute endowment income lump sum to satisfy interpersonal equity. This is the same as positing a one-consumer-equivalent economy. It highlights the efficiency aspects of the problem.

The Boiteux problem has general interest for public sector economics far beyond the theory of decreasing costs. It stands as the intellectual precursor to a considerable portion of all second-best tax and expenditure theory developed over the past 40 years. For instance, it turns out to be quite similar to the optimal commodity tax problem of Chapters 13 and 14. Boiteux's model can also be used as a basis for developing production decision rules for any public agency subject to a legislated budget constraint, whether or not the agency supplies decreasing-cost services. Since most governments do restrict agencies in this way, the Boiteux analysis obviously has far-reaching practical significance for government policy.

Analytics of the Boiteux Problem

The essence of the Boiteux problem can be described as follows. Let one production sector ("industry") of the economy be under the direct control (or complete regulation) of the government because it exhibits increasing-returns-to-scale production.[3] Assume that this particular government activity employs many inputs and produces many goods and services according to the implicit government production-possibilities relationship:

$$G(Z_1, \ldots, Z_i, \ldots, Z_N) = G\left(\vec{Z}\right) = 0 \qquad (21.1)$$

where $\vec{Z}$ is an $(N \times 1)$ vector of government inputs and supplies, with element Z_i. (The government need not literally employ all inputs and produce all goods and services in the economy, but it is analytically convenient to use the most general formulation possible. Some [perhaps most] of the Z_i will be identically equal to zero for any given application.) Assume further that government production is twice constrained:

1. The government must buy all inputs and sell all outputs at the vector of producer prices, $\vec{p} = (p_1, \ldots, p_i, \ldots, p_N)$, faced by the economy's perfectly competitive private sector firms. These prices reflect private sector marginal costs (or values of marginal products). Since there is no taxation in this model, $\vec{p}$ also serves as the vector of consumer prices.

---

[3] As will become evident, the increasing-returns-to-scale assumption merely provides a convenient motivation for government regulation or control. It is not a necessary condition for any of the theorems derived in this chapter.

2. Government purchases and sales must satisfy an overall budget constraint of the general form:

$$\sum_{i=1}^{N} p_i \, Z_i = B \qquad (21.2)$$

where B is set by some legislative body. Setting $B = 0$ is the natural interpretation for the regulated decreasing cost firms in the United States. Revenue from the sale of all government goods and services at actual market prices must equal the total cost of production. This can be thought of as the average- or full-cost pricing philosophy applied to a multiservice firm (with the allowable return to investors set at the opportunity cost of capital).

The problem, then, is to derive optimal production decision rules for the government control variables, the $\vec{Z}$, given the government's production function and its self-imposed budget constraint.

This problem can be analyzed quite easily using the loss-minimization technique. Assume a one-consumer (equivalent) economy in which all relevant information about the consumer is summarized by the expenditure function:

$$M(\vec{p}; \overline{U}) = \sum_{i=1}^{N} p_i \, X_i^{comp}(\vec{p}; \overline{U}) \qquad (21.3)$$

Assume, further, that private production exhibits general technology with constant returns to scale (CRS), summarized by the profit function:

$$\pi(\vec{p}) = \sum_{i=1}^{N} p_i \, y_i(\vec{p}) \qquad (21.4)$$

Since production occurs in the private and public sectors, market clearance must also be specified as:[4]

$$M_i(\vec{p}; \overline{U}) = \pi_i(\vec{p}) + Z_i \qquad i = 2, \ldots, N \qquad (21.5)$$

Recall that all markets cannot clear in terms of compensated demand (supply) functions. Therefore, let the first market remain uncleared, with compensation occurring in terms of good 1. The first good also serves as the numeraire ($p_1 \equiv 1$). Finally, as a matter of convenience, define the government's production function such that $\partial G / \partial Z_1 = G_1 = 1$, or $Z_1 = -g$ $(Z_2, \ldots, Z_N)$, with inputs measured negatively. ($\partial g / \partial Z_k \equiv g_{Z_k}$ measures the marginal product of Z_k in producing Z_1 as a positive number.)[5]

---

[4] Recall that $M_i = X_i^{comp}(\vec{p}; \overline{U})$ and $\pi_i = Y_i(\vec{p})$.

[5] Since Z_1 and Z_k can be either goods or factors, g_{Z_k} can also be interpreted as a technical rate of substitution or a marginal rate of transformation.

Loss is defined as the lump-sum income required to keep the consumer at utility level $\overline{U}$ less all sources of lump-sum income for any given values of the Z_i. In general,[6]

$$L\left(\vec{Z}\right) = M\left(\vec{p}; \overline{U}\right) - \pi(\vec{p}) - \sum_{i=1}^{N} p_i\, Z_i - B \tag{21.6}$$

Loss must be minimized with respect to the Z_i, subject to the constraints that $\sum_{i=1}^{N} p_i Z_i = B$ and government production. Formally:[7]

$$\min_{(Z_i)} M\left(\vec{p}; \overline{U}\right) - \pi(\vec{p}) - \sum_{i=1}^{N} p_i Z_i - B$$

$$\text{s.t.} \quad \sum_{i=1}^{N} p_i\, Z_i = B$$

$$Z_1 = -g(Z_2, \ldots, Z_N)$$

Alternatively, directly incorporating the government production function into the government budget constraint,

$$\min_{(Z_i)} M\left(\vec{p}; \overline{U}\right) - \pi(\vec{p}) + p_1 g\left(\vec{Z}\right) - \sum_{i=2}^{N} p_i\, Z_i - B$$

$$\text{s.t.} \quad - p_1 g\left(\vec{Z}\right) + \sum_{i=2}^{N} p_i\, Z_i = B$$

The corresponding Lagrangian is

$$\min_{(Z_i)} M\left(\vec{p}; \overline{U}\right) - \pi(\vec{p}) + p_1 g\left(\vec{Z}\right) - \sum_{i=2}^{N} p_i\, Z_i - B$$

$$+ \lambda\left[-p_1 g\left(\vec{Z}\right) + \sum_{i=2}^{N} p_i\, Z_i - B\right]$$

The producer prices p_i are functions of the Z_i with general technology. Therefore, the first-order conditions with respect to the Z_k are (with $p_1 = 1$):

$$\sum_{i=2}^{N} M_i \frac{\partial p_i}{\partial Z_k} - \sum_{i=2}^{N} \pi_i \frac{\partial p_i}{\partial Z_k} + p_1 g_{Z_k} - \sum_{i=2}^{N} Z_i \frac{\partial p_i}{\partial Z_k} - p_k$$

$$+ \lambda\left[-p_1 g_{Z_k} + \sum_{i=2}^{N} Z_i \frac{\partial p_i}{\partial Z_k} + p_k\right] = 0 \qquad k = 2, \ldots, N \tag{21.7}$$

---

[6] With CRS production ($\pi(\vec{p}) = 0$) and the requirement that $\sum_{i=1}^{N} p_i Z_i = B$, the loss function can be simplified to $L(\vec{Z}) = M(\vec{p}; \overline{U})$. The expanded version of loss will be maintained for generality in deriving the optimal production and pricing rules.

[7] Following the practice in Chapter 14, the market clearance equations will be kept outside the loss-minimization framework. In this example, they solve for the prices $\vec{p}$ once the loss-minimizing $\vec{Z}$ has been determined. Also, recall that $p_1 = 1$.

From market clearance,

$$M_i = \pi_i + Z_i \qquad i = 2, \ldots, N \tag{21.8}$$

Multiply Eq. (21.8) by $\partial p_i / \partial Z_k$ and sum over all $(N - 1)$ equations to obtain:

$$\sum_{i=2}^{N} M_i \frac{\partial p_i}{\partial Z_k} = \sum_{i=2}^{N} \pi_i \frac{\partial p_i}{\partial Z_k} + \sum_{i=2}^{N} Z_i \frac{\partial p_i}{\partial Z_k} \tag{21.9}$$

Thus, Eq. (21.7) simplifies to:

$$p_1 g_{Z_k} - p_k + \lambda \left(-p_1 g_{Z_k} + \sum_{i=2}^{N} Z_i \frac{\partial p_i}{\partial Z_k} + p_k \right) = 0, \tag{21.10}$$

$$k = 2, \ldots, N$$

or

$$(\lambda - 1)\left(-p_1 g_{Z_k} + p_k\right) + \lambda \sum_{i=2}^{N} Z_i \frac{\partial p_i}{\partial Z_k} = 0 \qquad k = 2, \ldots, N \tag{21.11}$$

To interpret Eq. (21.11), use the market clearance equations to substitute out the price derivatives, $\partial p_i / \partial Z_k$. Differentiate each of the market clearance equations, Eq. (21.8), with respect to Z_i to obtain:

$$\sum_{j=2}^{N} (M_{ij} - \pi_{ij}) \frac{\partial p_j}{\partial Z_k} = a_{ik} = \begin{array}{cc} \to 0, & i \neq k \\ \to 1, & i = k \end{array} \tag{21.12}$$

Differentiating the market clearance relationships with respect to all other Z_i, $i = 2, \ldots, k - 1, k + 1, \ldots, N$; and writing the results in matrix notation yields:

$$(M_{ij} - \pi_{ij})\left(\frac{\partial p}{\partial Z}\right) = I \tag{21.13}$$

where:

M_{ij} = an $(N - 1) \times (N - 1)$ matrix of derivatives $\partial M_i / \partial p_j$.
π_{ij} = an $(N - 1) \times (N - 1)$ matrix of derivatives $\partial \pi_i / \partial p_j$.
$\partial p / \partial Z$ = an $(N - 1) \times (N - 1)$ matrix of derivatives $\partial p_i / \partial Z_j$.
I = the $(N - 1) \times (N - 1)$ identity matrix.

Thus,

$$\frac{\partial p}{\partial Z} = (M_{ij} - \pi_{ij})^{-1} \tag{21.14}$$

Using Eq. (21.14), the entire set of first-order conditions, Eq., (21.11), can be expressed in matrix notations as:

$$(\lambda - 1)(-p_1 g_Z + p) + \lambda (M_i - \pi_i)(M_{ij} - \pi_{ij})^{-1} = 0 \tag{21.15}$$

where:

M_i is the $1 \times (N - 1)$ vector $(M_2, \ldots, M_N)$.

$\pi_i =$ the $1 \times (N - 1)$ vector $(\pi_2, \ldots, \pi_N)$, and

$$(M_i - \pi_i) = Z_i$$

$g_z =$ the $1 \times (N - 1)$ vector $(g_{Z_2}, \ldots, g_{Z_N})$.

Multiplying Eq. (21.15) by $(M_{ij} - \pi_{ij})$ yields:

$$(\lambda - 1)(-p_1 g_z + p)(M_{ij} - \pi_{ij}) + \lambda(M_i - \pi_i) = 0 \qquad (21.16)$$

Select the kth relationship from Eq. (21.16):

$$(\lambda - 1)\sum_{i=2}^{N}(-p_1 g_{Z_i} + p_i)(M_{ik} - \pi_{ik}) + \lambda(M_k - \pi_k) = 0 \qquad (21.17)$$

Rearranging terms:

$$\frac{\sum_{i=2}^{N}(-p_1 g_{Z_i} + p_i)(M_{ik} - \pi_{ik})}{M_k - \pi_k} = \frac{-\lambda}{\lambda - 1} \qquad k = 2, \ldots, N \qquad (21.18)$$

where the right-hand side is a constant independent of k. Written in this form, the first-order conditions can be given an interpretation remarkably similar to the optimal commodity tax rules of Chapters 13 and 14.

As originally defined, the problem asks us to interpret the first-order conditions of Eq. (21.11) as decision rules for the government production variables, the Z_i—that is, as government "investment" rules. Using Eq. (21.18), they can also be given a pricing interpretation if one thinks of the government as making "competitive" production decisions in the usual manner. Given a production function $Z_1 = -g(Z_2, \ldots, Z_N) = 0$ and a vector of fixed *shadow* prices for the inputs and outputs $\theta = (\theta_2, \ldots, \theta_i, \ldots, \theta_N)$, a profit-maximizing firm equates $g_i/g_j = \theta_i/\theta_j$, all $i, j = 2, \ldots, N$. Furthermore, if the shadow prices reflect true social opportunity costs for the inputs and outputs, the firm's decision rule is pareto optimal. Conditions (21.18) describe, in effect, how to define the optimal shadow prices for the government sector. To see this, let $\vec{p} = \vec{\theta} + \vec{t}$, with elements p_i, θ_i, and t_i, respectively, where $\vec{p}$ is the vector of actual market prices; $\vec{\theta}$, the vector of optimal shadow prices; and $\vec{t}$, a vector of *implicit* taxes driving a wedge between the two sets of prices. Given our normalization, $p_1 \equiv \theta_1$, $t_1 = 0$. Substituting for the p_i in Eq. (21.18),

$$\frac{\sum_{i=2}^{N}(\theta_i + t_i - p_1 g_{Z_i})(M_{ik} - \pi_{ik})}{M_k - \pi_k} = \frac{-\lambda}{\lambda - 1} = C \qquad (21.19)$$

$$k = 2, \ldots, N$$

But, if the government sector is using the θ_i as shadow prices,

$$\theta_i = p_1 g_{z_i} \qquad i = 2, \ldots, N \qquad (21.20)$$

Equation (21.20) says, for example, that the government producer hires an input until the value of its marginal product just equals its shadow price. Substituting Eq. (21.20) into (21.19) yields:

$$\frac{\sum_{i=2}^{N} t_i (M_{ik} - \pi_{ik})}{M_k - \pi_k} = C \qquad k = 2, \ldots, N \qquad (21.21)$$

which is virtually identical to the optimal commodity tax rule of Chapters 13 and 14.

Equations (21.21) say that the government should define a new set of shadow prices for use in production decisions by establishing a set of implicit taxes having the following properties (in Boiteux's words): "[The taxes] are proportionate to the infinitesimal variations in price, that, when accompanied by compensating variations in incomes, entail the same proportional change in the demands (supplies) of the goods produced (consumed) by the nationalized sector."[8] Boiteux's interpretation follows directly from the symmetry of the demand and production derivatives, $M_{ik} = M_{ki}$ and $\pi_{ik} = \pi_{ki}$, so that Eq. (21.21) can be rewritten as:

$$\frac{\sum_{i=2}^{N} t_i (M_{ki} - \pi_{ki})}{M_k - \pi_k} = C \qquad k = 2, \ldots, N \qquad (21.22)$$

M_{ki} gives the change in the compensated demand (supply) for good (factor) k in response to a change in the ith consumer price. Similarly, π_{ki} gives the change in supply (demand) of good (factor) k in private production in response to a change in the ith price. Consequently, $(M_{ki} - \pi_{ki})$ gives the change in government supply (demand) of good (factor) k required to maintain compensated market clearance in response to a change in the ith price. The denominator $(M_k - \pi_k) = Z_k$, from market clearance. Thus, Eq. (21.22) gives the familiar equal percentage rule, except that the conditions apply only to percentage changes entirely within the government sector.

The crux of the matter, then, can be viewed as defining a correct set of shadow prices on which to base standard "competitive" government production decisions. This suggests that the original problem could have been

---

[8] M. Boiteux, "On the Management of Public Monopolies," *Journal of Economic Theory*, September 1971, p. 230. Equation (21.21) also points out that our formulation of G( ) implies that the government retains control over all prices in the economy, an assumption we have been using all along. If the government is constrained from changing some distorted price–cost margins in the private sector, these additional constraints would change the optimal decision rules, both here and elsewhere in the text. Formally, the new constraints could be represented as $q_i = k_i p_i$, for some i, with k_i constant for good i, and they would have Lagrangian multipliers associated with them in the loss-minimization problem.

formulated as a tax–price problem rather than as a quantity problem. Viewed in this way, the problem is indistinguishable from the problem of designing a set of optimal commodity taxes on part of production, to be paid by the producer. The partial tax problem was first described for a single tax in the discussion of corporate tax incidence in Chapter 16 using the two-good, two-factor Harberger model. It can be easily generalized for $(N - 1)$ goods and factors by dividing the profit function into two sectors, one taxed and the other untaxed, and using the loss-minimization technique. Consumer and producer prices would differ only in the taxed sector. In the Boiteux problem, the taxes $\vec{t}$ are implicit and the $\vec{\theta}$ are shadow prices. They are not actually observed in the market. In contrast, the taxes in the partial tax problem are real, so that the $\vec{\theta}$ define observed gross-of-tax prices (for factors) or net-of-tax prices (for goods) to the firm.

Public Agencies and Private Markets

Whether or not these implicit valuations in the Boiteux formulation affect actual market prices depends upon the relationship of the government producer to the entire market. There are a number of possibilities. Suppose, for example, that the government is merely one of thousands of firms hiring a particular factor of production. It would then be reasonable to assume that its implicit tax had no effect on actual market prices, a situation depicted in Fig. 21.1. The government sets an implicit tax t_k on the purchase of X_k, which drives the factor's shadow price to X_k from p_k^0 to θ_{gk}^F. However, because it is small relative to the total market of X_k, the price of X_k remains at p_k^0 for all other firms and all consumers.

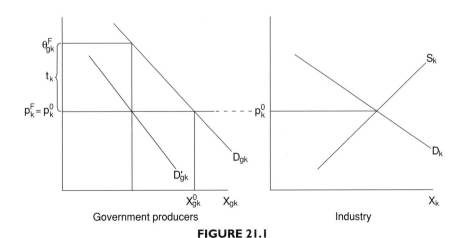

FIGURE 21.1

In fact, Fig. 21.1 is misleading because the government need not design implicit taxes in markets for which the tax does not affect market prices. Consider the kth equation of Eq. (21.11). If Z_k is "small" relative to the entire market for good (factor) k such that $\partial p_i/\partial Z_k = 0$, all $i = 2, \ldots, N$, then Eq. (21.11) becomes:

$$(\lambda - 1)(-p_1 g_{Z_k} + p_k) = 0 \qquad (21.23)$$

which is satisfied if $t_k = 0$. In other words, the government should use the actual market price of p_k in deciding how much Z_k to employ (supply).

Suppose, however, that the government is the only supplier of a particular output X_j. In this case, the implicit tax is virtually identical to a real tax. Refer to Fig. 21.2. The shadow price θ_j equals the firm's actual marginal costs at X_j^F, but because of the implicit tax the firm charges the consumer p_j^F, equal to measured marginal costs plus the implicit tax t_j. Thus, the consumer is indifferent between the implicit tax or a real partial tax (with lump-sum return of the revenues). (Notice that, although the firm receives p_j^F for each unit, it pretends it is receiving only θ_j for the purposes of implicit "competitive" profit maximization.)

These results indicate that the first-order conditions for optimal implicit taxes, Eq. (21.22), may be much easier to approximate than it appears at first pass, certainly much easier than the optimal tax rules for the economy as a whole. In many cases, the government producer will be supplying a few services that are unique to it and buying general factors whose prices are set in large national markets. Thus, it only need determine implicit taxes on its services. In effect, then, Eq. (21.22) tells the government how to raise prices above measured marginal costs on each of its services in order to satisfy

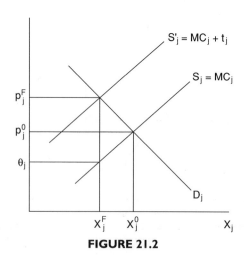

FIGURE 21.2

an overall budget constraint. Viewed in this way, Eq. (21.22) provides an efficient second-best algorithm for applying full or "average cost" pricing to the multiproduct firm.

The U.S. Postal Service

The full-cost interpretation of the Boiteux tax rules found its way into the setting of U.S. postal rates, in the form of the Inverse Elasticity Rule (IER). The Postal Service delivers four main classes of mail: first class (letters and post cards); second class (primarily magazines); third class (circulars and other "junk" mail); and fourth class (parcel post). The rates on each class of mail are adjusted periodically in an administrative proceeding presided over by an administrative law judge. The Postal Service proposes a new set of rates to the judge, who then receives testimony from the Postal Service and other interested parties before determining the final rate changes.

The Postal Service claims that its operation exhibits substantial economies of scope: That is, the total cost of delivering all four classes of mail is less than the combined total costs of delivering each class of mail under separate enterprises. The claim is controversial but difficult to prove or disprove because a large component of Postal Service costs is common to more than one class of service. In any event, the Postal Service argues that the costs that can be attributed to each class of mail are much less than the full operating cost of the Postal Service. Therefore, it has to propose rates on each class of mail that will be sufficient to cover its full operating cost, consistent with the structure of the Boiteux problem.

The Postal Service introduced the Inverse Elasticity Rule in the 1974 hearings as justification for its rate proposals. In particular, it sought a relatively large increase in the first-class rate and a small increase in the parcel-post rate and argued that its request was efficient because it was in line with the IER. The demand for first-class mail was relatively inelastic. Congress had granted the Postal Service a monopoly on delivering first-class mail and it had no serious competitors at the time. There were no fax machines or e-mails. In contrast, the demand for parcel post was relatively elastic because it faced stiff competition from United Parcel Service (UPS). The IER did not carry the day in 1974, but it was used as the basis for setting rates on the four classes of mail in the 1977 hearings.

United Parcel Service always objected strenuously to the use of the IER. It argued that the Postal Service seriously under-attributed costs to the various classes of mail, especially to parcel post, and was in effect using the IER to cross-subsidize parcel post with its revenues from first-class mail.[9] The

---

[9] The IER was first proposed by William Vickrey in the 1974 hearings as a means of determining postal rates on the various classes of mail (Docket No. R74–1). Also see "Postal Rate and Fee Increases," Docket No. R75–1.

opposition to the IER finally proved persuasive to the administrative law judge. In 1980, the Judge abandoned explicit use of the IER for setting postal rates.

Frank Scott undertook an independent study of the costs of the four classes of mail in 1980.[10] Based on his cost and demand estimates, he determined the rates that were consistent with the IER. He concluded that only the first-class rate was approximately equal to the IER rate. The second-class rate was close to marginal cost, the third-class rate was above the IER rate, and the fourth-class rate was below the IER rate. He estimated that aggregate consumer surplus would have been $14.5 million higher had all the rates been at IER levels, a rather modest increase. The gain in moving to the IER rates was small because the first-class rate was already at the IER rate and first-class mail accounted for 65% of the total revenues of the Postal Service in 1980. Of course, Scott's conclusions are only as accurate as his cost and demand estimates. As noted above, attributing costs to the various classes of mail requires a fair amount of judgment because of the large amount of common costs.

CONSTRAINED GOVERNMENT AGENCIES

Although Boiteux's analysis was motivated by an attempt to develop optimal second-best rules for public monopolies, the resulting decision rules, Eqs. (21.11) or (21.22), are directly applicable to any government agency subject to a legislated budget constraint. That this is so is obvious from our original formulation of the Boiteux problem, in which the government is constrained to meet a given revenue target B from the purchase and sales of inputs and outputs at actual market prices $(p_1, \ldots, p_i, \ldots, p_N)$, or $\sum_{i=1}^{N} p_i Z_i = B$. The government has a production function, $Z_1 = -g(Z_2, \ldots, Z_N)$, but there are no formal restrictions on $g(\vec{Z})$ (other than that it be continuous and twice differentiable). It does not even have to be a homogeneous function. Clearly, then, the original formulation is a fairly general problem covering any constrained public agency engaged in the production of goods and services. Conditions (21.22) suggest that constrained agencies should follow standard competitive production decision rules, based on shadow prices determined by the solution of Eq. (21.22). Once again, the number of shadow prices to be determined depends upon the importance of the agency relative to the national markets for its outputs and inputs. Finally, Boiteux was able to prove as an extension of his results that if there is more than one such constrained sector (agency), each sector has its own set of rules similar to Eq. (21.22).[11] This result

[10] F. Scott, Jr., "Assessing USA Postal Ratemaking: An Application of Ramsey Prices," *The Journal of Industrial Economics*, March 1986.

[11] M. Boiteux, "On the Management of Public Monopolies," *Journal of Economic Theory*, September 1971, p. 231.

is obviously of some importance since most government agencies operate under imposed budget constraints, but we will not exhibit it here.

REFERENCES

Baumol, W., and Bradford, D., "Optimal Departures from Marginal Cost Pricing," *American Economic Review*, June 1970.

Boiteux, M., "On the Management of Public Monopolies Subject to Budgetary Constraints," *Journal of Economic Theory*, September 1971 (translated from French in *Econometrica*, January 1956).

Dreze, J., "Some Post-War Contributions of French Economists to Theory and Public Policy," *American Economic Review*, June 1964 (suppl.).

"Postal Rate and Fee Increases," *Docket No. R75–1; Docket No. R74–1.*

Scott, Jr., F., "Assessing USA Postal Ratemaking: An Application of Ramsey Prices," *The Journal of Industrial Economics*, March 1986.

22

GENERAL PRODUCTION RULES IN A SECOND-BEST ENVIRONMENT

   Chapter 22 concludes our survey of second-best public expenditure theory by exploring some fairly general propositions about government production in an environment made second best because of distorting taxation. A major goal of the chapter is to integrate our previous results on second-best tax theory with second-best public expenditure theory. Therefore, all the analysis in Chapter 22 employs essentially the same set of assumptions regarding government activity and the underlying structure of the private sector that we have been using time and again.

   Regarding the government sector, the government is making a set of production decisions under two constraints: (1) it must buy inputs and sell outputs at the established private sector producer prices, and (2) it must cover any resulting deficit (surplus) with distorting commodity taxes levied on the consumer. Otherwise, government production is fully general. The government may buy or sell any inputs or outputs, including those traded in the private sector, and there are no restrictions on the form of the aggregate government production function other than the exclusion of externalities. Following Chapter 21, the government's production function is specified as $G(Z) = 0$, or $Z_1 = -g(Z_2, \ldots, Z_N)$, where Z spans (potentially) the entire set of the economy's inputs and outputs. The only difference between the specification of the government sector in this chapter and the specification employed in the Boiteux analysis is that the government taxes (subsidizes) all consumer transactions to cover its deficits (surpluses), not just those between the consumers and the government.

Regarding the private sector, all markets are assumed to be perfectly competitive and private production exhibits general technology with constant returns to scale (CRS). There can be no pure profits or losses from private production. We also assume that the consumers have no other sources of lump-sum income. All income derives from the sale of variable factors. These assumptions about the private sector are not necessary, but they greatly facilitate the analysis. In sum, the only distortions in the economy that render the analysis second best are the distorting commodity taxes used to cover government production deficits.

Given this analytical framework, the first problem to be considered is the so-called Diamond–Mirrlees problem, which Peter Diamond and James Mirrlees set out in their two-part article in the 1971 *American Economic Review* entitled "Optimal Taxation and Public Production."[1] By 1968, when their paper was drafted and widely circulated, the optimal tax rule for a one-consumer (equivalent) economy was well known, but only under the assumption that the government simply raised revenue to be returned lump sum to the consumer. Diamond and Mirrlees added government production to the standard second-best general equilibrium tax model and asked two questions:

1. How does the existence of government production affect the optimal tax rule? In particular, if the revenue is raised to cover a government production deficit under the conditions set forth above, what form do the tax rules take? They found that the optimal tax rule was unchanged. This result could have been anticipated since it was well known by then that the tax rules as originally derived did not contain any production terms even when *private* production exhibited general technology.

2. Turning the question around: What effect does distorting taxation have on government production rules? Their answer to this question most definitely was unanticipated. They proved that as long as the taxes are set optimally, the government should follow the standard *first-best* production rules, using the private sector producer prices and equating these price ratios to marginal rates of transformation. Distorting taxation necessarily forces society underneath its utility-possibilities frontier, but it should remain on the production-possibilities frontier. This is one of the strongest results in all of second-best theory.

Having established the Diamond and Mirrlees production result, the chapter then generalizes their analysis to consider government production

---

[1] P. Diamond and J. Mirrlees, "Optimal Taxation and Public Production" (2 parts, Part I: Production Efficiency, Part II: Tax Rules), *American Economic Review*, March, June 1971.

rules under conditions of nonoptimal distorting taxation. As one might suspect, production efficiency no longer holds. In fact, the production rules become fairly complicated. This is especially unfortunate because real-world taxes are likely to be far from optimal.

Any analysis incorporating both second-best tax and expenditure theory is bound to be complex, although the assumptions on the private sector help somewhat in simplifying the analysis. To simplify even further and highlight the efficiency aspects of taxation and government production, we begin the analysis in the context of a one-consumer (equivalent) economy using the technique of loss minimization. We will then conclude the chapter by reworking one of the production exercises in a many-person economy to suggest how equity considerations modify the one-consumer rules.[2]

THE DIAMOND–MIRRLEES PROBLEM: ONE-CONSUMER ECONOMY

Let us establish the general equilibrium framework for the Diamond–Mirrlees problem with some care since we will be using this same analytical structure throughout most of the chapter.

The Private Sector

The private sector consists of a single consumer and a set of perfectly competitive producers with general technologies and CRS production. Loss minimization requires that the consumer's decisions be represented by the expenditure function:

$$M(\vec{q}; \overline{U}) = \sum_{i=1}^{N} q_i X_i^{comp}(\vec{q}; \overline{U}) \qquad (22.1)$$

where:

$\vec{q}$ is the $(N \times 1)$ vector of consumer prices with element q_i (gross of tax for outputs, net of tax for inputs).

$\vec{X}^{comp} = \vec{M}_i$ the $(N \times 1)$ vector of demand and factor supplies, with element X_i^{comp} (or M_i).

Let private production be represented by an aggregate profit function:

$$\pi(\vec{p}) = \sum_{i=1}^{N} p_i Y_i(\vec{p}) \qquad (22.2)$$

---

[2] These analyses draw heavily from two papers by Robin Boadway: R. Boadway, "Cost–Benefit Rules and General Equilibrium," *Review of Economic Studies*, July 1975; and R. Boadway, "Integrating Equity and Efficiency in Applied Welfare Economics," *Quarterly Journal of Economics*, November 1976. We also benefited from a set of unpublished class notes provided by Peter Diamond.

where:

$\vec{p}$ = the (N × 1) vector of producer prices with element p_i (gross of tax for inputs, net of tax for outputs).

$\vec{Y} = \vec{\pi}_i$ = the (N × 1) vector of private supplies and factor demands, with element Y_i (or π_i).

With CRS, $\pi(\vec{p}) \equiv 0$.

The Government Sector

The government has an (N × 1) vector of production decision variables, $\vec{Z}$, with element Z_i, related by the aggregate government production function:

$$G\left(\vec{Z}\right) = 0 \quad \text{or} \quad Z_1 = -g(Z_2, \dots, Z_N) \tag{22.3}$$

Since it buys and sells at the private producer prices, the resulting deficit (surplus) from government production is

$$D = \sum_{i=1}^{N} p_i \, Z_i \tag{22.4}$$

with inputs measured negatively following the usual convention. The government covers the deficit (surplus) by using an (N × 1) vector of unit "commodity" taxes $\vec{t}$, with element t_i, placed on the consumer, such that $\vec{q} = \vec{p} + \vec{t}$. The revenue raised at the compensated equilibrium[3] is $\sum_{i=1}^{N} t_i \, M_i$, so that the government's budget constraint has the generalized form:

$$\sum_{i=1}^{N} t_i \, M_i + \sum_{i=1}^{N} p_i \, Z_i = B \tag{22.5}$$

If B is not equal to zero, the resulting surplus or deficit is returned lump sum to the consumer.

Market Clearance

With two sources of production and general production technology, market clearance must be introduced explicitly into the analysis. We know, however, that all markets cannot clear at the compensated with-tax equilibrium.[4] Therefore, specify:

$$M_i\left(\vec{q}; \overline{U}\right) = \pi_i(\vec{p}) + Z_i \qquad i = 2, \dots, N \tag{22.6}$$

and assume that compensation occurs in terms of good 1. Let good 1 also serve as the untaxed numeraire so that $q_1 \equiv p_1 \equiv 1$, $t_1 = 0$. This completes all the relevant elements of the general equilibrium framework. The govern-

---

[3] Recall from the discussion of the optimal tax problem that loss minimization requires measurement at the compensated equilibrium.

[4] Refer to Chapter 14 for a discussion of the compensated market clearance relationships.

ment has $(2N - 2)$ control variables at its disposal, $(Z_2, \ldots, Z_N)$ and $(t_2, \ldots, t_N)$.

Loss Minimization

The loss function the government minimizes with respect to these control variables has the general form:

$$L\left(\vec{t}; \vec{Z}\right) = M\left(\vec{q}; \overline{U}^0\right) - \sum_{i=2}^{N} t_i M_i - \sum_{i=1}^{N} p_i Z_i - \pi(\vec{p}) \tag{22.7}$$

where, with general technology,

$$\vec{q} = q\left(\vec{t}; \vec{Z}\right) \quad \text{and} \quad \vec{p} = p\left(\vec{t}; \vec{Z}\right) \tag{22.8}$$

Loss equals the lump-sum income required to keep the consumer indifferent to the gross of tax prices less all sources of lump-sum income resulting from decisions on the government control variables. In this model, lump-sum income derives from two sources: pure economic profits (losses) from private production and the remaining government surplus after taxes have been collected. With CRS, the profit term need not be included. Similarly, if tax revenues just cover government production deficits, the second and third terms could be dropped as well, with loss defined simply as $M(\vec{q}; \overline{U}^0)$. In the interest of generality, however, all these terms are retained in the subsequent analysis.

Loss is minimized subject to government production technology and the government budget constraint. Formally, the problem is

$$\min_{(\vec{t}, \vec{Z})} M\left(\vec{q}; \overline{U}^0\right) - \sum_{i=2}^{N} t_i M_i - \sum_{i=1}^{N} p_i Z_i - \pi(\vec{p})$$

$$\text{s.t.} \sum_{i=2}^{N} t_i M_i + \sum_{i=1}^{N} p_i Z_i = B$$

$$Z_1 = -g(Z_2, \ldots, Z_N)$$

Incorporating the government production constraint directly into the analysis and noting that $\vec{q} = \vec{p} + \vec{t}$, the problem can be restated as:

$$\min_{(\vec{t}, \vec{Z})} M\left(\vec{p} + \vec{t}; \overline{U}^0\right) - \sum_{i=2}^{N} t_i M_i + p_1 g(Z_2, \ldots, Z_N) - \sum_{i=2}^{N} p_i Z_i - \pi(\vec{p})$$

$$\text{s.t.} \sum_{i=2}^{N} t_i M_i - p_1 g(Z_2, \ldots, Z_N) + \sum_{i=2}^{N} p_i Z_i = B$$

Also, $q_1 \equiv p_1 \equiv 1$ for $t_1 = 0$, so that there are $(2N - 2)$ control variables, $(t_2, \ldots, t_N)$ and $(Z_2, \ldots, Z_N)$.

Finally, the market clearance equations are used to simplify the first-order conditions. Formally, they solve for $\vec{p}$ given the solution for $\vec{t}$ and $\vec{Z}$. The Lagrangian for this problem is

$$\min_{(\vec{t}, \vec{z})} L = M\left(\vec{p} + \vec{t}; \overline{U}^0\right) - \sum_{i=2}^{N} t_i M_i + p_1 g(Z_2, \dots, Z_N)$$

$$- \sum_{i=2}^{N} p_i Z_i - \pi(\vec{p}) + \lambda \left[\sum_{i=2}^{N} t_i M_i - p_1 g(Z_2, \dots, Z_N) + \sum_{i=2}^{N} p_i Z_i - B\right]$$

Optimal Taxation

To derive the Diamond–Mirrlees results, begin by considering the first-order conditions with respect to t_k and computing $\partial L/\partial t_k$ as an intermediate step:

$$\frac{\partial L}{\partial t_k} = M_k + \sum_{i=2}^{N} M_i \frac{\partial p_i}{\partial t_k} - M_k - \sum_{i=2}^{N} t_i \left(M_{ik} + \sum_{j=2}^{N} M_{ij} \frac{\partial p_j}{\partial t_k}\right)$$

$$- \sum_{i=2}^{N} Z_i \frac{\partial p_i}{\partial t_k} - \sum_{i=2}^{N} \pi_i \frac{\partial p_i}{\partial t_k} \qquad k = 2, \dots, N$$

(22.9)

Multiply each market clearance Eq. (22.6) by $\partial p_i/\partial t_k$ and sum over all $(N-1)$ relationships to obtain:

$$\sum_{i=2}^{N} M_i \frac{\partial p_i}{\partial t_k} = \sum_{i=2}^{N} \pi_i \frac{\partial p_i}{\partial t_k} + \sum_{i=2}^{N} Z_i \frac{\partial p_i}{\partial t_k}$$

(22.10)

Therefore, Eq. (22.9) simplifies to:

$$\frac{\partial L}{\partial t_k} = -\sum_{i=2}^{N} t_i \left(M_{ik} + \sum_{j=2}^{N} M_{ij} \frac{\partial p_j}{\partial t_k}\right) \qquad k = 2, \dots, N$$

(22.11)

Next, differentiate the government budget constraint with respect to t_k:

$$\frac{\partial B}{\partial t_k} = M_k + \sum_{i=2}^{N} t_i \left(M_{ik} + \sum_{j=2}^{N} M_{ij} \frac{\partial p_j}{\partial t_k}\right) + \sum_{i=2}^{N} Z_i \frac{\partial p_i}{\partial t_k} \qquad k = 2, \dots, N$$

(22.12)

From Eq. (22.11):

$$\frac{\partial B}{\partial t_k} = -\frac{\partial L}{\partial t_k} + \left(M_k + \sum_{i=2}^{N} Z_i \frac{\partial p_i}{\partial t_k}\right)$$

(22.13)

With CRS in private production, $\sum_{i=1}^{N} \pi_i(\partial p_i/\partial t_k) = 0$. But $\partial p_1/\partial t_k = 0$, so:

$$\sum_{i=2}^{N} \pi_i \frac{\partial p_i}{\partial t_k} = 0$$

(22.14)

Hence, from Eq. (22.10):

$$\sum_{i=2}^{N} Z_i \frac{\partial p_i}{\partial t_k} = \sum_{i=2}^{N} M_i \frac{\partial p_i}{\partial t_k} \tag{22.15}$$

Given Eq. (22.15), (22.13) can be rewritten as:

$$\frac{\partial B}{\partial t_k} = -\frac{\partial L}{\partial t_k} + \left(M_k + \sum_{i=2}^{N} M_i \frac{\partial p_i}{\partial t_k} \right) \tag{22.16}$$

Combining Eq. (22.11) and (22.16) and incorporating the Lagrangian multiplier λ, the first-order conditions with respect to t_k are

$$(1 - \lambda) \frac{\partial L}{\partial t_k} + \lambda \left(M_k + \sum_{i=2}^{N} M_i \frac{\partial p_i}{\partial t_k} \right) = 0 \qquad k = 2, \ldots, N \tag{22.17}$$

But Eq. (22.17) is identical to Eq. (14.28), the first-order conditions when revenue was simply raised for its own sake and returned lump sum. Applying the manipulations of Chapter 14, these conditions imply the standard optimal commodity tax rule, Eq. (13.32), or

$$\frac{\sum_{i=2}^{N} t_i M_{ik}}{M_k} = \frac{\lambda}{1 - \lambda} = C \qquad k = 2, \ldots, N \tag{22.18}$$

Thus, introducing government production into the analysis does not alter the optimal tax rules, the first of the two main Diamond–Mirrlees results. As was noted in Chapter 14, this result depends crucially on the assumption of CRS in private production.

Optimal Government Production

To derive their second, more striking result, differentiate the first-order conditions with respect to the Z_k. As before, begin with a preliminary consideration of $\partial L/\partial Z_k$:

$$\frac{\partial L}{\partial Z_k} = \sum_{i=2}^{N} M_i \frac{\partial p_j}{\partial Z_k} - \sum_{i=2}^{N} \sum_{j=2}^{N} t_i M_{ij} \frac{\partial p_j}{\partial Z_k} + p_1 g_{Z_k} - p_k$$
$$- \sum_{i=2}^{N} Z_i \frac{\partial p_i}{\partial Z_k} - \sum_{i=2}^{N} \pi_i \frac{\partial p_i}{\partial Z_k} \qquad k = 2, \ldots, N \tag{22.19}$$

Multiplying the market clearance Eq. (22.6) by $\partial p_i/\partial Z_k$ and summing over all $(N - 1)$ relationships yield:

$$\sum_{i=2}^{N} M_i \frac{\partial p_i}{\partial Z_k} = \sum_{i=2}^{N} \pi_i \frac{\partial p_i}{\partial Z_k} + \sum_{i=2}^{N} Z_i \frac{\partial p_i}{\partial Z_k} \tag{22.20}$$

Hence, Eq. (22.19) simplifies to:

$$\frac{\partial L}{\partial Z_k} = -\sum_{i=2}^{N}\sum_{j=2}^{N} t_i M_{ij} \frac{\partial p_j}{\partial Z_k} + p_1 g_{Z_k} - p_k \qquad k = 2, \ldots, N \qquad (22.21)$$

Next, consider $\partial B/\partial Z_k$:

$$\frac{\partial B}{\partial Z_k} = \sum_{i=2}^{N}\sum_{j=2}^{N} t_i M_{ij} \frac{\partial p_j}{\partial Z_k} - p_1 g_{Z_k} + p_k + \sum_{i=2}^{N} \frac{\partial p_i}{\partial Z_k} \qquad k = 2, \ldots, N$$

$$(22.22)$$

From market clearance and CRS in private production, Eq. (22.22) can be restated as:

$$\frac{\partial B}{\partial Z_k} = \sum_{i=2}^{N}\sum_{j=2}^{N} t_i M_{ij} \frac{\partial p_j}{\partial Z_k} - p_1 g_{Z_k} + p_k + \sum_{i=2}^{N} M_i \frac{\partial p_i}{\partial Z_k} \qquad (22.23)$$

Thus,

$$\frac{\partial B}{\partial Z_k} = -\frac{\partial L}{\partial Z_k} + \sum_{i=2}^{N} M_i \frac{\partial p_i}{\partial Z_k} \qquad k = 2, \ldots, N \qquad (22.24)$$

Combining Eqs. (22.21) and (22.24) and incorporating λ, the first-order conditions with respect to the Z_k are

$$(1-\lambda)\frac{\partial L}{\partial Z_k} + \lambda\sum_{i=2}^{N} M_i \frac{\partial p_i}{\partial Z_k} \qquad k = 2, \ldots, N \qquad (22.25)$$

Substituting the expression for $\partial L/\partial Z_k$ and changing the summation index on the $M_i \partial p_i/\partial Z_k$ terms, Eq. (22.25) becomes:

$$(1-\lambda)\left[-\sum_{i=2}^{N}\sum_{j=2}^{N} t_i M_{ij} \frac{\partial p_j}{\partial Z_k} - p_k + p_1 g_{Z_k} \right]$$

$$(22.26)$$

$$+ \lambda\sum_{j=2}^{N} M_j \frac{\partial p_j}{\partial Z_k} = 0 \qquad k = 2, \ldots, N$$

To consider the effect that optimal taxation has on these rules, rewrite (22.26) as:

$$\sum_{j=2}^{N}\left[(1-\lambda) - \sum_{i=2}^{N} t_i M_{ij} + \lambda M_j \right] \frac{\partial p_j}{\partial Z_k}$$

$$(22.27)$$

$$+ (1-\lambda)\left(p_k - p_1 g_{Z_k} \right) = 0 \qquad k = 2, \ldots, N$$

But, if commodity taxes are set optimally in accordance with Eq. (22.18):

$$-(1-\lambda) - \sum_{i=2}^{N} t_i M_{ij} + \lambda M_j = 0 \qquad j = 2, \ldots, N \qquad (22.28)$$

Thus, the government production rule is simply:

$$p_k - p_1 g_{Z_k} = 0 \qquad k = 2, \ldots, N \qquad (22.29)$$

or

$$p_k = p_1 g_{Z_k} \qquad k = 2, \ldots, N \qquad (22.30)$$

Equation (22.30) is the standard first-best rule for production efficiency in competitive markets. Alternatively,

$$\frac{p_k}{p_j} = \frac{g_{Z_k}}{g_{Z_j}} = MRT_{Z_k, Z_j} \qquad k, j = 2, \ldots, N \qquad (22.31)$$

with the government using the competitively determined producer prices as shadow prices in its production decisions.

This may well be the most striking result in all of second-best public expenditure theory, one of the precious few examples of a simple second-best decision rule. It implies overall production efficiency for the economy[5] or that the economy should remain on its aggregate production-possibilities frontier. Of course, with distorting taxation the economy cannot also be on its first-best utility-possibilities frontier. A final implication in an intertemporal context is that government investment decisions should use the private sector's gross-of-tax returns to capital as the rate of discount in present value calculations (recall that p_k is a gross-of-tax price for an input such as capital).[6] Since the U.S. marginal corporate tax rate is 34 or 35% for most firms in the United States, this implies a fairly high government rate of discount, the rate of return the government must beat to justify public investment at the expense of private investment. We will return to this point in Part IV when discussing the rate of discount in cost–benefit analysis.

PRODUCTION DECISIONS WITH NONOPTIMAL TAXES

The Diamond–Mirrlees problem provides a clear example of just how far removed second-best theory often is from the complexities of the real world, even though it contains elements that are more realistic than the traditional first-best assumptions. Taxes are distorting in this model, but assuming that current tax rates are (even approximately) at their optimal values is every bit as heroic as assuming that taxes are (approximately) lump sum, which first-best theory requires. We can move somewhat closer to reality by assuming explicitly that the current rates are nonoptimal and asking how this affects the

---

[5] Recall that the private sector is assumed to be perfectly competitive and therefore first-best pareto efficient.

[6] Intertemporally, all budget constraints in the general equilibrium framework must balance in terms of present value, not year by year, and there must be perfect capital markets for borrowing and lending.

government's production decision rules. Formally, this assumption is equivalent to adding further constraints to the original Diamond–Mirrlees problem of the form that a subset of the tax rates are predetermined at nonoptimal levels. Given these predetermined rates, the first-order conditions of the new problem indicate how the government can adjust its production decisions to minimize loss.

Unfortunately, the resulting production rules are extremely complex. They have a plausible interpretation, but it is doubtful whether any government would have sufficient information to implement them. Furthermore, this problem is still far removed from reality, for it retains the assumption of a perfectly competitive CRS private production sector. Were we to introduce monopoly elements in private production and/or decreasing or increasing returns to scale with pure profits or losses, the optimal production rules would change once again. Consequently, the normative policy content of this model is not especially compelling either. Nonetheless, it is instructive to explore the production decision rules when taxes are nonoptimal if only to give a flavor for this kind of analysis.

To keep the notation as simple as possible, rewrite the loss function entirely in vector notation as:

$$L(t; Z) = M\left(q; \overline{U}^0\right) - t'M_i + p_1 g(Z) - (q - t)' Z - \pi(q - t) \quad (22.32)$$

Written in this form the loss function incorporates every relevant constraint except for the market clearance equations, Eq. (22.6), expressed in vector notation as:

$$M_i\left(q; \overline{U}^0\right) = \pi_i(q - t) + Z \quad (22.33)$$

The nonoptimal tax and production rules are derived by totally differentiating the loss function with respect to t and Z, and using Eq. (22.33) to simplify the resulting expression:

$$dL(t; Z) = M'_i \frac{\partial q}{\partial t} dt + M'_i \frac{\partial q}{\partial Z} dZ - M'_i dt - t'M_{ij} \frac{\partial q}{\partial t} dt$$

$$- t'M_{ij} \frac{\partial q}{\partial Z} dZ + p_1 g_z dZ - Z' \frac{\partial q}{\partial t} dt + Z' dt - Z' \frac{\partial q}{\partial Z} dZ \quad (22.34)$$

$$- (q - t)' dZ - \pi'_i \frac{\partial q}{\partial t} dt - \pi'_i \frac{\partial q}{\partial Z} dZ + \pi' dt$$

From market clearance:

$$M'_i dt = \pi'_i dt + Z' dt \quad (22.35)$$

$$M'_i \frac{\partial q}{\partial t} dt = \pi'_i \frac{\partial q}{\partial t} dt + Z' \frac{\partial q}{\partial t} dt \quad (22.36)$$

and

$$M'_i \frac{\partial q}{\partial Z} dZ = \pi'_i \frac{\partial q}{\partial Z} dZ + Z' \frac{\partial q}{\partial Z} dZ \qquad (22.37)$$

Also,

$$(q - t)' = p' \qquad (22.38)$$

Using Eqs. (22.35) to (22.38), Eq. (22.34) simplifies to:

$$dL(t; Z) = -t'M_{ij} \frac{\partial q}{\partial t} dt - t'M_{ij} \frac{\partial q}{\partial Z} dZ + p_1 g_Z dZ - p' dZ \qquad (22.39)$$

Next, totally differentiate Eq. (22.8), obtaining:

$$dq = \frac{\partial q}{\partial t} dt + \frac{\partial q}{\partial Z} dZ \qquad (22.40)$$

Substituting Eq. (22.40) into (22.39) yields:

$$dL(t; Z) = -t'M_{ij} dq + p_1 g_Z dZ - p' dZ \qquad (22.41)$$

The first point to notice is that the Diamond–Mirrlees production rules follow directly from Eq. (22.41). Suppose taxes are set optimally. Since setting taxes is equivalent to setting consumer prices, this means that the vector dq is also optimal. But at the optimum, $dL = 0$. Hence, optimal taxation implies a dq such that the first term in Eq. (22.41) is zero ($dL = -t'M_{ij}dq = -t'dX = 0$ at the optimum, t*). The vector dZ must also be compatible with $dL = 0$.
Hence,

$$p_1 g_Z dZ - p' dZ = 0 \qquad (22.42)$$

or

$$p_1 g_Z = p' \qquad (22.43)$$

Tax Rules

If taxes are not optimal, however, the decision rules for government production are more complex, since changes in Z change q, thereby indirectly affecting dL through the (nonzero) tax term in Eq. (22.41). The separate effects of taxes and government production on loss in the general case can be obtained by totally differentiating the market clearance equations, solving for dq in terms of dt and dZ, and substituting the resulting expression for dq into the first term of Eq. (22.41), as follows:

$$M_{ij} dq = \pi_{ij} dq - \pi_{ij} dt + dZ \qquad (22.44)$$

$$dq = \left(-\pi_{ij} dt + dZ\right) E^{-1} \qquad (22.45)$$

where:

$E = [M_{ij} - \pi_{ij}]$, the matrix of compensated demand and private production price derivatives (as defined in Chapter 14).

Substituting Eq. (22.45) into (22.41) and rearranging terms:

$$dL = t'\left(M_{ij}\right)E^{-1}\pi_{ij}dt - \left(-p_1 g_Z + p' + t'M_{ij}E^{-1}\right)dZ \qquad (22.46)$$

Equation (22.46) can be used to compute the change in loss, or welfare, resulting from any combination of changes in t and Z, with the remaining t and Z held constant. One immediate and important implication of Eq. (22.46) is that the addition of government production does not affect any of the theorems in Chapter 14 on the dead-weight loss from changes in tax rates. In this sense, the welfare effects of government production are separable from the welfare effects of distorting taxes. The term $[t'M_{ij}E^{-1}\pi_{ij}]dt$ is identical to the right-hand side (RHS) of Eq. (14.17) in Chapter 14, with:

$$M_{ij} = \frac{\partial X^{comp}}{\partial q} \quad \text{and} \quad \pi_{ij} = \frac{\partial Y}{\partial p}$$

As indicated in that chapter, the marginal loss from a small increase in a distorting tax can be interpreted as a change in consumer and producer surpluses, where consumer surplus is defined in terms of compensated demand curves. This result continues to hold in the presence of government production because with $dZ = 0$, the market clearance derivatives imply $dq = -\pi_{ij}E^{-1}dt$, or

$$dL(t; Z) = t'M_{ij}dq = t'\frac{\partial X}{\partial q}dq = t'dX = (q - p)'dX \qquad (22.47)$$

exactly as in Chapter 14.

Production Rules

The government's production rules can be stated in a number of different ways depending upon the manner in which the control variables are manipulated. The most straightforward example to consider is the welfare implication of marginally increasing one of the inputs, say Z_k, in order to increase output of Z_1 through the marginal product relationship g_{Z_k}, all other Z and the tax rates constant. According to Eq. (22.46), the change in loss from this move would be

$$dL(\bar{t}; Z) = -\left(-p_1 g_{Z_k} + p_k + t'M_{ik}E^{-1}\right)dZ_k \qquad (22.48)$$

The *optimal* adjustment of Z_k is one for which $dL = 0$, or

$$-\left(-p_1 g_{Z_k} + p_k + t'M_{ik}E^{-1}\right)dZ_k = 0 \qquad (22.49)$$

In a first-best environment, the government would hire Z_k until its price equaled the value of its marginal product, or $p_1 g_Z = p_k$ (recall that Z_k enters negatively in g(z)). With distorting and nonoptimal taxes, however, Eq. (22.49) implies that the true social costs of hiring Z_k are $(p_k + t'M_{ik}E^{-1})$. Hence, the government should use these true costs as the shadow price for decision making and equate them to the value of marginal product. In other words, set:

$$p_1g_Z = (p' + t'M_{ij}E^{-1}) \tag{22.50}$$

The term $t'M_{ij}E^{-1}$ turns out to have an intuitively appealing interpretation. With taxes held constant, $dt = 0, dq = dp$, and the market clearance derivatives, Eq. (22.44), become:

$$M_{ij}dq = \pi_{ij}dp + dZ \tag{22.51}$$

Substituting $dq = dp$ and solving for dZ yield:

$$dZ = (M_{ij} - \pi_{ij})dq = Edq \tag{22.52}$$

Substituting Eq. (22.52) into the last term of Eq. (22.46) and letting only Z_k change:

$$-(-p_1g_{Z_k}dZ_k + p_kdZ_k + t'M_{ik}dq) = 0 \tag{22.53}$$

Rearranging terms:

$$p_1g_{Z_k} = \left(p_k + t'M_{ik}\frac{dq}{dZ_k}\right) \tag{22.54}$$

But,

$$t'M_{ik}\frac{dq}{dZ_k} = t'\frac{\partial X}{\partial q}\frac{dq}{dZ_k} = t'dX \tag{22.55}$$

the change in tax revenues caused by a change in Z_k at constant tax rates. This revenue change represents an additional dead-weight burden to the consumer because, with nonzero taxes, changes in market equilibria change the sum of producers' and consumers' surpluses lost as a result of the tax distortions.

Figure 22.1 illustrates this point. X_0 is the original no-tax equilibrium, and X_1 is the equilibrium with taxes (and government production), with loss equal to triangle ABC. If a marginal increase in Z_k shifts X again, generating a new equilibrium, X_2, then the loss area in the market for X increases by the trapezoidal area EBCD, which is approximately equal to $t'dX$ for small changes. The full social opportunity costs of using Z_k, then, are the standard market opportunity costs as represented by p_k plus the additional excess burden implied by the tax revenue response to changes in Z_k. Finally, since this result holds for all k, the production rule can be expressed in the traditional format as $MRT_{i,j} = \theta_i/\theta_j$, for $j = 2, \ldots, N$, where $\theta_i = p_i + t'M_{ji}(dq/dZ_i)$, the optimal shadow price for good (factor) i.

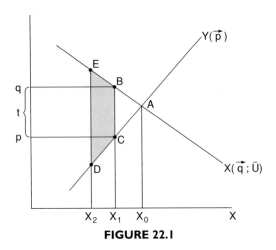

FIGURE 22.1

Special Cases

The government production shadow prices $\theta_k = (p_k + t'M_{ik}E^{-1})$ have a very appealing weighted-average interpretation if one assumes, as an approximation, that all cross-price derivatives in demand and private production are zero.[7] With this assumption, the shadow price simplifies to:

$$\theta_k = p_k + t_k \frac{\partial X_k}{\partial q_k}\left[\frac{\partial X_k}{\partial q_k} - \frac{\partial Y_k}{\partial p_k}\right]^{-1} \tag{22.56}$$

$$\theta_k = p_k + (q_k - p_k)\frac{\partial X_k}{\partial q_k}\left[\frac{\partial X_k}{\partial q_k} - \frac{\partial Y_k}{\partial p_k}\right]^{-1} \tag{22.57}$$

Rearranging the second term on the RHS of Eq. (22.57) yields:

$$\theta_k = p_k + (q_k - p_k)\left[\frac{1}{1 - \dfrac{\dfrac{\partial Y_k}{\partial p_k}}{\dfrac{\partial X_k}{\partial q_k}}}\right] \tag{22.58}$$

---

[7] This assumption is not tenable for either the compensated demand derivatives or the production derivatives. At least one M_{ij}, for $i \neq j$, and one π_{ij}, for $i \neq j$, must be positive. Thus, the assumption can only be approximately true. See R. Boadway, "Cost–Benefit Rules and General Equilibrium," *Review of Economic Studies*, July 1975, pp. 365, 366, and 370.

Let:

$$\alpha = \frac{\dfrac{\partial Y_k}{\partial p_k}}{\dfrac{\partial X_k}{\partial q_k}}$$

Therefore:

$$\theta_k = p_k + (q_k - p_k)\left[\frac{1}{1-\alpha}\right] \qquad (22.59)$$

Rearranging terms:

$$\theta_k = q_k\left(\frac{1}{1-\alpha}\right) + p_k\left(\frac{-\alpha}{1-\alpha}\right) \qquad (22.60)$$

Equation (22.60) says that the optimal shadow price for the input Z_k is a weighted average of the consumer and producer prices, with the weights equal to the proportions in which the increased Z_k comes at the expense of either decreased demand for the input by the private sector or increased supply of the input from consumers. Given market clearance, these are the only possibilities.

Consider the extreme cases as an aid to intuition. If, on the one hand, the entire increase in Z_k comes from an increase in consumer supply, $\partial Y_k/\partial p_k = 0$, $\alpha = 0$, and $\theta_k = q_k$. The only opportunity cost of increasing Z_k is the private opportunity cost to the consumer of supplying the additional Z_k. If, on the other hand, the entire increase in Z_k comes from a decrease in private demand, $\partial X_k/\partial q_k = 0$, $\alpha \to \infty$, and $\theta_k = p_k$, the market opportunity cost for Z_k. This is effectively what happens with optimal taxation—all changes in government production come entirely at the expense of private production.

The case of $\partial X_k/\partial q_k = 0$ also applies for linear technologies with fixed producer prices. All changes in government production must come entirely at the expense of private production when private production input demands and output supplies are perfectly elastic at the fixed producer prices. Indeed, we would expect the optimal shadow prices to equal the producer prices, $\vec{p}$ even if cross-price derivatives are nonzero. That this is so can be seen directly from Eq. (22.41). With $\vec{p}$, constant, $dq = dt$ and Eq. (22.41) becomes:

$$dL = -t'M_{ij}dt + (p_1 g_Z - p')dZ \qquad (22.61)$$

Even with nonoptimal distorting taxes, then, the government should use the competitive private sector producer prices as shadow prices to avoid any additional increases in dead-weight loss.

Balanced-Budget Changes in t and Z

Thus far, government production variables have been allowed to change without any reference to the government's budget constraint. Any changes in the budget surplus (deficit) are simply returned to the consumer lump sum. If, in fact, the government is required to maintain budgetary balance, then increasing Z_k may require a simultaneous change in at least one of the tax rates. One can imagine the following policy: Suppose the government increases Z_k (and, implicitly, Z_1) and simultaneously changes the jth tax, t_j, to maintain a balanced budget. Under these circumstances, what is the appropriate shadow price for Z_k?

The solution is straightforward given Eq. (22.46). Totally differentiate the government's budget, $t'M_i - p_1 g(Z) + p'Z = B$, with respect to t_j and Z_k to determine the required change in t_j for any given (small) change in Z_k, and substitute the resulting solution $dt_j^* = f' \cdot dZ_k$ into Eq. (22.46) to obtain an expression for the change in loss solely as a function of dZ_k. The optimal shadow price is then computed by setting $dL = 0$. Without actually carrying out the calculations, the effect of the budget constraint on the optimal shadow prices can be seen from Eq. (22.46):

$$\frac{dL}{dZ_k} = t'M_{ij}E^{-1}\pi_{ij}\frac{dt_j^*}{dZ_k} - \left(-p_1 g_{Z_k} + p_k + t'M_{ik}E^{-1}\right) = 0 \qquad (22.62)$$

where:

$\dfrac{dt_j^*}{dZ_k}$ is the required change in t_j for maintaining budgetary balance.

Note that $\dfrac{dt_j^*}{dZ_k}$ is not the only possibility; any number of tax changes could be used to keep the budget in balance as Z_k changes. The analysis must specify exactly how the tax rates are being changed. In any event, the new shadow price to be equated to the value of marginal product $p_1 g_{Z_k}$ is

$$\theta_k = p_k + t'M_{ik}E^{-1} - t'M_{ij}E^{-1}\pi_{ij}\frac{dt_j^*}{dZ_k} = p_1 g_{Z_k} \qquad (22.63)$$

There are now two necessary adjustments to p_k, the private opportunity costs, to obtain the full social opportunity costs of Z_k. The first is the additional dead-weight loss as tax revenues adjust directly to the change in Z_k, measured at constant tax rates, the effect described above. The second is the additional dead-weight loss resulting from the required increase in t_j to maintain budgetary balance. Since marginal changes in different Z's affect the budget equation differently, this second source of additional burden is, in general, unique to each Z. Quite obviously, governments are going to have a most difficult time computing these optimal shadow taxes, unless the distorting taxes are optimal or technology is linear. As we have seen, in either of these cases the optimal shadow prices are just the p_k. Note also that using p_k implies that the government's budget constraint necessarily holds. If $p_1 g_{Z_k} = p_k$, then

$$-p_1 g_{Z_k} dZ_k + p_k dZ_k = 0 \qquad k = 2, \ldots, N \qquad (22.64)$$

implies

$$-p_1 dZ_1 + p_k dZ_k = 0 \qquad k = 2, \ldots, N \qquad (22.65)$$

SECOND-BEST PRODUCTION RULES WHEN EQUITY MATTERS

Assuming a one-consumer-equivalent economy in second-best analysis is always somewhat contradictory. Unless consumers' tastes are severely restricted, one-consumer equivalence implies that the government is optimally redistributing income lump sum in accordance with the first-best interpersonal equity conditions, thereby equilibrating social marginal utilities of income. But if the government can do this, why would it ever have to use distorting taxes?

The more natural approach in a second-best framework is to deny the existence of optimal income redistribution and assume explicitly that social marginal utilities of income are unequal. This means, however, that the optimal shadow prices for government production decisions depend upon both efficiency and equity considerations, just as the many-person optimal tax and nonexclusive goods decision rules were seen to incorporate both efficiency and equity terms. This is doubly discouraging for policy purposes, as we noted when discussing those problems. Not only are optimal prices further complicated by the addition of equity terms, but also society may not agree on the proper equity weights for each individual. Thus, the analysis runs the risk of becoming totally subjective, since different sets of ethical weights imply different optimal shadow prices. Nonetheless, if society can agree on a ranking of social marginal utilities of income (a big if), then the proper shadow prices for government production can be determined. Furthermore, the shadow prices can be expressed as a simple combination of distinct equity and efficiency effects, at least for the particular government production decisions and second-best distortions being considered in this chapter.

To relate the many-person results as closely as possible to the one-person rules, we will assume away all sources of lump-sum income by requiring that all factor supplies are variable and private production exhibits CRS. A further assumption is that the government budget exactly balances. These assumptions greatly simplify the analysis, while capturing the flavor of many-person second-best analysis.[8]

The government's objective function, then, is:

$$W = W[V^h(\vec{q})] = V(\vec{q}) \qquad (22.66)$$

---

[8] With only minor changes, the analysis of this section is taken directly from R. Boadway, "Integrating Equity and Efficiency in Applied Welfare Economics," *Quarterly Journal of Economics*, November 1976.

where W is the agreed-upon individualistic Bergson–Samuelson social welfare function whose arguments are the individuals' indirect utility functions $V^h(\vec{q})$. Differentiating totally,

$$dW = \sum_{h=1}^{H} \sum_{i=1}^{N} \frac{\partial W}{\partial V^h} \frac{\partial V^h}{\partial q_i} dq_i = -\sum_{h=1}^{H} \sum_{i=1}^{N} \beta^h X_{hi} dq_i \qquad (22.67)$$

from Roy's Identity and the definition of an individual's social marginal utility of income as $\beta^h = (\partial W/\partial V^h)\alpha^h$, where $\alpha^h =$ the private marginal utility of income for person h. It will be convenient to express the change in social welfare in terms of Martin Feldstein's distributional coefficient for X_i:

$$R_i = \sum_{h=1}^{H} \beta^h \frac{X_{hi}}{X_i} \qquad i = 1, \ldots, N \qquad (22.68)$$

to work with aggregate consumption.[9] R_i is a weighted average of the individuals' social marginal utilities of income, with the weights equal to the proportion of good (factor) i consumed (supplied) by person h. Substituting Eq. (22.68) into (22.67) yields:

$$dW = -\sum_{i=1}^{N} R_i X_i dq_i \qquad (22.69)$$

The problem is to define dW in terms of the government control variables $\vec{t} = (t_2, \ldots, t_N)$ and $\vec{Z} = (Z_2, \ldots, Z_N)$, given the following constraints:

1. Private production possibilities, $F(Y_1, \ldots, Y_N) = 0$, assumed to exhibit CRS.
2. The government production function, $G(Z_1, \ldots, Z_N) = 0$, or $Z_1 = -g(Z_2, \ldots, Z_N)$, with inputs measured negatively.
3. The government budget constraint, $\sum_{i=2}^{N} t_i X_i + \sum_{i=1}^{N} p_i Z_i = 0$.
4. N market clearance relationships, $X_i(\vec{q}) = Y_i(\vec{p}) + Z_i$, for $i = 1, \ldots, N$. All markets clear in the actual general equilibrium.
5. $\vec{q} = \vec{p} + \vec{t}$, with $q_1 \equiv p_1 \equiv 1$, and $t_1 \equiv 0$.

As always, the first good serves as the untaxed numeraire.

The analysis proceeds much as in the one-consumer case. Begin by totally differentiating the market clearance equations:

$$dX_i = dY_i + dZ_i \qquad i = 1, \ldots, N \qquad (22.70)$$

Multiply each equation by $q_i = (p_i + t_i)$ and sum over all N equations to obtain:

---

[9] M. Feldstein, "Distributional Equity and the Optimal Structure of Public Prices," *American Economic Review*, March 1972. Also see our discussion of Feldstein's distributional coefficient in Chapter 14.

$$\sum_{i=1}^{N} q_i dX_i = \sum_{i=1}^{N} (p_i + t_i) \, dY_i + \sum_{i=1}^{N} (p_i + t_i) \, dZ_i \qquad (22.71)$$

Equation (22.71) can be simplified as follows. Totally differentiate the individual consumers' budget constraints $\sum_{i=1}^{N} q_i X_{hi} = 0$, all $h = 1, \ldots, H$, and sum over all individuals to obtain:

$$\sum_{i=1}^{N} q_i dX_i = -\sum_{i=1}^{N} X_i dq_i \qquad (22.72)$$

Next, differentiate the aggregate private production possibilities $F(\vec{Y}) = 0$,

$$\sum F_i dY_i = 0 \qquad (22.73)$$

But, if markets are perfectly competitive,

$$\frac{F_i}{F_1} = \frac{p_i}{p_1} = p_i, \quad \text{with } p_1 \equiv 1 \qquad i = 2, \ldots, N \qquad (22.74)$$

Therefore:

$$\sum_{i=1}^{N} F_i dY_i = 0 = F_1 \sum_{i=1}^{N} p_i dY_i \qquad (22.75)$$

or

$$\sum_{i=1}^{N} p_i dY_i = 0 \qquad (22.76)$$

Substituting Eqs. (22.72) and (22.76) into (22.71) yields:

$$-\sum_{i=1}^{N} X_i dq_i = \sum_{i=1}^{N} t_i dY_i + \sum_{i=1}^{N} t_i dZ_i + \sum_{i=1}^{N} p_i dZ_i \qquad (22.77)$$

Using Eq. (22.70), Eq. (22.77) can be expressed as:

$$-\sum_{i=1}^{N} X_i dq_i = \sum_{i=1}^{N} t_i dX_i + \sum_{i=1}^{N} p_i dZ_i \qquad (22.78)$$

Substituting Eq. (22.78) into (22.69) yields:

$$dW = -\sum_{i=1}^{N} R_i X_i dq_i + \sum_{i=1}^{N} X_i dq_i + \sum_{i=1}^{N} t_i dX_i + \sum_{i=1}^{N} p_i dZ_i \qquad (22.79)$$

or

$$dW = \sum_{i=1}^{N} (1 - R_i) X_i dq_i + \sum_{i=1}^{N} t_i dX_i + \sum_{i=1}^{N} p_i dZ_i \qquad (22.80)$$

Next, incorporate the government production function, $Z_1 = -g\,(Z_2, \ldots, Z_N)$, and note that $t_1 \equiv 0, dq_1 = 0$, to rewrite Eq. (22.80) as:

$$dW = \sum_{i=2}^{N} (1 - R_i)X_i dq_i + \sum_{i=2}^{N} t_i dX_i + \sum_{i=2}^{N} (-p_1 g_{Z_i} + p_i) dZ_i \qquad (22.81)$$

To eliminate the dX_i, totally differentiate the individual demand (factor supply) functions $X_{hi} = X_{hi}(\vec{q})$, $h = 1, \ldots, H$, and sum over all individuals to obtain:

$$dX_i = \sum_{j=2}^{N} \frac{\partial X_i}{\partial q_j} dq_j \qquad i = 1, \ldots, N \qquad (22.82)$$

Substituting Eq. (22.82) into (22.81) and rearranging terms yield:

$$dW = \sum_{i=2}^{N} \sum_{j=2}^{N} \left[(1 - R_i)X_i + t_j \frac{\partial X_j}{\partial q_i} \right] dq_i + \sum_{i=2}^{N} (-p_1 g_{Z_i} + p_i) dZ_i \qquad (22.83)$$

Finally, use the market clearance equations:

$$X_i(\vec{q}) = Y_i(\vec{q} - \vec{t}) + Z_i \qquad i = 1, \ldots, N \qquad (22.84)$$

to express dq_i in terms of the control variables dt_i and dZ_i, as follows. From Walras' law, only $(N - 1)$ of these relationships are independent. Since good 1 is the numeraire, eliminate the first equation and totally differentiate equations $2, \ldots, N$ to obtain:

$$\sum_{j=2}^{N} \frac{\partial X_i}{\partial q_j} dq_j = \sum_{j=2}^{N} \frac{\partial Y_i}{\partial p_j} dq_j - \sum_{j=2}^{N} \frac{\partial Y_i}{\partial p_j} dt_j + dZ_i \qquad i = 2, \ldots, N \qquad (22.85)$$

Writing all $(N - 1)$ equations in matrix notation:

$$\left(\frac{\partial X}{\partial q} \right) dq = \left(\frac{\partial Y}{\partial p} \right) dq - \left(\frac{\partial Y}{\partial p} \right) dt + dZ \qquad (22.86)$$

(All matrices have dimension $(N - 1) \times (N - 1)$; all vectors have dimension $((N - 1) \times 1)$.) Solving Eq. (22.86) for dq yields:

$$dq = E^{-1} \left[-dt' \left(\frac{\partial Y}{\partial p} \right) + dZ \right] \qquad (22.87)$$

where:

$$E = \left[\left(\frac{\partial X}{\partial q} \right) - \left(\frac{\partial Y}{\partial p} \right) \right]$$

Substituting Eq. (22.87) into (22.83), rearranging terms, and writing the resulting equation in matrix notation yield:

$$dW = - \left[\left[\left[(1 - R)' \cdot X \right] + t' \frac{\partial X}{\partial q} \right] E^{-1} \left(\frac{\partial Y}{\partial p} \right) \right] dt$$
$$+ \left[\left[(1 - R)' \cdot X \right] E^{-1} + t' \frac{\partial X}{\partial q} E^{-1} - p_1 g z + p' \right] dZ \qquad (22.88)$$

Equation (22.88) gives the change in social welfare for any given (marginal) changes in the government control variables, evaluated at the existing levels of each t and Z.

Notice that if the distribution of income were optimal so that $\beta^h = \beta$, for all $h = 1, \ldots, H$, then $R_i = \sum_{h=1}^{N} \beta_h X_{hi}/X_i = \beta$, all $i = 1, \ldots, N$, the common social marginal utility of income. Since W can be defined such that $\beta = 1$, by setting $\partial W/\partial V^h = 1/\alpha^h$, all $h = 1, \ldots, H$, dW simplifies to:

$$dW|_{\beta^h=\beta=1} = -\left(t'\frac{\partial X}{\partial q}\right)E^{-1}\left(\frac{\partial Y}{\partial p}\right)dt$$

$$+\left[t'\left(\frac{\partial X}{\partial q}\right)E^{-1} - p_1 g_Z + p'\right]dZ \tag{22.89}$$

But Eq. (22.89) is identical to Eq. (22.46), with $dW|_{\beta^h=\beta=1} = -dL$, $(\partial X/\partial q) = M_{ij}$, and $(\partial Y/\partial p) = \pi_{ij}$ (i.e., assuming away income effects so that actual and compensated demands and factor supplies are identical). Since Eq. (22.46) captures all the efficiency implications of distorting taxation, Eq. (22.88) can be viewed as a simple linear combination of the efficiency and equity effects of tax distortion, where the latter are embodied in the coefficients $[(1 - R)' \cdot X]' E^{-1}(\partial Y/\partial p)$ for changes in tax rates, and $[(1 - R)' \cdot X]'E^{-1}$ for changes in the government production variables. Thus, if the government were able to estimate the efficiency effects of the tax distortions and if it could provide an acceptable set of social marginal utilities of income, adjusting tax and production decision rules for equity considerations would be a relatively straightforward exercise. These are two huge ifs, however. Although it is appealing to be able to separate the equity and efficiency effects of government policies in principle, there is still no reason to suppose that a society will be able to agree on a set of distributional coefficients, R_i, much less that the government can compute the efficiency distortions with any confidence.

To make matters worse, the full social costs (benefits) for public sector inputs and outputs in a many-person environment generally consist of the coefficients on (some of) the dt terms as well as the coefficients on the appropriate dZ terms. To see why, suppose that the government increases its purchase of input Z_k, thereby increasing production of Z_1 through g_{Z_k}. It is tempting to conclude that the social cost for Z_k is p_k plus the appropriate terms in $[[(1 - R)' \cdot X]E^{-1} + t'(\partial X/\partial q) \cdot E^{-1}]$, to be equated to $p_1 g_{Z_k}$, the value of marginal product for Z_k. But, this ignores the fact that the government's budget must remain in balance. When computing the dq as functions of dt and dZ in Eq. (22.86), we invoked Walras' law to eliminate the market clearance equation for good 1. But the N market clearance equations are dependent only if all consumers are on their budget constraints, all firms are maximizing profits, *and* the government budget always remains in balance. Thus, although the government budget constraint was never explicitly mentioned in deriving the expression for dW, the solution for dq in Eq. (22.86) and for dX_i in Eq. (22.82) implicitly assumed that it holds, since lump-sum income was held constant. Therefore, any policy experiments evaluated with Eq. (22.88) must be consistent with maintaining the government's budget constraint. Were the government to follow the optimal shadow price for Z_k derived above, the budget will surely not remain in balance, since this would require $p_1 g_{Z_k} = p_k$, or $p_1 dZ_1 = p_k dZ_k$. In general, then, the government must vary at least one of the tax rates to maintain budgetary balance, in which case the full social cost of Z_k contains terms of the form:

$$\left[\left[(1 - R)' \cdot X \right] + t' \frac{\partial X}{\partial q} \right] E^{-1} \left(\frac{\partial Y}{\partial p} \right) \frac{dt^*}{dZ_k}$$

As before, the dt^*/dZ_k are the tax changes necessary to keep:[10]

$$\sum_{i=2}^{N} t_i X_i + \sum_{i=1}^{N} p_i Z_i = 0$$

The only simple case for optimal shadow prices occurs when the producer prices, $\vec{p}$ are fixed, such as with linear technologies or for a small country facing perfectly elastic supplies (input demand) at world prices. With $dq = dt$, Eq. (22.83) becomes:

$$dW|_{p=\bar{p}} = \sum_{i=2}^{N} \sum_{j=2}^{N} \left[(1 - R_i) X_i + t_j \frac{\partial X_j}{\partial q_i} \right] dt_i$$
$$+ \sum_{i=2}^{N} \left(-p_1 g_{Z_i} + p_k \right) dZ_i \tag{22.90}$$

The optimal shadow prices are just the private sector or producer prices p_k, exactly as in the one-consumer (equivalent) economy. With perfectly elastic supplies (input demands), changes in government production variables do not change consumer prices. Therefore, they have no equity effects and no efficiency implications other than the requirement that government producers do just as well as the private opportunity costs reflected in the price p_k. Furthermore, as noted in the preceding sections, with $p_1 g_{Z_k} = p_k$, or $p_1 dZ_1 = p_k dZ_k$, all $k = 2, \ldots, N$, marginal changes in government production are always self-financing, so that the government's budgetary balance is automatically maintained.

Concluding Comments

Equation (22.88) provides a fairly comprehensive guideline for government decision making. The many-person problem considered above imposes no restrictions on the form of the government production function and allows

---

[10] The budget could remain in balance without changing taxes if many Z's change simultaneously, but budgetary balance is unlikely to be maintained without changing some taxes.

the government to tax all goods and factors. Furthermore, the tax incidence analysis of Chapter 14 showed that it makes no difference whether distorting per-unit taxes are levied on producers or consumers. Finally, Eq. (22.88) holds at the existing values of all government tax and production control variables.

It is important to realize, however, that the analysis is not fully general. There are, for example, no externalities arising from the government's activity, private production is assumed to be perfectly competitive and exhibit CRS, and the government is free to vary all price–cost margins. Changes in any or all of these assumptions can be expected to alter the implied optimal shadow prices for public production.[11] Nonetheless, we will refer to Eq. (22.88) in the discussion of cost–benefit analysis in Part IV as representative of a large portion of existing second-best public expenditure theory.

REFERENCES

Boadway, R., "Cost–Benefit Rules and General Equilibrium," *Review of Economic Studies*, July 1975.

Boadway, R., "Integrating Equity and Efficiency in Applied Welfare Economics," *Quarterly Journal of Economics*, November 1976.

Diamond, P. A., and Mirrlees, J., "Optimal Taxation and Public Production" (2 parts; Part I: Production Efficiency, Part II: Tax Rules), *American Economic Review*, March June 1971.

Dreze, J. and Stern, N., "The Theory of Cost–Benefit Analysis," in A. Auerbach and M. Feldstein, Eds., *Handbook of Public Economics*, vol. II, Elsevier/North-Holland, Amsterdam, 1985, chap. 14.

Feldstein, M., "Distributional Equity and the Optimal Structure of Public Prices," *American Economic Review*, March 1972.

[11] Jean Dreze and Nicholas Stern undertake a more general analysis that incorporates some of these complicating factors in J. Dreze and N. Stern, "The Theory of Cost–Benefit Analysis," in A. Auerbach and M. Feldstein, Eds., *Handbook of Public Economics*, vol. II, Elsevier/North-Holland, Amsterdam, 1985, chap. 14.

PART **IV**

COST–BENEFIT ANALYSIS

23

INTRODUCTION: THE ISSUES OF COST–BENEFIT ANALYSIS

Cost–benefit analysis is the practitioner's art, the application of normative public sector theory to an imperfect world that does not conform to the underlying assumptions of any one theoretical model. Strictly speaking, it refers to the systematic evaluation of government *investment* projects, as distinguished from transfer programs or consumption-oriented allocational expenditures such as judicial services.

What criteria should the government employ to determine whether or not a particular investment project is worthwhile? If funds are limited for some reason, which of a number of worthwhile projects should be chosen? How can the government compare investments meant to serve different purposes that might have very different kinds of benefits and costs— for example, building a new highway versus subsidizing private manpower development training programs? Practical questions such as these are the substance of cost–benefit analysis. They tend not to have clear-cut answers, but attempts to answer them should recognize three fundamental principles.

THREE PRINCIPLES OF COST–BENEFIT ANALYSIS

The Limits of Analytical Rigor

The first principle merely reaffirms the notion that cost–benefit analysis is as much an art as a science, for which reasoned judgment is every bit as important as strict analytical rigor. Our theoretical knowledge of project costs and benefits comes from two sources: (1) first-best models, in which all markets are perfectly competitive and government policy responses to particular problems are totally unrestricted; and (2) second-best models, which have taken only the smallest steps in accounting for the vast array of real-world imperfections and complexities. Second-best theory has also shown us just how sensitive normative policy prescriptions are to both the form and the number of restrictions added to the basic first-best general equilibrium framework. Consequently, analytical rigor cannot be the sole arbiter in practical policy deliberations. At best, these theoretical models provide a consistent analytical framework for thinking about practical problems, with their results serving as guidelines to the policymaker.

The essence of any cost–benefit study derives from the assumptions it chooses. To this end, the most important prior consideration is whether or not first-best assumptions are reasonable for analyzing a given investment project and, if not, what specific second-best assumptions are appropriate to the analysis. As might be expected, the first-best assumptions greatly simplify the analysis in most instances, but there is no sense using them if they are clearly unreasonable. To give but one example, can the policymaker reasonably assume that the distribution of income is (approximately) optimal? The answer to this one question is central to a whole host of practical issues.

One of the main goals of Part IV is to indicate how the choice between first- and second-best assumptions dictates the approach to each of the practical problems being considered. For the most part, we will simply be recalling theoretical results from Parts II and III and reflecting upon their application to specific problems. It makes little sense to push forward with new second-best models in our view unless absolutely necessary, especially since no new second-best theoretical model can capture all the elements of reality in any event. Of course, no such modeling decision arises if the first-best assumptions are deemed appropriate because first-best theory offers a single, well-defined set of policy guidelines for any given problem. There is only one possible set of first-best assumptions.

Quantifying the Present Value Formula

The second principle is that a cost–benefit analysis of government investments proceeds exactly as the analysis of private investments undertaken by firms. Both analyses center around the present value formula, which is necessary to render all benefits and costs commensurate over time. Let the present value of a government project be defined as:

$$PV = -I_0 + \sum_{n=1}^{N} \frac{R_n}{(1+r)^n} \tag{23.1}$$

where:

PV = the present value of the investment,
I_0 = initial investments costs,
R_n = a measure of net benefits (benefits − costs) in period n,
r = the appropriate rate of discount (assumed constant over time),
N = the endpoint of the planning horizon,

exactly as for private sector investments.[1] The same decision rules apply for the government as well:

1. The government should accept all investments, and only those investments, that have a positive present value. This is the meaning of a "worthwhile" project.[2]
2. If funds are limited for some reason, the goal is to select the subset of projects that maximizes aggregate present value subject to the budget constraint. The solution to this problem requires programming techniques and may leave some of the funds unexpended, depending on the size of each individual project.

Ideally, the government should subject all potential investments to these present value tests regardless of their purpose.

The present value formula, Eq. (23.1), represents an addition to the theoretical tools developed in Parts II and III which ignored the investment aspect of government expenditures entirely by adopting a one-period, static, general equilibrium framework, but it is only a trivial addition in and of itself. Our previous models can easily be modified to incorporate government investments by appropriately time-subscripting all variables and writing all budget constraints (profit functions) in present value form.

The underlying analytical framework for cost–benefit analysis, then, is perfectly straightforward. All the interesting issues lie in trying to quantify each element in the present value formula. The same can be said of private investment analysis.

---

[1] If the one-year discount rate varies over time, the formula is $PV = -I_0 + \sum_{n=1}^{N} R_n \prod_{i=1}^{n} \frac{1}{(1+r_i)}$, where r_i is the appropriate rate of discount for year i.
[2] If a subset of these investments contains mutually exclusive projects, the project with the highest present value within the subset should be chosen.

The Full Employment Assumption

The final principle is that cost–benefit analysis implicitly assumes a fully employed economy, unless specifically stated otherwise. It is intended primarily as an exercise in microeconomic analysis, designed to help governments select among alternative uses of scarce resources. One immediate implication of the full-employment assumption is that government investment projects not only compete directly among themselves for scarce resources. Each project must also dominate all alternative private sector uses of the same scarce resources to be deemed worthwhile.

The formal structures of public sector cost–benefit and private sector investment analysis may be identical, but the former is ultimately more difficult and, in many ways, more subjective than the latter. Broadly speaking, the differences between them in application center around the point that market prices do not always reflect marginal *social* values. Private investment analysis typically ignores this fact, but the government's cost–benefit analysis cannot. Indeed, the very name "cost–benefit analysis" suggests that government project evaluation goes well beyond the calculation of profits at current and expected future market prices and interest rates that one normally associates with private sector investment analysis. Profitability is generally not the proper criterion for selecting among alternative public sector projects.

In trying to evaluate the present value formula, government policymakers face the same issues that beset private investment analysts, plus another whole set of difficult issues unique to the public sector. The common issues are the choice of an appropriate rate of discount and the general problem of uncertainty. Even so, their solutions are often markedly different. Let us consider each of them briefly by way of introduction.

ISSUES COMMON TO COST–BENEFIT AND PRIVATE INVESTMENT ANALYSIS

The Discount Rate

By inspection of Eq. (23.1), it is obvious that choosing the proper rate of discount is crucial to any investment analysis. Using a rate that is too low (high) introduces two types of errors. One is that too many (few) projects pass the present value test. The other is that the present value formula biases selection toward projects whose net returns occur later (earlier) rather than earlier (later), given equal undiscounted streams of returns. Furthermore, project selection tends to be very sensitive to even small absolute errors as a general rule. Choosing a discount rate of 5% when the "true" rate is 10% or

15% may cause the government to choose far too many projects, especially those whose returns occur far into the future.[3]

It is well accepted that the rate of discount for private investments should reflect the returns generally available to the owners of the firm on alternative investments of equal risk. That is to say, r defines the opportunity cost of capital for the firm.

The role of the discount rate in cost–benefit analysis is less clear cut, however, and is the subject of considerable disagreement among public sector economists. All economists would agree that, in theory, the so-called *public rate of discount* is just another price in a general equilibrium setting, the price that links the future and present values of economic variables. What value this price should have is difficult to say, however, because it depends on the underlying model used to describe the economy. The appropriate rate of discount can be highly complex and almost impossible to compute if a second-best model is chosen. The practical problem, therefore, is to choose a simplified way of thinking about the rate of discount, one that the policymaker can use. Two well-defined positions have emerged in the literature.

One position holds that the public rate of discount should be thought of as the opportunity cost of funds just as in private investment analysis (Harberger, Sjaastad, and Wisecarver, for example).[4] The opportunities foregone are the private consumption and investment that the public funds displace, and the opportunity cost equals the returns generally available on these two forms of private sector activity. The practical challenge for this position is selecting a numerical value for r that accurately reflects the returns generally available in the private sector.

A second position maintains that the discount rate in cost–benefit analysis has nothing whatsoever to do with opportunity cost (Marglin, Arrow, and Feldstein, for example).[5] Rather, it reflects the *social marginal rate of*

---

[3] These comments ignore the problem that any one project may have multiple internal yields, defined as a rate of discount that just sets PV = 0. With multiple internal yields, a project may pass the present value test over numerous regions of r, so that applying higher (lower) rates of discount may not generate a bias against (in favor of) the project.

[4] A. C. Harberger, *Project Evaluation: Collected Papers*, Markham Publishing Chicago, 1974. See also, "The Opportunity Costs of Public Investment Financed by Borrowing," in R. Layard, Ed., *Cost–Benefit Analysis*, Penguin Education, Penguin Books, Ltd., Harmondsworth, Middlesex, England, 1972; and L. Sjaastad and D. Wisecarver, "The Social Cost of Public Finance," *Journal of Political Economy*, June 1977.

[5] K. J. Arrow, "Discounting and Public Investment Criteria," in A. Kneese and S. Smith, Eds., *Water Resources Research*, Johns Hopkins University Press, Baltimore, 1966; M. Feldstein, "The Inadequacy of Weighted Discount Rates," in R. Layard, Ed., *Cost–Benefit Analysis* Penguin Education, Penguin Books, Ltd., Harmondsworth, Middlesex, England, 1972; S. Marglin, "The Opportunity Costs of Public Investment," *Quarterly Journal of Economics*, May 1963.

substitution, the interest rate that society deems appropriate for discounting any stream of consumption over time. The social MRS is commonly referred to as the *social rate of time preference*. According to this view, the net benefits resulting from any given project should simply be considered an addition to the stream of consumption available to society. The fact that public investment causes society to forego private consumption and investment opportunities is relevant but is properly accounted for by applying an appropriate shadow price to the initial investment costs, I_0 (and any subsequent *cash* deficits [surpluses] that may arise throughout the life of the project). The practical challenge for this position is determining the proper relationship between the consumers' private rates of time preference and the social rate of time preference.

To date, a full reconciliation of these conflicting positions has not been achieved. This is a matter of some importance, since the social rate of time preference is likely to be well below any rate reflecting the opportunity cost of funds in the private sector and, as noted above, present value calculations are extremely sensitive to the rate of discount chosen. These issues will be discussed at length in Chapter 24.

Uncertainty

Uncertainty is obviously a fundamental problem for any investment analysis. No one can know for sure what the stream of net benefits will be for any project nor the appropriate rate of discount in each future time period. All such estimates have probability distributions associated with them.

We have no intention of undertaking a detailed analysis of decision making under uncertainty in this section of the text. Parts II and III assumed perfect certainty when developing the normative theories of public expenditure and taxation, and the chapters on cost–benefit analysis will generally continue in this vein. Chapter 25 presents some general recommendations for accounting for uncertainty. Its main focus, however, is on a remarkable theorem attributed to Kenneth Arrow and Robert Lind, which shows that under fairly plausible conditions government investment analysis can actually *ignore* uncertainty.[6] Their proof uses nothing more sophisticated than the definition of a derivative, and their results hold not only in a first-best environment but for a broad range of second-best environments as well. The Arrow–Lind theorem also provides a striking exception to the general rule that public sector investment analysis is more difficult than private sector investment analysis, for it can also be used to demonstrate that private sector investment analysis cannot ignore uncertainty in general.

---

[6] K. J. Arrow and R. C. Lind, "Uncertainty and the Evaluation of Public Investment Decisions," *American Economic Review*, June 1970.

PROBLEMS UNIQUE TO COST–BENEFIT ANALYSIS

Chapters 26 and 27 consider two exceedingly complex issues for cost–benefit analysis that are not likely to be of much consequence for private investment analysis. Chapter 26 analyzes a broad set of measurement problems relating to both costs and benefits that arise whenever market prices do not reflect marginal social values. Chapter 27 considers a number of issues relating to the distribution of project costs and benefits when the distribution of income is nonoptimal.

Measurement Problems

The most common measurement problems associated with government projects can be grouped into four broad categories: intangibles, lumpiness, resources or services that are either drafted or given away, and the computation of shadow prices for government inputs and outputs. As a practical matter, resolving any one of them necessarily involves large doses of judgment and common sense, with theoretical analysis offering only broad guidelines to the policymaker.

Intangibles are costs or benefits that are impossible to evaluate in dollar terms, such as the increase in national security derived from a particular weapons system or the almost certain loss of lives when building a bridge. Private industry may occasionally consider intangibles such as "goodwill" in its investment analysis, but such items are bound to be peripheral. By and large, private sector projects are accepted or rejected on more objective, and measurable, grounds, such as the expected profitability of the investment or its projected effect on the firm's market share. In contrast, both proponents and opponents of public projects often view the presence of intangibles as the decisive factor in accepting or rejecting the project. This, of course, is devastating to objective cost–benefit analysis, because the present value formula is useful only to the extent that its various elements can be quantified. By the same token, however, certain legitimate benefits and costs of public projects may well be intangible. This does not render them any less relevant to the overall evaluation of the project.

Lumpiness refers to the fact that a government project may be large enough to have a significant impact on the economy, meaning that the project will change the general equilibrium vector of consumer and producer prices. For example, a hydroelectric project might significantly lower the price of electricity for an entire region of the country. In contrast, private investment analysis can usually assume that any one project is "small" enough so that it will not affect prices. The two situations are compared in Fig. 23.1.

In the case of the private sector firm, its additional capacity is so small relative to the overall market that the firm's demand curve essentially remains horizontal at P_0. Thus, the benefits of its investment projects are simply the

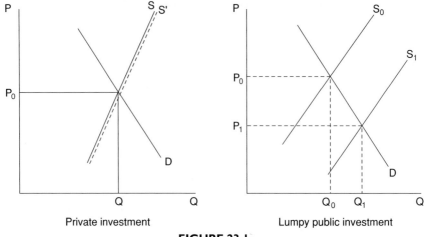

FIGURE 23.1

additional revenues at the existing (and expected future) market price(s). In the case of the public sector project, however, the supply curve shifts significantly, changing the equilibrium prices from P_0 to P_1. Normative theory may suggest that P_1 is the correct price to charge for the project's output. But if this project is being compared with other projects, there remains the problem of placing a dollar value on the benefits derived from the lower price and increased output. Neither $P_0(Q_1 - Q_0)$ nor $P_1(Q_1 - Q_0)$, two obvious *revenue* measures, is a reasonable approximation of the benefits in this market. Furthermore, if the project is expected to change the price within this market, prices in other markets are likely to change as well. As we have discovered throughout the text, public sector theory offers specific guidelines for measuring benefits and costs when prices change, but computing the appropriate measures with real-world data is almost never an easy task.

Whenever the government *commandeers resources* (e.g., military conscription) or offers *benefits of certain projects free of charge* (e.g., flood control benefits from a hydroelectric project), two issues arise. The first concerns the propriety of setting a zero price—is it justified or not? The second concerns the method of computing costs or benefits when price is zero. Obviously, the zero price by itself offers no useful information on costs or benefits.

Although only the second issue appears to be directly relevant to a cost–benefit study, the answer to the first question in part determines how the benefits and costs should be evaluated. For example, suppose the price of some service is zero because the short-run marginal costs for providing the service are zero. In this case, the zero price is consistent with first-best assumptions, and the cost–benefit study might reasonably employ the simpler first-best framework. If marginal costs differ from zero, however, the analytical framework must necessarily be second best. In formal terms, setting the price equal to zero acts as a binding constraint on the range of possible government policy responses, and this (additional) constraint must be incorporated into the analysis.

The final measurement problem, establishing appropriate *shadow prices* for government inputs and outputs, is a catch-all residual category that applies generally to any analysis using second-best assumptions. The theoretical analysis in Chapters 21 and 22 showed that if there are market imperfections throughout the economy or if government policy responses are constrained in any way, such as by the use of distorting taxes to finance government production, then the evaluation of costs and benefits generally requires the computation of shadow prices that differ from observed market prices. The nature of the second-best restrictions determines exactly how the shadow prices are to be computed, so that a cost–benefit study employing second-best assumptions must carefully specify the assumed policy environment. Unfortunately, for most real-world situations the information required to compute these shadow prices is difficult, if not impossible, to obtain. This helps explain the widespread appeal of first-best assumptions in cost–benefit analysis, even though they are often not very realistic. Observed market prices are the basic data for all benefit and (opportunity) cost measures in a first-best environment.[7]

The Distribution of Income

The distribution question is certainly unique to the evaluation of government projects. Private investment analysis quite properly ignores the fact that profits from investments accrue to the firm's owners in proportion to the distribution of ownership rights. Management's only concern is the aggregate present value for each project.

Governments, in contrast, are concerned with the equity implications of their policy actions. Consequently, the present value of the aggregate benefits and costs, which can be taken as an indicator of the efficiency of a project, may well be an incomplete measure of the project's contribution to social welfare. Given a choice between two projects, the government might be justified in selecting the project with lower present value if the distribution of its discounted benefits and costs is more equitable.

This is an extremely uncomfortable possibility, however, since all distributional evaluations are inherently subjective. The purpose of cost–benefit analysis is to provide the policymaker with objective measures of project costs and benefits, which can then be applied consistently to all government

---

[7] As noted in Chapter 22, Jean Dreze and Nicholas Stern have written an excellent survey of the theory of cost–benefit analysis in a second-best environment for the *Handbook of Public Economics*: J. Dreze and N. Stern, "The Theory of Cost–Benefit Analysis," in A. Auerbach and M. Feldstein, Eds., *Handbook of Public Economics*, Vol. II, Elsevier/North-Holland, Amsterdam, 1985, Chap. 14.

investments. But complete objectivity is virtually impossible to maintain if the distribution of costs and benefits matters. Consequently, many cost–benefit studies ignore distributional considerations entirely and attempt to measure only aggregate present values. Ignoring the distribution problem does not solve it, however. It merely consigns to cost–benefit analysis the more modest task of determining the relative efficiency of government projects, rather than ranking projects according to their contributions to social welfare. Perhaps this is all cost–benefit analysis can hope to achieve.

Chapter 27 explores two fundamental questions relating to the distribution of costs and benefits. First, under what conditions can the distribution question safely be ignored in cost–benefit analysis? Second, if these conditions do not exist, how should distributional considerations enter into the analysis? We will consider some suggestions for incorporating the distribution of the net benefits that have appeared in the literature. Unfortunately, none of them avoids the problem of subjectivity. One can almost always design a set of subjective distributional weights that overwhelm whatever objective efficiency information a cost–benefit study might contain, no matter what approach is taken.

PITFALLS IN COST–BENEFIT ANALYSIS

Chapter 28 concludes Part IV by discussing a number of common pitfalls in cost–benefit analysis. It may seem odd to spend time on false claims, but the sad truth is that public debate on government projects all too often focuses on irrelevancies and misconceptions. Roland McKean long ago labeled these errors "secondary benefits" (costs), implying that people find new sources of benefits (costs) to add to the true benefits (costs) in order to make the project seem all the more attractive (unattractive).[8] Unfortunately, these secondary, bogus benefits (costs) can be many times greater than the project's true benefits (costs).

We will consider five of the more common pitfalls:

1. *The chain-reaction game*, in which profits (losses) generated throughout the economy as a result of a government project are indiscriminately attached to the benefits (costs) of the project.

2. *The regional multiplier game*, in which Keynesian-type multipliers are used to enhance the benefits (costs) of the project.

3. *The labor game*, a variation of (1) and (2) in which the employment effects of the project are viewed as one of its major benefits, perhaps even the principal benefit. This error has become a matter of law. Federal and state legislation often requires that cost–benefit studies explicitly consider the

---

[8] R. N. McKean, *Efficiency in Government through Systems Analysis*, Wiley, New York, 1958, chaps. 8 and 9.

employment effects of the projects, which the politicians then focus on instead of the true benefits and costs.

4. *Double counting*, in which the same benefits (costs) appear twice in the analysis.

5. *The public sector bias charge*, which says that public investments have an unfair advantage over private investments because they do not have to make a profit. This charge is intended as an additional implicit cost for all government projects.

Many of these items contain the proverbial germ of truth, but they are commonly misused to the point of being totally misleading. Hence, it is fitting to conclude Part IV with a fair warning of these practices. They may arise because the public simply misunderstands the nature of true costs and benefits, but it is easy to be skeptical. Partisans always stand ready to exploit them for their own ends.

CONCLUSION

Chapters 24–28 do not pretend to be an exhaustive treatise on cost–benefit analysis; many excellent books, filled with detailed and illustrative examples, have already been written on the subject.[9] Rather, these chapters are meant to highlight the major problems that the policy analyst is likely to encounter when evaluating a project and indicate the extent to which public sector theory can help resolve them. In our view, if a cost–benefit analysis pays close attention to the issues raised in Chapters 24–27 and the theory underlying them, and avoids the pitfalls discussed in Chapter 28, then the analysis will enlighten public policy discussions. The inverse is equally true.

REFERENCES

Arrow, K. J., "Discounting and Public Investment Criteria," in A. Kneese and S. Smith, Eds., *Water Resources Research*, Johns Hopkins University Press, Baltimore, 1966.
Arrow, K. J., and Lind, R., "Uncertainty and the Evaluation of Public Investment Decisions," *American Economic Review*, June 1970.

[9] We especially recommend any of the following: R. Layard and S. Glaister, Eds., *Cost–Benefit Analysis*, second ed., Cambridge University Press, New York, 1994; an excellent compilation of articles on all aspects of cost–benefit analysis, written at the Ph.D. level. R. McKean, *Efficiency of Government through Systems Analysis*, Wiley, New York, 1958. E. J. Mishan, *Cost–Benefit Analysis*, Praeger Publishers, New York, 1976; comprehensive, but at times unconventional, with excellent references throughout. E. Stokey and R. Zeckhauser, *A Primer for Policy Analysis*, W. W. Norton, New York, 1978; not strictly a treatise on cost–benefit analysis but an excellent methods and tools text. Finally, J. N. Wolfe, Ed., *Cost–Benefit and Cost–Effectiveness: Studies and Analysis*, George Allen & Unwin, Ltd., London, 1973.

Dreze, J., and Stern, N., "The Theory of Cost–Benefit Analysis," in A. Auerbach and M. Feldstein, Eds., *Handbook of Public Economics*, Elsevier/North-Holland, Amsterdam, 1985, chap. 14.

Feldstein, M., "The Inadequacy of Weighted Discount Rates," in R. Layard, Ed., *Cost–Benefit Analysis*, Penguin Education, Penguin Books, Ltd., Harmondsworth, Middlesex, England, 1972.

Harberger, A., "The Opportunity Costs of Public Investment Financed by Borrowing," in R. Layard, Ed., *Cost–Benefit Analysis*, Penguin Education, Penguin Books, Ltd., Harmondsworth, Middlesex, England, 1972.

Harberger, A., *Project Evaluation: Collected Papers*, Markham Publishing, Chicago, 1974.

Layard, R., and Glaister, S., Eds., *Cost–Benefit Analysis*, second ed., Cambridge University Press, New York, 1994.

Marglin, S., "The Opportunity Costs of Public Investment," *Quarterly Journal of Economics*, May 1963.

McKean, R., *Efficiency in Government through Systems Analysis*, Wiley, New York, 1958.

Mishan, E., *Cost–Benefit Analysis*, Praeger Publishers, New York, 1976.

Stokey, E., and Zeckhauser, R., *A Primer for Policy Analysis*, W.W. Norton, New York, 1978.

Sjaastad, L., and Wisecarver, D., "The Social Cost of Public Finance," *Journal of Political Economy*, June 1977.

Wolfe, J., Ed., *Cost–Benefit and Cost–Effectiveness: Studies and Analysis*, George Allen Unwin, Ltd., London, 1973.

24

THE RATE OF DISCOUNT FOR PUBLIC INVESTMENTS

What rate of discount should the government use for computing the present values of various investment alternatives? As indicated in Chapter 23, this question has stirred considerable debate among public sector economists, one which goes far beyond attaching a particular numerical value to the public rate of discount. There is a fundamental conceptual disagreement over exactly what the public discount rate is meant to represent.

Roughly speaking, the division within the profession is threefold. One group, following Arnold Harberger,[1] believes that the rate of discount for public projects ought to reflect the opportunity cost of public funds, much as the discount rate for private investments measures the opportunity cost of capital to the firm. A second group, following Stephen Marglin and Martin Feldstein,[2] argues that the discount rate, *per se*, has nothing whatsoever to do with opportunity cost. It simply reflects society's rate of time preference, the social marginal rate of substitution between the present and future. The opportunity cost of public funds is relevant, but is properly accounted for by means of a separate shadow price applied directly to these funds. It is not relevant for discounting a future stream of net benefits. A final group remains eclectic (e.g., Peter Diamond, Roland McKean),[3] arguing that it is pointless to associate the rate of discount with any one concept such as opportunity cost or time preference. Rather, the rate of discount is simply one shadow price among many in a second-best environment that depends, as do all shadow prices, on the structure of that environment. Under some assumptions, the appropriate discount rate will appear to represent the opportunity cost of public funds; under different assumptions, society's rate of time preference. Yet it is always possible to describe reasonable assumptions under which there is no obvious relationship between the discount rate and either concept.

The eclectic view is unassailable on strictly theoretical grounds. The public rate of discount is determined by equations such as Eqs. (22.46) or (22.88), appropriately modified to have an intertemporal interpretation. But it bears reemphasizing that most issues in cost–benefit analysis cannot be decided by appealing strictly to theory. Ultimately governments must chose some rate of discount to apply consistently to all projects. Proponents in each of the first two groups would undoubtedly concede the theoretical point that the appropriate rate of discount is model sensitive. Nonetheless, they argue that their principles offer reasonable and practical guidelines for real-world policy evaluation. In contrast, attempts to estimate equations such as Eqs. (22.46) and (22.88) are bound to be loaded with assumptions, to be highly subjective, and unlikely to produce a consensus public rate of discount.

Despite their differences of opinion, virtually all public sector economists agree that the present value of government projects depends crucially upon

---

[1] A. Harberger, *Project Evaluation: Collected Papers*, Markham Publishing Chicago, 1974. See also "The Opportunity Costs of Public Investment Financed by Borrowing," in R. Layard, Ed., *Cost-Benefit Analysis*, Penguin Education, Penguin Books, Ltd., Harmondsworth, Middlesex, England, 1972.

[2] M. Feldstein, "The Inadequacy of Weighted Discount Rates," in R. Layard Ed., *Cost–Benefit Analysis*; S. Marglin, "The Opportunity Costs of Public Investment," *Quarterly Journal of Economics*, May 1963.

[3] P. Diamond, "The Opportunity Costs of Public Investment: Comment," *Quarterly Journal of Economics*, November 1968; R. McKean, "Tax Wedges and Cost–Benefit Analysis," *Journal of Public Economics*, February 1974.

three factors: (1) the opportunity cost of public funds, (2) the degree to which the net benefits of government projects are reinvested or consumed, and (3) the social rate of time preference. The disagreement arises over the emphasis placed on each of these factors and their precise role in the present value formula.

We begin with an intuitive discussion of these common factors to bring some structure to the controversy. We then consider what the theoretical models of public expenditure and tax theory developed in Parts II and III can tell us about the public rate of discount. It turns out that they do not settle the debate, by any stretch of the imagination. Therefore, we present a model developed by Bradford that is specifically designed to highlight the three factors listed above, and use it as a vehicle for comparing the conflicting views on the appropriate rate of discount. The chapter concludes with two empirical pieces: a survey of economists on the appropriate public rate of discount for global climate change, and an overview of discounting practices within the federal government.

THREE FACTORS RELEVANT TO PRESENT VALUE CALCULATIONS

The Opportunity Cost of Public Funds

Given the full-employment assumption, there is no question that bringing resources into the public sector for investment projects entails an opportunity cost, equal to the value of those resources if left in the private sector. What public sector economists cannot agree on is how the present value formula should account for these opportunity costs. In particular, should they affect the rate of discount or simply be reflected in the initial investment costs, I_0 in Eq. (23.1) (and any subsequent cash deficits that may arise)? Regardless of one's view on this issue, there remains the question of how to evaluate these opportunity costs, which we turn to first.

The major conceptual problem in evaluating the opportunity cost of public funds is that there are two natural claimants of scarce resources in the private sector: private consumption and private investment (ignoring the foreign sector). An extra dollar of government spending (in this case, government investment) implies either a dollar decrease in consumption spending or a dollar decrease in private investment spending, or some combination of the two adding to one dollar. Consequently, the opportunity cost of public funds must be a combination of at least three factors: (1) a rate of return that reflects the opportunity cost of consumption, (2) a rate of return that reflects the opportunity cost of private investment, and (3) the proportions by which an extra dollar of government investment comes at the expense of consumption and private investment.

The Marginal Rate of Substitution

To the extent government investment comes at the expense of private consumption, the government is, in effect, forcing consumers to save now in exchange for a specific stream of future consumption in the form of the net benefits from the government investment. Conceptually, then, we seek a rate of return sufficient to induce consumers to save now for future consumption. For any one consumer, this is simply the (private) marginal rate of substitution between present and future consumption, which we will assume is constant over time. For purposes of illustration, suppose a consumer has an initial endowment, Y, which he will convert to a stream of consumption over his lifetime.[4] A utility-maximizing consumer solves the following problem:

$$\max_{(C_t)} U(C_1, \ldots, C_t, \ldots, C_N)$$

$$\text{s.t.} \quad \sum_{t=1}^{N} \frac{C_t}{(1 + r_c)^t} = Y$$

where:

C_t = consumption at time t, a composite commodity with price equal to 1.

Y = initial endowment income.

r_c = the one-period rate of return on savings, net of tax, assumed constant over time.

N = the last year of life.

For any two consecutive periods, the first-order conditions imply:

$$\frac{U_{C_t}}{U_{C_{t+1}}} \equiv MRS_{C_t, C_{t+1}} = 1 + r_c \qquad (24.1)$$

where the left-hand side (LHS) of the equation is the marginal rate of substitution between the future and the present. Graphically, the consumer would be at point A in Fig. 24.1, with the slope of the budget line equal to $(1 + r_c)$. The relevant point for public investment analysis is that, if the government is going to force a (marginal) reduction in C_t to finance a government project (say, by means of taxation), the project should guarantee the consumer at least $(1 + r_c)$ units of consumption next period to compensate for each unit of C_t.

The analysis is straightforward enough, but selecting a single number from observable data to represent the marginal rate of substitution between present and future consumption is extremely difficult. There are hundreds of

---

[4] The example assumes no final bequest, although this is easily accounted for by assuming that the bequests the final act of consumption. We are also assuming that the consumer can borrow or lend at rate r_c, and that interest on borrowing is tax deductible.

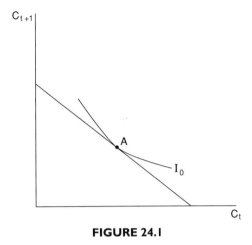

FIGURE 24.1

different savings instruments, real and financial, each with a specific array of characteristics, such as function, liquidity, return, risk, term to maturity, and so forth. There are millions of consumers, each with his or her own set of preferences. Actually, the large number of consumers would not matter so much except that various capital market imperfections force different groups of consumers into vastly different savings opportunity sets. Generally speaking, high-income savers tend to have more options than low-income savers, especially for real assets, and greater access to borrowed funds. Consumers also face varying marginal income tax rates, so that different consumers receive different effective returns on any given asset. Finally, some consumers, especially the poor, do not save at all, and are often liquidity constrained from borrowing. To protect their interests, the government must presumably finance only projects that exceed the net-of-tax returns available to these people if it is going to ask them to forego current consumption for future benefits. Ideally, one would want some weighted average of returns available to various subgroups of consumers.

Despite these difficulties, there does appear to be a consensus among public sector economists that relatively small rates of return, in the 3–6% range, accurately reflect consumers' marginal rates of substitution between present and future consumption in the United States.[5] The 3–6% estimate reflects the range of *net-of-tax returns* available on assets, since the after-tax return is the relevant rate for consumers' savings decisions under an income tax. These are also real rates of return, net of the expected rate of inflation. If there is an expected rate of inflation, e, the discount factor would simply be multiplied by $(1 + e)$. The stream of returns would also be adjusted by the

---

[5] We have never seen an estimate outside this range.

expected rate of inflation, however, so for purposes of this discussion it does not matter if we consider present value in nominal or real terms.

The Marginal Rate of Transformation

To the extent government investment comes at the expense of private investment, society is foregoing the productivity of the private investment alternatives. In line with the consumer example, think of competitive private sector producers transforming current consumption into future consumption by means of an aggregate production function:

$$F(C_1, \ldots, C_i, \ldots, C_N) = 0$$

Their goal is to maximize the present value of profits, $\sum_{t=1}^{N} C_t/(1 + r_p)^t$, subject to $F(C_i) = 0$, where r_p is the opportunity cost of funds to the firm, the rate of return available elsewhere to the firms' stockholders, assumed constant. For any two consecutive periods, the first-order conditions imply:

$$\frac{F_{C_t}}{F_{C_{t+1}}} \equiv MRT_{C_t, C_{t+1}} = 1 + r_p \tag{24.2}$$

The LHS is the marginal rate of transformation between the future and the present, the productivity of private investment on the margin. The production equilibrium is at point B in Fig. 24.2, with the slope of the intertemporal production-possibilities frontier equal to $(1 + r_p)$ the opportunity cost of a dollar of current consumption.

Selecting a single number to represent the marginal productivity of private sector investment is every bit as difficult as selecting a representative marginal rate of substitution. There are thousands of business firms in the

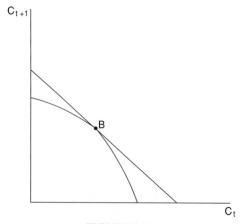

FIGURE 24.2

United States, each one with its own distinct set of investment alternatives, subject to varying degrees of risk and earning quite different rates of return. One can only be confident of two points. First, the appropriate measure of a firm's marginal productivity is its *gross-of-tax* return on investment at the equilibrium. By taxing these returns, the government is merely sharing in the distribution of the benefits. Thus, r_p is the gross-of-tax rate of return available to the stockholders. Second, returns to capital are fairly heavily taxed in the United States. Returns in the corporate sector are taxed twice, first by the federal (and some state) corporate income taxes and again by federal (and some state and local) personal income taxes as they are distributed.[6] The tax rates are substantial. The federal marginal corporate rate is 34% for most corporations, and marginal personal income tax rates may be well in excess of 40% with the combination of federal and state taxes. Inflation introduces a further bias against income from capital (see Chapter 11 for a discussion of this point). Hence, if rates of 3 to 6% are taken as reasonable estimates of the marginal rate of substitution between present and future consumption, then the private marginal rate of transformation is likely to be many times higher, in the 10 to 25% range. Estimates of private sector productivity vary considerably among public sector economists, but the majority are within this range.[7]

The Consumption–Investment Mix

The large difference between the MRS and MRT for the United States presents a serious problem, because the third factor relevant to the opportunity cost of public funds is the proportions by which increases in government investment come at the expense of consumption and private investment. At this point, think of the opportunity cost of government investment as a simple weighted average of the MRS and MRT, with the weights equal to the proportions in which government investment displaces consumption and private investment on the margin. This is the public rate of discount proposed by Harberger, and it is the appropriate rate under certain assumptions. We will discuss these points at length further along in the chapter.

Unfortunately, it is virtually impossible to determine what the mix is likely to be for any one project. Suppose one were willing to assume that each dollar of some government investment requires an additional dollar of taxes. The problem remains that there are many different kinds of taxes, each presumably implying a different consumption–investment sacrifice. Furthermore, it is generally impossible to relate specific taxes to specific projects.

---

[6] While unincorporated businesses escape the corporate tax, the more successful ones will be subjected to fairly high personal income tax rates.

[7] Feldstein's 1977 estimates of the MRS and MRT in the United States have been widely cited. He placed the MRS^{US} at 5% and the MRT^{US} at 12%. See M. Feldstein, "Does the United States Save Too Little?" *American Economic Association Papers and Proceedings*, February 1977, pp. 116–117.

All this would hardly matter if the marginal rates of substitution and transformation were approximately equal, but with the former in the 3 to 6% range and the latter between 10 and 25%, the consumption–investment mix is obviously crucial.

The point takes on even more force to the extent one agrees with Harberger *et al.*, that the public rate of discount ought to reflect the opportunity cost of funds. Lacking precise information on the consumption–investment mix, the government could try a range of values for the public rate of discount and hope that the same projects pass and fail each time. But this is unlikely to happen. Discounting at rates varying from 3 to 25% generally produces very different recommendations. As discussed in Chapter 23, the lower rates will tend to favor far more investments, and those whose net benefits occur farther in the future.

Reinvestment of Project Benefits

The goal of normative public sector theory is the maximization of an individualistic social welfare function, which depends ultimately upon the consumption possibilities available to consumers over time. Viewed in these terms, the essence of public sector investment is that it changes the stream of aggregate consumption, presumably to the benefit of society. For instance, the opportunity cost of taking scarce resources from the private sector can be thought of as the stream of aggregate consumption that would have arisen had those resources been left in the private sector. To the extent private investment is foregone, the entire future stream of consumption is necessarily altered simply by extracting resources for the initial public investment.

The repercussions of public projects do not end with the original source of the funds. The future stream of net benefits from the government investment also affects the future paths of private consumption and investment if government benefits are either substitutes for or complements to either component of private sector demand. Moreover, these future effects may well differ from the future effects of private investment, and these differences must be accounted for in determining the present value of public investment. Unfortunately, determining the private consumption and investment repercussions of project benefits is every bit as difficult as determining the consumption–investment mix of the source of funds. There are a number of problems. Suppose, for example, one could safely assume that the benefits from a certain project, say, a park, were in the nature of a consumption good. Even so, it remains uncertain whether such public consumption is a substitute or complement to private consumption, or unrelated. There is precious little econometric evidence on this score. Another problem is that the benefits from private investment are typically not so specific as those of most public projects. They typically accrue in the form of additional income, out of which consumers decide either to save or consume. That is to say, the time stream of future consumption resulting from private investments depends largely upon consumers' marginal propensity to consume (save). Yet the MPC (MPS) is unlikely to be relevant for highly specific public benefits. This merely underscores the point that different consumption effects from public and displaced private investment are almost certain to arise. Finally, we expect private firms to save some of the returns in order to replace depreciated capital. Can we also expect governments to save some of the benefits from their projects in the form of capital consumption allowances, or will the public insist on consuming all the net benefits as they arise? If the public benefits are not financial, will the government levy additional taxes earmarked for the replacement of public capital? Whatever the answers to these questions, it is reasonable to suppose that private and public sector depreciation practices differ, still another factor that generates different future consumption effects from the returns of public and private investments.

The Social Rate of Time Preference

The final issue concerns a possible divergence between consumers' private marginal rates of substitution over time and the appropriate social marginal rate of substitution over time, the so-called *social rate of time preference*. There is a consensus within the profession that the stream of additional consumption available to society as the result of a worthwhile government project ought to be discounted at the social rate of time preference. For instance, any formal intertemporal model of social welfare maximization would be cast in present value terms, with the maximand and all relevant constraints discounted at the social rate of time preference. The only source of controversy is whether this social marginal rate of substitution should simply reflect the consumers' private marginal rates of substitution or be adjusted to reflect additional social considerations. Harberger has argued in favor of the former position, but he would appear to be in the minority.[8] Most economists addressing this issue favor an adjusted MRS_{soc} that is below the private after-tax market rate. Two arguments have been advanced in favor of the adjusted rate.

The first is a distributional point, that private individuals tend to ignore the utility of unborn generations, whereas the government should not do so. Specifically, by ignoring future generations, the current population consumes too much, leaving too little capital for the future. Hence, the argument is that the government should counteract this tendency by using a lower MRS, thereby increasing the stock of public capital.

[8] A. Harberger, *Project Evaluation: Collected Papers*, Markham Publishing, Chicago, 1974.

The second point in favor of a socially adjusted MRS is due to Amartya Sen and Stephen Marglin.[9] They argue that saving has a Samuelsonian public good aspect to it that the government should take into consideration, just as it would any intratemporal externality. It is essentially the intertemporal version of the issue of pareto-optimal redistributions discussed in Chapter 10. Namely, the benefits received by future generations from any one individual's saving are twofold: (1) a direct benefit arising from the increased income of the individual's own heirs, plus (2) an external benefit arising because the returns are taxed and distributed throughout the population, thereby increasing the income of others' heirs. To the extent people receive utility from the indirect effect, Sen and Marglin show that a social contract in which all are forced to save for the future is generally pareto superior to the situation of privately determined savings, from the current generation's point of view. Without presenting the details, the essence of the proof is identical to that for any external economy: Subsidizing any activity that generates external economies yields net benefits otherwise unexploited by private decision making. In this instance, the subsidy implies setting MRS_{soc} below MRS_{priv} for purposes of project evaluation.

THEORETICAL CONSIDERATIONS FROM NORMATIVE PUBLIC EXPENDITURE AND TAX THEORY

Before proceeding to a model specifically designed to incorporate these three features, let us briefly consider the implications of the theoretical models of public expenditures and taxation developed in Parts II and III. They describe a number of special cases for which computing the rate of discount would be relatively straightforward, but the assumptions each time are so stringent that these results may not have much practical value.

The First-Best Environment

One "easy" case occurs if the economic and policy environment can reasonably be assumed to be first best. This would greatly simplify computations of the discount rate because the MRS and MRT between the present and future would be equal for investments of equal risk. Hence, the consumption–investment mix would be irrelevant. Optimal income distribution would render the economy equivalent to a one-consumer economy and, with perfect markets everywhere, the economy would reach an equilibrium such as point A in Fig. 24.3, at which the common MRS just equals the common MRT.

[9] S. Marglin, "The Social Rate of Discount and the Optimal Rate of Investment," *Quarterly Journal of Economics*, February, 1963; A. Sen, "The Social Time Preference Rate in Relation to the Market Rate of Interest," in R. Layard, Ed., *Cost–Benefit Analysis*, Penguin Education, Penguin Books, Ltd., Middlesex, England, 1972; A. Sen, "Isolation, Assurance, and the Social Rate of Discount," *Quarterly Journal of Economics*, February, 1967.

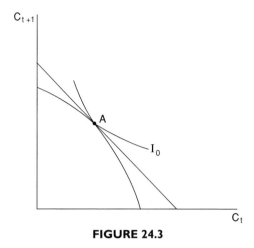

FIGURE 24.3

Hence, the MRS_{soc} *is* the opportunity cost of public funds, so that the two opposing pragmatic views on the public rate of discount coincide.[10]

As usual, the first-best assumptions make life easy, but they are clearly inappropriate for computing the public rate of discount in any of the developed market economies. As noted above, the MRS and MRT are driven far apart by taxation in the United States. Thus, determining the proper discount rate must fall within the domain of the second best, for which there is an uncomfortably wide range of possibilities.

The Second-Best Environment

To interpret our previous second-best models intertemporally, think of the economy as consisting of a single good produced and consumed over N time periods rather than N goods and factors in a single time period, and let the good in period N serve as the untaxed numeraire. The good can be consumed directly or used to produce additional units of the good in future periods. The objective function is the present value of social welfare, discounted at the MRS_{soc}. The consumers' MRS_{priv} equals the ratio of the consumer prices q_j: $(U_j/U_{j+1} = q_j/q_{j+1} = 1 + r_c)$. Similarly, the private producers' MRT equals the ratio of the producer prices p_j: $(f_j/f_{j+1} = p_j/p_{j+1} = 1 + r_p)$. In addition, the government's production function $Z_N = -g(Z_1, \ldots, Z_{N-1})$ defines the public sector's rate of transformation over time, with $g_{Z_j}/g_{Z_{j+1}}$ equal to the one-period rate of discount for public projects. Finally, all budget constraints

---

[10] I_0 in Fig. 24.3 is meant to be a social indifference curve under the first-best assumption of optimal income distribution. If $MRS_{priv} > MRS_{soc}$ because of a Sen-Marglin intergenerational savings externality, the private market MRT is the proper rate of discount, not the private market MRS. At a first-best optimum, $MRS_{priv} > MRS_{soc} = MRT$, with the saving externality incorporated into the social indifference curves.

(profit functions) are satisfied in terms of present value over the entire N periods, not period by period, discounted at the MRS_{soc}. Hence, $\sum_{i=1}^{N} p_i Z_i$ refers to the present value of the government deficit, and $\sum_{i=1}^{N} t_i M_i$ the present value of (compensated) tax collections. Requiring period-by-period balance, or $t_j M_j = p_j Z_j, j = 1, \ldots, N$, would add N constraints to the models, implying entirely different tax and expenditure rules.

Given this interpretation, let us simply recall the main results from Chapter 22:

1. Surely the most striking result is the Diamond–Mirrlees theorem, which says that the appropriate public rate of discount is the private sector's MRT between present and future outputs, the gross-of-tax producer prices for inputs, if two conditions hold: (a) private production exhibits constant returns to scale (CRS), and (b) the government uses per-unit distorting taxes to finance government expenditures and sets the taxes optimally. Although the first condition may be reasonable to assume, the second is unlikely to hold even approximately.

2. Given the same model, but assuming nonoptimal distorting taxation, Eq. (22.46) applies, reproduced here as Eq. (24.3) with the numeraire changed from the first to the N_{th}. good:[11]

$$
dL = \left[t' \frac{\partial X}{\partial p} E^{-1} \frac{\partial Y}{\partial p} \right] dt - \left[-p_N g_Z + p' + t' \frac{\partial X}{\partial q} E^{-1} \right] dZ \qquad (24.3)
$$

Equation (24.3) underscores the important theoretical point that the government's rate of discount is simply another shadow price defined in a temporal context.[12] Thus, all the difficulties of determining optimal shadow prices discussed in Chapter 22 apply directly to the computation of the proper social rate of discount.

As we discovered, there are only three relative easy cases. The first applies to optimal taxation, already mentioned above. Additionally, if private sector production technology is linear, then the constant producer prices are the optimal shadow prices for public production. This implies discounting government investments at the private marginal rate of transformation.[13] Finally,

---

[11] We are assuming an optimal distribution of income among all living persons to focus on the public rate of discount.

[12] See R. McKean, "Tax Wedges and Cost–Benefit Analysis," *Journal of Public Economics*, February 1974, for further discussion of this point.

[13] Diamond and Mirrlees later generalized this result, proving that, in all private sectors exhibiting CRS production, the shadow prices must be such that profits in these sectors equal zero calculated at the shadow prices. This holds true for any vector of distorting "commodity" taxes. Their theorem implies, for example, that if there are $(N - 1)$ CRS industries, each using one input, then the shadow prices are the producer prices (the social rate of discount is the MRT in an intertemporal context). See P. A. Diamond and J. Mirrlees, "Private Constant Returns and Public Shadow Prices," *Review of Economic Studies*, February 1976.

if all cross-price derivatives over time are zero, then the rate of discount in any given period (with respect to period N) is a straight weighted average of the MRS and MRT specific to that period. Reinterpret Eq. (22.60) as:

$$r^j_{pub} = \left(\frac{-\alpha}{1-\alpha}\right)MRT_j + \left(\frac{1}{1-\alpha}\right)MRS_j \qquad (24.4)$$

where:

$$\alpha = \frac{\dfrac{\partial Y_j}{\partial p_j}}{\dfrac{\partial X_j}{\partial q_j}}$$

Y_j = private sector production (use) of the good (factor) in period j.
P_j = the producer price in period j $\equiv MRT_j \equiv f_j/f_N$.
X_j = consumption (supply) of the good (factor) in period j.
q_j = the consumer price in period j $\equiv MRS_j \equiv U_j/U_N$.

Hence, if $\partial X_j/\partial q_j = 0$, or the government's investment comes entirely at the expense of private production (investment), $r_{pub} = MRT$, as expected, and vice versa if $\partial Y_j/\partial p_j = 0$.

Equation (24.4) is the formula recommended by Harberger. It obviously corresponds to the notion that r_{pub} should reflect the opportunity cost of extracting scarce resources from the private sector.[14]

THE BRADFORD MODEL OF THE PUBLIC SECTOR RATE OF DISCOUNT

The simplest cases from our second-best models appear to imply that the appropriate public rate of discount is biased toward the private MRT, but that would be a hasty conclusion. David Bradford developed a second-best model that highlights the relationship between the public rate of discount and the three factors discussed above: the opportunity cost of public funds, the reinvestment of project benefits, and the social rate of time preference. His model led him to conclude that the consumers' MRS_{priv} is probably closer to the true public rate.[15]

[14] A. Harberger, "The Opportunity Costs of Public Investment Financed by Borrowing," in R. Layard, Ed., *Cost–Benefit Analysis*, Penguin Education, Penguin Books, Ltd., Middlesex, England, 1972. He also presents an alternative formula which aggregates across consumers and firms who face different MRS's and MRT's, respectively. Finally, it should be noted that Harberger equates MRS_{soc} with MRS_{priv}. He does not believe there is a significant divergence between the two.

[15] D. Bradford, "Constraints on Government Investment Opportunities and the Choice of the Discount Rate," *American Economic Review*, December 1975. Bradford's principal

Bradford's model is more general than the ones we have been using because it permits any underlying market structure. Furthermore, his model does not necessarily require the existence of distorting taxation, nor even that the government's budget constraint must balance, assumptions that we used repeatedly in the theoretical chapters on second-best expenditure theory. Rather, his analysis is second-best simply because the government has certain investment opportunities that are not open to the private sector. In terms of our previous models, if the government produces some output Z_i, there cannot be a corresponding private sector output Y_i. Of course, our previous models were general enough to consider this possibility, but they placed a considerable number of restrictions on the underlying policy environment. Bradford avoids any specific restrictions by defining the relationship between private investment and the future stream of consumption broadly enough to encompass any specific set of market or policy assumptions one might choose to make.

Following Bradford, let V_t = the present value of the stream of consumption, discounted at the social MRS, that is generated by $1 of private investment at time t. The stream of consumption benefits begins in time $t + 1$. Presumably, V_t could be calculated for any specific model, such as those in Parts II and III of this text. The calculations may be extremely complex, but V_t would nonetheless be well defined for any given intertemporal general equilibrium model.

Bradford completes his model by assuming that:

1. The one-period rate of return on private investment, the MRT, is constant over time at rate r. $1 of private investment at time t yields $(1 + r)$ of income in time $t + 1$.

2. The government's objective function is the discounted stream of aggregate consumption over time, where the discount rate is the social MRS, equal to i. Assume that the government's MRS_{soc} equals the consumer's private MRS_{priv}. Specifically, Bradford assumes that the objective function is additively separable over time with constant undiscounted marginal utilities. That is,

$$U(C_1, \ldots, C_N) = \sum_{j=1}^{N}(1+i)^{-j}\phi^j(C_j) \qquad (24.5)$$

with

$$\frac{\partial \phi^j}{\partial C_j} = k \qquad j = 1, \ldots, N$$

---

contribution is that his model includes the reinvestment of project benefits. In other respects, his approach was already well represented in the literature (e.g., S. Marglin, "The Opportunity Costs of Public Investment"; M. Feldstein, "The Inadequacy of Weighted Discount Rates").

Maximizing Eq. (24.5) is equivalent to maximizing the stream of consumption discounted at i. These assumptions may seem particularly severe, but they are commonly employed in intertemporal economic analysis. They are, however, more restrictive than what we were implicitly assuming above when we considered the intertemporal specification of the one-consumer equivalent models in Chapter 22.

One-Period Government Investments

Given the concept V_t and Bradford's assumptions with respect to private investment, the government's objective function, and the government's investment opportunities, Bradford is able to derive specific expressions for the public rate of discount. To capture the flavor of his analysis, consider first the simple example of a government project which costs $1 in period t, yields $(1 + \rho)$ of income in period $(t + 1)$, and nothing thereafter. Think of ρ as a variable equal to the internal yield on the government investment, and ask: How large must ρ be to justify the project? The answer, ρ^*, defines the appropriate rate of discount for the project.

From our earlier discussion of the opportunity cost of public funds, we know that i (the MRS), r (the MRT), and the percentage decreases in C_t and I_t resulting from the financing of each dollar of government investment are all relevant to the calculation of ρ^*. Given Bradford's framework, we can also easily incorporate the future repercussions on both consumption and private investment, $(C_{t+1}, \ldots, C_{t+N})$ and $(I_{t+1}, \ldots, I_{t+N})$, resulting from the $(1 + \rho)$ of benefits generated by the government project in period $(t + 1)$. This is the reinvestment factor.

Let a_t = the fraction of each dollar of government investment that comes at the expense of private investment in time t. Hence, $(1 - a_t)$ represents the decrease in C_t. Similarly, let α_{t+1} be the fraction of each dollar of the net benefits from the government project that is saved (invested) in time $(t + 1)$. Hence, $(1 - \alpha_{t+1})$ is the increase in C_{t+1} per dollar of net benefits. This specification assumes either that the government investment generates returns in the form of income rather than as in-kind benefits or that consumers base their saving decision on the sum of their private incomes plus the dollar value of the in-kind benefits from government projects.

Since the government's objective function is just the stream of discounted consumption over time, its investment decision rule is straightforward. ρ must be such that the increase in the discounted stream of consumption arising from the net benefits of the government project is at least as large as the discounted stream of consumption sacrificed by having to finance the project. The point of equality, or indifference, defines ρ^*, the public rate of discount.

Using the concept V_t, the loss in discounted consumption per dollar of government investment can be represented as:

$$L_C = (1 - a_t) + a_t V_t \tag{24.6}$$

The first term equals the direct loss in C_t. The second term represents the indirect consumption loss caused by the decrease in I_t. a_t dollars of I_t translate, through V_t, into a loss of discounted consumption equal to $a_t V_t$.

Similarly, the gain in discounted consumption per dollar of government investment is

$$G_C = \frac{1}{(1 + i)} \left[(1 - \alpha_{t+1})(1 + \rho) + (1 + \rho)(\alpha_{t+1} V_{t+1}) \right] \tag{24.7}$$

The first term in brackets is the direct gain in $C_t + 1$ arising from $\$(1 + \rho)$ of benefits. The second term is the indirect gain in discounted consumption arising from an increase of $\alpha_{t+1}(1 + \rho)$ dollars of I_{t+1}. Because these benefits accrue in $(t + 1)$, they must be discounted by $(1 + i)$ to make them commensurate with L_C.

The investment criterion is simply $G_C \geq L_C$, or:

$$\frac{(1 + \rho)}{(1 + i)} \left[(1 - \alpha_{t+1}) + \alpha_{t+1} V_{t+1} \right] \geq \left[(1 - a_t) + a_t V_t \right] \tag{24.8}$$

Rearranging terms:

$$\frac{(1 + \rho)}{(1 + i)} \geq \frac{(1 - a_t) + a_t V_t}{(1 - \alpha_{t+1}) + \alpha_{t+1} V_{t+1}} \tag{24.9}$$

n-Period Government Investments

The generalization of Eq. (24.9) to government projects whose costs and benefits occur over all n periods is straightforward.

Let:

$e_t = (1 - a_t) + a_t V_t$ be the present value, *at time t*, of the decrease in consumption occasioned by \$1 of costs incurred by a government project at time t.

$\beta_t = (1 - \alpha_t) + \alpha_t V_t$ is the present value, *at time t*, of the increase in consumption arising from \$1 of benefits associated with a government project at time t.

$\delta_t = \dfrac{1}{(1 + i)^t}$, the discount factor for time t.

$b_t =$ the total dollar value of the project's benefits at time t.

E_t is the total dollar value of the project's costs at time t.

Given these definitions, the present value rule for government investments is

$$PV = \sum_{t=0}^{N} \delta_t (b_t \beta_t - E_t e_t) > 0 \tag{24.10}$$

Suppose $\beta_t = \beta$, all t and $e_t = e$ (for very long-lived projects). Then,[16]

$$PV = \sum_{t=0}^{N} \delta_t \left(b_t - E_t \frac{e}{\beta} \right) > 0 \tag{24.11}$$

Equation (24.11) implies that the government should discount all projects by the MRS, but scale the costs by the factor:

$$\frac{e}{\beta} = \frac{1 - a + aV}{1 - \alpha + \alpha V} \tag{24.12}$$

The evaluation of V is the key to understanding why Bradford favors discounting at δ. Suppose there is a constant savings rate, s, and that $1 of I_t yields $(1 + r)$ of income in time $(t + 1)$. Of this, $(1 - s)$ is consumed in $(t + 1)$ and s is saved and invested. The amount saved and invested yields $(1 + r)$ dollars of additional income in time $(t + 2)$, of which $(1 - s)$ is consumed and s is saved and invested, and so on. Hence,

$$V_t = \frac{(1 + r)(1 - s)}{(1 + i)} + \frac{s(1 + r)^2(1 - s)}{(1 + i)^2} + \frac{s^2(1 + r)^3(1 - s)}{(1 + i)^3} + \cdots \tag{24.13}$$

Factoring out $[(1 + r)/(1 + i)] \cdot (1 - s)$ yields:

$$V_t = \frac{(1 + r)}{(1 + i)} (1 - s) \left[1 + \frac{s(1 + r)}{(1 + i)} + \frac{s^2(1 + r)^2}{(1 + i)^2} + \cdots + \frac{S^N(1 + r)^N}{(1 + i)^N} \right] \tag{24.14}$$

Letting $\gamma = [(1 + r)/(1 + i)] > 1$, and taking the limit as $N \to \infty$:

$$V_t = \gamma(1 - s) \left[\frac{1}{1 - s\gamma} \right] > \gamma \tag{24.15}$$

Equation (24.15) permits a simple calculation of V_t. For example, setting $i = 0.05, r = 0.15$, and $s = 0.10$ as reasonable values for the MRS, MRT, and the rate of savings, respectively, in United States, $V_t = 1.11$. Bradford, in fact, believes $V_t = 1.05$ is even more plausible for the United States. Given that V is close to unity, Bradford reasonably concludes that discounting by the MRS is a safe rule of thumb on the grounds that the "*extreme* range for [the scale] factor $[e/\beta]$ is $1/V \geq e/\beta \geq V$, with $e/\beta = 1/V$ for $a_t = 0, \alpha_t = 1$, and $e/\beta = V$ for $a_t = 1, \alpha_t = 0$."[17] With $V = 1.11$ (Bradford: 1.05), the errors

---

[16] In the two-period government project analyzed in the preceding section, $E_t = \$1, E_{t+1} = 0, b_t = 0, b_{t+1} = (1 + \rho)$, so that

$$PV = -[(1 - a_t) + a_t V_t] + \frac{1 + \rho}{1 + i}(1 - \alpha_{t+1} + \alpha_{t+1} V_{t+1}) > 0 \tag{24.11N}$$

which is equivalent to Eq. (24.9).

[17] Bradford, "Constraints on Government Investment Opportunities and the Choice of the Discount Rate," *American Economic Review*, December 1975. p. 897.

from assuming $e/\beta = 1$ are within a range of $\pm 11\%$ (Bradford: 5%). Errors of this magnitude are probably within the range of cost estimation errors, as Bradford contends.

OTHER VIEWS ON THE APPROPRIATE RATE OF DISCOUNT

Bradford's conclusion is hardly the last word on the appropriate rate of discount. Indeed, we have already presented a number of theoretical cases in which the appropriate discount factor is either the MRT or a weighted average of the MRS and MRT. Furthermore, Bradford's V_t calculation assumes a simple model in which there is essentially only one good and a constant savings rate out of private sector income. Preferences are also severely restricted in other ways. More importantly, he assumes in calculating V that private investment yields returns r for one period only, and nothing thereafter. Hence, the maximum value of V, which occurs if all returns are consumed $(s = 0)$, is $(1 + r)/(1 + i)$, a number still reasonably close to one. Many economists' using his basic framework (e.g., Marglin, Feldstein, Sjaastad, and Wisecarver[18]) assume private investment is a perpetuity yielding r forever, which implies a $V = r/i$ with zero savings. This V is almost certainly much greater than 1, perhaps in the 2.5–4.0 range. Hence, under the perpetuity assumption, one would certainly not be willing to ignore the scaling factor e/β. The "best" assumption for private investment undoubtedly lies somewhere between the extremes of one-period and perpetual yields. In any event, results such as the Diamond–Mirrlees theorem suggest that the limits implied for the scaling factor in Bradford's model may be wide of the mark for many second-best environments, especially those with variable savings rates. This merely reemphasizes the general proposition demonstrated throughout the text that second-best results can be extremely sensitive to underlying assumptions.

Despite these reservations, Bradford's model is comprehensive enough to serve as a convenient vehicle for presenting some of the conflicting views in the literature.

Marglin–Feldstein: The Social Rate of Time Preference

The Marglin–Feldstein view that the appropriate present value calculation consists of discounting project benefits at the social rate of time preference and adjusting project costs by a shadow price reflecting second-best distor-

---

[18] S. Marglin, "The Opportunity Costs of Public Investment," *Quarterly Journal of Economics*, May 1963; M. Feldstein, "The Inadequacy of Weighted Discount Rates," in R. Layard, Ed., *Cost–Benefit Analysis*, Penguin Education, Penguin Books, Ltd., Middlesex, England, 1972; L. Sjaastad and D. Wisecarver, "The Social Cost of Public Finance," *Journal of Political Economy*, June 1977.

tions follows directly from Eq. (24.11). To see this, suppose all investment costs occur immediately and yield a stream of benefits forever. Under these assumptions, $e_t = 0$, $t \geq 1$, and Eq. (24.11) becomes;

$$PV = \sum_{t=1}^{N} \delta^t b_t - \frac{e}{\beta} E_0 > 0 \qquad (24.16)$$

This is essentially the original Marglin result,[19] with the shadow price of project costs equal to Bradford's scale factor, e/β. The only difference is that Marglin is not so willing to ignore the shadow price, given his assumption that private investment is a perpetuity. For instance, ignoring reinvestment ($\alpha = 0$), and assuming all private benefits are consumed,

$$\frac{e}{\beta} = e = (1 - a) + aV = (1 - a) + a\frac{r}{i} \qquad (24.17)$$

which may differ substantially from 1.

Feldstein extended Marglin's analysis to include cash deficits whenever they occur.[20] His recommended procedure also follows immediately from Eq. (24.11), although care must be taken to distinguish between true project costs and out-of-pocket costs. Suppose that some project benefits are sold and some costs are paid for by the government each period.

Let:

b_t = true project benefits in time t.
E_t = true project costs in time t.
R_t = project revenues in time t.
C_t = project cash payments in time t.

Net consumption benefits are $(b_t - R_t)$, and net transfers to consumers are $(C_t - E_t)$. The cash deficit is $(C_t - R_t)$, to which the shadow price of funds must be applied. Assuming no reinvestment of net project benefits ($\alpha = 0$), Feldstein's version of Bradford's formula is

$$PV = \sum_{t=0}^{\infty} \delta^t \Big[(b_t - R_t) + (C_t - E_t)$$
$$- ((1 - a) + aV_t)(C_t - R_t) \Big] > 0 \qquad (24.18)$$

Rearranging terms:

$$PV = \sum_{t=0}^{\infty} \delta^t \Big[(b_t - E_t) - (V - 1)a(C_t - R_t) \Big] > 0 \qquad (24.19)$$

[19] S. Marglin, "The Opportunity Costs of Public Investment," *Quarterly Journal of Economics*, May 1963; Marglin uses a continuous time model.

[20] M. Feldstein, "The Inadequacy of Weighted Discount Rates," in R. Layard, Ed., *Cost–Benefit Analysis*, Penguin Education, Penguin Books, Ltd., Middlesex, England, 1972.

One immediate implication of Eq. (24.19) is that the benefits of self-financing projects should be discounted at the social rate of time preference, with no further corrections applied.[21]

Harberger and Sjaastad–Wisecarver: The Opportunity Cost of Funds

Harberger's opportunity cost point of view, that the rate of discount should be a weighted average of r and i, with weights equal to a and $(1 - a)$, respectively, can also be derived from Eq. (24.11) under special assumptions. For instance, it has long been known that the two-period model generates this result.[22] The two-period version of Eq. (24.11) can be represented by Eq. (24.9) under the assumption that all project costs are incurred immediately, and all project benefits occur in period 1, equal to $1 + \rho$. Since life ends in period 1, all benefits from public *and* private investments are entirely consumed in period 1. Hence, $\alpha = 0$, $V_0 = (1 + r)/(1 + i)$, with $s = 0$. Therefore, Eq. (24.9) becomes:

$$\frac{1+\rho}{1+i} \geq (1 - a) + a\frac{(1+r)}{(1+i)} \tag{24.20}$$

Rearranging terms:

$$(1 + \rho) \geq (1 - a)(1 + i) + a(1 + r) \tag{24.21}$$

or

$$\rho \geq (1 - a)i + ar \tag{24.22}$$

which is the Harberger formula.

Larry Sjaastad and Daniel Wisecarver believe that using Eq. (24.22) is always appropriate no matter how long the investment horizon.[23] Consider, first, the extreme case in which both public and private investments are perpetuities, yielding ρ and r, respectively. Under this assumption, it is reasonable to assume that all benefits are consumed as they arise, since capital never depreciates. Thus, $1 of public investment at time 0 causes a loss in consumption equal to:

$$L_C = (1 - a) + a\frac{r}{i} \tag{24.23}$$

and a gain equal to:

$$G_C = \frac{\rho}{i} \tag{24.24}$$

---

[21] Equation (24.19) is also obviously consistent with Eqs. (24.16) and (24.11), assuming $\alpha = 0$, $R_t = 0$ and $C_t = E_t$.

[22] See, for example, P. Diamond, "The Opportunity Costs of Public Investment: Comment," *Quarterly Journal of Economics*, November 1968.

[23] L. Sjaastad and D. Wisecarver, "The Social Cost of Public Finance," *Journal of Political Economy*, June 1977.

in present value terms. $G_C \geq L_C$ implies:

$$\frac{\rho}{i} \geq (1 - a) + a\frac{r}{i} \tag{24.25}$$

or

$$\rho \geq (1 - a) i + ar \tag{24.26}$$

Notice that Eq. (24.26) is the Marglin–Feldstein rule, so that the two rules are equivalent for perpetuities.

In a world of finite investments, the Harberger opportunity cost and Marglin–Feldstein social rate of time preference with shadow price approaches differ. Yet Sjaastad and Wisecarver believe the former is still the appropriate technique. To compare the two, return to the special case of the Bradford model given by Eq. (24.9) in which all costs of public investment are incurred immediately and all the returns from the public project occur in period 1, but life continues beyond period 1 so reinvestment is possible. Under these assumptions, Eq. (24.9) does not necessarily imply Eq. (24.22), the Harberger opportunity cost rule, but Sjaastad and Wisecarver believe that appropriate assumptions on the functioning of capital markets and the treatment of public sector capital depreciation generate the opportunity cost rule. In effect, they argue that the reinvestment parameter, α, in Eq. (24.9) must be such as to generate Eq. (24.22); α is not free to assume an arbitrary value.

Their argument is as follows. $(1 + \rho)$ measures the gross returns to public investment, of which \$1 is depreciation. The key question is whether or not society will choose to consume the depreciation or save it in an attempt to maintain the stock of public capital. They believe it is natural to assume that society will try to save the \$1 and view the true benefits of the project as ρ, the net benefits. But the attempt to inject an additional dollar of savings into the capital market lowers interest rates and discourages some saving such that only \$a of saving and reinvestment actually result. \$(1 − a) are consumed. Notice that the \$a of saving is precisely the amount required to restore the total capital stock. Private investment declined by \$a in the initial period, and the \$1 of public investment fully depreciated by \$1. Furthermore, with the private capital stock remaining constant, the future investment effects on consumption beyond period 1 cancel, so all one need do is compare the direct consumption effects over the two periods. The immediate loss is

$$L_C = (1 - a) \tag{24.27}$$

The consumption gain in the first period is[24]

---

[24] The displacement of \$a of private investment at time 0 causes a loss of consumption equal to \$ar in period 1. This loss does not recur in subsequent periods once the capital stock is restored to its original level in period 1.

$$G_C = \frac{\rho - ar + (1 - a)}{1 + i} \tag{24.28}$$

$G_C = L_C$ implies:

$$\frac{\rho - ar + (1 - a)}{1 + i} \geq (1 - a) \tag{24.29}$$

$$\rho \geq (1 - a)i + ar \tag{24.30}$$

which is the Harberger formula once again.

Sjaastad and Wisecarver are able to show that this example is not a special case. As long as interest rate effects change \$1 of intended saving into \$a of actual saving, and society saves the depreciation on public capital, the weighted-average formula applies to all public projects yielding returns over any finite number of periods (with one insignificant adjustment).[25] Of course, it is problematic whether capital markets function as the authors posit or whether society adjusts its saving for public capital depreciation, assumptions crucial to their result. At the same time, ignoring saving for public depreciation and the interest rate effects on intended saving, a common feature of other models, is equally suspect.[26]

Conclusion

It is difficult to know what to make of the debate over the appropriate rate of discount for public projects. More than anything else, the debate reemphasizes the frustrating point that no single "rule of thumb" derived from a particular second-best model is likely to be very robust to changes in the underlying policy and market environment. We have presented many different rules in just these few pages that recommend a wide range of public discount rates.[27] Even so, the entire discussion ignored one final caveat, the *intragenerational* distribution of income.[28] It may seem natural to ignore distributional considerations when modeling the rate of discount. If the underlying distribution is nonoptimal, however, an equation such as

[25] See L. Sjaastad and D. Wisecarver, "The Social Cost of Public Finance," *Journal of Political Economy*, June 1977, pp. 524–528, for the development of their adjusted formula.

[26] Diamond has shown that models such as Marglin's that posit a constant marginal propensity to save, a constant stream of returns from private investment, and utility of consumption diminishing at a constant geometric rate over time generate the MRS_{soc} discounting rule. See P. Diamond, "The Opportunity Costs of Public Investment: Comment," *Quarterly Journal of Economics*, November 1968.

[27] The situation is actually worse than represented. Bradford demonstrates special cases for which the discount rate lies outside the range of rates bounded by the MRS_{soc} and the MRT. See D. Bradford, "Constraints on Government Investment Opportunities and the Choice of the Discount Rate," *American Economic Review*, December 1975, pp. 891–892.

[28] The *intergenerational* distribution is embodied in the social rate of time preference, however.

Eq. (22.88) applies to the rate of discount, as it does to all government shadow prices. Hence, intratemporal social welfare rankings may possibly overwhelm the pure efficiency aspects of the public discount rate, which are all these models consider.

EMPIRICAL EVIDENCE ON THE PUBLIC RATE OF DISCOUNT

What Do the Experts Say?

Martin Weitzman conducted a survey of economists in which he asked them what single real interest rate they would recommend for discounting the benefits and costs of environmental projects that are designed to reduce the harmful effects of changes in global climate. He received 2160 replies from economists in 48 different countries. The replies demonstrated a large difference of opinion among economists about the appropriate rate of discount. The vast majority of replies were from 1 to 6%, but the overall range was -3 to 27%. The mode was 2%, the mean just under 4%, and the standard deviation just under 3%.[29]

Weitzman observed that the distribution of responses was reasonably well approximated by the gamma distribution truncated at zero (only three responses were negative). This led him to propose a declining discount rate over time by the following argument.

Let:

$Z(t)$ = net project benefits at time t
$A(t)$ = the discount factor at time t.

Assuming a continuous time framework (to conform with the continuous gamma distribution), the present value of the investment is

$$PV = \int_0^\infty A(t)Z(t)dt \qquad (24.31)$$

With a single constant discount rate x, which all respondents were asked to assume, the discount factor would be

$$A(t) = e^{-xt} \qquad (24.32)$$

But given uncertainty over the appropriate discount rate from the economists' replies, Weitzman argues that it makes sense to think of each

---

[29] M. Weitzman, "Gamma Discounting," *American Economic Review*, March 2001. The sample statistics are reported on p. 268, with the complete distribution of responses listed in Table 1, p. 268. Weitzman notes that many economists were reluctant to name a single rate, probably because they understand that the appropriate rate is model dependent. Weitzman persisted in asking them to select a single rate, which most of the economists were willing to do.

economist's answer as a single draw, x_j, from the probability density function of rates $f(x)$. According to this view, the appropriate discount factor is

$$A(t) = \int_0^\infty e^{-xt} f(x) dx \tag{24.33}$$

The discount factor is a weighted-average function of the various rates proposed by the economists. The weights are the probabilities that each rate is the correct rate, with the probabilities given by the density function of the proposed rates, in this case the gamma distribution. The gamma distribution has the form:

$$f(x) = \frac{\beta^\alpha}{\Gamma(\alpha)} x^{\alpha-1} e^{-\beta x} \tag{24.34}$$

Thus,

$$A(t) = \frac{\beta^\alpha}{\Gamma(\alpha)} \int_0^\infty x^{\alpha-1} e^{-(\beta+t)x} dx \tag{24.35}$$

The value of the integral is such that $A(t)$ has the simple form:

$$A(t) = \left(\frac{\beta}{\beta+t}\right)^\alpha \tag{24.36}$$

For the gamma distribution,

$$\mu = \frac{\alpha}{\beta} \tag{24.37}$$

$$\sigma^2 = \frac{\alpha}{\beta^2} \tag{24.38}$$

Therefore,

$$\alpha = \frac{\mu^2}{\sigma^2} \tag{24.39}$$

$$\beta = \frac{\mu}{\sigma^2} \tag{24.40}$$

and

$$A(t) = \frac{1}{\left(1 + t\sigma^2/\mu\right)^{\frac{\mu^2}{\sigma^2}}} \tag{24.41}$$

The instantaneous flow rate of discount $R(t)$ is

$$R(t) = \frac{-\dot{A}(t)}{A(t)} \tag{24.42}$$

which from Eq. (24.41) is

$$R(t) = \frac{\mu}{1 + t\sigma^2 / \mu} \tag{24.43}$$

Equation (24.43) implies that the appropriate instantaneous rate of discount should decline over time if there is any uncertainty surrounding the appropriate rate. This is true even if all economists believe the rate should be constant over time, as they were asked to assume.[30] In particular, the instantaneous rate begins at rate μ at time zero and then declines toward zero as $t \to \infty$. For the sample of responses in Weitzman's survey, the (approximate) discount rates for future time periods turn out to be[31]

1–5 years	4%
6–25 years	3%
26–75 years	2%
76–300 years	1%
> 300 years	0%

The intuition behind the declining rates can be seen from Eq. (24.33). As time increases, the present value of the weighted higher rates necessarily decreases in importance relative to the weighted lower rates.

Discounting Within the Federal Government

The "experts'" uncertainty about the appropriate public rate of discount is apparently shared by federal policymakers. Bazelon and Smetters recently published an overview of discounting practices within the federal government. They characterized the range of discount rates in use as "striking."[32] One would hope that a common discount rate (or set of declining rates *a la* Weitzman), would be used to evaluate all government investment projects, but this turns out to be not even approximately true.

The Office of Management and Budget (OMB) appears to inject some uniformity in the area of cost–benefit analysis. Its regulation OMB-94 instructs all federal agencies to undertake a cost–benefit analysis using a 7% real discount rate for its investments and regulations. The 7% rate was chosen

---

[30] Notice that $R(t) = \mu$ for all time periods if $\sigma^2 = 0$, that is, if all economists were to pick the same rate μ.

[31] M. Weitzman, "Gamma Discounting," *American Economic Review*, March 2001, Table 2, p. 270.

[32] C. Bazelon and K. Smetters, "Discounting Inside the Washington, D.C. Beltway," *Journal of Economic Perspectives*, Fall 1999. The characterization is on p. 219.

as OMB's estimate of the pretax rate of return in the private sector in recent years preceding 1994.[33]

The OMB's directive probably does not have much force, however. One reason why not is that it can be overridden by Congressional legislation. A prominent example, noted in Chapter 8, is the enabling legislation for water and air antipollution regulations, which specifically forbid an analysis of abatement costs in applying command-and-control strategies. In addition, the federal agencies receive conflicting instructions from other overview bodies. For example, General Accounting Office (GAO) guidelines recommend the use of very low discount rates when projects have effects on human life in distant generations. The Congressional Budget Office generally uses a social rate of time preference in its social welfare analysis. Bazelon and Smetters point out still other instances when different discount rates are used, such as in the sale of government assets. They also note that budgetary planning is cash-flow based with a 5- to 10-year window. The spending and revenue implications of government policies that occur beyond 10 years into the future are essentially discounted at an infinite rate. In conclusion, discounting practices within the federal government really are quite varied and somewhat haphazard in application.

Concluding Observations

In our view, one would be hard-pressed to mount a decisive case for or against any public rate of discount over a range of 3 to 20 or even 25%. Nor is the argument Weitzman makes for declining discount rates over time entirely compelling. Why should the distribution of economists' opinions necessarily reflect the probabilities of correctness? A better approach might be to try to achieve a consensus about the appropriate underlying economic and policy environment and then select a single rate of discount based on the consensus. Perhaps Weitzman's approach is a good proxy of the alternative approach; perhaps not. All one can say for certain is that whatever rate the government selects, it should be applied equally to all potential investment projects (standardizing for risk; see Chapter 25). We have seen, however, that consistent project evaluation does not occur at the federal level, and one can guess that it does not occur at the state or local level, either.

REFERENCES

Bazelon, C., and Smetters, K., "Discounting Inside the Washington, D.C. Beltway," *Journal of Economic Perspectives*, Fall 1999.

[33] C. Bazelon and K. Smetters, "Discounting Inside the Washington, D.C. Beltway," *Journal of Economic Perspectives*, Fall 1999, p. 221. The discussion of federal discounting practices on which the remainder of this paragraph is based appears on pp. 219–226.

Bradford, D., "Constraints on Government Investment Opportunities and the Choice of the Discount Rate," *American Economic Review*, December 1975.

Diamond, P., "The Opportunity Costs of Public Investment: Comment," *Quarterly Journal of Economics*, November 1968.

Diamond, P., and Mirrlees, J., "Private Constant Returns and Public Shadow Prices," *Review of Economic Studies*, February 1976.

Feldstein, M., "The Inadequacy of Weighted Discount Rates," in R. Layard, Ed., *Cost–Benefit Analysis*, Penguin Education, Penguin Books, Ltd., Harmondsworth, Middlesex, England, 1972.

Feldstein, M., "Does the United States Save Too Little?," *American Economic Association Papers and Proceedings*, February 1977.

Harberger, A., "The Opportunity Costs of Public Investment Financed by Borrowing," in R. Layard, Ed., *Cost–Benefit Analysis*, Penguin Education, Penguin Books, Ltd., Harmondsworth, Middlesex, England, 1972.

Harberger, A., *Project Evaluation: Collected Papers*, Markham Publishing, Chicago, 1974.

Haveman, R., "Policy Analysis and the Congress: An Economist's View," in R. Haveman and J. Margolis, Eds., *Public Expenditure and Policy Analysis*, second ed., Rand-McNally College Publishing, Chicago, 1977.

Layard, R., Ed., *Cost–Benefit Analysis*, Penguin Education, Penguin Books, Ltd., Harmondsworth, Middlesex, England, 1972.

Marglin, S., "The Social Rate of Discount and the Optimal Rate of Investment," *Quarterly Journal of Economics*, February 1963.

Marglin, S., "The Opportunity Costs of Public Investment," *Quarterly Journal of Economics*, May 1963.

McKean, R., "Tax Wedges and Cost–Benefit Analysis," *Journal of Public Economics*, February 1974.

Sen, A., "Isolation, Assurance, and the Social Rate of Discount," *Quarterly Journal of Economics*, February 1967.

Sen, A., "The Social Time Preference Rate in Relation to the Market Rate of Interest," in R. Layard, Ed., *Cost–Benefit Analysis*, Penguin Education, Penguin Books, Ltd., Harmondsworth, Middlesex, England, 1972.

Sjaastad, L., and Wisecarver, D., "The Social Cost of Public Finance," *Journal of Political Economy*, June 1977.

Weitzman, M., "Gamma Discounting," *American Economic Review*, March 2001.

25

UNCERTAINTY AND THE ARROW– LIND THEOREM

When speaking of the rate of return or internal yield on an investment in the preceding chapter we were obviously referring only to a project's expected return. Given uncertainty about the future, the actual returns have an entire probability distribution associated with them defined over the possible states of nature that can occur.

Uncertainty presents a problem for investment analysis, public or private, because people are generally risk averse, not risk neutral. They would be willing to pay a premium to change an asset's uncertain stream of returns into a certain return. The difference between the expected or mean value of the asset and the risk premium is the certainty equivalent value of the asset. If society consists mainly of risk-averse consumers, and the government acts on the basis of individuals' preferences, then cost–benefit analysis of government projects would be expected to incorporate society's risk aversion. The expected net benefits should be reduced by an appropriate risk premium so that all projects are compared on the basis of their certainty equivalent values. The typical suggestion in the literature is to account for the risk premium through the public rate of discount: Calculate the expected benefits and costs over time, and then adjust the discount rate for the appropriate degree of risk.

The goal of this chapter is not to offer a comprehensive discussion of investment analysis under uncertainty. Instead, the chapter is centered around a remarkable theorem by Arrow and Lind.[1] They proved that the government can *ignore* risk under certain fairly broad conditions. That is, the aggregate risk premium under these conditions is zero. Since the conditions are not likely to apply to private investment projects, this is perhaps the one instance in which cost–benefit analysis may be conceptually easier than private investment analysis.

THE ARROW-LIND THEOREM

Kenneth Arrow and Robert Lind proved that government policy analysts can ignore risk under two conditions that may well be approximated by many public projects:

1. The net benefits of a government project are distributed independently of national income.
2. The net benefits of the project are each spread over a sufficiently large population.

Under these two conditions, the risk premium that society *in the aggregate* would be willing to pay to convert a stream of uncertain returns into a certain return goes to zero in the limit.

The Arrow–Lind theorem is especially powerful because it makes no assumptions about the underlying market environment. For instance, it need not be perfectly competitive. Also, there are no restrictions imposed on the government other than the two conditions assumed about the net benefits of the government's projects. Hence, their result is applicable to a wide range of second-best policy environments (as well as the first-best environment).

The only potentially unrealistic feature of their model concerns the distribution of project costs and benefits. Arrow and Lind guarantee that the first independence condition holds by assuming that the government pays all the costs of the investment, receives all the benefits, and then distributes the net benefits lump sum to each individual. They assume further that the project's net benefits are free of tax. Thus, there can be no further fiscal repercussions of the project that could lead indirectly to a correlation between its net benefits and each consumer's disposable income. These assumptions are clearly not meant to be realistic. Arrow and Lind use them merely as an analytically convenient way of satisfying the independence condition. They turn out not to be innocuous, however. L. Foldes and R. Rees contend

[1] K. Arrow and R. Lind, "Uncertainty and the Evaluation of Public Investment Decisions," *American Economic Review*, June 1970.

that it may not be possible to satisfy the independence condition for very many projects in the context of an actual fiscal system.[2] The Foldes–Rees objection follows the Arrown–Lind theorem.

Proof of the Arrow–Lind Theorem

The proof of the Arrow–Lind theorem requires nothing more sophisticated than the definition of a derivative and some properties of the expected value operator. Begin by assuming that society consists of N identical consumers, each of whom has initial income equal to A, where A is a random variable. In line with accepted practice in uncertainty analysis, assume further that each consumer maximizes expected utility. (The assumption that the consumers are identical is not necessary to the proof but greatly simplifies the derivation.) Let B = the total net returns from some government project. Assume B is also a random variable, equal to its expected value, $\overline{B}$, and a random component X with zero mean:

$$B = \overline{B} + X \tag{25.1}$$

with:

$$E[X] = 0$$

Finally, assume that B and A are independently distributed (the first condition) and that each of the N identical individuals receives an equal share of the returns B. Thus, each person's share is s = 1/N.

Under these assumptions, an individual's income without the project is A. With the project, the individual receives $A + sB = A + s\overline{B} + sX$. The corresponding expected utilities with and without the project are $E[U(A + s\overline{B} + sX)]$ and $E[U(A)]$

Define each person's expected utility with the project as a function of s, or

$$W(s) = E\left[U\left(A + s\overline{B} + sX\right)\right] \tag{25.2}$$

Differentiate W(s) with respect to s and evaluate the derivative at s = 0:

$$W'(s) = E\left[U'\left(A + s\overline{B} + sX\right)\left(\overline{B} + X\right)\right] \tag{25.3}$$

Hence:

$$W'(0) = E\left[U'(A)\left(\overline{B} + X\right)\right] = \overline{B}E[U'(A)] + E[U'(A) \cdot X] \tag{25.4}$$

But, if A and X are independently distributed,

$$E[U'(A) \cdot X] = E[U'(A)] \cdot E[X] = 0 \tag{25.5}$$

[2] L. Foldes and R. Rees, "A Note on the Arrow–Lind Theorem," *American Economic Review*, March 1977.

with:

$$E[X] = 0$$

Therefore:

$$W'(0) = \overline{B}E[U'(A)] \tag{25.6}$$

By the definition of a derivative, Eq. (25.6) implies that:

$$\lim_{s \to 0} \frac{E[U(A + s\overline{B} + sX) - U(A)]}{s} = \overline{B}E[U'(A)] \tag{25.7}$$

Substituting $s = 1/N$ into Eq. (25.7) yields:

$$\lim_{N \to \infty} N \cdot E\left[U\left(A + \frac{\overline{B}}{N} + \frac{X}{N}\right) - U(A)\right] = \overline{B}E[U'(A)] \tag{25.8}$$

Next, incorporate the idea of a risk premium leading to certainty equivalence. Assuming each individual is risk averse, there exists a number $k(N)$ such that the individual is indifferent between accepting the risky stream of returns $\overline{B}/N + X/N$ and paying $k(N)$ to receive $\overline{B}/N$ with certainty. Hence, define $k(N)$ such that:

$$E\left[U\left(A + \frac{\overline{B}}{N} + \frac{X}{N}\right)\right] = E\left[U\left(A + \frac{\overline{B}}{N} - k(N)\right)\right] \tag{25.9}$$

Substituting the certainty equivalent, Eq. (25.9), into Eq. (25.8) yields:

$$\lim_{N \to \infty} N \cdot E\left[U\left(A + \frac{\overline{B}}{N} - k(N)\right) - U(A)\right] = \overline{B}E[U'(A)] \tag{25.10}$$

But,

$$\lim_{N \to \infty} \frac{\overline{B}}{N} - k(N) = 0 \tag{25.11}$$

Clearly, as N becomes large without limit, each individual's share of the return and the risk approach zero. The fact that exposure to risk approaches zero in turn implies that the risk premium any individual would be willing to pay to convert the returns into a certain stream also approaches zero. But, if $\lim_{N \to \infty} \overline{B}/N - k(N) = 0$, then by the definition of a derivative,

$$\lim_{N \to \infty} \frac{E\left[U\left(A + \frac{\overline{B}}{N} - k(N)\right) - U(A)\right]}{\frac{\overline{B}}{N} - k(N)} = E[U'(A)] \tag{25.12}$$

Dividing Eq. (25.10) by (25.12) yields:

$$\lim_{N \to \infty} N \cdot \left[\frac{\overline{B}}{N} - k(N)\right] = \overline{B} \tag{25.13}$$

or

$$\lim_{N \to \infty} N \cdot k(N) = 0 \qquad (25.14)$$

Equation (25.14) says that the risk premium society in the aggregate would be willing to pay goes to zero, or that the value to society of the risky stream of returns B is simply its expected value, $\overline{B}$. A cost–benefit analysis can ignore the project's risk.

Implications of the Theorem

The Arrow–Lind theorem has two important policy implications. First, there is no need to adjust project benefits or costs, or the riskless rate of discount, because of uncertainty. Second, the government can simply compare alternative investments on the basis of their expected returns no matter how risky each of them may be. Furthermore, the risk-spreading phenomenon is likely to apply uniquely to public sector projects. Even if the returns on some private investment happen to be distributed independently of national income, they would generally not be spread over a sufficiently "large" population to render the theorem applicable. Thus, the response to uncertainty may be the only instance in which government investment analysis is conceptually easier than private investment analysis.

The Arrow–Lind theorem is surely one of the more uplifting results in all of public sector theory. The question remains how broadly applicable it may be, and this is somewhat of an open question. One can advance the following arguments in support of the theorem. First, projects at the national or (large) state level ought to satisfy the second condition, that the population be sufficiently large. The only obvious exceptions are investments for which the costs or benefits are narrowly targeted. Second, if the typical cost–benefit assumption of full employment is retained, it might be argued that the level of (real) national income is not a random variable but a given number determined independently of any one project. The full employment income is assured either by the corrective actions of monetary and fiscal policy or by the workings of a perfectly competitive market system. Hence, the first condition is also likely to hold. These arguments are not airtight, however. Public sector economists have advanced a number of caveats to accepting the theorem. We will briefly consider three of them.

Caveat: Single Versus Multiple Projects

Estelle James points out that the Arrow–Lind theorem may be limited because it applies to a single investment project.[3] Suppose it happened that each of M projects would be accepted if analyzed individually, in part

---

[3] E. James, "A Note on Uncertainty and the Evaluation of Public Investment Decisions," *American Economic Review*, March 1975.

because the Arrow–Lind risk-spreading effect removes the aggregate risk associated with each project. Nonetheless, society still could be in a position of wanting to reject the entire set of projects if they were analyzed collectively. In other words, the piecemeal or marginal decision process might not generate a global optimum.

To see how this anomaly can arise, assume that the returns and risks associated with each project are identical and that their returns are perfectly correlated. In this case, the returns accruing to any one consumer from the entire set of projects is $M \cdot \overline{B}/N$, and the consumer's exposure to risk is $M \cdot X/N$. For purposes of illustration, assume $M = N$ (the population is finite and the set of projects is extremely large). In this case, individual consumers receive returns $\overline{B}$, with risk X, exactly as if they received the entire returns and bore the entire risk associated with any one of the M projects. If the consumer's risk premium k exceeds $\overline{B}$ under these conditions, society should reject all M projects even though it would accept each of them if analyzed individually. In short, a sufficiently large number of projects with perfectly correlated returns can negate the Arrow–Lind risk-spreading effect.

The anomaly can be avoided if the returns on the M projects are independently distributed, in which case the aggregate risk premium is reduced by a second effect, the risk pooling or dispersion effect. This effect says that the risk premium associated with a portfolio of assets whose returns are independently distributed goes to zero as the number of assets becomes large without limit.

Even if society consisted of a single individual so that risk spreading is impossible, the individual might be willing to accept all M projects collectively if M were large enough and the returns on each project were independently distributed. Clearly, then, risk pooling supports risk spreading and reduces the chances of an anomaly with independent projects. In general, the likelihood of an anomaly occurring depends upon the values of M and N, and the extent to which the returns on individual projects are correlated. One suspects that the net benefits of projects coming from different government agencies may not be very highly correlated.

A final point is that private investors can benefit from risk pooling through portfolio diversification, even if they cannot take advantage of risk spreading. Private sector diversification is unlikely to reduce private sector risk premia to zero, however, especially in the absence of complete insurance markets for all risks. Consequently, public projects have one advantage over private projects if their net benefits are spread broadly throughout the population, in line with the Arrow–Lind conditions.

Caveat: Externalities

A second caveat concerns the population condition. The condition is not simply that the population be sufficiently large. Embedded in the proof of the theorem is the additional condition that the individuals' expected net benefits, $\overline{B}/N$, approach zero as $N \to \infty$. Arrow and Lind guarantee this result by assuming that the expected benefits are bounded, but this might not be true if externalities are present. For example, if the government is financing a Samuelsonian nonexclusive public good, each person consumes the entire "benefit" stream. If these benefits are positive for all individuals (as they would be for identical individuals, assuming the project is worthwhile), they are not bounded as $N \to \infty$. Hence, $\lim_{N \to \infty} \overline{B}/N - k(n) \neq 0$ and Eq. (25.11) does not hold. Given that externalities are a major justification for government intervention, this point is troublesome. The theorem may only be broadly applicable to investments in decreasing cost services.[4]

Caveat: Actual Fiscal Systems

A final caveat concerns the first condition, the assumed independence between project benefits and national income. It is natural to assume that national income is a random variable in an uncertain world even under the standard assumption of full employment as, indeed, Arrow and Lind assume. Corrective monetary and fiscal policy, or perfectly competitive markets, can only guarantee that the *expected value* of income is the full employment level. But, if national income is a random variable, one can easily identify many government projects for which the returns might well be correlated with national income in violation of the first condition, projects such as dams, recreational facilities, transportation infrastructures, education, research and development, and job training programs.

Even if the returns on some government projects have a particular form that turns out not to be correlated with national income (defense, possibly), the fiscal system itself can create a statistical dependence between income and the returns on *any* project. Arrow and Lind preclude this possibility by their assumption that the government pays all the costs and distributes the benefits lump sum, with no further taxation of the benefits. But, realistically, the net benefits of many projects are subject to income taxation, simply because they increase each person's income. Furthermore, if the government simultaneously adjusts the tax rate on other income to maintain budgetary balance given that net benefits are taxed, then the independence between individuals' disposable incomes without the project and the project's returns may be destroyed, even though gross incomes and project returns are independent. The relevant arguments of each individual's utility function are the share of the project's net benefits and each person's *disposable income* without the project.

---

[4] Anthony Fisher first made this point in A. Fisher, "A Paradox in the Theory of Public Investment," *Journal of Public Economics*, Vol. 2, 1973. See also the discussion in L. Foldes and R. Rees, "A Note on the Arrow–Lind Theorem," *American Economic Review*, March 1975.

Consider two distinct cases. First, with identical individuals, or a one-consumer-equivalent economy, changes in the income tax rate to offset the taxation of project net benefits cannot matter with a balanced government budget. If gross incomes and total project returns are independent, so too must be each person's disposable income and share of net benefits, because the income tax reductions just equal the revenues from taxing the benefits. This no longer holds with nonidentical individuals, however. An individual's disposable income and share of the benefits may be correlated if the government varies income taxes to meet an aggregate budget constraint. Thus, the "convenience" of lump-sum distributions of untaxed net benefits and identical individuals may disguise the relevant point that for most realistic fiscal structures the assumed independence between project benefits and disposable income is extremely unlikely.

The Foldes–Rees Analysis

To see this, consider the following fiscal system, a simplified version of a model suggested by Foldes and Rees.[5] Imagine an initial situation in which the government provides a nonexclusive public good G^0 each year which it finances with an income tax at rate t^0 on total income A. $A = \sum_{i=1}^{N} A_i$ where A_i is the gross income of person i before the project, assumed to be a random variable. The government's budget constraint without the project is

$$G^0 = t^0 A \qquad (25.15)$$

and each consumer's disposable income is initially:

$$D_i = (1 - t^0)A_i + G^0 \qquad (25.16)$$

Suppose the government then undertakes a project with net benefits B which are distributed independently of the A_i and subject to taxation at rate λ. If G^0 is unchanged, and the government's budget constraint continues to hold, the government has to adjust t^0 to offset the increased tax revenues on the project's benefits. The new government budget constraint is now:

$$G^0 = t^1 A + \lambda B \qquad (25.17)$$

Let person i's share of the net benefits be B_i, where $B = \sum_{i=1}^{N} B_i$. Each consumer's disposable income with the project is, therefore:

$$r_i + D_i = (1 - t^1)A_i + G^0 + (1 - \lambda)B_i \qquad i = 1, \ldots, N \qquad (25.18)$$

where r_i is the net benefit from the project. Combining Eqs. (25.15) and (25.16), and defining $a_i = A_i/A$, disposable income without the project can be expressed as:

[5] L. Foldes and R. Rees, "A Note on the Arrow–Lind Theorem," *American Economic Review*, March 1975.

$$D_i = a_i(A - G^0) + G^0 = \frac{(Na_i)(A - G^0)}{N} + \frac{G^0}{N} \cdot N \qquad (25.19)$$

Substituting Eq. (25.16) into (25.18) to solve for r_i yields:

$$r_i = (t^0 - t^i)A + (1 - \lambda)B_i \qquad (25.20)$$

Next, combine Eq. (25.15) and (25.17) to solve for $(t^0 - t^1)$:

$$t^0 A = t^1 A + \lambda B \qquad (25.21)$$

or

$$(t^0 - t^1) = \frac{\lambda B}{A} \qquad (25.22)$$

Substituting for $(t^0 - t^1)$ in Eq. (25.20) yields:

$$r_i = \frac{\lambda B A_i}{A} + (1 - \lambda)B_i \qquad (25.23)$$

or

$$r_i = a_i \lambda B + (1 - \lambda)B_i \qquad (25.24)$$

Finally, multiply Eq. (25.24) by N to obtain:

$$Nr_i = (Na_i)\lambda B + N(1 - \lambda)B_i \qquad (25.25)$$

For nonidentical individuals, the Arrow–Lind theorem requires that D_i and Nr_i converge to finite limits as $N \to \infty$, and that D_i and Nr_i be independently distributed.[6] Assume all the elements of D_i and Nr_i do converge, as required. By inspection of Eqs. (25.19) and (25.25), however, D_i and Nr_i will generally be statistically *dependent* because each contains the term Na_i. Independence can be preserved in only one of two ways:

1. Na_i is constant across all possible states of nature. This condition would be satisfied if $a_i = 1/N$, that is, if all consumers had identical initial incomes, as Arrow and Lind assume. With nonidentical individuals, however, Na_i almost certainly varies with the state of nature. This result highlights the point that the Arrow–Lind assumption of identical individuals is no longer innocuous once a more realistic fiscal structure is assumed.

2. The limits of the coefficients on Na_i approach zero as $N \to \infty$, in either Eq. (25.19) or (25.25), or both. But, this condition is not plausible for Eq. (25.19). It would imply either that $(A - G_0) \to 0$, which in turn implies a 100% tax rate t^0, or that $A/N \to 0$. For any realistic economy, however, A/N is obviously quite different from zero. Thus, the only remaining possibility is that $\lim_{N \to \infty} \lambda B = 0$, from Eq. (25.25). Since B is certainly finite, this implies

[6] See L. Foldes and R. Rees, "A Note on the Arrow–Lind Theorem," *American Economic Review*, March 1975, p. 190, for a proof.

that $\lim_{N \to \infty} \lambda = 0$, or that the benefits from the project are untaxed. While this is possible, it is unlikely to apply for very many government projects in an economy with income taxation, in which case the Arrow–Lind theorem would not be applicable.

These results provide yet another clear example of the general principle on second-best modeling emphasized repeatedly throughout Part III of the text, that there can never be an ultimate second-best model. One can always place additional effective constraints on any second-best model in the name of realism, after which the policy implications of the model are likely to change. In this particular instance, Foldes and Rees imposed a more realistic fiscal structure on the basic Arrow–Lind model, which was already second best, and were able to generate quite different results. The Foldes–Rees attack on Arrow–Lind would appear to be fairly devastating for many government projects, but there is always the possibility that some clever person will define a new set of realistic constraints that, when attached to the Foldes–Rees model, recapture the Arrow–Lind theorem. Any second-best model is potentially vulnerable in this way.

Further Reflections on the Arrow–Lind Theorem

Suppose that the two conditions on the Arrow–Lind Theorem do apply. Two additional implications of the theorem deserve comment.

First, the point that the government can take the expected value of government projects as the measure of their true value to society regardless of their riskiness facilitates comparisons among various government investment alternatives, but it does not eliminate the problem of uncertainty when comparing all government projects to private sector alternatives.[7] Uncertainty within the private sector still tends to obscure the proper value for the public sector's rate of discount. We alluded to this point earlier.

To illustrate, assume a Diamond–Mirrlees optimal taxation environment, in which the proper rate of discount is the productivity of private sector investments, the marginal rate of transformation between present and future consumption. As noted in Chapter 24, the MRT can be reasonably approximated by observed gross-of-tax returns on private investments. The problem, as noted earlier, is that *observed* private rates of return undoubtedly have risk premiums built into them. This implies that the government's true social rate of discount is *not* the observed MRT but the observed MRT less the private risk premium, or:

$$MRT_{\text{government opportunity cost}} = MRT_{\text{observed}} - \text{risk premium} \qquad (25.26)$$

The fact that the government can spread risk in a manner unavailable to the private sector is a real cost advantage which the public sector ought to

---

[7] We are assuming that the possibilities for risk pooling in the private sector are limited.

exploit by using a lower rate of discount on its projects. This advantage is substantial in the United States. The interest rate on U.S. Treasury bills, notes, and bonds is generally considered to be the risk-free rate of return for any given time period. The rate of return on equities has typically been 6 to 8 percentage points above the rate on Treasury securities. Discounting the expected net benefits of public sector projects at a real rate of, say, 3% would accept far more projects than discounting at 10 or 11%.[8]

A second important implication of the Arrow–Lind analysis is that if the net benefits (costs) of a project accrue to a small subset of the population, then an additional risk premium should be applied to them. The appropriate risk premium is suggested by the capital asset pricing model (CAPM). CAPM says that the expected return on an asset, i, exceeds the risk-free rate because of two factors: (1) a market or systematic risk that all investments share, and (2) a specific or unsystematic risk particular to the asset. The CAPM formula is

$$E(r_i) = r_f + (E(r_m) - r_f)\beta_i \qquad (2.27)$$

where:

$E(r_i)$ = the expected return on the asset
r_f = the risk-free rate of return
$E(r_m)$ = the expected rate of return on the broad market portfolio of assets, reflecting the market or systematic risk
β_i = the slope coefficient in the regression of r_i on r_m, that is, the $\dfrac{\text{Cov}(r_i, r_m)}{\sigma_m^2}$.

β_i is the measure of the specific or unsystematic risk associated with the asset.

$\beta_i = 1$ if the asset's returns are perfectly correlated with the broad market's return.

$\beta_i = 0$ if the asset's returns are uncorrelated with the broad market's return.

$\beta_i < 0$ if the asset's returns are negatively correlated with the broad market's return.

---

[8] More generally, the government's public rate of discount depends on the gross-of-tax (MRT) and net-of-tax (MRS) returns available in the private sector. To the extent these returns incorporate risk premiums, some adjustment in them is required when computing the public sector rate. If, in contrast, one agrees with Stephen Marglin and David Bradford that the discount rate ought to equal the social rate of time preference, risk premiums would only be reflected in the shadow price of project deficits. Perhaps both kinds of adjustments make sense, although the proper adjustment undoubtedly depends upon the underlying general equilibrium model being assumed. Theory is unlikely to reveal a single correct method. See R. Boadway, *Public Sector Economics* Winthrop Publishers, Cambridge, MA, 1979, pp. 202–205, for an analysis of various approaches and their justifications.

The expected net benefits of a public project that are narrowly distributed should be discounted at the risk-free rate only if the project's $\beta = 0$. Assume, instead that the project's $\beta > 0$. The project's benefits should then be discounted at a rate exceeding the risk-free rate since risk-adverse individuals prefer the expected benefits with certainty to the uncertain stream of benefits. Conversely, the project's costs should be discounted at a rate below the risk-free rate since risk-adverse individuals prefer the uncertain stream of costs to the expected costs with certainty.

These adjustments to the risk-free rate provide some solace for those who dislike projects that are narrowly conceived to benefit (harm) particular interest groups, since they must pass a more stringent test to be judged worthwhile. Note, however, that the adjustments have nothing whatsoever to do with the distribution question, *per se*. They are strictly a consequence of uncertainty, applicable to any subset of a risk-averse population, whether its members happen to have high or low social marginal utilities of income.

A practical difficulty is knowing exactly what adjustments to make. CAPM implies that different discount rates should be applied to different projects depending on the values of β, which may be difficult to determine for many, if not most, government projects.

A final point is simply to reemphasize that Arrow–Lind's call for ignoring the risks of public projects whose net benefits are broadly received has not been accepted by all economists. To give one further example beyond the caveats already noted, Bazelon and Smetters argue that federal agencies should add a risk premium into their discount rates. They believe that many private financial market inefficiencies that may have given the government a risk-spreading advantage in 1970 when the Arrow–Lind theorem appeared have since been removed or substantially reduced. They also worry about the distorting effect of taxation. They conclude:[9]

> "there is little evidence supporting the argument that government should price risks at less than the private market. Indeed, the distorting costs of taxation and the positive long-run correlation between stocks and wages suggest that the government should possibly *overprice* risks relative to the private market."

Arrow and Lind had considered the possibility that the risk-spreading effect might apply to large corporations, such that they should discount their investment opportunities at the risk-free rate in the interests of their stockholders. Nonetheless, given the high return to equity, it appears that corporate managers add a substantial risk premium to their discount rates. Arrow and Lind speculate that this may reflect the managers' perception of their own particular risks, namely their job security. In this case, Arrow and Lind argue that the government should use the risk-free rate in the interests of its

---

[9] C. Bazelon and K. Smetters, "Discounting Inside the Washington, D.C. Beltway," *Journal of Economic Perspectives*, Fall 1999, p. 216. Their discussion comparing government and private sector risks is on pp. 214–216.

citizens, but only if the public investment replaces consumption.[10] Public investments should not replace private investments that have higher returns since the risk associated with the private investments is also negligible. The second-best problem here is that the managerial perception of risk leads to too little private investment. Once again we are led to the conclusion that the appropriate public rate of discount is entirely model dependent.

REFERENCES

Arrow, K., and Lind, R., "Uncertainty and the Evaluation of Public Investment Decisions," *American Economic Review*, June 1970.

Bazelon, C., and Smetters, K., "Discounting Inside the Washington, D.C. Beltway," *Journal of Economic Perspectives*, Fall 1999.

Boadway, R., *Public Sector Economics*, Winthrop Publishers, Cambridge, MA, 1979.

Fisher, A., "A Paradox in the Theory of Public Investment," *Journal of Public Economics*, Vol. 2, 1973.

Foldes, L., and Rees, R., "A Note on the Arrow–Lind Theorem," *American Economic Review*, March 1977.

James, E., "A Note on Uncertainty and the Evaluation of Public Investment Decisions," *American Economic Review*, March 1975.

[10] K. Arrow and R. Lind, "Uncertainty and the Evaluation of Public Investment Decisions," *American Economic Review*, June 1970, pp. 375–376.

MEASUREMENT PROBLEMS IN COST–BENEFIT ANALYSIS

The problems discussed in Chapters 24 and 25—the proper rate of discount and adjusting for uncertainty—are shared by both private and public sector investment analysis. Chapter 26 explores a set of problems associated with the measurement of public sector costs and benefits that are unlikely to arise in the private sector. They derive either from the nature of the government projects themselves or the underlying policy and economic environment.

Generally speaking, private investment analysis attempts to measure the expected profitability on an investment, the difference between revenues and costs evaluated at current and expected future market prices. In contrast, profitability is usually not the proper criterion for project selection in public sector cost–benefit analysis. Market prices always convey useful information, but they often must be combined with other evaluative concepts to determine government project costs and benefits.

Chapter 23 identified four common sources of measurement problems in cost–benefit analysis:

1. Some of the benefits or costs may be intangibles.

2. Government projects are often lumpy, representing discrete, not marginal additions to an existing market environment.

3. Project benefits are sometimes given away free of charge or at least priced below marginal costs; similarly, project resources are sometimes commandeered, or bought at prices below marginal opportunity costs. In addition, some project benefits do not have direct market values, such as the reduction in air or water pollution. Their values have to be imputed in some way.

4. The presence of a second-best market or policy distortion requires the computation of shadow prices that differ from existing market prices.

With the exception of intangibles, most of the tools for analyzing these problems have been developed in Parts I–III of the text. Therefore, Chapter 26 will simply be recalling past results for the most part. There will be a considerable shift in perspective, however, because of the clear distinction between optimal normative policy prescription and policy evaluation. The former, which was the focus of the theoretical analysis, tells the government what it ought to do given specific and highly stylized policy and economic environments. Policy evaluation, in contrast, is concerned with measuring the costs and benefits of policies *actually* undertaken by the government regardless of whether they are optimal. As such, its orientation is towards beneficial policy reforms rather than optimality. It must also confront the staggering complexities of real-world economies, which are far removed from the stylized economies of our theoretical models. Cost–benefit analysis, then, requires a shift in emphasis away from theorems derived in tightly controlled policy environments toward the development of reasonable guidelines for the practitioner.

At the same time, however, the guidelines have to relate to the theoretical normative results if they are to aid policymakers in the pursuit of efficiency and equity. Consequently, the theoretical tools necessary for developing "reasonable" guidelines are the same as those used in developing the normative theory, concepts such as the expenditure function, general equilibrium profit function, and individualistic social welfare function. Furthermore, the assumed underlying economic and policy environment is as important to cost–benefit evaluation as it is to notions of optimality. It matters whether first-best or second-best assumptions are seen as reasonable and, if the latter, exactly what makes the environment second best. Perhaps the outstanding example in this regard concerns the distribution of income. If the underlying distribution is optimal, either by accident or through application of optimal first-best lump-sum taxes and transfers, then the measurement of costs and benefits is a relatively straightforward exercise, at least in principle. A nonoptimal distribution, in contrast, adds a layer of subjectivity to cost–benefit analysis along with a number of complicating factors. Therefore, it will pay to discuss the measurement problems listed above under the assumption of an optimal distribution of income. This is the only fruitful way of analyzing the implications of these problems in and of themselves. The distribution issues will then be considered in Chapter 27.

INTANGIBLES

Intangibles are the most intractable of the measurement problems. An *intangible* is a benefit or cost for which there is no obvious method of assigning a dollar value. Examples are easy to come by: national security in defense, the loss of life in constructing public works projects such as bridges and dams, the boost to national prestige of being the first nation to put a man on the moon, the United States' supposed love affair with passenger rail travel, and so forth.

By their very nature, economic analysis can offer little by way of guidance on intangibles. Indeed, if they are thought to be the major benefit (cost) of a particular project, as they undoubtedly are in many defense applications, there is no sense even attempting a full cost–benefit study. Cost–benefit analysis is useful only if costs and benefits can be reasonably quantified.

It is not surprising, therefore, that cost–benefit analysis is not used to evaluate alternative advanced weapons systems. Rather, the Department of Defense determines certain military objectives, requests proposals for weapons designed to meet these objectives, and then awards contracts on the basis of three broadly defined criteria: ability to meet the objectives, time to completion of the project, and cost.[1] The military objectives are the benefits, but they are simply assumed at the outset and not subjected to much further analysis in the awarding of contracts. There is an obvious loss of accountability and objectivity with this approach because the military itself largely determines the relevant objectives, but there is probably no other practical alternative.

Valuing a Life

The increased or decreased probability of death (or illness, or serious injury) associated with many nondefense projects (e.g., nuclear power plants, public inoculation programs, interstate highways) is another example of an external diseconomy (economy) that may well be intangible. Public sector economists universally agree that this type of externality ought to be included as a true project cost (benefit), but there is widespread disagreement over whether or

---

[1] Morton Peck and Frederic Scherer's book, *The Weapons Acquisition Process: An Economic Analysis*, remains the classic source on the evaluation procedures for military hardware. See M. Peck and F. Scherer, *The Weapons Acquisition Process: An Economic Analysis*, Division of Research, Graduate School of Business Administration, Harvard University, Boston, MA, 1962.

not the value of a person's life is measurable and, if so, how to do it. The following three methods of valuing a life illustrate the broad range of opinions on this issue.

The Economic Value of a Life

One popular method, generally attributed to Allen Kneese,[2] equates the value of life to the economic value of life. The economic value is the present discounted value of an individual's gross earnings over his lifetime, with each year's earnings weighted by the probability that the person will live through that year. Should the individual die unexpectedly as a result of a government project, the lost discounted earnings stream defines the cost of that death. This method of valuing a life is commonly used in U.S. legal proceedings.

The Subjective HCV

A second approach is associated with the British economist E. J. Mishan,[3] who rejects the discounted earnings approach in favor of computing each individual's subjective evaluation of Hicks' Compensating Variation (HCV) or Hicks' Equivalent Variation (HEV) required to offset his *involuntary* exposure to the increased risk of death (or disability) resulting from the project. According to Mishan, these subjective HCVs have three distinct components:

1. The compensatory payment required to offset the (subjectively determined) increased risk of death *per se*, either directly (e.g., direct exposure to radiation or working under dangerous conditions) or indirectly (e.g., the spread of an infectious disease originally contracted by someone else)
2. The psychic costs of bereavement over the increased risk of death to others
3. The financial gain or loss to the individual associated with the increased risk of death of others

These individual HCVs are then aggregated to determine the total costs (benefits) of the probable loss (savings) of life across the entire population.

Mishan distinguishes between involuntary and voluntary exposure to the increased risk of death, arguing that the latter is already built into the ordinary market demand and supply curves. For example, people's demand for a particular mode of transportation already includes an assessment of the subjective probability of incurring death (or injury) while traveling. Therefore, including the voluntary exposure to these risks in addition to the HCV

---

[2] A. Kneese, "Research Goals and Progress Toward Them," in H. Jarrett, Ed., *Environmental Quality in a Growing Economy*, Johns Hopkins Press, Washington, D.C., 1966.

[3] E. J. Mishan, "Evaluation of Life and Limb: A Theoretical Approach," *Journal of Political Economy*, March/April 1971.

computed directly from the market demand curves would entail double counting. Similarly, people's willingness to accept dangerous construction jobs is reflected in the increased wage required to hire them. The higher wage compensates workers for their voluntary exposure to the risks.

The *Ex Post* Versus *Ex Ante* Perspective

To cite one last opinion, John Broome[4] argues that it is virtually impossible to place a value on life as long as one believes that individuals view certain death as infinitely costly. The difference between his position and Mishan's is a matter of point of view. Broome argues that the government should adopt an *ex post* view of the loss of life, whereas Mishan adopts an *ex ante* view. Speaking directly to Mishan's position, Broome believes that each individual's subjective assessment of the increased probability of dying is irrelevant from a social perspective once one concedes that some people are virtually certain to die as a result of a project.

Suppose, for example, that the government is virtually certain that 3 out of 1000 workers will die during the construction of a suspension bridge. According to Mishan's *ex ante* point of view, each of the 1000 people might reasonably assume everyone's chances of death have increased by 3% and proceed to compute "Mishan" HCVs based on this assessment (although the wages on the job might already incorporate this assessment). According to Broome's *ex post* point of view, the fact that three workers are almost certain to die is the equivalent, from the *ex ante* perspective, of the government being able to name beforehand the three workers who will die. The aggregate "Mishan" HCVs would surely be much different in this case, presumably infinitely large. Broome argues that the latter calculation is the appropriate one if the government adopts an HCV approach to the valuation of life. From the government's point of view, the relevant facts are that three people *will* die with $\Pr \to 1$, each person views death with certainty as infinitely costly, and each individual HCV receives equal weight. The government's social welfare function is presumably impersonal. It may not care who dies, but it surely does care that three workers are virtually certain to die.

Of course, the *ex post* perspective leads immediately to the position that any project for which there is an expected loss of even one life should not be undertaken, a position Broome views as nonsensical.[5] His conclusion is that loss of life is a true intangible that cannot be subjected to a standard willingness-to-pay calculation. Public officials must simply make decisions in the presence of this intangible.

Broome's position has hardly carried the day. He was sharply criticized in a number of negative "Comments" to his paper, some supporting Mishan

[4] J. Broome, "Trying to Value a Life," *Journal of Public Economics*, February 1978.
[5] Or, any project that saves at least one life should be undertaken, an equally nonsensical position.

and others suggesting still different approaches to the evaluation of a person's life.[6] Even if one believes that the value of life is measurable in principle, however, there remains the difficult task of evaluating such concepts as Mishan's individual HCVs or Kneese's economic value of life. In that sense, Broome's general pessimism about valuing the loss of life is easily shared.

Limit Values of Intangibles

The real danger with true intangibles is that they can easily undermine objective cost–benefit analysis in nondefense areas when they are realistically only a fraction of overall benefits or costs. Proponents and opponents will undoubtedly be able to discover "substantial" intangible benefits or costs in any government project. By placing a sufficiently large implicit dollar value on some intangible element of a project, the project's present value can arbitrarily be made positive or negative. Cost–benefit analysis risks becoming a blatantly political exercise.

The presence of intangibles should not preclude undertaking a careful cost–benefit analysis. To the contrary, the only plausible way of obtaining a proximate valuation of the intangibles is by means of a cost–benefit analysis of the tangible project costs and benefits. The tangible data can then be used to place implicit lower or upper bounds on the value of the intangible elements. For example, suppose the government must choose between two mutually exclusive alternatives, A and B, with the following properties: The quantifiable present value of A is greater than the quantifiable present value of B, but B is perceived to contain some intangible benefits. For B to be chosen, the implicit dollar value of its intangible benefits must be at least $(PV_A - PV_B)$. One can then ask whether society would conceivably be willing to pay that much for the alleged intangible benefits. Placing even a lower (upper) bound on the value of intangible benefits (costs) is impossible without recourse to a careful cost–benefit study.

LUMPINESS

Suppose a private firm invests in a new machine that increases its annual production capacity by 1000 units. It typically measures the benefits of the machine as the increase in expected revenues from the 1000 units, equal to 1000 times the existing and expected future market price of the item each year for the projected life of the machine. The revenue measure $p\Delta X$ is usually

[6] J. M. Buchanan and R. L. Faith, "Trying Again to Value a Life"; M. W. Jones-Lee, "Trying To Value a Life: Why Broome Does Not Sweep Clean"; A. Williams, "A Note on 'Trying to Value a Life'"; and J. Broome, "Trying To Value a Life: A Reply," *Journal of Public Economics*, October 1979.

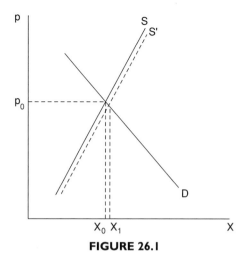

FIGURE 26.1

considered to be a reasonable approximation of the social benefits of the machine as long as the 1000 units represent a "small" increment to overall market capacity. As depicted in Fig. 26.1, $(X_1 - X_0 = 1000)$ is such a small addition to the overall market that it has virtually no effect on the market price.[7]

Government investments, in contrast, often represent substantial additions to existing market capacity, enough that they do affect prices. This situation is depicted in Fig. 26.2. Obvious examples include hydroelectric projects that substantially reduce the price of electricity to an entire region or large additions to a public transportation network in an urban area that substantially reduce travel and congestion costs. In these cases, $p\Delta X$ revenue calculations are no longer good approximations of the benefits. The proper benefit measures are a good deal more complex. They have been presented in Chapter 9 for measuring the benefits of decreasing-cost services and in Chapter 13 for measuring the loss from taxation. Our purpose here will be to collect and summarize these results in the context of benefit measurement when prices change discretely. The extension to cost measurement is straightforward.

First-Best Benefit Measures: A Single Price Change

As always in public sector analysis, it matters whether the underlying policy environment is considered first best or second best, although perhaps less so here than in other areas. To keep matters straight, however, we will assume to

[7] We are assuming a first-best environment in which consumers and producers face the same prices.

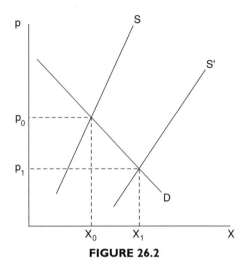

FIGURE 26.2

begin with that the environment is first best, that only a single price changes, and that there are no additional relevant supply effects from changes in production (e.g., linear or constant returns-to-scale [CRS] general technology). In addition, the economy is one consumer equivalent because of the assumption that income is continuously redistributed to satisfy the interpersonal equity conditions. Under these assumptions, we saw that the various benefit measures can be approximated by areas behind aggregate demand curves. Our previous analysis in Chapters 9 and 13 developed three such area measures, each depicted in Fig. 26.3. For purposes of discussion, assume price decreases from p_0 to p_1. Thus,

1. *Marshallian consumer surplus* is equal to the area behind the actual market demand curve, D^A, between the initial and final equilibrium prices p_0 and p_1, area p_0p_1 CA.

2. *Hicks' Compensating Variation (HCV)* is equal to the area behind the demand curve compensated at the original utility level, U^0, $D^C_{U=\overline{U}^0}$, between the prices p_0 and p_1, area p_0p_1 BA. This measures the lump-sum income the consumer would be willing to sacrifice in order to purchase X at the new lower price p_1. Notice that the quantity demanded with compensation at the original utility level exceeds the actual quantity demanded at prices greater than p_0, equals X_0^A at p_0, and is less than the actual quantity demanded at prices lower than p_0. At p_0, the required lump-sum income is the actual income because utility is U^0. At prices above p_0, the consumer would receive compensation to remain at U^0 so that his income is greater than actual income, and vice versa for prices less than P_0.

3. *Hicks' Equivalent variation (HEV)* is equal to the area behind the demand curve compensated at the new utility level U^1, $D^C_{U=\overline{U}^1}$, between the

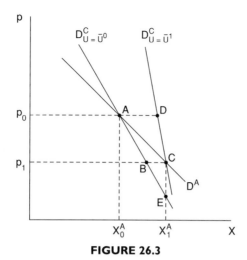

FIGURE 26.3

prices p_0 and p_1, area $p_0 p_1$ CD. This area represents the lump-sum income the consumer would require to return to the original price p_0 and remain at U_1. Notice that the quantity demanded with compensation at the new utility level exceeds the actual quantity demanded at prices greater than p_1, equals actual demand at p_1, and is less than the actual quantity demanded at prices less than p_1, by similar reasoning applied to the position of the demand curve compensated at U^0.

4. A fourth measure commonly employed in the literature, which we have not developed formally, is the *compensating surplus*. It equals the area under the demand curve compensated at the original utility level U^0, $D_{C_{U=\overline{U}^0}}$, between the initial and final equilibrium outputs, X_0^A and X_1^A, area $AEX_1^A X_0^A$. The measure represents the amount of the numeraire good the consumer would be willing to sacrifice to be able to consume (supply) the actual quantities of all other goods (factors) at the new equilibrium. In sacrificing the numeraire good, the consumer returns to the initial utility level.[8]

The differences in these areas clearly turn on income effects, since the consumer is paying or receiving different amounts of lump-sum income in each case. Therefore, to avoid having to choose among them and also because of data limitations, empirical researchers often assume away all income effects, so that all the compensated curves coincide with the actual market demand curve. Estimation of individual demand and supply curves offers no support for ignoring income effects, however.

---

[8] P. Diamond and D. McFadden, "Some Uses of the Expenditure Function in Public Finance," *Journal of Public Economics*, February 1974; W. Moss, "Some Uses of the Expenditure Function in Public Finance: A Comment," *Journal of Public Economics*, April–May 1976.

Researchers who assume income effects are faced with choosing among these alternative measures. Since they place different values on the benefits, they should choose one of them and apply it consistently across all projects.

In theory, measures 2 to 4 dominate measure 1 because the last three all have valid willingness-to-pay interpretations, whereas Marshallian consumer surplus does not. For example, the HEV is the difference between the consumer's expenditure function evaluated at the new utility level (U^1), and the prices with (p^1) and without (p^0) the project:

$$
\begin{aligned}
\text{HEV} &= M\left(P_1^0; \overline{P}_2, \ldots, \overline{P}_N; \overline{U}^1\right) - M\left(P_1^1; \overline{P}_2, \ldots, \overline{P}_N; \overline{U}^1\right) \\
&= \int_{p_1^1}^{p_1^0} \frac{\partial M\left(s; \overline{P}_2, \ldots, \overline{P}_N; \overline{U}^1\right)}{\partial s}\, ds \\
&= \int_{p_1^1}^{p_1^0} X_1\left(p_1; \overline{P}_2, \ldots, \overline{P}_N; \overline{U}^1\right) dp_1
\end{aligned}
\tag{26.1}
$$

assuming that only p_1 changes, with similar calculations for the HCV and the compensating surplus. Marshallian consumer surplus, on the other hand, is simply a money index of utility change that depends on the path taken by prices and income between the initial and final equilibrium.

In Chapter 9, we sided with Peter Hammond's position that applied researchers should reject Marshallian consumer surplus in favor of one of the appropriate willingness-to-pay measures. The reason is simply that the appropriate measures can be derived from the estimated market demand curve by means of Roy's Identity and numerical methods for solving ordinary differential equations that are easily handled by modern computing technology. Another possibility is the Jorgenson–Slesnick share estimation technique, described in Chapter 4, which estimates the parameters of the underlying (common) indirect utility function, but this approach requires much more data than the first option since it estimates an entire system of demand equations.

A Public Sector Bias?

A point worth emphasizing is that area measures of benefits for discrete price changes do not generate a bias for or against public sector projects relative to the standard private sector revenue measure, whatever area measure is chosen. $p\Delta X$ is also a willingness-to-pay measure under the assumption that ΔX is sufficiently small that it has no effect on prices. This can be seen directly by comparing $p\Delta X$ with the compensating surplus measure 4. Relative to the numeraire, $p_x = MRS_{X, \text{numeraire}}$, or the amount of the numeraire good the consumer would be willing to sacrifice in exchange for an additional unit of X. Hence, $p_x \Delta X$ gives the total amount of the numeraire the consumer would be willing to sacrifice for all additional units of X, under the assumption

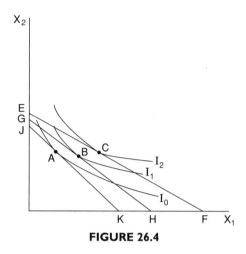

FIGURE 26.4

that p_x has not changed. But this is exactly what the compensating surplus measures, albeit for discrete changes in prices.

The Preference for the HEV

Many economists have expressed a preference for Hicks' Equivalent Variation if more than one project is being evaluated and the government for some reason can finance only a subset of all projects with positive present value.[9] All the willingness-to-pay measures indicate whether accepting any given project and moving to a new equilibrium is preferred to the original situation, but Hicks' Compensating Variation and the compensating surplus can be misleading with limited funds.

To see this, consider the example depicted in Fig. 26.4. The economy is at point A, and the government is considering two projects: One (B) will bring the economy to point B, and another (C) will bring the economy to point C. Suppose the government can finance only one of them. The government should choose project C.

Hicks' Equivalent Variation indicates that C is the preferred alternative since the same price line JK is first moved tangent to I_1 to evaluate B and then tangent to I_2 to evaluate C. At this common parallel, I_2 must be the farthest from the origin. Hicks' Compensating Variation, in contrast, first measures the distance from I_1 to I_0 at the parallel GH and then the distance from I_2 to I_0 at the parallel EF. The first distance measure could easily be greater than the second, falsely indicating a preference for B. A similar demonstration

[9] See, for example, J. Oiesen, "A Theoretical Justification of Cost–Benefit Analysis," *Staff Study: Report No. 55-213-U9-5*, U.S. Department of Transportation, Transportation Systems Center, Kendall Square, Cambridge, MA, pp. 29–30 (draft).

applies to the compensating surplus. The anomaly can arise because the distances are taken in different ways from one indifference curve to the next, thus the preference for Hicks' Equivalent Variation, which standardizes the distance measures by selecting the same parallel each time. In short, only the HEV provides a consistent money index of the utility function as prices change. By using the original prices and the new utility levels, its willingness-to-pay measure gives an appropriate monetary value to each utility level that is comparable across utilities.

First-Best Benefit Measures: Multiple Price Changes

The compensation measures easily generalize to situations in which more than one price changes. Hicks' Equivalent Variation is:

$$\text{HEV} = M\left(\vec{p}_0; \overline{U}^1\right) - M\left(\vec{p}_1; \overline{U}^1\right) \tag{26.2}$$

where:

$\vec{p}_0$ = the vector of consumer prices at the original equilibrium.
$\vec{p}_1$ = the vector of consumer prices at the final equilibrium.

and similarly for the other two measures. The multiple price change measures can also be interpreted as summations of areas under compensated demand (factor supply) curves in each market, as was shown in Chapters 9 and 13. Prices are assumed to change one at a time with each demand curve evaluated at a vector of prices containing the new prices for those markets for which areas have been computed and the initial prices in the remaining markets. The final value of the measure obtained in this manner is invariant to the order of summation because $\partial X_i^C / \partial p_j = \partial X_j^C / \partial p_i$, all i, j, for the compensated demands, and income is assumed constant. This again is the notion of path independence, that any assumed path of price changes from the initial to the final general equilibrium generates the same value for any of these measures. Path independence does not hold for Marshallian consumer surplus.[10]

[10] The following set of references provide an excellent overview of consumer surplus and, more generally, the welfare implications of price changes: P. Samuelson, "Social Indifference Curves," *Quarterly Journal of Economics*, February 1956. P. Samuelson, *Foundations of Economic Analysis*, Atheneum, New York, 1965. P. Samuelson, "Constancy of the Marginal Utility of Income," in O. Lange *et al.*, Eds., *Studies in Mathematical Economics and Econometrics: In Memory of Henry Schultz*, Books for Libraries Press, Plainview, NY, 1968. D. Patinkin, "Demand Curves and Consumer's Surplus," in C. Christ et. al., Eds., *Measurement in Economics*, Stanford University Press, Stanford, CA, 1963. A. Harberger, "Three Basic Postulates for Applied Welfare Economics," *Journal of Economic Literature*, September 1971. D. Richter, "Games Pythagoreans Play," *Public Finance Quarterly*, October 1977. A. Dixit, "Welfare Effects of Tax and Price Changes," *Journal of Public Economics*, February 1975. A. Dixit and K. Munk, "Welfare Effects of Tax and Prices Changes: A Correction," *Journal of Public Economics*, August

First-Best Benefit Measures: General Technology

We have been considering the lump-sum income the consumer would be willing to pay or give up for the price changes resulting from a lumpy government investment. This is only the demand side of the problem. The benefit measure must also include supply side effects, in particular, any changes in actual *pure economic profits* from private production in response to the government investment. Notice the emphasis on pure economic profits, a source of lump-sum income. Changes in factor incomes, including the opportunity returns to capital, are already incorporated in the consumer's expenditure function for all the factors whose supplies are variable (income changes accruing to factors in absolutely fixed supply can be considered part of the pure profits from private production).

Analytically, Eq. (26.2) is extended to incorporate the change in the value of the general equilibrium profit function at the final and initial producer prices. Hence, Hicks' Equivalent Variation measure of benefits for general technology is

$$HEV = [\pi(\vec{p}_1) - \pi(\vec{p}_0)] + \left[M\left(\vec{p}_0; \overline{U}^1\right) - M\left(\vec{p}_1; \overline{U}^1\right) \right] \qquad (26.3)$$

Equation (26.3) can be given one of two interpretations. As written, it compares the change in pure profits from production with the lump-sum income the consumer is willing to sacrifice to forego the change in prices. However, $M(\vec{p}_1; \overline{U}^1) = \pi(\vec{p}_1)$. Therefore,

$$HEV = M\left(\vec{p}_0; \overline{U}^1\right) - \pi(\vec{p}_0) \qquad (26.4)$$

which is interpreted as the lump-sum income the consumer requires to achieve the new utility level if faced with the original prices minus the pure profits the consumer receives at the original prices. Similar modifications apply to the HCV and the compensating surplus.

Benefit Measures: Second-Best Considerations

Equations (26.3) and (26.4) remain appropriate general equilibrium measures of the benefits of government projects in a second-best environment for one-consumer-equivalent economies. They may be incomplete in a second-best environment, however, if some additional constraint implies a further

1977. R. Willig, "Consumer's Surplus Without Apology," *American Economic Review*, September 1976. J. Seade, "Consumer's Surplus and Linearity of Engel's Curves," *Economic Journal*, September 1978. G. McKensie, "Measuring Gains and Losses," *Journal of Political Economy*, June 1976. G. McKenzie and I. Pearce, "Exact Measures of Welfare and the Cost of Living," *Review of Economic Studies*, October 1976. P. Hammond, "Theoretical Progress in Public Economics: A Provocative Assessment," *Oxford Economic Papers*, January 1990.

source of lump-sum income change—for example, a constraint that the government's budget deficit must be simultaneously decreased by a certain amount or maintained at some non-zero level. We saw this when analyzing the dead-weight loss from taxation, in which the budget deficit was part of the loss measure. Most second-best applications with budget constraints assume that the budget remains balanced at zero, in which case these equations are complete specifications of the net benefits from lumpy government investments. They incorporate all relevant general equilibrium reactions to an investment expressed in the form of lump-sum income changes.

The measures are straightforward enough in principle, but they may be difficult even to approximate in practice. For instance, will any researcher ever be able to estimate the full pattern of pure economic profits and losses in the private sector resulting from any given project? What adjustments will the government make to maintain a balanced budget as prices change? Beyond questions such as these, there is an additional serious conceptual problem with applying these measures. If compensation actually occurred and production exhibits general technology, the compensated general equilibrium price vector would differ from the actual observed general equilibrium price vector, so it is unclear how to evaluate equations such as Eq. (26.3). (Refer to the discussion of this point in Chapter 14.) This particular ambiguity has led Harberger to suggest an alternative method of evaluating price changes with distorted equilibria. Recall Eq. (13.11),[11] rewritten here as Eq. (26.5):

$$L(\vec{t}) = -\frac{1}{2}\sum_{i=2}^{N}\sum_{j=2}^{N}t_i t_j \frac{\partial X_i^C}{\partial q_j} \qquad (26.5)$$

Equation (26.5) approximates the total loss from a vector of distorting unit taxes, $\vec{t} = (t_2, \ldots, t_N)$, with constant producer prices by assuming that the compensated demand derivatives $\partial X_i^C/\partial q_j$ are constant over the relevant range of prices. The more general representation of loss for any policy variable leading to discrete changes in prices is

$$L(Z^*) = \int_{Z^0}^{Z^*}\sum_{i=1}^{N}D^i\left(\vec{Z}\right)\frac{\partial X_i}{\partial Z}d\vec{Z} \qquad (26.6)$$

where:

$\vec{Z}$ = a vector of policy variables (not necessarily unit taxes).
$D^i(\vec{Z})$ = the difference between the consumer and producer prices, $\vec{q}$ and $\vec{p}$, respectively, expressed as a function of $\vec{Z}$ ($= t_i$ when unit taxes are the policy variables and the only source of distortion).

Harberger recommends applying Eq. (26.5) or (26.6) for both linear *and* general technologies, in which the derivatives $\partial X_i/\partial Z$ represent changes in the

---

[11] Here, we adopt the convention in second-best analysis that q denotes consumer prices and p denotes producer prices.

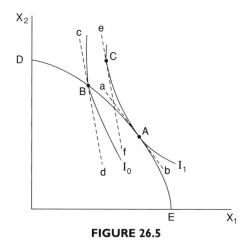

FIGURE 26.5

general equilibrium values of the quantities X_i given that the government acts in such a way as to keep all resources fully employed.[12] The practical advantage of Harberger's technique is that the loci of general equilibrium values of the X_i and their derivatives are observable. Notice, though, that his approach lacks strict theoretical justification. Compensation is occurring, but only to maintain production on the production possibilities frontier, not necessarily to keep the consumer at a particular utility level.

The difference is depicted in Fig. 26.5, with X_2 serving as the numeraire. Suppose the economy is originally at the undistorted equilibrium A, with $q_{x_1} (= p_{x_1})$ equal to (minus) the slope of the line segment ab. The government then levies a unit tax on X_1, raising q_{x_1} to (minus) the slope of line segment cd. Assume the government spends the revenues (and engages in further lump-sum distribution) in such a way as to keep society on its production-possibilities

---

[12] He argues his case most forcefully in A. Harberger, "Three Basic Postulates for Applied Welfare Economics," although his methodology is also spelled out in A. Harberger, "Taxation, Resource Allocation, and Welfare," in *The Role of Direct and Indirect Taxes in the Federal Revenue System*, National Bureau of Economic Research and The Brookings Institution, Princeton University Press, Princeton, NJ, 1964, A. Harberger, "The Measurement of Waste," *American Economic Association Papers and Proceedings*, May 1964. See also A. Harberger, *Taxation and Welfare*, Little, Brown & Company, Boston, MA, 1974, pp. 86–90. Harberger was also willing to ignore distributional considerations, the third of his three basic postulates for applied work in his 1971 paper. He backed off from this position somewhat in 1978, arguing that it was reasonable to give extra weight to net transfers to the poor providing that the efficiency loss was no greater than the minimum cost of effecting transfers to the poor through general taxes and transfers. His position left some discretion to the policymaker in choosing the poverty line for defining the poor and in selecting an efficiency cost of general transfers to the poor. Harberger thought a 20% efficiency cost was a reasonable maximum and seemed to prefer a lower percentage. See A. Harberger, "On the Use of Distributional Weights in Social Cost–Benefit Analysis," *Journal of Political Economy*, April 1978, part 2, section VII.

frontier DE, thereby establishing a new general equilibrium at B. The change from A to B is represented by $\sum_j (\partial X_i/\partial t_j)t_j$ in Eq. (26.5) and by $\int_{z^0}^{z^*} (\partial X_i/\partial Z)dZ$ in Eq. (26.6), the $\partial X_i/\partial t_i (\partial X_i/\partial Z)$ represent the (constant) marginal general equilibrium changes in X_i in response to the tax. Because of the nature of the X_i, Eq. (26.6) is a path-dependent money index of utility change.

Point C represents the fully compensated equilibrium, with the change from A to C given by $\sum_j (\partial X_i^c/\partial t_j)t_j \left(\int_{z^0}^{z^*} (\partial X_i^c/\partial Z)d\vec{Z} \right)$, where the $\partial X_i^c/\partial t_j$ $(\partial X_i^c/\partial Z)$ represent the (constant) Slutsky substitution terms evaluated at the utility level associated with I_1. The fully compensated loss measure would also incorporate the change in the value of pure economic profits as society moves from A to C. The two measures of loss clearly differ in general, begging the question of whether Harberger's approach is a reasonable practical compromise. Harberger obviously thinks that it is, but others may well disagree.[13]

NONMARKETED BENEFITS

When evaluating government services offered free of charge (e.g., toll-free bridges and highways, free access to over-the-air commercial and public television, free recreational facilities), the first consideration is whether the analysis can assume a first-best or second-best environment.[14] First-best assumptions are appropriate only if the service *ought* to have a zero price at the optimum, which is the case if short-run marginal cost is zero and there are no capacity constraints; otherwise, the zero price cannot possibly be first best. These supply characteristics are in addition to all the other conditions necessary for a first-best analysis, such as an optimal income distribution, perfectly competitive markets everywhere, and perfect information.

First-Best Environment

Some public services may actually approximate these supply conditions. The marginal cost of having another viewer turn on a television set is virtually zero no matter how many people are watching a particular program, nor are there any effective capacity constraints on over-the-air telecasts. Rural roads and bridges do not typically suffer congestion either, and maintenance costs on these facilities may be as much a function of weathering as travel. Clearly the marginal cost of a few additional vehicles is near zero for any given average traffic flow. Thus, offering over-the-air television free of charge to viewers and not charging tolls on rural highways and bridges can reasonably

---

[13] Don Richter provides a lucid critique of the Harberger loss measure in D. Richter, "Games Pythagoreans Play," *Public Finance Quarterly*, October 1977.

[14] The discussion in this section will be limited to benefits offered free of charge. The analysis is easily generalized to benefits that are underpriced in some meaningful sense or to conscripted resources.

be viewed as examples of first-best pricing. In these cases, the benefit measure is straightforward, equal to the area under an appropriate compensated demand curve over its full length less the total cost of providing the service (assuming the cost is covered through lump-sum taxes). If providing the services changes prices in other markets, then these price changes (and pure profit changes) would enter into the measure as well. In other words, these services are just another example of lumpy public projects, and equations such as Eq. (26.3) or (26.4) can be applied directly in measuring their net benefits.

These formulas may not be too useful, however, because the relevant demand curves cannot possibly be estimated if price has never been different from zero. All one can know is the zero-price point on the demand curve. Faced with this problem, economists have developed a number of techniques for indirectly estimating nonmarketed benefits (and costs). These techniques also apply to nonmarketed benefits such as environmental improvements. In fact, many of them were developed in an environmental context. We will briefly consider four of them:

1. Evaluating the underlying benefits that give rise to the demand curve
2. Making use of substitute products or defensive strategies to offset the damage from external diseconomies
3. The hedonic price technique
4. Surveys, also referred to as contingent valuation

The first three techniques are called *indirect market techniques* because they use market prices to evaluate nonmarketed benefits. Surveys are a direct and entirely nonmarket approach to evaluating nonmarketed benefits.

Evaluating the Underlying Benefits

Evaluating the underlying benefits that give rise to an unknown demand curve is a time-honored approach to the measurement of nonmarketed benefits. It is commonly employed in studies of transportation projects, among other applications. For instance, suppose the government builds a straight, four-lane superhighway between two small cities that had previously been connected only by a twisting, two-lane highway, an example relevant to many segments of the U.S. interstate highway system. In lieu of estimating an unknowable demand curve for the highway, the analyst could obtain estimates of projected travel demand at zero price and multiply this estimate by the per-trip value to the average user of having the new highway. The sources of value derive from factors such as increased safety, improved gasoline economy, reduced wear and tear on vehicles, and time saved per trip. Having identified these sources, one then tries to obtain reasonable dollar estimates of their value to the users. Accident records and medical expenses might be used to evaluate the safety factor (with some arbitrary valuation for each death prevented), and depreciation data on automobiles and trucks can be used to evaluate the "wear and tear" factor. Transportation economists typically choose the average wage rate, or some multiple thereof, to evaluate time saved, which turns out to be a major component of the total value in most studies. This practice stems from the neoclassical view of the labor–leisure choice, in which the $MRS_{labor, leisure}$ is equal to the wage. If the time savings are considerable, a multiple of the wage is sometimes used to reflect the value of inframarginal hours.[15]

Substitute Products and Defensive Behavior

If nonmarketed benefits happen to have close substitutes, then the value of the substitute products can serve as an estimate of the value of the benefits. An example would be using the price of bottled water as an estimate of the benefits of reducing pollution in a body of water to the point that it is drinkable. The estimate is precisely accurate if the two products are perfect substitutes, but this is unlikely.

The cost of behavior related to the benefits is another way of evaluating the benefits. For example, the cost of traveling to recreational sites has been used to estimate the benefits of the sites. Similarly, the costs of air pollution, such as more frequent painting of one's house or buying medicines to relieve respiratory distress, are used to estimate the benefits of pollution reduction.

The justification for the indirect use of defensive behavior to evaluate the benefits of pollution reduction is as follows. Suppose the harm, H, that people experience from some form of pollution, P, is a function of the amount of pollution and defensive behavior, D, taken against the pollution, according to the function $H = H(P,D)$. The price of D, P_D, is observed since the defensive inputs are purchased in the market. The marginal cost of pollution, P_P, is not observed even though people do implicitly place such a cost on their exposure to pollution (alternatively, a marginal value on reducing their exposure). With P_P in mind, individuals who engage in defensive behavior are in equilibrium when

$$\left(\frac{\frac{\partial H}{\partial P}}{\frac{\partial H}{\partial D}} \right) = MRS^H_{P,D} = \left(\frac{dD}{dP} \right)_{H=\bar{H}} = \frac{P_P}{P_D} \qquad (26.7)$$

or

$$P_P = P_D \left(\frac{dD}{dP} \right)_{H=\bar{H}} \qquad (26.8)$$

---

[15] A good reference on the valuation of time saved in transportation analysis is D. Tipping, "Time Savings in Transport Studies," *Economic Journal*, December 1968. See also E. Mishan, *Cost–Benefit Analysis*, Praeger Publishers, New York, 1976. Mishan analyzes various benefit and cost valuation problems through part V. Other useful general sources are R. Layard, Ed., *Cost–Benefit Analysis*, Penguin Education, Penguin Books, Ltd. Hammondsworth, Middlesex, England, 1972, R. Layard and S. Glaister, Eds., *Cost–Benefit Analysis*, second ed. Cambridge University Press, New York, NY, 1994.

$\left(\dfrac{dD}{dP}\right)_{H=\bar{H}}$ is a production relationship that presumably can be estimated, which then leads to an estimate of the unobserved P_P, the value that people are willing to pay for a marginal reduction in pollution.[16]

The Hedonic Price Technique

The values of some nonmarketed benefits are closely tied to marketed goods. Houses located in urban areas are a case in point: A household's exposure to air pollution or the benefit it receives from local public services depends to a great extent on the location of the house. Thus, the value of less polluted air or better local public services is likely to be capitalized into housing prices. For example, because of the prevailing westerly winds, the eastern suburbs of many U.S. cities experience much more polluted air than the western suburbs. For this reason alone, houses to the west of the city tend to command higher prices, and the higher income households tend to live in the western suburbs. Similarly, houses command a premium in the communities with the most desired public service bundles. Therefore, economists have tried to use housing market data to derive indirect estimates of the value that people place on cleaner air and local public services.

A house is a type of good that provides an entire array of services. The buyer pays a single price for the house, but that price reflects the separate values of a bundle of characteristics, including site values, such as the nature and location of the land and the size and design of the house; neighborhood effects, such as distance to public transportation, shopping, and a major central city and how safe the neighborhood is; the public services–tax mix in the community; and environmental effects such as the amount of exposure to air pollution. Kelvin Lancaster extended consumer theory to these types of goods to show how consumers incorporate the separate characteristics into a determination of how much they are willing to pay for each good.[17] Sherwin Rosen developed the econometric technique for estimating the value to consumers of each of the characteristics from data on the good's price.[18] The estimated values for the separate characteristic are called *hedonic prices*; hence, the estimating procedure is referred to as the *hedonic price technique*. The technique has been applied more successfully to evaluating air quality than to the demand for local public services so we will use air quality as the example.

[16] This example is from M. Cropper and W. Oates, "Environmental Economics: A Survey," *Journal of Economic Literature*, June 1992, p. 703. They also consider how to adjust the indirect valuation for nonmarginal changes in pollution. This excellent survey includes a discussion, with detailed references, of the four techniques presented in this section.

[17] K. Lancaster, *Consumer Demand: A New Approach*, Columbia University Press, New York, 1971.

[18] S. Rosen, "Hedonic Prices and Implicit Markets," *Journal of Political Economy*, January/February 1974.

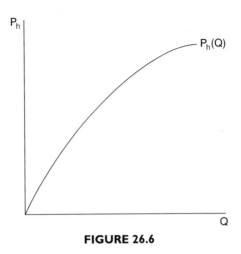

FIGURE 26.6

The hedonic price technique begins with the assumption that there exists a common house valuation function within a region whose arguments are the characteristics of each house. Consider three types of characteristics: site, neighborhood, and environmental. Let:

S_{is} = site characteristic s of house i, s = 1, ..., S
N_{in} = neighborhood characteristic n of house i, n = 1, ..., N
Q_i = the air quality where house i is located.

Then,

$$P_{hi} = P_h(S_{is}; N_{in}; Q_i) + e_i \tag{26.9}$$

where:

P_{hi} = the price of house i
$P_h(\ )$ = the common house valuation function
e_i = the error term, with zero mean

The first step is to estimate the function P_h from a sample of houses within the region. The estimate produces what urban economists call a *rent gradient* for each of the characteristics.[19] One would expect the other-things-equal rent gradient for air quality, $P_h(Q)$, to have a decreasing slope, as pictured in Fig. 26.6. The cleaner the air, the less people would be willing to pay on the margin for still cleaner air.

---

[19] Notice that the estimating equation (26.9) does not contain the individual characteristics of the homeowner because the set of potential buyers is assumed to be the same for each house. If housing markets segment by income within a region, then a separate $P_h(\ )$ function should be estimated for each subregion.

The slope of $P_h(Q)$, $P_Q(Q)$, is the hedonic price for cleaner air at every level of air quality, Q. The essence of Lancaster's theory is that consumers achieve an equilibrium with respect to each characteristic. In terms of air quality, consumers seek the air quality such that their marginal rate of substitution between cleaner air and the numeraire good (X) equals the hedonic price of cleaner air, $P_Q(Q)$. They purchase the house which has the bundle of characteristics that satisfy the equilibrium conditions MRS = the hedonic price for every characteristic.

Refer to the hedonic price function for cleaner air, pictured in Fig. 26.7. It looks like a demand curve for cleaner air but it is not. Instead, it is the locus of equilibrium points for all houses in the sample for which the buyers' $MRS_{Q,X} = P_Q(Q)$. It would be a demand function for cleaner air only if all the buyers were identical, which is certainly not the case in the market for housing. In general, separate supply and demand curves intersect at each point along the locus, as pictured in the figure.

The problem, then, is to estimate the underlying demand curves to determine the value that people place on cleaner air. This requires collecting additional data on the income and tastes of the households and estimating a demand curve for cleaner air such as:

$$Q_i = a + bP_{Q_i} + cY_i + d\vec{Z}_i + e_i \qquad (26.10)$$

where:

Q_i and P_{Q_i} are taken from the estimated $P_Q(Q)$ function given where the household lives.

Y_i = the income of household i.

$\vec{Z}_i$ = a vector of taste variables for household i.

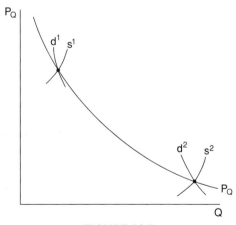

FIGURE 26.7

The way that the estimation proceeds depends on what is assumed about the supply of clean air across housing sites. One possibility is that land is plentiful, so that the supply of a given air quality is perfectly elastic in the vicinity of each site. In that case, the P_{Q_i} are exogenous and Eq. (26.10) can be estimated directly. Alternatively, the region could be highly developed with no more sites available. In this case, the Q_i are exogenous and an inverse demand function can be estimated. In general, the demand and supply functions for any characteristic such as air quality have to be estimated simultaneously.

Assuming that a demand function such as Eq. (26.10) can be estimated, it can then be used to measure the value that people place on either marginal or discrete improvements in air quality. For example, the shaded area in Fig. 26.8 is the Marshallian consumer surplus measure of the value household i places on an improvement in air quality from Q_1 to Q_2. The more appropriate Hicksian surplus measures can be derived from the estimated demand curve. The researcher might also choose to estimate these surplus measures at the mean values of Y and $\vec{Z}$.

The question remains whether the hedonic price technique can give a reasonably accurate estimate of how much people value cleaner air. In principle, economists might prefer the technique to surveys that ask people how much they would be willing to pay for some particular improvement in air quality, because people actually purchase the house. But the hedonic price technique has a number of practical problems. Foremost among them is the assumption that households are in equilibrium with respect to every characteristic of their house, including air quality. This assumption might be satisfactory for something such as an automobile with its various options that can be bundled independently, but it is unlikely to hold for houses.

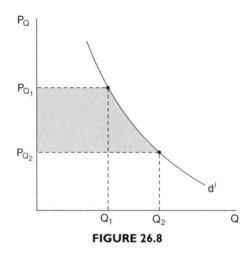

FIGURE 26.8

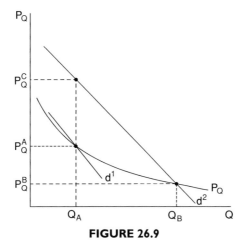

FIGURE 26.9

Suppose, for example, that a high-income household wants both clean air and close proximity to the central city with all its cultural amenities. If the central city is highly polluted, then the household cannot have both. Suppose it chooses the cultural amenities. Refer to Fig. 26.9. The household will be assigned the combination (Q_A, P_Q^A) for the demand estimation, as if it were on demand curve d^1. But its true demand curve is d^2. If the household could be in equilibrium with respect to air quality, it would choose Q_B and have a low marginal valuation of cleaner air, P_Q^B. Instead, it is forced to choose Q_A, at which its marginal valuation of cleaner air is P_Q^C, far above P_Q^A. It is unclear how much bias is introduced into the estimation by households being out of equilibrium with respect to air quality and other characteristics, as many surely are.

Finally, even if the estimated valuations for cleaner air were accurate they might not be of much use to the policymaker. Knowledge of the marginal benefits of reducing air pollutants still suffers from huge gaps in scientific understanding. The value people place on cleaner air might change considerably if they had better information on the hazards of different pollutants.

Surveys or Contingent Valuation

Economists resort to surveys to obtain values of nonmarketed benefits when indirect market techniques cannot be applied. The principal examples include the nonuse or existence values people place on preserving wilderness areas even if they never intend to visit them, or on preserving plant and animal species in the name of biodiversity. The cost of global warming is another possible application. The survey method is referred to as *contingent valuation* because the respondents' answers are contingent on the simulated environment presented in the survey.

Contingent valuation is highly controversial among economists, as one might expect. Some believe that it gives reliable measures of people's willingness to pay for nonmarketed benefits; others do not. The debate over contingent valuation heated up after the Exxon *Valdez* oil spill in 1989. Following the incident, Congress directed the National Oceanic and Atmospheric Administration (NOAA), a division of the Department of Commerce, to establish regulations for assessing the damages of such events. A particular concern was the reliability of contingent valuation for eliciting people's willingness to pay for nonuse or existence values, and the NOAA commissioned a panel of experts headed by Nobel laureates Kenneth Arrow and Robert Solow to address this issue. The panel concluded that contingent valuation was reliable providing that the surveys followed a large number of guidelines. One of the panel members, Paul Portney, listed the following seven guidelines as being especially important:

1. The surveyors must conduct personal interviews as opposed to telephone interviews or mailed questionnaires.

2. The surveyors should elicit the respondents' willingness to pay to prevent future incidents rather than events that have already occurred.

3. The survey should be in referendum format—that is, ask how the respondent would vote for a specific environmental benefit that would lead either to higher prices or higher taxes. This is a closed-ended evaluation rather than an open-ended evaluation in which people are asked how much they would be willing to pay for some environmental benefit. Closed-ended referendum questions were felt to reflect more accurately the types of decisions that people actually have to make.

4. The expected effects of an incident or program have to be clearly stated.

5. Respondents have to understand that a willingness to pay for something would reduce their disposable income.

6. Respondents should be made aware of substitutes for the object of the survey, such as wilderness sites other than the one they are being asked to evaluate.

7. Respondents should be given follow-up questions to be sure they understood what they were being asked to evaluate and to determine why they answered as they did.

Many economists disagree with the NOAA's panel of experts. They believe that surveys would not give accurate assessments of nonuse or existence values even if all the panel's guidelines were followed. MIT's Peter Diamond and Jerry Hausman are among the staunchest opponents of contingent valuation for assessing damages to wilderness areas. They argue that the surveys are not measuring what they claim to be measuring, primarily because people do not have well-formed preferences over existence values. They suspect that the surveys are picking up a generalized "warm glow" feeling that people should be in favor of protecting the environment rather than providing an accurate assessment of their willingness to pay to preserve a particular wilderness area. As evidence, they note that contingent valuations consistently fail the following subadditivity test which well-formed preferences ought to satisfy: The amount that people are willing to pay to preserve two wilderness areas should exceed the sum of the amounts they would be willing to pay to preserve each one individually, since the loss of two areas would leave fewer wilderness areas remaining. This test is almost never satisfied by existing studies. Their criticism is difficult to evaluate, however, since few if any of the existing studies meet the NOAA guidelines for validity. Even the proponents of contingent valuation admit that most of the existing surveys suffer from serious design flaws. In any event, the government does use contingent valuation to help assess the nonuse or existence value of wilderness areas.[20]

The econometric issues surrounding referendum-style surveys will be discussed in Chapter 31, where we consider how survey responses are used to estimate the demand for local public services. This is another area in which public sector economists have made frequent use of surveys.

Second-Best Analysis

So far we have been considering nonmarketed benefits under the first-best assumptions. Suppose, instead, that the policy environment is inherently second best, such as when services are given away even though their marginal costs are positive. This further complicates the valuation of the benefits because, as in all second-best analysis, valuation depends upon the complete specification of the second-best environment, and there are endless possibilities.

Fortunately, nonmarketed benefits are easily incorporated into the standard second-best models of government production that have been featured in this text. To illustrate this, let us return to the second-best model of Chapter 22 in which the government produces goods and services that may also be produced in the private sector and covers the resulting deficit with per-unit "commodity" taxes on the (one) consumer's goods demanded and factors supplied. It was also assumed that the government buys and sells all inputs and

---

[20] The Fall 1994 issue of the *Journal of Economic Perspectives* has three good articles on contingent valuation: P. Portney, "The Contingent Valuation Debate: Why Economists Should Care," is an excellent overview of the topic. The information on the guidelines recommended by the NOAA's panel of experts comes from here. Portney was a member of the panel. W. Hanemann, "Valuing the Environment Through Contingent Valuation," offers a defense of contingent valuation for measuring nonuse or existence values. P. Diamond and J. Hausman, "Contingent Valuation: Is Some Number Better than No Number?," presents the authors' critique of contingent valuation. Each article has extensive references to the literature on contingent valuation and the major surveys that have been undertaken.

outputs at the producer prices $\vec{p} = (p_1, \ldots, p_N)$. Recall that the measure of loss which the government sought to minimize was given by:

$$L\left(\vec{t}; \vec{Z}\right) = M\left(\vec{q}; \overline{U}\right) - \text{government surplus} - \pi(\vec{p}) \qquad (26.11)$$

where:

$\vec{t} = (t_2, \ldots, t_N)$, the vector of commodity taxes.
$\vec{Z} = (Z_i, \ldots, Z_N)$, the vector of government inputs and outputs.
$\vec{q} = \vec{p} + \vec{t} =$ the vector of consumer prices, with $q_1 \equiv p_1 \equiv 1, t_1 = 0$.
$\overline{U} =$ the utility level when $\vec{Z} = \vec{t} = \vec{0}$.
$\pi(\vec{p})$ the general equilibrium profit function.

and

$$\text{Government surplus} = \sum_{i=2}^{N} t_i M_i + \sum_{i=2}^{N} P_i Z_i - p_1 g(Z_2, \ldots, Z_N)$$

where:

$M_i =$ the compensated demand (supply) for good (factor) i.
$Z_1 = -g(Z_2, \ldots, Z_N)$ is the government's production function.

Since loss $= -$ benefits, the benefits from taxation and government production are simply:

$$B(t; Z) = \pi(\vec{p}) - M\left(\vec{q}; \overline{U}\right) + \text{government surplus} \qquad (26.12)$$

If the government's budget constraint balances at level zero, then:

$$B(t; Z) = \pi(\vec{p}) - M\left(\vec{q}; \overline{U}\right) \qquad (26.13)$$

which is just the HCV or HEV version of benefits with general private production technology, depending on which prices and utility levels are used to evaluate $M( )$.

The basic structure of this model can be maintained when some government outputs are given away (or resources drafted) under the following assumptions.[21] Suppose a subset $i = k + 1, \ldots, N$ of the Z_i is either given away or drafted. The remaining $i = 1, \ldots, k$, are bought and sold at the producer prices $(p_1, \ldots, p_k)$. To keep the analysis as general as possible, assume further that the goods (factors) given away (drafted) are routinely produced (purchased) in the private sector so that producer and consumer prices have been established for these goods (factors), and that the tax base to which the $\vec{t}$ apply is consumption (supply) less goods (factors) received free of charge (drafted) by the government. Write $\vec{Z} = [Z_1, \ldots, Z_k; \vec{0}]$ to represent the goods and factors bought and sold by the government, and $\vec{X} = [\vec{0}; X_{k+1}, \ldots, X_N]$ to represent the subset of goods (factors) given away

---

[21] The adaptation presented here appears in a set of unpublished class notes distributed by Peter Diamond.

(drafted) by the government. With this notation and the preceding assumptions, the government's budget surplus at the compensated equilibrium becomes:

$$S = \sum_{i=2}^{N} t_i(M_i - X_i) + \sum_{i=2}^{k} p_i Z_i - p_1 g\left(\vec{Z}; \vec{X}\right) \qquad (26.14)$$

where:

$Z_1 = -g(\vec{Z}; \vec{X})$, the government's production function incorporating both sold outputs (purchased inputs) and outputs (inputs) given away (drafted). Notice that the tax revenue has to be sufficient to cover the deficit on government goods and factors bought and sold and still produce the desired surplus. Goods (factors) given away (drafted) do not directly reduce (increase) the government's surplus (deficit) from production.

The total benefits, considering taxation, government production of bought and sold inputs and outputs, and goods (factors) given away (drafted) by the government are, therefore:

$$B\left(\vec{t}; \vec{Z}; \vec{X}\right) = \pi(\vec{p}) - \left[M(\vec{q}; \overline{U}) - \sum_{i=k+1}^{N} q_i X_i^{comp}\right] + S \qquad (26.15)$$

There are two differences in the benefits measure when goods are given away. First, the form of the government surplus equation changes. Second, the lump-sum income required to keep the consumer indifferent to the initial pregovernment situation is less than the value of the expenditure function by an amount equal to the value of the goods (factors) received from ("donated" to) the government free of charge, valued at the consumer prices $\vec{q}$ established in the private production and sale of these goods at the compensated equilibrium. Because the consumer simply receives (offers) these goods (factors) from (to) the government in amounts dictated by the government, the vector $\vec{X}$ is a lump-sum event from the consumer's point of view. Thus, it is appropriate to subtract its value in B, all the elements of which are in the form of lump-sum income.

The relatively minor adjustments in the benefits measure from the original model of government production with commodity taxation depend upon being able to retain the basic structure of that model. The modified model with free goods (factors) is fairly general and allows for second-best taxation, but it does contain some fairly restrictive assumptions that might not be applicable in real-life applications. It implicitly assumes optimal private and government production decisions so there is no distinction between short-run and long-run costs at the optimum. Thus, the model is inherently long run. It also requires private purchase (sale) of all goods (factors) which the government provides (drafts) free of charge in order to evaluate these goods. Finally, the one-consumer equivalent assumption prevents an analysis of the effect of rationing the X_i among different consumers. Removing any one of these assumptions would require significant modifications in the government production-tax model of Chapter 22. Nonetheless, the model as it stands remains a fairly general description of government policy in a second-best environment. It would appear to be applicable to government hydroelectric projects in which some of the benefits are sold (electricity) while others (recreational facilities) are given away even though they are routinely marketed in other contexts.

We leave it to the reader to derive and interpret the first-order conditions for this model. The normative policy rules yield a number of interesting conclusions. The existence of goods (factors) given away (drafted) does not change either the optimal tax rules or the result that with optimal taxation (and CRS in private production) the government should discount all *marketed* inputs and outputs at their marginal rate of transformation (the producer price). A different discount rate does apply to all *free* goods and *drafted* factors, however.

THE USE OF SHADOW PRICES FOR GOVERNMENT PROJECTS

The preceding sections discussed three problems commonly associated with government projects—intangibles, lumpiness, and nonmarketed benefits (costs)—that are unlikely to arise in private sector analysis. These problems need not always occur, however. In many instances government projects might be virtually identical to their private sector counterparts in the sense that they represent marginal additions to capacity and all inputs and outputs are bought and sold at competitive private sector prices.[22] Even when this occurs, however, there are still substantial differences between the evaluations of private and public sector costs and benefits, as a general rule.

As noted above, competitive producer prices are the proper values to attach to each unit of private inputs or outputs under these conditions, from society's point of view. $p\Delta X$ is an appropriate gross benefit measure for a private project in either a first- or second-best environment.

In contrast, Eq. (22.46), reproduced here as Eq. (26.16) (with a negative sign, since $B = -dL$),

$$dB = -t'(M_{ij})E^{-1}\pi_{ij}dt + \left(-p_1gz + p' + t'M_{ij}E^{-1}\right)dZ \qquad (26.16)$$

gives the proper *shadow prices* for government inputs and outputs in the one-consumer-equivalent, second-best economy of Chapter 22. The assumptions about government producers that underly Eq. (26.16) are the same as for private producers: The government buys and sells at competitive private

---

[22] One may wonder why the government is involved in the production of these services, but this is beside the point for cost–benefit analysis.

sector producer prices, and changes in government production are infinitesimal. Nonetheless, Eq. (26.16) indicates that the government should not use the competitive producer prices for project evaluation, in general, even though these prices are appropriate for evaluating "small" changes in private sector inputs and outputs. Rather, the government should use the shadow prices $p' + t'M_{ij}E^{-1}$.

These differences in public and private sector evaluation for similar kinds of production processes result from the underlying assumptions of the model in Chapter 22. Recall that the derivation of Eqs. (22.46) and (26.16) *assumed* that private sector production is first-best efficient, using competitive producer prices for its decisions, and satisfying pareto-optimal rules of the form:

$$-\frac{dY_j}{dY_k} = \frac{f_k}{f_j} = \frac{p_k}{p_j} \qquad \text{all } j, k = 1, \ldots, N \qquad (26.17)$$

where:

$\vec{Y} = (Y_1, \ldots, Y_N) = $ the vector of private sector inputs and outputs.
$f(\vec{Y}) = 0 = $ the aggregate production possibilities for the private sector.
$\vec{p} = (p_1, \ldots, p_N)$ the vector of competitively determined producer prices.

Given this assumed private sector behavior, if the government introduces distortions by means of per-unit taxes, it should also evaluate its own production decisions in accordance with Eq. (26.16). The cost coefficients on the $\vec{Z}$ equal $\vec{p}$ only for special cases, such as if the underlying environment is first best, the tax rates are optimal, or private sector production technology is linear.

Equation (26.16) applies to a specific second-best model; other models would generate different vectors of shadow prices. Nonetheless, the same general principle applies whatever the model: If the private sector is first-best efficient, changes in government production must be evaluated at shadow prices different from competitive producer prices, in general, given government induced second-best distortions. If the private sector is itself second best, then it would generally follow that the private sector also would not use the competitive prices $\vec{p}$ to evaluate the benefits and costs of its own projects. One would then expect the government shadow prices to differ from those in Eq. (26.16).[23]

These comments underscore the point that, when a cost–benefit analysis employs second-best assumptions, it must carefully specify all elements of the

---

[23] A case in point is the comprehensive analysis of shadow prices in Jean Dreze and Nicholas Stern's chapter on cost–benefit analysis in the *Handbook in Public Economics*. Their model is more comprehensive than the model in Chapter 22, including such features as private market distortions and rationed goods. Consequently, their equations for shadow prices differ from Eq. (26.16). See J. Dreze and N. Stern, "The Theory of Cost–Benefit Analysis," in A. Auerbach, and M. Feldstein, Eds., *Handbook of Public Economics*, Vol. II, Elsevier/North-Holland, Amsterdam, chap. 14.

underlying policy environment assumed to be second best. Neither normative decision rules nor cost–benefit evaluations generalize across second-best environments.

REFERENCES

Broome, J., "Trying To Value a Life," *Journal of Public Economics*, February 1978.

Broome, J., "Trying To Value a Life: A Reply," *Journal of Public Economics*, October 1979.

Buchanan, J., and Faith R., "Trying Again To Value a Life," *Journal of Public Economics*, October 1979.

Cropper, M., and Oates, W., "Environmental Economics: A Survey," *Journal of Economic Literature*, June 1992

Diamond, P., and Hausman, J., "Contingent Valuation: Is Some Number Better than No Number?," *Journal of Economic Perspectives*, Fall 1994.

Diamond, P., and McFadden, D., "Some Uses of the Expenditure Function in Public Finance," *Journal of Public Economics*, February 1974.

Dixit, A., "Welfare Effects of Tax and Price Changes," *Journal of Public Economics*, February 1975.

Dixit, A., and Munk, K., "Welfare Effects of Tax and Price Changes: A Correction," *Journal of Public Economics*, August 1977.

Dreze, J., and Stern, N., "The Theory of Cost–Benefit Analysis," in A. Auerbach and M. Feldstein, Eds., *Handbook of Public Economics*, Vol. II, Elsevier/North-Holland, Amsterdam, 1987, chap. 14.

Hammond, P., "Theoretical Progess in Public Economics: A Provocative Assessment," *Oxford Economic Papers*, January 1990.

Hanemann, W., "Valuing the Environment Through Contingent Valuation," *Journal of Economic Perspectives*, Fall 1994.

Harberger, A., "Taxation, Resource Allocation, and Welfare," in *The Role of Direct and Indirect Taxes in the Federal Revenue System*, National Bureau of Economic Research and The Brookings Institution, Princeton University Press, Princeton, NJ, 1964.

Harberger, A., "The Measurement of Waste," *American Economic Association Papers and Proceedings*, May 1964.

Harberger, A., "Three Basic Postulates for Applied Welfare Economics," *Journal of Economic Literature*, September 1971.

Harberger, A., *Taxation and Welfare*, Little, Brown & Co., Boston, MA, 1974.

Harberger, A., "On the Use of Distributional Weights in Social Cost–Benefit Analysis," *Journal of Political Economy*, April 1978, part 2.

Jones-Lee, M., "Trying To Value a Life: Why Broome Does Not Sweep Clean," *Journal of Public Economics*, October 1979.

Kneese, A., "Research Goals and Progress Toward Them," in H. Jarret, Ed., *Environmental Quality in a Growing Economy*, Johns Hopkins Press, Washington, D.C., 1966.

Lancaster, K., *Consumer Demand: A New Approach*, Columbia University Press, New York, 1971.

Layard, R., Ed., *Cost–Benefit Analysis*, Penguin Education, Penguin Books, Ltd., Harmondsworth, Middlesex, England, 1972.

Layard, R., and Glaister S., Eds., *Cost–Benefit Analysis*, second ed., Cambridge University Press, New York, 1994.

McKenzie, G., "Measuring Gains and Losses," *Journal of Political Economy*, June 1976.

McKenzie, G., and Pearce, I., "Exact Measures of Welfare and the Cost of Living," *Review of Economic Studies*, October 1976.

Mishan, E. J., "Evaluation of Life and Limb: A Theoretical Approach," *Journal of Political Economy*, March/April 1971.

Mishan, E. J., *Cost–Benefit Analysis*, Praeger Publishers, New York, 1976.

Moses, W., "Some Uses of the Expenditure Function in Public Finance: A Comment," *Journal of Public Economics*, April–May, 1976.

Oiesen, J., "A Theoretical Justification of Cost–Benefit Analysis," *Staff Study: Report No. 55-213-U9-5*, U.S. Department of Transportation, Transportation Systems Center, Kendell Square, Cambridge, MA, (draft).

Patinkin, D., "Demand Curves and Consumer's Surplus," in C. Christ *et al.*, Eds., *Measurement in Economics*, Stanford University Press, Stanford, CA, 1963.

Peck, M., and Scherer, F., *The Weapons Acquisition Process: An Economic Analysis*, Division of Research, Graduate School of Business Administration, Harvard University, Boston, MA, 1962.

Portney, P., "The Contingent Valuation Debate: Why Economists Should Care," *Journal of Economic Perspectives*, Fall 1994.

Richter, D., "Games Pythagoreans Play," *Public Finance Quarterly*, October 1977.

Rosen, S., "Hedonic Prices and Implicit Markets," *Journal of Political Economy*, January/February 1974.

Samuelson, P., "Constancy of the Marginal Utility of Income," in O. Lange *et al.*, Eds., *Studies in Mathematical Economics and Econometrics: In Honor of Henry Schultz*, Books for Libraries Press, Plainview, NY, 1968.

Samuelson, P., *Foundations of Economic Analysis*, Atheneum, New York, 1965.

Samuelson, P., "Social Indifference Curves," *Quarterly Journal of Economics*, February 1956.

Seade, J., "Consumer's Surplus and Linearity of Engel's Curves," *Economic Journal*, September 1978.

Tipping, D., "Time Savings in Transport Studies," *Economic Journal*, December 1968.

Williams, A., "A Note on 'Trying to Value a Life,'" *Journal of Public Economics*, October 1979.

Willig, R., "Consumer's Surplus without Apology," *American Economic Review*, September 1976.

27

COST–BENEFIT ANALYSIS AND THE DISTRIBUTION OF INCOME

JUSTIFICATIONS FOR IGNORING
    DISTRIBUTIONAL CONSIDERATIONS
JUSTIFICATIONS FOR INCLUDING
    DISTRIBUTIONAL CONSIDERATIONS
INCORPORATING DISTRIBUTIONAL PARAMETERS
    *Nonoptimal Income Distribution and Shadow Prices: The
        Boadway Framework*
    The Weisbrod Framework
CONCLUSION

Anyone undertaking a cost–benefit study faces a difficult question at the outset: Should cost–benefit analysis rank government projects strictly on the basis of their aggregate present value, or should the analysis consider the distribution of the project's benefits and costs as well? Normative theory argues strongly for the latter interpretation if the income distribution is nonoptimal. Ideally, cost–benefit analysis should rank projects according to their contributions to *social welfare*, and it can only do this if it includes the distributional consequences of the various projects.

Ignoring distributional considerations is vastly simpler, but it limits cost–benefit analysis to an exercise in efficiency. This may not be such a bad strategy. One long standing view of cost–benefit analysis holds that it is only meant to rank projects on the basis of their relative efficiency—that is, their aggregate present values. The feeling was that knowing the relative efficiency rankings of the proposed projects is useful information to the policymaker. But if society is not willing to choose projects on this basis alone, then cost–benefit analysis becomes only an intermediate step in the overall process of project selection. It leaves as an open question, from a social welfare perspective, the relative importance of the included efficiency information and the excluded distributional information.

Suppose, though, that the analyst decides to follow the recommendation of modern normative theory and consider the distribution of project costs and benefits. The difficult question then arises as to how this might be done in a consistent and practical manner. The normative analysis in Part III indicated time and again how distributional considerations complicate normative policy prescriptions relative to the one-consumer-equivalent case. This was true whatever the context—optimal commodity tax rules, optimal government responses to externalities, government production decision rules, and so forth. Furthermore, the normative policy rules became somewhat arbitrary and subjective, since the social welfare weights representing the distributional component were simply assumed to reflect the distributional preferences of society. Normative theory does not tell us how such preferences are actually determined or what they should be. Not surprisingly, cost–benefit analysis suffers an identical fate as an evaluative tool. Once distributional parameters are introduced into the evaluation, the present value calculations threaten to become so complex and so highly subjective that the analysis may well lose its ability to discriminate objectively among various investment alternatives.

So the distribution question poses a dilemma: Include distributional considerations and risk overwhelming complexity and subjectivity, or ignore distributional considerations in the name of practicality and capture only a part of each project's contribution to social welfare? As with all true dilemmas, there is no satisfactory resolution. All any analyst can do is decide in advance whether or not to include distributional considerations and attempt to justify the decision. Reasonable arguments can be offered in support of either choice

JUSTIFICATIONS FOR IGNORING DISTRIBUTIONAL CONSIDERATIONS

Four arguments might be used to justify ignoring distributional considerations, beyond the point that it greatly simplifies the analysis. One argument is in a negative vein and three are in a positive vein.

The negative argument is the one alluded to above, that incorporating distributional judgments into the analysis is so subjective that no useful information can possibly result.[1] This argument alone would suffice for ignoring distributional considerations, but then the question arises whether aggregate present value calculation is an appropriate criterion for project selection. Three reasonable arguments can be made that it is.

---

[1] Arnold Harberger argues for ignoring distributional considerations as one of his postulates for applied research in A. Harberger, "Three Postulates for Applied Welfare Economics," *Journal of Economic Literature*, September 1971. As noted in Chapter 26, he backed off somewhat from this position in 1978 (see p. 787, n. 12).

One could simply adopt the idealistic stance that the government should always be striving to reach Bator's first-best bliss point regardless of society's current position. Recall that the bliss point is represented by point B in Fig. 27.1, in which $U^2 — U^1$ is the first-best utility-possibilities frontier for persons 1 and 2, constrained only by the economy's underlying production technology and market clearance, and $W_0, W_1, \ldots$, are the social welfare indifference curves embodying society's distributional preferences. According to the social welfare rankings, B is distributionally the best of all efficient points on the utility-possibilities frontier.

Recall that attaining point B requires three conditions:

1. All markets are perfectly competitive, with perfect information.
2. Government policies may take any form required to satisfy the first-best pareto-optimal conditions.
3. The government can tax and transfer lump sum to satisfy the inter-personal equity conditions of the form $\dfrac{\partial W}{\partial U^h}\dfrac{\partial U^h}{\partial X_{hi}}$, all $h = 1, \ldots, H$, where $W = W[U^1(\ ), \ldots, U^H(\ )]$ is the Bergson–Samuelson individualistic social welfare function and X_i is any one of the goods or factors.

To promote the quest for the bliss point, therefore, the government must select all projects, and only those projects, with positive aggregate present value. This is just efficiency condition 2 applied to government investments. Accepting projects with aggregate present value less than zero because of their distributional consequences necessarily places society below the utility-possibilities frontier and thereby precludes attainment of the bliss point. As

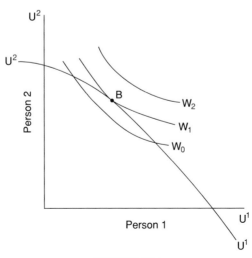

FIGURE 27.1

part of the quest, then, one must have faith that the government will tax and transfer to correct for unwanted distributional consequences arising from any given project. According to this view, cost–benefit analysis has a specific role, to ensure that the income or product to be distributed is as large as possible. Cost–benefit analysis must *not* be concerned with distributional implications.

A second possible justification is to argue that, for all practical purposes, the economy is equivalent to a one-consumer economy. This requires either that (1) all consumers have identical and homothetic preferences, or (2) the government is continuously redistributing income lump sum to satisfy the first-best interpersonal equity conditions so that social marginal utilities of income are identical for all people.[2] The second alternative would appear to be the most reasonable of these two conditions, if only because it relies partially on value judgments. Econometric evidence overwhelming rejects the first condition.

One is certainly free to argue that the underlying distribution of income is "about right" and that government redistributional policies tend to correct distributional imbalances if they happen to occur. Given this belief, the distributional implications of any one project are obviously irrelevant, and aggregate present value is the appropriate criterion. In effect, this position argues that failure to attain the first-best bliss point is solely a matter of existing inefficiencies, which choosing projects on the basis of their aggregate present value criterion can help to overcome.

A final possible justification for the aggregate present value criterion is an unabashed appeal to pragmatism. Even if one believes that the underlying distribution of income is nonoptimal and that there is virtually no hope of reaching the first-best bliss point, one could still argue that the distributional implications of any one government project are likely to be small relative to the distributional impact of the government's general tax and transfer policies. Policies such as indexing social security benefits to the cost of living, or removing some major "loopholes" from the federal personal income tax, no doubt have distributional impacts far beyond those of any ten government projects. Consequently, government projects *should* be chosen solely on the basis of relative efficiency by the aggregate present value criterion. It would be especially foolish to cloud the objective efficiency information that cost–benefit analysis can provide with subjective distributional judgments, given that the distributional implications of any one project are inconsequential for all intents and purposes.

---

[2] H. A. John Green developed another condition for one-consumer equivalence, that the covariance of the social marginal utility of income with the ratio X_{hk}/X_k is the same for all k. This condition is implausible, however. See J. Green, "Two Models of Optimal Taxation and Pricing," *Oxford Economic Papers*, November 1975.

JUSTIFICATIONS FOR INCLUDING DISTRIBUTIONAL CONSIDERATIONS

Each of the preceding positive arguments is fairly easy to counter. The first two are simply matters of personal taste and interpretation, on which there is bound to be disagreement. The first argument is suspect given that a substantial portion of all U.S. GDP is marketed under conditions far from the perfectly competitive ideal. Also, the major taxes and transfers are clearly not lump sum—they cannot be in a world of private information. Thus, it is equally reasonable to argue that the quest for the first-best bliss point is hopelessly idealistic and should not guide economic policy decisions. According to this view, policymaking is always a second-best undertaking. Regarding the second argument, many people believe that the distribution of income is far from optimal in the United States and is moving away from the optimum. The gap between the rich and the poor increased steadily from the late 1970s to the mid-1990s, and the distribution of wealth remains highly unequal. The income gap widened despite very large social insurance and public assistance programs, both cash and in-kind, and a progressive federal personal income tax.

Once it is conceded that the policy environment is second best, the third argument about the "smallness" of any one project's distributional implications is simply a red herring from a strictly theoretical point of view. After all, the efficiency gains from any one project are also "small." According to second-best public expenditure theory, society should take gains in social welfare where it can, and these gains include both efficiency and equity considerations. Hence, the proper decision rule for cost–benefit analysis involves ranking projects by their contribution to social welfare, not just to efficiency. The situation depicted in Fig. 27.2 is the relevant one for cost–benefit analysis.

Suppose B, the first-best bliss point, is unattainable. Suppose further that society is currently at point A and that the government can invest in only one of two projects, C or D, because of a (second-best) legislated budget constraint. C is presumably the more efficient project, the one with highest *aggregate* present value, because it brings society to its pareto-optimal utility-possibilities frontier. But according to the social welfare rankings, $W_0, \ldots, W_3$, which incorporate both efficiency and equity criteria, the government should choose project D. In effect, the superior equity implications of D are sufficient to override the smaller aggregate present value of D. C would be preferred only if the government could simultaneously tax and transfer lump sum to move society along the frontier to a point northeast of D. If such distributions are impossible, however, D is the preferred alternative. In short, just knowing the aggregate present value rankings of projects may not be so useful after all.

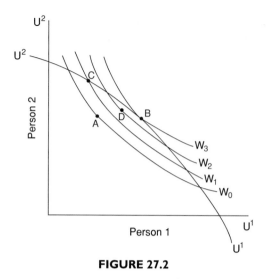

FIGURE 27.2

From a strictly theoretical point of view, then, if the policy environment is second best in part because the distribution of income is nonoptimal, and will remain so, then distributional considerations ought to enter cost–benefit analyses of government projects in a consistent manner. Unfortunately, normative theory offers precious few guidelines for consistent distributional evaluation that are practicable.

INCORPORATING DISTRIBUTIONAL PARAMETERS

The literature on cost–benefit analysis suggests a number of different ways of incorporating distributional considerations into cost–benefit calculations. The one that has been generally accepted by economists as theoretically appropriate was first formalized by Robin Boadway. We shall refer it as the new neoclassical position. It argues that the government should compute shadow prices for public sector inputs and outputs that incorporate the distributional preferences contained in society's social welfare function.

Boadway's shadow-price approach supplanted a number of older approaches that still have practical appeal. The best known of the older approaches, and the one most commonly used, says that individually perceived gains and losses should be weighted by each consumer's social marginal utility of income as given by society's social welfare function. This approach is most closely associated with Burton Weisbrod,[3] and we shall refer to it as

---

[3] B. Weisbrod, "Income Redistribution Effects and Benefit–Cost Analysis," in S. B. Chase, Jr., Ed., *Problems in Public Expenditure Analysis*, The Brookings Institution, Washington, D.C., 1968.

the standard neoclassical position. We will begin with a brief review of the Boadway approach.

Nonoptimal Income Distribution and Shadow Prices: The Boadway Framework[4]

The new neoclassical approach to nonoptimal income distribution accepts the idea that the goal of cost–benefit analysis is social welfare maximization. Rather than adjust individually perceived gains and losses for distributional considerations, however, it adjusts the second-best optimal shadow prices on government inputs and outputs. Hence, the required adjustment depends directly upon the ˜ature of the underlying second-best environment.

In Chapter 2ₓ, we derived the one-person and many-person shadow prices for a general model of government production with distorting taxation, government purchases and sales at private sector producer prices, and a government budget constraint. The relevant equations, Eqs. (22.46) and (22.88), are reproduced here as Eqs. (27.1) and (27.2) (with $dB = -dL$):

$$dB = -t'(M_{ij})E^{-1}\pi_{ij}dt + (-p_1gz + p' + t'M_{ij}E^{-1})dZ \qquad (27.1)$$

(one-consumer-equivalent economy)

$$
\begin{aligned}
dB = - &\left[[(1-R)'{\cdot}X] + t'M_{ij}\right]E^{-1}\pi_{ij}dt \\
&+ \left[-p_1gz + p' + [(1-R)'{\cdot}X]E^{-1} + t'M_{ij}E^{-1}\right]dZ
\end{aligned} \qquad (27.2)
$$

(many person economy with nonoptimal distribution)

where R is a matrix of Martin Feldstein's distributional coefficients for each good, with $R_i = \sum_{h=1}^{H}\beta^h\dfrac{X_{hi}}{X_i}$, $i = 1, \ldots, N$ and $\beta^h = \dfrac{\partial W}{\partial U^h}\dfrac{\partial U^h}{\partial Y_h}$, the social marginal utility of income for person h. E is a matrix of the compensated demand and general equilibrium supply derivatives, M_{ij} and Π_{ij}.

Recall that the optimal shadow prices are the terms following p_1g_z in the coefficients on the dZ, the vector of public sector inputs and outputs, with $p_1 \equiv 1$, the numeraire. Inspection of Eqs. (27.1) and (27.2) reveals that the many-person rules can be thought as a linear combination of an efficiency term, $p' + t'M_{ij}E^{-1}$ from Eq. (27.1) and an equity term $[(1-R)' \cdot X]E^{-1}$ from Eq. (27.2).[5] Recall also that if $\beta^h = \beta$, all $h = 1, \ldots, H$ (i.e., the distribution is optimal), then $R = 1$ and the many-person shadow prices are identical to the shadow prices for a one-consumer economy.

[4] R. Boadway, "Integrating Equity and Efficiency in Applied Welfare Economics," *Quarterly Journal of Economics*, November 1976.
[5] This is only approximately true if there are income effects, since the M_{ij} in (27.1) are compensated demand (factor supply) derivatives whereas the M_{ij} in (27.2) are the ordinary derivatives.

Equation (27.2) applied as a rule for project selection views the investment process as a straight production decision. Once the shadow prices are known, the government should simply try to maximize "pseudo" profits using these prices, subject to the government's production function. This yields the usual production rules: Inputs and outputs should be varied until $\theta_j dZ_j = \theta_i dZ_i$, all $i, j = 1, \ldots, N$, where θ_j and θ_i are the optimal shadow prices.

Applying Eq. (27.2) in practice is obviously fraught with a number of severe difficulties. Society must somehow determine the distributionally relevant subdivision of the population and the appropriate direct social marginal utilities of income for each relevant subgroup. Policy analysts also need to compute each subgroup's consumption and factor supply responses. That is, they would need to know the joint distribution of the social marginal utilities of income and demands (factor supplies) for the subgroups, along with a huge number of supply and demand elasticities for goods, services, and factors. The amount of data required is forbidding and unlikely to be known with much confidence. That said, economists would agree that the optimal shadow price approach is the proper guideline for incorporating distributional consideration from a theoretical standpoint.

The Weisbrod Framework

The standard neoclassical approach proposed by Weisbrod is in the spirit of first-best analysis. It views the distribution problem as computing a weighted average of individuals gains and losses resulting from government projects without reference to specific second-best constraints, other than that the distribution is nonoptimal.[6] It is entirely centered on the Bergson–Samuelson individualistic social welfare function.

Write the social welfare function as:

$$W = W(U^1, \ldots, U^H) = W(U^h) \tag{27.3}$$

Totally differentiating W( ) yields:

$$dW = \sum_{h=1}^{H} \frac{\partial W}{\partial U^h} dU^h \tag{27.4}$$

where $\dfrac{\partial W}{\partial U^h}$ is the marginal social welfare weight for person h. Thus, according to the standard view, the change in social welfare from a government project is a linear combination of the individuals' gains and losses, where the weights are the individual marginal social welfare weights based on the social welfare ranking W. Projects should be ranked according to dW in the usual manner: All projects having $dW > 0$ are acceptable because they increase

---

[6] Thus, the Weisbrod framework can be thought of as a restricted version of the more fully articulated Boadway framework.

social welfare. If there is a binding government budget constraint, the government should choose the affordable combination of projects yielding the highest dW. This guarantees the greatest increase in social welfare from any given set of projects.

The evaluation of the individual gains and losses, the dU^h, depends on whether the government project generates marginal or lumpy discrete changes in prices.

Marginal Changes

If the changes are marginal, the analysis typically proceeds by substituting the indirect utility functions $V^h(\vec{p}; \vec{z}; m^h)$ for the direct utility functions in W, where:

$\vec{p}$ = the vector of prices for the private goods and factors
$\vec{z}$ = the vector of publicly provided goods and services
m^h = the lump-sum income of person h

Assuming that the individuals are price takers in the private markets and that the $\vec{z}$ are exogenously determined by the government, the change in individual utility to a first order of approximation is (in vector notation):

$$dV^h = -\lambda^h x^h dp + \lambda^h q^h dz + \lambda^h dm^h \qquad (27.5)$$

where:

$\lambda^h = \dfrac{\partial V^h}{\partial m^h}$ is the private marginal utility of income for person h

q^h = the demand prices of person h for the fixed public goods. An example would be the Lindahl prices for a Samuelsonian nonexclusive good, equal to the MRS^h between the good and the numeraire private good.

The first term on the right-hand side (RHS) of Eq. (27.5) follows from Roy's Identity. The second term follows from Eqs. (16.12) and (16.14) in our analysis of nonexclusive public goods which imply that:

$$\frac{\partial V^h}{\partial z} = \frac{\partial V^h}{\partial m^h} MRS^h_{Z,\,numeraire} = \lambda^h q^h \qquad (27.6)$$

Therefore,

$$dW = \sum_{h=1}^{H} \frac{\partial W}{\partial U^h} dV^h \qquad (27.7)$$

or, from Eq. (27.5):

$$dW = \sum_{h=1}^{H} \beta^h \left(-xdp + q^h dz + dm^h \right) \qquad (27.8)$$

The researcher can estimate all the terms in the parentheses on the RHS of Eq. (27.8), at least in principle. It may be that only a few prices and z's will change.

Discrete Changes

Projects that generate discrete changes in prices and the z's require substituting an appropriate willingness-to-pay measure such as the HEV or the HCV for the dV^h in Eq. (27.7), as discussed in Chapter 26. These measures will presumably include each person's share of the changes in the general equilibrium profit functions, the discrete equivalent of the dm^h terms. The expenditure functions that form the basis of the HEV and HCV also have to include the initial and final values of each exogenous z.

Practical Difficulties

Decision rules (27.7) and (27.8) offer a straightforward and intuitively appealing method for combining efficiency and equity criteria in project selection Think of the dV^h in Eq. (27.7) or the terms in parentheses in Eq. (27.8) as the efficiency terms, the portion of the aggregate present value of a government project that accrues to each individual. If the distribution were optimal such that the β^h were equal (with reference to Eq. (27.8)), then dW would equal the aggregate present value of the project, the sum of the individual present values.

The simplicity of these decision rules is deceiving when the distribution is nonoptimal, however. They pose the same immense practical difficulties as does the Boadway approach. Some expansion of the remarks in the previous section is in order, since the analysis of applying distributional cost–benefit rules typically occurs within the Weisbrod framework.

The first problem is the inherent subjectivity of the rules. Applying a rule such as Eq. (27.8) requires a two-step procedure, both parts of which are highly subjective. First, the aggregate present value must be subdivided into the relevant distributional groupings, such that:

$$PV_{agg} = \sum_{i=1}^{I} PV_i \qquad (27.9)$$

where PV_i is the gain (loss) to subgroup i. Second, the appropriate social marginal utilities must be applied to each subgroup to compute the correct weighted-average present value:

$$PV^* = \sum_{i=1}^{I} \beta^i PV_i \qquad (27.10)$$

PV^* is equivalent to dW in Eq. (27.8). For consistent project evaluation, the present value of each project should be subdivided the same way, with the same social welfare weights applied to each subgroup in all projects.

The problem, of course, is that normative theory does not indicate how to perform either of these operations.

What is the relevant subgrouping? The government clearly will not compute gains and losses for every individual; therefore, how should it aggregate to form subgroups? Is income the only relevant consideration, so that the relevant subdivision is rich–poor or rich–middle income–poor? Is race or sex also important, such as under an affirmative action policy? If so, this would suggest increasing the subdivisions to include rich–white, rich–nonwhite, poor–white, and so forth, with perhaps further subdivisions by male–female.

Whatever subdivision society chooses, there remains the issue of an appropriate weighting scheme. For instance, should the social marginal utilities of the poorest group be equal to the social marginal utilities of all other groups (utilitarian social welfare), infinitely larger than any other group (Rawlsian social welfare), or some multiple (2, 10, 100) of the other groups?

Normative theory merely assumes that all these decisions have been made, adding only that the same subdivisions and weighting schemes should be applied consistently to all projects. Government agencies are not supposed to make separate determinations of these distributional factors. There is obviously an enormous range of indeterminacy here, since by suitable choice of the relevant subdivisions and social welfare weights, a set of N projects can receive virtually any ranking regardless of their relative aggregate present values. Therefore, unless society has agreed upon these distributional parameters, there is little point in computing each PV*. The computation would simply represent the distributional biases of the cost–benefit analyst. Yet ranking projects according to aggregate present value returns us to the other horn of the dilemma: Is a project ranking devoid of distributional considerations useful as a selection criterion?

Some economists have recommended the PV_{agg} ranking on the grounds that if $PV_{agg} > 0$, the gainers could compensate the losers and still experience a net increase in utility. This is the so-called Hicks–Kaldor criterion, which bases selection on a *potential* gain in social welfare. Given an individualistic social welfare function, the fact that some consumers could be made better off without others being made worse off would guarantee an increase in social welfare, *if the compensation actually took place*. The qualification in italics is crucial, because modern second-best analysis has developed a clear distinction between actual and potential gains in social welfare. Unfortunately, only actual gains and losses are relevant, not the potential for net social gain. In short, there can be no escaping the dilemma posed above.

A second difficulty is computing the actual changes in the private sector prices and the distribution of any changes in economic profits and losses. The difficulties here are obviously heightened for large projects that lead to discrete changes in the economy's general equilibrium. The researcher may have to estimate a huge array of supply and demand elasticities, a point noted in the previous section. Also, the social marginal utilities may change with discrete changes in individual gains and losses. In truth, a fully specified cost–benefit analysis is a hopeless task when the distribution is nonoptimal.[7] Policy analysts are forced to make many simplifying assumptions, yet they cannot really know whether their assumptions are entirely appropriate or reasonable.

CONCLUSION

No matter how one views the issue, a nonoptimal distribution of income poses grave difficulties for objective cost–benefit analysis. As indicated in the very first chapter of the text, normative theory has never been able to resolve the distribution question beyond the point of saying to the decision maker: "Tell us your distributional preferences and we will tell you what to do." To the extent society is unable to develop a consistent set of distributional preferences, cost–benefit analysis is firmly trapped in a dilemma. On the one hand, there is no obvious simple and practical way of incorporating distributional preferences into the analysis. On the other hand, there is no way of judging the value of an analysis which chooses to ignore distributional considerations. Indeed, if the distribution is nonoptimal, it may not even be possible to compute the *efficiency* implications for any given project because of various aggregation biases. Estimated market demand curves might yield highly inaccurate compensation measures of aggregate gains and losses. Finally, even if society's distributional preferences were well established, the data required to incorporate them consistently into the shadow prices for government projects are formidable, to say the least.

There is one apparent avenue for escaping the dilemma. The analyst can adopt the Jorgenson–Slesnick framework for estimating social welfare and social expenditure functions that we presented in Chapter 4. It is not a clean escape, however, because this framework avoids aggregation problems by assuming as a maintained hypothesis the so-called exact aggregation restrictions, which are restrictions on the parameters of the indirect utility functions. These are in addition to the many other restrictions taken from neoclassical consumer theory that are required for the estimation of the underlying system of expenditure share equations. Unfortunately, these restrictions are very likely to fail standard statistical tests in any application, which calls into question the reliability of their estimated indirect utility functions. There is no sure escape from the dilemma.

---

[7] Peter Hammond provides an excellent discussion of the difficulties of applied cost–benefit analysis that expands upon the discussion in the text in P. Hammond, "Theoretical Progress in Public Economics: A Provocative Assessment," *Oxford Economic Papers*, January 1990, sections 8–13. He includes some troubling econometric issues that we have ignored.

REFERENCES

Boadway, R., "Integrating Equity and Efficiency in Applied Welfare Economics," *Quarterly Journal of Economics*, November 1976.

Green, H., "Two Models of Optimal Taxation and Pricing," *Oxford Economic Papers*, November 1975.

Hammond, P., "Theoretical Progress in Public Economics: A Provocative Assessment," *Oxford Economic Papers*, January 1990.

Harberger, A., "Three Postulates for Applied Welfare Economics," *Journal of Economic Literature*, September 1971.

Weisbrod, B., "Income Redistribution Effects and Benefit–Cost Analysis," in S. B. Chase, Jr., Ed., *Problems in Public Expenditure Analysis*, The Brookings Institution, Washington, D.C., 1968.

28

COMMON PITFALLS IN COST–BENEFIT ANALYSIS

Cost–benefit analysis may be as much art as science, but any study that presents a careful discussion of the issues presented in Chapters 24–27—the public rate of discount, uncertainty, the various measurement problems, and the distribution of project costs and benefits—with all assumptions explicitly stated, cannot help but inform the decision-making process. Many cost–benefit studies stray from these central issues, however, and emphasize other factors that are essentially irrelevant to the fundamental question which cost–benefit analysis attempts to answer: Does a particular government investment constitute the best possible use of society's scarce resources? Once the peripheral issues gain prominence, cost–benefit analysis loses its ability to discriminate correctly among public investment alternatives.

It is hardly surprising that public forums such as congressional hearings and the media tend not to emphasize the proper economic issues. They are fairly technical and often difficult for the public to understand (with the possible exception of the distribution question). But since they happen to be the relevant issues, public discussions of the economic implications of proposed government projects are often badly misplaced, serving mainly to reinforce commonly held misconceptions.

Roland McKean's 1958 book, *Efficiency in Government Through Systems Analysis*, still remains one of the most comprehensive accounts of the various pitfalls in cost–benefit analysis and is filled with numerous entertaining examples.[1] We will highlight five of the most common misconceptions in this chapter, all of which share two characteristics. First, as with most popular misconceptions, they often contain a kernel of truth, but the kernel is blown up beyond all reasonable proportion to the point where the analysis becomes completely misleading. Whether this is done intentionally to support a particular cause or simply results from innocent misunderstanding is sometimes difficult to discern. Nonetheless, it clearly pays to exploit these misconceptions, because their second characteristic is that the errors they entail tend to be enormous. The dollar value of the benefits and/or costs attributed to these bogus issues, which McKean facetiously labels "secondary" benefits and costs, typically swamps any reasonable estimates of the true or "primary" benefits and costs. Consequently, emphasizing the secondary benefits and costs can be a very effective partisan gambit, if one can get away with it.

THE CHAIN REACTION GAME

In the chain-reaction game, people discover numerous sources of secondary profits (or losses) arising from the particular government project under study. Suppose the government builds a hydroelectric project for which the true benefits might include lowering the price of electricity to a large group of people, recreational benefits formed by damming a river, flood control, irrigation, and so forth. The lowered price of electricity is presumably the primary objective of the project, but these other benefits are legitimate technological external economies arising from the dam, and a careful analysis should try to evaluate them as part of the benefits. Proponents often go far beyond this, however, claiming as legitimate benefits the profits arising in other industries as a consequence of the dam. For example, profits in the region's construction industry are almost certain to rise, as well as profits in those industries supplying the construction materials. At the retail end of the spectrum, profits in the electric appliance industry are also likely to rise. So, too, will profits in all industries whose products are complements to electricity, and so on along the chain. With all these secondary profits added to the other benefits of the project listed above, the hydroelectric project is virtually assured of having a positive present value. Indeed, the value of the secondary profits may well exceed the dollar value of the true benefits.

---

[1] R. N. McKean, *Efficiency in Government Through Systems Analysis*, Wiley, New York, 1958, especially Chapters 8 and 9.

The kernel of truth in the chain-reaction game is that the change in the value of the general equilibrium profit function is a legitimate part of the true benefits measure. For example, recall that Hicks' Equivalent Variation measure of benefits in a one-consumer-equivalent economy with general technology is

$$\text{HEV} = [\pi(\vec{p}_1) - \pi(\vec{p}_0)] + \left[M\left(\vec{q}_0; \overline{U}^1\right) - M\left(\vec{q}_1; \overline{U}^1\right) \right] \tag{28.1}$$

where:

$(\vec{q}_0, \vec{p}_0)$ are the general equilibrium vectors of consumer and producer prices, respectively, at the initial equilibrium.

$(\vec{q}_1, \vec{p}_1)$ are the general equilibrium vectors of consumer and producer prices at the new equilibrium, which includes the project.

$M(\vec{q}; \overline{U}^1) = $ the consumer's expenditure function evaluated at the new utility level with the project.

$\pi(\vec{p}) = $ the general equilibrium profit function for the private sector.

Presumably, including the secondary profits arising from the project is meant to capture the change in the profit function, but there are two serious problems with this notion.

The most obvious flaw is that these secondary profits represent only a partial accounting of all secondary general equilibrium profit effects. The profit function measures aggregate profits and losses from *all* economic activity. If proponents of the project can develop a list of industries that experience increased profits as a result of the project, then the project's opponents can just as easily provide another list of industries that experience "secondary" losses as a result of the project. Roughly speaking, any activity that is in any way complementary to the construction of the hydroelectric project or to the true benefits derived from it can be expected to show increased profits. Conversely, all activities that bear a substitute relationship to the project and its benefits can be expected to show losses. For instance, gains in the electric appliance industry will be partially or wholly offset by decreased sales of gas and oil appliances. Bidding resources into the project may raise factor costs in other industries. The list of potential pure economic losses is no doubt as long as that of the pure economic profits.

The second flaw is that the profit function measures pure economic profits in a long-run equilibrium, whereas the gains and losses mentioned above are likely to be short-run effects. In the long run, the existence of pure profits or losses for the economy as a whole is essentially a function of production characteristics industry by industry, not changes in factor prices. Decreasing returns-to-scale production exhibits pure profits in the long run; increasing returns-to-scale production, pure losses. The short-run effects are not irrelevant, but it may be difficult to know how long they will continue in any given industry. In any event, one would not want to represent the short-run changes as recurring annually for the life of the project.

Once these two factors are admitted, it is easy to see that the secondary chain-reaction profit game is far overdone. We believe the safest strategy is simply to ignore profits and losses in other industries even though changes in the general equilibrium profit function are a legitimate part of benefits. Can any researcher really hope to trace through all the pure profits and losses arising from a given project, both in the short run and long run? The question, in effect, answers itself. The cost–benefit analyst would be well advised to accept the proposition that aggregate production exhibits (approximately) constant returns to scale (CRS) and assume no lasting pure profit effects in other industries. Assume, also, that short-run gains are completely offset by short-run losses as resources move throughout the economy.

At the same time, any pure profits or losses directly associated with the project ought to be included. The need to finance a decreasing-cost service in part out of general tax revenues, if price is set equal to marginal costs, is certainly a relevant project cost. Indeed, the government often invests in a particular industry precisely because it exhibits decreasing costs. Hence, it would be foolish to assume that government production necessarily exhibits CRS.

THE REGIONAL MULTIPLIER GAME

The regional multiplier game attaches a Keynesian-style multiplier analysis to the basic cost–benefit framework. Continuing with the example of the hydroelectric project, suppose the dam site was formerly a wilderness area. Presumably, the construction and continued operation of the dam will support all sorts of ancillary services. The people associated with the project have to be clothed, housed, and fed. Indeed, a small town might spring up around the dam site, generating a continual annual flow of income in a region formerly devoid of economic activity. By the very nature of the Keynesian multiplier, these secondary income effects will be a multiple of the project's direct costs and/or benefits. Therefore, if they are included as project benefits, the project would necessarily have a positive present value.

Something must be wrong here, for these regional multipliers appear to suggest that virtually any project placed in an underdeveloped region of a country will be worthwhile. The crux of the problem is that Keynesian multiplier analysis is simply irrelevant to the fundamental goal of cost–benefit analysis, which is to determine the best use of society's scarce resources. Cost–benefit analysis begins with a presumption of full employment so that, strictly speaking, it is concerned with the maximum expansion of society's production-possibilities frontier. Keynesian multiplier analysis, on the other hand, is concerned with moving an unemployed economy to its production-possibilities frontier. Hence, if the full-employment assumption is retained, the multiplied increases in income associated with any one project must be offset by multiplied decreases in income in other regions of the economy that lose resources to the project.

The kernel of truth here is that market economies are seldom fully employed and that cost–benefit analysis should be adjusted to account for unemployment. If a project generates a net gain in employment for the economy as a whole, this is a short-run benefit that can legitimately be included. But is it prudent to include these gains? A dam located in the wilderness of Colorado has obvious regional income effects, but a project of equal dollar amount located in the middle of New York City may well have the same regional income effects. They are just not as obvious. Is there any reason to suppose that one type of government project has a different multiplier from another type of project of equal size, especially given that the relevant measure is the aggregate economy-wide increase in income? Unless one can argue convincingly that some particular project has unusually strong multiplier effects for some reason, there would seem to be little point in attaching a Keynesian regional multiplier analysis to a cost–benefit study.

One reason these effects are so often emphasized is that the residents of Colorado and New York care very much indeed whether the federal government subsidizes a hydroelectric project in Colorado or an office building in New York City. But should the federal government care? Is regional development in and of itself a legitimate intangible benefit? Do the people of Colorado deserve some special consideration so that the issue becomes one of income distribution viewed in a peculiarly geographic fashion? Answers to questions such as these are largely a matter of taste. We happen to believe that the answers are likely to be "no."

THE LABOR GAME

The labor game is a popular variant of the regional multiplier game which focuses exclusively on the employment effects of particular projects. "The federal government should subsidize the production of a suspension bridge in part because it will employ 1000 construction workers for the next three years." Arguments such as this implicitly value the entire wages of these workers as a project benefit. This is an incredible proposition on face value, since wages are normally considered part of a project's *costs*, not its benefits. A project will almost certainly have a positive present value if a substantial portion of the project's costs can be moved to the benefits side of the ledger. Once again, the kernel of truth resides in the possibility of unemployment. Counting wages as benefits implicitly assumes that these workers are unemployed and unemployable in any other alternative occupation for the duration of the project. This is unlikely, to say the least.

A more careful accounting of labor's gains and losses would view the wage paid to each worker on a project as having three components:

1. The opportunity wage, equal to the wage received in the worker's next best alternative employment.

2. A component equal to the nuisance cost of changing jobs to work on the project. Labor can typically be bid away from alternative employment only by an offer of increased wages, but to the extent the increase just compensates the worker for the nuisance cost of moving it is a true cost of the project.

3. A pure wage rent.

Only the third component represents a true benefit. If labor receives a pure rent it is, in effect, directly capturing some of the legitimate benefits of the project.

It is true enough that a project undertaken in a high-unemployment area may have a higher pure-rent component than a project paying the same wages in a low-unemployment area and that this gives a legitimate advantage to the former project. But even projects in high-unemployment areas draw upon some currently employed resources, and not all unemployed workers hired would have been unemployed for long periods of time. The point is that computing pure wage rents is a far more subtle exercise than merely noting that X number of workers will be hired at a certain wage. Carried to its extreme, the labor game can lead to the following absurd conclusions:

1. Select larger projects over smaller projects because they employ more workers. If wages are viewed as benefits, large projects will tend to dominate.[2]

2. Subsidize industries no matter how unprofitable because failure to do so will lead to unemployment.

Arguments such as these deny the entire dynamic behind economic growth, whereby resources are continually reallocated to better alternatives at the expense of some short-run unemployment.

The emotional appeal of employment arguments is understandable, but they are seldom as relevant to project selection as they are made out to be. We would venture to guess that, as a first approximation, counting all wages as part of project costs is far more reasonable than counting all wages as pure wage rents for most projects. Nonetheless, the labor game is hugely popular in the Unites States. Sports fans well know that calls for public subsidies of new stadiums trumpet the employment effects of the stadiums. One can hardly blame the subsidies' proponents for they are merely following standard practice. Our experience is that cost–benefit analyses typically report the estimated employment effects. This is so even though most public projects of

---

[2] The bias toward larger projects also exists with the chain reaction and regional multiplier games.

comparable size are likely to have approximately the same employment effects. The truth is that public policy would be greatly served by a proper accounting of project wages.

PURE DOUBLE COUNTING

Double counting project costs or benefits is undoubtedly less common than the preceding three pitfalls, but McKean points out that it was once the official policy of the Bureau of Reclamation within the U.S. Department of the Interior.[3] The Bureau's manual on cost–benefit procedures required that the benefits of irrigated land be counted as the sum of:

1. the increase in the value of the land; and
2. the present value of the stream of net income obtained from farming the land.

McKean recounts a humorous exchange between a congressman and one of the Bureau's administrators in which the congressman wondered how the benefits of irrigated land could be so phenomenally large if no farmer was willing to pay that much for the land. The congressman was right, of course.

The quarrel here is not with counting irrigated land as a project benefit. Since irrigation changes the land's production function, the value of these changes is a legitimate technological externality. But landowners have only one of two choices, not both. They can farm the land themselves and take the gains as a stream of net income over time, or they can sell the land and let someone else farm it. Assuming a competitive market for land, the equilibrium sales price would just equal the discounted stream of net income from farming the land. Hence, the manual's recommended evaluation procedure represented a double counting of the benefits, pure and simple.

THE PUBLIC SECTOR BIAS CHARGE

Public sector investments are frequently accused of enjoying an advantage over private sector investments because they are not subjected to the discipline of the profit test. They do not have to earn a return to capital. But if cost–benefit analysis has been properly applied to all potential government investments, no such public sector bias exists. A primary goal of careful cost–benefit analysis is to ensure that government projects are selected if and only if they dominate private sector alternatives.

There are two common sources of confusion here. The first is that the government projects may be evaluated at a far lower rate of discount than

---

[3] R. McKean, *Efficiency of Government Through Systems Analysis*, Wiley, New York, 1958, pp. 153–154.

private sector investments. Managers of private sector enterprises are presumably discounting projects at the marginal rate of transformation (MRT) between the present and future, the gross-of-tax rate of return. As we discovered in Chapter 24, however, government projects need not necessarily be so productive. Under certain conditions the public rate of discount may be much lower than the MRT, possibly even less than consumers' marginal rate of substitution (MRS), or the net-of-tax return. Hence, the charge arises that government projects are subjected to less stringent criteria.

The source of confusion here lies in viewing private investments as the only alternative to public investments. Private consumption is another possible alternative, and consumers discount future consumption at the MRS, the net-of-tax return. Furthermore, the net benefits of public and private investments may generate different patterns of future private consumption and investment, which must be taken into consideration. Intertemporal externalities may also affect the public sector's rate of discount. Finally, Chapter 25 discussed how the government's ability to spread risk is a real cost advantage that is not necessarily shared by the private sector. All of these factors suggest that private and public investments may not have to earn equivalent internal rates of return to be judged as acceptable.

Determining the proper rate of discount for government projects is a devilishly complex task, but the principle is clear: Discounting government projects at the public rate of discount is the proper way to protect the interests of the private sector. Using any other rate of discount generates a bias that can favor either the public or the private sector.

The second possible source of confusion involves decreasing-cost projects. These services make losses with marginal cost pricing, whereas private sector projects must at least break even. But the losses are irrelevant in and of themselves. The appropriate all-or-none test is whether total benefits exceed total costs, where total benefits can be approximated by areas behind compensated demand curves. As was noted in Chapter 26, these area measures are needed because of the inherent lumpiness of decreasing cost services. They are altogether equivalent benefit measures to the revenues of private sector projects, given that private investments typically represent only marginal additions of output that do not change market prices. This is just another instance of a principle that is not widely appreciated: Profitability is not always the appropriate investment criterion for the public sector. To the contrary, forcing private sector profitability tests on public sector projects almost certainly generates an undue bias *against* the public sector.

For marginal public investments, we have seen that the government can be thought of as applying standard competitive, profit-maximizing input demand and output supply rules; for example: Use an input such that its price equals the value of its marginal product. But if the policy environment is second best, the government's demand and supply rules make use of shadow prices, not market prices, and the shadow prices can be very complex. Also, the public may have difficulty understanding the rationale for shadow prices, that they point the way toward maximizing efficiency or social welfare, not profit.

CONCLUSION

Put the remarks in this chapter to the test. Review numerous cost–benefit studies prepared by (or for) public agencies or read the congressional hearings or media accounts of proposed government projects (or subsidies for private investments), and see if the bogus "issues" discussed here predominate. Our experience is that they nearly always do. Careful cost–benefit analyses, highlighting the issues presented in Chapters 24–27, appear to be the exception.

REFERENCE

McKean, R., *Efficiency in Government Through Systems Analysis*, Wiley, New York, 1958.

PART V

FISCAL FEDERALISM

29

OPTIMAL FEDERALISM: SORTING THE FUNCTIONS OF GOVERNMENT WITHIN THE FISCAL HIERARCHY

Federalism refers to a hierarchical structure of governments in which each person is, simultaneously, a citizen of more than one government. The United States is an example, with its national government, 50 state governments, and over 89,000 local governmental entities, including cities, towns, counties, regional transportation authorities, metropolitan district commissions, and the like. Each person in the United States falls within the jurisdiction of at least three, and often four or more, distinct governmental bodies. The United States is hardly unique is this regard; all the industrialized market economies have a federalist structure.

A federalist structure adds considerable depth and complexity to normative public sector theory because of its layered jurisdictions. The fundamental principles of public expenditure and tax theory developed in Parts II and III of the text still apply under federalism. In particular, government intervention is still justified by the breakdown of the technical and market assumptions underlying a well-functioning competitive market system, to address such problems as externalities, decreasing cost production, private information, and market power. In addition, the goal of government intervention remains social welfare maximization, which, broadly speaking, translates into the pursuit of efficiency and equity (as always, stabilization problems will be ignored). As we have discovered, achieving a social welfare maximum is an incredibly difficult task for even a single government. Optimal public sector decision rules are easy enough to describe, but their application is often problematic at best. A federalist structure of governments significantly complicates both the theory and the application of public sector decision rules.

THE POTENTIAL FOR INCOMPATIBILITIES AND DESTRUCTIVE COMPETITION

The complications lie at the heart of a federalist system, that more than one government has jurisdiction over any one person. Given the layered structure, it is all too easy to envision potential inconsistencies and incompatibilities arising if each government simply tries to follow the single-government decision rules of public sector theory. This is so even if we were to assume that the population is stationary. For example, the national government may want to transfer income from person 1 to person 2, whereas the state government where the two people live may want to do exactly the opposite. Or, one state government may encourage expansion of a decreasing cost public utility which pollutes the air over a neighboring state that is trying to reduce air pollution.

People are highly mobile, not stationary, in the developed market economies and this gives rise to further complications. Mobility has a direct impact on a normative theory of the public sector because people move partly in response to government expenditure and tax policies and then become voters in their new jurisdictions. Hence, their movement can lead to a competition problem for lower level governments. Income redistribution is a common example. If wealthy residents of town A are asked to provide social services to the poor, they may well move to some other town, B, which has no such policy. People's ability to "vote with their feet" forces governments within a given level of the fiscal hierarchy into a competition with one another to attract and maintain a constituency. In general, optimal decision rules must be adjusted as people move in response to them.

Mobility and local competition turn out to introduce another avenue of potential inefficiency into the economy. They also raise the possibility that no stable equilibrium of localities exists. In short, a federalist structure of governments is unlikely to achieve a social welfare maximum when the population is mobile.

The Two Fundamental Sorting Questions of Fiscal Federalism

At the outset, therefore, federalism poses two fundamental sorting questions that a normative public sector theory must address. The first relates to the allocation of the legitimate functions of government throughout the fiscal hierarchy: Which governments should provide the various legitimate allocational and distributional functions of government so as to avoid potential incompatibilities and destructive competitions among the governments and achieve a social welfare maximum? The second question relates to the sorting of people among jurisdictions: How must people sort themselves among the various jurisdictions, again with the goal of avoiding incompatibilities and intergovernmental competitions and achieving a social welfare maximum? The attempt to answer these two questions is referred to as the *theory of fiscal federalism*.

The two questions of fiscal federalism are naturally interrelated. The sorting of the functions of government among jurisdictions in part determines how people move in response to government policies. In turn, the movement of the people in response to government policies determines in part how the functions should be allocated among jurisdictions.

Social Welfare within Fiscal Federalism

A final point of introduction is that the very meaning of social welfare maximization requires careful attention in a federalist system. A natural extension of the single-government model would be to assume that each autonomous government formulates its own distinct social welfare function that it attempts to maximize. As we have seen, a government has no political identity without a social welfare function in the mainstream normative theory of the public sector. Under this assumption, a natural characterization of an optimal federalism is one in which each government has maximized its own version of social welfare. This is the obvious extension of the standard single-government policy objective to a multigovernment environment and just as obviously is a very difficult objective to achieve.

This is not, however, the usual approach taken in the extensive theoretical literature on the optimal design of a federalist system. Most theoretical models of fiscal federalism assume that only the highest level (i.e., national) government in the fiscal hierarchy has a social welfare function. That is, only the national government concerns itself with the distribution question. The national government may also address allocational problems, but the key point is that all lower level governments (state, local, county, and so forth) concern themselves *only* with allocational problems. This modeling approach to fiscal federalism is a less complicated extension of the single government model than the assumption that all governments have social welfare functions. But it is a somewhat discomforting framework for a normative theory, since only the national government has a distinct political identity.[1]

In addition, many theoretical models of fiscal federalism employ the first-best technical, market, and policy assumptions to exploit the dichotomization of allocational and distributional issues inherent in first-best (but only first-best) models. The first-best assumptions allow the models to separate the allocational and distributional functions within the fiscal hierarchy. The separation would generally not be possible in a second-best environment.

SORTING THE FUNCTIONS OF GOVERNMENT WITHIN THE FISCAL HIERARCHY

The natural place to begin is with the sorting of functions throughout the fiscal hierarchy because it is the logically prior question. The sorting of people occurs mostly within a single layer of the hierarchy, such as among the localities within a state.

The assumption that only the national government has a social welfare function, when combined with a first-best policy environment, gives rise to a fundamental challenge for the theory of fiscal federalism, namely: What is the advantage of having a federalist structure?

The issue can best be seen as follows. Suppose the national government pursues the norm of social welfare maximization using the traditional first-best analytical framework developed in Chapter 2. In condensed form,

$$\max_{(X_{hi})} W\left[U^h(X_{hi})\right]$$

$$\text{s.t.} \quad F\left(\sum_{h=1}^{H} X_{hi}\right) = 0$$

where $h = 1, \ldots, H$ includes everyone in the society, and $F(\ )$ is the aggregate production-possibilities frontier. If the national government can achieve a set of policies consistent with the first-order conditions of this model in the presence of such problems as externalities, decreasing-cost production, and a nonoptimal distribution of income, what can lower level governments

---

[1] We will wait to pursue this point in detail until the last section of the chapter, in which we analyze distributional issues in the design of an optimal federalist system. Here we will follow the usual modeling approach in the literature.

possibly do to enhance the economic well being of society? Why not let the national government do everything?

Public sector economists have provided a variety of answers to this question, none entirely satisfactory. In considering them, keep in mind that each answer attempts to justify a role for lower level governments only with respect to the standard allocational or efficiency questions. Almost everyone concedes the distributional question to the national government. Social welfare issues are largely absent in lower level, or local, government decision making in the federalism literature.

Stigler's Prescription for an Optimal Federalism

George Stigler, in his short masterpiece "Tenable Range of Functions of Local Government" prepared for the Congressional Joint Economic Committee, adopted what amounts to an axiomatic resolution of this issue.[2] His justification for local (i.e., lower level) governments rests on two principles.

The first principle is that representative government works best the closer the government is to its constituency (presumably because local governments perceive the utilities or demands of their constituents better than a national government could, although this is unclear from his article). This principle is consistent with the notion that the democratic one-person-one-vote town meeting is the ideal form of government, a notion that has held considerable sway throughout the history of the United States.

The second principle is that subsets of people within a country have the right to vote different kinds and amounts of public services for themselves. This principle is the so-called doctrine of states' rights that was expounded so eloquently by various U.S. southern politicians in pre-Civil War days (absent, of course, the racial and slavery issues commonly associated with the doctrine during that period of U.S. history). A recent variant of the states' rights doctrine is that allowing for differences in public services encourages healthy experimentation and innovation in the public sector.

The growth in the size and influence of the national government in the U.S. has diminished somewhat the commitment to these principles. But it is fair to say that they remain persuasive even today, as seen by the current movement to devolve some of the functions that the national government had assumed back to the state and local governments. A recent example is replacement of the AFDC (Aid to Families with Dependent Children) public assistance program with TANF (Temporary Aid for Needy Families) in 1996. TANF gives the states much more discretion in how they choose to

---

[2] G. Stigler, "Tenable Range of Functions of Local Government," in *Federal Expenditure Policy for Economic Growth and Stability*, Joint Economic Committee, Subcommittee on Fiscal Policy, Washington, D.C., 1957, pp. 213–219.

assist poor families and make use of the federal funds they receive to support those families.

According to Stigler, these two principles imply that decision making should occur at the lowest level of government consistent with the goals of allocational efficiency and distributional equity. Notice that his conclusion provides, simultaneously, the justification for federalism and the norm for designing an optimal federalist system, one by which the various legitimate functions of government are best allocated among the governments within the fiscal hierarchy. In effect, Stigler has turned our original challenge to federalism on its head by asking: When is it appropriate to have anything but small, local governments?

His answer is that higher level governments may be necessary to achieve either allocational efficiency or distributional equity. In particular, he argues that the national government is the proper government for resolving the distribution question to avoid incompatibilities and competition among governments. As already noted, most other theorists have followed him on this point. In contrast, the responsibility for allocational functions throughout the fiscal hierarchy turns naturally on the geographic scope of both externalities and decreasing costs, the traditional allocational issues in first-best public sector theory. A governmental body must be sufficiently large to capture all decreasing costs from a particular decreasing cost service or to include all citizens affected by a particular externality generating activity, but it need not be any larger. Thus, the optimal size of a jurisdictional unit varies with each specific instance of a decreasing cost service or an externality.

Oates' Perfect Correspondence

Wallace Oates, in *Fiscal Federalism*, solidified Stigler's principle by proposing the notion of a perfect correspondence:[3]

> the optimal form of federal government to provide the set of *n* public goods would be one in which there exists a level of government for each subset of the population over which the consumption of a public good is defined. This would be sufficient to internalize the benefits from the provision of each good. Such a structure of government, in which the jurisdiction that determines the level of provision of each public good includes precisely the set of individuals who consume the good, I shall call a case of *perfect correspondence* in the provision of public goods. In the ideal model, each level of government, possessing complete knowledge of the tastes of its constitu-

---

[3] Excerpted from *Fiscal Federalism* by Wallace E. Oates, © 1972 by Harcourt Brace Jovanovich, Inc., pp. 34–35. Reprinted by permission of the publisher. Two points are worth noting with respect to Oates' definition of perfect correspondence. First, while he talks only of public goods, the principle clearly applies as well to any form of externality, or any decreasing cost industry. Second, Oates claims no originality for the notion of perfect correspondence, only for the terminology. Many other authors besides Stigler viewed the ideal federalist structure in a similar vein, including Albert Breton, Mancur Olson, and Vincent Ostron *et al.* See pp. 34 (note 4) and 35 in *Fiscal Federalism*.

ents and seeking to maximize their welfare, would provide the Pareto-efficient level of output and would finance this through benefit pricing.

That the allocation of resources resulting from our ideal case of a perfect correspondence is Pareto-efficient is, I think, clear [assuming no private sector inefficiencies].

Given the existence of a federalist system, the notion of a perfect correspondence sets a natural limit on the size of each local government. It is clearly a stringent requirement, leading one to question whether a perfect correspondence for even one public good or decreasing cost service actually exists, since political boundaries are never determined solely by the extent of externalities or decreasing costs. But a more fundamental theoretical issue turns on the usefulness of perfect correspondence as a policy norm for the public sector. Is it even worth pursuing by restructuring existing jurisdictional boundaries?

Oates is certainly correct when he says that a perfect correspondence generates a first-best social welfare optimum, assuming that local governments follow the first-best allocational decision rules. But we must return to our original challenge posed above. Given a first-best policy environment in which only the national government has a social welfare function, why is local decision making necessary at all, the existence of a perfect correspondence notwithstanding? Why cannot the national government note the extent of each externality or decreasing-cost service and make the appropriate policy response? There is something of an asymmetry here. A nonperfect correspondence can preclude local autonomy, but a perfect correspondence does not necessarily imply local autonomy in order to achieve a social welfare maximum. If we are to make a compelling theoretical argument for a federalist structure, something besides perfect correspondence is required.

Oates' Decentralization Theorem

Oates provides one possible justification by adding a new constraint to the basic first-best general equilibrium model.[4] Following Oates, assume that there are two subgroups of people, A and B, within the total population, such that all individuals within each subgroup have identical preferences but preferences vary across A and B. Suppose, in addition, that society produces two purely private goods, X and Y, that are both consumed by all members of the society. Y happens to be provided by a government, either national or local, despite its being a private good. Assume, finally, that the distribution of income is optimal, so that each subgroup can be viewed as containing a single individual. Under these assumptions, social welfare maximization is equivalent to achieving a pareto optimum, which can be represented as follows:

---

[4] Adapted from *Fiscal Federalism* by Wallace E. Oates, © 1972 by Harcourt Brace Jovanovich, Inc., p. 55, by permission of the publisher.

$$\max_{(X^A, Y^A, X^B, Y^B)} U^A(X^A, Y^A)$$

$$\text{s.t.} \quad U^B(X^B, Y^B) = \overline{U}$$

$$F(X^A + X^B; Y^A + Y^B) = 0$$

We know that the first-order conditions for this problem are

$$MRS^A_{X^A, Y^A} = MRS^B_{X^B, Y^B} = MRT_{X, Y} \qquad (29.1)$$

Moreover, with different tastes, $X^A \neq X^B$ and $Y^A \neq Y^B$ in general, at the optimum.

Given the model as it stands, it obviously makes no difference whether a single national government provides Y^A and Y^B according to Eq. (29.1), or whether each subgroup forms its own government and individually satisfies:

$$MRS^A_{X^A, Y^A} = MRT_{X, Y} \qquad (29.2)$$

and

$$MRS^B_{X^B, Y^B} = MRT_{X, Y} \qquad (29.3)$$

Suppose, however, that the national government is constrained to offer equal amounts of Y to each subgroup, so that $Y^A = Y^B$ with national provision of Y. Since, in general, $Y^A \neq Y^B$ at the social welfare optimum, this would represent an additional binding constraint on the formal general equilibrium model, implying a lower level of social welfare at the optimum. It is easy to show that the new first-order conditions become:

$$MRS^A_{X^A, Y^A} = MRS^B_{X^B, Y^B} = MRT_{X, Y} + \frac{\lambda_3}{\lambda_2 F_x} \qquad (29.4)$$

where:

λ_2 = the Lagrangian multiplier associated with society's production possibilities, $F(\ ) = 0$.

λ_3 = the Lagrangian multiplier associated with the new constraint, $Y^A = Y^B$.

Local autonomy is obviously the preferred structure under these conditions because it avoids subjecting society to an unnecessary constraint upon government decision making. Oates labels this result *the decentralization theorem:*[5]

> For a public good—the consumption of which is defined over geographical subsets of the total population, and for which the costs of providing each level of output of the good in each jurisdiction are the same for the central or the respective local government—it will always be more efficient (or at least as efficient) for local

[5] Excerpted from *Fiscal Federalism* by Wallace E. Oates, © 1972 by Harcourt Brace Jovanovich, Inc., p. 35. Reprinted by permission of the publisher.

governments to provide the Pareto-efficient levels of output for their respective jurisdictions than for the central government to provide *any* specified and uniform level of output across all jurisdictions.

The decentralization theorem does not solve the problem of justifying local level governments in a first-best policy environment. It is really an exercise in the theory of the second best, precisely because the national government is forced to offer equal service levels to all subsets of the population. Nonetheless, this is a compelling restriction in the context of the United States. U.S. citizens have expressed a longstanding fear of standardization if the national government provides public services. There are any number of examples. People have consistently and successfully argued for local autonomy over public elementary and secondary education on the grounds that a federal takeover, despite some financial advantages, would imply standardized education for all children. The Federal Communications Commission (FCC) has promoted local public television production to offset the standardized sitcom- and sports-dominated programming offered by the national networks. Chapter 8 discussed the major drawback to the federally legislated pollution control devices for all automobiles, that the level of pollution reduction obtained is almost certainly nonoptimal for all but a few localities. In that particular case, however, effective local initiatives against automobile pollution were difficult to imagine. Along these same lines, the national government is prohibited by the Constitution of the United States from varying certain taxes on a geographical basis. The point is that Oates' decentralization theorem strikes a responsive chord, at least in the United States. It is not just some arbitrary formal model that happens to be biased against national decision making.

Misperceived Preferences

Oates' justification for local autonomy is still somewhat unsettling because nationally provided services do not necessarily have to be standardized. A different approach that may be more appealing relies on a particular form of private information. It picks up on Stigler's idea that local officials know best their own constituents' demands for public services.

Suppose that the only allocational problem facing society is the existence of a Samuelsonian public good, X_g, the consumption of which happens to affect only a subset of the population. Let $h = 1, \ldots, k$ be the affected subset and $h = k + 1, \ldots, H$ be the unaffected subset. All other goods are pure private goods, and there is no other (e.g., decreasing costs) problem requiring government intervention for allocational reasons. The distribution of income is optimal and determined by the national government.

In a first-best world of perfect certainty, either the national government or a local jurisdiction comprising individuals $h = 1, \ldots, k$ could provide the proper level of X_g in accordance with the standard first-order condition:

$$\sum_{h=1}^{k} MRS_{g,1}^{h} = MRT_{g,1} \qquad (29.5)$$

where good 1 is one of the purely private goods. Suppose, however, that the local jurisdiction knows its citizens well in the sense that it knows any individual's $MRS_{g,1}^{h}$ with perfect certainty, whereas the national government knows each of these people less well in the sense that it observes each individual's marginal rate of substitution as a random variable:

$$M\hat{R}S_{g,1}^{h} = MRS_{g,1}^{h} + \alpha \qquad (29.6)$$

where:

$MRS_{g,1}^{h}$ = the true MRS as observed by the local jurisdiction.
α = a random variable, with $E(\alpha) = \bar{\alpha}$, possibly 0.

Under these conditions, social welfare is maximized, in general, by having the local jurisdiction form and decide the appropriate level of X_g, rather than letting the national government determine X_g according to the first-order condition:

$$\sum_{h=1}^{k} M\hat{R}S_{g,1}^{h} = MRT_{g,1} \qquad (29.7)$$

If $\bar{\alpha} \neq 0$, the national governments decision rule is clearly biased, implying either over- or underprovision of X_g. Even if $\bar{\alpha} = 0$, however, so that $M\hat{R}S_{g,1}^{h}$ is an unbiased estimate of $MRS_{g,1}^{h}$, a risk-averse society would prefer local provision of X_g. Expressed in terms of indirect utility functions:

$$V^h(\vec{q}; I^h; X_g^*) > E[V^h(\vec{q}; I^h; \overline{X}_g)] \qquad h = 1, \ldots, k \qquad (29.8)$$

where:

X_g^* = the optimal level of X_g, obtained with local provision.
$\overline{X}_g = X_g^* + \beta$, with $E(\beta) = 0$, obtained with national provision.

Assuming risk aversion, persons $h = 1, \ldots, k$ would be willing to pay a risk premium for local rather than national provision of X_g.

Proponents of federalism probably have this type of uncertainty in mind when they argue that local governments best know the interests of their own citizens. The sheer geographic distance from the central government to most of the people within a given society is bound to affect adversely the transmission of information.

Local Autonomy in a First-Best Environment?

Oates' decentralization theorem and the notion of misperceived preferences justify local autonomy by introducing second-best restrictions—standardization of national services or private information. The question remains whether local autonomy can be justified in a first-best environment when the national government is the only government allowed to make social welfare rankings, and it has perfect knowledge and access to whatever policy tools are necessary to generate first-best allocational decision rules. The answer would appear to be no, yet local autonomy does seem more appropriate for public services that are limited in scope, all the more so when Oates' perfect correspondence happens to obtain within jurisdictions that already exist. Stigler's twin axioms for allocating the functions of government— choose the lowest level jurisdictions consistent with allocational efficiency and preserve states' rights—remain compelling despite the formal implications of first-best theory. Is it possible, therefore, to resurrect fiscal federalism as an optimal governmental structure without introducing specific second-best assumptions? In our view, the answer is "yes:" Federalism can be justified on distributional grounds, but this involves a line of argument that has not received much attention in the theoretical literature on fiscal federalism.

OPTIMAL FEDERALISM AND THE DISTRIBUTION FUNCTION

The literature on the optimal structure of a federalist system of governments is virtually unanimous in assigning decisions on income distribution to the national government.[6] According to the conventional wisdom, allowing redistribution by lower level ("local") governments in the fiscal hierarchy is formally inconsistent with social welfare optimization, whether one assumes that people are immobile or fully mobile across local jurisdictions.

We happen to disagree with the conventional analysis on this point. In our view, a federalist system is not only formally consistent with social welfare maximization when it contains lower government redistributions, but it also *requires* local redistributions to have meaning as an optimal fiscal system from the mainstream perspective. A review and criticism of the conventional position is useful before developing our preferred model of federalism.

Redistribution, the Competition Problem, and Potential Incompatibilities

Assume first that people are mobile, and suppose that one local government tries to redistribute from its rich to its poor citizens, but only one.

---

[6] A notable exception is Mark Pauly, "Income Redistribution as a Local Public Good," *Journal of Public Economics*, Vol. 2, 1973. Pauly develops a model based on the Hochman and Rodgers notion of pareto-optimal redistributions (Chapter 10), in which, under certain

Neighboring governments do not attempt any redistribution. The wealthier citizens of the redistributing locality would have an incentive to move to the neighboring localities. This is the competition problem referred to earlier, and it is clearly in evidence in many metropolitan areas in the United States.

Such migration has two unfortunate implications. First, the government that tries to redistribute is totally frustrated. Not only are its poor not made significantly better off, but the total tax base of the community has declined and it becomes more difficult to maintain per-capita levels of public services. Second, if people move in response to taxation, this tends to increase the dead-weight loss arising from taxation (assuming for the moment that lump-sum redistributions are not viable). Thus, redistributions at the local level are seen to be inconsistent with the goal of maximizing social welfare in a federal system with mobile resources.

The competition problem reaches its full force under perfect mobility, in which people are free to move to any locality and mobility is costless. Local redistribution is impossible in this case since an equilibrium requires equal treatment of equals no matter where people live. The fiscal incidence on any one of its citizens is exogenous to each locality.

Even in a world without mobility, incompatibilities can arise throughout a federalist system if more than one government redistributes income. Suppose local government L wants to effect a redistribution from citizens in group A to citizens in group B, but the national government prefers a net redistribution from group B to group A. One can imagine an endless chain of redistributions as each government tries to have its way. Of course, this sort of game must be ruled out, and the most obvious way is to deny one government the right to redistribute.

To avoid the competition problem and potential incompatibilities, therefore, conventional analysis assigns redistribution policy solely to the national government. In an optimal federalist system, all lower level governments in the fiscal hierarchy perform only allocational functions, in accordance with the principles outlined in the preceding section. Furthermore, the prevailing model of optimal federalism stipulates that all local allocational expenditures be financed according to the benefits-received theory of taxation to avoid any unintended redistributions from their allocational decisions. An example would be financing local public goods by Lindahl taxes that equal each person's MRS between the public good and the numeraire good. Only the national government is allowed to tax on some basis other than benefits received, such as ability to pay, and then only to effect the goal of a just distribution. If local governments were to use some tax principle other than the benefits-received principle, then they would likely be redistributing, and

conditions, local government redistributions are optimal. In this chapter, we argue that local redistribution makes sense for a federalist system even if redistributions are based solely on interpersonal equity considerations without adding an externality component.

the problems of moving to escape taxes, excess burden, and incompatibility among governments are sure to arise. Oates is very clear on the point:[7]

> The most attractive solution to this whole [distribution] problem (at a formal level at least) is that suggested in Chapter One: let the central government resolve the distribution problem and allow decentralized levels of government to provide public services that they finance with benefit taxes. The use of ability-to-pay taxation by local government, instead of a national negative income tax, may well involve a very high cost both in terms of excess burden and the failure to realize distributional objectives.

According to Oates, this scheme produces a welfare optimum in an ideal world of perfect correspondence.

Two implications of the conventional model deserve mention. Models of fiscal federalism assume that mobile citizens search for localities offering their most preferred level and mix of public services. Roughly speaking, people choose among high service–high tax, medium service–medium tax, and low service–low tax localities along a broad spectrum. The public services would only be of the allocational kind, however. Distributional concerns would not enter into their locational decisions because all distributional issues are resolved by the national government. Another implication of the model in the ideal world of perfect correspondence is that there is no need for grants-in-aid among governments. Redistributions occur only among people, and at the instigation of the national government. According to Oates,[8]

> To achieve a just distribution of income among the individuals in a nation, a national program that redistributes income among individuals, not among jurisdictions, is the preferred alternative.

Criticisms of the Prevailing Model

To fix ideas on the meaning of a social welfare optimum in a federalist system, we assume a first-best economic and policy environment. This is the only fair way to assess the conventional position, since it was developed within a first-best context.

In our view, the conventional first-best analysis of optimal federalism is deficient in three respects. It has difficulties with decreasing-cost services, it has questionable political implications, and it flies in the face of reality.

Decreasing-Cost Services

The notion that taxation according to the benefits-received principle necessarily avoids redistributions is not correct, at least not with respect to decreasing-cost services. To preserve efficiency with decreasing-cost services,

---

[7] Excerpted from *Fiscal Federalism* by Wallace E. Oates, © 1972 by Harcourt Brace Jovanovich, Inc., p. 150. Reprinted by permission of the publisher.

[8] Excerpted from *Fiscal Federalism* by Wallace E. Oates, © 1972 by Harcourt Brace Jovanovich, Inc., p. 81. Reprinted by permission of the publisher.

which an optimal federalist system must surely do, correct benefits-received taxation or pricing implies that price must be set equal to marginal costs. Any other price cannot achieve a social welfare optimum. The problem is that setting price equal to marginal costs is not sufficient to cover full average costs if average costs are declining, so that the local government has to make up the deficit out of lump-sum taxes and transfers.[9] The question then arises: How is the local government supposed to finance the deficit if, as in the prevailing model, it is constrained from making redistributional decisions? Formally, this restriction implies that it is not allowed to have a social welfare function.

As we saw in Chapter 9, the decision to provide decreasing-cost services in an economy with a single government is inextricably tied to the lump-sum redistributions that satisfy the interpersonal equity conditions of social welfare maximization. The only modification is that the sum of all lump-sum taxes collected from individuals must exceed the sum of all lump-sum transfers to individuals by an amount sufficient to cover all deficits incurred by decreasing-cost industries. In this case, then, allocational and redistributional considerations are also inextricably bound together. A local government cannot, by itself, make what is essentially an allocational decision without simultaneously having some way of ranking individuals, such as by means of a social welfare function, to decide how to finance of the deficit. The alternative of reinterpreting the benefits principle of taxation to allow for average cost pricing is clearly illegitimate, because then the system of optimal federalism cannot achieve a welfare optimum. It cannot satisfy the pareto-optimality conditions of first-best theory.

One practical solution to the deficit problem would be to extend the benefits-received principle to the financing of the deficit. Have the local governments institute a two-part tariff, in which consumers pay a price equal to marginal costs to use the service, plus a one-time, lump-sum fee (which potential users would have to pay as well) sufficient to cover the resulting deficit. Believers in the benefits-received principle would be comfortable with this solution, but it is not especially compelling in the mainstream neoclassical model. Recall that the benefits-received principle has no standing as an equity principle in the mainstream model. It can only be applied to public pricing to achieve pareto-optimal allocations, such as setting a price equal to marginal cost for decreasing-cost services. The problem with applying it to the deficit is that it is not distributionally neutral. Therefore, it does not have any particular theoretical appeal if the local government cannot make distributional judgments. Why not have each

---

[9] Whether or not the service is privately or publicly owned is of little consequence. Decreasing-cost industries, if correctly priced, always involve a governmental decision because it is the government that must decide whether the benefit of having the service justifies the cost of financing the deficit.

locality charge just one of its citizens for the entire deficit, with the confidence that the national government's redistribution policies will correct any undue harm suffered by the individuals chosen?

A model of optimal federalism can sidestep the deficit problem by not allowing local governments to make decisions involving decreasing-cost services. These must also be the sole prerogative of the national government. One might counter that the local governments could decide on the level of service to be provided with the national government merely guaranteeing to cover whatever deficit ensues. But whether or not the service is worthwhile depends both upon the demands of the individuals using the service (assume no externalities) and upon the social welfare rankings of these people as determined by the national social welfare function. Since redistributions are the sole prerogative of the national government in the conventional model, the final decision rests in part with that government. Thus, the local governments cannot make a truly autonomous decision in this area if all the tenets of the prevailing model are to be preserved. This is not a devastating blow to that model, merely uncomfortable. Since it excludes decreasing-cost services from complete local autonomy, it probably excludes at least a number of transportation, recreational, and telecommunication services. One thinks immediately of mass transit systems, highways, parks (assuming no congestion), and television and internet cable transmissions. At this point it appears that local governments have only a single decision to make on their own, that of providing services with significant externalities among the local constituents.

Politics and the Social Welfare Function

A second, and more fundamental problem with the conventional solution to the distribution function was mentioned earlier in the chapter: Within the mainstream normative theory of the public sector, in what meaningful sense has an autonomous government been established if that government does not have the ability to determine a set of distributional rankings among its constituents, such as by means of a social welfare function? According to the normative theory, distributional rankings are the only element that the government itself brings to the analysis through a collective political decision; otherwise, it merely accepts consumers' preferences as paramount and acts, in effect, as their agent. Without the distribution function, an autonomous government can hardly be said to exist. The conventional analysis suggests that lower level governments have essentially a single set of decisions to make on their own, those relating to markets with significant externalities among the local constituents. In doing so they merely accept the distribution of income within their jurisdictions as determined by the combination of competitive market forces and national redistribution policies. They are agents pure and simple, sounding out the preferences of their constituents to satisfy conditions such as $\sum MRS = MRT$.

One begins to wonder why local governments should even bother with externalities. If the national government is engaging in lump-sum redistributions to achieve a just distribution of income in a first-best environment, then it is satisfying a set of first-order interpersonal equity conditions of the form:

$$\frac{\partial W}{\partial U^h} \frac{\partial U^h}{\partial X_{h1}} = \qquad \text{all } h = 1, \ldots, H$$

where:

$W = W(U^1, \ldots, U^H) =$ the social welfare function.
$U^1, \ldots, U^H$ is the utility functions of the H individuals in the society.
$X_{h1} =$ the consumption of good 1 by person h (one can think of good 1 as lump-sum income arising from a fixed factor of production).

But, if the national government knows enough to do this, it certainly knows enough to satisfy the pareto-optimal conditions within each jurisdiction to correct for local externalities. Put differently, if the national government is satisfying the distributional preferences of society, it might as well do everything else. The local governments are clearly not necessary.

We have reached an impasse. On the one hand, local governments have no political input into a formal model of the public sector without social welfare functions. On the other hand, redistributions at lower levels of government dictated by local social welfare functions can generate competition problems or incompatibilities among governments.

One might be tempted to resolve the impasse by permitting all governments to have social welfare functions but allowing only the national government to redistribute lump sum to pursue distributional goals. The problem with this solution is that the notion of a first-best social welfare optimum loses its meaning as a general rule. Consider the situation depicted in Fig. 29.1. Suppose locality L has two people. The curve U^1-U^2 depicts the utility-possibilities frontier for the two people. $L_1, L_2,$ and L_3 are the local government's social welfare indifference curves. Let ray 0C represent an optimal distribution of utility between the two people as determined by the national social welfare function. If forced to be on the ray 0C, the locality will choose point C, but this will not be a first-best optimum from its own citizens' point of view. It is forced into a second-best optimum. If it can redistribute, it will move to D, but then the social welfare function of the national government is not maximized. In either case, it is not clear that society has achieved a welfare optimum, since the citizens belong simultaneously to both governments. Moreover, a compromise solution between C and D on the utility-possibilities frontier obviously satisfies neither government.

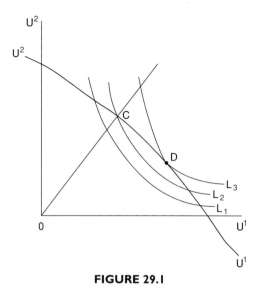

FIGURE 29.1

Redistributions in Reality

Our final criticism of the conventional analysis is simply an appeal to reality. State and local governments in the United States (or any other country) clearly do have distributional preferences. There are any number of examples. State and local governments provide public assistance and other social services to the poor. Questions of choosing among different taxes at all levels of government often consider their perceived incidence. States and localities are concerned about citizen mobility from a distributional perspective. States worry that increases in their public assistance payments will encourage in-migration of the poor from other states. High-income communities use zoning laws in the form of minimum lot sizes to prevent entry of low-income households. These examples all imply that states and localities make social welfare rankings.

It is also true that social welfare rankings differ among localities, states, and the national government. In general, the citizens in any given lower level government do not simply accept the national social welfare ranking as necessarily just, an assumption crucial to the conventional model. Furthermore, these differences in distributional preferences can be given a broader interpretation. People choose different jurisdictions not only because they demand different kinds of public allocational type services but also because they choose to live with people whom they deem compatible in terms of such factors as education, cultural background, and so forth. To deny the latter point is to deny an important justification for a federal system of governments. In essence, federalism supports fraternalism, the principle of states' rights applied to the distribution question in its broadest sense. We are not suggesting that people should pay heed to these factors. The ability to isolate oneself from "undesirables" which federalism allows may itself be viewed as undesirable. If one thought so, this would be a strong argument against establishing autonomous local governments. Federalism is not necessarily an optimal form of government.

The Need for Local Social Welfare Functions

In conclusion, we would argue that an optimal structure of fiscal federalism within the traditional theory of the public sector requires a schema whereby each government can simultaneously maximize its own social welfare function, subject to the usual generalized production constraints and market clearance. This is so for two reasons:

1. A truly autonomous government does not exist within the traditional normative theory of the public sector unless it has a social welfare function or some such means of deciding the relative ethical rankings of its constituents.

2. In a federalist system of governments, social welfare maximization by each government as defined above is the only acceptable meaning of an overall first-best social optimum.

Expanding on the second point, recall that the central theoretical problem in designing an optimal federalism is to divide the functions of the public sector among the governments so as to retain the maximum degree of local autonomy while avoiding conflicting decisions among the governments. One must accept the fact that people simultaneously pay allegiance to more than one government and that inconsistencies are almost certain to arise. One manifestation of this point already referred to is that governments will have different social welfare rankings, in general. Given this problem, the suggested definition of a first-best social welfare optimum is the only apparent possibility.

Optimal Redistribution in a Federalist System: An Alternative Model

The basic ingredients of our search for a formal model of federalism were presented in the preceding section. We seek a model in which:

1. Each government simultaneously maximizes an individualistic social welfare function subject only to generalized production constraints and market clearance. This serves as the definition of a first-best social welfare optimum in a federalist system.

2. Autonomy in the decision-making process is preserved at the lowest possible level of government. Without this assumption, the motivation for

developing a federalist system effectively collapses. One can always describe a model in which the national government does everything.

Assume a perfect correspondence so that externalities (and scale economies) are entirely contained (exhausted) within each jurisdiction.

A comment is in order before presenting the model. Potential incompatibility is a central feature of a federalist system because citizens are simultaneously members of more than one government. If condition 1 is satisfied, these inherent incompatibilities will have been dealt with in a particular way; they will not have disappeared. Therefore, the theoretical problem of determining an optimal federalist system can be restated as follows: What minimum restrictions must be placed on a federalist system of governments to ensure both of the above conditions? Clearly some restrictions must be placed on at least some governments. Incompatibilities are almost certain to arise if each government has the standard Bergson–Samuelson social welfare function used in single-government models. Each government cannot have social welfare functions whose arguments are the utility functions of their individual constituents.

The prevailing model places the restriction, unacceptable in our view, that no government but the national government can have a social welfare function. Our alternative model can be thought of as one with more acceptable restrictions.

In our opinion, the model that is consistent with federalism requires a dynastic set of social welfare functions, as follows:

> Each government has an individualistic social welfare function whose arguments are the social welfare functions of the governments *immediately* below it in the hierarchy of governments. The lowest level governments have individualistic social welfare functions whose arguments are the utility functions of their constituents—that is, the standard Bergson–Samuelson social welfare function.

In terms of the United States, the national government's social welfare function would contain as arguments the social welfare functions of the 50 states, each state's social welfare function would have as arguments the social welfare functions of the localities within the state, and each locality would have a social welfare function with the utility functions of its constituents as arguments.

To simplify notation, consider a two-tiered federalist system with a national government and L local governments.

Let:

$U^{hl}(X_k^{hl})$ be the utility function of person h living in locality l.
$h = 1, \ldots, H$
$l = 1, \ldots, L$

with X_k^{hl} the kth good consumed by person h living in locality l, for $k = 1, \ldots, N$.

(Note: there are only H people. People are double subscripted according to who they are and where they live.)

Also, let

$L^l[U^{hl}(X_k^{hl})]$ be the social welfare function of locality l, whose arguments contain the utility functions of all persons (or potential persons) living in locality l.

$F[L^l(U^{hl}(X_k^{hl}))]$ be the national social welfare function with L arguments, $L^1, \ldots, L^L$.

The restrictions on this model consist of the arguments that are allowed to appear in each government's social welfare function.

In this model, allocational decisions are determined exactly as in the prevailing model. The local governments make all decisions on services exhibiting economies of scale and/or externalities as long as the extent of the externalities or scale economies is contained within the local jurisdiction. The national government would provide those services with spillovers across localities, or design grants-in-aid to ensure efficient solutions at the local level (to be discussed in Chapter 31). Each government would maximize its own social welfare function subject to resource and generalized production constraints and market clearance. The usual first-best pareto-optimal conditions would emerge in each case because any social welfare terms drop out from this set of first-order conditions.

The difference with respect to the conventional model is that every government would also be engaged in lump-sum redistributions to satisfy the interpersonal equity conditions. Let good 1 be the good transferred lump sum. The lth local government must satisfy the following relationships:

$$\frac{\partial L^l}{\partial U^{hl}} \frac{\partial U^{hl}}{\partial X_1^{hl}} = \qquad \text{all h in l, every l} = 1, \ldots, L$$

The national government satisfies the following interpersonal equity conditions:

$$\frac{\partial F}{\partial L^l} \frac{\partial L^l}{\partial U^{hl}} \frac{\partial U^{hl}}{\partial X_1^{hl}} = \qquad \text{all h} = 1, \ldots, H$$

Notice, however, that the redistributions of the local governments ensure that the last two terms of the expression are equal for all people within a given locality, *l*. Therefore, all the national government need do is tax and transfer income lump-sum among localities until the entire term is equal for all people. At that point, its social welfare is also maximized.

As an example consider two localities, 1 and 2. By their actions,

$$\frac{\partial L^l}{\partial U^{hl}} \frac{\partial U^{hl}}{\partial X_1^{hl}} = \qquad \text{all h in 1}$$

and

$$\frac{\partial L^2}{\partial U^{h2}} \frac{\partial U^{h2}}{\partial X_1^{h2}} = \quad \text{all h in 2}$$

If $\partial F/\partial L^1(\ ) > \partial F/\partial L^2(\ )$, the national government would transfer income from 2 to 1 (and the localities would redistribute to maintain social equality on the margin within each jurisdiction). Presumably, the marginal social utility of income of the citizens of 1 would drop and that of 2 would rise (all from the national viewpoint). Redistribution continues until:

$$\frac{\partial F}{\partial L^1}(\ ) = \frac{\partial F}{\partial L^2}(\ ) \qquad (29.9)$$

The same schema holds for an n-tiered hierarchy of governments.

Comments on Our Alternative Model

The advantages of this model over the conventional model of optimal federalism are twofold. First, each government has an identity as traditionally defined in the theory of the public sector; that is, each government is allowed a social welfare function. Consequently, all governments provide important inputs into policy decisions and each retains the ability for truly autonomous decision making over the standard microeconomic functions assigned to the public sector. Second, the definition of a first-best social welfare optimum in a federalist system has been clarified and is consistent with the traditional definition of a first-best social welfare optimum with a single government. Both pareto optimality and the interpersonal equity conditions in terms of individuals are satisfied at all levels of government.

The major *operational* difference between the two models is that grants-in-aid among governments now play a central role, even if there exists a perfect correspondence for allocational functions. It is no longer true that redistributions among people at the national level are the "preferred alternative," as Oates claimed. In the alternative model presented here, only the lowest level governments redistribute among people. The higher governments use grants-in-aid to other governments exclusively in their redistributions.

The United States recognizes both models in its redistribution policies and cannot seem to decide which is the better approach to the distribution question. On the one hand, there are a number of national transfer programs, such as Social Security and Food Stamps, that transfer income directly to people. On the other hand, public assistance (welfare) was strictly a state and local initiative until the Great Depression forced the federal government to become involved. Despite the entry of the federal government, major elements of the U.S. public assistance effort remained essentially state programs. In particular, the states determined the level of monthly payments for the poor who qualified for assistance under the programs. The role of the federal government was primarily to offer financial assistance to the states, with the federal share of the costs dependent in part upon the relative fiscal capacities of the state governments. The replacement of AFDC with TANF further increased state autonomy in providing for impoverished families with dependent children. Public assistance, therefore, has always been structured in line with our alternative model. The United States cannot seem to decide which model for resolving the distribution question is the better approach.

Finally, notice that our alternative model avoids the two problems which proponents of the conventional model perceive as potentially devastating to the federalist system if lower level governments are allowed to redistribute income. Our alternative model obviously avoids the incompatibility problem with nonmobile populations, given the permissible arguments of each government's social welfare function. It also, at least formally, avoids the competition problem with mobile populations. Mobility of the kind that plagues U.S. cities today is a problem partly because the rich who leave do not adequately compensate those remaining behind for the loss in resources when they move out. The U.S. commitment to federalism (that is, to autonomous local governments) supports this phenomenon, which certainly contributes to inequality of opportunity in this country. A number of state supreme courts have questioned the legitimacy of local autonomy in ruling that financing education primarily through local property taxes is inherently discriminatory.

The conventional model suggests that the answer to unwanted inequality lies in stronger national redistributive policies. This may well work, but it represents a movement away from the federalist system. The alternative model presented here suggests an approach that would strengthen the federalist system. If the wealthy residents of city A move to suburb B because city A decides to redistribute income to its poor, presumably the state will insist upon a redistribution from B to A in order to maximize its own social welfare function. Upon knowing that such compensation is required, the incentive to move would diminish. Should the state fail to redistribute in this way, city A is the clear loser, but this is a matter of the state's preferences, not a formal inadequacy of our alternative model. If, as a practical matter, lower level governments within the federal hierarchy are seen to be acting perversely, then one would not want a federalist system in which lower level governments make truly autonomous decisions. There is certainly nothing sacred about a federalist system of governments. We have only suggested that our alternative model is consistent with the notion of a first-best social welfare optimum given the existence of a federalist system.

A final comment is that nothing can preserve complete local autonomy in a world of perfect mobility. Horizontal equity—equal treatment of equals— is the only possible equilibrium condition under perfect mobility no matter how society tries to structure its redistributive responsibilities. Therefore, all governments must accept the same degree of vertical equity—of inequality—

throughout the nation. Nonetheless, permitting local social welfare functions gives localities a say in determining how much inequality a society will allow. We will return to the effect of mobility on local redistributions in Chapter 30.

REFERENCES

Buchanan, J., "An Economic Theory of Clubs," *Economica*, February 1965.

Oates, W., *Fiscal Federalism*, Harcourt Brace Jovanovich, New York, 1972.

Pauly, M., "A Model of Local Government Expenditure and Tax Capitalization," *Journal of Public Economics*, October 1976.

Stigler, G., "Tenable Range of Functions of Local Government," *Federal Expenditure Policy for Economic Growth and Stability*, Joint Economic Committee, Subcommittee on Fiscal Policy, Washington, D.C., 1957.

30

OPTIMAL FEDERALISM: THE SORTING OF PEOPLE WITHIN THE FISCAL HIERARCHY

For a given distribution of the population throughout a nation, it is a reasonably simple exercise to define various examples of externalities and decreasing costs over subsets of the entire population and then describe an optimal set of local jurisdictions that can correct these problems in an optimal manner. But there remains the important question of whether people will naturally group into subsets congruent with the set of local jurisdictions required for a social welfare optimum.

Charles Tiebout,[1] the founding father of the mobility literature, was optimistic about federalism. He conjectured that the jurisdictions would form as required. Tiebout argued that the great advantage of federalism

---

[1] C. Tiebout, "A Pure Theory of Local Expenditures," *Journal of Political Economy*, October 1956. Tiebout's article is the seminal work, the first to consider the gains from local jurisdictions in a neoclassical framework.

compared with having a single government was that it permitted individuals to "vote with their feet," as they search for the combination of local services and taxes that maximizes their utility. Tiebout believed that if all people were free to search in this fashion, and packages of services and taxes were replicable, then social welfare would be maximized. This was so for two reasons. First, the ability to search for one's most preferred level of public goods avoids the free-rider problem associated with nonexclusive goods in the single-government model. People naturally reveal their preferences as they search among localities. Second, people with the same tastes will congregate together,[2] thereby providing a better match of preferences to the level of public services provided. Also, the public services will be offered at minimum cost. No cost differences can persist across localities offering identical services because people will naturally gravitate from high-cost to low-cost towns. In effect, the market for local public services will be perfectly competitive.

Tiebout spawned a huge literature that tested his conjecture using formal models, both positive and normative analysis. The positive analysis considers how people sort themselves among the localities. The normative analysis judges the outcomes of the sorting process using the standard efficiency and equity norms.

The literature has generally not supported Tiebout's conjecture; the problem of forming optimal jurisdictions turns out to be much more subtle than Tiebout had imagined. The positive analysis has shown that the sorting process may not reach an equilibrium—some people always want to move to another locality. Normative judgments are moot absent an equilibrium. Furthermore, even if the sorting process does reach an equilibrium, the outcome is often not optimal. The ability of people to move in response to government policies introduces another avenue for inefficiency even though it may produce a better match of preferences for the local public services. Tiebout's conjecture that federalism produces a social welfare optimum obtains only under highly specialized conditions that are unlikely to hold in most practical settings.

The literature on mobility following Tiebout is among the largest in all of public sector economics, so large that we cannot hope to do it justice here. Our more modest goal is to highlight some of the principal modeling techniques and results in the literature.

THE MODELING DIMENSIONS

Models of mobility under federalism vary along at least eight dimensions that influence the results predicted by the model. The dimensions include the

[2] As George Stigler put it, people would choose among high service–high tax, medium service–medium tax, and low service–low tax communities. See G. Stigler, "Tenable Range of Functions of Local Government," in *Federal Expenditure Policy for Economic Growth and Stability*, Joint Economic Committee, Subcommittee on Fiscal Policy, Washington, D.C., 1957.

underlying economic environment, the nature of the local government sector, and the information set available to citizens within a locality. The following list captures the main distinctions among the models in the literature, although by no means the only distinctions.

The Underlying Economic Environment

Flexible or Fixed Number of Communities

Models that assume a flexible number of communities typically envision people settling a new frontier that was previously uninhabited. Communities form and provide public services. If people do not like the outcome, they can join with other dissatisfied people and form another community offering a different mix of services. Communities continually form and break apart as people search for an equilibrium. The fixed-community models apply to more developed nations. In one variation, the number of communities is fixed but not their size. In another variation, both the number and the size of the communities are fixed. There are a given number of housing sites across all communities that just equals the total population, and equilibrium requires that people sort themselves among the existing houses such that no one wants to move again.

Endowment Income or Earned Income

Some models assume that people are endowed with a given amount of income that they bring with them as they move from one community to another. Some of the income is taxed to pay for the public services. Other models assume that the private and public goods have to be produced within each community, so that income is earned as a result of the production. The factors of production may be labor, land, and capital; just labor and land; or just labor. If just labor, there may be only one kind of homogenous labor or two classes of labor with different skill levels. Also, the output/income from production may be uncertain because of random shocks to the production function. The shocks may be favorable or adverse and either national in scope or idiosyncratic to localities. The produced income, or some portion of it, may be taxed to pay for the public services.

The Housing Market

The nature of the housing market is tied to the choice of flexible or fixed communities. The market for land is irrelevant in the frontier models because land is assumed to be available in unlimited amounts at a fixed or no charge. The housing services simply become part of the composite commodity. In contrast, the housing market can become a central feature of a fixed community model, especially if the number of housing sites is fixed. A housing market also allows for the possibility of financing the local public services with property taxes. As a general rule, the operation of housing markets

prevents an economy of fixed communities from reaching a first-best optimum. This is especially so in models with property taxes, since the property
tax itself is a distorting tax.

The Local Government Sector

The Government's Objective Function

There is quite a bit of variety here depending on whether the government
officials are utility or profit driven. A natural objective in a normative analysis
is to achieve a social welfare optimum, or at least a pareto optimum if the local
governments are denied social welfare functions, as they most often are. Profit-
driven models typically take one of two forms. In one version, the community
is controlled by local developers whose goal is to attract citizens so as to
maximize their profits. In another version, the community is controlled by
one subset of citizens, immobile landlords who own all the land (housing sites).
The landlords try to attract the mobile subset of the population who are
searching among communities and who pay rent to the landlords in their
chosen community. The landlords (developers) offer public services with the
goal of maximizing the rent (profit) they receive.

The Political System

The assumed political systems vary every bit as much as the governments' objective functions. One popular choice is voting for public services by
direct democracy—the town meeting model—along with the assumption that
the preferences of the median voter are decisive. The median voter is the one
whose preferences for the public services lie at the midpoint of the distribution of preferences among all the members of the community. Other models
assume a representative two-party system in which the majority party prevails. In models with profit- and rent-maximizing developers and landlords,
the developers and landlords are usually assumed to have complete control
over the public service and tax policies, although they have to pay attention
to the preferences of the mobile citizens they are trying to attract.

The Public Services

The public service is usually a Samuelsonian nonexclusive good, often
with the modification that the good may be subject to congestion. Congestion
means that the amount of the good's services available to each person
diminishes as the population increases. If the amount of the services per
person diminishes in direct proportion to the population, then the public
good has the same attributes as a private good. Hence the congestion feature
permits a specification of the public service that varies along the full spectrum
from a nonexclusive good to a private good. One important result in the
literature is that congestion of some form is necessary to justify local governments when nonexclusive goods are the only activity requiring public sector
intervention.

Taxes

The most common choices are a lump sum head tax, a property tax, and various kinds of income taxes, such as taxes on wage income or rents (profits). Not surprisingly, lump-sum taxes are often required for efficient outcomes.

The Knowledge Set

Nash or Other Behavior

The main distinction here is how savvy the individuals are within each community. Do they take the policies of other communities as given as they make their own decisions about public services and taxes? Or, do they assume that people in other communities react to their decisions in a utility-maximizing fashion? The distinction matters because decisions of any one community generate externalities for all other communities as people move in response to the decisions. As expected, federalism is more likely to achieve efficient outcomes if the mobility externalities are internalized. Note, also, that assumptions about people's reactions to policies in other communities are relevant only in the fixed-community models.

JURISDICTION FORMATION IN ACCORDANCE WITH THE THEORY OF CLUBS

The natural place to begin is with a model of mobility that generates a social welfare optimum, in line with Tiebout's conjecture. The assumption of flexible communities is the one most compatible with Tiebout's thinking, a frontier environment in which communities can form, break apart, and reform to generate the public service levels that subsets of people most prefer. The housing market is irrelevant in such a market, as are information assumptions.

Flexible-community models ask three interrelated questions:

1. Are there incentives for the formulation of local jurisdictions to provide traditional public services such as Samuelsonian nonexclusive public goods?
2. Will the resulting local public services be provided in accordance with standard first-best decision rules, such as $\sum MRS = MRT$?
3. Will jurisdictions form in such a manner that the public service is provided at least cost?

If the answer to all these questions is "yes", then the outcome can be a social welfare maximum with some additional assumptions.

The models used to analyze these questions draw heavily on Buchanan's theory of clubs.[3] Briefly, Buchanan argued that determining the optimal

---

[3] J. Buchanan, "An Economic Theory of Clubs," *Economica*, February, 1965.

membership of any club has an externality element to it. Think of a swim club. On the one hand, accepting new members reduces the direct out-of-pocket costs to the current members by spreading the costs associated with the swimming pool and clubhouse over more people. On the other hand, the new members generate external diseconomies in the form of a more crowded pool. Thus, the optimum-sized membership occurs when the marginal costs of the external diseconomies just equal the marginal savings from spreading total operating costs. A related issue is the optimal size of the pool for a given membership.

The theory of optimal clubs can be adapted quite easily to explain the optimal formation of local jurisdictions along with the provision of local public services. It can also be used to justify the existence of local jurisdictions. We will consider a simple model that Martin McGuire used to analyze this problem.[4]

To fix ideas, begin with a baseline model of a nonexclusive good that is consistent with the model in Chapter 6, a model that does not have club-like features. Suppose a country consists of H identical people whose preferences are defined over two goods, X, and Y^h, where:

X = a Samuelsonian nonexclusive public good provided by a government.

Y^h = the income of person h assumed fixed (alternatively, an endowment of a composite commodity with $P_y \equiv 1$).

Preferences are given by:

$$U^h(X, Y^h) \qquad \text{all } h = 1, \ldots, H \qquad (30.1)$$

Rather than defining a production function relating X and the Y^h, assume first-best production efficiency and posit a cost function for X:

$$C = C(X; \text{other arguments}) \qquad (30.2)$$

where C is measured in dollars, the same as the Y^h. If we assume that

1. Income is optimally distributed,
2. $C = C(X)$, with no other arguments, and
3. The costs of X are shared equally by all people by means of head taxes

then this representation of the Samuelsonian public good is equivalent to the formulation in Chapter 6.[5] To see this, note that the utility of each person h with equal cost sharing is

---

[4] M. McGuire, "Group Segregation and Optimal Jurisdictions," *Journal of Political Economy*, January/February, 1974.

[5] The assumption of equal cost sharing is convenient but unnecessary, as long as the cost sharing is lump sum.

$$U^h \left[X, Y^h - \frac{C(X)}{H} \right] \qquad h = 1, \ldots, H \qquad (30.3)$$

Since all people are identical and the distribution of income is optimal, all the government need do is maximize Eq. (30.3) with respect to X. The first-order conditions are

$$\frac{\partial U^h}{\partial X} - \frac{\partial U^h}{\partial y^h} \cdot \frac{\partial C}{\partial X} \cdot \frac{1}{H} = 0 \qquad (30.4)$$

where:

$$y^h = \left[Y^h - \frac{C(X)}{H} \right] \equiv \text{disposable income}$$

Rearranging terms:

$$H \cdot \frac{\dfrac{\partial U^h}{\partial X}}{\dfrac{\partial U^h}{\partial Y^h}} = \frac{\partial C}{\partial X} \qquad (30.5)$$

or $H \cdot MRS_{X,y^h} = MC_X = MRT_{X,y^h}$, with $P_y \equiv 1$. Equation (30.5) is the familiar first-best decision rule for public goods, implying national provision of X to all people within the country.

X must have two properties for local provision of the public good to be optimal and analogous to a club: excludability and congestion. Excludability means that if some locality provides an amount of X to its constituents, it can effectively prevent all other people from consuming its X. In terms of the theory of clubs, the services of the club are nonexclusive to its own members, but excludable to nonmembers. (i.e., only swim-club members can use the pool).

Excludability alone is not sufficient for optimal provision of X at the local level. The second requirement is that the good must be subject to congestion. As X is provided to more and more people, each person receiving X bears increased costs in some form.

The additional costs can be modeled in one of two ways. It may be that each person's enjoyment of X diminishes as more people consume it, along the lines of a straight consumer externality. This assumption implies that utility is a function of X, Y^h, *and* N, where N is the number of people consuming X, with $U_N < 0$. Alternatively, the direct costs of providing X could vary directly with N, so that $C = C(X, N)$, with $\partial C / \partial N = C_N > 0$.

With each person bearing some of the direct cost of providing X, it hardly matters in a formal sense which method is chosen. One can think of the cost function as including the external diseconomies of crowding, so that the two stories are virtually identical. All that matters is that each person's utility depends inversely upon N, the number of people consuming the public good. Examples might include police protection and education, in which the quantity of X commingles with certain quality attributes that vary with N to determine the cost of providing a unit of service. For example, police services can be replicated as more people move into a district, but the sheer increase in numbers may cause the costs of controlling criminal activity to increase more than proportionately.

In fact, McGuire chooses the direct cost approach, writing:

$$C = C(X, N) \qquad C_X, C_N > 0 \qquad\qquad (30.6)$$

With equal sharing of the costs, the utility of person h becomes $U^h[X, Y^h - C(X, N)/N]$. That is, each person pays the average costs of X where the average is defined relative to N for a given X. McGuire further assumes that the average costs are U-shaped, as depicted in Fig. 30.1. The spreading effects of having N in the denominator dominate up to some point, after which the marginal crowding costs (C_N) dominate, causing average cost to increase.

Under the twin assumptions of excludability and congestion, society has to determine the optimal provision of the good within each jurisdiction and the optimal size of each jurisdiction. Formally, society's problem becomes:

$$\max_{(X, N)} U^h \left[X, Y^h - \frac{C(X, N)}{N} \right]$$

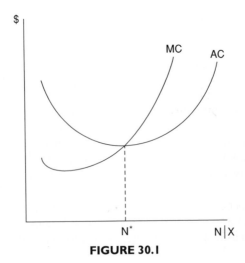

FIGURE 30.1

The first-order conditions are

$$X \text{ (optimal provision):} \quad \frac{\partial U^h}{\partial X} - \frac{\partial U^h}{\partial y^h} C_X \frac{1}{N} = 0 \qquad (30.7)$$

$$N \text{ (optimal size):} \quad \frac{\partial U}{\partial y^h} \left(\frac{-NC_N + C}{N^2} \right) = 0 \qquad (30.8)$$

Rearranging terms:

$$X: \quad N \cdot \left(\frac{\frac{\partial U}{\partial X}}{\frac{\partial U}{\partial y^h}} \right) = C_X \qquad (30.9)$$

$$N: \quad \frac{C}{N} = C_N \qquad (30.10)$$

Notice that Eqs. (30.9) and (30.10) are both functions of X and N, so that the provision of X within each jurisdiction and the optimal size of each jurisdiction are determined simultaneously. Nonetheless, each equation separately has a familiar interpretation. Equation (30.9) says that, given N, each jurisdiction should follow the usual public good decision rule, $\sum \text{MRS} = \text{MRT}$, to determine the optimal amount (or size) of X. Equation (30.10) says that, given X, people should form groups such that the average cost of X just equals the marginal costs of one additional person. This is the minimum efficient scale of operation, the long-run $\text{AC}_{\min}$ that occurs in competitive markets. As long as jurisdictions can be replicated, people can always regroup until $\text{AC}_{\min}$ obtains in each jurisdiction. No one should have to bear average costs higher than the minimum. Furthermore, Eqs. (30.9) and (30.10) imply equal-sized jurisdictions with identical people, H/N in number. National provision of a single X to all H people is no longer optimal, as long as $\text{AC}_{\min}$ occurs at $N^* < H$.[6]

McGuire also considers the case of a heterogeneous population consisting of homogeneous subgroupings. Without reproducing that model, it is

---

[6] The $\text{AC}_{\min}$ solution can be thought of as an instance of perfect correspondence even though Oates defined a perfect correspondence with respect to an externality that affected a distinct subset of people (firms). Here the additional costs associated with N vary continuously with N. Nonetheless, one can consider X as having two attributes, an externality associated with the public good quality of X and a decreasing cost element associated with the relationship of costs to N. For this good, a perfect correspondence occurs when the decreasing costs are exhausted. Since the X are exclusive to each jurisdiction, the externality associated with X automatically satisfies the perfect correspondence criterion once the jurisdictions have been set. Another point to note is that H/N* may not be an integer. This possibility causes minor technical problems that need not concern us. For a full analysis, see S. Scotchmer, "Public Goods and the Invisible Hand," in J. Quigley and E. Smolensky, Eds., *Modern Public Finance*, Harvard University Press, Cambridge, MA, 1994, chap. 4.

intuitive that each jurisdiction consists of people with like tastes, and that conditions (30.9) and (30.10) hold within each jurisdiction. X has to be provided to people of like tastes in order to maximize each person's net benefit of consuming and paying for X. The only substantive difference is that the level of X varies across jurisdictions, depending on tastes.

Curiously enough, although the McGuire model talks about the simultaneous problems of providing public goods and forming local jurisdictions, it does not necessarily imply local autonomy. The national government could still be the sole supplier of X. It would simply note that the costs of X vary with access to X, so that it would not be optimal to provide a national level of X with access to all, but rather exclusive subsets of X in accordance with conditions (30.9) and (30.10). With homogeneous populations, the amount of X provided to each subgroup would be equal, but these amounts would differ from the single amount of X provided if access did not affect direct costs or create external diseconomies. All McGuire has really done is complicate the nature of the production of X (or the externality associated with X). The national government could, in principle, anticipate this complication even though it is difficult to imagine national provision of local services such as police. Furthermore, local autonomy cannot guarantee by itself that the optimal conditions will obtain because people may not actually form subgroups in an optimal manner. Indeed, McGuire was forced to impose the following rather complex scenario to ensure that the pareto-optimal conditions obtain in the final equilibrium.

Reaching the Optimum

Imagine, at first, a single individual searching among local jurisdictions that have already been established, but only on a temporary basis. Suppose the individual currently belongs to "temporary" community j. In deciding whether to move from community j to some other community, k, the individual compares the benefits of the move with its costs. The benefits arise from the difference in the public goods provided in each community, X^k versus X^j. The costs depend upon the payment or tax scheme used by each town.

According to McGuire, a natural assumption is that each town asks a new member to pay the marginal costs of entry, so that no existing town member loses by having a new entrant. This is a standard assumption of mobility models. Thus, the cost comparison is $C_N^k(X^k, N^k)$ versus $C_N^j(X^j, N^j)$, where C_N is the marginal cost of X in terms of N.

Consider a move to a marginally different community. The *change* in costs can be represented as the total derivative of C_N:

$$dC_N = C_{NX}dX + C_{NN}dN \qquad (30.11)$$

Recall that N and X are simultaneously determined, so that a change in N changes the optimal level of X. Dividing Eq. (30.11) by dX defines the marginal cost/benefit ratio that is available to the individual if he moves:

$$\frac{dC_N}{dX} = C_{NX} + C_{NN} \left.\frac{dN}{dX}\right|_{\text{supply}} \qquad (30.12)$$

Equation (30.12) is the individual's ability to trade private goods for the public good on the margin.

Consider, next, the individual's preferences for such a move. The marginal rate of substitution between X and Y^h,

$$MRS^h_{X,\,Y^h} = \frac{dY^h}{dX} = -\frac{dC_N}{dX}$$

indicates the individual's willingness to trade private goods for the public good on the margin (an increase in costs subtracts, dollar for dollar, from private income Y^h). Hence, the individual searches until the willingness to trade equals the ability to trade, or

$$MRS^h_{X,\,Y^h} = C_{NX} + C_{NN} \left.\frac{dN}{dX}\right|_{\text{supply}} \qquad (30.13)$$

Homogeneous groupings naturally form if many people are searching under these conditions, since localities offering a given marginal cost/benefit ratio ultimately attract only those people whose $MRS_{X,\,Y^h}$ equals that ratio (assuming sufficient ability to form towns so that everyone is in equilibrium). Hence:

$$N \cdot MRS_{X,\,Y^h} = NC_{NX} + NC_{NN} \left.\frac{dN}{dX}\right|_{\text{supply}} \qquad (30.14)$$

must hold in the final equilibrium, where N represents the number of people in a particular homogeneous subgroup i.

McGuire argues next that the optimality conditions, (Eq. 30.10) ($C/N = C_N$), must necessarily hold in the final equilibrium if localities can be replicated sufficiently. With each person paying the marginal costs of entry, C_N, the only way that total tax payments can equal the total costs of providing X is if MC equals AC, or $C_N = C/N$. If C_N were temporarily in excess of C/N in some towns and below C/N in others, all of which offer equal levels of X, the people in the high-cost towns would move to the low-cost communities until all profits or rents to existing members disappear. In this sense, the search acts as a competitive market mechanism.

The McGuire search procedure, then, establishes two equilibrium conditions:

$$\frac{C}{N} = C_N \qquad (30.15)$$

and

$$N \cdot MRS_{X, Y^h} = NC_{NX} + NC_{NN} \left.\frac{dN}{dX}\right|_{supply} \tag{30.16}$$

Equation (30.15) is one of the two conditions for a welfare optimum. It remains to show that Eqs. (30.15) and (30.16) together imply the second pareto-optimal condition, the standard public goods decision rule, (Eq. 30.9).

To see that they do imply Eq. (30.9), totally differentiate Eq. (30.15) to obtain:

$$C_X dX + C_N dN = NC_{NX} dX + NC_{NN} dN + C_N dN \tag{30.17}$$

Rearranging terms:

$$(C_X - NC_{NX})dX = NC_{NN} dN \tag{30.18}$$

$$\frac{(C_X - NC_{NX})}{NC_{NN}} = \left.\frac{dN}{dX}\right|_{supply} \tag{30.19}$$

Substituting Eq. (30.19) into (30.16) and simplifying yields:

$$N \cdot MRS_{X, Y^h} = C_X \tag{30.20}$$

as required. Tiebout's conjecture holds true in McGuire's fluid, frontier model of fiscal federalism.

FIXED COMMUNITIES AND HOUSING SITES: ADDING THE HOUSING MARKET

McGuire's frontier model can reasonably ignore the housing market on the grounds that supply of land is perfectly elastic in frontier regions where jurisdictions are forming, breaking apart, and reforming, with each town replicating all others in the final equilibrium. The housing market cannot be ignored in models with a fixed number of jurisdictions, however, because then property values are necessarily tied to the provision of public services. Suppose some town offers a particularly attractive public services–tax mix. The demand for that town's services–tax mix might well cause property values there to rise as people try to move in. A final equilibrium cannot be achieved until the relative attractiveness of the town's services–tax mix is fully capitalized into the value of the town's property.

The Pauly Model of the Housing Market

In general, the housing market has an important impact on both the nature of the equilibrium and whether an equilibrium even exists. A model developed by Mark Pauly is instructive for exploring the various possibilities when the jurisdictions are fixed.[7] It lies at the opposite end of the spectrum from McGuire's frontier model in assuming a fixed number of communities along with a fixed number of housing sites.

Let:

X = a composite commodity whose price equals 1.

G = a bundle of public services, exclusive of taxes.

g = the unit price of (tax for) a public service, assumed constant across all jurisdictions.

R = the rental value of a standardized vector of property and housing services.

Y = lump-sum consumer income, assumed fixed for each individual.

Consumer utility is defined over X and G. Thus consumers solve the following "as if" maximization problem—that is, as if they could choose the value of G:

$$\max_{(X_h, G_h)} U^h(X_h, G_h)$$

$$\text{s.t.} \quad Y^h = X_h + gG_h + R \quad h = 1, \ldots, H$$

Assume initially that R is equal across all jurisdictions. The as-if maximization determines each person's most preferred amount of G which they will try to match as closely as possible with the set of Gs offered in the given communities.

Suppose the maximization generates a G_h^*. Person h, and all other consumers identical to h in terms of preferences and income, will want to form a jurisdiction providing exacting exactly G_h^* of public services, replicating if necessary to avoid any increases in R. If they could do so, preferences for public service bundles would be met exactly by homogeneous subgroupings of the population, and there would be no capitalization. This is the situation envisioned by the McGuire frontier model. Furthermore, g is essentially a head tax so that the subgroups would generate a pareto-optimal equilibrium.

Suppose, however, that there are a fixed number of localities, $\ell = 1, \ldots, L$, with the following characteristics:

1. Each locality offers a particular level of public services represented by the vector $\vec{G} = (G_1, \ldots, G_\ell, \ldots, G_L)$ in ascending order of G_ℓ;
2. Each town has a fixed number of properties, represented by the vector $\vec{H} = (H_1, \ldots, H_\ell, \ldots, H_L)$, such that $\sum_{\ell=1}^{L} H_\ell$ equals the entire population of individuals seeking a location; and

---

[7] M. Pauly, "A Model of Local Government Expenditure and Tax Capitalization," *Journal of Public Economics*, October 1976.

3. Rental values are specific to each locality, represented by the vector
$\vec{R} = (R_1, \ldots, R_\ell, \ldots, R_L)$

In this case it is possible that no individuals will find their preferred G_h^*, given the vectors of rental values and available public service bundles. All one can say is that individual h will locate in town ℓ_1 if:

$$V^h(G_{\ell 1}, R_{\ell 1}) > V^h(G_\ell, R_\ell), \text{ for } \ell \neq \ell_1 \qquad (30.21)$$

where $V^h(\ )$ is the indirect utility function of person h. G and R are parameters from the individuals' point of view. Together, they determine X_h, given Y^h, from the budget constraint.

Let $\eta(G_\ell) =$ the number of people who choose to locate in locality $\ell, \ell = 1, \ldots, L$. Equilibrium requires that:

$$\eta(G_\ell) = H_\ell \qquad \ell = 1, \ldots, L \qquad (30.22)$$

Everyone has to live somewhere.

There will be no capitalization of public service bundles in equilibrium only if $R_\ell = \overline{R}$, for $\ell = 1, \ldots, N$, holds as well. Return to the initial situation in which rental values are equal across all localities. Rental values can remain equal only if the search criterion, (Eq. 30.21), over all $h = 1, \ldots, H$, produces an exact matching of desired locations with the vector of locations available across all communities. Needless to say, a perfect matching without capitalization is unlikely. If it does not obtain, then the vector of rental values must change.

For example, suppose there existed a perfect matching that was upset by a sudden decline in G_1, the public services offered in the first locality. Some consumers in town 1, those who were closest to indifference between town 1 and 2, now prefer town 2 at the existing rental values. Their attempt to move to town 2 may drive up rental values there. But if rental values in town 2 begin to rise, some people in town 2, those closest to indifference between town 2 and town 3 at the initial equal rental values, now prefer town 3. Rental values in town 3 may begin to rise, and so on. The rental values in all towns may change. Another possibility is that R_1 decreases as G_1 increases and everyone stays put. In any event, equilibrium can only be restored if Eq. (30.22) is reestablished for all ℓ, and it will be an equilibrium with capitalization of public service bundles.

The equilibrium may never be restored, however. Pauly offers the following scenario as an intuitive counterexample relating to local educational services financed by local property taxes. Suppose there are two classes of otherwise identical families: small families with two or fewer children and large families with more than two children. Small families naturally want to live in towns with other small families; otherwise, the small families would be subsidizing the education of the large families for any given level of educational expenditures. Thus if a given community consists of, say, an equal mix of large and small families, the small families will search for communities with a higher percentage of small families. But large families also prefer communities with a higher proportion of small families because of the resulting educational subsidies. Hence, large families follow the small families in their search for communities with a higher percentage of small families. As rental values adjust, small families move once again, only to be followed by the large families, and so on.

The system may reach an equilibrium if rental values in mixed communities exactly capitalize the pattern of subsidies, which are absent in the homogeneous communities. That is, the rental values of small homes in mixed communities would have to be less than the rental values of small homes in a homogeneous community of small families (given equal education expenditures) to offset the subsidy paid by small families in the mixed communities. Conversely, the rental values of large homes in mixed communities would exceed their rental values in homogenous communities of large families.[8] But even if such capitalization occurred, there is no guarantee that Eq. (30.22) can be satisfied as required for a general equilibrium.

The Hohaus–Konrad–Thum Model of Housing Market Distortion

The housing market is both beneficial and harmful in models of federalism. Its beneficial function is the one described above, that it helps to bring the sorting of people across fixed communities to an equilibrium. At the same time, however, the housing market introduces two potential sources of inefficiency into the economy that preclude the achievement of a first-best social optimum. One is that it gives local officials the option of levying a property tax, which is the easiest tax to collect at the local level and therefore the one that localities use in the United States and elsewhere. Unfortunately, a property tax is not a lump-sum tax. It introduces a standard second-best tax distortion by increasing the relative price of housing services. The second, more subtle, distortion is that it can prevent localities from providing the level of public goods that maximizes social welfare. We will consider the second distortion here because it is the one inherent in the sorting process.

---

[8] Bruce Hamilton provides a similar example for high-income and low-income people. In his model, which uses a property tax, the low-income properties in mixed communities command a premium relative to their value in homogeneous communities, since their share of taxes declines in the mixed community for a given level of public services. The opposite holds for higher income properties in mixed communities. His model generates an equilibrium because properties can be expanded or contracted in each town, but it is not an efficient equilibrium. Because land values rise for low-income properties in the mixed communities, suppliers have an incentive to oversupply low-income housing in these communities. Consequently, low-income housing prices in mixed communities will no longer reflect the true value of the subsidies provided by the property taxes collected on the high-income properties. See B. Hamilton, "Capitalization of Intrajurisdictional Differences in Local Tax Prices," *American Economic Review*, December 1976.

Bolko Hohaus, Kai Konrad, and Marcel Thum analyzed this sorting distortion with a simple model patterned after Hotelling's model of optimal product differentiation.[9] The model has the following elements:

1. *Fixed communities and housing sites.* Hohaus, Konrad, and Thun posit two equal-sized communities, L and H, with just enough housing sites to accommodate the entire population. The entire population is defined as a continuum indexed from (0, 1), and half the population must choose to live in each community.

2. *The public sector and political system.* Each community provides a Samuelsonian nonexclusive public good, X, excludable to members outside the community. The preferences for X are ordered along the same (0, 1) continuum as the population. That is, person j prefers X_j. The political system that determines the amount of X in each community is a direct democracy, with the median voter decisive. When voting for the public good in each community, the median voter takes as given the amount of the public good in the other community.

The communities levy equal lump-sum head taxes to pay for the public good, whose total cost is C in each community. There is no tax distortion in the model.

3. *Social welfare.* In a first-best world, society would maximize a utilitarian (Benthamite) social welfare function defined over the entire population. This becomes the welfare standard against which the actual equilibrium is compared.

Preferences. The individuals have identical utility functions that depend on how closely the public good provided in their community matches their most preferred amount of the good. Letting X_H and X_L be the amounts of the public good in communities H and L, the utility functions of individual i in H and individual j in L are

$$U(X_H, X_i) = \alpha - \beta(X_H - X_i)^2 \tag{30.23}$$

and

$$U(X_L, X_j) = \alpha - \beta(X_L - X_j)^2 \tag{30.24}$$

Hohaus, Konrad, and Thum assume that the people have distributed themselves across the community such that those with the lowest preferences for X are in L, (0, 0.5), and those with the highest preferences are in H, (0.5, 1), hence the use of L and H to designate the low- and high-X communities. As we will see below, this distribution is the one that brings the provision of X in the actual equilibrium closest to the provision that maximizes social welfare. Also, with this distribution of the people, the head taxes are C/0.5 in each community, since

[9] B. Hohaus, K. Konrad, and M. Thum, "Too Much Conformity? A Hotelling Model of Local Public Goods Supply," *Economic Letters*, Vol. 44, No. 3, 1994, pp. 295–299.

$$\int\limits_{0}^{.5} (C/0.5)dX = C = \int\limits_{0.5}^{1} (C/0.5)dX \qquad (30.25)$$

The Housing Market Equilibrium

In deciding which community to choose, people compare the housing prices and the amounts of the public good in each community. The housing market equilibrium must be such that the person on the margin is just indifferent between the two towns. Given the ordering of X, this is the person whose preferred amount of X is 0.5. Therefore, in equilibrium the housing prices in the two communities, P_L and P_H, must satisfy:

$$P_L + \beta (X_L - 0.5)^2 = P_H + \beta (X_H - 0.5)^2 \qquad (30.26)$$

or

$$P_L - P_H = \beta (X_H - 0.5)^2 - \beta (X_L - 0.5)^2 \qquad (30.27)$$

The Median Voter

Given the assumed distribution of the population, the median voters in the two towns would prefer $X_L = 0.25$ and $X_H = 0.75$, absent any consideration of housing prices. But the natural assumption is that they do care about housing prices. In particular, they care about the difference in the housing prices in the two communities should they ever decide to move to the other community. They also understand that the amount of X they choose affects the difference in housing prices. Therefore, they choose their optimal amount of X upon considering both their preferred amount of X and the difference in housing prices.

Consider the median voter in L. Her goal is to maximize

$$U(X_H, X_L) = P_L(X_H, X_L) - P_H(X_H, X_L) + \alpha - \beta (X_L - 0.25)^2 - C/0.5 \qquad (30.28)$$

But the housing prices are given by Eq. (30.27). Substituting Eq. (30.27) into (30.28) yields:

$$U(X_H, X_L) = \beta (X_H - 0.5)^2 - \beta (X_L - 0.5)^2 + \alpha - \beta (X_L - 0.25)^2 - C/0.5 \qquad (30.29)$$

Taking X_H as given, the first-order conditions w.r.t. X_L are

$$\partial U/\partial X_L = -2\beta (X_L - 0.5) - 2\beta (X_L - 0.25) = 0 \qquad (30.30)$$

$$X_L = 0.375 \qquad (30.31)$$

Similar analysis of the median voter's decision in H yields $X_H = 0.625$. Notice from Eq. (30.27), that with X_L and X_H both 0.125 removed from 0.5, there is no difference in housing prices in the two communities in the voting equilibrium.

The Social Welfare Optimum

The social welfare optimum under a utilitarian social welfare function would be $X_L = 0.25$ and $X_H = 0.75$, the median voters' preferred amounts of X. With the optimal Xs each 0.25 from 0.5, they would also imply no difference in housing prices from Eq. (30.27). This is the result that Tiebout had in mind: People with the closest preferences for the local public good would live together and provide the best possible match of the public good to their preferences. Instead, the actual equilibrium produces too much conformity in X relative to the social welfare optimum. The distortion arises because the person whose preferences determine the housing market equilibrium differs from the median voter in each community.

Note, also, that the assumed distribution of people across the two communities produces the largest difference between X_L and X_H. Suppose, instead, that people were uniformly distributed across the communities, the opposite extreme from the assumed distribution. Then the preferred X by the median voters in both communities would be 0.5 which, from Eq. (30.30), would be the amount of X provided in each community. This total conformity is as far as possible from the social welfare optimum of $X_L = 0.25$ and $X_H = 0.75$.

Sophisticated Voters

The Hohaus–Konrad–Thum model is convenient for demonstrating a point made earlier in the chapter, that more sophisticated voters can often improve the outcome of the sorting mechanism. Consider again the median voter in L. Suppose this voter understands the structure of preferences well enough to realize that the voting equilibrium has to be symmetric around 0.5, so that $(X_H - 0.5) = (0.5 - X_L)$, or $X_H + X_L = 1$. This is hardly a great leap in sophistication, since Eq. (30.29) assumes that the voter understands how equilibrium is determined in the housing market. Substituting for X_H in Eq. (30.29) and maximizing yields $X_L = 0.25$. A similar understanding by the median voter in H yields $X_H = 0.75$. Hence, replacing the Nash assumptions with this additional degree of sophistication generates the social welfare optimum.

Empirical Estimates of Public Services Capitalization

The hedonic price technique described in Chapter 26 has been used to determine whether local public services and taxes are capitalized into housing prices as the Tiebout sorting theory suggests they should be. The results of these studies are mixed, and the technique fell out of favor as economists began to realize that no clear pattern of capitalization was ever likely to emerge.

With imperfect Tiebout sorting, there is no reason to expect any one pattern of coefficients on the public sector variables, either expenditures or taxes. They could be positive, negative, or zero, depending on people's preferences for expenditure–tax bundles relative to the bundles actually provided. If, for example, most communities in a given area are providing low service bundles, whereas most people prefer high service bundles, one would expect to find a positive correlation between property values and public services. If the situation were reversed, the regression coefficient would be negative. Worse yet, suppose most towns are offering either high or low levels of public services, whereas most people prefer a medium level of service. If the distribution of public services were symmetric across communities, a regression of property values on public services would yield a zero coefficient. Yet theory would suggest that rental values in the medium service communities would capitalize the excess demand for these services. Thus, even if capitalization is occurring, regression analysis may fail to discover it.[10]

Finally, if Tiebout sorting were perfect such that all households lived in communities with exactly the public service bundle they desired, then the hedonic price estimates on the public sector variables would again yield zero coefficients.[11] In short, economists realized that testing for capitalization with the hedonic price techniques was unlikely to generate useful information.

ANYTHING IS POSSIBLE

Theoretical models of fiscal federalism have shown that the sorting of people can lead to almost any outcome. We conclude this section with a simple model by Stiglitz that can produce a wide range of outcomes, from an efficient equilibrium to an inefficient equilibrium, multiple equilibria, or an equilibrium that can be improved upon by grants-in-aid from high-income to low-income communities.[12]

[10] This particular example is due to Pauly, although Bruce Hamilton has made essentially the same point. See M. Pauly, "A Model of Local Government Expenditure and Tax Capitalization," *Journal of Public Economics*, October 1976; B. Hamilton, "The Effects of Property Taxes and Local Public Spending on Property Values: A Theoretical Comment," *Journal of Political Economy*, June 1976.

[11] This point was made, and tested, by Matthew Edel and Elliot Sclar in "Taxes, Spending, and Property Values: Supply Adjustment in a Tiebout–Oates Model," *Journal of Political Economy*, September/October 1974.

[12] J. Stiglitz, "The Theory of Local Public Goods," in M. Feldstein and R. Inman (Eds.), *The Economics of Public Services: Proceedings of a Conference Held by the International Economic Association at Turin, Italy*, Macmillan, New York, 1977. Reproduced in abridged form in A. Aktinson and J. Stiglitz, *Lectures on Public Economics*, McGraw-Hill, New York, 1980, chap. 17.

The Stiglitz Model

Stiglitz' model is a variation of the McGuire model. Stiglitz posits a fixed number of communities, but with sufficient undeveloped land available in each community that expansion or contraction of the town has no effect on land prices. Thus he does not include a housing market. The main difference from the McGuire model is that income is generated by production in the communities, with each person supplying one unit of labor. There are no other factors of production. The output from production can take the form of a private good, X, and a Samuelsonian nonexclusive good G. A second difference from the McGuire model is that G is not subject to congestion. Its services are equally available to everyone in the town. Finally, mobility from community to community is costless, so that horizontal equity—equal treatment of equals—is the sorting equilibrium condition. Since the people are assumed to be identical, everyone must have the same utility in equilibrium.

Production

Let:

$$Y = f(N), f' > 0 \text{ and } f'' < 0 \tag{30.32}$$

define the total income or output generated by the N people in the community according to the production function f(N). Also,

$$f(N) = NX + G \tag{30.33}$$

where X is the amount of the private good received by each person.

Preferences

The identical individuals have utility functions defined over X and G:

$$U = U(X, G) \tag{30.34}$$

Also, Eq. (30.33) implies that the budget constraint for each individual is

$$f(N)/N = X + G/N \tag{30.35}$$

The first task is to describe the optimal levels of G and N.

The Optimal G

To determine the optimal amount of G for a given N, the individuals solve the following problem:

$$\max_{(X, G)} U(X, G)$$

$$\text{s.t.} \quad f(N)/N = X + G/N$$

with the corresponding Lagrangian:

$$\max_{(X,G)} L = U(X, G) + \lambda(f(N)/N - X - G/N)$$

The first-order conditions are

$$X: \ U_X - \lambda = 0 \tag{30.36}$$

$$G: \ U_G - \lambda(1/N) = 0 \tag{30.37}$$

Dividing Eq. (30.37) by (30.36) and rearranging terms yield:

$$N(U_G/U_X) = 1 \tag{30.38}$$

the standard $\sum MRS = MRT$ condition for nonexclusive goods.[13]

The Optimal N

In this model, N appears only in the budget constraint of the consumer problem. Therefore, the N that maximizes utility is the N that maximizes X for a given G (or vice versa). Write the budget constraint as:

$$X = (f(N) - G)/N \tag{30.39}$$

The maximum X for a given G is given by:

$$\partial X/\partial N = (Nf' - f(N) + G)/N^2 = 0 \tag{30.40}$$

or

$$Nf' - f(N) + G = 0 \tag{30.41}$$

or

$$f' = (f(N) - G)/N = X \tag{30.42}$$

Equation (30.42) says that the community should expand to the point at which the marginal product of the last person just equals his consumption. This is the equivalent of McGuire's idea that new entrants have to pay their marginal costs of entering a community so that the existing residents are willing to accept them. In the Stiglitz model, there is no reduction in G or in the private good available to anyone else if the last person in the community produces just enough to cover his own consumption. This is a common result in the literature.

The Henry George Theorem

Equation (30.41) points to another common result known as the Henry George theorem. Rewrite Eq. (30.41) as:

$$G = f(N) - Nf' \tag{30.43}$$

---

[13] The MRT is defined in terms of NX along the aggregate production-possibilities frontier, Eq. (30.33).

With labor paid its marginal product, the term Nf' on the RHS of Eq. (30.43) is the total wage bill, and the entire right-hand side (RHS) is the economic profit from production. Therefore, (Eq. 30.43) implies that the public good should be paid for by a 100% tax on economic profits, a nondistorting lump-sum tax. This result is called the Henry George theorem after Henry George, a New York City politician in the late 1800s who led a "single-tax movement" to finance local government spending with a tax on land. He argued that a tax on land, or equivalently on annual land rents, would be nondistorting since the supply of land is fixed. Taxing pure economic profits is equivalent to taxing land rents in the sense that they are both nondistorting. Many models of federalism with local production generate this result.

Community Formation: Varying N and G

As new people enter an existing community and join in production, the amount of X and G varies. A central feature of the model is that the opportunity locus of X and G available to each individual is concave as N varies. Fig. 30.2 illustrates.

The individual budget line for a given N is $X = f(N)/N - (1/N)G$, with slope $= -1/N$. As N increases, the maximum possible X, $f(N)/N$, decreases with $f'' < 0$ and the maximum amount of G, $f(N)$, increases. In addition, the maximum utility available to the individual along each budget line first increases and then decreases. At low N, utility is low because G is low. At high N, utility is low again because X is low. Congestion in this model occurs in terms of X, not G.

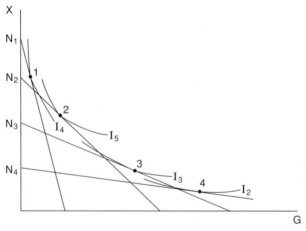

FIGURE 30.2

Possible Equilibrium Outcomes

Define V(N) as the maximum utility attainable at each N. Stiglitz illustrates different equilibrium outcomes depending on the precise shape of V(N), with each equilibrium satisfying horizontal equity across communities.

Efficient Equilibrium

Suppose V(N) is symmetric as in Fig. 30.3, reaching its peak at N*. The individuals will sort themselves in communities of size N*. If the total population is an even multiple of N*, then the sorting equilibrium is a pareto optimum. In order to compare the efficient case with the other possibilities, assume that the total population, $\overline{N}$, is twice N*, with two communities in equilibrium.

Inefficient Equilibrium

A variety of problems can arise if V(N) is asymmetric. Suppose that V(N) is as pictured in Fig. 30.4, and consider how the people will sort themselves into two communities. N_1 goes to the right and N_2 to the left, with $N_1 + N_2 = \overline{N}$. V(N) can no longer be maximized in both communities. The best outcome is point B with half the population in each community, but society may not get there. Suppose an initial sort occurs to the right of B, at N_1^1 and N_2^1. Utility is higher in community 1, so people will leave community 2 for community 1. The movement continues until everyone resides in community 1, with utility of A′. Similarly, if the initial sort is to the left of B, then everyone will move to community 2, with utility A″. A′ and A″ are both pareto inferior to B.

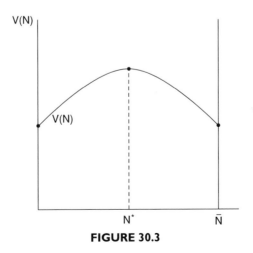

FIGURE 30.3

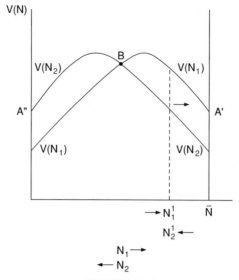

FIGURE 30.4

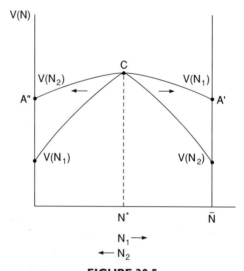

FIGURE 30.5

Efficient Equilibrium, But Unstable

Figure 30.5 pictures a variation of the previous case. Here, the best equilibrium is the pareto optimum C, with $N_1 = N_2 = N^*$, but it is not a stable equilibrium. The slightest movement away from C will lead everyone to reside in one community, with utilities A′ or A″. Instead of an optimal federalism, society is likely to get inefficient national provision of the public good.

Multiple Equilibria

Figure 30.6 illustrates the case of multiple equilibria, each with two communities. C is the best outcome, but B and B′ are the only stable equilibria. People move to B′ from anywhere to the left of C and to B from anywhere to the right of C.

Grants-in-Aid

The final example suggests a possible role for grants-in-aid among communities on efficiency grounds. Suppose the economy consists of two types of communities with different production technologies. V(N) for each community type is pictured as the two solid lines in Fig. 30.7. V(N) is symmetric, with a value of zero at $N = 0$ and at $\hat{N}$. There are no longer just two communities.

Everyone will live in a high-productivity town if there are enough such communities to accommodate everyone and give them utility greater than A, the maximum utility attainable in the low-productivity communities. If there are not enough high-productivity communities, however, a horizontal-equity equilibrium with utility of $A = A′$ in the two communities will obtain. The more productive community is the larger one. Society can do better if the more productive communities subsidize the less productive communities with a grant-in-aid, shifting the V(N) lines to the dotted lines in the figure. A new horizontal-equity equilibrium obtains with utility of $B = B′$, greater than

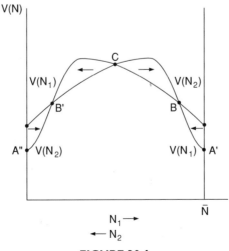

FIGURE 30.6

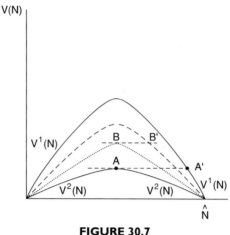

FIGURE 30.7

A = A'. The loss in income in the high-productivity communities from the grant-in-aid is more than compensated for by the movement of people to the low-productivity communities. This is another example of how a more sophisticated citizenry can improve the efficiency of the sorting process.

The ability of a simple model to generate such a variety of outcomes is unsettling and fairly devastating to Tiebout's optimistic conjecture about the potential advantages of a federalist system of government.[14,15] That said, Stiglitz's model produces three results that are common in the federalism literature, including:

1. The $\sum MRS = MRT$ rule for allocating the local public good
2. The last entrant into the community paying the marginal cost of his or her entry at the optimum
3. The Henry George Theorem, which calls for 100% taxation of economic profits or land rents to pay for the public good when the model includes local production.

[14] One ray of hope is that adding congestion of the public good to the Stiglitz model increases the likelihood of reaching a pareto optimum with two or more communities.

[15] Those interested in pursuing the sorting-of-people literature further might consult the following articles: T. Bewley, "A Critique of Tiebout's Theory of Local Public Expenditures," *Econometrica*, May 1981 (one of the first articles to formally question Tiebout's conjecture); D. Epple, R. Filimon, and T. Romer, "Existence of Voting and Housing Equilibrium in a System of Communities with Property Taxes," *Regional Science and Urban Economics*, November 1993; J. Henderson, "The Tiebout Model: Bring Back the Entrepreneurs," *Journal of Political Economy*, April 1985 (shows that profit maximization by local developers can be pareto optimal).

MOBILITY AND REDISTRIBUTION

We noted in Chapter 29 that the prevailing model of fiscal federalism calls for redistribution by the national government, in part because of the so-called competition problem. Mobility is seen to undermine the redistributional efforts of the lower level ("local") governments. A fairly large literature has evolved that explores in a positive vein the implications of local redistributions versus national redistribution when mobility is possible. The overall message from these studies is that mobility restricts but does not entirely destroy the possibilities for redistributions by lower level governments. These governments can likely engage in a considerable amount of redistribution even if mobility were costless. Furthermore, national redistribution is not necessarily preferred to local redistributions. We conclude this chapter with a discussion of three studies that highlight the main issues involved in comparing national versus local redistribution.

The Brown–Oates Model

Charles Brown and Wallace Oates published one of the first studies comparing local with national redistribution in 1987, a study that is still widely cited.[16] They adapted the pareto-optimal redistribution model of altruism to a federalist setting. In their model, each locality i consists of N_i nonpoor and P_i poor individuals. The nonpoor are altruistic to the poor—their utility depends upon their own income and the income of the poor. But the altruism of the nonpoor extends only to the poor within their locality; that is, redistribution is a local public good. This assumption generates a motivation for local redistribution (LR). Transfers are given equally to the poor within each locality and are financed by equal lump-sum taxes on the nonpoor. Thus, under LR the cost to each of the nonpoor of a dollar of transfer to each poor person in locality i is the ratio of the poor to the nonpoor, (P_i/N_i).

The poor care only about their own income, and they are the only mobile citizens in the model. Mobility is costly, consisting of one component, α, common to all the poor and another component that is specific to each poor person. Define C_k^i as the specific migration cost of person k in locality i. Poor person k will migrate from locality i to locality j if $T^j - T^i > C_k^i + \alpha$.

To isolate the effect of mobility on the possibilities for local redistributions, Brown and Oates assume that all nonpoor people have identical tastes and income and that all poor people also have identical tastes and income. Under these assumptions, differences in the amounts of transfer

[16] C. Brown and W. Oates, "Assistance to the Poor in a Federal System," *Journal of Public Economics*, April 1987.

across localities under LR depend only on the ratio (P_i/N_i) in each locality, the price of the transfer to the nonpoor. The transfer is determined by a majority vote, but the nonpoor are always assumed to be in the majority $(N_i > P_i$, all i). Finally, the nonpoor in each locality select their desired transfer to the poor under the Nash assumption that transfers in all the other localities remain at their current levels.

Local redistribution under these assumptions is compared with national or centralized redistribution (CR). Under CR, all the nonpoor are assessed equal head taxes to pay for transfers to all the poor. Thus, the price of a dollar of transfer to the poor is the same for all the nonpoor, equal to the ratio of the total poor population to the total nonpoor population, $\left(\dfrac{\sum_i P_i}{\sum_i N_i} \right)$. The poor everywhere receive the same transfer and there is no incentive for mobility.

The question Brown and Oates ask is whether the average level of transfers to the poor is lower under LR than CR in this model, and the answer is "not necessarily." Consider the case of just two localities. Under LR with the Nash assumption, mobility leads to a general incentive for the nonpoor to reduce the amount of transfer. An other-things-equal increase in locality i's transfer to the poor induces immigration of some poor from the other locality, j, which increases (P_i/N_i), the price of the transfer. The locality with the higher transfer, say i, experiences immigration of new poor, so the price actually does rise and the transfer falls. In locality j, however, the price of transferring (P_j/N_j) falls, which overcomes the general incentive not to raise the transfer and leads to an increase in its transfer. Therefore, with the transfer rising in one locality and falling in the other, the average level of transfers on LR could exceed the level of the transfers under CR.

Simulation Results

Brown and Oates perform a simulation with two localities to test whether LR is likely to reduce the average level of transfers. The nonpoor have a CES utility function defined over their own income and the income of the poor in their locality. The endowment income of the poor is set at 1/4 of the endowment income of the nonpoor. Initially 60% of the poor reside in one community and 40% in the other. The specific cost component of mobility, C_k^i, is assumed to be normally distributed with a mean and variance such as to distribute the population initially in the 60/40% ratio.

The simulations produce two expected results:

1. LR is likely to generate a lower average level of transfer than CR (this result requires that the elasticity of substitution of the nonpoor between their own income and the income of the poor be less than 1, which is the expected range).

2. Increased mobility leads to lower average levels of transfer under LR (mobility is increased by lowering the general mobility cost component α from ∞ (no mobility) to 0).

A more surprising result is that the average transfer is higher under CR than LR even with no mobility. This occurs because the price under CR, $(P_1 + P_2)/(N_1 + N_2)$, turns out to be lower than the average of the prices in the two localities, (P_1/N_1) and (P_2/N_2), in their simulation model (again, assuming that the elasticity of substitution in the CES utility function is < 1.)

Brown and Oates conclude that their simulations indicate a preference for CR over LR even when the motivation for redistribution is local. In addition to higher average transfers, CR avoids differential treatment of the poor across localities. Under LR, the amount of transfer differs considerably in the two localities in all their simulations. This differential treatment is unsettling since it depends so heavily on the initial distribution of the poor across the localities. One common objection to the U.S. public assistance programs is that the benefits that the poor receive depend on which state they happen to live in.

At the same time, however, the simulations suggest that LR can lead to substantial redistributions, even when the costs of mobility are as low as possible ($\alpha = 0$). The differences in the average levels of transfer under the two regimes are never huge. The case for national redistribution is suggestive but by no means conclusive.

Uncertain Incomes

In 1998, Kangoh Lee published a modification of the Brown–Oates model that allows for the possibility of uncertain incomes.[17] The uncertainty comes from favorable or adverse shocks to local production, which may be idiosyncratic to localities or national in scope, affecting production everywhere equally. Uncertain local income generates a further presumption in favor of national over local redistribution because national redistribution provides insurance against idiosyncratic shocks.

In Lee's model, each locality i consists of one rich person and N_i poor people, with the rich person being altruistic toward the poor within his or her own locality, as in the Brown–Oates model. Unlike the Brown–Oates model, however, the altruism of the rich toward the poor can vary across localities.

Production occurs in each locality according to the production function:

---

[17] K. Lee, "Uncertain Income and Redistribution in a Federal System," *Journal of Public Economics*, September 1998.

$$Y_i = \theta_i f(N_i) \tag{30.44}$$

θ_i is a random productivity shock that takes on the values $\underline{\theta}$ with probability p, and $\bar{\theta}$ with probability $(1 - p)$. The poor workers receive wages equal to their marginal products, $\theta_i f'(N_i)$. The rich person owns the production process (or an unnamed fixed factor) and receives the profits $g(N_i) = \theta_i(f(N_i) - f'(N_i))$. The output from production, Y_i, is a composite commodity whose price is 1.

Given that the preferences of the rich toward the poor can differ, Lee's benchmark presumption is that LR is preferred to CR in a world of no mobility and certain incomes. Pareto-optimal redistribution requires varying transfers across localities, which is not possible under CR, by assumption. As in the Brown–Oates model, CR implies equal transfers to all the poor.

Uncertainty greatly complicates the analysis. To capture the intuition of how the model works, consider the case of just two localities with equal numbers of workers, n, in each locality. Lee assumes that the local or centralized transfers to the poor are set before the production shocks are realized. Thus, the objective functions under LR and CR are

$$\text{LR: } \max E\big[U_i^R(Y_i, y_i)\big] \text{ in each locality,} \quad i = 1, 2$$
$$\text{CR: } \max E\big[U_1^R(Y_1, y_1)\big] + E\big[U_2^R(Y_2, y_2)\big]$$

where Y_i is the income of the rich person and y_i the income of each poor person in locality i. One important difference from the Brown–Oates model is that the tax to pay for the transfers is a tax on the income of the rich, a more realistic assumption.

No Mobility

Begin with the case of no mobility to focus on the insurance advantage of CR. Further, assume that the preferences of the rich are identical, so that the poor receive the same transfer under either LR or CR. (Recall that the transfers are set before the production shocks occur.) There is no efficiency advantage to LR absent uncertainty. Suppose, first, that the shocks are identical in the two localities, either adverse ($\underline{\theta}$) or favorable ($\bar{\theta}$) in both (a national shock). CR has no insurance advantage in this case, so society is indifferent between LR and CR under the given assumptions.

Suppose, instead, that the shocks are idiosyncratic, either $(\underline{\theta}_1, \bar{\theta}_2)$ or $(\bar{\theta}_1, \underline{\theta}_2)$. These outcomes happen with equal probability $p(1 - p)$. Since the transfers are set before the shock occurs, they are equal under LR or CR. Let the transfer be T per poor person.

Under LR, the rich in each locality pay taxes equal to nT regardless of the shock to the community. The total taxes paid by the rich are 2nT. Under CR, in contrast, the income tax payments to support the transfers vary according to the shocks:

$$\text{Adverse-shock locality: Tax} = 2nT\left(\frac{\theta}{\underline{\theta} + \bar{\theta}}\right) < nT$$

$$\text{Favorable-shock locality: Tax} = 2nT\left(\frac{\bar{\theta}}{\underline{\theta} + \bar{\theta}}\right) > nT$$

Since these two outcomes occur with equal probability, the expected tax of each rich person is nT, equal to the actual tax under LR. But by redistributing the tax burden from the adverse- to the favorable-shock locality, CR reduces the variation in the rich people's after-tax incomes relative to LR. Assuming the rich are risk averse, this mean-preserving contraction of their uncertain incomes increases their utility. CR is preferred to LR; it is the pareto-optimal solution.[18]

The insurance advantage of CR may not be enough to overcome the inherent efficiency advantage of LR if the altruistic preferences of the rich differ. In general, however, with no mobility and uncertain incomes, the following is true: CR is likely to be preferred to LR the more similar are the preferences of the altruistic rich and the more likely the shocks are idiosyncratic.

Mobility

Lee considers the case of perfect mobility of the poor, which implies horizontal equity. In the context of his model, the income of the poor including the transfer must be equal no matter where they live:

Horizontal Equity Condition:

$$\theta_i f'(N_i) + T_i = \qquad \text{all } i$$

Local redistribution has disadvantages and advantages relative to CR under costless mobility. On the one hand, LR gives rise to two forms of inefficiency that are absent under CR: production inefficiency and Nash inefficiency.

Production Inefficiency

Consider two localities i and j that receive the same production shock. Suppose the rich person in i is more altruistic than the rich person in j and sets $T_i > T_j$. The poor workers will migrate from j to i until the horizontal-equity condition holds, which implies that $\theta_i f'(N_i) < \theta_j f'(N_j)$. But output is maximized by equalizing the marginal products across the two localities. The unequal degrees of altruism generate a production inefficiency.

---

[18] If the tax rates were set prior to the shock rather than the transfer payment, then the insurance advantage would be received by the poor. Under CR, they receive equal transfers. Under LR, the transfers would be lower in the adverse-shock locality and higher in the favorable-shock locality given the budget constraint.

Nash Inefficiency

Lee adopts the usual Nash assumption that each rich person sets the transfer under the assumption that the transfers in all other localities are being held constant. The rich understand that higher transfers lead to immigration of some poor and a higher tax burden, which reduces the incentive to provide as much transfer. But they miss the externality that their transfer decision imposes on the other rich as the poor leave the other localities. The externality has two dimensions. The other rich face lower tax burdens with fewer poor, yet the income generated in the other localities is also lower. Ignoring this externality is the so-called Nash inefficiency under LR.

On the other hand, LR has two advantages relative to CR: a redistributional efficiency advantage and a particular kind of insurance advantage.

Redistributional Efficiency

LR permits unequal transfers across localities, which is in itself utility enhancing relative to the single transfer under CR if the altruistic preferences of the rich vary.

Insurance Advantage

The mobility of the poor in response to idiosyncratic shocks performs an income insurance function for the economy by reallocating resources from the adverse-shock communities to the favorable-shock communities. This insurance property of mobility greatly offsets the insurance advantage of CR, which operates through redistributing tax burdens among the rich in the presence of idiosyncratic shocks.

The net effect of the advantages and disadvantages of LR relative to CR is such that one regime is not necessarily preferred to the other. For example, Lee shows that CR may not be more efficient than LR even with identical preferences among the rich. Conversely, LR may not be more efficient than CR with varying preferences and identical (national) shocks because of the production and Nash inefficiencies that it gives rise to.

In general, Lee's analysis indicates that the case for CR versus LR with uncertain incomes turns on:

1. The extent of heterogeneity in the altruistic preferences of the rich across localities
2. The extent to which production shocks are national or idiosyncratic
3. The extent of the mobility of the poor in response to differences in transfers across localities

The Epple–Romer Model of Redistribution

The final model, by Dennis Epple and Thomas Romer, analyzes the possibilities for local redistribution in a much richer environment than the two previous models.[19] The Epple–Romer model is in the style of the Pauly model described earlier. They posit a set of households defined over a continuum of endowed income who must locate themselves within J local communities. Their utilities are a function of a numeraire composite commodity and housing. Although the number of communities is fixed, the supply of housing within each community is a variable, so that the number of people living in each community is endogenous. Mobility is costless.

The political process is a direct democracy with the median voter decisive. People in each community vote for a grant to be given equally to all residents, financed by a property (housing) tax. In deciding on the tax-transfer policy, voters are aware of its effect on housing prices, but they adopt the Nash assumption that their votes have no effect on the tax-transfer policies in the other communities. The other policies are taken as given. Notice that the redistributional motive in this model is entirely self-serving. The lower income residents can effect a redistribution from the higher income residents through the political process.

A model with all these features is highly complex. It requires that four conditions hold simultaneously for an equilibrium, three internal and one external. The internal equilibrium conditions are that, within each community, there must be:

1. *Housing market equilibrium*—The demand for housing must equal the supply of housing. The consumers' demand for housing is a function of the price of housing gross of the property tax, and the supply of housing is a function of the price of housing net of the tax.

2. *Budgetary balance*—The sum of the grants must equal the revenues collected from the property tax.

3. *Voting equilibrium*—The tax–transfer combination is that preferred by the median voter, and it must be consistent with the other equilibrium conditions.

The external equilibrium condition is that no one wants to move to another community.

Epple and Romer make some realistic assumptions about consumers' preferences that ensure the existence of a full equilibrium. They consider two versions of the model. In the first version, all households are renters who pay rent to absentee landlords. In the second version, some or all households are homeowners.

All Renters

Begin with the all-renters model first and consider the conditions on preferences that drive the results of the model. Utility is defined over a

---

[19] D. Epple and T. Romer, "Mobility and Redistribution," *Journal of Political Economy*, August 1991.

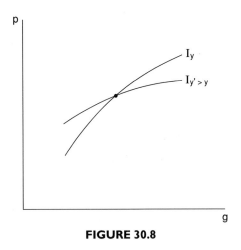

FIGURE 30.8

composite commodity (b) and housing (h). The budget constraint of a household living in community j is

$$y + g^j = p^j h + b \qquad (30.45)$$

where g^j is the per-household grant in community j, and p^j is the gross-of-tax price of housing. Utility maximization leads to an indirect utility function defined over y, p^j, and g^j. Assuming housing is a normal good, the indifferences curves for g and p are as pictured in Fig. 30.8. Furthermore, at any given (g, p) combination, the indifference curves are flatter the higher the household's income, also as pictured. This condition on the marginal rates of substitution is crucial to the results of the model.

To see why, refer to Fig. 30.9. Suppose the household with income y is indifferent between the combinations (g^i, p^i) and (g^j, p^j). Then, any household with income greater than y would prefer (g^i, p^i) to (g^j, p^j), as illustrated in the left-hand panel. Higher income households buy more housing and therefore require a bigger increase in g to compensate for the increase in p from p^i to p^j. Conversely, any household with income less than y would prefer (g^j, p^j) to (g^i, p^i), as illustrated in the right-hand panel. They require a smaller grant in compensation for the same increase in p.

Most households cannot achieve their most desired (g, p) combination with only a fixed number of communities to choose from. The following must be true, however, given the condition on the MRS: If two households with incomes y_1 and $y_2, y_2 > y_1$, most prefer community i with combination (g^i, p^i) from the J available choices, then all households with $y_1 < y < y_2$ also most prefer community i.

Finally, suppose that y_i is the highest income in community i and y_j is the highest income in community j. If $y_i > y_j$, then from the shape of the

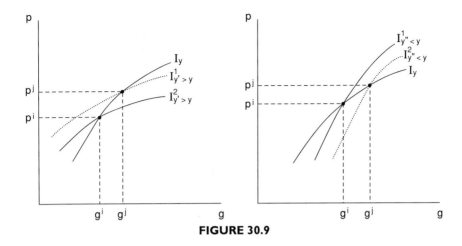

FIGURE 30.9

indifference curves, $g_i < g_j$ and $p_i < p_j$ in equilibrium. These considerations suggest the three principal results of the all-renter model:

1. The J communities stratify by income level.
2. Grants and property taxes are higher the lower the average income of the community. Lower income communities engage in more redistribution than higher income communities.
3. Even relatively high-income communities are likely to engage in some redistribution given that the preferences of the median voter are decisive. The Epple–Romer model has the property that the median voter over (g, p) within each community is the voter with the median income. Therefore, the median voter and all those with incomes below the median are likely to prefer some positive (g, p) even in very-high-income communities. Epple and Romer conclude that quite a lot of local redistribution is possible even if mobility is costless.

Homeowners

Adding homeowners to the model dramatically reduces the incentive to redistribute at all income levels because of the effect of the property tax on the net-of-tax price of housing. An increase in the property tax lowers the net-of-tax price of housing, which hurts the absentee landlords in the all-renter model. The amount of land that the landlords own is fixed, as is the number of communities, so they cannot respond to the taxes. They end up bearing some of the burden of the redistribution. Homeowners, however, now bear this burden as a capital loss, and they can influence the voting outcome. Their budget constraint is

$$y + g + \left(p^{net} - p_0^{net}\right)h_0 = ph + b \qquad (30.46)$$

where p and p^{net} are the gross- and net-of-tax housing prices, h_0 refers to the existing house, and p_0^{net} is the net-of-tax price paid originally for the house. The decline in p^{net} as taxes are raised to pay for the grant represents a capital loss, which homeowners take into consideration when voting on their preferred (g, p) combination. The capital loss flattens homeowners' indifference curves at every (g, p) combination relative to renters.

Simulation Results

Simulations of their model with three communities, roughly calibrated to the U.S. economy, generate all these results. In one version, Epple and Romer constrain the highest income community not to redistribute. In the all-renter case, the middle-income community imposes a 28% tax on housing services to finance a grant of $1676 against a mean income of $21,560. It is not true that the competition problem constrains only the lowest income communities to redistribute. Even more striking is the reduction of redistribution to trivial amounts in the all-homeowners version; grants fall to a range between $68 and $133. Epple and Romer conclude that home ownership and not mobility may be the biggest hindrance to local redistributions in a federalist system.

How applicable these findings are for the United States or any other developed market economy is difficult to say. One caveat is that the propensity to vote is inversely related to income, at least in the United States, so that the voter with the median preferences almost certainly does not have the median income in any community. Another is that local redistribution is not compared with centralized distribution. Finally, the Epple–Romer model lacks any degree of altruism toward the poor. These last two points make it difficult to compare the Epple–Romer model with the other two models above, a comment that applies generally to the federalism literature. Models of federalism have so many dimensions to choose from that no consensus model of federalism has emerged or is likely to emerge. At best we are left with a number of suggestive results, with no way yet of achieving a satisfactory synthesis.

REFERENCES

Aktinson, A., and Stiglitz, J., *Lectures on Public Economics*, McGraw-Hill, New York, 1980, chap. 17.

Bewley, T., "A Critique of Tiebout's Theory of Local Public Expenditures," *Econometrica*, May 1981.

Brown, C., and Oates, W., "Assistance to the Poor in a Federal System," *Journal of Public Economics*, April 1987.

Buchanan, J., "An Economic Theory of Clubs," *Economica*, February 1965.

Epple, D., and Romer, T., "Mobility and Redistribution," *Journal of Political Economy*, August 1991.

Epple, D., Filimon, R., and Romer, T., "Existence of Voting and Housing Equilibrium in a System of Communities with Property Taxes," *Regional Science and Urban Economics*, November 1993.

Hamilton, B., "The Effects of Property Taxes and Local Public Spending on Property Values: A Theoretical Comment," *Journal of Political Economy*, June 1976.

Hamilton, B., "Capitalization of Intrajurisdictional Differences in Local Tax Prices," *American Economic Review*, December 1976.

Henderson, J., "The Tiebout Model: Bring Back the Entrepreneurs," *Journal of Political Economy*, April 1985.

Hohaus, B., Konrad, K., and Thum, M., "Too Much Conformity? A Hotelling Model of Local Public Goods Supply," *Economic Letters*, Vol. 44, No. 3, 1994.

Lee, K., "Uncertain Income and Redistribution in a Federal System," *Journal of Public Economics*, September 1998.

McGuire, M., "Group Segregation and Optimal Jurisdictions," *Journal of Political Economy*, January/February 1974.

Pauly, M., "A Model of Local Government Expenditure and Tax Capitalization," *Journal of Public Economics*, October 1976.

Scotchmer, S., "Public Goods and the Invisible Hand," in J. Quigley and E. Smolensky, Eds., *Modern Public Finance*, Harvard University Press, Cambridge, MA, 1994, chap. 4.

Stigler, G., "Tenable Range of Functions of Local Government," *Federal Expenditure Policy for Economic Growth and Stability*, Joint Economic Committee, Subcommittee on Fiscal Policy, Washington, D.C., 1957.

Stiglitz, J., "The Theory of Local Public Goods," in M. Feldstein and R. Inman, Eds., *The Economics of Public Services: Proceedings of a Conference Held by the International Economic Association at Turin, Italy*, Macmillan, New York, 1977.

Tiebout, C., "A Pure Theory of Local Expenditures," *Journal of Political Economy*, October 1956.

31

THE ROLE OF GRANTS-IN-AID IN A FEDERALIST SYSTEM OF GOVERNMENTS

OPTIMAL FEDERALISM AND GRANTS-IN-AID: NORMATIVE ANALYSIS

First-Best Policy Environment

Whether grants-in-aid have any role in an optimal, first-best federalist system of governments depends upon the underlying model used to establish the notion of a social welfare optimum. Recall that in the conventional model of optimal federalism redistributional policy is the sole responsibility of the national government, whereas allocational functions reside in the lowest level governments consistent with pareto optimality. Consequently, only the national government is concerned with social welfare optimization as traditionally defined. The lower level governments care only about efficiency.

Grants-in-aid are unnecessary in this model, as long as the policy environment is truly first best and a perfect correspondence of jurisdictions exists for all allocational problems. The national government satisfies its interpersonal equity conditions with lump-sum taxes and transfers among individuals (and firms, with decreasing cost production), exactly as in the single-government model of the public sector. Similarly, all governments, whether national or "local," interact only with the individual consumers and firms within their jurisdictions when correcting for resource misallocations. Thus, they simply follow the normative decision rules derived under the assumption of a single government. There is no need for the grant-in-aid, because no government need be directly concerned with any other jurisdictions. In our view, this is yet another reason for rejecting the traditional model of optimal federalism. It seems implausible that intergovernmental relations would be of no consequence in a federalist system of governments, even under first-best assumptions.

Our alternative model of federalism, presented in Chapter 30, defined the social welfare optimum as an equilibrium in which each government maximized its own dynastic social welfare function, with the restriction that the arguments of each government's social welfare function are the social welfare functions of those governments immediately below it in the fiscal hierarchy. Grants-in-aid are required in this model to resolve the distribution question, since all but the lowest level governments must tax and transfer resources lump sum among the governments immediately below them in the fiscal hierarchy. In the parlance of grants-in-aid, these lump-sum grants would be *unconditional, nonmatching,* and *closed-ended*: unconditional, because one government cannot dictate to any other government how to dispose of the funds, the "states' rights" criterion; nonmatching and closed-ended, because the interpersonal equity conditions require straight resource transfers of some finite amount. Notice, too, that the "grants" are negative for those governments that must surrender resources.

Our alternative model shares with the conventional model the attribute that grants-in-aid are not required for allocational purposes in a first-best policy environment with a perfect correspondence of local functions. Simultaneously with satisfying all possible interpersonal equity conditions, satisfying all necessary pareto-optimal conditions proceeds government-by-government in the usual manner. To develop a further role for grants-in-aid, then, requires introducing some second-best distortion into the policy environment.

Second-Best Policy Environment

Imperfect Correspondence

A second-best restriction commonly analyzed in the literature is a maintained imperfect correspondence for an externality-generating activity, which causes each local government to follow the wrong decision rule. Imagine the following situation.[1] Community A, consisting of H_A individuals, provides a Samuelsonian nonexclusive public good in amount $\overline{X}_G$, the services of which are consumed directly by its own citizens. In determining the amount $\overline{X}_G$, the government of A follows the standard first-best decision rule:

$$\sum_{h_A=1}^{H_A} \mathrm{MRS}^{h_A}_{X_G, X_{h_A 1}} = \mathrm{MRT}_{X_G, X_1} \qquad (31.1)$$

where X_1 is a private good.

Suppose that H_B citizens of contiguous community B benefit from the existence of X_G in community A even though they cannot directly consume the services of X_G. For example, X_G may be police protection which has the spillover effect of reducing criminal activity in community B. In effect, then, X_G in community A becomes an aggregate external economy for the citizens of community B, entering into each person's utility function. The aggregate gain to community B's citizens on the margin can be represented as:

$$\sum_{h_B=1}^{H_B} \mathrm{MRS}^{h_B}_{X_G, X_{h_B 1}}$$

with each MRS^{h_B} measured positively. The true first-best pareto optimal conditions are, therefore:

$$\sum_{h_A=1}^{H_A} \mathrm{MRS}^{h_A}_{X_G, X_{h_A 1}} + \sum_{h_B=1}^{H_B} \mathrm{MRS}^{h_B}_{X_G, X_{h_B 1}} = \mathrm{MRT}_{X_G, X_1} \qquad (31.2)$$

Without any intervention from a higher level government in the fiscal hierarchy, X_G will be misallocated (presumably undersupplied), because community A ignores the second set of terms on the left-hand side of Eq. (31.2). The situation exemplifies the notion of an imperfect correspondence, since the jurisdictional boundaries of community A, which makes the allocational decision on X_G, do not encompass all citizens affected by the production and consumption of X_G.

There is no need for a grant-in-aid in this case. The next highest government in the fiscal hierarchy, one that includes the citizens of both A and B, could provide X_G to the citizens of A in accordance with Eq. (31.2). It does have the option, however, of allowing community A to decide on the level of X_G as before and influencing its decision with an appropriate grant-in-aid. Hence, its choice is fully analogous to that in single-government models of aggregate externalities, in which the government can either dictate the consumption of the good or use a Pigovian subsidy and maintain decentralization.

[1] A similar example appears in Wallace Oates, *Fiscal Federalism*, Harcourt Brace Jovanovich, New York, 1972, pp. 95–104. Oates's Chapter 3 and appendices provide an excellent analysis of the uses of grants-in-aid within the conventional model of fiscal federalism.

A society committed to federalism would presumably choose the grant-in-aid since it promotes decentralized local autonomy, much as a single government under capitalism would choose decentralized subsidies for aggregate externalities.

As discussed in Chapter 6, the appropriate subsidy is a per-unit subsidy, equal to the aggregate gain to the citizens of B on the margin, or:

$$s = \sum_{h_B=1}^{H_B} MRS^{h_B}_{X_G, X_{h_B1}}$$

which, in this case, is a grant-in-aid from the higher level government to community A. The grant, depicted in Fig. 31.1, would be *conditional, matching*, and *open-ended*: conditional on expenditures for X_G with a matching rate equal to the ratio s/P_G at the optimum, where P_G is the producer price of X_G (see Fig. 31.1), and open-ended because it is not optimal to limit the size of the grant to any value other than $s \cdot X_G^*$, where X_G^* is determined by the receiving government.

These simple grant-in-aid examples can be quite misleading, however. Localities tend to provide the same kinds of public services, so that the actual pattern of externalities is likely to be far more complex than depicted in our simple story. If community A's police expenditures generate external economies in community B (and, possibly, other neighboring communities), then community B's police expenditures can be expected to generate external economies for all its neighbors, including A. But, if this is so, then the spillover component of the externality is likely to be individualized by community, in which case the required pattern of grants-in-aid becomes extremely complex.

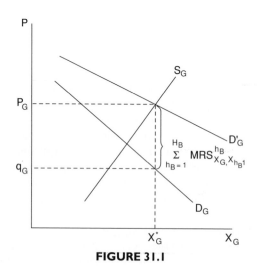

FIGURE 31.1

To see the possibilities, define $(X_{G_A}, X_{G_B}, \ldots, X_{G_C})$ as the vector of the individual community outputs, C in number, with $X_G = X_{G_A} + X_{G_B} + \cdots + X_{G_C}$ the aggregate output of X_G across all communities. If the aggregate X_G enters each person's utility function, then a single matching grant is appropriate, with $s = \sum_{\text{all } h} MRS^h_{X_G, X_{hl}}$. Referring again to police expenditures, the assumption is that the spillover effects on criminal activity within a region depend upon aggregate police expenditures across all communities within the region.

Although expenditures on police may give rise to an aggregate externality, each community is more likely to receive the most benefit from police expenditures in its contiguous communities and increasingly less benefit from police expenditures in ever more distant towns. If so, then the spillover externality remains individualized and pareto optimality requires a complex set of subsidies, one for each town. Moreover, the subsidies are interdependent, with each matching rate dependent upon police expenditures in every community. Thus, the situation is exactly analogous to case of individualized externalities arising from private sector activities.

We have seen that aggregate externalities admit to relatively simple solutions whereas individualized externalities do not. The existence of federalism, with imperfect correspondences, adds nothing to the complexity of the problem. Even if the next highest government in the fiscal hierarchy chose to provide X_G, it would still follow the same decision rules, providing, of course, that the direct services of each individual X_{G_i} are consumed exclusively by members of the corresponding community, as posited in our example. If there is not even a perfect correspondence for the direct consumption of these services, then a set of grants-in-aid is unlikely to be appropriate. In this case, the next highest government should decide upon the level of the aggregate $\overline{X}_G$ and its individual subcomponents. For instance, police services may be exclusive by town because the laws of each town forbid police to cross jurisdictions. But if there really is an imperfect correspondence here then these exclusions are arbitrary and nonoptimal. Fewer, larger police departments with a regional orientation would be the optimal solution, but these would have to be provided by the next highest government in the fiscal hierarchy.

Note finally that the analysis carries through in both the conventional model of federalism in which only the national government has a social welfare function, or in our alternative model in which each government possesses a social welfare function. As long as income is optimally distributed according to the interpersonal equity conditions of each model, allocational issues dichotomize from distributional concerns just as in single-government models.

These same points apply to externalities generated by private sector activity. Unless the direct component of the activity can be localized within a single community (say, a production externality arising at a particular site), grants-in-aid are unlikely to be pareto optimal. And even if pareto optimality could be achieved by the grants-in-aid, it may not be the most direct fiscal tool. Not surprisingly, grants-in-aid are most appropriate for publicly provided services.

Consider the example of a production site located in community A. Suppose its external diseconomies affect both citizens in A and those in other neighboring towns. If town A taxes the producer, it will undoubtedly base the tax on the marginal damages only to its own citizens. The next highest government could design a negative conditional matching grant (i.e., a tax) levied on town A that would optimally adjust for the broadened scope of the external diseconomy, but an additional direct tax on the producer would seem less cumbersome. Other more complex situations, such as the individualized pollution example in which production at multiple sites along a river generates external diseconomies for the other firms, can best be solved by producer taxes established by a higher level government and not by a set of grants-in-aid to a number of localities. There is no compelling reason to involve lower level governments as intermediaries in correcting for private sector externalities.

ALTERNATIVE DESIGN CRITERIA

That actual grants-in-aid bear little relationship to theoretical design criteria is hardly surprising, because the theory is so difficult to apply in this instance. In terms of our alternative model, distributional norms based on social welfare functions can never be more than suggestive to the policymaker. In terms of imperfect correspondences for externality-generating public services, varying matching formulas across "local" governments on the basis of marginal external benefit or harm may be unconstitutional. Faced with these realities, economists have resorted to developing practical design criteria that are at least roughly consistent with the underlying theory.

A surprising feature of the more practical literature is that it has tended to focus on distributional concerns, more in line with our alternative model of optimal distribution under federalism than with the mainstream position. A principal question is how to design grants to correct for perceived resource imbalances either across states (for federal grants) or across localities (for state grants). This focus makes sense at a practical level because many federal and state grants in the United States do attempt to direct aid disproportionately toward poorer states and localities. Examples are the federal grants to support states' public assistance payments under Temporary Assistance to Needy Families (TANF) and Medicaid and state grants to support local public school expenditures.

The LeGrand Guidelines

In the mid-1970s, Julian LeGrand suggested three sensible practical guidelines for grant-in-aid programs whose goals are redistributional.[2] First, the grants must be a function of the real income or wealth of the receiving government, commonly referred to as its fiscal capacity. LeGrand argues that jurisdictions with fiscal capacities below some target level should receive aid and jurisdictions above the target should pay a tax (receive a negative grant). In contrast, existing grant-in-aid programs always give something to all governments. The political motivations behind giving something to everyone are clear, but such grants tend by their very nature to have limited redistributional power. Note, also, that fiscal capacity accounts for differences in prices across communities, the relative expenditures required to achieve comparable levels of public services.

LeGrand's second guideline is that the amount of aid received (tax paid) should be independent of any expenditure decisions made by the receiving government. This guideline honors two principles: Redistributional policy ought properly be concerned with each government's overall initial level of resources, and, consistent with the federalist ideal, the grantor should not attempt to influence the specific spending decisions of lower level governments.

LeGrand's third guideline states that grants should vary directly with the receiving government's fiscal effort, the idea being that governments with less interest in providing public services should receive correspondingly less aid. This criterion is somewhat troublesome because it tends to contradict the second guideline. It implies that the grantor will try to influence the overall level of public services beyond the giving or taking of resources, although not the composition of these services. In any case, it is a commonly accepted principle. The U.S. Congress has frequently incorporated effort parameters into aid formulas.[3]

LeGrand shows that basing grants-in-aid on differences in fiscal capacity automatically incorporates each community's fiscal effort. To see this let:

T_i = total taxes per capita collected by government i.
P_i = a price index of public services provided by government i.
E_i = the effective tax rate in government i, the effort parameter
Y_i = the per capita tax base in government i.

---

[2] J. LeGrand, "Fiscal Equity and Central Government Grants to Local Authorities," *Economic Journal*, September 1975.

[3] When Congress replaced Aid to Families with Dependent Children (AFDC) with TANF it stipulated that the states could not reduce the expenditures on public assistance that they had been making under AFDC.

The fiscal capacity of government i is Y_i/P_i. LeGrand defines a purchasing power effort (PPE) ratio as:

$$PPE_i = \frac{T_i}{E_i P_i} \tag{31.3}$$

where purchasing power refers to the purchasing power of the taxes. But $T_i = E_i Y_i$. Therefore,

$$PPE_i = \frac{T_i}{E_i P_i} = \frac{E_i Y_i}{E_i P_i} = \frac{Y_i}{P_i} \tag{31.4}$$

LeGrand's PPE ratio is the same as fiscal capacity.

Under LeGrand's preferred grant-in-aid formula, the grantor picks a target PPE ratio or fiscal capacity, $PPE_T = Y_T/P_T$. The per-capita grant, G_i, is then designed to put all jurisdictions at that target PPE_T. Thus, G_i is such that:

$$\frac{T_i + G_i}{E_i P_i} = \frac{Y_i}{P_i} + \frac{G_i}{E_i P_i} = \frac{Y_T}{P_T} \tag{31.5}$$

or

$$G_i = E_i \left(\frac{P_i}{P_T} Y_T - Y_i \right) \tag{31.6}$$

The grant received (tax paid) depends upon a locality's fiscal effort as embodied in the tax rate, and its relative fiscal capacity, defined as the difference between its per-capita tax base and the target per-capita tax base adjusted by the differences in the prices of public services in the locality relative to the target community. Hence, all three of LeGrand's criteria are satisfied by this simple formula.

LeGrand's formula would lead to a substantial amount of redistribution, since richer than average towns would actually pay taxes. By including E_i, the formula also addresses a problem with federalism that many people find particularly inequitable; namely, wealthy communities can offer better public services than the poorest communities even though their tax rates are only a fraction of the tax rates in the poorest communities. LeGrand's formula doubly rewards the poor communities who have high tax rates. Finally, if one concedes that social welfare rankings may properly be functions of fiscal effort, among other things, this simple formula is reasonably consistent with the redistributional decision rules of our alternative model of fiscal federalism. It bears roughly the same relationship to these norms as the Haig–Simons ability-to-pay criterion does to the interpersonal equity conditions of single-government social welfare maximization. Both substitute income for utility, although the Haig–Simons criterion contains nothing comparable to the fiscal effort term.

Applying LeGrand's Principles: Bradbury et *al.*

LeGrand's grant formula is much too egalitarian to be politically acceptable. A more practical version of his proposal would be to close only a portion of the disparities in fiscal capacity:

$$G_i = kE_i \left(\frac{P_i}{P_T} Y_T - Y_i \right) \quad k < 1 \tag{31.7}$$

subject to the constraints:

$$G_i \geq 0 \quad \text{all i} \tag{31.8}$$

and

$$\sum_i G_i N_i = D \tag{31.9}$$

where D is the budget given to the distributional granting authority for the grants to reduce fiscal disparities (N_i is the population of locality i). Equation (31.8) ensures that no communities with fiscal capacities greater than Y_T/P_T would be taxed under the formula. The granting authority would maintain the budget constraint by varying k and the reference community Y_T. A high Y_T combined with a low k gives smaller amounts of aid to more communities, and vice versa. Taxes to support the grants would come from general tax revenues, not from levies on the high-fiscal-capacity communities.

In the early 1980s, Katherine Bradbury *et al.* were commissioned by the Massachusetts state government to design an equalizing grant program for distributing 5% of the state's grant budget, approximately $110 million, to the cities and towns with low fiscal capacities.[4] They approached the problem in the spirit of LeGrand, but they used a different measure of fiscal disparity in the aid formula. They based their formula on what they termed a community's fiscal gap, equal to:

$$\text{Gap}_i = \overline{E}C_i - \overline{t}B_i \tag{31.10}$$

where

$\overline{E}$ = the average per capita expenditures across all communities,
C_i = the cost of providing the average expenditures in community i
$\overline{t}$ = the average tax rate across all communities
B_i = the per-capita tax base in community i

In other words, a community's fiscal gap is the difference between what it would have to spend to provide the average local public service bundle and the tax revenues it would raise if it applied the average tax rate across all communities to its tax base.

---

[4] K. Bradbury, H. Ladd, M. Perrault, A. Reschovsky, and J. Yinger, "State Aid To Offset Fiscal Disparities Across Communities," *National Tax Journal*, June 1984.

A reference, or target, fiscal gap is defined in the same way:

$$\text{Gap}_* = \overline{E}C_{_T} - \bar{t}B_{_T} \tag{31.11}$$

The grant formula closes a portion of the difference between a community's fiscal gap and the reference fiscal gap,

$$A_i = k\,(\text{Gap}_i - \text{Gap}_T) = k\,[\overline{E}\,(C_i - C_T) - \bar{t}\,(B_i - B_T)] \qquad A_i \geq 0 \tag{31.12}$$

where A_i is the per-capita grant. The first term on the right-hand side (RHS) is the cost disadvantage suffered by community i relative to the reference community, and the second term is community i's tax-base disadvantage. The main deviation from LeGrand's principles is that the Bradbury *et al.* formula does not include an effort term.

Bradbury *et al.* argue that the average expenditure level $\overline{E}$ and the cost of providing the services C_i should be based on regression analysis. They also believe that the relative cost advantages or disadvantages should reflect only environmental factors that are beyond the immediate control of the communities, such as population density, the condition of the housing stock, and the crime rate. They posit a supply of expenditures function:

$$E_i = E_i\left(\vec{S}_i, \vec{P}_i, \vec{C}_i\right) \tag{31.13}$$

where

$\vec{S}_i$ = the vector of public services offered in community i
$\vec{P}_i$ = the vector of input prices for the factors used to produce the public
    service vector in community i
$\vec{C}_i$ = the vector of environmental factors that influence the cost of
    providing the public service in community i

The demand side of the model is a standard median voter model (described later) in which the median household solves an as-if maximization problem in terms of a numeraire private composite commodity and the vector of public services, subject to its individual budget constraints and the overall community budget constraint. The supply relationship, Eq. (31.13), enters as the expenditures in the overall community budget constraint. The analysis leads to a reduced-form equation for overall public expenditures (individual public service outputs are not measurable):

$$E_i = f\left(\overline{V}_i, \vec{A}_i, \vec{P}_i, \vec{D}_i, \vec{C}_i\right) \tag{31.14}$$

where:

$\overline{V}_i$ = the average (mean) property value in community i
$\vec{A}_i$ = a vector of other resources available to community i, such as other
    grants-in-aid
$\vec{D}_i$ = a vector of taste parameters, "demand" factors

The demand factors Bradbury *et al.* chose were per-capita income and the percentage of the population ≥ 65. The five environmental cost factors were population density, the condition of the housing stock, the ratio of children in the public schools to the entire population, the crime rate, and the poverty rate. They had no data on variation of input prices, $\vec{P}$, across the cities and towns. Equation (31.14) was estimated on a sample of 300 Massachusetts and towns.

To estimate $\overline{E}$ in the grant formula, Eq. (31.12), they set the values of all the explanatory variables in Eq. (31.14) equal to their average values across all 300 cities and towns. To compute the relative cost term C_i in their grant formula, they estimated $\hat{E}_i$ by setting the values of all the explanatory variables except $\vec{C}$ at their average values, and the values of the variables $\vec{C}$ at their actual values in community i. Then $C_i = \hat{E}_i/\overline{E}$ or $C_i\overline{E} = \hat{E}_i$ in the grant formula.

In applying the Bradbury *et al.* formula, the state:

1. Set the reference $\text{Gap}_T = 0$, to maximize the number of communities receiving aid.
2. Set an additional condition that every community receives a grant of at least \$5 per capita from the budget set aside for these grants.
3. Defined the fiscal gaps to include existing state aid, $\overline{A}$:

$$\text{Gap}_i = \overline{E}C_i - \bar{t}B_i - \overline{A}_i \tag{31.15}$$

Finally, since all grant, expenditure, and tax-base variables are in per-capita terms, the cities and towns received a proportion of the entire distribution budget equal to the product of their fiscal gaps and population divided by the sum of the fiscal gaps times populations of all the aided localities.

Bradbury *et al.* proposed that the aid be adjusted each year using the same estimating equation for E_i and just adjusting the values of the explanatory variables.

Redistributing Through Matching Grants

As our final example of practical grant design criteria we will consider Martin Feldstein's proposal for remedying unequal local public educational expenditures.[5] In the early and mid-1970s, a number of state supreme courts ruled that financing public educational expenditures entirely from local property taxes was inherently discriminatory, since wealthier communities could provide better education with less fiscal effort, that is, lower tax rates.[6] The states

---

[5] M. Feldstein, "Wealth Neutrality and Local Choice in Public Education," *American Economic Review*, March 1975.

[6] *Serrano v. Priest* in California was the landmark decision. Refer to *Serrano v. Priest*, L.A. 29820, Superior Court No. 938254.

were required to design a more equitable statewide financial arrangement which would somehow provide transfers from the wealthier to the poorer communities. Feldstein reasoned that the courts' decisions imply a fiscal solution which sets the elasticity of educational output with respect to wealth equal to zero ($E_{Ed, W} = 0$). He suggested using a matching grant for this purpose, in which the matching rate applied to any one community is inversely proportional to its wealth. To achieve this goal, one needs reliable econometric estimates of the price and income (wealth) elasticities of educational expenditures independent of a new grant program. These estimates can then be used to design the required matching rates.

To see how this would work, suppose it is possible to estimate a constant elasticity demand-for-education equation across communities of the form:

$$Ed = CP^{\alpha}W^{\beta} \tag{31.16}$$

where:

 Ed = a measure of educational output per capita.
 P = the price of a unit of educational output.
 W = a measure of per capita community wealth.
 α, β = the price and wealth elasticities.
 C = a constant term embodying all other factors influencing the demand for education.

Rewriting, Eq. (31.16) in log form:

$$\log Ed = C' + \alpha \log P + \beta \log W \tag{31.17}$$

Next, define a matching aid formula that makes the net-of-aid price a function of wealth according to the constant elasticity form:

$$P = W^{k} \tag{31.18}$$

or

$$\log P = k \log W \tag{31.19}$$

where:

 k = the elasticity of the net price with respect to wealth.

Substituting Eq. (31.19) into (31.17) yields:

$$\log Ed = C' + \alpha(k \log W) + \beta \log W = C' + (\alpha k + \beta) \log W \tag{31.20}$$

With this matching program:

$$\frac{\partial \log Ed}{\partial \log W} = E_{Ed, W} = \alpha k + \beta \tag{31.21}$$

Setting $E_{Ed, W} = 0$ implies:

$$k = -\beta/\alpha \tag{31.22}$$

Thus, the required matching rate elasticity just equals the ratio of the wealth and price elasticities of education within the state, at least for a log-linear demand for education function. Feldstein estimated an education equation for a cross section of Massachusetts communities to demonstrate his technique. The required matching rate elasticity for Massachusetts turned out to be between .33 and .37.[7]

It is worth repeating that matching grants for which the matching rate varies with respect to income or wealth have no role in the first-best theory of federalism and are at best only suggested by second-best considerations. Nonetheless, if the law requires neutralizing the effect of wealth on educational opportunity within states, then Feldstein's grant-in-aid formula provides a direct way of achieving this goal.

ESTIMATING THE DEMAND FOR STATE AND LOCAL PUBLIC SERVICES

The final issue in our analysis of grants-in-aid is an empirical one—the response of receiving governments to grants-in-aid. We have to begin with a detour, however, on the modeling of state and local governments' demands for the services that they offer. The reason is simply that any empirical analysis of how state and local governments respond to grants-in-aid is naturally embedded in a model of their demand for public services.

A number of different demand models exist in the literature, but it is fair to say that the median voter model has emerged over the past 25 years as the favored empirical model for estimating the determinants of state and local spending decisions. Its only serious competitor is the qualitative response model based on surveys that ask people questions about their desired increases or decreases in public spending. Therefore, we begin with a discussion of the median voter and survey models before turning to the response to grants-in-aid. Grants-in-aid will then be analyzed in the contest of the median voter model because it is by far the more widely used model.

The Median Voter Model

That the median voter model became so popular is testimony to the difficulties that economists face in trying to model state and local governments. In truth, the median voter model is highly problematic. It rests on extremely strong political and economic assumptions that are unlikely to hold for almost any state or locality. It also encounters some econometric problems that were not recognized in the earlier literature. These weaknesses notwithstanding, the

---

[7] M. Feldstein, "Wealth Neutrality and Local Choice in Public Education," *American Economic Review*, March 1975, p. 85.

median voter model is the predominant model for estimating the spending decisions of state and local governments.

The Political Assumptions

The model's name derives from its political assumptions. It is motivated by the direct democracy, one-person–one-vote, small town meeting, in which the citizens congregate periodically to discuss and vote on government spending and tax issues. A simple majority determines the outcome of the vote: A proposition wins if it gains 50% of the votes plus one. Under these rules, the preferences of the median voter are decisive so long as the preferences of the citizens are monotonic over the issue being voted on.

Panel (a) of Fig. 31.2 illustrates the case of a local public good G. The line G indicates the most preferred level of G for each citizen on the horizontal axis, ordered by their preferences for G. Assume an odd number of citizens so that the median voter is identified. G_{median} is the amount of G preferred by the median voter. Consider any $G < G_{median}$ such as G_1. In a vote for G_1 against a small increase in G, $G_1 + \Delta G$, the majority prefer $G_1 + \Delta G$. Similarly, for any $G > G_{median}$ such as G_2, the majority prefer a small decrease in G, $G_2 - \Delta G$. G_{median} is the only amount of G that can command the required 50% plus 1 vote majority against the next larger or smaller amount of G. The preferences of the median voter are decisive.

The idea that the median voter's preferences will be decisive in actual elections is difficult to accept for a number of reasons. First, the result relies crucially on preferences for public goods and services being monotonic. If, instead, the preferences for G are as pictured in panel (b) of Fig. 31.2, then G_1 wins a simple-majority election. The median voter prefers G_{max}, which cannot win a simple majority. More generally, democratic decision making runs up against Arrow's Impossibility Theorem. We showed in Chapter 4 that social preferences over a distinct set of choices can cycle and fail to establish a clear winner if individual preferences over the choices are not single peaked.

Cycling is almost certain to occur if people are asked to vote for choices that contain a bundle of two or more public goods, as is often the case. Town meeting members typically vote on entire budgets that include a variety of services: education, transportation, recreation, public safety, and so forth. Panel (c) of Figure 30.2 gives one example in which people are asked to vote for a combination of two public goods, G_1 and G_2. The points 1, 2, and 3 indicate the most preferred bundles for persons 1, 2, and 3, respectively. Utility declines with the distance from the most preferred choice in every direction, so that the indifference curves radiate from the most preferred choice in a circle-like pattern. In the example, the individual preferences for the three choices are as follows:

Person 1: 1 P 2 P 3
Person 2: 2 P 3 P 1
Person 3: 3 P 1 P 2

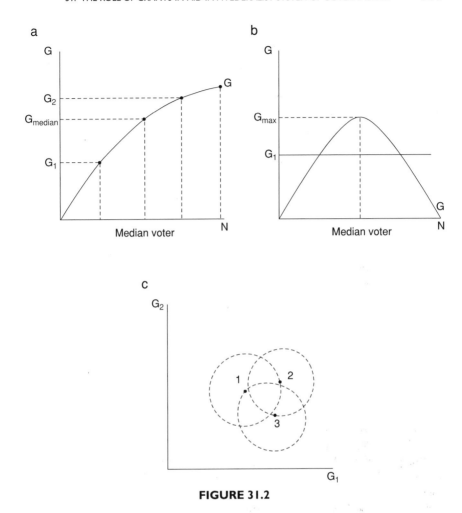

FIGURE 31.2

These are the same preferences as in Chapter 4, with the same intransitive results: Two of the three people prefer 1 to 2, 2 to 3, and 3 to 1. No clear winner emerges.

Add the political realities of representative democracy, political parties vying for votes, special interest groups lobbying legislators and members of the executive branch, and self-interested bureaucrats, and the idea that the median voter's preferences are likely to be decisive on any issue is problematic in the extreme. The median voter model can hardly be descriptive of any government except the very small towns that might still use the democratic town meeting to decide public issues. Nonetheless, researchers have used the median voter model as the basis for estimating even states' decisions.

The Economic Assumptions

The fundamental economic assumption of the model is the standard one in the federalism literature, that each household solves an as-if maximization problem to determine its most preferred level of public services.[8] The as-if maximization leads to an estimating equation that is then expanded to test a number of propositions about state and local public services of interest to economists. The model also requires a number of additional assumptions so that it can be estimated using readily available data. One of these assumptions ties the model to the political assumption that the median voter is decisive.[9]

As-If Maximization

Begin in the usual manner. Each household i has a fixed endowment of income, Y_i, that is spent on two goods, X_i and G_i. X_i is a private composite commodity and serves as the numeraire. G_i is the locally provided public good, which is purchased at price p_i. The household's as-if maximization problem is

$$\max_{(X_i, G_i)} U^i(X_i, G_i)$$

$$\text{s.t. } Y_i = X_i + p_i G_i$$

The resulting demand curve for the household's preferred G_i leads to the basic estimating equation (in log-linear form)

$$\ln G_i{}^* = a + b\ln Y_i + c\ln p_i + e_i \qquad (31.23)$$

where e_i is the error term.

The price p_i requires some explanation because households pay taxes and let the government buy the good on their behalf. They do not buy the public good directly. Consequently, the effective price depends on how the government collects taxes to pay for G. Assume that the model applies to localities that use a property tax. Then p_i turns out to be the product of two terms: the ratio of the value of household i's property, V_i, to the total property value in the locality, $V, (V_i/V)$; and the supply price of G, equal to q. This follows because household i pays a property tax equal to tV_i, where t is the property tax rate. Multiplying and dividing by V, the tax is

$$tV_i = tV(V_i/V) \qquad (31.24)$$

But the local government budget constraint requires that total taxes equal total expenditures, or:

---

[8] The household is the appropriate economic decision-making unit in the median voter model.

[9] The discussion in this section follows that of Atkinson and Stiglitz in A. Atkinson and J. Stiglitz, *Lectures on Public Economics*, McGraw-Hill, New York, 1980, pp. 322–326.

$$tV = qG \tag{31.25}$$

Substituting Eq. (31.25) into (31.24) yields:

$$tV_i = (V_i/V)qG \tag{31.26}$$

so that $p_i = (V_i/V)q$. Substituting for p_i in Eq. (31.23) yields the basic estimating equation:

$$\ln G_i{}^* = a + b\ln Y_i + c\ln(V_i/V) + c\ln q + e_i \tag{31.27}$$

Equation (31.27) is typically expanded and adjusted in the following ways to produce the final estimating equation.

Allowing for Congestion

The first adjustment is to allow for the possibility of congestion in the public good. Write:

$$G_i{}^* = G_i/N^\alpha \qquad \alpha = (0, 1) \tag{31.28}$$

where G_i is the actual G to be provided by the government. $\alpha = 0$ is the non-exclusive good; each household receives the full services of G. $\alpha = 1$ is the purely private good; it takes N units of G to provide one unit of G to household i. Expressing congestion in this way implies that the effective price of G to household i is

$$p_i{}^* = p_i N^\alpha \tag{31.29}$$

For example, household i has to pay for N units of G to get one effective unit of G if G is purely private; therefore, the effective price is N times the price as given by Eq. (31.23). Expressing Eqs. (31.28) and (31.29) in natural logs,

$$\ln G_i{}^* = \ln G_i - \alpha\ln N \tag{31.30}$$

$$\ln p_i{}^* = \ln p_i + \alpha\ln N \tag{31.31}$$

Substituting Eqs. (31.31) and (31.30) in Eq. (31.27) and rearranging terms yield the congestion-adjusted basic estimating equation:

$$\ln G_i = a + b\ln Y_i + c\ln(V_i/V) + c\ln q + \alpha(1 + c)\ln N + e_i \tag{31.32}$$

Expenditures per Person

Governments routinely publish data on expenditures rather than separate series on prices and outputs of their services. Indeed, defining the output of a school system or the police force is somewhat ambiguous and open to interpretation. With outputs ambiguous, so too are prices. Therefore, the dependent variable in the estimating equation is typically expenditures per capita for each category of public services. Write:

$$E_i/N = (qG_i)/N \tag{31.33}$$

or

$$\ln(E_i/N) = \ln q + \ln G_i - \ln N \tag{31.34}$$

Substituting for $\ln G$ in Eq. (31.32) and rearranging terms yields:

$$\ln(E_i/N) = a + b\ln Y_i + c\ln(V_i/V) + (1 + c)\ln q \\ + [\alpha(1 + c) - 1]\ln N + e_i \tag{31.35}$$

Other Determinants of G

The individual utility functions differ by a set of taste parameters, $\vec{Z}$, that reflect such things as differences in household composition and size, the households' inherent interest in supporting public education or public safety, and neighborhood characteristics such as population density and proximity to a major city. These parameters are simply added to the estimating equation (expressed here in log form):

$$\ln(E_i/N) = a + b\ln Y_i + c\ln(V_i/V) + (1 + c)\ln q \\ + [\alpha(1 + c) - 1]\ln N + \vec{d}\ln\vec{Z} + e_i \tag{31.36}$$

The Supply Price q

The supply price q presents a problem in estimating Eq. (31.35) because it is generally not observable. State and local governments do publish wage and salary data for the employees in each service category, however. Therefore, researchers typically substitute wages and salaries for the supply price by assuming that production is constant returns to scale and least-cost efficient and that the market for capital is national in scope.

To see the implication of these assumptions, assume that G is produced with capital (K) and labor (L) according to the CRS production function:

$$G = f(K, L) \tag{31.37}$$

If production is least-cost efficient, then:

$$f_K/f_L = r/w \tag{31.38}$$

where r is the cost of capital and w is the wage. Furthermore, the expansion path of capital and labor is linear given CRS. Therefore, if (K^*, L^*) is the optimal combination of capital and labor to produce G^*, then $(\lambda K^*, \lambda L^*)$ is also an optimal combination of capital and labor and produces $\lambda G^*[\lambda G^* = f(\lambda K^*, \lambda L^*)]$. But the total cost of production is

$$TC = rK + wL \tag{31.39}$$

Therefore,

$$\lambda TC = r(\lambda K) + w(\lambda L) \tag{31.40}$$

Since scaling capital and labor by λ scales both G and TC by λ for any r and w, the total cost function for G has the form:

$$TC = h(r, w)G \qquad (31.41)$$

Hence, marginal cost is

$$MC = h(r, w) \qquad (31.42)$$

Finally, assume that r is set in the national market and that the supply price, q, is equal to (or at least proportional to) marginal cost. Then q is proportional to the w, which varies across localities. This is the justification for substituting wages for q in the estimating equation, Eq. (31.36), yielding the final estimating equation:

$$\ln(E_i/N) = a + b \ln Y_i + c \ln(V_i/V) + (1 + c) \ln w$$
$$+ [\alpha(1 + c) - 1] \ln N + \vec{d} \ln \vec{Z} + e_i \qquad (31.43)$$

Whose Equation?

An equation such as Eq. (31.43) applies to each household as the solution to its as-if maximization problem. Each locality, however, supplies only one level of G (E/N) for each public service. The question, then, is whose G (E/N) obtains in the locality, and the answer is that of the median voter. But then what income and property value does the median voter have? The answer again is that the median voter resides in the household with the median income and the median property value. That is, the median voter has the median value of all the economic variables that vary by households. This heroic assumption is necessary because only median values of these variables are routinely available in the local (and state) Census of Governments. It permits estimation of the model with a cross section of data on localities (states).

An implication of this assumption is that preferences for public services are monotonic in incomes and property values. If not, then the median voter in terms of preferences for G will not necessarily have the median income or property value. One common test of this assumption is whether the full elasticity of G with respect to Y is positive (assuming public goods are normal goods). Let $(V_i/V) = t_i$ and write:

$$dG/dY = \partial G/\partial Y + (\partial G/\partial t_i)(\partial t_i/\partial Y) \qquad (31.44)$$

The first term is the direct effect of Y on G, and the second term is the indirect effect that works through the effect of Y on the value of the property (house) that people buy. To convert to elasticities, multiply all terms in Eq. (30.64) by Y/G and multiply the second term on the RHS by (t_i/t_i), yielding:

$$E_{G,Y}\,(\text{full}) = E_{G,Y}(\text{direct}) + E_{G,t_i} \cdot E_{t_i,Y} \qquad (31.45)$$

or

$$E_{G,Y}(\text{full}) = b + c \, E_{t_i, Y} \qquad (31.46)$$

from Eq. (31.43). $E_{t_i, Y}$ is the elasticity of the value of property (housing) with respect to income.

Further Conceptual Difficulties

The estimating model faces a number of additional difficulties even given all its heroic assumptions. A brief list would include the following.

Renters

The model essentially ignores renters by focusing on housing values. The median voter might not have anywhere close to the median house value when a locality contains a substantial percentage of renters, especially if renters have different demands for public services than homeowners.

Nonvoters

The model assumes that everyone votes. This is a terrible assumption for the United States, especially at the state and local level. The propensity to vote is known to be inversely related to income and education. Consequently, the median voter is likely to have income and property value well above the median.

Commercial and Industrial Property Taxes

The model should probably be adjusted for localities that levy taxes on commercial and industrial property as well as residential property, but it is not clear how. Expanding the tax base has the direct effect of lowering t_i. At the same time, however, commercial and industrial establishments increase the demand for certain kinds of public services. Therefore, the effective t_i of the median voter could rise or fall. What matters in any event is the median voter's perception of how commercial and industrial property taxation affects his or her t_i, whatever the truth might be.

Multiple-Service Budgets

The fact that votes are often taken on entire budgets strains the belief that voters can attach effective prices to each of the individual services. Do they really see the supply prices of the various services? If not, do they assume they are simply proportional to wages, and do they know the wages of the teachers, police, firefighters, sanitation workers, and so forth? More generally, do they know their share of the total property value in the community?

The Results

All these difficulties notwithstanding, the models have generated two results with a fair degree of consistency. One is that income elasticities exceed price elasticities (in absolute value), and often by a considerable margin. One

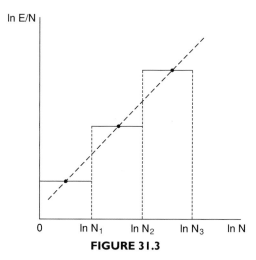

FIGURE 31.3

survey of the median voter literature concluded that the estimated income elasticity appears to be on the order of 2/3 and the estimated price elasticity somewhere between $-1/4$ and $-1/2$.[10] These estimates are roughly consistent with elasticities estimated using models other than the median voter model. The finding of very low price elasticities for local (and state) public services is the rule in the empirical federalism literature. The income and price elasticities are such that the full elasticity of public services with respect to income, Eq. (31.46), is positive, as expected.

The second consistent finding is that α is close to one for many public services; they appear to be much more like private goods than nonexclusive goods. Wallace Oates thinks this result may be an illusion, however. He believes that as populations increase in communities, many public services expand in discrete steps and become more complex, essentially different kinds of services, as illustrated in Fig. 31.3. If Oates is correct, then the public service could be nonexclusive within each step, as pictured. But the estimation will fit a line through the steps with a considerable slope (the dotted line), falsely suggesting a high degree of congestion (a high α).[11]

Econometric Problems: Tiebout Bias

Estimating an equation such as Eq. (31.43) with data on median incomes and property values across communities is almost certain to lead to biased

[10] T. Bergstrom, D, Rubinfeld, and P. Shaprio, "Micro-Based Estimates of Demand Functions for Local School Expenditures," *Econometrica*, September 1982, p. 1199 and Table IV, p. 1200.

[11] W. Oates, "On the Measurement of Congestion in the Provision of Local Public Goods," *Journal of Urban Economics*, July 1988.

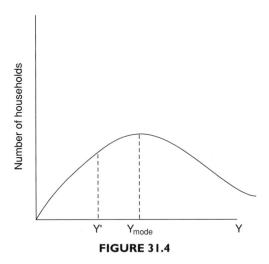

FIGURE 31.4

estimates of these coefficients. The bias occurs because households select communities on the basis of the public services in each community. For this reason, the bias is referred to as Tiebout bias. Tiebout bias is a specific instance of the estimation bias that results whenever economic agents select options on the basis of the dependent variable. Most of the existing empirical literature based on the median voter model makes no attempt to correct for Tiebout bias, certainly none before the mid–1980s. We will illustrate the bias with respect to income.[12]

Suppose that households solve their as-if maximization problems and there are enough towns so that all the households able to find their most preferred G. The matches are perfect. In this case, the estimation of G would proceed as it does for private households. Collect data on a random sample of individuals throughout the geographic region and estimate the equation (expressed here in level form):

$$G_i = a + bY_i + e_i \qquad (31.47)$$

Assume the error term e_i is normally distributed with mean zero and is uncorrelated with the independent variables. The estimate of b would be an unbiased estimate of the true b.

The matches are far from perfect, however, and this leads to the bias, as follows. Suppose the distribution of income throughout the entire region is unimodal as pictured in Fig. 31.4, and select an income Y' less than Y_{mode}. Households with income Y' have a distribution of tastes for G given by the error term in Eq. (31.47). Refer to Fig. 31.5. When $e = 0$, the number of

---

[12] The seminal article on Tiebout bias is G. Goldstein and M. Pauly, "Tiebout Bias on the Demand for Local Public Goods," *Journal of Public Economics*, Vol. 16, 1981, pp. 131–144.

households who want G' is f_0. G' is the level of G that corresponds to Y' according to the true relationship between G and Y.

Now consider the distribution of tastes for G by households with incomes equidistant from $Y', Y' - \delta$ and $Y' + \delta$. Refer to Fig. 31.6. G' is the preferred level of G for f_1 households with incomes $Y' - \delta$, and G' is the preferred level of G for f_2 households with incomes $Y' + \delta$. Given the unimodal distribution of Y throughout the region, f_2 is larger than f_1, as pictured. Since households are selecting communities on the basis of G, the median income of the community that offers G' is greater than Y'.

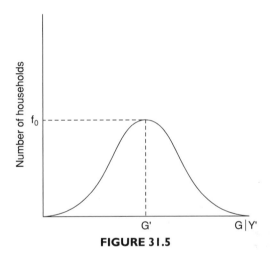

FIGURE 31.5

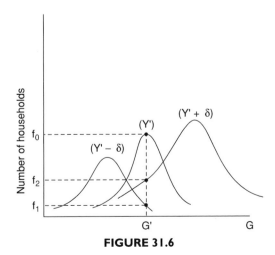

FIGURE 31.6

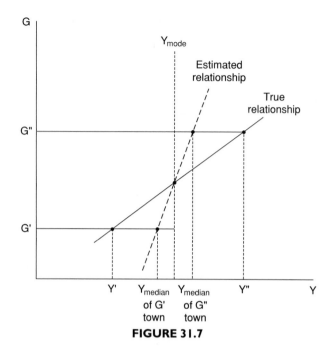

FIGURE 31.7

Similarly, select an income Y'' greater than the mode and consider the distribution of preferences for G'', the G associated with Y'' according to the true relationship between G and Y. By the same argument as above, the median income of the community that offers G'' is less than Y''.

The implication is that the estimated relationship between G and Y based on Y_{median} across localities is biased upward, as pictured in Fig. 31.7. The true relationship between G and Y is the solid line; the estimated relationship based on the median voter model is the dotted line.

Given the positive bias, the question arises whether the true income elasticities for public services really are much greater than the price elasticities, as is so commonly reported in the literature. Also, the receipt of exogenous grants-in-aid would be treated much like the receipt of income by the median voter. Therefore, estimates of the response to grants-in-aid may be biased upward as well.

Surveys

Economists also use surveys of individuals to estimate demand functions for state and local expenditures. The use of surveys was made possible by the development of the econometric theory for estimating qualitative response models.

The survey approach has two distinct advantages over the median voter model. One is that it avoids many of the unrealistic political and economic assumptions required to estimate the median voter model. Another is that it allows the researcher to collect detailed information on individual characteristics that are likely to affect households' demands for particular public services, such as the education and employment status of the head of household, the age composition of the household, race, ethnicity, the number of children in the public schools, and so forth. The principal disadvantage of the survey approach is concern about the reliability of the survey responses. Economists are inherently skeptical about surveys, having been trained to observe what people do rather than what they say. Surveys of large numbers of people are also quite time consuming and costly.

One of the earliest, and still best known, of the survey studies was by Theodore Bergstrom, Daniel Rubinfeld, and Perry Shapiro in the early 1980s.[13] We will use their study as an example of the survey approach.

Bergstrom, Rubinfeld, and Shapiro conducted a survey of 2001 people in Michigan to try to determine their demand for local school expenditures. They simply asked if people desired "more," "the same," or "less" spending. If respondents said "more," the surveyor noted that this would require higher taxes and asked if they still preferred more spending. If the answer was no, their responses were considered to be "the same." Twenty-five percent of the respondents said they would prefer "more" spending; 58%, "the same;" and 17%, "less."

To develop an estimating model, Bergstrom, Rubinfeld, and Shapiro adopted the standard assumption that people solve an as-if maximization problem to determine their desired spending levels for public services, which leads to an demand equation of the general form:

$$\ln G_i{}^* = a + b\ln Y_i + c\ln p_i + \vec{d}\ln \vec{Z}_i + \ln e_i \qquad (31.48)$$

where $G_i{}^*$ refers to the desired level of expenditures per pupil on public education rather than the output. The estimating equation mimics the estimating equation of the median voter model, other than containing a much richer vector of personal characteristics, $\vec{Z}$. For example, the relevant price p_i is the product of the respondent's tax share of an increased dollar of expenditure on education and the supply price of education. The supply price is proxied by the ratio of average teacher salaries to average salaries of all workers in the county in which the respondent resides. The distribution of $\ln e_i$ is assumed to be logistic because the estimating strategy is based on the probabilities of the responses, as explained below.

To see how the estimating model is developed, think of the demand function, Eq. (31.48), as the sum of its deterministic portion, labeled

---

[13] T. Bergstrom, D, Rubinfeld, and P. Shaprio, "Micro-Based Estimates of Demand Functions for Local School Expenditures," *Econometrica*, September 1982.

$\ln D(X_i)$, and the error term $\ln e_i$. Also, assume for the moment that there are only two categories: "more" spending and "less" spending. Finally, let G^A stand for the actual level of spending per pupil in a respondent's community.

The respondents will presumably say "more" if $G_i^* > G^A$ and "less" if $G_i^* < G^A$. The dependent variable G_i^* is unobserved, and the observed responses can only take on the two values "more" and "less" which can be represented as 1 ("more") and 0 ("less"). The limitation of the observed responses to 0 and 1 suggests a probabilistic interpretation of the model. The estimation framework should have the property that the probability of a "more" response increases the larger is $[\ln D(X_i) - \ln G^A]$, and approaches 1 as $[\ln D(X_i) - \ln G^A] \rightarrow \infty$. Conversely, the probability of a "less" response increases the larger is $[\ln G^A - \ln D(X_i)]$ and approaches 0 as $[\ln G^A - \ln D(X_i)] \rightarrow \infty$.

Consider the "more" response. $G_i^* > G^A$ implies that:

$$\ln D(X_i) + \ln e_i > \ln G^A \tag{31.49}$$

or

$$\ln e_i > \ln G^A - \ln D(X_i) \tag{31.50}$$

Giving Eq. (31.50) a probabilistic interpretation, the probability that the respondent will say more is the $\Pr(\ln e_i) > \ln G^A - \ln D(X_i)$. But, $\ln e_i$ has a logistic distribution, which is symmetric. Therefore, an equivalent statement is: The probability that the respondent will say "more" is the $\Pr(\ln e_i) < \ln D(X_i) - \ln G^A$. But, this is just the value of the logistic cumulative density function evaluated at $[\ln D(X_i) - \ln G^A]$, $F(\ln D(X_i) - \ln G^A)$, as pictured in Fig. 31.8. Similarly, the probability that the respondent will say "less" is $1 - F(\ln D(X_i) - \ln G^A)$.

The coefficients of Eq. (31.48) can be estimated by maximizing the likelihood function of the "more" and "less" responses expressed in terms of the binomial distribution (each response is considered to be one draw from the distribution):

$$\max L = \prod_{i=more} F\left(\ln D(X_i) - \ln G^A\right) \prod_{j=less}\left(1 - F\left(\ln D(X_j) - \ln G^A\right)\right) \tag{31.51}$$

The Threshold Effect

The response "the same" is accounted for by adding a threshold parameter, $\delta > 1$, such that the respondent replies "more" if $G_i^* > \delta G^A$, and "less" if $G_i^* < G^A/\delta$. This leads to three regions under the logistic cumulative density function:

$$\Pr(\text{"more"}): \quad \Pr(\ln e_i) < \ln D(X_i) - \ln G^A - \ln \delta$$
$$= F\left(\ln D(X_i) - \ln G^A - \ln \delta\right)$$

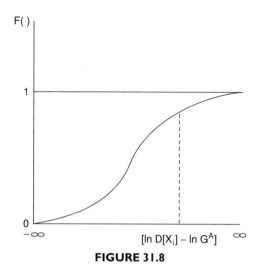

FIGURE 31.8

$$\text{Pr(“less”):} \quad \text{Pr}(\ln e_i) > \ln D(X_i) - \ln G^A + \ln\delta$$
$$= 1 - F\big(\ln D(X_i) - \ln G^A + \ln\delta\big)$$

$$\text{Pr (“the same”): } 1 - \text{Pr(“more”)} - \text{Pr(“less”)} = F(\ln D(X_i)$$
$$- \ln G^A + \ln\delta) - F\big(\ln D(X_i) - \ln G^A - \ln\delta\big)$$

The estimation maximizes a multinomial likelihood function with the three sets of product terms defined over the three responses.

The Results

Bergstrom, Rubinfeld, and Shapiro found a number of interesting results. One was that the estimated income and price elasticities, $E_y = 0.64$ and $E_p = -0.39$, were in the range of the estimates from the studies using the more aggregated median voter model. Another was that the ability of the survey approach to capture a broad set of individual characteristics was an important advantage. They found that respondents were more likely to want more spending on education if they were black, Jewish, renters, elderly, or a school employee or had children in the public schools. Conversely, respondents were more likely to want less spending if they were unemployed, retired, or disabled or sent their children to private schools. Finally, the estimated threshold effect was large, 1.5, suggesting perhaps that Tiebout searching leads to reasonably good matches of people's desired spending on public education.

Tiebout Bias

The survey approach is subject to Tiebout bias because the respondents selected their communities partly on the basis of the dependent variable.

Bergstrom, Rubinfeld, and Shapiro did not account for Tiebout bias in their original study, but Rubinfeld, Shapiro, and Judith Roberts published a follow-up study 5 years later on the same survey data that did try to account for the Tiebout bias.[14] Their results indicate that correcting the estimation for the bias is important. In particular, the new estimates produced very low income and price elasticities, both on the order of 0.1 (in absolute value). The very low income elasticity is really quite unusual in the local public sector empirical literature. The threshold effect also increased, to 1.65. In other words, spending on education would have to be 65% above or below its existing level before people would want less or more spending. They appear to be quite satisfied with the *status quo*, suggesting even more successful Tiebout matching of preferences than the earlier study.

THE RESPONSE TO GRANTS-IN-AID

The literature on the response to grants-in-aid has been motivated by two factors: (1) grants-in-aid have long been very important to state and local governments, and (2) governments receive many different kinds of grants-in-aid. Recall that grant formulas vary across three dimensions: conditional–unconditional, matching–nonmatching, and closed-ended–open-ended. Public sector economists have had a natural theoretical interest in the expected responses to the various possible combinations of formula parameters. Should it matter, for example, whether governments receive conditional or unconditional grants, matching or nonmatching grants, and so forth? On an empirical level, econometric analysis has tried to pinpoint the actual response to existing grants, both for its own sake and as a test of the theoretical analysis. Taken together, this body of literature is as extensive as any in public sector analysis, yet both the theoretical and empirical analysis of grant response have been far from conclusive.

The Flypaper Effect

The most consistent result in the empirical literature is that governments' responses to exogenous grants-in-aid far exceed their responses to exogenous increases in other resources, most particularly increases in the total wealth or income within the state or locality. This finding has been termed the *flypaper effect*, because grant funds appear to "stick where they hit."

The empirical analysis leading to the finding of a flypaper effect rests on two fundamental principles. The first, noted earlier, is that a model of how governments respond to grants-in-aid should be part of the same model used

---

[14] D. Rubinfeld, P. Shapiro, and J. Roberts, "Tiebout Bias and the Demand for Local Public Schooling," *Review of Economics and Statistics*, August, 1987.

to determine their demands for the various public services. Since the median voter model is the favored model for estimating the demand for state and local services, it is also the model used to estimate the response to grants-in-aid. This implies that the response of the median voter to the government's receipt of a grant determines how the government itself will respond to the grant, since the median voter is decisive. Consequently, the standard approach simply adds the grant parameters to the usual estimating equation of the median voter model. We will consider a truncated version of the full model that highlights the price and income terms, and write the basic estimating equation for spending category i to be adjusted for grants-in-aid as:

$$\ln(E/N)_i = a + b\ln Y_{med} + c\ln t_{med} + (1 + c)\ln q_i + \ldots + e_i \qquad (31.52)$$

where:

$(E/N)_i$ = expenditures per capita on category i

$t_{med} = (V_{med}/V)$ = the tax share of the median household, the ratio of its property value to the total property value in the community

q_i = the supply price of spending category i, proxied in the estimation by the wages and salaries of the employees in category i

The second principle is that the median voter should respond to a grant-in-aid exactly as a consumer would respond to an individual transfer payment. The operative question is how the median household perceives that the receipt of a grant-in-aid affects its own budget constraint. Assuming that the median household spends an endowment of income, Y_{med}, on a private numeraire good X and public good G_i, the median voter's budget constraint is

$$X + p_{med}G_i = Y_{med} \qquad (31.53)$$

or

$$X + t_{med}q_iG_i = Y_{med} \qquad (31.54)$$

The various transfer (grant) possibilities were discussed in Chapter 10 in the context of pareto-optimal redistributions. To review: If the median household's community receives an open-ended matching grant for G_i at a matching rate of m, the relevant net price of G_i to the median household becomes $P_{med}(1 - m)$. If the grant is closed-ended with a grant limit of A, the following possibilities arise:

1. *Unconditional, closed-ended grant that can be spent on any good—* Grants of this form are equivalent to increases in income to the recipient.

2. *Conditional, closed-ended grant targeted to good i—*As long as the receiving government spends more on good i than the amount of the grant, then the grant is equivalent to an unconditional grant, that is, to an increase

in income. The recipient can undo the conditions of the grant by adjusting its expenditures from its own resources on the aided and unaided items. The condition that the funds be spent on good i matters only if the recipient spends none of its own resources on good i, in which case it is forced to a corner solution on its budget constraint. This condition is virtually never satisfied for grants-in-aid and certainly not for any of the major grants. The receiving government always spends more than the maximum amount of the conditional grant under any of the major grants, such as the federal highway grants, the public assistance TANF grants, and the state education grants.

3. *Conditional, closed-ended matching grant*—This grant is also exogenous and equivalent to an unconditional grant so long as the receiving government reaches the limit of the aid. The matching rate is irrelevant beyond the limit; every additional dollar requires a dollar of funds from the locality's own resources. The grant acts as a price-reducing matching grant if the recipient remains within the matching region, which is unlikely. The possibilities suggest that all (important) grants other than open-ended matching grants should be equivalent to unconditional exogenous grants. Conditioning or targeting the grant to a specific type of expenditure should not matter. Therefore, an exogenous grant of A represents an increase in the resources of the median voter equal to $t_{med}A$, the household's share of the grant funds. The median household's budget constraint under an exogenous grant is

$$X + p_{med}G_i = Y_{med} + t_{med}A \tag{31.55}$$

Almost all federal grants are closed-ended conditional grants, matching or nonmatching, that are equivalent to an unconditional grants. The only exception is Medicaid, which is an open-ended matching grant to the states that reimburses them from 50 to 83% for whatever expenditures they incur under Medicaid, with the matching rates inversely related to state income. Most state grants to localities are also closed-ended conditional grants that are equivalent to unconditional grants. Therefore, researchers typically aggregate all exogenous grant funds and add them to the estimating equation on a per-capita basis. The grant-adjusted estimating equation incorporating open-ended matching and exogenous grants is

$$\ln(E/N)_i = a + b\ln Y_{med} + c\ln t_{med}(1 - m) + (1 + c)\ln q_i \\ + \ldots + f\ln(A/N) + e_i \tag{31.56}$$

where (A/N) equals total exogenous grants per capita, not just those targeted to good i.

The flypaper effect associated with the exogenous grants involves a comparison of the coefficient estimates of b and f. The exact comparison depends on how the median voter views (A/N).

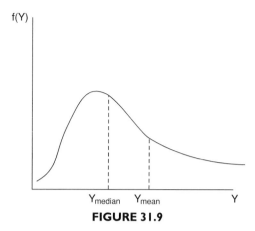

FIGURE 31.9

Since the median voter views the grant A as equivalent to an increase in its resources of $t_{med}A$, the expectation is that:[15]

$$\partial G_i/\partial(t_{med}A) = \partial G_i/\partial Y_{med} \qquad (31.57)$$

To represent the grants on a per capita basis, define $t^*_{med} = Nt_{med}$. Then

$$\partial G_i/\partial(t^*_{med}A/N) = \partial G_i/\partial Y_{med} \qquad (31.58)$$

If $t^*_{med} = 1$, then the median household treats the receipt of an exogneous per-capita grant as equivalent to an increase in income. But t^*_{med} is likely to be much less than 1 (equivalently, t_{med} is likely to be much less than 1/N), for two reasons. First, the distributions of income and most forms of wealth such as property values are almost always highly skewed toward the high end, as indicated in Fig. 31.9, such that the mean income or wealth is well above the median income or wealth. Hence, $t_{med} = (V_{med}/V)$ is likely to be less than 1/N in all states and localities, thus $t^*_{med} < 1$. In addition, localities are able to export some of their property tax burden to citizens outside the locality, which lowers the median voter's tax share even more. Estimates of the proportion of exported local tax revenues in the United States range from .65 to .85.

To test for a flypaper effect, therefore, rewrite Eq. (31.58) as:

$$\partial G_i/\partial(A/N) = t^*_{med}\,\partial G_i/\partial Y_{med} \qquad (31.59)$$

Convert Eq. (31.59) into elasticities consistent with the log-linear form of the estimating equation, Eq. (31.56), by multiplying both sides by $[Y_{med}(A/N)/G]$:

$$Y_{med}E_{G,(A/N)} = t^*_{med}(A/N)E_{G,Ymed} \qquad (31.60)$$

---

[15] Expressing the flypaper effect in terms of output instead of per-capita expenditure is less cumbersome. Only the output component of E/N changes as income or grants change.

$$f = [t^*_{med}(A/N)/Y_{med}]b \qquad (31.61)$$

Equation (31.61) indicates the expected equivalence in the median household's response to the community's receipt of a per-capita grant or to an increase in its income. A flypaper effect exists if $f > [t^*_{med}(A/N)/Y_{med}]b$. Since both t^*_{med} and $(A/N)/Y_{med}$ are less than one, f has to be greater than only a fraction of b to generate a flypaper effect. In fact, most estimates of equations such as Eq. (31.56) find that $f > b$; the flypaper effect appears to be very large. Governments respond much more to grants-in-aid than to an equivalent increase in income, that is, much more than the theory would predict. A strong flypaper effect is also typically found in estimating models other than the median voter model.

Possible Explanations of the Flypaper Effect

Economists have offered a number of possible explanations for the strong flypaper effect, all of them based on the idea that the grant-adjusted median voter model is somehow misspecified or incomplete. We will briefly consider two possibilities: fiscal illusion and the partial equilibrium nature of the model.

Fiscal Illusion

Wallace Oates believes that voters may suffer from a form of fiscal illusion. They may view exogenous grants as reducing the price of public services as well as increasing community resources because they confuse average and marginal prices. The average price of public services is the ratio of total tax collections to total expenditures (expressed as a vector):

$$P_{avg} = \left(\frac{\sum\limits_{i=1}^{N} T_i}{q \cdot G} \right) = \left(\frac{q \cdot G - A}{q \cdot G} \right) \qquad (31.62)$$

The perceived price effect introduces a bogus substitution effect that could help to explain the extra kick to public spending that grants appear to have. This explanation suffers from the normal skepticism of any theory based on people falling victim to illusions. In addition, the estimated price elasticities of local public goods are quite small, perhaps too small to explain the rather large flypaper effect, even if voters do suffer from average price illusion. At best, average price illusion appears to be only a partial explanation.

Combining Grant and Tax Effects

Ronald Fisher[16] has introduced a more promising explanation in our view, one that has not been adequately tested to date. Fisher argues that the

---

[16] R. Fisher, "Income and Grant Effects on Local Expenditures: The Flypaper Effect and Other Difficulties," *Journal of Urban Economics*, November 1982.

response to grants in the median voter model as described above is incomplete, in effect a partial equilibrium rather than a general equilibrium analysis. It views voters as savvy enough to see how the receipt of a grant by their community affects their own budget constraints in their as-if maximization problems. But if they are savvy enough to see this, then they are also savvy enough to realize that the grants have to be paid for by taxes collected from the higher level granting government. They would realize, in other words, that the net increase in resources to the community and to themselves is the grant less the taxes paid to finance the grant. Given the progressivity of the federal personal income tax, a grant to a high-income community from the federal government could easily represent a net decrease in resources to the community and the median voter.

In any event, to determine the effect of the grant on its budget constraint the median household should properly compare its share of the local property tax, t_{med}, with its share of federal taxes paid within the community to finance the grant nationwide, t_{med}^{fed}. The total response to the grant is

$$dG = (\partial G/\partial t_{med}A)d(t_{med}A) - (\partial G/\partial Y_{med})d\left(t_{med}^{fed}T^{fed}\right) \tag{31.63}$$

where T^{fed} are the total personal income taxes collected from the community to finance the grant program. Equation (31.63) indicates that a resource-neutral grant program from the community's point of view, $A = T^{fed}$, will not be resource neutral from the median household's point of view unless $t_{med} = t_{med}^{fed}$.

Fisher's general point is that the researcher has to get the model right before attempting to describe and estimate a flypaper effect.[17]

Project Grants and Bureaucrats

We conclude our discussion with the possibility of endogenous grant parameters. Most research on the response to grants-in-aid assumes that the grant parameters such as matching rates and grant limits are exogenous, equal to whatever the particular grant program describes them to be. This may not be true, however, if the bureaucrats administering the grants are pursuing their own agendas, in line with the public choice view of government officials. Howard Chernick pointed out long ago that the parameters of federal project grants to states and localities for such things as municipal waste treatment plants and community development initiatives were often subject to negotiation between the federal grant bureau and the potential recipients.[18] These

---

[17] Cheryl Holsley, "Price and Income Distortions Under Separate Spending and Taxing Decisions," *Journal of Public Economics*, January 1993, was one of the first economists to take a general equilibrium approach and consider the financing of the grants in analyzing the response to grants-in-aid.

[18] H. Chernick, "Price Discrimination and Federal Project Grants," *Public Finance Quarterly*, October 1981.

grants are almost always matching grants with a spending limit, and potential recipients apply for aid on specific projects. Chernick noted that federal administrators are often willing to make a portion of the grant fungible so that it could be spent on anything, in return for the recipients accepting lower matching rates. The administrators do this because they want to maximize the number of projects funded by their limited grant budgets, and they accept the results of the empirical grants literature that income elasticities were much higher than price elasticities for state and local expenditures. Exploiting the higher income elasticities with partially fungible grants is a way to stretch their budgets.

Renegotiations of this kind present a problem for researcher in trying to estimate the responses to grants because the parameters of the grant are endogenous and other than what they appear to be. Fig. 31.10 illustrates. It analyzes a matching grant to finance expenditures on some educational project. The community purchases education (Ed) and all other public goods and services (O), and the supply prices of Ed and O are set equal to 1 for convenience along the community's budget constraint DG. The community moves to point C as a result of the grant, receiving a grant of FC and paying EF from its own budget. The announced matching rate is FC/EC, so that the assumed effective net of grant price is EF/EC = (DE/EC).

Suppose, in fact, the grant bureau and the recipient negotiated a deal in which the recipient received a fungible grant in amount HD in return for accepting a lower matching rate, a combination that also placed the recipient at C after the grant. The true effective net-of-grant price as a result of the negotiation is HE/EC. The total grant, G, is still FC, equal to the fungible portion IC (=HD) plus the matching portion FI.

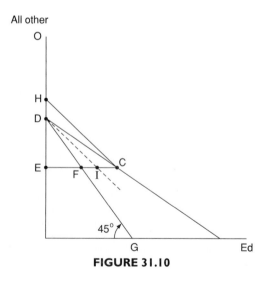

FIGURE 31.10

Martin McGuire developed a procedure for estimating the responses to grants of this type.[19] It requires the assumption that the exogenous fungible portion, G_Y, equals a portion θ of the total grant:

$$G_Y = \theta G \tag{31.64}$$

This implies that the effective net-of-grant price, $P = HE/EC$, equals:

$$P = \frac{DE + \theta G}{EF + FC} = \frac{E_{own} + \theta G}{E_{own} + G} \tag{31.65}$$

where E_{own} are expenditures by the community from its own resources. Adding and subtracting G in the numerator of Eq. (31.65), rearranging terms, and simplifying yields:

$$P = 1 + \frac{(\theta - 1)G}{E_{own} + G} = 1 + (\theta - 1)m \tag{31.66}$$

where $m = G/(E_{own} + G)$ is the assumed, observed matching rate.

Therefore, an estimating equation on education that includes the independent variables:

$$E = a(\text{exogenous grants}) + bP + \dots \tag{31.67}$$

becomes

$$E = a\theta G + b[1 + (\theta - 1)m] + \dots \tag{31.68}$$

with G and m are the observable total grant and matching rate, McGuire's estimating procedure allows for estimates of θ and the coefficients a and b. He finds that the price elasticities for these grants are negligible, thereby providing some justification for the federal administrators' willingness to negotiate.

The question remains why administrators in the recipient government have an incentive to negotiate in this manner. One possibility is that the receiving government happens to prefer having a portion of the grant with no strings attached, in line with the estimated income elasticities from the demand studies. Another possibility is more diabolical, in line with the public choice perspective that bureaucrats are aggressively self-serving. Suppose the local bureaucrats have private information about the negotiation and the project itself that they can hide from the legislature. They could then use their private information to their personal advantage as follows. Refer to Figure 31.11.

Suppose, to begin with, that the local bureaucrats can hide the fungible portion of the grant from the legislature but not the entire grant. They tell the

[19] M. McGuire, "An Econometric Model of Federal Grants and Local Fiscal Response," in R. Inman *et al.*, Eds., *Financing the New Fiscal Federalism*, Johns Hopkins University Press for Resources for the Future, Baltimore, MD, 1975, Chap. 5. Also, see M. McGuire, "The Analysis of Federal Grants into Price and Income Components," in P. Mieszkowski and W. Oakland, Eds., *Fiscal Federalism and Grants in Aid*, Urban Institute, Washington, D.C., 1979, Chap. 4.

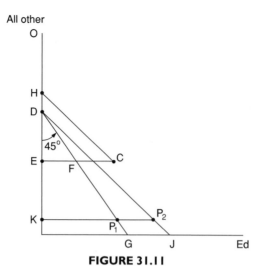

FIGURE 31.11

legislature that they were forced to accept the lower matching rate, but they do not mention the fungible portion. Therefore, they are pretending that the with-grant budget line is DJ, beginning from D but with the same slope (matching rate) as the true budget line beginning from H. A grant of FC on the *true* with-grant budget line is equal to a grant of P_1P_2 on the *pretend* with-grant budget line DJ. The bureaucrats tell the legislature that they are at point P_2 and require an amount KP_1 from the legislature to fund the recipient government's portion of the project. In fact, they only require EF from the legislature because they are really operating at C. Thus, they are able to pocket both the fungible portion of the grant plus the excess funds received from the government in the amount $(KP_1 - EF)$. Whether the bureaucrat's information concerning public projects is really so private that they could get away with such schemes is doubtful, of course. But the story is indicative of the general point that private information is likely to provide local bureaucrats with incentives to negotiate with federal administrators on grant parameters.

REFERENCES

Aktinson, A., and Stiglitz, J., *Lectures on Public Economics*, McGraw-Hill, New York, 1980, chap. 17.

Bergstrom, T., Rubinfeld, D., and Shaprio, P., "Micro-Based Estimates of Demand Functions for Local School Expenditures," *Econometrica*, September 1982.

Bradbury, K., Ladd, H., Perrault, M., Reschovsky, A., and Yinger, J., "State Aid to Offset Fiscal Disparities Across Communities," *National Tax Journal*, June 1984.

Chernick, H., "Price Discrimination and Federal Project Grants," *Public Finance Quarterly*, October 1981.

Feldstein, M., "Wealth Neutrality and Local Choice in Public Education," *American Economic Review*, March 1975.

Fisher, R., "Income and Grant Effects on Local Expenditures: The Flypaper Effect and Other Difficulties," *Journal of Urban Economics*, November 1982.

Goldstein, G., and Pauly, M., "Tiebout Bias on the Demand for Local Public Goods," *Journal of Public Economics*, Vol. 16, 1981, pp. 131–144.

Holsley, C., "Price and Income Distortions Under Separate Spending and Taxing Decisions," *Journal of Public Economics*, January 1993.

LeGrand, J., "Fiscal Equity and Central Government Grants to Local Authorities," *Economic Journal*, September 1975.

McGuire, M., "An Econometric Model of Federal Grants and Local Fiscal Response," in R. Inman *et al.*, Eds., *Financing the New Fiscal Federalism* Johns Hopkins University Press for Resources for the Future, Inc., Baltimore, MD, 1975, chap. 5.

McGuire, M., "The Analysis of Federal Grants into Price and Income Components," in P. Mieszkowski and W. Oakland, Eds., *Fiscal Federalism and Grants in Aid*, Urban Institute, Washington, D.C., 1979, chap. 4.

Oates, W., *Fiscal Federalism*, Harcourt Brace Jovanovich, New York, 1972.

Oates, W., "On the Measurement of Congestion in the Provision of Local Public Goods," *Journal of Urban Economics*, July 1988.

Rubinfeld, D., Shapiro, P., and Roberts, J., "Tiebout Bias and the Demand for Local Public Schooling," *Review of Economics and Statistics*, August, 1987.

Serrano v. Priest, L.A. 29820, Superior Court No. 938254.

INDEX